ACKNOWLEDGMENTS

There are many people who made great contributions to this project. I sincerely appreciate all their help. I especially want to thank my family. My wonderful husband, Mark, introduced me to the Web and taught me how to make it work for me. He helped me with the research and encouraged me throughout a seemingly endless project. Mark also took on many extra household jobs, so that I could stay at the computer. He even put up with the astronomical phone bills that I incurred in doing research for this publication. Our beautiful daughter, Madelon, helped me by playing alongside me at her own desk. She made me laugh and smile when I was discouraged during long days and nights of research and typing.

I am also eternally grateful to my mother, who suggested the project and put up with my phone calls and questions. Her expertise has been invaluable. My sister, Laura Pfeiffer, and Ancestry employee Paul Cannon helped complete the exhaustive research. My dad, my brother-in-law, John Sullivan, and our good friend Chris Hinson were my always-important "technical support and encouragement team." They upgraded, fixed, rehabilitated, and basically kept my computer up and running throughout this project and deserve special thanks. I also got a lot of moral support from my sisters and their families, and from my mother-in-law, Anne McWilliams. Last, but not least, I would like to thank Ancestry for giving me the opportunity to fulfill my dream of having a book published.

My thanks again to all.

THE
ANCESTRY
FAMILY HISTORIAN'S
ADDRESS
BOOK

2ND EDITION

A Comprehensive List of Local, State, and Federal
Agencies and Institutions and Ethnic and
Genealogical Organizations

Juliana Szucs Smith

Ancestry.

Library of Congress Cataloging-in-Publication Data

Smith, Juliana Szucs
   The ancestry family historian's address book : a comprehensive list of
local, state, and federal agencies and institutions, and ethnic and
genealogical organizations / by Juliana Szucs Smith.
      p. cm.
   ISBN 1-932167-99-4 (alk. paper)
   1. United States—Genealogy—Directories. I. MyFamily.com, Inc. II.
Title.

CS44.S65 2003
929'.1'02573--dc21
                                                                      2002156124

ISBN 0-932167-99-4

10   9   8   7   6   5   4   3   2

www.ancestry.com

CONTENTS

GENERAL RESOURCES

STATE ADDRESSES

PREFACE

The world is ever-evolving, and much has changed since the first edition of this book was released in 1997. As you would guess, many of the addresses—both street and Web—for genealogical societies, archives, and libraries have changed. It was the abundance of these changes that made this second edition of *The Ancestry Family Historian's Address Book* very necessary. In the course of the revision of the original manuscript each entry has been checked for accuracy, and necessary alterations were made. In addition, contact information has been added for many information repositories not included in the first edition.

As with the first edition, wherever possible, information was gathered directly from the archives, libraries, government offices, genealogical societies, and other agencies listed. In an attempt to make this the most complete collection of addresses for family and local historians, and in order to include even the more obscure addresses, a number of credible reference sources were also consulted. Time-consuming as this process was, it allowed us to provide you with the most up-to-date and complete collection of vital research source information.

Despite every effort to have the most up-to-date collection of listings, changes will occur. Offices and societies move, and area codes and ZIP codes change. Inadvertent omission is a possibility as well; we sincerely hope that we have not overlooked your society or favorite place to do research. Please contact Ancestry with any changes or corrections so that these can be included in future editions of this work. Meanwhile, as we did in the first edition, we have included some blank pages at the back of this book so that you can make notes and corrections, and add newly discovered sources.

While many of the organizations and agencies listed here can be found through their websites, the need still exists for a conventional, easy-to-use-everywhere address book with postal addresses and telephone numbers; not everyone wants to rely on a computer to look up an address. This book is intended for these users.

When I started this project so many years ago, I thought it would be useful to include the operating hours of the resources listed. After consulting with various organizations, libraries, and archives, and after visiting site after site on the Internet, however, I realized that hours of operation are often seasonal and are subject to change. I reasoned that it is far better to include telephone numbers, postal addresses, and web addresses so that you can call or write or visit the website before you make a trip. I have opted to do the same with this second edition. A word of advice: always find out what your options are before you plan a trip to any of these places. Sometimes local holidays, renovations, or other temporary problems cause unexpected closures and schedule adjustments, or affect the availability of collections. It is also wise to find out what the collections include and to make sure that the collection is relevant to your research.

The Internet is an especially useful tool for planning research. Websites usually provide a description of the particular source of interest, the access policy, up-to-date news about the collection, and notices about exhibits, conferences, and meetings. Some of these sites even have searchable databases that provide details and enable researchers to work from the comfort of their own homes. In some cases, you can obtain specific information by submitting an e-mail request; some states allow you to get vital records that way. Mailing lists are also a great way to find other people with similar research interests. (In the section titled "Helpful Websites for the Genealogist," I have included several websites that contain a variety of mailing lists and instructions on how to subscribe to them.) The people I have communicated with in the course of this project have been very generous. The chances are good that you will be able to find someone who can provide the missing pieces to your research problem.

The information in this book is divided into chapters by state. A separate chapter for "General Resources" contains some ethnic and religious societies and libraries. The individual state chapters include the following sections:

- State and National Archives
- Genealogical Societies
- Historical Societies
- Family History Centers of The Church of Jesus Christ of
    Latter-day Saints
- Archives/Libraries/Museums
- Major Newspaper Repositories
- Vital Records
- [State] on the Web (a list of particularly helpful or interesting Websites
    for each state)

The chapter on General Resources contains the following sections:

- National Societies
- National Archives/Libraries/Museums
- Military/Federal Government Agencies (includes National Archives)
- Ethnic /Ecclesiastical Societies, Resources, and Websites
    (both international and domestic in some cases)
- Helpful Websites for the Genealogist
    (includes some Search Engines and Directories)

I hope this book will prove to be as useful a tool in your genealogical pursuits as it has been in mine.

Juliana Szucs Smith

NATIONAL SOCIETIES

American Antiquarian Society
185 Salisbury Street
Worcester, MA 01609-1634
Tel: 508-755-5221
Fax: (508) 753-3311
http://www.americanantiquarian.org/

American Association for State and Local History
1717 Church Street
Nashville, TN 37203-2991
Phone: (615) 320-3203
Fax: (615) 327-9013
http://www.aaslh.org/
E-mail: history@aaslh.org

American Family Records Association
P.O. Box 15505
Kansas City, MO 64106
Tel: 816-373-6570

American Genealogical Lending Library
Genealogical Services
P.O. Box 244
Bountiful, UT 84011
Tel: 801-298-5358
800-760-AGLL
Fax: 801-298-5468
http://www.agll.com/

American Historical Association (AHA)
400 A Street, SE
Washington, DC 20003-3889
Tel: 202-544-2422
Fax: 202-544-8307
E-mail: aha@theaha.org
http://www.theaha.org/

Association for Professional Genealogists
P.O. Box 745729
Arvada, CO 80006-5729
Fax: 303-456-8825
E-mail: admin@apgen.org
http://www.apgen.org/

Augustan Society, Inc.
1510 Cravens Avenue
Torrance, CA 90501
Tel: 760-254-9223
Fax: 760-254-1953
Postal address
P.O. Box 75, Daggett, CA 92327-0075
E-mail: rcleve@msn.com
http://www.augustansociety.org/

Board for Certification of Genealogists
P.O. Box 14291
Washington, DC 20044
http://www.bcgcertification.org/

Colonial Dames of America
Dumbarton Oaks Museum
2715 Q Street, NW
Washington, DC 20007
Tel: 202-337-2288

Daughters of American Colonists-National Society
2205 Massachusetts Avenue, NW
Washington, DC 20008
Tel: 202-667-3076

Daughters of the American Revolution, National Society
1776 D Street, NW
Washington, DC 20006-5392
Tel: 202-628-1776
E-mail: dar@chesapeake.net
http://www.dar.org/natsociety/

Daughters of Union Veterans of the Civil War (DUV)
National Headquarters, DUV Registrar's Office
503 South Walnut Street
Springfield, IL 62704
Tel: 217-544-0616
E-mail: duvcw@comp.net
http://www.duvcw.org/

Descendants of the Signers of the Constitution, Society of
325 Chestnut Street
Philadelphia, PA 19106

Federation of Genealogical Societies
P.O. Box 200940
Austin, TX 78720-0940
Tel: 512-336-2731
888-FGS1500
Fax: 512-336-2732
888-380-0500
E-mail: fgs-office@fgs.org
http://www.fgs.org

GENTECH
A Division of the National Genealogical Society
4527 17th Street North
Arlington, Virginia 22207-2399
Tel. (703) 525-0050 or (800) 473-0060
Fax (703) 525-0052
E-mail info@gentech.org
http://www.gentech.org/ngsgentech/main/Home.asp/

Genealogical Society of Mayflower Descendants
P.O. Box 3297
Plymouth, MA 02361
URL (Unofficial Site):
http://members.aol.com/calebj/mayflower.html

General Society of the War of 1812
P.O. Box 106
Mendenhall, PA 19357-0106
Tel: 610-388-6015
http://www.societyofthewarof1812.org/

Grand Army of the Republic
Grand Army of the Republic Memorial Museum
78 East Washington Street
Chicago, IL 60602
Tel: 312-269-2926
http://suvcw.org/gar.htm

Immigrant Genealogical Society
Library and office:
1310-B Magnolia Blvd.
Burbank, CA 91510
Postal address:
P.O. Box 7369
Burbank, CA 91510
Tel: 818-848-3122
Fax: 818-716-6300
http://feefhs.org/igs/frg-igs.html

Immigration History Society
University of Cincinnati
3410 Bishop Street
Cincinnati, OH 45220
Tel: 513-861-7462
Fax: 513-556-7901
E-mail: alexanje@ucbeh.san.uc.edu

Ladies of the Grand Army of the Republic, National Organization
c/o Elizabeth Koch, National Secretary
119 N. Swarthmore Avenue, Apt. 1-H
Ridley Park, PA 19078
http://homepages.go.com/~aadar/nlgar.html

National Genealogical Society
4527 Seventeenth Street North
Arlington, VA 22207-2399
Tel: 703-525-0050 (Office)
800-473-0060 (Toll Free)
703-841-9065 (Library)
Fax: 703-525-0052
E-mail: ngs@ngsgenealogy.org
library@ngsgenealogy.org (library)
http://www.ngsgenealogy.org/

National Historical Society
6405 Flank Drive
Harrisburg, PA 17112
Tel: 717-657-9555

National Institute on Genealogical Research
Drawer HP, P.O. Box 14274
Washington, DC 20044-4274
E-mail: NatGenInst@juno.com
http://www.rootsweb.com/~natgenin/

National Maritime Historical Society
5 John Walsh Blvd.
P.O. Box 68
Peekskill, NY 10566
Tel: 914-737-7878
E-mail: nmhs@seahistory.org
http://www.seahistory.org

National Railway Historical Society
National Office and Library Location:
100 North 17th Street
Philadelphia, PA 19103
Postal Address: National Railway Historical Society
P.O. Box 58547
Philadelphia, PA 19102-8547
Tel: (215) 557-6606
Fax: (215) 557-6740
E-mail: services@nrhs.com
http://www.nrhs.com/

New England Historical and Genealogical Society (NEHGS)
101 Newbury Street
Boston, MA 02116-3007
Tel: 617-536-5740
888-AT-NEHGS (Membership & Education)
888-BY-NEHGS (Sales)
888-90-NEHGS (Library Circulation)
Fax: 617-536-7307
E-mail: nehgs@nehgs.org
http://www.nehgs.org/

Order of Descendants of Ancient Planters
http://tyner.simplenet.com/PLANTERS.HTM

Oregon-California Trails Association
P.O. Box 1019
Independence, MO 64051-0519
Tel: 816-252-2276
Fax: 816-836-0989
E-mail: octahqts@gvi.net
http://calcite.rocky.edu/octa/octahome.htm

Pilgrim Society
Pilgrim Hall Museum
75 Court Street
Plymouth, MA 02360
Tel: 508-746-1620
http://www.pilgrimhall.org/

Society of American Archivists
527 S. Wells St., 5th Floor
Chicago, IL 60607-3922
Tel: 312-922-0140
fax 312/347-1452
E-mail: info@archivists.org
http://www.archivists.org

Sons and Daughters of the Pilgrims, National Society
c/o Arthur Louis Finnell
3917 Heritage Hills Drive, #104
Bloomington, MN 55437
Tel: 612-893-9747
E-mail: ALFINNELL@compuserve.com
http://members.tripod.com/~NSSDP/

Sons of the American Revolution, National Society
1000 South Fourth Street
Louisville, KY 40203
Tel: 502-589-1776
http://www.sar.org/

Sons of Confederate Veterans
Maitland O. Westbrook III, Executive Director
PO Box 59
Columbia, TN 38402
Tel: 800-380-1896
Fax: 931-381-6712
Email exedir@scv.org
http://scv.org

Sons of Union Veterans of the Civil War
Post Office Box 1865
Harrisburg, Pennsylvania 17105
E-mail: YJNW42A@prodigy.com
http://suvcw.org/

Steamship Historical Society of America
University of Baltimore, Langsdale Library
1420 Maryland Avenue
Baltimore, MD 21201
Tel: 410-837-4334
http://www.ubalt.edu/archives/ship/ship.htm

United Daughters of the Confederacy (UDC)
UDC Memorial Building
328 North Boulevard
Richmond, VA 23220-4057
Tel: 804-355-1636
Fax: 804-355-1396
E-mail: hqudc@rcn.com
http://www.hqudc.org/

ARCHIVES, LIBRARIES, & MUSEUMS

Allen County Public Library
900 Webster Street
Fort Wayne, IN 46802
Tel: (219) 421-1200
Fax: (219) 422-9688
http://www.acpl.lib.in.us/

American Genealogical Society (AGS)
Depository and Headquarters
Samford University Library
Box 2296
800 Lakeshore Drive
Birmingham, AL 35229
Tel: 205-870-2749

Balch Institute for Ethnic Studies
Center for Immigrant Research
18 South 7th Street
Philadelphia, PA 19106-3794
Tel: 215-925-8090
E-mail: info@balchinstitute.org
http://www.libertynet.org/~balch/

Center for Migration Studies of New York, Inc.
209 Flagg Place
Staten Island, NY 10304-1199
Tel: 718-351-8800
Fax: 718-667-4598
http://www.cmsny.org/index.htm

Civil War Library and Museum
1805 Pine Street
Philadelphia, PA 19103
Tel: 215-735-8196
http://www.libertynet.org/~cwlm/

Cleveland Public Library
325 Superior Avenue
Cleveland, OH 44114-1271
Tel: 216-623-2800
Fax: 216-623-7015
E-mail: General.Reference@cpl.org
http://www.cpl.org/

Daughters of the American Revolution, National Society
1776 D Street, NW
Washington, DC 20006-5392
Tel: 202-628-1776
E-mail: dar@chesapeake.net
http://www.dar.org/natsociety/

David Library of the American Revolution
1201 River Road
P.O. Box 748
Washington Crossing, PA 18977
Tel: 215-493-6776
Fax: 215-493-9276
E-mail: dlar@libertynet.org
http://www.libertynet.org/~dlar

Denver Public Library
Genealogy Division
10W.Fourteenth Ave. Pkwy.
Denver, CO 80204-2731
Tel: 720-865-1821
TTY: 720-865-1825
http://www.denver.lib.co.us/

Detroit Public Library
Burton Historical Collection
5201 Woodward Avenue
Detroit, MI 48202
Tel: 313-833-1480
Fax: 313-832-0877
E-mail: jwhitso@detroit.lib.mi.us
http://www.detroit.lib.mi.us/special_collections.htm

Ellis Island Immigration Museum
American Family Immigration History Center
Liberty Island
New York, NY 10004
Tel: 212-363-3200
212-269-5755 (Circle Line Ferry for schedules/rates)
http://www.ellisisland.org/

Family History Library
Church of Jesus Christ of Latter-Day Saints
35 North West Temple Street
Salt Lake City, UT 84150-3400
Tel: 801-240-2331
FAX: 801-240-5551
E-mail: fhl@ldschurch.org
http://www.familysearch.org/

Genealogical Center Library (operates by mail)
P.O. Box 71343
Marietta, GA 30007-1343

Grand Army of the Republic War Museum/Ruan House Library
4278 Griscom Street
Philadelphia, PA 19124-3954
Tel: 215-289-6484
E-mail: GARMUSLIB@aol.com
http://suvcw.org/garmus.htm

Historical Trails Library
Route 1, Box 373
Philadelphia, MS 39350
Tel: 601-656-3506

Immigration History Research Center
University of Minnesota
311 Andersen Library
222 21st Avenue S.
Minneapolis MN 55455-0439
Phone: (612) 625-4800
Fax: (612) 626-0018
E-mail: ihrc@tc.umn.edu
http://www.umn.edu/ihrc/

Leo Baeck Institute
German-Jewish Families
15 West 16th St.
New York, NY 10011
E-mail: lbi1@lbi.com
Tel. (212) 744-6400
Fax (212) 988-1305
http://users.rcn.com/lbi1/

Library of Congress
Local History & Genealogy Divison
Thomas Jefferson Building, Room LJ G42
101 Independence Avenue, SE
Washington, DC 20540
Tel: (202) 707-5000
Reading Room: (202) 707-5537
Fax: (202) 707-1957
E-mail: lcweb@loc.gov
http://lcweb.loc.gov/
http://lcweb.loc.gov/rr/genealogy/

Los Angeles Public Library
History & Genealogy Department
630 West 5th Street, LL4
Los Angeles, CA 90071
Tel: 213-228-7400
Fax: 213-228-7409
E-mail: history@lapl.org
http://www.lapl.org/central/history.html

Mid-Continent Public Library
Genealogy and Local History
Department
317 West 24 Highway
Independence, MO 64050
Tel: 816-252-7228
E-mail: ge@mcpl.lib.mo.us
http://www.mcpl.lib.mo.us/gen.htm

National Genealogical Society/Library
4527 Seventeenth Street, North
Arlington, VA 22207-2399
Library: 1-800-473-0060 ext 331
Tel: 703-525-0050
Fax: 703-525-0052
E-mail: 76702.2417@compuserve.com
library@ngsgenealogy.org
http://www.ngsgenealogy.org/

New England Historical and Genealogical Society (NEHGS)
101 Newbury Street
Boston, MA 02116-3007
Tel: 617-536-5740
888-AT-NEHGS (Membership & Education)
888-BY-NEHGS (Sales)
888-90-NEHGS (Library Circulation)
Fax: 617-536-7307
E-mail: nehgs@nehgs.org
http://www.nehgs.org/

New York Public Library
The Irma and Paul Milstein Division of United States
    History, Local History and Genealogy
5th Avenue and 42nd Street, Room 121
New York, NY 10018-2788
Tel: (212) 930-0828
E-mail: histref@nypl.org
http://www.nypl.org/research/chss/lhg/genea.html

Newberry Library
60 West Walton Street
Chicago, IL 60610-3305
Tel: (312)943-9090 (Main)
(312)255-3506 (Reference)
(312)255-3512 (Genealogy)
Fax: (312) 255-3658
E-mail: genealogy@newberry.org
http://www.newberry.org/

St. Louis Public Library
History and Genealogy Department(Central Library)
1301 Olive Street
St. Louis, MO 63103
Tel: 314-241-2288
Fax: 314-539-0393
TDD: 314-539-0364
E-mail: webref@slpl.lib.mo.us
http://www.slpl.lib.mo.us/

Seattle Public Library
Humanities Department
1000 4th Avenue
Seattle, WA 98104
Tel: 206-386-4625
206-386-4629
E-mail: infospl@spl.org
http://www.spl.lib.wa.us/central/central.html

Smithsonian Institute
1000 Jefferson Drive
Washington, DC 20560
Tel: 202-357-2700
TTY: 202-357-1729
http://www.si.edu/

Steamship Historical Society of America
University of Baltimore, Langsdale Library
1420 Maryland Avenue
Baltimore, MD 21201
Tel: 410-837-4334
E-mail: ahouse@ubmail.ubalt.edu
http://www.ubalt.edu/www/archives/ship.htm

Sutro Library
480 Winston Drive
San Francisco, CA 94132
Tel: 415-731-4477
E-mail: sutro@library.ca.gov
MELVYL Catalog
http://www.melvyl.ucop.edu/?CSdb=cat

United States Civil War Center
Louisiana State University
Baton Rouge, LA 70803
Phone: (225) 578-3151
FAX: (225) 578-4876
http://www.cwc.lsu.edu/

United States Holocaust Memorial Museum
100 Rauol Wallenberg Place, SW
Washington, DC 20024-2126
Tel: 202-488-0400
E-mail: library@ushmm.org
archives@ushmm.org
http://www.ushmm.org/

Western Reserve Historical Society
Case Western Reserve University
History Library
10825 East Boulevard
Cleveland, OH 44106
Tel: 216-721-5722
Fax: (216) 725-5702
http://www.cwru.edu/UL/WHGC/pages/WRHS.html

Wisconsin, State Historical Society of
816 State Street
Madison, WI 53706
Tel: 608-264-6534
608-264-6535 (Reference)
608-264-6525 (Government Publications Reference)
http://www.shsw.wisc.edu/

ETHNIC & ECCLESIASTICAL RESOURCES

ACADIAN

Acadia University
Vaughan Memorial Library
Kirkconnell Room, Level B1 Room 216
Wolfville, Nova Scotia
Canada, B0P1X0
Tel: 902-585-1170
E-mail: reference.desk@acadiau.ca
http://www.acadiau.ca/vaughan/archives/

Acadian Archives
25 Pleasant Street
University of Maine at Fort Kent
Fort Kent, ME 04743
Tel: 207-834-7535
Fax: 207- 834-7518
E-mail: acadian@maine.edu
http://www.umfk.maine.edu/archives/main.htm

Acadian Cultural Society Page de la Maison
P.O. Box 2304
Fitchburg, MA 01420-8804
E-mail: ronfrazier@hotmail.com
http://www.angelfire.com/ma/1755/index.html

Acadian Genealogy Exchange
3265 Wayman Branch Rd.
Covington, KY 41015-4601
Phone, Fax and Modem: 859-356-9825
E-mail: info@acadiangenexch.com
http://www.acadiangenexch.com/

Action Cadienne (Cajun Action)
Action Cadienne
P.O. Box 60104
Lafayette, LA 70596-0104
info@actioncadienne.org
http://www.actioncadienne.org/

Creole-American Genealogical Society, Inc.
P.O. Box 2666, Church Street Station
New York, NY 10008

WEBSITES:

Acadian Genealogy Homepage
http://www.acadian.org/

ACADIAN GenWeb Site
http://www.geocities.com/Heartland/Acres/2162/

Acadian-Cajun Genealogy and History
http://www.genweb.net/acadian-cajun/

Genealogy of Acadia
http://www.francogene.com/

AFRICAN AMERICAN

African-American Cultural & Genealogical Society
314 North Main Street
P.O. Box 25251
Decatur, IL 62525
Tel: 217-429-7458
http://www.decaturnet.org/afrigenes.html

African American Genealogical Society of Northern California
P.O. Box 27485
Oakland, CA 94602-0985
Phone: (510) 496-2740 ext. 4144
Fax: (510) 496-2740 ext. 4144
E-mail: baobabtree@aagsnc.org
http://www.aagsnc.org/

African-American Genealogy Group (AAGG)
P.O. Box 1798
Philadelphia, PA 19105-1798
Tel: 215-572-6063
Fax: 215-885-7244
E-mail: aagg@libertynet.org
http://www.aagg.org/

AfriGeneas ~ African Ancestored Genealogy
Post Office Box 4906
Blue Mountain, Alabama 36204
Tel: 256-820-8794
Fax: 256-820-8339
http://www.afrigeneas.com/

Afro American Historical & Cultural Museum
7th and Arch Streets
Philadelphia, PA 19106
Tel: 215-574-0380
http://www.fieldtrip.com/pa/55740380.htm

Afro-American Historical and Genealogical Society
P.O. Box 73086
Washington, DC 20056
http://www.rootsweb.com/~mdaahgs/

Association for the Study of Afro-American Life and History
Mrs. Irena Webster, Executive Director
7961 Eastern Ave. Ste 301
Silver Spring, Md 20910
Tel:(301) 587-5900
Fax:(301) 587-5915
E-mail: asalh@earthlink.net
http://www.artnoir.com/asalh/default.html

Moorland-Spingarn Research Center
Founders Library
Howard University
Washington, DC 20059
Tel: 202-806-7480
http://www.founders.howard.edu/moorland-spingarn

W.E.B. Du Bois Institute for Afro-American Research
Harvard University
Cambridge, MA 02138
Tel: (617) 495-1000
http://webdubois.fas.harvard.edu/DuBois/Research/
　　Research.HTML

Schomburg Center for Research in Black Culture/Branch New York Public Library
515 Malcolm X Blvd.
New York, NY 10037-1801
Tel: 212-491-2200
http://www.nypl.org/research/sc/sc.html

WEBSITES:

Afrigeneas Homepage
http://www.afrigeneas.com/

Census Schedules and Black Genealogical Research:
One Family's Experience
http://www.colorado.edu/libraries/govpubs/debbie/cover.htm

Christine's Genealogy Website
http://www.ccharity.com/

ASIAN

Chinese Historical Society of America
644 Broadway Street, Suite 402
San Francisco CA 94133
Tel: 415 391-1188
Fax: 415 391-1150
E-mail: info@chsa.org
http://www.chsa.org/home.html

Filipino-American Historical Society
5462 S. Dorchester Ave.
Chicago, IL 60615-5309
Tel: 773-752-2156

Filipino American National Historical Society
810 18th Avenue, Room 100
Seattle, WA 98122
Tel: (206) 322-0203
Fax: (206) 461-4879
http://www.fanhs-national.org/index.html

Japanese American History Archives
1840 Sutter Street
San Francisco, CA 94115
Tel: 415-776-0661
http://www.amacord.com/fillmore/museum/jt/jaha/
　　jaha.html

Korean American Historical Society
10303 Meridian Avenue N., Suite 200
Seattle, Washington 98133-9483
Tel: 206-528-5784
Fax: 206-523-4340
E-mail: kahs@arkay-intl.com
http://www.kahs.org/

Morikami Museum and Japanese Gardens
4000 Morikami Park Rd.
Delray Beach, FL 33446
Tel: 561-495-0233
http://www.morikami.org/

National Japanese American Historical Society
1684 Post Street
San Francisco, CA 94115
Tel: 415.921.5007
Fax: 415.921.5087
E-mail: njahs@njahs.org
http://www.nikkeiheritage.org/

Pacific Asia Museum
46 North Los Robles Ave.
Pasadena, CA 91101
Tel: 626-449-2742
Fax 626-449-2754
http://www.pacasiamuseum.org/

AUSTRALIAN

Australian Institute of Genealogical Studies
P.O. Box 339
Blackburn, Victoria, 3130
Australia
Tel: (61 3) 9877 3789
Fax: (61 3) 9877 9066
E-mail: aigs@alphalink.com.au
http://www.alphalink.com.au/~aigs/

Military Historical Society of Australia
P.O. Box 30
Garran, ACT 2605
Australia
E-mail: astaunto@pcug.org.au
http://www.pcug.org.au/~astaunto/mhsa.htm

National Archives of Australia
PO Box 7425
Canberra Mail Centre ACT 2610
General inquiries
Tel: (02) 6212 3600
Fax: (02) 6212 3699
E-mail: archives@naa.gov.au
http://www.aa.gov.au/default.html

National Library Of Australia
Canberra, ACT 2600
AUSTRALIA
Tel: 61 2 6262 1111
Fax: 61 2 6257 1703
http://www.nla.gov.au/collect/

WEBSITES:

Australasian Federation of Family History Organisations Inc.
http://carmen.murdoch.edu.au/~affho/affho-04.htm

Australian Family History Compendium
http://www.cohsoft.com.au/afhc/

Genealogy in Australia
(Sponsored by the Canberra Dead Persons Society)
http://www.pcug.org.au/~mpahlow/welcome.html

BAPTIST

American Baptist Historical Society
P.O. Box 851
Valley Forge, PA 19482-0851
Tel: 610-768-2374
http://www.abc-usa.org/abhs/abhscontact.html

American Baptist Historical Society
Samuel Colgate Historical Library
1106 South Goodman Street
Rochester, NY 14620-2532
Tel: 716-473-1740
http://www.crds.edu/abhs/

North American Baptists Archives
1605 Euclid Avenue
Sioux Falls, SD 57105
Tel: 605-336-6588

BELGIAN/DUTCH

Archives of Mechelen
Stadsarchief
Hof van Habsburg
Goswin de Stassartstraat, 145,
B-2800 Mechelen
Belgium
Tel: (0)15/20.43.46 en (0)15/20.39.43
http://www.mechelen.be/archief/archiefe.htm

Belgian-American Heritage Association
1008 NE Marion Place
Bend, OR 97701-3727
E-mail: linghels@eosc.osshe.edu

Genealogical Society of Flemish Americans
18740 Thirteen Mile Road
Roseville, MI 48066
http://www.rootsweb.com/~gsfa/gsfainfo.html

Holland Library
112 Walton Street
Alexandria Bay, NY 13607
Tel: 315-482-2241

Holland Society of New York
122 E. 58th Street
New York, NY 10022
Tel: 212-758-1675
E-mail: info@hollandsociety.com
http://www.hollandsociety.com/contact.html

WEBSITES:

Belgium-Roots Project
http://belgium.rootsweb.com/index.html

Dutch-English Online Dictionary
http://www.travlang.com/languages/cgi-bin/langchoice.cgi

The Emigrants from Belgium to the United States and Canada
http://www.ping.be/picavet/

Genealogy in Belgium (Flanders)
http://users.skynet.be/sky60754/familiekunde/

Genealogy in Belgium (French)
http://www.francogene.com/

Holland America Historical Society
http://home.soneraplaza.nl/qn/prive/larryvanderlaan/hahs.html

Yvette's Dutch Genealogy Homepage
http://wwwedu.cs.utwente.nl/~hoitink/genealogy.html

CAJUN

(See Acadian/Cajun/Creole)

CANADIAN

American-Canadian Genealogical Society (ACGS)
4 Elm Street
P.O. Box 6478
Manchester, NH 03108
Tel. 603-622-1554
Fax 603-624-8843
E-mail: acgensoc@juno.com
http://www.acgs.org/

Canadian Federation of Genealogical and Family History Societies
227 Parkville Bay
Winnipeg, MB, R2M 2J6
Canada
http://www.geocities.com/Athens/Troy/2274/index.html

National Archives of Canada
Genealogy Reference Services
395 Wellington Street
Ottawa, Ontario K1A 0N3
Tel: 613-996-7458
Fax: 613-995-6274
http://www.archives.ca/

National Library of Canada
395 Wellington St.
Ottawa, ON K1A 0N4
Tel: (613) 995-9481 or 1-877-896-9481 (Toll free in Canada)
TTY: (613) 992-6969 or 1-866-299-1699 (Toll free in Canada)
Fax: (613) 943-1112
http://www.nlc-bnc.ca/services/genealogy/gnlogy-e.htm

WEBSITES:

Canada GenWeb Project
http://www.rootsweb.com/~canwgw/

Canadian Genealogy and History
http://www.islandnet.com/~jveinot/cghl/cghl.html

Sources for Genealogical Research in Canada
http://www.king.igs.net/~bdmlhm/cangenealogy.html

CATHOLIC

American Catholic Historical Association
Catholic University of America
Mullen Library, Room 318
Washington, DC 20064
Tel: 202-319-5079

Archdiocese for the Military Services
415 Michigan Ave. N.E.
Suite 300
Washington, DC 20017-1518
Phone: 202-269-9100
FAX: 202-269-9022
E-mail: info@milarch.org
http://www.milarch.org/

Catholic University of America
Department of Archives, Manuscripts, and Museum
Collections
Life Cycle Institute
Washington, DC 20064
Tel: 202-319-5065
E-mail: meagher@cua.edu
http://www.cua.edu/

U.S. Catholic Historical Society
The Catholic Center
1011 First Avenue
New York, NY 10022
Tel: 800-225-7999
E-mail: catholichistory@aol.com
http://www.catholic.org/uschs/

WEBSITES:

Local Catholic Church History Genealogical Research Guide
http://home.att.net/~Local_Catholic/

CHRISTIAN

Congregational Christian Historical Society
14 Beacon Street
Boston, MA 02108
Tel: 617-523-0470
Fax: 617-523-0491
http://www.14beacon.org/

THE CHURCH OF JESUS CHRIST OF LATTER-DAY SAINTS

Family History Library
Church of Jesus Christ of Latter-Day Saints
35 North West Temple
Salt Lake City, UT 84150
Tel: 801-240-2331
FAX: 801-240-5551
E-mail: fhl@ldschurch.org
http://www.familysearch.org

(See State Listings for Family History Centers)

Mormon History Association
2470 North 1000 West
Layton, UT 84041
Tel: 801-773-4620
Fax: 801-779-1348
E-mail: Suzfoster@bigplanet.com
http://www.mhahome.org/

CREOLE
(See Acadian/Cajun/Creole)

EASTERN EUROPEAN
(Also See German)

American Hungarian Historical Society/Library
215 East 82nd Street
New York, NY 10028
Tel: 212-744-5298

American Hungarian Foundation
300 Somerset Street P.O.Box 1084
New Brunswick, NJ 08903
Tel: 732-846-5777
Fax: 732-249-7033
E-mail: info@ahfoundation.org
http://www.ahfoundation.org/

Archives of the Moravian Church
41 W. Locust Street
Bethlehem, PA 18018
Tel: 610-866-3255

Carpatho/Rusyn Society
125 Westland Drive
Pittsburgh, PA 15217
E-mail: 76163.1402@compuserve.com
http://www.carpatho-rusyn.org/

Croatian Ethnic Institute
4851 South Drexel Blvd.
Chicago, IL 60615
Tel (773)373-4670
Fax 773-373-4746
E-mail: croetljubo@aol.com
http://www.croatian-institute.org/

Croatian Heritage Museum & Library
34900 Lake Shore Blvd.
Willoughby, OH 44095-2043
Tel: 440-946-2044

Czech Heritage Preservation Society
P.O. Box 3
Tabor, SD 57063

Czech & Slovak Museum & Library, National
30 - 16th Avenue SW
Cedar Rapids, Iowa 52404-5904
Phone: 319-362-8500
Fax: 319-363-2209
E-mail: dmuhlena@ncsml.org
http://www.ncsml.org/index.htm

Czechoslovak Heritage Museum
122 W. 22nd Street
OakBrook,IL60523-1557
Tel: 630-472-0500
Fax:630-472-1100
TollFree:1-800-543-3272
E-mail: lifecsa@aol.com

Czechoslovak Genealogical Society Intl., Inc.
P.O. Box 16225
St. Paul, MN 55116-0225
E-mail: cgsi@aol.com
http://cgsi.org

East European Genealogical Society
P.O. Box 2536
Winnipeg, MB
CANADA R3C 4A7Tel: (204) 989-3292
E-mail: info@eegsociety.org
http://www.eegsociety.org/member.html

Federation of East European Family History Societies (FEEFHS)
P.O. Box 510898
Salt Lake City, UT 84151-0898
E-mail: feefhs@feefhs.org
http://feefhs.org/

Hungarian-American Friendship Society
1035 Starbrook Drive
Galt, CA 95632
Tel: (209) 744-8099
Email:HAFS@dholmes.com
http://www.dholmes.com/hafs.html

Hungarian Genealogical Society
124 Esther Street
Toledo, OH 43605-1435

Lithuanian American Genealogical Society
c/o Balzekas Museum of Lithuanian Culture
6500 South Pulaski Road
Chicago, IL 60629-5136
Tel: 773-582-6500
http://www.feefhs.org/baltic/lt/frg-lags.html

Moravian Heritage Society
31910 Rd. 160
Visalia, CA 93292
http://www.czechusa.com/moravian/default.htm

Moravian Historical Society
214 E. Center Street
Nazareth, PA 18064
Tel: 610-759-5070
http://nazarethtoday.com/MHS/

Polish American Cultural Center
308 Walnut Street
Philadelphia, PA 19106
Tel: 215-922-1700
Fax: 215-922-1518
E-mail: mail@polishamericancenter.org
http://www.polishamericancenter.org/

Polish American Museum
16 Bellview Avenue
Port Washington, NY 11050
Tel: 516-883-6542
www.liglobal.com/t_i/attractions/museums/polish/

Polish Genealogical Society of America
Polish Museum of America
984 North Milwaukee Ave.
Chicago, IL 60622
Tel: 773-384-3352
E-mail: PGSAmerica@aol.com
http://www.pgsa.org/

Polish Museum of America
984 North Milwaukee Ave.
Chicago, IL 60622-4101
Tel: 312-384-3352

Romanian Folk Art Museum
2526 Ridgeway
Evanston, IL 60201-1160
Tel: 847-328-9099

Slovenian Genealogy Society
c/o Al Peterlin, Pres.
52 Old Farm Road
Harrisburg, PA 17011-2604
Tel: 717-731-8804
http://feefhs.org/slovenia/frg-sgsi.html

Ukrainian Fraternal Association
440 Wyoming Avenue
Scranton, PA 18503
Tel: 717-342-0937

Ukrainian Museum
203 Second Avenue
New York, NY 10003
Tel:(212) 228-0110
http://www.ukrainianmuseum.org

Ukrainian Museum/Archives
1202 Kenilworth Avenue
Cleveland, OH 44113-4417
Tel: 216-781-4329
http://www.umacleveland.org/

Ukrainian National Museum
2453 West Chicago Avenue
Chicago, IL 60622-4633
Tel: 312-421-8020

WEBSITES:

Alex Glendinning's Hungarian Pages
http://user.itl.net/~glen/Hungarianintro.html

Association of European Migration Institutions
http://users.cybercity.dk/~ccc13652

East Europe GenWeb
http://www.rootsweb.com/~easeurgw/

Eastern Slovakia, Slovak, and Carpatho-Rusyn Genealogy Resources
http://www.iarelative.com/slovakia.htm

Hungarian-English Online Dictionary
http://www.sztaki.hu/services/dictionary/index.html

PolishRoots
http://www.polishroots.org/index.htm

Radio Prague History Online
http://www.radio.cz/history/

EPISCOPAL

Episcopal Church Home Archives
505 Mount Hope Avenue
Rochester, NY 14620
Tel: 716-546-8400
Fax: 716-325-6553

Archives of the Episcopal Church USA
Research Office:
606 Rathervue Place
P.O. Box 2247
Austin, Texas 78768
Records Administration Office:
Episcopal Church Center
815 Second Avenue
New York, NY 10017-4594
Telephone: 512-472-6816
FAX: 512-480-0437
E-mail: Research@episcopalarchives.org
http://www.episcopalchurch.org/

FRENCH (ALSO ACADIAN, CAJUN, CREOLE, AND HUGUENOT)

American-French Genealogical Society
(Library at the First Universalist Church)
78 Earle Street
Woonsocket, RI 02895
Mail:
P.O. Box 830
Woonsocket, RI 02895
Tel/Fax: 401-765-6141
E-mail: rogerafgs@home.com
http://www.afgs.org/

WEBSITES:

Franco-American/Canadian Genealogy Home Page
http://www.francogene.com/

French-English Online Dictionary
http://dictionaries.travlang.com/FrenchEnglish/

GERMAN

American Historical Society of Germans from Russia
631 D Street
Lincoln, NE 68502-1199
Tel: 402-474-3363
Fax: 402-474-7229
E-mail: ahsgr@ahsgr.org
http://www.ahsgr.org/

Anglo-German Family History Society
20 Skylark Rise
Plymouth, Devon
ENGLAND, United Kingdom, PL6 7SN
Tel: 01752 310852
Fax: 01752 310852
E-mail: PeterTowey@compuserve.com
http://feefhs.org/uk/frgagfhs.html

Bukovina Society of the Americas/Museum
722 Washington
P.O. Box 81
Ellis, KS 67637
Tel: 913-625-9492
913-726-4568
E-mail: owindholz@ruraltel.net
http://members.aol.com/LJensen/bukovina.html

Federation of East European Family History Societies (FEEFHS)
P.O. Box 510898
Salt Lake City, UT 84151-0898
E-mail: feefhs@feefhs.org
http://feefhs.org/masteri.html

German-American Heritage Institute
7824 West Madison Street
Forest Park, IL 60130-1485
Tel: 708-366-0017

German-Bohemian Heritage Society
P.O. Box 822
New Ulm, MN 56073
Email address:lal@mnic.net
http://www.rootsweb.com/~gbhs/

Germans from Russia Heritage Society
1125 W. Turnpike Ave.
Bismarck, ND 58501
Tel: 701-223-6167
http://www.grhs.com/

Gluckstal Colonies Research Association
611 Esplanade
Redondo Beach, CA 90277-4130
Tel: 310-540-1872

Palatines to America Society
Library Address and Phone:
611 East Weber Road
Columbus, Ohio 43211-1097
Tel: 614-267-4700
Fax: 614-267-4888
E-mail: pal-am@juno.com
http://genealogy.org/~palam/

Society for German Genealogy in Eastern Europe
Box 905 Stn "M"
Calgary, AB T2P 2J3
Canada
http://www.sggee.org/index.html

WEBSITES:

Archives in Germany
http://www.bawue.de/~hanacek/info/earchive.htm

Association of European Migration Institutions
http://users.cybercity.dk/~ccc13652

German and American Sources for German Emigration to America
by Michael P. Palmer
http://www.genealogy.net/gene/misc/emig/index.html

German-English Online Dictionary
http://dictionaries.travlang.com/GermanEnglish/

German Genealogy Home Page
http://www.genealogy.net/

Internet Sources of German Genealogy
http://my.bawue.de/~hanacek/info/edatbase.htm

ODESSA...A German-Russian Genealogical Library
http://pixel.cs.vt.edu/library/odessa.html

Palatines to America: Immigrant Ancestor Register
Index
http://genealogy.org/~palam/ia_index.htm

GREEK

Archives Department of the Greek Orthodox
Archdiocese of America
8 East 79th Street
New York, NY 10021
Tel:(212) 570-3565
Fax:(212) 861-2183
http://www.goarch.org/goa/departments/archives/

Greek Family Heritage Committee
75-21 177th Street
Flushing, NY 11366
Tel: 718-591-9342

WEBSITES:

Greece GenWeb
http://mediterraneangenweb.org/greece/

GreekFamilies.com
Greek Genealogy Resources on the Internet
http://www.greekfamilies.com/

HISPANIC

American Portugese Genealogical & Historical Society,
Inc.
P.O. Box 644
Taunton, MA 02780-0644

Hispanic Genealogical Research Center-New Mexico
P.O. Box 51088
Albuquerque, NM 87181.
Tel: 505-836-5438
E-mail: HGRC@HGRC-NM.ORG
http://www.hgrc-nm.org/

Hispanic Genealogical Society
P.O. Box 231271
Houston, Texas 77223-1271
http://www.brokersys.com/~joguerra/

National Society of Hispanic Genealogy
P.O. Box 48147
Denver, CO 80204
http://www.hispanicgen.org/

Portugese Genealogical Society of Hawaii
810 North Vineyard Blvd., Room 11
Honolulu, HI 96817
Tel: 808-841-5044
E-mail: chism@hi.net
http://www.lusaweb.com/genealogy/html/phgs.cfm

Puerto Rican/Hispanic Genealogical Society
P.O. Box 260118
Bellerose, NY 11426-0118
Tel: (516) 834-2511
E-mail: prhgs@yahoo.com
http://www.rootsweb.com/~prhgs/

Society of Hispanic Historical and Ancestral Research
P.O. Box 490
Midway City, CA 92655-0490
Tel: 714-894-8161
Fax: 714-898-7063
http://members.aol.com/shhar/

Spanish American Genealogical Association
P O Box 794
Corpus Christi, TX 78403-0794
E-mail: SagaCorpus@aol.com
http://members.aol.com/sagacorpus/saga.htm

WEBSITES:

Basque Genealogy Homepage
http://www.primenet.com/~fybarra/

Hispanic Genealogy
http://home.att.net/~Alsosa/

Cuban Genealogy Resources
http://ourworld.compuserve.com/homepages/ee/

Hispanic Heraldry
http://www.ctv.es/artes/home.htm/home.html

Spanish-English Online Dictionary
http://dictionary.travlang.org/SpanishEnglish/

HUGUENOT

Huguenot Historical Society
88 Huguenot Street
New Paltz, NY 12561
Tel: (914) 255-6738
Fax: (914) 255-0376
E-mail: hhslib@ix.netcom.com
http://www.hhs-newpaltz.org/

Huguenot Society of America/Library
122 East 58th Street
New York, NY 10022
Tel: 212-755-0592

National Huguenot Society
9033 Lyndale Avenue, S. - Suite 108
Bloomington, MN 55420-3535
Tel: 952-885-9776
http://www.huguenot.netnation.com/general/

WEBSITES:

Huguenots
http://www.geocities.com/SoHo/3809/Huguen.htm

Ireland
(See United Kingdom - U.K.)

ITALIAN

Italian Genealogical Group, Inc.
P.O. Box 626
Bethpage, NY 11714-0626
E-mail: info@italiangen.org
http://www.italiangen.org/default.stm

Italian Genealogy Society of America
P.O. Box 8571
Cranston, RI 02920-8571

Italian Historical Society of America
111 Columbia Hts
Brooklyn, NY 11201
Tel: 718-852-2929
http://www.italianhistorical.org/

WEBSITES:

Italian Genealogy Homepage
http://www.italgen.com/

Italian Surname Database
http://www.italgen.com/surnames.htm

JEWISH

American Jewish Archives
Hebrew Union College/Jewish Institute of Religion
3101 Clifton Avenue
Cincinnati, OH 45220-2488
Tel: 513-221-7444 ext. 403
Fax: 513-221-7812
E-mail: AJA@cn.huc.edu
http://www.huc.edu/aja/Archive.htm

American Jewish Historical Society
2 Thornton Road
Waltham, MA 02453
Tel: 781-891-8110
Fax: 781-899-9208
http://www.ajhs.org/

Annenberg Research Institute
420 Walnut Street
Philadelphia, PA 19106
Tel: 215-238-1290
Fax: 215-238-1540

Association of Jewish Genealogical Society (AJGS)
P.O. Box 50245
Palo Alto, CA 94303
Tel: 415-424-1622
E-mail: RWeissJGS@aol.com
http://www1.jewishgen.org/ajgs/index.html

AVOTAYNU, Inc.
PO Box 99
Bergenfield, NJ 07621
Tel: 800-AVOTAYNU (U.S. and Canada)
Fax: 201-387-2855
E-mail: info@avotaynu.com
http://www.avotaynu.com/

Holocaust Library & Research Center
557 Bedford Avenue
Brooklyn, NY 11211
Tel: 718-599-5833

Institute for Jewish Research
1048 Fifth Avenue
New York, NY 10028

International Association of Jewish Genealogical Societies
Howard Margol, President
4430 Mt. Paran Parkway NW
Atlanta, Georgia 30327-3747
E-mail: HoMargol@aol,com
http://www.jewishgen.org/ajgs/

Jewish Genealogical Society, Inc.
15 West 16th Street
New York, NY 10011
Tel: 212-294-8326
http://www.jgsny.org/

JewishGen, Inc.
2951 Marina Bay Dr., Suite 130-472
League City, TX 77573
Phone: 713-940-0605
Fax: 281-535-0036
http://www.jewishgen.org

Leo Baeck Institute
German-Jewish Families
15 West 16th St.
New York, NY 10011
Tel: (212) 744-6400
Fax: (212) 988-1305
E-mail: lbi1@lbi.com
http://www.lbi.org/

National Museum of American Jewish History
55 North 5th Street
Independence Mall East
Philadelphia, PA 19106-2197
Tel: 215-923-3811
Fax: 215-923-0763
E-mail: nmajh@nmajh.org
http://www.nmajh.org/

Philadelphia Jewish Archives Center
Balch Institute for Ethnic Studies
18 South 7th Street
Philadelphia, PA 19106-3794
Tel: 215-925-8090
Fax: (215) 925-4413
Email pjac@balchinstitute.org
http://www.libertynet.org/pjac/index.html

Simon Wiesenthal Center Library and Archives
1399 South Roxbury Drive (third floor)
Los Angeles, CA 90035-4709
Tel: 310-772-7605
Fax: 310-277-6568
E- mail: library@wiesenthal.net
http://www.wiesenthal.com/library/index.cfm

United States Holocaust Memorial Museum
100 Raoul Wallenberg Place SW
Washington DC 20024-2126
Main telephone: (202) 488-0400
http://www.ushmm.org/

Yivo Institute for Jewish Research
15 West 16th Street (Sometime in 1997)
New York, NY 10011
Tel:(212) 294-6143
Fax: (212) 292-1892
E-mail: Archives@yivo.cjh.org.
http://www.yivoinstitute.org/

WEBSITES:

Jewish Resources on the Internet
http://www.opus1.com/emol/tucson/directory/jewish.html

LUTHERAN AND EVANGELICAL

Archdiocese of the Evangelical Lutheran Church in America
5400 Milton Parkway
Rosemont, IL
Mail:
8765 W. Higgins Road
Chicago, IL 60631
Tel: 800-638-3522
773-380-2818
Fax: 773-380-1465
E-mail: archives@elca.org
http://www.elca.org/os/archives/intro.html

Evangelical Covenant Church
Archives and Special Collections of
North Park University
3225 W. Foster Avenue
Chicago, Illinois 60625-4895
Telephone: (773) 244-6224
Fax: (773) 244-4891
E-mail: eengseth@northpark.edu
http://www.campus.northpark.edu/library/archives/
default.htm

Evangelical & Reformed Church, Historical Society of
Archives
West James Street and College Avenue
Lancaster, PA 17604
Tel: 717-393-0654

Lutheran Church in American Archives
1100 East 55th Street
Chicago, IL 60615
Tel: 773-667-3500

MENNONITE

Mennonite Family History Library
10 W. Main Street
Elverson, PA 19520-0171
Tel: 610-286-0258
Fax: 610-286-6860
http://feefhs.org/men/frg-mfh.html

Mennonite Heritage Center
565 Yoder Road
P.O. Box 82
Harleysville, PA 19438
Tel: 215-256-3020
Fax: 215-256-3023
E-mail: info@mhep.org
http://www.mhep.org/heritage.html

METHODIST

The General Commission on Archives and History
The United Methodist Church
P.O. Box 127, 36 Madison Avenue, Madison NJ 07940
Phone: (973) 408-3189
FAX: (973) 408-3909
E-mail: research@gcah.org
http://www.gcah.org/index.htm

Methodist Historical Center
326 New Street
Philadelphia, PA 19106

United Methodist Archives Center
Drew University
GCAH
P.O. Box 127
Madison, NJ 07940
Tel: 973-408-3189
E-mail: dpatters@drew.edu
http://depts.drew.edu/lib/uma.html

Native American

Anchorage Museum of History & Art
121 West 7th Avenue
P.O. Box 196650
Anchorage, AK 99519-6650
Tel: 907-343-4326
Fax: 907-343-6149
http://www.ci.anchorage.ak.us/Services/Departments/
    Culture/Museum/index.html

Baranov Museum
Kodiak Historical Society
101 Marine Way
Kodiak, AK 99615
Tel: 907-486-5920
Fax: 907-486-3166

Bishop Museum and Library/Archives
1525 Bernice Street
P.O. Box 19000-A
Honolulu, HI 96817-0916
Tel: 808-848-4147/8
808-848-4182/3
Fax: 808-841-8968
http://www.bishop.hawaii.org/bishop/library/library.html
http://www.bishop.hawaii.org/bishop/archives/arch.html

Bureau of Indian Affairs
U.S. Department of the Interior
Office of Public Affairs
1849 C Street, NW - MS-4542-MIB
Washington, DC 20240-0001
Tel: 202-208-3711
Fax: 202-501-1516
http://www.doi.gov/bureau-indian-affairs.html
Genealogy Resources
http://www.doi.gov/bia/ancestry/index.htm

Dacotah Prairie Museum
21 S. Main
Aberdeen, SD 57401
Tel: 605-626-7117
Fax: 605-626-4010
http://www.brown.sd.us/museum/

Daughters of Hawaii
Queen Emma's Summer Palace
2913 Pali Highway
Honolulu, HI 96817
Tel: 808-595-6291
808-595-3167
Fax: 808-595-4395
http://www.daughtersofhawaii.org/

Mashantucket Pequot Museum and Research Center
110 Pequot Trail
PO Box 3180
Mashantucket CT 06339-3180
Archives
Tel: 860-396-7001
Fax: 860-396-7004
http://www.mashantucket.com/update/rcais.html

Mescalero Apache Cultural Center
P.O. Box 227
Mescalero, NM 88340
Tel: 505-671-4494

Native American Heritage Museum at Highland Mission
1727 Elgin Rd.
Highland, KS 66035-9801
Tel: 913-442-3304
http://www.kshs.org/places/highland.htm

Pueblo Cultural Center
2401 12th Street, NW
Albuquerque, NM 87104
Tel: 505-843-7270
800-766-4405
Fax: 505-842-6959
http://www.indianpueblo.org/

Siouxland Heritage Museum
 200 W. 6th Street
Sioux Falls, SD 57104-6001
Tel: 605-367-4210
Fax: 605-367-6004

Tanana-Yukon Historical Society
Wickersham House Museum
Alaskaland Park, Airport Way
P.O. Box 71336
Fairbanks, AK 99707
Tel: 907-474-4013
E-mail: tyhs@polarnet.com
http://www.ptialaska.net/~tyhs/

Totem Heritage Center
601 Deermont Street
(Mailing Address: 629 Dock St.)
Ketchikan, AK 99901
Tel: 907-225-5900
Fax: 907-225-5602

Trading Post Historical Society/Museum
15710 N 4th St
Pleasanton, KS 66075
Tel: 913-352-6441

UCLA American Indian Studies Center
3220 Campbell Hall
Box 951548
Los Angeles, CA 90095-1548
Tel: 310-825-7315
Fax: 310-206-7060
E-mail: aisc@ucla.edu
http://www.sscnet.ucla.edu/indian/CntrHome.html

Ute Mountain Ute Tribal Research Archives Library
Tribal Compound
Box CC
Towaoc, CO 81334
Tel: 970-565-3751 x257
Fax: 970-565-7412
http://www.swcolo.org/Tourism/IndianCulture.html

Yupiit Piciryarait Cultural Center and Museum
420 Chief Eddie Hoffman State Highway
Mailing address:
AVCP, Inc.
P.O. Box 219
Bethel, AK 99559
Tel: 907-543-1819
Fax: 907-543-3596

WEBSITES:

Broken Threads
http://homepages.rootsweb.com/~snowdawn/

Index of Native American Resources on the Internet
http://hanksville.phast.umass.edu/misc/NAresources.html

Native American Genealogy
http://members.aol.com/bbbenge/front.html

Native American Resources
http://indy4.fdl.cc.mn.us/~isk/mainmenu.html

NativeWeb
http://www.nativeweb.org/

POLISH

See Eastern European

POLYNESIAN

Polynesian Voyaging Society
Pier 7, 191 Ala Moana Blvd.
Honolulu, HI 96813
Tel: (808) 536-8405
E-mail: pvs@lava.net
http://leahi.kcc.hawaii.edu/org/pvs/

PRESBYTERIAN

Presbyterian Historical Society
425 Lombard Street
Philadelphia, PA 19147
Tel: 215-627-1852
Fax: 215-627-0509
http://www.history.pcusa.org/contents.html

QUAKER

Haverford College
Magill Library, The Quaker Collection
370 Lancaster Avenue
Haverford, PA 19041-1392
E-mail: aupton@haverford.edu
http://www.haverford.edu/library/sc/sc.html

Earlham College
Lilly Library, Friends Collection
National Road West
Richmond, IN 47374
E-mail: tomh@earlham.edu
http://www.earlham.edu/%7Elibr/quaker/

National Society of Descendants of Early Quakers
Mrs. George W. Hallgren, St.
National Corresponding Clerk, NSDEQ
PO Box 453
Abingdon, MD 21009-0453
http://www.terraworld.net/mlwinton/index.htm#quaker

WEBSITES:

Quaker Corner
http://www.rootsweb.com/~quakers/records.htm

RUSSIAN

American Historical Society of Germans from Russia
631 D Street
Lincoln, NE 68502-1199
Tel: 402-474-3363
Fax: 402-474-7229
E-mail: ahsgr@ahsgr.org
http://www.ahsgr.org/

Russian Baltic Information Center - BLITZ
907 Mission Avenue
San Rafael, CA 94901
Tel: 415-453-3579
Fax: 415-453-0343
E-mail: enute@igc.apc.org
http://dcn.davis.ca.us/go/feefhs/blitz/frgblitz.html

Germans from Russia Heritage Society
1125 W. Turnpike Ave.
Bismarck, ND 58501
Tel: (701) 223-6167
Email:grhs@btigate.com
http://www.grhs.com/

WEBSITES:

Researching Russian Roots
http://www.mtu-net.ru/rrr/

RussiaGenWeb
http://www.rootsweb.com/~ruswgw/

Russian Heraldry
http://sunsite.cs.msu.su/heraldry/

SCANDINAVIAN

American-Swedish Historical Museum
(in Franklin Delano Roosevelt Park)
1900 Pattison Avenue
Philadelphia, PA 19145
Tel: 215-389-1776
E-mail: ashm@libertynet.org
http://www.libertynet.org/~ashm/

Concordia College
Carl B. Ylvisaker Library
Moorhead, MN 56562
Tel: 218-299-4239
218-299-3241 (Archives)
E-mail: library@cord.edu
http://home.cord.edu/dept/library/

The Danish Immigrant Museum
2212 Washington Street, P O Box 470
Elk Horn, IA 51531-0470
Tel: 712-764-7001
    800-759-9192
Fax: 712-764-7002
E-mail: dkmus@netins.net
http://dkmuseum.org

Finnish-American Heritage Center
Suomi College
Hancock, MI 49930
Tel: 906-487-7367
Fax: 906-487-7383
http://www.suomi.edu/Ink/FHC.html

Finnish-American Historical Archives
Suomi College
601 Quincy Street
Hancock, MI 49930
Tel: 906-487-7273
http://www.suomi.edu/06a.html

Finnish-American Historical Society, Minnesota
P.O. Box 34
Wolf Lake, MN 56593

Norwegian American Bygdelagenes Fellesraad
c/o Marilyn Somdahl, Pres.
10129 Goodrich Circle
Bloomington, MN 55437
Tel: 612-831-4409
E-mail: rsylte@ix.netcom.com
http://www.hfaa.org/bygdelag/

Norwegian-American Historical Association (NAHA)
1510 St. Olaf Avenue
Northfield, MN 55057
Tel:(507) 646 3221
Fax: 507-646-3734
E-mail: naha@stolaf.edu
http://www.naha.stolaf.edu/about.htm

Norwegian Emigrant Museum
Akershagan
2312 Ottestad
Norway
Tel. +47 62 57 48 50
Fax. +47 62 57 48 51
E-mail: museum@emigrant.museum.no
http://www.museumsnett.no/emigrantmuseum/

Norwegian Emigration Center
Strandkaien 31
N-4005 Stavenger
Norway
Tel: +47 51 53 88 60
Fax: +47 51 53 88 63
E-mail: detnu@online.no
http://www.utvandrersenteret.no/index_eng.html

Scandinavian American Genealogical Society (SAGS)
P.O. Box 16069
St. Paul, MN 55116-0069
http://www.mtn.org/mgs/branches/sags.html

Scandinavian Genealogical Society
8143 Olney St. SE
Salem, OR 97301
Tel: 503-749-2874

Swedish-American Historical Society/Library
5125 North Spaulding Avenue
Chicago, IL 60625-4816
Phone: (773)583-5722
E-mail: info@swedishamericanhist.org
http://www.swedishamericanhist.org/index.html

Swedish-American Museum Center
5211 N. Clark Street
Chicago, IL 60640-2101
Tel: 773-728-8111
E-mail: museum@samac.org
http://www.samac.org/index1.html

Swedish Colonial Society
C/o Doriney Seagers – Registrar
371 Devon Way
West Chester, PA 19380,
E-mail: DorineySeagers@ColonialSwedes.org
http://www.colonialswedes.org/

Swedish Finn Historical Society
5410 17th Ave. NW, Room 329
Seattle, WA 98107
Mailing address:
P.O. Box 17264
Seattle, WA 98107-0964
Tel: 206-706-0738
Fax: 206-782-5813
E-mail: sfhs@gte.net
http://sfhs.eget.net/

Swenson Swedish Immigration Research Center
Augustana College
639 38th Street
Rock Island, IL 61201-2296
Tel: 309-794-7204
Fax: 309-794-7443
E-mail: sag@augustana.edu
http://www2.augustana.edu/admin/swenson/

Vesterheim Genealogical Center and Naeseth Library
415 W. Main Street
Madison, WI 53703-3116
Phone: 608-255-2224
Fax: 608-255-6842
http://www.vesterheim.org/genealogy/

WEBSITES:

Association of European Migration Institutions
http://users.cybercity.dk/~ccc13652

Danish-English Online Dictionary
http://dictionaries.travlang.com/DanishEnglish/

Finnish-English Online Dictionary
http://dictionaries.travlang.com/finnish.html

NOIS - Norway Online Information Service
How to Trace Your Ancestors in Norway
http://www.norway.org/ancestor.htm

Nordic Notes
http://www.nordicnotes.com/

Norwegian Historical Data Centre
http://draug.rhd.isv.uit.no/rhd/indexeng.html

ODIN-Ministry of Foreign Affairs
http://odin.dep.no/ud/engelsk/index-b-n-a.html

How to Trace Your Ancestors in Norway
http://odin.dep.no/ud/publ/96/ancestors/

Sogn og Fjordane-Emigration Archives
http://www.sffarkiv.no/sffeng.htm

SCOTLAND
(See United Kingdom - U.K.)

SOUTH AFRICAN

Albany Museum: Ancestry Research-Genealogy
Somerset Street
GRAHAMSTOWN, 6139
South Africa
Int.Tel: +27 46 622-2312
Int.Fax: +27 46 622-2398
E-mail: W.Jervois@ru.ac.za
http://www.ru.ac.za/departments/am/geneal.html

Genealogical Institute of South Africa
115 Banghoek Road
STELLENBOSCH
Postal Address:
P.O. Box 3033
Matieland
7602
Telephone: (021) 887 5070
Fax: (021) 887 5031
E-mail: gisa@renet.sun.ac.za
http://www.sun.ac.za/gisa/index1.htm

Genealogical Society of South Africa
Suite 143, Postnet, X2600
HOUGHTON, 2041
Republic of South Africa
http://www.rootsweb.com/~zafgssa/Eng/

WEBSITES:

Afrikaans-English Online Dictionary
http://dictionaries.travlang.com/AfrikaansEnglish/

SWISS

Swiss Mennonite Cultural and Historical Association
109 East Hirschler
Moundridge, KS 67107
Tel: 316-345-2844

Swiss Society of Genealogy Studies
E-mail: nickj@3dplus.ch
http://www.3dplus.ch/~nickj/Engl_SSEG.html

WEBSITES:

Swiss Genealogy
http://www.mindspring.com/~philipp/che.html

Swiss Genealogy on the Internet
http://www.eye.ch/swissgen/gener-e.htm

UNITED KINGDOM - U.K (INCLUDING IRELAND AND SCOTLAND)

British Heritage Society
4177 Garrick Avenue
Warren, MI 48091
Tel: 810-757-4177
E-mail: Anton_The_Lord_Hartforth@msn.com

Clan MacDuff Society of America
Barbara Huff-Duff, Society Genealogist
237 Madeline Drive
Monrovia, CA 91016-2431
E-mail: huffduff@cco.caltech.edu
http://www.crimson.com/scots_austin/macduff.htm

Family Records Centre
1 Myddelton Street
London
EC1R 1UW
Tel: 020 8392 5300
Fax: 020 8392 5286
http://www.pro.gov.uk/about/frc/

Genealogical Society of Ireland
11 Desmond Avenue
Dun Laoghaire, Dublin
Ireland
Tel: 353.1.284 2711
Fax: 353.1.285 4020
E-mail: GenSocIreland@iol.ie
http://welcome.to/GenealogyIreland

General Register Office for Scotland
New Register House
3 West Register Street
Edinburgh
Scotland
EH1 3YT
Tel: 0131 334 0380
Fax: 0131 314 4400
http://wood.ccta.gov.uk/grosweb/grosweb.nsf/pages/home

Irish-American Cultural Institute
1 Lackawanna Place
Morristown NJ 07960
Tel: 973-605-1991
Fax: 973-605-8875
E-mail: irishwaynj@aol.com
http://www.irishaci.org/index.htm

Irish-American Heritage Center Museum and Art Gallery
4626 North Knox Avenue
Chicago, IL 60630-4030
Tel: 773-282-7035
http://www.irishamhc.com/

Irish American Heritage Museum
107 Washington Avenue
Albany, NY 12210
Tel: (518) 432-6598
Fax: (518) 449-2540
http://www.irishamericanhermuseum.org/

The Irish Ancestral Research Association (TIARA
Dept. W
P.O. Box 619
Sudbury, MA 01776
http://www.tiara.ie/

Irish Family History Forum, Inc.
PO Box 67
Plainview, New York 11803-0067
516-616-3587
http://www.ifhf.org/ifhfcntct.html

Irish Genealogical Society, Intl. (IGSI)
P.O. Box 16585
St. Paul, MN 55116-0585
http://www.rootsweb.com/~irish/

Jersey Archives Service
Clarence Road
St Helier, Jersey JE2 4JY
Tel: 01534-617441
Fax: 01534-66085
http://www.jerseyheritagetrust.org/

National Library of Scotland
George IV Bridge
Edinburgh, EH1 1EW
Scotland
http://www.nls.uk/

Office for National Statistics
1 Myddelton Street
London
EC1R 1UW
Tel: 0181 392 5300
Fax: 0181 392 5307

Public Record Office (PRO)
Ruskin Avenue
Kew
Surrey
TW9 4DU
Tel: 020 8392 5200
Fax: 020 8878 8905
enquiry@pro.gov.uk
http://www.pro.gov.uk/

Scotch-Irish Society of the U.S.A.
3 Parkway, 20th Floor
Philadelphia, PA 19102

Scottish Genealogy Society
15 Victoria Terrace
Edinburgh, EH1 2JL
Scotland
Tel: +44 0131 220 3677
E-mail: info@scotsgenealogy.com
http://www.sol.co.uk/s/scotgensoc/

Society of Genealogists
14 Charterhouse Buildings
Goswell Road
London EC1M 7BA
National (020) 7251 8799
International +44 20 7251 8799
http://www.sog.org.uk/

WEBSITES:

A Little Bit of Ireland
http://members.aol.com/LABATH/irish.htm

Channel Islands Genealogy
http://www.rootsweb.com/~jfuller/ci.html

Electric Scotland; Scottish Clans
http://www.electricscotland.com/webclans/index.html

Genealogical Guide to Ireland
http://www.bess.tcd.ie/roots/prototype/genweb2.htm

GENUKI
http://www.genuki.org.uk/

Irish Family History Foundation
http://www.irishroots.net/

Irish Genealogy
http://www.genealogy.org/~ajmorris/ireland/ireland.htm

IRLGEN: Tracing Your Irish Ancestors
http://www.ireland.com/ancestor/

National Archives of Ireland
http://www.nationalarchives.ie/

Scotland Genealogy: Tracing Your Scottish Ancestry
http://www.geo.edu.ac.uk/home/Scotland/genealogy.html

Scottish Reference Information (Database)
http://www.ktb.net/~dwills/13300-scottishreference.htm

MILITARY & FEDERAL GOVERNMENT AGENCIES

MILITARY

American Battle Monuments Commission
5119-5120 Pulaski Building
Courthouse Plaza II, Suite 500
2300 Clarendon Boulevard
Arlington, VA 22201
Tel: (703) 696-6897
http://www.usabmc.com/

American Merchant Marine Museum
U.S.M.M.A.
300 Steamboat Road
Kings Point, NY 11024
Tel: 516-773-5515
http://www.usmma.edu/museum/Default.htm

American Veterans Historical Museum
P.O. Box 115
Pleasantville, NY 10570
Tel: 914-769-5297

Archdiocese for the Military Services
415 Michigan Ave. N.E.
Suite 300
Washington, DC 20017-1518
Phone: 202-269-9100
FAX: 202-269-9022
E-mail: info@milarch.org
http://www.milarch.org/

Citadel
Daniel Library
171 Moultrie Street
Charleston, SC 29409
Tel: 843-953-2569 (Reference)
Fax: 843-953-5190
E-mail: reichardtk@citadel.edu
http://www.citadel.edu/library/

Dept. of Veterans Affairs
810 Vermont Avenue, NW
Washington, DC 20420
Tel: 202-233-4000
800-827-1000
http://www.vba.va.gov/

Marine Corps Historical Center
Washington Navy Yard, Building 58
Ninth and M Streets, SE
Washington, DC 20374-0580
Tel: 202-433-3483
http://www.usmc.mil/historical.nsf/table+of+contents

Military Heritage Museum
195 Washington Avenue
Albany, NY 12205
Tel: 518-436-0103

Military Order of the Loyal Legion of the United States
1805 Pine Street
Philadelphia, PA 19103
Tel: 215-735-8196 (Civil War Library)
E-mail: YJNW42A@prodigy.com
http://suvcw.org/mollus/molid.htm

National Cemetery System
Department of Veterans Affairs
810 Vermont Avenue, NW
Washington, DC 20420
Tel: 202-273-5221
E-mail: ncscss@mail.va.gov
http://www.va.gov/cemetery/index.htm

National Guard Association of the United States
Library
One Massachusetts Avenue, NW
Washington, DC 20001
Tel: 202-789-0031
http://www.ngaus.org/

National Museum of Health and Medicine/Archives
Walter Reed Army Medical Center
6900 Georgia Avenue and Elder St., NW
Building 54
Washington D.C. 20307-5001
Tel: 202-576-2334
http://www.natmedmuse.afip.org/collections/
    collections.html

National Personnel Records Center
Military Personnel Records
9700 Page Avenue
St. Louis, MO 63132-5100
Tel: 314-538-4243 (Air Force records)
Tel: 314-538-4261 (Army records)
Tel: 314-538-4141 (Navy, Marine Corps, Coast Guard
    records)
Fax: 314-538-4175
E-mail: center@stlouis.nara.gov (General information
    only, no email requests for records)
http://www.nara.gov/regional/stlouis.html

Naval Historical Center
Washington Navy Yard
805 Kidder Breese SE
Washington, D.C. 20374-5060
Library:
Tel: 202-433-4132
Fax: 202-433-9553
Museum:
Tel: 202-433-4882
Fax: 202-433-8200
Operational Archives:
Tel: (202) 433-3224
Fax: 202-433-2833
Ships History Branch:
Tel: 202-433-3643
Fax: 202-433-6677
http://www.history.navy.mil/

U.S. Air Force Historical Research Agency
Mail:
HQ AFHRA/RSA
600 Chennault Circle
Maxwell AFB, AL 36112-6424
Phone: (334) 953-2395
E-mail: AFHRANEWS@maxwell.af.mil
http://www.au.af.mil/au/afhra/

U.S. Army Center of Military History
Location:
Building 35
102 Fourth Avenue
Fort McNair
Washington, DC
Mail:
103 Third Avenue
Fort McNair, DC 20319-5058
Tel: 202-761-5413
E-mail: cmhweb@cmh-smtp.army.mil
http://www.army.mil/cmh-pg/

U.S. Army Command & General Staff College
Combined Arms Research Library
Attn: Ed Burgess
250 Gibbon Avenue
Fort Leavenworth, KS 66027
Tel: 913-758-3053
DSN 720-3155
http://www-cgsc.army.mil/carl/index.htm

U.S. Army Military History Institute
22 Ashburn Drive, Carlisle Barracks
Carlisle, PA 17013
Tel: 1-717-245-3971
FAX: 1-717-245-3711
http://carlisle-www.army.mil/usamhi/

U.S. Army Publications Center
2800 Eastern Boulevard
Baltimore, MD 21220-2896
Tel: 410-671-2272

U.S. Coast Guard Academy
Fifteen Mohegan Avenue
New London, CT 06320-4195
Tel: 860- 444-8511

U.S. Coast Guard Historian's Office (G-IPA-4)
 2100 2nd Street, SW
Washington, DC 20593
Tel: 202-267-0948
E-mail: rbrowning@comdt.uscg.mil
    sprice@comdt.uscg.mil
http://www.uscg.mil/hq/g-cp/history/collect.html

U.S. Maritime Administration
Department of Transportation
400 7th Street, SW
Washington, DC 20590
1-800-99-MARAD
E-mail: pao.marad@marad.dot.gov
http://marad.dot.gov/index.html

U.S. Military Academy/Museum and Archives
Olmsted Hall
Pershing Center
West Point, NY 10996-2099
Tel: (845) 938-2203/3590
E-mail: museum@www.usma.edu
http://www.usma.edu/Museum

U.S. Naval Academy
Nimitz Library
589 McNair Road
Annapolis, MD 21402-5029
Tel: 410-293-2220 (Special Collections)
410-293-2178 (Archives)
E-mail: cummings@nadn.navy.mil
http://www.nadn.navy.mil/Library

U.S. Naval Institute
U.S. Naval Academy Campus
291 Wood Road
Annapolis, MD 21402
Tel: 410-268-6110
Fax: 410-269-7940
http://www.usni.org/

U.S. Naval War College/Library
Code 1E3
686 Cushing Road
Newport, RI 02841-1207
Tel: 401-841-1435
401-841-3397
401-841-4345 (Government Documents)
E-mail: libref@nwc.navy.mil
http://www.nwc.navy.mil/

WEBSITES:

Army Awards and Decorations
http://www.usarotc.com/awards.htm

American Civil War-Resources on the Internet
http://www.dsu.edu/~jankej/civilwar.html

Master Index of Army Records
http://www.army.mil/cmh-pg/reference/records.htm

Medals of Honor Index
(List of Medal of Honor recipient by conflict with information about each honoree)
http://www.army.mil/cmh-pg/moh1.htm

U.S. Civil War Center
http://www.cwc.lsu.edu/

U.S. Internet Genealogical Society
http://www.usigs.org/library/military/index.htm

FEDERAL GOVERNMENT AGENCIES

Bureau of Indian Affairs
U.S. Department of the Interior
Office of Public Affairs
1849 C Street, NW - MS-4542-MIB
Washington, DC 20240-0001
Tel: 202-208-3711
Fax: 202-501-1516
http://www.doi.gov/bureau-indian-affairs.html
Genealogy Resources
http://www.doi.gov/bia/ancestry/index.htm

Bureau of Land Management (Headquarters)
1849 C Street
Washington, DC 20240
Phone: (202) 452-5125
Fax: (202) 452-5124
http://www.blm.gov/nhp/index.htm

Dept. of Veterans Affairs
810 Vermont Avenue, NW
Washington, DC 20420
Tel: 202-233-4000
800-827-1000
http://www.va.gov/

Office of Information and Privacy
 Suite 570, Flag Building
Department of Justice
Washington, D.C. 20530-0001
Tel: (202) 514-FOIA
http://www.usdoj.gov/oip/oip.html

Government Printing Office (GPO)
Washington, DC 20401
Tel: 888-293-6498
202-512-1530
Fax: 202-512-1262
E-mail: gpoaccess@gpo.gov
http://www.access.gpo.gov/
GPO Access Databases
http://www.access.gpo.gov/su_docs/aces/aaces003.html

Immigration and Naturalization Service (INS)
Historical Reference Library
425 I Street, NW
Room 5304
Washington, DC 20536
Tel: 800-755-0777
800-870-3676 (To request forms)
202-514-2837
http://www.ins.usdoj.gov/
Forms Download
www.ins.usdoj.gov/graphics/formsfee/forms/index.htm
Request Forms by Mail
http://www.ins.usdoj.gov/graphics/exec/forms/index.asp

INS REGIONAL OFFICES

Alaska
620 East 10th Avenue
Anchorage, AK 99501-7581

Arizona
2035 N. Central Avenue
Phoenix, AZ 85004

California
865 Fulton Mall
Fresno, CA 93721-2816

California
Chet Holifield Federal Building
24000 Avila Road
P.O. Box 30080
Laguna Niguel, CA 92607-0080

California
300 North Los Angeles Street
Los Angeles, CA 90012

California
650 Capitol Mall
Sacramento, CA 95814

California
880 Front Street
San Diego, CA 92188

California
630 Sansome Street
San Francisco, CA 94111-2280

California
280 South First Street, Room 1150
San Jose, CA 95113

Colorado
Albrook Center
4730 Paris Street
Denver, CO 80239-2804

Connecticut
Ribicoff Federal Building
450 Main Street
Hartford, CT 06103-3060

Florida
400 West Bay Street, Room G-18
P.O. Box 35029
Jacksonville, FL 32202

Florida
7880 Biscayne Blvd.
Miami, FL 33138

Florida
5509 W. Gray Street, Suite 113
Tampa, FL 33609

Georgia
77 Forsyth Street, SW
Room 284
Atlanta, GA 30303

Guam
801 Pacific News Building
238 O'Hara Street
Agana, Guam 96910

Hawaii
595 Ala Moana Blvd.
Honolulu, HI 96813

Illinois
10 West Jackson Blvd., 2nd Floor
Chicago, IL 60604

Indiana
Gateway Plaza
950 North Meridian, Suite 400
Indianapolis, IN 46204

Kentucky
Gene Snyder Courthouse
601 West Broadway
Louisville, KY 40202

Louisiana
Postal Service Building
701 Loyola Avenue, Room T-8005
New Orleans, LA 70113

Maine
176 Gannett Drive
South Portland, ME 04106

Maryland
Fallon Federal Building
31 Hopkins Plaza
Baltimore, MD 21201

Massachusetts
JFK Federal Building
Government Center
Boston, MA 02203

Michigan
Federal Building
333 Mt. Elliott Street
Detroit, MI 48207-4381

Minnesota
2901 Metro Drive, Suite 100
Bloomington, MN 55425

Minnesota
Bishop Henry Whipple Federal Building
One Federal Drive
Fort Snelling, MN 55111-4007

Missouri
9747 North Conant Avenue
Kansas City, MO 64153

Missouri
Robert A. Young Federal Building
1222 Spruce Street, Room 1100
St. Louis, MO 63101-2815

Montana
2800 Skyway Drive
Helena, MT 59602

Nebraska
3736 South 132nd Street
Omaha, NE 68144

Nebraska
Northern Service Center
850 S. Street
Lincoln, NE 68508

Nevada
3373 Pepper Lane
Las Vegas, NV 89120

Nevada
1351 Corporate Boulevard
Reno, NV 89502

New Jersey
Federal Building
970 Broad Street
Newark, NJ 07102

New Mexico
1720 Randolph Road SE
Albuquerque, NM 87106

New York
James T. Foley Federal Courthouse
445 Broadway, Room 220
Albany, NY 12207

New York
130 Delaware Avenue
Buffalo, NY 14202

New York
26 Federal Plaza
New York, NY 10278

North Carolina
210 E. Woodlawn Road
Building 6, Suite 138
Charlotte, NC 28217

Ohio
J.W. Peck Federal Building
550 Main Street, Room 4001
Cincinnati, OH 45202

Ohio
Anthony Celebreeze
Federal Building
1240 East 9th Street, Room 1917
Cleveland, OH 44199

Oklahoma
4149 Highline Blvd., Suite 300
Oklahoma City, OK 73108

Oregon
Federal Office Building
511 NW Broadway
Portland, OR 97209

Pennsylvania
1600 Callowhill Street
Philadelphia, PA 19130

Pennsylvania
Federal Building, Room 2130
1000 Liberty Avenue
Pittsburgh, PA 15222

Puerto Rico
P.O. Box 365068
San Juan, PR 00936

Rhode Island
200 Dyer Street
Providence, RI 02903

Tennessee
Suite 100
1341 Sycamore View Road
Memphis, TN 38134

Texas
8101 North Stemmons Freeway
Dallas, TX 75247

Texas
700 E. San Antonio Street
P.O. Box 9398
El Paso, TX 79984

Texas
1545 Hawkins Blvd., Suite 170
El Paso, TX 79925

Texas
P.O. Box 152122
Irving, TX 75105-0212

Texas
2102 Teege Road
Harlingen, TX 78550

Texas
126 Northpoint
Houston, Texas 77060

Texas
8940 Fourwinds Drive
San Antonio, TX 78239

Utah
5272 South College Drive
Murray, UT 84123

Vermont
Eastern Service Center
75 Lower Welden Street
St. Albans, VT 05479-0001

Vermont
70 Kimball Avenue
South Burlington, VT 05403-6813

Virginia
5280 Henneman Drive
Norfolk, VA 23513

Virginia
4420 North Fairfax Drive
Arlington, VA 22203

Washington
815 Airport Way, South
Seattle, WA 98134

Washington
691 U.S. Courthouse Building
Spokane, WA 99201

Wisconsin
517 E. Wisconsin Avenue
Milwaukee, WI 53202

Passport Office
Dept. of State
1111 19th Street, NW
Suite 200
Washington, DC 20524
Tel: 202-647-0518
http://travel.state.gov/passport_services.html

Social Security Administration
4 M 5 South Block
FOIA
300 N. Greene St.
Baltimore MD 21201
Tel: 410-965-1727
http://www.ssa.gov/
http://www.ssa.gov/foia/foia_guide.html

U.S. Census Bureau
1201 E. Tenth Street
P.O. Box 1545
Jeffersonville, IN 47132
Tel: (812) 218-3046
http://www.census.gov/
Census records after 1920

U.S. Geological Survey
Tel: 1-888-ASK-USGS
Fax on Demand: 703-648-4888
http://www.usgs.gov/

USGS REGIONAL LIBRARIES

U.S. Geological Survey Library
950 National Center
12201 Sunrise Valley
Reston, VA 20192
 Tel: 703-648-4302 (Reference)
703-648-6080 (History Project)
Fax: 703-648-6373
TDD: 703-648-4105
E-mail: library@usgs.gov
http://library.usgs.gov/reslib.html

U.S. Geological Survey Library
345 Middlefield Road, MS 955
Menlo Park, CA 94025-3591
Tel: (650) 329-5027
    Fax: 650-329-5132
TDD: 650-329-5094
E-mail: men_lib@usgs.gov
http://library.usgs.gov/menlib.html

U.S. Geological Survey Library
2255 N. Gemini Drive
Flagstaff, AZ 86001
Tel: 520-556-7272
Fax: 520-556-7156
E-mail: flag_lib@usgs.gov
http://library.usgs.gov/flaglib.html

U.S. Geological Survey Library
Denver Federal Center, Building 20
Box 25046, MS 914
Denver, CO 80225-0046
Tel: 303-236-1000
Fax: 303-236-0015
TDD: 303-236-0998
E-mail: dcn_lib@usgs.gov
http://library.usgs.gov/denlib.html

USGS Mapping Information: Geographic Names Information System
Online Data Base Query Form
http://geonames.usgs.gov/gnisform.html

U.S. Patent and Trademark Office Library
Crystal Park 3, Room 2C02
Washington, DC 20231
Tel: 800-786-9199 or 703-308-4357
Fax: 703-306-2654
URL;http://www.uspto.gov/web/offices/ac/ido/ptdl/
    index.html

Searchable Patent Database 1976-1997
http://www.uspto.gov/patft/index.html

NATIONAL ARCHIVES AND RECORDS ADMINISTRATION

National Archives and Records Administration (NARA)
Archives I
700 Pennsylvania Avenue, NW
Washington, DC 20408
Tel: 202-501-5410 (Genealogical Staff)
202-501-5400 (Record Availability)
Fax: 301-713-6905 (Fax-on-Demand Information)
E-mail: inquire@arch2.nara.gov
http://www.nara.gov/nara/dc/Archives1_directions.html

National Archives and Records Administration (NARA)
Archives II
8601 Adelphi Road
College Park, MD 20740
Tel: 202-501-5400 (Record Availability)
301-713-6800 (General Reference)
301-713-7040 (Cartographic Reference)
Fax: 301-713-6905 (Fax-on-Demand Information)
E-mail: inquire@arch2.nara.gov
http://www.nara.gov/nara/dc/Archives2_directions.html

NATIONAL RECORDS CENTERS

National Personnel Records Centers, NARA
http://www.nara.gov/regional/stlouis.html

Civilian Records Facility
111 Winnebago Street
St. Louis, MO 63118-4126
Tel: 314-538-5761
Fax: 314-425-5719
E-mail: center@cpr.nara.gov
http://www.nara.gov/regional/cpr.html

Military Records Facility
9700 Page Avenue
St. Louis, MO 63132-5100
Recorded Information Lines
314-538-4243 Air Force
314-538-4261 Army
314-538-4141 Navy/Marine/Coast Guard
Fax: 314-538-4175
E-mail: center@stlouis.nara.gov
http://www.nara.gov/regional/mpr.html

Pittsfield Federal Records Center, NARA
10 Conte Drive
Pittsfield, Massachusetts 01201-8230
Tel: 413-445-6885
Fax: 413-445-7305
E-mail: center@pittsfield.nara.gov
http://www.nara.gov/regional/pittsfie.html

Washington National Records Center, NARA
4205 Suitland Road
Suitland, MD 20746-8001
Tel: 301-457-7000
Fax: 301-457-7117
E-mail: center@suitland.nara.gov
http://www.nara.gov/records/wnrc.html

REGIONAL ARCHIVES

National Archives-Pacific Alaska Region (Anchorage)
654 W. Third Avenue
Anchorage, AK 99501-2145
Tel: 907-271-2443
Fax: 907-271-2442
E-mail: archives@alaska.nara.gov
http://www.nara.gov/regional/anchorag.html (Alaska)

National Archives-Central Plains Region
2312 East Bannister Road
Kansas City, MO 64131
Tel: 816-926-6920
Fax: 816-926-6982
E-mail: center@kansascity.nara.gov |
http://www.nara.gov/regional/kansas.html
(Iowa, Kansas, Minnesota, Missouri, Nebraska, North
    Dakota, and South Dakota)

National Archives-Great Lakes Region (Chicago)
7358 Pulaski Road
Chicago, IL 60629-5898
Tel: 773-581-7816
Fax: 312-886-7883
E-mail: chicago.archives@nara.gov
http://www.nara.gov/regional/chicago.html
(Illinois, Indiana, Michigan, Minnesota, Ohio, and
    Wisconsin)

National Archives-Mid Atlantic Region
900 Market Street
Philadelphia, PA 19107
Tel: 215-597-3000
Fax: 215-597-2303
E-mail: archives@philarch.nara.gov
http://www.nara.gov/regional/philacc.html
(Delaware, Maryland, Pennsylvania, Virginia, and West
    Virginia)

National Archives-Northeast Region (Boston)
Frederick C. Murphy Federal Center
380 Trapelo Road
Waltham, MA 02452-6399
Tel: 781-647-8104
Fax: 781-647-8088
E-mail: center@waltham.nara.gov
http://www.nara.gov/regional/boston.html
(Connecticut, Maine, Massachusetts, New Hampshire,
    Rhode Island, and Vermont)

National Archives-Northeast Region (New York)
201 Varick Street
New York, NY 10014
Tel: 212-337-1300
Fax: 212-337-1306
E-mail: archives@newyork.nara.gov
http://www.nara.gov/regional/newyork.html
(New Jersey, New York, Puerto Rico, and U.S. Virgin
    Islands)

National Archives-Pacific Alaska Region (Seattle)
6125 Sand Point Way, NE
Seattle, WA 98115-7999
Tel: 206-526-6501
Fax: 206-526-6575
E-mail: center@seattle.nara.gov
http://www.nara.gov/regional/seattle.html
(Idaho, Oregon, and Washington)

National Archives-Pacific Region (Laguna Niguel)
24000 Avila Road, First Floor-East Entrance
Laguna Niguel, California 92677-3497
P. O. Box 6719
Laguna Niguel, California 92607-6719
Tel: 949-360-2641
Fax: 949-360-2624
E-mail: archives@laguna.nara.gov
www.nara.gov/regional/laguna.html
(Arizona, Southern California, and Clark County, NV)

National Archives-Pacific Region (San Francisco)
1000 Commodore Drive
San Bruno, CA 94066
Tel: 650-876-9009
Fax: 650-876-9233
E-mail: archives@sanbruno.nara.gov
http://www.nara.gov/regional/sanfranc.html
(Northern California, Hawaii, Nevada-Except Clark
    County
Guam, American Samoa, and the Trust Territory of the
    Pacific Islands)

National Archives-Rocky Mountain Region
Building 48, Denver Federal Center
West 6th Avenue and Kipling Street
Denver, Colorado 80225
P. O. Box 25307
Denver, Colorado 80225-0307
Tel: 303-236-0804
Fax: 303-236-9297
E-mail: archives@denver.nara.gov
www.nara.gov/regional/denver.html
(Colorado, Montana, New Mexico, North Dakota, South
    Dakota, Utah, and Wyoming)

National Archives-Southeast Region
1557 St. Joseph Ave.
East Point, GA 30344-2593
Tel: 404-763-7474
Fax: 404-763-7059
E-mail: center@atlanta.nara.gov
www.nara.gov/regional/atlanta.html
(Alabama, Florida, Georgia, Kentucky, Mississippi, North
    Carlina, South Carolina, and Tennessee)

National Archives-Southwest Region
501 West Felix Street, Building 1
Fort Worth, Texas 76115-3405
P. O. Box 6216
Fort Worth, Texas 76115-0216
Telephone: 817-334-5525
Fax: 817-334-5621
E-mail: archives@ftworth.nara.gov
www.nara.gov/regional/ftworth.html
(Arkansas, Oklahoma, Louisiana, and Texas)

HELPFUL NARA WEBSITES

American Indians
http://www.nara.gov/publications/microfilm/amerindians/
indians.html

Black Studies
http://www.nara.gov/publications/microfilm/blackstudies/
blackstd.html

Census Records
http://www.nara.gov/publications/microfilm/census.html

Genealogical and Biographical Research
http://www.nara.gov/publications/microfilm/biographical/

Genealogical Searchable Database-NAIL
http://www.nara.gov/nara/nail/nailgen.html

Genealogy Page
http://www.nara.gov/genealogy/genindex.html

Immigrant and Passenger Arrivals
http://www.nara.gov/publications/microfilm/immigrant/

Microfilm Resources for Research
http://www.nara.gov/publications/microfilm/comprehensive/

Military Service Records
http://www.nara.gov/publications/microfilm/military.html

Naturalization Records
http://www.nara.gov/genealogy/natural.html

Post Office Records
http://www.nara.gov/genealogy/postal.html

Soundex Machine
http://www.nara.gov/genealogy/soundex/soundex.html

HELPFUL GENEALOGY WEBSITES

1895 Atlas Project
http://www.livgenmi.com/1895.htm

American Civil War Homepage
http://sunsite.utk.edu/civil-war/

American Immigrant Wall of Honor
http://www.wallofhonor.com/

Ancestry.com
http://www.ancestry.com/

The Attic-Genealogy Resources
http://www.geocities.com/TheTropics/1127/attic.html

Barrel of Genealogical Links
http://cpcug.org/user/jlacombe/mark.html

Biographical Database
http://s9.com/biography/

Calendar Index
http://www.earth.com/calendar

Cemetery Internment Lists on the Internet
http://www.interment.net/

Charlotte's Web Genealogical Gleanings
http://www.charweb.org/gen/

Charts for Reference in Genealogy Research
http://members.tripod.com/~Silvie/charts.html

Christine's Genealogy Website
http://ccharity.com/

Concentration of Surnames
http://www.hamrick.com/names/index.html

Cyndi's List of Genealogical Sites
http://www.cyndislist.com/

Directory of Underground Railroad Operators
http://www.ugrr.org/ur-names.htm

Emigration/Ships Lists and Resources
www.geocities.com/Heartland/5978/Emigration.html

FGS Society Hall
http://www.familyhistory.com/societyhall/main.asp

Genealogical Resources on the Internet
http://www.tc.umn.edu/~pmg/genealogy.html

Genealogical Websites of Societies and CIGs
http://genealogy.org/PAF/www/gwsc/

Genealogy Exchange & Surname Registry
http://www.genexchange.org/

Genealogy Home Page
http://genhomepage.com/

Genealogy.org
http://genealogy.emcee.com/

Genealogy's Most Wanted
http://www.citynet.net/mostwanted/

Geneanet (Surname Database)
http://www.geneanet.org/

Helms Genealogy Toolbox
http://www.genealogytoolbox.com/

International Internet Genealogical Society
http://www.iigs.org/

Land Records
http://www.ultranet.com/~deeds/

Library Card Catalogs
http://library.usask.ca/hytelnet/
http://www.libdex.com/

Lineages, Inc.
http://www.lineagesnet.com/

Mailing Lists, from Genealogy Resources on the Internet
http://www.rootsweb.com/~jfuller/gen_mail.html

Mapquest
http://www.mapquest.com/

Maritime History on the Internet
http://ils.unc.edu/maritime/home.shtml

Maritime History Virtual Archives
http://pc-78-120.udac.se:8001/WWW/Nautica/Nautica.html

Newsletter Library
http://pub.savvy.com/

Olive Tree
http://olivetreegenealogy.com/index.shtml

Online Genealogical Databases
http://www.gentree.com/

Oregon-California Trails Association
http://calcite.rocky.edu/octa3/octahome.htm

Political Graveyard
http://www.potifos.com/tpg/index.html

Railroad Historical
http://www.rrhistorical.com/index.html

Rand Genealogical Group
http://www.rand.org/personal/Genea

Rootsweb
http://www.rootsweb.com/

Roots-L Resources (State by state listings for resources)
http://www.rootsweb.com/roots-l/usa.html

Soundex Machine
http://www.nara.gov/genealogy/soundex/soundex.html

Travlang's Translating Dictionaries
http://dictionaries.travlang.com/

U.S. GenWeb Project
http://www.usgenweb.org/

U.S. Internet Genealogical Society
http://www.usigs.org/index.htm

WorldGenWeb
http://worldgenweb.org/

DIRECTORIES

555-1212
http://www.555-1212.com/

Big Book
http://www.bigbook.com/

Internet Address Finder
http://www.iaf.net/

NAIS Private Investigator's Link List (Lots of directories, search engines, and other goodies)
http://www.pimall.com/nais/links.html

Netscape White Pages
http://home.netscape.com/netcenter/whitepages.html?cp
=hop03hs8

Switchboard
http://www.switchboard.com/

Telephone Directories on the Net
http://www.procd.com/hl/direct.htm

Ultimate Directory - Infospace
http://www.infospace.com/

WhoWhere
http://www.whowhere.lycos.com/Phone

Yahoo People Search
http://www.yahoo.com/search/people/email.html

Yahoo's City to County Locator
http://local.yahoo.com/bin/get_local/

SEARCH ENGINES

Alta Vista
http://altavista.digital.com/

DejaNews
http://www.dejanews.com/

Excite
http://www.excite.com/

Hot Bot
http://www.hotbot.com/

Lycos
http://www.lycos.com/

Metacrawler
http://www.metacrawler.com/

NAIS Private Investigator's Link List (Lots of directories, search engines, and other goodies)
http://www.pimall.com/nais/links.html

Search Center
http://humansearch.w1.com/

Webcrawler
http://webcrawler.com

Yahoo
http://www.yahoo.com/

ALABAMA

ARCHIVES, STATE & NATIONAL

Alabama Department of Archives & History
624 Washington Avenue
Montgomery, AL
Mail to:
P.O. Box 300100
Montgomery AL 36130-0100
Tel: 334-242-4435
Fax: 334-240-3433
http://www.archives.state.al.us/index.html

National Archives-Southeast Region
1557 St. Joseph Ave.
East Point, GA 30344-2593
Tel: 404-763-7474
Fax: 404-763-7059
E-mail: center@atlanta.nara.gov
http://www.nara.gov/regional/atlanta.html

GENEALOGICAL SOCIETIES

Alabama Genealogical Society
AGS Depository and Headquarters
Samford University Library
Box 2296
800 Lakeshore Drive
Birmingham, AL 35229-0001

AlaBenton Genealogical Society
c/o Anniston-Calhoun Public Library, The Alabama Room
P.O. Box 308
Anniston, AL 36202
http://www.anniston.lib.al.us/alabenton.htm

Autauga Genealogical Society
P.O. Box 680668
Prattville, AL 36067-0668
http://www.rootsweb.com/~alags/

Baldwin County Genealogical Society
c/o Foley Public Library
319 East Laurel Avenue
Foley, AL 36535
334-937-9464

Birmingham Genealogical Society
P.O. Box 2432
Birmingham, AL 35201
http://www.birminghamgenealogy.org/

Butler County Historical and Genealogical Society
P.O. Box 561
Greenville, AL 36037

Central Alabama Genealogical Society
P.O. Box 125
Selma, AL 36701

Civil War Descendants Society
P.O. Box 233
Athens, AL 35611

Coosa River Valley Historical & Genealogical Society
P.O. Box 295
Centre, AL 35960

DeKalb County Genealogical Society
P. O. Box 681087
Fort Payne, AL 35968-1612
http://www.webspawner.com/users/dekalbsociety/

Genealogical Society of East Alabama
P.O. Drawer 1351
Auburn, AL 36830

Genealogical Society of Washington County
P.O. Box 399
Chatom, AL 36518
Tel: 334-847-3156
 or 334-847-2286
http://members.aol.com/JORDANJM2/WCGS.html

Lamar County Genealogical & Historical Society
P.O. Box 357, Hwy. 17
Vernon, AL 35592

Limestone County Genealogical Society
c/o Limestone County Historical Society
The Donnell House
601 South Clinton Street
P.O. Box 82
Athens, AL 35611

Lowndes County Historical and Genealogical Society
P.O. Box 266
Hayneville, AL 36040

Marengo County Genealogical Society
c/o Demopolis Public Library
2111 East Washington Street
Demopolis, AL 36732

Marion County Genealogical Society
P.O. Drawer O
Winfield, AL 35594

Mobile Genealogical Society
P.O. Box 6224
Mobile, AL 36660-6224
Tel: 334-432-MGS-4
E-mail: tjk5405@zebra.net
http://www.siteone.com/clubs/mgs/

Montgomery Genealogical Society, Inc.
P.O. Box 230194
Montgomery, AL 36123-0194
http://www.rootsweb.com/~almgs/

Morgan County Genealogical Society
624 Bank St.
Decatur, Al. 35601
http://pweb.netcom.com/~mocoarch/genealogy.html

Natchez Trace Genealogical Society
P.O. Box 420
Florence, AL 35631-0420

North Alabama Genealogical Society
3327 Danville Road, SW
Decatur, AL 35603-9027

North Central Alabama Genealogical Society
P.O. Box 13
Cullman, AL 35056-0013
http://home.hiwaay.net/~lthurman/society.htm

Northeast Alabama Genealogical Society
P.O. Box 8268
Gadsden, AL 35902
E-mail: AlwaysPS@aol.com
http://www.geocities.com/Heartland/Ranch/5952/

Pea River Historical and Genealogical Society
109 South Main
Enterprise, AL 36330

Pickens County Genealogical Society
P.O. Box 336
Gordo, AL 35466

Piedmont Historical and Genealogical Society
P.O. Box 47
Spring Garden, AL 36275

Pike County Historical & Genealogical Society
c/o Mrs. Karen C. Bullard, Treasurer
4041 Country Road 59
Troy, AL 36079

Rutherford Genealogical Society Online
14291 Hunter Road
Harvest, AL 35749
Tel: 256-233-3176

Sons and Daughters of the Province and Republic of West Florida
P.O. Box 82672
Baton Rouge, LA 70884-2672
http://cust2.iamerica.net/mmoore/sonsdau.htm

Southeast Alabama Genealogical Society (SEAGS)
P.O. Box 246
Dothan, Ala. 36302-0245

Southern Society of Genealogists
P.O. Box 295
Centre, AL 35960

Tennessee Valley Genealogical Society
P.O. Box 1568
Huntsville, AL 35807
http://hiwaay.net/~white/TVGS/tvgs.html

Tuscaloosa Genealogical Society
P.O. Box 020802
Tuscaloosa, AL 35402-0802

Walker County Genealogical Society
P.O. Box 3408
Jasper, AL 35502

Winston County Genealogical Society
P.O. Box 112
Double Springs, Al. 35553

HISTORICAL SOCIETIES

Alabama Historical Association
P.O. Box 2877
Tuscaloosa, AL 35486

Alabama Historical Commission
468 South Perry Street
P.O. Box 300900
Montgomery, AL 36130-0900
http://www.preserveala.org/

Arab Historical Society
Rt. 4, Box 418C
Arab, AL 35016

Auburn Heritage Association
P.O. Box 2248
Auburn, AL 36830

Autauga County Heritage Association
102 E. Main Street
Prattville, AL 36067

Baldwin County Historical Society
P.O. Box 69
Stockton, AL 36579

Bibb County Heritage Association
Route 1, Box 147
Brierfield, AL 35035

Birmingham Historical Society
1 Sloss Quarter
Birmingham, AL 35203

Blount County Historical Society
P.O. Box 45
Oneonta, AL 35121

Blount County Memorial Museum
204 2nd Street N.
Oneonta, AL 35121-1740
Tel: 205-625-6905

Blountsville Historical Society
P.O. Box 399
Blountsville, AL 35031
(205) 429-2535

Bullock County Historical Society
P.O. Box 663
Union Springs, AL 36089

**Butler County Historical and Genealogical
Society/Library**
309 Fort Dale Street
Greenville, AL 36037

Chilton County Historical Society and Archives, Inc.
Chilton/Clanton Public Library
P.O. Box 644
Clanton, Al 35046-0644

Citronelle Historical Preservation Society
18990-19000 South Center Street
P.O. Box 384
Citronelle, AL 36522

Clarke County Historical Society
P.O. Box 131
Jackson, AL 36545
Phone: 334-275-8684

Clay County Historical Society
P.O. Box 997
Ashland, Alabama 36251

Cleburne County Historical Society
120 Vickery St.
Room 105
Heflin, AL 36264

Coosa County Historical Society
P.O. Box 5
Rockford, AL 35136

Coosa River Valley Historical & Genealogical Society
P.O. Box 295
Centre, AL 35960

Covington County Historical Society
P.O. Box 1582
Andalusia, AL 36420

Cullman County Historical Society
1505 Pinecrest NW
Cullman, AL 35055

Dale County Historical Society
c/o Judge Val McGee
P.O. Box 1231
Ozark, AL 36361

Elmore County Historical Society
1384 Jug Factory Road
Wetumpka AL 36092

Escambia County Historical Society
P.O. Box 276
Brewton, AL 36427
Tel: 334-867-7382
E-mail: eschistsoc@acet.net

Etowah County Historical Society
P.O. Box 8131
Gadsden, Al 35901

Eufaula Heritage Association, Inc.
340 North Eufaula Avenue
P.O. Box 486
Eufaula, AL 36027-0846
http://www.snowhill.com/~clr/pilg/index.html

Fayette County Historical Society
P.O. Box 309
Fayette, AL 35555-0309

Geneva County Historical Society
P.O. Box 27
Geneva, AL 36340

Greene County Historical Society
P.O. Box 746
Eutaw, AL 35462

Henry County Historical Society
c/o Abbeville Memorial Library, History Room
P.O. Box 222
Abbeville, AL 36310

Historic Mobile Preservation Society, Inc.
300 Oakleigh Place
Mobile, AL 36604

Historic Chattahoochee Commission
P.O. Box 33
Eufaula, AL 36027
http://www.hcc-al-ga.org/index1.cfm

Hueytown Historical Society
310 South Parkway
Hueytown, AL 35023
http://www.hueytown.org/historical/

Jackson County Historical Association
P.O. Box 1494
Scottsboro, AL 35768

Lee County Historical Society
P.O. Box 206
Loachapoka, AL 36865

Limestone County Historical Society
The Donnell House
601 South Clinton Street
P.O. Box 82
Athens, AL 35611

**Lowndes County Historical
and Genealogical Society**
P.O. Box 266
Hayneville, AL 36040

The Montgomery County Historical Society
512 South Court Street, P. O. Box 1829
Montgomery, Alabama, 36102
Tel: 334-264-1837
Fax: 334-834-9292
http://www.mindspring.com/~mchs/#menu

Pea River Historical and Genealogical Society
P.o. Box 310628
108 South Main Street
Enterprise, Alabama 36331-0628
Tel:(334) 393-2901
Fax: (334)393-8204
http://www.rootsweb.com/~alprhgs/

Perry Co. Historical and Preservation Society
P.O. Box 257
Marion 36756

Piedmont Historical and Genealogical Society
P.O. Box 47
Spring Garden, AL 36275

Pike County Historical & Genealogical Society
c/o Mrs. Karen C. Bullard, Treasurer
4041 Country Road 59
Troy, AL 36079.

Russell County Historical Commission
801 Dillingham Street
Seale, AL 36875

Saint Clair Historical Society
c/o Ashville Museum and Archives
P.O. Box 1570
Ashville, Alabama 35953

**Selma-Dallas County Historical and Preservation
Society**
719 Tremont St
Selma, AL 36701

Shelby County Historical Society
1854 Old Courthouse
P.O. Box 457
Columbiana, AL 35051
Tel: 205-669-3912
http://www.rootsweb.com/~alshelby/schs.html

Society of Pioneers of Montgomery, Inc.
P.O. Box 413
Montgomery, AL 36101

Southern Society of Genealogists, Inc.
Stewart University
P.O. Box 295
Centre, AL 35960

Talladega County Historical Association
106 Broome Street
Talladega, AL 35160

Tennessee Valley Historical Society
P.O. Box 149
Sheffield, AL 35660
http://home.hiwaay.net/~krjohn/

Washington County Historical Society
P.O. Box 456
Chatom, AL 36518
http://members.aol.com/JORDANJM2/WCHS.htm

LDS Family History Centers

For locations of Family History Centers in this state, see the Family History Center locator at FamilySearch: www.familysearch.org/eng/Library/FHC/frameset_fhc.asp

Archives/Libraries/Museums

Abbeville Memorial Library
301 Kirkland Street
Abbeville, AL 36310
Tel: 334-585-2818

Aliceville Public Library
416 3rd Avenue North
Aliceville, AL 35442
Tel: 205-373-6691
E-mail: apl@pickens.net
http://www.pickens.net/~apl/

Andalusia Public Library
212 S. Three Notch Street
Andalusia, AL 36420-3799
Tel: 334-222-6612
http://www.andylibrary.com/

Anniston Calhoun County Public Library
(Liles Memorial Library)
The Alabama Room
108 E. 10th Street
P.O. Box 308
Anniston, AL 36202-0308
Tel: 205-237-8501
E-mail: tracks@prodigy.net
http://www.anniston.lib.al.us/alaroom.htm

Auburn University Library
Special Collections Department
231 Mell Street
Auburn, AL 36830
Tel: 334-844-1755
E-mail: fostecd@lib.auburn.edu
http://www.lib.auburn.edu/special/

Baldwin County Library Cooperative
P.O. Box 399
22743 Milwaukee St.
Robertsdale, AL 36567
http://www.gulftel.com/~bclc/home.html

Baldwin Heritage Museum Association
P.O. Box 1117
Foley, AL 36536

Birmingham Public Library
2100 Park Place
Birmingham, AL 35203
Tel: 205-226-3610
http://www.bham.lib.al.us/

Black Heritage Museum of West Alabama
Stillman College
P.O. Box 1430
Tuscaloosa, AL 35403
Tel: 205-349-4240

Blount County Memorial Museum
P.O. Box 45
204 2nd St N
Oneonta, AL 35121
Tel: 205-625-6905

Brent-Centreville Public Library
20 Library Street
Centreville, AL 35042
Tel: 205-926-4736

Butler County Historical Society/Library
309 Fort Dale Street
Greenville, AL 36037
Tel: 334-382-3216

Carrollton Public Library
P.O. Box 92
Carrollton, AL 35447
Tel: 205-367-2142
http://www.pickens.net/~cpl/info.html

Choctaw County Historical Museum
Alabama Hwy 17 and County Road 14 (Melvin Road)
P.O. Box 162
Gilbertown, AL 36908
334-843-2501 (Museum Office)
http://www.choctaw.net/museum/

Cullman County Library
200 Clarke Street NE
Cullman, AL 35055
Phone 256-736-2011
http://www.ccpls.com/spccollection.htm

Escambia County Library
700 E. Church Street
P.O. Box 1026
Atmore, AL 36504
Tel: 334-368-4130

Evergreen Conecuh Public Library
201 Park Street
Evergreen, AL 36401-2903
Tel: 334-578-2670

Florence-Lauderdale Public Library
218 N. Wood Avenue
Florence, AL 35630-4707
Phone: 256.764.6564
Fax: 256.764.6629
http://www.library.florence.org/

Foley Public Library
 319 East Laurel Avenue
Foley, AL 36535
http://gulftle.com/~bclc/bclibraries/foley.html

Gadsden Etowah County Library
254 College Street
Gadsden, AL 35999-3100
Tel: 205-549-4699
http://library.gadsden.com/index.html

Gordo Public Library
Main Street
P.O. Box 336
Gordo, AL 35466
Tel: 205-364-7148

Historic Mobile Preservation Society, Inc.
300 Oakleigh Place
Mobile, AL 36604
Tel: 334-432-6161

Horseshoe Bend Regional Library
207 N. West Street
Dadeville, AL 36853
Tel: 256-825-9232
http://www.mindspring.com/~hbrl/hbrl.html

Huntsville-Madison County Public Library
Huntsville Heritage Room
915 Monroe Street
Huntsville, AL 35801
Tel: 205-532-5940
205-532-5969 (Huntsville Heritage Room)
http://www.hsvchamber.org/guide/amenities/hsvlibrary.html

Interstate Library Contract
6030 Monticello Drive
Montgomery, AL 36130
Tel/Fax: 334-213-3900

Lawrence County Archives
Historic Bank of Moulton Building
698 Main Street
Moulton, AL 35650-0728
Tel: (256) 974-1757
FAX: (256) 974-2538
http://hometown.aol.com/LawCoArchives/

Limestone County Department of History and Archives
310 West Washington Street
Athens, AL 35611
Tel: (205)233-6404
http://fly.hiwaay.net/~gbf/limestone.html

Mobile Public Library
704 Government Street
Mobile, AL 36602-1402
Tel: 334-208-7093
http://www.mplonline.org/lhg.htm

Monroe County Heritage Museum
P.O. Box 1637
Monroeville, AL 36461
Tel: (334) 575-7433
http://www.tokillamockingbird.com/index.html

Museums of the City of Mobile
355 Government Street
Mobile, AL 36602-2315
Tel: 334-434-7569

Pickens County Cooperative Library
P.O. Box 489
Carrollton, AL 35447
Tel: 205-367-2142
www.pickens.net/~cpl

Reform Public Library
216 1st Street South
P.O. Box 819
Reform, AL 35481
Tel: 205-375-6240

Samford Univ. Institute of Genealogy and Historical Research
Samford University Library
800 Lakeshore Drive
Birmingham, AL 35229-7008
Tel: 205-870-2780
Fax: 205-870-2483
Libraryhttp://davisweb.samford.edu/
Special Collections:
http://www.samford.edu/schools/ighr/geninfo99.html
Institutehttp://www.samford.edu/schools/ighr/ighr.html

Scottsboro/Jackson County Heritage Center
Tel: 205-259-2122

Scottsboro Public Library
1002 S. Broad Street
Scottsboro, AL 35768-2512
Tel: 256-574-4335

Shelby County Museum and Archives
P.O. Box 457
Columbiana, AL 35051

Troy Public Library
300 N. Three Notch Street
Troy, Alabama 36081
(334) 566-1314

Tuscaloosa Public Library
1801 Jack Warner Parkway
Tuscaloosa, AL 35401
Tel: 205-345-5820

University of Alabama Library
William Stanley Hoole Special Collections Library
P.O. Box 870266
Tuscaloosa, AL 35487-0266
Tel: 205-348-0500
http://www.lib.ua.edu/hoole/

University of South Alabama
History Department
Humanities Building 344
Mobile, AL 36688
Main Office: 334/460-6210
Fax: 334/460-6750

University of South Alabama Archives
USA Springhill, Room 0722
Mobile, AL 36688
Phone: (334) 434-3800
Fax: (334) 434-3622
E-mail: archives@jaguar1.usouthal.edu
http://www.usouthal.edu/archives/archome.htm

Wallace State Community College Library
Family & Regional History Program
Wallace State Community College
801 Main Street
P.O. Box 2000
Hanceville, AL 35077-2000
Phone: 205-352-8265
http://home.hiwaay.net/~wdsmith/collect.htm

NEWSPAPER REPOSITORIES

Alabama Deptartment of Archives & History
Newspaper Program
624 Washington Avenue
Montgomery, AL 36130-0100
Tel: 334-242-4441
Fax: 334-242-4452
E-mail: ebridges@dsmd.dsmd.state.al.us
http://www.archives.state.al.us/newsp/newsp.html

VITAL RECORDS

Alabama Department of Archives & History
624 Washington Avenue
Montgomery, Alabama 36130-0100
Phone: (334) 242-4435
E-mail: dependlet@archives.state.al.us
http://www.archives.state.al.us/

Alabama Center for Health Statistics
P. O. Box 5625
Montgomery, Al 36103-5625
Tel: 334-206-5418
(Birth & Death, 1908-present, Marriage 1936-present,
    Divorce 1950-present)
http://www.alapubhealth.org/vital/vitalrcd.htm
Vital records information from the Alabama Department
    of Archives & History
(Includes addresses and availability for county-level
    records)
http://www.archives.state.al.us/referenc/vital.html

ALABAMA ON THE WEB

Alabama Ancestral Database
http://www.geocities.com/Heartland/Ranch/5952/

Alabama Department of Archives & History
http://www.archives.state.al.us/

Alabama GenWeb Project
http://www.rootsweb.com/~algenweb/index.html

Alabama Society, Sons of the American Revolution
http://www.sar.org/alssar/

Birmingham Public Library by A.C. Alexander
http://www.bham.lib.al.us/

Old Huntsville Magazine
http://www.oldhuntsville.com/

Travellers Southern Families
http://genealogy.traveller.com/genealogy/

ALASKA

ARCHIVES, STATE & NATIONAL

Alaska State Archives & Records Management Services
141 Willoughby Ave.
Juneau, AK 99801-1720
Tel: 907-465-2270
907-465-2317
Fax: 907-465-2465
E-mail: archives@eed.state.ak.us
http://www.archives.state.ak.us/

National Archives-Pacific Alaska Region
654 W. Third Avenue
Anchorage, AK 99501-2145
Tel: 907-271-2441
Fax: 907-271-2442
E-mail: archives@alaska.nara.gov
http://www.nara.gov/regional/anchorag.html

GENEALOGICAL SOCIETIES

Anchorage Genealogical Society
P.O.Box 242294
Anchorage, AK 99524-2294
http://www.rootsweb.com/~akags/

Fairbanks Genealogical Society
P.O. Box 60534
Fairbanks, AK 99706-0534
http://www.ptialaska.net/~fgs/

Gastineau Genealogical Society
3270 Nowell Avenue
Juneau, AK 99801
Tel: 907-586-3695

Genealogical Society of Southeastern Alaska
P.O. Box 6313
Ketchikan, AK 99901-1313

Kenai Totem Tracers
c/o Kenai Community Library
163 Main Street Loop
Kenai, AK 99611

Sons of the American Revolution
Alaska Society
3310 Checkmate Drive
Anchorage, Alaska 99508

Wrangell Genealogical Society
P.O. Box 928EP
Wrangell, AK 99929

HISTORICAL SOCIETIES

Alaska Historical Society
524 West Fourth Avenue, Suite 208
P.O. Box 100299
Anchorage, AK 99510-0299
Tel: 907-276-1596
E-mail: ahs@alaska.net
http://www.alaska.net/~ahs/index.htm

Anvik Historical Society and Museum
P.O. Box 110, Anvik, AK 99558
Telephone: (907) 663-6358

Chugiak-Eagle River Historical Society
P.O. Box 670573
Chugiak, Alaska 99567

Cook Inlet Historical Society
Anchorage Museum of History & Art
121 West 7th Avenue
P.O. Box 196650
Anchorage, AK 99519-6650
Tel: 907-343-4326
Fax: 907-343-6149
http://www.ci.anchorage.ak.us/Services/Departments/Cult
    ure/Museum/index.html

Copper Valley Historical Society
Mile 101 Old Richardson Highway
Copper Center Loop Road
P.O. Box 84
Copper Center, AK 99573
Tel: 907-822-5285

Cordova Historical Society
Cordova Historical Museum
Centennial Building
622 First Street
Box 391
Cordova, AK 99574
Tel: 907-424-6665
Fax: 907-424-6000 (City Hall)

Delta Historical Society
P.O. Box 1089
Delta Junction, AK 99737

Eagle Historical Society & Museum
Box 23
Eagle City, AK 99738
Tel: 907-547-2325
http://www.eagleak.org/

Gastineau Channel Historical Society
P.O. Box 21264
Juneau, AK 99802
Tel: 907-586-5235

Resurrection Bay Historical Society
336 3rd Ave.
P.O. Box 55
Seward, AK 99664-0055
Tel/Fax: 907-224-3902

Sealaska Heritage Foundation
One Sealaska Plaza, Suite 201
Juneau, AK 99801
Tel: 907-463-4844
http://www.shfonline.org/

Sitka Historical Society
Isabel Miller Museum
330 Harbor Drive
Sitka, AK 99835
Tel: 907-747-6455
Fax: 907-747-3739
http://www.sitka.org/historicalmuseum

Soldotna Historical Society & Museum, Inc.
Centennial Park Road
P.O. Box 1986
Soldotna, AK 99669
Tel: 907-262-3756
Fax: 907-262-8466

Talkeetna Historical Society
P.O. Box 76
Talkeetna, AK 99676
Tel/Fax: 907-733-2487

Tanana-Yukon Historical Society
Wickersham House Museum
Alaskaland Park, Airport Way
P.O. Box 71336
Fairbanks, AK 99707
Tel: 907-474-4013
E-mail: tyhs@polarnet.com
http://www2.polarnet.com/~tyhs/

Wasilla-Knik-Willow Creek Historical Society
Dorothy Page Museum & Old Wasilla Townsite Park
300 N. Boundary Street, Suite B
Wasilla, AK 99654
Tel: (907) 376-2005
Fax: 373-9072
E-mail: wkwchistorical@hotmail.com

LDS FAMILY HISTORY CENTERS

For locations of Family History Centers in this state, see the Family History Center locator at FamilySearch:
http://www.familysearch.org/eng/Library/FHC/
frameset_fhc.asp

ARCHIVES/LIBRARIES/MUSEUMS

Adak Community Museum
PSC 486, Box 1313
FPO AP 96506-1271
Tel/Fax: 907-592-8064

Alaska Historical Collections
Alaska State Library
8th Floor, State Office Building
333 Willoughby Ave.
P.O. Box 110571
Juneau, AK 99811-0571
Phone: 907-465-2925
Fax: 907-465-2990
E-mail: asl@muskox.alaska.edu
http://www.library.state.ak.us/hist/hist.html

Alaska Office of History and Archaeology
550 W 7th Ave., Ste. 1310
Anchorage, AK 99501-3565
(907) 269-8721
E-mail: oha@alaska.net
website: www.dnr.state.ak.us/parks/oha_web/

Alaska State Museum
395 Whittier Street
Juneau, AK 99801-1718
Tel: 907-465-2901
Fax: 907-465-2976
E-mail: bruce_kato@educ.state.ak.us
http://www.museums.ak.us/

Alpine Historical Park
Mile 61.5 Glenn Highway
P.O. Box 266
Sutton, AK 99674
Tel: 907-745-7000

Alutiiq Museum and Archaelogical Repository
215 Mission Road, Suite 101
Kodiak, AK 99615
Tel/Fax: 907-486-7004/7048
E-mail: alutiiq2@ptialaska.net
http://www.alutiiqmuseum.com

Anchorage Municipal Library
3600 Denali
Anchorage, AK 99503-6093
(907) 261-2975
http://www.ci.anchorage.ak.us/Services/Departments/
    Culture/Library/index.html

Anchorage Museum of History & Art
121 West 7th Avenue
P.O. Box 196650
Anchorage, AK 99519-6650
Tel: 907-343-4326
Fax: 907-343-6149
http://www.anchoragemuseum.org/

Baranov Museum
Kodiak Historical Society
101 Marine Way
Kodiak, AK 99615
Tel: 907-486-5920
Fax: 907-486-3166
E-mail: baranov@ptialaska.net
Web page: www.ptialaska.net/~baranov

Carrie McLain Memorial Museum
200 E. Front Street
Box 53
Nome, AK 99762
Telephone: (907) 443-6630
Fax: 443-7955
E-mail: museum@ci.nome.ak.us
http://www.nome100.com

Circle Historical Museum
Mile 128 Steese Highway
P.O. Box 1893
Central, AK 99730
Tel/Fax: 907-520-5312

Colony House Museum / Palmer Historical Society
316 East Elmwood Ave
Mailing address: P.O. Box 1925
Palmer, AK 99645-1925
Telephone: (907) 745-3703 (Historical Society)

Consortium Library Archives
University of Alaska, Anchorage
3211 Providence Drive
Anchorage, AK 99508

Cordova Historical Museum
622 First Street
Box 391
Cordova, AK 99574
Tel: 907-424-6665
Fax: 907-424-6000 (City Hall)

Dorothy Page Museum & Old Wasilla Townsite Park
Wasilla-Knik-Willow Creek Historical Society
323 Main Street
Wasilla, AK 99654
Telephone: (907) 373-9071
Fax: 373-9072
E-mail: museum@ci.wasilla.ak.us

Duncan Cottage Museum
Physical location: Tait Street
Mailing address: P.O. Box 8
Metlakatla, AK 99926
Telephone: (907) 886-4441 ex. 232
FAX (907) 886-7997
http://tours.metlakatla.net

Elmer E. Rasmuson Library
Alaska and Polar Regions Department
P.O. Box 756811
Fairbanks, AK 99775-6811
(907) 474-7261
http://www.uaf.edu/library/collections/apr/index.html

Eagle Historical Society & Museum
Box 23
Eagle City, AK 99738
Tel: 907-547-2325

George Ashby Memorial Museum
Copper Valley Historical Society
Mile 101 Old Richardson Highway
Copper Center Loop Road
P.O. Box 84
Copper Center, AK 99573
Tel: 907-822-5285

Heritage Library and Museum
National Bank of Alaska
301 W. Northern Lights Blvd.
P.O. Box 100600
Anchorage, AK 99510-0600
Tel: 907-265-2834
Fax: 907-265-2002

House of Wickersham Museum
213 Seventh Street
Mailing address: 400 Willoughby Ave.
Juneau, AK 99801
Telephone: (907) 586-9001

Isabel Miller Museum
Sitka Historical Society
330 Harbor Drive
Sitka, AK 99835
Tel: 907-747-6455
Fax: 907-747-3739
http://www.sitka.org/historicalmuseum

Juneau/Douglas City Museum
155 South Seward Street
Juneau, AK 99801
Tel: 907-586-3572
Fax: 907-586-3203
http://www.juneau.lib.ak.us/parksrec/museum/museum.htm

Kake Tribal Heritage Foundation
93009 Glacier Hwy.
P.O. Box 263
Juneau, AK 99801
Juneau Tel: 907-790-2214
Kake Tel: 907-785-3221
Fax: 907-785-6407

Kenitzee Indian Tribe, IRA
2255 Ames Street
P.O. Box 988
Kenai, AK 99611
Tel: 907-283-3633
Fax: 907-283-3052

Klondike Gold Rush National Historical Park
Second & Broadway
P.O. Box 517
Skagway, AK 99840
Tel: 907-983-2921
Fax: 907-983-2046
E-mail: Debra_Sanders@nps.gov
Web page:http://www.nps.gov/klgo

Kodiak Military History Museum
Ft. Abercrombie State Historical Park
Mailing address: 1623 Mill Bay Road, Kodiak, AK 99615
Telephone: (907) 486-7015
E-mail: wl7aml@arrl.net
Web page: www.kadiak.org

Museums Alaska
(Statewide Organization)
P.O. Box 242323
Anchorage, AK 99524
Tel/Fax: 907-243-4714
http://www.museumsalaska.org/

NANA Museum of the Artic
100 Shore Avenue
P.O. Box 49
Kotzebue, AK 99752
Tel: 907-442-3304
Fax: 907-442-2866

Pratt Museum
3779 Bartlett Street
Homer, AK 99603
Tel: 907-235-8635
Fax: 907-235-2764
E-mail: pratt@alaska.net
http://www.prattmuseum.org/

Resurrection Bay Historical Society/Seward Museum
336 3rd Ave.
P.O. Box 55
Seward, AK 99664-0055
Tel/Fax: 907-224-3902

Sheldon Jackson Museum
104 College Drive
Sitka, AK 99835-7657
Tel: 907-747-8981
Fax: 907-747-3004
E-mail: peter_corey@eed.state.ak.us
Web page: www.museums.state.ak.us/sjhome.html

Sheldon Museum & Cultural Center
Main & First Street
Box 269
Haines, AK 99827
Tel: 907-766-2366
Fax: 907-766-2368
http://www.sheldonmuseum.org/

Sitka National Historical Park
106 Metlakatla Street; Lincoln St.
P.O. Box 738
Sitka, AK 99835
Tel: 907-747-6281
Fax: 907-747-5938
E-mail: sue-thorsen@nps.gov
http://www.nps.gov/sitk/

Skagway Museum and Archives
Physical location: Seventh Ave. and Spring Street in the
            Historic District.
Mailing address: P.O. Box 521, Skagway, AK 99840
Telephone: (907) 983-2420 FAX (907) 983-3420
E-mail: skgmus@ptialaska.net

Soldotna Historical Society & Museum, Inc.
Centennial Park Road
P.O. Box 1986
Soldotna, AK 99669
Tel: 907-262-3756
Fax: 907-262-8466
http://www.geocities.com/soldotnamuseum/

Talkeetna Historical Society
P.O. Box 76
Talkeetna, AK 99676
Tel/Fax: 907-733-2487

Tongass Historical Museum
629 Dock Street
Ketchikan, AK 99901
Tel: 907-225-5600
Fax: 907-225-5602
E-mail: museumdir@city.ketchikan.ak.us
www.city.ketchikan.ak.us/ds/tonghist/index.html

Totem Heritage Center
601 Deermont Street
(Mailing Address: 629 Dock St.)
Ketchikan, AK 99901
Tel: 907-225-5900
Fax: 907-225-5602
www.city.ketchikan.ak.us/ds/tonghert/index.html

Trail of '98 City Museum
7th & Spring Streets
Box 415
Skagway, AK 99840
Tel: 907-983-2420
Fax: 907-983-2151

University of Alaska, Anchorage
Archives and Manuscripts Department, Consortium
    Library
University of Alaska Anchorage
3211 Providence Drive
Anchorage, AK 99508
Telephone: (907) 786-1849
Fax: (907) 786-1845
E-mail: ayarch@uaa.alaska.edu
http://asimov.lib.uaa.alaska.edu/archives/index.html

University of Alaska Fairbanks Museum
907 Yukon Drive
P.O. Box 756960
Fairbanks, AK 99775-6960
Tel: 907-474-7505
Fax: 907-474-5469
http://www.uaf.alaska.edu/museum/

Valdez Museum & Historical Archive
217 Egan Drive
Box 8
Valdez, AK 99686-0008
Tel: 907-835-2764
Fax: 907-835-4597 or 5800
E-mail: vldzmuse@alaska.net
http://www.alaska.net/~vldzmuse/index.html

Wickersham House Museum
Tanana-Yukon Historical Society
Alaskaland Park, Airport Way
P.O. Box 71336
Fairbanks, AK 99707
Tel: 907-474-4013
E-mail: tyhs@polarnet.com
http://www2.polarnet.com/~tyhs/

Wrangell Museum
318 Church Street
P.O. Box 1050
Wrangell, AK 99929
Tel/Fax: 907-874-3770
E-mail: museum@wrangell.com
Web page: http://www.wrangell.com/cultural/museum.htm

Yukon Archives
P.O. Box 2703
Whitehorse, Yukon Territory, Canada, Y1A 2C6
(403) 667-5641
http://www.gov.yk.ca/depts/education/libarch/yukarch.html

Yupiit Piciryarait Cultural Center and Museum
420 Chief Eddie Hoffman State Highway
 Mailing address:
AVCP, Inc.
P.O. Box 219
Bethel, AK 99559
Telephone: (907) 543-1819
FAX: 543-1885

NEWSPAPER REPOSITORIES

Alaska Newspaper Project
Alaska State Library
8th Floor, State Office Building
333 Willoughby Ave.
P.O. Box 110571
Juneau, AK 99811-0571
Phone: 907-465-2919
Fax: 907-465-2990
E-mail: maryn@muskox.alaska.edu
http://www.library.state.ak.us/hist/newspaper.html

Elmer E. Rasmuson Library
Rare Books, Archives and Manuscripts
University of Alaska, Fairbanks
Fairbanks, AK 99701
http://www.uaf.alaska.edu/library/libweb/

Fairbanks Genealogical Society
P.O. Box 60534
Fairbanks, AK 99706-0534
http://www.ptialaska.net/~fgs/

Vital Records

Department of Health & Social Services
Bureau of Vital Statistics
350 Main Street, Room 114 (location)
P.O. Box 110675 (mail)
Juneau, AK 99811-0675
Tel: 907-465-3392
Fax: 907-465-3618
(Birth 1890-present, Marriage & Death, 1913-present,
Divorce 1950-present)
http://health.hss.state.ak.us/htmlstuf/dph/vitals/vitalst.htm

Alaska on the Web

Alaska Genweb Project
http://www.akgenweb.org/

Alaska State Library
http://www.library.state.ak.us/

Fairbanks Genealogical Society
http://www.ptialaska.net/~fgs/

**Library of Congress exhibit on "The Russian Church
and Native Alaskan Cultures"**
http://lcweb.loc.gov/exhibits/russian/s1a.html

Yukon and Alaska Genealogy Centre
http://www.yukonalaska.com/pathfinder/gen/

ARIZONA

ARCHIVES, STATE & NATIONAL

Arizona Department of Library
Archives and Public Records
Archives Division
 State Capitol, Suite 342
1700 W. Washington St.
Phoenix, AZ 85007
Tel: 602-542-4159
Fax: 602-542-4402
E-mail: archive@lib.az.us
http://www.lib.az.us/archives/index.html

National Archives-Pacific Region (Laguna Niguel)
24000 Avila Rd., First Floor-East Entrance
P.O. Box 6719
Laguna Niguel, CA 92607-6719
Tel: 949-360-2641
Fax: 949-360-2624
E-mail: laguna.archives@nara.gov
http://www.nara.gov/regional/laguna.html

GENEALOGICAL SOCIETIES

Afro-American Historical & Genealogical Society
7739 East Broadway, Suite 195
Tucson, AZ 85710

Arizona First Families
4813 E. Flower Street
Phoenix, AZ 85018

Arizona Genealogical Advisory Board
P.O. Box 5641
Mesa, AZ 85211-5641
www.azgab.org

Arizona Genealogical Computer Interest Group
P.O. Box 51498
Phoenix, AZ 85076-1498
http://www.agcig.org/

Arizona Society of Genealogists
6565 East Grant Road
Tucson, AZ 85715

Arizona State Genealogical Society
P.O. Box 42075
Tucson, AZ 85733-2075
(520) 275-2747
http://www.rootsweb.com/~asgs/

Black Family History Society
P.O. Box 1515
Gilbert, AZ 85299-1515

Camp Verde
Historical Society
P.O. Box 182
Rimrock, AZ 86335

Cherokee Family Ties
516 North 38th Street
Mesa, AZ 85208

Cochise Genealogical Society
P.O. Box 68
Pirtleville, AZ 85626
http://www.mycochise.com/

Coconino County Genealogical Society
649 E. Edison
Williams, AZ 86046

Daughters of the American Revolution
Arizona Society
2622 Papago Trail
Sierra Vista, AZ 85635

Family History Society of Arizona
P.O. Box 63094
Phoenix, AZ 85082-3094
http://www.fhsa.org/

Genealogical Society of Arizona
P.O. Box 27237
Tempe, AZ 85282

Genealogical Society of Yuma Arizona
P.O. Box 2905
Yuma, AZ 85366-2905
http://www.lib.az.us/archives/index.html

Genealogical Workshop of Mesa
P.O. Box 6052
Mesa, AZ 85216-6052
http://members.home.net/gwom/

Genealogy Society of Pinal County
1128 North Kaduta Ave.
Casa Grande, AZ 85222

Green Valley Genealogical Society
P.O. Box 1009
Green Valley, AZ 85622-1009

Hispanic Family History Society
3607 S. Kenneth Place
Tempe, AZ 85282

Lake Havasu Genealogical Society
P.O. Box 953
Lake Havasu City, AZ 86405-0953
http://www.rootsweb.com/~azlhgs/

Mohave County Genealogical Society
400 West Beale Street
Kingman, AZ 86401

Monte Vista Genies
Monte Vista Village Resort
Pueblo Room
8865 E. Baseline Rd.
Mesa, AZ 85208-5309

Navajo County Genealogical Society
P.O. Box 1403
Winslow, AZ 86047

Northern Arizona Genealogical Society
P.O. Box 695
Prescott, AZ 86302
http://www.rootsweb.com/~aznags/index.htm

Northern Gila County Genealogical Society
P.O. Box 952
Payson, AZ 85547

Ohio Genealogical Society
Arizona Chapter
P.O. Box 677
Gilbert, AZ 85299-0677

Phoenix Genealogical Society
P.O. Box 38703
Phoenix, AZ 85069-8703

Polish Genealogical Interest Group of Arizona
2015 E. Redmon Dr.
Tempe, AZ 85283
http://www.azneighbors.com/212/Contact.wsi

Saddlebrooke Genealogy Club
38418 S. Golf Course Dr.
Tucson, AZ 85739-1113

Sedona Genealogy Club
P.O. Box 4258
Sedona, AZ 86340
http://www.rootsweb.com/~azsgc/

Sierra Vista Genealogical Society
P.O. Box 1084
Sierra Vista, AZ 85636-1084
http://www.rootsweb.com/~azsvgs/

Sun City Vistoso Genealogical Society
13763 N. Buster Spring Way
Tucson AZ 85737-4717

Tri-States Genealogical Society
P.O. Box 9689
Fort Mohave, AZ 86427

West Valley Genealogical Society
P. O. Box 1448
Sun City, AZ 85372
623-933-4945
http://www.rootsweb.com/~azwvgs/index.htm

HISTORICAL SOCIETIES

Arizona Historical Foundation
Hayden Library, ASU
P.O. Box 871006
Tempe, AZ 85287-1006
Phone: 480-965-3283
FAX: 480-966-1077
http://www.users.qwest.net/~azhistoricalfdn/

Arizona Historical Society
Central Arizona Division
1300 North College Avenue
Tempe, AZ 85281
Tel: 480-929-0292
Fax: 480-967-5450
http://www.tempe.gov/ahs/

Arizona Historical Society
Southern Arizona Division
949 E. Second Street
Tucson, AZ 85719
Tel: 520-628-5774
Fax: 520-628-5695
E-mail: azhist@azstarnet.com
http://www.tempe.gov/ahs/

Arizona Historical Society
Rio Colorado Division
Century House Museum
240 Madison Avenue
Yuma, AZ 85364
Phone: 520-782-1841
http://www.tempe.gov/ahs/yuma.htm

Arizona Jewish Historical Society
700 W. Edgewood
Mesa, AZ 85202.

Arizona Pioneers Historical Society
949 East Second Street
Tucson, AZ 85719

Graham County Historical Society
Box 127
Safford, AZ 85548
Tel: 520-348-3212 (at museum)
http://www.rootsweb.com/~azgraham/histsoc.html

Greenlee County Historical Society
P.O. Box 787
Clifton, AZ 85533
520 865 3115

Prescott Historical Society
Sharlot Hall Museum
415 W. Gurley Street
Prescott AZ 86301
520.445.3122
http://www.sharlot.org/

Southern Arizona Jewish Historical Society
4181 E. Pontatoc Canyon Dr.
Tucson, AZ 85718

LDS FAMILY HISTORY CENTERS

For locations of Family History Centers in this state, see
the Family History Center locator at FamilySearch:
http://www.familysearch.org/eng/Library/FHC
/frameset_fhc.asp

ARCHIVES/LIBRARIES/MUSEUMS

Apache County Historical Society Museum
180 W. Cleveland (P.O. Box 146)
St. Johns, AZ 85936
(520) 337-4737

Arizona State Library
Department of Library, Archives & Public Records
State Capitol
1700 West Washington
Phoenix, AZ 85007
Tel: (602) 542-3701
         (800) 228-4710
Fax: (602) 542-4400
http://www.lib.az.us/research/index.html
Archives Division:
Tel: 602-542-4159
       800-228-4710
Fax: 602-542-4402
http://www.lib.az.us/archives/index.html
E-mail: archive@lib.az.us
Research Division
E-mail: research@lib.az.us

Arizona State University
Hayden Library
P.O. Box 871006
Tempe, AZ 85287-1006
Mailing Address:
Arizona State University Libraries
Box 871006
Tempe AZ 85287-1006
Tel: (480) 965-6164
http://www.asu.edu/lib/hayden/

Bisbee Historical Society Museum
37 Main Street
Old Bisbee, AZ 85603

Bisbee Mining Historical Museum
5 Copper Queen Plaza
Old Bisbee, AZ 85603
Tel: 520-432-7071
http://www.amdest.com/az/Bisbee/bmining.html

Bloom Southwest Jewish Archives
1052 N. Highland Ave.
Tucson, AZ 85721
Tel: 520-621-5774
http://dizzy.library.arizona.edu/images/swja/swjalist.html

Graham County Historical Museum
Thatcher School Building
4th and Main
Thatcher, AZ 85552
http://www.rootsweb.com/~azgraham/museum.html

Heard Museum Library & Archives
2301 North Central Avenue
Phoenix, AZ 85004
Tel: 602-252-8848
Fax: 602-252-9757
http://www.heard.org/research/index.html

Sharlot Hall Museum
415 W. Gurley Street
Prescott AZ 86301
520.445.3122
http://www.sharlot.org/

University of Arizona Library
1510 E. University Blvd.
P.O. Box 210055
Tucson, AZ 85721-0055
Tel: 520-621-6441
http://www.library.arizona.edu/

NEWSPAPER REPOSITORIES

Research Division
Arizona State Library
Department of Library, Archives & Public Records
State Capitol
1700 West Washington
Phoenix, AZ 85007
Tel: (602) 542-3701
(800) 228-4710
Fax: (602) 542-4400
http://www.lib.az.us/research/index.html

Arizona Historical Society
Southern Arizona Division
949 E. Second Street
Tucson, AZ 85719
Tel: 520-628-5774
Fax: 520-628-5695
E-mail: azhist@azstarnet.com
http://www.tempe.gov/ahs/

University of Arizona Library
1510 E. University Blvd.
P.O. Box 210055
Tucson, AZ 85721-0055
Tel: 520-621-6441
http://www.library.arizona.edu/

VITAL RECORDS

Arizona Department of Health Services
Vital Records Section
2727 W. Glendale Avenue
P.O. Box 3887
Phoenix, AZ 85030-3887
Tel: (602) 364-1300
http://www.hs.state.az.us/vitalrcd/index.htm

State Historic Preservation Office (SHPO)
Arizona State Parks
1300 W. Washington
Phoenix, AZ 85007
Tel: 602-542-4009
http://www.pr.state.az.us/partnerships/shpo/shpo.html

ARIZONA ON THE WEB

Arizona Department of Library, Archives & Public Records,
Genealogical Research Page
http://www.lib.az.us/research/genealogy.htm

Arizona Genealogy Computer Interest Group
http://www.agcig.org/

Arizona USGenWeb
http://www.rootsweb.com/~azgenweb/

Arizona Historical Society
http://www.tempe.gov/ahs/

Arizona Internet Yellow Pages
http://www.amdest.com/az/yellow_pages.html

Arizona State Archives
http://www.lib.az.us/archives/index.html

Family History Society of Arizona
http://www.fhsa.org/

ARKANSAS

ARCHIVES, STATE & NATIONAL

Arkansas History Commission & State Archives
One Capitol Mall
Little Rock, AR 72201
Tel: 501-682-6900
http://www.ark-ives.com/ahc.html

National Archives-Southwest Region
501 W. Felix Street, Building 1
P.O. Box 6216
Fort Worth, TX 76115-0216
Tel: 817-334-5515
 Fax: 817-334-5511
E-mail: ftworth.archives@nara.gov
http://www.nara.gov/regional/ftworth.html

Southwest Arkansas Regional Archives
Old Washington Historic State Park
Hempstead County Courthouse
P.O. Box 98
Washington, AR 71862
Tel: 870-983-2684 (Mon-Fri)
870-983-2733 (Sat-Sun)
http://peace.saumag.edu/swark/sara/sara.html

GENEALOGICAL SOCIETIES

Afro-American Historical & Genealogical Society
Arkansas Chapter
14617 Sara Drive
Little Rock, AR 72206

Ancestors Unknown
P.O. Box 164
Conway, AR 72033-0164

Ark-La-Tex Genealogical Association, Inc.
P.O. Box 4462
Shreveport, LA 71104

Arkansas Family History Association
609 Colynwood
Sherwood, AR 72120
501-835-7502

Arkansas Genealogical Research
805 East 5th Street
Russellville, AR 72801

Arkansas Genealogical Society
4200 "A" Street
Little Rock, AR 72205
P.O. Box 908
Hot Springs, AR 71902-0908
http://www.rootsweb.com/~args/

Arkansas Genealogical Society
4200 A Street
Little Rock, AR 72205

Ashley County Genealogical Society
P.O. Drawer R
Crossett, AR 71635-1819
http://www.rootsweb.com/~arashley/
        AshleyCoRes.html#ACGS

Batesville Genealogical Society
P.O. Box 3883
Batesville, AR 72503-3883

Baxter County Historical & Genealogical Society
P.O. Box 1611
Mountain Home, AR 72654
http://www.geocities.com/Athens/2101/bchgs.html

Bradley County Genealogical Society
P.O. Box 837
Warren, AR 71671-0837

Clay County Genealogy Society
c/o Piggott Public Library
361 West Main
Piggott, AR 72454-2099

Conway County Genealogical Association
P. O. Box 865
Morrilton, AR 72110

Corbin Genealogical Society
RR 3, Box 86
Paris, AR 72855-9517

Crawford County Genealogical Society
P.O. Box 276
Alma, AR 72921

Crowley's Ridge Genealogical Society
P.O. Box 2091
State University, AR 72467

Dallas County Genealogical & Historical Society
c/o Dallas County Library
Fordyce, AR 71742

Daughters of the American Revolution
Enoch Ashley Chapter
2613 Dauphine Drive
Rogers, AR 72756

Frontier Researchers Genealogical Society
P.O. Box 2123
Fort Smith, AR 72902

Grand Prairie Genealogical Society
c/o Stuttgart Public Library
2002 So. Buerkle St.
Stuttgart, AR 72160
Phone: (870) 673- 1966
Fax: (870) 673-4295
http://www.rootsweb.com/~ararkans/grandpra.htm

Greene County Historical & Genealogical Society
c/o Greene County Library
120 N. 12th Street
Paragould, AR 72450
http://www.greenecountylibrary.com/library/brown/
    greene.htm

Hempstead County Genealogical Society
P.O. Box 1158
Hope, AR 71801

Heritage Club
218 Howard
Nashville, AR 71852

Heritage Seekers Genealogy Club
P.O. Box 532
 North Little Rock, AR 72115-0532

Hot Springs County Historical & Genealogical Society
P.O. Box 674
Malvern, AR 72104

Jefferson County Genealogical Society
P.O. Box 2215
Pine Bluff, AR 71613

Madison County Genealogical & Historical Society
P.O. Box 427
Huntsville, AR 72740
Tel: 501-738-6408
http://home.sprynet.com/sprynet/progers/mcghsinf.htm

Marion County, Arkansas Historic & Genealogical Society
c/o Marion County Library
P.O. Box 554
Yellville, AR 72687

Melting Pot Genealogical Society
P.O. Box 936
Hot Springs, AR 71902

Newton County Historical & Genealogical Society
P.O. Box 360
Jasper, AR 72641
Tel: 501-434-5931

Northwest Arkansas Genealogical Society
400 So. Walton Blvd.
Bentonville, AR 72712
P.O. Box K
Rogers, AR 72757
Tel: 501-273-3890

Ouachita-Calhoun Genealogical Society
P.O. Box 2092
Camden, AR 71711

Polk County Genealogical Society
P.O. Box 317
Hatfield, AR 71945
501-394-6355

Professional Genealogists of Arkansas, Inc.
P.O. Box 1807
Conway, AR 72033-1807

Pulaski County Historical Society
P.O. Box 653
Little Rock, AR 72203

Saline County Historical & Heritage Society
P.O. Box 221
Alexander, AR 72022-0221

Sevier County Genealogical Society, Inc.
717 N. Maple
De Queen, AR 71832

Sons of the American Revolution
Arkansas Society
1119 Scenic Way
Benton, AR 72015

Southeast Arkansas Genealogical Society
119 West College Street South Main Street
Monticello, AR 71655
870 367-7446

Southwest Arkansas Genealogical Society
1022 Lawton Circle
Magnolia, AR 71753

Stone County Genealogical Society
P.O. Box 1477
Mountain View, AR 72560
http://members.nbci.com/stonecoargen/index.htm

Texarkana USA Genealogical Society
Rte. 7, Box 466, BA7
Texarkana, AR 75501

Tri-County Genealogical Society
(Monroe, Phillips, & Lee Co.)
P.O. Box 580
Marvell, AR 72366

Union County Genealogical Society
Barton Library
200 East 5th Street
El Dorado, AR 71730
870-862-3198

Village Genealogical Society
5 Murcia Place
Hot Springs Village, AR 71909-4403
501-922-4560

Yell County Historical & Genealogical Society
P.O. Box 622
Dardanelle, AR 72834

HISTORICAL SOCIETIES

Arkansas Historical Association
History Department
Ozark Hall, 12, University of Arkansas
Old Main 416
Fayetteville, AR 72701
Tel: 501-575-5884
http://cavern.uark.edu/depts/histinfo/history/ARKQuart/index.html

Arkansas Historical Society
422 South Sixth Street
Van Buren, AR 72956

Arkansas History Commission
One Capitol Mall
Little Rock, AR 72201
Tel: 501-682-6900
http://www.ark-ives.com/

Baxter County Historical & Genealogical Society
P.O. Box 1611
Mountain Home, AR 72654
http://www.geocities.com/Athens/2101/bchgs.html

Benton County Historical Society
Peel Mansion
400 South Walton Boulevard
Bentonville, Arkansas
Mailing address:
P.O. Box 1034
Bentonville, AR 72712
Tel. 501-273-3890
http://www.uark.edu/depts/globmark/bchsark/

Carroll County Historical and Genealogical Society, Inc.
P.O. Box 249
Berryville, AR 72616-0249
Phone 870 423-6312
www.rootsweb.com/~arcchs

Clark County Historical Association
Box 516
Arkadelphia, AR 71923

Cleburne County Historical Society
Rt. 2, Box 326 K
Heber Springs, AR 72543

Craighead County Historical Society
P.O. Box 1011
Jonesboro, AR 72403-1011
http://www.insolwwb.net/~nlmatthews/newsletter.htm

Crawford County Historical Society
929 East Main Street
Van Buren, AR 72956

Dallas County Genealogical & Historical Society
c/o Dallas County Library
Fordyce, AR 71742

Desha County Historical Society
P.O. Box 432
McGehee, AR 71654

Drew County Historical Society
404 South Main Street
Monticello, AR 71655

Faulkner County Historical Society
P.O. Box 731
Conway, AR 72032
http://www.users.intellinet.com/~wmeriwet/faulkner.htm

Fort Smith Historical Society
61 South 8th Street
Fort Smith, AR 72901

Grand Prairie Historical Society
P.O. Box 122
Gilette, AR 72055

Greene County Historical & Genealogical Society
c/o Greene County Library
120 N. 12th Street
Paragould, AR 72450
http://www.greenecountylibrary.com/library/brown/
greene.htm

Hazen Historical Society
311 North Hazen Ave.
Hazen, AR 72064
870-255-4547

Hempstead County Historical Society
P.O. Box 1257
Hope, AR 71801

Hot Springs County Historical & Genealogical Society
P.O. Box 674
Malvern, AR 72104

Independence County Historical Society
P.O. Box 1412
Batesville, AR 72501

Izard County Arkansas Historical Society
c/o Izard County Historian
P.O. Box 84
Dolph, AR 72528

Johnson County Historical Society
P.O. Box 505
Clarksville, AR 72830

Lafayette County Historical Society
P.O. Box 180
Bradley, AR 71826

Lawrence County Historical Society
Powhatan Courthouse State Park
P.O. Box 93
Powhatan, AR 72458

Logan County Historical Society
P.O. Box 40
Magazine, AR 72943-0040

Madison County Genealogical & Historical Society
P.O. Box 427
Huntsville, AR 72740
Tel: 501-738-6408

Marion County, Arkansas Historical & Genealogical Society
c/o Marion County Library
P.O. Box 554
Yellville, AR 72687

Monroe County Historical & Cemetery Association
804 Walker Street
Clarendon, AR 72029-2438

Montgomery County Historical Society
P.O. Box 520
Mount Ida, AR 71957-0520
Tel: 870-867-3121

Newton County Historical & Genealogical Society
P.O. Box 360
Jasper, AR 72641
Tel: 870-434-5931

Orphan Train Heritage Society of America
614 E. Emma Ave., #115
Springdale, AR 72764
Tel: 501-756-2780
Fax: 501-756-0769
E-mail: mjohjnson@jcf.jonesnet.org

Ouachita County Historical Society
926 Washington NW
Camden, AR 71701

Poinsett County Historical Society
P.O. Box 424
Harrisburg, AR 72432

Pope County Historical Society
1120 North Detroit
Russellville, AR 72801

Pulaski County Historical Society
P.O. Box 653
Little Rock, AR 72203

Saline County History & Heritage Society
P.O. Box 221
Bryant, AR 72022-0221

Saline County Historical Commission
c/o Gunn Museum Saline County
218 South Market Street
Benton, AR 72015

Scott County Historical & Genealogical Society
P.O. Box 1560
Waldron, AR 72958

Sevier County Historical Society
509 West Heynecker
DeQueen, AR 71832

Van Buren County Historical Society/Museum
3rd & Poplar
P.O. Box 1023
Clinton, AR 72031
Tel: 501-745-4066
http://www.ntanet.net/nta/historical.html

Washington County Arkansas Historical Society
118 East Dickson Street
Fayetteville, AR 72701

Yell County Historical & Genealogical Society
108 West 18th
P.O. Box 356
Russellville, AR 72801-7119

LDS FAMILY HISTORY CENTERS

For locations of Family History Centers in this state, see the Family History Center locator at FamilySearch:
http://www.familysearch.org/eng/Library/FHC/
    frameset_fhc.asp

ARCHIVES/LIBRARIES/MUSEUMS

Arkansas Records Center
314 Vine Street
Newport, AR 72112

Arkansas State Library
One Capitol Mall
Little Rock, AR 72201-1081
Tel: 501-682-2053
http://www.asl.lib.ar.us/index.html

Arkansas State University
Dean B. Ellis Library
Arkansas Room
108 Cooley Drive
Jonesboro, AR 72467
P.O. Box 2040
State University, AR 72467
Tel: 870-972-3078
Main Office 870-972-3077
Reference Desk 870-972-3208
Circulation Desk 870-972-2460
Media Services 870-972-3432
E-mail: library@choctaw.astate.edu
http://www.library.astate.edu/

Central Arkansas Library System
The Butler Center
100 Rock Street
Little Rock, AR 72202
501-918-3056
http://www.cals.lib.ar.us/arkansas/index.html

Corning Library
613 Pine St.
Corning, AR 72422
Tel: 870-857-3453

Delta Cultural Center
114 Cherry Street
Helena, AR 72342
Tel: 870-338-4350
Fax: 870-338-4358
E-mail: INFO@DAH.STATE.AR.US
http://www.deltaculturalcenter.com/

Department of Arkansas Heritage
1500 Tower Building
323 Center Street
Little Rock, AR 72201
Voice: 501-324-9150
Fax: 501-324-9154
TDD: 501-324-9811
http://www.arkansasheritage.com/index.html
DeWITT PUBLIC LIBRARY
205 West Maxwell
DeWitt, AR 72042

Fayetteville Public Library/Ozarks Regional Library System
217 E. Dickson St.
Fayetteville, AR 72701
Tel: 501-442-2242
Fax: 501-442-5723
E-mail: publib@www.uark.edu
http://www.uark.edu/ALADDIN/publib/index.html

Fort Smith Public Library
Genealogy Department
3201 Rogers Avenue, Fort Smith, AR 72903
Tel: (501) 783-0229
E-mail: genealogy@fspl.lib.ar.us
http://www.fspl.lib.ar.us/genmain.html#contact

Greene County Library
120 N. 12th Street
Paragould, AR 72450
Tel: 870-236-8711
http://www.greenecountylibrary.com/library/brown/
    greene.htm

Historic Arkansas Museum
200 East Third Street
Little Rock, AR 72201-1608
Tel: 501-324-9351
Voice: 501-324-9345
Fax: 501-324-9811 TDD
E-mail: info@dah.state.ar.us
http://www.arkansashistory.com/

Hot Spring County Public Library
Ash & E Streets
Malvern, AR 72104
Tel: 501-332-5441

Lipscomb Room Greene County Library
120 North 12th Street
Paragould, AR 72450-4155

Little Rock Public Library
700 Louisiana Street
Little Rock, AR 72201
Tel: 501-370-5950

Morrilton-Conway County Library
101 W. Church
Morrilton, AR 72110
Tel: 501-354-5204

Northwest Arkansas Genealogical Library
400 S. Walton Boulevard
Bentonville, AR 72712

Orphan Train Riders Research Center
614 E. Emma Ave., #115
Springdale, AR 72764
Tel: 501-756-2780
Fax: 501-756-0769
E-mail: mjohjnson@jcf.jonesnet.org

Piggott Library
361 West Main St.
Piggott, AR 72454-2016
Tel: 870-598-3666

Pike County Archives
DeWayne Gray, President
c/o Happy Valley Grocery
Murfreesboro, AR 71958

The Pope County Library
116 East Third Street
Russellville, AR 72801

Powhatan Courthouse State Park
P.O. Box 93
Powhatan, AR 72458
Tel: 870-878-6794

Prescott-Nevada County Depot Museum
400 W. 1st Street South
P.O. Box 10
Prescott, AR 71857
Tel: 870-887-5821
http://wolfden.swsc.k12.ar.us/depot_museum/

Rector Library
121 W. 4th Street
Rector AR 72461-1309
(870) 595-2410
(870) 595-2410

Shiloh Museum of Ozark History
118 West Johnson Ave.
Springdale, AR 72764
Tel: 501-750-8165
Fax: 501-750-8171
http://www.uark.edu/ALADDIN/shiloh/

University of Arkansas Libraries
Special Collections Dept.
Fayetteville, AR 72701
Tel: 501-575-5417
E-mail: mdabrish@saturn.uark.edu
http://cavern.uark.edu/libinfo/speccoll/

NEWSPAPER REPOSITORIES

Arkansas History Commission
One Capitol Mall
Little Rock, AR 72201
Tel: 501-682-6900
http://www.ark-ives.com/

University of Arkansas Libraries
Special Collections Dept.
Mullins Library
Fayetteville, AR 72701
Tel: (501) 575-5577
FAX: (501) 575-6656
E-mail: mdabrish@saturn.uark.edu
http://www.uark.edu/libinfo/speccoll/

University of Arkansas at Little Rock
Special Collections Division
University Avenue at 33rd Street
Little Rock, AR 72704

VITAL RECORDS

Arkansas Department of Health
Division of Vital Records, Slot 44
4815 West Markham Street
Little Rock, AR 72205-3867
Tel: 501-661-2336
(Birth & Death 1914-present, Marriages 1917-present,
       Divorce 1923-present)
http://health.state.ar.us/htm/vr_faq.htm

ARKANSAS ON THE WEB

Arkansas Genweb Project
http://www.rootsweb.com/~argenweb/

Arkansas History Commission & State Archives
http://www.state.ar.us/ahc/index.htm

Original Arkansas Genealogy Project
http://www.couchgenweb.com/arkansas/

Persistence of the Spirit
African-American Experience in Arkansas
http://www.aristotle.net/persistence/

Travellers Southern Families
 http://genealogy.traveller.com/genealogy/

University of Arkansas, Fayetteville
http://cavern.uark.edu/libinfo/speccoll/index.html

CALIFORNIA

ARCHIVES, STATE & NATIONAL

California State Archives
Sacramento, CA 95814
Tel: 916-653-2246
Fax: 916-653-7363
E-mail: ArchivesWeb@ss.ca.gov
http://www.ss.ca.gov/archives/archives_b.htm

National Archives-Pacific Region (Laguna Niguel)
24000 Avila Rd., First Floor-East Entrance
P.O. Box 6719
Laguna Niguel, CA 92607-6719
Tel: 949-360-2626
Fax: 949-360-2624
E-mail: laguna.archives@nara.gov
http://www.nara.gov/regional/laguna.html

National Archives-Pacific Region (San Francisco)
1000 Commodore Drive
San Bruno, CA 94066
Tel: 650-876-9001
Fax: 650-876-9233
E-mail: sanbruno.archives@nara.gov
http://www.nara.gov/regional/sanfranc.html

GENEALOGICAL SOCIETIES

African American Genealogical Society of Northern California
P.O. Box 27485, Oakland, CA 94602-0985
Phone: (510) 496-2740 ext. 4144
Fax: (510) 496-2740 ext. 4144
E-mail: baobabtree@aagsnc.org
http://www.aagsnc.org/index.htm

Afro-American Genealogical Society
California Afro-American Museum
600 State Drive, Exposition Park
Los Angeles, CA 90037

Amador County Genealogical Society
322 Via Verde, Sutter Terrace
Sutter Creek, CA 95685

Antelope Valley Genealogical Society
P.O. Box 1049
Lancaster, CA 93534-1049
Tel: 805-942-4676

Association of Jewish Genealogical Societies
P.O. Box 50245
Palo Alto, CA 94303

Association of Professional Genealogists
Southern California Chapter (SCC-APG)
P.O. Box 9486
Brea, CA 92822-9486
http://www.cagenweb.com/sccapg/

Basin Research Associates, Inc.
1933 Davis Street
San Leandro, CA 94577
(510) 430-8441

Calaveras Genealogical Society
753 Main Street
P.O. Box 184
Angels Camp, CA 95222-0184

California African-American Genealogical Society
P.O. Box 8442
Los Angeles, CA 90008-0442

California Genealogical Society
1611 Telegraph Ave., Suite 200
Oakland, CA 94612-2152
Telephone: (510) 663-1358
http://www.calgensoc.org/

California Pioneers of Santa Clara County
P.O. Box 8208
San Jose, CA 95155

California Society of Colonial Pioneers
456 McAlister Street
San Francisco, CA 94102

California State Genealogical Alliance
P.O. Box 311
Danville CA 94526-0311
http://feefhs.org/csga/frg-csga.html

California State Society
Daughters of the American Revolution
http://members.home.net/swelch/cssdar/

Chester Genealogy Club
P.O. Box 107
Chester, CA 96020

Chula Vista Genealogical Society
c/o Chula Vista City Library
4th & F Streets
Chula Vista, CA 91910

Clan Diggers Genealogical Society
(Kern River Valley, Kern County)
P.O. Box 531
Lake Isabella, CA 93240
Tel: 619-376-6210

Coachella Valley Genealogical Society
P.O. Box 124
Indio, CA 92202

Colorado River-Blythe Quartsite Genealogical Society
P.O. Box 404
Blythe, CA 92226

Colusa County Genealogical Society
P.O. Box 973
Williams, CA 95987

Computer Rooters
P.O. Box 161693
Sacramento, CA 95816

Computer Genealogy Society of San Diego (CGSSD)
P.O. Box 370357
San Diego, CA 92137-0357
Tel: 619-670-0960
E-mail: cgssd-board@ucsd.edu.
http://www.cgssd.org/

Conejo Valley Genealogical Society
P.O. Box 1228
Thousand Oaks, CA 91358-1228
Tel: 805-497-8293
E-mail: cvgs@themall.net
http://home.earthlink.net/~hwallace/cvgspage/index.html

Contra Costa Genealogical Society
P.O. Box 910
Concord, CA 94522
http://www.geocities.com/Heartland/Plains/4335/cccgs/
        cccgs.html

Davis Genealogical Club/Library
Davis Senior Center
646 A Street
Davis, CA 95616
Tel: (916) 757-5696
http://feefhs.org/ghcsv/dgc/frg-dgcl.html

Delta Genealogical Interest Group
P.O. Box 157
Knightsen, CA 94548

East Bay Genealogical Society
405 14th St., Terrace Level (library)
P.O. Box 20417
Oakland, CA 94620-0417
Tel: 510-451-9599
http://www.katpher.com/EBGS/EBGS.html

East Kern Genealogical Society
9716 Irene Ave.
California, CA 93505-1329
Tel: 619-373-4728

El Dorado Research Society
P.O. Box 56
El Dorado, CA 95623

Escondido Genealogical Society
P.O. Box 2190
Escondido, CA 92025-2190
Tel: 619-743-6049

Fresno Genealogical Society
P.O. Box 1429
Fresno, CA 93716-1429
Tel: 209-488-3195

Genealogical Society of Hispanic America
Southern California Branch (GSHA-SC)
P.O. Box 2472
Santa Fe Springs, CA 90670-0472
http://www.gsha.net/sc/

German Research Association, Inc. (GRA)
P.O. Box 711600
San Diego, CA 92171-1600
http://www.feefhs.org/gra/frg-gra.html

German Genealogical Society
2125 Wright Avenue, C9
LaVerne, CA 91750

Glendora Genealogical Group
P.O. Box 1141
Glendora, CA 91740

Glenn Genealogy Group
1121 Marin
Orland, CA 95963
Grass Roots Genealogical Group
11350 McCourtney Road
Grass Valley, CA 95949-9759
http://www.nccn.net/leisure/crafthby/genealog.htm

Hadley Genealogical Society of Southern California
33210 Baily Park Dr.
Menifee, CA 92584

60

Hayward Area Genealogical Society
P.O. Box 754
Hayward, CA 94543

Hemet-San Jacinto Genealogical Society
1779 East Florida Ave, Unit C-1
Hemet, CA 92544
Mail:
P.O. Box 2516
Hemet, CA 92546-2516
Tel: 909-658-6153

Heritage Genealogical Society
12056 Lomica Dr.
San Diego, CA 92128
Tel: 619-485-6009

Hi Desert Genealogical Society
P.O. Box 1271
Victorville, CA 92393
Tel: 619-247-8835
http://vvo.com/comm/hdgs.htm

Hispanic Historical & Ancestral Research, Society of
P.O. Box 5294
Fullerton, CA 92635
E-mail: SHHARPres@AOL.com
http://members.aol.com/shhar/

Humboldt County Genealogical Society
2336 G Street
P.O. Box 882
Eureka, CA 95502

Immigrant Genealogical Society
1310-B Magnolia Blvd.
P.O. Box 7369
Burbank, CA 91510
Tel: 818-848-3122
Fax: 818-716-6300
E-mail: ted.hanft@panasia.com
http://feefhs.org/igs/frg-igs.html

Imperial County Genealogical Society
1573 Elam Street
El Centro, CA 92243-3133

Indian Wells Valley Genealogical Society
131 Los Flores
P.O. Box 2047
Ridgecrest, CA 93555

Intermountain Genealogical Society
P.O. Box 399
Burney, CA 96013

Jewish Genealogical Society of Los Angeles
P.O. Box 55443
Sherman Oaks, CA 91413
http://www.jewishgen.org/jgsla/

Jewish Genealogical Society of Orange County
2370-1D Via Mariposa,
Laguna Woods, CA 92653
949-855-4692
http://www.jewishgen.org/jgsoc/

Jewish Genealogical Society of Sacramento
2351 Wyda Way
Sacramento, CA 95825
(916) 486-0906 ext. 361
jgs_sacramento@hotmail.com
http://www.jewishgen.org/jgs-sacramento/

Jewish Genealogical Society of San Diego
255 South Rios Avenue
Solana Beach, CA 92075

Kern County Genealogical Society
P.O. Box 2214
Bakersfield, CA 93303
Tel: 805-831-7527

Lake County Genealogical Society/Museum
255 North Forbes Street
P.O. Box 1323
Lakeport, CA 95453
Tel: 707-263-4555

Lake Elsinore Genealogical Society (LEGS)
P.O. Box 807
Lake Elsinore, CA 92330
Tel: 909-674-5776

Leisure World Genealogical Workshop/Library
2300 Beverly Manor Road
Seal Beach, CA 90740

Livermore-Amador Genealogical Society (L-AGS)
P.O. Box 901
Livermore, CA 94551
Tel: 510-846-4265
510-447-9386
E-mail: webmaster@l-ags.org
http://www.l-ags.org/

Lompoc Valley Genealogical Society, Inc.
P.O. Box 81
Lompoc, CA 93438-0081

Los Angeles Westside Genealogical Society
P.O. Box 10447
Marina del Rey, CA 90295
E-mail: LAWGS@genealogy-la.com
http://www.genealogy-la.com/lawgs.shtml

Los Banos California Genealogical Society
16778 South Place
P.O. Box 1106
Los Banos, CA 93635
Tel: 209-826-4882

Los Californianos
P.O. Box 5155
San Francisco, CA 94101

Lucerne Valley Genealogy Association, Root Diggers
c/o Lucerne Valley Library
P.O. Box 408
Lucerne Valley, CA 92356

Madera Genealogical Society
P.O. Box 495
Madera, CA 93639-0495
Tel: 209-661-1219
http://www.cagenweb.com/madera/

Maidu Genealogical Society
Maidu Committee Center
1550 Maidu Drive
Roseville, CA 95661
Tel: 916-786-0186

Marin County Genealogical Society
P.O. Box 1511
Novato, CA 94948-1511
Tel: 415-435-2310
E-mail: MarinGenSoc@juno.com
http://www.maringensoc.org/

Mayflower Descendants Society of the State of California
405 Fourteenth Street, Terrace Level
Oakland, CA 94612
Telephone: 916-771-5094
Fax: 916-771-7461
http://www.mayflowersociety.com/

Mendocino Coast Genealogical Society
P.O. Box 762
Fort Bragg, CA 95437

Merced County Genealogical Society
P.O. Box 3061
Merced, CA 95344
Tel: 209-723-9019
E-mail: mcgs@usa.net
http://www.rootsweb.com/~camcgs/home.htm

Mission Oaks Genealogical Club
Mission Oaks Community Center
4701 Gibbons Dr.
Carmichael, CA 95609
Mail:
P.O. Box 216
Carmichael, CA 95609-0216
Tel: 916-482-8531

Mojave Desert Genealogical Society
P.O. Box 1320
Barstow, CA 92311

Monterey County Genealogical Society
P.O. Box 8144
Salinas, CA 93912-8144

Morongo Basin Genealogical Society
P.O. Box 234
Yucca Valley, CA 92284
http://www.yuccavalley.com/genealogy/

Mt. Diablo Genealogical Society
1938 Tice Blvd.
P.O. Box 4654
Walnut Creek, CA 94596
Tel: 415-932-4423

Napa Valley Genealogical & Biographical Society
1701 Menlo Avenue
P.O. Box 385
Napa, CA 94558
Tel: 707-252-2252
E-mail: nvgbs@napanet.net
http://www.napanet.net/~nvgbs/

Nevada County Genealogical Society
Dept. I
P.O. Box 176
Cedar Ridge, CA 95924
Tel: 619-257-3780
http://www.nccn.net/leisure/crafthby/genealog.htm

Genealogical Society of North Orange County
P.O. Box 706
Yorba Linda, CA 92885

North San Diego County Genealogical Society
P.O. Box 581
Carlsbad, CA 92018-0581
http://www.cagenweb.com/nsdcgs/

Norwegian Genealogy Group
c/o Sons of Norway Lodge
2006 East Vista Way
Vista, CA 92084-3321

Ohio Genealogical Society
Southern California Chapter
P.O. Box 5057
Los Alamitos, CA 90721-5057

**Orange County California Genealogical Society
(OCCGS)**
P.O. Box 1587
Orange, CA 92856-1587
http://www.occgs.com/welcome.html

Pajaro Valley Genealogical Society
53 North Drive
Freedom, CA 95019

Palm Springs Genealogical Society
P.O. Box 2093
Palm Springs, CA 92263-2093
E-mail: editor1@earthlink.net
http://www.ci.palm-springs.ca.us/Library/lgen.html

Paradise Genealogical Society
P.O. Box 460
Paradise, CA 95967-0460
Tel: 530-877-2330
E-mail: pargenso@jps.net
http://pweb.jps.net/~pargenso/index.html

Pasadena Genealogy Society
P.O. Box 94774
Pasadena, CA 91109-4774
Tel: 818-794-7973

Patterson Genies
525 Clover Avenue
Patterson, CA 95363

Placer County Genealogical Society
P.O. Box 7385
Auburn, CA 95604-7385
Tel: 530- 887-2646
E-mail: gunruh@pcgenes.com
http://www.webcom.com/gunruh/pcgs.html

Pocahontas Trail Genealogical Society
3628 Cherokee Lane
Modesto, CA 95356

Polish Genealogical Society of California (PGS CA)
P.O. Box 713
Midway City, CA 92655-0713
http://feefhs.org/pol/pgsca/frgpgsca.html

Pomona Valley Genealogical Society
P.O. Box 286
Pomona, CA 91769-0286
Tel: 909-599-2166
http://home.earthlink.net/~hazefam/PVGS.html

Questing Heirs Genealogical Society
P.O. Box 15102
Long Beach, CA 90815-0102
Tel: 310-596-8736
http://www.cagenweb.com/questing/

Rancho Bernardo Genealogy Group
c/o San Diego Public Library
Rancho Bernardo Branch
16840 Bernardo Center
San Diego, CA 92128
Tel: 619-485-6977

Redwood Genealogical Society
P.O. Box 645
Fortuna, CA 95540-0645
Tel: 707-725-3791

Renegade Root Diggers
9171 Fargo Avenue
Hanford, CA 93230

Riverside Genealogical Society
P.O. Box 2557
Riverside, CA 92516
http://www.geocities.com/Heartland/Woods/6250/

Root Cellar Sacramento Genealogical Society
P.O. Box 265
Citrus Heights, CA 95611
Tel: 916-481-4930

Sacramento Genealogical Association
P.O. Box 28297
Sacramento, CA 95828

Sacramento Genealogical Society
P.O.Box 265
Citrus Heights, CA 95611-0265

Sacramento German Genealogy Society
P.O. Box 660061
Sacramento, CA 95866-0061
http://www.feefhs.org/sggs/frg-sggs.html

**Sacramento Valley, Genealogical and Historical
Council of the**
P.O. Box 214749
Sacramento, CA 95821-0749
Tel: 916-331-4349
http://feefhs.org/ghcsv/frgghcsv.html

San Benito County Genealogical Society
1021 Peach Court
Hollister, CA 95023
Tel: 831-636-8229
Fax: 831-636-5350

San Bernardino Valley Genealogical Society
P.O. Box 26020
San Bernardino, CA 92406
Tel: 909-883-7468

San Diego African-American Genealogy Research Group
P.O. Box 740240
San Diego, CA 92174-0240

San Diego Genealogical Association
P.O. Box 422
Ramona, CA 92065

San Diego Genealogical Society
1050 Pioneer Way, Suite E
El Cajon, CA 92020-1943
Tel: 619-588-0065
E-mail: sdgs2000@yahoo.com
http://www.rootsweb.com/~casdgs/

San Diego Jewish Genealogical Society
P.O. Box 927089
San Diego, CA 92192-7089
http://www.homestead.com/sdjgs/

San Fernando Valley Genealogical Society
P.O. Box 3486
Winnetka, CA 91396-3486

San Francisco Bay Area Jewish Genealogical Society
P.O. Box 471616
San Francisco, CA 94147-1616

San Gorgonio Genealogical Society
1050 Brinton Ave.
Banning, CA 92220

San Joaquin Genealogical Society
P.O. Box 4817
Stockton, CA 95204-0817
http://www.rootsweb.com/~sjgs/index.htm

San Luis Obispo County Genealogical Society
P.O. Box 4
Atascadero, CA 93423-0004
Tel: 805-927-8172
http://www.slonet.org/vv/slocgs/genweb.html

San Mateo County Genealogical Society (SMCGS)
25 Tower Road
P.O. Box 5083
San Mateo, CA 94402
Tel: 650-572-2929
http://www.smcgs.org/

San Ramon Valley Genealogical Society
P.O. Box 305
Diablo, CA 94528
Tel: 510-837-8858

Santa Barbara County Genealogical Society
316 Castillo Street
P.O. Box 1303
Goleta, CA 93116-1303
Tel: 805-967-8954
E-mail address:sbcgs@juno.com
http://www.cagenweb.com/santabarbara/sbcgs/

Santa Clara Historical & Genealogical Society
2635 Homestead Road
Santa Clara, CA 95051-5387
Tel: 408-615-2986
http://www.katpher.com/SCCHGS/#Location

Santa Cruz County, Genealogical Society of
P.O. Box 72
Santa Cruz, CA 95063
Tel: 831-420-5794

Santa Maria Valley Genealogical Society
P.O. Box 1215
Santa Maria, CA 93456

Sequoia Genealogical Society
Tulare Public Library
113 North F Street
Tulare, CA 93274-3803

Shasta Genealogical Society
P.O. Box 994652
Redding, CA 96099-4652
http://www.rootsweb.com/~cascogs/

Siskiyou County Genealogical Society
P.O. Box 225
Yreka, CA 96097
Tel: 916-842-8175

Sloughhouse Area Genealogical Society
Rancho Murietta, CA 95683
Tel: 916-354-2807

Society of California Pioneers
300 Fourth Street San Francisco, CA 94107-1272
Tel 415.957.1849 Fax 415-957.9858
E-mail: shaas@californiapioneers.org.
http://www.californiapioneers.org/

Solano County Genealogical Society
Old Town Hall
620 E. Main St.
Vacaville, CA
Mail:
P.O. Box 2494
Fairfield, CA 94533-0249
(707) 446-6869
http://www.scgsinc.org/

Sonoma County Genealogical Society
P.O. Box 2273
Santa Rosa, CA 95405-0273
http://www.scgs.org/

South Bay Cities Genealogical Society
P.O. Box 11069
Torrance, California 90510-1069
E-mail: sbcgs@hotmail.com
http://www.rootsweb.com/~casbcgs/

South Humboldt Historical & Genealogical Society
P.O. Box 656
Garberville, CA 95440

South Orange County California Genealogy Society (SOCCGS)
P.O. Box 4513
Mission Viejo, CA 92690-4513
E-mail: soccgs@savoury.net
http://www.rootsweb.com/~casoccgs/

Southern California Genealogical Society (SCGS)
417 Irving Drive, Burbank, CA 91504
PHONE: 818-843-7247 or (818) THE-SCGS
FAX: 818-843-7262
E-mail: scgs@earthlink.net
http://www.scgsgenealogy.com/

Southern California Genealogical Society,Inc.
600 South Central Avenue
Glendale, CA 91204

Stanislaus County Genealogical Society
P.O. Box A
Modesto, CA 95352-3660
Tel: (209) 571-3227
http://www.cagenweb.com/lr/stanislaus/gssc.html

Sutter-Yuba Genealogical Society
P.O. Box 1274
Yuba City, CA 95991

TRW Genealogical Society
One Space Park R7/2214
Redondo Beach, CA 90278

Taft Area Genealogical Society
P.O. Box 1411
Taft, CA 93268

Tehama Genealogical & Historical Society
P.O. Box 415
Red Bluff, CA 96080

Temecula Valley Genealogical Society
27475 Ynez Rd., Ste. 291
Temecula, CA 92591

Tracy Area Genealogical Society
Lolly Hansen Senior Center
375 East 9th Street
Tracy, CA
Mailing Address:
1852 W. 11th Street, Box 632
Tracy, CA 95376

Tule Tree Tracers
Porterville Public Library
41 West Thurman Ave.
Porterville, CA 93257
Tel: 209-784-0177

Tuolumne County Genealogical Society
158 West Bradford Ave.
P.O. Box 3956
Sonora, CA 95370-3956
Tel: 209-532-1317
http://www.tchistory.org/gen_soc.html

Ukiah Tree Tracers Genealogical Society
P.O. Box 72
Ukiah, CA 95482

Universal Genealogical Society of Bellflower
8251 Cedar Street
Bellflower, CA 90706

Vallejo, Genealogy Society of
734 Marin Street
Vallejo, CA 94590-5913
707-748-1367
http://www.rootsweb.com/~cagsv/

Vandenberg Genealogical Society
P.O. Box 81
Lompoc, CA 93438-0081
Tel: 805-736-9637
    805-736-4778

Ventura County Genealogical Society
P.O. Box 24608
Ventura, CA 93002
Tel: 805-648-2715
    805-642-1242

Whittier Area Genealogical Society (WAGS)
P.O. Box 4367
Whittier, CA 90607-4367
Tel: 310-946-1758
http://www.cagenweb.com/kr/wags/

Yorba Linda Genealogical Society
4751 Libra Place
Yorba Linda, CA 92686

Yucaipa Valley Genealogical Society
P.O. Box 32
Yucaipa, CA 92399

HISTORICAL SOCIETIES

Alameda County Historical Society
484 Lake Park Avenue, #307
Oakland, CA 94610-2730
510-452-4474

Alameda Historical Society
2264 Santa Clara Avenue
Alameda, CA 94501

Alhambra Historical Society
1550 W. Alhambra Road (P.O. Box 6687)
Alhambra, CA 91802
626-300-8845

Alpine County Historical Society
P.O. Box 24
Markleeville, CA 96120

Altadena Historical Society
P.O. Box 144
Altadena, CA 91003
818-398-0760

Alvarado Adobe
#1 Alvarado Square
San Pablo, CA 94806

Amador-Livermore Valley Historical Society
603 Main Street
P.O. Box 573
Pleasanton, CA 94566
Tel: 510-462-2766

Amador County Historical Society
P.O. Box 761
Jackson, CA 95642
E-mail: amadorarchives@volcano.net
http://www.amadorarchives.org/achs.html

American Historical Association
Loyola Marymount-Dept. of History
Los Angeles, CA 90045
213-642-2805

American Historical Society of Germans from Russia
3233 North West
Fresno, CA 93705

Anaheim Historical Society
Anaheim Blvd. at Broadway
P.O. Box 927
Anaheim, CA 92815
Tel: 714-778-3301

Anderson Valley Historical Society
P.O. Box 676
Boonville, CA 95415
Tel: 707-895-3207

Association for Northern California Records & Research
P.O. Box 3024
Chico, CA 95927
E-mail: ANCRR@csuchico.edu
http://www.csuchico.edu/ancrr/

Atascadero History Society
6500 Palma
P.O. Box 1047
Atascadero, CA 93423
Tel: 805-466-8341
http://www.atascaderocofc.com/
    subitem.asp?parItemID=30

Augustan Society, Inc.
P.O. Box 75
Daggett, CA 92327-0075
Tel: 760-254-9223
FAX: 760-254-1953
E-mail: robertcleve@yahoo.com
http://www.augustansociety.org/

Azusa Historical Society, Inc.
City Hall Complex
213 E. Foothill Blvd.
Azusa, CA 91702

Baldwin Park Historical Society
4061 Sterling Way
Baldwin Park, CA 91706
626-338-7130

Belmont Historical Society
Historical Room
1225 Ralston Avenue
Belmont, CA 94002
http://www.belmont.gov/hist/index.html

Belvedere-Tiburon Landmarks Society
Archives
1550 Tiburon Blvd., Courtyard
P.O. Box 134
Tiburon, CA 94920
415-435-5490 (Archives)
415-435-1853 (Society)
http://www.weblink.com/landmarks/landmark.html

Berkeley Historical Society
1931 Center Street
P.O. Box 1190
Berkeley, CA 94701-1190
Tel: 510-848-0181
E-mail: berkhist@ix.netcom.com
http://www.ci.berkeley.ca.us/histsoc/

Big Bear Valley Historical Society
Big Bear City Park
P.O. Box 513
Big Bear City, CA 92314
Tel: 909-585-8100

Bishop Museum/Historical Society
P.O. Box 363
Bishop, CA 93514
Tel: 760-873-5950

Black Historical Society of Santa Clara
468 North 11th Street
San Jose, CA 95112
Tel: 408-295-9183

Boulder Creek Historical Society
12547 Highway 9
Boulder Creek, CA 95006
Tel: 831-338-6617

Burbank Historical Society
1015 W. Olive Avenue
Burbank, CA 91506
Tel: 818-841-6333
Fax: 818-841-0059

Butte County Historical Society
1480 Lincoln
Oroville, CA 95965
P.O. Box 2195
Oroville, CA 95965
Tel: 916-533-5316

Calabasas Historical Society
P.O. Box 8067
Calabasas, CA 91371
818-347-0470

Calaveras County Historical Society, Museum, & Archives
30 North Main Street
P.O. Box 723
San Andreas, CA 95249
Tel: 209-754-1058

California Council for the Promotion of History
P.O. Box 221476
Sacramento CA 95822
http://www.vcnet.com/sbra/ccph/

California Historical Society
678 Mission Street
San Francisco, CA 94105
Tel: 415-357-1848
Fax: 415-357-1850
http://www.californiahistoricalsociety.org/

California History Center & Foundation
21250 Stevens Creek Blvd.
Cupertino, CA 95014
Tel: 408.864.8712
Fax: 408.864.5486
E-mail: info@calhistory.org
http://www.calhistory.org/

California Mennonite Historical Society
4824 E. Butler
Fresno, CA 93727
http://www.fresno.edu/affiliation/cmhs/

California Pioneers of Santa Clara County
661 Empey Way
San Jose, CA 95128
408-998-1174

Californian Southern Division,
U.S. Mormon Battalion, Inc.
2510 Juan Street
San Diego, California 92110
Telephone (619) 298-3317
http://www.ldssocal.org/vc/mbvc.htm

Chinese Historical Society of America
965 Clay Street
San Francisco, CA 94108
Tel 415.391.1188
Fax 415.391.1150
E-mail: info@chsa.org
http://www.chsa.org/

Chinese Historical Society of Southern California
P.O. Box 862647
Los Angeles, CA 90086-2647
323.222.0856
http://www.chssc.org/

Chino Valley Historical Society
5493 B Street
P.O. Box 972
Chino, CA 91708
(909) 627-6464

City of San Bernardino Historical & Pioneer Society
P.O. Box 875
San Bernardino, CA 92402

Clayton Historical Society
6101 Main Street
P.O. Box 94
Clayton, CA 94517
Tel: 925-672-0240
http://94517.com/chs/

Coachella Valley Historical Society
P.O. Box 505
Indio, CA 92202-0505
Tel: 619-342-6651

Colfax Area Historical Society
P.O. Box 185
Colfax, CA 95713-0185
Tel: 530-346-2267
http://www.foothill.net/colfax/history/

Colusa County Historical Records Commission
c/o Colusa County Free Library
738 Market Street
Colusa, CA 95932
Tel: 530 -458-7671

**Commission for the Preservation
of Pioneer Jewish Cemeteries and Landmarks**
c/o Western Jewish History Center
Judah L. Magnes Memorial Museum
2911 Russell St.
Berkeley, CA 94710
Tel: 510-549-6932
http://www.magnesmuseum.org/cemecom.htm

Concord Historical Society
1601 Sutter St., Suites E and F
Mail: P.O. Box 404
Concord, CA 94522
Telephone: 925-827-3380
www.conhistsoc.org

Conejo Valley Historical Society
Stagecoach Inn Museum
51 South Ventu Park Road
Newbury Park, CA 91320
Tel: 805-498-9441
http://www.toguide.com/stagecoach/about.html

Conference of California Historical Societies
University of the Pacific
Stockton, CA 95211
Tel: 209-946-2169
http://www.cs.uop.edu/organizations/CCHSBROC.html

Contra Costa County Historical Society
610 Main Street
Martinez, CA 94553
Phone: (925) 229-1042
FAX : (925) 229 1772
http://www.cocohistory.com/

Coronado Historical Association
1100 Orange Avenue
Coronado, CA 92118
619-435-7242
E-mail: info@coronadohistory.org
http://www.coronadohistory.org/

Costa Mesa Historical Society
1870 Anaheim Ave.
P.O. Box 1764
Costa Mesa, CA 92628
Tel: 714-631-5918

Covina Historical Society
125 E. College St.
Covina, CA 91723
626-966-3976

Covina Valley Historical Society
300 N. Valencia Place
Covina, CA 91723

Crockett Museum and Historical Society
P.O. Box 194
Crockett, CA 94525
Tel: 510-787-2178
E-mail: keithglenn@home.com
http://pages.zdnet.com:8083/keithglenn/crockettmuseum/

Cupertino Committee for the Promotion of History
21250 Stevens Creek Blvd.
Cupertino, CA 95014

De Anza Trek Lancer Society
20739 Sunrise Drive
Cupertino, CA 95014

Del Mar Historical Society
240 10th St,
Del Mar, CA 92014
858-794-0029

Del Norte County Historical Society
577 H Street
Crescent City, CA 95531
707-464-3922

Delano Historical Society & Heritage Park
330 Lexington Street
Delano, CA 93215
Tel: 661-725-6730

Desert Hot Springs Historical Society
P.O. Box 1267
Desert Hot Springs, CA 92240
760-329-7610

Downey Historical Society and History Center
12540 S. Rives Ave.
Downey, CA 90242
(562) 862-2777
http://www.downeyca.org/visitor/hiscenter.htm

Duarte Historical Society
777 Encanto Parkway
P.O. Box 263
Duarte, CA 91009
626-357-9419
E-mail: margiloff@compuserve.com

Eagle Rock Valley Historical Society
Eagle Rock Cultural Center
2225 Colorado Blvd.
Eagle Rock, CA 90041
Tel: 323-226-1617

East Contra Costa Historical Society and Museum
3890 Sellers Ave.
Brentwood, California 94513
Tel: 925-625-3553
http://www.theschoolbell.com/history/

Echo Park Historical Society
P.O. Box 261022
Echo Park, CA 90026
323-860-8874
http://www.echopark.net/org/ephs.htm

El Cajon Historical Society
P.O. Box 1973
El Cajon, CA 92022-1973
http://www.cajon.k12.ca.us/echs/

El Monte Historical Society
3150 N. Tyler Ave.
El Monte, CA
P.O. Box 6307
El Monte, CA 91734
626-444-3813

Encino Historical Society
16756 Moorpark Street
Encino, CA 91436

Escondido Historical Society
321 N. Broadway
P.O. Box 263
Escondido, CA 92025
Tel: 760-743-8207
http://www.ci.escondido.ca.us/visitors/uniquely/historic/

Fallbrook Historical Society
260 Rocky Crest Road
P.O. Box 1375
Fallbrook, CA 92088-1375
760-723-4125
http://sd.znet.com/~schester/fallbrook/history/society/

Fillmore Historical Society & Museum
350 Main St
Fillmore, CA 93015
805-524-0948

Folsom Historical Society
823 Sutter Street
Folsom, CA 95630
Tel: 916-985-2707

Fort Crook Historical Society
P.O. Box 397
Fall River Mills, CA 96028

Fort Point National Historic Site
Long Avenue & Marine Drive
P.O. Box 29333
Presidio of San Francisco, CA 94129-0333
Tel: (415) 556-1693
http://www.nps.gov/fopo/index.htm

Fortuna Historical Commission
621 11th Street
Fortuna, CA 95540
http://www.chamber.sunnyfortuna.com/memberspages/
fortuna_historical_commission/

Fresno City & County Historical Society
7160 W. Kearney Boulevard
Fresno, CA 93706
telephone: 559-441-0862
fax: 559-441-1372
E-mail: FrHistSoc@aol.com
web sites: www.valleyhistory.org

Friends of the Adobes, Inc.
Rios Caladonia Adobe
San Miguel, CA 93451
805-467-3357

Friends of the Carrillo Adobe
P.O. Box 2843
Santa Rosa, CA 95405
http://www.carrilloadobe.org/index.htm

Garden Grove Historical Society
12174 Euclid Street
Garden Grove, CA 92640
Tel: 714-530-8871
http://ch.ci.garden-grove.ca.us/internet/gghsocty.html

Gilroy Historical Society
Gilroy Museum
195 5th St
Gilroy, CA 95021
(408)848-0470

Glendale Historical Society
P.O. Box 4173
Glendale, CA 91202
818-242-7447
http://www.glendalehistorical.org/

Glendora Historical Society
314 N. Glendora Avenue
P.O. Box 532
Glendora, CA 91740
626-963-0419

Goleta Valley Historical Society
304 North Los Carneros
Goleta, CA 93117
Tel: 805-964-4407
http://www.goletahistory.org/

Hayward Area Historical Society/Museum
22701 Main Street
Hayward, CA 94541
Tel: 510-581-0223

Healdsburg Historical Society
221 Matheson
Healdsburg, CA 95448
707-431-3325

Heritage Association of El Dorado County
P.O. Box 62
Placerville, CA 95667
http://www.geocities.com/RainForest/7589/

Hispanic Historical & Ancestral Research, Society of
P.O. Box 5294
Fullerton, CA 92635
E-mail: SHHARPres@AOL.com
http://members.aol.com/shhar/

Historical Society of Centinela Valley
7634 Midfield Avenue
Los Angeles, CA 90045
213-649-6272

Historical Society of Long Beach
428 Pine Avenue
P.O. Box 1869
Long Beach, CA 90801
Tel: 562-495-1210
Fax: 562-495-1281
E-mail: hslb@thegrid.net

Historical Society of Monterey Park
781 S. Orange Avenue (P.O. Box 172)
Monterey Park, CA 91754
626-307-1267

Historical Society of Southern California
200 East Avenue 43
Los Angeles, CA 90031
Tel: 323-222-0546
Fax: 323-222-0771
E-mail: HSSC@socalhistory.org
http://www.socalhistory.org/

Historical Society of the Upper Mojave Desert
P.O. Box 2001
Ridgecrest, CA 93556-2001
Tel: (760) 375-6900
archives are located at:
302 Station Street
Ridgecrest, CA
http://www.maturango.org/Hist.html

Humboldt County Historical Society
Street address: 703 8th St., Eureka
Mailing address: P.O. Box 8000
Eureka, CA 95502
telephone: 707-445-4342
fax: 707-445-4146
E-mail: hchs@reninet.com
http://www.humboldthistory.org/

Huntington Beach Historical Society
Newland House Museum
19820 Beach Blvd.
Huntington Beach, CA 92648
Tel: 714-962-5777
http://hb.quik.com/jperson/nwhouse.html or
http://www.stockteam.com/newland.html

Irvine Historical Society & Museum
5 Rancho San Joaquin
Irvine, CA 92717
Tel: 714-786-4112

Kern-Antelope Historical Society
P.O. Box 325
Rosamond, CA 93560
Tel: 805-943-3221

Kern County Historical Organizations & Museums
Kern County Historical Records Commission
3801 Chester
Bakersfield, CA 93301
Tel: 805-861-2132

Kern River Valley Historical Society
Kern Valley Museum
49 Big Blue Rd
P.O. Box 651
Kernville, CA 93238
(760)376-6683

Kern County Historical Society
P.O. Box 141
Bakersfield, CA 93302
http://www.kerncountylibrary.org/historicalsoc.html

La Habra Old Settlers Historical Society
600 Linden Lane
La Habra, CA 90631
Tel: (714) 870-6084

La Jolla Historical Society
7846 Eads Avenue
P.O. Box 2085
La Jolla, CA 92038
Tel: (858) 459-0226
http://www.lajolla.org/

La Mesa Historical Society
8369 University Ave.
P.O. Box 882
La Mesa, CA 91944-0882
Tel: 619-466-0197
http://www.grossmont.k12.ca.us/lmhs/

La Puente Valley Historical Society
16021 Gale Avenue
Hacienda Heights, CA 91745
(626) 336-7644

Lafayette Historical Society
P.O. Box 133
Lafayette, CA 94549
Archives located at:
Lafayette Public Library
952 Moraga Road
Lafayette, CA 94549
Tel: 510-283-3872
http://lhs.lafayette.ca.us/

Lake County Historical Society
Lake County Historical Courthouse Museum
255 N.Main St
Lakeport, CA
P.O. Box 1011
Lakeport, CA 95453
(707) 263-4555
http://www.museum.lake.k12.ca.us/

Lake Tahoe Historical Society
3058 Highway 50
P.O. Box 404
South Lake Tahoe, CA 95705
530-541-5458

Las Virgines Historical Society
P.O. Box 124
Agoura, CA 91301

Lakeside Historical Society
9906 Maine Ave.
Lakeside, CA 92040
Tel: 619-561-1886
E-mail: info@lakesidehistory.org
http://www.lakesidehistory.org/

Lassen County Historical Society
William H. Pratt Museum
105 North Weatherlow St.
P.O. Box 321
Susanville, CA 96130
Tel: 530-257-4584

Leisure World Historical Society of Laguna Hills
23522 Paseo de Valencia
P.O. Box 2220
Laguna Hills, CA 92654
Tel: 714-951-2330

Lemon Grove Historical
P.O. Box 624
Lemon Grove, CA 91946
Museum Tel: 619-460-4353
Office Tel: 619-462-6494
Fax: 619-462-8266
E-mail: ofield@mail.sdsu.edu
http://www.sandiegohistory.org/societies/lemongrove/

Little Landers Historical Society
10110 Commerce Ave.
Tujunga, CA 91042
818-352-3420
http://www.rootsweb.com/~casfvgs/bolton.html

Livermore Heritage Guild
P.O. Box 961
Livermore, CA 94551-0961
925-449-9927
E-mail: lhg@lhg.org
http://www.lhg.org/

Lomita Historical Society
P.O. Box 549
Lomita, CA 90717
(310) 325-6884
E-mail: babylonm@pacbell.net
http://www.restorationcentral.com/orgs/lomita/

Lompoc Valley Historical Society
P.O. Box 88
Lompoc, CA 93438

Los Angeles City Historical Society
P.O. Box 41046
Los Angeles, CA 90041
213-936-2912

Los Altos Historical Commission
1 North San Antonio Road
Los Altos Hills, CA 94022
Phone(650)948-1491
Fax(650)941-7419
http://www.ci.los-altos.ca.us/histcom.htm

Madera County Historical Society
210 West Yosemite Ave.
Madera, CA 93639
Tel: 559-673-0291
http://www.maderahistory.org/

Marin County Historical Society
1125 B Street
San Rafael, CA 94901
Tel: 415-454-8538
E-mail: infomchs@pacbell.net
http://www.marinhistory.org

Martinez Historical Society
1005 Escobar Street
Martinez, CA 94553
http://www.martinezhistory.org/

Mendocino County Historical Society
603 W. Perkins St.
Ukiah, CA 95482-4726
Tel: 707-462-6969
http://www.pacificsites.com/~mchs/

Mendocino Historical Research
Kelley House Museum
45007 Albion St.
P.O. Box 922
Mendocino, CA 95460
Tel: 707-937-5791
http://www.mcn.org/ed/CUR/liv/ind/mark/kell.htm

Menlo Park Historical Association
Menlo Park Library
800 Alma Street
Menlo Park, CA 94025
650-858-3368
www.pls.lib.ca.us/pls/mpl/HistAssoc.html

Merced County Historical Society
Old County Courthouse
21st and N Streets
Merced, CA 95340
Tel: 209-723-2401
FAX: 209-723-8029
http://www.mercedmuseum.org/

Millbrae Historical Society
Millbrae Museum
450 Poplar Ave
Millbrae, CA 94030
P.O. Box 511
Millbrae, CA 94030
Tel: 650-692-5786
650-692-3720

Mission San Miguel
775 Mission Street
P.O. Box 69
San Miguel, CA 93451
Museum: 805-467-3256
http://www.missionsanmiguel.org/index.html

Modoc County Historical Society and Museum
600 S. Main Street
Alturas, CA 96101
(530) 233-6328.
Mojave Desert Heritage & Cultural Association
P. O. Box 66
Essex, CA 92332-0066
E-mail: mdhca@juno.com
http://www.mdhca.org/

Mohave Historical Society
P.O. Box 21
Victorville, CA 92392
http://vvo.com/comm/mhs.htm

Mokelumne Hill Historical Society
8367 Center Street
Mokelumne Hill, CA 95245
Tel: 209-286-1770

Montecito History Committee
1469 East Valley Road
Montecito, CA 93108
(805) 969-1597

Monterey County Historical Society
333 Boronda Rd.
P.O. Box 3576
Salinas, CA 93912
Tel: 408-757-8085
http://users.dedot.com/mchs/

Monterey History & Art Association
5 Custom House Plaza
Monterey, CA 93940
(408) 372-2608
http://csumb.edu/academic/projects/mhaa/mhaa.htm

Moraga Historical Society and Archives
1500 St. Mary's Road
P.O. Box 103
Moraga, CA 94556
Phone: 925-377-8734
FAX: 925-377-0354
E-mail: mhistory@silcon.com
http://www.moragahistory.org/

Morgan Hill Historical Society
17860 Monterey Street
Morgan Hill, CA 95037
(408) 782-7191

Mountain Empire Historical Society
31130 Highway 94
Campo, CA 91906
P.O. Box 394
Campo, CA 92006
Tel: 619-478-5707

Mountain View Pioneer & Historical Association
P.O. Box 252
Mountain View, CA 94041
415-968-6595

Napa County Historical Society
Goodman Library Building
1219 First Street
Napa, CA 94559
Tel: 707-224-1739
http://www.napanet.net/organizations/nhs/

National Trust for Historic Preservation
Western Regional Office
8 California Street, Suite 400
San Francisco, CA 94111-4803
Tel: (415) 956-0610
Fax: (415) 956-0837
E-mail: wro@nthp.org
http://www.nationaltrust.org/about_the_trust/western.html

Native American Heritage Commission
915 Capitol Mall, Room 364
Sacramento, CA 95814
Tel: (916) 653-4082
Fax: (916) 657-5390
http://www.ceres.ca.gov/nahc/

Nevada County Historical Society
P.O. Box 1300
Nevada City, CA 95959
Tel: 916-265-5468
http://www.nccn.net/~histsoc/welcome.htm

Newport Beach Historical Society
c/o Sherman Library
2647 East Pacific Coast Highway
Corona del Mar, CA 92625
Tel: (949) 673-1880
Fax: (949) 675-5458
http://www.slgardens.org/

North Lake Tahoe Historical Society
130 West Lake Blvd.
Tahoe City, CA 96145-6141
P. O. Box 6141
Tahoe City, CA 96145
(530) 583-1762
nlths@tahoecountry.com
http://www.tahoecountry.com/nlths/

Ojai Valley Museum & Historical Society
130 W Ojai Ave
Ojai, CA 93023-3212
P.O. Box 204
Ojai, CA 93023
Phone: (805)640-1390

Olompali State Historical Park
P.O. Box 1016
Novato, CA 94948
Tel: 415-892-3383
http://www.marinij.com/entertainment/recreation/parks/
    olompali.html

Orange County Historical Commission
211 W. Santa Ana Boulevard
P.O. Box 4048
Santa Ana, CA 91702-4048
714-834-5560

Orange Community Historical Society
101 N. Center
P.O. Box 5484
Orange, CA 92613-5484
Tel: 714-532-0361

Orange County Historical Society
Historic Howe-Waffle House
120 West Civic Center Dr.
Santa Ana, CA 92701
Tel: 714-543-8282
http://www.santaanahistory.com/articles/ochs.html

Orland Historical & Cultural Society
P.O. Box 183
Orland, CA 95963
Tel: 916-865-1444
http://www.sierraii.com/orland/ohcs.htm

Pacific Beach Historical Society
P.O. Box 9200
San Diego, CA 92169
Tel: 858-272-6655

Pacific Grove Heritage Society
Laurel and 17th Streets
P.O. Box 1007
Pacific Grove, CA 93950
Tel: 831-372-2898
http://www.mbay.net/~heritage/#member

Pacific Palisades Historical Society
P.O. Box 1299
Los Angeles, CA 90272

Pajaro Valley Historical Association
261 East Beach Street
Watsonville, CA 95076
Tel: 831-722-0305

Palm Springs Historical Society
221 South Palm Canyon Drive
P.O. Box 1498
Palm Springs, CA 92263
Tel: 760-323-8297
Fax: 760-320-2561
palmspgshistory@aol.com
http://palmsprings.com/history/

Palo Alto Historical Association
P.O. Box 193
Palo Alto, CA 94302
650-329-2437
http://www.commerce.digital.com/palo-alto/
historical-assoc/home.html

Pasadena Heritage
651 South St. John Avenue
Pasadena, CA 91105
Tel: 626.441.6333
Fax: 626.441.2917
E-mail: preservation@pasadenaheritage.org
http://www.pasadenaheritage.org/index.html

Pasadena Historical Society and Museum
470 West Walnut St.
Pasadena, CA 91103
Tel: 626-577-1660
Fax: 626-577-1662
http://www.pasadenahistory.org/

Patterson Township Historical Society
P.O. Box 15
Patterson, CA 95363
http://www.patterson-ca.com/histsoc/

Pioneer Historical Society of Riverside
P.O. Box 246
Riverside, CA 92502

Placentia Historical Committee
401 East Chapman Ave.
Placentia, CA 92870
http://www.placentia.org/Historical%20Committee/
Historical%20Page.htm

Plumas County Historical Society
P.O. Box 695
Quincy, CA 95971

Pomona Valley Historical Society
1569 North Park
Pomona, CA 91768
(909) 620-0264
http://www.osb.net/Pomona/

Portuguese Historical & Cultural Society
P.O. Box 161990
Sacramento, CA 95816
http://www.dholmes.com/o-prog.html

Ramona Pioneer Historical Society, Inc.
645 Main Street
P.O. Box 625
Ramona, CA 92065
Tel: 760-789-7644

Rancho Santa Fe Historical Society
6036 La Flecha
Rancho Santa Fe, CA 92091
(858) 756-9291

Redlands Area Historical Society
P.O. Box 1024
Redlands, CA 92373
Tel: (909) 307-6060
http://www.rahs.org/

Redondo Beach Historical Society
P.O. Box 978
Redondo Beach, CA 90277
http://members.aol.com/rbhistsoc/

Reedley Historical Society
Reedley Museum
1752 10th Street
P.O. Box 877
Reedley, CA 93654
Tel: 559-638-1913
http://www.reedley.com/Lori/Community-Tourism/
lo-reedley_museum.htm

Rialto Historical Society
205 North Riverside Ave.
P.O. Box 413
Rialto, CA 92377
Tel: 714-875-1750
http://www.wemweb.com/traveler/towns/20rialto/
hstsoc.html

Ridge Route Communities Museum/Historical Society
P.O. Box 684
Frazier Park, CA 93225
Tel: 661-245-7747
http://www.frazmtn.com/~rrchs/mainie.html

Riverside County Historical Association
4600 Crestmore Rd.
P.O. Box 3507
Riverside, CA 92519
Tel: (909) 955-4310

Sacramento County Historical Society
P.O. Box 160065
Sacramento, CA 95816-0065
Phone: (916)443-6265

Sacramento Historical Museum
101 I Street
Sacramento, CA 95814
Tel: 916-449-2057

Sacramento Museum & History Commission
1930 J Street
Sacramento, CA 95814

Sacramento River Delta Historical Society
P.O. Box 293
Walnut Grove, CA 95690

Sacramento Valley, Genealogical and Historical Council of the
P.O. Box 214749
Sacramento, CA 95821-0749
Tel: 916-331-4349
http://feefhs.org/ghcsv/frgghcsv.html

Saddleback Area Historical Society
25151 Seranno Road
P.O. Box 156
El Toro, CA 92630
Tel: 949-586-8485

San Antonio Valley Historical Association
216 Grove Place
King City, CA 93930
Tel: 832 -385-3587

San Antonio Valley Historical Society/Museum
P.O. Box 21
Lodi, CA 95241

San Benito County Historical Society
498 Fifth Street
P.O. Box 357
Hollister, CA 95023
Phone: 1-831-635-0335
E-mail: sbchs@hollinet.com
http://www.sbchistoricalsociety.org/

San Clemente Historical Society
117 Avenida Cabrillo
P.O. Box 283
San Clemente, CA 92672
Tel: (949) 492-9684
http://www.ocnow.com/community/groups/sanclemente/

San Diego Historical Society
P.O. Box 81825
San Diego, CA 92138-1825
Tel: 619-232-6203 ext. 105
http://edweb.sdsu.edu/edweb_folder/sdhs/mainpages/
sdhsmission.htm

San Diego Military Heritage Society
P.O. Box 33672
San Diego, CA 92163

San Fernando Valley Historical Society
10940 Sepulveda Blvd.
Mission Hills, CA 91345
(818) 365-7810

San Francisco African American Historical & Cultural Society
Fort Mason Center, Bldg. C, Room 165
San Francisco, CA 94123
Tel: 415-441-0640

San Francisco Historical Society
P.O. Box 420569
San Francisco, CA 94142
Tel: (415) 775-1111
http://www.sfhistory.org/

San Gabriel Historical Association
546 West Broadway
San Gabriel, CA 91776
(626) 308-3223

San Joaquin County Historical Society/Museum
11793 N. Micke Grove Road
Lodi, CA 95240
Tel: 209-331-2055
Fax: 209-331-2057
E-mail: sjmuseum@softcom.net
http://www.sanjoaquinhistory.org/index2.htm

San Joaquin Pioneer & Historical Society
The Haggin Museum
1201 North Pershing Avenue
Stockton, CA 95203

San Juan Bautista Historical Society
P.O. Box 1
San Juan Bautista, CA 95045
http://archaeology.csumb.edu/sjbhs/

San Juan Capistrano Historical Society
31831 Los Rios Street
P.O. Box 81
San Juan Capistrano, CA 92675
Tel: 949-493-8444
http://www.sjchistoricalsociety.com/

San Leandro Library & Historical Commission
300 Estudillo Avenue
San Leandro, CA 94577
510-577-3980

San Luis Obispo Historical Society
696 Monterey Street
San Luis Obispo, CA
P. O. Box 1391
San Luis Obispo, CA 93406-1391
(805) 543-0638
http://www.slochs.org/

San Marcos Historical Society
270 W San Marcos Blvd
San Marcos, CA 92069
Tel: (760) 744-9025

San Marino Historical Society
P.O. Box 80222
San Marino, CA 91118-8222
Tel: 626-796-6023
http://www.smnet.org/comm_group/historical/

San Mateo Co. Historical Assn. & Museum
777 Hamilton Street
Redwood City, CA 94063
phone: (650) 299-0104
fax: (650) 299-0141
E-mail: Info@sanmateocountyhistory.com
http://www.sanmateocountyhistory.com/

San Pablo Historical Society and Museum
#1 Alvarado Square
San Pablo, CA 94806
510-215-3046
http://www.ci.san-pablo.ca.us/history/

San Ramon Valley Historical Society
P.O. Box 521
Danville, CA 94526

Santa Ana Mountain Historical Society
28192 Silverado Canyon Rd.
P.O. Box 301
Silverado, CA 92676
Tel: 714-649-2216

Santa Barbara Historical Society
136 E. De la Guerra Street
P.O. Box 578
Santa Barbara, CA 93102
Tel: 805-966-1601
http://www.tfaoi.com/newsm1/n1m643.htm

Santa Clara Historical & Genealogical Society
2635 Homestead Road
Santa Clara, CA 95051-5387
Tel: 408-984-3236
408-248-8205
http://www.katpher.com/SCCHGS/#Membership

Santa Clara Historical Heritage Commission
70 West Hedding Street
San Jose, CA 95110
(408) 358-3741

Santa Clarita Valley Historical Society
24107 San Fernando Road
P.O. Box 221925
Newhall, CA 91322
Tel: 805-254-1275
http://www.scvhs.org/

Santa Cruz Historical Society
P.O. Box 246
Santa Cruz, CA 95061

Santa Fe Springs Historical Committee
11710 Telegraph Road
Santa Fe Springs, CA 90670

Santa Maria Valley Historical Society
616 South Broadway
P.O. Box 584
Santa Maria, CA 93454
Tel: 805-922-3130
http://www.best1.net/~smmuseum/

Santa Monica Historical Society
P.O. Box 3059
Santa Monica, CA 90403
Santa Monica Historical Society

Santa Ynez Valley Historical Society
3596 Sagunto Street
Santa Ynez, CA 93460
(805) 688-7889
http://www.rootsweb.com/~casyhsmc/

Saratoga Historical Foundation
Saratoga Historical Museum
20450 Saratoga Los Gatos Road
Saratoga, CA 95070
(408) 867-4311

Sausalito Historical Society
Archive and Special Exhibits
Sausalito Civic Center
Top Floor
420 Litho Street
Sausalito, CA
Mailing address:
P.O. Box 352
Sausalito, CA 94966
415-289-4117
E-mail: shs@ci.sausalito.ca.us
http://www.ci.sausalito.ca.us/shs/contents.htm

Selma Museum Historical Society
1880 Art Gonzales Pkwy.
Selma, CA 93662
Tel: 209-896-8871

Shafter Historical Society
150 Central Valley Highway
P.O. Box 1088
Shafter, CA 93263
Tel: 805-746-1557

Shasta Historical Society
1449 Market St.
Redding, CA 96001
530-243-3720
http://www.shastahistory.org/

Sierra County Historical Society
P.O. Box 260
Sierra City, California 96125
Tel: 530-862-1310
http://www.sierracounty.org/schs_home.html

Sierra Madre Historical Society
P.O. Box 202
Sierra Madre, California 91025-0202
(626) 355-8129
http://www.sierramadre.lib.ca.us/smarchives/
    sierra_madre_historical_preserva.htm

Simi Valley Historical Society
Strathearn Historical Park
137 Strathearn Place
P.O. Box 351
Simi Valley, CA 93062
Tel: (805) 526-6453
http://www.cyber-pages.com/strathearn/

Siskiyou County Historical Society & Museum
910 South Main
Yreka, CA 96097
530-842-3836

Society of California Pioneers
300 Fourth Street San Francisco, CA 94107-1272
Tel 415.957.1849
Fax 415-957-9858
E-mail: shaas@californiapioneers.org.
http://www.californiapioneers.org/

Solano County Historic Records Commission
c/o Central Services
1745 Enterprise Drive
Building 2, Suite A
Fairfield, CA 94533

Solano County Historical Society
P.O. Box 922
Vallejo, CA 94590

Sonoma County Historical Society
P.O. Box 1373
Santa Rosa, CA 95402
http://www.sonomacountyhistory.org/

Sonoma Valley Historical Society
P.O. Box 861
Sonoma, CA 95476
http://www.vom.com/depot/

South San Francisco History Room
306 Walnut Avenue
South San Francisco, CA 94080
650-877-8533
http://www.pls.lib.ca.us/pls/ssf/ssfhist.html

Southern California, Historical Society of
200 East Avenue 43
Los Angeles, CA 90031
Tel: 323 222-0546
Fax: 323 222-0771
http://www.socalhistory.org/

Spanishtown Historical Society
505 Johnson Street
P.O. Box 62
Half Moon Bay, CA 94019
Tel: 650-726-7084
http://www.spanishtownhs.org/

**Sunnyvale Historical Society
and Museum Association**
235 E California Ave
P.O. Box 61301
Sunnyvale, CA 94086
408- 749-0220

Sutter County Historical Society
P. O. Box 1004
Yuba City, CA 95992

Tehama Genealogical & Historical Society
P.O. Box 415
Red Bluff, CA 96080
http://tco1.tco.net/tehama/museum/tcmgene.html

Tomales Regional History Center
26701 Highway 1
Tomales, CA 94971
(707)878-9443

Torrance Historical Society
1345 Post Avenue
Torrance, CA 90501
http://www.ci.torrance.ca.us/city/councils/histsoc.htm
http://www.visittorrance.com/historical.htm

Trinity County Historical Society
508 Main Street
P.O. Box 333
Weaverville, CA 96093
Tel: 530- 623-5211
http://www.trinitycounty.com/museum.htm

Truckee-Donner Historical Society
P.O. Box 893
Truckee, CA 96160
http://www.tahoenet.com/tdhs/tpnewslt.html#intro

Tulare County Historical Society
P.O. Box 295
Visalia, CA 93279
http://www.calhist.org/frost2/tulare/tulareindex2.html

Tuolumne County Historical Society
158 West Bradford Avenue
Sonora, CA
Mailing address:
P.O. Box 695
Sonora, CA 95370-0695
(209) 532-1317
http://www.tchistory.org/

Tustin Area Historical Society
395 El Camino Real
P.O. Box 185
Tustin, CA 92681
Tel: 714-731-5701
http://www.tustinhistory.org/

Twenty-Nine Palms Historical Society
P.O. Box 1926
Twenty-Nine Palms, CA 92277
http://www.virtual29.com/societys/histsoc.html

Villa Park Historical Society
City Hall of Villa Park
Villa Park, CA 92861

Vista Ranchos Historic Society, Inc.
651 E. Vista Way, Suite A
P.O. Box 1032
Vista, CA 92085-1032
760-630-0444

Walnut Creek Historical Society
Shadelands Ranch Historical Museum
2660 Ygnacio Valley Road
P.O. Box 4562
Walnut Creek, CA 94596
Tel: (925) 935-7871
http://www.ci.walnut-creek.ca.us/wchs.html

Washington Township Historical Society
P.O. Box 3045
Fremont, CA 94539
Tel: 510-656-3761

Western Sonoma County Historical Society
261 S. Main St.
Sebastopol, CA 95472
707-829-6711
http://www.wschs-grf.pon.net/

Whittier Historical Society
6755 Newlin Avenue
Whittier, CA 90601
Tel: 562-945-3871
Fax: 562-945-9106
http://www.whittiermuseum.org/

Willow Creek/China Flat Museum
P.O. Box 102
Willow Creek, CA 95573
Tel: 530-629-2653
http://www.bfro.net/NEWS/wcmuseum.htm

Windsor Square-Hancock Park Historical Society
542 1/2 North Larchmont Blvd.
Los Angeles, CA 90004

Yolo County Historical Society
P.O. Box 1447
Woodland, CA 95776
(530) 661-2212
http://www.yolo.net/ychs/

LDS FAMILY HISTORY CENTERS

For locations of Family History Centers in this state, see the Family History Center locator at FamilySearch: http://www.familysearch.org/eng/Library/FHC/ frameset_fhc.asp

ARCHIVES/LIBRARIES/MUSEUMS

A.K. Smiley Public Library /Museum
125 W. Vine St.
Redlands, CA. 92373
Tel: (909) 798-7632
E-mail: archives@akspl.org
http://www.akspl.org/heritage.html

Alpine County Museum
School Street
P.O. Box 517
Markleeville, CA 96120
Tel: 530-694-2317
E-mail: alpinecountymuseum@gbis.com
http://www.co.alpine.ca.us/dept/museum/museum.htm

Amador County Archives
38 Summit Street (location)
Jackson, California
Mailing Address:
500 Argonaut Ln.
Jackson, CA 95642
Tel: 209-223-6389
E-mail: archives@amadorarchives.org
http://www.amadorarchives.org/archives.html

Amador County Library
530 Sutter St.
Jackson, CA 95642.
Tel: 209-223-6401.
E-mail: amalib@cdepot.net.

Amador County Museum
225 Church Street
Jackson, CA 95642
Tel: 209-223-6386
http://www.amadorarchives.org/museum.html

American Victorian Museum
203 S Pine St
Nevada City, CA 95959
(530)265-5804

Anderson Valley Historical Museum
12340 Highway 128
P.O. Box 676
Boonville, CA 95415
707-895-3207

Angel Island State Park
P.O. Box 318
San Francisco, CA 94920
415-435-1915
http://www.angelisland.com/
or
Angel Island Association
http://www.angelisland.org/

Archives of the Archdiocese of San Francisco
St. Patrick's Seminary
320 Middlefield Road
Menlo Park, CA 94025
Tel: 650-328-6502
http://www.stpatricksseminary.org/index.html

Archival Center
San Fernando Mission
15151 San Fernando Mission Blvd
Mission Hills, CA 91345
818-361-0186

Association for Northern California Records & Research
P.O. Box 3024
Chico, CA 95927
Tel: 916-898-62137
http://www.csuchico.edu/ancrr/

Atherton Heritage Association
Atherton Town Hall
91 Ashfield Road
Atherton, CA 94027
Tel: 415-688-6540
http://www.ci.atherton.ca.us/heritage.html

Autry Museum of Western Heritage
4700 Western Heritage Way
Los Angeles, CA 90027
Telephone: 323-667-2000
Fax: 323-660-5721
http://www.autry-museum.org

Bancroft Library
University of California-Berkeley
Berkeley, CA 94720
Tel: 510-642-6481
http://www.lib.berkeley.edu/BANC/

Belmont Historical Society
Historical Room
1225 Ralston Avenue
Belmont, CA 94002
http://www.belmont.gov/hist/index.html

Benicia Capitol State Historic Park
115 West G Street
P.O. Box 5
Benicia, CA 94510
707-745-3385
http://cal-parks.ca.gov/default.asp?page_id=475

Berkeley Historical Society Museum
Veterans Memorial Building
1931 Center Street
P.O. Box 1190
Berkeley, CA 94701-1190
Tel: 510-848-0181
http://www.ci.berkeley.ca.us/histsoc/

Bidwell Mansion Association
525 Esplanade
Chico, CA 95926
Tel: 530-895-6144
http://www.norcal.parks.state.ca.us/bidwell_mansion_asso
ciation.htm

Bishop Museum-Historical Society
P.O. Box 363
Bishop, CA 93514
Tel: 760-873-5950

Boulder Creek Historical Society
12547 Highway 9
Boulder Creek, CA 95006
Tel: 831-338-6617

Burlingame Historical Society
Washington Park
P.O. Box 144
Burlingame, CA 94011
Tel: 415-340-9960
http://www.best.com/~spectrum/history/history.html

Butte County Historical Society
Ehmann Home
1480 Lincoln Street
Oroville, CA 95965
P.O. Box 2195
Oroville, CA 95965.
Tel: (530) 533-9418

Cabrillo National Monument
1800 Cabrillo Memorial Drive
San Diego, CA 92106
Tel: 619-557-5450
http://www.nps.gov/cabr/
http://edweb.sdsu.edu/cab/

**Calaveras County Historical Society,
Museum, & Archives**
30 North Main Street
P.O. Box 723
San Andreas, CA 95249
Tel: 209-754-3918

California Afro-American Museum
Afro-American Genealogical Society
600 State Drive, Exposition Park
Los Angeles, CA 90037
Tel: 213- 744-7432
http://www.caam.ca.gov/

California Department of Parks and Recreation
Office of Historic Preservation
P.O. Box 942896
Sacramento, CA 94296-0001
Tel: 916-653-6624
Fax: 916-653-9824
E-mail: calshpo@ohp.parks.ca.gov
http://ohp.parks.ca.gov/

California Ethnic and Multicultural Archives (CEMA)
Davidson Library
University of California
Santa Barbara, CA 93106
Tel: 805-893-8563
805-893-3062
Fax: 805-893-4676
http://www.library.ucsb.edu/speccoll/cema/

California Genealogical Society Library
1611 Telegraph Ave, Suite 200
Oakland, CA 94612-2152
Tel: 510-663-1358
Fax: 510-663-1596
E-mail: library@calgensoc

California Historical Society Library
North Baker Research Library
678 Mission Street
San Francisco, CA 94105
Fax: 415.357.1850
http://www.californiahistoricalsociety.org/

California History Center Foundation
21250 Stevens Creek Blvd.
Cupertino, CA 95014
Tel: 408-864-8712
Fax: 408.864.5486
E-mail: info@calhistory.org
http://www.calhistory.org/chc.html

California State Capitol Museum
10th and L Streets
State Capitol Room 124
Sacramento, CA 95814
Tel: 916-324-0333
http://www.assembly.ca.gov/museum/

California State Indian Museum
2618 K Street
Sacramento, CA 95816
Tel:916-324-0971
http://cal-parks.ca.gov/default.asp?page_id=486

California State Library
California History Room
900 N Street, Room 200
Sacramento, CA 95814
Tel: 916-654-0176
E-mail: csl-adm@library.ca.gov
http://www.library.ca.gov/html/genealogy.html

California State Univ. L.A. History
5151 State University Drive
Los Angeles, CA 90032

Campbell Historical Museum
51 N. Central Ave.
Campbell, CA 95008
Tel: 408-866-2119
Fax: 408-866-2795
http://www.ci.campbell.ca.us/communityandarts/muse-
um.htm

Capitola Historical Museum
410 Capitola Ave.
Capitola, CA 95010-3318
Tel: 831-464-0322
http://www.capitolamuseum.org/

Carlsbad City Library
1250 Carlsbad Village Dr.
Carlsbad, CA 92008-1991
Genealogy Desk: 760-434-2931
Reference Desk: 760-434-2871
http://www.ci.carlsbad.ca.us/cserv/library.html

Carnegie History and Cultural Arts Center
424 South C Street
Oxnard, CA 93030
(805) 385-8157
http://www.vcnet.com/carnart/history.html

Casa de Rancho Cucamonga/Rains' House
8810 Hemlock
Rancho Cucamonga, CA 91730
Tel: 909-989-4970
http://www.citivu.com/rc/hist1.html

Catalina Island Museum Society, Inc.
Casino Building
P.O. Box 366
Avalon, CA 90704
Tel: 213-510-2414
Fax: 310-510-2780
E-mail: museum@catalinas.net
http://www.catalina.com/museum.html

Center for Museum Studies
John F. Kennedy University
1717 17th Street
San Francisco, CA 94103

Chaffey Communities Cultural Center
525 W. 18th Street
P.O. Box 772
Upland, CA 91785-0772
Tel: 909-982-8010
E-mail: mavb@worldnet.att.net
http://www.culturalcenter.org/

Chaffey-Garcia House
7150 Etiwanda Ave.
Rancho Cucamonga, CA 91739
Tel: 909-899-1209

Charles W. Bowers Museum
2002 North Main
Santa Ana, CA 92706
714-567-3600
http://www.bowers.org/

Cherokee Heritage and Museum Association
Route 7, Box 297
Cherokee, CA 95965

Cherokee Museum Association
4227 Cherokee Road
Oroville, CA 95965
Tel: 530-533-1849

Chico Museum
141 Salem Street
Chico, CA 95926
Tel: 530-891-4336

Chula Vista City Library
365 F St.
Chula Vista, CA 91910
619-691-5069
http://www.ci.chula-vista.ca.us/library.htm

Chula Vista Heritage Museum
360 3rd Ave
Chula Vista, CA 91910-3932
619-476-5373
http://www.chulavista.lib.ca.us/museum/

Clarke Memorial Museum
240 E Street
Eureka, CA 95501
Tel: 707-443-1947

Colton Hall Museum & Old MOnterey
Pacific & Jefferson
Monterey, CA 93940
Tel: 831-646-5640
Fax: 831-646-3917
E-mail: klusmire@ci.monterey.ca.us
http://www.monterey.org/museum

Colusa County Archives
Colusa County Clerk
546 Jay Street
Colusa, CA 95932
Tel: 530-458-5146
http://www.colusacountyclerk.com/doc.asp?ID=8

Colusa County Historical Records Commission
c/o Colusa County Free Library
738 Market Street
Colusa, CA 95932
Tel: 530-458-7671

Community Memorial Museum of Sutter County
1333 Butte House Road
P. O. Box 1555
Yuba City, CA 95992
Tel: 530-822-7141
E-mail: museum@syix.com.
http://www.syix.com/museum/

Cooper Regional History Museum
217 East A Street
P.O. Box 772
Upland, CA 91785-0722
Tel: 909-982-8010
http://www.culturalcenter.org/museum.htm

Crockett Museum and Historical Society
P.O. Box 194
Crockett, CA 94525
Tel: 510-787-2178
E-mail: keithglenn@home.com

Delano Historical Society & Heritage Park
330 Lexington Street
Delano, CA 93215
Tel: 805-725-6730

Depot Park Museum
P.O. Box 861
Sonoma, CA 95476
http://www.vom.com/depot/

Discovery Museum of Orange County
3101 West Harvard Street
Santa Ana, CA 92704
714-540-0404
http://www.discoverymuseumoc.org/index.html

East Bay Genealogical Society
P.O. Box 20417
Oakland, CA 94620-0417
Tel: 510-451-9599
http://www.katpher.com/EBGS/EBGS.html

East Contra Costa Historical Society
P. O. Box 202
3890 Sellers Avenue
Brentwood CA 94513
Tel: 925-634-3553
http://www.theschoolbell.com/history

El Pueblo de Los Angeles Historic Park
845 North Alameda
Los Angeles, CA 90012
213- 680-2381
http://www.olvera-street.com/olvera_street.html

El Dorado County Historical Museum
104 Placerville Drive
Placerville, CA 95667
Tel: (530) 621-5865
Fax: (530) 621-6644
http://www.co.el-dorado.ca.us/
        generalservices/museum.html

Escondido Public Library
Pioneer Room
247 S. Kalmia St.
Escondido, CA 92025
Tel: 760-839-4315
http://www.ci.escondido.ca.us/library/

Ferndale Museum
P.O. Box 431
Ferndale, CA 95536
Tel: 707-786-4466
http://www.gingerbread-mansion.com/
        ferndalemuseum.html

First American Title Insurance Historical Library
114 East 5th Street
Santa Ana, CA 92701
714-558-3211
or
949-495-4050

Folsom History Museum
823 Sutter Street
Folsom, CA 95630
Tel: 916-985-2707
http://www.folsom.ca.us/activities/tour.html

Fontana Historical Society/Library
8459 Wheeler Ave.
P.O. Box 426
Fontana, CA 92334
Tel: 909-823-1733

Fort Crook Historical Society/Museum
Fort Crook Ave. and Highway 299
P.O. Box 397
Fall River Mills, CA 96028
Tel: 530-336-5110

Fort Humboldt State Historic Park
3431 Fort Avenue
Eureka, CA 95501
Tel: 707-445-6567
http://www.humboldtredwoods.org/forthumboldt.htm

Fort Point & Army Museum Association
P.O. Box 29333
Presidio of San Francisco, CA 94129-0333
or
Fort Point NHS
Long Avenue & Marine Drive
Presidio of San Francisco, CA 94129
Tel: 415-556-1693
Fax: 415-561-4390
http://www.nps.gov/fopo/

Fort Ross State Historic Park
19005 Coast Highway 1
Jenner, CA 95450
Tel: 707-847-3286
http://www.parks.sonoma.net/fortross.html

Fresno Metropolitan Museum
1515 Van Ness
Fresno, CA 93721
Tel: 559-441-1444
http://www.fresnomet.org/

Gilroy Historical Museum
195 Fifth Street
Gilroy, CA 95020
Tel: 408-848-0470

Harrison Memorial Library
The Henry Meade Williams
Local History Department
Mission Avenue and Sixth Street
Carmel-by-the-Sea, CA 93921
Tel: 831-624-1615
Fax: 831-624-0407
http://www.hm-lib.org/7a.htm

Hayward Area Historical Society/Museum
22701 Main Street
Hayward, CA 94541
Tel: 510-581-0223

Healdsburg Museum
221 Matheson
Healdsburg, CA 95448
http://carnegie-libraries.org/california/regions/
      northcoast/healdsburg.html

Held-Poage Library
Mendocino County Historical Society
603 West Perkins
Ukiah, CA 95482-4726
Tel: 707-462-6969
      707-462-2039
http://www.pacificsites.com/~mchs/heldpoage.htm

Hemet-San Jacinto Genealogical Society Library
P.O. Box 2516
Hemet, CA 92546-2516
Tel: 909-925-1130

Heritage Association of El Dorado County
P.O. Box 62
Placerville, CA 95667
Tel: 916-622-8388
      916-621-5793
http://www.geocities.com/RainForest/7589/index.html

Heritage Park
12100 Mora Drive
Santa Fe Springs, CA 90670
Tel: 562-946-6476
http://www.santafesprings.org/hpark.htm

Holt-Atherton Special Collections
University of the Pacific Library
3601 Pacific Avenue
Stockton, CA 95211
Tel: 209-946-2945
Fax: 209-946-2942http://jarda.cdlib.org/guides.html

Honnold/Mudd Library of the Claremont Colleges
Special Collections
800 North Dartmouth
Claremont, CA 91711
Tel: 909-621-8000
http://voxlibris.claremont.edu/sc/default.html

Huntington Beach Public Library
7111 Talbert Ave.
Huntington Beach, CA 92648-1296
Tel: 714- 842-4481

Imperial Valley College Museum and Society
11 Frontage Road
Octillo, CA 92259
Mailing address: P.O. Box 430
Octillo CA 92259
Tel: 760-358-7016
Fax: 760-358-7827
http://www.imperial.cc.ca.us/ivc-dm/

Indian Grinding Rock State Historic Park
14881 Pine Grove-Volcano Road
Pine Grove, CA 95665
Tel: 209-296-7488
http://www.sierra.parks.state.ca.us/igr/igr_main.htm

Irish Cultural Center Library
2700 45th Street
San Francisco, CA 94116-2696
Tel: 415-661-2700
Fax: 415-661-8620
http://www.irishcentersf.org/

Irvine Historical Society & Museum
5 Rancho San Joaquin
Irvine, CA 92717

Japanese American History Archives
1840 Sutter Street
San Francisco, CA 94115
Tel: 415-776-0661
http://www.amacord.com/fillmore/museum/jt/jaha/
     jaha.html

Judah L. Magnes Memorial Museum/
Blumenthal Library
2911 Russell Street
Berkeley, CA 94705
Tel: 510-849-2710
510-549-6950
http://www.magnesmuseum.org/

Julian Pioneer Museum
2811 Washington St.
Julian, CA 92036
Tel: 760-765-0227
http://www.orangebook.com/julian/pioneer.php3

Karl A. Vollmayer Local History Room
1044 Middlefield Road
Redwood City, CA 94063
Tel: 650-780-7030
http://www.ci.redwood-city.ca.us/library/rcpl.html

Kern County Museum
3801 Chester Avenue
Bakersfield, CA 93301
Tel: 661-852-5000
Fax: 661-322-6415
http://www.kcmuseum.org/visit

Kern River Valley Historical Society & Museum
49 Big Blue Road
P.O. Box 651
Kernville, CA 93238
Tel: 760-376-6683
http://www.kernvalley.com/news/museum.htm

Lake County Genealogical Society/Museum
255 N. Main St.
Lakeport, CA 95453
Tel: 707-263-4555
http://www.museum.lake.k12.ca.us/

Lake Oroville State Historic Site
400 Glen Drive
Oroville, CA 95965
530-538-2200

Lake Tahoe Museum
3058 South Highway 50
P.O. Box 404
South Lake Tahoe, CA 95705
Tel: 530-541-5458

Lassen Historical Museum
105 North Weatherlow St.
P.O. Box 321
Susanville, CA 96130
Tel: 916-257-6551

Los Altos History Museum
51 So. San Antonio Road
Los Altos, CA 94022
Tel 650-948-9427
Fax 650-559-0268
http: //www.losaltoshistory.org/

Los Angeles Public Library
History & Genealogy Department
630 West 5th Street, LL4
Los Angeles, CA 90071
Tel: 213-228-7400
Fax: 213-228-7409
E-mail: history@lapl.org
http://www.lapl.org/central/history.html

Malki Museum
Morongo Indian Reservation
11-795 Fields Road
Banning, CA 92220
Tel: 909-849-7289
909-849-3549
http://www.malkimuseum.org/

Mandeville Special Collections Library
UCSD Libraries 0175S
9500 Gilman Drive
La Jolla, CA 92093-0175
Tel: (858)534-2533
Fax: (858)534-5950
E-mail: spcoll@ucsd.edu
http://orpheus.ucsd.edu/speccoll/

Marin Museum of the American Indian
2200 Novato Blvd.
P.O. Box 864
Novato, CA 94948
Tel: 415-897-4064
http://www.marinindian.com/

Mariposa Museum and History Center
5119 Jessie Street
P.O. Box 606
Mariposa, CA 95338
Tel: 209-966-2924

Maturango Museum
100 E. Las Flores Ave.
Ridgecrest, CA 93555
Tel: 760-375-6900
Fax: 760-375-0479
E-mail: matmus@ridgecrest.ca.us
http://www.maturango.org/

Mayflower Society Library
405 14th Street
Oakland, CA 94612
Tel: 916-771-5094
Fax: 916-771-7461
http://www.mayflowersociety.com/join.htm

McHenry Museum
1402 I Street
Modesto, CA 95354
http://www.mchenrymuseum.org/museum/

McPherson Center for Art & History
705 Front Street
Santa Cruz, CA 95062
Tel: 831-429-1964
Fax: 831-429-1954
http://www.santacruzmah.org/

Menlo Park Library
Menlo Park Historical Association
800 Alma Street
P.O. Box 1002
Menlo Park, CA 94026-1002
http://www.pls.lib.ca.us/pls/mpl/mpl.html

Meriam Library Special Collections at
California State University, Chico
Chico, CA 95929-0295
Tel: 530-898-6342
http://www.csuchico.edu/lbib/spc/iepages/home.html

Mill Valley Public Library
Historical Records Section
375 Throckmorton Ave.
Mill Valley, CA 94941
Tel: 415-389-4292
http://millvalleylibrary.org/

Mission Inn Museum
3696 Main Street
Riverside, CA 92501
Tel: 909-788-9556
http://www.missioninnmuseum.com/m_top.html

Mission Santa Cruz
Mission Plaza
High Street (At Emmet St.)
Santa Cruz, CA 95060
Tel: 831-426-5686
Fax: 831-423-7183
http://www.geocities.com/Athens/Aegean/7151/

Mission San Antonio de Padua
Mission Creek Road
P.O. Box 803
Jolon, CA 93928
Tel: 832-385-4478
http://www.missionsanantoniopadua.com/

Mission San Carlos Borromeo
3080 Rio Road
Carmel, CA 93921
Tel: 831-624-3600
info@carmelmission.org
http://www.carmelmission.org/

Mission Viejo Library
25209 Marguerite Parkway
Mission Viejo, CA 92692
Tel: 949-830-7100
http://cmvl.org/

Modoc County Historical Society and Museum
600 S. Main Street
Alturas, CA 96101
Tel: 530-233-6238

Mojave River Valley Museum Association
270 E. Virginia Way
P.O. Box 1282
Barstow, CA 92312-1282
Tel: 760-256-5452
http://www.1stoptravelguide.com/calif/923xx/barstow/
mojrvmus/mojrvmus.htm

Monterey Public Library
History Room
625 Pacific Street
Monterey, CA 93940
831-646-3932
http://www.monterey.org/library/cahist.html

Montclair Library
9955 Fremont Ave
Montclair, CA 91763
Tel: 909-624-4671

Moraga Historical Society and Archives
1500 St. Mary's Road
P.O. Box 103
Moraga, CA 94556
Tel: 510-376-6952

Morgan Hill Historical Museum
600 W Main Ave
Morgan Hill Ca 95037
(408)779-5755
http://www.geocities.com/SoHo/Veranda/4103/
morgan.html

Museum of Cultural History
University of California
Box 951549
Los Angeles, CA 90095-1549
Tel: 310-825-4361
http://www.fmch.ucla.edu/

Museum of History & Art
225 South Euclid Ave.
Ontario, CA 91762
Tel: 909-983-3198

Museum of San Diego History
Historical & Research Archives
Casa de Balboa
1649 El Prado
P.O. Box 81825
San Diego, CA 92138
Tel: 619-232-6203
http://edweb.sdsu.edu/edweb_folder/SDHS/mainpages/
locate2.htm

Museum of the City of San Francisco
2801 Leavenworth St. (at Jefferson)
San Francisco, CA 94133
Mailing Address:
PMB 423
945 Taraval Street
San Francisco, CA 94116
Tel: 415-928-0289
http://www.sfmuseum.org/

Museum of Local History
190 Anza Street
Fremont, CA 94539
Tel: 510-623-7907
http://www.infolane.com/fremontmuseum/index.html

Museum of Russian Culture
2450 Sutter Street
San Francisco, CA 94115
Tel: 415-921-4082

National City Public Library
Hollingsworth Local History Room
200 E. 12th Street
National City CA 91954
Tel: 619-336-4280

National Maritime Museum Association & Library
Fort Mason Center, Building E
900 Beach Street
P.O.Box 470310
San Francisco, CA 94147-0310
Tel: 415-556-9870 Library
415-556-3002
415-556-8177 Museum
E-mail: members@maritime.org
http://www.maritime.org/

Newbury Park Branch Library
2331 Borchard Road
Newbury Park, CA 91320
Tel: 805-498-2139
http://www.tol.lib.ca.us/1newbury.html

Novato History Museum and Archives
815 Delong Ave.
Novato, CA 94945
Mail:
900 Sherman Ave.
Novato, CA 94945
Tel: 415-897-4320
Fax: 415-892-9136

Oakland Museum-History Dept.
1000 Oak Street
Oakland, CA 94607
1-888-625-6873 [OAK-MUSE]
www.museumca.org

Ojai Valley Museum & Historical Society
130 West Ojai Avenue
P.O. Box 204
Ojai, CA 93023
Phone: 805-640-1390

Old Mission San Jose Museum
43300 Mission Boulevard
P.O. Box 3159
Fremont, CA 94539
Tel: 510-657-1797

Old Mission San Luis Obispo de Tolosa
P.O. Box 1483
San Luis Obispo, CA 93406

Ontario City Library
Model Colony Room
215 East C Street
Ontario, CA 91764
Tel: 909.395.2004
http://www.ci.ontario.ca.us/library/main.htm

Orange County Library
Cypress Branch
5331 Orange Ave.
Cypress, CA 90630-2985
Tel: 714-826-0350
http://www.ocpl.org/cypress/Cypres.htm

Orange County Library
El Toro Branch
24672 Raymond Way
Lake Forest, CA 92630-4489
Tel: 949-855-8173
http://www.ocpl.org/eltoro/Eltoro.htm

Orange County Library
Garden Grove Regional Library
11200 Stanford Ave.
Garden Grove, CA 92840-5398
Tel: 714-530-0711
http://www.ocpl.org/ggregnal/ggreg.htm

Orange County Library
Tustin Branch Library
345 E. Main Street
Tustin, CA 92780-4491
Tel: 714-544-7725
http://www.ocpl.org/tustin/tustin.htm

Pacific Asia Museum
46 North Los Robles Ave.
Pasadena, CA 91101
Tel: 626-449-2742
http://www.pacificasiamuseum.org/

Pajaro Valley Historical Association
261 East Beach Street
Watsonville, CA 95076-4830
Tel: 831-722-0305

Palm Springs Public Library
300 S. Sunrise Way
Palm Springs, CA 92262
Tel: 760-322-7323

Palmdale City Library
700 E. Palmdale Blvd.
Palmdale, CA 93550-4742
Tel: 661-267-5600
http://palmdale.lib.ca.us/

Palo Alto Main Library
1213 Newell Road
Palo Alto, CA 94303
Tel: 650-329-2436
650-329-2664
http://www.city.palo-alto.ca.us/library/about/main.html

Palos Verdes Library District
2400 Via Campesina
Palos Verdes Estates CA 90274
Mailing address: 701 Silver Spur Road
Rolling Hills Estates, CA 90274
Tel: (310) 377-9584 ext. 550 or 549
http://www.palos-verdes.lib.ca.us/

Paradise Fact & Folklore
P.O. Box 1696
Paradise, CA 95967
Tel: 916-877-3699

Pardee Home Museum
672 11th Street
Oakland, CA 94607
Tel: 510-444-2187
http://www.pardeehome.org/

Pasadena Historical Museum
470 W. Walnut Street
Pasadena, CA 91103-3594
Tel: 626-577-1660
Fax: 626-577-1662
www.pasadenahistory.org

Pasadena Public Library
Centennial Room
285 E. Walnut St.
Pasadena, CA 91101
Tel: 626-744-4052
http://www.ci.pasadena.ca.us/library/

Petaluma Museum & Historical Library
20 4th Street
Petaluma, CA 94952
Tel: 707-778-4398
http://www.petaluma.net/historicalmuseum/

Petaluma State Historic Park
3325 Adobe Road
Petaluma, CA 94952
Tel: 707-762-4871
http://www.parks.sonoma.net/adobe.html

Pleasanton Library
400 Old Bernal Ave.
Pleasanton, CA 94566
Tel: 925-931-3400
http://www.ci.pleasanton.ca.us/library.html

Plumas County Museum
500 Jackson Street
Quincy, CA. 95971
Tel: 530-283-6320
http://www.countyofplumas.com/museum/

Porterville Public Library
41 West Thurman Ave.
Porterville, CA 93257
Tel: 559-784-0177
http://www.sjvls.lib.ca.us/sjvls/hrln/members/ppubl.html

Presidio of Monterey Museum
Corporal Ewing Road, Bldg. 113
Presidio of Monterey, CA 93944
Tel: 831-646-3456
Fax: 831-646-3917
http://www.monterey.org/museum/pom/

Presidio Army Museum
William Penn Mott Jr. Visitor Center
Building 102, Montgomery Street
San Francisco, CA 94129
Tel: 415-561-4323
http://www.nps.gov/prsf/

Ramona Museum of California History
4580 North Figueroa St.
Los Angeles, CA 90065

Rancho Los Cerritos Historic Site
4600 Virginia Road
Long Beach, CA 90807
562-570-1755
http://bixbyland.com/rancho.htm

Redding Museum of Art & History
56 Quartz Hill Road
Caldwell Park
P.O. Box 992360
Redding, CA 96099-2360
Tel: 530-243-8801
     1-800-TURTLEBAY (1-800-887-8532)
Fax: 530-243-8929
Redwood City Public Library
http://www.turtlebay.org/

Richmond Museum
400 Nevin Avenue
P.O. Box 1267
Richmond, CA 94802
Tel: 510-235-7387
http://www.ci.richmond.ca.us/~library/
     richmond_museum_of_history.htm

Ridge Route Communities Museum/Historical Society
P.O. Box 684
Frazier Park, Ca. 93225
Tel: 661-245-7747
http://www.frazmtn.com/~rrchs/mainie.html

Riverside City/County Library
3581 Mission Inn Avenue
P.O. Box 468
Riverside, CA 92502
Tel: 909-826-5213
Fax: 909-826-5407
http://www.ci.riverside.ca.us/library/

Riverside Municipal Museum
3580 Mission Inn Avenue
Riverside, CA 92501
Tel: 909-826-5273
Fax: 909-369-4970
http://www.ci.riverside.ca.us/museum/

Rosemead Library
8800 Valley Blvd.
Rosemead, CA 91770
Tel: 626-573-5220
http://www.colapublib.org/libs/rosemead/

Sacramento Archives and Museum Collection Center (SAMCC)
551 Sequoia Pacific Blvd.
Sacramento, CA 95814
916-264-7072
http://www.sacramenities.com/history/

Sacramento Valley Museum Association
1491 E Street(Route 1, Box 290)
Williams, CA 95987
Tel: 916-473-2978

San Bernardino County Archives
777 E. Rialto
San Bernardino, CA 92415-0795
Tel: 909-387-2030

San Bernardino County Historical Archives
104 West Fourth Street
San Bernardino, CA 92415

San Bernardino County Museum
2024 Orange Tree Lane
Redlands, CA 92374
Tel: 909) 307-2669
http://www.co.san-bernardino.ca.us/museum/

San Bruno Local History Room
701 West Angus Ave.
San Bruno, CA 94066
Tel: (650) 616-7078
Fax: (650) 876-0848
E-mail: sbpl@pls.lib.ca.us
http://www.ci.sanbruno.ca.us/Library/library.html

San Carlos Historical Museum
533 Laurel Street
San Carlos, CA 94070
Tel: (650) 802-4354
http://www.ci.san-carlos.ca.us/is/display/
       0,1124,deptid-31_isid-112,00.html

Santa Cruz Museum of Art and History
705 Front Street
Santa Cruz, CA 95060
Phone: (831) 429-1964
Fax: (831) 429-1954
http://www.santacruzmah.org/index.html

San Diego Historical Society Library
Casa de Balboa, LL
1649 El Prado
San Diego, CA 92101-1621
Tel: 619-232-6203 ext. 105
http://edweb.sdsu.edu/edweb_folder/sdhs/mainpages/sdhs
       mission.htm

San Diego Maritime Museum
1492 North Harbor Drive
San Diego, CA 92101
Tel: (619) 234-9153
http://www.sdmaritime.com/

San Diego Public Library
820 E Street
San Diego, CA 92101
Tel: 619-236-5800
http://www.sannet.gov/public-library/

San Francisco Maritime Natl. Historic Park
Building E, Fort Mason Center
San Francisco, CA 94123
Tel: 415-556-3002

San Francisco Public Library-Main Branch
San Francisco Archives
100 Larkin Street
San Francisco, CA 94102
Tel: 415-557-4400
http://sfpl.lib.ca.us/

San Jacinto Valley Museum Association
P.O. Box 922
San Jacinto, CA 92383

San Joaquin County Historical Society/Museum
11793 N. Micke Grove Road
Lodi, CA 95240
Tel: 209-331-2055
Fax: 209-331-2057
http://www.sanjoaquinhistory.org/index2.htm

San Jose Historical Museum/Archives
Chinese Historical & Cultural Project
Kelley Park
1600 Senter Road
San Jose, CA 95112-2599
Tel: 408-287-2290
408-277-4017
http://www.dnai.com/~rutledge/CHCP_museum.html

San Jose Public Library
180 W. San Carlos Street
San Jose, CA 95113-2005
Tel: 408-277-4846
http://www.sjpl.lib.ca.us/

San Leandro Library & Historical Commission
300 Estudillo Avenue
San Leandro, CA 94577
Tel: (510) 577-3971
Fax: (510) 577-3967
http://www.ci.san-leandro.ca.us/sllibrarylocations.html

San Luis Obispo Historical Society Museum
696 Monterey Street
P.O. Box 1391
San Luis Obispo, CA 93406-1391
Tel: 805-543-0638
http://www.slochs.org/

San Mateo County Historical Museum
1700 West Hillside
San Mateo, CA 94403
Tel: 415-877-5344

San Mateo County Library-San Carlos
610 Elm St., San Carlos CA 94070
Tel: 650-591-0341
Fax: 650-591-1585
http://www.sancarloslibrary.org/

San Mateo County Genealogical Society Library
25 Tower Road
San Mateo, CA 94402-4000
http://www.smcgs.org/

San Pablo Historical Society and Museum
#1 Alvarado Square
San Pablo, CA 91806
510-215-3046
http://www.ci.san-pablo.ca.us/history/

Santa Ana Public Library
26 Civic Center Plaza
Santa Ana, CA 92701-4010
Tel: 714-647-5250
http://www.ci.santa-ana.ca.us/departments/library/
default.htm

Santa Clara Central Library
Santa Clara County Historical & Genealogical Society
2635 Homestead Road
Santa Clara, CA 95051-5387
Tel: 408-615-2900 Reference Desk;
408-615-2986 Santa Clara County Historical &
Genealogical Society (Voice mail)
http://www.library.ci.santa-clara.ca.us/

Santa Cruz Mission State Historic Park
144 School Street
Santa Cruz, CA 95060-3726
Tel: 831-425-5849
http://cal-parks.ca.gov/default.asp?page_id=548

Santa Cruz Public Library
Central Branch
224 Church Street
Santa Cruz, CA 95060
831-420-5700
http://www.santacruzpl.org/index.html

Santa Fe Springs City Library
11700 Telegraph Rd.
Santa Fe Springs, CA 90670
Phone: 562-868-7738
http://www.santafesprings.org/libindex.htm

Santa Monica Heritage Square Museum
2612 Main Street
Santa Monica, CA 90405

Searls Historical Library
214 Church Street
Nevada City, CA 95959
Tel: 530-265-5190
http://www.nevadacitycalifornia.com/Museums/
earlsHistoricalLibrary/searlshistlibrary.htm

Seaver Center of Western History Research
900 Exposition Blvd.
Los Angeles, CA 90007
Tel: 213-763-3359
http://www.nhm.org/research/history/seaver_center.html

Sharpsteen Museum
1311 Washington
P.O. Box 573
Calistoga, CA 94515
Phone: 707-942-5911
Fax: 707-942-6325
E-mail: admin@sharpsteen-museum.org
http://www.sharpsteen-museum.org/

Shasta State Historic Park
P.O. Box 2430
Shasta, CA 96087

Silverado Museum
1490 Library Lane
Saint Helena, CA 94574
Tel: 707-963-3757

Simi Valley Historical Society
Strathearn Historical Park
137 Strathearn Place
Simi Valley, CA 93065
Tel: 805-526-6453
http://www.cyber-pages.com/strathearn/

Siskiyou County Historical Society & Museum
910 South Main
Yreka, CA 96097
530-842-3836
http://www.siskiyoucounty.com/museum/

Siskiyou Public Library
719 Fourth Street
Yreka, CA 96097
http://www.snowcrest.net/siskiyoulibrary/

Society of California Archivists
University of California, Berkeley
Berkeley, CA 94720-1111
Tel: 714-643-4241
http://dlis.gseis.ucla.edu/society_of_california_archivists/

Sonoma County Library/Santa Rosa
Local History and Genealogy Annex
Behind Central Library
Third & E Streets
Santa Rosa, CA 95404
Tel: 707-545-0831 ext. 562
http://www.sonoma.lib.ca.us/index.html

Sonoma County Museum
425 7th Street
Santa Rosa, CA 95401
Tel: (707) 579-1500
Fax: (707) 579-4849
http://www.sonomacountymuseum.com/

Sonoma State Historic Park
20 East Spain Street
Sonoma, CA 95476
http://www.napanet.net/~sshpa/

Sonoma State University Library
1801 East Cotati Avenue
Rohnert Park, CA 94928
http://libweb.sonoma.edu/default.html

Sourisseau Academy for State & Local History
San Jose State University, WLN 606
San Jose, CA 95192
Tel: 408-924-6510
http://www.sjsu.edu/depts/history/resource/sourisseau.htm

South San Francisco Public Library
South San Francisco History Room
306 Walnut Street
San Francisco, CA 94080
Tel: 650-829-3872
http://www.ssflibrary.org/

Spanishtown Historical Society
P.O. Box 62
505 Johnson Street
Half Moon Bay, CA 94019
Tel: 650-726-7084
http://www.spanishtownhs.org/

Stanford House State Historic Park
802 N Street
Sacramento, CA 95814
Tel: 916-324-0575

Stanford University
Cecil H. Green Library
557 Escondido Mall
(behind Hoover Tower)
Stanford, CA 94305-6004
Tel: (650) 725-1492
http://www-sul.stanford.edu/depts/green/

Sutro Library
480 Winston Drive
San Francisco, CA 94132
Tel: 415-731-4477
MELVYL Cataloghttp://www.melvyl.ucop.edu/

Sutter's Fort State Historic Park
2701 L Street
Sacramento, CA 95814
Tel: 916-445-4422

Tehama County Museum Foundation
P.O. Box 275
Tehama, CA 96090
Museum Address:
C & 3rd. Streets
Tehama, CA
http://www.tco.net/tehama/museum/

Thousand Oaks Library
1401 E. Janss Road
Thousand Oaks, CA 91362
Tel: 805-449-2660
http://www.tol.lib.ca.us/1library.html

Tomales Regional History Center
26701 State Route 1
P.O. Box 262, Tomales, CA 94971
Tel: 707-878-9443
E-mail address: info@tomaleshistory.org
http://www.tomaleshistory.org/

Tulare County Public Library
Annie R. Mitchell History Room
200 W. Oak Ave.
Visalia, CA 93291
Phone: 559-733-6954
Fax: 559-737-4586

Tulare Public Library
113 North F Street
Tulare, CA 93274-3803
Phone: 559-685-2341
Genealogy: 559-685-2342
Fax: 559-685-2345
http://www.sjvls.org/tularepub/

Union City Historical Museum
3841 Smith Street
Union City, CA 94587
http://members.xoom.com/ucmuseum

University of California
P.O. Box 5900
Riverside CA 92517-5900
Tel: (909)787-3220
Special Collections:(909)787-3233
E-mail: bm.ehs@rlg.org
http://library.ucr.edu/

Upland Public Library
450 North Euclid Ave.
Upland, CA 91786
Tel: 909-931-4200
http://uplandpl.lib.ca.us/index.html

Vacaville Museum
213 Buck Avenue
Vacaville, CA 95688
Tel: 707-447-4513
Fax: 707-447-2661
E-mail Vacmuseum@aol.com
http://www.vacavillemuseum.org/index.html

Vallejo Naval & Historical Museum
734 Marin Street
Vallejo, CA 94590
Tel: 707-643-0077
Fax: 707-643-2443
http://www.vallejomuseum.org/

Ventura County Museum of History & Art
100 East Main Street
Ventura, CA 93001
Tel: 805-653-0323
Fax: 805-653-5267
http://www.vcmha.org/

Victorville Branch Library
15011 Circle Drive
Victorville, CA 92392
Tel: 760-245-4222
Fax: 760-245-2273
http://vvo.com/comm/sbclvv.htm

Walter W. Stiern Library
California State University-Bakersfield
Special Collections, Room 102
9001 Stockdale Highway
Bakersfield, CA 93311-1099
Reference: 661-664-3231
Archives: 661-664-6127
Fax: 805-664-3339
http://www.lib.csub.edu/

Weaverville Joss House State Historic Park
South West corner of Highway 299 and Oregon Street
Weaverville, CA 96093
Mailing Address:
Northern Buttes Cascade Sector
P.O. Box 2430
Shasta, CA, 96087-2430
Tel: (530) 623-5284
http://www.norcal.parks.state.ca.us/weaverville.htm

Wells Fargo Bank History Museum
420 Montgomery St.
San Francisco, CA 94104
Tel: 415 396-2619

Western Jewish History Center
2911 Russell Street
Berkeley, CA 94705
Tel: 510-549-6956

William H. Pratt Museum
Lassen Historical Museum
105 North Weatherlow St.
P.O. Box 321
Susanville, CA 96130
Tel: 916-257-6551

William S. Hart Museum
24151 San Fernando Road
Newhall, CA 91321
Tel: 661-254-4584
E-mail: information@hartmuseum.org.
www.hartmuseum.org

Willow Creek-China Flat Museum
P.O. Box 102
Willow Creek, CA 95573

Yolo County Historical Museum
512 Gibson Road
Woodland, CA 95695
Tel: 530-666-1045
http://yolo.net/vme/ychm/

Yuba-Feather Museum
19096 New York Flat Road
Forbestown, CA 95941
Tel: 530-675-1025
http://www.yfhmuseum.org/

NEWSPAPER REPOSITORIES

California State Library
California History Room
900 N Street, Room 200
Sacramento, CA 95814
Tel: 916-654-0176
E-mail: cslcal@library.ca.gov
http://www.library.ca.gov/

Sutro Library
480 Winston Drive
San Francisco, CA 94132
Tel: 415-731-4477
MELVYL Cataloghttp://www.melvyl.ucop.edu/

University of California
P.O. Box 5900
Riverside CA 92517-5900
Tel: (909)787-3220
Offices of California Newspaper Project:(909)787-2388
http://www.cbsr.ucr.edu/cnp/index.html

VITAL RECORDS

California State Department of Health Services
Office of Vital Records and Statistics
304 S Street
Sacramento, CA 95814
Fax: 800-858-5553
(July 1905-present)
(Order by fax on forms available at site)
http://www.dhs.cahwnet.gov/org/hisp/chs/vorder.htm
County Health Officials, Registrars and Recorders
http://www.dhs.cahwnet.gov/org/hisp/chs/vsreg.htm

CALIFORNIA ON THE WEB

California Genealogical Resources
by James Stevenson Publ.
Http://www.jspub.com/~jsp/genresor.html

California Genealogical Society
http://www.calgensoc.org/

California Genweb Project
http://www.cagenweb.com/

California Historical Society
http://www.californiahistoricalsociety.org/

California Pioneer Project
http://www.cagenweb.com/cpl/

Computer Genealogical Society of San Diego
http://www.cgssd.org/

The Great American Gold Rush
http://www.acusd.edu/~jross/goldrush.html

L.A. as Subject
http://www.usc.edu/isd/archives/arc/lasubject/

NORCAL Genealogy Index
http://homepages.rootsweb.com/~yvonne/
     NORCAL%20index/

Southern California Chapter-Association of Professional Genealogists
http://www.cagenweb.com/sccapg/

Southern California Libraries
http://home.earthlink.net/~jsmog/library0.html

Colorado

ARCHIVES, STATE & NATIONAL

Colorado State Archives
Centenniel Building
1313 Sherman Street, Rm. 1B-20
Denver, CO 80203
Tel: 303-866-2358
303-866-2390
800-305-3442 (Toll-free in Colorado only)
Fax: 303-866-2257
E-mail: archives@state.co.us
http://www.archives.state.co.us/index.html

National Archives-Rocky Mountain Region
Denver Federal Center, Building 48
West 6th Avenue and Kipling Street
Denver, CO 80225-0307
Mailing Address:
P.O. Box 25307
Denver, Colorado 80225-0307
Tel: 303-236-0817
E-mail: denver.archives@nara.gov
Fax: 303-236-9297
http://www.nara.gov/regional/denver.html

GENEALOGICAL SOCIETIES

Archuleta County Genealogical Society
P.O. Box 1611
Pagosa Springs, CO 81147
http://www.rootsweb.com/~cosjhs/acgs.htm

Aurora Genealogical Society of Colorado
1298 Peoria Street
P.O. Box 31732
Aurora, CO 80041-0732

Black Genealogy Search Group
P.O. Box 40674
Denver, CO 80204-0674
http://www.coax.net/people/lwf/bgsg_den.htm

Boulder Genealogical Society
P.O. Box 3246
Boulder, CO 80307-3246
http://www.rootsweb.com/~bgs/

Brighton Genealogy Society
343 S. 21st Street
Brighton, CO 80602-2525

Colorado Association of Professional Genealogists
P.O. Box 740637
Arvada, CO 80006-0637

Colorado Cornish Cousins
7945 S. Gaylord Way
Littleton, CO 80122
http://users.idcomm.com/trevithick/

Colorado Council of Genealogical Societies
P.O. Box 24379
Denver, CO 80224-0379
http://www.rootsweb.com/~coccgs/

Colorado Genealogical Society
P.O. Box 9218
Denver, CO 80209-0218
Tel: 303-571-1535
http://www.rootsweb.com/~cocgs/index.htm

Colorado Genealogical Society
Computer Interest Group
http://www.rootsweb.com/~cocgs/cigmain.htm

Columbine Genealogical and Historical Society
P.O. Box 2074
Littleton, CO 80161-2074
http://www.rootsweb.com/~cocghs/

Czech and Slovak Search Group
209 S. Ogden
Denver, CO 80209-2321

Estes Park Genealogical Society
2598 Big Thompson
Drake, CO 80515

Foothills Genealogical Society
P.O. Box 150382
Lakewood, CO 80215-0382
http://www.rootsweb.com/~cofgs/

Four Corners Genealogy Society
P.O. Box 2636
Durango, CO 81302

Fore-Kin Trails Genealogical Society
8508 High Mesa Road
Olathe, CO 81425

Fremont County Genealogical Society
1836 Flora Court
Canon City, CO 81212

Fremont County Genealogy Society
Canon City Public Library
516 Macon Ave
Canon City, CO 81218

Genealogical Research Society of Durango
2720 Delwood
Durango, CO 81301

Genealogical Society of Hispanic America
P.O. Box 9606
Denver, CO 80209-0606
http://members.aol.com/mrosado007/co.htm

Jewish Genealogical Society of Colorado
6965 E. Girard Ave.
Denver, CO 80224
http://www.jewishgen.org/jgs-colorado/index.html

Larimer County Genealogical Society
P.O. Box 9502
Fort Collins, CO 80525-9502
http://jymis.com/~lcgs/index.htm

Longmont Genealogical Society
P.O. Box 6081
Longmont, CO 80501-2077
http://www.rootsweb.com/~colgs/index.htm/

Mesa County Genealogical Society
P.O. Box 1506
Grand Junction, CO 81502-1506
Tel: (970)242-0971
E-mail: webmaster@MCGS
http://www.gj.net/mcgs/

Mountain Genealogists
19637 Hill Drive
Morrison, CO 80465

Ohio Genealogical Society
Colorado Chapter
P.O. Box 1106
Longmont, CO 80502-1106
http://www.ogs.org/chap.htm

Palatines to America
Colorado Chapter
4612 Hampshire St.
Boulder, CO 80301-4211
Tel: 303-530-9525

Pikes Peak Genealogical Society, Inc.
P.O. Box 1262
Colorado Springs, CO 80901
http://www.familyhistory.com/societyhall/
      viewmember.asp?societyid=160

Prowers County Genealogical Society
P.O. Box 928
Lamar, CO 81052-0928

Sedgewick County Genealogical Society
P.O. Box 86
Julesburg, CO 80737
http://www.rootsweb.com/~cosedgwi/society.htm

Slovenian Genealogy Society
Colorado Chapter
837 Swiggler Road
Jefferson, CO 90456-9732

Southeastern Colorado Genealogy Society, Inc.
P.O. Box 4207
Pueblo, CO 81003-0207

Weld County Genealogical Society
P.O. Box 278
Greeley, CO 80632
http://www.rootsweb.com/~cowcgs/

WISE Search Group (Wales, Ireland, Scotland, England)
P.O. Box 48226
Denver CO 80204-8226

Yuma County Genealogical Society
P.O. Box 24
Yuma, CO 80759

HISTORICAL SOCIETIES

American Historical Society of Germans from Russia
Denver Metro Research Room and Library
2727 Bryant Street, Room L4
Denver, CO 80211
Tel: (303) 455-2727
http://www.ahsgr.org/codenver.htm

American Historical Society of Germans from Russia
Northern Colorado Chapter
1476 43rd Avenue
Greeley, CO 80634
Tel: 970-353-3612
http://www.ahsgr.org/conorthe.html

Colorado Historical Society
Stephen H. Hart Library
1300 Broadway
Denver, CO 80203
Tel: 303-866-3682
http://www.coloradohistory.org/

Douglas County Historical Society
620 Lewis
Castle Rock, CO 80104

Eagle County Historical Society
P.O. Box 192
Eagle, CO 81631

Fort Collins Historical Society
121 North Grant Ave.
Fort Collins, CO 80521

Fort Morgan Museum
414 Main Street
Fort Morgan, CO 80701
Tel: 970-867-6331
http://www.ftmorganmus.org/

Frontier Historical Society
1001 Colorado Avenue
Glenwood Springs, CO 81601
http://www.glenwoodguide.com/museum/

High Plains Historical Society/Museum
775 3rd Street, P.O. Box 122
Nunn, Colorado 80648
Tel: 970-897-2215
http://highplainshistory.homestead.com/

Johnstown Historical Society
701 Charlotte St.
Johnstown, Colorado 80534
Tel: 970-587-0278
http://www.geocities.com/johnstownhistoricalsociety/

La Plata County Historical Society
P.O. Box 3384, Durango, CO 81302
Tel: 970-259-2402
http://www.frontier.net/~animasmuseum/about.html

Larimer County Historic Alliance
3711 N. Taft Hill Road
Fort Collins, CO 80524

Mesa County Historical Society
P.O. Box 841
Grand Junction, CO 81502

Museum of Western Colorado
Research Center and Special Library
462 Ute Ave.
Grand Junction, CO 81501
Mailing Address:
P. O. Box 20000 81502-5020
Tel: 970-242-0971
Fax: 970-242-3960
http://www.wcmuseum.org/

**Negro Historical Association of Colorado Springs
(NHACS)**
5180 Mountain Villa Grove
Colorado Springs, CO 80917
Tel: 719-574-8332

Old Colorado City Historical Society
One South 24th Street
Colorado Springs, CO 80904-3319
Tel: 719-636-1225
E-mail: history@oldcolo.com
http://history.oldcolo.com/

Phillip S. Miller Branch Library
961 South Plum Creek Boulevard
Castle Rock, CO 80104
Tel: (303) 814-0795
Fax: (303) 688-1942
E-mail: dpldlhc@mail.douglas.lib.co.us
http://history.douglas.lib.co.us/lhcinfo/index.htm

Pioneer Association/Pioneer Women
Donath Lake Farm
8420 South Co. Road 13
Fort Collins, CO 80525

Pueblo County Historical Society
Vail Hotel
217 South Grand
Pueblo, CO 81003
Tel: 719-543-6772
http://www.puebloonline.com/pchs/

Scottish Society of Northern Colorado
3200 Silverthorn Dr.
Fort Collins, CO 80526

South Park Historical Foundation
South Park City Museum
100 Fourth Street
P.O. Box 634
Fairplay, CO 80440
Tel: 719-836-2387

Summit County Historical Society
309 North Main
Breckenridge, CO 97045-9022

Wheat Ridge Historical Society
4610 Robb St.
Wheat Ridge, CO
Mail: P.O. Box 1833
Wheat Ridge, CO 80034
Tel: 303-467-0023
E-mail: Cworth1234@aol.com
http://www.virtualref.com/_slic/126.htm

LDS FAMILY HISTORY CENTERS

For locations of Family History Centers, see the Family
History Center locator at: http://www.familysearch.org/eng/
Library/FHC/frameset_fhc.asp

ARCHIVES/LIBRARIES/MUSEUMS

Animas Museum
31st Street & West Second Avenue
Durango, CO 81301
Mailing address:
Box 3384
Durango, CO 81302
Tel: (970) 259-2402
http://www.frontier.net/~animasmuseum/index.html

Aurora History Museum/Library
15001 E. Alameda Drive
Aurora, CO 80012
Tel: 303-739-6660
http://www.ci.aurora.co.us/index.cfm?fuseaction=sec_sub
_articles&sectionid=1&SubSectionid=92

Berthoud Public Library
236 Welch Ave
P.O. Box 1259
Berthoud, CO 80513
Tel: (970)532-2757
Fax: (970)532-4372
http:/pyramid.cudenver.edu/Berthoud

Boulder Museum of History
1206 Euclid Ave.
Boulder, CO 80302
Tel: 303-449-3464
http://bcn.boulder.co.us/arts/bmh/

Boulder Public Library
1000 Canyon Blvd.
Boulder, CO 80302
Tel: 303-441-3100
http://www.boulder.lib.co.us/

Buena Vista Heritage Museum
512 E. Main
P.O. Box 1414
Buena Vista, CO 81211
Tel: 719-395-8458

Buena Vista Public Library
131 Linderman Ave.
Buena Vista, CO 81211
Tel: 719-395-8700

Carnegie Branch Library
Local History Research Center
1125 Pine Street
Boulder, CO 80302
Tel: 303-441-3110
http://www.boulder.lib.co.us/branch/carnegie.html

Chautauqua Association
Archive and History Room
Administration Building
900 Baseline Road
Boulder, CO 80302
Tel: 303-442-3282
Fax: 303-449-0790
http://www.chautauqua.com/

Colorado College
Tutt Library
1021 N. Cascade Ave.
Colorado Springs, CO 80903-2165
Circulation: (719) 389-6184
Reference: (719) 389-6662
Fax: (719) 389-6859
E-mail: tuttref@coloradocollege.edu
http://www.coloradocollege.edu/Library/

Colorado Historical Society
Stephen H. Hart Library
1300 Broadway
Denver, CO 80203
Tel: 303-866-3682
http://www.coloradohistory.org/

Colorado Springs Pioneers Museum
215 South Tejon Street
Colorado Springs, CO 80903
Tel: 719-385-5990
Fax: 719-385-6545
http://www.springsgov.com/SectionIndex.asp?SectionID=9

Colorado State Library
201 E. Colfax Ave.
Denver, CO 80203
Tel: 303-866-6900
Fax: 303-866-6940
http://www.cde.state.co.us/index_library.htm

Colorado State University
Special Collections & Archives
Fort Collins, CO 80523
Tel: 970-491-3977 Information
970-491-1841 Social Sciences/Humanities
970-491-1882 Government Documents
970-491-1844 Archives-Voice
Fax:970-491-1195
http://manta.library.colostate.edu/

Cortez Center
25 North Market Street
Cortez, CO 81321
Tel: 970-565-1151
Fax: 970-565-4075
E-mail: cultural@fone.net
http://www.cortezculturalcenter.org/

Denver Public Library
10 West 14th Avenue Pkwy.
Denver, CO 80204
Tel: 720-865-1111
Western History Genealogy Department: 720-865-1821
http://dpl20.denver.lib.co.us/

Edwin A. Bemis Library
6014 S. Datura Street
Littleton, CO 80120
Tel: 303-795-3961
http://www.littletongov.org/bemis/

Estes Park Area Historical Museum
200 Fourth Street
Estes Park, CO 80517
Tel: 970-586-6256
http://www.estesnet.com/Museum/

Estes Park Public Library
P.O. Box 1687
335 East Elkhorn Ave.
Estes Park, CO 80517
Tel: 970-586-8116
http://estes.lib.co.us/

Fort Collins Museum
200 Mathews
Fort Collins, CO 80524
Tel: 970-221-6738
http://www.ci.fort-collins.co.us/museum/

Fort Collins Public Library
201 Peterson Street
Fort Collins, CO 80524
Tel: 970-221-6380 Reference
970-221-6688 Local History
http://fcgov.com/library/

Golden Library
1019 Tenth Street
Golden, CO 80401
Tel: 303-279-4585
http://jefferson.lib.co.us/

Greeley Museums Office
Municipal Archives
919 Seventh Street
Greeley, CO 80631
Tel: 970/350-9220
Fax: 970/350-9570
http://www.ci.greeley.co.us/1phase/Cultural/museums.html

Gunnison County Public Library
Ann Zugelder Library
307 North Wisconsin
Gunnison, CO 81230
Tel: (970) 641-3485
Fax: (970) 641-4653
http://www.co.gunnison.co.us/Library/library.html

High Plains Historical Society/Museum
775 3rd Street, P.O. Box 122
Nunn, Colorado 80648
Tel: 970-897-2215
http://highplainshistory.homestead.com/

Lakewood Library
10200 W. 20th Ave.
Lakewood, CO 80215
Tel: 303-232-9507
http://jefferson.lib.co.us/

Loveland Museum and Gallery
503 N. Lincoln Ave.
Loveland, CO 80537
Tel: 970-962-2410
http://www.ci.loveland.co.us/museum.htm

Loveland Public Library
300 N. Adams Avenue
Loveland, CO 80537
Tel: 970-962-2665
http://www.ci.loveland.co.us/Library/libmain.htm

Montrose Public Library
320 South 2nd Street Montrose, CO 81401
http://www.colosys.net/montrose/#

Morrison Heritage Museum
501 Highway 8
P.O. Box 564
Morrison, CO 80465
Tel: 303-697-1873
http://town.morrison.co.us/historical/mhm.html
Historic Morrison website:
http://town.morrison.co.us/historical/families.html

Norlin Library
184 UCB
University of Colorado
Boulder, CO 80309-0184
Tel: 303-492-8705; 303-492-8834 (Government
Publications Library)
E-mail: libweb@colorado.edu
http://www.libraries.colorado.edu/ps/nor/frontpage.htm

Penrose Public Library
20 N. Cascade
Colorado Springs, CO 80903
Tel: 719-531-6333
Fax: 719-528-5289
http://library.ppld.org/SpecialCollections/default.asp

Pueblo Regional Library
100 Abriendo Ave.
Pueblo, CO 81004
Tel: 719-543-9600

Salida Museum
Salida Chamber of Commerce
406 W. Highway 50
Salida, CO 81201
Tel: 719-539-2068

Salida Regional Library
405 E Street
Salida, CO 81201
Tel: 719-539-4826

Sisson Memorial Library
811 San Juan
P.O. Box 849
Pagosa Springs, CO 81147
Tel: 970-264-2209
http://www.frontier.net/~ruby/

Southern Peaks Public Library
423 Fourth Street
Alamosa, CO 81101
Tel: 719-589-6592

Southern Ute Community Library
330 Burns Avenue
Ignacio, CO 81137-0348
Tel: 970-563-0235
Fax: 970-563-0382

Stagecoach Library
1840 S. Wolcott Ct.
Denver, CO 80219
Tel: (303)922-8856

Standley Lake Library
8485 Kipling Street
Arvada, CO 80005
Tel: 303-456-0806
http://jefferson.lib.co.us/

University of Colorado at Boulder Archives
Campus Box 184
Basement, Norlin Library
Boulder, CO 80309
Tel: 303-492-7242
Fax: 303-492-3960
E-mail: arv@colorado.edu
http://www.libraries.colorado.edu/ps/arv/

Ute Mountain Ute Tribal Research Archives Library
Tribal Compound
Box CC
Towaoc, CO 81334
Tel: 970-565-3751 x257
Fax: 970-565-7412
http://www.swcolo.org/Tourism/IndianCulture.html

Weld County Library
2227 23rd Avenue
Greeley, CO 80634
Tel: 970-330-7691
http://www.weld.lib.co.us/

Wellington Public Library
3800 Wilson Avenue
Wellington, CO 80549
Tel: 970-568-3040

NEWSPAPER REPOSITORIES

Colorado Historical Society
Stephen H. Hart Library
1300 Broadway
Denver, CO 80203
Tel: 303-866-3682
http://www.coloradohistory.org/

Denver Public Library
10 West 14th Avenue Pkwy.
Denver, CO 80204
Tel: 720-865-1111
Western History Genealogy Department: 720-865-1821
http://dpl20.denver.lib.co.us/

Norlin Library
184 UCB
University of Colorado
Boulder, CO 80309-0184
Tel: 303-492-8705
      303-492-8834 (Government Publications Library)
E-mail: libweb@colorado.edu
http://www.libraries.colorado.edu/ps/nor/frontpage.htm

VITAL RECORDS

Colorado Dept of Health
4300 Cherry Creek Dr South
Denver, CO 80246-1530
Recorded message: (303) 756-4464
Phone request: (303) 692-2224
Fax: (800) 423-1108
http://www.cdphe.state.co.us/hs/certs.asp
County Sources
http://www.cdphe.state.co.us/hs/countysources.asp
For genealogists and family historians
http://www.cdphe.state.co.us/hs/genealogy.html
Births, Deaths, Marriages, and Divorces Online
http://www.cdphe.state.co.us/hs/marriagedivorce.asp

COLORADO ON THE WEB

Census Schedules and Black Genealogical Research:
One Family's Experience
http://www.colorado.edu/libraries/govpubs/debbie/cover.htm

Colorado Civil War Casualties Index
http://www.archives.state.co.us/ciwardea.html

Colorada GenWeb Project
http://www.rootsweb.com/~cogenweb/comain.htm

Colorado Veterans' Grave Registrations 1862-1949
http://www.archives.state.co.us/grave_dir/cograv.html

Colorado Volunteers in the Spanish American War (1898)
http://www.archives.state.co.us/spamwar.html

Denver Public Library's Gopher
Colorado 1861 Territorial Election
Colorado Civil War GAR members
Colorado State Reformatory Prisoner Records 1887-1939
Denver Obituary Index
Pre-1963 Colorado Mining Fatalities
http://dpl20.denver.lib.co.us/ref/refmain.html
(Genealogy Resources - Colorado Resources)

Colorado State Archives Genealogy Resources
http://www.archives.state.co.us/geneal.html

CONNECTICUT

ARCHIVES, STATE & NATIONAL

Connecticut State Archives
Connecticut State Library
231 Capitol Avenue
Hartford, CT 06106
Tel: 860-757-6595
Fax: 860-757-6542
E-mail: MJones@cslib.org
http://www.cslib.org/archives.htm

National Archives-Northeast Region (Boston)
Frederick C. Murphy Federal Center
380 Trapelo Road
Waltham, MA 02154-8104
Tel: 781-647-8104
Fax: 781-647-8088
E-mail: waltham.center@nara.gov
http://www.nara.gov/regional/boston.html

GENEALOGICAL SOCIETIES

Connecticut Ancestry Society, Inc.
P.O. Box 249
Stamford, CT 06904-0249

Connecticut Professional Genealogists Council
P.O. Box 4273
Hartford, CT 06147-4273
http://www.rootsweb.com/~ctpgc/

Connecticut Society of Genealogists
175 Maple Street
East Hartford, CT 06118
Mail: P.O. Box 435
Glastonbury, CT 06033-0435
Tel: 860-569-0002
http://www.csginc.org/

Descendants of the Founders of Ancient Windsor
P.O. Box 39
Windsor, CT 06095-0039
http://www.societyct.org/windsor.htm

French Canadian Genealogical Society of Connecticut
P.O. Box 928
53 Tolland Green
Tolland, CT 06084
Tel: 860-872-2597
http://www.fcgsc.org/

Jewish Genealogical Society of Connecticut
22 Marilyn Rd
South Windsor, CT 06074
http://www.geocities.com/jgsct/JGSCT.html

Killingly Historical and Genealogical Society, Inc.
196 Main Street
P.O. Box 6000
Danielson, CT 06239
Tel: 860- 779-7250
http://www.qvctc.commnet.edu/brian/KHS/kilz1.html

Middlesex Genealogical Society
P.O. Box 1111
Darien, CT 06820-1111
http://www.darien.lib.ct.us/mgs/default.htm

New England Historic Genealogical Society
101 Newbury Street
Boston, MA 02116-3007
Tel: 617-536-5740
888-296-3447
Fax: 617-536-7307
http://www.nehgs.org/

Polish Genealogical Society of Connecticut
8 Lyle Road
New Britain, CT 06053
http://www.pgsctne.org/

Society of Mayflower Descendants in Connecticut
39 Butternut Lane
Vernon, CT 06066
http://www.ctmayflower.org/index.htm

Sons of the American Revolution
Connecticut Society (CTSSAR)
P.O. Box 411
East Haddam, CT 06423
http://www.ctssar.org/

Southington Genealogical Society
Southington Historical Center
239 Main Street
Southington, CT 06489
Tel: 860-628-7831

HISTORICAL SOCIETIES

Amity and Woodbridge Historical Society
Thomas Darling House
1907 Litchfield Turnpike
Woodbridge, CT 06525
Tel: 203-387-2823
http://www.woodbridgehistory.org/

Andover Historical Society
Bunker Hill Road
Andover, CT 06232
Tel: 860-742-6796

The Avon Historical Society, Inc.
P. O. Box 448
Avon, CT 06001
Tel: 860-678-1043
http://www.avonct.com/historicalsociety/

Bantam Historical Society
P.O. Box 436
Bantam, CT 06750-0436
http://www.museumsusa.org/data/museums/CT/75539.htm

Barkhamsted Historical Society
P.O. Box 94
Pleasant Valley, CT 06063
http://www.barkhamstedhistory.org/feedback.html

Beacon Falls Historical Commissions
10 Maple Ave.
Beacon Falls, CT 06403
Tel: 203-729-4340

Berlin Historical Society
305 Main St. (on the corner)
Berlin, CT 06037
http://berlincthistorical.org/

Branford Historical Society
Harrison House
124 Main Street
P.O. Box 504
Branford, CT 06405
Tel: 203-488-4828
http://members.aol.com/dtrofatter/histsoc.htm

Bridgewater Historical Society
Main Street
Bridgewater, CT 06752
http://www.newmilford-chamber.com/towns/
    bridgewater. htm

Brookfield Historical Society
Whisconier Road
P.O. Box 5231
Brookfield, CT 06804
Tel: 203-740-8140
http://www.danbury.org/org/brookhc/index.htm

Brooklyn Historical Society
25 Canterbury Road
P.O. Box 90
Brooklyn, CT 06234
Tel: 860-774-7728

Canton Historical Society
11 Front Street
Collinsville, CT 06019
Tel: 860-693-2793
http://www.cantonmuseum.org/pages/homepage.html

Chatham Historical Society of East Hampton
Bevin Boulevard
East Hampton, CT 06424

Cheshire Historical Society
Hitchcock-Phillips House
43 Church Drive
P.O. Box 281
Cheshire, CT 06410
Tel: 203-272-2574
http://users.rcn.com/andersonel/chs.htm

Chester Historical Society
4 Liberty
Chester, CT 06412
http://www.wuzzup.com/lowctriver/chester/historical.html

Colchester Historical Society
P.O. Box 13
Colchester, CT 06415

Colebrook Historical Society
Colebrook Center
558 Colebrook Road
P.O. Box 85
Colebrook, CT 06021
Tel: 860-738-3142

Connecticut Historical Commission
59 South Prospect Street
Hartford, CT 06106
Tel: 203-566-3005
Fax: 860-566-5078
E-mail: cthist@neca.com
http://www.cthistorical.com/

Connecticut Historical Society
1 Elizabeth Street at Asylum Avenue
Hartford, CT 06105
Tel: 860-236-5621
Fax: 860-236-2664
E-mail: ask_us@chs.org General Information
libchs@chs.org Library and Genealogy
http://www.hartnet.org/chs/

Connecticut League of History Organizations
940 Whitney Avenue
Hamden, CT 06517-4002
Tel: (203) 624-9186
Fax: (203) 773-0107
http://www.clho.org/

Cornwall Historical Society
Pine Street
P.O. Box 115
Cornwall, CT 06753

Coventry Historical Society
P. O. Box 534
Coventry, CT 06238
http://www.geocities.com/coventrycthistory/index.html

Danbury Museum & Historical Society
43 Main Street
Danbury, CT 06810
Tel: 203-743-5200
http://www.danburyhistorical.org/

Darien Historical Society
Bates-Scofield Homestead
45 Old King's Highway, North
Darien, CT 06820
Tel: 203-655-9233
http://www.darien.lib.ct.us/historical/default.htm

Denison Society
P.O. Box 42
Mystic, CT 06355
http://freepages.genealogy.rootsweb.com/
~denisonsociety/index.htm

Derby Historical Society
37 Elm Street
Ansonia, CT 06401
Mail: P.O. Box 331
Derby, CT 06418
Tel: 203-735-1908
E-mail: Derbyhistoricalsoc@juno.com
http://electronicvalley.org/derby/history/derbyhist.htm

Durham Historical Society
Main Street
P.O. Box 345
Durham, CT 06422

East Haddam Historical Society
264 Town Street
East Haddam, CT 06423
Tel: 860-873-3944

East Hartford, Historical Society of
P.O. Box 380166
East Hartford, CT 06138-0166
Tel: 860-568-7645
http://www.hseh.org/

East Haven Historical Society
P.O. Box 120052
East Haven, CT 06512

East Windsor Historical Society
Scantic Road
P. O. Box 363
East Windsor Hill, CT 06028
http://eastwindsorhistory.home.att.net/

Easton Historical Society
P.O. Box 121
Easton, CT 06612
Tel: 203-261-4622
http://www.tomorrowseaston.com/guestwebpages/
historicalsociety/historicalsociety.htm

Enfield Historical Society
1294 Enfield Street
Enfield, CT 06083
Tel: 860-745-1729
http://home.att.net/~mkm-of-enfct/

Essex Historical Society
The Pratt House
West Avenue
P.O. Box 123
Essex, CT 06426
Tel: 860-767-0681

Fairfield Historical Society
636 Old Post Road
Fairfield, CT 06430-6647
Tel: 203-259-1598
Fax: 203-255-2716
E-mail: info@fairfieldhs.org
http://www.fairfieldhistoricalsociety.org/

Falls Village-Canaan Historical Society
Main Street
P.O. Box 206
Falls Village, CT 06031
860-824-0707

Farmington Historical Society
71 Main St
P.O. Box 1645
Farmington, CT 06034
Tel: 860-678-1645

Gaylordsville Historical Society
P.O. Box 25
Gaylordsville, CT 06755
Tel: 860-350-0300
http://www.gaylordsville.org/

Glastonbury Historical Society
1944 Main Street
P.O. Box 46
Glastonbury, CT 06033
Tel: 860-633-6890
http://www.glasct.org/hissoc/home.htm

Goshen Historical Society
21 Old Middle Road (Rte. 63)
Goshen, CT 06756-2001
Tel: 860- 491-9610

Greater Bristol Historical Society
54 Middle Street
P.O. Box 1393
Bristol, CT 06010
Tel: 860-583-6309
http://www.museumsusa.org/data/museums/CT/75833.htm

Greenwich, Historical Society of
39 Strickland Road
Cos Cob, CT 06807
Tel: 203-869-6899
http://www.hstg.org/

Griswold Historical Society
P.O. Box 261
Jewett City, CT 06351
http://hometown.aol.com/caseywilkz/griswold/griswold.htm

Guilford Keeping Society
171 Boston Street
P.O. Box 363
Guilford, CT 06437
Tel: 203-453-3176
http://www.guilfordkeepingsociety.com/

Haddam Historical Society
P.O. Box 97
Haddam, CT 06438-0097

Hamden Historical Society
P.O. Box 5512
Hamden, CT 06518-0512
http://www.museumsusa.org/data/museums/CT/77107.htm

Hampton Antiquarian & Historical Society
Main Street
P.O. Box 12
Hampton, CT 06247

Hartland Historical Society
141 Center Street
East Hartland, CT 06027
Tel: 860-653-3055
http://vvv.munic.state.ct.us/hartland/historical.htm

Harwinton Historical Society
P.O. Box 84
Harwinton, CT 06791
http://www.museumsusa.org/data/museums/CT/76449.htm

Huntington Historical Society
P.O. Box 2155
Shelton, CT 06484
Tel: 203-925-1803

The Jewish Historical Soc. of Greater New Haven
P.O. Box 3251
New Haven, CT 06515-0351
Tel: 203-392-6125 (Office)
203-392-5860 (Archives)
203-392-6126 (FAX)
http://pages.cthome.net/hirsch/

Killingly Historical and Genealogical Society, Inc.
196 Main Street
P.O. Box 6000
Danielson, CT 06239
Tel: 860-779-7250
http://www.qvctc.commnet.edu/brian/khs/kilz1.html

**Lebanon Historical Society Museum
And Visitors Center**
856 Trumbull Highway, on the Historic Lebanon Green
P.O. Box 151
Lebanon CT 06249
Tel: 860-642-6579
Fax: 860-642-6583
E-mail: lebanon.hist.soc@snet.net
http://www.lebanonct.org/visitor_services.html

Litchfield Historical Society
7 South Street
Litchfield, CT 06759
Tel: 860-567-4501
http://www.litchfieldct.com/twn/lhistsoc.html

Lyme Historical Society/Archives
Florence Griswold Museum
96 Lyme Street
Old Lyme, CT 06371-1426
Tel: 860-434-5542
http://www.flogris.org/index.htm

Madison Historical Society
853 Boston Post Road
Madison, CT 06443

Manchester Historical Society
126 Cedar Street
Manchester, CT 06040
Mailing Address:
106 Hartford Road
Manchester, CT 06040
Tel: 860-647-9983
http://www.manchesterhistory.org/

Mansfield Historical Society
P.O. Box 145
Storrs, CT 06268
Tel: 860-429-6575
http://www.mansfield-history.org/

Marlborough Historical Society
P.O. Box 281
Marlborough, CT 06447
Tel: 860-295-8106

Mattatuck Historical Society/Museum
144 West Street
Waterbury, CT 06702
Tel: 203-753-0381
Fax: 203-756-6283
E-mail: info@mattatuckmuseum.org
http://www.mattatuckmuseum.org/main/main.htm

Middlebury Historical Society
P.O. Box 104
Middlebury CT 06762
http://www.middlebury-ct.org/historical.shtml

Middlesex County Historical Society
151 Main Street
Middletown, CT 06457
Tel: 860-346-0746

Milford Historical Society
34 High Street
Milford, CT 06460
Tel: 203-874-2664
http://www.geocities.com/SiliconValley/Park/3831/

Monroe Historical Society
Wheeler and Old Tannery Road
P. O. Box 212
Monroe, CA 06468
Tel: 203-261-1383
http://www.monroehistoricsociety.org/

Morris Historical Society
South Street
P.O. Box 234
Morris, CT 06763

Mystic River Historical Society
Old New London Rd. and High Street
P.O. Box 245
Mystic, CT 06355
Tel: 860-536-4779

Naugatuck Historical Society
P.O. Box 317
Water Street
Naugatuck, CT 06770
Tel: 203-729-9039
http://naugatuckhistory.com/

New Canaan Historical Society
13 Oenoke Ridge
New Canaan, CT 06840
Tel: 203-966-1776
Fax(203)972-5917
E-mail: newcanaan.historical@snet.net
www.nchistory.org

New England Historic Genealogical Society
101 Newbury Street
Boston, MA 02116-3007
Tel: 617-536-5740
888-296-3447
Fax: 617-536-7307
http://www.nehgs.org/

New Fairfield Historical Society
Fairfield Public Library
Route 39
Mailing Address:
2 Brush Hill Rd., P.O. Box F
New Fairfield, CT 06812
Tel: 203-312-5679

New Hartford Historical Museum/Library
367 Main Street
Pine Meadow, CT 06061
Mailing Address:
Box 41
New Hartford, CT 06057
Tel: 860-379-6894
http://www.town.new-hartford.ct.us/nhhs/index.html

New Haven Colony Historical Society
114 Whitney Avenue
New Haven, CT 06510
Phone: (203) 562-4183
Fax: (203) 562-2002

New London County Historical Society
11 Blinman Street
New London, CT 06320
Tel: 860-443-1209
http://www.rootsweb.com/~ctnewlon/nlhs.html

New Milford Historical Society & Museum
6 Aspetuck Ave.
P.O. Box 566
New Milford, CT 06776
Tel: 860-354-3069
http://www.nmhistorical.org/

Newington Historical Society & Trust
679 Willard Ave.
Newington, CT 06111
Tel: 860-666-7118

Newtown Historical Society
44 Main Street
P.O. Box 189
Newtown, CT 06470
http://www.newtownhistorical.b3.nu/

Noank Historical Society/Museum
17 Sylvan St.
P.O. Box 9454
Groton, CT 06340
Tel: 860-536-5021
860-536-7026

Norfolk Historical Society
Village Green
Norfolk, CT 06058
Tel: 860-542-5761

North Haven Historical Society
27 Broadway
North Haven, CT 06473
Tel: 203-239-7722
http://www.geocities.com/northhavenhistoricalsociety/
home.htm

North Stonington Historical Society
1 Wyassup Road
P.O. Box 134
North Stonington, CT 06359
http://www.nostoningtonhistsoc.homestead.com/

Norwalk Historical Society
The Mill Hill Historic Park and Museum
P.O. Box 335, 2 East Wall St.
Norwalk, CT 06852
Tel: (203) 846-0525
http://www.geocities.com/Heartland/Trail/8030/

Old Bethlehem Historical Society
P.O. Box 132
Bethlehem, CT 06751
Tel: 203-266-5196
http://www.ci.bethlehem.ct.us/OBHSI/old.htm

Old Saybrook Historical Society
Archival Section
Gen. William Hart House
350 Main Street
P.O. Box 4
Old Saybrook, CT 06475
Tel: 860-395-1635
http://www.oldsaybrook.com/History/society.htm

Old Woodbury Historical Society
P.O. Box 705
405 Main Street South
Woodbury, CT 06798
Tel: 203- 263-2595
http://www.see-ct.com/?place=OldWoodburyHistorical
Society

Orange Historical Society
The Academy Museum
605 Orange Center Road
The Stone-Otis House
615 Orange Center Road
P.O. Box 784
Orange, CT 06477
Tel: 203-795-3106
203-795-6465
http://www.orangehistory.org/

Oxford Historical Society
154 Bowers Hill Road
Oxford, CT 06478
Tel: 203-888-0363
http://www.oxford-ct.com/civicgroups/OxfordHistorical
Society.shtml

Plainville Historical Society
Plainville Historical Center
Farmington Canal Room
29 Pierce Street
P.O. Box 464
Plainville, CT 06062
Tel: 860-747-6577

Plymouth Historical Society
572 Main Street
P.O. Box 176
Plymouth, CT 06782
Tel: 860-585-7040

Pomfret Historical Society
P.O. Box 152
Pomfret, CT 06259

Portland Historical Society
P.O. Box 98
Portland, CT 06480
http://www.geocities.com/portlandhistsoc/

Prospect Historical Society
Center Street
Mail: 31 Summit Road
Prospect, CT 06712

Ridgefield Historical Society
Scott House
Sunset Lane and Grove Street
Ridgefield, CT 06877
Tel: 203-438-2282
http://www.ridgefieldct.org/history/history.htm

Rocky Hill Historical Society/Academy Hall Museum
785 Old Main Street
Rocky Hill, CT 06067
Tel: 860-563-8710
860-563-6704 (museum)
http://www.rockyhillhistory.org/

Rowayton Historical Society
177 Rowayton Ave.
P.O. Box 106
Rowayton, CT 06853
http://www.rowayton.org/

Roxbury Historical Society
South Street (behind the Old Town Hall)
Roxbury, CT 06783

Salisbury Association
Scoville Library, History Room
38 Main Street
P.O. Box 516
Salisbury, CT 06068-0516
Tel: 860-435-2838
http://www.biblio.org/scoville/

Salmon Brook Historical Society
208 Salmon Brook Street
Granby, CT 06035
Tel: 860-653-9713
http://www.salmonbrookhistorical.org/

Seymour Historical Society
59 West Street
Seymour, CT 06483
Tel: 203-888-7471
    203-888-0037

Sharon Historical Society
The Gay-Hoyt House
18 Main Street
Sharon, CT 06069
Tel: 860-364-5688
www.sharonhist.org

Sherman Historical Society
10 Route 37 Center
Sherman, CT 06784
Tel: 860-354-3083
E-mail: info@shermanhistorical.org
http://www.shermanhistorical.org/

Simsbury Historical Society
Massacoh Plantation
800 Hopmeadow Street
P.O. Box 2
Simsbury, CT 06070
Tel: 860-628-2500
http://www.simsburyhistory.com/

The Somers Historical Society, Inc.
11 Battle Street
P.O. Box 652
Somers, CT 06071
Tel: 860-749-3219
http://www.somershistoricalsociety.org/

South Windsor Historical Society
P.O. Box 216
South Windsor, CT 06074
http://southwindsorhistory.home.att.net/

Southbury Historical Society
P.O. Box 124
Southbury, CT 06488
Tel: 203-264-2993
http://www.southburyhistorical.org/default.htm

Southington Historical Society
Southington Historical Center
239 Main Street
Southington, CT 06489
Tel: 860-621-4811
http://www.southington.com/

Sprague Historical Society
1 Main Street
Baltic, CT 06330

Stafford Historical Society
11 Murphy Road
P.O. Box 56
Stafford Springs, CT 06075
Tel: 860-684-9189

Stamford Historical Society/Library/Museum
1508 High Ridge Road
Stamford, CT 06903
Tel: 203-329-1183
Fax: 203-322-1607
http://www.stamfordhistory.org/main.htm

Stonington Historical Society
Wadawanuck Square
P.O. Box 103
Stonington, CT 06378-0103
Tel: 860-535-1131
http://www.stoningtonhistory.org/index.html

Stratford Historical Society
Judson House & Catherine B. Mitchell Museum
967 Academy Hill
P.O. Box 382
Stratford, CT 06615-0382
Tel: 203-378-0630
http://www.stratfordhistoricalsociety.com/

Suffield Historical Society
232 South Main Street
P.O. Box 893
Suffield, CT 06078
Tel: 203-668-5286
http://www.suffield-library.org/localhistory/king.htm

Thomaston Historical Society
158 Main Street
Thomaston, CT 06787
Tel: 860-283-2159
860-283-9474

Thompson Historical Society
Thompson Hill Road and Chase
P.O. Box 47
Thompson, CT 06277
Tel: 860-923-3200
http://www.thompsonhistorical.org/

Tolland Historical Society
P.O. Box 107
Tolland, CT 06084

Torrington Historical Society
192 Main Street
Torrington, CT 06790
Tel: 860-482-8260

Trumbull Historical Society
1856 Huntington Tpke.
Trumbull, CT 06611
Tel: 203-377-6620
http://trumbull.ct.us/history/

Union Historical Society
583 Buckly Highway
Union, CT 06076
Tel: 860-684-7078

Voluntown Historical Society
P.O. Box 130
Voluntown, CT 06384
Tel: 860-376-9563

Wallingford Historical Society
Samuel Parsons House
180 South Main Street
Wallingford, CT 06492

Waterford Historical Society
P.O. Box 117
Waterford, CT 06385-0117

Watertown Historical Society
22 DeForest Street
Watertown, CT 06795
Tel: 860-274-1634

West Hartford Historical Society/Noah Webster Foundation
227 South Main Street
West Hartford, CT 06107
Tel: 860-521-5362
http://www.ctstateu.edu/noahweb/

Weston Historical Society
104 Weston Road
P.O. Box 1092
Weston, CT 06883
Tel: 203-226-1804
http://www.wvfd.com/whs.htm

Westport Historical Society
Wheeler House
25 Avery Place
Westport, CT 06880
Tel: 203-222-1424
http://www.westporthistory.org/

Wethersfield Historical Society
150 Main Street
Wethersfield, CT 06109
Tel: 860-529-7656
Fax: (860) 529-1905
E-mail: weth.hist.society@snet.net
http://www.wethhist.org/main.html

Willington Historical Society
48 Red Oak Hill
West Willington, CT 06279
Tel: 860-429-2656
http://www.willingtonct.org/whs.html

Wilton Historical Society
Wilton Library, History Room
137 Old Ridgefield Road
Tel: 203-762-3950
http://www.wiltonlibrary.org/histroom.asp

Windsor Historical Society/Library
96 Palisado Avenue
Windsor, CT 06095
Tel: 860-688-3813
Fax: 860-687-1633
http://historicalsocietyct.com/windsor2/

Windsor Locks Historical Society
Noden-Reed Park
58 West Street
Windsor Locks, CT 06096
Tel: 860-627-9212
http://www.cnctb.org/detail.cfm?ID=365

Wintonbury Historical Society
151 School Street
Bloomfield, CT 06002
Tel: 860-243-1531

Woodstock Historical Society
523 Route 169
Woodstock, CT 06281
Tel: 860-928-1035

LDS FAMILY HISTORY CENTERS

For locations of Family History Centers in this state, see the Family History Center locator at FamilySearch: http://www.familysearch.org/eng/Library/FHC/frameset_fhc.asp

ARCHIVES/LIBRARIES/MUSEUMS

Abington Social Library
536 Hampton Road
Abington, CT 06230
Tel: 860-974-0415

Academy Hall Museum
Rocky Hill Historical Society
785 Old Main Street
Rocky Hill, CT 06067
Tel: 860-563-8710
860-563-6704 (museum)
http://www.rockyhillhistory.org/

Beardsley and Memorial Library
40 Munroe Place
Winsted, CT 06098-1423
Tel: 860-379-6043
http://www.beardsleyandmemorial.org/

Bridgeport Public Library
Burroughs Library Building
Historical Collection, 3rd Floor
925 Broad Street
Bridgeport, CT 06604
Tel: 203-576-7403
http://www.futuris.net/bpl/welcome.htm

Bristol Public Library
5 High Street
Bristol, CT 06010
Tel: 860-854-7787
http://www.ci.bristol.ct.us/Library/MainLibrary/LibraryMain.htm

Canton Historical Museum
11 Front Street
Collinsville, CT 06022
Tel: 860-693-2793
http://www.cantonmuseum.org/pages/homepage.html

Connecticut College
Shain Library
270 Mohegan Avenue
New London, CT 06320-4196
Tel: 860-439-2659
E-mail: libref@conncoll.edu
http://www.conncoll.edu/is/info-resources/

Connecticut Historical Society
1 Elizabeth Street at Asylum Avenue
Hartford, CT 06105
Tel: 860-236-5621
Fax: 860-236-2664
E-mail: libchs@chs.org (library and genealogy)
http://www.chs.org/

Connecticut Polish American Archive
Elihu Burritt Library
Central Connecticut State University
1615 Stanley Street
New Britain, CT 06050
Tel: 860-832-2055
Fax: 860-832-2118
http://wilson.ctstateu.edu/lib/archives/polish/

Connecticut State Library
History & Genealogy Unit
231 Capitol Avenue
Hartford, CT 06106
Tel: 860-757-6580
Fax: 860-757-6521
http://www.cslib.org/handg.htm

Cyrenius H. Booth Library
25 Main Street
Newtown, CT 06470
Tel: 203-426-4533
http://www.biblio.org/chbooth/index.htm

Danbury Public Library
170 Main Street
Danbury, CT 06810-7835
Tel: 203-797-4505
http://danburylibrary.org/

Danbury Museum & Historical Society
43 Main Street
Danbury, CT 06810
Tel: 203-743-5200
http://www.danburyhistorical.org/

Darien Historical Society
Bates-Scofield Homestead
45 Old King's Highway, North
Darien, CT 06820
Tel: 203-655-9233
http://www.darien.lib.ct.us/historical/default.htm

Darien Library
35 Leroy Avenue
Darien, CT 06820-4497
Tel: 203-655-1234
http://www.darien.lib.ct.us/lib/

Dodd Research Center
University of Connecticut
405 Babbidge Road
Storrs, CT 06269-1205
http://www.lib.uconn.edu/DoddCenter/

East Hartford Public Library
840 Main Street
East Hartford, CT 06108
Tel: 860-289-6429
Fax: 860-291-9166
http://www.easthartford.lib.ct.us/

Fairfield Historical Society Library
Fairfield Historical Society
636 Old Post Road
Fairfield, CT 06430-6647
Tel: 203-259-1598
Fax: 203-255-2716
E-mail: info@fairfieldhs.org
http://www.fairfieldhistoricalsociety.org/

Fairfield Public Library
1080 Old Post Road
Fairfield, CT 06430
Tel: 203-256-3155
http://www.fairfieldpubliclibrary.org/

Farmington Museum
37 High Street
Farmington, CT 06032
http://www.farmington.lib.ct.us/

Ferguson Library
One Public Library Plaza
Stamford, CT 06904
Tel: 203-964-1000
http://www.futuris.net/ferg/

Godfrey Memorial Library
134 Newfield Street
Middletown, CT 06457
Tel: 860-346-4375
Fax: 860-347-9874
E-mail: godfrey@connix.com
http://www.godfrey.org/

Greenwich Library
101 West Putnam Avenue
Greenwich, CT 06830
Tel: 203-622-7900
http://www.greenwich.lib.ct.us/

Groton Public Library
52 Newtown Road, Route 117
Groton, CT 06340
Tel: 860-441-6750
http://www.town.groton.ct.us/Library/library.htm

Gunn Memorial Library
5 Wykeham Road
P.O. Box 1273
Washington, CT 06793
Tel: 860-868-7586
860-868-7756 (museum)
http://www.biblio.org/gunn/

Hartford Public Library
500 Main Street
Hartford, CT 06103
Tel: 860-543-8628
http://www.hartfordpl.lib.ct.us/

Indian and Colonial Research Center
Main Street (Route 27)
Old Mystic, CT 06372
Tel: 860-536-9771
http://www.geocities.com/icrc06372/

Kent Memorial Library
Historical Room
50 North Main Street
Suffield, CT 06078-2117
Tel: 860-668-3896
E-mail: kentlib@tiac.net
http://www.suffield-library.org/

Killingly Historical and Genealogical Society, Inc.
196 Main Street
P.O. Box 6000
Danielson, CT 06239
Tel: 860-779-7250
http://www.qvctc.commnet.edu/brian/khs/kilz1.html

Lebanon Historical Society Museum
and Visitors Center
856 Trumbull Highway, on the Historic Lebanon Green
P.O. Box 151
Lebanon CT 06249
Tel: 860-642-6579
Fax: 860-642-6583
E-mail: lebanon.hist.soc@snet.net
http://www.lebanonct.org/visitor_services.html

Litchfield Historical Society
7 South Street
Litchfield, CT 06759
Tel: 860-567-4501
http://www.litchfieldct.com/twn/lhistsoc.html

Living Museum of Avon
8 East Main Street
Avon, CT 06001
Tel: 860-678-1043
http://www.avonct.com/historicalsociety/living.html

Lyme Historical Society/Archives
Florence Griswold Museum
96 Lyme Street
Old Lyme, CT 06371-1426
Tel: 860-434-5542
http://www.flogris.org/index.htm

Mattatuck Historical Society/Museum
144 West Street
Waterbury, CT 06702
Tel: 203-753-0381
Fax: 203-756-6283
E-mail: info@mattatuckmuseum.org
http://www.mattatuckmuseum.org/main/main.htm

Museum of Connecticut History
Connecticut State Library
231 Capitol Avenue
Hartford, CT 06106
Tel: 860-757-6535
Fax: 860-757-6533
http://www.cslnet.ctstateu.edu/museum.htm

Mystic and Noank Library
40 Library Street
Mystic, CT 06355-2418
Tel: 860-536-7721
860-536-3019
Fax: 860-536-2350
http://www.mysticnoanklibrary.com/

Mystic Seaport
P.O. Box 6000
75 Greenmanville Ave.
Mystic, CT 06355
Tel: 860-572-0711
860-572-5315
http://www.mysticseaport.org/

New Britain Public Library
20 High Street
New Britain, CT 06051
Phone:(860) 224-3155
Fax:(860) 223-6729
http://www.nbpl.lib.ct.us/

New Canaan Historical Society/Library
13 Oenoke Ridge
New Canaan, CT 06840
Tel: 203-966-1776
Fax: (203) 972-5917
E-mail: newcanaan.historical@snet.net
http://www.montrealservers.com/~mycro/nchistory/

New England Historic Genealogical Society
101 Newbury Street
Boston, MA 02116-3007
Tel: 617-536-5740; 888-296-3447
Fax: 617-536-7307
http://www.nehgs.org/

New Hartford Historical Museum/Library
The Licia & Mason Beekley Community Library
P.O. Box 247
10 Central Avenue
New Hartford, CT 06057
Tel: 860-379-7235
http://www.libct.org/newhartfordpl/

New Haven Colony Historical Society
114 Whitney Avenue
New Haven, CT 06510
Phone: (203) 562-4183
FAX (203) 562-2002

New Haven Free Public Library
Local History Room
133 Elm Street
New Haven, CT 06510
Tel: 203-946-8130
http://www.nhfpl.lib.ct.us/

New London Public Library
63 Huntington Street
New London, CT 06320-6194
Tel: 860-447-1411
http://www.lioninc.org/newlondon/

New Milford Historical Society & Museum
6 Aspetuck Ave.
P.O. Box 566
New Milford, CT 06776
Tel: 860-354-3069
http://www.nmhistorical.org/

Noah Webster Memorial Library
West Hartford Public Library
20 S. Main Street
West Hartford, CT 06107
Tel: 860-523-3279
http://www.west-hartford.com/library/

Noank Historical Society/Museum
17 Sylvan St.
P.O. Box 9454
Groton, CT 06340
Tel: 860-536-5021
860-536-7026

Old Saybrook Historical Society
Archival Section
Gen. William Hart House
350 Main Street
P.O. Box 4
Old Saybrook, CT 06475
Tel: 860-395-1635
http://www.oldsaybrook.com/History/society.htm

Oliver Wolcott Library
160 South Street
P.O. Box 187
Litchfield, CT 06759
Tel: 860-567-8030
http://www.owlibrary.org/

Otis Library
261 Main Street
Norwich, CT 06360
Tel: 860-889-2365
Fax: 860-886-4744
http://www.lioninc.org/norwich/otis_home.htm

Pequot Library
720 Pequot Avenue
Southport, CT 06490
Tel: 203-259-0346
Fax: 203-259-5602
http://www.pequotlibrary.org/

Phoebe Griffin Noyes Library
2 Library Lane
Old Lyme, CT 06371
Tel: 860-434-1684
Fax: 860-434-9547
http://www.oldlyme.lioninc.org/

Ridgefield Library and Historical Assn.
Historical Collection
472 Main Street
Ridgefield, CT 06877
Tel: 203-438-2282
http://www.biblio.org/rdgfld/rdgfld.htm

Russell Library
123 Broad Street
Middletown, CT 06457
Tel: 860-347-2528
860-347-2520
Fax: 860-347-4048
http://russelllibrary.org/

Salmon Brook Historical Society
208 Salmon Brook Street
Granby, CT 06035
Tel: 860-653-9713
http://www.salmonbrookhistorical.org/

Scoville Library, History Room
38 Main Street
P.O. Box 516
Salisbury, CT 06068-0516
Tel: 860-435-2838
http://www.biblio.org/scoville/

Seymour Public Library
46 Church Street
Seymour, CT 06483-2612
Tel: 203-888-3903
Fax: 203-888-4099
http://www.electronicvalley.org/seymour/lib/seymour.htm

Simsbury Genealogical & Historical Research Library
749 Hopmeadow Street
P.O. Box 484
Simsbury, CT 06070

Southington Public Library
255 Main Street
Southington, CT 06489-2509
Tel: 860-628-0947
http://www.munic.state.ct.us/SOUTHINGTON/library.htm

Stamford Historical Society/Library/Museum
1508 High Ridge Road
Stamford, CT 06903
Tel: 203-329-1183
Fax: 203-322-1607
http://www.stamfordhistory.org/main.htm

Sterling Memorial Library
Yale University
120 High Street
New Haven, CT 06511
Tel: 203-432-1775
http://www.library.yale.edu/rsc/sml/

Stratford Historical Society
Judson House & Catherine B. Mitchell Museum
967 Academy Hill
P.O. Box 382
Stratford, CT 06615-0382
Tel: 203-378-0630
http://www.stratfordhistoricalsociety.com/

Trinity College
Watkinson Library
300 Summit Street
Hartford, CT 06106
Tel: 860-297-2268
http://www.trincoll.edu/depts/library/watkinson/
watk_intro.html

U.S. Coast Guard Academy
Coast Guard Museum
Fifteen Mohegan Avenue
New London, CT 06320-4195
Tel: 860-444-8511
http://www.uscg.mil/hq/g%2Dcp/museum/museuminfo.html

Wadsworth Atheneum Auerbach
600 Main Street
Hartford, CT 06103-2990
Tel: 860-278-2670
Fax: 860-527-0803
http://www.wadsworthatheneum.org/index.htm

Wesleyan University
Olin Memorial Library
Special Collection & Archives
252 Church Street
Middletown, CT 06459
Tel: 860-685-2660
http://www.wesleyan.edu/libr/olinhome/olinhome.htm

West Hartford Public Library
20 South Main Street
West Hartford, CT 06107
http://www.west-hartford.com/library/

Westport Historical Society
Wheeler House
25 Avery Place
Westport, CT 06880
Tel: 203-222-1424
http://www.westporthistory.org/

Wilton Historical Society
Wilton Library, History Room
137 Old Ridgefield Road
Tel: 203-762-3950
http://www.wiltonlibrary.org/histroom.asp

Windsor Historical Society/Library
96 Palisado Avenue
Windsor, CT 06095
Tel: 860-688-3813
Fax: 860-687-1633
http://historicalsocietyct.com/windsor2/

Wood Memorial Library
783 Main Street
P. O. Box 131
South Windsor, CT 06074
Tel: 860-289-1783
Fax: 860-289-4178
E-mail: wood.memorial.lib@snet.net
http://pages.cthome.net/wood.memorial.lib/

Yale University Library
Manuscripts & Archives
Sterling Memorial Library
120 High Street and 128 Wall Street
New Haven, CT 06520
Tel: 203-432-1744
http://www.library.yale.edu/mssa/home1.htm

NEWSPAPER REPOSITORIES

Connecticut Historical Society
1 Elizabeth Street at Asylum Avenue
Hartford, CT 06105
Tel: 860-236-5621
Fax: 860-236-2664
E-mail: libchs@chs.org (library and genealogy)
http://www.chs.org/

Connecticut State Library
History & Genealogy Unit
231 Capitol Avenue
Hartford, CT 06106
Tel: 860-757-6524
Fax: 860-757-6503
E-mail: JCullinane@cslib.org
http://www.cslib.org/cnp.htm

VITAL RECORDS

State of Connecticut
Department of Public Health
Vital Records Section
410 Capitol Avenue
P.O. Box 340308
MS#11VRS
Hartford, CT 06134-0308
Tel: 860-509-7896
Fax: 860-509-7964
 (July 1,1897-present)
http://www.dph.state.ct.us/OPPE/hpvital.htm

Connecticut State Library
History & Genealogy Unit
Barbour Collection
231 Capitol Avenue
Hartford, CT 06106
Tel: 860-757-6500
Fax: 860-757-6503
http://www.cslib.org/vitals.htm

CONNECTICUT ON THE WEB

Barbour Collection of Connecticut Vital Records
http://www.cslib.org/barbour.htm

Charles R. Hale Collection
http://www.cslib.org/halecol.htm

Connecticut Genweb Project
http://www.rootsweb.com/~ctgenweb/

DELAWARE

ARCHIVES, STATE & NATIONAL

Delaware Public Archives
121 Duke of York Street
Dover, DE 19901
Tel: 302-739-5318
E-mail: archives@state.de.us
http://www.state.de.us/sos/dpa/

National Archives-Mid Atlantic Region
900 Market Street
Philadelphia, A 19107-4292
Tel: 215-597-3000
Fax: 215-597-2303
E-mail: philadelphia.archives@nara.gov
http://www.nara.gov/regional/philacc.html

GENEALOGICAL SOCIETIES

Delaware Genealogical Society
505 N. Market Street Mall
Wilmington, DE 19801-3091
http://delgensoc.org/

Lower Delmarva Genealogical Society (LDGS)
P.O. Box 3602
Salisbury, MD 21802-3602
http://bay.intercom.net/ldgs/index.html

Sons of the American Revolution
Delaware Society
P.O. Box 2169
Wilmington, DE 19899
http://www.sar.org/dessar/default.htm

HISTORICAL SOCIETIES

Afro-American Historical Society of Delaware
512 East 4th Street
Wilmington, DE 19801
Tel: 302-571-1699
Fax: 302-571-9300

Brandywine Historical Society
18 Third Ave.
Claymont, DE 19703
Tel: 302-792-2724

Bridgeville Historical Society
102 South Williams Street
Bridgeville, DE 19933
Tel: 302-337-7600

Chester County Historical Society
225 North High Street
West Chester, PA 19380
Tel: 215-692-4800
http://www.chestercohistorical.org/

Delaware, Historical Society of
Old Town Hall
505 Market Street
Wilmington, DE 19801
Tel: 302-655-7161
Fax: 302-655-7844
E-mail: hsd@hsd.org
http://www.hsd.org/

Fort Delaware Society
(Ferry Dock in Delaware City off route 1)
P.O. Box 553
Delaware City, DE 19706
Tel: 302-834-1630
Fax: 302-836-7256
E-mail: FtDSociety@del.net
http://www.del.net/org/fort/

Georgetown Historical Society
510 S. Bedford Street
Georgetown, DE 19947
Tel: 302-855-9660
http://www.marvelmuseum.org/2index2.html

Historical Society of Pennsylvania
1300 Locust Street
Philadelphia, PA 19107
Tel: 215-732-6200
http://www.hsp.org/index.html

Jewish Historical Society of Delaware
c/o Historical Society of Delaware
505 Market Street
Wilmington, DE 19801
Tel: 302-655-6232
http://www.hsd.org/jhsd.htm

Laurel Historical Society
502 East 4 Street
Laurel, DE 19956
Tel: 302-875-1344

Lewes Historical Society
110 Shipcarpenter Street
Lewes, DE 19958-1210
Tel: 302-645-7670
http://www.beach-net.com/lewestour/ltour15.html

Nanticoke Indian Association
R.D. 4, Box 107A
Millsboro, DE 19966
Tel: 302-945-3400
302-945-7022 (museum)

New Castle Historical Society
Two East Fourth Street
New Castle, Delaware 19720
Tel: 302-322-2794
Fax: 302-322-8923
http://www.newcastlecity.net/nc_hs/nc_hs.html

Presbyterian Historical Society
425 Lombard Street
Philadelphia, PA 19147-1516
Tel: 215-627-1852
Fax: 215-627-0509
http://www.history.pcusa.org

Rehoboth Beach Historical Society
Anna Hazzard Museum
17 Christian Street
P.O. Box 42
Rehoboth Beach, DE 19971
Tel: 302-227-6111
302-226-1119
http://www.cityofrehoboth.com/history.htm

Seaford Historical Society
Ross Plantation
North Pine Street
Box 393
Seaford, DE 19973
Tel: 302-628-9500
Fax: 302-628-9501
http://www.seafordde.com/history.html

LDS FAMILY HISTORY CENTERS

For locations of Family History Centers in this state, see
the Family History Center locator at FamilySearch:
http://www.familysearch.org/eng/Library/FHC/
frameset_fhc.asp

ARCHIVES/LIBRARIES/MUSEUMS

Barratt's Chapel and Museum/Research Library
6362 Bay Road
Frederica, DE 19946
Tel: 302-335-5544
E-mail: Barratts@aol.com
http://users.aol.com/Barratts/home.html

Corbit-Calloway Memorial Library
115 High Street
P.O. Box 128
Odessa, DE 19730
Tel: 302-378-8838
Fax: 302-378-7803
http://www.dla.lib.de.us/Dir_Data/Library63.html

Delaware Division of Libraries
Department of Community Affairs
43 South Dupont Highway
Dover, DE 19901
Tel: 302-739-4748
Fax: 302-739-6787
http://www.state.de.us/sos/library.htm

Delaware State University
William C. Jason Library-Learning Center
1200 N. Dupont Highway
Dover, Delaware 19901-2277
Tel: 302-739-3571
http://www.dsc.edu/library/library.html

Dover Public Library
45 South State Street
Dover, DE 19901
Tel: 302-736-7030
http://www.cityofdover.com/library.html

**Edward H. Nabb Research Center for DelMarVa
History & Culture**
Power Professional Bldg, Room 190
Salisbury, MD 21801
Tel: 410-543-6312
http://nabbhistory.salisbury.edu/

Episcopal Church
Diocese of Delaware
400 Burnt Mill Road
Centerville, DE 19807
Tel: 302 254-2222
http://www.dioceseofdelaware.net/index.htm

Hagley Museum/Library
298 Buck Road East
P.O. Box 3630
Wilmington, DE 19807-0630
Tel: 302-658-2400 (weekdays)
302-658-4674 (weekends)
Fax: 302-658-0568
http://www.hagley.lib.de.us/

Hendrickson House Museum & Old Swedes Church
606 North Church Street
Wilmington, DE 19801-4421
Tel: 302-652-5629
http://www.oldswedes.org/

Historical Society of Delaware Library/Museum
Old Town Hall
505 Market Street
Wilmington, DE 19801
Tel: 302-655-7161
302-656-0637 (museum)
Fax: 302-655-7844
E-mail: hsd@hsd.org
http://www.hsd.org/

Holy Trinity (Old Swedes) Episcopal Church
606 Church Street
Wilmington, DE 19801
Tel: 302-652-5629
http://www.oldswedes.org/

Laurel Public Library
101 E. Fourth Street
Laurel, DE 19956-1547
Tel: 302-875-3184
Fax: 302-875-4519
http://www.dla.lib.de.us/Dir_Data/Library184.html

Lewes Chamber of Commerce
Fisher Martin House
120 Kings Highway
P.O. Box 1
Lewes, DE 19958
Tel: 302-645-8073
Fax: 302-645-8412
http://www.leweschamber.com/

Lewes Public Library
111 Adams Ave.
Lewes, DE 19958
Tel: 302-645-2733
http://www.leweslibrary.org/

Meetinghouse Galleries
316 S. Governors Ave.
Dover, DE 19904-6706
Tel: 302-739-3260

Milford Public Library
11 S.E. Front Street
Milford, DE 19963-1941
Tel: 302-422-8996
http://www.cityofmilford.com/library.cfm

New Castle Public Library
501 Delaware Street
New Castle, DE 19720
Tel: 302-328-2392

Preservation Delaware, Inc.
Library
1405 Greenhill Ave.
Wilmington, DE 19806
Tel: 302-651-9617
Fax: 302-651-9603
http://www.preservationde.org/index.html

Redmen Nanticoke Tribe
Route 113
Georgetown, DE 19947
Tel: 302-856-2405

Rockwood Museum
610 Shipley Road
Wilmington, DE 19809-3609
Tel: 302-761-4340
E-mail: info@rockwood.org
http://www.fieldtrip.com/de/27614340.htm

Roman Catholic Archives
Diocese of Wilmington
P.O. Box 2030
1925 Delaware Ave
Wilmington, DE 19899
Tel: 302-573-3100
Fax: 302-573-2391
http://www.cdow.org/index.html

Seaford District Library
402 North Porter Street
Seaford, DE 19973
Tel: 302-629-2524
Fax: 302-629-9181
http://www.dla.lib.de.us/Dir_Data/Library262.html

Smyrna Public Library
107 South Main Street
Smyrna, DE 19977
Tel: 302-653-4579
Fax : (302) 653 - 2650
E-mail: smypublib58@yahoo.com
http://smyrnapubliclibrary.mybravenet.com/

State of Delaware Division of Libraries
43 S. DuPont Highway
Dover, DE, 19901
Tel: 302-739-4748
Fax: 302-739-6787
http://www.state.de.us/sos/library.htm

University of Delaware
Morris Library
Special Collections Department
181 South College Avenue
Newark, DE 19717-5267
Tel: 302-831-2229
302-831-2231
Fax: 302-831-1046
http://www.lib.udel.edu/

Wesley College
Parker Library
College Square
Dover, DE 19901
Tel: 302-736-2413
Fax: 302-736-2533
http://www.wesley.edu/library/index_library.html

Wicomico County Free Library
122 South Division Street
Salisbury, MD 21801-4929
Tel: 410-749-5171
410-749-3612
http://www.wicomicolibrary.org/

Widener University School of Law
Legal Information Center
Brandywine Valley Historical Collection
4601 Concord Pike
P.O. Box 7475
Wilmington, DE 19803
Tel: 302-477-2063
Fax: 302-477-2240
http://www.law.widener.edu/Law-Library/

Wilmington Institute Free Library
10 S. Market Street
P.O. Box 2303
Wilmington, DE 19899-2303
Tel: 302-571-7416
Fax: 302-654-9132
http://www.wilmlib.org/index.html

Winterthur Museum, Gardens, and Library
Winterthur Museum Archives
Winterthur, DE 19735
Tel: 302-888-4600
Fax: 302-888-4870
http://www.winterthur.org/

NEWSPAPER REPOSITORIES

Delaware, Historical Society of
Old Town Hall
505 Market Street
Wilmington, DE 19801
Tel: 302-655-7161
Fax: 302-655-7844
E-mail: hsd@dca.net
http://www.hsd.org/

Delaware State Archives
Hall of Records
121 Duke of York St., Suite 1
Dover, DE 19901
Tel: 302-744-5000
Fax 302-739-2578
http://www.state.de.us/sos/archives.htm

University of Delaware Libraries
181 South College Avenue
Newark, DE 19717-5267
Tel: 302-831-2229
http://www.lib.udel.edu/

VITAL RECORDS

Delaware State Archives
Hall of Records
Bureau of Archives and Records Management
121 Duke of York Street
Dover, DE 19901
Tel: 302-744-5000
E-mail: archives@state.de.us (Requests accepted)
(Births, Deaths, and Marriages 1913-present)
http://www.state.de.us/sos/dpa/

DELAWARE ON THE WEB

Delaware Genealogical Society
http://delgensoc.org/

Delaware Genweb Project
http://www.geocities.com/Heartland/8074/state_de.htm

Delaware State Library
http://www.lib.de.us/

Historical Society of Delaware
http://www.hsd.org/

Lower DelMarVa Genealogical Society
http://bay.intercom.net/ldgs/index.html

District of Columbia

Archives, State & National

District of Columbia Archives
1300 Naylor Court, NW
Washington, DC 20001-4225
Tel: 202-727-2054

Maryland State Archives
Hall of Records Building
350 Rowe Blvd.
Annapolis, MD 21401
Tel: 410-260-6400
    800-235-4045 MD toll free
Fax: 410-974-3895
E-mail: archives@mdarchives.state.md.us
www.mdarchives.state.md.us

National Archives and Records Administration (NARA)
Archives I
700 Pennsylvania Avenue, NW
Washington, DC 20408
Tel: 202-501-5410 (Genealogical Staff)
202-501-5400 (Record Availability)
Fax: 301-713-6905 (Fax-on-Demand Information)
E-mail: inquire@arch1.nara.gov
http://www.nara.gov/nara/dc/Archives1_directions.html

National Archives and Records Administration (NARA)
Archives II
8601 Adelphi Road
College Park, MD 20740
Tel: 202-501-5400 (Record Availability)
301-713-6800 (General Reference)
301-713-7040 (Cartographic Reference)
Fax: 301-713-6905 (Fax-on-Demand Information)
E-mail: inquire@arch2.nara.gov
http://www.nara.gov/nara/dc/Archives2_directions.html

National Archives and Records Administration (NARA)
Washington National Records Center
Shipping Address:
4205 Suitland Road
Suitland, MD 20746-8001
Mail:
4205 Suitland Road
Washington, DC 20409-0002
Tel: 301-457-7000
Fax: 301-457-7117
E-mail: center@suitland.nara.gov
http://www.nara.gov/nara/dc/wnrc.html

Genealogical Societies

African-American Historical & Genealogical Society
P.O. Box 73086
Washington, DC 20056-3086
http://www.rootsweb.com/~mdaahgs/

African-American National Capital Area Historical
Genealogical Society
P. O. Box 60632
Washington, DC 20039-0632

District of Columbia Genealogical Society
P.O. Box 63467
Washington, DC 20029-3467

Jewish Genealogy Society of Greater Washington
P.O. Box 31122
Bethesda, MD 20824-1122
Library collection located at:
Isaac Franck Jewish Public Library
4928 Wyaconda Road
Rockville, MD 20852
Tel: 301-255-1970.
http://www.jewishgen.org/jgsgw/

National Genealogical Society
4527 Seventeenth Street North
Arlington, VA 22207-2399
Tel: 703-525-0050 (Office)
800-473-0060 (Toll Free)
703-841-9065 (Library)
Fax: 703-525-0052
E-mail: ngs@ngsgenealogy.org
   library@ngsgenealogy.org (library)
http://www.ngsgenealogy.org/

National Society-Daughters of American Colonists
2205 Massachusetts Avenue, NW
Washington, DC 20008
E-mail: NSDAC@excite.com
http://www.nsdac.org/index.html

National Society, Daughters of the American Revolution
Memorial Continental Hall
1776 D Street NW
Washington, DC 20006-5303
Tel: 202-628-1776
http://www.dar.org/natsociety/

HISTORICAL SOCIETIES

Historical Society of Washington, DC
The Heurich House Museum
1307 New Hampshire Avenue, NW
Washington, DC 20036
Tel: 202-785-2068
E-mail: HSWDC@aol.com
http://www.hswdc.org/

U.S. Capitol Historical Society
200 Maryland Avenue, NE
Washington, DC 20002
Tel: 202-543-8919
800-887-9318
Fax: 202-544-8244
E-mail: uschs@uschs.org
http://www.uschs.org/

White House Historical Association
740 Jackson Place, NW
Washington, DC 20503
Tel: 202-737-8292
Fax: 202-789-0440
http://www.whitehousehistory.org/

LDS FAMILY HISTORY CENTERS

For locations of Family History Centers in this state, see
the Family History Center locator at FamilySearch:
http://www.familysearch.org/eng/Library/FHC/
frameset_fhc.asp

ARCHIVES/LIBRARIES/MUSEUMS

Anderson House Library & Museum, Society of Cincinnati at
2118 Massachusetts Avenue, NW
Washington, DC 20008
Tel: 202-785-2040
http://www.dkmuseums.com/cincin.html

Catholic University of America
Department of Archives, Manuscripts, and Museum
     Collections
101 Life Cycle Institute
The Catholic University of America
Washington, DC 20064
Tel: 202-319-5065
Fax: 202-319-6554
http://libraries.cua.edu/archives.html

District of Columbia Archives Division
1300 Naylor Court, NW
Washington, DC 20001
Telephone: (202) 671-1105
Fax: (202) 727-6076
http://os.dc.gov/info/pubrec/pubrec.shtm#archives

Georgetown Branch Library
Peabody Room
3260 R Street, N.W.
at Wisconsin Avenue, N.W.
Washington, D.C. 20007
Tel: 202-282-0220
http://www.dclibrary.org/branches/geo/

Georgetown University
Lauinger Library
Special Collections
37th and N Streets N.W., Fifth floor
Washington, DC 20057
Tel: 202-687-7444
http://gulib.lausun.georgetown.edu/

Library of Congress
Local History & Genealogy Division
Thomas Jefferson Building, Room LJ G42
101 Independence Avenue, S.E.
Washington, D.C. 20540-4660
http://lcweb.loc.gov

Martin Luther King Memorial Library
Washingtoniana Division and the Washington Star
     Collection
901 G Street NW, Washington, D.C. 20001
Room 307 (3rd Floor)
Tel: 202-727-1213
http://www.dclibrary.org/washingtoniana/index.html

George Washington University
Melvin Gelman Library
2130 H Street NW
Washington, DC 20052
Tel: 202-994-6455
http://www.gwu.edu/gelman/

National Society, Daughters of the American Revolution
Memorial Continental Hall
1776 D Street NW
Washington, DC 20006-5303
Tel: 202-628-1776
http://www.dar.org/natsociety/

Smithsonian Institute
1000 Jefferson Drive
Washington, DC 20560
Tel: 202-357-2700
TTY: 202-357-1729
http://www.si.edu/

United States Holocaust Memorial Museum
100 Rauol Wallenberg Place, SW
Washington, DC 20024-2126
Tel: 202-488-0400
http://www.ushmm.org/

NEWSPAPER REPOSITORIES

Library of Congress
Local History & Genealogy Division
Thomas Jefferson Building, Room LJ G42
101 Independence Avenue, S.E.
Washington, D.C. 20540-4660
http://lcweb.loc.gov

Martin Luther King Memorial Library
Washingtoniana Division and the Washington Star
    Collection
901 G Street NW, Washington, D.C. 20001
Room 307 (3rd Floor)
Tel: 202-727-1213
http://www.dclibrary.org/washingtoniana/index.html

VITAL RECORDS

Vital Records Division
State Center for Health Statistics,
825 North Capitol Street NE
Washington, DC 20024.
Tel: 202-442-9009
202-645-5962.
http://dchealth.dc.gov/services/vital_records/index.shtm
(For Births from 1874, and Deaths from 1855.)

DC Superior Court Marriage License Bureau
500 Indiana Avenue, NW, Room 4485
Washington, DC 20001-2131
Tel: 202-879-4850
(Marriage records from 1811.)

DC Archives and Records Center
1300 Naylor Court, NW
Washington, DC 20001-4225
Tel: 202-727-2054
Fax: 202-727-6076
(Uncertified copies)

National Archives and Records Administration (NARA)
Archives I
700 Pennsylvania Avenue, NW
Washington, DC 20408
Tel: 202-501-5410 (Genealogical Staff)
202-501-5400 (Record Availability)
Fax: 301-713-6905 (Fax-on-Demand Information)
E-mail: inquire@arch1.nara.gov
http://www.nara.gov/nara/dc/Archives1_directions.html

D.C. ON THE WEB

District of Columbia GenWeb Project
http://www.rootsweb.com/~dcgenweb/

FLORIDA

ARCHIVES, STATE & NATIONAL

Florida State Archives
 Bureau of Archives Management
Division of Library & Information Services
Public Services Section
R.A. Gray Building
500 South Bronough Street
Tallahassee, FL 32399-0250
Tel: (850) 245-6700
http://dlis.dos.state.fl.us/barm/fsa.html

National Archives-Southeast Region
1557 St. Joseph Avenue
East Point, GA 30344
Tel: 404-763-7474
Fax: 404-763-7059
E-mail: atlanta.center@nara.gov
http://www.nara.gov/regional/atlanta.html

GENEALOGICAL SOCIETIES

**Afro-American Historical and Genealogical Society, Inc.
(AAHGS) Central Florida Chapter**
P.O. Box 1347
Orlando, FL 32802
http://www.rootsweb.com/~flcfaahg/

Alachua County Genealogical Society
P.O. Box 12078, University Station
Gainesville, FL 32604-0078
http://www.afn.org/~acgs/

Amelia Island Genealogical Society
P.O. Box 6005
Fernandina Beach, FL 32035-6005
http://www.net-magic.net/biz-directory/genelogy.htm

Bay County Genealogical Society
P.O. Box 662
Panama City, FL 32402

Bonita Springs Genealogy Club
P.O. Box 366471
Bonita Springs, FL 34136

Brevard Genealogical Society
P.O. Box 1123
Cocoa, FL 32923-1123
http://www.rootsweb.com/~flbgs/

Broward County Genealogical Society
P.O. Box 485
Fort Lauderdale, FL 33302
http://www.rootsweb.com/~flgsbc/

Central Florida Genealogical Society
P.O. Box 536309
Orlando, FL 32853-6309
E-mail: cfgs@geocities.com
http://www.geocities.com/Heartland/Ranch/4580/index.html

Charlotte County Genealogical Society
P.O. Box 2682
Port Charlotte, FL 33949-2682

Citrus County Genealogical Society
P.O. Box 2211
Inverness, FL 34451-2211

Clay County Genealogical Society
P.O. Box 1071
Green Cove Springs, FL 32043

Collier County, Genealogical Society of
P.O. Box 7933
Naples, FL 34101-7933
http://aps.naples.net/community/nfnwebpages/story-
    board.cfm?StoryBoardNum=8&PageNum=1

East Central Florida Genealogical Society Co-op
1300 Airport Blvd #473
Melbourne, FL 32901-2969
http://www.rootsweb.com/~flecfgsc/index.htm

Florida State Genealogical Society, Inc.
P.O. Box 10249
Tallahassee, FL 32302-2249
http://www.rootsweb.com/~flsgs/

Geneva Historical & Genealogical Society
P.O. Box 91
Geneva, FL 32732

Golden Gate-Naples Genealogical Society
1689 Bonita Court
Naples, FL 33962

Greater Miami, Genealogical Society of
P.O. Box 162905
Miami, FL 33116-2905
http://www.rootsweb.com/~flgsgm/

Halifax Genealogical Society of Ormond Beach
P. O. Box 5081
Ormond Beach, FL 32175-5081

Hernando County, Genealogy Society of
P.O. Box 1793
Brooksville, FL 34605-1793
http://www.rootsweb.com/~flhernan/#GSHC

Highlands County Genealogical Society
Sebring Public Library
319 W. Center Avenue
Sebring, FL 33870
http://www.heartlineweb.org/hcgs/

Huxford Genealogical Society
P.O. Box 595
Homerville, GA 31634
Tel: 912-487-2310
E-mail: hgs@huxford.com
http://www.huxford.com/

Imperial Polk Genealogical Society
P.O. Box 10
Kathleen, FL 33849-0010
http://www.ipgs.org/index.html

Indian River Genealogical Society, Inc.
P.O. Box 1850
Vero Beach, FL 32961-1850
http://www.rootsweb.com/~flindigs/

Jacksonville Genealogical Society
P.O. Box 60756
Jacksonville, FL 32236-0756
Tel: 904-781-9300
http://users2.fdn.com/~jgs/

Jewish Genealogical Society of Broward County
P.O. Box 17251
Fort Lauderdale, FL 33318

Jewish Genealogical Society of Central Florida
P.O. Box 520583
Longwood, FL 32752

Jewish Genealogical Society of Greater Miami
P.O. Box 560432
Miami, FL 33156-0432
Tel: (305) 266-3350

Jewish Genealogical Society of Greater Orlando
P.O. Box 941332
Maitland, FL 32794-1332
Fax: 407-671-7485
http://members.aol.com/JGSGO/

Jewish Genealogical Society of Palm Beach County
P.O. Box #7796
Delray Beach, FL 33482-7796
http://www.jewishgen.org/jgspbci/

Keystone Genealogical Society
695 E. Washington Street (library)
P.O. Box 50
Monticello, FL 32344
Tel: 850-997-3304
E-mail: canesyrup@aol.com

Lake County Kinseekers Genealogical Society
P.O. Box 492711
Leesburg, FL 32749-2711

Lee County Genealogical Society
P.O. Box 150153
Cape Coral, FL 33915-0153

Lehigh Acres Genealogical Society
P.O. Box 965
Lehigh Acres, FL 33970-0965

Lemon Bay Historical & Genealogical Society
P.O. Box 236
Englewood, FL 33533

Manasota Genealogical Society
Historical Records Library
1405 4th Avenue, W
Bradenton, FL 34205-7507
Tel: (941) 741- 4070
http://www.rootsweb.com/~flmgs/

Martin County Genealogical Society
P. O. Box 275
Stuart, FL 34995

Mayflower Society of Florida
Florida State Society
Punta Gorda, Florida 33950
http://www.geocities.com/flmayflower/

North Brevard, Genealogical Society of (GSNB)
P.O. Box 897
Titusville, FL 32781-0897
http://www.nbbd.com/npr/gsnb/index.html

Ocala/Marion County Genealogical Society
P.O. Box 1206
Ocala, FL 34478-1206

Ohio Genealogical Society
Florida Chapter
15550 Burnt Store Road #46
Punta Gordo, FL 33955-9336
http://www.ogs.org/chap.htm

Okaloosa County, Genealogical Society of
P.O. Box 1175
Fort Walton Beach, FL 32549
http://www.rootsweb.com/~flwalton/gsoc.txt

Okeechobee, Genealogical Society of
P.O. Box 371
Okeechobee, FL 34973-0371

Genealogy Club Of Osceola County
P.O. Box 701295,
St Cloud, FL 34770-1295
http://www.rootsweb.com/~flosceol/osceola.htm

Palm Beach County Genealogical Society
P.O. Box 1746
West Palm Beach, FL 33402-1746
Tel: 561-832-3279
http://www.gopbi.com/community/groups/pbcgensoc/

Pasco County Genealogical Society
P.O. Box 2072
Dade City, FL 33526-2072

Pinellas Genealogy Society, Inc.
c/o Largo Public Library
351 East Bay Drive
P.O. Box 1614
Largo, FL 33779-1614
http://www.rootsweb.com/~flpgs/

Putnam County Genealogical Society
P.O. Box 2354
Palatka, FL 32178-2354

Ridge Genealogical Society
P.O. Box 477
Babson Park, FL 33827

Roots & Branches Genealogical Society
P.O. Box 612
DeLand, FL 32721-0612

St. Augustine Florida Genealogical Society
c/o St. Johns County Public Library
1960 N. Ponce de Leon Blvd.
St. Augustine, FL 32084
http://www.geocities.com/glwilson_us/Stauggen.html

Sarasota Genealogical Society
P.O. Box 1917
Sarasota, FL 34230-1917
http://www.rootsweb.com/~flgss/

Seminole County, Genealogical Group of
P.O. Box 2148
Casselberry, FL 32707

Sons and Daughters of the Province and Republic of West Florida
P.O. Box 82672
Baton Rouge, LA 70884-2672
http://homepages.xspedius.net/mmoore/lghs/sonsdau.htm

Sons of the American Revolution
http://www.flssar.org/index.html

South Bay Genealogy Club
P.O. Box 5202
Sun City Ctr., FL 33571

South Brevard County, Genealogical Society of
P.O. Box 786
Melbourne, FL 32901-0786

South Hillsborough Genealogists
Route 1, Box 400
Palmetto, FL 33561

Southeast Volusia County, Genealogical Society of
New Smyrna Beach Public Library
1001 S. Dixie Freeway
New Smyrna Beach FL 32168
(904) 424-2910

Southern Genealogists Exchange Society, Inc.
6215 Sauterne Drive
P.O. Box 2801
Jacksonville, Florida 32203-2801
Tel: 904-387-9142
http://www.angelfire.com/fl/sges/

Suncoast Genealogy Society
P.O. Box 1294
Palm Harbor, FL 34682-1294

Suwannee Valley Genealogical Society, Inc.
P.O. Box 967
Live Oak, FL 32064
Tel: 386-330-0110
http://www.rootsweb.com/~flsvgs/svgs.htm

Tallahassee Genealogical Society
P.O. Box 4371
Tallahassee, FL 32315
http://www.rootsweb.com/~fltgs/

Treasure Coast Genealogical Society
P.O. Box 12582
Fort Pierce,
Saint Lucie County
Florida, 34979-2582
http://www.rootsweb.com/~fltcgs/

Villages Genealogical Society
1910 Del Norte Drive
Lady Lake, FL 32159-9220
http://www.angelfire.com/fl3/genie3/new_index.html

Volusia Genealogical & Historical Society
P.O. Box 2039
Daytona Beach, FL 32015

West Florida Genealogical Society
P.O. Box 947
Pensacola, FL 32594-0947
http://www.rootsweb.com/~flescamb/wfgs2.htm

West Pasco Genealogical Society
P.O. Box 1142
Port Richey, FL 34673
http://homepages.rootsweb.com/~wpcgs/wpsgmember.htm

HISTORICAL SOCIETIES

Baker County Historical Society
P.O. Box 856
Macclenny, FL 32063
http://rootsweb.com/~flbaker/books.html

Broward County Historical Commission
151 S.W. 2nd Street
Fort Lauderdale, Florida 33301
Tel: 954-765-4670
http://www.co.broward.fl.us/history.htm

Clearwater Historical Society
1644 Cleveland Street
Clearwater, 33756
Tel: 727-443-3139
http://www.zipmall.com/proswap/arts/arts-tampabay/
    fulllist.dbm?ln=(45)

Dunedin Historical Society/Museum
349 Main Street
P.O. Box 2393
Dunedin, FL 34697-2393
Tel: 727-736-1176
727-529-3307
http://www.ci.dunedin.fl.us:/dunedin/
    historical-society.htm

East Hillsborough Historical Society
Quintilla Geer Bruton Archives Center
605 North Collins Street
Plant City, FL 33566
Tel: 813-754-7031
http://www.rootsweb.com/~flqgbac/ehhs.html

Florida Baptist Historical Society
Stetson University
P.O. Box 8353
Deland, FL 32720
Telephone: 904-822-7175
Fax: 904-822-7199

Florida Historical Society
1320 Highland Avenue
Melbourne, FL 32935
Tel: (321) 254-9855
http://www.florida-historical-soc.org/

Geneva Historical & Genealogical Society
P.O. Box 91
Geneva, FL 32732

Halifax Historical Society
252 S. Beach St.
Daytona Beach, FL 32114-4407
Tel: 386-255-6976
Fax: 386-255-7605
http://www.halifaxhistorical.org/

Hillsborough County Historical Commission
Museum, Historical & Genealogical Library
Tampa Bay History Center
Tampa Convention Center Annex
225 S. Franklin St.
Tampa Bay, FL 33602
Phone: 813-228-0097
Fax: 813-223-7021
http://www.tampabayhistorycenter.org/

Indian River County Historical Society
Vero Beach Railroad Station
2336 14th Avenue
Vero Beach, FL
Mail:
P.O. Box 6535
Vero Beach, FL 32961

Jacksonville Historical Society
317 A. Philip Randolph Blvd.
Jacksonville, FL 32202-2217
Tel: 904-396-6307
Fax: 904-398-4647
http://jaxhistory.com/

Lake County Historical Society
317 West Main Street
Tavares, FL 32778
Tel: 352-343-9600
Fax: 352-343-9696

Loxahatchee Historical Society/Museum
805 N. U.S. Highway 1
Jupiter Beach, FL 33477
Tel: 407-747-6639

Maitland Historical Society
840 Lake Lily Drive
P.O. Box 941001
Maitland, FL 32751-5613
Tel: 407-644-2451
http:http://www.home.mpinet.net/maiths/

Martin County, Historical Society of
825 NE Ocean Boulevard
Hutchinson Island
Stuart, FL 34996-1696
Tel: 407-225-1961
http://www.classicar.com/museums/histmart/histmart.htm

Micanopy Historical Society/Museum
706 NE Cholokka Blvd.
P.O. Box 462
Micanopy, FL 32667
E-mail: micanopy@afn.org
http://www.afn.org/~micanopy/

North Brevard Historical Society
301 S. Washington Avenue
P.O. Box 6199
Titusville, FL 32782-6199
Tel: 321-269-3658
http://www.nbbd.com/godo/history/

Orange County Historical Society/Museum
Orange County Regional History Center
65 East Central Boulevard
Orlando, FL 32801
Tel: (407) 836-8500
http://www.thehistorycenter.org/home.html

Palm Beach County Historical Society
400 North Dixie Highway
West Palm Beach, FL 33401
Tel: 561-832-4164
Fax: 561-832-7965
http://www.gopbi.com/community/groups/pbchistory/

Pensacola Historical Society/Museum
117 East Government Street
Pensacola, FL 32501
Tel: (850)434-5455
http://www.pensacolahistory.org/

St. Augustine Historical Society
271 Charlotte Street
St. Augustine, FL 32084-5033
Tel: 904-824-2872
E-mail: oldhouse@aug.com
http://www.oldcity.com/oldhouse/historical.html

Sebastian Area Historical Society
700 Main Street
Post Office Box 781348
Sebastian, Florida 32978-1348
Tel: 561-589-9741

South Brevard Historical Society
615 N. Riverside
Indialantic, FL 32903
Tel: 407-723-6835 (also fax)

Tampa Historical Society
245 S. Hyde Park Ave.
Tampa, FL 33606
Tel: 813-259-1111

LDS FAMILY HISTORY CENTERS

For locations of Family History Centers in this state, see the Family History Center locator at FamilySearch:
http://www.familysearch.org/eng/Library/FHC/frameset_fhc.asp

ARCHIVES/LIBRARIES/MUSEUMS

The Alma Clyde Field Library of Florida History
435 Brevard Avenue
Historic Cocoa Village, 32922
Tel: (321) 690-1971 or (321) 690-0099
http://www.florida-historical-soc.org/

Amelia Island Museum of History
233 South Third Street
Fernandina Beach, FL 32034
Tel: 904-261-7378
http://www.ameliaisland.com/pix/MOSAIC/museum.htm

Bay County Public Library
25 West Government St.
Caller Box 2625
Panama City, FL 32402
Tel: (850) 872-7500
Fax : (850) 872-7507
http://www.nwrls.lib.fl.us/localhistory/index.html

Black Archives
Florida A&M University
Tallahassee, FL 32307
Tel: 850-599-3020
http://www.famu.edu/acad/archives/

Black Archives History Foundation
5400 NW 22nd Ave.
Miami, FL 33142
Tel: 305-636-2390
Fax: 305-636-2391

Bonita Springs Public Library
26876 Pine Avenue
Bonita Springs, FL 34135
Tel: (239) 992-0101
TTY (239) 992-1043
Fax: (239) 992-6680
http://www.lee-county.com/library/
    library/branches/bn.htm

Brevard Community College
Learning Resource Centers
Tel: 321-632-1111 ext. 62963 (Genealogy)
Cocoa Campus
BCC/UCF Joint Use Library
1519 Clearlake Rd.
Cocoa, FL 32922-6597
http://www.brevard.cc.fl.us/lrc/libc.htm
Palm Bay Campus
Florida Advanced Technology Center
250 Grassland Road, SE
Palm Bay, FL 32909-2299
http://www.brevard.cc.fl.us/lrc/libp.htm
Melbourne Campus
Philip F. Nohrr Learning Resources Center
3865 North Wickham Road
Melbourne, FL 32935-2399
http://www.brevard.cc.fl.us/lrc/libm.htm
Titusville Campus
Dr. Frank Elbert Williams Learning Resources Center
1311 North U.S. 1
Titusville, FL 32796-2192
http://www.brevard.cc.fl.us/lrc/libt.htm

Brevard County Public Library-Melbourne
540 Fee Avenue
Melbourne, FL 32901
Tel: 321-952-4514
http://manatee.brev.lib.fl.us/locations/mla/mla.htm

Broward County Library
100 S. Andrews Ave.
Fort Lauderdale, FL 33301
Tel: (954) 357-7444
Fax: (954) 357-7399
http://www.broward.org/library/

Cape Coral Public Library
921 SW 39th Terrace
Cape Coral, FL 33914-5721
Tel: (239) 542-3953
TTY (239) 542-4429
Fax: (239) 542-2711
http://www.lee-county.com/library/library/
     branches/cc.htm

Cedar Key Historical Society Museum
2nd Street at SR 24
P.O. Box 222
Cedar Key, FL 32625
Tel: 904-543-5549

Central Brevard Library & Reference Center
308 Forrest Avenue
Cocoa, FL 32922
Tel: 321-633-1792
http://manatee.brev.lib.fl.us/locations/cla/cla.htm

Clearwater Public Library
100 North Osceola Ave.
Clearwater, FL 33755-4083
Tel: 727-462-6800
Fax: 727-462-6420
http://www.clearwater-fl.com/cpl/

Collier County Museum/Margaret T. Scott Library
3301 Tamiami Trail, East
Naples, FL 34112
Tel: 941-774-8476
Fax: 941-774-8580
http://www.colliermuseum.com/main/index.htm

Collier County Public Library
2385 Orange Blossom Drive
Naples, FL 34109
Reference: (941) 593-0177

Cooper Memorial Library
620 Montrose Street
Clermont, FL 34711
Tel: 352-394-4265
http://www.lakeline.lib.fl.us/cmlintro.htm

Cornell Museum
Delray Beach Historical Society Archives
51 N. Swinton Ave.
Delray Beach, FL 33444
Tel: 561-274-9578
http://www.delraybeachhistoricalsociety.org/index.html

DeLand Public Library
130 E. Howry Ave.
DeLand, FL 32724-5517
Tel: (386) 822-6430

Florida Atlantic University
S.E. Wimberly Library
777 Glades Road
Boca Raton, FL 33431-0991
Tel: 561-297-3779
http://www.fau.edu/library/homehome.htm

Florida Division of Historical Resources
500 S. Bronough Street
Tallassee, FL 32399
Tel: 904-488-1480
http://dhr.dos.state.fl.us/index.html

Florida State University Library
Strozier Library
Tallahassee, FL 32306-2047
Tel: 904-644-2706 (Reference)
http://www.fsu.edu/~library/brdept/strozier.html

Fort Myers-Lee County Public Library
2050 Lee Street
Fort Myers, FL 33901
Tel: 239-479-4635
TTY 239-479-4633
FAX 239-479-4634
http://www.lee-county.com/library/library/
    branches/fm.htm

Gainesville Public Library
401 East University Avenue
Gainesville, FL 32601
Tel: 352-334-3900
http://www.acld.lib.fl.us/acld-new/branches/hq/hq.html

Genealogical Society of Broward County Library
6500 Parkside Drive
Parkland, FL 33067
http://www.rootsweb.com/~flgsbc/library.html

Halifax Historical Society
252 S. Beach St.
Daytona Beach, FL 32114-4407
Tel: 386-255-6976
Fax: 386-255-7605
http://www.halifaxhistorical.org/

Haydon Burns Library
Jacksonville Public Library
122 N. Ocean Street
Jacksonville, FL 32202
Tel: 904-630-2665
904-630-2409 (Genealogy)
904-630-2410 (Florida Collection)
http://jpl.coj.net/english/welcome.html

Helen B. Hoffman Library
Genealogy Room
501 N. Fig Tree Lane
Plantation, FL 33317-1849
Tel: 954-797-2140

Historical Museum of Southern Florida
101 West Flagler Street
Miami, FL 33130
Tel: 305-375-1492
E-mail: hasf@historical-museum.org
http://www.historical-museum.org/

Holocaust Memorial & Resource Center of Central Florida
851 North Maitland Avenue
Maitland, Florida 32794
P.O. Box 941508
Maitland, FL 32794
Tel: 407-628-0555
Fax: 407-628-1079
E-mail: info@holocaustedu.org

Homestead Branch Library
700 N. Homestead Blvd.
Homestead, FL 33030
Tel: 727-587-6715
http://www.largo.com/library/liby.htm

Indian River County Main Library
Julian W. Lowenstein Florida History & Genealogy
Department
1600 21st Street
Vero Beach, FL 32960
Tel: 561-770-5060
Fax: 561-770-5066
http://www.rootsweb.com/~flindian/ircl/

Jackson County Florida Library
413 North Green Street
Maryanna, FL 32446

Jacksonville Public Library
Haydon Burns Library
122 N. Ocean Street
Jacksonville, FL 32202
Tel: 904-630-2665
904-630-2409 (Genealogy)
904-630-2410 (Florida Collection)
http://jpl.coj.net/english/welcome.html

Lake County Historical Museum
317 West Main Street
Tavares, FL 32778
Tel: 352-343-9600
Fax: 352-343-9696

Largo Library
351 East Bay Drive
Largo, FL 33770
Tel: 813-586-7410
E-mail: bpotters@largo.com
http://www.largo.com/departments/library/library.html

Loxahatchee Historical Society/Museum
805 N. U.S. Highway 1
Jupiter Beach, FL 33477
Tel: 407-747-6639

Maitland Historical Museum
221 Packwood Avenue
P.O. Box 941001
Maitland, FL 32794
Tel: 407-644-1364
http://www.home.mpinet.net/maiths/museumsframed.htm

Manatee County Central Library
1301 Barcarrota Blvd., W
Bradenton, FL 34205-7599
Tel: 941-748-5555
Fax: 941-749-7191
http://www.co.manatee.fl.us/service/library/index.html

Melbourne Public Library
540 East Fee Avenue
Melbourne, FL 32901
Tel: 321-952-4514
http://manatee.brev.lib.fl.us/locations/mla/mla.htm

Metro-Dade Cultural Resource Center
111 NW 1st Street
Miami, FL 33128-1902
Tel: 305-375-4635

Miami-Dade Public Library
Main Library
101 West Flagler St.
Miami, FL 33130
Tel: 305-375-2665
http://www.mdpls.org/

Micanopy Historical Society/Museum
706 NE Cholokka Blvd.
P.O. Box 462
Micanopy, FL 32667
E-mail: micanopy@afn.org
http://www.afn.org/~micanopy

Mission San Luis de Apalachee
Division of Historical Resources
2020 Mission Road
Tallahassee, FL 32304-1624
Tel: 850-487-3655
http://dhr.dos.state.fl.us/bar/san_luis/

Morikami Museum and Japanese Gardens
4000 Morikami Park Rd.
Delray Beach, FL 33446
Tel: 561-495-0233
http://www.pbol.com/arts_ent/a_emmjg.htm

Museum of Florida History
Division of Historical Resources
500 S. Bronough Street
Tallahassee, FL 32399
Tel: 850-245-6400
Fax: 850-245-6433
http://www.dos.state.fl.us/dhr/museum/c_r.html

North Brevard Historical Society Museum
301 S. Washington Avenue
P.O. Box 6199
Titusville, FL 32782-6199
Tel: 321-269-3658
http://www.nbbd.com/godo/history/

North Brevard Public Library
2121 Hopkins Ave.
Titusville, FL 32780
Tel: 321-264-5026
Fax: 321-264-5030
http://manatee.brev.lib.fl.us/locations/nba/nba.htm

North Indian River County Library
1001 Country Road 512
Sebastian, FL 32958
Tel: 561-589-1355
Fax: 561-388-3697
http://indian-river.fl.us/library/north/

Orange County Historical Society/Museum
Orange County Regional History Center
65 East Central Boulevard
Orlando, FL 32801
Tel: (407) 836-8500
http://www.thehistorycenter.org/home.html
http://www.inusa.com/tour/fl/orlando/orange.htm

Orlando Public Library
101 East Central Blvd.
Orlando, FL 32801
Tel: 407-835-7323
http://www.ocls.lib.fl.us/

Ormond Beach Public Library
30 S. Beach Street
Ormond Beach, FL 32174-6380
Tel: 386-676-4191
http://www.vcpl.lib.fl.us/

Palm Beach County Historical Society
400 North Dixie Highway
West Palm Beach, FL 33401
Tel: 561-832-4164
Fax: 561-832-7965
http://www.gopbi.com/community/groups/pbchistory/

Palm Harbor Library
2330 Nebraska Avenue
Palm Harbor, FL 34683
Tel: 727-784-3332
Fax: 727-785-6534
727-787-8388 (reference fax)
http://207.22.150.67/phl/default.htm

Pensacola Historical Society/Museum
115 E. Zaragosa St.
Tel: 850-433-1559
http://www.pensacolahistory.org/museum.htm

Polk County Historical & Genealogical Library/ Museum
Historic Courthouse
100 East Main Street
Bartow, FL 33830
Tel: 863-534-4380
863-534-4386 (Museum)
Fax: 863-534-4382
http://www.polk-county.net/library.html

Safety Harbor Public Library
101 Second Street, N
Safety Harbor, FL 34695
Tel: 727-724-1525
Fax: 727-724-1533
http://snoopy.tblc.lib.fl.us/shpl/

St. Augustine Historical Society/Research Library
271 Charlotte Street
St. Augustine, FL 32084-5033
Tel: 904-824-2872
E-mail: oldhouse@aug.com
http://www.oldcity.com/oldhouse/historical.html

St. Johns County Public Library
1960 Ponce de Leon Blvd.
St. Augustine, FL 32084-2620
Tel: 904-823-2650
Fax: 904-823-2656
http://www.sjcpls.org/welcome.htm

St. Petersburg Public Library
3745 9th Avenue North
St. Petersburg, FL 33713
Tel: 727-893-7724
727-893-7928
http://st-petersburg-library.org/

Sanibel Public Library
770 Dunlop Road
Sanibel, FL 33957
Tel: 941-472-2483
Fax: 941-472-9524
http://www.sanlib.org/

Selby Public Library
1331 First Street
Sarasota, FL 34236-4807
Tel: 941-316-1181/3
941-951-5501/2
http://suncat.co.sarasota.fl.us/selby/selby.html

Southern Genealogists Exchange Society
6215 Sauterne Drive
Jacksonville, FL 32203
http://www.angelfire.com/fl/sges/

State Library of Florida
Florida Collection
Division of Library & Information Services
R.A. Gray Building
500 South Bronough Street
Tallahassee, FL 32399-0250
Tel: 850-245-6600
http://dlis.dos.state.fl.us/stlib/flcoll.html

Tampa Bay History Center
Tampa Convention Center Annex
225 S. Franklin St.
Tampa Bay, FL 33602
Phone: 813-228-0097
Fax: 813-223-7021
http://www.tampabayhistorycenter.org/

Tampa Bay Library Consortium
1202 Tech Blvd Ste 202
Tampa, FL 33619-7864
Tel: (813) 622-8252
Fax: (813) 628-4425
E-mail: helpdesk@tblc.org
http://snoopy.tblc.lib.fl.us/

Tampa-Hillsborough Public Library System
Main Library
Special Collections-Genealogy Collection
900 North Ashley Drive
Tampa, FL 33602
Tel: 813-273-3652
http://www.thpl.org/

University of Central Florida Library
P.O. Box 162666
Orlando, FL 32816
(407) 823-2562
http://library.ucf.edu/Special/

University of Florida
P.K. Yonge Library of Florida History
Smathers Library East, 2nd Floor
P. O. Box 117007
Gainesville, FL 32611-7001
Tel: 352-392-9075, ext. 306
http://web.uflib.ufl.edu/spec/pkyonge/

University of Miami
Otto G. Richter Library
1300 Memorial Dr., P.O. Box 248214
Coral Gables, Florida 33124-0320
Tel: 305-284-3551
Fax: 305-284-4027
http://www.library.miami.edu/library/archives.html

University of South Florida Library, LIB 407
Special Collections Department
4202 East Fowler Avenue
Tampa, FL 33620
Tel: 813-974-2731
Fax: 813-974-5153
http://www.lib.usf.edu/spccoll/

University of West Florida
John Chandler Pace Library, Room 006
11000 University Parkway
Pensacola, FL 32514-5750
Tel: 850-474-2213
http://library.uwf.edu/SpecialCollections/index.shtml

Volusia County Public Library
City Island
Daytona Beach, FL 32114
Tel: 386-257-6036
http://merlin.vcpl.lib.fl.us/

NEWSPAPER REPOSITORIES

Amelia Island Museum of History
233 South Third Street
Fernandina Beach, FL 32034
Tel: 904-261-7378
http://www.ameliaisland.com/pix/MOSAIC/museum.htm

Palm Beach County Historical Society
400 North Dixie Highway
West Palm Beach, FL 33401
Tel: 561-832-4164
Fax: 561-832-7965
http://www.gopbi.com/community/groups/pbchistory/

St. Augustine Historical Society/Research Library
271 Charlotte Street
St. Augustine, FL 32084-5033
Tel: 904-824-2872
E-mail: oldhouse@aug.com
http://www.oldcity.com/oldhouse/historical.html

State Library of Florida
Florida Collection
Division of Library & Information Services
R.A. Gray Building
500 South Bronough Street
Tallahassee, FL 32399-0250
Tel: 850-245-6600
http://dlis.dos.state.fl.us/stlib/flcoll.html

University of Florida
P.K. Yonge Library of Florida History
Smathers Library East, 2nd Floor
P. O. Box 117007
Gainesville, FL 32611-7001
Tel: 352-392-9075, ext. 306
http://web.uflib.ufl.edu/spec/pkyonge/

VITAL RECORDS

State of Florida Dept. of Health & Rehabilitative Services
Vital Statistics
1217 Pearl Street (location)
P.O. Box 210 (mail)
Jacksonville, FL 32231
Tel: 904-359-6900 Ext. 9000
Fax: 904-359-6993
(Births from 1865, Deaths from 1877, Marriage from June 1927)
http://www9.myflorida.com/planning_eval/vital_statistics/index.html

FLORIDA ON THE WEB

Dayna's Southern Genealogy Page
http://home.texoma.net/~mmcmullen/welcome.html

Florida GenWeb Project
http://www.rootsweb.com/~flgenweb/index.html

Florida State Archives Photographic Collection (Over 790,000 photographs)
http://www.dos.state.fl.us/fpc/

Traveller Southern Families
http://misc.traveller.com/genealogy/3

GEORGIA

ARCHIVES, STATE & NATIONAL

Georgia Department of Archives and History
Office of Secretary of State
330 Capitol Avenue, SE
Atlanta, GA 30334
Tel: (404) 656-2350
E-mail: reference@sos.state.ga.us
http://www.sos.state.ga.us/archives

National Archives-Southeast Region
1557 St. Joseph Avenue
East Point, GA 30344
Tel: 404-763-7474
Fax: 404-763-7059
E-mail: atlanta.center@nara.gov
http://www.nara.gov/regional/atlanta.html

GENEALOGICAL SOCIETIES

African-American Family History Association
P.O. Box 115268
Atlanta, GA 30310

Augusta Genealogical Society/Library
1109 Broad Street
P.O. Box 3743
Augusta, GA 30914-3743
Tel: 706-722-4073
http://www.augustagensociety.org/

Bartow County Genealogical Society/Research Library
425 W. Main Street
P.O. Box 993
Cartersville, GA 30120-0993
Tel: 770-606-0706
http://www.geocities.com/Heartland/Park/9465/bartowco-ga.html

Butts County Genealogical Society
P.O. Box 1297
Jackson, GA 30233
http://www.lofthouse.com/USA/ga/butts/#society

Carroll County Genealogical Society
P.O. Box 576
Carrollton, GA 30117
Tel: 770-832-7746
E-mail: mfword@aol.com
http://ccgs.westgeorgia.org/

Central Georgia Genealogical Society
P.O. Box 2024
1600 Elberta Rd
Warner Robins, GA 31093-1516
http://www.cggs.org/

Clarke-Oconee Genealogical Society
P.O. Box 6403
Athens, GA 30604
http://www.rootsweb.com/~gacogs/

Cobb County Georgia Genealogical Society
P.O. Box 1413
Marietta, GA 30061-1413
http://www.rootsweb.com/~gaccgs/

Colonial Dames of America in the State of Georgia
329 Abercorn Street
Savannah, GA 31401
Tel: 912-233-6854
Fax: 912-338-1828
http://www.andrewlow.com/location.html

Coweta County Genealogical Society
Old Passenger Train Depot in Historic
Corner of West Broad and Main Streets
Grantville, Georgia
Mailing Address:
P.O. Box 1014
Newnan, GA 30264
Tel: 770-251-2877
http://members.tripod.com/~CowetaGS/

Daughters of the American Revolution
Georgia State Society
Meadow Garden
1320 Independence Dr.
Augusta, GA
Tel: 706-724-4174
http://www.geocities.com/Heartland/Ridge/4935/index.html

Delta Genealogical Society
504 McFarland Avenue
Rossville, GA 30741
Tel: 706-866-1368
Fax: 706-858-0251
http://www.rootsweb.com/~gadgs/

Douglas County Genealogical Society
P.O. Box 5667
Douglasville, Ga 30154
http://www.douglascountygenealogicalsociety.org/

East Georgia Genealogical Society
P. O. Box 117
Winder, GA 30680
http://www.rootsweb.com/~gaeggs/

Etowah Valley Family Tree Climbers
Bartow County Courthouse
115 West Cherokee Avenue
P.O. Box 1886
Cartersville, GA 30120
Tel: 770-606-8862
E-mail: evhs@evhsonline.org
http://www.evhsonline.org/index.shtml

Fayette County Historical Society
195 Lee Street
P.O. Box 421
Fayetteville, GA 30214
Tel: 770-716-6020
E-mail: Fayhistsoc@aol.com
http://www.historyfayettecoga.org/

First Families of Georgia, 1733-1797
1604 Executive Park Lane, NE
Atlanta, GA 30329-3115
Tel: 404- 634-9866
Fax: 404- 634-9866

Genealogy Unlimited Society
P.O. Box 3013
Valdosta, GA 31604-3013
http://www.rootsweb.com/~gagus/

Georgia Genealogical Society
P.O. Box 54575
Atlanta, GA 30308-0575
E-mail: ggs@gagensociety.org
http://www.gagensociety.org/

Georgia Salzburger Society
2980 Ebenezer Road
Rincon, GA 31326
Tel: 912-754-7001
http://www.gasalzburgers.org/

Henry and Clayton Counties, Genealogical Society of
P.O. Box 1296
McDonough, GA 30253
Tel: 770-954-1456
E-mail: GENSOCIETY@ATT.NET
http://www.rootsweb.com/~gagshcc/

Huxford Genealogical Society
P.O. Box 595
Homerville, GA 31634
Tel: 912-487-2310
Fax: 912-487-3881
http://www.huxford.com/

Jamestowne Society
First Georgia Company
2310 Bohler Rd. N. W.
Atlanta, GA 30327
http://www.jamestowne.org/company.htm

Jewish Genealogical Society of Georgia, Inc.
P.O. Box 681022
Marietta, GA 30068-0018
http://www.jewishgen.org/jgsg/

Muscogee Genealogical Society
P.O. Box 761
Columbus, GA 31902
Tel/Fax: 706-561-5831
http://www.muscogeegenealogy.com/

Northeast Georgia Historical and Genealogical Society
P.O. Box 907643 NLS
Gainesville, GA 30501
http://www.rootsweb.com/~gahall/nega/

Northwest Georgia Historical and Genealogical Society
P.O. Box 5063
Rome, GA 30162
http://www.rootsweb.com/~ganwhags/index.html

Okefenokee Historical and Genealogical Society, Inc.
1617 Ball Street
Waycross, GA 31503

Original Muscogee County, Genealogical Society of
W.C. Bradley Memorial Library
1120 Bradley Drive
Columbus, GA 31906
Tel: (706) 649-0780

Rockdale County Genealogical Society
c/o Nancy Guinn Memorial Library
864 Green Street
Conyers, GA 30012
Tel: 770-388-5040
Fax: 770-388-5043
URL (newsletter):
http://mtf.home.mindspring.com/newsltr.htm

Savannah Area Genealogical Association
P.O. Box 15385
Savannah, GA 31416
http://www.rootsweb.com/~gasaga/

Savannah River Valley Genealogical Society
P.O. Box 895
Hartwell, GA 30643
http://www.srvgs.org/

Smyrna Historical and Genealogical Society
2861 Atlanta Street
Smyrna, Georgia 30082
Tel: 770-435-7549
Fax: 770-431-2858
http://www.rootsweb.com/~gashgs/

Sons and Daughters of the Province and Republic of West Florida
P.O. Box 82672
Baton Rouge, LA 70884-2672
http://cust2.iamerica.net/mmoore/sonsdau.htm

Sons of the American Revolution
http://www.sar.org/gassar/

Sons of Confederate Veterans
Georgia Division
http://www.georgiascv.com/

Southwest Georgia Genealogical Society
P.O. Box 4672
Albany, GA 31706
http://www.swggs.org/

Taylor County Historical-Genealogical Society
P.O. Box 1925
Butler, GA 31006

Warren County Genealogical Society
103 Memorial Drive
P.O. Box 47
Warrenton, GA 30828

HISTORICAL SOCIETIES

Alma-Bacon County Historical Society
406 Mercer St.
Alma, GA 31510
Tel: 912-632-8450

Alpharetta Historical Society
1835 Old Milton Parkway
Alpharetta, GA 30004
Tel: 770-475-4663
Fax: 770-475-0091
http://www.ahsga.org/

Athens Historical Society
P.O. Box 7745
Athens, GA 30604-7745

Atlanta Historical Society
Atlanta History Center
130 West Paces Ferry Road, NW
Atlanta, GA 30305-1366
Tel: 404-814-4101
Fax: 404-814-4186
http://www.atlhist.org/

Banks County Historical Society
P.O. Box 473
Homer, GA 30547
http://www.rootsweb.com/~gabchs/html/

Barnesville-Lamar County Historical Society
P.O. Box 805
Barnesville, GA 30204
Tel: 770-358-0150 (museum)
Fax: 770-358-5149
http://www.rootsweb.com/~galamar/society.html

Barrow County Historical Society
Athens Street
P.O. Box 277
Winder, GA 30680
Tel: 770-307-1183

Bonaventure Historical Society
1317 East 55th Street
Savannah, GA 31404-4615
http://home.earthlink.net/~bonaventure/

Brantley County Historical & Preservation Society
P.O. Box 1096
Nahunta, GA 31553
http://www.rootsweb.com/~gabrantl/branco-home.html

Brooks County Historical Society
P.O. Box 676
Quitman, GA 31643

Bulloch County Historical Society
P.O. Box 42
Statesboro, GA 30459

Butts County Historical Society
Highway 42, Indian Spring
P.O. Box 215
Jackson, GA 30233
Tel: 770-775-6734

Byron Area Historical Society
P.O. Box 755
Byron, GA 31008
Tel: 912-956-3600

Carroll County Historical Society
West Avenue
Carrollton, GA 30117
Tel: 770-834-3081
Fax: 770-836-6626

Catoosa County Historical Society
P.O. Box 113
Ringgold, GA 30736
Tel: 706-965-3056

Cave Spring Historical Society
13 Cedartown Road
P.O. Box 715
Cave Spring, GA 30124
Tel: 706-777-8865

Charlton County Historical Society
P.O. Box 575
Folkston, GA 31537-0575
Tel: (912) 496-4578

Chattahoochee Valley Historical Society
3419 Twentieth Avenue
Valley, AL 36854
Tel: 334- 768-2050
Fax: 334-768-7272

Chattooga County Historical Society
P.O. Box 626
Summerville, GA 30747
http://www.rootsweb.com/~gachatto/cchs.htm

Cherokee County Historical Society
P.O. Box 1287
Canton, GA 30114
http://www.rockbarn.org/

Coastal Georgia Historical Society
101 12th Street
P.O. Box 21136
St. Simons Island, GA 31522-0636
Tel: 912-638-4666
Fax: 912-638-6609
http://www.saintsimonslighthouse.org/

Cobb Landmarks and Historical Society
Root House Museum
145 Denmeade Street
Marietta, GA 30060
Tel: 770-426-4982
http://www.roothousemuseum.com/

College Park Historical Society
City Hall
3667 Main Street
P.O. Box 87137
College Park, GA 30337
Tel:404-761-8932
http://collegeparkga.com/

Columbia County Historical Society
P.O. Box 203
Appling, GA 30802

Crawford County Historical Society
Crawford County Business Development Center
Roberta, GA 31078
Tel: 478-836-5753
Fax: 478- 836-2355

Dawson County Historical and Genealogical Society
P.O. Box 1074
Dawsonville, GA 30534

Decatur County Historical Society
P.O.Box 682
119 W. Water St.
Bainbridge, GA 31717
912-248-1719

DeKalb Historical Society
Old Courthouse on the Square
101 East Court Square
Decatur, GA 30030
Tel: 404-373-1088
Fax: 404-378-8287
http://www.dekalbhistory.org/

Early County Historical Society
P.O. Box 564
Blakely, GA 31723
http://www.rootsweb.com/~gaearly/misc/
early_historical_society.htm

East Point Historical Society
1685 Norman Berry Drive
P.O. Box 90675
East Point, GA 30364-0675

Eatonton-Putnam County Historical Society
104 Church Street
Eatonton, GA 31024
Tel: 706-485-4532

Elbert County Historical Society
One Deadwyler Street
P.O. Box 1033
Elberton, GA 30635

Eleventh Circuit Historical Society
P.O. Box 1556
Atlanta, GA 30301

Etowah Valley Historical Society
Bartow County Courthouse
115 West Cherokee Avenue
P.O. Box 1886
Cartersville, GA 30120
Tel: 770-606-8862
E-mail: evhs@evhsonline.org
http://www.evhsonline.org/index.shtml

Fayette County Historical Society
195 Lee Street
P.O. Box 421
Fayetteville, GA 30214
Tel: 770-716-6020
http://www.historyfayettecoga.org/

Forsyth County, Historical Society of
P.O. Box 1334
Cumming, GA 30028

Fort Gaines Historical Society
P.O. Box 6
Fort Gaines, GA 31751

Foxfire Fund/Museum
P.O. Box 541
Mountain City, GA 30562
Tel: 706-746-5828
Fax: 706-746-5829
http://www.foxfire.org/

Franklin County Historical Society
P.O. Box 482
Carnesville GA 30521
Tel: 706-384-4361

Georgia Historical Society
Hodgson Hall Archives and Library
501 Whittaker Street
Savannah, GA 31499
Tel: 912-651-2125
912-651-2128
Fax: 912-651-2831
E-mail: ghslib@georgiahistory.com
http://www.georgiahistory.com/

Gordon County Historical Society
P.O. Box 342
Calhoun, GA 30701
Tel: 706-629-1515
Fax: 706-629-4510

Grady County Historical Society
P.O. Box 586
Cairo, GA 31728

Greene County Historical Society
201 Green Street
P.O. Box 238
Greensboro, GA 30642
Tel: 706-453-2588
Fax: 706-453-4970

Griffin-Spalding Historical Society
P.O. Box 196
Griffin, GA 30224
Tel: 770-229-2432
Fax: 770-227-5586

Guale Historical Society
P.O. Box 398
St. Marys, GA 31558
Tel: 912-882-4587

Guyton Historical Society
205 Lynn Bonds Avenue
P.O. Box 99
Guyton, GA 31312
Tel: 912-772-3353
Fax: 912-772-3152

Gwinnett Historical Society
P.O. Box 261
Lawrenceville, GA 30046
Tel: 770-822-5174
Fax: 770-237-5616
E-mail: ghs@gwinnetths.org
http://www.gwinnetths.org/

Habersham County Historical Society
P.O. Box 1552
Clarkesville, GA 30523

Hahira Historical Society
102 South Church, Street
Hahira, GA 31632
Phone 912-794-2330
Fax 912 794-9310
http://www.hahira.ga.us/historicalsociety.htm

Hall County Historical Society
380 Green Street Historic District
P.O. Box 2999
Phone: 770-503-1319
Fax: 770-536-7072
Gainesville, GA 3050
E-mail: Hchs@Hallcountyhistoricalsociety.Org
http://www.hallcountyhistoricalsociety.org/index.html

Hapeville Historical Society
P.O. Box 82055
Hapeville, GA 30354

Haralson County Historical Society
Old Haralson County Courthouse
P.O. Box 585
Buchanan, GA 30113
http://www.rootsweb.com/~gahchs/

Hart County Historical Society
31 East Howell Street
P.O. Box 96
Hartwell, GA 30643
Tel: 706-376-6330
Fax: 706-376-1456

Heard County Historical Society
161 Shady Street
P.O. Box 990
Franklin, GA 30217
Tel: 706-675-6507

Historic Oglethorpe County, Inc.
P.O. Box 1793
Lexington, GA 30648
Tel: (706) 546-1850

Historical Effingham Society
1002 Pine Street
P.O. Box 665
Springfield, GA 31329
Tel: 912-826-4770

Jackson County Historical Society
c/o Crawford W. Long Museum
28 College Street
Jefferson, GA 30549
Tel: 706-367-5307

Jefferson County Historical Society
P.O. Box 491
Louisville, GA 30434-0491
Tel: (478) 625-7673

Jenkins County Historical Society
Chamber of Commerce
548 Cotton Street
Millen, GA 30442
Tel: (478) 982-5799
Fax: 912-982-5512

Johnson County Historical Society
Harlie Fulford Library (Johnson County)
301 Elm Street
Wrightsville, GA 31096
Phone: 1-478-864-3940
Fax: 1-478-864-0626

Kennesaw Historical Society
2829 Cherokee Street
Kennesaw, GA 30144
Tel: 770-975-0887
http://www.mindspring.com/~robertcjones/khs/khs.htm

Laurens County Historical Society
Dublin-Laurens Museum
311 Academy Avenue
P.O. Box 1461
Dublin, GA 31040
Tel: 478-272-9242
http://organizations.nlamerica.com/historical/

Lee County Historical Society
Lee County Public Library
245 Walnut Street
P. O. Box 393
Leesburg, GA 31763-0049
Tel: 229-759-2369

Liberty County Historical Society
P.O. Box 982
Hinesville, GA 31310
Records housed at
Midway Museum
Highway 17
Midway, GA 31320
Tel: 912-884-5837

Louisville Historical Society
P.O. Box 491
Louisville, GA 30434-0491

Lower Altamaha Historical Society
P.O. Box 1405
Darien, GA 31305
Tel: 912- 280-9547
Fax: 912- 437-5479
E-mail: bsullivan@ocean.nos.noa.gov

Lowndes County Historical Society/Museum
305 W. Central Avenue
P.O. Box 434
Valdosta, GA 31603
Tel: 229-247-4780
Fax: 229-247-2840
http://www.surfsouth.com/~lownhist/

Lumpkin County Historical Society
The Old Jail
P.O. Box 894
Dahlonega, GA 30533
Tel: 706-864-3668
http://www.dahlonega.org/historicalsociety/
    historicalsociety.html

Macon County Historical Society
North Dooly Street
P.O. Box 571
Montezuma, GA 31063
Tel: (478) 472-5038

Madison County Heritage Association
P.O. Box 74
Danielsville, GA 30633
Tel: 706-795-2017

Marble Valley Historical Society
Main Street
P.O. Box 815
Jasper, GA 30143
Tel: (706) 268-3311
http://www.marblevalley.org/

McDuffie County Historical Society
633 Hemlock Drive
P.O. Box 1816
Thomson, GA 30824
Tel: 706-595-3548
Fax: 706-595-4710

Middle Georgia Historical Society
Sidney Lanier Cottage
935 High Street
P.O. Box 13358
Macon, GA 31208-3358
Tel: 478-743-3851
http://www.cityofmacon.net/Living/slcottage.htm

Monroe County Historical Society
East Johnston Street
P.O. Box 401
Forsyth, GA 31029
Tel: 478-994-5070

Moreland Community Historical Society
P.O. Box 128
Moreland, GA 30259

Morgan County Historical Society
277 South Main Street
Madison, GA 30650
Tel: 706-342-9627
Fax: 706-342-1154

National Society of Andersonville
P.O. Box 65
Andersonville, GA 31711
Tel: (229) 924-2558

Newnan-Coweta Historical Society
Male Academy Museum
30 Temple Avenue
P.O. Box 1001
Newnan, GA 30264
Tel/Fax: 770-251-0207
http://newnan.com/nchs/

Newton County Historical Society
Chamber of Commerce Building
2100 Washington Street
P.O. Box 2415
Covington, GA 30210
Tel: 770-786-7510
Fax: 770-786-1294

North Georgia Methodist Historical Society
Depository: Pitts Theology Library
Emory University
Atlanta, GA 30322
http://www.gcah.org/Conference/umcdirectory.htm

Northeast Georgia Historical and Genealogical Society
Hall County Public Library
127 Main Street NW
P.O. Box 907643
Gainesville, GA 30501
http://www.rootsweb.com/~gahall/nega/

Northwest Georgia Historical and Genealogical Society
P.O. Box 5063
Rome, GA 30162
Tel: 706-236-4607
Fax: 706-236-4605
http://www.rootsweb.com/~ganwhags/

Old Campbell County Historical Society
P.O. Box 342
Fairburn, GA 30213-0342

Old Capitol History Society
P.O. Box 4
Milledgeville, GA 31061
Tel: 478-453-9049
478- 445-6795

Old Clinton Historical Society
154 Randolph Street
Gray, GA 31032

Paulding County Historical Society
P.O. Box 333
Dallas, GA 30132
Tel: 770-948-5915
http://www.rootsweb.com/~gapauldi/historicalsociety/
hsociety.html

Perry Area Historical Society
P.O. Drawer D
Perry, GA 31069

Polk County Historical Society
205 N. College Avenue
P.O. Box 203
Cedartown, GA 30125
Tel: 770-748-0073
http://polkhist.home.mindspring.com/

Rabun County Historical Society
P.O. Box 921
Clayton, GA 30525
http://www.rootsweb.com/~garchs/

Randolph Historical Society
P. O. Box 472
Cuthbert, GA 31740
Tel: 229-732-6574

Richmond County Historical Society
c/o Reese Library, Augusta College
2500 Walton Way
Augusta, GA 30904-2200
Tel: 706-737-1532
Fax: 706-667-4415
http://www.downtownaugusta.com/heroes-overlook/
    heroes-overlook.htm

Rockdale County Historical Society
967 Milstead Avenue
P.O. Box 351
Conyers, GA 30207
Tel: 770-483-4398

Rome Area History Museum
303-305 Broad Street
Rome, GA 30161
Tel: 706-235-8051
http://rahm.roman.net/index.html

Roswell Historical Society
City Of Roswell Research Library And Archives
950 Forrest Street
Roswell, GA 30075
Tel: 770-594-6405
Fax: 770-594-6402
http://www.roswellgov.com/

Schley County Historical Society
P.O. Box 326
Ellaville, GA 31806

Seminole County Historical Society
P.O. Box 713
Donalsonville, GA 31759
Tel: 229- 524-2588

Senoia Area Historical Society
P.O. Box 301
Senoia, GA 30276
Tel: 770- 599-6457

Seven Springs Historical Society
3901 Brownsville Road
P.O. Box 4
Powder Springs, GA 30073
Tel: 770-943-7949

Smyrna Historical and Genealogical Society
2861 Atlanta Street
Smyrna, Georgia 30082
Tel: 770-435-7549
Fax: 770-431-2858
http://www.rootsweb.com/~gashgs/

Society of Georgia Archivists
P.O. Box 133085
Atlanta, GA 30333
http://www.soga.org/

Sparta-Hancock County Historical Society
P. O. Box 762
Sparta, GA 31087-0762
Tel: 706-444-6411

Stephens County Historical Society
313 S. Pond Street
Toccoa, GA 30577
Tel: 706-282-5055

Suwanee Historical Association
P.O. Box 815
Suwanee, GA 30174

Taliaferro County Historical Society
P.O. Box 32
Crawfordville, GA 30631

Taylor County Historical-Genealogical Society
P.O. Box 1925
Butler, GA 31006

Terrell County Restoration Society
P.O. Box 63
Dawson, GA 31742
Tel: 229-995-2125
Fax: 229-995-4000
E-mail: eduskin@surfsouth.com

Thomas County Historical Society
725 N. Dawson Street
P.O. Box 1922
Thomasville, GA 31799
Tel: 229-226-7664
Fax: 229-226-7466
http://www.rose.net/~history/

Toombs County Historical Society
P.O. Box 2825
Vidalia, GA 30474
Tel: 912-537-2779

Towns County Historical and Genealogical Society
Post Office Box 932
Hiawassee, GA 30546
Tel: 706- 896-7369
http://www.rootsweb.com/~gatowns/histsoc.txt

Treutlen County Historical Society
Treutlen County Museum of Local History
Soperton, GA 30457

Troup County Historical Society and Archives
136 Main Street
P.O. Box 1051
LaGrange, GA 30241
Tel: 706-884-1828
Fax: 706-884-1840
http://www.trouparchives.org/

Tybee Island Historical Society
30 Meddin Drive, Fort Screven
Tybee Island, Ga 31328
Tel: 912-786-5801
Fax: 912-786-6538
http://www.tybeelighthouse.org/

Union County Historical Society
Courthouse Square
P.O. Box 35
Blairsville, GA 30514-0035
Tel: 706-745-5493
http://www.ngeorgia.com/uchs.html

Upson Historical Society
P.O. Box 363
Thomaston, GA 30286
Tel: 706-647-6839
Fax: 706-646-3524
http://www.rootsweb.com/~gauhs/index.html

Walker County Historical Society
305 South Duke Street
LaFayette, GA 30728-2936
http://www.geocities.com/Heartland/Prairie/6370/walker/wchs.html

Washington County Historical Society
129 Jones Street
P.O. Box 6088
Sandersville, GA 31082
Tel: 478-552-6965
Fax: 478-552-1449
http://www.rootsweb.com/~gawashin/
washingtoncounty002.htm

Wayne County Historical Society
125 NE Broad Street
Jesup, GA 31545-5516
Tel: 912-427-3233

White County Historical Society
Courthouse Square
P.O. Box 1139
Cleveland, GA 30528
Tel: 706-865-3225
http://www.georgiamagazine.com/counties/white/wchs/

Whitfield-Murray Historical Society
Crown Garden and Archives
715 Chattanooga Avenue
Dalton, GA 30720
Tel: 706-278-0217
http://www.geocities.com/wmhs1976/WMHS.html

Worth County Historical Society
P.O. Box 5073
Sylvester, GA 31791
Tel: (229) 776-4481

LDS FAMILY HISTORY CENTERS

For locations of Family History Centers in this state, see the Family History Center locator at FamilySearch:
http://www.familysearch.org/eng/Library/FHC/frameset_fhc.asp

ARCHIVES/LIBRARIES/MUSEUMS

Andersonville National Historic Site
Route 1, Box 800
Andersonville, GA 31711
Tel: 229-924-0343
Fax: 229-928-9640
http://www.nps.gov/ande/

Andrew College Archives
Pitts Library
413 College Street
Cuthbert, GA 31740
Tel: 229- 732-5944
Fax: 229- 732-5957
http://www.andrewcollege.edu/

Appling County Heritage Center
Thomas & Harvey Streets
P.O. Box 87
Baxley, GA 31513
Tel: 912-367-8133
Fax: 912-367-8133

Athens Regional Library
Heritage Room
2025 Baxter Street
Athens, GA 30606
Tel: 706-613-3650 ext. 350
Fax: 706-613-3660
http://www.clarke.public.lib.ga.us/

Atlanta-Fulton Public Library
Georgia History & Genealogy Department
1 Margaret Mitchell Square
Atlanta, GA 30303-1089
Tel: 404-730-1700
http://www.af.public.lib.ga.us/central/gagen/index.html

Atlanta History Center
130 West Paces Ferry Road, NW
Atlanta, GA 30305-1366
Tel: 404-814-4000
Fax: 404-814-4186
http://www.atlhist.org/

Atlanta University Center
Robert W. Woodruff Library
Emory University
111 James P. Brawley Drive, S.W.
Atlanta, GA 30314
Phone: 404-522-8980
Fax: 404-577-5158
http://www.auctr.edu/

Auburn Avenue Research Library
101 Auburn Avenue, NE
Atlanta, GA 30303
Tel: 404-730-4001
Fax: 404-730-5879
http://aarl.af.public.lib.ga.us/

Augusta Genealogical Society/Library
1109 Broad Street
P.O. Box 3743
Augusta, GA 30914-3743
Tel: 706-722-4073
http://www.augustagensociety.org/

Augusta-Richmond County Public Library
East Central Georgia Regional Library
902 Greene Street
Augusta, GA 30901-2294
Tel: 706-821-2600
Fax: 706-724-6762
http://www.ecgrl.public.lib.ga.us/default.htm

Augusta State University
Reese Library
Special Collections
2500 Walton Way
Augusta, GA 30904-2200
Tel: 706-737-1744
Fax: 706-737-1475
http://www.aug.edu/library/departments.html

Austell City Museum
2716 Broad Street
Austell, GA 30001
Tel: 770-944-4309
Fax: 770-944-4311

Barnesville-Lamar County Historical Society
P.O. Box 805
Barnesville, GA 30204
Tel: 770-358-0150 (museum)
Fax: 770-358-5149
http://www.rootsweb.com/~galamar/society.html

Bartow County Genealogical Society/Research Library
425 W. Main Street
P.O. Box 993
Cartersville, GA 30120-0993
Tel: 770-606-0706
http://www.geocities.com/Heartland/Park/9465/
    bartowcoga.html

Bartow County Public Library
429 W. Main Street
Cartersville, GA 30120
Tel: 770-382-4203
http://www.bartowlibraryonline.org/

Bartram Trail Regional Library
204 E. Liberty Street
Washington, GA 30673
Tel: 706-678-7736
Fax: 706-678-1474
http://ptquattlebaum.com/library/

Bradley Memorial Library
Chattahoochee Valley Regional Library
1120 Bradley Drive
Columbus, GA 31906-2800
Tel: 706-649-0780
Fax: 706-649-1914
E-mail: holdenm@mail.muscogee.public.lib.ga.us

Brooks County Public Library
404 Tallokas Road
Quitman, GA 31643
Tel: 912-263-4412
Fax: 912-263-8002

Brunswick Regional Library
208 Gloucester Street
Brunswick, GA 31521
Tel: 912-267-1212

Bryan-Lang Historical Library
P. O. Box 725
311 Camden Avenue
Woodbine, GA 31569
Tel: 912-576-5841

Carter-Coile Country Doctors Museum
111 Marigold Lane
P.O. Box 306
Winterville, GA 30683
Tel: 706-742-8600
Fax: 706-742-5476

Catholic Archdiocese of Atlanta Archives
680 West Peachtree St., NW
Atlanta, GA 30308-1984
Tel: 404-885-7253
Fax: 404-885-7230
http://www.archatl.com/archives/

Catholic Diocese of Savannah Archives
601 E. Liberty Street
Savannah, GA 31401-5196
Tel: 912-201-4070
http://www.dioceseofsavannah.org/Home/default.asp

Chatham-Effingham-Liberty Regional Library
2002 Bull Street
Savannah, GA 31401
Tel: 912-652-3600
Fax: 912-652-3638
http://www.celrl.org/

Chattahoochee Valley State Community College
Learning Resource Center
2602 College Drive
Phenix City, AL 36869
Tel: (334) 291-4978
Fax: (334) 291-4980
http://www.cvcc.cc.al.us/library/

Chattooga County Library System
360 Farrar Drive
Summerville, GA 30747-2016
Tel: 706-857-2553
Fax: 706-857-7841

Cherokee Regional Library
Lafayette-Walker County Library
Georgia History & Genealogy Room
305 S. Duke Street
P.O. Box 707
LaFayette, GA 30728
Tel: 706-638-2992
Fax: 706-638-4028
http://www.walker.public.lib.ga.us

Chieftains Museum
800 Riverside Parkway
P.O. Box 373
Rome, GA 30162
Tel/Fax: 706-291-9494
http://www.romegeorgia.com/chiefmus.html

Chipley Historical Center of Pine Mountain
P.O. Box 1055
146 North McDougald Avenue
Pine Mountain, GA 31822
Tel: 770-663-4044

Clayton County Library System
Genealogy & Local History Room
865 Battlecreek Road
Jonesboro, GA 30236
Tel: 770-473-3850
Fax: 770-473-3858
http://www.clayton.public.lib.ga.us/

Coastal Plain Regional Library
2014 Chestnut Street
P.O. Box 7606
Tifton, GA 31793-7606
Tel: 229-386-3400
Fax: 229-386-7007
http://www.tift.public.lib.ga.us/

Cobb County Public Library
The Georgia Room
266 Roswell Street
Marietta, GA 30060-2004
Tel: 770-528-2333
Fax: 770-528-2367
http://library.cobbcat.org/?

Cobb Memorial Archives
3419 Twentieth Avenue
Valley, AL 36854
Tel: 334-768-2161
Fax: 334-768-7272

Columbia Theological Seminary
John Bulow Campbell Library
701 Columbia Drive
Decatur, GA 30030
Tel: 404-378-8821
Fax: 404-377-9696
http://www.ctsnet.edu/

Commerce Public Library
Heritage Room
1344 S. Broad Street
Commerce, GA 30529
Tel: 706-335-5946

Cordele-Crisp Carnegie Library
115 East 11th Avenue
Cordele, GA 31015
Tel: 912-276-1300
http://www.lbrl.org/cordele.html

Crawford W. Long Museum
Jackson County Historical Society
28 College Street
Jefferson, GA 30549
Tel: 706-367-5307

Crescent Farm Historical Center
Cherokee County Historical Society
P.O. Box 1287
658 Marietta Highway
Canton, GA 30114
(770) 345-3288
http://www.rockbarn.org/facilities.htm

Crown Garden and Archives
Whitfield-Murray Historical Society
715 Chattanooga Avenue
Dalton, GA 30720
Tel: 706-278-0217
http://www.geocities.com/wmhs1976/WMHS.html

Dahlonega Courthouse Gold Museum
Public Square
P.O. Box 2042
Dahlonega, GA 30533
Tel: 706-864-2257
http://www.dahlonega.org/museum/goldmuseum.html

DeKalb County Public Library System
Decatur Library
215 Sycamore Street
Decatur, GA 30030
Tel: 404-370-3070
Fax: 404-370-3081
http://www.dekalb.public.lib.ga.us

DeSoto Trail Regional Library
145 E. Broad Street
Camilla, GA 31730
Tel: 229-336-8372
Fax: 229-336-9353
E-mail: mitchelg@mail.mitchell.public.lib.ga.us

Dougherty County Public Library
Genealogy Room
300 Pine Avenue
Albany, GA 31701
Tel: 229-420-3200
229-420-3218 (Genealogy Room)
http://www.docolib.org/

Dublin-Laurens Museum
Laurens County Historical Society
311 Academy Avenue
P.O. Box 1461
Dublin, GA 31040
Tel: 478-272-9242
http://organizations.nlamerica.com/historical/

Elbert County Public Library
345 Heard Street
Elberton, GA 30635
Tel: 706-283-5375
Fax: 706-283-5456
E-mail: suddethp@mail.elbert.public.lib.ga.us

Ellen Payne Odom Genealogy Library
Moultrie-Colquitt County Library
204 Fifth Street, SE
P.O. Box 2828
Moultrie, GA 31776-2828
Tel: 912-985-6540
Fax: 912-985-0936

Emory University
Pitts Theology Library
Archives and Manuscripts
505 Kilgo Circle
Atlanta, GA 30322
Tel: 404-727-4166
Fax: 404-727-1219
http://www.pitts.emory.edu/

Emory University
R.W. Woodruff Library
Special Collections and Archives Department
540 Asbury Circle
Atlanta, GA 30322-2870
Tel: 404-727-6887
Fax: 404-727-0360
E-mail: speccollref@emory.edu
http://info.library.emory.edu/Special/default.html

Factor's Walk Military Museum
P.O. Box 10041
Savannah, GA 31412
Tel: 912-232-8003
Fax: 912-232-5457

Fayette County Library
1821 Heritage Park Way
Fayetteville, GA 30214-2131
Tel: 770-461-8841
http://www.admin.co.fayette.ga.us/public_library/
    library.htm

First African Baptist Church Museum
23 Montgomery Street
Savannah, GA 31401
Tel: 912-233-2244
Fax: 912-234-7950
http://www.oldestblackchurch.org/index.htm

Fitzgerald-Ben Hill County Library
123 N. Main Street
Fitzgerald, GA 31750
Tel: 229-426-5080
http://www.fitzgeraldga.org/comm6.mfr.html

Flint River Regional Library
800 Memorial Drive
Griffin, GA 30223-4499
Tel: 770-412-4770
Fax: 770-412-4773
http://www.spalding.public.lib.ga.us/

Forsyth County Public Library
585 Dahlonega Road
Cumming, GA 30040
Tel: 770-781-9840
http://www.forsyth.public.lib.ga.us/

Fort Frederica National Monument
Route 9, Box 286-C
St. Simons Island, GA 31522-9710
Tel/Fax: 912-638-3639
E-mail: fofr_superintendent@nps.gov
http://www.nps.gov/fofr/

Fort McAllister Historic Park
3894 Fort McAllister Road
Richmond Hill, GA 31324
Tel: 912-727-2339
http://fortmcallister.org/

Foxfire Fund/Museum
P.O. Box 541
Mountain City, GA 30562
Tel: 706-746-5828
Fax: 706-746-5829
http://www.foxfire.org/

Genealogical Center Library (operates by mail)
P.O. Box 71343
Marietta, GA 30007-1343
E-mail: gencenlib@aol.com
http://homepages.rootsweb.com/~gencenlb/

Georgia Agrirama Development Authority
P.O. Box Q
Tifton, GA 31793
Tel: 229-386-3344
Fax: 229-386-3386

Georgia Baptist Historical Society Archives
Mercer University
Jack Tarver Library
1300 Edgewood Ave.
Macon, GA 31207
Tel: 478-301-2055
http://tarver.mercer.edu/special_collections/default.htm

Georgia College
Ina Dillard Russell Library
Campus Box 043
Georgia College & State University
Milledgeville, GA 31061
Tel: 478-445-5573
http://library.gcsu.edu/~reference/about.html

Georgia Historical Society
Hodgson Hall Archives and Library
 501 Whittaker Street
Savannah, GA 31499
Tel: 912-651-2125
912-651-2128
Fax: 912-651-2831
E-mail: ghslib@georgiahistory.com
http://www.georgiahistory.com/Lib_and_Archives.html

Georgia State Library
Capitol Hill Station
330 Capitol Ave SE
Atlanta, GA 30334
Tel: 404-656-2392

Georgia State University
Pullen Library
Special Collections Dept.
100 Decatur Street, SE
Atlanta, GA 30303-3202
Tel: 404-651-2477
Fax: 404-651-2476
E-mail: LIBSC@LANGATE.GSU.EDU
http://www.library.gsu.edu/spcoll/

Gwinnett County Public Library
1001 Lawrenceville Highway
Lawrenceville, GA 30045
Tel: 770-822-4522
Fax: 770-822-5379
http://www.gcpl.public.lib.ga.us/

Gwinnett History Museum
455 S. Perry Street
Lawrenceville, GA 30045
Tel: 770-822-5178
Fax: 770-822-8835
http://www.gogwinnett.com/gwinnetthistorymuseum/

Hall County Library
127 Main Street
Gainesville, GA 30505-2399
Tel: 770-532-3311
Fax: 770-532-4305
E-mail: dbronson@crls.hall.public.lib.ga.us
http://www.hall.public.lib.ga.us/

Hart County Library
150 Benson Street
Hartwell, GA 30643-1392
Tel: 706-376-4655
Fax: 706-376-1157
E-mail: hartl0@mail.hart.public.lib.ga.us
http://www.hartwellga.com/hclibrary/

Houston County Public Libraries
1201 Washington Ave.
Perry, GA 31069-2599
Tel: 478-987-3050
Fax: 478-987-4572
E-mail: goldenj@mail.houston.public.lib.ga.us

Huxford Genealogical Society Library
Municipal Complex
P.O. Box 595
Homerville, GA 31634
Tel: 912-487-2310
http://www.huxford.com/

Jarrell Plantation State Historic Site
711 Jarrell Plantation Road
Juliette, GA 31046
Tel: 478-986-5172
E-mail: jarrell_plantation_park@mail.dnr.state.ga.us
http://www.mylink.net/~jarrell/index.html

Jefferson County Library
306 E. Broad Street
Louisville, GA 30434-1624
Tel: 478-625-3751
Fax: 478-625-7683
E-mail: rogersc@mail.jefferson.public.lib.ga.us

Kennesaw Civil War Museum
2829 Cherokee Street
Kennesaw, GA 30144
Tel: 770-427-2117
Fax: 770-429-4559
http://thegeneral.org/

Kennesaw Mountain National Battlefield Park
Kennesaw Mountain Historical Association
900 Kennesaw Mountain Drive
Kennesaw, GA 30152
Phone: 770-422-3696
Fax: 770-423-1890
http://www.kmha.org/

Kennesaw State University
Horace W. Sturgis Library
1000 Chastain Road
Kennesaw, GA 30144
Tel: 770-423-6186
Fax: 770-499-3376
http://www.kennesaw.edu/library/

Kinchafoonee Regional Library
913 Forrester Drive
Dawson, GA 31742
Tel: 912-995-6331
Fax: 912-995-3383
http://www.terrell.public.lib.ga.us/KRL_system.htm

Ladson Genealogical & Historical Foundation Library
119 Church Street
Vidalia, GA 30474
Mail: c/o Ohoopee Regional Library System
610 Jackson Street
Vidalia, GA 30474
Tel/Fax: 912-537-8186
E-mail: ladsonl@mail.toombs.public.lib.ga.us
http://www.toombs.public.lib.ga.us/ladson.htm

Lake Blackshear Regional Library
307 E. Lamar Street
Americus, GA 31709
Tel: 912-924-8091
Fax: 912-928-4445
http://www.lbrl.org/

Lower Muskogee Creek Tribe
Tama Creek Tribal Town
107 Long Pine Drive
Whigham, GA 31797
Tel/Fax: 229-762-3165
http://www.rose.net/~mvr/

Lowndes County Historical Society/Museum
305 W. Central Avenue
P.O. Box 434
Valdosta, GA 31603
Tel: 229-247-4780
Fax: 229-247-2840
http://www.surfsouth.com/~lownhist/

Lumpkin County Library
342 Courthouse Square
Dahlonega, GA 30533
Phone 706-864-3668
Fax 706-864-3937
http://www.dahlonega.org/library/library.html

Mercer University
Jack Tarver Library
1300 Edgewood Ave.
Macon, GA 31207
Tel: 478-301-2055
http://tarver.mercer.edu/

Methodist Museum
Epworth-by-the-Sea
100 Arthur J. Moore Drive
St. Simons Island, GA 31522
Tel: 912-638-4050
http://www.epworthbythesea.org/

Midway Museum
U.S. Highway 17
P.O. Box 195
Midway, GA 31320
Tel: 912-884-5837
http://www.libertyconnection.com/midway/museum.html

Morgan County African-American Museum
156 Academy Street
P.O. Box 482
Madison, GA 30650
Tel: 706-342-9191
Fax: 706-342-7806

Morgan County Library
1131 East Avenue
Madison, Georgia 30650
Tel. (706) 342-1206
Fax (706) 342-0883
http://www.uncleremus.org/morgan.htm

Morgan County Records Archives
Hancock Street
P.O. Box 130
Madison, GA 30650
Tel: 706-342-3605
Fax: 706-342-7806

Mountain Regional Library
698 Miller Street
P.O. Box 159
Young Harris, GA 30582
Tel: 706-379-3732
Fax: 706-379-2047
E-mail: haymoret@mail.towns.public.lib.ga.us

Nancy Guinn Memorial Library
Conyers-Rockdale Library System
864 Green Street
Conyers, GA 30012
Tel: 770-388-5040
Fax: 770-388-5043
http://www.rockdale.public.lib.ga.us/default.html

National P.O.W. Museum
Andersonville National Historic Site
496 Cemetery Road
Andersonville, GA 31711
Tel: 229-924-0343
http://www.nps.gov/ande/pphtml/facilities.html

Neva Lomason Memorial Library
West Georgia Regional Library
710 Rome Street
Carrollton, GA 30117-3046
Tel: 770-836-6711
http://www.carroll.public.lib.ga.us/Branches/Carrollton/
nlpl.htm

Newnan-Coweta Historical Society
Male Academy Museum
30 Temple Avenue
P.O. Box 1001
Newnan, GA 30264
Tel/Fax: 770-251-0207
http://newnan.com/mam/index.html

Newton County Library
7116 Floyd Street, NE
Covington, GA 30014
Tel: 770-787-3231
Fax: 770-784-2092

Newton County Library System
1174 Monticello Street
Covington, GA 30209
Tel: 770-784-2090
Fax: 770-784-2092
E-mail: soltisl@mail.newton.public.lib.ga.us

Northeast Georgia Regional Library
P.O. Box 2020
Clarksville, GA 30523
Tel: 706-754-4413
Fax: 706-754-3479
E-mail: e_murphy@cyberhighway.net

Northwest Georgia Regional Library
310 Cappes Street
Dalton, GA 30720-4123
Tel: 706-272-2974
Fax: 706-272-2977
http://www.whitfield.public.lib.ga.us/

Ocmulgee Regional Library System
505 Second Avenue
P.O. Box 4369
Eastman, GA 31203
Tel: 478-374-4711
Fax: 478-374-5646
http://www.orls.org/

Oconee Regional Library
801 Bellevue Avenue
P.O. Box 100
Dublin, GA 31040
Tel: 478-272-5710
Fax: 478-272-5381
http://www.laurens.public.lib.ga.us/

Ohoopee Regional Library System
610 Jackson Street
Vidalia, GA 30474-2835
Tel: 912-537-9283
Fax: 912-537-3735
http://www.toombs.public.lib.ga.us/

Okefenokee Regional Library System
401 Lee Avenue
P.O. Box 1669
Waycross, GA 31501
Tel: 912-287-4978
Fax: 912-287-4981
http://www.ware.public.lib.ga.us/

Peach Public Libraries
315 Martin Luther King Jr. Drive
Fort Valley, Georgia 31030
Tel: 478-825-1640
Fax: 478-825-2061
http://www.peach.public.lib.ga.us/

Piedmont Regional Library
189 Bell View Street
Winder, GA 30680
Tel: 770-867-2762
Fax: 770-867-7483
http://library.barrow.public.lib.ga.us/

Pine Mountain Regional Library
218 Perry Street
P.O. Box 709
Manchester, GA 31816
Tel: 706-846-3851
Fax: 706-846-9632
http://www.meriwether.public.lib.ga.us/Lib_Hours.shtml

Roddenbery Memorial Library
320 North Broad Street
Cairo, GA 31728-2199
Tel: 229-377-3632
Fax: 229-377-7204
www.grady.public.lib.ga.us/

Rossville Public Library
504 McFarland Ave.
Rossville, GA 30741
Tel: 706-866-1368
Fax: 706-858-0251
http://www.walker.public.lib.ga.us/branches/rossville.html

Roswell Research Library and Archives
Roswell Historical Society
950 Forrest Street
Roswell, GA 30075
Tel: 770-594-6405
Fax: 770-594-6402

Sara Hightower Regional Library
Rome-Floyd County Library
Special Collections Department
205 Riverside Parkway
Rome, GA 30161-2913
Tel: 706-236-4607
Fax: 706-236-4631
E-mail: gentryt@mail.floyd.public.lib.ga.us
http://www.floyd.public.lib.ga.us/

Satilla Regional Library
201 S. Coffee Avenue
Douglas, GA 31533
Tel: 912-384-4667
Fax: 912-389-4365
E-mail: schildb@mail.coffee.public.lib.ga.us

Savannah Jewish Archives
@ Georgia Historical Society
501 Whitaker Street
Savannah, GA 31401
Phone: (912) 651-2125
Fax: (912) 651-2831
http://www.georgiahistory.com/sja.htm

Screven-Jenkins Regional Library
106 South Community Drive
Sylvania, GA 30467-2055
Tel: 912-564-7526
Fax: 912-564-7580
http://www.sjrls.public.lib.ga.us/index.htm

R.T. Jones Memorial Library
Sequoyah Regional Library
116 Brown Industrial Parkway
Canton, GA 30114
Tel: 770-479-3090
Fax: 770-479-3069
http://168.8.195.81/sequoyah/

Signal Archives
Command Historian
U.S. Army Signal Center and Fort Gordon
Attn: ATZH-MH, Fort Gordon
Fort Gordon, GA 30905
Tel: 706-791-5212
Fax: 706- 679-5777

Sixth Cavalry Museum
#2 Barnhardt Circle
Fort Oglethorpe, GA 30742
Tel: 706-861-2860

Smyrna Museum
Smyrna Historical and Genealogical Society
2861 Atlanta Street
Smyrna, GA 30082
Tel: 770-435-7549
Fax: 770-431-2858
http://www.rootsweb.com/~gashgs/

South Georgia Regional Library
300 Woodrow Wilson Drive
Valdosta, GA 31602-2592
Tel: 229-333-0086
http://www.sgrl.org/

Southwest Georgia Regional Library
Genealogy Room
301 South Monroe Street
Bainbridge, GA 31717
Tel: 229-248-2665
Fax: 229-248-2670
http://www.decatur.public.lib.ga.us/openpage.htm

State University of West Georgia
Ingram Library
Carrollton, GA 30118
Tel: 770-830-2350
http://www.westga.edu/~library/

Statesboro Regional Library
124 S. Main Street
Statesboro, GA 30458
Tel: 912-764-1337
http://www.srls.public.lib.ga.us/

Thomas College Library Archives
1501 Millpond Road
Thomasville, GA 31792
Tel: 229-226-1621
Fax: 229-226-1679
http://www.thomasu.edu/

Thomas County Public Library System
201 North Madison Street
Thomasville, GA 31792
Tel: 229-225-5252
Fax: 229-225-5258
http://www.thomas.public.lib.ga.us/

Thomaston-Upson Archives
301 S. Carter Street
P.O. Box 1137
Thomaston, GA 30286
Tel: 706-646-2437
Fax: 706-646-3524
http://www.tuarch.org/

Thomasville Genealogical, History, and Fine Arts Library
135 North Broad Street
Thomasville, GA 31792
Tel: 229-226-9640
Fax: 229-226-3199
E-mail: glibrary@rose.net
http://www.rose.net/~glibrary/

Thomasville Landmarks
312 N. Broad Street
P.O. Box 1285
Thomasville, GA 31799
Tel: 229-226-6016
Fax: 229-226-6672
E-mail: tli@rose.net
http://members.aol.com/shuknnjivn/CommPresProj.html

Troup County Historical Society and Archives
136 Main Street
P.O. Box 1051
LaGrange, GA 30241
Tel: 706-884-1828
Fax: 706-884-1840
E-mail: info@trouparchives
http://www.trouparchives.org/

Troup-Harris-Coweta Regional Library
115 Alford Street
LaGrange, GA 30240
Tel: 706-882-7784
Fax: 706-882-7342
http://www.thclibrary.net/

Uncle Remus Regional Library
1131 East Avenue
Madison, GA 30650
Tel: 706-342-4974
Fax: 706-342-4510
http://www.morgan.public.lib.ga.us/unclehom.htm

Union County Historical Society
P.O. Box 35
Blairsville, GA 30514-0035
Tel: 706-745-5493
http://www.ngeorgia.com/uchs.html

U.S. Navy Supply Corps Museum
1425 Prince Avenue
Athens, GA 30606-2205
Tel: 706-354-7349
Fax: 706-354-7239
http://www.nscs.com/activities/museum.asp

University of Georgia
Department of Archives
Main Library
Athens, GA 30602
Tel: 706-542-8151
Fax: 706-542-4144
http://www.libs.uga.edu/

University of Georgia
Hargrett Library
Athens, GA 30602-1641
Tel: 706-542-7123
706-542-7131
Fax: 706-542-4144
http://www.libs.uga.edu/hargrett/speccoll.html

University of Georgia
Richard B. Russell Library
Athens, GA 30602-1642
Tel: 706-542-5788
Fax: 706-542-4144
E-mail: sbvogt@uga.cc.uga.edu
  pdean@uga.cc.uga.edu
http://www.libs.uga.edu/russell/

Valdosta State University Archives
Odum Library
Valdosta, GA 31698
Tel: (229) 333-7150
Fax: (229) 333-5862
http://books.valdosta.peachnet.edu/arch/archives.html

Vann House State Historical Park
82 Highway 225 N
Chatsworth GA 30705
Tel: 706-695-2598
Fax: 706-517-4255
http://www.alltel.net/~vannhouse/

Washington Memorial Library
Middle Georgia Regional Library/Archives
Genealogical & Historical Room
1180 Washington Avenue
Macon, GA 31208-6334
Tel: 478-744-0800 (library)
478-744-0851 (archives)
Fax: 478-744-0893
http://www.co.bibb.ga.us/library/Default.htm

West Georgia Museum of Tallapoosa
8 Lyon Street
P.O. Box 725
Tallapoosa, GA 30176
Tel: 404-574-3125
http://www.cyberspacemuseum.com/n7_8.html

West Georgia Regional Library
710 Rome Street
Carrollton, GA 30117
Tel: 770-836-6711
Fax: 770-836-4787
E-mail: cooperj@mail.carroll.public.lib.ga.us
http://www.carroll.public.lib.ga.us/

William Breman Jewish Heritage Museum
Ida Pearle & Joseph Cuba Jewish Archives &
Genealogical Center
1440 Spring Street
Atlanta, GA 30309
Tel: 404-873-1661
Fax: 404-874-7043
http://www.jewishculture.org/jewishmuseums/breman.htm

Young Harris College
Duckworth Libraries
Young Harris, GA 30582
Tel: 706-379-4313
Fax: 706-379-4314
E-mail: bobrich@yhc.edu
http://hoboken.yhc.edu:80/dept/lib/

NEWSPAPER REPOSITORIES

Chatham-Effingham-Liberty Regional Library
2002 Bull Street
Savannah, GA 31401
Tel: 912-652-3600
Fax: 912-652-3638
http://www.celrl.org/

Commerce Public Library
Heritage Room
1344 S. Broad Street
Commerce, GA 30529
Tel: 706-335-5946

Etowah Valley Historical Society
P.O. Box 1886
Cartersville, GA 30120
http://www.evhsonline.org/index.shtml

Oconee Regional Library
801 Bellevue Avenue
P.O. Box 100
Dublin, GA 31040
Tel: 478-272-5710
Fax: 478-272-5381
http://www.laurens.public.lib.ga.us/

Rossville Public Library
504 McFarland Ave.
Rossville, GA 30741
Tel: 706-866-1368
Fax: 706-858-0251
http://www.walker.public.lib.ga.us/branches/rossville.html

University of Georgia
Department of Archives
Georgia Newspaper Project
Athens, GA 30602
Tel: 706-542-2131
Fax: 706-542-4144
http://www.libs.uga.edu/gnp/

VITAL RECORDS

Georgia Department of Human Resources
Vital Records Unit, Room 217-H
2600 Skyland Drive NE
Atlanta, GA 30319-3640
Tel: (404) 679-4701
http://health.state.ga.us/programs/vitalrecords/
Birth: http://health.state.ga.us/programs/vitalrecords/
    birth.shtml
Death 1919-present: http://health.state.ga.us/programs/
    vitalrecords/ death.shtml
Marriage 1952-present: http://health.state.ga.us/pro-
    grams/ vitalrecords/marriage.shtml
Divorce (For records, see county clerk)http://
    health.state.ga.us/programs/vitalrecords/
    divorce.shtml

GEORGIA ON THE WEB

Genealogical Computer Society of Georgia
http://www.mindspring.com/~noahsark/gcsga.html

Georgia GenWeb Project
http://www.rootsweb.com/~gagenweb/

Georgia HomePLACE
http://www.public.lib.ga.us/homeplace/

State of Georgia, Office of Secretary of State
Georgia Department of Archives and History
http://www.sos.state.ga.us/archives

State of Georgia, Office of Secretary of State
Historical Organizations and Resources Directory
http://www.sos.state.ga.us/archives/ghrab/dir/ghor.htm

Travellers Southern Families
http://misc.traveller.com/genealogy/

HAWAII

ARCHIVES, STATE & NATIONAL

Hawaii State Archives
Iolani Palace Grounds
Kekauluohi Building
King & Richards Streets
Honolulu, HI 96813
Tel: 808-586-0313
808-586-0329
Fax: 808-586-0330
http://www.hawaii.gov/dags/archives/welcome.html

National Archives-Pacific Region (San Francisco)
1000 Commodore Drive
San Bruno, CA 94066
Tel: 650-876-9001
Fax: 650-876-0920
E-mail: sanbruno.archives@nara.gov
http://www.nara.gov/regional/sanfranc.html

GENEALOGICAL SOCIETIES

Daughters of Hawaii
Queen Emma's Summer Palace
2913 Pali Highway
Honolulu, HI 96817
Tel: 808-595-6291
808-595-3167
Fax: 808-595-4395
http://www.daughtersofhawaii.org/daughters/about.shtml

Hawaii County Genealogical Society
P.O. Box 831
Keaau, HI 96749-0831

Maui Genealogical Society
38A Alania Place
Kihei, HI 96753
http://www.maui.net/~mauifun/mgs.htm

Portuguese Genealogical Society of Hawaii
810 North Vineyard Blvd., Room 11
Honolulu, HI 96817
Tel: 808-841-5044
http://www.lusaweb.com/genealogy/html/phgs.cfm

Sandwich Islands Genealogical Society
P.O. Box 235039
Honolulu, HI 96823-3500
Manoa Gardens Community Center
2790 Kahaloa Drive
Manoa Gardens, HI 96822
http://www.hpcug.org/ancestors/sigs.html

HISTORICAL SOCIETIES

Hawaiian Historical Society/Library
560 Kawaiahao Street
Honolulu, HI 96813
Tel: 808-537-6271
http://www.hawaiianhistory.org/

Kaua'i Historical Society
P.O. Box 1778
Lihu'e, HI 96766
Tel: 808-245-3373
Fax: 808-245-8693
http://www.kauaihistoricalsociety.org/

Kona Historical Society/Museum
Highway 11
Kealakekua, HI
Mail: P.O. Box 398
Captain Cook, HI 96704
Tel: 808-323-3222
http://www.jcch.com/index.html

Maui Historical Society/Library
2375 A Main Street
P.O. Box 1018
Wailuku, HI 96793
Tel: 808-244-3326
Fax: 808-242-4878
http://www.mauimuseum.org/

Polynesian Voyaging Society
Pier 7, 191 Ala Moana Blvd.
Honolulu, HI 96813
Tel: (808) 536-8405
Fax: (808) 536-1519
E-mail: pvs@lava.net
http://pvs.hawaii.org/

LDS FAMILY HISTORY CENTERS

For locations of Family History Centers in this state, see the Family History Center locator at FamilySearch: http://www.familysearch.org/eng/Library/FHC/ frameset_fhc.asp

ARCHIVES/LIBRARIES/MUSEUMS

Bishop Museum and Library/Archives
1525 Bernice Street
P.O. Box 19000-A
Honolulu, HI 96817-0916
Tel: 808-848-4147/8
808-848-4182/3
Fax: 808-841-8968
http://www.bishopmuseum.org/research/cultstud/libarch/

Brigham Young University Hawaii Campus Archives
Joseph F. Smith Library
55-220 Kulanui Street
Laie, HI 96762-1266
Tel: 808-293-3869
Fax: 808-293-3877
http://www.byuh.edu/library/

Central Union Church Archives
1660 So. Beretania St.
Honolulu, HI 96826
Tel: (808) 941-0957
Fax: (808) 941-9124

Cooke Library
Punahou School Archives
1601 Punahou Street
Honolulu, HI 96822
Tel:(808) 943-3225
Fax: (808) 944-5766
http://www.punahou.edu:591/index4.html

Daughters of Hawaii
Queen Emma's Summer Palace
2913 Pali Highway
Honolulu, HI 96817
Tel: 808-595-6291
808-595-3167
Fax: 808-595-4395
http://www.daughtersofhawaii.org/daughters/about.shtml

Episcopal Church in Hawaii
229 Queen Emma Square
Honolulu, HI 96813
Tel: 808-536-7776
FAX: 808-538-7194
http://ecusa.anglican.org/hawaii/

Hana Cultural Center & Museum
4974 Uakea Road
P.O. Box 27
Hana, HI 96713-0027
Tel: 808-248-8622
Fax: 808-248-8620
E-mail: hccm@aloha.net
http://planet-hawaii.com/hana/

Hawaii Chinese History Center
111 North King Street, Room 410
Honolulu, HI 96817
Tel: 808-521-5948

Hawaii Maritime Center Library & Photo Archives
Pier 7
Honolulu, HI 96813
Tel: 808-523-6151
808-536-6373
Fax: 808-536-1519
http://holoholo.org/maritime/

Hawaii Plantation Village
94-695 Waipahu St.
Waipahu, HI 96797
Tel: (808) 677-0110
Fax: (808) 676-6727

Hawaii State Library
478 South King Street
Honolulu, HI 96813
Tel: 808-586-3535 (Hawaii & Pacific Section)
Tel: 808-586-3499 (Language, Literature, & History Section)
http://www.hcc.hawaii.edu/hspls/hsl/hslov.html

Hawaiian Historical Society/Library
560 Kawaiahao Street
Honolulu, HI 96813
Tel/Fax: 808-537-6271
http://www.hawaiianhistory.org/lib/libmain.html

Hawaiian Mission Children's Society Library
553 South King Street
Honolulu, HI 96813-3002
Tel: 808-531-0481
Fax: 808-545-2280
http://www.lava.net/~mhm/hmcs.htm

Honolulu City and County
Municipal Reference and Records Center
City Hall Annex
558 S. King Street
Honolulu, HI 96813
Tel: (808) 523-4044
Fax: (808) 523-4985
http://www.co.honolulu.hi.us/csd/lrmb/ references.htm#records

Japanese Cultural Center of Hawaii
2454 So. Beretania St.
Honolulu, Hawaii 96826.
Tel:(808) 945-7633
Fax:(808)944-1123
http://www.jcch.com/index.html

Kauai Museum
4428 Rice Street
P.O. Box 248
Lihue, HI 96766
Tel: 808-245-6931
Fax: 808-245-6864

Kona Historical Society/Museum
Highway 11
Kealakekua, HI
Mail: P.O. Box 398
Captain Cook, HI 96704
Tel: 808-323-3222
http://www.jcch.com/index.html

Lahaina Restoration Foundation
120 Dickenson Street
Lahaina, Hawaii 96761
Phone (808) 661-3262
Fax (808) 661-9309
http://www.lahainarestoration.org/

Lyman House Memorial Museum
276 Haili Street
Hilo, HI 96720
Tel: 808-935-5021
Fax: 808-969-7685
http://www.lymanmuseum.org/

Maui Historical Society/Library
2375 A Main Street
P.O. Box 1018
Wailuku, HI 96793
Tel: 808-244-3326
Fax: 808-242-4878
http://www.mauimuseum.org/

Palama Settlement Archives
810 No. Vineyard Blvd.
Honolulu, Hawaii 96817
Tel:(808) 845-3945
Fax:(808) 847-2873

Roman Catholic Diocese of Honolulu
1184 Bishop Street
Honolulu, HI   96813
Tel: 808-533-1791
Fax: 808-521-8428

University of Hawaii at Hilo
Edwin Mookini Library
200 West Kawili Street
Hilo, HI 96720
Tel: 808-974-7346
http://library.uhh.hawaii.edu/

University of Hawaii at Manoa
Sinclair and Hamilton Libraries
2550 McCarthy Mall
Honolulu, HI 96822
Tel: 808-956-8264
Fax: 808-956-5968
http://www2.hawaii.edu/~speccoll/arch/hours.htm

NEWSPAPER REPOSITORIES

Bishop Museum and Library/Archives
1525 Bernice Street
P.O. Box 19000-A
Honolulu, HI 96817-0916
Tel: 808-848-4147/8
808-848-4182/3
 Fax: 808-841-8968
http://www.bishopmuseum.org/

Hawaii State Archives
Iolani Palace Grounds
Kekauluohi Building
King & Richards Streets
Honolulu, HI 96813
Tel: 808-586-0313
808-586-0329
Fax: 808-586-0330
http://www.hawaii.gov/dags/archives/welcome.html

Hawaiian Historical Society/Library
560 Kawaiahao Street
Honolulu, HI 96813
Tel/Fax: 808-537-6271
http://www.hawaiianhistory.org/lib/libmain.html

University of Hawaii at Manoa
University of Hawaii at Manoa
Sinclair and Hamilton Libraries
2550 McCarthy Mall
Honolulu, HI 96822
Tel: 808-956-8264
Fax: 808-956-5968
http://www2.hawaii.edu/~speccoll/
http://libweb.hawaii.edu/hnp/index.shtml

VITAL RECORDS

Hawaii State Department of Health
Issuance/Vital Statistics Section
1250 Punchbowl Street, First Floor, Room 103, (location)
P.O. Box 3378 (mail)
Honolulu, HI 96801
Tel: 808-586-4533
E-mail: mailto:vr-info@mail.health.state.hi.us
(Births, Marriages, and Deaths 1896 to present, with
    some earlier)
http://www.state.hi.us/health/records/vr_howto.html

HAWAII ON THE WEB

Hawaii GenWeb Project
http://www.rootsweb.com/~higenweb/

Hawaiian Oral Genealogies
http://home.earthlink.net/~motuahina/hawaiian_genealogy/

Pearl Harbor Casualty List
ftp://ftp.rootsweb.com/pub/usgenweb/hi/military/pearl.txt

IDAHO

ARCHIVES, STATE & NATIONAL

Idaho State Historical Library & Archives
325 W. State Street
Boise, ID 83702
Tel: 208-334-2150
Fax: 208-334-4016
http://www.lili.org/isl/

National Archives-Pacific Alaska Region (Seattle)
6125 Sand Point Way, NE
Seattle, WA 98115-7999
Tel: 206-526-6501
Fax: 206-526-6575
E-mail: seattle.archives@nara.gov
http://www.nara.gov/regional/seattle.html

GENEALOGICAL SOCIETIES

Bonner County Genealogical Society
P.O. Box 221
Kootenai ID 83840
http://www.rootsweb.com/~idbcgs/

Caldwell Genealogical Group
3504 S. Illinois Street
Caldwell, ID 83605

Friends of the Idaho Genealogical Library
9846 Westview Drive
Boise, ID 83704
E-mail: dyingst@rmci.net
http://www.rmci.net/idaho/genidaho/

Idaho Genealogical Society
P.O. Box 1854
Boise, ID 83701-1854
(208) 384-0542
http://www.lili.org/idahogenealogy/index.htm

Kamiah Genealogical Society
P.O. Box 322
Kamiah, ID 83536

Kootenai County Genealogical Society
Hayden Lake Library
8385 N. Government Way
Hayden Lake, ID 83835
http://www.rootsweb.com/~idkooten/kcgs.htm

Latah County Genealogical Society
327 E. Second Street
Moscow, ID 83843
Tel: 208-882-5943

Pocatello Branch Genealogical Society
156 South 6th Avenue
P.O. Box 4272
Pocatello, ID 83201

Shoshone County Genealogical Society
P.O. Box 182
Kellogg, ID 83837
http://www.rootsweb.com/~idshosho/scghs.htm

Snake River Genealogical Society of Southeastern Idaho
122 North Front Street
P.O. Box 30
Sugar City, ID 83448-0030
Tel: 208-356-7072

Twin Rivers Genealogical Society
P.O. Box 386
Lewiston, ID 83501

Valley County Genealogical Society
P.O. Box 111
Cascade, ID 83611-0111

HISTORICAL SOCIETIES

Adams County Historical Society
P.O. Box 352
New Meadows, ID 83654

Bannock Historical Society/Museum
Upper Level of Ross Park
3000 Alvord Loop
Pocatello, ID 83204
Tel: 208-233-0434
http://www.ohwy.com/id/b/bannochm.htm

Bonner County Historical Society/Museum
609 S. Ella Ave.
P.O. Box 1063
Sandpoint, ID 83864
Tel: 208-263-2344

Bonneville County Historical Society
Corner of Northeastern Ave and Elm
P.O. Box 1784
Idaho Falls, ID 83403
http://www.idahofallsmuseum.org/

Boundary County Historical Society/Free Museum
7229 Main Street
P.O. Box 808
Bonners Ferry, ID 83805
Tel: 208-267-7720

Camas County Historical Society
General Delivery
Fairfield, ID 83327

Canyon County Historical Society
1200 Front Street
P.O. Box 595
Nampa, ID 83651
Tel: (208) 467-7611

Caribou County Historical Society
c/o County Courthouse
Soda Springs, ID 83276

Cassia County Historical Society/Museum
E. Main Street & Hiland
P.O. Box 331
Burley, ID 83318
Tel: 208-678-7172
http://www.cassiacounty.org/
       historical-society/museum.htm

Clearwater County Historical Society/Museum
315 College Ave
P.O. Box 1454
Orofino, ID 83544
Tel: 208-476-5033
http://home.valint.net/chmuseum/

Crane Historical Society
Crane House
Main Street
P.O. Box 152
Harrison, ID 83833
Tel: 208-689-3032

Elmore County Historical Foundation
P.O. Box 204
Mountain Home, ID 83647

Fremont County Historical Society
St. Anthony, ID 83445

Gem County Historical Society
501 East 1st Street
Emmett, ID 83617
Tel: 208-365-9530 or 208-365-4340
E-mail: gemcohs@bigskytel.com
www.gemcohs.org

Gooding County Historical Society/Museum
210 Main St
P. O. Box 580
Gooding, ID 83330

The Hagerman Valley Historical Society
100 South State Street
Hagerman, ID 83332
Tel: 208-837-6288

Idaho State Historical Society
1109 Main Street, Suite 250
Boise, ID 83702-5642
Tel: 208-334-2682
Fax: 208-334-2774
http://www.state.id.us/ishs/index.htm

Ilo-Vollmer Historical Society (Lewis County)
Box 61
Craigmont, ID 83523
Tel: 208-924-5474

Jerome County Historical Society
220 North Lincoln
P.O. Box 50
Jerome, ID 83338
Tel: 208-324-5641
Fax: 208-324-7694
Http://Www.Historicaljeromecounty.Com/Index.Dsp

Latah County Historical Society
Centennial Annex
327 East 2nd St.
Moscow, ID 83843
Tel: 208-882-1004
http://users.moscow.com/lchs/

Lewis County Historical Society
Route 2 - Box 10
Kamiah, ID 83536

Minidoka County Historical Society
100 East Baseline
P.O. Box 21
Rupert, ID 83350

Nez Perce Historical Society/ Museum
 0306 Third Street
Lewiston, ID 83501
Tel: 208-743-2535
http://www.idahohighway12.com/pages/lewiston/
       npmuseumpoint.html

Old Fort Boise Historical Society
Old Fort Boise Park
Parma, ID 83660

Payette County Historical Society
90 South Ninth Street
P.O. Box 476
Payette, ID 83661
http://www.geocities.com/payettehistory/
homepage.html?1019771915660

Shoshone Genealogical and Historical Society
Box 182
Kellogg, ID 83837
http://www.rootsweb.com/~idshosho/scghs.htm

South Bannock County Historical Society/Museum
110 East Main Street
Lava Hot Springs, ID 83246
http://www.lavahotsprings.com/history.html

South Custer County Historical Society
P.O. Box 355
MacKay, ID 83251

Spirit Lake Historical Society
Spirit Lake, ID 83869

Upper Snake River Valley Historical Society/Library
51 N. Center St.
P.O. Box 244
Rexburg, ID 83440
Tel: 208- 356-9101

Wood River Historical Society
P.O. Box 552
Ketchum, ID 83340

LDS FAMILY HISTORY CENTERS

For locations of Family History Centers in this state, see
the Family History Center locator at FamilySearch:
http://www.familysearch.org/eng/Library/FHC/
frameset_fhc.asp

ARCHIVES/LIBRARIES/MUSEUMS

Aberdeen Public Library
76 E. Central Ave.
P.O. Box 207
Aberdeen, ID 83210
Tel: 208-397-4427
http://www.lili.org/aberdeen/

Ada Community Library
10664 West Victory Road
Boise, ID 83709
Tel: 208-362-0181
Fax: 208-362-0303
http://www.adalib.org/

Albertson College of Idaho
Terteling Library
College Campus
Caldwell, ID 83605
Tel: 208-459-5505
Fax: 208-459-5299
http://www.albertson.edu/library/

Appaloosa Museum & Heritage Center
2720 W Pullman Rd
Moscow, ID 83843
Tel: (208) 882-5578, ext. 279
Fax: (208) 882-8150
E-mail: museum@appaloosa.com
http://www.appaloosamuseum.org/

Bannock Historical Society/Museum
Upper Level of Ross Park
3000 Alvord Loop
Pocatello, ID 83204
Tel:208-233-0434
http://www.ohwy.com/id/b/bannochm.htm

Bicentennial Historical Museum
305 N. College Street
Rt. 2, Box 500
Grangeville, ID 83530
Tel: 208-983-2573
http://www.grangevilleidaho.com/historical_museum.htm

Bingham County Historical Museum
190 N. Shilling Ave.
Blackfoot, ID 83221
Tel: 208-785-8065
208-785-8040

Blackfoot Library
129 N. Broadway
P.O. Box 610
Blackfoot, ID 83221
Tel: 208-785-8628

Blaine County Historical Museum
N. Main Street
P.O. Box 124
Hailey, ID 83333-0124
Tel: 208-788-1801
208-788-4185

Boise Basin District Library
P.O. Box BL
404 Montgomery Street
Idaho City, ID 83631
Tel: 208-392-4558
Fax: 208-392-4974
http://boisebasin.lib.id.us/

Boise Basin Historical Museum
402 Montgomery
P.O. Box 325
Idaho City, ID 83631

Boise Basque Museum and Cultural Center
611 Grove Street
Boise, ID 83702
Tel: 208-343-2671
http://www.basquemuseum.com/

Boise Public Library
715 S. Capitol Blvd.
Boise, ID 83702
Tel: 208-384-4076
http://www.boisepubliclibrary.org/

Boise State University
Albertsons Library
1910 University Drive
P.O. Box 46
Boise, ID 83725
Tel: 208-385-1235
http://library.boisestate.edu/

Bonner County Historical Society/Museum
609 S. Ella Ave.
P.O. Box 1063
Sandpoint, ID 83864
Tel: 208-263-2344

Boundary County Historical Society/Free Museum
7229 Main Street
P.O. Box 808
Bonners Ferry, ID 83805
Tel: 208-267-7720

Boundary County Public Library
6370 Kootenai
P.O. Box Y
Bonners Ferry, ID 83805-1276
Tel: 208-267-3750

Bureau of Land Management
Information Access Center
Idaho State Office
1387 S. Vinnell Way
Boise, ID 83709
Phone: (208) 373-3889
http://www.id.blm.gov/information/data/iac.htm

Caldwell Public Library
1010 Dearborn
Caldwell, ID 83605
Tel: 208-459-3242

Canyon County Historical Museum
1200 Front Street
Nampa, ID 83651
Tel: 208-467-7611

Cascade Public Library
105 Front Street
P.O. Box 10
Cascade, ID 83611
Tel: 208-382-4757
http://www.lili.org/cascade/

Cassia County Historical Society/Museum
E. Main Street & Hiland
P.O. Box 331
Burley, ID 83318
Tel: 208-678-7172
http://www.cassiacounty.org/
            historical-society/museum.htm

Centennial Library
215 W. North Street
Grangeville, ID 83530
Tel: 208-983-0951
Fax: 208-983-2336
E-mail: info@centennial-library.org
http://www.centennial-library.org/

Clearwater County Museum
315 College Ave
P.O. Box 1454
Orofino, ID 83544
Tel: 208-476-5033
http://home.valint.net/chmuseum/

Coeur d'Alene Public Library
201 Harrison Avenue
Coeur d'Alene, ID 83814
Tel: 208-769-2315
Fax: 208-769-2381
E-mail: cdapl@dmi.net
http://www.dmi.net/cdalibrary/

Craigmont City Library
112 W. Main St.
P.O. Box 144
Craigmont, ID 83523
Tel: 208-924-5510

Crane Historical Society
Crane House
Main Street
P.O. Box 152
Harrison, ID 83833
Tel: 208-689-3032

Eagle Public Library
100 North Stierman Way
Eagle, ID 83616-5162
Tel: 208-939-6814
http://www.eaglepubliclibrary.org/

Elmore County Historical Museum
180 South, 3 East Mountain
Home, ID 83647
Tel: 208-587-6847

Garden City Library
201 East 50
Boise, ID 83714
Tel: 208-377-2180
http://www.gardencitylibrary.org/moving.htm

Garden Valley Library
342 Village Circle
Garden Valley, ID 83622
Tel: 208-462-3317
http://www.lili.org/gardenvalley/

Glenns Ferry Historical Museum
211 West Cleveland
Glenns Ferry, ID 83623
Tel: 208-366-2760

Hayden Branch, Kootenai-Shoshone Area Library
8385 N. Government Way
Hayden, ID 83835
Tel: 208-772-5612
Fax: 208-772-2498
http://www.nicon.org/ksal/hayden.htm

Horseshoe Bend Library
392 Highway 55
Horseshoe Bend, ID 83629-9701
Tel: 208-793-2460
Tel: 208-392-4550

Idaho State Historical Society
Historic Sites Office
Old Idaho Penitentiary
2445 Old Penitentiary Road
Boise, ID 83712-8254
Tel: 208-334-2844
Fax: 208-334-3225
http://www.state.id.us/ishs/index.htm

Idaho State Library
325 West State Street
Boise, ID 83702
Tel: 208-334-2150
Fax: 208-334-4016
http://www.lili.org/isl/

Idaho State Historical Museum
610 North Julia Davis Drive
Boise, ID 83702-7695
Tel: 208-334-2120
Fax: 208-334-4059
http://www.state.id.us/ishs/museum.htm

Idaho State Historical Society
Library & Archives
450 North Fourth Street
Boise, ID 83702-6027
Tel: 208-334-3356
Fax: 208-334-3198
http://www.state.id.us/ishs/library.htm

Idaho State Historical Society
Oral History Center
450 N. Fourth St.
Boise, ID 83702
Tel: 208-334-3863
Fax: 208-334-3198
http://www.state.id.us/ishs/oralhist.htm

Idaho State University
E.M. Oboler Library
850 S. Ninth Street
P.O. Box 8089
Pocatello, ID 83209-0009
Tel: 208-282-2958
Fax: 208-282-5847
http://www.isu.edu/departments/library/home.htm

Jerome County Historical Society/Museum
220 North Lincoln
P.O. Box 50
Jerome, ID 83338
Tel: 208-324-5641
Fax: 208-324-7694
http://www.historicaljeromecounty.com/index.dsp

Kamiah Library
505 Main
P.O. Box 846
Kamiah, ID 83536
Tel: 208-935-0428

Kuna Public Library
P.O. Box l29, 457 N. Locust
Kuna, ID 83634
Tel: 208-922-1025
Fax: 208-922-1026

Latah County Historical Society
Centennial Annex
327 East 2nd St.
Moscow, ID 83843
Tel: 208-882-1004
http://users.moscow.com/lchs/

Lewis-Clark State College Library
500 8th Avenue
Lewiston, ID 83501
Tel: 208-799-2397 (Collections)
208-799-2395 (Reference)
208-799-2394 (Periodicals)
Fax: 208-799-2831
http://www.lcsc.edu/Library/

Lewiston City Library
428 Thain Road
Lewiston, ID 83501-5399
Tel: 208-743-6519
http://www.cityoflewiston.org/library/

Massacre Rocks State Park
3592 N. Park Lane
American Falls, ID 83211
Tel: 208-548-2672
http://www.idahoparks.org/parks/massacre.html

McCall City Library
218 Park Street
P.O. Box 848
McCall, ID 83638-0848
Tel: 208-634-5522

McKay Library
Brigham Young University Idaho
25 South Center Street
Rexburg, ID 83460-0405
Tel: 208-496-2351
http://abish.byui.edu/SpecialCollections/

Middleton Public Library
307 E. Main
P.O. Box 519
Middleton, ID 83644
Tel: 208-585-3931

Mountain Home Public Library
790 North, 10 East
Mountain Home, ID 83647
Tel: 208-587-4716
http://www.mhlibrary.org/

Nampa Public Library
101 11th Avenue South
Nampa, ID 83651
Tel: 208-465-2263
http://www.lili.org/nampa/

Nez Perce Historical Society/Museum
0306 Third Street
Lewiston, ID 83501
Tel: 208-743-2535
http://www.idahoshighway12.com/pages/lewiston/
npmuseumpoint.html

Nez Perce National Historical Park
39063 U.S. Highway 95
Spalding, ID 83540-9715
Tel: 208-843-2261
http://www.nps.gov/nepe/

North Bingham County District Library
197 W. Locust
Shelley, ID 83274
Tel: 208-357-7801
http://www.lili.org/bingham/

North Idaho College
Molstead Library
1000 West Garden Avenue
Coeur d'Alene, ID 83814
Tel: 208-769-3355
Fax: 208-769-3428
http://www.nic.edu/library/

Our Memories Museum
1122 Main Street
Caldwell, ID 83605
Tel: 208-459-1413

Owyhee County Historical Museum
Bassey Street
P.O. Box 67
Murphy, ID 83650
Tel: 208-495-2319

Payette Public Library
24 South Tenth
Payette, ID 83661-2861
Tel: 208-642-6029
E-mail: payettelib@earthlink.net

Prairie Community Library
508 King Street
P.O. Box 65
Cottonwood, ID 83522
Tel: 208-962-3714

Rails and Trails Museum
The National Oregon/California Trail Center
P.O. Box 323
320 North 4th Street
Montpelier, ID 83254
Tel: (208) 847-3800
Fax: (208) 847-3801
http://www.oregontrailcenter.org/
siteoverview.html#anchor39486

160

St. Gertrude's Library/Museum
Hc 3 Box 121
Cottonwood, ID 83522
Tel: 208-962-7123
208-962-3224
Fax: 208-962-8647
http://www.historicalmuseumatstgertrude.com/index.html

Shoshone-Bannock Library/Museum
HRDC Building
Bannock and Pima Streets
P.O. Box 306
Fort Hall, ID 83203
Tel: 208-238-3882
208-237-9791
Fax: 208-237-0797

South Bannock County Historical Society/Museum
110 East Main Street
Lava Hot Springs, ID 83246
http://www.lavahotsprings.com/history.html

Three Island Crossing State Park
P.O. Box 609
Glenns Ferry, ID 83623
http://www.idahoparks.org/parks/threeisland.html

University of Idaho Library
Special Collections and Archives
Moscow, ID 83844-2351
Tel: 208-885-7951
http://www.lib.uidaho.edu/special-collections/

Upper Snake River Valley Historical Society/Library
51 N. Center St.
P.O. Box 244
Rexburg, ID 83440

Wilder Public Library
207 A Avenue
P.O. Box 128
Wilder, ID 83676-0128
Tel: 208-482-7880

Newspaper Repositories

Boundary County Public Library
6370 Kootenai
P.O. Box Y
Bonners Ferry, ID 83805-1276
Tel: 208-267-3750

Idaho Historical Society
Idaho State Historical Library & Archives Bldg.
325 W. State Street
Boise, ID 83702
Mail: Idaho State Historical Library & Archives
450 North 4th Street
Boise, ID 83702
Tel: 208-334-3356/7
http://www.rmci.net/idaho/genidaho/contents.htm

Idaho State Library
325 West State Street
Boise, ID 83702
Tel: 208-334-2150
Fax: 208-334-4016
http://www.lili.org/isl/

Lewis-Clark State College Library
500 8th Avenue
Lewiston, ID 83501
Tel: 208-799-2397 (Collections)
208-799-2395 (Reference)
208-799-2394 (Periodicals)
Fax: 208-799-2831
http://www.lcsc.edu/Library/

Payette Public Library
24 South Tenth
Payette, ID 83661-2861
Tel: 208-642-6029
E-mail: payettelib@earthlink.net

Vital Records

Vital Statistics Unit
Department of Health & Welfare
450 West State Street, 1st Floor
P.O. Box 83720
Boise, ID 83720-0036
Tel: 208-334-5980
(Births & Deaths since 1911, Marriages since 1947)
http://www2.state.id.us/dhw/

Idaho on the Web

Genealogical Records in Idaho
http://www.lib.uidaho.edu/special-
collections/genealgl.htm

Genealogy Idaho
http://home.rmci.net/dyingst/index.htm

Historical Archive Collection of Nez Perce People
http://www.nezperce.com/npeindex.html

Idaho GenWeb Project
http://www.rootsweb.com/~idgenweb/

ILLINOIS

ARCHIVES, STATE & NATIONAL

Illinois State Archives
Reference Unit
Margaret Cross Norton Building
Capitol Complex
Springfield, IL 62756
Tel: 217-782-3556
Fax: 217-524-3930
http://www.cyberdriveillinois.com/departments/
archives/serv_sta.html

National Archives-Great Lakes Region
7358 Pulaski Road
Chicago, IL 60629
Tel: 773-581-7816
Fax: 312-886-7883
E-mail: chicago.archives@nara.gov
http://www.nara.gov/regional/chicago.html

Illinois Regional Archives Depository (IRAD)
Illinois State Archives
Reference Unit
Margaret Cross Norton Building
Capitol Complex
Springfield, IL 62756
Tel: 217-785-1266
Fax: 217-524-3930
http://www.cyberdriveillinois.com/departments/
archives/irad/iradhome.html

Eastern Illinois University
Booth Library
600 Lincoln Avenue
Charleston, IL 61920
Tel: 217-581-6093
http://www.eiu.edu/~booth/
Serves the following counties: Clark, Clay, Coles,
Crawford, Cumberland, Douglas, Edgar, Edwards,
Effingham, Jasper, Lawrence, Moultrie, Richland,
Shelby, Wabash, Wayne.

Illinois State University
Williams Hall
Campus Box 5500
Normal, IL 61790-5500
Tel: 309-452-6027
Serves the following counties: Champaign, DeWitt, Ford,
Grundy, Iroquois, Kankakee, Livingston, Logan,
Marshall, McLean, Piatt, Tazewell, Vermilion,
Woodford.

Northeastern Illinois University
Ronald Williams Library
5500 N. St. Louis Avenue
Chicago, IL 60625-4699
Tel: 773-442-4506
http://www.neiu.edu/~neiulib/
Serves Cook County.

Northern Illinois University
Swen Parson Hall, Room 155
DeKalb, IL 60115
Tel: 815-753-1807
Serves the following counties: Boone, Bureau, Carroll,
DeKalb, DuPage, Jo Daviess, Kane, Kendall, Lake,
LaSalle, Lee, McHenry, Ogle, Putnam, Stephenson,
Whiteside, Will, Winnebago.

Southern Illinois University
Morris Library
Special Collections
Carbondale, IL 62901-6632
Tel: 618-453-3040
http://www.lib.siu.edu/
Serves the following counties: Alexander, Clinton,
Franklin, Gallatin, Hamilton, Hardin, Jackson,
Jefferson, Johnson, Madison, Marion, Massac,
Monroe, Perry, Pope, Pulaski, Randolph, St. Clair,
Saline, Union, Washington, White, Williamson.

University of Illinois at Springfield
Brookens Library
P.O. Box 19243
Springfield, IL 62794
Tel: 217- 206-6520
Fax: 217-786-6633
http://www.uis.edu/library/lib-arch/
Serves the following counties: Bond, Cass, Christian,
Fayette, Greene, Jersey, Macon, Macoupin, Mason,
Menard, Montgomery, Morgan, Sangamon, Scott.

Western Illinois University
University Library
Archives & Special Collections
1 University Circle
Macomb, IL 61455
Tel: 309-298-2717/8
E-mail: mfgrl@WIU.edu
http://www.wiu.edu/library/
Serves the following counties: Adams, Brown, Calhoun,
Fulton, Hancock, Henderson, Henry, Knox,
McDonough, Mercer, Peoria, Pike, Rock Island,
Schuyler, Stark, Warren.

GENEALOGICAL SOCIETIES

African-American Cultural & Genealogical Society
314 North Main Street
P.O. Box 25251
Decatur, IL 62525
Tel: 217-429-7458
http://www.decaturnet.org/afrigenes.html

African-American Genealogical and Historical Society (AAHGS)
Little Egypt
207 Lendview Drive
Carbondale, IL 62901

African-American Genealogical and Historical Society (AAHGS)
Patricia Liddell Researchers
P. O. Box 438652
Chicago, Il 60643
E-mail: sirqulate@aol.com

Bishop Hill Old Settlers Association
Descendants of the Bishop Hill Colonists
Box 68 Bishop
Hill, IL 61419

Blackhawk Genealogical Society
P.O. Box 3912
Rock Island, IL 61204-3912
http://www.rootsweb.com/~ilbgsrim/

Bond County Genealogical Society
P.O. Box 172
Greenville, IL 62246
http://www.greenville-chamber.com/bcgs/

Bureau County Genealogical Society
P.O. Box 402
Princeton, IL 61356-0402
http://www.rootsweb.com/~ilbcgs/

Carroll County Genealogical Society
P.O. Box 354
Savanna, IL 61074
E-mail: kcebrunner@essex1.com
        gmarken@internetni.com
http://homepages.rootsweb.com/~haliotis/

Cass County Historical & Genealogical Society
P.O. Box 11
Virginia, IL 62691
http://www.rootsweb.com/~ilcchgs/

Champaign County Genealogical Society
Champaign County Historical Archives
201 South Race Street
Urbana, IL 61801-3235
http://www.rootsweb.com/~ilccgs/

Chicago Genealogical Society
P.O. Box 1160
Chicago, IL 60690-1160
Tel: 773-725-1306
773-834-7491 (library)
http://www.chgogs.org/

Christian County Genealogical Society
P.O. Box 28
Taylorville, IL 62568-0028
http://homepage.macomb.com/~tkuntz/christianco.htm

Clark County Genealogical Society
309 Maple Street
P.O. Box 153
Marshall, IL 62441

Clay County Genealogical Society
P.O. Box 94
Louisville, Il 62858
http://www.rootsweb.com/~ilclay/ccgs.htm

Coles County Genealogical Society
P.O. Box 592
Charleston, IL 61920-0592
http://www.rootsweb.com/~iltccgs/

Council of Northeastern Illinois Genealogical Societies
820 Lisdowney Dr.
Lockport, IL 60441

Crawford County Genealogical Society
P.O. Box 120
Robinson, IL 62454

Cumberland County Genealogical Society
P.O. Box 393
Greenup, IL 62428

Czech & Slovak American Genealogy Society of Illinois
P.O. Box 313
Sugar Grove, IL 60554
http://www.csagsi.org/

Decatur Genealogical Society/Library
356 North Main Street
P.O. Box 1548
Decatur, IL 62525-1548
Tel: 217-429-0135
E-mail: DecaturGenealogicalSociety@msn.com
http://www.rootsweb.com/~ildecgs/

DeKalb County Historical-Genealogical Society
P.O. Box 295
Sycamore, IL 60178-0295

Des Plaines Genealogical Questors
Des Plaines Historical Society
789 Pearson
Des Plaines, IL 60016-4506
Tel: 847-391-5399

DeWitt County Genealogical Society
P.O. Box 632
Clinton, IL 61727

Douglas County Genealogical Society
P.O. Box 113
Tuscola, IL 61953

Dunton Genealogical Society
Arlington Hieghts Memorial Library
500 North Dunton
Arlington Heights, IL 60004-5966
Tel: 847-392-0100

DuPage County, Illinois, Genealogical Society
P.O. Box 3
Wheaton, IL 60189-0003
http://www.dcgs.org/

Edgar County Genealogical Society
408 N. Main
P.O. Box 304
Paris, IL 61944-0304
Tel: 217-463-4209

Effingham County Genealogical Society
P.O. Box 1166
Effingham, IL 62401

Elgin Genealogical Society
P.O. Box 1418
Elgin, IL 60121-1418
E-mail: jvandusn@foxvalley.net
http://nsn.nslsilus.org/elghome/egs/

Elmhurst, Genealogical Forum of
120 East Park Avenue
Elmhurst, IL 60126
E-mail: FORUM@nsn.org
http://www.elmhurstexpress.com/FORUM/

Farmer City Genealogical & Historical Society
P.O. Box 173
Farmer City, IL 61842

Fayette County Genealogical Society
P.O. Box 177
Vandalia, IL 62471

Fox Valley Genealogical Society
705 North Brainerd St.
P.O. Box 5435
Naperville, IL 60567-5435
E-mail: fvgs1@aol.com
http://members.aol.com/fvgs1/

Frankfort Area Genealogical Society
P.O. Box 427
West Frankfort, IL 62896-0427

Franklin County Genealogical Society
P.O. Box 524
West Frankfort, IL 62896

Freeburg Genealogical & Historical Society
P.O. Box 69
Freeburg, IL 62243

Fulton County Historical & Genealogical Society
45 North Park Drive
P.O. Box 583
Canton, IL 61520

Grayslake Genealogical Society
Grayslake Historical Municipal Museum
164 Hauley Street
P.O. Box 185
Grayslake, IL 60030-0185
Tel: 847-223-7663

Great River Genealogical Society
Quincy Public Library
526 Jersey Street
Quincy, IL 62301-3996
E-mail: jeankay@adams.net
http://www.outfitters.com/~grgs/

Green Hills Genealogical Society
Green Hills Library
8611 West 103rd Street
Palos Hills, IL 60465
Tel: 708-598-8446 (Library)
Fax: 708-598-0856
http://www.greenhills.lib.il.us/

Greene County Genealogical & Historical Society
P.O. Box 137
Carrollton, IL 62016
http://www.rootsweb.com/~ilgreene/gcgs.htm

Griggsville Area Genealogical & Historical Society
P.O. Box 75
Griggsville, IL 62340

Hancock County Genealogical & Historical Society
P.O. Box 68
Carthage, IL 62321

Hardin County Historical & Genealogical Society
P.O. Box 72
Elizabethtown, IL 62931

Henry County Genealogical Society
P.O. Box 346
Kewanee, IL 61443
http://www.rootsweb.com/~ilhcgs/

Henry Historical & Genealogical Society
610 North Street
Henry, IL 61537

Illiana Genealogical & Historical Society
215 West North Street
P.O. Box 207
Danville, IL 61834-0207
E-mail: ighs@danville.net
http://www.danvillevirtual.com/vcclients/danville/
IllianaGene/

Illinois Mennonite Historical & Genealogical Society
P.O. Box 819
Metamora, IL 61548

Illinois State Genealogical Society
P.O. Box 10195
Springfield, IL 62791-0195
http://www.rootsweb.com/~ilsgs/

Iroquois County Genealogical Society
Old Courthouse
103 West Cherry Street
Watseka, IL 60970
Tel: 815-432-3730
E-mail: iroqgene@techinter.com
http://www.rootsweb.com/~ilicgs/

Jacksonville Area Genealogical & Historical Society
416 S. Main Street
Jacksonville, IL 62650-2904
Tel: 217-245-5911
217-245-9623
E-mail: jaghs@csj.net
http://www.japl.lib.il.us/community/clubs/jaghs/

Jasper County Genealogical & Historical Society
Newton Public Library
100 South Van Buren
Newton, IL 62448

Jefferson County Genealogical Society
C.E. Brehm Memorial Library
101 South Seventh Street
Mt. Vernon, IL 62864-4187

Jersey County Genealogical Society
P.O. Box 12
Jerseyville, IL 62052

Jewish Genealogical Society of Illinois
P.O. Box 515
Northbrook, IL 60065-0515
Tel: 847-657-7576
E-mail: jrfraz@core.com
http://www.jewishgen.org/jgsi/

Jewish Genealogical Society, South Suburban Branch
3416 Ithaca
Olympia Fields, IL 60461

Kane County Genealogical Society
P.O. Box 504
Geneva, IL 60134-0504
E-mail: bowl12x@aol.com
http://www.rootsweb.com/~ilkcgs/

Kankakee Valley Genealogical Society
P.O. Box 442
Bourbonnais, IL 60914-0442
http://www.kvgs.org/

Kendall County Genealogical Society
P.O. Box 123
Yorkville, IL 60560-0123

Knox County Genealogical Society
P.O. Box 13
Galesburg, IL 61401-0013

LaHarpe Historical & Genealogical Society
P.O. Box 289
LaHarpe, IL 61450
http://www.outfitters.com/illinois/hancock/laharpe/ lhgs/

Lake County, Illinois, Genealogical Society
P.O. Box 721
Libertyville, IL 60048-0721
http://www.rootsweb.com/~illcgs/

LaSalle County Genealogical Guild
115 West Glover Street
Ottawa, IL 61350
Tel: 815-433-5261

Lawrence County Genealogical Society
RR 1, Box 44
Bridgeport, IL 62417

Lee County Genealogical Society
213 South Peoria Avenue
Dixon, IL 61021-0063
Tel: 815-288-6702
E-mail: bucaneer@essex1.com
http://www.rootsweb.com/~illee/

Lexington Genealogical & Historical Society
318 W. Main Street
Lexington, IL 61753

Lithuanian American Genealogical Society
Balzekas Museum of Lithuanian Culture
6500 South Pulaski Road
Chicago, IL 60629-5136
Tel: 773-582-6500
http://feefhs.org/baltic/lt/frg-lags.html

Logan County Genealogical & Historical Society
P.O. Box 283
Lincoln, IL 62656
http://www.rootsweb.com/~illogan/logangh.htm

Macoupin County Genealogical Society
P.O. Box 95
Staunton, IL 62088-0095
E-mail: smckenzi@midwest.net
http://www.rootsweb.com/~ilmacoup/m_gensoc.htm

Madison County Genealogical Society
P.O. Box 631
Edwardsville, IL 62025
Tel: 618-692-7556
http://library.wustl.edu/~spec/archives/aslaa/
        madison-genealogy.html

Marion County Genealogical & Historical Society
217 W Main Street
P.O. Box 342
Salem, IL 62881

Marissa Genealogical & Historical Society
P.O. Box 47
Marissa, IL 62257-0047
Tel: 618-295-2562

Mason County Genealogical & Historical Society
P.O. Box 446
Havana, IL 62644
http://www.havana.lib.il.us/community/mcghs.html

Massac County Genealogical Society
P.O. Box 1043
Metropolis, IL 62960
E-mail: mcgscontact@earthlink.net
http://www.rootsweb.com/~ilmcgs/

McDonough County Genealogical Society
P.O. Box 202
Macomb, IL 61455
http://www.macomb.com/mcgs/

McHenry County, Illinois, Genealogical Society
P.O. Box 184
Crystal Lake, IL 60039-0184

McLean County Genealogical Society
P.O. Box 488
Normal, IL 61761-0488

Mercer County Genealogical & Historical Society
RR 2
Aledo, IL 61231

Meredosia Area Historical & Genealogical Society
P.O. Box 304
Meredosia, IL 62665

Montgomery County Genealogical Society
P.O. Box 212
Litchfield, IL 62056

Morgan Area Genealogical Association
P.O. Box 84
Jacksonville, IL 62651-0084
http://www.rootsweb.com/~ilmorgan/maga.html

Moultrie County Genealogical & Historical Society
P.O. Box MM
Sullivan, IL 61951

Mt. Vernon Genealogical Society
Mt. Vernon Public Library
101 South Seventh Street
Mt. Vernon, IL 62864

North Central Illinois Genealogical Society
P.O. Box 4635
Rockford, IL 61110-4635
http://www.rootsweb.com/~ilwinneb/ncengen.htm

North Suburban Genealogical Society
Winnetka Public Library
768 Oak Street
Winnetka, IL 60093-2583
Tel: 847-446-7220
http://www.wpld.alibrary.com/nsgs.htm

Northern Will County Genealogical Society
603 Derbyshire Lane
Bolingbrook, IL 60439

Northwest Suburban Council of Genealogists
P.O. Box AC
Mt. Prospect, IL 60056-9019
http://www.mtprospect.org/nsgs/

Odell Prairie Trails Historical & Genealogical Society
P.O. Box 82
Odell, IL 60460

Ogle County Genealogical Society
P.O. Box 251
Oregon, IL 61061

Palatines to America, Illinois Chapter
P.O. Box 9638
Peoria, IL 61612-9368
Tel: 309-691-0292

Peoria Genealogical Society
P.O. Box 1489
Peoria, IL 61655

Piatt County Genealogical & Historical Society
P.O. Box 111
Monticello, IL 61856
http://www.monticello.net/html/genealogy.html

Pike/Calhoun Counties Genealogical Society
P.O. Box 104
Pleasant Hill, IL 62366

Polish Genealogical Society of America
984 North Milwaukee Avenue
Chicago, IL 60622
Tel: 773-384-3352
E-mail: PGSAmerica@aol.com
http://www.pgsa.org

Poplar Creek Genealogical Society
200 Kosan Circle
Streamwood, IL 60103

Randolph County Genealogical Society/Library
600 State Street, Suite 306
Chester, IL 62233
Tel: 618-826-3807
E-mail: vlchas@mindspring.com
http://www.rootsweb.com/~ilrcgs/

Richland County Genealogical & Historical Society
P.O. Box 202
Olney, IL 62450

St. Clair County Genealogical Society
P.O. Box 431
Belleville, IL 62222
http://www.compu-type.net/rengen/stclair/ stchome.htm

Saline County Genealogical Society
P.O. Box 4
Harrisburg, IL 62946

Sangamon County Genealogical Society
P.O. Box 1829
Springfield, IL 62705

Schaumburg Genealogical Society
Schaumburg Public Library
32 West Library
Lane Schaumburg, IL 60194

Schuyler-Brown Genealogical & Historical Society
Schuyler Jail Museum
200 South Congress
Rushville, IL 62681

Shelby County Genealogical & Historical Society
South First and South Washington Streets
Shelbyville, IL 62565
E-mail: shgensoc@bmmhnet.com
http://www.shelbycohistgen.org/

Sons of the American Revolution
State of Illinois
http://www.execpc.com/~sril/

South Suburban Genealogical and Historical Society
320 East 161st Place
P.O. Box 96
South Holland, IL 60473-0096
Tel: 708-333-9474
http://www.rootsweb.com/~ssghs/

Southern Illinois, Genealogy Society of
John A. Logan College
700 Logan College Road
Carterville, IL 62918-9599
http://www.jal.cc.il.us/Gssi_org.html

Stark County Genealogical Society
P.O. Box 83
Toulon, IL 61483-0083
http://www.rootsweb.com/~ilscgs/

Stephenson County Genealogical Society
P.O. Box 514
Freeport, IL 61032-0514
E-mail: stephcogensoc@yahoo.com
http://www.rootsweb.com/~ilstephe/
    HISTORYand MUSEUMS/GenSociety.html

Tazewell County Genealogical & Historical Society
Ehrlicher Research Center
719 N. Eleventh Street
P.O. Box 312
Pekin, IL 61555-0312
Tel: 309-477-3044
http://www.rootsweb.com/~iltcghs/

Tinley Moraine Genealogical Society
P.O. Box 521
Tinley Park, IL 60477-0521

Tri-State Genealogical Society
Willard Library
21 First Avenue
Evansville, IN 47710
Tel: 812-425-4309
E-mail: mylines@evansville.net
http://www.rootsweb.com/~intsgs/

Union County Genealogical & Historical Society
101 East Spring Street
Anna, IL 62906

Versailles Area Genealogical & Historical Society
P.O. Box 92
Versailles, IL 62378

Warren County Genealogy Society
Genealogy Room
58 Public Square
P.O. Box 761
Monmouth, IL 61462-0761
http://www.maplecity.com/~wcpl/genhome.html

Waverly Genealogical & Historical Society
157 E. Tremont
Waverly, IL 62692

Western Springs Genealogical Society
Western Springs Historical Society
916 Hillgrove Avenue
4211 Grand Avenue
P.O. Box 139
Western Springs, IL 60558-0139
Tel: 708-246-9230

Whiteside County Genealogists
P.O. Box 145
Sterling, IL 61081
http://www.serve.com/bmosher/WSCGen/ wscgen.htm

Will/Grundy Counties Genealogical Society
P.O. Box 24
Wilmington, IL 60481-0024

Winnebago/Boone Counties Genealogical Society
P.O. Box 10166
Rockford, IL 61131-0166

Zion Genealogical Society
Zion Benton Public Library
2400 Gabriel Avenue
Zion, IL 60099-2296
http://wkkhome.northstarnet.org/zion/

Historical Societies

Adams and Quincy County Historical Society
425 South 12th
Quincy, IL 62301
Tel: 217-222-1835
http://library.wustl.edu/units/spec/archives/aslaa/
    directory/quincy.html

African-American Genealogical and Historical Society (AAHGS)
Little Egypt
207 Lendview Drive
Carbondale, IL 62901

African-American Genealogical and Historical Society (AAHGS)
Patricia Liddell Researchers
P. O. Box 438652
Chicago, IL 60643
E-mail: sirqulate@aol.com

American Historical Society of Germans from Russia (AHSGR)
Northern Illinois Chapter
208 Cold Spring Ct.
Palatine, IL 60067
E-mail: Cgorr@aol.com
http://www.ahsgr.org/ilnorthe.html

Arlington Heights, Historical Society of
Arlington Heights Museum
110 West Fremont
Arlington Heights, IL 60004-5912
Tel: 847-255-1225
http://www.ahmuseum.org/

Barrington Area Historical Society
212-218 West Main Street
Barrington, IL 60010
Tel: 847-381-1730
http://bakhome.northstarnet.org/BHS/

Bartlett Historical Society
128 S. Main Street, Village Hall
P.O. Box 8257
Bartlett, IL 60103-8257
Tel: 630-837-0800

Berwyn Historical Society
P.O. Box 479
Berwyn, IL 60402-0479
Tel: 708-484-0020

Blue Island Historical Society
Blue Island Public Library
2433 York Street
Blue Island, IL 60406-2094
Tel: 708-371-8546; 708-388-1078 (Library)
http://www.blueisland.org/Historical.html

Bureau County Historical Society/Library & Museum
109 Park Avenue West
Princeton, IL 61356
Tel: 815-875-2184

Calumet City Historical Society
760 Wentworth Avenue
Calumet City, IL 60409
Tel: 708-832-9390
http://www.thetimesonline.com/org/cchs/

Chicago & East Illinois Railroad Historical Society
P.O. Box 606
Crestwood, IL 60445-0606
http://cei.justnet.com/

Chicago & Northwestern Railroad Historical Society
P.O. Box 1436
Elhurst, IL 60126-9998
E-mail: cnwhs@cnwhs.org
http://www.cnwhs.org/

Chicago Heights Historical Society
25 West 15th Street & Chicago Road
Chicago Heights, IL 60411
Tel: 708-754-0323

Chicago Historical Society
Clark Street at North Avenue
Chicago, IL 60614-6099
Tel: 312-642-4600
Fax: 312-266-2077
E-mail: info@chicagohistory.org
http://www.chicagohs.org/

Chicago Jewish Historical Society
618 South Michigan Avenue
Chicago, IL 60605
Tel: 312-580-2020

Cicero, Historical Society of
2423 South Austin Boulevard
Cicero, IL 60650-2695
Tel: 708-652-8305

Clinton County Historical Society
1091 Franklin Street
Carlyle, IL 62231

Croatian Ethnic Institute
4851 South Drexel Blvd.
Chicago, IL 60615
Tel: 773-373-4670
Fax 773-373-4746
E-mail: croetljubo@aol.com
http://www.croatian-institute.org/

Cumberland County Historical Society
RR 2, Box 39
Greenup, IL 62428

DeKalb County Historical-Genealogical Society
P.O. Box 295
Sycamore, IL 60178-0295

Des Plaines Historical Society/Museum/Library
789 Pearson
Des Plaines, IL 60016-4506
Tel: 847-391-5399
http://www.northstarnet.org/dpkhome/DPHS/

East Side Historical Society
3658 East 106th Street
Chicago, IL 60617-6611
Tel: 773-721-7948

Edgewater Historical Society
5358 N. Ashland Avenue
Chicago, IL 60660-4410
Tel: 773-334-5609
E-mail: Info@EdgewaterHistory.org
http://www.edgewaterhistory.org/

Elk Grove Historical Society
399 Biesterfield Road
Elk Grove, IL 60007-3625
Tel: 847-439-3994
http://www.elkgrove.org/heritage/About.htm

Elmwood Park, Historical Society of
Elmwood Park Library
1 Conti Parkway
Elmwood Park, IL 60707
Tel: 708-453-7645
Fax: 708-453-4671
E-mail: eps@sls.lib.il.us
http://www.epcusd.w-cook.k12.il.us/eppl/

Evanston Historical Society/Museum & Library
225 Greenwood Street
Evanston, IL 60201-4713
Tel: 847-475-3410
Fax: 847-475-3599
http://www.evanstonhistorical.org/

Farmer City Genealogical & Historical Society
P.O. Box 173
Farmer City, IL 61842

Filipino-American Historical Society
5462 S. Dorchester Avenue
Chicago, IL 60615-5309
Tel: 312-752-2156

Flagg Creek Historical Society
502 Chicago Road
P.O. Box 254
Newark, IL 60541-0254

Forest Park, Historical Society of
400 Lakewood Boulevard
Park Forest, IL 60466
Tel: 708-748-3731
http://www.lincolnnet.net/users/lrpfhs/

Freeburg Genealogical & Historical Society
P.O. Box 69
Freeburg, IL 62243

Fulton County Historical & Genealogical Society
45 North Park Drive
P.O. Box 583
Canton, IL 61520

Glencoe Historical Society
999 Green Bay Road
Glencoe, IL 60022-1263
http://www.glencoevillage.org/GCKHisS.html

Glenview Area Historical Society
1121 Waukegan Road
Glenview, IL 60025-3036
Tel: 847-724-2235

Greene County Genealogical & Historical Society
P.O. Box 137
Carrollton, IL 62016
http://www.rootsweb.com/~ilgreene/gcgs.htm

Griggsville Area Genealogical & Historical Society
P.O. Box 75
Griggsville, IL 62340

Grove Heritage Association
P.O. Box 484
Glenview, IL 60025-0484
Tel: 847-299-6096

Hancock County Genealogical & Historical Society
P.O. Box 68
Carthage, IL 62321

Hardin County Historical & Genealogical Society
P.O. Box 72
Elizabethtown, IL 62931

Henry Historical & Genealogical Society
610 North Street
Henry, IL 61537

Historic Pullman Foundation, Inc.
11111 S. Forrestville Avenue
Chicago, IL 60628-4649
Tel: 773-785-8181

Homewood Historical Society
2035 West 183rd Street
P.O. Box 1144
Homewood, IL 60430
Tel: 708-799-1896
http://home.nyc.rr.com/johnmiller/hmwd.html

Hyde Park Historical Society
5529 South Lake Park
Chicago, IL 60637-1916
Tel: 773-493-1893
E-mail: alice@hydeparkhistory.orgu
http://www.HydeParkHistory.org/

Illiana Genealogical & Historical Society/Library
215 West North Street
P.O. Box 207
Danville, IL 61834-0207
E-mail: ighs@danville.net
http://www.danvillevirtual.com/vcclients/danville/
    IllianaGene/

Illinois Heritage Association
602 1/2 East Green Street
Champaign, IL 61820
Tel: 217-359-5600
E-mail: plmxiha@prairienet.org
http://www.prairienet.org/iha/

Illinois Mennonite Historical & Genealogical Society
P.O. Box 819
Metamora, IL 61548

Illinois State Historical Society
210 South Sixth Street, Suite 210
Springfield, IL 62701-1507
Tel: 217-782-2635
217-782-4286
Fax: 217-524-8042
E-mail: ishs@eosinc.com
http://www.historyillinois.org/

Illinois Labor History Society
28 East Jackson Blvd.
Chicago, IL 60604-2215
Tel: 312-663-4107
http://www.kentlaw.edu/ilhs/

Illinois Postal History Society
P.O. Box 546
Wilmette, IL 60091

Irving Park Historical Society
4122 North Kedvale
Chicago, IL 60641-2245

Jackson County Historical Society
1616 Edith Sreet
P.O. Box 7
Murphysboro, IL 62956
http://www.iltrails.org/jackson/jchs.htm

Jacksonville Area Genealogical & Historical Society
416 S. Main Street
Jacksonville IL 62650-2904
Tel: 217-245-5911
217-245-9623
E-mail: jaghs@csj.net
http://www.japl.lib.il.us/community/clubs/jaghs/

Jasper County Genealogical & Historical Society
Newton Public Library
100 South Van Buren
Newton, IL 62448

LaGrange Area Historical Society
444 South LaGrange Road
LaGrange, IL 60525-2448
Tel: 708-482-4248

LaHarpe Historical & Genealogical Society
P.O. Box 289
LaHarpe, IL 61450
http://www.outfitters.com/illinois/hancock/laharpe/ lhgs/

Lansing Historical Society
2750 Indiana Avenue
P.O. Box 1776
Lansing, IL 60438-0633
Tel: 708-474-6160

Lemont Area Historical Society/Museum
306 Lemont Street
P.O. Box 126
Lemont, IL 60439-0126
Tel: 630-257-2972
http://www.township.com/lemont/historical/

Lexington Genealogical & Historical Society
318 W. Main Street
Lexington, IL 61753

Leyden Historical Society
P.O. Box 506
Franklin Park, IL 60131

Logan County Genealogical & Historical Society
P.O. Box 283
Lincoln, IL 62656
http://www.rootsweb.com/~illogan/logangh.htm

Lyons Historical Commission
7801 West Ogden Avenue
Lyons, IL 60534
Tel: 708-447-8886
http://www.northstarnet.org/lyshome/hoffman/

Macoupin County Historical Society/Library & Museum
920 West Breckenridge Street
P.O. Box 432
Carlinville, IL 62626
Tel: 217-854-2850

Maine West Historical Society
Maine West High School
1755 S. Wolf Road
Des Plaines, IL 60018-1994
Tel: 847-827-6176

Marissa Genealogical & Historical Society
P.O. Box 47
Marissa, IL 62257-0047
Tel: 618-295-2562

Marshall County Historical Society
314 Fifth Street
P.O. Box 123
Lacon, IL 61540-0123
http://www.rootsweb.com/~ilmarsha/mphs.htm

Mason County Genealogical & Historical Society
P.O. Box 446
Havana, IL 62644
http://www.havana.lib.il.us/community/mcghs.html

Matteson Historical Society/Museum
813 School Avenue
Matteson, IL 60443
Tel: 708-748-3033

Maywood Historical Society
202 South 2nd Avenue
Maywood, IL 60153-2304
Tel: 708-344-4282

McLean County Historical Society
Old Courthouse Museum
200 N. Main Street
Bloomington, IL 61701
Tel: 309-827-0428
Fax: 309-827-0100
http://www.mchistory.org/

Melrose Park Historical Society
P.O. Box 1453
Melrose Park, IL 60160

Mercer County Genealogical & Historical Society
RR 2
Aledo, IL 61231

Meredosia Area Historical & Genealogical Society
P.O. Box 304
Meredosia, IL 62665

Midlothian Historical Society
14609 Springfield
Midlothian, IL 60445
Tel: 708-389-0200

Morton Grove Historical Society/Museum
Haupt-Yehl House
Harrer Park
6240 Dempster Street
P.O. Box 542
Morton Grove, IL 60053-2946
Tel: 847-965-1200
847-965-0203 (Museum)
http://mgkhome.northstarnet.org/parkdist/html/
    historical.html

Moultrie County Genealogical & Historical Society
P.O. Box MM
Sullivan, IL 61951

Mt. Greenwood Historical Society
Mt. Greenwood Public Library
11010 South Kedzie
Avenue Chicago, IL 60655-2222

Mt. Prospect Historical Society/Museum
101 South Maple Street
P.O. Box 81
Mt. Prospect, IL 60056-0081
Tel: 847-392-9006
Fax: 847-392-8995
E-mail: mphist@aol.com
http://www.mphist.org/mphshome.htm

National Baha'i Archives
1233 Central Street
Evanston, IL 60201
Tel: 847-869-9039

National Railway Historical Society
Chicago Chapter
P.O. Box 53
Oak Park, IL 60303-0053
Tel: 708-579-1905
Fax: 708-354-1753
http://www.chicagonrhs.com/

Neponset Township Historical Society/Museum
Neponset, IL 61345
Tel: 309-594-2197

North Eastern Illinois Historical Council
7007 Fargo Avenue
Niles, IL 60714-3719

Northbrook Historical Society
1776 Walters Avenue
P.O. Box 2021
Northbrook, IL 60065
E-mail: nbhsoc@nsn.org
http://www.northstarnet.org/nbkhome/nbhsoc/

Norwood Park Historical Society
5624 North Newark Avenue
Chicago, IL 60631-3137
Tel: 773-631-4633

Oak Forest Historical Society
15440 South Central Avenue
Oak Forest, IL 60452-2104
Tel: 708-687-4050

Oak Lawn Historical Society
9526 South Cook Avenue
Oak Lawn, IL 60453
Mail:
4332 West 109th Street
Oak Lawn, IL 60453

Oak Park and River Forest,
Historical Society/Museum of
217 Home
P.O. Box 771
Oak Park, IL 60303-0771
Tel: 708-848-6755
E-mail: flipo@enteract.com
http://www.oprf.com/oprfhist/

Odell Prairie Trails Historical
& Genealogical Society
P.O. Box 82
Odell, IL 60460

O'Fallon Historical Society/Museum
101 West State Street
P.O. Box 344
O'Fallon, IL 62269
Tel: 618-624-8409
E-mail: ohs@ofallonhistory.org
http://www.ofallonhistory.org/

Old Edgebrook Historical Society
6173 North McClellan
Chicago, IL 60646-4013

Orland Historical Society
14228 Union Avenue
Orland Park, IL 60462-2011

Palatine Historical Society
224 E Palatine Road
P.O. Box 134
Palatine, IL 60078-0134
Tel: 847-991-6460

Palos Heights Historical Society
7607 College Drive
Palos Heights, IL 60463

Palos Historical Society
12332 Forest Glen Boulevard
Palos Park, IL 60464-1707

Park Forest Historical Society
400 Lakewood Blvd.
Park Forest, IL 60466-1684
Tel: 708-748-3731

Park Ridge Historical Society
41 West Prairie Avenue
Park Ridge, IL 60068

Perry County Historical Society
Perry County Jail Museum
108 W. Jackson Street
Pinckneyville, IL 62274
Tel: 618-357-2225
http://www.fnbpville.com/perrycounty.html

Piatt County Genealogical & Historical Society
P.O. Box 111
Monticello, IL 61856
http://www.monticello.net/html/genealogy.html

Putnam County Historical Society
P.O. Box 74
Hennepin, IL 61327
http://www.rootsweb.com/~ilputnam/pchs.htm

Ravenswood-Lakeview Historical Society
4455 N. Lincoln Avenue
Chicago, IL 60625-2192

Richland County Genealogical & Historical Society
P.O. Box 202
Olney, IL 62450

Ridge Historical Society
10621 South Seely Avenue
Chicago, IL 60643-2618

Riverdale Historical Society
Riverdale Library
208 West 144th Street
Riverdale, IL 60627-2788
Tel: 708-841-3311 (Library)

Robbins Historical Society
13822 S. Central Park Avenue
P.O. Box 1561
Robbins, IL 60472-1561
Tel: 708-389-5393

Rock Island County Historical Society
Rock Island Historical House
822, 11th Avenue
Moline, IL 61265-1221
Tel: 309-764-8590
http://www.netexpress.net/~richs/

Rogers Park Historical Society
2555 West Farwell
Chicago, IL 60645-5422

St. Clair County Historical Society
P.O. Box 431
Belleville, IL 62222-0431
Tel: 618-234-0600
http://www.compu-type.net/rengen/stclair/ stchome.htm

Schiller Park Historical Society
9526 Irving Park Road
Schiller Park, IL 60176
Tel: 847-678-2550

Sheffield Historical Society/Museum
235 Reed Street
Sheffield, IL 61361-0103

Shelby County Genealogical & Historical Society
South First and South Washington Streets
Shelbyville, IL 62565
E-mail: shgensoc@bmmhnet.com
http://www.shelbycohistgen.org/

Skokie Historical Society
8031 Floral
Skokie, IL 60077
Tel: 847-675-3674

Society of American Archivists
527 S. Wells Street, 5th Floor
Chicago, IL 60607-3922
Tel: 312-922-0140
Fax: 312-347-1452
http://www.archivists.org/

South Holland Historical Society/Museum
South Holland Public Library
16250 Wausau Avenue, Lower Level
P.O. Box 48
South Holland, IL 60473-0048
Tel: 708-596-2722
        708-331-5262 (Library)
Fax: 708-331-6557
http://www.southhollandlibrary.org/

South Suburban Genealogical and Historical Society
320 East 161st Place
P.O. Box 96
South Holland, IL 60473-0096
Tel: 708-333-9474
http://www.rootsweb.com/~ssghs/

South Suburban Heritage Association
17130 67th Ct
Tinley Park, IL 60477
Tel: 708-614-8713

Stone Park Historical Association
Village Hall
1629 N. Mannheim Road
Stone Park, IL 60165-1118

Streamwood Historical Society/Museum
Hoosier Grove Park
700 West Irving Park Rd.
Streamwood, IL 60107
Tel: 630-372-7275

Swedish-American Historical Society/Library
5125 North Spaulding Avenue
Chicago, IL 60625-4816
Tel: 773-583-5722
E-mail: info@swedishamericanhist.org
http://www.swedishamericanhist.org/

Thornton Historical Society/Library and Museum
114 N Hunter Street
P.O. Box 34
Thornton, IL 60476
Tel: 708-877-6569
http://www.thornton60476.com/
    historical%20society.htm

Tinley Park Historical Society/Museum
6727 West 174th Street
P.O. Box 325
Tinley Park, IL 60477-0325
Tel: 708-429-4210
E-mail: lrtphist@lincolnnet.net

Triton Community History Organization
Triton College
2000 5th Avenue
River Grove, IL 60171-1995
Tel: 708-456-0300 ext. 245

Union County Genealogical & Historical Society
101 East Spring Street
Anna, IL 62906

Versailles Area Genealogical & Historical Society
P.O. Box 92
Versailles, IL 62378

Washington County Historical Society
326 S. Kaskaskia
St. Nashville, IL 62263

Waverly Genealogical & Historical Society
157 E. Tremont
Waverly, IL 62692

West Side Historical Society
Chicago Public Library
Legler Branch
115 South Pulaski Road
Chicago, IL 60624
Tel: 312-746-7730
Fax: 312-746-7750
E-mail: tward@chipublib.org

Westchester Historical Society
10332 Bond Street
Westchester, IL 60154-4361
Tel: 708-865-1972

Western Springs Historical Society/Museum
916 Hillgrove Avenue
4211 Grand Avenue
P.O. Box 139
Western Springs, IL 60558-0139
Tel: 708-246-9230

Wheeling Historical Society
251 North Wolf Road
P.O. Box 3
Wheeling, IL 60090-0003

White County Historical Society
Ratcliff Inn (library)
P.O. Box 121
Carmi, IL 62821
http://www.rootsweb.com/~ilwcohs/

Williamson County Historical Society
105 S. Van Buren
Marion, IL 62959
Tel: 618-997-5863

Wilmette Historical Society
555 Hunter Road
Wilmette, IL 60091-2209

Winnetka Historical Society
1140 Elm Street
Winnetka, IL 60093-2563
Tel: 847-501-6025

LDS FAMILY HISTORY CENTERS

For locations of Family History Centers in this state, see the Family History Center locator at FamilySearch. http://www.familysearch.org/eng/Library/FHC/ frameset_fhc.asp

ARCHIVES/LIBRARIES/MUSEUMS

AASR Valley of Chicago
915 North Dearborn Street
Chicago, IL 60610
Tel: 312-787-7605 ext. 9
http://www.valleyofchicago.org/

Algonquin Area Public Library
2600 Harnish Drive
Algonquin, IL 60102
Tel: 847-458-6060
Fax: 847-658-0179
http://www.aapld.org/

American Police Center and Museum
1926 S Canalport Ave
Chicago, IL 60616
Tel: 312-455-8709

Arlington Heights Historical Museum
110 W. Fremont
Arlington Heights, IL 60004-5912
Tel: 847-255-1225
http://www.ahmuseum.org/

Arlington Heights Memorial Library
500 North Dunton
Arlington Heights, IL 60004-5966
Tel: 847-392-0100
Fax: 847-392-0136
http://www.ahml.lib.il.us/

Assumption Public Library
205 N Oak Street
Assumption, IL 62510
Tel: 217-226-3915

Augustana College Library
639 38th Street
Rock Island, IL 61201-2296
Tel: 309-794-7317
Fax: 309-794-7230
E-mail: libraryinfo@augustana.edu
http://www.augustana.edu/library/

Avalon Branch of the Chicago Public Library
8828 South Stony Island
Chicago, IL 60617
Tel: 312-747-5234

Balzekas Museum of Lithuanian Culture
6500 South Pulaski Road
Chicago, IL 60629-5136
Tel: 773-582-6500
Fax: 773-582-5133
http://centerstage.net/other/balzekas.html

Belleville Public Library
Genealogy Section
121 E. Washington St., #4114
Belleville, Il 62220-2205
Tel: 618-234-0441
Fax: 618-234-9474
http://www.compu-type.net/rengen/stclair/BPL.htm

Blue Island Public Library
2433 York Street
Blue Island, IL 60406-2094
Tel: 708-388-1078
708-371-8546 (Hist. Soc.)
Fax: 708-388-1143
E-mail: bis@sls.lib.il.us
http://www.blueislandlibrary.org/

Bourbonnais Public Library
250 W. Casey Drive
Bourbonnais, IL 60914
Tel: 815-933-1727
Fax: 815-933-1961

Brehm Memorial Library
101 South Seventh Street
Mount Vernon, IL 62864
Tel: 618-242-6322
Fax: 618-242-0810
E-mail: kendik@shawls.lib.il.us
http://www.sirin.lib.il.us/docs/bml/docs/lib/

Bryan-Bennett Library
217 West Main Street
Salem, IL 62881
Tel: 618-548-7784
Fax: 618-548-9593
http://www.sirin.lib.il.us/docs/bbl/docs/lib/

Bureau County Historical Society/Library & Museum
109 Park Avenue West
Princeton, IL 61356
Tel: 815-875-2184

Calumet City Historical Society Museum
760 Wentworth Avenue
Calumet City, IL 60409
Tel: 708-832-9390
http://www.thetimesonline.com/org/cchs/

Champaign County Historical Archives
Champaign County Genealogical Society
201 South Race Street
Urbana, IL 61801-3235
http://www.rootsweb.com/~ilccgs/

Charleston Carnegie Public Library
712 6th Street
Charleston, IL 61920
Tel: 217-345-4913
Fax: 217-348-5616
http://www.charlestonlibrary.org/

Chicago & Northwestern Railroad Historical Society/Archives
P.O. Box 1436
Elhurst, IL 60126-9998
E-mail: cnwhs@cnwhs.org
http://www.cnwhs.org/

Chicago Heights Public Library
25 West 15th Street
Chicago, IL 60411
Tel: 708-754-0323
Fax: 708-754-0325
http://www2.sls.lib.il.us/CHS/

Chicago Historical Society
Clark Street at North Avenue
Chicago, IL 60614-6099
Tel: 312-642-4600
Fax: 312-266-2077
E-mail: info@chicagohistory.org
http://www.chicagohs.org/

Chicago Lawn Library
6120 Kedzie Avenue
Chicago, IL 60629-4638
Tel: 312-747-0639
Fax: 312-747-6182

Chicago Municipal Reference Library
City Hall, Room 1004
121 North LaSalle Street
Chicago, IL 60602

Chicago Public Library
Harold Washington Center
Special Collections Department
400 South State Street, 9th Floor
Chicago, IL 60605
Tel: 312-747-4999
312-747-4875 (Special Collections)
TDD: 312-747-4969
http://www.chipublib.org/

Chicago Tribune Archives
Tribune Tower
435 North Michigan Avenue, Rm. 1231
Chicago, IL 60611
http://pqasb.pqarchiver.com/chicagotribune/

Collinsville Memorial Public Library
Collinsville Historical Museum
408 West Main Street
Collinsville, IL 62234
Tel: 618-344-1112
Fax: 618-345-6401

Cook Memorial Library
413 N. Milwaukee Avenue
Libertyville, IL 60048
Tel: 847-362-2330
Fax: 847-362-2354
http://www.cooklib.org/

Crystal Lake Public Library
126 W. Paddock Street
Crystal Lake, IL 60014
Tel: 815-459-1687
Fax: 815-459-9581
http://www.crystallakelibrary.org/

Czechoslovak Heritage Museum, Library and Archives
CSA Fraternal Life
122 W. 22nd Street
Oak Brook, IL 60521
Tel: 630-472-0500
800-543-3272 (Toll Free)
Fax: 630-472-1100
E-mail: lifecsa@aol.com
http://www.csafraternallife.org/museum.htm

Danville Public Library
319 N. Vermilion Street
Danville, IL 61832
Tel: 217-477-5220
Fax: 217-477-5230
http://www.danville.lib.il.us/

Decatur Genealogical Society/Library
356 North Main Street
P.O. Box 1548
Decatur, IL 62525-1548
Tel: 217-429-0135
E-mail: DecaturGenealogicalSociety@msn.com
http://www.rootsweb.com/~ildecgs/

DePaul University Archives
Administrative Offices
2350 N Kenmore Avenue
Chicago, IL 60614
Tel: 312-362-6922
E-mail: kdegraff@depaul.edu
http://www.lib.depaul.edu/speccoll/uarchive.htm

Des Plaines Historical Society/Museum/Library
789 Pearson
Des Plaines, IL 60016-4506
Tel: 847-391-5399
http://www.northstarnet.org/dpkhome/DPHS/

Des Plaines Public Library
1501 Ellinwood Street
Des Plaines, IL 60016
Tel: 847-827-8551
http://www.dppl.org/

DuPage County Historical Museum
102 East Wesley Street
Wheaton, IL 60187
Tel: 630-682-7343
http://www.dupageco.org/museum/

DuQuoin Public Library
28 S. Washington Street
DuQuoin, IL 62832-1396
Tel: 618-542-5045

DuSable Museum of African-American History/Archives
740 East 56th Place
Chicago, IL 60637-1408
Tel: 773-947-0600
http://www.dusablemuseum.org/

Edwardsville Public Library
Madison County Genealogical Society Library
112 S. Kansas Street
Edwardsville, IL 62025
Tel: 618-692-7556
Fax: 618-692-9566
E-mail: ede@lcls.org
http://edwardsvillelibrary.org/

Elmhurst Historical Museum
120 East Park Avenue
Elmhurst, IL 60126-3420
Tel: 630-833-1457
http://www.elmhurst.org/elmhurst/museum/

Elkwood House Museum
509 N. First Street
DeKalb, IL 60115

Elmwood Park Library
4 Conti Parkway
Elmwood Park, IL 60707
Tel: 708-453-7645
Fax: 708-453-4671
http://centerstage.net/literature/libraries/
    elmwood-park.html

Episcopal Diocese of Chicago
St. James Cathedral
65 East Huron
Chicago, IL 60611
Tel: 312-751-4200
Fax: 312-787-4534
http://www.epischicago.org/

Evangelical Covenant Church of America
5101 N. Francisco Avenue
Chicago, IL 60625
Tel: 773-784-3000
Fax: 773-784-4366
E-mail: webster@covchurch.org
http://www.covchurch.org/cov/

Evans Public Library
215 S. 5th Street
Vandalia, IL 62471
Tel: 618-283-2824
Fax: 618-283-2705
http://www.sirin.lib.il.us/docs/epl/docs/lib/

Evanston Historical Society/Museum & Library
225 Greenwood Street
Evanston, IL 60201-4713
Tel: 847-475-3410
Fax: 847-475-3599
http://www.evanstonhistorical.org/

Flagg Creek Historical Museum
Pleasantdale Park District
7425 South Wolf Road
Burr Ridge, IL 60525
http://www.pleasantdaleparks.org/vial_house.htm

Fossil Ridge Library
386 Kennedy Road
Braidwood, IL 60408
Tel: 815-458-2187
Fax: 815-458-2042
http://www.fossilridge.org/

Franklin Park Historical Museum
Franklin Park Public Library
10311 Grand Avenue
Franklin Park, IL 60131
Tel: 847-455-6016

Freeport Public Library
314 W. Stephenson Street
Freeport, IL 61031
Tel: 815-233-3000

Gale Borden Public Library
200 N. Grove Avenue
Elgin, IL 60120
Tel: 847-742-2411
Fax: 847-742-0485
TDD: 847-742-2455
http://www.elgin.lib.il.us/

Galena Historical Museum
211 South Bench Street
Galena, IL 61036
Tel: 815-777-9129

Galena Public Library
601 S. Bench Street
Galena, IL 61036
Tel: 815-777-0200
Fax: 815-777-0219

Galesburg Public Library
40 East Simmons Street
Galesburg, IL 61401
Tel: 309-343-6118
Fax: 309-343-4877
E-mail: director@galesburglibrary.org
http://www.galesburglibrary.org/

Glenview Public Library
1930 Glenview Road
Glenview, IL 60025
Tel: 847-729-7500
Fax: 847-729-7682
TDD: 847-729-7529
E-mail: info@glenview.lib.il.us
http://www.glenview.lib.il.us/

Glencoe Historical Museum
Glencoe Historical Society
999 Green Bay Road
Glencoe, IL 60022-1263
Tel: 847-835-4935

Glenview Area Historical Museum and Library
Glenview Historical Society
1121 Waukegan Road
Glenview, IL 60025-3036
Tel: 847-724-2235

Grayslake Historical Municipal Museum
164 Hauley Street
P.O. Box 185
Grayslake, IL 60030-0185
Tel: 847-223-7663 (Historical Society)

Green Hills Library
8611 West 103rd Street
Palos Hills, IL 60465
Tel: 708-598-8446
Fax: 708-598-0856
http://www.greenhills.lib.il.us/

Grove National Historic Landmark
1421 Milwaukee Avenue
Glenview, IL 60025-1436
Tel: 847-299-6096

Hellenic Museum and Cultural Center
168 North Michigan Avenue, 4th Floor
Chicago, IL 60601
Tel: 312-726-1234
Fax: 312-726-8539
http://www.hellenicmuseum.org/

Homewood Historical Museum
2035 West 183rd Street
Homewood, IL 60430-1044
Tel: 708-799-1896

Illiana Genealogical & Historical Society/Library
215 West North Street
P.O. Box 207
Danville, IL 61834-0207
E-mail: ighs@danville.net
http://www.danvillevirtual.com/vcclients/danville/
    IllianaGene/

**Illinois Association for the Preservation of
Historic Arms and Armaments, Inc.**
1800 Western Avenue
Flossmoor, IL 60422-0339

Illinois State Historical Society
210 South Sixth Street, Suite 210
Springfield, IL 62701-1507
Tel: 217-782-2635
217-782-4286
Fax: 217-524-8042
E-mail: ishs@eosinc.com
http://www.historyillinois.org/

Illinois State Library
300 South Second Street
Springfield, IL 62701-1796
Tel: 217-785-5600
800-665-5576 (in Illinois only)
TDD: 800-665-5576
http://www.cyberdriveillinois.com/library/isl/ isl.html

Illinois Veteran's Home Library
1707 North 12th Street
Quincy, IL 62301
Tel: 217-222-8641 ext. 248
Fax: 217-222-0139
http://www.quincynet.com/ivh/museum.htm

**Irish-American Heritage Center Museum
and Art Gallery**
4626 North Knox Avenue
Chicago, IL 60630-4030
Tel: 773-282-7035
http://www.irishamhc.com/

Italian Cultural Center
1621 North 39th Avenue
Stone Park, IL 60165-1105
Tel: 708-345-3842
Fax: 708-345-3891
http://www.mobilito.com/icc/

Jacob & Bernard Hostert Log Cabins
West Avenue and 147th Street
14228 Union Avenue
Orland Park, IL 60462-2011
Tel: 708-349-0046

James P. Fitzgibbons Historical Museum
Calumet Park Fieldhouse
9800 Avenue G
Chicago, IL 60675

John Crerar Library
University of Chicago
5730 South Ellis Avenue
Chicago, IL 60637
Tel: 312-225-2526
E-mail: crerar-reference@lib.uchicago.edu
http://www.lib.uchicago.edu/e/crerar/

John Mosser Public Library
106 West Meek Street
Abingdon, IL 61410-1450
Tel/Fax: 309-462-3129

Joliet Public Library
150 N. Ottawa Street
Joliet, IL 60431
Tel: 815-740-2660
Fax: 815-740-6161
http://joliet.lib.il.us/

Kankakee County Historical Museum
Kankakee County Historical Society
801 South 8th Avenue
Kankakee, IL 60901
Tel: 815-932-5279
http://www.kankakeecountymuseum.com/

Kankakee Public Library
304 S. Indiana Avenue
Kankakee, IL 60901
Tel: 815-939-4564
Fax: 815-939-9057
http://www.lions-online.org/

Kenilworth Historical Museum and Library
415 Kenilworth Avenue
P.O. Box 181
Kenilworth, IL 60043-1134
Tel: 847-251-2565

Knox College
Seymour Library
2 Cedar Street
P.O. Box 500
Galesburg, IL 61401-0500
Tel: 309-341-7246
Fax: 309-343-9292
http://library.knox.edu/

LaGrange Area Historical Museum and Library
444 South LaGrange Road
LaGrange, IL 60525-2448
Tel: 708-482-4248

LaGrange Public Library
10 West Cossitt
LaGrange, IL 60525
Tel: 708-352-0576
Fax: 708-352-1620
http://www.lagrangelibrary.org/

Lansing Historical Museum
2750 Indiana Avenue
Lansing, IL 60438-0633
Tel: 708-474-6160

Lemont Area Historical Society/Museum
306 Lemont Street
P.O. Box 126
Lemont, IL 60439-0126
Tel: 630-257-2972
http://www.township.com/lemont/historical/

Lincoln Library
Sangamon Valley Collection
326 South Seventh Street
Springfield, IL 62701
Tel: 217-753-4900 ext. 234
Fax: 217-753-5329
TDD: 217-753-4947
http://lincolnlibrary.rpls.lib.il.us/llhome5.htm

Litchfield Carnegie Library
400 N. State Street
P.O. Box 212
Litchfield, IL 62056-0212
Tel: 217-324-3866
Fax: 217-324-3884

Little Rock Township Public Library
North Center Street
Plano, IL 60545

Loyola University Archives
6525 Sheridan Road
Chicago, IL 60626
Tel: 773-274-3000 ext. 791
http://www.luc.edu/info/keyfacts/welcome.html

Lutheran Church in American Archives
321 Bonnie Lane
Elk Grove Village, IL 60007
Tel: 847-690-9410
E-mail: archives@elca.org
http://www.elca.org/os/archives/intro.html

Lyons Public Library
4209 Joliet Avenue
Lyons, IL 60534
Tel: 708-447-3577
Fax: 708-447-3589
E-mail: lys@sls.lib.il.us
http://www.lyons.lib.il.us/

Macomb Public Library
Local History/Genealogy Room
235 South Lafayette
P.O. Box 220
Macomb, IL 61455
Tel/Fax: 309-833-2714
E-mail: maco@mail.alsrsa.org
http://www.macomb.lib.il.us/library/

Madison County Historical Museum and Library
Madison County Historical Society
715 North Main Street
Edwardsville, IL 62025
Tel: 618-656-7562
http://www.plantnet.com/museum/

Malcolm X College
1900 West Van Buren Street
Chicago, IL 60612-3145
Tel: 312-850-7000
http://www.ccc.edu/malcolmx/

Matson Public Library
Bureau County Genealogical Society Collection
15 Park Avenue, West
2nd Floor
Princeton, IL 61356
Tel: 815-875-1331
Fax: 815-875-1376
E-mail: birdcs@matsonpubliclibrary.org
http://matsonpubliclibrary.org/

Matteson Historical Society/Museum
813 School Avenue
Matteson, IL 60443
Tel: 708-748-3033

Mattoon Public Library
1600 Charleston Avenue
P.O. Box 809
Mattoon, IL 61938-0809
Tel: 217-234-2621
Fax: 217-234-2660
http://www.ltls.org/mtn.html

McHenry Public Library
809 N. Front St.
McHenry, IL 60050
Tel: 815-385-0036
Fax: 815-385-7035

McLean County Genealogical Society
P.O. Box 488
Normal, IL 61761-0488

Midwest Archives Conference (MAC) Archives
Northwestern University Library Archives
1935 Sheridan Road
Evanston, IL 60201
Tel: 847-491-3354
Fax: 847-467-4110
E-mail: archives@northwestern.edu
http://www.library.northwestern.edu/archives/

Mitchell Indian Museum at Kendall College
2600 Central Park Avenue
Evanston, IL 60201-2899
Tel: 847-475-1030
E-mail: mitchellmuseum@mindspring.com
http://www.mitchellmuseum.org/

Moody Bible Institute Library
820 North LaSalle
Chicago, IL 60610
Tel: 312-329-4000
Fax: 312-329-2155
http://www.moody.edu/

Morton B. Weiss Museum of Judaica
K.A.M. Isaiah Israel Congregation
1100 East Hyde Park Boulevard
Chicago, IL 60615-2899
Tel: 773-924-1234
Fax: 773-924-1238
http://www.kamii.org/

Morton Grove Historical Society/Museum
Haupt-Yehl House
Harrer Park
6240 Dempster Street
P.O. Box 542
Morton Grove, IL 60053-2946
Tel: 847-965-1200
847-965-0203 (Museum)
http://mgkhome.northstarnet.org/parkdist/html/
    historical.html

Morton Grove Public Library
6140 Lincoln Avenue
Morton Grove, IL 60053
Tel: 847-965-4220
TDD: 847-965-4236
Fax: 847-965-7903
E-mail: refdesk@mgk.nslsilus.org
http://www.northstarnet.org/mgkhome/library/
    mgplmenu.html

Mt. Greenwood Public Library
11010 South Kedzie Avenue
Chicago, IL 60655-2222

Mt. Prospect Historical Society/Museum
101 South Maple Street
P.O. Box 81
Mt. Prospect, IL 60056-0081
Tel: 847-392-9006
Fax: 847-392-8995
E-mail: mphist@aol.com
http://www.mphist.org/mphshome.htm

Mt. Prospect Public Library
10 South Emerson Street
Mt. Prospect, IL 60056-3251
Tel: 847-253-5675
Fax: 847-253-0642
E-mail: mgenther@mppl.org
http://www.mppl.org/

Mt. Vernon Public Library (C.E. Brehm Library)
101 South Seventh
Mount Vernon, IL 62864-4187
Tel: 618-242-6322
Fax: 618-242-0810
E-mail: kendik@shawls.lib.il.us
http://www.sirin.lib.il.us/docs/bml/docs/lib/

Mundelein College Archives-Chicago
6363 Sheridan Road
Chicago, IL 60660
Tel: 773-262-8100

Newberry Library
60 West Walton Street
Chicago, IL 60610-3305
Tel: 312-943-9090 (Main)
312-255-3506 (Reference)
312-255-3512 (Genealogy)
E-mail: furmans@newberry.org
http://www.newberry.org/

Niles Historical Society/Museum
8970 Milwaukee Avenue
Niles, IL 60714-1737
Tel: 847-390-0160
E-mail: ContactUs@vniles.com

Northeastern Illinois University Library
Ronald Williams Library
5500 North St. Louis
Chicago, IL 60625
Tel: 773-583-4050 ext. 479
773-794-6279
http://www.neiu.edu/~neiulib/

Northwestern University Library
Special Collections-Archives
633 Clark Street
Evanston, IL 60201
Tel: 847-491-7658
Fax: 847-491-8306
E-mail: library@northwestern.edu
http://www.library.northwestern.edu/

Oak Lawn Public Library
9427 South Raymond Avenue
Oak Lawn, IL 60453
Tel: 708-422-4990
http://www.lib.oak-lawn.il.us/

Oak Park and River Forest, Historical Society/Museum of
217 Home
P.O. Box 771
Oak Park, IL 60303-0771
Tel: 708-848-6755
E-mail: flipo@enteract.com
http://www.oprf.com/oprfhist/

Oak Park Public Library
834 Lake Street
Oak Park, IL 60301
Tel: 708-383-8200
Fax: 708-383-6384
http://www.oppl.org/

O'Fallon Historical Society/Museum
101 West State Street
P.O. Box 344
O'Fallon, IL 62269
Tel: 618-624-8409
E-mail: ohs@ofallonhistory.org
http://www.ofallonhistory.org/

Paarlberg Farmstead Homestead
172nd Place and Paxton Avenue
P.O. Box 48
South Holland, IL 60473-0048
Tel: 708-596-2722

Palatine Park District
250 East Wood Street
Palatine, IL 60078
Tel: 847-991-0333
Fax: 847-847-9127
http://www.palatineparkdistrict.com/

Parlin-Ingersoll Library
205 West Chestnut
Canton, IL 61520-2499
Tel: 309-647-0328
Fax: 309-647-8117
E-mail: parlin@parliningersoll.org
http://www.parliningersoll.org/

Peoria Public Library
107 NE Monroe Street
Peoria, IL 61602
Tel: 309-497-2000
http://www.peoria.lib.il.us/

Plainfield Public Library
705 N. Illinois Street
Plainfield, IL 60544
Tel: 815-436-6639
Fax: 815-439-2878
http://plainfield.lib.il.us/home.htm

Polish Museum of America
984 North Milwaukee Avenue
Chicago, IL 60622-4101
http://pma.prcua.org/

Poplar Creek Public Library District
1405 South Park Avenue
Streamwood, IL 60107-2997
Tel: 630-837-6800
http://www.poplarcreek.lib.il.us/

Quincy Public Library
526 Jersey Street
Quincy, IL 62301-3996
Tel: 217-223-1309
Fax: 217-222-3052
http://www.quincylibrary.org/main.htm

Randolph County Genealogical Society/Library
600 State Street, Suite 306
Chester, IL 62233
Tel: 618-826-3807
E-mail: vlchas@mindspring.com
http://www.rootsweb.com/~ilrcgs/

Reddick Library
1010 Canal Street
Ottawa, IL 61350
Tel: 815-434-0509
Fax: 815-434-2634
E-mail: vtrupiano@reddicklibrary.org
http://reddicklibrary.org/

Riverdale Library
208 West 144th Street
Riverdale, IL 60627-2788
Tel: 708-841-3311
E-mail: rds@sls.lib.il.us
http://www2.sls.lib.il.us/RDS/

Riverside Historical Museum
Longommon and Pine Roads
27 Riverside Road
Riverside, IL 60546-2264

Rock Island Public Library
401 19th Street
Rock Island, IL 61201
Tel: 309-732-7323
http://www.rbls.lib.il.us/rip/

Rockford Public Library
215 N. Wyman Street
Rockford, IL 61101
Tel: 815-965-6731
TDD: 815-965-3007
Fax: 815-965-0866
http://www.rpl.rockford.org/Locations/main.htm

Saint Peter Lutheran Church Museum
208 East Schaumburg Rd.
Schaumburg, IL 60194

Schaumburg Public Library
130 S. Roselle Road
Schaumburg, IL 60193
Tel: 847-985-4000
TDD: 847-985-1462
http://www.stdl.org/

Schuyler Jail Museum
200 South Congress
P.O. Box 96
Rushville, IL 62681

Sheffield Historical Society/Museum
235 Reed Street
Sheffield, IL 61361-0103

Southeast Side Historical Museum
Calumet Park Fieldhouse
9801 Avenue G.
Calumet Park, IL 60617
Tel: 773-721-7948

South Holland Historical Society/Museum
South Holland Public Library
16250 Wausau Avenue, Lower Level
P.O. Box 48
South Holland, IL 60473-0048
Tel: 708-596-2722
708-331-5262 (Library)
Fax: 708-331-6557
http://www.southhollandlibrary.org/

South Suburban Genealogical and Historical Society
320 East 161st Place
P.O. Box 96
South Holland, IL 60473-0096
Tel: 708-333-9474
http://www.rootsweb.com/~ssghs/

Spertus Museum
618 South Michigan Avenue
Chicago, IL 60605-1901
Tel: 312-322-1747
Fax: 312-922-3934
http://www.spertus.edu/

Staunton Public Library
George and Santina Sawyer Genealogy Room
306 West Main
Staunton, IL 62088
Mail:
Macoupin County Genealogical Society
P.O. Box 95
Staunton, IL 62088-0095
E-mail: smckenzi@midwest.net
http://www.rootsweb.com/~ilmacoup/m_gensoc.htm

Streamwood Historical Society/Museum
Hoosier Grove Park
700 West Irving Park Rd.
Streamwood, IL 60107
Tel: 630-372-7275

Swedish-American Historical Society/Library
5125 North Spaulding Avenue
Chicago, IL 60625-4816
Tel: 773-583-5722
E-mail: info@swedishamericanhist.org
http://www.swedishamericanhist.org/

Swedish-American Museum Center
5211 N. Clark Street
Chicago, IL 60640-2101
Tel: 773-728-8111
http://www.samac.org/

Swenson Swedish Immigration Research Center
Augustana College
639 38th Street
Rock Island, IL 61201-2273
Tel: 309-794-7204
Fax: 309-794-7443
E-mail: swsa@augustana.edu
http://www.augustana.edu/administration/SWENSON/

Thornton Historical Society/Library and Museum
114 N Hunter Street
P.O. Box 34
Thornton, IL 60476
Tel: 708-877-6569
http://www.thornton60476.com/historical%20society.htm

Three Rivers Public Library
25207 W. Channon Dr.
P.O. Box 300
Channahon, IL 60410-0300
Tel: 815-467-6200
Fax: 815-467-4012
http://www.three-rivers-library.org/

Tinley Park Historical Society/Museum
6727 West 174th Street
P.O. Box 325
Tinley Park, IL 60477-0325
Tel: 708-429-4210
E-mail: lrtphist@lincolnnet.net

Trailside Museum
738 Thatcher Avenue
River Forest, IL 60305
Tel: 708-366-6530

Ukrainian National Museum
721 North Oakley Blvd.
Chicago, IL 60612
Tel: 312-421-8020
E-mail: info@ukrntlmuseum.org
http://www.ukrntlmuseum.org/

University of Chicago
Joseph Regenstein Library
1100 East 57th Street
Chicago, IL 60637
E-mail: reg-reference@lib.uchicago.edu
http://www.lib.uchicago.edu/e/reg/

University of Illinois at Urbana-Champaign
University Archives
1408 W. Gregory Drive
Urbana, IL 61801
Tel: 217-333-0798 (Archives)
217-333-8400 (General Information)
Fax: 217-333-2214
E-mail: illiarch@uiuc.edu
http://web.library.uiuc.edu/ahx/

University of Illinois at Chicago
801 S. Morgan, Room 220
P.O. Box 8198
Chicago, IL 60607
Tel: 312-996-2756
http://www.uic.edu/depts/lib/

Urbana Free Library
201 South Race Street
Urbana, IL 61801-3283
Tel: 217-367-4057
Fax: 217-367-4061
http://urbanafreelibrary.org/

Vogel Genealogical Research Library
305 1st Street, Box 132
Holcomb, IL 64043

Warren County Library
60-62 Public Square
Monmouth, IL 61462
Tel: 309-734-3166
Fax: 309-734-5955
E-mail: wcpl@maplecity.com
http://www.maplecity.com/~wcpl/

Western Springs Historical Society/Museum
916 Hillgrove Avenue
4211 Grand Avenue
P.O. Box 139
Western Springs, IL 60558-0139
Tel: 708-246-9230

Wheaton Public Library
225 N. Cross Street
Wheaton, IL 60187
Tel: 630-668-1374
Fax: 630-668-1465
http://www.wheaton.lib.il.us/library/wpl.html

Wheeling Historical Museum
251 North Wolf Road
P.O. Box 3
Wheeling, IL 60090-0003

Wilmette Historical Museum
609 Ridge Road
Wilmette, IL 60091-2209
Tel: 847-853-7666
Fax: 847-853-7706
http://www.wilmette.com/museum/

Winnetka Historical Museum and Library
Winnetka Historical Society
P.O. Box 365
Winnetka, IL 60093
Tel: 847-501-6025
Fax: 847-501-3221
http://www.winnetkahistory.org/

Winnetka Public Library
768 Oak Street
Winnetka, IL 60093-2583
Tel: 847-446-7220
Fax: 847-446-5085
http://www.wpld.alibrary.com/

Woodlands Native American Indian Museum/Art Gallery
6384 West Willow Wood Drive
Palos Heights, IL 60463-1847
Tel: 708-614-0334

Woodson Regional Library
9525 South Halsted
Chicago, IL 60628
Tel: 312-747-6900
TDD: 312-747-0121
Fax: 312-747-3396
http://cpl.lib.uic.edu/002branches/woodson/
woodson.html

Wyanet Historical Society
109 East Main Street
Wyanet, IL 61379

Zion Benton Public Library
2400 Gabriel Avenue
Zion, IL 60099-2296
Tel: 847-872-4680
E-mail: sclark@zblibrary.org
http://www.zblibrary.org/

NEWSPAPER REPOSITORIES

Belleville Public Library
Genealogy Section
121 E. Washington St., #4114
Belleville, IL 62220-2205
Tel: 618-234-0441
Fax: 618-234-9474
http://www.compu-type.net/rengen/stclair/BPL.htm

Chicago Historical Society
Clark Street at North Avenue
Chicago, IL 60614-6099
Tel: 312-642-4600
Fax: 312-266-2077
E-mail: info@chicagohistory.org
http://www.chicagohs.org/

Illinois State Archives
Norton Building
Capitol Complex
Springfield, IL 62756
Tel: 217-782-4682
Fax: 217-524-3930
http://www.cyberdriveillinois.com/departments/
archives/archives.html

Illinois State Historical Library
Newspaper Library
1 Old State Capitol
Springfield, IL 62701
Tel: 217-785-7941
http://www.state.il.us/hpa/lib/Microfilm.htm

Joliet Public Library
150 N. Ottawa Street
Joliet, IL 60431
Tel: 815-740-2660
Fax: 815-740-6161
http://joliet.lib.il.us/

Plainfield Public Library
705 N. Illinois Street
Plainfield, IL 60544
Tel: 815-436-6639
Fax: 815-439-2878
http://plainfield.lib.il.us/home.htm

University of Illinois at Urbana-Champaign
University Archives
1408 W. Gregory Drive
Urbana, IL 61801
Tel: 217-333-0798 (Archives)
217-333-8400 (General Information)
Fax: 217-333-2214
E-mail: illiarch@uiuc.edu
http://web.library.uiuc.edu/ahx/

VITAL RECORDS

Illinois State Vital Records Office
Division of Vital Records
605 West Jefferson Street
Springfield, IL 62702-5097
Tel: 217-782-6553
Fax: 217-523-2648
http://www.vitalrec.com/il.html

ILLINOIS ON THE WEB

Genealogy-Family History Research in Illinois
http://www.outfitters.com/illinois/history/family/

IlGenWeb Project
http://www.rootsweb.com/~ilgenweb/

Illinois Gateway - Genealogy Feature
http://www.sos.state.il.us/departments/archives/
services.html

Illinois in the Civil War
http://www.illinoiscivilwar.org/

Illinois Public Domain Land Sales Search
http://www.cyberdriveillinois.com/departments/archives/
data_lan.html

Indiana

Archives, State & National

Indiana State Archives
6440 E. 30th St.
Indianapolis, IN 46219
Tel: 317-591-5222
E-mail: arc@icpr.state.in.us
http://www.ai.org/icpr/webfile/archives/homepage. html

National Archives-Great Lakes Region
7358 Pulaski Road
Chicago, IL 60629-5898
Tel: 773-581-7816
Fax: 312-886-7883
E-mail: chicago.archives@nara.gov
http://www.nara.gov/regional/chicago.html

Genealogical Societies

African-American Historical & Genealogical Society (AAHGS)
502 Clover Terrace
Bloomington, IN 47404-1809

Alexandria/Monroe Township Genealogy Society
302 West Tyler Street
Alexandria, IN 46001

Allen County Genealogical Society (ACGSI)
P.O. Box 12003
Fort Wayne, IN 46802
E-mail: MunsonJo@aol.com
http://www.ipfw.edu/ipfwhist/historgs/acgsi.htm

Bartholomew County Genealogical Society
P.O. Box 2455
Columbus, IN 47202-2455

Blackford-Wells Genealogy Society
P.O. Box 54
Bluffton, IN 46714-0054
http://www.rootsweb.com/~inwells/society.html

Brown County Genealogical Society
P.O. Box 1202
Nashville, IN 47448

Cass County Genealogical Society
P.O. Box 373
Logansport, IN 46947
http://www.rootsweb.com/~inccgs/

Clay County Genealogical Society/Library
309 Main Street
P.O. Box 56
Center Point, IN 47840-0056
Tel: 812-835-5005
E-mail: research@ccgsilib.org
http://www.ccgsilib.org/

Clinton County Genealogical Society
609 N. Columbia Street
Frankfort, IN 46041

County Seat Genealogy Society
310 Urban Street
Danville, IN 46122

Crawford County Historical & Genealogical Society
P.O. Box 133
Leavenworth, IN 47137

Daviess County Genealogical Society
703 Front Street
Washington, IN 47501

Dubois County Genealogical Society
P.O. Box 84
Ferdinand, IN 47532-0084

Elkhart County Genealogical Society
P.O. Box 1031
Elkhart, IN 46515-1031
http://www.rootsweb.com/~inelkhar/ecgs.htm

Fountain County Genealogical Society
2855 S. Kingman Road
Kingman, IN 47952
Tel: 765-294-4954
E-mail: focogensoc@netscape.net
http://glenmar.com/~emoyhbo/fcgs.html

Grant County Genealogical Society
P.O. Box 1951
Marion, IN 46952

Grant County Genealogy Club
1419 W. 11th Street
Marion, IN 46952

Hendricks County Genealogical Society
Danville Public Library
101 South Indiana Street
Danville, IN 46122
Tel: 317-745-2604
Fax: 317-745-0756

Howard County Genealogical Society
P.O. Box 2
Oakford, IN 46965
E-mail: morris@netusa1.net
http://www.rootsweb.com/~inhoward/gensoc.html

Illiana Genealogical & Historical Society
215 West North Street
P.O. Box 207
Danville, IN 61834-0207
Tel: 217-431-8733
E-mail: ighs@danville.net
http://www.danvillevirtual.com/vcclients/danville/
        IllianaGene/

Indiana Genealogical Society
P.O. Box 10507
Fort Wayne, IN 46852
http://www.indgensoc.org/

Jackson County Genealogical Society
415 Walnut Street
Seymour, IN 47274

Jay County Genealogical Society
P.O. Box 1086
Portland, IN 47371

Jennings County Genealogical Society
RR 1, Box 227
Scipion, IN 47273

LaPorte Genealogical Society
904 Indiana Avenue
LaPorte, IN 46350
E-mail: opearson1@attbi.com
http://www.rootsweb.com/~inlcigs/

Lawrence County Historical & Genealogical Society
12 Court House Museum
Bedford, IN 47421
Tel: 812-275-4141

Marion-Adams Historical and Genealogical Society
308 Main Street
Sheridan, IN 46069

Marshall County Genealogical Society
Marshall County Historical Society
123 N. Michigan Street
Plymouth, IN 46563

Martin County Genealogical Society
P.O. Box 45
Shoals, IN 47581

Miami County Genealogical Society
P.O. Box 542
Peru, IN 46970
http://www.rootsweb.com/~inmiami/gensoc.html

Monroe County Genealogical/Historical Society
Genealogy Library
202 East 6th Street
Bloomington, IN 47408
Tel: 812-332-2517
E-mail: monroehistsoc@hotmail.com
http://www.kiva.net/~mchm/monroe2.htm

Morgan County History and Genealogy Association, Inc.
P.O. Box 1012
Martinsville, IN 46151-1012
http://www.rootsweb.com/~inmchaga/mchagai.html

Noble County Genealogical Society
P.O. Box 162
Albion, IN 46701
http://www.nobgensoc.org/

North Central Indiana Genealogical Society
2300 Canterbury Drive
Kokomo, IN 46901

Northwest Indiana Genealogical Society
P.O. Box 595
Griffith, IN 46319
http://www.rootsweb.com/~inlake/nwigs.htm

Northwest Territory Genealogical Society
Lewis Historical Library
Vincennes University LRC-22
Vincennes, IN 47591
E-mail: rking@indian.vinu.edu
http://www.vinu.edu/lewis.htm

Orange County Genealogical Society
P.O. Box 344
Paoli, IN 47454
http://www.usgennet.org/usa/in/county/orange/
        gensoc.htm

Owen County Historical and Genealogical Society
P.O. Box 569
Spencer, IN 47460
Tel: 812-829-3392
E-mail: peterson@ccrtc.com
http://www.owen.in.us/owenhist/owen.htm

Palatines to America, Indiana Chapter
P.O. Box 40435
Indianapolis, IN 46240-0435
Tel: 317-875-7210

Porter County Public Library Genealogical Group
103 Jefferson Street
Valparaiso, IN 46383

Pulaski County Genealogical Society
Pulaski County Library
121 South Riverside Dr.
Winamac, IN 46996

Putnam County Genealogy Club
Rte. 1, Box 28
Bainbridge, IN 46105

Randolph County Genealogical Society
Route 3, Box 61
Winchester, IN 47394

Scott County Genealogical Society
P.O. Box 23
Scottsburg, IN 47170-0023

Shelby County Genealogical Society
Grover Museum
52 West Broadway
Shelbyville, IN 46176

South Bend Area Genealogical Society
The Mishawaka-Penn-Harris Public Library
209 Lincoln Way East
Mishawaka, Indiana 46544
http://www.rootsweb.com/~insbags/

Southern Indiana Genealogical Society
P.O. Box 665
New Albany, IN 47151

Southern Indiana Genealogical Society
RR 1
Leavenworth, IN 47137

Starke County Genealogical Society
Henry F. Schricker Library
152 West Culver Road
Knox, IN 46534
http://www.maplewoodfarm.com/strkctygen.htm

Tippecanoe County Area Genealogical Society
909 South Street
Lafayette, IN 47901
http://www.tcha.mus.in.us/

Tri-County Genealogy Society
23184 Pocket Road, W
P.O. Box 118
Batesville, IN 47006

Tri State Genealogical Society
Willard Library
21 First Avenue
Evansville, IN 47710
Tel: 812-425-4309
E-mail: mylines@evansville.net
http://www.rootsweb.com/~intsgs/

Wabash Valley Genealogical Society
P.O. Box 85
Terre Haute, IN 47808

Wayne County Genealogical Society
P O Box 2599
Richmond IN 47375-2599
http://www.waynet.org/nonprofit/WCGS.htm

White County Genealogy Society
P.O. Box 149
Monticello, IN 47960

Whitley County, Genealogical Society of
P.O. Box 224
Columbia City, IN 46725-0224
http://home.whitleynet.org/genealogy/

HISTORICAL SOCIETIES

Adams County Historical Society
420 W. Monroe Street
P.O. Box 262
Decatur, IN 46733-0262
Tel: 260-724-2341

African-American Historical & Genealogical Society (AAHGS)
502 Clover Terrace
Bloomington, IN 47404-1809

Alexandria-Monroe Township Historical Society
313 N. Harrison Street
Alexandria, IN
http://www.rootsweb.com/~inmadiso/ alexandria.htm

Allen County-Fort Wayne Historical Society/ Museum & Archives
302 E. Berry Street Fort Wayne, IN 46802
Tel: 219-426-2882
Fax: 219-424-4419

Anson Wolcott Historical Society
P.O. Box 294
Wolcott, IN 47995

Bartholomew County Historical Society
524 Third Street
Columbus, IN 47201
Tel: 812-372-3541
http://bchs.hsonline.com/

Besancon Historical Society
15533 Lincoln Highway East
New Haven, IN 46774
Tel: 219-749-4525
http://www.ipfw.edu/ipfwhist/historgs/besanco.htm

Blackford County Historical Society/Museum
321 North High Street
P.O. Box 264
Hartford City, IN 47348
http://www.bchs-in.org/

Boone County Historical Society
P.O. Box 141
404 W. Main Street
Lebanon, IN 46052-0141
Tel: 765-483-9414
http://www.bccn.boone.in.us/bchs/

Brown County Historical Society
P.O. Box 668
Nashville, Indiana 47448
Tel: 812-988-6089
http://www.browncounty.org/bchistoric.html

Carmel-Clay Historical Society
211 First Street Southwest
Carmel, Indiana 46032
Tel: 317-846-7117
http://www.digitalrainllc.com/CCHS.htm

Carroll County Historical Society/Museum
P.O. Box 277
Delphi, IN 46923
Tel: 765-564-3152
Fax: 1-765-564-3624
E-mail: cchs@dcwi.com
http://dcwi.com/~cchs/cchs.html

Cass County Historical Society
1004 E. Market Street
Logansport, IN 46947
Tel: 219-753-3866

Cedar Lake Historical Association
Lake of the Red Cedars Museum
P.O. Box 421
Cedar Lake, IN 46303
Tel: 219-374-6157

Clark County Historical Society
Howard Steamboat Museum, Inc.
1101 East Market Street
P.O. Box 606
Jeffersonville, IN 47130-0606
Tel: 812-283-3728

Clark's Grant Historical Society
P.O. Box 423
Charlestown, IN 47111

Clay County Historical Society
100 E. National Road
Brazil, IN 47834
Tel: 812-446-4036

Clinton County Historical Society/Museum
301 E. Clinton
Frankfort, IN 46041
Tel: 765-659-2030
Fax: 765-654-7773
E-mail: cchsm@geetel.net
http://srv1.geetel.net/~cchsm/

Crawford County Historical & Genealogical Society
P.O. Box 133
Leavenworth, IN 47137

Daleville Historical Society
P.O. Box 586
Daleville, IN 47334

Daviess County Historical Society/Museum
Donaldson Road
Washington, IN 47501
Tel: 812-254-5122
http://www.honest-abe.com/Museum/
or
http://www.artcom.com/museums/nv/af/ 47501.htm

Dearborn County Historical Society
Courthouse
215 West High Street
Lawrenceburg, IN 47025
Tel: 812-537-4075

Decatur County Historical Society
222 East Franklin
P.O. Box 143
Greensburg, IN 47240

Decatur Township Historical Society
P.O. Box 42 West
Newton, IN 46183

DeKalb County Historical Society
Box 686
Auburn, IN 46706

Delaware County Historical Alliance/Heritage Library
120 East Washington
P.O. Box 1266
Muncie, IN 47308
Tel: 317-282-1550
E-mail: dcha@iquest.net
http://www.iquest.net/~dcha/

Dolan Historical Society
New Prospect Baptist Church
6055 North Old State Road 37
Dolan, IN 47401

Dubois County Historical Society
737 W. 8th Street
Jasper, IN 47546

Duneland Historical Society
P.O. Box 809
Chesterton, IN 46304

Dyer Historical Society
Dyer Town Hall
One Town Square
Dyer, IN 46311
Tel: 219-865-6108
E-mail: history@dyeronline.com
http://www.dyeronline.com/history/

East Chicago Historical Society
2401 East Columbus Drive
East Chicago, IN 46312
Tel: 219-397-2453

Elkhart County Historical Society/Museum
304 West Vistula Street
P.O. Box 434
Bristol, IN 46507
Tel: 219-848-4322

Ferdinand Historical Society
Box 194
Ferdinand, IN 47532

Floyd County Historical Society
P.O. Box 455
New Albany, IN 47151-0455

Fort Benjamin Harrison Historical Society
P.O. Box 269597
Indianapolis, IN 46226-9597
E-mail: fortben@msn.com
http://www.msnusers.com/FortBenjaminHarrison
    HistoricalSociety/homepage.msnw

Fort Wayne Railroad Historical Society, Inc.
P.O. Box 11017
Fort Wayne, IN 46855
Tel: 219-493-0765
E-mail: mguptail@765.org
http://www.765.org/

Fountain County Historical Society
724 S. Layton
P.O. Box 148
Kingman, IN 47952

Franklin County Historical Society/Museum
P.O. Box 342
Brookville, IN 47012

Franklin Township Historical Society
P.O. Box 39015
Indianapolis, IN 46239

Fulton County Historical Society
37 East, 375 North
Rochester, IN 46975
Tel: 574-223-4436
http://www.icss.net/~fchs/

Garrett Historical Society
300 N Randolph Street
P.O. Box 225
Garrett, IN 46738
http://www.garretthistoricalsociety.org/

Gary Historical & Cultural Society
P.O. Box M-603
Gary, IN 46404
Tel: 219-882-3311
E-mail: ghcsinc@yahoo.com
http://members.tripod.com/~ghcs/

Gas City Historical Society
505 E. South F Street
P.O. Box 192
Gas City, IN 46933

Gibson County Historical Society
P.O. Box 516
Princeton, IN 47670

Goshen Historical Society
P.O. Box 701
Goshen, IN 46526

Grant County Historical Society
1713 North Quarry Road
P.O. Box 1951
Marion, IN 46952

Greene County Historical Society
P.O. Box 301
Bloomfield, IN 47424-0301

Griffith Historical Society
P.O. Box 678
Griffith, IN 46319
E-mail: DepotKaren@aol.com
http://www.thetimesonline.com/org/griffithhistsoc/table.htm

Guilford Township Historical Society
Plainfield Public Library
1120 Stafford Road
Plainfield, IN 46168
Tel: 317-839-6602

Hamilton County Historical Society
Old Sheriff's Residence and Jail
P.O. Box 397
Noblesville, IN 46060
Tel: 317-770-0775
E-mail: hamcohmsn@aol.com
http://www.rootsweb.com/~inhchs/
or
http://www.noblesville.com/history.htm

Hammond Historical Society
Hammond Public Library
564 State Street
Hammond, IN 46320
Tel: 219-931-5100
E-mail: longs@hammond.lib.in.us
http://www.hammondindiana.com/society_ page.html

Hancock County Historical Society
P.O. Box 375
Greenfield, IN 46140
Tel: 317-462-7780

Harrison County Historical Society
117 Beaver Street
Corydon, IN 47112

Hebron Historical Society, Inc.
P.O. Box 675
Hebron, IN 46341

Hendricks County Historical Society/Museum
170 South Washington
Danville, IN 46122

Henry County Historical Society/Museum
606 South 14th Street
New Castle, IN 47362
Tel: 765-529-4028
http://www.kiva.net/~hchisoc/museum.htm

Heritage Society of Northwest Indiana
P.O. Box 508
Chesterton, IN 46304-0508

Hessville Historical Society
7205 Kennedy Avenue
Hammond, IN 46323
Tel: 219-844-5666

Highland Historical Society
Bank of Highland
2611 Highway Avenue
Highland, IN 46322
http://www.rootsweb.com/~inlake/highland.htm

Historic Forks of the Wabash, Inc.
P.O. Box 261
Huntington, IN 46750
Tel: 219-356-1903
E-mail: dericsson@huntcol.edu
http://www.historicforks.org/

Hobart Historical Society
Mariam Library
706 East Fourth Street
P.O. Box 24
Hobart, IN 46342
Tel: 219-942-0970

Howard County Historical Society/Museum
1200 W. Sycamore Street
Kokomo, IN 46901
Tel: 765-452-4314
http://www.howardcountymuseum.org/

Huntington County Historical Society
1041 South Jefferson Street
P.O. Box 1012
Huntington, IN 46750

Indiana German Heritage Society
401 East Michigan Street
Indianapolis, IN 46204
http://www.ulib.iupui.edu/kade/ighstran.html

Indiana Historical Bureau
140 North Senate Avenue, Room 408
Indianapolis, IN 46204
Tel: 317-232-2535
Fax: 317-232-3728
E-mail: ihb@statelib.lib.in.us
http://www.statelib.lib.in.us/WWW/ihb/ihb.HTML

Indiana Historical Society/Library
450 W. Ohio Street
Indianapolis, IN 46202
Tel: 317-232-1882
 317-232-1879 (Library)
http://www.indianahistory.org/

Indiana Jewish Historical Society
203 W. Wayne Street #312
Fort Wayne, IN 46802

Indiana Religious History Association
P.O. Box 88267
Indianapolis, IN 46208

Irvington Historical Society
Benton House
312 South Downey Avenue
Indianapolis, IN 46219
Tel: 317-357-0318

Jackson County Historical Society
115 N. Sugar Street
Brownstown, IN 47220

Jay County Historical Society
P.O. Box 1282
Portland, IN 47371
Tel: 219-726-4323
http://www.rootsweb.com/~injay/research/ jayhist.htm

Jefferson County Historical Society
Madison Railroad Station
615 West First Street
Madison, IN 47250
Tel: 812-265-2335
Fax: 812-273-5023
E-mail: jchs@seidata.com
http://www.seidata.com/~jchs/jchs.htm

Johnson County Historical Society
135 North Main Street
Franklin, IN 46131
Tel: 317-736-4655

Kennard Historical Society
P.O. Box 227
Kennard, IN 47351

Kosciusko County Historical Society/Library
Kosciusko County Jail Museum
P.O. Box 1071
Warsaw, IN 46580-1071
Tel: 219-269-1078
http://culture.kconline.com/kchs/

LaGrange County Historical Society
P.O. Box 134
LaGrange, IN 46761

Lake County Historical Society/Museum
5131 Canterbury Avenue
Portage, IN 46368
Tel: 219-662-3975
http://www.crownpoint.net/museum.htm

Lake Station Historical Society
P.O. Box 5253
Lake Station, IN 46405-2232

LaPorte Historical Society/Museum
809 State Street
LaPorte, IN 46350-3329
Tel: 219-326-6808 ext. 276
E-mail: history@lapcohistsoc.org
http://www.lapcohistsoc.org/

Lawrence County Historical & Genealogical Society
12 Court House Museum
Bedford, IN 47421
Tel: 812-275-4141

Lexington Historical Society
P.O. Box 238
Lexington, IN 47138-0238

Ligonier Historical Society
300 South Main Street
Ligonier, IN 46767-1812
Tel: 219-894-4511
Fax: 219-894-4509

Linden-Madison Township Historical Society
P.O. Box 154
Linden, IN 47955
Tel: 765-339-7245
http://www.tctc.com/~weaver/depot.htm

Madison County Historical Society
1931 Brown Street, Suite 2
Anderson, IN 46016
Tel: 765-683-0052
http://www.rootsweb.com/~inmadiso/mchs.htm#top

Marion-Adams Historical and Genealogical Society
308 Main Street
Sheridan, IN 46069

Marion County-Indianapolis Historical Society
P.O. Box 2223
Indianapolis, IN 46206

Marshall County Historical Society, Inc.
123 N. Michigan Street
Plymouth, IN 46563
Tel: 574-936-2306
Fax: 574-936-9306
http://www.mchistoricalsociety.org/

Martin County Historical Society
P.O. Box 564
Shoals, IN 47581

Merrillville-Ross Township Historical Society
6975 Broadway
Merrillville, IN 46410

Miami County Historical Society
Courthouse, Room 102
51 North Broadway
Peru, IN 46970
Tel: 765-473-9183
Fax: 765-476-3880
http://www.miamicountymuseum.org/society.html

Michiana Jewish Historical Society
P.O. Box 11074
South Bend, IN 46634-0074

Michigan City Historical Society
P.O. Box 512
Michigan City, IN 46360
Tel: 219-872-6133
http://www.michigancity.com/MCHistorical/

Middletown-Fall Creek Township Historical Society
707 West Mill Street
Middletown, IN 47356

Monon Historical Society
P.O. Box 193
Monon, IN 47959

Monroe County Genealogical/Historical Society
Genealogy Library
202 East 6th Street
Bloomington, IN 47408
Tel: 812-332-2517
E-mail: monroehistsoc@hotmail.com
http://www.kiva.net/~mchm/monroe2.htm

Montgomery County Historical Society
212 Water Street
Crawfordsville, IN 47933
Tel: 765-362-3416

Montpelier Historical Society, Inc.
109 West Huntington Street
Montpelier, IN 47359

Morgan County Historic Preservation Society
P.O. Box 1377
Martinsville, IN 46151

**Morgan County History
and Genealogy Association, Inc.**
P.O. Box 1012
Martinsville, IN 46151-1012
http://www.rootsweb.com/~inmchaga/mchagai.html

Munster Historical Society
Townhall
1005 Ridge Road
Munster, In 46321
Tel: 219-838-3296
E-mail: oldmunster@aol.com
http://members.aol.com/_ht_a/oldmunster/
mhstree/Page_1x.html

New Paris Historical Society
P.O. Box 101
New Paris, IN 46553

Noble County Historical Society
P.O. Box 152
Albion, IN 46701

North Manchester Historical Society
P.O. Box 361
North Manchester, IN 46962
http://mcs.k12.in.us/histsoc/

Northern Indiana Historical Society
808 West Washington Blvd.
South Bend, IN 46601
Tel: 219-235-9664
http://www.nd.edu/~crush/hist.html

Ohio County Historical Society
212 South Walnut Street
Rising Sun, IN 47040
Tel: 812-438-4915

Ogden Dunes, Historical Society of
101 Ogden Dunes
Portage, IN 46368-1268
Tel: 219-762-1268
http://members.tripod.com/~Ogden_Dunes/

Orange County Historical Society
Thomas Elwood Lindley House
P.O. Box 454
Paoli, IN 47454
http://www.rootsweb.com/~inochs/ocmuseum.htm

Osceola Historical Society
P.O. Box 14
Osceola, IN 46561

Owen County Historical and Genealogical Society
P.O. Box 569
Spencer, IN 47460
Tel: 812-829-3392
E-mail: peterson@ccrtc.com
http://www.owen.in.us/owenhist/owen.htm

Palmyra Historical Society
Palmyra Historical Museum
Palmyra Commercial Building
Palmyra, IN 47164

Park County Historical Society
503 E. Oak Drive
P.O. Box 332
Rockville, IN 47872
Tel: 765-569-2223

Perry County Historical Society
538 Eleventh Street
Tell City, IN 47586

Pike County Historical Society
Pike County Public Library
1104 Main Street
Petersburg, IN 47567

Porter County, Historical Society of
Old Jail Museum
153 Franklin
Valparaiso, IN 46383
Tel: 219-465-3595
http://home.attbi.com/~hspc/

Portage Community Historical Society
2100 Willowcreek Road
Portage, IN 46368

Posey County Historical Society
P.O. Box 171 Mount
Vernon, IN 47620
http://www.rootsweb.com/~inposey/society.htm

Pulaski County Historical Society
400 South Market
Street Winamac, IN 46996

Putnam County Historical Society
Roy O. West Library
Archives & Special Collections
DePauw University
Greencastle, IN 46135
Tel: 765-658-4406
Fax: 765-658-4423
E-mail: archives@depauw.edu
http://www.depauw.edu/library/archives/
　　archiveshome.htm

Randolph County Historical Society/Museum
416 South Meridian
Winchester, IN 47394

Ripley County Historical Society
Local History & Genealogical Library
125 Washington Street
P.O. Box 525
Versailles, IN 47023
Tel: 812-689-3031
E-mail: rchslib@seidata.com
http://www.seidata.com/~rchslib/

Rush County Historical Society
614 N. Jackson
P.O. Box 302
Rushville, IN 46173

St. John Historical Society
P.O. Box 134
St. John, IN 46373

Schererville Historical Society
P.O. Box 333
Schererville, IN 46375

Scotland Historical Society, Inc.
P.O. Box 173
Scotland, IN 47457

Scott County Historical Society
P.O. Box 245
Scottsburg, IN 47170

Shawnee Historical Association
5501 East 200 North
Lafayette, IN 47905
Tel: 765-589-8049

Shelby County Historical Society
52 West Broadway
P.O. Box 74
Shelbyville, IN 46176
Tel: 317-392-4634

Shirley Centennial Historical Society, Inc.
Historic Shirley Museum
P.O. Box 69
Shirley, IN 47384-0069

Southwestern Indiana Historical Society
435 S. Spring Street
Evansville, IN 47714-1550

Spencer County Historical Society
Rockport-Ohio Township Public Library
210 Walnut Street
Rockport, IN 47635
E-mail: middletonb@rockport-spco.lib.in.us
http://www.rockport-spco.lib.in.us/page5.html

Starke County Historical Society/Museum
401 South Main Street
Knox, IN 46534
Tel: 574-772-5393

Stones Trace Historical Society
4946 North SR 5
Ligonier, IN 46767

Sugar Creek Historical Society
P.O. Box 23
Thorntown, IN 46071
Tel: 765-436-2202
E-mail: llwhite@bccn.boone.in.us
http://www.bccn.boone.in.us/tpl/schs/

Sullivan County Historical Society
P.O. Box 326
Sullivan, IN 47882
Tel: 812-268-6253
http://www.rootsweb.com/~inschs/

Swiss Heritage Society, Inc.
1200 Swissway Road
P.O. Box 88
Berne, IN 46711
Tel: 219-589-8007

Switzerland County Historical Society
P.O. Box 201
Vevay, IN 47043
Tel: 812-427-3560
http://www.switzcpl.lib.in.us/historicalsociety.html

Tell City Historical Society
516 Main Street
Tell City, IN 47586

Three Creeks Historical Association
Lowell Public Library
1505 Commercial Avenue
Lowell, IN 46356
Tel: 219-696-7704
http://www.lowellpl.lib.in.us/

Tippecanoe County Historical Association/Museum
909 South Street
Lafayette, IN 47901
Tel: 765-476-8411
Fax: 765-476-8414
E-mail: mail@tcha.mus.in.us
http://www.tcha.mus.in.us/

Topeka Area Historical Society
123 Indiana Street
P.O. Box 33
Topeka, IN 46571

United Methodist Historical Society
P.O. Box 331
Greencastle, IN 46135

Upland Area Historical Society
P.O. Box 577
Upland, IN 46989

Vanderburgh County Historical Society
P.O. Box 2626
Evansville, IN 47728-0626

Vermillion County Historical Society
220 E. Market Street
P.O. Box 273
Newport, IN 47966
Tel: 765-492-3570
http://vcihs.homestead.com/

Vigo County Historical Society/Museum
1411 South Sixth Street
Terre Haute, IN 47807
Tel: 812-235-9717
E-mail: vchs@iquest.net
http://web.indstate.edu/community/vchs/home.html

Wabash County Historical Society
Memorial Hall
89 West Hill Street
Wabash, IN 46992
Tel: 219-563-0661

Wakarusa Historical Society
P.O. Box 2
Wakarusa, IN 46573

Warren County Historical Society
P.O. Box 176
Williamsport, IN 47993

Washington County Historical Society
307 E. Market Street
Salem, IN 47167
Tel: 812-883-6495
http://165.138.44.13/washington/wacohiso.htm

Wayne County Historical Association
Wayne County Historical Museum
1150 North A Street
Richmond, IN 47374
Tel: 765-962-5756
http://www.waynet.org/nonprofit/historical_museum.htm

Wayne Township Historical Society
1220 S. High School Road
Indianapolis, IN 46241

Wells County Historical Society/Museum
420 West Market Street
P.O. Box 143
Bluffton, IN 46714-0143
Tel: 219-824-9956
E-mail: pbender@parlorcity.com
http://wchs-museum.org/

West Baden Historical Society
P.O. Box 6
West Baden Springs, IN 47469

Whiting-Robertsdale Historical Society
1610 119th Street
Whiting, IN 46394
Tel: 219-659-1432

Whitley County Historical Society/Museum
108 West Jefferson Street
Columbia City, IN 46725
Tel: 219-244-6372
Fax: 219-244-6384
http://home.whitleynet.org/historical/wch.htm

Winona Lake Historical Society
101 Fourth Street
Winona Lake, IN 46590

Zionsville Historical Society
714 Sugarbush Drive
Zionsville, IN 46077

LDS FAMILY HISTORY CENTERS

For locations of Family History Centers in this state, see the Family History Center locator at FamilySearch. http://www.familysearch.org/eng/Library/FHC/frameset_fhc.asp

ARCHIVES/LIBRARIES/MUSEUMS

Akron Carnegie Public Library
205 East Rochester Street
P.O. Box 428
Akron, IN 46910-0428
Tel/Fax: 219-893-4113
http://www.akron.lib.in.us/

Alameda McCullough Library
Wetherill Historical Resource Center
1001 South Street
Lafayette, IN 47901
Tel: 765-476-8407
Fax: 765-476-8414
E-mail: library@tcha.mus.in.us
http://www.tcha.mus.in.us/library.htm

Alexandria Public Library
117 E. Church Street
Alexandria, IN 46001

Alexandrian Public Library
115 West Fifth Street
Mount Vernon, IN 47620
Tel: 812-838-3286
Fax: 812-838-9639
http://www.apl.lib.in.us/

Allen County Public Library
900 Webster Street
P.O.Box 2270
Fort Wayne, IN 46802
Tel: 260-421-1200
Fax: 260-422-9688
E-mail: sfortriede@acpl.lib.in.us
http://www.acpl.lib.in.us/

Anderson Public Library
111 E. 12th Street
Anderson, IN 46016
Tel: 765-641-2456
Fax: 765-641-2468
http://www.and.lib.in.us/

Andrews/Dallas Township Public Library
63 Madison
P.O. Box 367
Andrews, IN 46702
Tel: 219-786-3574

Angola-Carnegie Public Library
322 S. Wayne Street
Angola, IN 46703
Tel: 219-665-3362

Atlanta/Jackson Township Public Library
100 S. Walnut Street
P.O. Box 68
Atlanta, IN 46031
Tel: 765-292-2521

Attica Public Library
305 S. Perry Street
Attica, IN 47918
Tel: 765-764-4194
http://glenmar.com/~emoyhbo/atticalb.html

Aurora Public Library
414 Second Street
Aurora, IN 47001
Tel: 812-926-0646
http://www.seidata.com/~aurplib/

Avon-Washington Township Public Library
498 N. State Road 267
Avon, IN 46168
Tel: 317-272-4818
http://www.avonlibrary.org/books/

Ball State University
Bracken Library
Muncie, IN 47306
Tel: 765-285-1101
765-285-5078 (Archives & Special Collections)
http://www.bsu.edu/library/indexjs.html

Bartholomew County Public Library
536 Fifth Street
Columbus, IN 47201
Tel: 812-379-1255
http://www.barth.lib.in.us/MainLib.html

Batesville Memorial Public Library
131 N. Walnut Street
Batesville, IN 47006
Tel: 812-934-4706
Fax: 812-934-6288
E-mail: mkruse@ind.net
http://www.bmpl.cnz.com/

Bedford Public Library
1323 K Street
Bedford, IN 47421
Tel: 812-275-4471
http://www.bedlib.org/

Beech Grove Public Library
1102 W. Main Street
Beech Grove, IN 46107
Tel: 317-788-4203
E-mail: diane@bgpl.lib.in.us
http://www.bgpl.lib.in.us/Library/

Bell Memorial Public Library
306 N. Broadway
P.O. Box 368
Mentone, IN 46539
Tel: 219-353-7234

Benton County Public Library
102 N. Van Buren Avenue
Fowler, IN 47944
Tel: 765-884-1720
E-mail: bentoncountypl@hotmail.com
http://www.mwprairienet.lib.in.us/Social_ Services/ben-
ton.htm

Berne Public Library
166 N. Sprunger
Berne, IN 46711
Tel: 219-589-2809

Bicknell/Vigo Township Public Library
201 W. Second Street
Bicknell, IN 47512
Tel: 812-735-2317
Fax: 812-735-2018
E-mail: director@bicknell-vigo.lib.in.us
http://bicknell-vigo.lib.in.us/

Blackford County Historical Society/Museum
321 North High Street
P.O. Box 264
Hartford City, IN 47348
http://www.bchs-in.org/

Bloomfield-Eastern Greene County Public Library
125 S. Franklin Street
Bloomfield, IN 47424
Tel: 812-384-4125
Fax: 812-384-0820
E-mail: Bloomfield@bloomfield.lib.in.us
http://www.bloomfield.lib.in.us/

Bluffton/Wells County Public Library
200 West Washington
Bluffton, IN 46714
Tel: 260-824-1612
http://www.wellscolibrary.org/bluffton.html

Boonville Public Library
611 W. Main Street
Boonville, IN 47601
Tel: 812-897-1500

Boswell-Grant Township Public Library
101 East Main Street
P.O. Box 315
Boswell, IN 47921
Tel: 765-869-5428
E-mail: boswelllib@hotmail.com
http://www.mwprairienet.lib.in.us/boswell-lib/

Bourbon Public Library
307 N. Main Street
Bourbon, IN 46504
Tel: 219-342-5655

Brazil Public Library
204 N. Walnut Street
Brazil, IN 47834
Tel: 812-448-1981

Bremen Public Library
304 N. Jackson St.
P.O. Box 130
Bremen, IN 46506
Tel: 219-546-2849
E-mail: bremenpl@bremen.lib.in.us
http://www.bremen.lib.in.us/

Bristol Public Library
505 N. Vistula Street
Bristol, IN 46507
Tel: 574-848-7458
http://www.bristol.lib.in.us/

Brook-Iroquois Township Public Library
100 West Main
P.O. Box 155
Brook, IN 47922
Tel: 219-275-2471
Fax: 219-275-8471
http://www.brook.lib.in.us/

Brookston-Prairie Township Library
111 West Second Street
Brookston, IN 47923
Tel: 765-563-6511
Fax: 765-563-6833
E-mail: bptpl@dcwi.com
http://dcwi.com/~bptpl/Welcome.html

Brookville Township Public Library
919 Main Street
Brookville, IN 47012
Tel: 765-647-4031

Brown County Public Library
205 Locust Lane
P.O. Box 8
Nashville, IN 47448
Tel: 812-988-2850
Fax: 812-988-8119
TDD: 812-988-2850
http://www.browncounty.lib.in.us/

Brownsburg Public Library
450 S. Jefferson Street
Brownsburg, IN 47112-1310
Tel: 317-852-3167
http://www.brownsburg.lib.in.us/

Butler-Carnegie Library
340 South Broadway
Butler, Indiana 46721
Tel: 260-868-2351
Fax: 260-868-5491
http://www.butler.lib.in.us/

Cambridge City Public Library
33 W. Main Street
Cambridge, IN 47327

Camden-Jackson Township Public Library
258 Main Street
P.O. Box 24
Camden, IN 46917
Tel: 219-686-2120

Cannelton Public Library
210 S 8th Street
Cannelton, IN 47520
Tel: 812-547-6028

Carmel Clay Public Library
515 East Main Street
Carmel, IN 46032
Tel: 317-844-3361
http://www.carmel.lib.in.us/

Carthage Public Library
102 North Main
P.O. Box 35
Carthage, IN 46115
Tel: 765-565-6631

Cedar Lake Historical Association
Lake of the Red Cedars Museum
P.O. Box 421
Cedar Lake, IN 46303
Tel: 219-374-6157

Centerville Township Public Library
115 West Main Street
Centerville, IN 47330
Tel: 765-855-5223
Fax: 765-855-2009
E-mail: cctpl@infocom.com

Charlestown/Clark County Public Library
51 Clark Road
Charlestown, IN 47111
Tel: 812-256-3337

Churubusco Public Library
116 N. Mulberry Street
Churubusco, IN 46723
Tel: 260-693-6466
http://buscolibrary.whitleynet.org/

Clay County Genealogical Society/Library
309 Main Street
P.O. Box 56
Center Point, IN 47840-0056
Tel: 812-835-5005
E-mail: research@ccgsilib.org
http://www.ccgsilib.org/

Clayton/Liberty Township Public Library
5199 Iowa Street
P.O. Box E
Clayton, IN 46118
Tel: 317-539-2991
Fax: 317-539-2050
E-mail: cltpl@indy.tds.net
http://personalpages.tds.net/~cltpl/

Clinton County Historical Society/Museum
301 E. Clinton
Frankfort, IN 46041
Tel: 765-659-2030
Fax: 765-654-7773
E-mail: cchsm@geetel.net
http://srv1.geetel.net/~cchsm/

Clinton Public Library
313 S. 4th Street
Clinton, IN 47842
Tel: 765-832-8349
Fax: 765-832-3823
E-mail: clinpl@holli.com
http://www.netcontrol.net/themata-new/141005/

Coatesville Public Library
North Milton Street
P.O. Box 147
Coatesville, IN 46121-0147
Tel: 765-386-2355
Fax: 765-386-2355

Colfax Public Library
207 S Clark Street
P.O. Box 308
Colfax, IN 46035
Tel: 765-324-2915
http://www.tctc.com/~library/conHome.htm

Corydon Public Library
117 W. Beaver Street
Corydon, IN 47112
Tel: 812-738-4110

Covington Public Library
622 5th Street
Covington, IN 47932
Tel: 765-793-2572
http://glenmar.com/~emoyhbo/covlib.html

Crawford County Public Library
203 Indiana Avenue
P.O. Box 159
English, IN 47118
Tel: 812-338-2606

Crawfordsville District Public Library
222 S. Washington Street
Crawfordsville, IN 47933
Tel: 317-362-2242
Fax: 317-362-7986
http://www.cdpl.lib.in.us/

Crown Point Library
214 S. Court Street
Crown Point, IN 46307
Tel: 219-663-0270

Culver-Union Township Public Library
415 Lake Shore Drive
Culver, IN 46511
Tel: 574-842-2941
Fax: 574-842-3441
E-mail: cutpl@culcom.net
http://www.culcom.net/~cutpl/

Danville Township Public Library
101 S. Indiana Street
Danville, IN 46122
Tel: 317-745-2604
E-mail: dplind@dpl.lib.in.us
http://www.dpl.lib.in.us/genealogy.html

Darlington Public Library
203 W. Main Street
Darlington, IN 47940
Tel: 765-794-4813
Fax: 765-794-4813

Daviess County Historical Society/Museum
Donaldson Road
Washington, IN 47501
Tel: 812-254-5122
http://www.honest-abe.com/Museum/
or
http://www.artcom.com/museums/nv/af/ 47501.htm

Decatur Public Library
128 South 3rd Street
Decatur, IN 46733
Tel: 260-724-2605

Delphi Public Library
222 East Main Street
Delphi, IN 46923
Tel: 765-564-2929
Fax: 765-564-4746
E-mail: dplibrar@carlnet.org
http://www.carlnet.org/dpl/

DeMotte Public Library
901 Birch Street SW
DeMotte, IN 46310
Tel: 219-987-2221
Fax: 219-987-2220

DePauw University
Archives & Special Collections
Greencastle, IN 46135
Tel: 765-658-4406
Fax: 765-658-4423
E-mail: archives@depauw.edu
http://www.depauw.edu/library/archives/
    archiveshome.htm

Dublin Public Library
2249 East Cumberland
P.O. Box 188
Dublin, IN 47335
Tel: 765-478-6206

Earl Park Public Library
East Fifth Street
P.O. Box 97
Earl Park, IN 47942
Tel: 219-474-6932
E-mail: eplib@ffni.com
http://www.mwprairienet.lib.in.us/Social_Services/
    eplib.html

Earlham College
Earlham College Libraries
Arthur & Kathleen Postle Archives and Friends
Collection
Richmond, IN 47374
Tel: 765-983-1200 (Main Switchboard)
http://www.earlham.edu/~libr/

East Chicago Public Library
2401 E. Columbus Drive
East Chicago, IN 46312
Tel: 219-397-2453
http://www.ecpl.org/

Eckhart Public Library
603 South Jackson Street
Auburn, IN 46706
Tel: 260-925-2414
Fax: 260-925-9376
http://www.epl.lib.in.us/

Edinburgh Public Library
119 West Main Cross Street
Edinburgh, IN 46124
Tel: 812-526-5487
Fax: 812-526-7057
E-mail: chamm@edinburgh.lib.in.us
http://www.edinburgh.lib.in.us/library/

Elkhart County Historical Society/Museum
304 West Vistula Street
P.O. Box 434
Bristol, IN 46507
Tel: 219-848-4322

Elkhart County Public Library
300 South Second Street
Elkhart, IN 46516
Tel: 219-522-2665
E-mail: webmastr@elkhart.lib.in.us
http://www.elkhart.lib.in.us/

Elwood-North Madison County Public Library
1600 Main Street
Elwood, IN 46036-2023
Tel: 765-552-5001
http://165.138.170.44/

Evansville Public Library
22 SE Fifth Street
Evansville, IN 47708
Tel: 812-428-8200
Fax: 812-428-8215
http://www.evcpl.lib.in.us/

Fairmount Public Library
205 South Main Street
P.O. Box 27
Fairmount, IN 46928
Tel: 765-948-3177

Farmland Public Library
116 S. Main Street
P.O. Box 189
Farmland, IN 47340
Tel: 765-468-7292

Fayette County Public Library
828 Grand Avenue
Connersville, IN 47331
Tel: 765-827-0883
Fax/TDD: 765-825-4592
http://www.fcplibrary.com/

Flora-Monroe Public Library
109 North Center Street
Flora, IN 46929
Tel: 574-967-3912
Fax: 574-967-3671
http://www.carlnet.org/floralib/

Fort Branch Public Library
107 E. Locust Street
Fort Branch, IN 47648
Tel: 812-753-4212

Francesville-Salem Public Library
P.O. Box 577
Francesville, IN 47947
Tel: 219-567-9433

Frankfort Public Library
208 West Clinton Street
Frankfort, IN 46041
Tel: 765-654-8746
TDD: 765-659-3047
Fax: 765-654-8747
E-mail: fcpl@accs.net
http://www.accs.net/fcpl/

Fremont Public Library
3145 East North Street
P.O. Box 7
Fremont, IN 46737-0007
Tel: 219-495-7157

Fulton County Public Library
320 West Seventh Street
Rochester, IN 46975
Tel: 219-223-2713
Fax: 219-223-5102

Garrett Public Library
107 West Houston Street
Garrett, IN 46738
Tel: 260-357-5485
Fax: 260-357-5170
http://www.gpl.lib.in.us/

Gary Public Library
220 West Fifth Avenue
Gary, IN 46402
Tel: 219-886-2484
Fax: 219-886-6829
http://www.gary.lib.in.us/

Gas City/Mill Township Public Library
135 East Main Street
Gas City, IN 46933
Tel: 765-674-4718
Fax: 765-674-5176

Geneva Public Library
305 East Line Street
P.O. Box 187
Geneva, IN 46740
Tel: 219-368-7270
http://www.genevapl.lib.in.us/

Goodland-Grant Township Public Library
111 South Newton Street
P.O. Box 405
Goodland, IN 47948
Tel/Fax: 219-297-4431
http://www.mwprairienet.lib.in.us/Social_Services/
    goodlib.html

Goshen Public Library
601 South Fifth Street
Goshen, IN 46526
Tel: 574-533-9531
Fax: 574-533-5211
E-mail: gpl@goshenpl.lib.in.us
http://www.goshenpl.lib.in.us/

Gosport History Museum
Owen County State Bank
P.O. Box 56
Gosport, IN 47433
Tel: 812-879-4450

Greenfield Public Library
700 Broadway
Greenfield, IN 46140
Tel: 317-462-5141
http://www.hancockpub.lib.in.us/

Greentown Public Library
421 South Harrison Street
Greentown, IN 46936
Tel: 765-628-3534
Fax 765-628-3957
http://www.eastern.k12.in.us/gpl/Grentown.htm

Greenwood Public Library
310 South Meridian
Greenwood, IN 46143
Tel: 317-881-1953
Fax: 317-881-1963
E-mail: mhamltn@iquest.net
http://www.greenwood.lib.in.us/

Hagerstown Public Library
10 West College
Hagerstown, IN 47346
Tel: 765-489-5632
Fax: 765-489-5808
E-mail: info@hagerstown.lib.in.us
http://www.hagerstown.lib.in.us/

Hammond Public Library
564 State Street
Hammond, IN 46320
Tel: 219-931-5100
E-mail: infodesk@hammond.lib.in.us
http://www.hammond.lib.in.us/

Hartford City Public Library
314 N. High Street
Hartford City, IN 47348
Tel: 765-348-1720
http://birch.palni.edu/~jkieffer/hcpl/libhome.htm

Hartman House
901 West Maumee Street
Angola, IN 46703

Hayden Historical Museum, Inc.
P.O. Box 58
Hayden, IN 47245
Tel: 812-346-8212
E-mail:haydenmu@seidata.com
http://www.seidata.com/~haydenmu/

Hebron Public Library
201 E. Sigler Street
P.O. Box 97
Hebron, IN 46341
Tel: 219-996-3684
http://www.pcpls.lib.in.us/brhebron.htm

Hendricks County Historical Society/Museum
170 South Washington
Danville, IN 46122

Henry County Historical Society/Museum
606 South 14th Street
New Castle, IN 47362
Tel: 765-529-4028
http://www.kiva.net/~hchisoc/museum.htm

Howard County Historical Society/Museum
1200 W. Sycamore Street
Kokomo, IN 46901
Tel: 765-452-4314
http://www.howardcountymuseum.org/

Howard Steamboat Museum, Inc.
Clark County Historical Society
1101 East Market Street
Jeffersonville, IN 47130-0606
Tel: 812-283-3728
http://homepages.ius.edu/Special/OralHistory/
     HSYmuseum.htm

Huntingburg Public Library
419 Jackson Street
Huntingburg, IN 47542
Tel: 812-683-2052
Fax: 812-683-2056
http://www.huntingburg.lib.in.us/

Hussey Memorial Public Library
250 W. Hawthorne Street
P.O. Box 840
Zionsville, IN 46077
Tel: 317-873-3149
Fax: 317-873-8339
http://www.zionsville.lib.in.us/

IUPUI University Library
Ruth Lilly Special Collections and Archives
755 West Michigan Street
Indianapolis, IN 46202-5195
Tel: 317-274-0464
Fax: 317-278-2331
E-mail: speccoll@iupui.edu
http://www.ulib.iupui.edu/special/

Indiana Historical Society/Library
450 W. Ohio Street
Indianapolis, IN 46202
Tel: 317-232-1882
317-232-1879 (Library)
http://www.indianahistory.org/

Indiana State Library
140 N. Senate Avenue, Room 250 (Gen. Section)
Indianapolis, IN 46204
Tel: 317-232-3675
Fax: 317-232-3728
TDD: 317-232-7763
http://www.statelib.lib.in.us/

Indiana University - Bloomington
Main Library
1320 E. 10th Street
Bloomington, IN 47405-1801
Tel: 812-855-8028 (Reference)
812-855-8084 (Subject and Area Librarians)
812-855-3722 (Government Publications)
E-mail: libref@indiana.edu
http://www.indiana.edu/~librcsd/

Indiana State University
Cunningham Memorial Library
650 Sycamore Street
Terre Haute, IN 47809
Tel: 812-237-2580
E-mail: librbsc@cml.indstate.edu
http://library.indstate.edu/orhttp://odin.indstate.edu/

Indiana University - School of Medicine
Ruth Lilly Medical Library
975 W. Walnut Street
Indianapolis, IN 46202-5121
Tel: 317-274-2076
Fax: 317-278-2349
E-mail: billings@iupui.edu
http://www.medlib.iupui.edu/hom/

Indianapolis-Marion County Public Library
40 East St. Clair Street
P.O. Box 211
Indianapolis, IN 46206
Tel: 317-269-1700
http://www.imcpl.org/

Jackson County Public Library
303 West 2nd Street
Seymour, IN 47274
Tel: 812-522-3412
Fax: 812-522-5456
TDD: 812-522-3412 Ext.244
E-mail: thill@japl.lib.in.us
http://www.japl.lib.in.us/

Jasper Public Library
116 Main Street
Jasper, IN 47546
Tel: 812-482-2712

Jay County Public Library
315 N. Ship Street
Portland, IN 47371
Tel: 260-726-7890
Fax: 260-726-7317
http://www.jaycpl.lib.in.us/library/

Jefferson County Historical Society
Madison Railroad Station
615 West First Street
Madison, IN 47250
Tel: 812-265-2335
Fax: 812-273-5023
E-mail: jchs@seidata.com
http://www.seidata.com/~jchs/jchs.htm

Jeffersonville Township Public Library
211 East Court Avenue
P.O. Box 1548
Jeffersonville, IN 47131
Tel: 812-282-7765
812-285-5632
http://jefferson.lib.in.us/

Jennings County Public Library
2375 North State Hwy 3
North Vernon, IN 47265
Tel: 812-346-2091
Fax: 812-346-2127
E-mail: jlibrary@seidata.com
http://seidata.com/~jlibrary/

Johnson County Public Library
401 South State Street
Franklin, IN 46131
Tel: 317-738-2833
Fax: 317-738-9635
E-mail: webmaster@jcplin.org
http://www.jcpl.lib.in.us/

Jonesboro Public Library
124 E. Fourth Street
Jonesboro, IN 46938
Tel: 765-677-9080

Kendallville Public Library
126 West Rush Street
Kendallville, IN 46755
Tel: 260-347-2768
Fax: 260-374-5314
E-mail: kpl@kendallvillelibrary.org
http://www.kendallvillelibrary.org/

Kentland-Jefferson Township Library
201 East Graham Street
Kentland, IN 47951
Tel: 219-474-5044
Fax: 219-474-5351
E-mail: robdew@ffni.com
http://www.mwprairienet.lib.in.us/Kent-lib/

Kewanna Public Library
210 E. Main Street
P.O. Box 365
Kewanna, IN 46939-0365
Tel: 219-653-2011

Kirklin Public Library
P.O. Box 8
Kirklin, IN 46050
Tel: 765-279-8258
E-mail: kirklinpl@accs.net
http://www.accs.net/kirklinpl/kirklin.htm

Knox County Public Library
502 N. Seventh Street
Vincennes, IN 47591
Tel: 812-886-4380
http://www.kcpl.lib.in.us/

Knox County Records Library
819 Broadway
Vincennes, IN 47591
Tel: 812-885-2557

Kokomo-Howard County Public Library
Genealogy and Local History Dept.
220 North Union
Kokomo, IN 46901
Tel: 765-457-3242
Fax: 765-457-3683
E-mail: khcpl@kokomo.lib.in.us
http://www.kokomo.lib.in.us/genealogy/

Kosciusko County Historical Society/Library
Kosciusko County Jail Museum
P.O. Box 1071
Warsaw, IN 46580-1071
Tel: 219-269-1078
http://culture.kconline.com/kchs/

Ladoga Public Library
128 Main Street
P.O. Box 248
Ladoga, IN 47954
Tel: 765-942-2456

Lake County Public Library
1919 West 81st Avenue
Merrillville, IN 46406
Tel: 219-769-3541
Fax: 219-756-9358
http://www.lakeco.lib.in.us/

LaGrange Public Library
203 West Spring Street
LaGrange, IN 46761-1845
Tel/Fax: 260-463-2841
E-mail: info@lagrange.lib.in.us
http://www.lagrange.lib.in.us/

LaPorte County Public Library
904 Indiana Avenue
LaPorte, IN 46350
Tel: 219-362-6156
http://www.lapcat.org/
      orhttp://lcpl2.lpco.lib.in.us/

LaPorte Historical Society/Museum
809 State Street
LaPorte, IN 46350-3329
Tel: 219-326-6808 ext. 276
E-mail: history@lapcohistsoc.org
http://www.lapcohistsoc.org/

Lawrence County Historical & Genealogical Society
12 Court House Museum
Bedford, IN 47421
Tel: 812-275-4141

Lawrenceburg Public Library
123 West High Street
Lawrenceburg, IN 47025
Tel: 812-537-2857
Fax: 812-537-2810
http://www.lpld.lib.in.us/

Lebanon Public Library
104 East Washington
Lebanon, IN 46052
Tel: 765-482-3460
http://www.bccn.boone.in.us/LPL/

Ligonier Public Library
300 South Main Street
Ligonier, IN 46767-1812
Tel: 219-894-4511
Fax: 219-894-4509
http://www.ligtel.com/~library1/

Linden-Carnegie Public Library
102 South Main Street
P.O. Box 10
Linden, IN 47955
Tel: 765-339-4239

Logansport Public Library
616 East Broadway
Logansport, IN 46947
Tel: 219-753-6383
http://www.logan.lib.in.us./

Loogootee Public Library
410 North Line Street
Loogootee, IN 47553
Tel: 812-295-3713

Madison-Jefferson County Public Library
420 West Main Street
Madison, IN 47250
Tel: 812-265-2744
http://www.madison-jeffco.lib.in.us/

Mariam Library
Hobart Historical Society
706 East Fourth Street
P.O. Box 24
Hobart, IN 46342
Tel: 219-942-0970

Marion Public Library
600 South Washington Street
Marion, IN 46953
Tel: 765-668-2900
Fax: 765-668-2911
http://www.marion.lib.in.us/

Melton Public Library
8496 West College Street
French Lick, IN 47432
Tel: 812-936-2177
http://www.melton.lib.in.us/

Mennonite Historical Library
1700 S. Main
Goshen, IN 46526
Tel: 574-535-7418
Fax: 574-535-7438
E-mail: mhl@goshen.edu
http://www.goshen.edu/mhl/

Michigan City Public Library
100 E. Fourth Street
Michigan City, IN 46360
Tel: 219-873-3044
E-mail: reference@mclib.org
http://www.mclib.org/

Milford Public Library
101 North Main Street
P.O. Box 247
Milford, IN 46542
Tel: 574-658-4312
Fax: 574-658-9454
http://www.milford.lib.in.us/

Mishawaka Public Library
209 Lincoln Way E.
Mishawaka, IN 46544
Tel: 574-259-5277
http://www.mppl.lib.in.us/

Mitchell Community Public Library
804 W. Main Street
Mitchell, IN 47446
Tel: 812-849-2412
E-mail: mitlib@mitlib.org
http://www.mitlib.org/

Monon Town & Township Public Library
427 N. Market Street
P.O. Box 305
Monon, IN 47959
Tel: 219-253-6517
Fax: 219-253-8373
E-mail: jminnick@urhere.net
http://dcwi.com/~nhartman/monon.htm

Monroe County Genealogical/Historical Society
Genealogy Library
202 East 6th Street
Bloomington, IN 47408
Tel: 812-332-2517
E-mail: monroehistsoc@hotmail.com
http://www.kiva.net/~mchm/monroe2.htm

Monroe Public Library
Indiana Room
303 E. Kirkwood Avenue
Bloomington, IN 47408
Tel: 812-349-3080
812-349-3050
E-mail: pgrayove@monroe.lib.in.us
http://www.monroe.lib.in.us/

Monterey-Tippecanoe Public Library
P.O. Box 38
Monterey, IN 46960-0038
Tel: 574-542-2171

Montpelier Public Library
300 South Main Street
Montpelier, IN 47359
Tel: 765-728-5969

Mooresville Public Library
Indiana Library
220 West Harrison
Mooresville, IN 46158
Tel: 317-831-7323
http://www.mooresvillelib.org/

Morgan County Public Library
Genealogy Section
110 South Jefferson Street
Martinsville, IN 46151
Tel: 765-342-3451
Fax: 765-342-9992
E-mail: morglib@scican.net
http://www.scican.net/~morglib/libweb.html

Morrison-Reeves Public Library
80 N. 6th Street
Richmond, IN 47374
Tel: 765-966-8291
Fax: 765-962-1318
E-mail: library@mrl.lib.in.us
http://mrl.lib.in.us/

Muncie Public Library
301 East Jackson St.
Muncie, IN 47305
Tel: 765-747-8200
http://www.munpl.org/

Nappanee Public Library
157 N. Main Street
Nappanee, IN 46550-1956
Tel: 574-773-7919
http://www.nappanee.lib.in.us/

New Albany/Floyd County Public Library
180 W. Spring Street
New Albany, IN 47150
Tel: 812-949-3527
Fax: 812-949-3532
http://www.nafcpl.lib.in.us/

New Carlisle Public Library
124 E. Michigan Street
P.O. Box Q
New Carlisle, IN 46552
Tel: 219-654-3046
Fax: 219-654-8260
E-mail: stephen@ncpl.lib.in.us
http://www.ncpl.lib.in.us/

New Castle Public Library
376 South 15th Street
P.O. Box J
New Castle, IN 47362
Tel: 765-529-0362
http://www.nchcpl.lib.in.us/

Noblesville Southeastern Public Library
One Library Plaza
Noblesville, IN 46060
Tel: 317-773-1384
http://www.nspl.lib.in.us/

North Judson Public Library
208 Keller Avenue
North Judson, IN 46366
Tel: 219-896-2841
http://www.njwt.lib.in.us/

North Manchester Public Library
405 North Market Street
North Manchester, IN 46962
Tel: 260-982-4773
Fax: 260-982-6342
E-mail: nmpl@nman.lib.in.us
http://www.nman.lib.in.us/

Notre Dame Archives
607 Hesburgh Library
Notre Dame, IN 46556
Tel: 574-631-6448
Fax: 574-631-7980
E-mail: archives.1@nd.edu
http://archives1.archives.nd.edu/guidecon.htm

Oakland City Public Library
210 South Main Street
Oakland City, IN 47660
Tel: 812-749-3559

Odon Winkelpleck Memorial Library
202 West Main Street
Odon, IN 47562
Tel: 812-636-4949

Ohio County Public Library
100 North High Street
Rising Sun, IN 47040
Tel: 812-438-2257

Ohio Township Public Library
23 West Jennings Street
Newburgh, IN 47630
Tel: 812-853-5468
Fax: 812-853-6377
http://www.ohio.lib.in.us/

Orleans Public Library
174 N. Maple Street
Orleans, IN 47452
Tel: 812-865-3270

Osgood Public Library
136 West Ripley
Osgood, IN 47037
Tel: 812-689-4011
http://www.geocities.com/Athens/Pantheon/6269/

Otterbein Public Library
29 South Main Street
P.O. Box 550
Otterbein, IN 47970
Tel: 765-583-2107

Owen County Public Library
10 South Montgomery Street
Spencer, IN 47460
Tel: 812-829-3392
Fax: 812-829-6165
http://www.owenlib.org/

Owensville-Carnegie Public Library
110 Main Street
P.O. Box 219 Owensville, IN 47665
Tel: 812-724-3335

Oxford Public Library
201 East Smith Street
P.O. Box 6
Oxford, IN 47971
Tel: 765-385-2177
http://www.mwprairienet.lib.in.us/Social_Services/
oxford.html

Paoli Public Library
NE Court Square
Paoli, IN 47454
Tel: 812-723-3841

Patrick Henry Sullivan Museum & Genealogy Library
225 W. Hawthorne Street
Zionsville, IN 46077
Tel: 317-873-4900
http://www.artcom.com/museums/nv/mr/46077-16.htm

Peabody Library
1160 East Hwy 205
P.O. Box 406
Columbia City, IN 46725
Tel: 219-244-5541
http://ppl.lib.in.us/

Pennville Public Library
195 N. Union
P.O. Box 206
Pennville, IN 47369
Tel: 260-731-3333

Peru Public Library
102 East Main Street
Peru, IN 46970
Tel: 765-473-3069
Fax:765-473-3060
E-mail: ppl@peru.lib.in.us
http://www.peru.lib.in.us/

Pierceton Public Library
P.O. Box 328
Pierceton, IN 46562
Tel: 219-594-5474

Pike County Public Library
Barrett Memorial Library
1104 Main Street
Petersburg, IN 47567
Tel: 812-354-6257
Fax: 812-354-6259
http://www.pikeco.lib.in.us/

Plainfield Public Library
1120 Stafford Road
Plainfield, IN 46168-2230
Tel: 317-839-6602
Fax: 317-839-4044
E-mail: plpl.plpl@incolsa.palni.edu
http://www.plainfield.lib.in.us/

Plymouth Public Library
201 N. Center Street
Plymouth, IN 46563
Tel: 219-936-2324
http://www.plymouth.lib.in.us/

Poseyville Public Library
55 South Cale Street
P.O. Box 220
Poseyville, IN 47633
Tel/Fax: 812-874-3418
E-mail: library2@ccsi.tds.net
http://www.geocities.com/area51/capsule/6374/

Princeton Public Library
124 South Hart
Princeton, IN 47670
Tel: 812-385-4464

Pulaski County Public Library
121 South Riverside Drive
Winamac, IN 46996
Tel: 574-946-3432
Fax/TDD: 574-946-6981

Putnam County Public Library
103 East Poplar Street
Greencastle, IN 46135
Tel: 765-653-2755
http://www.greencastle.com/pcpl/

Randolph County Historical Society/Museum
416 South Meridian
Winchester, IN 47394

Remington-Carpenter Township Library
105 Ohio Street
P.O. Box 65
Remington, IN 47977
Tel: 219-261-2543
http://www.mwprairienet.lib.in.us/Social_Services/
    remlib.html

Rensselaer Public Library
208 West Susan Street
Rensselaer, IN 47978
Tel: 219-866-5881
Fax: 219-866-7378
E-mail: jcplref@netnitco.net
http://www.jasperco.lib.in.us/

Ridgeville Public Library
P.O. Box 63
Ridgeville, IN 47380
Tel: 765-857-2025

Ripley County Historical Society
Local History & Genealogical Library
125 Washington Street
P.O. Box 525
Versailles, IN 47023
Tel: 812-689-3031
E-mail: rchslib@seidata.com
http://www.seidata.com/~rchslib/

Ripley County Historical Society Museum
Main and Water Streets
Versailles, IN 47023
E-mail: rchslib@seidata.com
http://www.seidata.com/~rchslib/

Roachdale Public Library
P.O. Box 278
Roachdale, IN 46172

Roann-PawPaw Public Library
P.O. Box 248
Roann, IN 46974
Tel: 765-833-5231

Roanoke Public Library
126 N. Main Street
P.O. Box 249
Roanoke, IN 46783
Tel: 219-672-3306

Rockville Public Library
106 N. Market Street
Rockville, IN 47872
Tel: 765-569-5544

Royal Center/Boone Township Public Library
P.O. Box 459
Royal Center, IN 46978
Tel: 574-643-3185

Rushville Public Library
130 West 3rd Street
Rushville, IN 46173
Tel: 765-932-3496
Fax: 765-932-4528
http://www.rushcounty.com/library/

St. Joseph County Public Library
1150 East Kern Road
South Bend, IN 46614
Tel: 574-251-3700
E-mail: m.waterson@gomail.sjcpl.lib.in.us
http://www.sjcpl.lib.in.us/

Salem Public Library
212 N. Main Street
Salem, IN 47167
Tel: 812-883-5600

Scott County Public Library
108 S. Main Street
Scottsburg, IN 47170
Tel: 812-752-2751

Shelbyville Public Library
57 West Broadway
Shelbyville, IN 46176
Tel: 317-398-7121
Fax: 317-398-4430
http://www.sscpl.lib.in.us/library/

Sheridan Public Library
214 S. Main Street
Sheridan, IN 46069
Tel: 317-758-5201
http://www.sheridan.lib.in.us/

Shoals Public Library
Fourth and High Street
P.O. Box 909
Shoals, IN 47581-0909
Tel: 812-247-3838

Speedway Public Library
5633 W. 25th Street
Speedway, IN 46224
Tel: 317-243-8959
Fax: 317-243-9373
http://www.speedway.lib.in.us/

Spencer County Public Library
210 Walnut Street
Rockport, IN 47635
Tel: 812-649-4866
Fax: 812-649-4018
E-mail: reference@rockport-spco.lib.in.us
http://www.rockport-spco.lib.in.us/

Spencer-Owen Public Library
110 E. Market Street
Spencer, IN 47460
Tel: 812-829-3392

Spiceland Public Library
106 Main Street
Spiceland, IN 47385
Tel: 765-987-7472

Sullivan County Public Library
100 S. Crowder Street
Sullivan, IN 47882
Tel: 812-268-4957
E-mail: rcole@sullivan.lib.in.us
http://www.sullivan.lib.in.us/

Swayzee Public Library
301 South Washington
P.O. Box 307
Swayzee, IN 46986-0307
Tel: 765-922-7526

Switzerland County Public Library
205 Ferry Street
P.O. Box 133
Vevay, IN 47043
Tel: 812-427-3363
Fax: 812-427-3654
E-mail: info@switzcpl.lib.in.us
http://www.switzcpl.lib.in.us/

Syracuse Public Library
115 E. Main Street
Syracuse, IN 46567
Tel: 574-457-3022
http://www.syracuse.lib.in.us/

Thorntown Public Library
124 N. Market Street
Thorntown, IN 46071
Tel: 765-436-7348
Fax: 765-436-7011
E-mail: tpl@bccn.boone.in.us
http://www.bccn.boone.in.us/tpl/

Tippecanoe County Historical Association/Museum
909 South Street
Lafayette, IN 47901
Tel: 765-476-8411
Fax: 765-476-8414
E-mail: mail@tcha.mus.in.us
http://www.tcha.mus.in.us/

Tippecanoe County Public Library
627 South Street
Lafayette, IN 47901
Tel: 765-429-0100
http://www.tcpl.lib.in.us/

Tipton County Public Library
127 E. Madison Street
Tipton, IN 46072
Tel: 765-675-8761
Fax: 765-675-4475
E-mail: tipton@tiptonpl.lib.in.us
http://www.tiptonpl.lib.in.us/

Union City Public Library
408 N. Columbia Street
Union City, IN 47390
Tel: 765-964-4748

Union County Public Library
2 East Seminary Street
Liberty, IN 47353
Tel: 765-458-5355

University of Southern Indiana
David L. Rice Library
Evansville, IN 47712
E-mail: Libweb@usi.edu
http://www.usi.edu/library/library.asp

Valparaiso/Porter County Public Library
103 Jefferson Street
Valparaiso, IN 46383
Tel: 219-462-0524
Fax: 219-477-4866
TDD: 219-462-4948
http://www.pcpls.lib.in.us/

Veedersburg Public Library
408 North Main Street
Veedersburg, IN 47987
Tel: 765-294-2808
http://glenmar.com/~emoyhbo/vburglib.html

Vermillion County Public Library
385 East Market Street
P.O. Box 97
Newport, IN 47966
Tel: 765-492-3555
http://www.rootsweb.com/~invermil/library.htm

Vigo County Historical Society/Museum
1411 South Sixth Street
Terre Haute, IN 47807
Tel: 812-235-9717
E-mail: vchs@iquest.net
http://web.indstate.edu/community/vchs/home.html

Vigo County Public Library
One Library Square
Terre Haute, IN 47807
Tel: 812-232-1113
http://www.vigo.lib.in.us/

Vincennes University
Lewis Historical Library
1002 N. 1st Street
Vincennes, IN 47591
Tel: 812-885-4330
E-mail: rking@indian.vinu.edu
http://www.vinu.edu/lewis.htm

Wabash County Historical Museum
89 West Hill Street
Wabash, IN 46992

Wabash-Carnegie Public Library
188 West Hill Street
Wabash, IN 46992
Tel: 260) 563-2972
Fax: 260-563-0222
E-mail: general@wabash.lib.in.us
http://www.wabash.lib.in.us/index.htm

Wabash Valley Historical Museum
1411 South Sixth Street
Terre Haute, IN 47802
Tel: 812-235-9717

Wakarusa Public Library
124 N. Elkhart
P.O. Box 485
Wakarusa, IN 46573
Tel: 219-862-2465
Fax: 219-862-4156
E-mail: joneill@wakarusa.lib.in.us

Walkerton/Lincoln Township Public Library
300 North Michigan Street
Walkerton, IN 46574
Tel: 219-586-2933

Walton-Tipton Township Public Library
103 E. Bishop
P.O. Box 406
Walton, IN 46994
Tel: 574-626-2234
E-mail: waltonlibrary@hotmail.com
http://web.incolsa.net/~cmcclosk/

Wanatah Public Library
104 N. Main Street
P.O. Box 299
Wanatah, IN 46390
Tel: 219-733-9303

Warren Public Library
123 E. Third Street
P.O. Box 327
Warren, IN 46792
Tel: 219-375-3450

Warrick County Museum
217 N 1st Street
Boonville, IN 47601
Tel: 812-897-3100

Warsaw Public Library
315 E. Center Street
Warsaw, IN 46580
Tel: 574-267-6011
Fax: 574-269-7739
http://www.wcpl.lib.in.us/

Washington-Carnegie Public Library
300 West Main Street
Washington, IN 47501
Tel: 812-254-4586

Waveland/Brown Township Public Library
P.O. Box 158
Waveland, IN 47989
Tel: 765-435-2700

West Lafayette Public Library
208 West Columbia Street
West Lafayette, IN 47906-3096
Tel: 765-743-2261
Fax: 765-743-2063
http://www.wlaf.lib.in.us/

Westchester Public Library
200 W. Indiana Avenue
Chesterton, IN 46304
Tel: 219-926-7696
http://wpl.lib.in.us/

Westfield Public Library
333 W. Hoover Road
Westfield, IN 46074
Tel: 317-896-9391
Fax: 317-896-3702
http://www.westfieldlibrary.lib.in.us/Library/

Westville-New Durham Public Library
153 Main Street
P.O. Box 789
Westville, IN 46391
Tel: 219-785-2015

White County Historical Museum
101 S. Bluff
Monticello, IN 47960
Tel: 219-583-3998

Whiting Public Library
1735 Oliver Street
Whiting, IN 46394
Tel: 219-659-0269
Fax: 219-659-5833
E-mail: cyh@whiting.lib.in.us
http://www.whiting.lib.in.us/

Willard Library
21 North First Avenue
Evansville, IN 47710
Tel: 812-425-4309
Fax: 812-421-9742
E-mail: willard@willard.lib.in.us
http://www.willard.lib.in.us/

Williamsport/Washington Township Public Library
9 Fall Street
Williamsport, IN 47993
Tel: 765-762-6555
Fax: 765-762-6588
E-mail: wwtpl@incolsa.net
http://www.wwtpl.lib.in.us/

Winchester Public Library
125 N. East Street
Winchester, IN 47394
Tel: 765-584-4824

Wolcott Public Library
101 E. North Street
P.O. Box 376
Wolcott, IN 47995
Tel: 219-279-2695
E-mail: wolclib@ffni.com
http://www.mwprairienet.lib.in.us/Social_Services/
    wollib.html

Worthington Public Library
26 N. Commercial Street
Worthington, IN 47471
Tel: 812-875-3815

York Township Public Library
8908 West 845 North
Earl Park, IN 47942-8701

NEWSPAPER REPOSITORIES

Batesville Memorial Public Library
131 N. Walnut Street
Batesville, IN 47006
Tel: 812-934-4706
Fax: 812-934-6288
E-mail: mkruse@ind.net
http://www.bmpl.cnz.com/

Indiana Historical Society/Library
450 W. Ohio Street
Indianapolis,IN 46202
Tel: 317-232-1882
317-232-1879 (Library)
http://www.indianahistory.org/

Indiana State Library
140 N. Senate Avenue, Room 250 (Gen. Section)
Indianapolis, IN 46204
Tel: 317-232-3675
Fax: 317-232-3728
TDD: 317-232-7763
http://www.statelib.lib.in.us/

Indiana University - Bloomington
Main Library
1320 E. 10th Street
Bloomington, IN 47405-1801
Tel: 812-855-8028 (Reference)
812-855-8084 (Subject and Area Librarians)
812-855-3722 (Government Publications)
E-mail: libref@indiana.edu
http://www.indiana.edu/~librcsd/

St. Joseph County Public Library
1150 East Kern Road
South Bend, Indiana 46614
Tel: 574-251-3700
E-mail: m.waterson@gomail.sjcpl.lib.in.us
http://www.sjcpl.lib.in.us/

VITAL RECORDS

Indiana State Department of Health
Vital Records Department
2 North Meridian Street
Indianapolis, IN 46204
Tel: 317-233-2700
317-233-1325 (Local Health Departments Assistance)
http://www.state.in.us/doh/vital/vr1.html

INDIANA ON THE WEB

Allen County Public Library
http://www.acpl.lib.in.us/

Index of Indiana Marriages Through 1850
http://www.statelib.lib.in.us/www/indiana/
genealogy/mirr.html

Indiana GenWeb Project
http://www.ingenweb.org/

Indiana Historical Society/Library
http://www.indianahistory.org/

Indiana History
http://www.ipfw.edu/ipfwhist/indihist.htm

Indiana in the Civil War
http://www.IndianaintheCivilWar.com/cwrt/cwrt.htm

Indiana State Archives
http://www.state.in.us/icpr/webfile/archives/

Indiana State Library
http://www.statelib.lib.in.us/

Morgan County Public Library
http://www.scican.net/~morglib/genasist/genasist.html

Underground Railroad Operators Directory - Indiana
http://www.ugrr.org//names/map-in.htm

Iowa

Archives, State & National

Iowa State Archives
State Historical Society of Iowa
Capitol Complex
State of Iowa Historical Building
600 East Locust
Des Moines, IA 50319
Tel: 515-281-6200
http://www.iowahistory.org/

National Archives-Central Plains Region
2312 East Bannister Road
Kansas City, MO 64131
Tel: 816-926-6920
Fax: 816-926-6982
E-mail: kansascity.archives@nara.gov
http://www.nara.gov/regional/kansas.html

Genealogical Societies

Adams County Genealogical Society
P.O. Box 117
Prescott, IA 50859

Ankeny Genealogical Chapter
P.O. Box 136
Ankeny, IA 50021

Appanoose County Genealogy Society
1601 S. 16th Street
Centerville, IA 52544

Boone County Genealogical Society
P.O. Box 453
Boone, IA 50036
http://www.rootsweb.com/~iabcgs/

Botna Valley Genealogical Society of East Pottawattamie County
P.O. Box 633
Oakland, IA 51560

Bremer County Genealogical Society
Route 1, Box 132
Plainfield, IA 50666

Buchanan County Genealogical Society
P.O. Box 4
Independence, IA 50644-0004
Tel: 319-334-9333
http://www.rootsweb.com/~iabuchan/gen.htm

Buena Vista Genealogical Society/Library
221 West Railroad Street
Storm Lake, IA 50588
Tel: 712-732-7111

Butler County Genealogy Society
Clarksville Public Library
103 West Greene Street
Clarksville, IA 50619

Carroll County Genealogical Society
P.O. Box 21
Carroll, IA 51401
http://www.rootsweb.com/~iacarrol/CarGenie.html

Cass County Genealogical Society
Atlantic Public Library
507 Poplar Street
Atlantic, IA 50022

Central Iowa Genealogical Society
P.O. Box 945
Marshalltown, IA 50158
http://www.marshallnet.com/~manor/genea/cigs.html

Chickasaw County Genealogical Society
P.O. Box 434
New Hampton, IA 50659
http://www.rootsweb.com/~iachicka/CK_CCGS.htm

Clayton County Genealogical Society
P.O. Box 846
Elkader, IA 52043
http://www.rootsweb.com/~iaccgs/

Clarke County Genealogical Society
Osceola Public Library
300 South Fillmore
Osceola, IA 50213

Clinton County Gateway Genealogical Society
P.O. Box 2256
Clinton, IA 52733-2256
Tel: 563-242-4712
http://www.clintongatewaygensoc.homestead.com/

Crawford County Genealogical Society
P.O. Box 26
Vail, IA 51465

Dallas County Genealogical Society
P.O. Box 264
Dallas Center, IA 50063-0264

Decorah Genealogy Association
Decorah Public Library
202 Winnebago Street
Decorah, IA 52101
Tel: 563-382-8559
Fax: 563-382-4524
E-mail: ddiggers@hotmail.com
http://www.rootsweb.com/~iawinnes/dga.htm

Des Moines County Genealogical Society
P.O. Box 493
Burlington, IA 52601

Dubuque County-Key County Genealogical Society
P.O. Box 13
Dubuque, IA 52004-0013
E-mail: dckcgs_library@hotmail.com
http://www.rootsweb.com/~iadckcgs/

Fayette County Genealogical Society
Fayette County Historical Center
100 North Walnut
West Union, IA 52175
Tel: 563-422-5797
http://www.rootsweb.com/~iafayett/iafirst6.htm

Forest City Municipal Library
115 East L Street
Forest City, IA 50436
Tel: 641-585-4542

Franklin County Genealogical Society
Hampton Public Library
4 Federal Street South
Hampton, IA 50441
E-mail: yankeez@willowtree.com
http://www.willowtree.com/~yankeez/fcgs/page1.htm

Fremont County Genealogical Society
P.O. Box 671
Sidney, IA 51652-0337

Greater Sioux County Genealogical Society
Sioux Center Public Library
327 First Avenue, NE
Sioux Center, IA 51250
Tel: 712-722-2138
E-mail: scplsilo@mtcnet.net
http://www.mtcnet.net/~citysc/library.htm

Greene County Genealogical Society
P.O. Box 133
Jefferson, IA 50129
http://www.rootsweb.com/~iagreene/gcgs.htm

Grundy County Genealogical Society
18419 205th Street
Grundy Center, IA 50638-8733

Guthrie County Genealogical Society
P.O. Box 96B
Jamaica, IA 50128-0096
http://www.rootsweb.com/~iaguthri/html/society.html

Hamilton Heritage Hunters Genealogical Society
P.O. Box 364
Webster City, IA 50595

Hancock County Genealogical Society
P.O. Box 81
Klemme, IA 50449

Hardin County Genealogical Society
P.O. Box 252
Eldora, IA 50627

Harrison County Genealogical Society
Merry Brook School Museum
212 Lincoln Way
Woodbine IA
Tel: 712-647-2593
E-mail:hcgsl@pionet.net
http://www.rootsweb.com/~iaharris/hcgs/

Henry County Genealogical Society
P.O. Box 81
Mt. Pleasant, IA 52641

Howard-Winneshiek Genealogy Society
P.O. Box 362
Cresco, IA 52136
http://www.rootsweb.com/~iawinnes/wcgs.htm

Humboldt County Genealogical Society
Humboldt Public Library
30 6th Street North
Humboldt, IA 50548

Iowa City Genealogical Society
P.O. Box 822
Iowa City, IA 52244
http://www.rootsweb.com/~iajohnso/icgensoc.htm

Iowa Genealogical Society/Library
IGS-NET
6000 Douglas Avenue
P.O. Box 7735
Des Moines, IA 50322-7735
Tel: 515-276-0287
Fax: 515-727-1824
E-mail: igs@iowagenealogy.org
http://www.iowagenealogy.org/library.htm

Iowa Lakes Genealogy Society
Spencer Public Library
21 East 3rd Street
Spencer, IA 51301
Tel: 712-580-7290
Fax: 712-580-7468
http://spencerlibrary.com/genealogy.htm

Jackson County Genealogical Chapter (IGS)
P.O. Box 1065
Maquoketa, IA 52060

Jasper County Genealogical Society
P.O. Box 163
Newton, IA 50208
Tel: 641-792-1522
http://www.usgennet.org/usa/ia/county/jasper1/jcgs/
      jcgs.htm

Jefferson County Genealogical Society
Route 1
Fairfield, IA 52556

Jones County Genealogical Society
P.O. Box 174
Anomosa, IA 52205

**Keomah Genealogical Society
(Keokuk and Mahaska Counties)**
P.O. Box 616
Oskaloosa, IA 52577-0616
Tel: 641-673-9373
http://www.geocities.com/Heartland/Acres/2263/

Lee County Genealogical Society
P.O. Box 303
Keokuk, IA 52632-0303
http://www.rootsweb.com/~ialeecgs/

Lime Creek/Winnebago County Genealogical Society
115 East L Street
Forest City, IA 50436
Tel: 641-585-4542
http://www.pafways.org/genealogy/societies/winnebago.htm

Linn County Genealogical Society
813 1st Avenue SE
P.O. Box 175
Cedar Rapids, IA 52406
Tel: 319-369-0022
http://www.usgennet.org/usa/ia/county/linn/ gen_soc.htm

Louisa County Genealogical Society
607 Highway 61 North
P.O. Box 202
Wapello, IA 52653
http://www.rootsweb.com/~ialcgs/

Lucas County Genealogical Society
Chariton Free Public Library
Family History Room
803 Braden Avenue
Chariton, IA 50049
Tel: 515-774-5514
Fax: 515-774-8695
E-mail: lucasgene@hotmail.com
http://www.lucasco.net/cityhall/Library.html

Madison County Genealogy Society
P.O. Box 26
Winterset, IA 50273-0026

Marion County Genealogical Society
P.O. Box 385
Knoxville, IA 50138
E-mail: severns@harenet.net
http://www.rootsweb.com/~iamcgs/Index.html

Mid-American Genealogical Society
P.O. Box 316
Davenport, IA 52801

Mills County Genealogical Society
Glenwood Public Library
109 North Vine Street
Glenwood, IA 51534
Tel: 712-527-5252
Fax: 712-527-3619
E-mail: crawford@glenwood.lib.ia.us
http://www.glenwood.lib.ia.us/

Monroe County Genealogical Society
Albia Public Library
203 Benton Avenue, E
Albia, IA 52531
http://www.iamonroe.org/monroeco.htm

Montgomery County Genealogical Society
320A Coolbaugh
Red Oak, IA 51566

Nishnabotna Genealogical Society of Shelby County
847 Rd M56
Harlan, IA 51537
http://www.rootsweb.com/~iashelby/scgs.htm

North Central Iowa Genealogical Society
P.O. Box 237
Mason City, IA 50402-0237
http://www.pafways.org/genealogy/societies/
      northcentraliowa/

Northeast Iowa Genealogical Society
Grout Museum
503 South Street
Waterloo, IA 50701-1517
http://www.iowa-counties.com/blackhawk/gene.htm

Northwest Iowa Genealogical Society
LeMars Public Library
46 First Street, SW
LeMars, IA 51031
E-mail: jwintger@pionet.net
http://www.homestead.com/genealogynwia/gen.html

Old Fort Genealogical Society
P.O. Box 1
Fort Madison, IA 52627
http://freepages.genealogy.rootsweb.com/~oldfort/

Page County Genealogical Society
RR 2, Box 236
Shenandoah, IA 51610

Palo Alto County Genealogical Society
Emmetsburg Public Library
707 N Superior Street
Emmetsburg, IA 50536
http://www.rootsweb.com/~iapaloal/pageone.htm

Pioneer Sons & Daughters Genealogical Society, Polk County
P.O. Box 13133
Des Moines, IA 50310-0133

Pottawattamie County Genealogical Society
P.O. Box 394
Council Bluffs, IA 51502
E-mail: pcgs@qwest.net
http://www.rootsweb.com/~iapottaw/PCGS.htm

Poweshiek County Historical and Genealogical Society
206 North Mill Street
P.O. Box 280
Montezuma, IA 50171
Tel: 641-623-3322
E-mail: leon429@netins.net
http://showcase.netins.net/web/powshk/

Sac County Genealogical Society
P.O. Box 54
Sac City, IA 50583
http://www.rootsweb.com/~iasac/gensociety/ gensoc.htm

Scott County Genealogical Society/Library
P.O. Box 3132
Davenport, IA 52808-3132
Tel: 563-326-7902 (Library)
http://www.rootsweb.com/~iascott/scigs.htm

Story County Chapter (IGS)
Chamber of Commerce
1601 Golden Aspen Dr. Suite 110
Ames, IA 50010
http://www.rootsweb.com/~iastory/chapter.htm

Tama County Tracers Genealogical Society
200 North Broadway
Toledo, IA 52342

Taylor County Genealogical Society
RR 3
Bedford, IA 50833

Tree Stumpers
P.O. Box 247
Cleghorn 51014-0247

Union County Genealogical Society
Gibson Memorial Library
200 West Howard
Creston, IA 50801-2339
Tel: 641-782-2277
E-mail: jbriley@aea14.k12.ia.us
http://lserver.aea14.k12.ia.us/SWP/jbriley/ucgen/
    ucgenhome.html

Wapello County Genealogical Society/Library
Amtrack Depot
210 W. Main Street
P.O. Box 163
Ottumwa, IA 52501-0163
Tel: 515-682-8676
E-mail: dhull@franklin.se-iowa.net
http://www.rootsweb.com/~iawapegs/

Warren County Genealogical Society
306 W. Salem
Indianola, IA 50125-2438
E-mail: marieta51@aol.com

Washington County Genealogical Society
P.O. Box 446
Washington, IA 52353-0446
E-mail: washlib@lisco.net
http://www.rootsweb.com/~iawashin/wcgs.htm

Wayne County Genealogical Society
304 North Franklin
Corydon, IA 50060-1330
E-mail: lecompte@netins.net

Webster County Genealogical Society
P.O. Box 1584
Fort Dodge, IA 50501-1584
E-mail: joanewing@dodgenet.com
http://www.rootsweb.com/~iawebste/webgenso.htm

Winneshieck County Genealogical Society
P.O. Box 344
Decorah, IA 52101-0344
E-mail: djsowers@powerbank.net

Woodbury County Genealogical Society
P.O. Box 624
Sioux City, IA 51102-0624
E-mail: moonbeam157@juno.com

Wright County Genealogical Searchers
P.O. Box 225
Clarion, IA 50525-0225
E-mail: gramstad@trvnet.net

HISTORICAL SOCIETIES

Benton County Historical Society
612 First Avenue
Vinton, IA 52349-1705

Boone County Historical Society
602 Story Street
Boone, IA 50036
Tel: 515-432-1907
E-mail: bchs@opencominc.com
http://homepages.opencominc.com/bchs/

Central Community Historical Society
RR 2, Box 98
DeWitt, IA 52742

Cherokee County Historical Society
P.O. Box 247
Cleghorn, IA 51014-0247

Fayette County Helpers Club & Historical Society
100 North Walnut
West Union, IA 52175
Tel: 563-422-5797
http://www.rootsweb.com/~iafayett/iafirst6.htm

Iowa, State Historical Society of
In Des Moines:
600 E. Locust
Des Moines, IA 50319-0290
Tel: 515-281-5111 (Museum)
http://www.iowahistory.org/
In Iowa City:
402 Iowa Avenue
Iowa City, IA 52240-1806
Tel: 319-335-3916
http://www.iowahistory.org/

Johnson County Historical Society
310 5th Street
P.O. Box 5081
Coralville, IA 52241
Tel: 319-351-5738

Kellogg Historical Society/Museum
218 High Street
P.O. Box 295
Kellogg, IA 50135-0295
Tel: 641-526-3430

Linn County Heritage Society
P.O. Box 175
Cedar Rapids, IA 52406

Linn County Historical Society/Museum
101 8th Avenue, SE
Cedar Rapids, IA 52401
Tel: 319-362-1501

Louisa County Historical Society
609 Highway 61 North
Wapello, IA 52653

Pella Historical Society/Village
507 Franklin Street
Pella, IA 50219
Tel: 641-628-4311
Fax: 641-628-9192
E-mail: pellatt@kdsi.net
http://www.kdsi.net/~pellatt/

Pottawattamie County, Historical Society of
226 Pearl Street
Council Bluffs, IA 51503
E-mail: dencatd@aol.com
http://www.geocities.com/Heartland/Plains/5660/

Poweshiek County Historical and Genealogical Society
206 North Mill Street
P.O. Box 280
Montezuma, IA 50171
Tel: 641-623-3322
E-mail: leon429@netins.net
http://showcase.netins.net/web/powshk/

LDS FAMILY HISTORY CENTERS

For locations of Family History Centers in this state, see the Family History Center locator at FamilySearch.
http://www.familysearch.org/eng/Library/FHC/frameset_fhc.asp

ARCHIVES/LIBRARIES/MUSEUMS

Ames Public Library
515 Douglas Avenue
Ames, IA 50010-6215
Tel: 515-239-5630
Fax: 515-232-4571
E-mail: dhayslet@ames.lib.ia.us
http://www.ames.lib.ia.us/

Buena Vista Genealogical Society/Library
221 West Railroad Street
Storm Lake, IA 50588
Tel: 712-732-7111

Burlington Public Library
501 North Fourth Street
Burlington, IA 52601
Tel: 319-753-1647
http://www.burlington.lib.ia.us

Carnegie-Eldon Public Library
608 West Elm Street
Eldon, IA 52554-0430
Tel: 641-652-7517

Carnegie-Montezuma Public Library
200 South 3rd
P.O. Box 158
Montezuma, IA 50171
Tel: 641-623-3417
641-623-3339

Carnegie-Stout Public Library
360 W. 11th Street
Dubuque, IA 52001
Tel: 563-589-4225
Fax: 563-589-4217
http://www.dubuque.lib.ia.us/

Carnegie-Vierson Public Library
823 Broadway
Pella, IA 50219
Tel: 641-628-4268
E-mail: cvpublib@central.edu

Carroll Public Library
118 E. 5th Street
Carroll, IA 51401
Tel: 712-792-3432
Fax: 712-792-0141
http://www.carrolliowa.com/library.htm

Cedar Falls Public Library
524 Main Street
Cedar Falls, IA 50613
Tel: 319-273-8643
Fax: 319-273-8648
E-mail: cfpljohn@iren.net
http://www.iren.net/cfpl/

Cedar Rapids Historical Archives
1201 6th Street, SW
Cedar Rapids, IA 52404
Tel: 319-398-0419

Cedar Rapids Public Library
500 1st Street, SE
Cedar Rapids, IA 52401
Tel: 319-398-5123
Fax: 319-398-0476
http://www.crlibrary.org/

Chariton Free Public Library
803 Braden Avenue
Chariton, IA 50049
Tel: 641-774-5514
Fax: 641-774-8695
E-mail: library@lucasco.net
http://www.lucasco.net/cityhall/Library.html

Clinton Public Library
306 8th Avenue, S
Clinton, IA 52732
Tel: 563-242-8441
Fax: 563-242-8162
E-mail: silo@cis.net (Genealogy)
http://users.cis.net/danh/

Conrad Public Library
102 E. Grundy
Conrad, IA 50621
Tel: 641-366-2583
Fax: 641-366-3105

Danish Immigrant Museum
2212 Washington Street
P.O. Box 178
Elk Horn, IA 51531
Tel: 800-759-9192

Davenport Public Library
321 N. Main Street
Davenport, IA 52801
Tel: 563-326-7832
Fax: 563-326-7809
http://www.rbls.lib.il.us/lib/dpa.html

Decorah Public Library
202 Winnebago Street
Decorah, IA 52101
Tel: 563-382-8559
563-382-3717
Fax: 563-382-4524
E-mail: dpllib@decorah.lib.ia.us
http://www.decorah.lib.ia.us/

Des Moines Public Library
100 Locust
Des Moines, IA 50309
Tel: 515-283-4152
Fax: 515-237-1654
E-mail: pldmdirector@pldminfo.org
http://www.desmoineslibrary.com/orhttp://www.pldmifo.org

Donnellson Public Library
Family History Department
500 Park
Donnellson, IA 52625
E-mail: localfamilyhistory@hotmail.com
http://homepages.rootsweb.com/~donnlibr/

Drake University
Cowles Library
2507 University Avenue
Des Moines, IA 50311-4505
Tel: 515-271-3993 (Administrative)
515-271-2113 (Reference Questions)
Fax: 515-271-3933
http://www.lib.drake.edu/

Eckels Memorial Library
207 S. Highway
P.O. Box 519
Oakland, IA 51560
Tel: 712-482-6668

Elgin Public Library
214 Main Street
P.O. Box 36
Elgin, IA 52141
Tel/Fax: 563-426-5313

Elliott Public Library
401 Main Street
P.O. Box 306
Elliott, IA 51532
Tel: 712-767-2355

Emmetsburg Public Library
707 Superior
Emmetsburg, IA 50536
Tel: 712-852-4009
Fax: 712-852-3785
E-mail: skroesche@ilcc.cc.ia.us
http://www.emmetsburg.com/qualitylife/ Library1.htm

Ericson Public Library
702 Greene Street
Boone, IA 50036
Tel: 515-432-3727
Fax: 515-432-1103
E-mail: rsanders@boone.lib.ia.us
http://www.booneiowa.homestead.com/ericsonlibrary.html

Fairfield Public Library
104 West Adams
Fairfield, IA 52556
Tel: 641-472-6551
Fax: 641-472-3249
E-mail: library@fairfield.com
http://www.fairfield.lib.ia.us/

Fort Dodge Public Library
424 Central Avenue
Fort Dodge, IA 50501
Tel: 515-573-8167
Fax: 515-573-5422
http://www.fortdodge.lib.ia.us/

Frontier Heritage Library
622 Fourth Street
P.O. Box 394
Council Bluffs, IA 51502-0394

Glenwood Public Library
109 N. Vine
Glenwood, IA 51534
Tel: 712-527-5252
Fax: 712-527-3619
E-mail: crawford@glenwood.lib.ia.us
http://www.glenwood.lib.ia.us/

Greenfield Public Library
P.O. Box 328
Greenfield, IA 50849
Tel: 641-743-6120

Grout Museum of History & Science
Hans J. Chryst Archival Library
503 South Street
Waterloo, IA 50701
Tel: 319-234-6357
Fax: 319-236-0500
E-mail: grout@cedarnet.org
http://www.groutmuseumdistrict.org/

Grundy Center Public Library
708 7th Street
Grundy Center, IA 50638
Tel: 319-824-3607
Fax: 319-824-5863

Guthrie Center Public Library
507 State Street
Guthrie Center, IA 50115
Tel/Fax: 641-747-8110

Hampton Public Library
4 Federal Street South
Hampton, IA 50441
Tel: 641-456-4451
Fax: 641-456-2377
E-mail: Hampublib@hampton-dumont.k12.ia.us

Harlan Community Library
718 Court Street
Harlan, IA 51537
Tel: 712-755-5934
Fax: 712-755-3952
E-mail:harlanpl@harlannet.com
http://www.harlan.lib.ia.us/

Hawkins Memorial Library
308 Main
LaPorte, IA 50651
Tel/Fax: 319-342-3025
http://www.cedarnet.org/library/laport.html

Independence Public Library
210 2nd Street, NE
Independence, IA 50644
Tel/Fax: 319-334-2470
E-mail: Indeelibrary@trxinc.com
http://city.trxinc.com/ia/independence/library/

Indianola Public Library
207 North B Street
Indianola, IA 50125
Tel: 515-961-9418
E-mail: info@indianola.lib.ia.us
http://www.indianola.lib.ia.us/

Iowa City Public Library
123 South Linn Street
Iowa City, IA 52240-1820
Tel: 319-356-5200
TDD: 319-356-5494
E-mail: mclark@wade.iowa-city.lib.ia.us
http://www.jeonet.com/city/library.htm

Iowa Genealogical Society/Library
IGS-NET
6000 Douglas Avenue
P.O. Box 7735
Des Moines, IA 50322-7735
Tel: 515-276-0287
Fax: 515-727-1824
E-mail: igs@iowagenealogy.org
http://www.iowagenealogy.org/library.htm

Iowa Masonic Library
The Grand Lodge of Iowa, A.F. & A.M.
813 First Avenue SE
P.O. Box 279
Cedar Rapids, IA 52406-0279
Tel: 319-365-1438
Fax: 319-365-1439
E-mail: Librarian@gl-iowa.org
http://showcase.netins.net/web/iowamasons/ library.html

Iowa, State Historical Society of
In Des Moines:
600 E. Locust
Des Moines, IA 50319-0290
Tel: 515-281-5111 (Museum)
http://www.iowahistory.org/
In Iowa City:
402 Iowa Avenue
Iowa City, IA 52240-1806
Tel: 319-335-3916
http://www.iowahistory.org/

Iowa, State Library of
1112 East Grand Avenue
Des Moines, IA 50319
Tel: 515-281-4105
E-mail: siloweb@www.silo.lib.ia.us
http://www.silo.lib.ia.us

Iowa State University
Parks Library
Osborn and Morrill
Ames, IA 50011
Tel: 515-294-2345
Fax: 515-294-1885
http://www.lib.iastate.edu/

Janesville Public Library
227 Main Street
P.O. Box 328
Janesville, IA 50647
Tel/Fax: 319-987-2925
http://www.cedarnet.org/library/janesvil.html

Kellogg Historical Society/Museum
218 High Street
P.O. Box 295
Kellogg, IA 50135-0295
Tel: 641-526-3430

Kendall Young Library
1201 Wilson Avenue
Webster City, IA 50595
Tel: 515-832-9100
Fax: 515-832-9102
E-mail: info@kendall-young.lib.ia.us
http://www.kendall-young.lib.ia.us/

Keokuk Public Library
210 N. 5th
Keokuk, IA 52632
Tel: 319-524-1483
Fax: 319-524-2320
E-mail: keokukpl@keokuk.lib.ia.us
http://www.interl.net/~keokukpl/LibPages/Hrs.html

Kinney Memorial Library
214 Main Street
Hanlontown, IA 50444
Tel/Fax: 641-896-2888

Knoxville Public Library
213 E. Montgomery
Knoxville, IA 50138
Tel/Fax: 641-828-0585
http://www.youseemore.com/knoxville/

LeMars Public Library
46 First Street, SW
LeMars, IA 51031
Tel: 712-546-5004
Fax: 712-546-5797

Linn County Historical Society/Museum
101 8th Avenue, SE
Cedar Rapids, IA 52401
Tel: 319-362-1501

Livermore Public Library
402 5th Street and 4th Avenue
Livermore, IA 50558
Tel: 515-379-2078
Fax: 515-379-1002
E-mail: livplib@trvnet.net
http://www.trvnet.net/~livplib/

Living History Farms
2600 NW 111th Street
Urbandale, IA 50322
Tel: 515-278-5286
       515-278-2400 (24-hour/event info)
E-mail: info@lhf.org
http://www.lhf.org/

Loras College
Wahlert Memorial Library
1450 Alta Vista
Dubuque, IA 52001
Tel: 319-588-7189
Fax: 319-588-7292
http://www.loras.edu/~LIB/

Lost Nation Public Library
301 Pleasant Street
Lost Nation, IA 52254-0397
Tel/Fax: 563-678-2114

Manchester Public Library
300 N. Franklin
Manchester, IA 52057
Tel: 563-927-3719
Fax: 563-927-3058
http://www.manchesteriowa.org/libraryl.htm

Marshalltown Public Library
36 N. Center Street
Marshalltown, IA 50158
Tel: 641-754-5738
Fax: 641-754-5708
E-mail: library@marshallnet.com
http://www.marshallnet.com/library.htm

Mason City Public Library
225 2nd Street, SE
Mason City, IA 50401
Tel: 641-421-3668
Fax: 641-423-2615
E-mail: librarian@mcpl.org
http://www.mcpl.org/

Matilda J. Gibson Memorial Library
200 W Howard Street
Creston, IA 50801
Tel: 641-782-2277
Fax: 641-782-4604
E-mail: cstanger@aea14.k12.ia.us

Merry Brook Museum
212 Lincoln Way
Woodbine, IA 51579
Tel: 712-647-2593

Montgomery Memorial Library
711 Main Street
P.O. Box 207
Jewell, IA 50130
Tel: 515-827-5112
E-mail: jewell_public.lib@s-hamilton.k12.ia.us

Musser Public Library
304 Iowa Avenue
Muscatine, IA 52761-3875
Tel: 563-263-3472
Fax: 563-264-1033
E-mail: mtate@libby.rbls.lib.il.us
http://www.rbls.lib.il.us/mus/orhttp://www.muscatineli-
       brary.org

Newberry Library
60 West Walton Street
Chicago, IL 60610-3305
Tel: 312-943-9090 (Main)
312-255-3506 (Reference)
312-255-3512 (Genealogy)
E-mail: furmans@newberry.org
http://www.newberry.org/

Northwestern Community College
Ramaker Library
101 7th Street, SW
Orange City, IA 51041-1996
Tel: 712-707-7000
http://www.nwciowa.edu/dept/library/

Oelwein Public Library
22 1st Avenue, NW
Oelwein, IA 50662
Tel/Fax: 319-283-1515
E-mail: publiclibrary@oelwein.com

Onawa Public Library
707 Iowa Avenue
Onawa, IA 51040
Tel: 712-423-1733
Fax: 712-423-3828

Orange City Public Library
112 Albany Street, SE
Orange City, IA 51041
Tel: 712-737-4302
Fax: 712-737-4431
E-mail: floydj@worf.netins.net
http://showcase.netins.net/web/nwc-iowa/ OCPubLib/

Osage Public Library
406 Main Street
Osage, IA 50461
Tel; 641-732-3323
Fax: 641-732-4419
E-mail: osagepl@osage.net
http://www.osage.net/~osagepl/

Oskaloosa Public Library
301 South Market
Oskaloosa, IA 52577
Tel: 641-673-0441
Fax: 641-673-6237
E-mail: OPL@wmpenn.edu
http://www.wmpenn.edu/PennWeb/OPL/OPL.html

Ottumwa Public Library
102 West Fourth Street
Ottumwa, IA 52501
Tel: 641-682-7563
http://www.ottumwalibrary.com/

Pella Historical Society/Village
507 Franklin Street
Pella, IA 50219
Tel: 641-628-4311
Fax: 641-628-9192
E-mail: pellatt@kdsi.net
http://www.kdsi.net/~pellatt/

Pioneer Heritage Public Library
204 N. Vine Street
P.O. Box 188
LeGrand, IA 50142
Tel/Fax: 641-479-2122

Pocahontas Public Library
14 Second Avenue, NW
Pocahontas, IA 50574
Tel/Fax: 712-335-4471
E-mail: pokypl@ncn.net
http://www.ncn.net/~pokypl/

Putnam Museum of History and Natural Science
Putnam Museum Library
1717 West 12th Street
Davenport, IA 52807
Tel: 563-324-1933
Fax: 563-324-6638
http://www.putnam.org/

Red Oak Public Library
400 N. 2nd Street
Red Oak, IA 51566
Tel: 712-623-6516
Fax: 712-623-6518
http://www.redoakiowa.com/ropl/

Richardson-Sloane Genealogical Library
1019 Mound Street, Suite 301
Davenport, IA 52803
Tel: 563-383-0007
800-828-4363
Fax: 319-383-0008

Scott County Genealogical Society/Library
P.O. Box 3132
Davenport, IA 52808-3132
Tel: 563-326-7902 (Library)
http://www.rootsweb.com/~iascott/scigs.htm

Scott County Library System
215 N. 2nd Street
Eldridge, IA 52748
Tel: 563-285-4794
Fax: 563-285-4743

Shelby County Historical Museum
1805 Morse
Harlan, IA 51537
Tel: 712-755-2437

Sidney Public Library
604 Clay Street
P.O. Box 479
Sidney, IA 51652
Tel: 712-374-2223

Sioux Center Public Library
327 First Avenue, NE
Sioux Center, IA 51250
Tel: 712-722-2138
E-mail: scplsilo@mtcnet.net
http://www.mtcnet.net/~citysc/library.htm

Sioux City Public Library
529 Pierce Street
Sioux City, IA 51101
Tel: 712-255-2933
Fax: 712-279-6432
E-mail: questions@mail.sc.lib.ia.us
http://www.sc.lib.ia.us/

Spencer Public Library
21 E. Third Street
Spencer, IA 51301
Tel: 712-264-7290
Fax: 712-580-7468
E-mail: info@spencerlibrary.com
http://spencerlibrary.com/

Storm Lake Public Library
609 Cayuga Street
Storm Lake, IA 50588
Tel: 712-732-8026
Fax: 712-732-7609
E-mail: slpl@stormlake.org
http://www.stormlake.org/city/pages/library.htm

Tama Public Library
901 McClellan
P.O. Box 308 Tama, IA 52339
Tel/Fax: 515-484-4484

University of Iowa
100 Main Library
Iowa City, IA 52242
Tel: 319-335-5299
Fax: 319-335-5900
http://www.lib.uiowa.edu/

University of Northern Iowa
Rod Library
Cedar Falls, IA 50613-3675
Tel: 319-273-2838
Fax: 319-273-2913
TTY: 319-273-7299
http://www.library.uni.edu/

Urbandale Public Library
3520 86th Street
Urbandale, IA 50322
Tel: 515-278-3945
Fax: 515-278-3918
E-mail: reference@urbandale.org
http://www.urbandalelibrary.org/

Vesterheim Norwegian American Museum/Library
523 W. Water Street
P.O. Box 379
Decorah, IA 52101
Tel: 563-382-9681
Fax: 563-382-8828
E-mail: vesterheim@vesterheim.org
http://www.vesterheim.org/

Waterloo Public Library
415 Commercial Street
Waterloo, IA 50701
Tel: 319-291-4521
     319-291-4476 (information)
Fax: 319-291-6736
http://www.wplwloo.lib.ia.us/wpl.html

Waukon Municipal Library
401 1st Avenue
Waukon, IA 52172
Tel/Fax: 563-568-4424

Webb Shadle Memorial Library
301 W. Dallas
Pleasantville, IA 50225
Tel: 515-848-5617

NEWSPAPERS REPOSITORIES

Iowa Genealogical Society/Library
IGS-NET
6000 Douglas Avenue
P.O. Box 7735
Des Moines, IA 50322-7735
Tel: 515-276-0287
Fax: 515-727-1824
E-mail: igs@iowagenealogy.org
http://www.iowagenealogy.org/library.htm

Iowa, State Historical Society of
In Des Moines:
600 E. Locust
Des Moines, IA 50319-0290
Tel: 515-281-5111 (Museum)
http://www.iowahistory.org/
In Iowa City:
402 Iowa Avenue
Iowa City, IA 52240-1806
Tel: 319-335-3916
http://www.iowahistory.org/

VITAL RECORDS

Iowa Department of Public Health
Bureau of Vital Records
Lucas State Office Building, 1st Floor
Des Moines, IA 50319-0075
Tel: 515-281-4944
    515-281-5787
http://www.idph.state.ia.us/pa/vr.htm

IOWA ON THE WEB

Iowa Genweb Project
http://iagenweb.org/

Iowa Historical Information
http://www.iowa-counties.com/historical/index.shtml

North Central Iowa Genealogy Connection
http://www.pafways.org/

Underground Railroad Operators-Iowa
http://www.ugrr.org//names/map-ia.htm

Kansas

Archives, State & National

Kansas State Archives
Kansas State Historical Society/Library & Archives
The Kansas History Center
6425 SW Sixth Street
Topeka, KS 66615-1099
Tel: 785-272-8681
TTY: 785-272-8683
Fax: 785-272-8682
E-mail: Webmaster@kshs.org
http://www.kshs.org/archives/index.htm

National Archives-Central Plains Region
2312 East Bannister Road
Kansas City, MO 64131
Tel: 816-926-6920
Fax: 816-926-6982
E-mail: kansascity.archives@nara.gov
http://www.nara.gov/regional/kansas.html

Genealogical Societies

Atchison County Genealogical Society
Atchison Library
401 Kansas Avenue
P.O. Box 303
Atchison, KS 66002
Tel: 913-367-1902
http://skyways.lib.ks.us/genweb/society/atchison/
ackgs.htm

Barton County Genealogical Society, Inc.
Great Bend Public Library
1409 Williams Street
P.O. Box 425
Great Bend, KS 67530
Tel: 620-792-2409
http://www.ckls.org/~gbpl/

Bluestem Genealogical Society
P.O. Box 582
Eureka, KS 67045

Branches and Twigs Genealogical Society
Kingman Carnegie Library
445 North Main
Kingman, KS 67068
Tel: 620-532-3061
Fax: 620-532-2528
http://skyways.lib.ks.us/library/kingman/

Bukovina Society of the Americas/Museum
722 Washington
P.O. Box 81
Ellis, KS 67637
E-mail: owindholz@ruraltel.net
http://members.aol.com/LJensen/bukovina.html

Chanute Genealogical Society
1010 South Allen
Chanute, KS 66720
http://www.rootsweb.com/~kscgs/

Cherokee County Kansas Genealogical/Historical Society
100 South Tennessee
P.O. Box 33
Columbus, KS 66725-0033
Tel: 620-429-2992
E-mail: cckghs@columbus-ks.com
http://skyways.lib.ks.us/genweb/cherokee/society/
cckghs.html

Cloud County Genealogical Society
P.O. Box 202
Concordia, KS 66901
E-mail: CloudGen@care2.com
http://www.dustdevil.com/towns/concordia/history/ ccgs/

Coffey County Genealogical Society
712 Sanders
Burlington, KS 66839
Tel: 620-364-8795

Cowley County Genealogical Society
P.O. Box 102
Arkansas City, KS 67005
Tel: 620-442-6750

Crawford County Genealogical Society
Pittsburg Public Library
308 North Walnut
Pittsburg, KS 66762
Tel: 620-231-8110
Fax: 620-232-2258
http://skyways.lib.ks.us/library/pittsburg/

Decatur County Genealogical Society
258 South Penn
Oberlin, KS 67749-2245
Tel: 785-475-2712

Douglass County Genealogical Society, Inc.
P.O. Box 3664
Lawrence, KS 66046-0664
http://skyways.lib.ks.us/genweb/douglas/dckgs.htm

Family Researchers
Geary County Historical Society
530 North Adams
P.O. Box 1161
Junction City, KS 66441
Tel: 785-238-1666

Finney County Genealogical Society
P.O. Box 592
Garden City, KS 67846-0592
Tel: 620-272-3680
Fax: 620-272-3682
E-mail: yolen@hotpop.com

Flint Hills Genealogical Society
P.O. Box 555
Emporia, KS 66801-0555
Tel: 316-343-2719
E-mail: lyoncoks@bigfoot.com
http://www.rootsweb.com/~ksfhgslc/

Fort Hays Genealogical Society
Fort Hays State University
Forsyth Library, Western Collection Room
600 Park Street
Hays, KS 67601
E-mail: semk@fhsuvm.fhsu.edu
http://www.fhsu.edu/forsyth_lib/specoll1.htm

Four State Genealogy Society
Galena Public Library
22 Galena Avenue
Galena, KS 66739
Tel: 620-783-5132

Franklin County Genealogical Society
P.O. Box 353
Ottawa, KS 66067
http://www.ukans.edu/~hisite/franklin/fcgs/

Genealogical Researchers
Dickinson County Historical Society's Heritage Center
412 South Campbell
Abilene, KS 67410
Tel: 785-263-2681
http://www.ku.edu/heritage/abilene/herctr.html

Harper County Genealogical Society
P.O. Box 224
Freeport, Kansas 67049
Tel: 620-896-2959 (Harper Public Library)
http://skyways.lib.ks.us/kansas/genweb/society/ harper/

Heritage Genealogical Society
Rankin Memorial Library
502 Indiana
Neodesha, KS 66757
Tel: 620-325-3275
http://skyways.lib.ks.us/kansas/genweb/wilson/
rankin.html

Hodgeman County Genealogical Society
P.O. Box 441
Jetmore, KS 67854

Jefferson County Genealogical Society
P.O. Box 174
Oskaloosa, KS 66066-0174
Tel: 785-863-2070
E-mail: jcgs1979@yahoo.com

Johnson County Genealogical Society/Library
8700 Shawnee Mission Parkway
P.O. Box 12666
Shawnee Mission, KS 66282
E-mail: kenl@sky.net
http://www.johnsoncountykansasgenealogy.org/

Kansas Council of Genealogical Societies
P.O. Box 3858
Topeka, KS 66604-6858
E-mail: mphil@parod.com
http://skyways.lib.ks.us/genweb/kcgs/

Kansas Genealogical Society, Inc.
Village Square Mall, Lower Level
2601 Central Avenue
P.O. Box 103
Dodge City, KS 67801
Tel: 620-225-1951
http://www.dodgecity.net/kgs/

Leavenworth County Genealogical Society
http://skyways.lib.ks.us/genweb/society/leavenwo/

Midwest Historical and Genealogical Society
1203 North Main
P.O. Box 1121
Wichita, KS 67201-1121
Tel: 316-264-3611
http://skyways.lib.ks.us/kansas/genweb/mhgs/

Montgomery County Genealogy Society
P.O. Box 444
Coffeyville, KS 67337

Morris County Genealogical Society
P.O. Box 114
White City, KS 66872

North Central Kansas Genealogical Society
P.O. Box 251
Cawker City, KS 67430
Tel: 785-781-4925 (Cawker City Library)
http://skyways.lib.ks.us/kansas/towns/Cawker/
    library.html#society

Northwest Kansas Genealogical and Historical Society
Oakley Library
700 West 3rd
Oakley, KS 67748
Tel: 785-672-4776

Norton County Genealogical Society
101 East Lincoln
Norton, KS 67654
Tel: 785-877-2481 (Library)

Old Fort Genealogical Society
of Southeastern Kansas, Inc.
502 South National
Fort Scott, KS 66701
Tel: 620-223-3300
http://skyways.lib.ks.us/genweb/society/ftscott/

Osborne County Genealogical
and Historical Society, Inc.
Osborne Public Library
325 West Main
Osborne, KS 67473
Tel: 785-346-5486

Phillips County Genealogical Society
P.O. Box 114
Phillipsburg, KS 67661
Tel: 785-543-5325
http://skyways.lib.ks.us/genweb/phillips/plgensoc. html

Rawlins County Genealogical Society
Atwood Public Library
102 South Sixth
Atwood, KS 67730
Tel: 785-626-3805
Fax: 785-626-3670
E-mail: atwoodli@ruraltel.net
http://skyways.lib.ks.us/genweb/rawlins/library.html

Reno County Genealogical Society
Hutchinson Public LIbrary
901 North Main Street
P.O. Box 5
Hutchinson, KS 67504
Tel: 620-663-5441
http://www.hplsck.org/200.htm

Riley County Genealogical Society/Library
2005 Claflin Road
Manhattan, KS 66502
Tel: 785-565-6495
http://www.rileycgs.com/

Santa Fe Trail Genealogical Society
P.O. Box 528
Syracuse, KS 67878

Smoky Valley Genealogical Society
211 West Iron Street, Suite 205
Salina, Kansas 67401
Tel: 785-825-7573
http://skyways.lib.ks.us/kansas/genweb/ottawa/
    smoky.html

Southeast Kansas Genealogy Society
Iola Public Library
218 E. Madison
P.O. Box 393
Iola, KS 66749
Tel: 620-365-3262
Fax: 620-365-5137
E-mail: iolaref@alltel.net
http://www.iola.lib.ks.us/

Stafford County Historical and Genealogical Society
100 South Main
P.O. Box 249
Stafford, KS 67578
Tel: 620-234-5664
http://home.earthlink.net/~mjhathaway61/

Tonganoxie Genealogical Society
Tonganoxie Public Library
305 S Bury Street
P.O. Box 354
Tonganoxie, KS 66086
Tel: 913-845-3281
E-mail: beckie@tongie.lib.ks.us
http://skyways.lib.ks.us/library/tongie/

Topeka Genealogical Society/Library
2717 SE Indiana Avenue
P.O. Box 4048
Topeka, KS 66604
Tel: 785-233-5762
E-mail: TGS@networksplus.net
http://www.networksplus.net/donno/

Washington County Historical and Genealogical Society
P.O. Box 31
Washington, KS 66968-0031
Tel: 785-325-2198

Wichita Genealogical Society
P.O. Box 3705
Wichita, KS 67201-3705
E-mail: wardm@mail.dec.com
http://www.ukans.edu/kansas/wgs/

Woodson County Genealogical Society
608 North Prairie
Yates Center, KS 66783

HISTORICAL SOCIETIES

Albany Historical Society, Inc.
415 Grant
Sabetha, KS 66534

Allen County Historical Society/Library
207 North Jefferson
Iola, KS 66749
Tel: 620-365-3051

Anderson County Historical Society/Library
6th and Maple
Garnett, KS 66032

Argonia and Western Sumner County Historical Society
221 West Garfield
Argonia, KS 67004

Arkansas City Historical Society
1400 North 3rd
Arkansas City, KS 67005

Atchison County Historical Society/Museum
200 South Main
P.O. Box 201
Atchison, KS 66002
Tel: 913-367-6238
http://www.atchisonkansas.net/Tourism/ HistSoct.htm

Augusta Historical Society/Museum
303 State Street
P.O. Box 545
Augusta, KS 67010
Tel: 316-775-5655
http://www.augusta-ks.org/Museum.htm

Barton County Historical Society/Museum
85 South Highway 281
P.O. Box 1091
Great Bend, KS 67530
Tel: 620-793-5125
E-mail: shorock@midusa.net

Baxter Springs Historical Society/Museum
740 East Avenue
P.O. Box 514
Baxter Springs, KS 66713
Tel: 620-856-2385
http://home.4state.com/~heritagectr/gallery.html

Brown County Historical Society/Library
611 Utah Street
Hiawatha, KS 66434
Tel: 785-742-3330

Butler County Historical Society/Museum
383 East Central
P.O. Box 696
El Dorado, KS 67042
Tel: 316-321-9333

Butterfield Trail Association &
Historical Society of Logan County, Kansas, Inc.
Highway 25 and Museum Drive
P.O. Box 336
Russell Springs, KS 67755
Tel: 785-751-4242
E-mail: wardtayl@st-tel.net
http://www.windyplains.com/butterfield/

Caney Valley Historical Society
4th & Wood
P.O. Box 354
Caney, KS 67333
Tel: 620-879-2210

Chase County Historical Society/Library/Museum
301 Broadway
P.O. Box 375
Cottonwood Falls, KS 66845
Tel: 620-273-8500

Cherokee County Kansas Genealogical/Historical Society
100 South Tennessee
P.O. Box 33
Columbus, KS 66725-0033
Tel: 620-429-2992
E-mail: cckghs@columbus-ks.com
http://skyways.lib.ks.us/genweb/cherokee/society/
        cckghs.html

Cheyenne County Historical Society
West Highway 36
P.O. Box 611
St. Francis, KS 67756
Tel: 785-332-2504

Clark County Historical Society
Pioneer-Krier Museum
430 West 4th
P.O. Box 862
Ashland, KS 67831
Tel: 620-635-2227

Clay County Historical Society
Clay County Museum
2121 7th Street
Clay Center, KS 67432
Tel: 785-632-3786

Clearwater Historical Society
149 North 4th
P.O. Box 453
Clearwater, KS 67026
Tel: 620-584-2444

Clifton Historical Society
Clifton Museum
108 Clifton Street
Clifton, KS 66937
Tel: 785-455-3555

Clinton Lake Historical Society
261 North 851 Diag. Road
Overbrook, KS 66524
Tel: 785-748-9836

Cloud County Historical Society
Cloud County Historical Museum
635 Broadway
Concordia, KS 66901
Tel: 785-243-2866

Comanche County Historical Society, Inc.
410 South Baltimore
P.O. Box 177
Coldwater, KS 67029

Cowley County Historical Society/Library
1011 Mansfield
Winfield, KS 67156
Tel: 620-221-4811

Crawford County Historical Society/Museum
651 South Highway 69
Pittsburg, KS 66762
Tel: 620-231-1440

Dickinson County Historical Society
Heritage Center
412 South Campbell
Abilene, KS 67410
Tel: 785-263-2681
http://history.cc.ukans.edu/heritage/abilene/
    herctr.html

Doniphan County Historical Society
Library District #1
105 North Main
Troy, KS 66087
Tel: 785-985-2597

Douglas County Historical Society
Watkins Community Museum of History
1047 Massachusetts
Lawrence, KS 66044
Tel: 785-841-4109
E-mail: wcmhist@sunflower.com
http://www.ci.lawrence.ks.us/museums/watkins.html

Downs Carnegie Library, Historical Society of
504 South Morgan
Downs, KS 67437
Tel: 785-454-3821

Edwards County Historical Society
Highway 56
Kinsley, KS 67547
Tel: 620-659-2420

Elk County Historical Society
Caney Valley Ranch
Route 1
Grenola, KS 67346

Ellis County Historical Society
100 West 7th Street
Hays, KS 67601
Tel: 785-628-2624

Ellsworth County Historical Society
104 West Main
Ellsworth, KS 67439
Tel: 785-472-3059
http://www.cityofellsworth.org/Historical%20 Society.htm

Eudora Area Historical Society
620 Elm
P.O. Box 370
Eudora, KS 66025

Finney County Historical Society
Finnup Park
403 South 4th
P.O. Box 796
Garden City, KS 67846
Tel: 620-272-3664

First National Black Historical Society of Kansas
601 North Water
P.O. Box 2695
Wichita, KS 67201
Tel: 316-262-7651

Florence Historical Society
408 West 7th Street
Florence, KS 66851
Tel: 620-878-4474 (Harvey House)

Ford County Historical Society
P.O. Box 131
Dodge City, KS 67801
http://www.ku.edu/kansas/ford/

Fort Larned Historical Society, Inc.
Santa Fe Trail Center
Route 3
Larned, KS 67550
Tel: 620-285-2054
Fax: 620-285-7491
E-mail: trailctr@larned.net
http://www.larned.net/trailctr/

Fort Leavenworth Historical Society
Frontier Army Museum Gift Shop
100 Reynolds Avenue
Fort Leavenworth, KS 66027
Tel: 913-651-7440

Franklin County Historical Society/Library
315 S Main Street
P.O. Box 145
Ottawa, KS 66067
Tel: 785-242-1232
http://www.ukans.edu/~hisite/franklin/fchs/

Frederic Remington Area Historical Society
P.O. Box 133
Whitewater, KS 67154
E-mail: aharder@southwind.net
http://skyways.lib.ks.us/towns/Brainerd/

Geary County Historical Society
530 North Adams
P.O. Box 1161
Junction City, KS 66441
Tel: 785-238-1666

Graham County Historical Society
Graham County Public Library Building
414 North West
Hill City, KS 67642
Tel: 785-674-5601
http://www.geocities.com/RainForest/Vines/5320/

Grant County Museum and Historical Society
300 East Oklahoma Avenue
P.O. Box 906
Ulysses, KS 67880
Tel: 620-356-3009

Greeley County Historical Society/Library
P.O. Box 231
Tribune, KS 67879
Tel: 620-376-4996

Greenwood County Historical Society/Library/Museum
120 West 4th Street
Eureka, KS 67045-1445
Tel: 620-583-6682
E-mail: gwhistory@correct-connect.com
http://skyways.lib.ks.us/kansas/genweb/greenwoo/gchs.htm

Halstead Historical Society
116 East First
P.O. Box 88
Halstead, KS 67056
Tel: 316-835-2267
http://www.halsteadkansas.com/historical.html

Harper City Historical Society
Harper Public Library
1002 Oak
Harper, KS 67058
Tel: 620-896-2959

Harvey County Historical Society/Library
203 N. Main
P.O. Box 4
Newton, KS 67114
Tel: 316-283-2221
http://www.infonewtonks.org/tourism/h_society.htm

Haskell County Historical Society
Fairgrounds
P.O. Box 101
Sublette, KS 67877
Tel: 620-675-8344

Heritage of the Plains Historical Society
Arnold, KS 67515

Hillsboro Historical Society
Adobe House Museum
501 South Ash
Hillsboro, KS 67063
Tel: 620-947-3775

Historic Preservation Association of Bourbon County
117 South Main
Fort Scott, KS 66701

Hodgeman County Historical Society
Route 2
P.O. Box 114
Jetmore, KS 67854

Humboldt Historical Society
P.O. Box 63
Humboldt, KS 66748

Inman Heritage Association
P.O. Box 217
Inman, KS 67546

Iron Horse Historical Society
P.O. Box 8
Parsons, KS 67357
Tel: 620-421-1959

Jackson County Historical Society/Library
Jackson County Museum
4th and New
P.O. Box 104
Holton, KS 66436
Tel: 785-364-2087

Jefferson County Historical Society/library
Old Jefferson Town
Highway 59
P.O. Box 146
Oskaloosa, KS 66066
Tel: 785-863-2070

Jewell County Historical Society
201 North Commercial
Mankato, KS 66956
http://skyways.lib.ks.us/towns/Mankato/ museum.html

Kansas State Historical Society/Library & Archives
The Kansas History Center
6425 SW Sixth Street
Topeka, KS 66615-1099
Tel: 785-272-8681
Fax: 785-272-8682
TTY: 785-272-8683
E-mail: Webmaster@kshs.org
http://www.kshs.org/places/khcenter.htm

Kearny County Historical Society and Museum
111 South Buffalo Street
P.O. Box 329
Lakin, KS 67860
Tel: 620-355-7448
http://skyways.lib.ks.us/towns/Lakin/museum.html

Kingman County Historical Society/Library/Museum
400 North Main
P.O. Box 281
Kingman, KS 67068
Tel: 620-532-5274
http://skyways.lib.ks.us/towns/Kingman/museum/

Lake Region Historical Society
121 East 2nd
Ottawa, KS 66067

Lane County Historical Society/Museum
333 North Main
P.O. Box 821
Dighton, KS 67839
Tel: 620-397-5652

Lansing Historical Society
115 East Kansas Avenue
P.O. Box 32
Lansing, KS 66043

Leavenworth County Historical Society/Museum
1128 5th Avenue
Leavenworth, KS 66048
Tel: 913-682-7759
Fax: 913-682-2089
http://leavenworth-net.com/lchs/

Lecompton Historical Society
P.O. Box 372
Lecompton, KS 66050
Tel: 785-887-6285
785-887-6148

Lenexa Historical Society
Legler Barn Museum
14907 West 87th Street Pkwy.
Lenexa, KS 66215
Tel: 913-492-0038
E-mail: lhskc@kc.net
http://www.idir.net/~lhskc/

Lincoln County Historical Society
214 West Lincoln Avenue
Lincoln, KS 67455

Linn County Historical Society
Dunlap Park
P.O. Box 137
Pleasanton, KS 66075
Tel: 913-352-8739

Luray Historical Society/Library
P.O. Box 134
Luray 67649-0134

Lyon County Historical Society/Museum
118 East 6th Avenue
Emporia, KS 66801-3922
Tel: 620-342-0933
http://slim.emporia.edu/resource/lchs/LyonCo.htm

Marquette Historical Society, Inc.
202 North Washington
Marquette, KS 67464
Tel: 785-546-2205 (City Hall)

Marshall County Historical Society
1207 Broadway
Marysville, KS 66508
Tel: 785-562-5012

Medicine Lodge Historical Society
Highway 160
Medicine Lodge, KS 67104
Tel: 620-886-3417 (Chamber of Commerce)

Miami County Historical Society/Library
North Side of Square
P.O. Box 393
Paola, KS 66071

Midwest Historical and Genealogical Society
1203 North Main
P.O. Box 1121
Wichita, KS 67201-1121
Tel: 316-264-3611
http://skyways.lib.ks.us/kansas/genweb/mhgs/

Milan Historical Society
Park House Museum
Milan, KS 67105

Mitchell County Historical Society/Museum
402 West 8th
Beloit, KS 67420
Tel: 785-738-5355
Fax: 785-738-9503
http://members.nckcn.com/mchs/

Morris County Historical Society
Council Grove Public Library
303 West Main
Council Grove, KS 66846
Tel: 620-767-5716

Morton County Historical Society
U.S. Highway 56
P.O. Box 1248
Elkhart, KS 67950
Tel: 620-697-2833
E-mail: mtcomuseum@elkhart.com
http://www.mtcoks.com/museum/museum.html

Moundridge Historical Association
P.O. Box 69
Moundridge, KS 67107

Mulvane Historical Society
Mulvane Historical Museum
300 West Main
P.O. Box 117
Mulvane, KS 67110
Tel: 316-777-0506

Nemaha County Historical Society/Library
6th and Nemaha
Seneca, KS 66538
http://www.ku.edu/kansas/seneca/gensoc/ gensoc.html

Ness County Historical Society
Ness County Historical Museum
123 South Pennsylvania Avenue
Ness City, KS 67560
Tel: 785-798-3298
http://skyways.lib.ks.us/towns/NessCity/ museum.html

Nicodemus Historical Society
P.O. Box 131
Bogue, KS 67625
Tel: 785-674-3311

Northwest Kansas Genealogical and Historical Society
Oakley Library
700 West 3rd
Oakley, KS 67748
Tel: 785-672-4776

Northwest Kansas Heritage Center
401 Kansas Street
P.O. Box 284
Brewster, KS 67732
Tel: 785-694-2891

Norton County Historical Society
105 East Lincoln
P.O. Box 303
Norton, KS 67654
Tel: 785-877-5107
E-mail: bullock1@ruraltel.net
http://www.nex-tech.com/clients/nchistory/

Olathe Historical Society
12466 Twilight
Olathe, KS 66062

Old Fort Bissell/Phillips County Historical Society, Inc.
City Park
Route 2
P.O. Box 18A
Phillipsburg, KS 67661
Tel: 785-543-6212

Onaga Historical Society
310 East 2nd
Onaga, KS 66521

Osage County Historical Society
631 Topeka
P.O. Box 361
Lyndon, KS 66451
Tel: 785-828-3477

Osage Mission/Neosho County Historical Society
P.O. Box 113
St. Paul, KS 66771
Tel: 620-449-2320

Osborne County Genealogical and Historical Society, Inc.
Osborne Public Library
325 West Main
Osborne, KS 67473
Tel: 785-346-5486

Oswego Historical Society/Museum
410 Commercial
Oswego, KS 67356
Tel: 620-795-4500

Parsons Historical Society
401 South Corning
Parsons, KS 67357
Tel: 620-421-3382

Peabody Historical Society
Route 2
Peabody, KS 66866

Pratt County Historical Society/Library
208 South Ninnescah
Pratt, KS 67124
Tel: 620-672-7874

Rawlins County Historical Society/Museum
308 State
Atwood, KS 67730
Tel: 785-626-3885

Reno County Historical Society, Inc.
100 South Walnut
P.O. Box 664
Hutchinson, KS 67504-0664
Tel: 620-662-1184

Republic County Historical Society
West Highway 36
P.O. Box 218
Belleville, KS 66935
Tel: 785-527-5971

Rice County Historical Society
Coronado Quivira Museum
105 West Lyon
Lyons, KS 67554
Tel: 620-257-3941
http://skyways.lib.ks.us/towns/Lyons/museum/

Riley County Historical Society
2309 Claflin Road
Manhattan, KS 66502
Tel: 785-565-6490

Rock Creek Valley Historical Society
P.O. Box 13
Westmoreland, KS 66549

Rooks County Historical Society/Museum
Frank Walker Museum
921 South Cedar
Stockton, KS 67669
Tel: 785-425-7217
http://www.rookscounty.net/museum.htm

Rush County Historical Society, Inc.
Post Rock Museum
202 West First
P.O. Box 473
LaCrosse, KS 67548
Tel: 785-222-2719

Russell County Historical Society/Library
331 N Kansas Street
Russell, KS 67665
Tel: 785-483-3637

St. Marys Historical Society/Library
106 East Mission
St. Marys, KS 66536
Tel: 913-437-6600

Saline County Historical Society
216 West Bond Street
Salina, KS 67401

Santa Fe Trail Historical Society
P.O. Box 443
Baldwin, KS 66006

Seward County Historical Society
567 East Cedar
Liberal, KS 67901
Tel: 620-624-7624

Shawnee County Historical Society
P.O. Box 2201
Topeka, KS 66601

Shawnee Historical Society
P.O. Box 3042
Shawnee, KS 67740

Sheridan County Historical Society
County Courthouse
817 Royal Avenue
P.O. Box 274
Hoxie, KS 67740
Tel: 785-675-3501

Sherman County Historical Society
P.O. Box 684
Goodland, KS 67735
Tel: 785-899-5461
http://skyways.lib.ks.us/genweb/sherman/shchs.html

Smith County Historical Society
P.O. Box 38
Kensington, KS 66951

Smoky Valley Historical Association
Lindsborg Community Library
111 South Main
Lindsborg, KS 67456
Tel: 785-227-2710

Stafford County Historical and Genealogical Society
100 South Main
P.O. Box 249
Stafford, KS 67578
Tel: 620-234-5664
http://home.earthlink.net/~mjhathaway61/

Stanton County Historical Society
104 East Highland
P.O. Box 806
Johnson, KS 67855
Tel: 620-492-1526

Sumner County Historical Society
P.O. Box 213
Mulvane, KS 67110

Swiss Mennonite Cultural and Historical Association
109 East Hirschler
Moundridge, KS 67107
Tel: 620-345-8320 (Edan Church Office)
http://www.swissmennonite.org/

Thomas County Historical Society
1905 South Franklin Avenue
Colby, KS 67701
Tel: 785-462-4590

Tonganoxie Community Historical Society
P.O. Box 325
Tonganoxie, KS 66086

Trading Post Historical Society/Museum
15710 N 4th Street
P.O. Box 145A
Pleasanton, KS 66075
Tel: 913-352-6441

Trego County Historical Society
Highway 283
P.O. Box 132
WaKeeney, KS 67672
Tel: 785-743-2964
http://skyways.lib.ks.us/towns/WaKeeney/museum.html

Tri-County Historical Society/Archives/Museum
Railroad Baggage Car Annex
800 South Broadway
P.O. Box 9
Herington, KS 67449
Tel: 785-258-2842

Valley Center Historical and Cultural Society
112 North Meridian
P.O. Box 173
Valley Center, KS 67147
Tel: 316-755-7340 (Chamber of Commerce)

Valley Falls Historical Society
310 Broadway
Valley Falls, KS 66088

Wabaunsee County Historical Society
227 Missouri Street
P.O. Box 387
Alma, KS 66401
Tel: 785-765-2200

Wamego Historical Society/Museum
P.O. Box 84
Wamego, KS 66547
Tel: 785-456-2040

Washington County Historical and Genealogical Society
P.O. Box 31
Washington, KS 66968-0031
Tel: 785-325-2198

Wichita County Historical Society, Inc.
201 North 4th Street
Leoti, KS 67861
Tel: 620-375-2316

Wilson County Historical Society/Library/Museum
420 North 7th
Fredonia, KS 66736
Tel: 620-378-3965

Woodson County Historical Society/Library
Route 1
P.O. Box 16
Yates Center, KS 66783

Wyandotte County Historical Society
Museum and Harry M. Trowbridge Research Library
631 North 126th
Bonner Springs, KS 66012
Tel: 913-721-1078
http://www.kumc.edu/wcedc/museum/ wcmuseum.html

LDS FAMILY HISTORY CENTERS

For locations of Family History Centers in this state, see
the Family History Center locator at FamilySearch.
http://www.familysearch.org/eng/Library/FHC/
frameset_fhc.asp

ARCHIVES/LIBRARIES/MUSEUMS

Allen County Historical Society/Library
207 North Jefferson
Iola, KS 66749
Tel: 620-365-3051

Anderson County Historical Society/Library
6th and Maple
Garnett, KS 66032

Anthony Public Library
624 E Main Street
Anthony, KS 67003
Tel: 620-842-5344

Arkansas City Public Library
120 E. 5th Avenue
Arkansas City, KS 67005
Tel: 620-442-1280
Fax: 620-442-4277
E-mail: arkcitypl@acpl.org
http://www.acpl.org/

Atchison County Historical Society/Museum
200 South Main
P.O. Box 201
Atchison, KS 66002
Tel: 913-367-6238
http://www.atchisonkansas.net/Tourism/ HistSoct.htm

Atchison Public Library
401 Kansas Avenue
Atchison, KS 66002
Tel: 913-367-1902

Atwood Public Library
102 South 6th Street
Atwood, KS 67730
Tel: 785-626-3805
Fax: 785-626-3670
http://skyways.lib.ks.us/genweb/rawlins/library.html

Augusta Historical Society/Museum
303 State Street
P.O. Box 545
Augusta, KS 67010
Tel: 316-775-5655
http://www.augusta-ks.org/Museum.htm

Baker University Archives
P.O. Box 65
Baldwin, KS 66006
Tel: 785-594-6451 ext. 380
E-mail: Brenda.Day@bakeru.edu
http://www.bakeru.edu/library/archives/

Barton County Historical Society/Museum
85 South Highway 281
P.O. Box 1091
Great Bend, KS 67530
Tel: 620-793-5125
E-mail: shorock@midusa.net

Baxter Springs Historical Society/Museum
740 East Avenue
P.O. Box 514
Baxter Springs, KS 66713
Tel: 620-856-2385
http://home.4state.com/~heritagectr/gallery.html

Boot Hill Museum and Front Street
Front Street
Dodge City, KS 67801
http://www.boothill.org/

Brown County Historical Society/Library
611 Utah Street
Hiawatha, KS 66434
Tel: 785-742-3330

Bukovina Society of the Americas/Museum
722 Washington
P.O. Box 81
Ellis, KS 67637
E-mail: owindholz@ruraltel.net
http://members.aol.com/LJensen/bukovina.html

Butler County Historical Society/Museum
383 East Central
P.O. Box 696
El Dorado, KS 67042
Tel: 316-321-9333

Cassoday Historical Museum
133 South Washington & Beaumont
Cassoday, KS 66842
Tel: 620-735-7286

Cawker City Public Library
802 Locust Street
Cawker City, KS 67430
Tel: 785-781-4925
E-mail: ejluckey@nckcn.com
http://skyways.lib.ks.us/kansas/towns/Cawker/library.html

Chanute Genealogical Society
1010 South Allen
Chanute, KS 66720
http://www.rootsweb.com/~kscgs/

Chase County Historical Society/Library/Museum
301 Broadway
P.O. Box 375
Cottonwood Falls, KS 66845
Tel: 620-273-8500

Cherokee County Kansas Genealogical/Historical Society
100 South Tennessee
P.O. Box 33
Columbus, KS 66725-0033
Tel: 620-429-2992
E-mail: cckghs@columbus-ks.com
http://skyways.lib.ks.us/genweb/cherokee/society/
      cckghs.html

Cherokee Strip Land Rush Museum
South Summit Street
P.O. Box 1002
Arkansas City, KS 67005
Tel: 620-442-6750
http://www.sckstourism.com/counties/cities/
      arkcitylandrush.html

Chetopa Historical Museum
419 Maple
P.O. Box 135
Chetopa, KS 67336
http://skyways.lib.ks.us/towns/Chetopa/ museum.html

Chisholm Trail Museum
502 N. Washington Avenue
Wellington, KS 67152
Tel: 620-326-3820
http://skyways.lib.ks.us/towns/Wellington/museum.html

Clay County Historical Society
Clay County Museum
2121 7th Street
Clay Center, KS 67432
Tel: 785-632-3786

Coffey County Historical Museum
1101 Neosho
Burlington, KS 66839
Tel: 620-364-2653
E-mail: artifacts@kans.com
http://www.coffeycountymuseum.org/

Coffeyville Historical Museum, Inc.
113 East Eighth
P.O. Box 843
Coffeyville, KS 67337

Columbus Public Library
205 N. Kansas
Columbus, KS 66725-1297
Tel: 620-429-2086
Fax: 620-429-1950
E-mail: collib@columbus-ks.com
http://skyways.lib.ks.us/library/columbus/

Combined Arms Research Library
Eisenhower Hall
250 Gibbon Ave
Leavenworth, KS 66027-2314
Tel: 913-758-3053
http://www.cgsc.army.mil/carl/

Council Grove Library
303 W. Main Street
Council, KS 66846
Tel: 620-767-5716
Fax: 620-767-7312
E-mail: cglib@cgtelco.net
http://skyways.lib.ks.us/norcen/cgrove

Cowley County Historical Society/Library
1011 Mansfield
Winfield, KS 67156
Tel: 620-221-4811

Crawford County Historical Society/Museum
651 South Highway 69
Pittsburg, KS 66762
Tel: 620-231-1440

Decatur County Museum
258 South Penn
Oberlin, KS 67749
Tel: 785-475-2712

Dickinson County Historical Society
Heritage Center
412 South Campbell
Abilene, KS 67410
Tel: 785-263-2681
http://history.cc.ukans.edu/heritage/abilene/herctr.html

Dodge City Public Library
1001 Second Avenue
Dodge City, KS 67801
http://www.dcpl.info/

Douglass Historical Museum
314 S. Forest
Douglass, KS 67039

Downs Carnegie Library
504 South Morgan
Downs, KS 67437
Tel: 785-454-3821

Emmett Kelly Historical Museum
Main Street
Sedan, KS 67361
Tel: 620-725-3470

Emporia Public Library
110 E. 6th Avenue
Emporia, KS 66801
Tel: 620-342-6524
Fax: 620-342-2633
http://skyways.lib.ks.us/library/emporia/

Fort Hays State University
Forsyth Library
600 Park Street
Hays, KS 67601
Tel: 785-628-4431
http://www.fhsu.edu/forsyth_lib/

Fort Larned National Historic Site
Route 3
Larned, KS 67550
Tel: 620-285-6911
http://www.nps.gov/fols/

Fort Wallace Memorial Association
Highway 40
Wallace, KS 67761
Tel: 785-891-3564

Franklin County Historical Society/Library
315 S Main Street
P.O. Box 145
Ottawa, KS 66067
Tel: 785-242-1232
http://www.ukans.edu/~hisite/franklin/fchs/

Friends University
Quaker Room Archives
Special Collections
2100 University
Wichita, KS 67213
Tel: 316-295-5000
http://www.friends.edu/library/SpecialCollections/

Frederic Remington Area Historical Society
P.O. Box 133
Whitewater, KS 67154
E-mail: aharder@southwind.net
http://skyways.lib.ks.us/towns/Brainerd/

Frontier Army Museum
Department of the Army
Commander, HQ CAC LVN, ATTN ATZL GCT M
100 Reynolds Avenue
Fort Leavenworth, KS 66027-5072
Tel: 913-684-3191
913-684-3767
Fax: 913-684-3624
http://leav-www.army.mil/museum/

Galena Public Library
City Municipal Building
315 W. 7th Street
Galena, KS 66739
Tel: 620-783-5132

Garden City Public Library
210 North 7th
Garden City, KS 67846

Geary County Historical Society
530 North Adams
P.O. Box 1161
Junction City, KS 66441
Tel: 785-238-1666

Grant County Museum and Historical Society
300 East Oklahoma Avenue
P.O. Box 906
Ulysses, KS 67880
Tel: 620-356-3009

Great Bend Public Library
1409 Williams Street
Great Bend, KS 67530
Tel: 620-792-2409
Emai: jswan@ckls.org
http://www.ckls.org/~gbpl/

Greeley County Historical Society/Library
P.O. Box 231
Tribune, KS 67879
Tel: 620-376-4996

Greenwood County Historical Society/Library/Museum
120 West 4th Street
Eureka, KS 67045-1445
Tel: 620-583-6682
E-mail: gwhistory@correct-connect.com
http://skyways.lib.ks.us/kansas/genweb/greenwoo/gchs.htm

Hamilton County Library
102 West Avenue C.
P.O. Box 1307
Syracuse, KS 67878
Tel: 620-384-5622
Fax: 620-384-5623
E-mail: hamcolib@yahoo.com
http://skyways.lib.ks.us/library/hamilton/

Hamilton County Museum
108 E. Highway 50
P.O. Box 923
Syracuse, KS 67878
Tel: 620-384-7496

Harper Public Library
1002 Oak
Harper, KS 67058
Tel: 620-896-2959

Harvey County Historical Society/Library
203 N. Main
P.O. Box 4
Newton, KS 67114
Tel: 316-283-2221
http://www.infonewtonks.org/tourism/h_society.htm

Hays Masonic Bodies (A.F. & A.M.)
107 W. 11th
Hays, KS 67601
Tel: 785-625-3127
http://spidome.net/~masons/index.html

Hays Public Library
1205 Main Street
Hays, KS 67601-3693
Tel: 785-625-9014
Fax: 785-625-8683
http://www.hayspublib.org/

High Plains Museum
1717 Cherry
Goodland, KS 67735
Tel: 785-899-4595
http://www.goodlandnet.com/museum/

Hutchinson Public Library
901 N. Main
Hutchinson, KS 67501
Tel: 620-663-5441
E-mail: Webmaster@hplsck.org
http://www.hplsck.org/200.htm

Iola Public Library
218 E. Madison Avenue
Iola, KS 66749
Tel: 620-365-3262
Fax: 620-365-5137
E-mail: iolaref@alltel.net
http://www.iola.lib.ks.us/

Jackson County Historical Society/Library
Jackson County Museum
4th and New
P.O. Box 104
Holton, KS 66436
Tel: 785-364-2087

Jefferson County Historical Society/library
Old Jefferson Town
Highway 59
P.O. Box 146
Oskaloosa, KS 66066
Tel: 785-863-2070

Johnson County Genealogical Society/Library
8700 Shawnee Mission Parkway
P.O. Box 12666
Shawnee Mission, KS 66282
E-mail: kenl@sky.net
http://www.johnsoncountykansasgenealogy.org/

Johnson County Library
9875 W. 87th Street
Overland, KS 66212
Tel: 913-495-2400
TDD: 913-495-2433
http://www.jocolibrary.org/

Johnson County Museum of History
6305 Lackman Road
Shawnee Mission, KS 66217
Tel: 913-631-6709

Johnston Public Library
210 W. 10th
Baxter Springs, KS 66713
Tel: 620-856-5591

Kansas Center for Historical Research
6425 SW 6th Avenue
Topeka, KS 66615
Tel: 785-272-8681 ext. 117
Fax: 785-272-8682
TTY: 785-272-8683
http://www.kshs.org/places/chr.htm

Kansas City Public Library
625 Minnesota Street
Kansas City, KS 66101
Tel: 913-551-3280
Fax: 913-279-2032
E-mail: refinfo@kckpl.lib.ks.us
http://www.kckpl.lib.ks.us/

Kansas Genealogical Society, Inc.
Village Square Mall, Lower Level
2601 Central Avenue
P.O. Box 103
Dodge City, KS 67801
Tel: 620-225-1951
http://www.dodgecity.net/kgs/

Kansas Heritage Center
1000 2nd Avenue
P.O. Box 1207
Dodge City, KS 67801-1207
Tel: 620-227-1616
E-mail: info@ksheritage.org
http://ksheritage.org/

Kansas State Historical Society/Library & Archives
The Kansas History Center
6425 SW Sixth Street
Topeka, KS 66615-1099
Tel: 785-272-8681
Fax: 785-272-8682
TTY: 785-272-8683
E-mail: Webmaster@kshs.org
http://www.kshs.org/places/khcenter.htm

Kansas State Library
300 S.W. Tenth Avenue, Room 343-N
Topeka, KS 66612-1593
Tel: 785-296-3296
800-432-3919 (In Kansas)
Fax: 785-296-6650
http://skyways.lib.ks.us/kansas/KSL/

Kansas State University
Morse Department of Special Collections
323 Seaton Hall
Manhattan, KS 66506
Tel: 785-532-7456 (Archives)
E-mail: archives@ksu.edu
http://www.lib.ksu.edu/depts/spec/

Kearny County Historical Society and Museum
111 South Buffalo Street
P.O. Box 329
Lakin, KS 67860
Tel: 620-355-7448
http://skyways.lib.ks.us/towns/Lakin/museum.html

Kingman Carnegie Library
455 North Main
Kingman, KS 67068-1395
Tel: 620-532-3061
Fax: 620-532-2528
E-mail: kingc1lb@websurf.net
http://skyways.lib.ks.us/library/kingman/

Kingman County Historical Society/Library/Museum
400 North Main
P.O. Box 281
Kingman, KS 67068
Tel: 620-532-5274
http://skyways.lib.ks.us/towns/Kingman/museum/

Lane County Historical Society/Museum
333 North Main
P.O. Box 821
Dighton, KS 67839
Tel: 620-397-5652

Last Indian Raid Museum
132 South Penn Avenue
Oberlin, KS 67749
E-mail: decaturmuseum@nwkansas.com
http://www.indianraidmuseum.org/

Lawrence Public Library
707 Vermont Street
Lawrence, KS 66044
Tel: 785-843-3833
Fax: 785-843-3368
http://www.lawrence.lib.ks.us/

Leavenworth County Historical Society/Museum
1128 5th Avenue
Leavenworth, KS 66048
Tel: 913-682-7759
Fax: 913-682-2089
http://leavenworth-net.com/lchs/

Leavenworth Public Library
417 Spruce Street
Leavenworth, KS 66048
Tel: 913-682-5666
http://skyways.lib.ks.us/library/leavenworth/

Liberal Memorial Library
519 N. Kansas Avenue
Liberal, KS 67901
Tel: 620-626-0180
Fax: 620-626-0182
http://skyways.lib.ks.us/library/liberal/

Lindsborg Community Library
111 South Main
Lindsborg, KS 67456
Tel: 785-227-2710

Luray Historical Society/Library
P.O. Box 134
Luray 67649-0134

Lyndon Carnegie Library
127 E. 6th
P.O. Box 563
Lyndon, KS 66451
Tel: 785-828-4520
Fax: 785-828-4565
E-mail: lyndlibrary@lyndon.lib.ks.us
http://skyways.lib.ks.us/towns/Lyndon/library/

Lyon County Historical Society/Museum
118 East 6th Avenue
Emporia, KS 66801-3922
Tel: 620-342-0933
http://slim.emporia.edu/resource/lchs/LyonCo.htm

Marion Historical Museum
Main at Central Park
Marion, KS 66861
Tel: 620-382-3432
http://www.marionks.com/museum.html

Marshall County Historical Society
1207 Broadway
Marysville, KS 66508
Tel: 785-562-5012

Mary Cotton Public Library
915 Virginia
P.O. Box 70
Sabetha, KS 66534
Tel: 785-284-3160

McPherson County Old Mill Museum and Park
120 Mill Street
P.O. Box 94
Lindsborg, KS 67456
Tel: 785-227-3595
Fax: 785-227-2810
E-mail: oldmillmuseum@hotmail.com
http://www.oldmillmuseum.org/

Meade County Historical Museum
200 East Carthage
P.O. Box 893
Meade, KS 67864
Tel: 620-873-2359

Mennonite Library and Archives
Bethel College
300 East 27th
North Newton, KS 67117
Tel: 316-283-2500
E-mail: mla@bethelks.edu
http://www.bethelks.edu/services/mla/

Miami County Historical Society/Library
North Side of Square
P.O. Box 393
Paola, KS 66071

Midwest Historical and Genealogical Society
1203 North Main
P.O. Box 1121
Wichita, KS 67201-1121
Tel: 316-264-3611
http://skyways.lib.ks.us/kansas/genweb/mhgs/

Mitchell County Historical Society/Museum
402 West 8th
Beloit, KS 67420
Tel: 785-738-5355
Fax: 785-738-9503
http://members.nckcn.com/mchs/

Morrill Public Library
431 Oregon
Hiawatha, KS 66434
Tel: 785-742-3831
http://skyways.lib.ks.us/towns/Hiawatha/ library.html

Native American Heritage Museum at Highland Mission
1727 Elgin Road
P.O. Box 152C
Highland, KS 66035
Tel: 785-442-3304
http://www.kshs.org/places/highland.htm

Nemaha County Historical Society/Library
6th and Nemaha
Seneca, KS 66538
http://www.ku.edu/kansas/seneca/gensoc/ gensoc.html

North Central Kansas Genealogical Society
P.O. Box 251
Cawker City, KS 67430
Tel: 785-781-4925 (Cawker City Library)
http://skyways.lib.ks.us/kansas/towns/Cawker/
    library.html#society

Northwest Kansas Heritage Center
401 Kansas Avenue
P.O. Box 284
Brewster, KS 67732
Tel: 785-694-2891

Oakley Library
700 West 3rd
Oakley, KS 67748
Tel: 785-672-4776

Olathe Public Library
201 E. Park Street
Olathe, KS 66061-3456
Tel: 913-764-2259
913-393-6888 (Reference Desk)
http://olathe.lib.ks.us/

Osborne Public Library
325 W. Main Street
Osborne, KS 67473
Tel: 785-346-5486
http://skyways.lib.ks.us/towns/Osborne/library.html

Oswego Historical Society/Museum
410 Commercial
Oswego, KS 67356
Tel: 620-795-4500

Ottawa County Historical Museum
110 S. Concord
Minneapolis, KS 67467
Tel: 785-392-3621
http://www.cyberspacemuseum.com/n3_3.html

Ottawa Public Library
105 S. Hickory
Ottawa, KS 66067
Tel: 785-242-3080
http://www.ottawa.lib.ks.us/

Pioneer-Krier Museum
430 West 4th
P.O. Box 862
Ashland, KS 67831
Tel: 620-635-2227
http://skyways.lib.ks.us/towns/Ashland/ museums.html

Pittsburg Public Library
308 North Walnut
Pittsburg, KS 66762
Tel: 620-231-8110
Fax: 620-232-2258
http://skyways.lib.ks.us/library/pittsburg/

Pratt County Historical Society/Library
208 South Ninnescah
Pratt, KS 67124
Tel: 620-672-7874

Rawlins County Historical Society/Museum
308 State
Atwood, KS 67730
Tel: 785-626-3885

Riley County Genealogical Society/Library
2005 Claflin Road
Manhattan, KS 66502
Tel: 785-565-6495
http://www.rileycgs.com/

Russell County Historical Society/Library
331 N Kansas Street
Russell, KS 67665
Tel: 785-483-3637

St. Mary College
DePaul Library
Leavenworth, KS 66048
Tel: 913-758-6306
Fax: 913-758-6200
E-mail: lonergan@hub.smcks.edu
http://www.smcks.edu/library/

St. Marys Historical Society/Library
106 East Mission
St. Marys, KS 66536
Tel: 913-437-6600

Saline County Historical Society/Library
216 West Bond Street
Salina, KS 67401

Santa Fe Trail Center
Route 3
Larned, KS 67550
Tel: 316-285-2054
Fax: 316-285-7491
E-mail: trailctr@larned.net
http://www.awav.net/trailctr/

Scandia Museum
Main Street
Scandia, KS 66966
Tel: 785-335-2271
http://www.nckcn.com/homepage/republic_co/muse-
um1.htm

Seneca Free Library
606 Main
Seneca, KS 66538
Tel: 785-336-2377
Fax: 785-336-3699
E-mail: khaus66538@yahoo.com
http://skyways.lib.ks.us/library/seneca/

Smoky Valley Genealogical Society/Library
211 West Iron Street, Suite 205
Salina, Kansas 67401
Tel: 785-825-7573
http://skyways.lib.ks.us/kansas/genweb/ottawa/smoky.html

Stafford County Historical and Genealogical Society
100 South Main
P.O. Box 249
Stafford, KS 67578
Tel: 620-234-5664
http://home.earthlink.net/~mjhathaway61/

Topeka and Shawnee County Public Library
1515 SW 10th Avenue
Topeka, KS 66604-1374
Tel: 785-580-4400
E-mail: tscpl@tscpl.lib.ks.us
http://www.tscpl.org/

Topeka Genealogical Society/Library
2717 SE Indiana Avenue
P.O. Box 4048
Topeka, KS 66604
Tel: 785-233-5762
E-mail: TGS@networksplus.net
http://www.networksplus.net/donno/

Trading Post Historical Society/Museum
15710 N 4th Street
P.O. Box 145A
Pleasanton, KS 66075
Tel: 913-352-6441

Tri-County Historical Society/Archives/Museum
Railroad Baggage Car Annex
800 South Broadway
P.O. Box 9
Herington, KS 67449
Tel: 785-258-2842

U.S. Cavalry Museum
Building 205
P.O. Box 2160
Fort Riley, KS 66442
Tel: 785-239-2737

W.A. Rankin Memorial Library
Wilson County Kansas
502 Indiana
Neodosha, KS 66757
Tel: 620-325-3275

Watkins Community Museum of History
1047 Massachusetts
Lawrence, KS 66044
Tel: 785-841-4109
E-mail: wcmhist@sunflower.com
http://www.ci.lawrence.ks.us/museums/ watkins.html
Wichita City Library
223 South Main Street
Wichita, KS 67202
Tel: 316-261-8509
E-mail: webmaster@wichita.lib.ks.us
http://www.wichita.lib.ks.us/

Wichita/Sedgwick County Historical Museum
204 South Main
Wichita, KS 67202
Tel: 316-265-9314
Fax: 316-265-9319
E-mail: wschm@onemain.com
http://www.wscribe.com/history/

Wichita State University
Wichita State University Libraries
Department of Special Collections
1845 Fairmount
Wichita, KS 67260-0068
Tel: 316-978-3590
Fax: 316-978-3048
E-mail: mary.nelson@wichita.edu
http://specialcollections.wichita.edu/

Wilson County Historical Society/Library/Museum
420 North 7th
Fredonia, KS 66736
Tel: 620-378-3965

Woodson County Historical Society/Library
Route 1
P.O. Box 16
Yates Center, KS 66783

Wyandotte County Historical Society
Museum and Harry M. Trowbridge Research Library
631 North 126th
Bonner Springs, KS 66012
Tel: 913-721-1078
http://www.kumc.edu/wcedc/museum/ wcmuseum.html

Young Historical Library
2770 Avenue I
Little River, KS 67457
Tel: 620-897-6236

NEWSPAPERS REPOSITORIES

Kansas State Historical Society/Library & Archives
The Kansas History Center
6425 SW Sixth Street
Topeka, KS 66615-1099
Tel: 785-272-8681
Fax: 785-272-8682
TTY: 785-272-8683
E-mail: Webmaster@kshs.org
http://www.kshs.org/places/khcenter.htm

VITAL RECORDS

Office Vital Statistics
1000 S W Jackson, Suite 110
Topeka, KS 66612
Tel: 785-296-1500
    785-296-3253
Fax: 785-357-4332
E-mail: info@kdhe.state.ks.us
http://www.kdhe.state.ks.us/

KANSAS ON THE WEB

Kansas Collection
http://kuhttp.cc.ukans.edu/carrie/kancoll/

Kansas GenWeb Project
http://skyways.lib.ks.us/kansas/genweb/

Kansas Pioneers Project
http://history.cc.ukans.edu/heritage/pioneers/
    pion_main.html

Kansas State Historical Society
http://www.kshs.org/

Orphan Trains of Kansas
http://www.ku.edu/carrie/kancoll/articles/orphans/

Plains and Emigrant Tribes of Kansas
http://history.cc.ukans.edu/heritage/old_west/indian.html

Underground Railroad Operators Directory—Kansas
http://www.ugrr.org//names/map-ks.htm

KENTUCKY

ARCHIVES, STATE & NATIONAL

Kentucky Department for Libraries and Archives
Public Records Division
Archives Research Room
300 Coffee Tree Road
P.O. Box 537
Frankfort, KY 40602-0537
Tel: 502-564-8300
Fax: 502-564-5773
http://www.kdla.state.ky.us/

National Archives-Southeast Region
1557 St. Joseph Avenue
East Point, GA 30344
Tel: 404-763-7474
Fax: 404-763-7059
E-mail: atlanta.center@nara.gov
http://www.nara.gov/regional/atlanta.html

GENEALOGICAL SOCIETIES

Adair County Genealogical Society
P.O. Box 613
Columbia, KY 42728
http://www.rootsweb.com/~kyacgs/

Ballard-Carlisle Historical & Genealogical Society
P.O. Box 279
Wickliffe, KY 42087
Tel: 270-335-5059
E-mail: bcmilner@wk.net
http://www.ballardconet.com/bchgs/

Boyle County Genealogical Association
2825 Shakertown Road
Danville, KY 40422
Tel: 859-332-7313
E-mail: crabtree@mis.net

Breathitt County Genealogical & Historical Society
121 Turner Drive
Jackson, KY 41339
http://www.breathittcountylibrary.com/
    Community/History.html

Bullitt County Genealogical Society
P.O. Box 960
Shepherdsville, KY 40165
http://www.bcplib.org/genealogy/

Butler County Historical & Genealogical Society
P.O. Box 146
Morgantown, KY 42261

Campbell County Historical & Genealogical Society Library
19 East Main Street
Alexandria, KY 41001
Tel: 606-635-6417
E-mail: cchistoricalsoc@sprynet.com

Carter County Historical & Genealogical Society
P.O. Box 1128
Grayson, KY 41143

Christian County Genealogical Society
1101 Bethel Street
Hopkinsville, KY 42240

Clay County Genealogical & Historical Society, Inc.
P.O. Box 394
Manchester, KY 40962-0394
Tel: 606-598-5507
http://members.tripod.com/~Sue_1/clay.html

Crittenden County Genealogical Society
South Crittenden County Library
P.O. Box 61
Marion, KY 42064

Eastern Kentucky Genealogical Society
P.O. Box 1544
Ashland, KY 41105-1544

Estill County Historical and Genealogical Society
P.O. Box 221
Ravenna, KY 40472
http://www.rootsweb.com/~kyestill/echgs.htm

Fayette County Genealogical Society
P.O. Box 8113
Lexington, KY 40533-8113
http://www.rootsweb.com/~kyfcgs/

Floyd County Historical & Genealogical Society
P.O. Box 217
Auxier, KY 41602
E-mail: shatcher@kymtnnet.org
http://www.geocities.com/Heartland/Ridge/2060/

Fulton County Genealogical Society
P.O. Box 1031
Fulton, KY 42041

Graves County Genealogical Society
P.O. Box 245
Mayfield, KY 42066
http://www.rootsweb.com/~kygraves/gravesghs.html

Hancock County, Genealogical Society of
Old Courthouse
Hawesville, KY 42348

Harlan County Genealogical Society
P.O. Box 1498
Harlan, KY 40831

Harlan Heritage Seekers
P.O. Box 853
Harlan, KY 40831

Harrodsburg Historical Society
Genealogical Committee
220 Chiles Street
P.O. Box 316
Harrodsburg, KY 40330
Tel: 859-734-5985
http://www.rootsweb.com/~kymercer/hhs/

Henderson County Genealogical & Historical Society
132-B Green Street
P.O. BOX 303
Henderson, KY 42419- 0303
Tel: 270-830-7514
E-mail: hendersoncounty@hotmail.com
http://www.rootsweb.com/~kyhender/Henderson/
    HCHGS/HCHGSpg.htm

Hopkins County Genealogical Society
P.O. Box 51
Madisonville, KY 42431
http://www.rootsweb.com/~kyhopkin/hcgs/

Jewish Genealogical Society of Louisville
Israel T. Namani Library
3600 Dutchmans Lane
Louisville, KY 40205

Johnson County Historical & Genealogical Society
Johnson County Public Library
P.O. Box 788
Paintsville, KY 41240
http://www.rootsweb.com/~kyjchs/johnson.html

Kentucky Genealogical Society
P.O. Box 153
Frankfort, KY 40602
E-mail: kygs@aol.com
http://www.kygs.org/

KYOWVA Genealogical Society
232 Main Street, Guyandotte
Huntington, WV
Tel: 304-525-4367
http://www.rootsweb.com/~wvkgs/

Lee County Historical & Genealogical Society
P.O. Box V
Beattyville, KY 41311

Letcher County Historical & Genealogical Society
P.O. Box 312
Whitesburg, KY 41858
http://www.rootsweb.com/~kyletch/lchgs/lchgs.htm

Louisville Genealogical Society
200 Cambridge Station Road
Louisville, KY 40223-3337
E-mail: lougensoc@yahoo.com
http://www.rootsweb.com/~kylgs/

Marshall County Historical & Genealogical Society
P.O. Box 373
Benton, KY 42025
Tel: 270-527-4749
E-mail: marcoky@vci.net

Mason County Genealogical Society
P.O. Box 266
Maysville, KY 41056

McCracken County Genealogical Society
4640 Buckner Lane
Paducah, KY 42001

Menifee County Roots
P.O. Box 114
Frenchburg, KY 40322

Muhlenberg County Genealogical Society
Harbin Memorial Library
117 S. Main Street
Greenville, KY 42345

Nelson County Genealogical Roundtable
P.O. Box 409
Bardstown, KY 40004

Pendleton County Historical & Genealogical Society
Route 5, Box 280
Falmouth, KY 41040

Perry County Genealogical & Historical Society
148 Chester Street
Haxard, KY 41701

Scott County Genealogical Society
Scott County Public Library
104 South Bradford Lane
Georgetown, KY 40324
E-mail: jog1@ix.netcom.com
http://www.rootsweb.com/~kyscott/scgs.htm

South Central Kentucky Historical/Genealogical Society
P.O. Box 157
Glasgow, KY 42142-0157
E-mail: sgorin@glasgow-ky.com
http://www.rootsweb.com/~kybarren/society.html

Southern Kentucky Genealogical Society
P.O. Box 1782
Bowling Green, KY 42102
E-mail: gail.j.miller@kytnresearch.com
http://members.aol.com/kygen/skgs/gen-1.htm

Tri-State Genealogical Society
Willard Library
21 First Avenue
Evansville, KY 47710
Tel: 812-425-4309

Washington County Genealogical Society
210 E. Main Street
Springfield, KY 40069

Wayne County Historical & Genealogical Society
Wayne County Public Library
159 S. Main Street
P.O.Box 320
Monticello, KY 42633
Tel: 606-348-8565 (Library)
Fax: 606-348-3829
http://www.rootsweb.com/%7Ekywayne/hist-soc.html

Webster County Historical & Genealogical Society
P.O. Box 215
Dixon, KY 42409-0215
http://www.rootsweb.com/~kywebste/wch_gs.htm

West-Central Kentucky Family Research Association
P.O. Box 1932
Owensboro, KY 42302
E-mail: wckfra@yahoo.com
http://www.rootsweb.com/~kywckfra/

HISTORICAL SOCIETIES

Ancestral Trails Historical Society
P.O. Box 573
Vine Grove, KY 40175
http://www.aths.com/

Ballard-Carlisle Historical & Genealogical Society
P.O. Box 279
Wickliffe, KY 42087
Tel: 270-335-5059
E-mail: bcmilner@wk.net
http://www.ballardconet.com/bchgs/

Bell County Historical Society
207 North 20th Street
P.O. Box 1344
Middlesboro, KY 40965
Tel: 606-242-0005
http://www.geocities.com/bellhistorical/

Bracken County Historical Society
207 Madison Street
P.O. Box 307
Brooksville, KY 41004
Tel: 606-735-3337
http://www.rootsweb.com/~kybchs/bracken.html

Breathitt County Genealogical & Historical Society
121 Turner Drive
Jackson, KY 41339
http://www.breathittcountylibrary.com/Community/
History.html

Breckinridge County Historical Society
Breckinridge County Clerk
Courthouse Square
P.O. Box 498
Hardinsburg, KY 40143-0538
Tel: 270-756-2246
Fax: 270-756-5444

Butler County Historical & Genealogical Society
P.O. Box 146
Morgantown, KY 42261

Caldwell County Historical Society
P.O. Box 1
Princeton, KY 42445

Campbell County Historical & Genealogical Society Library
19 East Main Street
Alexandria, KY 41001
Tel: 606-635-6417
E-mail: cchistoricalsoc@sprynet.com

Carter County Historical & Genealogical Society
P.O. Box 1128
Grayson, KY 41143

Clark County Historical Society
122 Belmont Avenue
Winchester, KY 40391

Clay County Genealogical & Historical Society, Inc.
P.O. Box 394
Manchester, KY 40962-0394
Tel: 606-598-5507
http://members.tripod.com/~Sue_1/clay.html

Estill County Historical and Genealogical Society
P.O. Box 221
Ravenna, KY 40472
http://www.rootsweb.com/~kyestill/echgs.htm

Filson Club Historical Society
1310 South Third Street
Louisville, KY 40208
Tel: 502-635-5083
Fax: 502-635-5086
E-mail: MarkWeth@filsonhistorical.org (Director)
http://www.filsonhistorical.org/

Floyd County Historical & Genealogical Society
P.O. Box 217
Auxier, KY 41602
E-mail: shatcher@kymtnnet.org
http://www.geocities.com/Heartland/Ridge/2060/

Fulton County Historical Society
P.O. Box 1031
Fulton, KY 42041

Garrard County Historical Society
208 Danville Street
Lancaster, KY 40444

Grayson County Historical Society
P.O.Box 84
Leitchfield, KY 42754

Green County Historical Society
P.O. Box 276
Greensburg, KY 42743

Harrodsburg Historical Society
Genealogical Committee
220 Chiles Street
P.O. Box 316
Harrodsburg, KY 40330
Tel: 859-734-5985
http://www.rootsweb.com/~kymercer/hhs/

Hart County Historical Society/Museum
Chapline Building
Main Street
P.O. Box 606
Munfordville, KY 42765
Tel: 270-524-0101
http://www.historichart.org/museum.htm

Henry County Historical Society
P.O. Box 570
New Castle, KY 40050

Hickman County Historical Society
Route 3, Box 255
Clinton, KY 42031

Johnson County Historical & Genealogical Society
Johnson County Public Library
P.O. Box 788
Paintsville, KY 41240
http://www.rootsweb.com/~kyjchs/johnson.html

Kentucky Historical Society/Library/Museum
Old Capitol Annex
Corner of Broadway and Lewis Streets
P.O. Box 1792
Frankfort, KY 40602-1792
Tel: 502-564-3016
Fax: 502-564-4701

Knott County Historical Society
P.O. Box 1023
Hindman, KY 41822
Tel: 606-785-5751
Fax: 606-785-0700
http://www.geocities.com/Athens/Oracle/5468/

Knox County Historical Society, Inc.
P.O. Box 528
Barbourville, KY 40906

Laurel County Historical Society/Library
1 Old City Hall
Broad Street & West 3rd Street
P.O. Box 816
London, KY 40741
Tel: 606-864-0607
E-mail: lchistsoc@kih.net
http://www.users.kih.net/~lchistsoc/histsoc/

Lee County Historical & Genealogical Society
P.O. Box V
Beattyville, KY 41311

Letcher County Historical & Genealogical Society
P.O. Box 312
Whitesburg, KY 41858
http://www.rootsweb.com/~kyletch/lchgs/lchgs.htm

Lewis County Historical Society
P.O. Box 212
Vanceburg, KY 41179

Lyon County Historical Society
P.O. Box 894
Eddyville, KY 42038

Madison County Historical Society
P.O. Box 5066
Richmond, KY 40476
Tel: 606-622-2820
   606-622-1792
E-mail: mchs@iclub.org
http://www.iclub.org/kentucky/madison/history/

Magoffin County Historical Society/Library
213 South Church Street
P.O. Box 222
Salyersville, KY 41465
Tel: 606-349-1607
Fax: 606-349-1353
http://www.rootsweb.com/~kymhs/

Marshall County Historical & Genealogical Society
P.O. Box 373
Benton, KY 42025
Tel: 270-527-4749
E-mail: marcoky@vci.net

Metcalfe County Historical Society
Box 910
Edmonton, KY 42129
http://www.rootsweb.com/~kymetca2/historicalsociety.htm

Ohio County Historical Society
P.O. Box 44
Hartford, KY 42347

Pendleton County Historical & Genealogical Society
Route 5, Box 280
Falmouth, KY 41040

Perry County Genealogical & Historical Society
148 Chester Street
Haxard, KY 41701

Pulaski County Historical Society
Pulaski County Public Library Building
107 N. Main Street
P.O. Box 36
Somerset, KY 42502
Tel: 606-679-8401
http://www.rootsweb.com/~kypchs/

Red River Historical Society
P.O. Box 195
Clay City, KY 40312

Rockcastle County Historical Society
P.O. Box 930
Mt. Vernon, KY 40456

Rowan County Historical Society
P.O. Box 60
Morehead, KY 40351

Simpson County Historical Society/Library and Archives
206 N. College Street
Franklin, KY 42134
Tel: 270-586-4228
Fax: 270-586-4429
E-mail: Information@SimpsonCountyKyArchives.com
http://www.rootsweb.com/~kyschs/

South Central Kentucky Historical/Genealogical Society
P.O. Box 157
Glasgow, KY 42142-0157
E-mail: sgorin@glasgow-ky.com
http://www.rootsweb.com/~kybarren/society.html

Taylor County Historical Society
P.O. Box 14
Campbellsville, KY 42719

Trimble County Historical Society
2926 Patton's Creek
Pendleton, KY 40055
http://www.ole.net/~maggie/trimble/histsoc.htm

Union County Historical Society/Museum
221 W. McElroy
Morganfield, KY 42437

Vanlear Historical Society
P.O. Box 12
Vanlear, KY 41265

Woodford County Historical Society
121 Rose Hill
Versailles, KY 40383
Tel: 859-873-6786
http://www.woodfordkyhistory.org/

LDS FAMILY HISTORY CENTERS

For locations of Family History Centers in this state, see
   the Family History Center locator at FamilySearch.
http://www.familysearch.org/eng/Library/FHC/
   frameset_fhc.asp

ARCHIVES/LIBRARIES/MUSEUMS

Adair County Public Library
307 GReensburg Street
Columbia, KY 42728
Tel: 270-384-2472

Bath Memorial Library
24 West Main Street
P.O. Box 380
Owingsville, KY 40360
Tel: 606-674-2531
E-mail: bcml@mail.state.ky.us
http://bathcountylibrary.tripod.com/

Boyd County Public Library
Eastern Kentucky Genealogy Room
1740 Central Avenue
Ashland, KY 41101
Tel: 606-329-0090
Fax: 606-329-0578
http://www.thebookplace.org/

Breathitt County Public Library
1024 College Avenue
Jackson, KY 41339
Tel: 606-666-5541
Fax: 606-666-8166
E-mail: library@tgtel.com
http://www.breathittcountylibrary.com/

Breckinridge County Public Library
Special Collections
112 South Main Street
Hardinsburg, KY 40143
Tel: 270-756-2323
Fax: 270-756-5634

Buffalo Trace/Fleming County Public Library
303 South Main Cross Street
Flemingsburg, KY 41041
Tel: 606-845-7851
    606-845-9571
http://members.tripod.com/~edneyj/index-2.html

Bullitt County Public Library
Ridgway Memorial Library
127 North Walnut
P.O. Box 146
Shepherdsville, KY 40165
Tel: 502-543-7675
    502-543-5487

Campbell County Historical & Genealogical Society Library
19 East Main Street
Alexandria, KY 41001
Tel: 606-635-6417
E-mail: cchistoricalsoc@sprynet.com

Campbellsville University
American Civil War Institute
1 University Drive
Campbellsville, KY 42718-2799
Tel: 270-789-5000
http://www.campbellsvil.edu/campbellsville/civilwar/

Clark County Public Library
370 South Burns Avenue
Winchester, KY 40391-1876
Tel: 859-744-5661

Cincinnati Public Library
800 Vine Street
Cincinnati, OH 45202-2071
Tel: 513-369-6900
http://www.cincinnatilibrary.org/

Crittenden County Library
204 West Carlisle Street
Marion, KY 42064
Tel: 270-965-3354

Cynthiana-Harrison County Public Library
110 North Main Street
Cynthiana, KY 41031
Tel: 859-234-4881
Fax: 859-234-0059
E-mail: sellis@harrisonlibrary.org
http://harrisonlibrary.org/

Department of Military Affairs
Military Records & Research Branch
Pine Hill Plaza
1121 Louisville Road
Frankfort, KY 40601
Tel: 502-564-4873
Fax: 502 564-4437
http://www.state.ky.us/agencies/military/mrrb.htm

Eastern Kentucky University
Libraries Complex, Room 126
Special Collections & Archives
521 Lancaster Avenue
Richmond, KY 40475-3121
Tel: 859-622-1792
Fax: 859-622-1174
http://www.library.eku.edu/SCA/

Elizabethtown Community College
Media Center/Microfilm
600 College Street
Elizabethtown, KY 42701
Tel: 270-769-2371 ext. 240
Fax: 270-769-1618
http://www.elizabethtowncc.com/ecdweb/Library/

Filson Club Historical Society
1310 South Third Street
Louisville, KY 40208
Tel: 502-635-5083
Fax: 502-635-5086
E-mail: MarkWeth@filsonhistorical.org   (Director)
http://www.filsonhistorical.org/

Fulton County Public Library
312 Main Street
Fulton, KY 42041
Tel: 270-472-3439
Fax: 270-472-6241

Gallatin Free Public Library
209 W. Market Street
P.O. Box 258
Warsaw, KY 41095
Tel/Fax: 859-567-2786
E-mail: Info@GallatinCountyLibrary.org
http://gallatincountylibrary.org/

Garrard County Public Library
101 Lexington Street
Lancaster, KY 40444
Tel: 859-792-3424
Fax: 859-792-2366
E-mail: garlib@hotmail.com
http://millennium.fortunecity.com/paddington/739/

George Coon Public Library
114 South Harrison Street
P.O. Box 230
Princeton, KY 42445
Tel: 270-365-2884
Fax: 270-365-2892

Graves County Public Library
601 North 17th Street
Mayfield, KY 42066
Tel: 270-247-2911
Fax: 270-247-2990
http://www.gcpl.org/

Green County Public Library
116 South Main Street
Greensburg, KY 42743
Tel: 270-932-7081

Greenup County Public Library
614 Main Street
Greenup, KY 41144
Tel: 606-473-6514

Harvey Helm Memorial Library
301 Third Street
Stanford, KY 40484
Tel: 606-365-7513

Henderson Public Library
101 South Main Street
Henderson, KY 42420
Tel: 270-826-3712

Henry M. Caudill Memorial Library
220 Main Street
Whitesburg, KY 41858
Tel: 606-633-7547

Hickman County Memorial Public Library
209 Mayfield Road
Clinton, KY 42031
Tel/Fax: 270-653-2225

Israel T. Namani Library
3600 Dutchmans Lane
Louisville, KY 40205

Jackson County Public Library
David Street
P.O. Box 160
McKee, KY 40447-0160
Tel: 606-287-8113
Fax: 606-287-7774

John Fox Memorial Library
Duncan Tavern Shrine
323 High Street
Paris, KY 40361
Tel: 859-987-1788
http://www.mindspring.com/~jogt/johnfoxjr.htm

Kenton County Public Library
502 Scott Boulevard
Covington, KY 41011
Tel: 859-491-7610
http://www.kenton.lib.ky.us/

Kentucky Department for Libraries and Archives
Public Records Division
Archives Research Room
300 Coffee Tree Road
P.O. Box 537
Frankfort, KY 40602-0537
Tel: 502-564-8300
Fax: 502-564-5773
http://www.kdla.state.ky.us/pubrec/archbr.htm

Kentucky Historical Society/Library/Museum
Old Capitol Annex
Corner of Broadway and Lewis Streets
P.O. Box 1792
Frankfort, KY 40602-1792
Tel: 502-564-3016
Fax: 502-564-4701

Laurel County Historical Society/Library
1 Old City Hall
Broad Street & West 3rd Street
P.O. Box 816
London, KY 40741
Tel: 606-864-0607
E-mail: lchistsoc@kih.net
http://www.users.kih.net/~lchistsoc/histsoc/

Laurel County Public Library
116 East 4th Street
London, KY 40741
Tel: 606-864-5759
Fax: 606-864-9061

Lee County Public Library
123 Center Street
P.O. Box V
Beattyville, KY 41311
Tel: 606-464-8014
Fax: 606-464-2052
E-mail: lcpl01@tgtel.com
http://www.geocities.com/Athens/Olympus/2942/

Leslie County Public Library
P.O. Box 498
Hyden, KY 41749

Lexington Public Library
140 East Main
Lexington, KY 40507
Tel: 859-231-5520
859-231-5530
http://www.lexpublib.org/

Louisville Free Public Library
301 York Street
Louisville, KY 40203
Tel: 502-574-1611
http://www.lfpl.org/

Magoffin County Historical Society/Library
213 South Church Street
P.O. Box 222
Salyersville, KY 41465
Tel: 606-349-1607
Fax: 606-349-1353
http://www.rootsweb.com/~kymhs/

Marion County Free Public Library
201 East Main
Lebanon, KY 40033
Tel: 270-692-4698

Martin County Public Library
Main Street
P.O. Box 1318
Inez, KY 41224
Tel: 606-298-7766

Mary Wood Weldon Memorial Library
107 W. College Street
Glasgow, KY 42141
Tel: 270-651-2824
http://www.glasgowbarren.com/commun/library/
     library.htm

Menifee County Library
P.O. Box 237
Frenchburg, KY 40322
Tel: 606-768-2212

Morehead State University
Camden-Carroll Library
Special Collections
150 University Blvd.
Morehead, KY 40351
Tel: 606-783-2829
     606-783-5107
http://www.morehead-st.edu/units/library/collections/

Morganfield Public Library
Union County Public Library
126 South Morgan Street
Morganfield, KY 42437
Tel: 270-389-1696
Fax: 270-389-3935

Mt. Sterling/Montgomery County Library
241 W. Locust Street
Mt. Sterling, KY 40353
Tel: 859-498-2404

Nelson County Government Library
90 Court Square
Bardstown, KY 40004
Tel: 502-348-3714

Nicholas County Library
223 N. Broadway Street
Carlisle, KY 40311
Tel: 859-289-5595
http://www.nicholascountylibrary.com/

Ohio County Library
413 Main Street
Hartford, KY 42347
Tel: 270-298-3790

Owen County Public Library
118 North Main Street
Owenton, KY 40359
Tel: 502-484-3450
http://www.owentonky.com/LIBRARY/library.html

Owensboro/Daviess County Public Library
Kentucky Room, Local History & Genealogy
450 Griffith Avenue
Owensboro, KY 42301
Tel: 270-684-0211
http://www.dcpl.lib.ky.us/

Owsley County Public Library
#2 Medical Plaza
P.O. Box 280
Booneville, KY 41314
Tel: 606-593-5700
Fax: 606-593-5708

Perry County Public Library
479 High Street
P.O. Box 928
Hazard, KY 41701
Tel: 606-436-2475
Fax: 606-436-0191
E-mail: pcpl479@gte-mail.net
http://www.geocities.com/pcpl479/

Pikeville Public Library
119 College Street
P.O. Box 471
Pikeville, KY 41502-0471
Tel: 606-432-1285

Pulaski County Public Library
107 N. Main
Somerset, KY 42501
Tel: 606-679-8401
E-mail: libinfo@hyperaction.net
http://www.pcpl.lib.ky.us/

Robertson County Public Library
407 East Walnut Street
P.O. Box 282
Mt. Olivet, KY 41064
Tel: 606-724-5746
http://www.rcpl.state.ky.us/

Rockcastle County Public Library
60 Ford Drive
Mt. Vernon, KY 40456
Tel: 606-256-2388
Fax: 606-256-5460
E-mail: rcpl@kih.net
http://www.rockcastlelibrary.com/

Rowan County Public Library
129 Trumbo Road
Morehead, KY 40351
Tel: 606-784-7137

Rufus M. Reed Public Library
P.O. Box 359
Lovely, KY 41231
Tel/Fax: 606-395-5809

Scott County Public Library
104 South Bradford Lane
Georgetown, KY 40324
Tel: 502-863-3566
http://www.scottpublib.org/

Secretary of State Land Office
700 Capital Avenue Suite 152
State Capitol
Frankfort, KY 40601
Tel: 502-564-3490
Fax: 502-564-5687
http://www.sos.state.ky.us/

Simpson County Historical Society/Library and Archives
206 N. College Street
Franklin, KY 42134
Tel: 270-586-4228
Fax: 270-586-4429
E-mail: Information@SimpsonCountyKyArchives.com
http://www.rootsweb.com/~kyschs/

Union County Historical Society/Museum
221 W. McElroy
Morganfield, KY 42437

University of Kentucky
Margaret I. King Library
Special Collection and Archives
Lexington, KY 40506
Tel: 859-257-8611
http://www.uky.edu/Libraries/Special/

Wayne County Public Library
159 S. Main Street
Monticello, KY 42633
Tel: 606-348-8565
Fax: 606-348-3829

Western Kentucky University
DLSC/Kentucky Library
Kentucky Building, Room 206
1 Big Red Way
Bowling Green, KY 42101-3576
Tel: 270-745-5083
Fax: 270-745-6264
E-mail: library.web@wku.edu
http://www.wku.edu/Library/dlsc/ky_lib.htm

NEWSPAPER REPOSITORIES

Filson Club Historical Society
1310 South Third Street
Louisville, KY 40208
Tel: 502-635-5083
Fax: 502-635-5086
E-mail: MarkWeth@filsonhistorical.org   (Director)
http://www.filsonhistorical.org/

Kentucky Historical Society/Library/Museum
Old Capitol Annex
Corner of Broadway and Lewis Streets
P.O. Box 1792
Frankfort, KY 40602-1792
Tel: 502-564-3016
Fax: 502-564-4701

Lexington Public Library
140 East Main
Lexington, KY 40507
Tel: 859-231-5520
    859-231-5530
http://www.lexpublib.org/

Murray State University
Pogue Library
Special Collections
208 Waterfield Library
Murray, KY 42071-3307
Tel: 270-762-2291
http://www.murraystate.edu/msml/Pogue.html

St. Joseph County Public Library
304 South Main Street
South Bend, IN 46601
Tel: 219-282-4646
E-mail: m.waterson@gomail.sjcpl.lib.in.us
http://sjcpl.lib.in.us/homepage/LocalHist/
    Genealogy.html

University of Kentucky
Margaret I. King Library
Special Collection and Archives
Lexington, KY 40506
Tel: 859-257-8611
http://www.uky.edu/Libraries/Special/

University of Louisville
Archives and Records Center
Ekstrom Library Building
Louisville, KY 40292
Tel: 502-852-6674
Fax: 502-852-6673
E-mail: archives@louisville.edu
http://www.louisville.edu/library/uarc/

VITAL RECORDS

Office of Vital Statistics
275 East Main Street
Frankfort, KY 40601
Tel: 502-564-4212
Fax: 502-227-0032
http://publichealth.state.ky.us/vital.htm

KENTUCKY ON THE WEB

First Kentucky Brigade, CS, "The Orphan Brigade"
http://www.rootsweb.com/~orphanhm//

Kentucky Biographies Project
http://www.starbase21.com/kybiog/

Kentucky Explorer (Magazine)
http://kentuckyexplorer.com/

Kentucky GenWeb Project
http://www.rootsweb.com/~kygenweb/

Kentucky in the Civil War
http://www.myoldkentuckyroots.com/CIVILWAR.html

Kentucky Vital Records Index
http://ukcc.uky.edu/~vitalrec/

Ohio River Valley Families
http://orvf.com/

Travellers Southern Families
http://misc.traveller.com/genealogy/

LOUISIANA

ARCHIVES, STATE & NATIONAL

Louisiana State Archives
3851 Essen Lane
Baton Rouge, LA 70809-2137
Tel: 225-922-1000
E-mail: archives@sec.state.la.us
http://www.sec.state.la.us/archives/archives/ archives-
   index.htm

National Archives-Southwest Region
501 West Felix Street
Building 1, Dock 1
P.O. Box 6216
Fort Worth, TX 76115-0216
Tel: 817-334-5515
Fax: 817-334-5511
E-mail: ftworth.archives@nara.gov
http://www.nara.gov/regional/ftworth.html

GENEALOGICAL SOCIETIES

Allen Genealogical and Historical Society
P.O. Box 789
Kinder, LA 70648

Amite Genealogical Club
739 West Oak
P.O. Box 578
Amite, LA 70422-2734

Ark-La-Tex Genealogical Association
P.O. Box 4462
Shreveport, LA 71134

Baton Rouge Genealogical and Historical Society
SE Station
P.O. Box 80565
Baton Rouge, LA 70898-0565
http://www.intersurf.com/~rcollins/brg.htm

Cajun Clickers Computer Club
10120 Red Oak Drive
Baton Rouge, LA 70815
Tel: 225-273-7113
Fax: 225-273-7713
http://www.clickers.org/

Central Louisiana Genealogical Society
P.O. Box 12206
Alexandria, LA 71315-2006
http://www.rootsweb.com/~laclgs/

East Ascension Genealogical and Historical Society
P.O. Box 1006
Gonzales, LA 70707-1006

Evangeline Genealogical and Historical Society
P.O. Box 664
Ville Platte, LA 70586-0664

Florida Parishes Genealogical Society
P.O. Box 520
Livingston, LA 70754-0520

Friends of Genealogy
P.O. Box 17835
Shreveport, LA 71138

GENCOM PC User Group of Shreveport
9913 Dagger Point
Shreveport, LA 71115
E-mail: hr50@softdisk.com

Genealogy West, Inc.
West Bank of the Mississippi
5644 Abbey Drive
New Orleans, LA 70131-3808

**German-Acadian Coast Historical and Genealogical
Society**
P.O. Box 517
Destrahan, LA 70047-0517
http://www.rootsweb.com/~lastjohn/geracadn.htm

Imperial/St. Landry Genealogical and Historical Society
P.O. Box 118
Opelousas, LA 70571-0118
http://www.imperialstlandry.org/

Jefferson Genealogical Society
P.O. Box 961
Metairie, LA 70004-0961
http://www.gnofn.org/~jgs/

Jennings Genealogical Society
136 Greenwood Drive
Jennings, LA 70546

Jewish Genealogical Society of New Orleans
P.O. Box 7811
Metairie, LA 70010-7811
Tel: 504-888-3817
http://www.jewishgen.org/jgsno/

Lafayette Genealogical Society
1021 Rosedown Lane
Lafayette, LA 70532-5832

Le Comite des Archives de la Louisiane
Capitol Station
P.O. Box 44370
Baton Rouge, LA 70804-4370

Louisiana Genealogical and Historical Society
P.O. Box 82060
Baton Rouge, LA 70884
E-mail: LGHS@aol.com
http://www.rootsweb.com/~la-lghs/

Louisiana Roots
P.O. Box 383
Marksville, LA 71351
Tel: 318-253-5413
Fax: 318-253-7223
http://www.geocities.com/BourbonStreet/5978/

Natchitoches Genealogical and Historical Association
P.O. Box 1349
Natchitoches, LA 71458
Tel: 318-357-2235
E-mail: ngha@wnonline.net
http://www.rootsweb.com/~lanatchi/ngl.htm

New Orleans, Genealogical Research Society of
P.O. Box 51791
New Orleans, LA 70150-1791
http://www.rootsweb.com/~lagrsno/

North Louisiana Genealogical Society
P.O. Box 324
Ruston, LA 71270

Plaquemines Deep Delta Genealogical Society
Plaquemines Parish Library
203 Highway 11 South
Buras, LA 70041
Tel: 985-657-7121

Pointe de l'Eglise Genealogical and Historical Society
P.O. Box 160
Church Point, LA 70525
E-mail: ffwp26e@prodigy.com

St. Bernard Genealogical Society
P.O. Box 271
Chalmette, LA 70044-0271
http://www.ccugpc.org/sbgs/sbgs.htm

St. Mary Genealogical and Historical Society
P.O. Box 662
Morgan City, LA 70381

St. Tammany Genealogical Society
310 West 21st Street
P.O. Box 1904
Covington, LA 70434-1904
Tel: 985-893-6280

Sons and Daughters of the Province and Republic of West Florida 1763-1810
P.O. Box 82672
Baton Rouge, LA 70884-2672

Southwest Louisiana Genealogical Society
P.O. Box 5652
Lake Charles, LA 70606-5652
http://homepages.xspedius.net/mmoore/calcasie/swlgs.htm

Terrebonne Genealogical Society
Station 2, Box 295
Houma, LA 70360-0295
http://www.rootsweb.com/~laterreb/tgs.htm

Vermilion Genealogical Society
307 N. Main Street
P.O. Box 117
Abbeville, LA 70511-0117

Vernon Genealogical and Historical Society
P.O. Box 159
Anacoco, LA 71403

Vicksburg Genealogical Society
P.O. Box 1161
Vicksburg, MS 39181-1161
http://www.rootsweb.com/~msvgs/

West Bank Genealogy Society
P.O. Box 872
Harvey, LA 70059-0872
http://www.geocities.com/heartland/forest/7425/

West Baton Rouge Genealogical Society
P.O. Box 1126
Port Allen, LA 70767

Winn Parish Genealogical and Historical Society
P.O. Box 652
Winnfield, LA 71483-0652
E-mail: peggy@winnsurf.net
http://www.rootsweb.com/~lawpgha/

HISTORICAL SOCIETIES

Allen Genealogical and Historical Society
P.O. Box 789
Kinder, LA 70648

Action Cadienne (Cajun Action)
P.O. Box 60104
Lafayette, LA 70596-0104
E-mail: info@actioncadienne.org
http://www.actioncadienne.org/

Baton Rouge Genealogical and Historical Society
SE Station
P.O. Box 80565
Baton Rouge, LA 70898-0565
http://www.intersurf.com/~rcollins/brg.htm

East Ascension Genealogical and Historical Society
P.O. Box 1006
Gonzales, LA 70707-1006

Edward Livingston Historical Association
P.O. Box 67
Livingston, LA 70754-0067

Evangeline Genealogical and Historical Society
P.O. Box 664
Ville Platte, LA 70586

Feliciana History Committee
P.O. Box 8341
Clinton, LA 70722

Feliciana Historical Society
P.O. Box 338
St. Francisville, LA 70775

German-Acadian Coast Historical and Genealogical Society
P.O. Box 517
Destrahan, LA 70047-0517
http://www.rootsweb.com/~lastjohn/geracadn.htm

Imperial/St. Landry Genealogical and Historical Society
P.O. Box 118
Opelousas, LA 70571-0118
http://www.imperialstlandry.org/

Lafourche Heritage Society
412 Menard Street
P.O. Box 913
Thibodaux, LA 70302

Louisiana Genealogical and Historical Society
P.O. Box 82060
Baton Rouge, LA 70884
E-mail: LGHS@aol.com
http://www.rootsweb.com/~la-lghs/

Natchitoches Genealogical and Historical Association
P.O. Box 1349
Natchitoches, LA 71458
Tel: 318-357-2235
E-mail: ngha@wnonline.net
http://www.rootsweb.com/~lanatchi/ngl.htm

North Caddo, Historical Society of
100 SW Front Street
P.O. Box 31
Vivian, LA 71082
http://pages.prodigy.net/scollier/hsnc/

St. Augustine Historical Society
P.O. Box 39
Melrose, LA 71456
Tel: 318-357-0602
E-mail: colsonj@nsula.edu
http://members.tripod.com/creoles/

St. Helena Historical Society
Route 1, Box 131
Amite, LA 70422-9415

St. Mary Genealogical and Historical Society
P.O. Box 662
Morgan City, LA 70381

St. Tammany Parish Historical Society
P.O. Box 1001
Mandeville, LA 70470-1001

Southeast Louisiana Historical Society
P.O. Box 789
Hammond, LA 70401-0789

Tangipahoa Parish Historical Society
77139 N. River Road
Kentwood, LA 70444

Vermillion Historic Foundation
1600 Surrey Street
P.O. Box 2266
Lafayette, LA 70502-2266
Tel: 337-233-4077
800-99-BAYOU

Vernon Genealogical and Historical Society
P.O. Box 159
Anacoco, LA 71403

West Feliciana Historical Society/Museum
Ferdinand Street
P.O. Box 338
St. Francisville, LA 70775
Tel: 225-635-6330

Winn Parish Genealogical and Historical Society
P.O. Box 652
Winnfield, LA 71483-0652
E-mail: peggy@winnsurf.net
http://www.rootsweb.com/~lawpgha/

LDS FAMILY HISTORY CENTER

For locations of Family History Centers in this state, see the Family History Center locator at FamilySearch. http://www.familysearch.org/eng/Library/FHC/frameset_fhc.asp

ARCHIVES/LIBRARIES/MUSEUMS

Amistad Research Center
Tilton Hall
Tulane University
6823 St. Charles Avenue
New Orleans, LA 70118
Tel: 504-865-5535
Fax: 504-865-5580
E-mail: arc@tcs.tulane.edu
http://www.tulane.edu/~amistad/

Ascension Parish Library
708 S. Irma Avenue
Gonzales, LA 70707-1006
Tel: 225-647-3955
http://www.ascension.lib.la.us/apl

Assumption Parish Library
293 Napoleon Avenue
Napoleonville, LA 70390
Tel: 985-369-7070
Fax: 985-369-6019
E-mail: apl1@pelican.state.lib.la.us

Avoyelles Parish Library
101 North Washington Street
Marksville, LA 71351-2496
Tel: 318-253-7559
Fax: 318-253-6361
E-mail: xxx1137@ucs.usl.edu

Beauregard Parish Library
205 S. Washington Avenue
DeRidder, LA 70634
Tel: 337-463-6217
800-524-6239
http://www.beau.lib.la.us/lib/

Bogalusa Branch/Washington Parish Library
304 Avenue F
Bogalusa, LA 70427
Tel: 985-735-1961

Centenary College of Louisiana
Magale Library
2911 Centenary Blvd.
P.O. Box 41188
Shreveport, LA 71134
Tel: 318-869-5170
Fax: 318-869-5094
http://www.centenary.edu/lib_tech/index2.html

East Baton Rouge Parish Library
7711 Goodwood Blvd.
Baton Rouge, LA 70806 U.S.A.
Tel: 225-231-3700
225-231-3750
http://www.ebr.lib.la.us/

Iberville Parish Library
24605 J. Gerald Berret Blvd.
P.O. Box 736
Plaquemine, LA 70764-0736
Tel: 225-687-2520
Fax: 225-687-9719
E-mail: dball@pelican.state.lib.la.us (Director)
http://www.iberville.lib.la.us/

Jackson Barracks Military Library
Office of the Adjutant General
Building 53, Jackson Barracks
New Orleans, LA 70146-0330
Tel: 504-278-8241
Fax: 504-278-6554

Jefferson Parish Library
4747 West Napoleon Avenue
Metairie, LA 70001
Tel: 504-838-1100
Fax: 504-838-1110
http://www.jefferson.lib.la.us/

Lafayette Parish Public Library
301 West Congress Street
P.O. Box 3427
Lafayette, LA 70502-3427
Tel: 337-261-5775
Fax: 337-261-5782
http://www.lafayette.lib.la.us/

Lafourche Parish Library
303 West 5th Street
Thibodaux, LA 70301
Tel: 985-446-1163
Fax: 985-446-3848
E-mail: lpl1@pelican.state.lib.la.us
http://www.lafourche.lib.la.us/

Lincoln Parish Library
509 West Alabama
Ruston, LA 71270
P.O. Box 637
http://www.lincoln.lib.la.us/

Louisiana State Library
Louisiana Section
701 North 4th Street
P.O. Box 131
Baton Rouge, LA 70821-0131
Tel: 225-342-4914
E-mail: ladept@pelican.state.lib.la.us
http://www.state.lib.la.us/

Louisiana State Museum Historical Center
751 Chartres Street
P.O. Box 2448
New Orleans, LA 70116-2448
Tel: 504-568-6968
504-568-4995 (Receptionist)
E-mail: lsm@crt.state.la.us
http://lsm.crt.state.la.us/

Louisiana State University
Hill Memorial Library
Special Collections Public Services
Baton Rouge, LA 70803-3300
Tel: 225-388-6568 (Reference Desk)
225-578-6544 (Public Services Desk)
Fax: 225-578-9425
E-mail: lbyspc@lsuvm.sncc.lsu.edu
http://www.lib.lsu.edu/special/

Louisiana State University/Shreveport
Noel Memorial Library
Shreveport, LA 71115
Tel: 318-797-5069
http://www.lsus.edu/library/

Natchitoches Parish Library
450 Second Street
Natchitoches, LA 71457
Tel: 318-357-3280
Fax: 318-357-7073
http://www.youseemore.com/Natchitoches/

New Orleans Public Library
219 Loyola Avenue
New Orleans, LA 70112-2044
Tel: 504-529-READ
        504-596-2610 (Louisiana Division)
http://nutrias.org/~nopl/welcome.html

Ouachita Parish Public Library
Genealogy Room
1800 Stubbs Avenue
Monroe, LA 71201-5787
Tel: 318-327-1490
Fax: 318-327-1373
E-mail: eileenk@ouachita.lib.la.us
http://www.ouachita.lib.la.us/

Plaquemines Parish Library
35572 Highway 11
Buras, LA 70041-1625
Tel: 985-657-7121
985-657-7122
Fax: 985-657-6175
E-mail: admin.s1pq@pelican.state.lib.la.us
http://www.plaquemines.lib.la.us/

Pointe Coupee Library
201 Clairborne Street
New Roads, LA 70760-3403
Tel: 225-638-7593
225-638-9841
Fax: 225-638-9847

Rapides Parish Library
Red Carpet Van Service
411 Washington Street
Alexandria, LA 71301-8338
Tel: 318-445-2411 Ext. 221
318-445-6436
Fax: 318-445-6478
318-445-6196 (Administrarion Office)
E-mail: l_fandries@hotmail.com
http://www.rpl.org/

St. James Parish Library
1879 West Main Street
Lutcher, LA 70071-9704
Tel: 225-869-3618
Fax: 225-869-8435
http://www.stjames.lib.la.us/

St. John the Baptist Parish Library
1334 West Airline Highway
LaPlace, LA 70068
Tel: 985-652-6857
Fax: 985-652-2114
E-mail: rdesoto@stjohn.lib.la.us
http://www.stjohn.lib.la.us/

St. Martin Parish Library
201 Porter Street
P.O. Box 79
St. Martinsville, LA 70582-0079
Tel: 337-394-2207
Fax: 337-394-2248
E-mail: admin.b1mt@pelican.state.lib.la.us
http://www.stmartin.lib.la.us/

Shreve Memorial Library
424 Texas Street
P.O. Box 21523
Shreveport, LA 71120
Tel: 318-226-5897 (Genealogy)
E-mail: e_refsml@yahoo.com
http://www.shreve-lib.org/

Shreveport Exhibit Museum
3015 Greenwood Road
Shreveport, LA 71109
Tel: 318-632-2020
318-632-2019
E-mail: lsem@sec.state.la.us
http://www.sec.state.la.us/museums/shreve/shreveindex.htm

Southwest Louisiana Genealogical Library
Calcasieu Parish Public Library
411 Pujo Street
Lake Charles, LA 70601
Tel: 337-437-3490
Fax: 337-437-4198
http://www.calcasieu.lib.la.us/genealogy.htm

Tangipahoa Parish Library
200 East Mulberry Street
Amite, LA 70422
Tel: 985-748-7559
Fax: 985-748-2812
E-mail: admin.c1tg@pelican.state.lib.la.us
http://www.tangipahoa.lib.la.us/

Terrebonne Parish Library
424 Roussell Street
Houma, LA 70360
Tel: 985-876-5861
Fax: 985-876-5864
E-mail: main.b1tb@pelican.state.lib.la.us
http://www.terrebonne.lib.la.us/

Tulane University
Howard/Tilton Memorial Library
Special Collections
New Orleans, LA 70118
Tel: 504-865-5643
Fax: 504-865-6773
E-mail: meneray@mailhost.tcs.tulane.edu
http://www.tulane.edu/~lmiller/

University of Southwest Louisiana
Edith Garland Dupre' Library
Jefferson Caffery Louisiana Room
302 E. St. Mary Street
Lafayette, LA 70504
Tel: 337-482-6396
337-482-6030 (Reference Desk)
Fax: 337-482-5841
http://www.louisiana.edu/InfoTech/Library/

Vernon Parish Library
1401 Nolan Trace
Leesville, LA 71446-4331
Tel: 337-239-2027
800-737-2231
Fax: 337-238-0666
E-mail: vernonpl@alpha.nsula.edu
http://www.vernon.lib.la.us/

Washington Parish Library
825 Free Street
Franklinton, LA 70438
Tel: 985-839-7806
Fax: 985-839-7808

West Baton Rouge Museum
845 N. Jefferson
Port Allen, LA 70767
Tel: 225-336-2422
http://www.lapage.com/wbrm/

West Baton Rouge Parish Library
830 N. Alexander
Port Allen, LA 70767-2327
Tel: 225-342-7920
Fax: 225-342-7918
E-mail: pawbr1@Unix1.sncc.lsu.edu
http://www.wbr.lib.la.us/

West Feliciana Historical Society/Museum
Ferdinand Street
P.O. Box 338
St. Francisville, LA 70775
Tel: 225-635-6330

West Feliciana Parish Library
Audubon Library
11865 Ferdinand Street
St. Francisville, LA 70775
Tel: 225-635-3364

Xavier University
1 Drexel Drive
New Orleans, LA 70125
Tel: 504-483-7305
Fax: 504-485-7917
E-mail: library@xula.edu
http://www.xula.edu/Library_Services/library.html

NEWSPAPER REPOSITORIES

Louisiana State University
Hill Memorial Library
Special Collections Public Services
Baton Rouge, LA 70803-3300
Tel: 225-388-6568 (Reference Desk)
225-578-6544 (Public Services Desk)
Fax: 225-578-9425
E-mail: lbyspc@lsuvm.sncc.lsu.edu
http://www.lib.lsu.edu/special/

New Orleans Public Library
219 Loyola Avenue
New Orleans, LA 70112-2044
Tel: 504-529-READ
504-596-2610 (Louisiana Division)
http://nutrias.org/~nopl/welcome.html

VITAL RECORDS

Louisiana Department of Health
Vital Records Registry Office of Public Health
325 Loyola Avenue
P.O. Box 60630
New Orleans, LA 70160
Tel: 504-568-8353
Fax: 504-568-6909
E-mail: vitalweb@dhh.state.la.us
http://oph.dhh.state.la.us/recordsstatistics/vitalrecords/

LOUISIANA ON THE WEB

Acadian Genealogy Homepage
http://www.acadian.org/

Louisiana GenWeb Project
http://www.lagenweb.org/

Traveller Southern Families
http://misc.traveller.com/genealogy/search/

U.S. Civil War Center
http://www.cwc.lsu.edu/civlink.htm

MAINE

ARCHIVES, STATE & NATIONAL

Maine State Archives
84 State House Station
Augusta, ME 04333-0084
Phone: 207-287-5795
Fax: 207-287-5739
http://www.state.me.us/sos/arc/

National Archives—New England Region
Frederick C. Murphy Federal Center
380 Trapelo Road
Waltham, MA 02154-8104
Tel: 781-647-8104
Fax: 781-647-8088
E-mail: waltham.center@nara.gov
http://www.nara.gov/regional/boston.html

GENEALOGICAL SOCIETIES

Lincoln County Genealogical Society
P.O. Box 61
Wiscasset, ME 04578
http://www.rootsweb.com/~wvlincol/LCGS.html

Maine Genealogical Society
P.O. Box 221
Farmington, ME 04938
http://www.rootsweb.com/~megs/MaineGS.htm

New England Historical and Genealogical Society (NEHGS)
101 Newbury Street
Boston, MA 02116-3007
Tel: 617-836-5740
888-296-3447 (Membersip and Sales)
888-906-3447 (Library Circulation)
Fax: 617-536-7307
E-mail: nehgs@nehgs.org
http://www.newenglandancestors.org/

HISTORICAL SOCIETIES

Acton/Shapleigh Historical Society
P.O. Box 545
Acton ME 04001-0545

Alexander-Crawford Historical Society
216 Pokey Road
Alexander, ME 04694

Allagash Historical Society
Rte. 161
St. Francis, ME 04774
Tel: 207-398-3335
207-398-3347
http://aroostook.me.us/allagash/historical.html

Alna Historical Society
Old Alna Meeting House
Route 218
Alna, ME 04535

Androscoggin Historical Society
2 Turner
Auburn, ME 04210
Tel: 207-784-0586
http://www.rootsweb.com/~meandrhs/

Bangor Historical Society/Museum
159 Union Street
Bangor, ME 04401
Tel: 207-942-5766

Bar Harbor Historical Society/Museum
34 Mt. Desert Street
Bar Harbor, ME 04609
Tel: 207-288-4245

Bath Historical Society
Patten Free Library
33 Summer Street
Bath, ME 04530-2687
Tel: 207-443-5141
Fax: 207-443-3514
http://www.biddeford.com/~pfl/shgr.htm

Bethel Historical Society/Museum
14 Broad Street
P.O. Box 12
Bethel, ME 04217
Tel: 207-824-2908
Fax: 207-824-0882
E-mail: info@bethelhistorical.org
http://www.bethelhistorical.org/

Biddeford Historical Society
McArthur Library
270 Main Street
P.O. Box 200
Biddeford, ME 04005-0200
Tel: 207-283-4706
http://www.mcarthur.lib.me.us/bidhisso.htm

Blue Hill Historical Society
Holt House
Water Street
Blue Hill, ME 04614

Boothbay Region Historical Society
70 Oak Street
P.O. Box 272
Boothbay Harbor, ME 04538-0272
Tel: 207-633-0820
http://www.boothbayregister.maine.com/1998-06-25/
    historical_society.html

Border Historical Society
Washington Street
P.O. Box 95
Eastport, ME 04631
Tel: 207-853-2328

Brewer Historical Society
Clewley Museum
199 Wilson Street
Brewer, ME 04412
Tel: 207-989-7468
Fax: 207-989-1769
E-mail: Joshcham@agate.net

Bridgton Historical Society/Museum
Gibbs Avenue
P.O. Box 44
Bridgton, ME 04009
Tel: 207-647-3699
E-mail: bhs@megalink.net
http://www.megalink.net/~bhs/index.html

Brooksville Historical Society/Museum
Route 176
Brooksville, ME 04617
Phone: 207-326-8681
E-mail: mcmillen@acadia.net

Buckfield Historical Society
R.R. 4, Box 780
Turner, ME 04282-9604
http://www.sad39.k12.me.us/zadoc/society.html

Camden Historical Society
80 Mechanic Street
Camden, ME 04843

Camden-Rockport Historical Society
Old Conway Complex & Museum
P.O. Box 747
Camden, ME 04843
Tel/Fax: 207-236-2257
E-mail: chmuseum@mint.net
http://members.mint.net/chmuseum/

Caribou Historical Society
P.O. Box 1058
Caribou, ME 04736
Tel: 207-498-2556

Chebeague Island Historical Society
RR 1 Box 16
Chebeague Island, ME 04017
E-mail: Etta137@aol.com

Cherryfield-Narraguagus Historical Society
Main Street
P.O. Box 96
Cherryfield, ME 04622

Cushing Historical Society/Museum
P.O. Box 110
Cushing, Maine 04563
Tel: 207-354-8262
800-261-1369
http://www.rootsweb.com/~usgenweb/me/knox/cushing.htm

Dead River Area Historical Society
172 Main Street
Stratton, ME 04982

Dexter Historical Society
P.O. Box 481
Dexter, Maine 04930
Tel: 207-924-5721
E-mail: dexhist@panax.com
http://www.dextermaine.org/museum/

Dixfield Historical Society
63 Main Street
P.O. Box 182
Dixfield, ME 04224
E-mail: btowle@megalink.net

Dresden Historical Society
Dresden Brick School House
Route 128
Dresden, ME 04342

Durham Historical Society
15 Cyr Road
Durham, ME 04222

Easton Historical Society
Station Road
Easton, ME 04740
Tel: 207-488-6652
http://www.historiceaston.org/

Falmouth Historical Society
Falmouth Memorial Library
5 Lunt Road
Falmouth, ME 04105
Tel: 207-781-2351
Fax: 207-781-4094
E-mail: mdevine1@maine.rr.com
http://www.falmouth.lib.me.us/historical.html

Franklin Historical Society
Sullivan Road, Rt. 200
Franklin, ME
Tel: 207-565-3635

Freeport Historical Society
Enoch Harrington House
45 Main Street
Freeport, ME 04032
Tel: 207-865-0477

Fryeburg Historical Society/Museum
96 Main Street
Fryeburg, ME 04037-1126
Tel: 207-935-4192
Fax: 207-935-4192
E-mail: museum@landmarknet.net
http://www.geocities.com/fryeburghs/

Gouldsboro Historical Society
Old Town House
Route 1
Gouldsboro, ME 04443

Guilford Historical Society
North Main Street
Guilford, ME 04443
Tel: 207-876-2787

Hampden Historical Society
Kinsley House Museum and Archives
83 Main Road
Hampden, ME 04444
Tel: 207-862-2027

Hancock Historical Society
Hancock Corner
Hancock, ME 04640

Harpswell Historical Society
1334 Harpswell Islands Road
Orr's Island, ME 04066
Tel: 207-833-5873
E-mail: gyork@clinic.net
http://www.curtislibrary.com/hhs/

Harrison Historical Society
121 Haskell Hill Road
Harrison, ME 04040
Tel: 207-583-6225
http://www.caswell.lib.me.us/histsoc.html

Island Falls Historical Society
Burley Street
Island Falls, ME 04037
Tel: 207-463-2264

Islesboro Historical Society
Old Town Hall/School
Main Road
P.O. Box 301
Islesboro, ME 04848
Tel: 207-734-6733

Jay Historical Society
Holmes-Crafts Homestead
Rt. 4, Jay Hill
North Jay, ME 04262
Tel: 207-645-2732

Kennebec Historical Society
61 Winthrop Street
P.O. Box 5582
Augusta, Maine 04332-5582
Tel: 207-622-7718
http://www.kennebechistorical.org/

Kennebunkport Historical Society
Town House School
135 North Street
P.O. Box 1173
Kennebunkport, ME 04046
Tel: 207-967-2751
Fax: 207-967-1205
E-mail: KportHS@gwi.net
http://www.kporthistory.org/

Lee Historical Society/Museum
P.O. Box 306
Lee, ME 04455
Tel: 207-738-4125

Liberty Historical Society
Old Octagonal Post Office
Main Street, Route 173
Liberty, ME 04949

Lincoln County Historical Association
15 Federal Street
Wiscasset, ME 04578
Tel: 207-882-6817
http://bradford.wiscasset.net/LCHA/

Lincolnville Historical Society/Museum
P.O. Box 211
Lincolnville ME 04850
Tel: 207-789-5445
http://www.booknotes.com/lhs/

Lisbon Historical Society
14 High Street
Lisbon, ME 04250

Lovell Historical Society
P.O. Box 166
Lovell, ME 04051-0166
Tel: 207-925-3234
Fax: 207-925-2792
E-mail: lovellhist@landmarknet.net

Machiasport Historical Society
Gates House
Route 92
P.O. Box 301
Machiasport, ME 04655
Tel: 207-255-8461

Madawaska Historical Society
Library Building
Main Street
Madawaska, ME 04756

Maine Historical Society
Center for Maine History
489 Congress Street
Portland, ME 04101
Tel: 207-774-1822
Fax: 207-775-4301
E-mail: info@mainehistory.org
http://www.mainehistory.org/

Maine Military Historical Society/Museum
Camp Keyes
Upper Winthrop Street
Augusta, ME 04330
Tel: 207-626-4338
http://www.me.ngb.army.mil/About%20Us/History/
    Museum.htm

Maine's Swedish Colony
P.O. Box 50
New Sweden, ME 04762
Tel: 207-896-5624
207-896-3199
Fax: 207-896-3120
E-mail: duncan@ainop.com
http://www.geocities.com/maineswedishcolony/

Monmouth Historical Society
Monmouth Museum
P.O. Box 352
Monmouth, ME 04259-0352
Tel: 207-933-2287
E-mail: agriffit@abacus.bates.edu
http://www.rootsweb.com/~mekenneb/monmouth/
    monhs.htm

Moosehead Historical Society
P.O. Box 1116
Greenville, Maine 04441-1116
Tel: 207-695-2909
E-mail: history@midmaine.com
http://www.mooseheadhistory.org/

Mt. Desert Island (MDI) Historical Society/Museum
P.O. Box 653
Mt. Desert, ME 04660
Tel: 207-244-5045

Naples Historical Society/Museum
P.O. Box 1757
Naples, ME 04055
Phone: 207-693-4297
E-mail: nhs@pivot.net

New England Historical and Genealogical Society (NEHGS)
101 Newbury Street
Boston, MA 02116-3007
Tel: 617-836-5740
888-296-3447 (Membersip and Sales)
888-906-3447 (Library Circulation)
Fax: 617-536-7307
E-mail: nehgs@nehgs.org
http://www.newenglandancestors.org/

Nobleboro Historical Society
Center Street
P.O. Box 122
Nobleboro, ME 04555
Tel: 207-563-5874

Norridgewock Historical Society
Mercer Road
Norridgewock, ME 04957
Tel: 207-634-4243

Norway Historical Society/Museum
232 Main Street
Norway, ME 04268
Tel: 207-743-7377

Old Berwick Historical Society
Main and Liberty Streets
P.O. Box 296
South Berwick, ME 03908
Tel: 207-384-0000
E-mail: pirsig@attbi.com

Old Orchard Beach Historical Society/Museum
Harmon Memorial
4 Portland Avenue
Old Orchard Beach, ME 04064
Tel: 207-934-9319

Old York Historical Society/Museum
207 York Street
P.O. Box 312
York, ME 03909
Tel: 207-363-4974
207-351-1083
Fax: 207-363-4021
E-mail: oyhs@oldyork.org
http://www.oldyork.org/

Orland Historical Society
Main Street, Rt. 175
Orland, ME 04472
Tel: 207-469-2476

Otisfield Historical Society
Otisfield Town Office Building
Route 121, Oxford Road
Otisfield, ME 04270
Tel: 207-539-2664
Mail: 105 Cape Road
Otisfield, ME 04270
http://www.rootsweb.com/~mecotisf/otis8.htm

Oxford Historical Society
683 Main Street
Oxford, ME 04270

Paris Cape Historical Society/Museum
19 Park Street
South Paris, ME 04281

Parsonfield/Porter Historical Society
Main Street
Porter, ME 04068

Pejepscot Historical Society/Museum
159 Park Row
Brunswick, ME 04011
Tel: 207-729-6606
Fax: 207-729-6012
E-mail: pejepscot@gwi.net
http://www.curtislibrary.com/pejepscot.htm

Pemaquid Historical Society
Rt. 2, Box 4000-314
Damariscottta 04543-9766

Phillips Historical Society
Pleasant Street
Phillips, ME 04966

Pittsfield Historical Society
Depot House Museum
Railroad Plaza
Pittsfield, ME 04967

Presque Isle Historical Society
16 3rd Street
Presque Isle, ME 04769
Tel: 207-762-1151

Rangeley Lakes Region Historical Society
Route 16, Dead River Road
P.O. Box 740
Rangeley, ME 04970

Raymond-Casco Historical Society
Main Street
Raymond, ME 04071

Readfield Historical Society
P.O. Box 354
Readfield, ME 04355
http://www.rootsweb.com/~mecreadf/rdfldrhs.htm

Richmond Historical Society
7 Gardiner Street
Richmond, ME 04357

Rumford Area Historical Society
Area Historical Museum
Rt. 2
Rumford, ME, 04276
Tel: 207-364-4007
http://www.rumfordmaine.net/history.htm

St. Croix Historical Society
245 Main Street
Calais, ME 04619

Ste. Agatha Historical Society
P.O. Box 237
St. Agatha, ME 04772
Tel: 207-543-6364
http://www.stagatha.com/society.html

Salmon Brook Historical Society of Washburn
Main Street
P.O. Box 68
Washburn, ME 04786
Tel: 207-455-5339
Fax: 207-455-4339
E-mail: smnbrkhs@smnbrkhs.sdi.agate.net

Scarborough Historical Society
649 U.S. Route One
P.O. Box 156
Scarborough ME 04070-0156
http://www.scarboroughmaine.com/historical/

Searsport Historical Society
Main Street, Rt. 1
Searsport, ME 04974

Sedgwick/Brooklin Historical Society/Museum
Route 172
P.O. Box 63
Sedgwick, ME 04676
E-mail: oblong @ hypernet.com

Southern Maine Technical College
Portland Harbor Museum
2 Fort Road
South Portland, ME 04106
Tel: 207-799-6337
E-mail: phm@gwi.net
http://www.portlandharbormuseum.org/

Standish Historical Society
Oak Hill Road
Standish, ME 04084
Tel: 207-642-5170 (Old Red Church)

Stockholm Historical Society
280 Main Street
Stockholm, ME 04783

Strong Historical Society
Vance & Dorothy Hammond Museum
Main Street
Strong, ME 04983

Sweden Historical Society
RR 1, Box 230
Bridgton, ME 04009
E-mail: sueblack@nbridgton.lib.me.us

Thomaston Historical Society
P.O. Box 384
Thomaston, ME 04861
Tel: 207-354-2295
http://www.mint.net/thomastonhistoricalsociety/

Vassalboro Historical Society/Museum
Rt. 32
East Vassalboro 04935
Tel: 207-923-3533

Vinalhaven Historical Society/Museum
High Street
P.O. Box 339
Vinalhaven, ME 04863
Tel: 207-863-4410
E-mail: vhhissoc@midcoast.com
http://www.midcoast.com/~vhhissoc/

Waldoboro Historical Society/Museum
Rt. 220 South
P.O. Box 110
Waldoboro, ME 04572

Waterford Historical Society/Museum
P.O. Box 201
Waterford, ME 04088

Waterville Historical Society
Redington Museum
64 Silver
Waterville, ME 04901
Tel: 207-872-9439

Weld Historical Society
P.O. Box 31
Weld, Maine 04285

Wells Historical Society
Meetinghouse Museum
Genealogical & Historical Research Library
Rt. 1, Post Road
Wells, ME 04090
Tel: 207-646-4775

Windham Historical Society
26 Dutton Hill
Road Gray, ME 04039
Tel: 207-892-9667

Winslow Historical Society
16 Benton Avenue
Winslow, ME 04902

Winterport Historical Association
760 North Main
Winterport, ME 04496
Phone: 207-223-5556
Fax: 207-223-4035
E-mail: dtweston@aol.com

Woodstock Historical Society/Museum
70 South Main Street
Bryant Pond, ME 04219

Woolwich Historical Society
Route 1 and Nequasset Road
P.O. Box 98
Woolwich ME 04579
Tel: 207-443-4833
E-mail: whs@gwi.net
http://www.woolwichhistory.org/

Yarmouth Historical Society
Museum of Yarmouth History &
Merrill Memorial Library
Main Street
Yarmouth, ME 04096
Tel: 207-846-6259

LDS FAMILY HISTORY CENTERS

For locations of Family History Centers in this state, see the Family History Center locator at FamilySearch. http://www.familysearch.org/eng/Library/FHC/frameset_fhc.asp

ARCHIVES/LIBRARIES/MUSEUMS

Acadia National Park
Mount Desert Island
P.O. Box 177
Bar Harbor, ME 04609
Tel: 207-288-5459
Fax: 207-288-5507

Acadian Village
Rt. 1
Van Buren, ME 04785
Tel: 207-868-5042
http://themainelink.com/acadianvillage/

Aroostook County Historical & Art Museum
109 Main Street
Houlton, ME 04730
Tel: 207-532-4216

Auburn Public Library
49 Spring Street
Auburn, ME 04210
Tel: 207-782-3191
Fax: 207-782-1859
E-mail: e-mail@auburn.lib.me.us
http://www.auburn.lib.me.us/

Bangor Public Library
145 Harlow Street
Bangor, ME 04401
Tel: 207-947-8336
Fax: 207-945-6694
E-mail: bplill@bpl.lib.me.us
http://www.bpl.lib.me.us/

Bethel Historical Society/Museum
14 Broad Street
P.O. Box 12
Bethel, ME 04217
Tel: 207-824-2908
Fax: 207-824-0882
E-mail: info@bethelhistorical.org
http://www.bethelhistorical.org/

Bowdoin College
Hawthorne-Longfellow Library
Archives and Special Collections
3000 College Station
Brunswick, ME 04011-8421
Tel: 207-725-3288 (Special Collections)
207-725-3096 (Archives)
http://library.bowdoin.edu/

Brewer Historical Society
Clewley Museum
199 Wilson Street
Brewer, ME 04412
Tel: 207-989-7468
http://www.agate.net/~joshcham/

Bridgton Historical Society/Museum
Gibbs Avenue
P.O. Box 44
Bridgton, ME 04009
Tel: 207-647-3699
E-mail: bhs@megalink.net
http://www.megalink.net/~bhs/index.html

Brooksville Historical Society/Museum
Route 176
Brooksville, ME 04617
Phone: 207-326-8681
E-mail: mcmillen@acadia.net

Camden-Rockport Historical Society
Old Conway Complex & Museum
P.O. Box 747
Camden, ME 04843
Tel/Fax: 207-236-2257
E-mail: chmuseum@mint.net
http://members.mint.net/chmuseum/

Cary Library
Genealogy Room
107 Main Street
Houlton, ME 04730
Tel: 207-532-1302
Fax: 207-532-4350
E-mail: bettyf@cary.lib.me.us
http://www.cary.lib.me.us/

Chebeague Island Library
511 South Road
Chebeague, ME 04017
Tel: 207-846-4351
http://www.chebeague.org/library/librarysite/

Curtis Memorial Library
23 Pleasant Street
Brunswick, ME 04011
Tel: 207-725-5242
Fax: 207-725-6313
E-mail: info@curtislibrary.com
http://www.curtislibrary.com/home.html

Cushing Historical Society/Museum
P.O. Box 110
Cushing, ME 04563
Tel: 207-354-8262
800-261-1369
http://www.rootsweb.com/~usgenweb/me/knox/cushing.htm

Dexter Historical Society
P.O. Box 481
Dexter, ME 04930
Tel: 207-924-5721
E-mail: dexhist@panax.com
http://www.dextermaine.org/museum/

Ellsworth Public Library
20 State Street
Ellsworth, ME 04605
Tel: 207-667-6363
Fax: 207-667-4901
E-mail: pat@ellsworth.lib.me.us
http://www.ellsworth.lib.me.us/

Falmouth Memorial Library
5 Lunt Road
Falmouth, ME 04105
Tel: 207-781-2351
Fax: 207-781-4094
E-mail: mdevine1@maine.rr.com
http://www.falmouth.lib.me.us/historical.html

Farmington Public Library
117 Academy Street
Farmington, ME 04938
Tel: 207-778-4312
E-mail: cutler@saturn.caps.maine.edu
http://www.farmington.lib.me.us/

Fryeburg Historical Society/Museum
96 Main Street
Fryeburg, ME 04037-1126
Tel: 207-935-4192
Fax: 207-935-4192
E-mail: museum@landmarknet.net
http://www.geocities.com/fryeburghs/

Gardiner Public Library
Community Room
152 Water Street
Gardiner, ME 04345
Tel: 207-582-3312
E-mail: webmaster@gpl.lib.me.us
http://www.gpl.lib.me.us/hist.htm

Hampden Historical Society
Kinsley House Museum and Archives
83 Main Road
Hampden, ME 04444
Tel: 207-862-2027

Islesford Historical Museum
Little Cranberry
Islesford, ME 04646
Tel: 207-288-3338

Kennebunk Free Library
112 Main Street
Kennebunk, ME 04043
Tel: 207-985-2173
http://www.kennebunk.lib.me.us/

Kittery Historical and Naval Museum
Rogers Road
P.O. Box 453
Kittery, ME 03904
Tel: 207-439-3080

Lawrence Public Library
Lawrence Avenue
Fairfield, ME 04937
Tel: 207-453-6867
Fax: 207-453-9345
E-mail: Plibrary@Lawrence.lib.me.us
http://www.lawrence.lib.me.us/

Lee Historical Society/Museum
P.O. Box 306
Lee, ME 04455
Tel: 207-738-4125

Lewiston Public Library
200 Lisbon Street
Lewiston, ME 04240
Tel: 207-784-0135
Fax: 207-784-3011
http://www.avcnet.org/lpl/

Lincolnville Historical Society/Museum
P.O. Box 211
Lincolnville ME 04850
Tel: 207-789-5445
http://www.booknotes.com/lhs/

Maine Historical Society
Center for Maine History
489 Congress Street
Portland, Maine 04101
Tel: 207-774-1822
Fax: 207-775-4301
E-mail: info@mainehistory.org
http://www.mainehistory.org/

Maine Military Historical Society/Museum
Camp Keyes
Upper Winthrop Street
Augusta, ME 04330
Tel: 207-626-4338
http://www.me.ngb.army.mil/About%20Us/History/
    Museum.htm

Maine State Library
LMA Building
64 State House Station
Augusta, ME 04333-0064
Tel: 207-287-5600
http://www.state.me.us/msl/

Maine State Museum
LMA Building
83 State House Station
Augusta, ME 04333-0083
Tel: 207-287-2132
207-287-2301
Fax: 207-287-6633
http://www.cyberspacemuseum.com/n8_20.html

McArthur Library
270 Main Street
P.O. Box 346
Biddeford, ME 04005
Tel: 207-284-4181
E-mail: reference@mcarthur.lib.me.us
http://www.mcarthur.lib.me.us/

Mt. Desert Island (MDI) Historical Society/Museum
P.O. Box 653
Mt. Desert, ME 04660
Tel: 207-244-5045

Naples Historical Society/Museum
P.O. Box 1757
Naples, ME 04055
Phone: 207-693-4297
E-mail: nhs@pivot.net

New England Historical and Genealogical Society (NEHGS)
101 Newbury Street
Boston, MA 02116-3007
Tel: 617-836-5740
888-296-3447 (Membersip and Sales)
888-906-3447 (Library Circulation)
Fax: 617-536-7307
E-mail: nehgs@nehgs.org
http://www.newenglandancestors.org/

New Sweden Historical Museum
Capitol Hill Road
New Sweden, ME 04762
Tel: 207-896-3018

Norway Historical Society/Museum
232 Main Street
Norway, ME 04268
Tel: 207-743-7377

Nylander Museum
657 Main Street
P. O. Box 1062
Caribou, ME 04736
Tel: 207-493-4209
207-493-4474
http://www.nylandermuseum.org/

Oakfield Historical Museum
Oakfield, ME 04763
Tel: 207-757-8575

Old Orchard Beach Historical Society/Museum
Harmon Memorial
4 Portland Avenue
Old Orchard Beach, ME 04064
Tel: 207-934-9319

Old Town Historical Museum
North Fourth Ext.
Old Town, ME 04468
Tel: 207-827-7256

Orono Public Library
Goodridge Drive
Orono, ME 04473
Tel: 207-866-5060
E-mail: kwhedon@orono.lib.me.us
http://www.caps.maine.edu/~molloy/

Otisfield Historical Society
Otisfield Town Office Building
Route 121, Oxford Road
Otisfield, ME 04270
Tel: 207-539-2664
Mail: 105 Cape Road
Otisfield, ME 04270
http://www.rootsweb.com/~mecotisf/otis8.htm

Paris Cape Historical Society/Museum
19 Park Street
South Paris, ME 04281

Patten Free Library
Sagadahoc History & Genealogy Room
33 Summer Street
Bath, ME 04530
Tel: 207-443-5141
Fax: 207-443-3514
E-mail: pfl@patten.lib.me.us
http://www.biddeford.com/~pfl/shgr.htm

Pejepscot Historical Society/Museum
159 Park Row
Brunswick, ME 04011
Tel: 207-729-6606
Fax: 207-729-6012
E-mail: pejepscot@gwi.net
http://www.curtislibrary.com/pejepscot.htm

Penobscot Marine Museum
Stephen Phillips Memorial Library
Church Street at U.S. Route 1
P.O. Box 498
Searsport, ME 04974
Tel: 207-548-2529
Fax: 207-548-2520
E-mail: museumoffices@penobscotmarinemuseum.org
http://www.acadia.net/pmmuseum/

Penobscot Nation Museum
5 Center Street
Old Town, ME 04468
Tel: 207-827-4153

Portland Public Library
5 Monument Square
Portland, ME 04101
Tel: 207-871-1700
Fax: 207-871-1703
E-mail: skaye@www.portland.lib.me.us
http://www.portlandlibrary.com/

Redington Museum
Waterville Historical Society
64 Silver
Waterville, ME 04901
Tel: 207-872-9439

Sedgwick/Brooklin Historical Society/Museum
Route 172
P.O. Box 63
Sedgwick, ME 04676
E-mail: oblong @ hypernet.com

University of Maine/Fort Kent
Acadian Archives
25 Pleasant Street
Fort Kent, ME 04743
Tel: 207-834-7535
Fax: 207-834-7518
E-mail: acadian@maine.edu
http://www.umfk.maine.edu/infoserv/archives/

University of Maine/Orono
Fogler Library
Special Collections
Orono, ME 04469
Tel: 207-581-1661
Fax: 207-581-1653
E-mail: spc@umit.maine.edu
http://www.library.umaine.edu/speccoll/

University of Maine/Orono
Maine Folklife Center
South Stevens 5773
Orono, ME 04469-5773
Tel: 207-581-1891
Fax: 207-581-1823
E-mail: folklife@maine.edu
http://www.umaine.edu/folklife/

University of Maine/Presque Isle
Library/Special Collections
181 Main Street
Presque Isle, ME 04769
Tel: 207-768-9591
E-mail: young@polaris.umpi.maine.edu
http://www.umpi.maine.edu/info/lib/specol.htm

Vassalboro Historical Society/Museum
Rt. 32
East Vassalboro 04935
Tel: 207-923-3533

Vinalhaven Historical Society/Museum
High Street
P.O. Box 339
Vinalhaven, ME 04863
Tel: 207-863-4410
E-mail: vhhissoc@midcoast.com
http://www.midcoast.com/~vhhissoc/

Waldoboro Historical Society/Museum
Rt. 220 South
P.O. Box 110
Waldoboro, ME 04572

Walker Memorial Library
800 Main Street
Westbrook, ME 04092

Waponahki Resource Center & Sipayik Museum
Rt. 190
Pleasant Point
Perry, ME 04667
Tel: 207-853-4001

Waterford Historical Society/Museum
P.O. Box 201
Waterford, ME 04088

Wells Historical Society
Meetinghouse Museum
Genealogical & Historical Research Library
Rt. 1, Post Road
Wells, ME 04090
Tel: 207-646-4775

Wiscasset Public Library
21 High Street
P. O. Box 367
Wiscasset ME 04578
Tel: 207-882-7161
Fax: 207-882-6698
E-mail: wpl@wiscasset.lib.me.us
http://www.wiscasset.lib.me.us/

Woodstock Historical Society/Museum
70 South Main Street
Bryant Pond, ME 04219

Yarmouth Historical Society
Museum of Yarmouth History &
Merrill Memorial Library
Main Street
Yarmouth, ME 04096
Tel: 207-846-6259

Young Institute Museum/Dyer Library
371 Main Street
Saco, ME 04072
Tel: 207-283-3861

NEWSPAPER REPOSITORIES

Maine Historical Society
Center for Maine History
489 Congress Street
Portland, ME 04101
Tel: 207-774-1822
Fax: 207-775-4301
E-mail: info@mainehistory.org
http://www.mainehistory.org/

Maine State Library
LMA Building
64 State House Station
Augusta, ME 04333-0064
Tel: 207-287-5600
http://www.state.me.us/msl/

University of Maine/Orono
Fogler Library
Special Collections
Orono, ME 04469
Tel: 207-581-1661
Fax: 207-581-1653
E-mail: spc@umit.maine.edu
http://www.library.umaine.edu/speccoll/

VITAL RECORDS

Maine Department of Human Services
Office of Vital Records
221 State Street, Station 11
Augusta, ME 04333-0011
Tel: 207-287-3181
http://www.vitalrec.com/me.html

MAINE ON THE WEB

Acadian Genealogy Homepage
http://www.acadian.org/

Colonial Massachusetts and Maine Genealogies
http://home.earthlink.net/~anderson207/

Index to Maine Marriages
http://thor.ddp.state.me.us/archives/plsql/
        archdev. Marriage_Archive.search_form

Maine GenWeb Project
http://www.rootsweb.com/~megenweb/

Maine State Archives
http://www.state.me.us/sos/arc/

Maine State Archives/Civil War Page
http://www.state.me.us/sos/arc/archives/military/
        civilwar/civilwar.htm

E Travel Maine
http://www.etravelmaine.com/museums/museums.html

MARYLAND

ARCHIVES, STATE & NATIONAL

Maryland State Archives
Hall of Records Building
350 Rowe Blvd.
Annapolis, MD 21401
Tel: (410) 260-6400
(800) 235-4045 MD toll free
fax: (410) 974-3895
E-mail: archives@mdarchives.state.md.us
www.mdarchives.state.md.us

National Archives—Mid Atlantic Region
900 Market Street
Philadelphia, PA 19107-4292
Tel: 215-597-3000
Fax: 215-597-2303
E-mail: philadelphia.archives@nara.gov
http://www.nara.gov/regional/philacc.html

GENEALOGICAL SOCIETIES

**Afro-American Historical & Genealogical
Society/Baltimore (AAHGS)**
P.O. Box 9366
Baltimore, MD 21229-3125
E-mail: rolandmills@netzero.net

**Afro-American Historical & Genealogical
Society/Central Maryland (AAHGS)**
P. O. Box 648
Columbia, MD 21045
E-mail: gourdinr@home.com

**Afro-American Historical & Genealogical Society
Prince George's County (AAHGS)**
P.O. Box 44722
Fort Washington, MD 20744-9998
E-mail: cbwoods@erols.com
http://www.rootsweb.com/~mdaahgs/pgcm/

Allegany County Genealogical Society
P.O. Box 3103
LaVale, MD 21502

Allegheny Regional Family History Society (ARFHS)
P.O. Box 1804
Elkins, WV 26241
http://www.swcp.com/~dhickman/arfhs.html

Anne Arundel Genealogical Society
P.O. Box 221
Pasadena, MD 21123
http://www.geocities.com/Yosemite/Trails/4256/gensoc.htm

Baltimore Genealogical Society
P.O. Box 10085
Towson, MD 21285-0085
http://www.serve.com/bcgs/bcgs.html

Calvert County Genealogical Committee
Calvert County Historical Society
P.O. Box 358
Prince Frederick, MD 20678
Tel: 410-535-2452
Fax: 410-535-1747

Calvert County Genealogy Society
P.O. Box 9
Sunderland, MD 20689
Tel: 410-535-0839

Carroll County Genealogical Society
P.O. Box 1752
Westminster, MD 21158
http://www.carr.lib.md.us/ccgs/ccgs.html

Catonsville Historical & Genealogical Society
Townsend House
1824 Frederick Road
P.O. Box 9311
Catonsville, MD 21228-0311
Tel: 410-744-3034
E-mail: chistory@catonsvillehistory.com
http://www.catonsvillehistory.org/

Cecil County Genealogical Society
P.O. Box 11
Charlestown, MD 21914

Frederick County Genealogical Society
P.O. Box 324
Monrovia, MD 21770

Genealogical Council of Maryland
Bible Records Chair
P.O. Box 10096
Gaithersburg, MD 20898-0096

Harford County Genealogical Society
P.O. Box 15
Aberdeen, MD 21001
http://www.rtis.com/reg/md/org/hcgs/default.htm

Howard County Genealogical Society
P.O. Box 274
Columbia, MD 21045-0274
E-mail: rwbush@worldnet.att.com
http://users.aol.com/castlewrks/hcgs/

Jewish Genealogy Society of Greater Washington, DC
P.O. Box 31122
Bethesda, MD 20824-1122
Tel: 301-530-3511
http://www.jewishgen.org/jgsgw/

Lower DelMarVa Genealogical Society
P.O. Box 3602
Salisbury, MD 21802-3602
http://bay.intercom.net/ldgs/

Lower Shore Genealogical Society
1133 Somerset Avenue
Princess Anne, MD 21853

Maryland Genealogical Society
Maryland Historical Society
201 West Monument Street
Baltimore, MD 21201-4674
Tel: 410-685-3750
Fax: 410-385-2105
http://www.mdgensoc.org/

Montgomery County Historical Society/Genealogy Club/Library
111 West Montgomery Avenue
Rockville, MD 20850
Tel: 301-340-2974
E-mail: info@montgomeryhistory.org
http://www.montgomeryhistory.org/Genealogy.htm

Prince George's County Genealogical Society
P.O. Box 819
Bowie, MD 20718-0819
http://www.rootsweb.com/~mdpgcgs/

Saint Mary's County Genealogical Society
P.O. Box 1109
Leonardtown, MD 20650-1109

Upper Shore Genealogical Society of Maryland
P.O. Box 275
Easton, MD 21601
http://www.chronography.com/usgs/center.html

HISTORICAL SOCIETIES

Accohannock Tribe
P.O. Box 404
Marion, MD 21838
Tel: 410-623-2660
E-mail: accohannock@crisfield.md
http://skipjack.net/le_shore/accohannock/

Afro-American Historical & Genealogical Society/ Baltimore(AAHGS)
P.O. Box 9366
Baltimore, MD 21229-3125
E-mail: rolandmills@netzero.net

Afro-American Historical & Genealogical Society/ Central Maryland (AAHGS)
P. O. Box 648
Columbia, MD 21045
E-mail: gourdinr@home.com

Afro-American Historical & Genealogical Society Prince George's County (AAHGS)
P.O. Box 44722
Fort Washington, MD 20744-9998
E-mail: cbwoods@erols.com
http://www.rootsweb.com/~mdaahgs/pgcm/

Allegany County Historical Society
218 Washington Street
Cumberland, MD 21502
http://www.historyhouse.allconet.org/

Anne Arundel Historical Society
P.O. Box 385
Linthicum, MD 21090

Baltimore County Historical Society
Agriculture Building
9811 Van Buren Lane
Cockeysville, MD 21030
Tel: 410-666-1878

Calvert County Historical Society
P.O. Box 358
Prince Frederick, MD 20678
Tel: 410-535-2452
Fax: 410-535-1747
http://www.somd.lib.md.us/CALV/cchs/

Caroline County Historical Society
Preston, MD 21655

Carroll County Historical Society
210 East Main Street
Westminster, MD 21157
E-mail:hscc@carr.org
http://www.carr.lib.md.us/hscc/

Catonsville Historical & Genealogical Society
Townsend House
1824 Frederick Road
P.O. Box 9311
Catonsville, MD 21228-0311
Tel: 410-744-3034
E-mail: chistory@catonsvillehistory.com
http://www.catonsvillehistory.org/

Cecil County Historical Society
135 East Main Street
Elkton, MD 21921
Tel: 410-398-1790
E-mail: history@cchistory.org
http://cchistory.org/

Dorchester County Historical Society
902 LaGrange Avenue
Cambridge, MD 21613
Tel: 410-228-7953
Fax: 410-228-2947
E-mail: dchs@fastol.com
http://www.intercom.net/npo/dchs/

Dundalk Patapsco Neck Historical Society
43 Shipping Place
P.O. Box 9235
Dundalk, MD 21222
Tel: 410-284-2331

Essex and Middle River, Heritage Society of
516 Eastern Blvd.
Essex, MD 21221-6701
Tel: 410-574-6934

Frederick County Historical Society
24 East Church Street
Frederick, MD 21701
Tel: 301-663-1188
http://www.fwp.net/hsfc/

Garrett County Historical Society/Museum
107 South Second Street
P.O. Box 28
Oakland, MD   21550
Tel: 301-334-3226
http://www.deepcreektimes.com/gchs.html

Harford County Historical Society
143 N. Main Street
P.O. Box 366
Bel Air, MD 21014-0366
Tel: 410-838-7691
E-mail: harchis@msn.com
http://www.harfordhistory.net/

Howard County Historical Society/Library
8324 Court Avenue
Ellicott City, MD 21043-4506
Tel: 410-461-1050
410-750-0370 (Library)

Jewish Historical Society of Maryland
Jewish Heritage Center
15 Lloyd Street
Baltimore, MD 21202
Tel: 410-732-6400
Fax: 410-732-6451
E-mail: info@jewishmuseummd.org
http://www.jhsm.org/

Kent County Historical Society
101 Church Alley
Chestertown, MD 21620
Tel: 410-778-3499
Fax: 410-778-3747
E-mail: hskcmd@friend.ly.net
http://www.hskcmd.com/

Maryland Historical Society
201 West Monument Street
Baltimore, MD 21201-4674
Tel: 410-685-3750
Fax: 410-385-2105
http://www.mdhs.org/

Middletown Valley Historical Society
305 W. Main Street
P.O. Box 294
Middletown, MD 21769-8022

Montgomery County Historical Society/Genealogy Club/Library
Beall Dawson House
111 West Montgomery Avenue
Rockville, MD 20850
Tel: 301-340-2974
http://www.montgomeryhistory.org/

Prince George's County Historical Society
P.O. Box 14
Riverdale, MD 20738-0014
E-mail: info@pghistory.org
http://www.pghistory.org/

Queen Anne's County Historical Society
Wright's Chance
121 South Commerce Street
Centreville, MD 21617
Tel: 410-758-0980

Saint Mary's City Historical Society
11 Courthouse Drive
P.O. Box 212
Leonardtown, MD 20650

Somerset County Historical Society
P.O. Box 181
Princess Anne, MD 21853
Tel: 410-651-2238

Talbot County Historical Society
25 Washington Street
P.O. Box 964
Easton, MD 21601
Tel/Fax: 410-822-0773
http://www.hstc.org/

Washington County Historical Society
The Miller House
135 West Washington Street
Hagerstown, MD 21740
http://www.rootsweb.com/~mdwchs/miller.html

Wicomico County Historical Society
Pemberton Drive
P.O. Box 573
Salisbury, MD 21803-0573
Tel: 410-860-0447
E-mail: history@shore.intercom.net
http://skipjack.net/le_shore/whs/

Worcester County Historical Society
3 E. 2nd Street
Pocomoke City, MD 21851

LDS FAMILY HISTORY CENTERS

For locations of Family History Centers in this state, see
the Family History Center locator at FamilySearch.
http://www.familysearch.org/eng/Library/FHC/
frameset_fhc.asp

ARCHIVES/LIBRARIES/MUSEUMS

Allegany Community College
Appalachian Collection
Willowbrook Road
Cumberland, MD 21502
Tel: 301-784-5005
http://www.ac.cc.md.us/

Anne Arundel County Public Library
5 Harry S. Truman Pkwy.
Annapolis, MD 21401
Tel: 410-222-7371
http://web.aacpl.lib.md.us/

Baltimore City Archives
2165 Druid Park Drive
Baltimore, MD 21211
Tel: 410-396-0306

Banneker-Douglass Museum
Mount Moriah A.M.E. Church
84 Franklin Street Annapolis, MD 21401
Tel: 410-974-2553
http://www.hometownannapolis.com/tour_banneker.html

Bowie State University
Thurgood Marshall Library
14000 Jericho Park Road
Bowie, MD 20715-9465
Tel: 301-860-4000
http://www.bowiestate.edu/library/

C. Burr Artz/Frederick County Public Library
110 E. Patrick Street
Frederick, MD 21701
Tel: 301-694-1630
Fax: 301-631-3789
TDD: 301-663-6999
E-mail: fcplweb@fcpl.org
http://www.fcpl.org/

Caroline County Public Library
100 Market Street
Denton, MD 21629
Tel: 410-479-1343
Fax: 410-479-1443
TDD: 410-479-2468
http://www.caro.lib.md.us/library/

Catonsville Branch/Baltimore County Public Library
1100 Frederick Road
Catonsville, MD 21228-5092
Tel: 410-887-0951
Fax: 410-788-8166
E-mail: catonsvi@bcpl.net
http://www.bcpl.lib.md.us/branchpgs/ca/cahome.html

Cecil County Public Library
301 Newark Avenue
Elkton, MD 21921-5441
Tel: 410-996-5600
Fax: 410-996-5604
TDD: 410-996-5609
http://www.ebranch.cecil.lib.md.us/

Charles County Public Library
Charles & Garrett Streets
P.O. Box 490
LaPlata, MD 20646-0490
Tel: 301-870-3520
Fax: 301-934-2297
TDD: 301-934-9090
http://www.ccplonline.org/

Cheasapeake Bay Maritime Museum
Mill Street
P.O. Box 636
St. Michaels, MD 21663
Tel: 410-745-2916
Fax: 410-745-6088
http://www.cbmm.org/

Dorchester County Public Library
303 Gay Street
Cambridge, MD 21613
Tel: 410-228-7331
Fax: 410-228-6313
TDD: 410-228-0454
E-mail: dorch@mail.esrl.lib.md.us
http://www.dorchesterlibrary.org/

Enoch Pratt Free Library
400 Cathedral Street
Baltimore, MD 21201
Tel: 410-396-5300
410-396-5430
Fax: 410-396-1441
E-mail:GenInfo@mail.pratt.lib.md.us
http://www.pratt.lib.md.us/

Harford County Library
100 East Pennsylvania Avenue
Bel Air, MD 21014
Tel: 410-638-3151
Fax: 410-638-3155
TDD: 410-838-3371
http://www.harf.lib.md.us/

Issac Franck Jewish Public Library
Board of Jewish Education of Greater Washington
4928 Wyaconda Road
Rockville, Maryland 20852
Tel: 301-255-1970
Fax: 301-230-0267
E-mail: bje@bjedc.org
http://www.bjedc.org/bje/library/library.cfm

John Hopkins University
Arthur Friedheim Library
Peabody Archives
1 East Mt. Vernon Place
Baltimore, MD 21202-2397
Tel: 410-659-8257
Fax: 410-727-5101
E-mail: archives@mse.jhu.edu
http://www.peabody.jhu.edu/lib/archives.html

Kuethe Library
Historical & Genealogical Research Center
5 Crain Highway SE
Glen Burnie, MD 21061
Tel: 410-760-9679

Maryland Historical Trust Library
100 Community Place
Crownsville, MD 21032
Tel: 410-514-7655
http://www.MarylandHistoricalTrust.net/

Maryland State Law Library
Court of Appeals Building
361 Rowe Boulevard
Annapolis, MD 21401
Tel: 410-260-1430
Fax: 410-974-2063
TTY: 410-260-1571
http://www.lawlib.state.md.us/

Montgomery County Historical Society/Genealogy Club/Library
111 West Montgomery Avenue
Rockville, MD 20850
Tel: 301-340-2974
E-mail: info@montgomeryhistory.org
http://www.montgomeryhistory.org/

Queen Anne's County Free Library
121 S. Commerce Street
Centreville, MD 21617
Tel: 410-758-0980
http://www.quan.lib.md.us/

Reistertown Branch/Baltimore County Public Library
History Room, 2nd floor
21 Cockeys Mill Road
Reistertown, MD 21136-1285
Tel: 410-887-1165
Fax: 410-833-8756
E-mail: reisters@bcpl.net
http://www.bcpl.lib.md.us/branchpgs/re/rehome.html

Rockville Regional Library/Montgomery County Public Library
99 Maryland Avenue
Rockville, MD 20850
Tel: 240-777-0140
TTY: 240-777-0902
http://www.mont.lib.md.us/branchinfo/ro.asp

Ruth Enlow Branch/Garrett County Library
6 North 2nd Street
Oakland, MD 21550-1316
Tel/TDD: 301-334-3996
Fax: 301-334-4152
E-mail: info@relib.net

St. Mary's College
Library
St. Mary's City, MD 20686
Tel: 301-862-0264
http://www.smcm.edu/library/

St. Mary's County Memorial Library
Route 1, Box 9E
Leonardtown, MD 20650-9601
Tel: 301-475-2846
Fax: 301-884-4415
TDD: 301-475-8003
E-mail: webexpert@somd.lib.md.us
http://www.stmalib.org/

Salisbury State University
Nabb Research Center for DelMarVa History & Culture
1101 Camden Avenue, PP 190
Salisbury, MD 21801
Tel: 410-543-6312
E-mail: rcdhac@salisbury.edu
http://nabbhistory.salisbury.edu/

Snow Hill Branch/Worcester County Public Library
Worcester Room
307 N. Washington Street
Snow Hill, MD 21863
Tel: 410-632-2600
Fax/TDD: 410-632-1159
E-mail: worc-sh@worc.lib.md.us
http://www.worc.lib.md.us/library/home.html

Talbot County Free Library
Maryland Room
100 W. Dover Street
Easton, MD 21601-2620
Tel: 410-822-1626
Fax: 410-820-8217
TDD: 410-822-8735
http://www.esrl.lib.md.us/counties/talbot/library/home.html

Towson Branch/Baltimore County Public Library
320 York Road
Towson, MD 21204-5179
Tel: 410-887-6166
Fax: 410-887-3170
http://www.bcplonline.org/branches/branch_to.html

University of Baltimore
Langsdale Library
1420 Maryland Avenue
Baltimore, MD 21201
Tel: 410-837-4260
E-mail: swheeler@ubmail.ubalt.edu
http://langsdale.ubalt.edu/

University of Maryland/Baltimore County
Albin O. Kuhn Library
5401 Wilkens Avenue
Catonsville, MD 21228
Tel: 301-455-2232
http://www.umbc.edu/aok/main/

University of Maryland/College Park
McKeldin Library
College Park, MD 20742
Tel: 301-405-9212
E-mail: marylandia@umail.umd.edu
http://www.lib.umd.edu/MCK/mckeldin.html

Washington County Free Library
100 S. Potomac Street
Hagerstown, MD 21740
Tel: 301-739-3250
TDD: 301-739-3253
http://www.wash.lib.md.us/wcfl/

Westminster Branch/Carroll Public Library
50 E. Main
Westminster, MD 21157
Tel: 410-848-4250
410-876-6018

Wicomico County Free Library
Maryland Room and Genealogical Collection
122-126 S. Division Street
P.O. Box 4148
Salisbury, MD 21801
Tel: 410-749-5171
http://www.wicomicolibrary.org/

NEWSPAPER REPOSITORIES

Maryland State Archives
Hall of Records Building
350 Rowe Blvd.
Annapolis, MD 21401
Tel: 410-974-3914
Fax: 410-974-2525
E-mail: archives@mdarchives.state.md.us
http://www.mdarchives.state.md.us/

VITAL RECORDS

State of Maryland Department of Health & Mental Hygiene
Division of Vital Records
Department of Health and Mental Hygiene
6550 Reisterstown Avenue
P.O. Box 68760
Baltimore, MD 21215-0020
Tel: 410-764-3089
    800-832-3277

MARYLAND ON THE WEB

Cindy's Genealogy on the Eastern Shore of MD, DE, & VA
http://www.shoreweb.com/cindy/index.html

Handley's Eastern Shore Genealogy Project
http://bay.intercom.net/handley/index.html

Maryland Catholics on the Frontier
http://www.pastracks.com/mcf/

Maryland GenWeb Project
http://www.mdgenweb.org/

Maryland Loyalists and the American Revolution
http://www.erols.com/candidus/index.htm

U.S. Colored Troops Resident in Baltimore at the time of the 1890 Census
http://www.mdarchives.state.md.us/msa/speccol/
    3096/html/00010001.html

Massachusetts

Archives, State & National

Massachusetts Archives
Reference Supervisor
220 Morrissey Blvd.
Boston, MA 02125
Tel: 617-727-2816
Fax: (617) 288-8429
E-mail: archives@sec.state.ma.us
http://www.state.ma.us/sec/arc/arcidx.htm

National Archives-Northeast Region (Boston)
Reference Supervisor
220 Morrissey Blvd.
Boston, MA 02125
Tel: 617-727-2816
Fax: (617) 288-8429
E-mail: archives@sec.state.ma.us
http://www.state.ma.us/sec/arc/arcidx.htm

Genealogical Societies

Acadian Cultural Society
P.O. Box 2304
Fitchburg, MA 01460-8804
http://www.angelfire.com/ma/1755/index.html

**American Portuguese Genealogical
& Historical Society, Inc.**
P.O. Box 644
Taunton, MA 02780-0644
http://www.tauntonma.com/apghs/

Association for Gravestone Studies
278 Main Street
Greenfield, MA 01301
Tel: 413-772-0836
E-mail: info@gravestonestudies.org
http://www.gravestonestudies.org/

Berkshire Family History Association
P.O. Box 1437
Pittsfield, MA 01201
http://www.berkshire.net/~bfha/

Cape Cod Genealogical Society
P.O. Box 1394
East Harwich, MA 02645
http://www.capecodgensoc.org/

Central Massachusetts Genealogical Society
P.O. Box 811
Westminster, MA 01473-0811

Colonial Society of Massachusetts
87 Vernon Street
Boston, MA 02108
Tel: 617-227-2782

Essex County Society of Genealogists
18 Summer Street
P.O. Box 313
Lynnfield, MA 01940-0313
http://www.esog.org/

Falmouth Genealogical Society
P.O. Box 2107
Teaticket, MA 02536
http://www.rootsweb.com/~mafgs/Default.htm

Genealogical Round Table
812 Main St.
Concord, MA 01742

General Society of Mayflower Descendants
Mayflower Society Museum
4 Winslow Street
P.O. Box 3297
Plymouth, MA 02361
Tel: 508-746-3188
508-746-2590
http://www.mayflower.org/

Irish Ancestral Research Association (TIARA)
Dept. W
P.O. Box 619
Sudbury, MA 01776
http://www.tiara.ie/

Jewish Genealogical Society of Greater Boston
P.O. Box 610366
Newton, MA 02461-0366
Tel: 617-796-8522
E-mail: info@jgsgb.org
http://www.jewishgen.org/jgsgb/

Massachusetts Genealogical Council
P.O. Box 5393
Cochituate, MA 01778
http://home.attbi.com/~sages/mgc/

Massachusetts Society of Genealogists, Inc.
P.O. Box 215
Ashland, MA 01721
Tel: 508-792-5066
E-mail: sgoodwin@massed.net
http://www.rootsweb.com/~masgi/msog/

Massachusetts Society of Mayflower Descendants
100 Boylston St. Suite #750
Boston, MA 02116
E-mail: msmd@massmayflower.org
http://www.massmayflower.org/

New England Historical and Genealogical Society (NEHGS)
101 Newbury Street
Boston, MA 02116-3007
Tel: 617-836-5740
888-296-3447 (Membersip and Sales)
888-906-3447 (Library Circulation)
Fax: 617-536-7307
E-mail: nehgs@nehgs.org
http://www.newenglandancestors.org/

Plymouth Colony Genealogists
60 Sheridan Street
Brockton, MA 02402-2852

Polish Genealogical Society of Massachusetts
P.O. Box 381
Northampton, MA 01061-0381
E-mail: Jskibiski@aol.com
http://www.rootsweb.com/~mapgsm/

South Shore Genealogical Society
P.O. Box 396
Norwell, MA 02061-0396

Western Massachusetts Genealogical Society
Forest Park Station
P.O. Box 206
Springfield, MA 01108
http://www.rootsweb.com/~mawmgs/

HISTORICAL SOCIETIES

American Antiquarian Society/Library
185 Salisbury Street
Worcester, MA 01609
Tel: 508-755-5221
Fax: 508-753-3311
E-mail: ladams@mwa.org
http://www.americanantiquarian.org/

American Jewish Historical Society
2 Thornton Road
Waltham, MA 02154
Tel: 781-891-8110
Fax: 781-899-9208
http://www.ajhs.org/

American Portuguese Genealogical & Historical Society, Inc.
P.O. Box 644
Taunton, MA 02780-0644
http://www.tauntonma.com/apghs/

Amherst Historical Society
Strong House Museum
67 Amity Street
Amherst, MA 01002
Tel: 413-256-0678
http://www.amhersthistory.org/

Andover Historical Society
97 Main Street
Andover, MA 01810
Tel: 978-475-2236
Fax: 978-470-2741
E-mail: info@andhist.org
http://www.ultranet.com/~andhists/

Arlington Historical Society
7 Jason Street
Arlington, MA 02174
Tel: 781-648-4300

Ashland Historical Society
2 Myrtle Street
Ashland, MA 01721
Tel: 508-881-8183

Association for Gravestone Studies
278 Main Street
Greenfield, MA 01301
Tel: 413-772-0836
E-mail: info@gravestonestudies.org
http://www.gravestonestudies.org/

Barre Historical Society
18 Common Street
Barre, MA 01005

Bay State Historical League
The Vale Lyman Estate
185 Lyman Street
Waltham, MA 02254-9998
Tel: 781-899-3920
Fax: 781-893-7832
http://www.masshistory.org/

Berkley Historical Society
725 Berkley Street
Berkley, MA 02779

Berkshire County Historical Society
780 Holmes Road
Pittsfield, MA 01201
Tel: 413-442-1793
Fax: 413-443-1449

Berlin Art & Historical Society
Woodward Avenue
Berlin, MA 01503

Beverly Historical Society/Museum
117 Cabot Street
Beverly, MA 01915
Tel: 978-922-1186
E-mail: info@beverlyhistory.org
http://www.beverlyhistory.org/

Bolton Historical Society
Sawyer House
676 Main Street
Bolton, MA 01740
Tel: 978-779-6392

Bostonian Society
Old State House
206 Washington Street
Boston, MA 02109-1713
Tel: 617-720-1713
Fax: 617-720-3289
http://www.bostonhistory.org/

Bourne Historical Society
P.O. Box 3095
Bourne, MA 02532-0795
Tel: 508-759-8167
http://www.bournehistoricalsoc.org/

Braintree Historical Society
786 Washington Street
Braintree, MA 02184
Tel: 781-848-1640
http://www.key-biz.com/ssn/Braintree/hist_soc.html

Brockton Historical Society/Museum
216 N. Pearl Street, Rte. 27
Brockton, MA 02401
Tel: 508-583-1039
E-mail: gerryb@brocktonma.com
http://www.brocktonma.com/bhs/bhs_mus.html

Brookline Historical Society
347 Harvard Street
Brookline, MA 02146
Tel: 617-566-5747

Burlington Historical Commission/Museum
Corner of Bedford and Cambridge Streets
Burlington, MA 01803
Tel: 781-272-0606

Cambridge Historical Society
159 Brattle Street
Cambridge, MA 02138
Tel: 617-547-4252
Fax: 617-661-1623
http://www.pastconnect.com/cambridge/Default.htm

Canton Historical Society
1400 Washington Street
Canton, MA 02021
http://www.geocities.com/Heartland/Hills/1496/canton.html

Cape Ann Historical Association/Library
27 Pleasant Street
Gloucester, MA 01930
Tel: 978-283-0455

Centerville Historical Society
513 Main Street
Centerville, MA 02632
Tel: 508-775-0331

Charlestown Historical Society
Bunker Hill Museum
43 Monument Square
Charlestown, MA 02129

Chatham Historical Society
347 Stage Harbor Road
Chatham, MA 02633
Tel: 508-945-2493
Fax: 508-945-1205
E-mail: chs2002@msn.com
http://www.atwoodhouse.org/

Chelmsford Historical Society
40 Byam Road
Chelmsford, MA 01824
Tel: 978-256-2311
http://www.chelmhist.org/

Chesterfield Historical Society
The Bisbee Mill Museum
66 East Street
Chesterfield, MA 01012
Tel: 413-296-4750
http://www.bisbeemillmuseum.org/historical.html

Cohasset Historical Society
14 Summer Street
Cohasset, MA 02025

Congregational Christian Historical Society
14 Beacon Street
Boston, MA 02108

Danvers Historical Society
13 Page Street
P.O. Box 381
Danvers, MA 01923
Tel: 978-777-1666
Fax: 978-777-5028
E-mail: dhs@danvershistory.org
http://www.danvershistory.org/

Dedham Historical Society
612 High Street
P.O. Box 215
Dedham, MA 02027-0215
Tel: 781-326-1385
E-mail: society@DedhamHistorical.org
http://dedhamhistorical.org/

Dennis Historical Society
Dennis Memorial Library Association
Old Bass River Road
Dennis, MA 02638
Tel: 508-385-2255

Dighton Historical Society
1217 Williams
Dighton, MA 02715

Dorchester Historical Society
195 Boston Street
Boston, MA 02125
Tel: 617-265-7802

Duxbury Rural & Historical Society, Inc.
P.O. Box 2865
Duxbury, MA 02331
Tel: 781-934-6106
http://www.duxburyhistory.org/

Eastham Historical Society, Inc.
P.O. Box 8
Eastham, MA 02642

Essex Historical Society
Essex Shipbuilding Museum
66 & 28 Main Street
P.O. Box 277
Essex, MA 01929
Tel: 978-768-7541
Fax: 978-768-2541
E-mail: info@essexshipbuildingmuseum.org
http://www.essexshipbuildingmuseum.org/society. html

Fall River Historical Society
451 Rock Street
Fall River, MA   02720
Tel: 508-679-1071

Falmouth Historical Society
55 Palmer Ave # 65
Falmouth, MA 02541
Tel: 508-548-4857

Fitchburg Historical Society
50 Grove Street
Fitchburg, MA 01420
Tel: 978-345-1157

Framingham Historical and Natural History Society
Old Academy Building
16 Vernon Street
Framingham, MA 01701
Tel: 508-872-3780

Freetown Historical Society/Museum
1 Slab Bridge Road
P.O. Box 253
Assonet, MA 02702
Tel: 508-644-5310
http://freetownhistory.8m.com/

Greenfield, Historical Society of
43 Church Street
Greenfield, MA 01301

Groton Historical Society
172 Main Street
Groton, MA 01450
Tel: 508-448-2046

Hardwick Historical Society
Hardwick Common
Hardwick, MA 01037

Harvard Historical Society
Still River Road
Still River, MA 01467
Mail:
P.O. Box 542
Harvard, MA 01451
Tel: 978-456-3148
E-mail: hhs@ma.ultranet.com
http://www.harvard.ma.us/hhs.htm

Harwich Historical Society
Brooks Academy Museum
80 Parallel Street
P.O. Box 17
Harwich, MA 02645
Tel: 508-432-8089
http://history.capecod.com/harwich/Default.htm

Haverhill Historical Society
Buttonwoods Museum
240 Water Street
Haverhill, MA 01830
Tel: 978-374-4626
http://www.haverhillhistory.org/Home%20Page.htm

Hingham Historical Society
Old Ordinary
21 Lincoln Street
Hingham, MA 02043
Tel: 781-749-0013

Ipswich Historical Society
John Heard House
54 South Main Street
Ipswich, MA 01938
Tel: 978-356-2811
http://www.ipswichma.com/directory/ihs/

Jones River Village Historical Society
Major John Bradford House
Maple Street & Landing Road
Kingston, MA 02364
Tel: 781-585-6300

Lawrence and Its People, Historical Society of
Immigrant City Archives
6 Essex Street
Lawrence, MA 01840
Tel: 978-686-9230

Leverett Historical Society
North Leverett Road
Leverett, MA 01054

Lexington Historical Society
Munroe Tavern
1332 Massachusetts Avenue
P.O. Box 514
Lexington, MA 02173
Tel: 781-862-1703
Fax: 781-862-4920
E-mail: info@lexingtonhistory.org
http://www.lexingtonhistory.org/

Longmeadow Historical Society
697 Longmeadow Street
Longmeadow, MA 01106
Tel: 413-567-3600
http://www.longmeadow.org/hist_soc/histsoc_ main.html

Longyear Historical Society/Museum
120 Seaver Street
Brookline, MA 02146

Lynn Historical Society/Library & Museum
125 Green Street
Lynn, MA 01902
Tel: 781-592-2465

Manchester Historical Society
10 Union Street
Manchester, MA 01944
Tel: 978-526-7230

Marblehead Historical Society
170 Washington Street
Marblehead, MA 01945
Tel: 781-631-1768

Marlborough Historical Society
377 Elm Street
Marlborough, MA 01752
Tel: 508-485-4763
http://www.marlborough.com/historical/

Martha's Vineyard Historical Society
Cooke & School Street
P.O. Box 1310
Edgartown, MA 02539
Tel: 508-627-4441
Fax: 508-627-4436
http://www.marthasvineyardhistory.org/

Massachusetts Historical Commission
220 Morrissey Blvd.
Boston, MA 02125
Tel: 617-727-8470
Fax: 617-727-5128
TDD: 800-392-6090
E-mail: mhc@sec.state.ma.us
http://www.state.ma.us/sec/mhc/

Massachusetts Historical Society
1154 Boylston Street
Boston, MA 02215
Tel: 617-536-1608
http://www.masshist.org/

Mattapoisett Historical Society
5 Church Street
Mattapoisett, MA 02739
Tel: 508-758-2844

Medford Historical Society
10 Governors Avenue
Medford, MA 02155

Middleborough Historical Association, Inc.
Jackson Street
P.O. Box 304
Middleborough, MA 02346
Tel: 508-947-1969

Middleton Historical Society
Lura Watkins Museum
Pleasant Street
Middleton, MA 01949

Milton Historical Society
1370 Canton Avenue
Milton, MA 02186
Tel: 617-333-0644
http://world.std.com/~ssn/Milton/mhs.html

Nantucket Historical Association
5 Washington Street
P.O. Box 1016
Nantucket, MA 02554
Tel: 508-228-1894
E-mail: nhainfo@nha.org
http://www.nha.org/

Narragansett Historical Society
The Common
Templeton, MA 01468

Natick Historical Society/Museum
Bacon Free Library Building, Lower Level
58 Eliot Street
South Natick, MA 01760
Tel: 508-647-4841
E-mail: eliot@ixl.net
http://www.ixl.net/~natick/

Needham Historical Society
53 Glendoon Road
Needham, MA 02192

New England Historical and Genealogical Society (NEHGS)
101 Newbury Street
Boston, MA 02116-3007
Tel: 617-836-5740
    888-296-3447 (Membersip and Sales)
    888-906-3447 (Library Circulation)
Fax: 617-536-7307
E-mail: nehgs@nehgs.org
http://www.newenglandancestors.org/

Newton Historical Society
Jackson Homestead
527 Washington Street
Newton, MA 02158
Tel: 617-552-7238
Fax: 617-552-7228
E-mail vfelson@ci.newton.ma.us
http://www.ci.newton.ma.us/jackson/default.htm

North Andover Historical Society
153 Academy Road
North Andover, MA 01845
Tel: 978-686-4035

Northampton Historical Society
Historic Northampton
46 Bridge Street
Northampton, MA 01060
Tel: 413-584-6011

Northborough Historical Society, Inc.
50 Main Street
Northborough, MA 01532

Old Abington Historical Society
Dyer Memorial Library
25 Centre Avenue (Route 123)
Abington, MA 02351
Tel: 781-878-8480

Old Bridgewater Historical Society
Memorial Building
162 Howard Street
West Bridgewater, MA 02379
Tel: 508-559-1510

Old Colony Historical Society
66 Church Green
Taunton, MA 02780
Tel: 508-822-1622
http://www.oldcolonyhistoricalsociety.org/

Old Dartmouth Historical Society
New Bedford Whaling Museum
18 Johnny Cake Hill
New Bedford, MA 02740
Tel: 508-997-0046

Old Newbury, Historical Society of
98 High Street
Newburyport, MA 01950
Tel: 978-462-2681

Old Yarmouth, Historical Society of
11 Strawberry Lane
Yarmouth Port, MA 02675
Tel: 508-362-3021
http://www.hsoy.org/

Osterville Historical Society, Inc.
155 Bay Road
Osterville, MA 02655
Tel: 508-428-5861

Peabody Historical Society
35 Washington Street
Peabody, MA 01960
http://www.peabodyhistorical.org/

Pembroke Historical Society, Inc.
116 Center Street
Pembroke, MA 02359
Tel: 781-293-9083

Petersham Historical Society, Inc.
North Main Street
Petersham, MA 01366

Pilgrim Society
Pilgrim Hall Museum
75 Court Street
Plymouth, MA 02360
Tel: 508-746-1620
http://www.pilgrimhall.org/plgrmhll.htm

Plymouth Antuquarian Society
P.O. Box 1137
Plymouth, MA 02360
Tel: 508-746-0012

Quincy Historical Society
Adams Academy Building
8 Adams Street
Quincy, MA 02169
Tel: 617-773-1144
http://ci.quincy.ma.us/htm/qhist/

Ramapogue Historical Society
70 Park Street
West Springfield, MA 01089
Tel: 413-734-8322

Rowe Historical Society
Kemp-McCarthy Memorial Museum
Zoar Road
Rowe, MA 01966
Tel: 413-339-4238

Rowley Historical Society
233 Main Street
Rowley, MA 01969
Tel: 978-948-7483

Roxbury Historical Society
189 Roxbury Street, John Eliot Square
Roxbury, MA 02119
Tel: 617-445-3399

Rumford Historical Association
90 Elm Street
North Woburn, MA 01801

Sandwich Historical Society
Sandwich Glass Museum
Town Hall Square
129 Main Street
Sandwich, MA 02563
Tel: 508-888-0251
Fax: 508-888-4941
http://www.sandwichglassmuseum.org/

Sandy Bay Historical Society & Museums, Inc.
40 King Street
Rockport, MA 01966
Tel: 978-546-9533

Santuit and Cotuit, Historical Society of
1148 Main Street
Cotuit, MA 02635
Tel: 508-428-0461

Scituate Historical Society
Laidlaw Historical Center
43 Cudworth Road
Scituate, MA 02066
Tel: 781-545-1083

Somerville Historical Society/Museum
1 Westwood Road
Somerville, MA 02143
Tel: 617-666-9810

Stoughton Historical Society
Lucius Clapp Memorial, Stoughton Center
6 Park Street
Stoughton, MA 02072
Tel: 781-344-5456
E-mail: davidl@user1.channel1.com

Swampscott Historical Society
99 Paradise Road
Swampscott, MA 01907
Tel: 781-599-1297
http://www.usgennet.org/usa/ma/town/swampscott/
docs/histsoc.html

Topsfield Historical Society
One Howlett Street
Topsfield, MA 01983

Wakefield Historical Society
American Civic Center
467 Main Street
Post Office Box 1902
Wakefield, MA 01880
http://www.wakefieldma.org/society.html

Waltham Historical Society
190 Moody Street
Waltham, MA 02154
Tel: 781-891-5815

Wayland Historical Society
12 Cochituate Road
Wayland, MA 01778
Tel: 508-358-7959

Wellesley Historical Society, Inc.
229 Washington Street
Wellesley Hills, MA 02181
Tel: 781-235-6690

Wellfleet Historical Society/Museum
266 Main Street
Wellfleet, MA 02667
Tel: 508-349-9157

Wenham Historical Association
132 Main Street, Route 1A
Wenham, MA 01984
Tel: 978-468-2377

Weston Historical Society
P.O. Box 343
Weston, MA 02493

Williamstown House of Local History
David and Joyce Milne Public Library
1095 Main Street
Williamstown, MA 01267
http://www.williamstown.net/house_of_local_history.htm

Winchendon Historical Society
50 Pleasant Street
Winchendon, MA 01475
Tel: 978-297-0300

Winchester Historical Society
1 Copley Street
P.O. Box 127
Winchester, MA 01890-0127
E-mail: president@WinchesterHistoricalSociety.org
http://www.winchesterhistoricalsociety.org/

LDS FAMILY HISTORY CENTERS

For locations of Family History Centers in this state, see the Family History Center locator at FamilySearch.
http://www.familysearch.org/eng/Library/FHC/frameset_fhc.asp

ARCHIVES/LIBRARIES/MUSEUMS

Acton Public Library
486 Main Street
Acton, MA 01720
Tel: 978-264-9641
Fax: 978-635-0073

Afro American History, Museum of
Administrative Office
14 Beacon Street, Suite 719
Boston, MA 02108
Tel: 617-725-0022
Fax: 617-720-5225
E-mail: history@afroammuseum.org
http://www.afroammuseum.org/

Agawam Public Library
750 Cooper Street
Agawam, MA 01001
Tel: 413-789-1550
Fax: 413-789-1552

American Antiquarian Society/Library
185 Salisbury Street
Worcester, MA 01609
Tel: 508-755-5221
Fax: 508-753-3311
E-mail: library@mwa.org
http://www.americanantiquarian.org/

Amesbury Public Library
149 Main Street
Amesbury, MA 01913
Tel: 978-388-8148
Fax: 978-388-2662
E-mail: todd@mvlc.lib.ma.us
http://www.amesburylibrary.org/

Archdiocese of Boston Archives
2121 Commonwealth Avenue
Boston, MA 02135
Tel: 617-746-5797
Fax: 617-783-5642
http://www.rcab.org/archives/welcome.htm

Armenian Library and Museum of America
65 Main Street
Watertown, MA 02172
Tel: 617-926-2562
http://www.almainc.org/

Attleboro Public Library
74 North Main Street
Attleboro, MA 02703
Tel: 508-222-0157
Fax: 508-226-3326
http://www.sailsinc.org/Attleboro/apl.htm

Bacon Free Public Library
58 Eliot Street
Natick, MA 01760
Tel: 508-653-6730

Bedford Free Public Library
7 Mudge Way
Bedford, MA 01730
Tel: 781-275-9440
Fax: 781-275-6347
TDD: 781-275-6347
E-mail: bedford@mln.lib.ma.us
http://www.bedfordlibrary.net/

Belmont Public Library
336 Concord Avenue
P.O. Box 125
Belmont, MA 02178
Tel: 617-489-2000
Fax: 617-489-5725
http://www.belmont.lib.ma.us/

Berkshire Athenaeum
1 Wendell Avenue
Pittsfield, MA 01201
Tel: 413-499-9486
Fax: 413-499-9489

Beverly Historical Society/Museum
117 Cabot Street
Beverly, MA 01915
Tel: 978-922-1186

Boston Athenaeum
10 1/2 Beacon Street
Boston, MA 02108
Tel: 617-227-0270
Fax: 617-227-5266

Boston Public Library
Central Library
700 Boylston Street
Boston MA 02117
Tel: 617-536-5400
E-mail: info@bpl.org
http://www.bpl.org/

Bostonian Society
Old State House
206 Washington Street
Boston, MA 02109-1713
Tel: 617-720-1713
Fax: 617-720-3289
http://www.bostonhistory.org/

Bourne Public Library
19 Sandwich Road
Bourne, MA 02532
Tel: 508-759-0644
Fax: 508-759-0647
http://www.bournelibrary.org/

Bridgewater Public Library
15 South Street
Bridgewater, MA 02324
Tel/TDD: 508-697-3331
Fax: 508-279-1467
E-mail: bwpl@ma.ultranet.com
http://www.ultranet.com/~bwpl/index.shtml

Bridgewater State College
Clement C. Maxwell Library
Special Collections, 3rd Floor
Bridgewater, MA 02325
Tel: 508-697-1756
E-mail: smbates@bridgew.edu
http://www.bridgew.edu/depts/maxwell/speccoll.htm

Brockton Historical Society/Museum
216 N. Pearl Street, Rte. 27
Brockton, MA 02401
Tel: 508-583-1039
E-mail: gerryb@brocktonma.com
http://www.brocktonma.com/bhs/bhs_mus.html

Brockton Public Library
(Temporary Location)
155 W. Elm St.
Brockton, MA 02301
Tel: 508-580-7890
Fax: 508-580-7898
E-mail: brpublib@tiac.net
http://www.brocktonpubliclibrary.org/

Brookline Public Library
333 Washington Street
Brookline, MA 02445
Tel: 617-730-2360
617-730-2375
Fax: 617-232-7146
http://www.town.brookline.ma.us/library/

Brooks Academy Museum
80 Parallel Street
P.O. Box 17
Harwich, MA 02645
Tel: 508-432-8089

Burlington Historical Commission/Museum
Corner of Bedford and Cambridge Streets
Burlington, MA 01803
Tel: 781-272-0606

Buttonwoods Museum
240 Water Street
Haverhill, MA 01830
Tel: 978-374-4626
http://www.haverhillhistory.org/Home%20Page.htm

Caleb Lothrop House
14 Summer Street
Cohasset, MA 02025

Cambridge Public Library
449 Broadway
Cambridge, MA 02138
Tel: 617-349-4040
Fax: 617-349-4028
TTY: 617-349-4421
http://www.ci.cambridge.ma.us/~CPL/

Cape Ann Historical Association/Library
27 Pleasant Street
Gloucester, MA 01930
Tel: 978-283-0455

Cary Memorial Library
1874 Massachusetts Avenue
Lexington, MA 02173
Tel: 781-862-6288
http://www.carylibrary.org/governan.html

Chelmsford Public Library
25 Boston Road
Chelmsford, MA 01824
Tel: 978-256-5521
Fax: 978-256-4368
E-mail: chelmsfordlib@netway.com
http://www.chelmsfordlibrary.org/

Concord Free Public Library
129 Main Street
Concord, MA 01742
Tel/TTY: 978-318-3300
Fax: 978-318-3344
E-mail: bpowell@mln.lib.ma.us
http://www.concordnet.org/library/

Congregational Library and Archives
14 Beacon Street
Boston, MA 02108
Tel: 617-523-0470

Connecticut Valley Historical Museum
220 State Street
Springfield, MA 01103-9942
Tel: 413-263-6800
http://www.quadrangle.org/CVHM.htm

Danvers Archival Center
Peabody Institute Library
15 Sylvan Street
Danvers, MA 01923
Tel: 978-774-0554
http://etext.lib.virginia.edu/salem/witchcraft/Collection.html

Dennis Memorial Library Association
1020 Old Bass River Road
Dennis, MA 02638
Tel: 508-385-2255

Dyer Memorial Library
25 Centre Avenue (Route 123)
Abington, MA 02351
Tel: 781-878-8480

East Bridgewater Public Library
32 Union Street
East Bridgewater, MA 02333
Tel: 508-378-1616
Fax: 508-378-1617
E-mail: mgreeley@sailsinc.org

Eastham Public Library
190 Samoset Road
RR 1, Box 338
Eastham, MA 02642
Tel: 508-240-5950
Fax: 508-240-0786
E-mail: mail@easthamlibrary.org
http://www.easthamlibrary.org/

Edwards Memorial Museum
3 North Road
Chesterfield, MA 01012
Tel: 413-296-4750

Edwin Smith Historical Museum
6 Elm Street
Westfield, MA 01085
Tel: 413-568-7833

Eldredge Public Library
564 Main Street
Chatham, MA 02633
Tel: 508-945-5170
Fax: 508-945-5173
E-mail: igillies@clams.lib.ma.us
http://www.eldredgelibrary.org/

Essex Shipbuilding Museum
66 Main Street
Essex, MA 01929
Tel: 978-768-7541
Fax: 978-768-2541
E-mail: info@essexshipbuildingmuseum.org
http://www.essexshipbuildingmuseum.org/

Falmouth Public LIbrary
123 Katharine Lee Bates Road
Falmouth, MA
Tel: 508-457-2555
http://www.falmouthpubliclibrary.org/

Fitchburg Public Library
Willis Room
610 Main Street
Fitchburg, MA 01420
Tel: 978-345-9635
Fax: 978-345-9631
http://www.net1plus.com/users/fpl

Fobes Memorial Library
Historical Room
4 Maple Street
Oakham, MA 01068
Tel: 508-882-3372

Forbes Library
20 West Street
Northampton, MA 01060
Tel: 413-587-1011
http://www.forbeslibrary.org/

Freetown Historical Society/Museum
1 Slab Bridge Road
P.O. Box 253
Assonet, MA 02702
Tel: 508-644-5310
http://freetownhistory.8m.com/

Goodnow Public Library
21 Concord Road
Sudbury, MA 01776
Tel: 978-443-1035
Fax: 978-443-1036

Harvard University
Graduate School of Business Administration
Baker Library, Historical Collection Dept.
Soldiers Field
Boston, MA 02163
Tel: 617-495-6397
Fax: 617-496-3811
E-mail: refquest@hbs.edu
http://library.hbs.edu/collmu.htm#Historical Collections

Haverhill Public Library
99 Main Street
Haverhill, MA 01830
Tel: 978-373-1586
Fax: 978-373-8466
http://www.haverhillpl.org/

Heard House Museum
54 South Main Street
Ipswich, MA 01938
Tel: 978-356-2811

Hingham Public Library
66 Leavitt Street
Hingham, MA 02043
Tel: 781-741-1405
Fax: 781-749-0956
E-mail: kleahy@ocln.org
http://www.hingham-ma.com/html/public_ library.html

Holyoke Public Library/Museum
335 Maple Street
Holyoke, MA 01040
Tel: 413-534-2211

Hyannis Public Library
401 Main Street
Hyannis, MA 02601-3903
Tel: 508-775-2280
http://www.hyannislibrary.org/

J.V. Fletcher Library
50 Main Street
Westford, MA 01886
Tel: 978-692-5555
Fax: 978-692-4418
E-mail: mwf@mailserv.mvlc.lib.ma.us
http://www.westfordlibrary.org/library.htm

Jackson Homestead
527 Washington Street
Newton, MA 02158
Tel/Fax: 617-552-7238
http://www.ci.newton.ma.us/jackson/default.htm

Jones Library, Inc.
Boltwood Local History & Genealogy Collection
43 Amity Street
Amherst, MA 01002
Tel: 413-256-4090
Fax: 413-256-4096
E-mail: joneslib@cwmars.org
http://www.joneslibrary.org/

Joshua Hyde Public Library
Local History Room
306 Main Street
Sturbridge, MA 01566
Tel: 508-347-2512
Fax: 508-347-2872
E-mail: library@town.sturbridge.ma.us
http://www.town.sturbridge.ma.us/
        Public_ Documents/SturbridgeMA_Depts/library

Kemp-McCarthy Memorial Museum
282 Zoar Road
Rowe, MA 01966
Tel: 413-339-4238

Kendall Whaling Museum
27 Everett Street
Sharon, MA 02067
Tel: 781-784-5642
http://www.artcom.com/museums/nv/gl/02067-10.htm

Lawrence Free Public Library
51 Lawrence Street
Lawrence, MA 01841
Tel: 978-682-1727
Fax: 978-688-3142

Longyear Historical Society/Museum
120 Seaver Street
Brookline, MA 02146

Lucius Beebe Memorial Library
345 Main Street
Wakefield, MA 01880-5093
Tel: 781-246-6334
Fax: 781-246-6385
E-mail: wakefieldlibrary@noblenet.org
http://www.noblenet.org/wakefield/

Lynn Historical Society/Library & Museum
125 Green Street
Lynn, MA 01902
Tel: 781-592-2465

Lynn Public Library
5 North Common Street
Lynn, MA 01902
Tel: 781-595-0567
Fax: 781-592-5050
E-mail: lynlib@shore.net
http://www.noblenet.org/lynn/

Lynnfield Public Library
18 Summer Street
Lynnfield, MA 01940
Tel: 781-334-5411
Fax: 781-334-2164
E-mail: lfd@noblenet.org
http://www.noblenet.org/lynnfield/

Malden Public Library
36 Salem Street
Malden, MA 02148
Tel: 781-324-0218
http://mbln.lib.ma.us/malden/index.htm

Marlborough Public Library
35 West Main Street
Marlborough, MA 01752
Tel: 508-624-6900
Fax: 508-485-1494
http://www.marlborough.com/library/index.html

Massachusetts College Of Liberal Arts
Freel Library, Special Collections
375 Church Street
P.O. Box 9250
North Adams, MA 01247
Tel: 413-662-5321
http://www.nasc.mass.edu/web/resources/library/
     page20.htm

Massachusetts Historical Society
1154 Boylston Street
Boston, MA 02215
Tel: 617-536-1608
http://www.masshist.org/

Massachusetts Society of Mayflower Descendants
100 Boylston St. Suite #750
Boston, MA 02116
E-mail: msmd@massmayflower.org
http://www.massmayflower.org/

Massachusetts State Library
341 State House
Beacon Street
Boston, MA 02133
Tel: 617-727-2590
Fax: 617-727-5819
TTD/TTY: 617-727-0917
http://www.state.ma.us/lib/homepage.htm

Mayflower Society Museum
4 Winslow Street
P.O. Box 3297
Plymouth, MA 02361
Tel: 508-746-2590

Melrose Public Library
69 West Emerson Street
Melrose, MA 02176-3173
Tel: 781-665-2313
Fax: 781-662-4229
E-mail: mel@noblenet.org
http://www.noblenet.org/melrose/

Memorial Hall Library
Andover Room
Elm Square
Andover, MA 01810
Tel: 978-623-8401
Fax: 978-623-8407
E-mail: webmaster@mhl.org
http://www.mhl.org/

Milford Public Library
80 Spruce Street
Milford, MA 01757
Tel: 508-473-2145
Fax: 508-473-8651
http://www.infofind.com/library/

Millicent Library
45 Center Street
P.O. Box 30
Fairhaven, MA 02719 U.S.A.
Tel: 508-992-5342
Fax: 508-993-7288
E-mail: millie@ma.ultranet.com
http://www.millicentlibrary.org/

Milton Public Library
476 Canton Avenue
Milton, MA 02186
Tel: 617-698-5757
E-mail: miref@ocln.org
http://www.miltonlibrary.org/

Morrill Memorial Library
33 Walpole Street
P.O. Box 220
Norwood, MA 02062
Tel: 781-769-0200
E-mail: norwood@mln.lib.ma.us
http://www.ci.norwood.ma.us/library/

Morse Institute
14 E. Central Street
Natick, MA 01760
Tel: 508-647-6520

Museum of Our National Heritage
33 Marrett Road
Lexington, MA 02173
Tel: 781-861-6559
781-861-9638
Fax: 781-861-9846
TTY: 781-274-8539
http://www.monh.org/

Needham Free Public Library
1471 Highland Avenue
Needham, MA 02194
Tel: 781-455-7559
781-455-7562 (Reference)
Fax: 781-449-4569
http://www.town.needham.ma.us/

New Bedford Free Public Library
613 Pleasant Street
New Bedford, MA 02740-6203
Tel: 508-991-6275
Fax: 508-979-1481
http://www.ci.new-bedford.ma.us/SERVICES/LIBRARY/
        library2.htm

**New England Historical and Genealogical Society
(NEHGS)**
101 Newbury Street
Boston, MA 02116-3007
Tel: 617-836-5740
888-296-3447 (Membersip and Sales)
888-906-3447 (Library Circulation)
Fax: 617-536-7307
E-mail: nehgs@nehgs.org
http://www.newenglandancestors.org/

Newburyport Public Library
94 State Street
Newburyport, MA 01950
Tel: 978-465-4428
Fax: 978-463-0394
E-mail: msavage@mailserv.mvlc.lib.ma.us
http://www.newburyportpl.org/

Newton Free Public Library
330 Homer Street
Newton, MA 02159
Tel: 617-552-7145
http://www.ci.newton.ma.us/Library/

Northborough Free Library
34 Main Street
Northborough, MA 01532
Tel: 508-393-5025

Norwell Public Library
64 South Street
Norwell, MA 02061
Tel: 781-659-2015
E-mail: dianek@ocln.org
http://www.ssec.org/idis/norwell/nplnew/joanne/ npl.htm

Peabody Essex Museum
Phillips Library
East Indian Square
Salem, MA 01970
Tel: 978-745-9500
Fax: 978-744-6776
E-mail: pem@pem.org
http://www.pem.org/phillips.html

Pilgrim Hall Museum
75 Court Street
Plymouth, MA 02360
Tel: 508-746-1620
Fax: 508-747-4228
E-mail: pegbaker@pilgrimhall.org
http://www.pilgrimhall.org/plgrmhll.htm

Plymouth Public Library
Plymouth Collection
132 South Street
Plymouth, MA 02360
Tel: 508-830-4250
TTY: 508-747-5882
E-mail: ppl@pcix.com
http://www.gis.net/~ppl/

Pollard Memorial Library
401 Merrimack Street
Lowell, MA 01852
Tel: 978-970-4120
Fax: 978-970-4117
TDD: 978-970-4129
http://www.pollardml.org/

Randall Library
380 Great Road
Stow, MA 01775
Tel: 978-897-8572

Reading Public Library
64 Middlesex Avenue
Reading, MA 01867
Tel: 617-944-0840
Fax: 781-942-9106
E-mail: readingpl@noblenet.org
http://www.noblenet.org/reading/

Rockland Memorial Library
20 Belmont Street
Rockland, MA 02370
Tel: 617-878-1236
E-mail: roill@ocln.org

Salem Maritime National Historic Site
174 Derby Street
Salem, MA 01970
Tel: 978-740-1660
Fax: 978-740-1685
http://www.nps.gov/sama/

Salem Public Library
370 Essex Street
Salem, MA 01970
Tel: 978-744-0860
Fax: 978-745-8616
E-mail: sal@noblenet.org
http://www.peabodylibrary.org/libraries/salem.shtml

Salem Witch Museum
19 1/2 Washington Square, North
Salem, MA 01970
Tel: 508-744-1692
E-mail: facts@salemwitchmuseum.com
http://www.salemwitchmuseum.com/

Salisbury Public Library
17 Elm Street
Salisbury, MA 01952
Tel: 978-465-5071
E-mail: msa.@mvlc.lib.ma.us

Sandy Bay Historical Society & Museums, Inc.
40 King Street
Rockport, MA 01966
Tel: 978-546-9533

Scituate Town Library
85 Branch Street
Scituate, MA 02066
Tel: 781-545-8727
Fax: 781-545-8728
E-mail: sclib@ocln.org
http://www.scituatetownlibrary.org/

Sharon Public Library
11 North Main Street
Sharon, MA 02067
Tel: 781-784-1578
Fax: 781-784-4728
E-mail: sharon@gateway.sharon.lib.ma

Shrewsbury Free Public Library
609 Main Street
Shrewsbury, MA 01545
Tel: 508-842-0081

Somerville Public Library
Local History Room
79 Highland Avenue
Somerville, MA 02143
Tel: 617-623-5000
TTY: 617-625-8808
E-mail: somerville@mln.lib.ma.us
http://www.ultranet.com/~somlib/

Springfield Libraries & Museums
Genealogy and Local History Library
220 State Street
Springfield, MA 01103
Tel: 413-263-6800 ext. 311
http://www.springfieldlibrary.org

Strong House Museum
67 Amity Street
Amherst, MA 01002
Tel: 413-256-0678

Sturgis Library
3090 Main Street, Rte. 6A
P.O. Box 606
Barnstable, MA 02630
Tel: 508-362-6636
Fax: 508-362-5467
E-mail: sturgislib@attbi.com
http://home.capecod.net/~sturgis/

Swansea Free Public Library
69 Main Street
Swansea, MA 02777
Tel: 508-674-9609

Taft Public Library
Main Street
P.O. Box 35
Mendon, MA 01756-0035
Tel: 508-473-3259
Fax: 508-473-7049

University of Massachusetts/Amherst
W.E.B. DuBois Library
Special Collections
Amherst, MA 01003
Tel: 413-545-0150
http://www.library.umass.edu/spcoll/spec.html

Ventress Memorial Library
15 Library Plaza
Marshfield, MA 02050
Tel: 781-834-5535
Fax: 781-837-8362
E-mail: eriboldi@ocln.org
http://www.ventresslibrary.org/

Vineyard Haven Library
Main Street
Vineyard Haven, MA 02568
Tel: 508-696-4211
Fax: 508-696-7495
http://www.vhlibrary.org/

Martha's Vineyard Historical Society/Museum
P.O. Box 1310
Edgartown, MA 02539
Tel: 508-627-4441
Fax: 508-627-4436
http://www.vineyard.net/org/mvhs/

Watertown Free Public Library
123 Main Street
Watertown, MA 02172
Tel: 617-972-6431
Fax: 617-924-5471
E-mail: lcole@ci.watertown.ma.us
http://www.watertownlib.org/

Wayland Public Library
5 Concord Road
Wayland, MA 01778
Tel: 508-358-2311
http://www.wayland.ma.us/library/

Wenham Public Library
138 Main Street
Wenham, MA 01984
Tel: 978-468-5527
E-mail: mwn@mvlc.lib.ma.us

Westborough Public Library
55 West Main Street
Westborough, MA 01581
Tel: 508-366-3050
Fax: 508-366-3049
http://www.westboroughlib.org/

Weston Public Library
87 School Street
Weston, MA 02193
Tel: 617-893-3312
Fax: 617-893-9142
E-mail: weston@mln.lib.ma.us

Williamstown House of Local History
Williamstown Public Library
Elizabeth S. Botsford Memorial Building
762 Main Street, 2nd Floor
Williamstown, MA 01267
http://bcn.net/~willieb/hlh.html

Winchester Public Library
80 Washington Street
Winchester, MA 01890
Tel: 781-721-7171
Fax: 781-721-7170
http://www.winchestermass.org/lib.html

Woburn Public Library
45 Pleasant Street
P.O. Box 298
Woburn, MA 01801
Tel: 617-933-0148
Fax: 617-938-7860
E-mail: info@woburnpubliclibrary.org
http://www.woburnpubliclibrary.org/

Worcester Public Library
Local History/Worcester Room
3 Salem Square
Worcester, MA 01608
Tel: 508-799-1655
http://www.worcpublib.org/

Yarmouth Library
297 Main Street
Yarmouthport, MA 02675

NEWSPAPER REPOSITORIES

Boston Public Library
Central Library
700 Boylston Street
Boston, MA 02117
Tel: 617-536-5400
E-mail: info@bpl.org
http://www.bpl.org/

Massachusetts State Library
341 State House
Beacon Street
Boston, MA 02133
Tel: 617-727-2590
Fax: 617-727-5819
TTD/TTY: 617-727-0917
http://www.state.ma.us/lib/homepage.htm

VITAL RECORDS

Massachusetts Department of Public Health
150 Mount Vernon Street, 1st Floor
Dorchester, MA 02125-3105
Tel: 617-740-2600
http://www.state.ma.us/dph/bhsre/rvr/rvr.htm

MASSACHUSETTS ON THE WEB

America's Homepage—Plymouth
http://pilgrims.net/plymouth/

Colonial Massachusetts & Maine Genealogies
http://home.earthlink.net/~anderson207/

Historical Records of Tisbury, Massachusetts
http://www.vineyard.net/vineyard/history/index.html

Massachusetts GenWeb Project
http://www.rootsweb.com/~magenweb/

Mayflower Web Pages
http://members.aol.com/calebj/mayflower.html

MICHIGAN

ARCHIVES, STATE & NATIONAL

Michigan State Archives
Michigan Library and Historical Center
717 West Allegan Street
Lansing MI 48918-1800
(517) 373-3559
TDD 1-800-827-7007
http://www.sos.state.mi.us/history/archive/ archive.html

National Archives—Great Lakes Region
7358 Pulaski Road
Chicago, IL 60629
Tel: 773-581-7816
Fax: 312-886-7883
E-mail: chicago.archives@nara.gov
http://www.nara.gov/regional/chicago.html

GENEALOGICAL SOCIETIES

Bay County Genealogical Society
P.O. Box 27
Essexville, MI 48732

Bigelow Genealogical Society
P.O. Box 4115
Flint, MI 48504

Branch County Genealogical Society
P.O. Box 443
Coldwater, MI 49036
http://www.geocities.com/TheTropics/1050/
Gensociety.html

Calhoun County Genealogical Society
P.O. Box 879
Marshall, MI 49068
E-mail: AnitaStuever@voyager.net
http://www.rootsweb.com/~micalhou/ccgs.htm

Charlevoix County Genealogical Society
Boyne District Libary
201 E. Main Street
Boyne City, MI 49712
Tel: 231-582-7861
Fax: 231-582-2998
E-mail: boynec1@northland.lib.mi.us
http://www.rootsweb.com/~micharle/cx-03.htm

Cheboygan County Genealogical Society
P.O. Box 51
Cheboygan, MI 49721
http://www.rootsweb.com/~miccgs/CCGSmainx. html

Dearborn Genealogical Society
P.O. Box 1112
Dearborn, MI 48121-1112
E-mail: dearbrown2@aol.com
http://www.rootsweb.com/~midgs/

Detroit Society for Genealogical Research
Detroit Public Library
Burton Historical Collection
5201 Woodward Avenue
Detroit, MI 48202
Tel: 313-833-1480
http://www.dsgr.org/

Dickinson County Genealogical Society
401 Iron Mountain Street
Iron Mountain, MI 49801
http://www.upclics.org/dcgs/

Downriver Genealogical Society
1394 Cleophus
P.O. Box 476
Lincoln Park, MI 48146
http://www.rootsweb.com/~midrgs/drgs.htm

Eaton County Genealogical Society
1885 Courthouse
Charlotte, MI 48813
Tel: 517-543-8792
Fax: 517-543-6999
http://userdata.acd.net/mmgs/ecgs.html

Farmington Genealogical Society
23500 Liberty
Farmington, MI 48024
http://www.metronet.lib.mi.us/FCL/genealsoc.html

Flemish Americans, Genealogical Society of
18740 Thirteen Mile Road
Roseville, MI 48066
http://www.rootsweb.com/~gsfa/

Flint Genealogical Society
P.O. Box 1217
Flint, MI 48501
E-mail: ldnelson@tir.com
http://www.rootsweb.com/~mifgs/

Ford Genealogy Club
Ford Motor Credit Company Building, Room 1491
(meetings only)
P.O. Box 1652
Dearborn, MI 48121-1652
E-mail: miprofgenie@wwnet.net (President)
http://www.wwnet.net/~krugman1/fgc/

Four Flags Area Genealogical Society
P.O. Box 414
Niles, MI 49120

French-Canadian Heritage Society of Michigan
9513 Whipple Shores Drive
Clarkston, MI 48348
http://habitant.org/fchsm/

French-Canadian Heritage Society of Michigan
Lansing Chapter
P.O. Box 10028
Lansing, MI 48901-0028
http://habitant.org/fchsm/

French-Canadian Heritage Society of Michigan
http://habitant.org/fchsm/

Gaylord Fact-Finders Genealogical Society
P.O. Box 1524
Gaylord, MI 49735
http://www.otsego.org/factfinders/

Grand Haven Genealogical Society
Loutit Library
407 Columbus
Grand Haven, MI 49417
Tel: 616-842-5560
E-mail: ghgs_2000@yahoo.com
http://www.geocities.com/ghgs_2000/Grand_Haven_Gene
    alogical_Society.html

Grand Traverse Area Genealogical Society
P.O. Box 2015
Traverse City, MI 49685
http://www.rootsweb.com/~migtags/gtag.htm

Gratiot County Historical & Genealogical Society
P.O. Box 73
Ithaca, MI 48847
http://www.rootsweb.com/~migratio/gchgs/

Harrison Area Genealogical Society
P.O. Box 796
Harrison, MI 48625
http://www.rootsweb.com/~miclare/harrison.htm

Holland Genealogical Society
Herrick Pubic Library
300 River Avenue
Holland, MI 49423

Huron County Genealogical Society
2843 Electric Avenue
Port Huron, MI 48060

Huron Shores Genealogical Society
Robert J. Parks Public Library
6010 N. Skeel Avenue
Oscoda, MI 48750
Tel: 517-362-5425
      517-739-3650
E-mail: klenowr@alpena.cc.mi.us
      shermanaj@hotmail.com
http://www.rootsweb.com/~miiosco/huronpage.html

Huron Valley Genealogical Society
1100 Atlantic
Milford, MI 48042
http://milford.lib.mi.us/mcin/groups/hvgs.htm

Ionia County Genealogical Society
3011 Knoll Road,
Portland, MI 48875
E-mail lfox@mvcc.com
http://www.rootsweb.com/~miionia/icgshome.htm

Jackson County Genealogical Society
Jackson District Library
244 West Michigan Avenue
Jackson, MI 49201
http://www.rootsweb.com/~mijackso/jcgs.htm

Jewish Genealogical Society of Michigan
P.O. Box 1361
Royal Oak, MI 48068

**Jewish Historical Society of Michigan,
Genealogical Branch**
3345 Buckingham Trail
West Bloomfield, MI 48033

Kalamazoo Valley Genealogical Society
P.O. Box 405
Comstock, MI 49041
E-mail: 76635.231@compuserve.com
    or tptm71a@prodigy.com
http://www.rootsweb.com/~mikvgs/

Kalkaska Genealogical Society
P.O. Box 353
Kalkaska, MI 49646
http://hometown.aol.com/fiddlerben/kasgensoc.html

Lapeer County Genealogical Society
Lapeer County Library/Marguerite deAngeli Branch
921 Nepressing Street
Lapeer, MI 48446
Tel: 810-664-6971
Fax: 810-664-5581
http://www.library.lapeer.org/deAngeli/mdeangeli. htm

Lenawee County Genealogical Society
P.O. Box 511
Adrain, MI 49221

Livingston County Genealogical Society
P.O. Box 1073
Howell, MI 48844-1073
http://www.livgenmi.com/lcgslogo.htm

Luce-Mackinac Genealogical Society
P.O. Box 113
Engadine, MI 49827-0113
http://www.rootsweb.com/~miluce/luce-mac.htm

Lyon Township Genealogical Society
Lyon Township Public Library
P.O. Box 326
27005 Milford Road
New Hudson, MI 48165
Tel: 248-437-8800
Fax: 248-437-4621
E-mail: lyonlibrary@yahoo.com
http://www.lyon.lib.mi.us/

Macomb County Genealogy Group
Mount Clemens Public Library
150 Cass Avenue
Mount Clemens, MI 48043
Tel: 810-469-6200
http://www.macomb.lib.mi.us/mountclemens/genealog.htm

Marquette County Genealogical Society
Peter White Public Library
217 North Front Street
Marquette, MI 49855
E-mail: MQTCGS@aol.com
http://members.aol.com/MQTCGS/MCGS/mcgs.html

Mason County Genealogical Society
P.O. Box 352
Ludington, MI 49431

Michigan Genealogical Council
P.O. Box 80953
Lansing, MI 48908
http://www.geocities.com/Heartland/Meadows/2192/

Mid-Michigan Genealogical Society
P.O. Box 16033
Lansing, MI 48901
http://userdata.acd.net/mmgs/mmgssoc.html

Midland Genealogical Society
Grace A. Dow Library
1710 West St. Andrews Drive
Midland, MI 48640

Monroe County, Genealogical Society of
P.O. Box 1428
Monroe, MI 48161
http://www.tdi.net/havekost/gsmc.htm

Muskegon County Genealogical Society
Hackley Library
316 W. Webster Avenue
Muskegon, MI 49440
Tel: 231-722-7276

National Society, Daughters of the Union 1861-1865, Inc.
http://personal.atl.bellsouth.net/sdf/c/s/cseales/home.htm

North Oakland Genealogical Society
Orion Township Public Library
825 Joslyn Rd.
Lake Orion, MI 48362
Tel: 810-693-3000
http://tln.lib.mi.us/~pont/genealog.htm

Northeast Michigan Genealogical Society
Jesse Besser Museum
491 Johnson Street
Alpena, MI 49707
http://members.aol.com/alpenaco/migenweb/genealog.htm

Northville Genealogical Society
P.O. Box 932
Northville, MI 48167-0932
http://www.rootsweb.com/~mings/

Oakland County Genealogical Society
P.O. Box 1094
Birmingham, MI 48012
http://www.rhpl.org/OCGS/

Ogemaw Genealogical & Historical Society
West Branch Public Library
119 North Fourth Street
West Branch, MI 48661
Tel: 989-345-2235

Osceola County Genealogical Society
(formerly Reed City Area Genealogical Society)
P.O. Box 27
Reed City, MI 49677-0027

Polish Genealogical Society of Michigan
Detroit Public Librar
Burton Historical Collection
5201 Woodward Avenue
Detroit, MI 48202
http://feefhs.org/pol/frgpgsmi.html

Pontiac Area Historical & Genealogical Society
P.O. Box 430901
Pontiac, MI 48343-0901

Presque Isle County Genealogical Society
Onaway Library
20774 State Street
P.O. Box 742
Onaway, MI 49765
Tel: 989-733-6621
Fax: 989-733-7842
E-mail: onaway1@northland.lib.mi.us

Roseville Historical & Genealogical Society
Roseville Public Library
29777 Gratiot Avenue
Roseville, MI 48066
http://www.macomb.lib.mi.us/roseville/
        historical_ genealogical_society.htm

Saint Clair County Family History Group
P.O. Box 611483
Port Huron, MI 48061-1483

Saginaw Genealogical Society
Saginaw Public Library
505 Janes Avenue
Saginaw, MI 48507

Shiawassee County Genealogical Society
P.O. Box 841
Owosso, MI 48867
http://www.shianet.org/community/orgs/scgs/

Southwestern Michigan, Genealogical Association of
P.O. Box 573
St. Joseph, MI 49085

Sterling Heights Genealogical & Historical Society
P.O. Box 1154
Sterling Heights, MI 48311-1154
http://www.rootsweb.com/~mishghs/

Van Buren Regional Genealogical Society
P.O. Box 143
Decatur, MI 49045
http://woodlands.lib.mi.us/van/vbrgs.htm

Washtenaw County, Genealogical Society of
P.O. Box 7155
Ann Arbor, MI 48107

Western Michigan Genealogical Society
Grand Rapids Public Library
111 Library Street NE
Grand Rapids, MI 49503-3268
E-mail: wmgs@wmgs.org
http://www.wmgs.org/

Western Wayne County Genealogical Society
P.O. Box 53
Livonia, MI 48152

HISTORICAL SOCIETIES

Albion Historical Society
Gardner House Museum
509 South Superior Street
Albion, MI 49224
Tel: 517-629-5100
E-mail:history@forks.org
http://www.forks.org/history/albion.htm

Ann Arbor Historical Foundation
312 South Division Street
Ann Arbor, MI 48104
Tel: 313-996-3008

Bellaire Area Historical Society
P.O. Box 1016
Bellaire, MI 49615

Benzie Area Historical Society
6941 Traverse Avenue
P.O. Box 185
Benzonia, MI 49616

Berrien County Historical Association
313 North Cass Street
P.O. Box 261
Berrien Springs, MI 49103
Tel: 616-471-1202
Fax: 616-471-7412
http://www.berrienhistory.org/

Branch County Historical Society
P.O. Box 443
Coldwater, MI 49036

Chelsea Area Historical Society
125 Jackson Road
Chelsea, MI 48118
Tel: 734-475-9330

Elk Rapids Area Historical Society
401 River Street
P.O. Box 2
Elk Rapids, MI 49629
http://www.ole.net/~maggie/antrim/elk.htm

Elsie Historical Society
P.O. Box 125
Elsie, MI 48831
http://www.rootsweb.com/~migratio/elsiehiso/ elsiehist-
        soc.html

Flat River Historical Society
P.O. Box 188
Greenville, MI 48838

Flat Rock Historical Society
P.O. Box 386
Flat Rock, MI 48134

Fraser Historical Society
P.O. Box 26155
Fraser, MI 48026
http://www.ci.fraser.mi.us/library/part/historical.html

Grand Traverse Pioneer and Historical Society
232 Front Street
P.O. Box 1108
Traverse City, MI 49685

Grass Lake Area Historical Society
P.O. Box 53
Grass Lake, MI 49240

Gratiot County Historical & Genealogical Society
P.O. Box 73
Ithaca, MI 48847
http://www.rootsweb.com/~migratio/gchgs/

Grosse Ile Historical Society
P.O. Box 131
Grosse Ile, MI 48138
Tel: 734-675-1250

Huron County Historical Society
223 Third Street
Harbor Beach, MI 48441

Huron Valley RR Historical Society
3487 Broad Street
Dexter, MI 48130
Tel: 734-426-5100

Ionia County Historical Society
P.O. Box 1776
Ionia, MI 48846
http://www.mrwcreative.com/Historical/

Iosco Bay Historical Society
405 E Bay Street
P.O. Box 144
East Tawas, MI 48730
Tel: 989-362-8911

Jewish Historical Society of Michigan, Genealogical Branch
3345 Buckingham Trail
West Bloomfield, MI 48033

Keweenaw County Historical Society
HC-1, Box 265L
Eagle Harbor, MI 49950
http://www.keweenawhistory.org/

Lake Odessa Historical Society
Page Building
839 4th Avenue
Lake Odessa, MI 48849

Lincoln Park Historical Society
P.O. Box 1776
Lincoln Park, MI 48146

Little Traverse Historical Society/Museum
P.O. Box 162
Petoskey, MI 49770
Tel: 231-347-2620
http://members.tripod.com/~deemamafred/lths.html

Livonia Historical Society
38125 Eight Mile Road
Livonia, MI 48152

Marine Historical Society of Detroit
Dept. W
606 Laurel Avenue
Port Clinton, OH 43452
http://www.mhsd.org/

Marquette County Historical Society
John M. Longyear Research Library
213 North Front Street
Marquette, MI 49855
http://www.geocities.com/Heartland/Plains/5666/
    Marhistsoc.html

Mason County Historical Society
1687 South Lake Shore Drive
Ludington, MI 49431

Michigan Historical Commission
505 State Office Building
Lansing, MI 48913

Michigan, Historical Society of
1305 Abbott Rd.
East Lansing, MI 48823
Tel: 517-324-1828
Fax: 517-324-4370
E-mail: hsm@hsmichigan.org
http://www.hsofmich.org/

Midland County Historical Society
Midland Center for the Arts
1801 West Andrews Drive
Midland, MI 48640

Northville Historical Society
P.O. Box 71
Northville, MI 48167

Northwest Oakland County Historical Society
306 South Saginaw Street
Holly, MI 48442

Oakland County Pioneer & Historical Society/Archives
405 Oakland Avenue
Pontiac, MI 48342
Tel: 248-338-6732
Fax: 248-338-6731
http://www.wwnet.net/~ocphs/

Ogemaw Genealogical & Historical Society
119 N. 4th Street
West Branch, MI 48661

Plymouth Historical Society
155 South Main Street
Plymouth, MI 48170
Tel: 734-455-8940
Fax: 734-455-7797
http://www.plymouth.lib.mi.us/~history/
E-mail: plymouthhistoricalmuseum@netzero.net

Pontiac Area Historical & Genealogical Society
P.O. Box 430901
Pontiac, MI 48343-0901
http://members.tripod.com/ginblock/pahags.html

Rockwood Area Historical Society
P.O. Box 68
Rockwood, MI 48173

Romulus Historical Society
Romulus Public Library
11121 Wayne Road
Romulus, MI 48174

Rose City Area Historical Society, Inc.
Ogemaw District Library
107 West Main
P.O. Box 427
Rose City, MI 48654

Roseville Historical & Genealogical Society
Roseville Public Library
29777 Gratiot Avenue
Roseville, MI 48066
http://www.macomb.lib.mi.us/roseville/
        historical_genealogical_society.htm

Saginaw River Marine Historical Society
Dept. W
P.O. Box 2051
Bay City, MI 48707
http://www.boatnerd.com/museums/srmhs/

Sanilac County Historical Society
228 North Ridge Street
Port Sanilac, MI 48469
Tel: 810-622-9946

Washtenaw County Historical Society
500 North Main Street
Ann Arbor, MI 48104
Tel: 313-662-9092

Wayne Historical Society
1 Town Square
Wayne, MI 48184

Ypsilanti Historical Society/Museum/Archives
220 North Huron Street
Ypsilanti, MI 48197
Tel: 734-482-4990
E-mail: barr@hvcn.org
http://www.hvcn.org/info/libyhma.html

Zeeland Historical Society
P.O. Box 165
Zeeland, MI 49464

LDS FAMILY HISTORY CENTERS

For locations of Family History Centers in this state, see
the Family History Center locator at FamilySearch.
http://www.familysearch.org/eng/Library/FHC/
frameset_fhc.asp

ARCHIVES/LIBRARIES/MUSEUMS

Adrian Public Library
143 E. Maumee Street
Adrian, MI 49221
Tel: 517-265-2265
Fax: 517-265-8847
http://woodlands.lib.mi.us/adrian/adrian.htm

Albion Public Library
501 S. Superior Street
Albion, MI 49224
Tel: 517-629-3993
TDD: 517-629-3994
E-mail: director@albionlibrary.org
http://www.albionlibrary.org/

Allen County Public Library
900 Webster Street
Fort Wayne, IN 46802
Tel: 260-421-1200
http://www.acpl.lib.in.us/

Alpena County Library
George N. Fletcher Public Library
211 North First Avenue
Alpena, MI 49707
Tel: 989-356-6188
Fax: 989-356-2765
E-mail: alpena1@northland.lib.mi.us
http://members.aol.com/alpenaco/migenweb/
    library.htm

Ann Arbor Public Library
343 South 5th Avenue
Ann Arbor, MI 48104
Tel: 734-994-2333

Archdiocese of Detroit
Archives Department
1234 Washington Road
Detroit, MI 48226-1875
Tel: 313-237-5846
Fax: 313-237-4643
http://www.archdioceseofdetroit.org/

Bacon Memorial District Library
45 Vinewood
Wyandotte, MI 48192
Tel: 734-246-8357
Fax: 734-282-1540
http://www.wyandotte.lib.mi.us/

Bay County Library
708 Center Avenue
Bay City, MI 48708
Tel: 989-893-9566
Fax: 989-893-9799
TDD: 989-893-9566
http://www.baycountylibrary.org/

Bay County Library/Sage Branch
4101 East Wilder Road
Bay City, MI 48706
Tel: 989-892-8555
Fax: 989-892-2575
http://www.baycountylibrary.org/bsa.htm

Bay County Library-South Side Branch
311 Lafayette Avenue
Bay City, MI 48708
Tel: 989-893-1287
Fax: 989-894-0505
http://www.baycountylibrary.org/bss.htm

Birmingham Public Library
300 W. Merrill Street
Birmingham, MI 48009
Tel: 248-647-1700

Boyne City Public Library
201 E. Main St.
Boyne City, MI 49712
Tel: 231-582-7861
Fax: 231-582-2998
E-mail: boynec1@northland.lib.mi.us
http://nlc.lib.mi.us/members/boyne_c.htm

Branch District Library
10 E. Chicago Street
Coldwater, MI 49036
Tel: 517-278-2341
Fax: 517-279-7134
E-mail: Director@brnlibrary.org
http://www.brnlibrary.org/

Cadillac and Wexford County Public Library
411 South Lake Street
Cadillac, MI 49601
Tel: 231-775-6541

Central Michigan University
Clarke Historical Library
Central Michigan University
Mount Pleasant, MI 48859
Tel: 989-774-3352
    989-774-3471 (Reference)
Fax: 989-774-2160
E-mail: clarke@cmich.edu
http://www.lib.cmich.edu/clarke/clarke.htm

Cheboygan Area Public Library
107 S. Ball Street
Cheboygan, MI 49721
Tel: 231-627-2381
Fax: 231-627-2381
E-mail: cheboy1@northland.lib.mi.us
http://nlc.lib.mi.us/members/cheboyga.htm

Comstock Township Library
6130 King Highway
Comstock, MI 49001
Tel: 616-345-0136
http://www.comstocktownshiplib.org/

Detroit Public Library
Burton Historical Collection
5201 Woodward Avenue
Detroit, MI 48202
Tel: 313-833-1000
Fax: 313-832-0877
E-mail: dporemba@detroit.lib.mi.us
http://www.detroit.lib.mi.us/burton/

Dexter Area Museum
3433 Inverness
Dexter, MI 48130
Tel: 734-426-2519
E-mail: DexMuseum@aol.com
http://www.hvcn.org/info/dextermuseum/

Dickinson County Library
401 Iron Mountain Street
Iron Mountain, MI 49801
Tel: 906-774-1218
Fax: 906-774-4079
http://www.dcl-lib.org/

Ecorse Public Library
4184 Jefferson Avenue
Ecorse, MI 48229
Tel/TDD: 313-389-2030
Fax: 313-389-2032
http://tln.lib.mi.us/~ecor/index.htm

Farmington Community Library
32737 West 12 Mile Road
Farmington Hills, MI 48334
Tel: 248-553-0300
http://www.farmlib.org/

Finnish-American Heritage Center
Finland University
601 Quincy Street
Hancock, MI 49930
Tel: 906-487-7367
Fax: 906-487-7383
http://www.finlandia.edu/fahc.html

Flint Public Library
1026 E. Kearsley Street
Flint, MI 48502
Tel: 810-232-7111
Fax: 810-232-8360
http://www.flint.lib.mi.us/

Galesburg Memorial Library
188 E. Michigan
Galesburg, MI 49053
Tel: 616-665-7839
Fax: 616-345-0138

Grace A. Dow Library
1710 West St. Andrews Drive
Midland, MI 48640
Tel: 517-835-9599

Grand Rapids Public Library
1100 Hynes Avenue S.W., Suite B
Grand Rapids, MI 49507
Tel: 616-988-5400
http://www.grapids.lib.mi.us/

Hackley Public Library
316 W. Webster Avenue
Muskegon, MI 49440
Tel: 616-722-7276
http://www.remc4.k12.mi.us/muskegon/library/
    hackley.htm

Hall-Fowler Memorial Library
126 E. Main Street
Ionia, MI 48846
Tel: 616-527-3680
Fax: 616-527-6210
http://ionia.llcoop.org/

Harrison Community Library
105 West Main Street
P.O. Box 380
Harrison, MI 48625
Tel: 989-539-6711
Fax: 989-539-6301
E-mail: harrlib@hotmail.com
http://www.geocities.com/Athens/Ithaca/4577/

Herrick Public Library
300 South River Avenue
Holland, MI 49423
Tel: 616-355-1400

Howell Carnegie District Library
314 W. Grand River
Howell, MI 48843
Tel: 517-546-0720
Fax: 517-546-1494
http://hcdl.howell-carnegie.lib.mi.us/

Iosco-Arenac District Library
951 Turtle Road
Tawas City, MI 48763
Tel: 989-362-2651

Jesse Besser Museum
491 Johnson
Street Alpena, MI 49707
Tel: 989-356-2202
http://www.oweb.com/upnorth/museum/

Kalamazoo Public Library
315 South Rose Street (under construction until Dec. 1997)
121 West South (Temporary Address)
Kalamazoo, MI 49007
Tel: 616-342-9837
    616-342-5745 (Local History Room)
Fax: 616-342-8342
http://www.kpl.gov/

Lansing Public Library
401 South Capitol
P.O. Box 40719
Lansing, MI 48901
Tel: 517-367-6350
Fax: 517-367-6333
E-mail: morrowl@mlc.lib.mi.us
http://www.cadl.org/Branches/lansing_library.htm

Lapeer County Library/Marguerite deAngeli Branch
921 West Nepressing
Lapeer, MI 48446
Tel: 810-664-6971
Fax: 810-664-5581
http://www.library.lapeer.org/deAngeli/mdeangeli. htm

Mackinac Island Public Library
Box C
Mackinac Island, MI 49757
Tel: 906-847-3421
E-mail: MackPLIB@aol.com
http://cterwilliger.com/HTML/Mackinac/library.html

Mackinaw Public Library
528 West Central Avenue
P.O. Box 67
Mackinaw City, MI 49701-0067
Tel: 616-436-5451
Fax: 616-436-7344
E-mail: mackina3@northland.lib.mi.us
http://nlc.lib.mi.us/members/mackinaw.htm

Mancelona Public Library
202 East State Street
Mancelona, MI 49659
Tel: 231-587-9451

Manistee Public Library
95 Maple Street
Manistee, MI 49660
Tel: 231-723-2519

Marquette County Historical Society
John M. Longyear Research Library
213 North Front Street
Marquette, MI 49855
http://www.geocities.com/Heartland/Plains/5666/
    Marhistsoc.html

McKay Memorial Library
105 S. Webster
Augusta, MI 49012
Tel: 616-731-4000

Michigan Library & Historical Center
Library of Michigan
Genealogical & Local History Collection
717 Allegan Street
P.O. Box 30007
Lansing, MI 48909
Tel: 517-373-1580
http://www.libofmich.lib.mi.us/

**Michigan Technological University Archives and
The Copper County Historical Collection**
J. Robert Van Pelt Historical Collection
1400 Townsend Drive
Houghton, MI 49931-1295
Tel: 906-487-2508
Fax: 906-487-2357
E-mail: wwwlib@mtu.edu
http://www.lib.mtu.edu/

Milan Public Library
151 Wabash Street
Milan, MI 48160
Tel: 734-439-1240
Fax: 734-439-5625
E-mail: milan@monroe.lib.mi.us
http://woodlands.lib.mi.us/milan/

Milford Township Library
1100 Atlantic Street
Milford, MI 48381
Tel: 248-684-0845
E-mail: milford@tln.lib.mi.us
http://milford.lib.mi.us/

Mitchell Public Library
22 N. Manning Street
Hillsdale, MI 49242
Tel: 517-437-2581
Fax: 517-437-2583

Monroe County Library System
Ellis Reference and Information Center
3700 S. Custer Road
Monroe, MI 48161
Tel: 734-241-5277
Fax: 734-241-4722
http://monroe.lib.mi.us/

Mount Clemens Public Library
150 Cass Avenue
Mount Clemens, MI 48043
Tel: 586-469-6200
http://www.macomb.lib.mi.us/mountclemens/

North Berrien Historical Museum
300 Coloma Avenue
Coloma, MI 49038-9724
Tel: 616-468-3330

Northville District Library
212 W. Cady Street
Northville, MI 48167
Tel: 248-349-3020
Fax: 248-349-8250
http://tln.lib.mi.us/~nort/

Northwestern Michigan College
Helen and Mark Osterlin Library
1701 E. Front Street
Traverse City, MI 49686
Tel: 231-922-1060
231-995-1540 (Reference Desk)
E-mail: library@elmo.nmc.edu
http://www.nmc.edu/~library/

Novi Public Library
45245 West Ten Mile Road
Novi, MI 48375
Tel: 248-349-0720
Fax/TDD: 248-349-6520
http://www.novi.lib.mi.us/

Ogemaw District Library
107 West Main
P.O. Box 427
Rose City, MI 48654

Onaway Library
P.O. Box 742
Onaway, MI 49765

Parchment Community Library
401 S. Riverview
Parchment, MI 49004
Tel: 616-343-7747
http://parlib.tripod.com/

Peter White Public Library
217 North Front Street
Marquette, MI 49855
Tel: 906-228-9510
http://www.uproc.lib.mi.us/pwpl/

Petoskey Public Library
451 E. Mitchell Street
Petoskey, MI 49770
Tel: 231-347-4211
Fax: 231-348-8662
E-mail: library@petoskeylibrary.org
http://www.petoskeylibrary.org/

Portage Public Library
300 Library Lane
Portage, MI 49002
Tel: 616-329-4544

Reed City Public Library
410 West Upton Avenue
Reed City, MI 49677
Tel: 231-832-2131

Rochester Hills Public Library
Local History Room
500 Olde Towne Road
Rochester, MI 48307-2043
Tel: 248-656-2900
http://www.rhpl.org/

Romulus Public Library
11121 Wayne Road
Romulus, MI 48174
Tel/TDD: 313-942-7589
Fax: 313-941-3575
http://www.romulus.lib.mi.us/

Roseville Public Library
29777 Civic Center Blvd.
Roseville, MI 48066
Tel: 586-445-5407

Royal Oak Public Library
222 E. Eleven Mile Rd.
P.O. Box 494
Royal Oak, Michigan 48068-0494
Tel: 248-246-3700
E-mail: cwindorf@tln.lib.mi.us
http://www.ci.royal-oak.mi.us/library/

Saint Clair County Library
Michigan Room
210 McMorran Blvd.
Port Huron, MI 48060-4098
Tel: 810-987-7323

Saint Clair Shores Library
22500 East 11 Mile Road
St. Clair Shores, MI 48081
Tel: 586-771-9020

Saint Joseph Public Library
500 Market Street
St. Joseph, MI 49085
Tel: 616-983-7167

Saginaw Public Library
Hoyt Main Branch
505 Janes Avenue
Saginaw, MI 48607
Tel: 989-755-0904
Fax: 989-755-9829
http://www.saginaw.lib.mi.us/

Schoolcraft Community Library
330 N. Centre
Schoolcraft, MI 49087
Tel: 616-679-5959

Spies Public Library
940 First Street
Menominee, MI 49858
Tel: 906-863-3911
Fax: 906-863-5000
http://www.uproc.lib.mi.us/spies/

Sturgis Public Library
255 North Street
Sturgis, MI 49091
Tel: 616-659-7224
Fax: 616-651-4534

Three Rivers Public Library
920 West Michigan Avenue
Three Rivers, MI 49093
Tel: 616-273-8666
Fax: 616-279-9654
http://www.threeriverslibrary.org/

Trenton Veterans Memorial Library
2790 Westfield
Trenton, MI 48183
Tel: 734-676-9777
Fax: 734-676-9895
TDD: 734-676-9773
http://tln.lib.mi.us/~tren/

Troy Public Library
510 Big Beaver Road
Troy, MI 48084
Tel: 248-524-3538

University of Michigan/Ann Arbor
Bentley Historical Library
1150 Beall Avenue
Ann Arbor, MI 48109-2113
Tel: 734-764-3482
Fax: 734-936-1333
http://www.umich.edu/~bhl/

University of Michigan/Flint
Frances Willson Thompson Library
Genesee History Collection Center
Flint, MI 48502
Tel: 810-762-3400
Fax: 810-762-3133
http://lib.umflint.edu/archives/

Van Buren District Library
200 North Phelps Street
Decatur, MI 49045
Tel: 616-423-4771
Fax: 616-423-8373
E-mail: dtate@monroe.lib.mi.us
http://woodlands.lib.mi.us/van/vanburen.htm

Vicksburg District Library
215 S. Michigan
Vicksburg, MI 49097
Tel: 616-649-1648
Fax: 616-649-3666
http://www.youseemore.com/vicksburg/

Wayne State University
Walter P. Reuther Library
5401 Cass Avenue
Detroit, MI 48202
Tel: 313-577-4024
Fax: 313-577-4300
TDD: 313-993-7573
http://www.reuther.wayne.edu/

Western Michigan University
Archives and Regional History Collection
Room 111, East Hall
Mail:
Archives and Regional History Collections
Western Michigan University
1903 W. Michigan Avenue
Kalamazoo, MI 49008-5081
Tel: 616-387-8490
Fax: 616-387-8484
E-mail: arch_collect@wmich.edu
http://www.wmich.edu/library/depts/archives/

Willard Library
7 W. Van Buren
Battle Creek, MI 49017
Tel: 616-968-8166
http://www.willard.lib.mi.us/

Ypsilanti District Library/Peters Branch
1165 Ecorse Road
Ypsilanti, MI 48198
Tel: 734-482-5025
Fax: 734-482-0122
http://tln.lib.mi.us/directory/members/petr/

Ypsilanti Historical Society/Museum/Archives
220 North Huron Street
Ypsilanti, MI 48197
Tel: 734-482-4990
E-mail: barr@hvcn.org
http://www.hvcn.org/info/gswc/society/socypsilanti.htm

NEWSPAPER REPOSITORIES

Detroit Public Library
Burton Historical Collection
5201 Woodward Avenue
Detroit, MI 48202
Tel: 313-833-1000
Fax: 313-832-0877
E-mail: dporemba@detroit.lib.mi.us
http://www.detroit.lib.mi.us/burton/

Grand Rapids Public Library
1100 Hynes Avenue S.W., Suite B
Grand Rapids, MI 49507
Tel: 616-988-5400
http://www.grapids.lib.mi.us/

Michigan Library & Historical Center
Library of Michigan
Genealogical & Local History Collection
717 Allegan Street
P.O. Box 30007
Lansing, MI 48909
Tel: 517-373-1580
http://www.libofmich.lib.mi.us/

University of Michigan/Ann Arbor
Bentley Historical Library
1150 Beall Avenue
Ann Arbor, MI 48109-2113
Tel: 734-764-3482
Fax: 734-936-1333
http://www.umich.edu/~bhl/

VITAL RECORDS

Michigan Department of Community Health
Sixth Floor, Lewis Cass Building
320 South Walnut Street
Lansing, MI 48913
Tel: 517-373-3500
TDD: 517-373-3573
E-mail: arias@michigan.gov
http://www.michigan.gov/mdch

MICHIGAN ON THE WEB

Michigan County Clerks Genealogical Directory
http://www.sos.state.mi.us/history/archive/archgene.html

Michigan GenWeb Project
http://www.rootsweb.com/~migenweb

Michigan in the Civil War
http://users.aol.com/dlharvey/cwmireg.htm

Michigan Library & Historical Center
http://www.libofmich.lib.mi.us/genealogy/genealogy.html

Native Genealogy
http://www.rootsweb.com/~minatam/

Sons of Union Veterans of the Civil War, Department of Michigan
http://www.centuryinter.net/suvcw.mi/index.html

MINNESOTA

ARCHIVES, STATE & NATIONAL

Minnesota State Archives
Minnesota Historical Society Research Center
345 Kellogg Boulevard
St. Paul, MN 55102
Tel: 651-296-6126
http://www.mnhs.org/index.html

National Archives—Central Plains Region
2312 East Bannister Road
Kansas City, MO 64131
Tel: 816-926-6920
Fax: 816-926-6982
E-mail: kansascity.archives@nara.gov
http://www.nara.gov/regional/kansas.html

National Archives—Great Lakes Region
7358 Pulaski Road
Chicago, IL 60629
Tel: 773-581-7816
Fax: 312-886-7883
E-mail: chicago.archives@nara.gov
http://www.nara.gov/regional/chicago.html

GENEALOGICAL SOCIETIES

Anoka County Genealogical Society
2135 Third Avenue North
Anoka, MN 55303-2421
Tel: 763-421-0600
http://freepages.genealogy.rootsweb.com/relativememory/

Carlton County, Genealogical Society of
P.O. Box 204
Cloquet, MN 55720

Chippewa County Genealogical Society
P.O. Box 303
Montevideo, MN 56265

Chisago County Genealogical Society
Chisago Historical Society
P.O. Box 360
Center City, MN 55012

Clarks Grove Area Heritage Society
P.O. Box 188
Clarks Grove, MN 56016

Crow River Genealogical Society
380 School Road, North
Hutchinson, MN 55350

Crow Wing County Genealogical Society
2103 Graydon Avenue
Brainerd, MN 56401

Czechoslovak Genealogical Society International
P.O. Box 16225
St. Paul, MN 55116-0225
Tel: 612-645-4585
http://members.aol.com/CGSI/index.html

Dakota County Genealogical Society
P.O. Box 74
South St. Paul, MN 55075
E-mail: VAlbu@mediaone.net
http://www.geocities.com/Heartland/Flats/9284/

Danish American Genealogical Group
Minnesota Genealogical Society
5768 Olson Memorial Highway
Golden Valley MN 55422
Tel: 763-595-9347
http://mngs.org/

Dodge County Genealogical Society
P.O. Box 683
Dodge Center, MN 55927

Douglas County Genealogical Society
P.O. Box 505
Alexandria, MN 56308
http://www.rootsweb.com/~mndougla/

English Genealogical Society
Minnesota Genealogical Society
5768 Olson Memorial Highway
Golden Valley MN 55422
Tel: 763-595-9347
http://mngs.org/

Freeborn County Genealogical Society
P.O. Box 403
Albert Lea, MN 56007
E-mail: rflisran@smig.net
http://fox.co.net/austin/arts/geneal.html

Fulda Heritage Society
P.O. Box 303
Fulda, MN 56131

German-Bohemian Heritage Society
P.O. Box 822
New Ulm, MN 56073
E-mail: rpaulgb@skypoint.com
http://www.rootsweb.com/~gbhs/

Germanic Genealogical Society
Minnesota Genealogical Society
5768 Olson Memorial Highway
Golden Valley MN 55422
Tel: 763-595-9347
http://mngs.org/

Heart-O-Lakes Genealogical Society
P.O. Box 622
Detroit Lakes, Minnesota 56502-0622
E-mail: holgs2002@hotmail.com
http://www.angelfire.com/mn/HOLGS/

Irish Genealogical Society
P.O. Box 16585
St. Paul, MN 55116-0585
http://www.rootsweb.com/~irish/

Itasca County Genealogical Society
P.O. Box 261
Bovey, MN 55709

Jackson/Cottonwood Genealogical Group
307 North Highway 86
P.O. Box 238
Lakefield, MN 56150
Tel: 507-662-5505

Kandiyohi County, Heritage Searchers of
P.O. Box 175
Willmar, MN 56201-0175

Martin County Genealogical Society
Martin County Public Library
110 North Park Street
Fairmont, MN 56031
Tel: 507-238-4207
Fax: 507-238-4208
http://www.co.martin.mn.us/Library/Library.htm

Meeker County Genealogical Society
308 Marshall Avenue, North
Litchfield, MN 55355

Minnesota Genealogical Society
5768 Olson Memorial Highway
Golden Valley MN 55422
Tel: 763-595-9347
http://mngs.org/

Minnesota, Genealogical Society of
4105-41 st Avenue, South
Minneapolis, MN 55406
Tel: 612-724-2101
http://www.tc.umn.edu/~smith213/

Minnkota Genealogical Society
P.O. Box 12744
Grand Forks, ND 58208
http://www.rootsweb.com/~minnkota/

Mower County Genealogical Society
P.O. Box 145
Austin, MN 55912
Tel: 507-437-6082

Nobles County Genealogical Society
407 12th Street, Suite 2
Worthington, MN 56187-2411

Norwegian American Bygdelagenes Fellesraad
10129 Goodrich Circle
Bloomington, MN 55437
Tel: 612-831-4409
http://www.mtn.org/mgs/branches/naga/nagaindx. htm

Olmsted County Genealogical Society
P.O. Box 6411
Rochester, MN 55903
Tel: 507-282-9447
E-mail: ochs@olmstedhistory.com
http://olmstedhistory.com/ocgs.htm

Otter Tail County Genealogical Society
1110 Lincoln Avenue, West
Fergus Falls, MN 56537
Tel: 218-736-6038

Pipestone County Genealogical Society
Pipestone County Museum
113 South Hiawatha
Pipestone, MN 56164
Tel: 507-825-2563
E-mail: pipctymu@rconnect.com
http://www.pipestoneminnesota.com/museum/

Polish Genealogical Society of Minnesota
Minnesota Genealogical Society
5768 Olson Memorial Highway
Golden Valley MN 55422
Tel: 763-595-9347
http://www.rootsweb.com/~mnpolgs/pgs-mn.html

Prairieland Genealogical Society
Southwest Historical Center, Room 141
Southwest State University
Marshall, MN 56258
Tel: 507-537-7373
E-mail: cmolitor@starpoint.net

Rainy River Valley Genealogical Society
P.O. Box 1032
International Falls, MN 56649

Range Genealogical Society
P.O. Box 388
Chisholm, MN 55719

Red River Valley Genealogical Society
P.O. Box 9284
Fargo, ND 58106

Renville County Genealogical Society
211 North Main Street
P.O. Box 331
Renville, MN 56284
http://ci.renville.mn.us/rcgs/

Rice County Genealogical Society
408 Division Street
Northfield, MN 55057

St. Cloud Area Genealogist, Inc.
P.O. Box 213
St. Cloud, MN 56302
Tel: 320-252-6673
E-mail: annettedt@astound.net
http://www.rootsweb.com/~mnscag/SCAG/

Scandinavian American Genealogical Society
Minnesota Genealogical Society
5768 Olson Memorial Highway
Golden Valley MN 55422
Tel: 763-595-9347

South Central Minnesota Genealogical Society
110 North Park Street
Fairmont, MN 56031

Stevens County Genealogical Society
West 6th and Nevada
Morris, MN 56267

Swedish Genealogical Group of Minnesota
Minnesota Genealogical Society
5768 Olson Memorial Highway
Golden Valley MN 55422
Tel: 763-595-9347

Traverse des Sioux Genealogical Society/Mankato
815 Nicollet Avenue
North Mankato, MN 56001

Traverse des Sioux Genealogical Society/St. Peter
Treaty Site History Center
1851 North Minnesota Avenue
St. Peter, MN 56082

Twin Ports Genealogical Society
P.O. Box 16895
Duluth, MN 55806

Waseca Area Genealogical Society
P.O. Box 364
Waseca, MN 56093
Tel: 507-835-7700

White Bear Lake Genealogical Society
P.O. Box 10555
White Bear Lake, MN 55110

Wilkin County Historical Society, Genealogy Committee
704 Nebraska Avenue
Breckenridge, MN 56520
Tel: 218-643-1303

Winona County Genealogical Roundtable/Society
P.O. Box 363
Winona, MN 55987

Wright County Genealogical Society
911 2nd Avenue, South
Buffalo, MN 55313

Yankee Genealogical Society
Minnesota Genealogical Society
5768 Olson Memorial Highway
Golden Valley, MN 55422
Tel: 763-595-9347
http://www.mtn.org/mgs/branches/yankee.html

HISTORICAL SOCIETIES

Afton Historical Society
P.O. Box 178
Afton, MN 55001
Tel: 651-436-3500

Aitkin County Historical Society
20 Pacific Street, SW
P.O. Box 215
Aitkin, MN 56431
Tel: 218-927-3348
E-mail: achs@mlecmn.net
http://www.aitkin.com/achs/

Albany Historical Society
P.O. Box 25
Albany, MN 56307

Alden Community Historical Society
P.O. Box 323
Alden, MN 56009

American Historical Society of Germans from Russia (AHSGR)
North Star Chapter - Minnesota
175 Spring Valley Drive
Bloomington, MN 55420-5337
E-mail: dochaas@isd.net
http://www.ahsgr.org/mnnostar.html

Anoka County Historical Society/Library
2135 Third Avenue North
Anoka, MN 55303-2421
Tel: 763-421-0600
http://www.ac-hs.org/

Atwater Area History Society
108 N. 3rd Street
Atwater, MN 56209
Tel: 320-974-8284

Barnesville Heritage Society
P.O. Box 126
Barnesville, MN 56514

Bay Area Historical Society
Outer Drive
P.O. Box 33
Silver Bay, MN 55614
Tel: 612-226-4870

Becker County Historical Society
P.O. Box 622
Detroit Lakes, MN 56502
Tel: 218-847-2938
Fax: 218-847-5048
E-mail: bech39@beckercountyhistory.org
http://www.beckercountyhistory.org/

Belle Plaine Historical Society
South Cedar Avenue
P.O. Box 73
Belle Plaine, MN 56011
Tel: 952-873-6109

Beltrami County Historical Society
County Fairgrounds T.H. #71
P.O. Box 683
Bemidji, MN 56601
Tel: 218-444-3376
E-mail: depot@paulbunyan.net
http://www.paulbunyan.net/users/depot/

Benton County Historical Society
218 1st Street, North
P.O. Box 245
Sauk Rapids, MN 56379
Tel: 320-253-9614

Big Stone County Historical Society
RR 2, Box 31
Ortonville, MN 56278
Tel: 320-839-3359

Bloomington Historical Society
10200 Penn Avenue, South
Bloomington, MN 55431
Mail:
2525 W. Old Shakopee Road
Bloomington, MN 55431
Tel: 612-948-8881

Blue Earth County Historical Society/Museum
415 Cherry Street
Mankato, MN 56001
Tel: 507-345-5566

Brooklyn Center Historical Society
P.O. Box 29345
Brooklyn Center, MN 55429

Brown County Historical Society
2 North Broadway
P.O. Box 116
New Ulm, MN 56073
Tel: 507-354-2016

Browns Valley Historical Society
514 3rd Street, South
Browns Valley, MN 56219

Cannon Falls Area Historical Society
P.O. Box 111
Cannon Falls, MN 55009
Tel: 507-263-4080

Canosia Historical Society
5762 North Pike Lake
Duluth, MN 55811

Carlton County Historical Society
History & Heritage Center
406 Cloquet Avenue
Cloquet, MN 55720
Tel: 218-879-1938
E-mail: CCHS@cpinternet.com
http://www.carltoncountyhs.org/snews/vxv1/pg4.htm

Carver County Historical Society
555 West 1st Street
Waconia, MN 55387
Tel: 612-442-4234

Cass County Historical Society
P.O. Box 505
Walker, MN 56484
Tel: 218-547-3300 ext. 251

Center City Historical Society
P.O. Box 366
Center City, MN 55012

Chaska Historical Society
City Hall
205 East 4th Street
Chaska, MN 55318
Tel: 612-448-6077
612-448-4458

Chatfield Historical Society
RR 1
Chatfield, MN 55923

Chippewa County Historical Society
151 Pioneer Drive
P.O. Box 303
Montevideo, MN 56265
Tel: 320-269-7636
E-mail: CCHS.June@juno.com
http://www.montechamber.com/cchs/cchshp.htm

Chisago County Historical Society
30495 Park Street
P.O. Box 146
Lindstrom, MN 55045-0146
Tel: 651-257-5310

Chisago County Historical Society, North Chapter
51245 Fairfield Avenue
Rush City, MN 55609

Clarks Grove Area Heritage Society
P.O. Box 188
Clarks Grove, MN 56016

Clay County Historical Society
Heritage Hjemkomst Interpretive Center
202 First Avenue, North
P.O. Box 501
Moorhead, MN 56560
Tel: 218-233-4604
E-mail: mpeihl@delphi.com
http://www.gps.com/Pioneer_Spirit/THEN/authors.htm

Clearwater County Historical Society
112 2nd Avenue
P.O. Box 241
Bagley, MN 56621
Tel: 218-785-2000
http://www.rrv.net/bagleymn/histSoc.htm

Cokato-Finnish American Society
10783 County Road 3, SW
Cokato, MN 55321
E-mail: lpoko@xtratyme.com
http://www.cokato.mn.us/org/fahs.html

Cokato Historical Society
Cokato Museum & Library Building
175 4th Street West
P.O. Box 269
Cokato, MN 55321
Tel: 320-286-2427
E-mail: cokatomuseum@cmgate/com
http://www.cokato.mn.us/org/chs.html

Comfrey Area Historical Society
P.O. Box 218
Comfrey, MN 56019

Cook County Historical Society
Lightkeepers House
4 Broadway
P.O. Box 1293
Grand Marais, MN 55604
Tel: 218-387-2314

Coon Rapids Historical Society
11155 Robinson Drive
Coon Rapids, MN 55433
Tel: 763-755-2880

Cottonwood Area Historical Society
Cottonwood Library
86 Main Street West
P.O. Box 106
Cottonwood, MN 56229-0106
Tel: 507-423-6488
Fax: 507-423-5638

Cottonwood County Historical Society
Museum and Research Library
812 4th Avenue
Windom, MN 56101
Tel: 507-831-1134
http://www.rootsweb.com/~mncotton/cchs.htm

Crosslake Area Historical Society
P.O. Box 369
Crosslake, MN 56442

Crow Wing Historical Society
320 Laurel Street
P.O. Box 722
Brainerd, MN 56401
Tel: 218-829-3268
E-mail: cwchistsoc@brainerdonline.com
http://www.brainerdonline.com/museum/

Cuyuna Range Historical Society
101 1st Street, NE
P.O. Box 128
Crosby, MN 56441
Tel: 218-546-6178

Dakota County Historical Society
130 3rd Avenue, North
South St. Paul, MN 55075
Tel: 651-552-7548
Fax: 651-552-7265
http://www.dakotahistory.org/DCHS%20Home%20Page.asp

Dodge County Historical Society
P.O. Box 433
Mantorville, MN 55955
Tel: 507-635-5508

Douglas County Historical Society
1219 South Nokomis
Alexandria, MN 56308
Tel: 320-762-0382
http://www.rea-alp.com/~historic/

East Grand Forks, Heritage Foundation of
218 NW 4th Street
P.O. Box 295
East Grand Forks, MN 56721
Tel: 218-773-7481

East Otter Tail Historical Society
349 2nd Avenue,
SE Perham, MN 56573

Eden Prairie Historical Society
Eden Prairie City Hall
8950 Eden Prairie Road
Eden Prairie, MN 55344
Tel: 612-944-2486

Edina Historical Society
4711 West 70th St.
Edina, MN 55424
Tel: 952-920-8952

Ellendale Area Historical Society
P.O. Box 334
Ellendale, MN 56026

Ely-Winton Historical Society
1900 Camp Street
Ely, MN 55731
Tel: 218-365-3226

England Prairie Pioneer Club
P.O. Box 127
Verndale, MN 56481

Esko Historical Society
5 Elizabeth Avenue
Esko, MN 55733

Evansville Historical Foundation
P.O. Box 337
Evansville, MN 56326
Tel: 218-948-2010

Excelsior/Lake Minnetonka Historical Society
P.O. Box 305
Excelsior, MN 55331

Faribault County Historical Society
405 E. Sixth Street
Blue Earth, MN 56013
Tel: 507-526-5421

Fillmore County Historical Society
Route 1, Box 81-D
Fountain, MN 55935
Tel: 507-268-4449

Finland Historical Society
P.O. Box 583
Finland, MN 55603

Finnish-American Historical Society, Minnesota
P.O. Box 34
Wolf Lake, MN 56593

Freeborn County Historical Society
1031 Bridge Avenue
P.O. Box 105
Albert Lea, MN 56007
Tel: 507-373-8003
E-mail: rflisran@wolf.co.net

Fridley Historical Society
5273 NE Horizon
Drive Fridley, MN 55432

Golden Valley Historical Society
7800 Golden Valley Road
Golden Valley, MN 55427

Goodhue Area Historical Society
P.O. Box 141
Goodhue, MN 55027

Goodhue County Historical Society
1166 Oak Street
Red Wing, MN 55066
Tel: 651-388-6024
Fax: 651-388-3577
E-mail: goodhuecountyhis@qwest.net
http://www.goodhuehistory.mus.mn.us/

Goodridge Area Historical Society
Goodridge City Hall
P.O. Box 171
Goodridge, MN 56725

Grant County Historical Society
P.O. Box 1002
Elbow Lake, MN 56531
Tel: 218-685-4864

Hastings Historical Society
109 1/2 2nd Street, East
Hastings, MN 55033

Hennepin County Historical Society
Hennepin History Museum
2303 3rd Avenue, South
Minneapolis, MN 55404
Tel: 612-870-1329
Fax: 612-870-1320
E-mail: hhmuseum@mtn.org
http://www.hhmuseum.org/

Hesper/Mabel Area Historical Society
P.O. Box 56
Mable, MN 55954

Hibbing Historical Society
400 E. 23rd Street
Hibbing, MN 55746
Tel: 218-263-8522
http://www.uslink.net/~hibbhist/

Hill Farm Historical Society
28 Meadowlark Lane
North Oaks, MN 55127

Hollandale Area Historical Society
P.O. Box 184
Hollandale, MN 56045

Hopkins Historical Society
Hopkins Community Center
33 14th Street, North
Hopkins, MN 55343
Mail: 1010 1st Street, South
Hopkins, MN 55343
Tel: 952-979-0447
http://www.hopkinsmn.com/communityfacilities/
historicalsociety.htm

Houston County Historical Society
Museum on the fairgrounds
P.O. Box 173
Houston, MN 55943
Tel: 507-724-3884

Hubbard County Historical Society
Hubbard County Historical Museum
301 Court Avenue
P.O. Box 327
Park Rapids, MN 56470
Tel: 218-732-5237

Irish-American Cultural Institute
683 Osceola Avenue
St. Paul, MN 55105
Tel: 651-962-6040
Fax: 651-962-6043

Iron Range Historical Society
Gilbert City Hall, 2nd Floor
P.O. Box 786
Gilbert, MN 55741
Tel: 218-749-3150
http://www.angelfire.com/mn3/gilbert/
ironrangehistoricalsociety.html

Isanti County Historical Society
139 East 1st Avenue
P.O. Box 525
Cambridge, MN 55008
Tel: 763-689-4229
http://www.rootsweb.com/~mnisanti/Isanti/historical.html

Itasca County Historical Society
105th Street, NW
P.O. Box 664
Grand Rapids, MN 55744
Tel: 218-326-6431

Jackson County Historical Society
307 North Highway 86
P.O. Box 238
Lakefield, MN 56150
Tel: 507-662-5505

Jasper Historical Society
217 2nd Street, SE
Jasper, MN 56144

Jewish Historical Society of the Upper Midwest
1554 Midway Parkway
St. Paul, MN 55108
Tel: 651-637-0202 ext. 202
E-mail: history@jhsum.org
http://www.tc.umn.edu/~schlo006/

Kanabec County Historical Society
P.O. Box 113
Mora, MN 55051

Kandiyohi County Historical Society
617 NE Hwy 71
Willmar, MN 56201
Tel: 320-235-1881
E-mail: kandhist@wecnet.com
http://freepages.genealogy.rootsweb.com/~kchs123/

Kenyon Area Historical Society
Gunderson House
107 Gunderson Blvd.
Kenyon, MN 55946
Tel: 507-789-5954

Kittson County Historical Society
P.O. Box 100
Lake Bronson, MN 56734
Tel: 218-754-4100

Koochiching County Historical Society
Smoky Bear Park
214 6th Avenue.
P.O. Box 1147
International Falls, MN 56649
Tel: 218-283-4316

Lac Qui Parle County Historical Society
South T.H. 75
P.O. Box 124
Madison, MN 56256
Tel: 320-598-7678

La Societe Canadienne Française du Minnesota
4895 Bryant Avenue
Inver Grove Heights, MN 55075

Lake Benton Historical Society
115 1/2 South Center Street
P.O. Box 218
Lake Benton, MN 56149-0218
Tel: 507-368-4214

Lake City Historical Society
City Hall
205 W Center Street
Lake City, MN 55041

Lake County Historical Society
Railroad Depot Museum
P.O. Box 313
Two Harbors, MN 55616
Tel: 218-834-4898

Lake Crystal Historical Society
132 North Grove
Lake Crystal, MN 56055

Lake of the Woods County Historical Society
County Museum
119 8th Avenue, SE
P.O. Box 808
Baudette, MN 56623
Tel: 218-634-1200

Lake Park Area Historical Society
RR 1, Box 124A
Lake Park, MN 56544

Lakeville Area Historical Society
20195 Holyoke Avenue
Lakeville, MN 55044
Tel: 952-985-4406
952-985-2700
http://www.rootsweb.com/~mnlahs/

Lamberton Area Historical Society
110 2nd Avenue, West
Lamberton, MN 56152

Lanesboro Historical Society
105 Parkway, South
P.O. Box 354
Lanesboro, MN 55949

Le Sueur County Historical Society
P.O. Box 240
Elysian, MN 56028
Tel: 507-627-4620

Le Sueur Historians
709 North 2nd Street
Le Sueur, MN 56058
Tel: 507-665-2050

Lincoln County Historical Society
610 West Elm
Hendricks, MN 56136
Mail:
406 Brooks Street
Hendricks, MN 56136
Tel: 507-275-3537

Lindstrom Historical Society
P.O. Box 12
Lindstrom, MN 55045

Little Canada Historical Society
515 East Little Canada Road
Little Canada, MN 55117
Tel: 651-766-4029
Fax: 651-766-4048
http://hometown.aol.com/littlecanadamn/
HomePage-index.html

Lyon County Historical Society
114 North Third Street
Marshall, MN 56258
Tel: 507-537-6580

Madison Lake Area Historical Society
525 Main Street
Madison Lake, MN 56063

Mahnomen County Historical Society
P.O. Box 123
Mahnomen, MN 56557
Tel: 218-935-5490

Marine Historical Society
Stone House Museum
5th & Oak Streets
Marine on St. Croix, MN 55047

Marshall County Historical Society
Historical Visitor Center
P.O. Box 103
Warren, MN 56762
Tel: 218-745-4803

Martin County Historical Society
304 East Blue Earth Avenue
Fairmont, MN 56031
Tel: 507-235-5178
http://www.co.martin.mn.us/mchs/

Masonic Historical Society and Museum, Minnesota
200 E. Plato Blvd.
St. Paul, MN 55107
Tel: 651-222-6051
Fax: 651-222-6144
http://mn-mason.org/mmhsm.html

McLeod County Historical Society
380 North School Road
Hutchinson, MN 55350
Tel: 320-587-2109

Meeker County Historical Society
308 Marshall Avenue, North
Litchfield, MN 55355
Tel: 320-693-8911

Menahga Area Historical Society
P.O. Box 299
Menahga, MN 56464

Mendota/West St. Paul Historical Society
1160 Dodd Road
Mendota Heights, MN 55118

Military Historical Society of Minnesota
Minnesota Military Museum
15000 Highway 115
Little Falls, MN 56345-4173
Tel: 320-632-7374
Fax: 320-632-7702
http://www.dma.state.mn.us/cpripley/SpecFeatures/
     muse1.htm

Mille Lacs County Historical Society
Depot Museum
101 South 10th Avenue
Princeton, MN 55371
Tel: 763-389-1296
http://mlchs.tripod.com/mlchshome.html

Minnesota Historical Society
345 Kellogg Boulevard
St. Paul, MN 55102-1906
Tel: 651-296-2143
Fax: 651-297-7436
E-mail: reference@mnhs.org
http://www.mnhs.org/

Minnesota Lake Area Historical Society
Kremer House
P.O. Box 225
Minnesota Lake, MN 56068
Tel: 507-462-3420
http://www.minnesotalake.com/Tourism/kremer. html

Minnetonka Historical Society
Burwell House
13209 McGinty Road, East
Minnetonka, MN 55343
Tel: 952-933-1611
E-mail: mhs@ci.minnetonka.mn.us
http://www.minnetonka-history.org/

Missabe Railroad Historical Society
506 W. Michigan Street
Duluth, MN 55802
E-mail: missabe@chartermi.net
http://www1.minn.net/~mspanton/

Moose Lake Historical Society
Village Hall Museum
205 Elm
Moose Lake, MN 55767
Tel: 218-485-4680

Morrison County Historical Society
The Charles A. Weyerhaeuser Memorial Museum
P.O. Box 239
2151 South Lindberg Drive
Little Falls, MN 56345
Tel: 320-632-4007
http://www.upstel.net/~johns/History/MorrisonCo.html

Morristown Historical Society
P.O. Box 113
Morristown, MN 55052

Mower County Historical Society
Mower County Fairgrounds
1303 SW 6th Avenue
P.O. Box 804
Austin, MN 55912
Tel: 507-437-6082
http://www2.smig.net/mchistory/

Murray County Historical Society
2480 29th Street
P.O. Box 61
Slayton, Minnesota 56172
Tel: 507-836-6533
E-mail: society@frontiernet.net
http://murray-countymn.com/museum.htm

New Brighton Area Historical Society
850 Emerald Court
New Brighton, MN 55112

New York Mills/Finnish American Society
P.O. Box 316
New York Mills, MN 56567
Tel: 218-385-2085

Nicollet County Historical Society
Treaty Site History Center
1851 North Minnesota Avenue
St. Peter, MN 56082
Tel: 507-931-2160
Fax: 507-931-0172
E-mail: wea13@mnic.net
http://emuseum.mnsu.edu/history/treatycenter/

Nobles County Historical Society
407 12th Street, Suite 2
Worthington, MN 56187
Tel: 507-376-3125
E-mail: demuth@worthington.mn.frontiercomm.net

Norman County Historical Society
409 East 1st Avenue
Ada, MN 56510
Tel: 218-784-4989

North St. Paul Historical Society
2666 E. 7th Avenue
North St. Paul, MN 55109
Tel: 651-779-6402

Northfield Historical Society
408 Division Street
Northfield, MN 55057
Tel: 507-645-9268
http://www.northfieldhistory.org/

Norwegian-American Historical Association (NAHA)
1510 St. Olaf Avenue
Northfield, MN 55057
Tel: 507-646-3452 (Reference)
Fax: 507-646-3734
E-mail: naha@stolaf.edu
http://www.naha.stolaf.edu/

Olmsted County Historical Society
Mayowood Mansion
1195 County Road 22, SW
Rochester, MN 55902
Tel: 507-282-9447
E-mail: ochs@olmstedhistory.com
http://olmstedhistory.com/

Otter Tail County Historical Society
1110 W. Lincoln
Fergus Falls, MN 56537
Tel: 218-736-6038
Fax: 218-739-3075
E-mail: otchs@yahoo.com
http://www.fergusfalls.com/tourism/museum.html

Paul Bunyan Historical Society
Route 2, Box 131
Akeley, MN 56433

Paynesville Historical Society
570 River Street
Paynesville, MN 56362

Pennington County Historical Society
Peder Engelstad Pioneer Village
Oakland Park Road
P.O. Box 127
Thief River Falls, MN 56701
Tel: 218-681-5767
http://pvillage.org/

Pine County Historical Society
305 Governors Way
Sandstone, MN 55704

Pipestone County Historical Society
Pipestone County Museum
113 South Hiawatha
Pipestone, MN 56164
Tel: 507-825-2563
E-mail: pipctymu@rconnect.com
http://www.pipestoneminnesota.com/museum/

Plymouth Historical Society
3605 Fernbrook Lane
Plymouth, MN 55447
Mail:
3400 Plymouth Blvd.
Plymouth, MN 55447
Tel: 763-559-9201

Polk County Historical Society
US Hwy. 2
P.O. Box 214
Crookston, MN 56716
Tel: 218-281-1038
http://crookston.net/Museum/

Pope County Historical Society
809 S. Lakeshore Drive
Glenwood, MN 56334
Tel: 320-634-3293

Preston Historical Society
Houston & Preston Streets
Preston, MN 55965

Ramsey County Historical Society
75 West 5th Street, Room 323
St. Paul, MN 55102
Tel: 651-222-0701
Fax: 651-223-8539
E-mail: info@rchs.com
http://www.rchs.com/

314

Red Lake County Historical Society
Lake Pleasant School House
Route 1, Box 298
Red Lake Falls, MN 56750

Redwood County Historical Society
RR 2, Box 12
Redwood Falls, MN 56283
Tel: 507-637-3329

Renville County Historical Society
441 North Park Drive
P.O. Box 266
Morton, MN 56270
Tel: 507-697-6147

Rice County Historical Society
Museum and Genealogical Research Center
1814 NW 2nd Avenue
Faribault, MN 55021
Tel: 507-332-2121

Richfield Historical Society
6900 Lyndale Avenue, South
P.O. Box 23304
Richfield, MN 55423
Tel: 612-869-2049

Rock County Historical Society
Hinkly House
P.O. Box 741
Luverne, MN 56156
http://www.rockartsrock.com/rchs.htm

Rockford Area Historical Society
Ames-Florida-Stork House
8131 Bridge Street
P.O. Box 186
Rockford, MN 55373
Tel: 763-477-5383

Roseau County Historical Society
Roseau County Museum and Center
505 2nd Avenue, NE
Roseau, MN 56751
Tel: 218-463-1918
http://www.roseaucohistoricalsociety.org/

Rosemount Area Historical Society
15335 Danbury Avenue
Rosemount, MN 55068
E-mail: rosemounthistory@hotmail.com
http://www.rootsweb.com/~mnrahs/

Roseville Historical Society
110 2nd Avenue N.E.
Roseau, MN 56751

Royalton Historical Society
P.O. Box 196
Royalton, MN 56373

Rushford Area Historical Organization
403 East North Street
Rushford, MN 55971

Sacred Heart Area Historical Society
Rural Route 2
Sacred Heart, MN 56285

St. Francis Historical Society
22731 Rum River Blvd., NW
St. Francis, MN 55070
Tel: 763-753-1224

St. Louis County Historical Society
506 West Michigan Street
Duluth, MN 55802-1505
Tel: 218-727-8025
E-mail: steve@thehistorypeople.org
http://www.thehistorypeople.org/

St. Louis Park Historical Society
Jovig Park
6210 West 37th Street
St. Louis Park, MN 55426

Sauk Centre Area Historical Society
1725 Sinclair Lewis Avenue
Sauk Centre, MN 56378

Schroeder Area Historical Society
9248 W. Highway 61
Schroeder, MN 55613

Scott County Historical Society
235 South Fuller
Shakopee, MN 55379
Tel: 952-445-0378
Fax: 952-445-4154
E-mail: info@scottcountyhistory.org
http://www.scottcountyhistory.org/

Sherburne County Historical Society
13122 First Street
Becker, MN 55308
Tel: 763-261-4433
E-mail: schs@sherbtel.net
http://www.rootsweb.com/~mnschs/home.htm

Sibley County Historical Society
700 Main Street
P.O. Box 407
Henderson, MN 56044
Tel: 507-248-3434
http://history.sibley.mn.us/

Sleepy Eye Historical Society
316 Walnut, SE
Sleepy Eye, MN 56085

South St. Paul Historical Society
345 7th Avenue, South
South St. Paul, MN 55075

Spencer Brook Historical Society
RR 3
Princeton, MN 55371

Spring Valley Community Historical Society, Inc.
112 South Washington Avenue
Spring Valley, MN 55975
Mail:
909 South Broadway
Spring Valley, MN 55975

Stearns County Historical Society
Stearns County Heritage Center
235 33rd Avenue, South
P.O. Box 702
St. Cloud, MN 56302
Tel: 320-253-8424

Steele County Historical Society
1448 Austin Road
Owatonna, MN 55060
Tel: 507-451-1420

Stevens County Historical Society
West 6th & Nevada
Morris, MN 56267
Tel: 320-589-1719
E-mail: history@infolink.morris.mn.us

Swift County Historical Society
2135 Minnesota Avenue
Building #2
Benson, MN 56215
Tel: 320-843-4467

Taylors Falls Historical Society
505 Folsom Street
Taylors Falls, MN 55084
Tel: 651-465-3125

Territorial Pioneers
1395 McKinley
St. Paul, MN 55108

Todd County Historical Society
333 Central Avenue
Long Prairie, MN 56347

Tofte Historical Society
P.O. Box 2312
Tofte, MN 55615-2312

Tower Soudan Historical Society
Train Coach
P.O. Box 413
Tower, MN 55790
Tel: 218-753-3039

Traverse County Historical Society
RR 1, Box 42
Wheaton, MN 56396

Upsala Area Historical Society
Borgstrom House
Highway 238
P.O. Box 35
Upsala, MN 56384
Tel: 320-573-4208
http://www.upstel.net/~johns/History/History.html

Verndale Historical Society
North 3rd Street & Main Street
Verndale, MN 56481

Virginia Area Historical Society
P.O. Box 736
Virginia, MN 55792
Tel: 218-741-1136

Wabasha County Historical Society
503 West Center Street
Lake City, MN 55041

Wabasso County Historical Society
564 South Street
Wabasso, MN 56293

Wadena County Historical Society
603 North Jefferson
Wadena, MN 56482

Warroad Historical Society
Warroad Heritage Center
202 Main Avenue, NE
P.O. Box 688
Warroad, MN 56763
Tel: 218-386-1283

Waseca County Historical Society
315 2nd Avenue, NE
P.O. Box 314
Waseca, MN 56093
Tel: 507-835-7700
http://www.historical.waseca.mn.us/

Washington County Historical Society
602 North Main Street
P.O. Box 167
Stillwater, MN 55082
Tel: 651-439-5956
http://www.wchsmn.org/

Watonwan County Historical Society
423 Dill Avenue, SW
P.O. Box 126
Madelia, MN 56062
Tel: 507-642-3247
http://www.rootsweb.com/~mnwatonw/wchs.htm

Wawina Area Historical Society
P.O. Box 102
Wawina, MN 55794

Wayzata Historical Society
At the Depot
402 East Lake Street
Wayzata, MN 55391
http://www.wayzatahistory.org/

Welcome Historical Society
109 Hulseman
Welcome, MN 56181
Tel: 507-728-8806

West Concord Historical Society
P.O. Box 346
West Concord, MN 55985

West Side Historical Society
625 Stryker Avenue
St. Paul, MN 55107

Western Hennepin County Pioneers Association
1953 West Wayzata Blvd.
P.O. Box 332
Long Lake, MN 55356
Tel: 952-473-6557

Westonka Historical Society
3740 Enchanted Lane
Mound, MN 55364

Wilkin County Historical Society
704 Nebraska Avenue
P.O. Box 212
Breckenridge, MN 56520
Tel: 218-643-1303

Winnebago Historical Society/Museum
P.O. Box 35
Winnebago, MN 56098
Tel: 507-893-4660

Winona County Historical Society
160 Johnson Street
Winona, MN 55987
Tel: 507-454-2723
Fax: 507-454-0006
http://www.winona.msus.edu/historicalsociety/

Wright County Historical Society
2001 Highway 25, North
Buffalo, Mn 55313
Tel: 763-682-7323

Yellow Medicine County Historical Society
Junction T.H. 67 & 23
P.O. Box 145
Granite Falls, MN 56241
Tel: 320-564-4479
E-mail: ymchs@kilowatt.net
http://www.kilowatt.net/ymchs/index.html

LDS FAMILY HISTORY CENTERS

For locations of Family History Centers in this state, see the Family History Center locator at FamilySearch.
http://www.familysearch.org/eng/Library/FHC/frameset_fhc.asp

ARCHIVES/LIBRARIES/MUSEUMS

Amador Heritage Center
Route 2, Box 191
North Branch, MN 55056

American Swedish Institute
2600 Park Avenue
Minneapolis, MN 55407-1090
Tel: 612-871-4907
Fax: 612-871-8682
http://www.americanswedishinst.org/

Anoka County/Northtown Central Library
707 Highway 10, NE
Blaine, MN 55434
Tel: 612-784-1100
Fax: 612-784-3233
TDD: 612-784-7013

Archdiocese of St. Paul & Minneapolis
226 Summit Avenue
St. Paul, MN 55102
Tel: 651-291-4400
E-mail: communications@archspm.org
http://www.archspm.org/

Austin-Mower County Public Library
323 4th Avenue NE
Austin, MN 55912
Tel: 507-433-2391
Fax: 507-433-8787
TTY: 507-433-8665
E-mail: austinmnpl@selco.lib.mn.us
http://www.spamtownusa.com/apl/

Bemidji State University
A.C. Clark Library
1500 Birchmont Drive, NE
Bemidji, MN 56601
Tel: 218-755-3342
Fax: 218-755-2051
E-mail: library@beaver.bemidji.msus.edu
http://www.bemidjistate.edu/library/

Bethel Theological Seminary Library/Archives
3949 Bethel Drive
St. Paul, MN 55112
Tel: 651-638-6180
http://www.bethel.edu/Welcome.html

Blue Earth County Historical Society/Museum
415 Cherry Street
Mankato, MN 56001
Tel: 507-345-5566

Carleton College
Lawrence McKinley Gould Memorial Library
Northfield, MN 55057-4097
Tel: 507-646-4260
Fax: 507-646-4087
http://www.library.carleton.edu/

Cleveland Historical Center
303 Broadway
Cleveland, MN 56017
Tel: 507-931-1510

Concordia College
Carl B. Ylvisaker Library
Moorhead, MN 56560
Tel: 218-299-4239
http://home.cord.edu/dept/library/

Dakota County Library
1340 Wescott Road
Eagan, MN 55123
Tel: 651-688-1500
Fax: 651-688-1515
http://www.co.dakota.mn.us/library/

Duluth Public Library
520 West Superior Street
Duluth, MN 55802
Tel: 218-723-3800
Fax: 218-723-3815
http://www.duluth.lib.mn.us/

Ethnic Cultural Center of Minnesota
400 Third Avenue, South
South St. Paul, MN 55075
Tel: 651-455-4449

Gustavus Adolphus College
Folke Bernadotte Memorial Library
800 W. College Avenue
St. Peter, MN 56082
Tel: 507-933-7556
http://www.gac.edu/oncampus/academics/library/

Hamline University
School of Law Library
1536 Hewitt Avenue
St. Paul, MN 55104
Tel: 651-523-2125
http://www.hamline.edu/law/library/

Henderson Public Library
110 South 6th Street
Henderson, MN 56044
Tel: 507-248-3880

Hennepin County Historical Society
Hennepin History Museum
2303 3rd Avenue, South
Minneapolis, MN 55404
Tel: 612-870-1329
Fax: 612-870-1320
E-mail: hhmuseum@mtn.org
http://www.hhmuseum.org/

Hennepin County Public Library/Southdale
7001 York Avenue
Edina, MN 55435
Tel: 952-847-5900
http://www.hennepin.lib.mn.us/

Heritage/Hjemkomst Interpretive Center
202 1st Avenue, North
Moorhead, MN 56560
Tel: 218-233-5604
http://www.artcom.com/museums/vs/gl/56560-19.htm

Immigration History Research Center
University of Minnesota
College of Liberal Arts
311 Andersen Library
222-21st Avenue S.
Minneapolis MN 55455-0439
Tel: 612-625-4800
Fax: 612-626-0018
http://www.umn.edu/ihrc/

Iron Range Research Center
Ironworld Complex
Highway 169 West
P.O. Box 392
Chisholm, MN 55719
Tel: 218-254-7959
E-mail: yourroots@ironworld.com
http://www.ironrangeresearchcenter.org/

Kanabec History Center
805 West Forest Avenue
P.O. Box 113
Mora, MN 55051
Tel: 320-679-1665
Fax: 320-679-1673
http://www.kanabechistory.com/

Luther Seminary
Gullixson Hall
Region 3 Archives, 3rd floor
2481 Como Avenue
St. Paul, MN 55108
Tel: 651-641-3456
Fax: 651-523-1609
http://www.luthersem.edu/archives/

Mankato State University
Memorial Library
Southern Minnesota Historical Center
Maywood and Ellis
MSU #19, P.O. Box 8419
Mankato, MN 56002
Tel: 507-389-5952
507-389-5953
Fax: 507-389-5155
E-mail: libweb@mankato.msus.edu
http://www.lib.mankato.msus.edu/

Masonic Historical Society and Museum, Minnesota
200 E. Plato Blvd.
St. Paul, MN 55107
Tel: 651-222-6051
Fax: 651-222-6144
http://mn-mason.org/mmhsm.html

Mayo Foundation Archives & Historical Area
200 1st Street, SW
Rochester, MN 55901
Tel: 507-282-2511 ext. 2585

Minneapolis Public Library
Minneapolis Collection
300 Nicollet Mall
Minneapolis, MN 55401
Tel: 612-630-6000
http://www.mpls.lib.mn.us/

Minneapolis Regional Native American Center
1530 East Franklin Avenue
Minneapolis, MN 55404
Tel: 612-879-1750

Minnesota Alliance of Local Historical Museums
Stearns County Historical Society
P.O. Box 702
St. Cloud, MN 56302
Tel: 320-253-8424

Minnesota Genealogical Society
5768 Olson Memorial Highway
Golden Valley, MN 55422
Tel: 763-595-9347
http://mngs.org/

Minnesota Historical Society
345 Kellogg Boulevard
St. Paul, MN 55102-1906
Tel: 651-296-2143
Fax: 651-297-7436
E-mail: reference@mnhs.org
http://www.mnhs.org/

Minnesota Military Museum
Camp Ripley
15000 Highway 115
Little Falls, MN 56345-4173
Tel: 320-632-7374
Fax: 320-632-7702
E-mail: mnmuseum@brainerd.net
http://www.dma.state.mn.us/cpripley/SpecFeatures/
    muse1.htm

Minnesota State Law Library
Minnesota Judicial Center Room G25
25 Constitution Avenue
St. Paul, MN 55155-6122
Tel: 651-296-2775
Fax: 651-296-6740
TDD: 651-282-5352
http://www.state.mn.us/courts/library/

Monastic Heritage Museum
Saint Benedict's Monastery
104 Chapel Lane
St. Joseph, MN 56374-0220
Tel: 320-363-7100
Fax: 320-363-7130
E-mail: pruether@csbsju.edu (General Inquiries)
rboedigheim@csbsju.edu (Archives)
http://www.sbm.osb.org/

Moorhead State University
Livingston Lord Library
Northwest Minnesota Historical Center
1104 7th Avenue, South
Moorhead, MN 56563
Tel: 218-236-2461
E-mail: shoptaug@mhdli.moor
http://www.moorhead.msus.edu/library/

Nicollet County Historical Society
Treaty Site History Center
1851 North Minnesota Avenue
St. Peter, MN 56082
Tel: 507-931-2160
Fax: 507-931-0172
E-mail: wea13@mnic.net
http://emuseum.mnsu.edu/history/treatycenter/

Nobles County Library & Information Center
407 12th Street
Worthington, MN 56187

Old Home Town Museum
608 5th Street
P.O. Box 593
Stephen, MN 56757
Tel: 218-478-3092

Olmsted County Historical Society
Mayowood Mansion
1195 County Road 22, SW
Rochester, MN 55902
Tel: 507-282-9447
E-mail: ochs@olmstedhistory.com
http://olmstedhistory.com/

Osakis Heritage Center
Todd County Highway 46E
P.O. Box 327
Osakis, MN 56360
Tel: 320-859-3777

Otter Tail County Genealogical Society
1110 Lincoln Avenue, West
Fergus Falls, MN 56537
Tel: 218-736-6038

Owatonna Public Library
105 N. Elm
Owatonna, MN 55060
Tel: 507-444-2460
TDD: 507-444-2480
Fax: 507-444-2465
E-mail: info@owatonna.lib.mn.us
http://www.owatonna.lib.mn.us/index.php

Polish American Cultural Institute of Minnesota
514 22nd Avenue N.E.
Minneapolis, MN 55429
http://polamlibrary.homestead.com/

Ramsey County/Roseville Public Library
2180 N. Hamline Avenue
Roseville, MN 55113
Tel: 651-628-6803
E-mail: lwyman@ramsey.lib.mn.us
http://www.ramsey.lib.mn.us/detrv.htm

Renville County Genealogical Society
211 North Main Street
P.O. Box 331
Renville, MN 56284
http://www.ci.renville.mn.us/rcgs/

Rice County Historical Society
Museum and Genealogical Research Center
1814 NW 2nd Avenue
Faribault, MN 55021
Tel: 507-332-2121

Rochester Public Library
101 2nd Street, SE
Rochester, MN 55904
Tel: 507-285-8000
E-mail: judith@selco.lib.mn.us
http://www.rochesterpubliclibrary.org/

St. Cloud State University
Learning Resources Services
Central Minnesota Historical Center
720 Fourth Avenue, South
St. Cloud, MN 56301
Tel: 320-255-2084
Fax: 320-255-4778
E-mail: webteam@stcloudstate.edu
http://lrs.stcloudstate.edu/

St. John's University
Alcuin Library
P.O Box 2500
Collegeville, MN 56321-2500
Tel: 612-363-2122
Fax: 612-363-2126
http://www.csbsju.edu/library/index.html

St. Olaf College
Rolvaag Memorial Library
Northfield, MN 55057
Tel: 507-646-3452 (Reference)
507-646-3229 (Archives)
http://www.stolaf.edu/library/

St. Paul Public Library
90 West 4th
Street St. Paul, MN 55102
Tel: 651-292-6311
Fax: 651-292-6141
http://www.stpaul.lib.mn.us/

Sandstone History and Art Center
4th and Main
P.O. Box 398
Sandstone, MN 55072
Tel: 320-245-2271

South St. Paul Public Library
106 Thrid Avenue, North
South St. Paul, MN 55075
Tel: 651-554-3240
Fax: 651-554-3241
http://www.southstpaul.org/library/library.htm

Southwest State University
Center for Rural and Regional Studies
1501 State Street ·
Marshall, MN 56258
Tel: 507-537-6226
Fax: 507-537-6147
E-mail: CRRS@southwest.msus.edu
http://www.southweststate.edu/regional/

Stillwater Library
223 N Fourth Street
Stillwater, MN 55082
Tel: 651-439-1675
http://www.ci.stillwater.mn.us/library/index.htm

Todd County Historical Museum
333 Central Avenue
Long Prairie, MN 56347
Tel: 320-732-4426

United Methodist Church
Commission on Archives and History
122 West Franklin Avenue
Minneapolis, MN 55404
Tel: 612-870-0058
Fax: 612-870-1260
E-mail: gary@mumac.org
http://www.mumac.org/

University of Minnesota/Duluth
Northeast Minnesota Historical Center
Library 375
10 University Drive
Duluth, MN 55812-2495
Tel: 218-726-8526
      218-726-8100
Fax: 218-726-6205
E-mail: pmaus@d.umn.edu
http://www.d.umn.edu/lib/collections/nemn.html

University of Minnesota/Minneapolis
Government Publications Library
409 Wilson Library
309 19th Avenue, South
Minneapolis, MN 55455
Tel: 612-624-5073
E-mail: Govref@tc.umn.edu
http://www.lib.umn.edu/gov/

University of Minnesota/Minneapolis
Law Library
Walter F. Mondale Hall
229 - 19th Ave. So.
Minneapolis, MN 55455
Tel: 612-625-4300
Fax: 612-625-3478
http://www.law.umn.edu/library/home.html

University of Minnesota/Morris
Rodney A. Briggs Library
West Central Minnesota Historical Center
600 E. 4th Street
Morris, MN 56267
Tel: 320-589-6180
Fax: 320-589-6168
http://www.mrs.umn.edu/library/

University of Minnesota/St. Paul
Magrath Library
1984 Buford Avenue
St. Paul, MN 55108
Tel: 612-624-1212
Fax: 612-624-3793
E-mail: stpref@zazu.lib.umn.edu
http://magrath.lib.umn.edu/gov/

Waseca-LeSueur Regional Library
408 North State
Waseca, MN 56093
Tel: 507-835-2910
Fax: 507-835-3700
E-mail: wastlr@tds.lib.mn.us

William Mitchell College of Law
Warren E. Burger Law Library
875 Summit Avenue
St. Paul, MN 55105
Tel: 651-290-6424
Fax: 651-290-6318
http://www.wmitchell.edu/library/

Winona State University
Maxwell Library
P.O. Box 5838
Winona, MN 55987-5838
Tel: 507-457-5146
Fax: 507-457-5586
E-mail: Refdesk@vax2.winona.msus.edu
http://www.winona.msus.edu/is-f/library-f/libhome.htm

NEWSPAPER REPOSITORIES

Mankato State University
Memorial Library
Southern Minnesota Historical Center
Maywood and Ellis
MSU #19, P.O. Box 8419
Mankato, MN 56002
Tel: 507-389-5952
507-389-5953
Fax: 507-389-5155
E-mail: libweb@mankato.msus.edu
http://www.lib.mankato.msus.edu/

Minnesota Historical Society
345 Kellogg Boulevard
St. Paul, MN 55102-1906
Tel: 651-296-2143
Fax: 651-297-7436
E-mail: reference@mnhs.org
http://www.mnhs.org/

Moorhead State University
Livingston Lord Library
Northwest Minnesota Historical Center
1104 7th Avenue, South
Moorhead, MN 56563
Tel: 218-236-2461
E-mail: shoptaug@mhdli.moor
http://www.moorhead.msus.edu/library/

St. Cloud State University
Learning Resources Services
Central Minnesota Historical Center
720 Fourth Avenue, South
St. Cloud, MN 56301
Tel: 320-255-2084
Fax: 320-255-4778
E-mail: webteam@stcloudstate.edu
http://lrs.stcloudstate.edu/

Southwest State University
Center for Rural and Regional Studies
1501 State Street
Marshall, MN 56258
Tel: 507-537-6226
Fax: 507-537-6147
E-mail: CRRS@southwest.msus.edu
http://www.southweststate.edu/regional/

University of Minnesota/Duluth
Northeast Minnesota Historical Center
Library 375
10 University Drive
Duluth, MN 55812-2495
Tel: 218-726-8526
218-726-8100
Fax: 218-726-6205
E-mail: pmaus@d.umn.edu
http://www.d.umn.edu/lib/collections/nemn.html

University of Minnesota/Morris
Rodney A. Briggs Library
West Central Minnesota Historical Center
600 E. 4th Street
Morris, MN 56267
Tel: 320-589-6180
Fax: 320-589-6168
http://www.mrs.umn.edu/library/

VITAL RECORDS

Minnesota Department of Health
P.O. Box 64975
St. Paul, MN 55164-0975
Tel: 651-215-5800
http://www.health.state.mn.us/

MINNESOTA ON THE WEB

Minnesota GenWeb Project
http://www.rootsweb.com/~mngenweb/

Minnesota Historical Society
http://www.mnhs.org/

**Pig's Eye's Notepad—Historical Encyclopedia
of St. Paul, MN 1830-1850**
http://www.lareau.org/pep.html

MISSISSIPPI

ARCHIVES, STATE & NATIONAL

Mississippi Department of Archives and History
War Memorial Building
100 South State Street
Jackson, MS 39201
P.O. Box 571
Jackson, MS 39205-0571
Tel: 601-359-6850
Administration fax (601) 359-6975
Archives and Library Division fax (601) 359-6964
Historic Preservation Division fax (601) 359-6955
E-mail: webmaster@mdah.state.ms.us
http://www.mdah.state.ms.us/

National Archives—Southeast Region
1557 St. Joseph Avenue
East Point, GA 30344
Tel: 404-763-7474
Fax: 404-763-7059
E-mail: atlanta.center@nara.gov
http://www.nara.gov/regional/atlanta.html

GENEALOGICAL SOCIETIES

Aberdeen Genealogical Society
General Delivery
Aberdeen, MS 39730

Adams County, Genealogical Society of
P.O. Box 187
Washington, MS 39190

Alcorn County Genealogical Society
P.O. Box 1808
Corinth, MS 38835

Calhoun County Historical and Genealogical Society
P.O. Box 114
Pittsboro, MS 38951
E-mail: thallum@teclink.htm
http://personalpages.tds.net/~rosediamond/
    societymainpage.html

Central Mississippi, Family Research Association of
P.O. Box 13334
Jackson, MS 39236

Chickasaw County Historical & Genealogical Society
P.O. Box 42
Houston, MS 38851
E-mail: tommyg@network-one.com
http://www.rootsweb.com/~mschchgs/

Claiborne/Jefferson County Genealogical Society
P.O. Box 1017
Port Gibson, MS 39150

Columbus-Lowndes Genealogical Society
314 Seventh Street, North
Columbus, MS 39701

Dancing Rabbit Genealogical Society
Carthage Leake Library
114 East Franklin Street
Carthage, MS 39051
Fax: 601-267-7874
E-mail: drgs@netdoor.com
http://drgs.org/

DeSoto County, Genealogical Society of
P.O. Box 607
Hernando, MS 38632-0607
Tel: 662-429-1310
E-mail: GSDCMS@hotmail.com
http://www.rootsweb.com/~msdesoto/gsdcm.htm

Jackson County Genealogical Society
1803 Jackson Avenue
P.O. Box 984
Pascagoula, MS 39567
Tel: 662-841-9013

Jones County Genealogical And Historical Organization
P.O. Box 2644
Laurel, MS 39442-2644
http://freepages.genealogy.rootsweb.com/~msjones/jcgh.htm

Lowndes County Genealogical Society
Lowndes County Library System
314 7th Street, North
Columbus, MS 39701
Tel: 662-329-5300

Mississippi, Family Research Association
P.O. Box 13334
Jackson, MS 39236

Mississippi Coast Genealogical and Historical Society
P.O. Box 513
Biloxi, MS 39530

Mississippi Genealogical Society
P.O. Box 5301
Jackson, MS 39216-5301

Mississippi, Historical and Genealogical Association of
618 Avalon Road
Jackson, MS 39206

Northeast Mississippi Historical and Genealogical Society
Lee County Library
219 Madison Avenue
P.O. Box 434
Tupelo, MS 38802-0434
Tel: 662-841-9013

Ocean Springs Genealogical Society
P.O. Box 1765
Ocean Springs, MS 39566-1765
http://www.rootsweb.com/~msosgs/

Panola County, Historical and Genealogical Society of (Pan Gens)
105 Church Street
Batesville, MS 38606

Pontotoc County Pioneers
207 North Main Street
Pontotoc, MS 38863

Skipwith Historical and Genealogical Society, Inc.
P.O. Box 1382
Oxford, MS 38655
http://www.rootsweb.com/~mslafaye/books.htm

South Mississippi Genealogical Society
Southern Station
P.O. Box 15271
Hattiesburg, MS 39404
E-mail: CLARISE@prodigy.net
http://www.smsgs.org/

Tate County Genealogical and Historical Society
P.O. Box 974
Senatobia, MS 38668
Tel: 662-562-0390

Tippah County Historical and Genealogical Society
308 North Commerce Street
Ripley, MS 38663
Tel: 662-837-7773

Vicksburg Genealogical Society, Inc.
P.O. Box 1161
Vicksburg, MS 39181-1161
http://www.rootsweb.com/~msvgs/

Wayne County Genealogy Organization
Waynesboro-Wayne County Library System
712 Wayne Street
Waynesboro, MS 39367
Tel: 601-735-2268
866-735-2268
Fax: 601-735-6407
E-mail: wlib@wwcls.lib.ms.us
http://www.wwcls.lib.ms.us/

West Chickasaw County Genealogy and Historical Society
P.O. Box 42
Houston, MS 38851

Winston County Genealogical and Historical Society
P.O. Box 387
Louisville, MS 39339

HISTORICAL SOCIETIES

Bolivar County Historical Society
1615 Terrace Road
Cleveland, MS 38732

Calhoun County Historical and Genealogical Society
P.O. Box 114
Pittsboro, MS 38951
E-mail: thallum@teclink.htm
http://personalpages.tds.net/~rosediamond/societymain-page.html

Hancock County Historical Society
108 Cue Street
Bay St. Louis, MS 39520
Tel: 228-467-4090

Itawamba County Historical Society
P.O. Box 7
Mantachie, MS 38855
Tel: 662-282-7664
E-mail: robfra@network-one.com
http://www.rootsweb.com/~msichs/

Marshall County Historical Society
220 East College Avenue
P.O. Box 806
Holly Springs, MS 38635

Mississippi Baptist Historical Society
Mississippi College Library
P.O. Box 4024
Clinton, MS 39058
Tel: 601-925-3434
Fax: 601-925-3435
E-mail: mbnc@mc.edu

Mississippi Coast Genealogical and Historical Society
P.O. Box 513
Biloxi, MS 39530

Mississippi, Historical and Genealogical Association of
618 Avalon Road
Jackson, MS 39206

Mississippi Historical Society
100 South State Street
Jackson, MS 39205

Northeast Mississippi Historical and Genealogical Society
Lee County Library
219 Madison Avenue
P.O. Box 434
Tupelo, MS 38802-0434
Tel: 662-841-9013

Noxubee County Historical Society
P.O. Box 392
Macon, MS 39341
http://www.rootsweb.com/~msnoxube/society.htm

Panola County, Historical and Genealogical Society of (Pan Gens)
105 Church Street
Batesville, MS 38606

Pearl River Historical Group
Books & Things
120 Tate Street
Picayune, MS 39466
http://www.gulfcoastplus.com/histsoc/pearlriv.htm

Pontotoc County Pioneers
207 North Main Street
Pontotoc, MS 38863

Rankin County Historical Society
P.O. Box 841
Brandon, MS 39042
http://therankincountyhistoricalsociety.org/

Skipwith Historical and Genealogical Society, Inc.
P.O. Box 1382
Oxford, MS 38655
http://www.rootsweb.com/~mslafaye/books.htm

Sunflower County Historical Society, Inc.
201 Cypress Drive
Indianola, MS 38751

Tate County Genealogical and Historical Society
P.O. Box 974
Senatobia, MS 38668
Tel: 662-562-0390

Tippah County Historical and Genealogical Society
308 North Commerce Street
Ripley, MS 38663
Tel: 662-837-7773

Tishomingo County Historical and Genealogical Society
204 North Main Street
P.O. Box 437
Iuka, MS 38852
Tel: 662-423-1971
Fax: 662-423-2543
E-mail: brendaw@sixroads.com
http://www.rootsweb.com/%7Emstchgs/

Vicksburg and Warren County Historical Society
Old Court House Museum
1008 Cherry Street
Vicksburg, MS 39180
Tel: 601-636-0741

Webster County Historical Society
Route 3, Box 14
Elepora, MS 39744

West Chickasaw County Genealogy and Historical Society
P.O. Box 42
Houston, MS 38851

Wilkinson County Historical Society
Wilkinson County Museum
P.O. Box 1055
Woodville, MS 39669
E-mail: Wilkmuseum@aol.com

Winston County Genealogical and Historical Society
P.O. Box 387
Louisville, MS 39339

Woodville Civic Club
Friends of the Museum
P.O. Box 814
Woodville, MS 39669

Yalobusha County Historical Society
P.O. Box 258
Coffeeville, MS 38922-0258

Yazoo Historical Society
332 North Main Street
P.O. Box 575
Yazoo City, MS 39194
Tel: 662-746-2273

LDS FAMILY HISTORY CENTERS

For locations of Family History Centers in this state, see the Family History Center locator at FamilySearch. http://www.familysearch.org/eng/Library/FHC/frameset_fhc.asp

ARCHIVES/LIBRARIES/MUSEUMS

Attala County Library
201 South Huntington Street
Kosciusko, MS 39090
Tel: 662-289-5141
Fax: 662-289-9983
E-mail: attala@midmissregional.lib.ms.us

Batesville Public Library
206 Highway 51 North
Batesville, MS 38606
Tel: 662-563-1038
Fax: 662-563-6640
http://www.first.lib.ms.us/page3.html

Biloxi Public Library
139 Lameuse Street
P.O. Box 467
Biloxi, MS 39530-4298
Tel: 228-374-0330
Fax: 228-374-0375
http://www.harrison.lib.ms.us/libraries/bc_lib.htm

Bolivar/Robinson-Carpenter Memorial Library
401 S. Court Street
Cleveland, MS 38732
Tel: 662-843-2774

Carnegie Public Library
114 Delta Avenue
Clarksdale, MS 38614
Tel: 662-624-4461

Carthage Leake Library
114 East Franklin Street
Carthage, MS 39051
Tel: 601-267-7821

Center for the Study of Southern Culture
University of Mississippi
University, MS 38677
Tel: 662-915-5993
Fax: 662-915-5814
E-mail: cssc@olemiss.edu
http://www.olemiss.edu/depts/south/

Columbus Public Library
314 North 7th Street
Columbus, MS 39701
Tel: 662-329-5300

Corinth/Northeast Regional Library
1023 N. Fillmore Street
Corinth, MS 38834
Tel: 601-287-2441

DeKalb Library
Kemper Newton Regional Library
P.O. Box 710
DeKalb, MS 39328
Tel: 601-743-5981
E-mail: lynlong@kemper.lib.ms.us

Evans Memorial Library
105 N. Long Street
Aberdeen, MS 39730
Tel: 662-369-4601

Forrest Library
329 Hardy Street
Hattiesburg, MS 39401
Tel: 601-582-4461
http://www.hpfc.lib.ms.us/

Greenville/Percy Memorial Library
341 Main Street
Greenville, MS 38701
Tel: 662-335-2331

Greenwood/Leflore Public Library
405 W. Washington Street
Greenwood, MS 38930
Tel: 662-453-3634
Fax: 662-453-0683
E-mail: sharris@greenwood.lib.ms.us

Gulfport Public Library
1300 21st Avenue
P.O. Box 4018
Gulfport, MS 39501
Tel: 228-863-6411
Fax: 228-868-8413
http://www.harrison.lib.ms.us/libraries/gm_lib.htm

Harriet Person Memorial Library
P.O. Box 1017
Port Gibson, MS 39150
Tel: 601-437-5202

Historical Trails Library
Route 1, Box 373
Philadelphia, MS 39350
Tel: 601-656-3506

Iuka Library
204 North Main Street
Iuka, MS 38852
Tel: 662-423-6300
E-mail: iu@nereg.lib.ms.us

Jefferson County Public Library
428 North Main
Fayette, MS 39069
Tel: 601-786-3982

Jennie Stephens Smith Library
219 King Street
New Albany, MS 38652
Tel: 662-534-1991
http://www.newalbanymainstreet.com/library.htm

Judge George W. Armstrong Library
220 Commerce Street
Natchez, MS 39120
Tel: 601-445-8862

Lauderdale County, Dept. of Archives and History
Courthouse Annex
P.O. Box 5511
Meridian, MS 39302

Laurel/Jones County Library
530 Commerce Street
Laurel, MS 39440
Tel: 601-428-4313
Fax: 601-428-4314
http://www.laurel.lib.ms.us/

Lauren Rogers Memorial Library/Museum
5th and 7th Streets
P.O. Box 1108
Laurel, MS 39440

Lee County Library
219 North Madison
Tupelo, MS 38801
Tel: 662-841-9029

Lincoln Public Library
100 S. Jackson Street
Brookhaven, MS 39601
Tel: 601-833-3369

Lowndes County Library System
314 7th Street, North
Columbus, MS 39701
Tel: 662-329-5300

Marks/Quitman County Library
315 East Main
Marks, MS 38646
Tel: 662-326-7141

McComb Public Library
1022 Virginia Avenue
Mccomb, MS 39648
Tel: 601-684-2661

Meridian Public Library
2517 7th Street
Meridian, MS 39301
Tel: 601-693-6771
http://www.meridian.lib.ms.us/

Mississippi State University
Mitchell Memorial Library/Special Collections
Starkville, MS 39759
Tel: 662-325-7679
E-mail: sp_coll@library.msstate.edu
http://library.msstate.edu/sc/

Noxubee County Library
103 King Street
Macon, MS 39341
Tel: 662-726-5461

Oxford/Lafayette County Public Library
401 Bramlett Boulevard
Oxford, MS 38655
Tel: 662-234-5751

Pascagoula Public Library
3214 Pascagoula Street
Pascagoula, MS 39567
Tel: 601-769-3000

Philadelphia/Neshoba County Library
230 Beacon Street
Philadelphia, MS 39350
Tel: 601-656-4911

Ripley Public Library
308 North Commerce
Ripley, MS 38663
Tel: 662-837-7773

Starkville/Oktibbeha County Public Library
326 University Drive
P.O. Box 1406
Starkville, MS 39759
Tel: 662-323-2766
Fax: 662-323-9140
http://www.starkville.lib.ms.us/

Sunflower County Library
201 Cypress Drive
Indianola, MS 38751
Tel: 662-887-2298
Fax: 662-887-2153
http://www.sunflower.lib.ms.us/sunflower/default.asp

Union County Library
219 King Street
P.O. Box 846
New Albany, MS 38652

Union Public Library
101 Peachtree
Union, MS 39365
E-mail: lcweb@loc.gov

University of Mississippi
Department of Archives and Special Collections
University, MS 38677
Tel: 601-234-6091
Fax: 601-234-6381
E-mail: libweb@www.olemiss.edu
http://www.olemiss.edu/depts/general_library/files/archives/

University of Southern Mississippi
McCain Library
Southern Station Box 5053
Hattiesburg, MS 39406-5053
Tel: 601-266-4241
http://www.lib.usm.edu/mccain.html

Vicksburg/Warren Public Library
700 Veto Street
P.O. Box 511
Vicksburg, MS 39181-0511
Tel: 601-636-6411

William Carey College
L.W. Anderson Genealogical Library
1856 Beach Drive,
Gulfport, MS 39507
Tel: 228-897-7213
http://library.wmcarey.edu/

NEWSPAPER REPOSITORIES

Mississippi Department of Archives and History
War Memorial Building
120 North State Street
P.O. Box 571
Jackson, MS 39205-0571
Tel: 601-359-6850
Fax: 601-359-6964
E-mail: refdesk@mdah.state.ms.us
http://www.mdah.state.ms.us/

VITAL RECORDS

State Department of Health
Vital Records
2423 North State
Street Jackson, MS 39216
Tel: 601-960-7981
http://www.msdh.state.ms.us/msdhsite/

MISSISSIPPI ON THE WEB

Christine's Genealogy Website
http://ccharity.com/

Mississippi Civil War History Sources
http://www.misscivilwar.org/resources/list-hx.html

Mississippi GenWeb Project
http://www.insolwwb.net/~rholler/ms/

Southern Roots
http://www.gower.net/bclayton/index.html

Traveller Southern Families
http://misc.traveller.com/genealogy/

MISSOURI

ARCHIVES, STATE & NATIONAL

Missouri State Archives
600 W. Main
P.O. Box 1747
Jefferson City, MO 65102
Telephone: (573) 751-3280
E-mail:archref@sosmail.state.mo.us
http://mosl.sos.state.mo.us/rec-man/arch.html

National Archives—Central Plains Region
2312 East Bannister Road
Kansas City, MO 64131
Tel: 816-926-6920
Fax: 816-926-6982
E-mail: kansascity.archives@nara.gov
http://www.nara.gov/regional/kansas.html

GENEALOGICAL SOCIETIES

Afro-American Historical and Genealogical Society (AAHGS)
Landon Creek
P.O. Box 23804
St. Louis, MO 63121-0804
www.rootsweb.com/~mdaahgs/chapters.html

Afro-American Historical and Genealogical Society (AAHGS)
Magic
3700 Blue Parkway
Kansas City, MO 64130

American Family Records Association
P.O. Box 15505
Kansas City, MO 64106

Audrain County Area Genealogical Society
Mexico/Audrain County Public Library
305 West Jackson Street
Mexico, MO 65265

Barry County Genealogical Society
P.O. Box 291
Cassville, MO 65625
http://www.rootsweb.com/~mobarry/society.html

Boone County Historical Society/Museum
3801 Ponderosa Drive
P.O. Box 26
Columbia, MO 65205
Tel: 573-443-8936
E-mail: KTEH59A@prodigy.com
www.rootsweb.com/~ilboone/histmusm.htm

Butler County, Genealogical Society of
P.O. Box 426
Poplar Bluff, MO 63901

Campbell Area Genealogical and Historical Society
P.O. Box 401
Campbell, MO 63933-0401

Cape Girardeau County Genealogical Society
Riverside Regional Library
204 South Union Avenue
P.O. Box 389
Jackson, MO 63755
Tel: 573-243-8141
Fax: 573-243-8142
http://www.showme.net/rrl/general/hours.html

Carthage Genealogical Society
Southwest Missouri Genealogical Library
Route 3, Box 117
Carthage, MO 64836

Dade County Genealogical Society
P.O. Box 155
Greenfield, MO 65661

Daughters of Old Westport
8124 Pennsylvania Lane
Kansas City, MO 64114

Douglas County Historical and Genealogical Society
P.O. Box 986
Ava, MO 65608

Dunklin County Genealogical Society
Dunklin County Library
209 North Main
Kennett, Missouri 63857
Tel: 573-888-3561
573-888-2261
Fax: 573-888-6393
http://dunklin-co.lib.mo.us/

Excelsior Springs Genealogical Society
1000 Magnolia West
Excelsior, MO 64024

Family Tree Climbers
P.O. Box 422
Lawson, MO 64062

Genealogy Friends of the Library
P.O. Box 314
Neosho, MO 64850

Gentry County Genealogical Society
802 E. Canady
Albany, MO 64402

Grundy County Genealogical Society
P.O. Box 223
Trenton, MO 64683

Harrison County Genealogical Society
2307 Central Street
P.O. Box 65
Bethany, MO 64424
http://www.rootsweb.com/~moharris/hcgen.html

Heart of America Genealogical Society
Kansas City Public Library, Valley Room
311 East 12th Street
Kansas City, MO 64106
Tel: 816-701-3400
Fax: 816-701-3401
http://www.kclibrary.org/

Howard County Genealogical Society
206 North Linn Avenue, Rte. 1
Fayette, MO 65248

Jackson County Genealogical Society
420 S Main Street
P.O. Box 2145
Independence, MO 64055
Tel: 816-252-8128

Jefferson County Genealogical Society
Jefferson County Library
3033 High Ridge Blvd.
High Ridge, MO 63049
Tel: 636-677-8186

Jewish Genealogical Society of St. Louis (JGSSTL)
United Hebrew Congregation
One Gudder Campus
13788 Conway Road
Creve Coeur, MO 63141
E-mail: letvak@aol.com
http://uahc.org/congs/mo/mo005/

Joplin Genealogical Society
Joplin Public Library
300 South Main Street
P.O. Box 152
Joplin, MO 64802
Tel: 417-623-7953

Laclede County Genealogical Society
P.O. Box 350
Lebanon, MO 65536

Lincoln County Genealogical Society
P.O. Box 192
Hawk Point, MO 63349

Linn County Genealogy Researchers
771 Tomahawk
Brookfield, MO 64628

Livingston County Genealogical Society
450 Locust Street
Chillicothe, MO 64601-2597

Mid-Missouri Genealogical Society
109 Madison Street
P.O. Box 715
Jefferson, MO 65102

Mississippi County Genealogical Society
P.O. Box 5
Charleston, MO 63834

Missouri State Genealogical Association
P.O. Box 833
Columbia, MO 65205-0833
E-mail: mosga@mac.com
http://www.mosga.org/

Native Sons of Kansas City
P.O. Box 10046
Kansas City, MO 64113

Newton County Historical Society/Genealogy Study Group
P.O. Box 675
Neosho, MO 64850

Nodaway County Genealogical Society
P.O. Box 214
Maryville, MO 64468
http://www.rootsweb.com/~monodawa/ncgs.htm

Northeast Missouri Genealogical Society
614 Clark Street
Canton, MO 63435
http://www.rootsweb.com/~monemgs/

Northwest Missouri Genealogical Society
Buchanan County Research Center
412 Felix Street
P.O. Box 382
St. Joseph, MO 64502
Tel: 816-233-0524
http://www.rootsweb.com/~monwmgs/

Oregon County Genealogical Society
P.O. Box 324
Alton, MO 65606
http://www.geocities.com/SiliconValley/Park/3507/
ogensoc.htm

Ozarks Genealogical Society/Library
534 West Catalpa
P.O. Box 3945 G.S.
Springfield, MO 65808
Tel: 417-831-2773
E-mail: society@mail.orion.org
http://www.rootsweb.com/~ozarksgs

Phelps County Genealogical Society
P.O. Box 571
Rolla, MO 65402
Tel: 573-364-5977
E-mail: pcgs@rollanet.org
http://www.rollanet.org/~pcgs/

Pike County Genealogical Society
P.O. Box 364
Bowling Green, MO 63334
http://www.pastracks.com/pcgs/welcome.htm

Platte County Genealogical Society
P.O. Box 103
Platte City, MO 64079
Tel: 816-431-5121 (Museum)

Pulaski County, Genealogy Society of
P.O. Box 226
Crocker, MO 65452

Ray County Genealogical Association
901 W. Royle Street
Richmond, MO 64085
http://www.rootsweb.com/~moray/rcga/

Reynolds County Genealogy and Historical Society
P.O. Box 281
Ellington, MO 63638

Ripley County Historical and Genealogical Society
101 Washington Street
Doniphan, MO 63935

St. Charles County Genealogical Society
Historic Courthouse
Third and Jefferson, Room 106
P.O. Box 715
St. Charles, MO 63302-0715
Tel: 314-947-1762
http://www.rootsweb.com/~mosccgs/

St. Louis Genealogical Society
9011 Manchester Road,
Ste. 3 St. Louis, MO 63144

Santa Fe Trail Researchers Genealogical Society
RR 1, Box 84
Franklin 65250

Seeking 'n Searching Ancestors
Route 1, Box 52
St. Elizabeth, MO 65075

South-Central Missouri Genealogical Society
939 Nichols Drive
West Plains, MO 65775

South Vernon Genealogical Society
Route 2, Box 280
Sheldon, MO 64784

Southwest Missouri Genealogical Society
Carthage Public Library
612 South Garrison Avenue
Carthage, MO 64836
http://carthage.lib.mo.us/

Texas County Genealogical and Historical Society
P.O. Box 12
Houston, MO 65483

Thrailkill Genealogical Society
2018 Gentry Street
North Kansas City, MO 64116

Vernon County Genealogical Society
Nevada Public Library
225 West Austin
Nevada, MO 64772

Warren County Genealogical Society
401 Oak Drive
Warrenton, MO 63383

Webb City Area Genealogical Society
101 South Liberty Street
Webb City, MO 64870

West Central Missouri Genealogical Society/Library
705 Broad
Warrensburg, MO 64093

Wright County Historical and Genealogical Society
101 E Rolla Street
P.O. Box 66
Hartville, MO 65667
Tel: 417-741-6265

HISTORICAL SOCIETIES

Adair County Historical Society/Library
308 South Franklin Street
Kirksville, MO 63501

African Historical Society
P.O. Box 4964
St. Louis, MO 63106

Afro-American Historical and Genealogical Society (AAHGS)
Landon Creek
P.O. Box 23804
St. Louis, MO 63121-0804
 www.rootsweb.com/~mdaahgs/chapters.html

Afro-American Historical and Genealogical Society (AAHGS)
Magic
3700 Blue Parkway
Kansas City, MO 64130

Andrew County Historical Society/Museum
P.O. Box 12
Savannah, MO 64485
Tel: 816-324-4720

Ash Grove Historical Society
606 West Boone
Ash Grove, MO 65604

Audrain County Historical Society
P.O. Box 398
Mexico, MO 65265
Tel: 573-581-3910

Augusta Historical Society
498 Schell Road
Augusta, MO 63332

Boone County Historical Society/Museum
Wilson-Huff History and Genealogical Library
3801 Ponderosa Drive (Nifong Park)
Columbia, MO 65201
Tel: 573-443-8936

Boone-Duden Historical Society
3565 Mill Street
P.O. Box 82
New Melle, MO 63365
E-mail: bdhissoc@norn.org
http://www.rootsweb.com/~moboonhs

Boonslick Historical Society of Cooper and Howard Counties
811 7th Street Terrace
P.O. Box 324
Booneville, MO 65233
Tel: 660-882-6370

Campbell Area Genealogical and Historical Society
P.O. Box 401
Campbell, MO 63933-0401

Cass County Historical Society
400 East Mechanic
P.O. Box 406
Harrisonville, MO 64701
Tel: 816-887-2393

Centralia Historical Society, Inc.
319 East Sneed
Centralia, MO 65240
Tel: 573-682-5711

Chariton County Historical Society
115 E. Second
Salisbury, MO 65281
Tel: 660-388-5941

Clay County Historical Society/Museum
14 North Main Street
Liberty, MO 64068
Tel: 816-792-1849

Cole County Historical Society/Museum
109 Madison Street
Jefferson City, MO 65101
Tel: 573-635-1850

Cooper County Historical Society
111 Roe Street
P.O. Box 51
Pilot Grove, Mo. 65276
http://www.mid-mo.net/cchs/

Dallas County Historical Society
P.O. Box 594
Buffalo, MO 65622

DeKalb County Historical Society
P.O. Box 477
Maysville, MO 64469

Douglas County Historical and Genealogical Society
P.O. Box 986
Ava, MO 65608

Florissant Valley Historical Society
1 Taille de Noyer
P.O. Box 298
Florissant, MO 63032
Tel: 314-524-1100

Foristell Area Historical Society
626 Ball Street
Wentzville, MO 63385

Franklin County Historical Society
P.O. Box 352
Washington, MO 63090

Friends of Florida
Route 1
Stoutsville, MO 65283

Friends of Historic Boonville
614 E. Morgan
P.O. Box 1776
Boonville, MO 65233
Tel: 660-882-7977

Friends of Keytesville, Inc.
408 Bridge Street
Keytesville, MO 65261

Friends of the Neosho Library, Genealogy
P.O. Box 314
Neosho, MO 64850

Friends of Rocheport
P.O. Box 122
Rocheport, MO 65279

Glascow Area Historical and Preservation Society
100 Market
Glascow, MO 65254
Tel: 660-338-2377

Graham Historical Society
417 South Walnut
Marysville, MO 64468

Green County Missouri Historical Society
P.O. Box 3466 G.S.
Springfield, MO 65808
E-mail: gsociety@mail.orion.org
http://www.rootsweb.com/~gcmohs/

Henry County Historical Society/Genealogy Library
203 West Franklin Street
P.O. Box 65
Clinton, MO 64735
Tel: 660-885-8414

Heritage League of Greater Kansas City
Newcomb Hall
5100 Rockhill
P.O. Box 10366
Kansas City, MO 64171
http://www.heritageleaguekc.org/index.shtml

Higbee Area Historical Society
P.O. Box 38
Higbee, MO 65257

Huntsville Historical Society
107 North Main
Huntsville, MO 65259

Iron County Historical Society
Iron County Historical Museum
123 West Wayne Street
Irontown, MO 63650

Johnson County Historical Society
Heritage Library
302 North Main
Warrensburg, MO 64093
Tel: 660-747-6480

Kimmswick Historical Society
6000 Third Street
P.O. Box 41
Kimmswick, MO 63053

Kingdon of Callaway Historical Society
331 West 7th Street
P.O. Box 6073
Fulton, MO 65251

Lawrence County Historical Society
P.O. Box 406
Mt. Vernon, MO 65712

Lewis County Historical Society, Inc.
614 Clark Street
Canton, MO 63435

Lincoln County Historical Society
Court and Collier Streets
P.O. Box 29
Troy, MO 63370

Macon County Historical Society
120 Bennett Avenue
Macon, MO 63552

Madison County Historic Society
HCR 78, Box 427
Fredericktown, MO 63645

Maries County, Historical Society of
P.O. Box 289
Vienna, MO 65582

Missouri Historical Society
225 S. Skinker
P.O. Box 11940
St. Louis, MO 63112-0040
Tel: 314-746-4599
http://www.mohistory.org/

Missouri Methodist Historical Society
10516 E. 35th Terrace
Independence, MO 64052
http://www.cmc.edu/library/Archives/
        Historical%20society.html

Missouri Pacific Historical Society
P. O. Box 456
Ballwin, MO 63022-0456
E-mail: Mo-pac1@netwitz.net (Archivist)
http://mopac.org/

Missouri State Historical Society
Ellis Library Building
1020 Lowry Street
Columbia, MO 65201
Tel: 573-882-7083
Fax: 573-882-4950
E-mail: shsofmo@ext.missouri.edu
http://www.system.missouri.edu/shs/

Missouri Territorial Pioneers
3929 Milton Drive
Independence, MO 64055

Moniteau County Historical Society
P.O. Box 263
California, MO 65018

Montgomery County Historical Society/Museum
112 West Second Street
Montgomery City, MO 63361

Morgan County Historical Society
P.O. Box 177
Versailles, MO 65084

Newton County Historical Society
P.O. Box 675
Neosho, MO 64850

Northern Cherokee Nation
578 E Highway 7
Clinton, MO 64735-9511
Tel: 660-885-7779
Fax: 660-885-4257
http://northerncherokee.net/

O'Fallon Historical Society
Civic Park Drive
O'Fallon, MO 63366

Old Mines Area Historical Society
Route 1, Box 300Z
Cadet, MO 63630

Osage County Historical Society
402 East Main Street
P.O. Box 402
Linn, MO 65051
Tel: 573-897-2932

Perry County Historical Society
P.O. Box 97
Perryville, MO 63775

Phelps County Historical Society
Dillon Log Cabin/Phelps County Museum
302 Third Street
P.O. Box 1535
Rolla, MO 65402
Tel: 573-364-5977
http://web.umr.edu/~whmcinfo/pchs/

Randolph County Historical Society
P.O. Box 116
Moberly, MO 65270

Ray County Historical Society
P.O. Box 2
Richmond, MO 64085

Reynolds County Genealogy and Historical Society
P.O. Box 281
Ellington, MO 63638

Ripley County Historical and Genealogical Society/Library
Current River Heritage Museum
101 Washington Street
Doniphan, MO 63935

St. Charles Historical Society/Archives
101 South Main Street
St. Charles, MO 63301
Tel: 636-946-9828

Saline County Historical Society
P.O. Box 4028
Marshall, MO 65340
Tel: 816-886-8013
http://www.salinecountymo.com/

Scotland County Historical Society
P.O. Box 263
Memphis, MO 63555

South Howard County Historical Society
P.O. Box 13
New Franklin, MO 65274

Stone County Historical Society
Stone County Library
P.O. Box 63
Galena, MO 65656

Texas County Genealogical and Historical Society
P.O. Box 12
Houston, MO 65483

Union Cemetery Historical Society
2727 Main Street, Suite 120
Kansas City, MO 64108

Vernon County Historical Society
Bushwacker Museum
231 North Main Street
Nevada, MO 64772
http://www.bushwhacker.org/

Warren County Historical Society/Museum and History Library
Walton and Market St.
P.O. Box 12
Warrenton, MO 63383
Tel: 636-456-3820

Washington Historical Society
314 West Main Street
P.O. Box 146
Washington, MO 63090
Tel: 636-239-0280

Wentzville Community Historical Society/Archives
506 South Lynn Avenue
P.O. Box 122
Wentzville, MO 63385

White River Valley Historical Society
P.O. Box 555
Point Lookout, MO 65726
http://homepages.rootsweb.com/~moarwrv/wrvhs. html

Wright County Historical and Genealogical Society
101 E Rolla Street
P.O. Box 66 Hartville, MO 65667
Tel: 417-741-6265

LDS FAMILY HISTORY CENTERS

For locations of Family History Centers in this state, see the Family History Center locator at FamilySearch.
http://www.familysearch.org/eng/Library/FHC/frameset_fhc.asp

ARCHIVES/LIBRARIES/MUSEUMS

Adair County Historical Society/Library
308 South Franklin Street
Kirksville, MO 63501

Adair County Public Library
One Library Lane
Kirksville, MO 63501
Tel: 660-665-6038
Fax: 660-627-0028
http://adair.lib.mo.us/

Barry County/Cassville Branch Library
1007 Main Street
Cassville, MO 65625
Tel: 417-847-2121

Boone County Historical Society/Museum
Wilson-Huff History and Genealogical Library
3801 Ponderosa Drive (Nifong Park)
Columbia, MO 65201
Tel: 573-443-8936

Boonslick Regional Library
219 West 3rd Street
Sedalia, MO 65301
Tel: 660-827-7111
http://204.185.183.77/

Callaway County Public Library
710 Court Street
Fulton, MO 65251-1992
Tel: 573-642-7261
TDD: 573-642-0662

Central Missouri, Genealogical Society of
3801 Ponderosa Drive
P.O. Box 26
Columbia, MO 65205
Tel: 573-443-8936
E-mail: tazcat69@yahoo.com
http://www.gscm.gen.mo.us/

Clay County Archives and Historical Library
210 East Franklin Street
P.O. Box 99
Liberty, MO 64068
Tel/Fax: 816-781-3611
E-mail: info@claycountyarchives.org
http://www.claycountyarchives.org/

Clay County Museum/Library
14 North Main Street
Liberty, MO 64068

Cole County Historical Society/Museum
109 Madison Street
Jefferson City, MO 65101
Tel: 573-635-1850

Concordia Historical Institute
301 DeMun Avenue
St. Louis, MO 63105

Dallas County Library
219 W. Main
Buffalo, MO 65622

Daniel Boone Regional Library
100 W. Broadway
P.O. Box 1267
Columbia, MO 65201
Tel: 573-443-3161
E-mail: dbrlpr@coin.org
http://dbrl.library.missouri.org/

Doniphan/Ripley County Public Library
207 Locust Street
Doniphan, MO 63935
Tel: 573-996-2616

Dunklin County Library
226 N. Main
Kennett, MO 63857
Tel: 573-888-3561
Fax: 573-888-6393
http://dunklin-co.lib.mo.us/

Frenchtown Museum
1400 North Second Street
St. Charles, MO 63301
Tel: 636-946-2865
http://home.stlnet.com/~tgodwin/vinson.html

Garst Memorial Library
219 West Jackson Street
Marshfield, MO 65706
Tel: 417-468-3335
http://webstercounty.lib.mo.us/library_home.htm

Henry County Historical Society/Genealogy Library
203 West Franklin Street
P.O. Box 65
Clinton, MO 64735
Tel: 660-885-8414

Heritage Library
302 N Main Street
Warrensburg, MO 64093
Tel: 660-747-6480

Jefferson County Library
3033 High Ridge Blvd.
High Ridge, MO 63049
Tel: 636-677-8186

Johnson County Historical Society
Heritage Library
P.O. Box 825
302 North Main Warrensburg, MO 64093
Tel: 660-747-6480

Joplin Public Library
300 S. Main Street
Joplin, MO 64801
Tel: 417-624-5465
417-623-7953
Fax: 417-624-5217
http://www.joplinpubliclibrary.org/

Kansas City Public Library
Local History Research/Special Collections
311 East 12th Street
Kansas City, MO 64106
Tel: 816-701-3505
http://www.kcpl.lib.mo.us/sc/default.htm

Keytesville Library
406 W. Bridge Street
Keytesville, MO 65261
Tel: 660-288-3204

Livingston County Library
450 Locust
Chillicothe, MO 64601
Tel: 660-646-0547
Fax: 660-646-5504
http://www.livcolibrary.org/

Maryville Public Library
Genealogy Division
509 N. Main
Maryville, MO 64468
Tel: 660-582-5281

Mercer County Library
601 Grant
Princeton, MO 64673
Tel: 660-748-3725

Mexico/Audrain County Public Library
Audrain County Area Genealogical Society Section
305 West Jackson Street
Mexico, MO 65265
Tel: 573-581-4939
Fax: 573-581-7510
http://maain.com/library/

Mid-Continent Public Library
Genealogy and Local History Department
317 West 24 Highway
Independence, MO 64050
Tel: 816-252-0950
E-mail: ge@mcpl.lib.mo.us
http://www.mcpl.lib.mo.us/gen.htm

Missouri State Library
600 West Main Street Jefferson City, MO 65101
P.O. Box 387
Tel: 573-751-3615
Fax: 573-526-1142
E-mail: libref@sosmail.state.mo.us

Montgomery County Historical Society/Museum
112 West Second Street
Montgomery City, MO 63361

Neosho City/County Library
201 W Spring Street
Neosho, MO 64850
Tel: 417-451-4231

Newton County Museum/Library
121 N. Washington
P.O. Box 675
Neosho, MO 64850
Tel: 417-451-4940

Northwest Missouri Genealogical Society
Buchanan County Research Center
412 Felix Street
P.O. Box 382
St. Joseph, MO 64502
Tel: 816-233-0524
http://www.smartnet.net/~stjoed/nwmgs.html

Ozarks Genealogical Society/Library
534 West Catalpa
P.O. Box 3945 G.S.
Springfield, MO 65808
Tel: 417-831-2773

Phelps County Archives
Phelps County Courthouse, Room 315
200 North Main
Rolla, MO 65401
Tel: 573-364-1891

Phelps County Historical Society
Dillon Log Cabin/Phelps County Museum
302 Third Street
P.O. Box 1535
Rolla, MO 65402
Tel: 573-364-5977
http://web.umr.edu/~whmcinfo/pchs/

Putnam County Library
1618 Main Street
P.O. Box 305
Unionville, MO 63565
Tel: 660-947-3192

Richland Library
111 W Camden Avenue
P.O. Box 340
Richland, MO 65556
Tel: 573-765-3642

Ripley County Historical and Genealogical Society/Library
Current River Heritage Museum
101 Washington Street
Doniphan, MO 63935

Riverside Regional Library
204 South Union Avenue
P.O. Box 389
Jackson, MO 63755
Tel: 573-243-8141
http://www.showme.net/rrl/home2.html

St. Charles County Genealogical Society
Historic Courthouse
Third and Jefferson, Room 106
P.O. Box 715
St. Charles, MO 63302-0715

St. Charles Historical Society/Archives
101 South Main Street
St. Charles, MO 63301
Tel: 314-946-9828

St. Charles Library/Kathryn Linneman Branch
Kathryn Linnemann Branch Library
2323 Elm Street
St. Charles, MO 63301
Tel: 636-946-6294
636-723-0232
E-mail: aking01@mail.win.org
http://www.win.org/library/services/lhgen/
    cinmenu.htm

St. Joseph Museum/Library
1100 Charles Street
St. Joseph, MO 64501
Tel: 816-232-8471
Fax: 816-232-8482

St. Louis Public Library
1301 Olive Street
St. Louis, MO 63103
Tel: 314-241-2288
Fax: 314-539-0393
TDD: 314-539-0364
E-mail: webmaster@slpl.lib.mo.us
http://www.slpl.lib.mo.us/

Scenic Regional Library/New Haven Branch
901 Maupin
New Haven, MO 63068
Tel: 573-237-2189

Shelbina/Carnegie Public Library
102 North Center Street
P.O. Box 247
Shelbina, MO 63468
Tel: 573-588-2271
http://www.shelbinalibrary.org/

Southeast Missouri State University
Kent Library
1 University Plaza Cape
Girardeau, MO 63701
Tel: 573-651-2235
Fax: 573-651-2666
http://library.semo.edu/

Southwest Missouri Genealogical Library
Route 3, Box 117
Carthage, MO 64836

Southwest Missouri State University
Meyer Library/Lena Wills Collection
901 S. National
Springfield, MO 65804
Tel: 417-836-4535 (Reference/Information)
417-836-4532 (Govt. Documents)
Fax: 417-836-6799
TDD: 417-836-6794
http://library.smsu.edu/

Springfield Public Library
Midtown Carnegie Branch
397 East Central Street
Springfield, MO 65802
Tel: 417-837-5000
417-869-0320
http://thelibrary.springfield.missouri.org/index.html/

Stephens Museum
411 Central Methodist Square
Fayette, MO 65248
Tel: 660-248-3391
http://www.cmc.edu/

Summers Memorial Library
135 Harwood Lebanon, MO 65536
Tel: 417-532-2148
Fax: 417-532-7424
E-mail: llclref@llion.org
http://lebanon.laclede.library.missouri.org/summers.html

University City Library
6701 Delmar Blvd.
University City, MO 63130
Tel: 314-968-2763

University of Missouri/Columbia
Western Historical Manuscript Collection
23 Ellis Library
Columbia, MO 65201
Tel: 573-882-6028
Fax: 573-884-4950
E-mail: whmc@ext.missouri.edu
http://www.system.missouri.edu/whmc/

University of Missouri/Kansas City
Western Historical Manuscript Collection
302 Newcomb Hall
5100 Rockhill Road
Kansas City, MO 64110
Tel: 816-235-1543
E-mail: WHMCKC@umkc.edu
http://www.umkc.edu/WHMCKC/

University of Missouri/Rolla
Western Historical Manuscript Collection
Curtis Laws Wilson Library
1870 Miner Circle
Rolla, MO 65409-0060
Tel: 573-341-4874
E-mail: whmcinfo@umr.edu
http://web.umr.edu/~whmcinfo/

University of Missouri/St. Louis
Western Historical Manuscript Collection
Thomas Jefferson Library, Room 221
8001 Natural Bridge Road
St. Louis, MO 63121
Tel: 314-516-6034 (Information)
314-516-5060 (Reference)
Fax: 314-516-5853
TDD: 314-516-5212
E-mail: whmc@umsl.edu
http://www.umsl.edu/~whmc/

Warren County Historical Society/Museum and History Library
Walton and Market St.
P.O. Box 12
Warrenton, MO 63383
Tel: 636-456-3820

Waynesville Library
306 Route 66
Waynesville, MO 65583
Tel: 573-774-2965
Fax: 573-774-2965

Westminster College
Winston Churchill Memorial Library
501 Westminster
Fulton, MO 65251
Tel: 573-592-5369
http://www.westminster-mo.edu/cm/

Wright County Library
Courthouse
Main Street
P.O. Box 70
Hartville, MO 65667
Tel: 417-741-7595

NEWSPAPER REPOSITORIES

State Historical Society of Missouri
1020 Lowry Street
Columbia, MO 65201
Tel: 573-882-7083
Fax: 573-882-4950
E-mail: shsofmo@ext.missouri.edu
http://www.system.missouri.edu/shs/

VITAL RECORDS

Missouri Department of Health
Bureau of Vital Records
930 Wildwood
P.O. Box 570
Jefferson, MO 65102
Tel: 573-751-6400
http://www.vitalrec.com/mo.html

University of Missouri/Kansas City
Western Historical Manuscript Collection
302 Newcomb Hall
5100 Rockhill Road
Kansas City, MO 64110
Tel: 816-235-1543
E-mail: WHMCKC@umkc.edu
http://www.umkc.edu/WHMCKC/

MISSOURI ON THE WEB

COIN Genealogy Center
http://www.coin.org/community/genealogy/

**Directory of Archives and Manuscript Repositories
in the St. Louis Area**
http://library.wustl.edu/units/spec/archives/aslaa/
 directory/

Missouri GenWeb Project
http://www.rootsweb.com/~mogenweb/mo.htm

Missouri Pioneers
http://www.rootsweb.com/~mopionee/

Osage County Missouri Genealogy Resources
http://www.mindspring.com/~mgentges/

●

MONTANA

ARCHIVES, STATE & NATIONAL

Montana State Archives
Montana Historical Society
Memorial Building
225 N. Roberts St.
P.O. Box 201201
Helena, MT 59620-1201
Tel: 800-243-9900
406-444-4774/5
Fax: 406-444-5297
E-mail: archives@state.mt.us
http://www.montanahistoricalsociety.org/departments/archives/index.html

National Archives—Rocky Mountain Region
Bldg. 48, Denver Federal Center
West 6th Avenue and Kipling Street
Denver, Colorado 80225-0307
Mailing Address:
P.O. Box 25307
Denver, Colorado 80225-0307
Phone: 303-236-0817
Fax: 303-236-9297
E-mail: denver.archives@nara.gov
http://www.nara.gov/regional/denver.html

GENEALOGICAL SOCIETIES

Beaver-Head-Hunters Genealogical Society
Beaverhead County Museum
15 South Montana
P.O. Box 830
Dillon, MT 59725
http://www.rootsweb.com/~mtbhhgs/

Big Horn County Genealogical Society
P.O. Box 51
Hardin, MT 59034

Bitterroot Genealogical Society
702 S. Fifth Street
Hamilton, MT 59840
http://www.rootsweb.com/~mtbgs/

Broken Mountains Genealogical Society
P.O. Box 261
Chester, MT 59522

Fort Assiniboine Genealogical Society
P.O. Box 321
Havre, MT 59501

Gallatin Genealogical Society
P.O. Box 1783
Bozeman, MT 59771-1783

Great Falls Genealogy Society
1400 1st Avenue North
Great Falls, MT 59401
E-mail: GFGS@mcn.net

Lewis and Clark County Genealogical Society
P.O. Box 5313
Helena, MT 59604
Tel: 406-447-1690 ext. 28

Lewistown Genealogy Society
701 West Main
Lewitton, MT 59457

Miles City Genealogical Society
Miles City Public Library
1 South 10th Street
P.O. Box 711
Miles City, MT 59301
Tel: 406-232-1496

Montana State Genealogical Society
P.O. Box 555
Chester, MT 59522
http://www.rootsweb.com/~mtmsgs/

Park County Genealogy Society
Park County Public Library
228 West Callender Street
Livingston, MT 59047

Powder River Genealogical Society
P.O. Box 394
Broadus, MT 59317
E-mail: emmov@rangeweb.net
http://www.rangeweb.net/~emmov/prgs/prgs.html

Powell County Genealogical Society
912 Missouri Avenue
Deer Lodge, MT 59722

Root Diggers Genealogical Society
P.O. Box 249
Glasgow, MT 59230

Western Montana Genealogical Society
Missoula Public Library
301 East Main
Missoula, MT 59801
http://www.rootsweb.com/~mtwmgs/

Yellowstone Genealogy Forum
Parmly Billings Library
510 North Broadway
Billings, MT 59101
Tel: 406-657-8259
http://www.billings.lib.mt.us/

HISTORICAL SOCIETIES

Anaconda Deer Lodge County Historical Society
401 E. Commercial Street
Anaconda, MT 59711-2327
Tel: 406-563-2220
http://www.mtech.edu/silverbow/deerlodge.htm

Carbon County Historical Society
P.O. Box 881
Red Lodge, MT 59068

Cascade County Historical Society/Museum
422 2nd Avenue SW
Great Falls, MT 59404
Tel/Fax: 406-452-3462

Gallatin County Historical Society/Pioneer Museum
Old County Jail
317 W. Main Street
Bozeman, MT 59715-4576
Tel: 406-582-3195

Mineral County Historical Society
P.O. Box 38
Superior, MT 59872

Montana Historical Society
225 North Roberts Street
P.O. Box 201201
Helena, MT 59601
Tel: 406-444-2694
Fax: 406-444-2696
http://www.his.state.mt.us/

Phillips County Historical Society/Museum
431 Hwy 2 East
Malta, MT 59538
Tel: 406-654-1037

Stumptown Historical Society
500 Depot Street Suite 101
Whitefish, MT 59937
Tel: 406-862-0067
http://www.whitefishmt.com/stumphis/

Upper Blackfoot Valley Historical Society
P.O. Box 922
Lincoln, MT 59639
Tel: 406-362-4099

Upper Musselshell Historical Society/Museum
11 S. Central Avenue
Harlowton, MT 59036
Tel: 406-632-5519

LDS FAMILY HISTORY CENTERS

For locations of Family History Centers in this state, see the Family History Center locator at FamilySearch.
http://www.familysearch.org/eng/Library/FHC/frameset_fhc.asp

ARCHIVES/LIBRARIES/MUSEUMS

Beaverhead County Museum
15-25 South Montana
P.O. Box 830
Dillon, MT 59725
Tel: 406-683-5027

Big Horn County Historical Museum
P.O. Box 1206A
Hardin, MT 59034
Tel: 406-665-1671

Blackfoot Cultural Program
P.O. Box 850
Browning, MT 59417
Tel: 406-338-7406

Bureau of Land Management
Granite Tower
222 North 32nd Street
P.O. Box 36800
Billings, MT 59107
Tel: 406-255-2939

Butte/Silver Bow County Archives
17 West Quartz Street
Tel: 406-497-6226
E-mail: buttearchives@in-tch.com
http://www.co.silverbow.mt.us/archives.htm

Butte/Silver Bow County Public Library
226 W. Broadway Street
Butte, MT 59701
Tel: 406-723-8262
Fax: 406-782-6637

Carter County Library
Ekalaka, MT 59324
Tel: 406-775-6336

Cascade County Historical Museum
Paris Gibson Square
1400 First Avenue, North
Great Falls, MT 59401
Tel/Fax: 406-452-3462

Crow Tribal Council
P.O. Box 159
Crow Agency, MT 59022
Tel: 406-638-2601

Daniels County Museum
7 Country Road
P.O. Box 133
Scobey, MT 59263
Tel: 406-487-5965

Diocese of Great Falls
121 23rd Street, South
P.O. Box 1399
Great Falls, MT 59403
Tel: 406-727-6683
Fax: 406-454-3480
http://cf.disciplesnow.com/dnc_dio.cfm?dio=GFBs

Diocese of Helena
515 North Ewing
P.O. Box 1729
Helena, MT 59624
Tel: 406-442-5820
http://www.diocesehelena.org/pages/home.htm

Fallon County Library
6 West Fallon Avenue
P.O. Box 1037
Baker, MT 59313
Tel: 406-778-2883

Flathead Cultural Committee
P.O. Box 418
St. Ignatius, MT 59865
Tel: 406-745-4572

Fort Missoula Historical Museum
Fort Missoula Building 322
Missoula, MT 59804
Tel: 406-728-3476
Fax: 406-543-6277
E-mail: ftmslamuseum@marsweb.com
http://www.montana.com/ftmslamuseum/

Gallatin County Historical Society/Pioneer Museum
Old County Jail
317 W. Main Street
Bozeman, MT 59715-4576
Tel: 406-582-3195

Glasgow Library
408 Third Avenue, South
Glasgow, MT 59230
Tel: 406-228-2731
http://www.mtgl.mtlib.org/

Great Falls Public Library
301 2nd Avenue, North
Great Falls, MT 59401
Tel: 406-453-0349
http://www.greatfallslibrary.org/

Hardin Historical Museum
East of Hardin
Hardin, MT 59034
Tel: 406-665-1671

Havre/Hill County Library
402 3rd Street
P.O. Box 1151
Havre, MT 59501
Tel: 406-265-2123
http://www.mtha.mt.lib.org/

Kootenai Cultural Center
77406 Hwy 93
Elmo, MT 59915
Tel: 406-849-5541

Lewis & Clark Library
120 Last Chance Gulch
Helena, MT 59601
Tel: 406-447-1690
Fax: 406-447-1687
E-mail: pdunham@mtlib.org
http://www.mth.mtlib.org/

Libby Heritage Museum
1367 U.S. Highway 2, South
Libby, MT 59923-9011
Tel: 406-293-7521
http://www.lincolncountylibraries.com/museum/

Lincoln County Library/Eureka Branch
318 Dewey Avenue
Eureka, MT 59917
Tel/Fax: 406-296-2613
http://www.lincolncountylibraries.com/
    eureka_ library.html

Miles City Public Library
1 South 10th Street
P.O. Box 711
Miles City, MT 59301

Mineral County Historical Society
P.O. Box 38
Superior, MT 59872

Missoula Public Library
301 East Main
Missoula, MT 59802
Tel: 406-721-2665
Fax: 406-728-5900
E-mail: mslaplib@missoula.lib.mt.us
http://www.missoula.lib.mt.us/

Mon Dak Heritage Center
120 3rd Avenue, SE
Sidney, MT 59270-4324
Tel: 406-482-3500

Montana Historical Society
225 North Roberts Street
P.O. Box 201201
Helena, MT 59601
Tel: 406-444-2694
Fax: 406-444-2696
http://www.his.state.mt.us/

Montana State Library
1515 East Sixth Avenue
P.O. Box 201800
Helena, MT 59620-1800
Tel: 406-444-3115
Fax: 406-444-5612
http://www.msl.state.mt.us/

Montana State University/Billings
Library
1500 North 30th
Street Billings, MT 59101
Tel: 406-657-2011
http://www.msubillings.edu/library/

Montana State University/Bozeman Library
Renne Library
P.O. Box 173320
Bozeman, MT 59717-3320
Tel: 406-994-3119
Fax: 406-994-2851
http://www.lib.montana.edu/collect/spcoll/

Montana State University/Northern
Vande Bogard Library
P.O. Box 7751
Havre, MT 59501
Tel: 406-265-3706
Fax: 406-265-3550
http://www.msun.edu/infotech/library/

Montana Tech, The University of Montana
1300 West Park Street
Butte, MT 59701
Tel: 406-496-4284
http://www.mtech.edu/library/

Northern Cheyenne Cultural Center
Dull Knife Community College
P.O. Box 98
Lame Deer, MT 59043
Tel: 406-477-6215

O'Fallon Historical Museum
723 S. Main
Baker, MT 59313
Tel: 406-778-3265

Old Trail Museum
823 North Main Street
Choteau, MT 59422
Tel: 406-466-5332
http://www.oldtrailmuseum.org

Park County Public Library
228 West Callender Street
Livingston, MT 59047

Parmly Billings Library
510 North Broadway
Billings, MT 59101
Tel: 406-657-8259
http://www.billings.lib.mt.us/

Phillips County Historical Society/Museum
431 Hwy 2 East
Malta, MT 59538
Tel: 406-654-1037

Powder River Historical Museum
P.O. Box 573
Broadus, MT 59317
Tel: 406-436-2977
http://www.mcdd.net/museum/

Powell County Museum
1119 Main Street
Deer Lodge, MT 5972
Tel: 406-846-3111
Fax: 406-846-3156
http://www.montanaoldprisonmuseums.com/

Rocky Mountain College
Paul M. Adams Memorial Library
1511 Poly Drive
Billings, MT 59102
Tel: 406-657-1087
Fax: 406-259-9751

Sheridan County Library
100 West Laurel Avenue
Plentywood MT 59254
Tel: 406-765-2317
Fax: 406-765-2629
E-mail: library@co.sheridan.mt.us
http://www.co.sheridan.mt.us/library.htm

University of Montana/Missoula
32 Campus Drive #9936
Missoula, MT 59812-9936
Tel: 406-243-6866
Fax: 406-243-4067
E-mail: mullin@selway.umt.edu
http://www.lib.umt.edu/

Upper Musselshell Historical Society/Museum
11 S. Central Avenue
Harlowton, MT 59036
Tel: 406-632-5519

Valley County Pioneer Museum
Box 44
Glasgow, MT 59230
Tel: 406-228-8697

Victor Heritage Museum
Blake and Main
Victor, MT 59875
Tel: 406-642-3997

Western Heritage Center
2822 Montana Avenue
Billings, MT 59101
Tel: 406-256-6809
Fax: 406-256-6850
http://www.ywhc.org/

NEWSPAPER REPOSITORIES

Montana Tech, The University of Montana
1300 West Park Street
Butte, MT 59701
Tel: 406-496-4284
http://www.mtech.edu/library/

Montana Historical Society
225 North Roberts Street
P.O. Box 201201
Helena, MT 59601
Tel: 406-444-2694
Fax: 406-444-2696
http://www.his.state.mt.us/

VITAL RECORDS

Department of Public Health and Human Services (DPHHS)
111 North Sanders
P.O. Box 4210
Helena, MT 59604-4210
http://www.dphhs.state.mt.us/home.htm

MONTANA ON THE WEB

Montana GenWeb
http://www.rootsweb.com/~mtgenweb/

Native American Research in Montana
http://www.rootsweb.com/~mtgenweb/native.html

Nebraska

Archives, State & National

Nebraska State Historical Society/State Archives Division
1500 R Street
P.O. Box 82554
Lincoln, NE 68501
Tel: 402-471-3270
402-471-4771 (library)
Fax: 402-471-3100
http://www.nebraskahistory.org/

National Archives—Central Plains Region
2312 East Bannister Road
Kansas City, MO 64131
Tel: 816-926-6272
Fax: 816-926-6982
E-mail: archives@kansascity.nara.gov
http://www.nara.gov/nara/regional/06nsgil.html

Genealogical Societies

Adams County Genealogical Society
1330 N. Burlington
P.O. Box 424
Hastings, NE 68902
Tel: 402-463-5838
E-mail: achs@inebraska.com
http://incolor.inebraska.com/achs/acgs.html

Arnold Kinseekers
P.O. Box 135
Arnold, NE 69120

Boone-Nance County Genealogical Society
P.O. Box 231
Belgrade, NE 68623
http://www.rootsweb.com/~nenance/bngensoc.html

Cairo Roots
Route 1, Box 42
Cairo, NE 68824

Chase County Genealogical Society
P.O. Box 303
Imperial, NE 69033

Cherry County Genealogical Society
P.O. Box 380
Valentine, NE 69201

Cheyenne County Genealogical Society
P.O. Box 802
Sidney, NE 69162

Cozad Genealogy Club
Wilson Public Library
910 Meridian
Cozad, NE 69130

Dakota County Genealogical Society
P.O. Box 18
Dakota City, NE 68850

Dawson Genealogical Society
514 E. 8th Street
Cozad, NE 69130

Eastern Nebraska Genealogical Society
P.O. Box 541
Fremont, NE 68025
http://www.connectfremont.org/CLUB/ENGS.HTM

Fillmore Heritage Genealogical Society
Route 2, Box 28
Exeter, NE 68351

Flatwater Genealogical Society
P.O. Box 324
Gibbon, NE 68840

Fort Kearney Genealogical Society
P.O. Box 22
Kearney, NE 68847
E-mail: cottonmill@kearney.net
http://rootsweb.com/~nebuffal/fkgs.htm

Frontier County Genealogical Society
P.O. Box 507
Curtis, NE 69025

Furnas County Genealogical Society
P. O. Box 391
Beaver City, NE 68926
http://www.rootsweb.com/~nefurnas/
    GenSocResources.html

Genealogical Seekers
871 West 6th
Wahoo, NE 68066

Greater Omaha Genealogical Society
P.O. Box 4011
Omaha, NE 68104-0011
E-mail: GrOmahaGenSoc@aol.com
http://hometown.aol.com/gromahagensoc/
　　myhomepage/index.html

Greater York Area Genealogical Society
Kilgore Memorial Library
6th and Nebraska
York, NE 68467

Holdrege Area Genealogical Club
Phelps County Museum/Library
P.O. Box 778
Holdrege, NE 68949
E-mail: rs55453@navix.net
http://www.rootsweb.com/~nephelps/ phelpsgen.html

Holt County Genealogical Society
P.O. Box 376
O'Neill, NE 68763

Hooker County Genealogical Society
P.O. Box 280
Mullen, NE 69152

Howard County Kinquesters
317 7th Street
St. Paul, NE 68873

Jefferson County Genealogical Society
P.O. Box 163
Fairbury, NE 68352-0163
E-mail: eb72539@navix.net
http://www.rootsweb.com/~nejeffgs/

Lexington Genealogical Society
P.O. Box 778
Lexington, NE 68850

Lincoln/Lancaster County Genealogy Society
P.O. Box 30055
Lincoln, NE 68503-0055

Madison County Genealogical society
P.O. Box 347
Norfolk, NE 68701

Nebraska D.A.R./Library
202 West 4th Street
Alliance, NE 69301

Nebraska S.A.R.
6731 Summer
Street Lincoln, NE 68506

Nebraska State Genealogical Society
P.O. Box 5608
Lincoln, NE 68505

Nemaha Valley Genealogy Society
Nemaha Valley Museum
P.O. Box 25
Auburn, NE 68305

Northern Central Nebraska Genealogical Society
P.O. Box 362
O'Neill, NE 68763

North Platte Genealogical Society
P.O. Box 1452
North Platte, NE 69101

Northeastern Nebraska Genealogical Society (NENGS)
P.O. Box 169
Lyons, NE 68038

Northern Antelope County Genealogical Society
P.O. Box 267
Orchard, NE 68764

Northwest Genealogical Society
P.O. Box 6
Alliance, NE 69301-0006

Nuckolls County Genealogical Society
P.O. Box 441
Superior, NE 68978-0441

Pawnee Genealogy Scouters
P.O. Box 112
Albion, NE 68620

Perkins County Genealogical Society
P.O. Box 418
Grant, NE 69140

Plains Genealogical Society
Kimball Public Library
208 South Walnut Street
Kimball, NE 69145
Tel: 308-235-4523
http://www.ci.kimball.ne.us/library.htm

Platte Valley Kinseekers
P.O. Box 153
Columbus, NE 68601

Prairie Pioneer Genealogical Society
P.O. Box 1122
Grand Island, NE 68802

Ravenna Genealogical Society
105 Alba Street
Ravenna, NE 68869

Rebecca Winters Genealogical Society
1121 Avenue L
P.O. Box 323
Scottsbluff, NE 69361

Saline County Genealogical Society
P.O. Box 24
Crete, NE 68333

Sarpy County Genealogical Society
2402 Sac Place
Bellevue, NE 68005

Saunders County Genealogy Seekers
462 E. 13th
Wahoo, NE 68066

Seward County Genealogical Society
P.O. Box 72
Seward, NE 68434

South Central Genealogical Society
Route 2, Box 57
Minden, NE 68959

Southeast Nebraska Genealogical Society
P.O. Box 562
Beatrice, NE 68310-0562

Southwest Nebraska Genealogical Society
P.O. Box 156
McCook, NE 69001

Thayer County Genealogical Society
P.O. Box 388
Belvidere, NE 68315

Thomas County Genealogical Society
P.O. Box 136
Thedford, NE 69166

Tri-State Corners Genealogical Society
Falls City Public Library
Falls City, NE 68355

Valley County Genealogical Society
619 South 10th
Ord, NE 68862

Wahoo Genealogical Seekers
871 West 6th
Wahoo, NE 68066

Washington County Genealogical Society
Blair Public Library
210 South 17th Street
Blair, NE 68008

HISTORICAL SOCIETIES

Adams County Historical Society/Archives
1330 N. Burlington
P.O. Box 102
Hastings, NE 68902
Tel: 402-463-5838
http://incolor.inebraska.com/achs/

American Historical Society of Germans from Russia (AHSGR)
Lincoln Chapter
631 D Street
Lincoln, NE 68502
Tel: 402-474-3363
Fax: 402-474-7229
E-mail: ahsgr@ahsgr.org
http://www.ahsgr.org/nelincol.html

American Historical Society of Germans from Russia (AHSGR)
Northeast Nebraska Chapter
314 S. 13th Place
E-mail: ruthelaine@uswest.net (Jan-Apr)
     ruthelaine@cableone.net (May-Dec)
http://www.ahsgr.org/nenorthe.html

Brownville Historical Society
131 Main
Brownville, NE 68321
Tel: 402-825-6001

Butler County Historical Society
1125 3rd Street
David City, NE 68632
Tel: 402-367-3500

Cheyenne County Historical Association
6th and Jackson
Sidney, NE 69162
Tel: 308-254-2150

Custer County Historical Society, Inc./Museum & Archives
445 South 9th Avenue
P.O. Box 334
Broken Bow, NE 68822
Tel: 308-872-2203
http://www.rootsweb.com/~necuster/

Dakota County Historical Society
RR 1
Chadron, NE 68731-9801
Tel: 402-698-2288

Dawson County Historical Society
P.O. Box 369
Lexington, NE 68850

Dodge County Historical Society
1643 N. Nye
P.O. Box 766
Fremont, NE 68026-0766

Douglas County Historical Society
Fort Omaha
5730 N. 30 St, #11B
Omaha, NE 68111-1657
Tel: 402-455-9990
Fax: 402-453-9448
http://www.omahahistory.org/fort_omaha.htm

Gage County Historical Society
2nd and Court Streets
P.O. Box 793
Beatrice, NE 68310
Tel: 402-228-1679
http://www.infoanalytic.com/gage/

High Plains Historical Society/Museum
413 Norris Avenue
McCook, NE 69001-2003
Tel: 308-345-3661

Holt County Historical Society
P.O. Box 231
O'Neill, NE 68763

Naponee Historical Society
P.O. Box 128
Naponee, NE 68960
http://www.alltel.net/~ps60313/naponeehist.html

Nebraska State Historical Society
1500 R Street
P.O. Box 82554
Lincoln, NE 68501-2554
Tel: 402-471-3270
     402-471-4771 (library)
Fax: 402-471-3100
http://www.nebraskahistory.org/

Phelps County Historical Society
North Burlington
Holdrege, NE 68949
Tel: 308-995-5015

Platte County Historical Society/Museum
2916 16th Street
Columbus, NE 68601
Tel: 402-564-1856

Railroad Station Historical Society
430 Ivy Avenue
Crete, NE 68333

Saunders County Historical Society
240 N. Walnut Street
Wahoo, NE 68066
Tel: 402-443-3090
http://www.co.saunders.ne.us/saumuseum.htm

Thurston County Historical Society
General Delivery
Pender, NE 68047

Washington County Historical Association
102 N 14th Street
P.O. Box 25
Fort Calhoun, NE 68023
Tel: 402-468-5740

LDS FAMILY HISTORY CENTERS

For locations of Family History Centers in this state, see
     the Family History Center locator at FamilySearch.
http://www.familysearch.org/eng/Library/FHC/
     frameset_fhc.asp

ARCHIVES/LIBRARIES/MUSEUMS

Adams County Historical Society/Archives
1330 N. Burlington
P.O. Box 102
Hastings, NE 68902
Tel: 402-463-5838
http://incolor.inebraska.com/achs/

Alice M. Farr Library
1603 L Street
Aurora, NE 68818
E-mail: afl@hamilton.net
http://www.cityofaurora.org/library.html

Alliance Public Library
1750 Sweetwater Avenue
Alliance, NE 69301
Tel: 308-762-1387

Antelope County Historical Museum
Antelope County Historical Society
305 K Street
Neligh, NE 68756

Bayard Public Library
509 Avenue A
P.O. Box B
Bayard, NE 69334

Beatrice Public Library
100 N. 16th Street
Beatrice, NE 68310
Tel: 402-223-3584

Bennett Martin Public Library
136 South 14th Street
Lincoln, NE 68508
Tel: 402-441-8500
Fax: 402-441-8586
E-mail: library@ci.lincoln.ne.us
http://www.lcl.lib.ne.us/

Big Springs Public Library
P.O. Box 192
Big Springs, NE 69122
Tel: 308-889-3482

Black Americana Historical Museum
1240 S. 13th Street
Omaha, NE 68108
Tel: 402-341-6908
http://www.omaha.org/oma/orans.htm

Blair Public Library
210 S. 17th Street
Blair, NE 68008
Tel: 402-426-3617
E-mail: library@huntel.net
http://www.blairpubliclibrary.com/

Bridgeport Public Library
722 Main
P.O. Box 940
Bridgeport, NE 69336
Tel: 308-262-0326

Broadwater Public Library
Route 2
Box 64
Broadwater, NE 69125

Cass County Historical Museum
646 Main Street
Plattsmouth, NE 68048
Tel: 402-296-4770

Catholic Chancery Office
Diocese of Lincoln
3400 Sheridan Blvd.
Lincoln, NE 68506
Tel: 402-488-0921

Chadron Public Library
507 Bordeaux Street
Chadron, NE 69337
Tel: 308-432-0531
Fax: 308-432-0534
http://members.panhandle.net/chadronpublic library/

Chadron State College
Mari Sandoz Heritage High Plains Center
Chadron, NE 69337
http://www.csc.edu/alumni/sandoz.asp

Chadron State College
Chadron State College King Library
300 East 12th Street
Chadron Nebraska 69337
Tel: 308-432-6271
http://www.csc.edu/l/library/kingweb/

Chappell Public Library
289 Babcock Avenue
P.O. Box 248
Chappell, NE 69129
Tel: 308-874-2626

Columbus Public Library
2504 14th Street
Columbus, NE 68601
Tel: 402-564-7116
http://www.megavision.com/~cisweb/columbus/
    cpl.htm

Cozad Public Library
910 Meridian Avenue
Cozad, NE 69130
Tel: 308-784-2019

Crawford Public Library
601 2nd Street
Crawford, NE 69339
Tel: 308-665-1780

Creighton University
Reinert/Alumni Library
2500 California Plaza
Omaha, NE 68178
Tel: 402-280-2927
    402-280-2746 (Archives)
Fax: 402-280-2435
http://reinert.creighton.edu/archives.htm

Crete Public Library
305 E. 13th Street
P.O. Box 156
Crete, NE 68333-0156
Tel: 402-826-3809

Dalton Public Library
306 Main Street
P.O. Box 206
Dalton, NE 69131

Dana College
C.A. Dana/LIFE Library
2848 College Drive
Blair, NE 68008
Tel: 402-426-7300
Fax: 402-426-7332
http://www.dana.edu/library/

Dawes County Historical Museum
RR 1
Chadron, NE 69337
Tel: 308-432-4999

Douglas County Historical Society
Fort Omaha
5730 N. 30 St, #11B
Omaha, NE 68111-1657
Tel: 402-455-9990
Fax: 402-453-9448
http://www.omahahistory.org/fort_omaha.htm

Garfield County Historical Museum
737 H Street
RR1 Box 66
Burwell, NE 68823

Geneva Public Library
1043 G Street
Geneva, NE 68361
Tel: 402-759-3416
http://www.ci.geneva.ne.us/General.htm#library

Gering Public Library
1055 P Street
Gering, NE 69341
Tel: 308-436-7433
http://www.gering.org/library/

Gordon Public Library
101 W. 5th Street
Gordon, NE 69343
Tel: 308-282-1198

Gothenburg Public Library
1104 Lake Avenue
Gothenburg, NE 69138
Tel: 308-537-2591
http://www.ci.gothenburg.ne.us/library.htm

Grand Island/Edith Abbott Memorial Library
211 South Washington
Grand Island, NE 68801
Tel: 308-385-5333
Fax: 308-385-5339
http://www.gi.lib.ne.us/

Hay Springs/Cravath Memorial Library
243 North Main Street
P.O. Box 309
Hay Springs, NE 69347
Tel: 308-638-4541

Hemingford Public Library
812 Box Butte Avenue
Alliance, NE 69301
Tel: 308-487-3454

High Plains Historical Society/Museum
413 Norris Avenue
McCook, NE 69001-2003
Tel: 308-345-3661

Holdrege Area Genealogical Club
Phelps County Museum/Library
P.O. Box 778
Holdrege, NE 68949
E-mail: rs55453@navix.net
http://www.rootsweb.com/~nephelps/ phelpsgen.html

Kearney Public Library
2020 1st Avenue
Kearney, NE 68847
Tel: 308-233-3282
Fax: 308-233-3291
http://www.kearneylib.org/

Keene Memorial Library
1030 North Broad Street
Fremont, NE 68025
Tel: 402-727-2694
Fax: 402-727-2826
E-mail: info@keene.lib.ne.us

Kilgore Memorial Library
520 Nebraska Avenue
York, NE 68467
Tel: 402-363-2620
http://www.ci.york.ne.us/communit.htm#kilgore

Kimball Public Library
208 South Walnut Street
Kimball, NE 69145
Tel: 308-235-4523
http://www.ci.kimball.ne.us/library.htm

Lewellen Public Library
P.O. Box 58
Lewellen, NE 69147
Tel: 308-778-5421

Lexington Public Library
103 E. Tenth Street
P.O. Box 778
Lexington, NE 68850
Tel: 308-324-2151

Lincoln County Historical Museum
2403 N. Buffalo
North Platte, NE 69101
Tel: 308-534-5640

Lincoln Public Library
Heritage Room Bennett Martin Public Library
136 South 14th Street
Lincoln, NE 68508

Lisco Library
P.O. Box 137
Lisco, NE 69148

Lydia Brun Woods Memorial Library
120 E. 18th Street
Falls City, NE 68355
Tel: 402-245-2913

Lyman Public Library
313 Jeffers Avenue
P.O. Box 384
Lyman, NE 69352
Tel: 308-787-1366

Mitchell Public Library
1447 Center Avenue
Mitchell, NE 69357
Tel: 308-623-2222

Minatare Public Library
405 Main
P.O. Box 483
Minatare, NE 69356
Tel: 308-783-1414

Morrill Public Library
119 E. Webster
P.O. Box 402
Morrill, NE 69358
Tel: 308-247-2611

Nancy Fawcett Memorial Library
P.O. Box 318
Lodgepole, NE 69149
Tel: 308-483-5714

Nebraska D.A.R./Library
202 West 4th Street
Alliance, NE 69301

Nebraska Library Commission
The Atrium
1200 N. Street, Suite 120
Lincoln, NE 68508-2023
Tel: 402-471-2045
     800-307-2665 (in Nebraska only)
Fax: 402-471-2086
http://www.nlc.state.ne.us/

Nebraska State Law Library
State Capitol Bldg.
15th & K Streets
P.O. Box 98931
Lincoln, NE 68509-8931
Tel: 402-471-3189
Fax: 402-471-1011
E-mail:nsc_lawlib@nsc.state.ne.us
http://court.nol.org/library/lawlibindex.htm

Nebraska United Methodist Archives & History Center
5000 St. Paul Avenue
Lincoln, NE 68504
Tel: 402-465-2175

Nebraska Veterans Administration Office
5631 S. 48th Street
Lincoln, NE 68516
Tel: 402-420-4023
     402-420-4021

Nemaha Valley Museum
P.O. Box 25
Auburn, NE 68305

Norfolk Public Library
308 Prospect Avenue
Norfolk, NE 68701
Tel: 402-644-8711
Fax: 402-370-3260
http://www.ci.norfolk.ne.us/library/

Omaha Public Library
215 South 15th Street
Omaha, NE 68102
Tel: 402-444-4800
     402-444-4826 (Genealogy Dept.)
http://www.omaha.lib.ne.us/

Oshkosh Public Library
P.O. Box 140
Oshkosh, NE 69154
Tel: 308-772-4554

Platte County Historical Society/Museum
2916 16th Street
Columbus, NE 68601
Tel: 402-564-1856

Potter Public Library
333 Chestnut
P.O. Box 317
Potter, NE 69156
Tel: 308-879-4345

Ralston Archives/Museum
8311 Park Drive
Ralston, NE 68127

Rushville Public Library
207 Sprague Street
P.O. Box 473
Rushville, NE 69360
Tel: 308-327-2740

Scottsbluff Public Library
1809 3rd Avenue
Scottsbluff, NE 69361
Tel: 308-630-6250
http://city.scottsbluff.net/

Stuhr Museum of the Prairie Pioneer
3133 W. U.S. Highway 34
Grand Island, NE 68801-7280
Tel: 308-385-5316
http://www.gionline.net/arts/stuhr/

Thurston County Historical Museum
500 Ivan Street
Pender, NE 68047
Tel: 402-385-3210

Union College Library
3800 South 48th Street
Lincoln, NE 68506
Tel: 402-486-2514
http://www.ucollege.edu/library/library.htm

University of Nebraska/Kearney
Calvin T. Ryan Library
905 W. 25th Street
Kearney, NE 68849
Tel: 308-865-8535
    308-865-8544 (Archives/Special Collections)
Fax: 308-865-8722
E-mail: lillis@platte.unk.edu
http://rosi.unk.edu/

University of Nebraska/Lincoln
Archives and Special Collections
P.O. Box 880410
Lincoln, NE 68588-0410
Tel: 402-472-2531
Fax: 402-472-5131
http://www.unl.edu/libr/libs/spec/regulations.html

University of Nebraska/Omaha
University Library
Omaha, NE 68182-0237
Tel: 402-554-2661 (Information)
    402-554-3202 (Government Documents)
    402-554-2884 (Special Collections)
http://revelation.unomaha.edu/

Washington County Historical Museum
102 North 14th
Fort Calhoun, NE 68023
Tel: 402-468-5740
http://www.newashcohist.org/museum.asp

Wayne Public Library
410 Main Street
Wayne, NE 68787
Tel: 402-375-3135

Webster County Historical Museum
721 W. 4th Avenue
Red Cloud, NE 68970-2221
Tel: 402-746-2444

Western Heritage Museum
801 South 10th Street
Omaha, NE 68108
Tel: 402-444-5071
Fax: 402-444-5397
E-mail: info@dwhm.org
http://www.dwhm.org/

NEWSPAPER REPOSITORIES

Lincoln/Lancaster County Genealogy Society
P.O. Box 30055
Lincoln, NE 68503-0055

Nebraska State Genealogical Society
P.O. Box 5608
Lincoln, NE 68505

Nebraska State Historical Society
1500 R Street
P.O. Box 82554
Lincoln, NE 68501-2554
Tel: 402-471-3270
    402-471-4771 (library)
Fax: 402-471-3100
http://www.nebraskahistory.org/

University of Nebraska/Lincoln
Archives and Special Collections
P.O. Box 880410
Lincoln, NE 68588-0410
Tel: 402-472-2531
Fax: 402-472-5131
http://www.unl.edu/libr/libs/spec/regulations.html

VITAL RECORDS

Nebraska Department of Health & Human Services/Vital Records
P.O. Box 95065
Lincoln, NE 68509-5065
Tel: 402-471-2871
http://www.hhs.state.ne.us/

NEBRASKA ON THE WEB

Andreas' History of the State of Nebraska (publ. 1885)
http://www.ukans.edu/carrie/kancoll/andreas_ne/

Nebraska GenWeb Project
www.rootsweb.com/~negenweb/

Nebraska State Government Publications Online
(Guide to Genealogical Research &
Historical Society Reference Information Guide)
http://www.nlc.state.ne.us/docs/pilot/pilot.html

NEVADA

ARCHIVES, STATE & NATIONAL

National Archives—Pacific Southwest Region
24000 Avila Rd., First Floor-East Entrance
P.O. Box 6719
Laguna Niguel, CA 92607-6719
Tel: 949-360-2626
Fax: 949-360-2624
E-mail: laguna.archives@nara.gov
http://www.nara.gov/regional/laguna.html
(Serves Clark County)

National Archives—Pacific Sierra Region
1000 Commodore Drive
San Bruno, CA 94066
Tel: 650-876-9001
Fax: 650-876-9233
E-mail: sanbruno.archives@nara.gov
http://www.nara.gov/regional/sanfranc.html
(Serves Nevada, except for Clark County)

Nevada State Library and Archives
100 N. Stewart Street
Carson City, NV 89710
Tel: 702-687-5160 (Library)
702-687-5210 (Archives)
http://dmla.clan.lib.nv.us/docs/nsla/

GENEALOGICAL SOCIETIES

Churchill County Historical & Genealogical Society
Churchill County Museum & Archives
1050 South Main Street
Fallon, NV 89406
Tel: 775-423-3677
Fax: 775-423-3662
E-mail: ccmuseum@phonewave.net
http://www.ccmuseum.org/

Clark County Genealogical Society
P.O. Box 1929
Las Vegas, NV 89125-1929
Tel: 702-225-5838
Fax: 702-258-4099
http://www.rootsweb.com/~nvccngs/

Humboldt County Genealogical Society
Humboldt County Library
85 East 5th Street
Winnemucca, NV 89445
Tel: 775-623-6388
http://www.clan.lib.nv.us/polpac/library/clan/HCL/
    humtest.htm

Jewish Genealogical Society of Las Vegas, Nevada
P.O. Box 29342
Las Vegas, NV 89126-3342
E-mail: carmont7@juno.com

Nevada State Genealogical Society
P.O. Box 20666
Reno, NV 89515
http://www.rootsweb.com/~nvsgs/

Northeastern Nevada Genealogical Society
1515 Idaho Street
Elko, NV 89801
http://www.rootsweb.com/~nvnengs/

HISTORICAL SOCIETIES

Carson Valley Historical Society
1477 U.S. Highway 395 North
Gardnerville, NV 89410
http://www.carsonvalleymuseums.com/

Central Nevada Historical Society
P.O. Box 326
Tonopah, NV 89049

Churchill County Historical & Genealogical Society
Churchill County Museum & Archives
1050 South Main Street
Fallon, NV 89406
Tel: 775-423-3677
Fax: 775-423-3662
E-mail: ccmuseum@phonewave.net
http://www.ccmuseum.org/

Eureka County Historical Society
Eureka Sentinel Museum
P.O. Box 284
Eureka, NV 89316
Tel: 775-237-5010
Fax: 775-237-6040

Goldfield Historical Society
P.O. Box 178
Goldfield 89013

Inter-Tribal Council History Project
680 Greenbrae Drive
Sparks, NV 89431
Tel: 775-355-0600
http://itcn.org/itcn/itcn.html

Nevada Historical Society/Library
1650 North Virginia Street
Reno, NV 89503
Tel: 775-688-1190
Fax: 775-688-2917
http://dmla.clan.lib.nv.us/docs/museums/reno/
his-soc.htm

Nevada State Museum and Historical Society
State Mall Complex
700 Twin Lakes Drive
Las Vegas, NV 89158
Tel: 702-486-5205
Fax: 702-486-5172
http://dmla.clan.lib.nv.us/docs/museums/lv/ vegas.htm

North Central Nevada Historical Society
Humboldt County Museum
P.O. Box 819
Winnemucca, NV 89445
Tel: 775-623-2912

North Lake Tahoe Historical Society
P.O. Box 6141
Tahoe City, CA 96145
Tel: 530-583-1762
E-mail: nlths@tahoecountry.com
http://www.tahoecountry.com/nlths/

Southern Nevada Historical Society
P.O. Box 1358
Las Vegas, NV 89101

White Pine Historical and Archaeological Society
P.O. Box 1117
Ely, Nevada 89315
http://www.webpanda.com/white_pine_county/
historical_society/

LDS FAMILY HISTORY CENTERS

For locations of Family History Centers in this state, see the Family History Center locator at FamilySearch.
http://www.familysearch.org/eng/Library/FHC/
frameset_fhc.asp

ARCHIVES/LIBRARIES/MUSEUMS

African American Museum and Research Center
The Walker Foundation
705 W. Van Buren Avenue
Las Vegas, NV 89106
Tel: 702-647-2242

Boulder City Historical Association/Museum
444 Hotel Plaza
P.O. Box 60516
Boulder City, NV 89006
Tel: 702-294-1988
http://www.accessnv.com/bcmha/

Boulder City Library
701 Adams Boulevard
Boulder City, NV 89005
Tel: 702-293-1281
Fax: 702-293-0239
E-mail: duncan@accessnv.com
http://www.bclibrary.org/

Churchill County Museum & Archives
1050 South Main Street
Fallon, NV 89406
Tel: 775-423-3677
http://www.ccmuseum.org/

Clark County Museum
1830 South Boulder Highway
Henderson, NV 89015
Tel: 702-455-7955

Douglas County Library
1625 Library Lane
P.O. Box 337
Minden, NV 89423
Tel: 702-782-9841
E-mail: ldeacy@douglas.lib.nv.us
http://douglas.lib.nv.us/

East Ely Railroad Depot Museum
1100 Avenue
P.O. Box 151100
Ely, NV 89301
Tel: 775-289-1663
Fax: 775-289-1664
http://dmla.clan.lib.nv.us/docs/museums/ely/ely.htm

Eureka Sentinel Museum
P.O. Box 284
Eureka, NV 89316
Tel: 775-237-5010
Fax: 775-237-6040

Humboldt County Library
85 East 5th Street
Winnemucca, NV 89445

Humboldt County Museum
P.O. Box 819
Winnemucca, NV 89445
Tel: 775-623-2912

Las Vegas Public Library
833 Las Vegas Blvd., North
Las Vegas, NV 89101
Tel: 702-382-3493
http://www.lvccld.org/

Lincoln County Museum
69 Main Street
Box 515
Pioche, NV 89043
Tel: 775-962-5207

Lost City Museum
721 S. Moapa Valley Blvd.
P.O. Box 807
Overton, NV 89040
Tel: 702-397-2193
Fax: 702-397-8987
E-mail: Lostcity@comnett.net
http://dmla.clan.lib.nv.us/docs/museums/lost/
lostcity.htm

Lyon County Museum
215 South Main
Yerington, NV 89447
Tel: 775-463-2245
Fax: 775-463-3369

Mineral County Museum
P.O. Box 1584
Hawthorne, NV 89415

Nevada Historical Society/Library
1650 North Virginia Street
Reno, NV 89503
Tel: 775-688-1190
Fax: 775-688-2917
http://dmla.clan.lib.nv.us/docs/museums/reno/
his-soc.htm

Nevada State Museum
600 North Carson
Carson City, NV 89710
Tel: 775-687-4810
Fax: 775-687-4333

Nevada State Museum and Historical Society
State Mall Complex
700 Twin Lakes Drive
Las Vegas, NV 89158
Tel: 702-486-5205
Fax: 702-486-5172
http://dmla.clan.lib.nv.us/docs/museums/lv/egas.htm

Northeastern Nevada Museum
1515 Idaho Street
P.O. Box 503
Elko, NV 89801
Tel: 775-738-3418
Fax: 774-778-9318
E-mail: museum@nenv-museum.org
http://www.nenv-museum.org/

Sparks Heritage Foundation/Museum
820 Victorian Avenue
Sparks, NV 89431
Tel: 775-355-1144

University of Nevada/Las Vegas (UNLV)
4505 Maryland Parkway
Las Vegas, NV 89154
Tel: 702-895-3285
http://www.library.unlv.edu/speccol/

University of Nevada/Reno
Getchell Library
Special Collections Dept. 322
Reno, NV 89557
Tel: 775-784-6500
E-mail: specarch@unr.edu
http://www.library.unr.edu/specoll/

Washoe Archive and Cultural Resource Center
861 Crescent Drive
Carson City, NV 89701
Tel: 775-888-0936

Washoe County Library
301 South Center
P.O. Box 2151
Reno, NV 89501
Tel: 775-785-4190
Fax: 775-785-4692
E-mail: jkup@washoe.lib.nv.us
http://www.washoe.lib.nv.us/

Western Railroaders Hall of Fame & Museum
2533 N. Carson Street
Carson City, NV 89706

White Pine Public Museum
2000 Aultman Street
Ely, NV 89301
Tel: 702-289-4710
http://www.webpanda.com/white_pine_county/ museum/

NEWSPAPER REPOSITORIES

Nevada Historical Society/Library
1650 North Virginia Street
Reno, NV 89503
Tel: 775-688-1190
Fax: 775-688-2917
http://dmla.clan.lib.nv.us/docs/museums/reno/
his-soc.htm

Nevada State Library and Archives
100 N. Stewart Street
Carson City, NV 89710
Tel: 775-687-5160 (Library)
775-684-3360
Fax: 775-684-3330
TDD: 775-687-8338
E-mail: cmathwig@clan.lib.nv.us
http://dmla.clan.lib.nv.us/docs/NSLA/

University of Nevada/Las Vegas (UNLV)
4505 Maryland Parkway
Las Vegas, NV 89154
Tel: 702-895-3285
http://www.library.unlv.edu/speccol/

University of Nevada/Reno
Getchell Library
Special Collections Dept. 322
Reno, NV 89557
Tel: 775-784-6500
E-mail: specarch@unr.edu
http://www.library.unr.edu/specoll/

VITAL RECORDS

State Office of Vital Records
Capitol Complex
505 E. King Street, Room 102
Carson City, NV 89710
Tel: 775-684-4242
Fax: 775-684-4156
http://www.vitalrec.com/nv.html

NEVADA ON THE WEB

Nevada GenWeb Project
http://www.rootsweb.com/~nvgenweb/

Pony Express Home Page
http://www.xphomestation.com/

NEW HAMPSHIRE

ARCHIVES, STATE & NATIONAL

National Archives-Northeast Region (Boston)
Frederick C. Murphy Federal Center
380 Trapelo Road
Waltham, MA 02154-8104
Tel: 781-647-8104
Fax: 781-647-8088
E-mail: waltham.center@nara.gov
http://www.nara.gov/regional/boston.html

New Hampshire Division of Records Management and Archives
771 South Fruit Street
Concord, NH 03301
Tel: 603-271-2236
Fax: 603-271-2272
http://www.state.nh.us/state/index.html

GENEALOGICAL SOCIETIES

American Canadian Genealogical Society/Library
378 Notre Dame Avenue
P.O. Box 668
Manchester, NH 03105

American-Canadian Genealogical Society (ACGS)
4 Elm Street
P.O. Box 6478
Manchester, NH 03108
Tel: 603-622-1554
Fax: 603-624-8843
http://www.acgs.org/

Grafton County Historic & Genealogy Society
P.O. Box 1163
Ashland, NH 03217
E-mail: rbhicks@cyberportal.net

New England Historical and Genealogical Society (NEHGS)
101 Newbury Street
Boston, MA 02116-3007
Tel: 617-836-5740
    888-296-3447 (Membersip and Sales)
    888-906-3447 (Library Circulation)
Fax: 617-536-7307
E-mail: nehgs@nehgs.org
http://www.newenglandancestors.org/

New Hampshire Society of Genealogists
30 Park Street
P.O. Box 2316
Concord, NH 03302-2316
Tel: 603-225-3381
E-mail: milliken@tiac.net
http://nhsog.org/

Piscataqua Pioneers
University of New Hampshire
Milne Special Collections and Archives
UNH Library
18 Library Way
Durham, NH 03824-3592
Tel: 603-862-2714 (Special Collections)
    603-862-2956 (University Archives)
Fax: 603-862-1919
E-mail: library.special.collections@unh.edu
    or archives@unh.edu
http://www.izaak.unh.edu/

Rockingham Society of Genealogists
P.O. Box 81
Exeter, NH 03833-0081

HISTORICAL SOCIETIES

Acworth Historical Society
Acworth Silsby Library
Acworth, NH 03601

Alton Historical Society
P.O. Box 536
Alton, NH 03809

Amherst, Historical Society of
P.O. Box 717
Amherst, NH 03031

Andover Historical Society
P.O. Box 167
Andover, NH 03216

Ashland Historical Society
P.O. Box 175
Ashland, NH 03217

Association of Historical Societies of New Hampshire
11 Ironwood Lane
Atkinson, NH 03811

Atkinson Historical Society
3 Academy Avenue
P.O. Box 863
Atkinson, NH 03811
http://www.town-atkinsonnh.com/
        historical_society.htm

Bedford Historical Society
24 N. Amherst Road
Bedford, NH 03110
http://www.geocities.com/bedfordhistoricalsociety/

Bennington Historical Society
P.O. Box 50
Bennington, NH 03442

Boscawen Historical Society
P.O. Box 3067
Boscawen, NH 03303

Brentwood Historical Society
1 Dalton Road
Brentwood, NH 03833

Canaan Historical Society/Museum
P.O. Box 38
Canaan, NH 03741

Candia Historical Society
P.O. Box 300
Candia, NH 03034
http://www.geocities.com/candianh/HistoricalPage.html

Canterbury Historical Society
P.O. Box 206
Canterbury, NH 03224

Center Harbor Historical Society
P.O. Box 98
Center Harbor, NH 03226

Charlestown Historical Society
P.O. Box 253
Charlestown, NH 03603

Cheshire County, Historical Society & Archives
246 Main Street
P.O. Box 803
Keene, NH 03431
Tel: 603-352-1895

Chester Historical Society
P.O. Box 34
Chester, NH 03036
Phone: 603-887-4545
E-mail:chesterhistorical@yahoo.com
http://www.geocities.com/chesterhistorical/

Chesterfield Historical Society
P.O. Box 204
Chesterfield, NH 03443

Chichester Historical Society
Chichester Library
Main Street
Chichester, NH 03263

Claremont Historical Society
26 Mulberry Street
Claremont, NH 03743
Tel: 603-543-1400

Colebrook Area Historical Society
P.O. Box 32
Colebrook, NH 03576

Conway Historical Society
100 Main Street
P.O. Box 1949
Conway, NH 03818
Tel: 603-447-5551
http://www.conwayhistory.org/

Cornish Historical Society
RR 2, Box 416
Cornish, NH 03745

Deerfield Heritage Commission
60 South Road
Deerfield, NH 03037

Deering Historical Society
RR 1, Box 69
Deering, NH 03244

Derry Historical Society/Museum
65 Birch Street
Derry, NH 03038

Durham Historic Association
P.O. Box 305
Durham, NH 03824
Tel: 603-868-5436

Effingham Historical Society
P.O. Box 33
South Effingham, NH 03882
Tel: 603-539-6715

Epping Historical Society
P.O. Box 348
Epping, NH 03042

Exeter Historical Society
47 Front Street
P.O. Box 924
Exeter, NH 03833
Tel: 603-778-2335

Franklin Historical Society
P.O. Box 43
Franklin, NH 03235

Gilmanton Historical Society
P.O. Box 236
Gilmanton, NH 03237

Gilsum Historical Society
P.O. Box 205
Gilsum, NH 03448

Goffstown Historical Society
18 Parker Station Road
P.O. Box 284
Goffstown, NH 03045
Tel: 603-497-4306

Grafton County Historic & Genealogy Society
P.O. Box 1163
Ashland, NH 03217
E-mail: rbhicks@cyberportal.net

Greenland Historical Society
459 Portsmouth Avenue
Greenland, NH 03840

Hampton Historians, Inc.
3 Thomsen Road
Hampton, NH 03842

Hancock Historical Society
7 Main Street
P.O. Box 138
Hancock, NH 03049
Tel: 603-525-9379
E-mail: hancockhistsoc@monad.net
http://www.mv.com/ipusers/hancocknh/hhs/
hhs_home.htm

Hanover Historical Society
P.O. Box 142
Hanover, NH 03755

Harold Gilman Historical Museum
Rt. 140 & Main Street
P.O. Box 659
Alton, NH 03809
Tel: 603-875-2161

Hawke Historical Society of Danville
P.O. Box 402
Danville, NH 03819

Henniker Historical Society
P.O. Box 674
Henniker, NH 03242
http://www.hennikerhistory.org/

Hill Historical Society
P.O. Box 193
Hill, NH 03243

Hillsborough Historical Society
P.O. Box 896
Hillsboro, NH 03244
Tel: 603-478-3165
E-mail: c_chadwick@conknet.com

Hinsdale Historical Society
RR 2, River Street, Box 9
Hinsdale, NH 03451

Holderness Historical Society
P.O. Box 319
Holderness, NH 03245

Hollis Historical Society
Ruth E. Wheeler house
20 Main Street
P.O. Box 754
Hollis, NH 03049
Tel: 603-465-3935
http://www.hollis-history.org/

Jackson Historical Society
P.O. Box 8
Jackson, NH 03846
Tel: 603-383-4060
http://www.jacksonnhhistory.org/ recentadditions.html

Jaffrey Historical Society
123 Main Street
Jaffrey, NH 03452

Kensington Historical Society
Kensington Public Library
126 Amesbury Road
Kensington, NH 03833
Tel: 603-772-5022
E-mail: kensingtonlibrary@attbi.com
http://town.kensington.nh.us/library/

Laconia Historical Society
P.O. Box 1126
Laconia, NH 03247

Lancaster Historical Society
226 Main Street
P.O. Box 473
Lancaster, NH 03584
Tel: 603-788-3004

Lee Historical Society
Lee Town Hall
7 Mast Road
Lee, NH 03824

Littleton Area Historical Society
1 Cottage Street
Littleton, NH 03561

Londonderry Historical Society
P.O. Box 136
Londonderry, NH 03053

Madbury Historical Society
13 Town Hall Road
Madbury, NH 03820

Madison Historical Society
P.O. Box 335
Madison, NH 03849

Manchester Historic Association
129 Amherst Street
Manchester, NH 03101
Tel: 603-622-7531
E-mail: history@manchesterhistoric.org
http://www.mv.com/org/mha/

Marlborough Historical Society, Inc.
P.O. Box 202
Marlborough, NH 03455

Meredith Historical Society
P.O. Box 920
Meredith, NH 03253
Tel: 603-279-8704

Merrimack Historical Society
P.O. Box 1525
Merrimack, NH 03054

Milford Historical Society
P.O. Box 609
6 Union Street
Milford, NH 03055
Tel: 603-673-3385
http://www.milfordnh.com/history/

Milton Township Historical Society
P.O. Box 621
Milton, NH 03851

Moultonborough Historical Society
P.O. Box 6549
Moultonborough, NH 03254

Nashua Historical Society
5 Abbott Street
Nashua, NH 03060

New England Historical and Genealogical Society (NEHGS)
101 Newbury Street
Boston, MA 02116-3007
Tel: 617-836-5740
      888-296-3447 (Membersip and Sales)
      888-906-3447 (Library Circulation)
Fax: 617-536-7307
E-mail: nehgs@nehgs.org
http://www.newenglandancestors.org/

New Hampshire Antiquarian Society
300 Main Street
Hopkinton, NH 03229
Tel: 603-746-3825

New Hampshire Historical Society/Library
30 Park Street
Concord, NH 03301-6384
Tel: 603-228-6688
Fax: 603-224-0463
E-mail: swilding@aol.com
http://www.nhhistory.org/

New Hampton Historical Society
P.O. Box 422
New Hampton, NH 03256
E-mail: ronocal@lr.net
http://www.rugreview.com/nhhs/nhhsind.htm

New London Historical Society
P.O. Box 965
New London, NH 03257
http://www.newlondonhistoricalsociety.org/

Newmarket Historical Society
Granite Street
Newmarket, NH 03857
Tel: 603-659-7420
http://www.seacoastnh.com/dct/newmarket.html

Newbury Historical Society
P.O. Box 176
Newbury, NH 03255

Newfields Historical Society
P.O. Box 126
Newfields, NH 03856

Northwood Historical Society
P.O. Box 114
Northwood, NH 03261
http://www.rootsweb.com/~nhnhs/

Nottingham Historical Society
P.O. Box 241
Nottingham, NH 03290

Ossipee Historical Society
P.O. Box 245
Ossipee, NH 03864
http://groups.msn.com/OssipeeHistoricalSociety/
_homepage.msnw?pgmarket=en-us

Pelham Historical Society
8 Nashua Road
Pelham, NH 03076

Peterborough Historical Society
Grove Street
P.O. Box 58
Peterborough, NH 03458
Tel: 603-924-3235

Piermont Historical Society
P.O. Box 273
Piermont, NH 03779

Pittsburg Historical Society
P.O. Box 128
Pittsburg, NH 03592

Plainfield Historical Society
P.O. Box 107
Plainfield, NH 03781

Plaistow Historical Society
P.O. Box 434
Plaistow, NH 03865

Raymond Historical Society
P.O. Box 94
Raymond, NH 03077

Rindge Historical Society
South Main Street
Rindge, NH 03461

Rochester Historical Society
P.O. Box 65
Rochester, NH 03867

Rye Historical Society
P.O. Box 583
Rye, NH 03870

Salem Historical Society
79 Brady Avenue
Salem, NH 03079

Sanbornton Historical Society
P.O. Box 2
Sanbornton, NH 03269

Sandown Historical Society/Museum
P.O. Box 300
Sandown, NH 03873

Sandwich Historical Society/Museum
Maple Street
P.O. Box 106
Center Sandwich, NH 03227
Tel: 603-284-6269

Seabrook, Historical Society of
P.O. Box 500
Seabrook, NH 03874

Stoddard Historical Society
120 South Street
Munsonville, NH 03457
http://www.stoddardnh.org/shs.html

Strafford Historical Society
P.O. Box 33
Center Strafford, NH 03815

Stratham Historical Society
P.O. Box 39
Stratham, NH 03885

Somersworth Historical Society
6 Drew Road
Somersworth, NH 03878

Sutton Historical Society
P.O. Box 503
South Sutton, NH 03273

Tamworth Historical Society
P.O. Box 13
Tamworth, NH 03886

Temple Historical Society
P.O. Box 114
Temple, NH 03084
http://templenh.info/historicalsociety.htm

Thompson/Ames Historical Society
P.O. Box 7404
Gilford, NH 03247-7404
http://www.villagebanknh.com/html/
thompson-ames.html

Tilton Historical Society
P.O. Box 351
Tilton, NH 03276

Tuftonboro Historical Society
P.O. Box 372
Melvin Village, NH 03850

Wakefield/Brookfield Historical Society
P.O. Box 795
Brookfield, NH 03872

Walpole Historical Society
P.O. Box 292
Walpole, NH 03608

Warner Historical Society
15 Main Street
P.O. Box 189
Warner, NH 03278
http://www.warnerhistorical.org/

Warren Historical Society
P.O. Box 114
Warren, NH 03279

Washington Historical Society
P.O. Box 90
Washington, NH 03280
http://www.ultimate.com/washington/whs/

Weare Historical Society
P.O. Box 33
Weare, NH 03281

Wilmot Historical Society
Town Office Building
Wilmot Flat, NH 03287

Windham Historical Society
P.O. Box 441
Windham, NH 03087

Wolfeboro Historical Society
Pleasant Valley Schoolhouse
P.O. Box 1066
Wolfeboro, NH 03894
Tel: 603-569-4997

LDS FAMILY HISTORY CENTERS

For locations of Family History Centers in this state, see the Family History Center locator at FamilySearch.
http://www.familysearch.org/eng/Library/FHC/frameset_fhc.asp

ARCHIVES/LIBRARIES/MUSEUMS

Acworth Silsby Library
P.O. Box 88
South Acworth, NH 03607
Tel: 603-835-2150
E-mail: honeybrook@usaexpress.net
http://www.sover.net/~acworthl/

American Canadian Genealogical Society/Library
378 Notre Dame Avenue
P.O. Box 668
Manchester, NH 03105

American Independence Museum
One Governers Lane
Exeter, NH 03833-2420
Tel: 603-772-2622
Fax: 603-772-0861
E-mail: info@IndependenceMuseum.org
http://www.independencemuseum.org/

Cheshire County, Historical Society & Archives
246 Main Street
P.O. Box 803
Keene, NH 03431
Tel: 603-352-1895

Chichester Library
161 Main Street
Chichester, NH 03234
Tel: 603-798-5613

Conant Public Library/Historical Museum
Main Street
P.O. Box 6
Winchester, NH 03470
Tel: 603-239-4331
http://adam.cheshire.net/~conantlibrary/ home.htm

Dartmouth College Archives
Rauner Library
6065 Webster Hall
Hanover, NH 03755-3519
Tel: 603-646-2037
        603-646-0538 (Reference)
Fax: 603-646-0447
E-mail: Rauner.Ref@dartmouth.edu
http://www.dartmouth.edu/~speccoll/noframes/
        index_n.html

Dover Public Library
73 Locust Street
Dover, NH 03820
Tel: 603-516-6050
http://www.dover.lib.nh.us/

Exeter Public Library
1 Founders Park
Exeter, NH 03833
Tel: 603-772-3101
Fax: 603-772-7548
http://www.exeterpl.org/

Fiske Free Library
108 Broad Street
Claremont, NH 03743
Tel: 603-542-7017
Fax: 603-542-7029
E-mail: marilyn@fiske.lib.nh.us
http://www.fiske.lib.nh.us/

Gilsum Public Library
Main Street
P.O. Box 57
Gilsum, NH 03448
Tel: 603-357-0320

Keene Public Library
Wright Room
60 Winter Street
Keene, NH 03431
Tel: 603-352-0157
Fax: 603-352-1101
http://www.ci.keene.nh.us/library/

Kensington Social and Public Library
126 Amesbury Road
Exeter, NH 03833
Tel: 603-772-5022
E-mail: kensingtonlibrary@attbi.com

Lane Memorial Library
2 Academy Avenue
Hampton, NH 03842
Tel: 603-926-3368
Fax: 603-926-1348
E-mail: library@hampton.lib.nh.us
http://www.hampton.lib.nh.us/

Manchester Library
Carpenter Memorial Building
405 Pine Street
Manchester, NH 03104
Tel: 603-624-6550

New England Historical and Genealogical Society (NEHGS)
101 Newbury Street
Boston, MA 02116-3007
Tel: 617-836-5740
    888-296-3447 (Membersip and Sales)
    888-906-3447 (Library Circulation)
Fax: 617-536-7307
E-mail: nehgs@nehgs.org
http://www.newenglandancestors.org/

New Hampshire Historical Society/Library
30 Park Street
Concord, NH 03301-6384
Tel: 603-225-3381
Fax: 603-224-0463
E-mail: Library@nhhistory.org
http://nhhistory.library.net/

New Hampshire Museum of History
6 Eagle Square
Concord, NH 03301
Tel: 603-226-3189
http://www.nhhistory.org/museum.html

New Hampshire State Library
20 Park Street
Concord, NH 03301
Tel: 603-271-2144
    603-271-2239
Fax: 603-271-6826
E-mail: tepare@lilac.nhsl.lib.nh.us
http://www.state.nh.us/nhsl/

Pelham Public Library
5 Main Street
Pelham, NH 03076
Tel/Fax: 603-635-7581
E-mail: library@pelham-nh.com
http://www.pelham-nh.com/library/

Pillsbury Free Library
18 East Main Street
P.O. Box 299
Warner, NH 03278
Tel: 603-456-2289
Fax: 603-456-3177
E-mail: infowarner.lib.nh.us
http://warner.lib.nh.us/

Plymouth Historical Museum
Court Street
Plymouth, NH 03264
Tel: 603-536-2337
E-mail: plymouthhistoricalmuseum@netzero.net

Portsmouth Athenaeum
9 Market Square
Portsmouth, NH 03801
Tel: 603-431-2538
http://www.tfaoi.com/newsmu/nmus108.htm

Sandown Historical Society/Museum
P.O. Box 300
Sandown, NH 03873

Sandwich Historical Society/Museum
Maple Street
P.O. Box 106
Center Sandwich, NH 03227
Tel: 603-284-6369

Silsby Free Public Library
226 Main Street
P.O. Box 307
Charlestown, NH 03603
Tel: 603-826-7793
http://www.keenenh.com/towns/libraries/ charlestown.asp

Strawbery Banke Museum
Thayer Cumings Library and Archives
454 Court Street
P.O. Box 300
Portsmouth, NH 03802-0300
Tel: 603-433-1100
Fax: 603-433-1115
http://www.strawberybanke.org/museum/
cummings.html

Sugar Hill Historical Museum
Village Green
Sugar Hill, NH 03585
Tel: 603-823-5336

University of New Hampshire
Milne Special Collections and Archives
UNH Library
18 Library Way
Durham, NH 03824-3592
Tel: 603-862-2714 (Special Collections)
603-862-2956 (University Archives)
Fax: 603-862-1919
E-mail: library.special.collections@unh.edu
or archives@unh.edu
http://www.izaak.unh.edu/

Westmoreland Public Library
New England Collection
South Village Road
Westmoreland, NH 03467
Tel: 603-399-7750
http://www.keenenh.com/towns/libraries/
westmoreland.asp

Wolfeboro Historical Society
Pleasant Valley Schoolhouse
P.O. Box 1066
Wolfeboro, NH 03894
Tel: 603-569-4997

Wolfeboro Public Library
259 South Main Street
P.O. Box 710
Wolfeboro, NH 03894
Tel: 603-569-2428
Fax: 603-569-8180
E-mail: wolfelib@worldpath.net
http://www.worldpath.net/~wolfelib/

NEWSPAPER REPOSITORIES

Dartmouth College Archives
Rauner Library
6065 Webster Hall
Hanover, NH 03755-3519
Tel: 603-646-2037
603-646-0538 (Reference)
Fax: 603-646-0447
E-mail: Rauner.Ref@dartmouth.edu
http://www.dartmouth.edu/~speccoll/specoll/
archives.html

New Hampshire Historical Society/Library
20 Park Street
Concord, NH 03301
Tel: 603-271-2144
603-271-2239
Fax: 603-271-6826
E-mail: tepare@lilac.nhsl.lib.nh.us
http://www.state.nh.us/nhsl/

New Hampshire State Library
20 Park Street
Concord, NH 03301
Tel: 603-271-2144
603-271-2239
Fax: 603-271-2205
E-mail: tepare@lilac.nhsl.lib.nh.us
http://www.state.nh.us/nhsl/

VITAL RECORDS

Bureau of Vital Records
6 Hazen Drive
Concord, NH 03301
Tel: 800-852-3345 ext. 4651
E-mail: vitalrecords@dhhs.state.nh.us
http://www.vitalrec.com/nh.html

NEW HAMPSHIRE ON THE WEB

Irish in 19th-Century Portsmouth, New Hampshire
http://www.fortunecity.com/bally/limerick/123/ports/
dir.htm

New Hampshire GenWeb Project
http://www.rootsquest.com/~usgwnhus/

NEW JERSEY

ARCHIVES, STATE & NATIONAL

National Archives—Northeast Region
201 Varick Street
New York, NY 10014-4811
Phone: 212-337-1300
Fax: 212-337-1306
E-mail: newyork.archives@nara.gov
http://www.nara.gov/regional/newyork.html

New Jersey State Archives
225 West State Street-Level 2
Department of State Building
P.O. Box 307
Trenton, NJ 08625-0307
Tel: (609) 292-6260 (general information)
     (609) 633-8334 (administrative office)
Fax: (609) 396-2454
E-mail: info@archive.sos.state.nj.us
http://www.state.nj.us/state/darm/archives.html

GENEALOGICAL SOCIETIES

Afro-American Historical & Genealogical Society
145 Van Nostrand Avenue
Jersey City, NJ 07305
Tel: 201-547-5262
E-mail: b104216m1121p@cs.com

Bergen County Genealogy Society
P.O. Box 432
Midland Park, NJ 07432
http://www.rootsweb.com/~njgsbc/

Burlington County Genealogy Club
Woodlane Road
P.O. Box 2449, RD 2
Mount Holly, NJ 08060

Cape May Historical & Genealogical Society/Library
504 Route 9
Cape May Courthouse, NJ 08210-3070
Tel: 609-465-3535
http://www.cmcmuseum.org/library.htm

Central Jersey Genealogy Club
P.O. Box 9903
Hamilton, NJ 08650
http://www.rootsweb.com/~njcjgc/

Genealogical Society of New Jersey
P.O. Box 1291
New Brunswick, NJ 08903
http://www.rootsweb.com/~njgsnj/main.htm

Jewish Genealogical Society of North Jersey
1 Bedford Road
Pompton Lakes, NJ 07442
E-mail: EStolb7395@aol.com
http://community.nj.com/cc/jgsnorthjersey

Mayflower Descendants in New Jersey
142 N. Chestnut Street
Westfield, NJ 07090
E-mail: Pmahansen@aol.com

Metuchen/Edison Genealogy Club
The Metuchen-Edison Historical Society
P.O. Box 61
Metuchen, NJ 08840-0061
http://www.jhalpin.com/metuchen/metgen99.htm

Monmouth County Genealogical Club
Monmouth County Historical Association
70 Court Street
Freehold, NJ 07728
Tel: 732-462-1466
Fax: 732-462-8346
http://home.infi.net/~kjshelly/mcgs.html

Morris Area Genealogy Society
P.O. Box 105
Convent Station, NJ 07961

New Jersey Historical Society/Library
Genealogy Club
230 Broadway Newark, NJ 07104
Tel: 973-483-3939
Fax: 973-483-1988

Ocean County Genealogical Society
135 Nautilus Drive
Manahawkin, NJ 08050

Passaic County Genealogy Club
Passaic County Historical Society
Lambert Castle, Valley Road
Paterson, NJ 07503
Tel: 973-247-0085
Fax: 973-357-1070
http://www.rootsweb.com/~njpchsgc/

Salem County, Genealogical Society of
P.O. Box 231
Woodstown, NJ 08098
http://www.rootsweb.com/~njsalem/gsscnj.html

Warren County Historical & Genealogical
Society/Museum & Library
313 Mansfield Street
P.O. Box 313
Belvidere, NJ 07823
Tel: 908-475-4246
Fax: 908-475-4246

West Fields, Genealogical Society of the
Westfield Memorial Library
550 East Broad Street
Westfield, NJ 07090
Tel: 908-789-4090
E-mail: gswf@westfieldnj.com
http://www.westfieldnj.com/gswf/index.htm

HISTORICAL SOCIETIES

Absecon Historical Society
618 Franklin Blvd.
Absecon, NJ 08201

Afro-American Historical & Genealogical Society
145 Van Nostrand Avenue
Jersey City, NJ 07305
Tel: 201-547-5262
E-mail: b104216m1121p@cs.com

Alexandria Township Historical Society
174 Warsaw Road
Frenchtown, NJ 08825

Allendale Historical Society
P.O. Box 294
Allendale, NJ 07401

Allentown/Upper Freehold Historical Society
76 North Main Street
P.O. Box 328
Allentown, NJ 08501

Alpine Historical Society
P.O. Box 59
Alpine, NJ 07620

American-Italian Historical Association
Historic Dorothea's House
120 John Street
Princeton, NJ 08540

Andover Boro, Historical Society of
189 Main Street
Andover, NJ 07821

Association of New Jersey County Cultural & Heritage
Agencies
Camden County Cultural & Heritage Commission
Hopkins House
250 S. Park Drive
Haddon Township, NJ 08108
Tel: 609-858-0040
http://arts.camden.lib.nj.us/

Atlantic County Cultural & Heritage Commission
40 Farragut Avenue
Mays Landing, NJ 08330
Tel: 609-625-2776

Atlantic County Historical Society/Library & Museum
907 Shore Road
P.O. Box 301
Somers Point, NJ 08244
Tel: 609-927-5218
http://www.aclink.org/achs/

Atlantic Highlands Historical Society
27 Prospect Avenue
P.O. Box 108
Atlantic Highlands, NJ 07716
Tel: 732-291-1861

Audubon Historical Society
238 Washington Terrace
Audubon, NJ 08106

Barnegat Light Historical Society
West 5th & Central Avenue
P.O. Box 386
Barnegat Light, NJ 08006
Tel: 609-494-8578

Battleground Historical Society
P.O. Box 61
Tennent, NJ 07763

Bay Head Historical Society
P.O. Box 127
Bay Head, NJ 08742

Bayonne Historical Society
P.O. Box 3034
Bayonne, NJ 07002

Belleville Historical Society
Belleville Public Library
221 Washington Avenue
Belleville, NJ 07109-3189
Tel: 973-450-3434
Fax: 973-450-9518
http://www.intac.com/~bpllibn/

Bergen County Division of Cultural & Historic Affairs
Administration Building
Court Plaza South
21 Main Street
Hackensack, NJ 08601-7000
Tel: 201-646-2786

Bergen County Historical Society
120 Main Street
P.O. Box 55
River Edge, NJ 07661
Tel: 201-343-9492
        201-487-1739 (Steuben House)
http://apollo.carroll.com/bchs/

Berkeley Heights, Historical Society of
P.O. Box 237
Berkeley Heights, NJ 07922

Berkeley Township Historical Society
759 U.S. Highway 9
Bayville, NJ 08721
Tel: 732-269-9527

Bethlehem Township Historical Society
P.O. Box 56
Asbury, NJ 08802

Bloomfield, Historical Society of
90 Broad Street
Bloomfield, NJ 07003
E-mail: BloomfHist@aol.com

Blue Hills Historical Society
311 West End Avenue
North Plainfield, NJ 07060

Boonton Historic Society
210 Main Street
Boonton, NJ 07005
Tel: 973-402-8840 (taped information)
E-mail: eamarlatt@att.net
http://www.boonton.org/historical/

Boonton Township, Historical Society of
RD 2, Box 152
Boonton, NJ 07005

Bordentown Historical Society
302 Farnsworth Avenue
P.O. Box 182
Bordentown, NJ 08505
Tel: 609-298-1740

Bradley Beach Historical Society
Bradley Beach Library
511 4th Avenue
Bradley Beach, NJ 07720
Tel: 732-776-2995
Fax: 732-774-4591
http://www.bradleybeachlibrary.org/

Brick Township Historical Society
P.O. Box 160
Brick, NJ 08723
Tel: 732-477-4513

Brigantine Historical Society
470 West Shore Drive
Brigantine, NJ 08203

Burlington City Historical Society
City Hall
Burlington City, NJ 08016
Tel: 609-386-3993

Burlington County Cultural & Heritage Department
49 Rancocas Road
Mount Holly, NJ 08060
Tel: 609-265-5068

Burlington County Historical Society
451 High Street
Burlington City, NJ 08016-4514
Tel: 609-386-4773
Fax: 609-386-4828
http://08016.com/bchs.html

Byram Township Historical Society
10 Mansfield Drive
Byram Township, NJ 07874

Califon Historical Society
25 Academy Street
P.O. Box 424
Califon, NJ 07830
Tel: 908-832-0878
http://www.califonhistoricalsociety.org/

Camden County Cultural & Heritage Commission
250 South Park Drive
Haddon Township, NJ 08108
Tel: 856-858-0040
http://arts.camden.lib.nj.us/

Camden County Historical Society/Library
1900 Park Blvd.
Collingswood, NJ 08108-0378
Mail:
P.O. Box 378
Camden, NJ 08103-3697
Tel: 856-964-3333
http://www.cchsnj.com/library.shtml

Cape May County, Department of Culture & Heritage
Cape May Court House
4 Moore Road
Cape May Court House, NJ 08210
Tel: 609-463-6370
Fax: 609-463-6335
http://cmcculture.org/

Cape May Historical & Genealogical Society/Library
504 Route 9
Cape May Courthouse, NJ 08210-3070
Tel: 609-465-3535
http://www.cmcmuseum.org/library.htm

Cedar Grove Historical Society
903 Pompton Avenue
P.O. Box 461
Cedar Grove, NJ 07009
Tel: 973-239-5414

Chatham Historical Society
P.O. Box 682
Chatham, NJ 07928

Chester Historical Society
245 W. Main Street
P.O. Box 376
Chester, NJ 07930
Tel: 908-879-2761
E-mail: ChesterHist20@aol.com
http://chesterbicentennial.gti.net/

Chesterfield Township Historical Society
P.O. Box 86
Crosswicks, NJ 08515

Clark Historical Society
Municipal Building, Room 18
430 Westfield Avenue
Clark, NJ 07066
http://www.geocities.com/CapitolHill/Congress/
6576/organiza/histsoc.htm

Colts Neck Historical Society
15 Enclosure
Colts Neck, NJ 07722

Cranbury History & Preservation Society
4 Park Place, E
Cranbury, NJ 08512
Tel: 609-655-2611

Cranford Historical Society
38 Springfield Avenue
Cranford, NJ 07016
Tel: 908-276-0082
E-mail: bdevlin@bobdevlin.com
http://www.bobdevlin.com/crhshis.html

Cumberland County Cultural & Heritage Commission
422 Rhonda Drive
Millville, NJ 08332
Tel: 856-825-9662
http://www.co.cumberland.nj.us/govtserv/
departments/culture_heritage/

Cumberland County Historical Society
Gibbon House
960 Ye Greate Street
P.O. Box 16
Greenwich, NJ 08323
Tel: 856-455-4055
http://www.rootsweb.com/~njcumber/ cumbernj.html

Dennis Township Historical Society
P.O. Box 109
South Dennis, NJ 08245
Tel: 609-861-2925

Denville Historical Society
Diamond Spring Road
P.O. Box 466
Denville, NJ 07834
Tel: 973-625-1165

Dover Area Historical Society
P.O. Box 609
Dover, NJ 07801

Dunellen Historical Society
322 Whittier Avenue
Dunellen, NJ 08812

East Brunswick Historical Association
43 Sullivan Way
East Brunswick, NJ 08816

East Hanover Historical Society
181 Mount Pleasant Avenue
East Hanover, NJ 07936

Eatontown Historical Committee/Museum
75 Broad Street
Eatontown, NJ 07724
Tel: 732-542-4026

Edison Township Historical Society
328 Plainfield
Edison, NJ 08817

Egg Harbor City Historical Society
533 London Avenue
Egg Harbor City, NJ 08215
Tel: 609-965-9073

Elmwood Park Historical Society
210 Lee Street
Elmwood Park, NJ 07407

Englewood Historical Society
500 Liberty Street
Englewood, NJ 07631

English Neighborhood Historical Society
656 Elm Street
Maywood, NJ 07607

Essex County, Department of Parks, Recreation, Cultural & Historic Affairs
115 Clifton Avenue
Newark, NJ 07104
Tel: 973-268-3500
Fax: 973-481-5302

Essex Fells Historical Society
96 Forest Way
Essex Fells, NJ 07021

Evesham Historical Society
10 Madison Court
Marlton, NJ 08053
Tel: 856-988-0995

Ewing Township Historical Preservation Society/Library
27 Federal City Road
Ewing, NJ 08638
Tel: 609-530-1220

Fair Haven Historical Society
P.O. Box 72
Fair Haven, NJ 07704
Tel: 732-842-4453

Fairfield Historical Society
221 Hollywood Avenue
Fairfield, NJ 07006

Farmingdale Historical Society
2 Goodenough Road
Farmingdale, NJ 07727

Florham Park, Historical Society of
P.O. Box 193
Florham, NJ 07932

Fort Lee Historical Society
Borough Hall
309 Main Street
Fort Lee, NJ 07024
Tel: 201-592-3580

Fortescue Historical Society
Pier #1, Bayside
Fortescue, NJ 08321

Frenchtown Historical Association
Borough Hall
2nd Street Frenchtown, NJ 08825

Garfield Historical Society
204 Outwater
Lane Garfield, NJ 07026

Glen Ridge Historical Society
P.O. Box 164
Glen Ridge, NJ 07028
http://www.glenridge.org/org/grhs.html

Glen Rock Historical & Preservation Society
Municipal Building, Borough Hall
Glen Rock, NJ 07452

Gloucester County Cultural & Heritage Commission
406 Swedesboro Road
Gibbstown, NJ 08027

Gloucester County Historical Society/Library
17 Hunter Street
Woodbury, NJ 08096
Tel: 856-845-4771
http://www.rootsweb.com/~njglouce/gchs/

Great Egg Harbor Township Historical Society
Township Hall
RD 1, Box 262
Linwood, NJ 08221

Greater Cape May Historical Society
Colonial House
643 Washington Street
P.O. Box 495
Cape May, NJ 08204
Tel: 609-884-9100
http://www.beachcomber.com/Capemay/ histsoc.html

Green Township Historical Society
P.O. Box 203
Tranquility, NJ 07879

Griggstown Historical Society
RD 1, Canal Road
Princeton, NJ 08554

Hackettstown Historical Society
106 Church Street
Hackettstown, NJ 07840
Tel: 908-852-8797

Haddon Heights Historical Society
Haddon Heights Library
608 Station Avenue
Haddon Heights, NJ 08035
Tel: 856-547-7132

Haddon Township Historical Society
109 Emerald Avenue
Westmont, NJ 08108

Haddonfield Historical Society
Greenfield Hall
343 Kingshighway East
Haddonfield, NJ 08033
Tel: 609-429-7375

Hamilton Township Historical Society
2200 Kuser Road
Trenton, NJ 08650
Tel: 609-585-1686

Hammonton Historical Society
767 Central Avenue
Hammonton, NJ 08037

Harding Township Historical Society
Village & Millbrook Roads
P.O. Box 1777
New Vernon, NJ 07976
Tel: 973-292-0161
        973-292-3661 (Archives Office)

Hardwick Township Historical Society
P.O. Box 722
Blairstown, NJ 07925

Hardyston Heritage Society
North Woods Trail
P.O. Box 434
Stockholm, NJ 07460

Harrington Park Historical Society
10 Herring Street
Harrington Park, NJ 07640

Harrison Township Historical Society
62 South Main Street
P.O. Box 4
Mullica Hill, NJ 08062
Tel: 856-478-4949

Hazlet Township Historical Society
Municipal Offices
319 Middle Road
Hazlet, NJ 07730

Helmetta Historical Society
Municipal Offices
60 Main Street
Helmetta, NJ 08828

Highland Park Historical Commission
P.O. Box 1330
Highland Park, NJ 08904
Tel: 908-572-3400

Highlands, Historical Society of
P.O. Box 13
Highlands, NJ 07732

Hightstown/East Windsor Historical Society
164 North Main Street
Hightstown, NJ 08520
Tel: 609-371-9580

Hillsborough Historical Society
P.O. Box 720
Neshanic, NJ 08853
Tel: 603-478-3165
E-mail: c_chadwick@conknet.com

Hillside Historical Society
111 Conant Avenue
Hillside, NJ 07205
Tel: 908-353-8828

Holland Township Historical Society
P.O. Box 434
Milford, NJ 08848
Tel: 908-995-9197

Holmdel Historical Society
P.O. Box 282
Holmdel, NJ 07733

Hope Historical Society
High Street
P.O. Box 52
Hope, NJ 07844

Hopewell Valley Historical Society
State Highway 579 & 601
P.O. Box 371
Pennington, NJ 08534
Tel: 609-737-7751
http://www.rootsweb.com/~njhvhs/

Howell Historical Society
427 Lakewood Farmingdale Road
Howell, NJ 07731
Tel: 732-938-2212
http://www.howellnj.com/historic/

Hudson County Division of Cultural & Heritage Affairs
Murdoch Hall
114 Clifton Place
Jersey City, NJ 07304
Tel: 201-434-1316

Hunterdon County Cultural & Heritage Commission
3 Chorister Place
P.O. Box 2900
Flemington, NJ 08822-2900
Tel: 908-788-1256
http://www.co.hunterdon.nj.us/depts/c&h/c&h.htm

Hunterdon County Historical Society
Hiram E. Deats Memorial Library
114 Main Street
Flemington, NJ 08822
Tel: 908-782-1091
http://members.aol.com/njysprez/hchs.htm

Indian Mills Historical Society
Atsion Road
RD 5, Box 252
Vincentown, NJ 08088

Irvington Historical Society
34 Clinton Terrace
Irvington, NJ 07111
Tel: 201-374-7500

Island Heights Cultural & Heritage Association
105 Simpson Avenue
P.O. Box 670
Island Heights, NJ 08732
http://www.islandhts.org/new_page_5.htm

Jamesburg Historical Association
203 Buckelew Avenue
Jamesburg, NJ 08831
Tel: 732-521-2040

Jefferson Township Historical Society
Dover Milton Road
P.O. Box 1776
Oak Ridge, NJ 07438
Tel: 973-697-0258
http://www.hicom.net/~jefferson/hisindex.html

Jewish Historical Society of Central Jersey
228 Livingston Avenue
New Brunswick, NJ 08901
Tel: 732-249-4894
E-mail: jhscj@cs.com
http://www.jewishgen.org/jhscj/

Jewish Historical Society of MetroWest
901 Route 10 East
Whippany, NJ 07981
Tel: 973-884-4800 ext. 565
Fax: 973-428-4720
E-mail: jsettanni@ujfmetrowest.org
http://www.fiengroup.com/jhs/jhs.htm

Jewish Historical Society of Northern New Jersey
1205 McBride Avenue
P.O. Box 708
West Paterson, NJ 07424

Jewish Historical Society of Trenton
865 Lower Ferry Road
Trenton, NJ 08628
Tel: 609-883-2228

Kearny Cottage Historical Association
63 Catalpa Avenue
Perth Amboy, NJ 08861
Tel: 732-826-1826

Keyport Historical Society
2 Broad Street
P.O. Box 312
Keyport, NJ 07735
Tel: 732-739-6390

Kingwood Township Historical Society
Kingwood Township Municipal Building
P.O. Box 199
Baptistown, NJ 08803

Kinnelon Historical Commission
25 Kiel Avenue
Kinnelon, NJ 07405
Tel: 973-838-0185
http://www.kinnelonboro.org/
     KINNELON%20HISTORICAL%20COMMISSION.htm

Lacey Historical Society
P.O. Box 412
Forked River, NJ 08731
http://lhs.laceytownship.net/

Lake Hopatcong Historical Society
Lake Hopatcong Historical Museum
P.O. Box 668
Landing, NJ 07850
Tel: 973-398-2616
E-mail: lhhistory@att.net
http://www.hopatcong.org/museum/

Lakehurst Historical Society
505 Oak Street
Lakehurst, NJ 08733
http://www.fieldtrip.com/nj/86577209.htm

Lambertville Historical Society
62 Bridge Street
P.O. Box 2
Lambertville, NJ 08530
Tel: 609-397-0770
E-mail: info@lambertvillehistoricalsociety.org
http://www.lambertvillehistoricalsociety.org/

Lawnside Historical Society
P.O. Box 608
Lawnside, NJ 08045-0608

Lawrence Historical Society
P.O. Box 6025
Lawrenceville, NJ 08648
Tel: 609-895-1728
http://salinas.princeton.edu/~oberst/lhs/

League of Historical Societies of New Jersey
P.O. Box 909
Madison, NJ 07940
http://scils.rutgers.edu/~macan/leaguelist.html

Leonia Historical Society
199 Christie Street
Leonia, NJ 07605

Linwood Historical Society
16 Poplar Avenue
Linwood, NJ 08221
Tel: 609-927-8293
http://www.linwoodnj.org/

Little Falls Township Historical Society
8 Douglas Drive
Little Falls, NJ 07424

Little Silver Historical Society
Borough Hall
480 Prospect Avenue
Little Silver, NJ 07739
Tel: 732-842-2400

Livingston Historical Society
P.O. Box 220
Livingston, NJ 07039

Long-a-Coming Historical Society
59 S. White Horse Pike
Berlin, NJ 08009
Tel: 609-767-6221

Long Beach Island Historical Association
Engelside & Beach Avenue
P.O. Box 1222
Beach Haven, NJ 08008
Tel: 609-492-0700
E-mail: lbiha@att.net
http://www.nealcomm.com/nonprof/lbimusm.html

Long Branch Historical Museum
1260 Ocean Avenue
Long Branch, NJ 07740
Tel: 908-222-9879

Long Hill Township Historical Society
1336 Valley Road
Stirling, NJ 07087

Longport Historical Society
Borough Hall
2305 Atlantic Avenue
Longport, NJ 08403
Tel: 609-823-1115

Lumberton Historical Society
P.O. Box 22
Lumberton, NJ 08048
http://www.lumberton.com/club.orgs/historical/

Lyndhurst Historical Society
P.O. Box 135
Lyndhurst, NJ 07071
Tel: 201-804-2513

Madison Township Historical Society
Box 150 Morristown
Road Matawan, NJ 07747

Mahwah Historical Society
310 Forest Road
Mahwah, NJ 07430

Manchester Historical Society
18 Bowie Drive
Whiting, NJ 08759

Mansfield Township Historical Society
3121 Route 206
Columbus, NJ 08022-9530

Maple Shade Historical Society
P.O. Box 368
Maple Shade, NJ 08052

Matawan Historical Society
94 Main Street
P.O. Box 41
Matawan, NJ 07747
Tel: 732-566-5605

Mauricetown Historical Society
1229 Front Street
Mauricetown, NJ 08329
Tel: 856-785-0457

Medford Historical Society
275 Church Road
Medford, NJ 08055
Tel: 609-654-7767

Mercer County Cultural & Heritage Commission
640 S. Broad Street
Trenton, NJ 08650
Tel: 609-989-6899

Merchantville Historical Society
1 West Maple Avenue
Merchantville, NJ 08109

Metuchen/Edison Regional Historical Society
Genealogy Club
P.O. Box 61
Metuchen, NJ 08840
http://www.jhalpin.com/metuchen/met-ed.htm

Middlesex County Cultural & Heritage Commission
703 Jersey Avenue
New Brunswick, NJ 08901
Tel: 732-745-4489
http://www.cultureheritage.org/

Middletown Township Historical Society
Leonardville Road
Leonardo, NJ 07737
Mail:
P.O. Box 434
Middletown, NJ 07748
Tel: 732-291-8739

Midland Park Historical Society
212 Park Avenue
Midland Park, NJ 07432

Millburn/Short Hills Historical Society
4 Fox Hill Lane
P.O. Box 243
Short Hills, NJ 07078
Tel: 973-564-9519
Fax: 973-564-9519
E-mail: MSHHS2002@cs.com
http://community.nj.com/cc/millburn-shhistsoc

Milltown Historical Society
P.O. Box 96
Milltown, NJ 08850

Millville Historical Society
200 East Main Street
Millville, NJ 08332
Tel: 856-825-7000 Ext. 275
http://www.cccnj.net/~taktani/millville.htm

Monmouth County Historical Association
70 Court Street
Freehold, NJ 07728
Tel: 732-462-1466
Fax: 732-462-8346
E-mail: mchalib@aol.com
http://www.monmouth.com/~mcha/

Monmouth County Historical Commission
27 E. Main Street
Freehold, NJ 07728
Tel: 908-431-7413
Fax: 732-409-4820
http://www.visitmonmouth.com/historicalcomm/

Monroe Township Historical Society
Hall Street
P.O. Box 474
Williamstown, NJ 08094
Tel: 609-728-0458

Montclair Historical Society
Terhune Library
108 Orange Road
Montclair, NJ 07043
Tel: 973-744-1796
http://www.montclairhistorical.org/

Montville Historical Society
415 Boyd Street
P.O. Box 497
Boonton, NJ 07005

Moorestown, Historical Society of
Smith-Cadbury Mansion
12 High Street
P.O. Box 477
Moorestown, NJ 08057
Tel: 856-235-0353
E-mail: historical@moorestown.com
http://www.moorestown.com/community/history/

Morris County Heritage Commission
300 Mendham Road
P.O. Box 900
Morristown, NJ 07963-0900
Tel: 973-829-8117
Fax: 973-829-8114
http://www.co.morris.nj.us/Heritage/

Morris County Historical Society/Research Library
Acorn Hall
68 Morris Avenue
P.O. Box 170M Morristown, NJ 07960
Tel: 973-267-3465
http://www.acornhall.org/

Mount Holly Historical Society
Park Drive
P.O. Box 4081
Mount Holly, NJ 08060
Tel: 609-267-8844

Neptune Township Historical Society/Museum
25 Neptune Blvd.
P.O. Box 1125
Neptune, NJ 07753
Tel: 732-775-8241

New Egypt Historical Society
P.O. Box 295
New Egypt, NJ 08533

New Jersey Graveyard Preservation Society
P.O. Box 5
East Brunswick, NJ 08816

New Jersey Historical Society/Library
230 Broadway
Newark, NJ 07104
Tel: 973-483-3939
Fax: 973-483-1988

New Providence Historical Society
Memorial Library
377 Elkwood Avenue
New Providence, NJ 07974
http://www.daddezio.com/society/locals/nphs.html

Newfield Historical Society
Newfield Borough Hall
107 N.E. Blvd.
Newfield, NJ 08344
Tel: 856-697-1100

North Arlington Historical Society
89 Canterbury Avenue
North Arlington, NJ 07032
Tel: 201-998-6290

North Brunswick Historical Society
690 Cranbury Crossroad
North Brunswick, NJ 08902

North Jersey Highlands Historical Society
P.O. Box 248
Ringwood, NJ 07456
http://www.northjerseyhistory.org/

Nutley Historical Society
65 Church Street
Nutley, NJ 07110
Tel: 973-667-1528

Oakland Historical Society
Van Allen House
P.O. Box 296
Oakland, NJ 07436
Tel: 201-825-9049

Ocean City Historical Society/Museum
1735 Simpson Avenue
Ocean City, NJ 08226
Tel: 609-399-1801

Ocean County Cultural & Heritage Commission
101 Hooper Avenue, Room 225
CN 2191
Toms River, NJ 08754-2191
Tel: 732-929-4779
Fax: 732-288-7871
http://www.co.ocean.nj.us/Cultural/

Ocean County Historical Society
Strickler Research Library
26 Hadley Avenue
P.O. Box 2191
Toms River, NJ 08754
Tel: 908-341-1880
http://www.islandhts.com/ochs.htm
or
http://www.fieldtrip.com/nj/83411880.htm

Ocean Gate Historical Society/Museum
Cape May and Asbury Avenues
P.O. Box 895
Ocean Gate, NJ 08740
http://www.fieldtrip.com/nj/82693468.htm

Ocean Grove, Historical Society of
50 Pitman Avenue
P.O. Box 446
Ocean Grove, NJ 07756
Tel: 732-774-1869
Fax: 732-774-1685
http://www.oceangrovehistory.org/

Ogdensburg Historical Society
15 Richards Street
Ogdensburg, NJ 07439

Old Randolph Historical Society
P.O. Box 1776
Ironia, NJ 07845
Tel: 973-989-7095
     973-989-7057
http://www.gti.net/randolph/hsor/

Old Schralenburgh Historical Society
43 Overlook Road
Dumont, NJ 07628

Old Wall Historical Society
1701 New Bedford Road
Wall, NJ 07719
Tel: 732-974-1430

Oldman Township Historical Society
Railroad Avenue
P.O. Box 158208
Pedricktown, NJ 08067

Oliver Cromwell Black History Society
Afri-Mail Institute
348 High Street
Burlington, NJ 08016
Tel: 609-387-8133
Fax: 609-387-8144

Oxford Historical Society
P.O. Box 277
Oxford, NJ 07863

Paramus Historical and Preservation Society
650 E. Glen Avenue
Ridgewood, NJ 07450
Tel: 201-447-3242

Parsippany Historical Society
93 Intervale Road
Boonton, NJ 07005

Pascack Historical Society
19 Ridge Avenue
Park Ridge, NJ 07656
Tel: 201-573-0307

Passaic County Cultural & Heritage Council
Passaic County College
College Blvd.
Paterson, NJ 07509
Tel: 973-684-6555
Fax: 973-684-5444
E-mail: apapazian@pccc.cc.nj.us

Passaic County Historical Society/Library
Lambert Castle
Valley Road
Paterson, NJ 07503
Tel: 973-881-2761
http://www.geocities.com/pchslc/library.html

Pennsauken Historical Society
9201 Burrough Dover Lane
P.O. Box 56
Pennsauken, NJ 08110
Tel: 856-662-3002

Pennsville Township Historical Society
86 Church Landing Road
Pennsville, NJ 08070
Tel: 856-678-4453
http://www.pvhistorical.njcool.net/

Perth Amboy Historical Society
1 Lewis Street
Perth Amboy, NJ 08861

Phillipsburg Area Historical Society
675 Corliss Avenue
Phillipsburg, NJ 08865
Tel: 908-454-5500 ext. 353
E-mail: pburghistory@yahoo.com

Piscataway Historical & Heritage Society
1001 Maple Avenue
Piscataway, NJ 08854

Plainfield, Historical Society of
Drake House Museum
602 West Front Street
Plainfield, NJ 07060-1004
Tel: 908-755-5831

Plainsboro Historical Society
641 Plainsboro Road
P.O. Box 278
Plainsboro, NJ 08536
Tel: 609-799-0909
http://www.plainsboro.com/historical/

Pohatcong Historical Society
Rte. 1, Box 251
Phillipsburg, NJ 08865
Tel: 908-995-7107

Point Pleasant Historical Society
P.O. Box 1273
Point Pleasant Beach, NJ 08742
Tel: 732-892-3091
http://home.att.net/~ppbhist/pphs.htm

Port Republic Historical Society
City Hall
143 Main Street
Port Republic, NJ 08241

Princeton Historical Society/Library
158 Nassau Street
Princeton, NJ 08542
Tel: 609-921-6748
E-mail: PHS@injersey.com
http://www.princetonhistory.org/

Rahway Historical Society
1632 Saint Georges Avenue
P.O. Box 1842
Rahway, NJ 07065
Tel: 732-381-0441

Ramsey Historical Association
538 Island Road
Ramsey, NJ 07446
Tel: 201-825-1126

Red Bank Historical Society
P.O. Box 712
Red Bank, NJ 07701

Riverfront Historical Society
P.O. Box 175
Beverly, NJ 08010

Riverside Township Historical Society
220 Heulings Avenue
Riverside, NJ 08075

Riverton, Historical Society of
405 Midway
Riverton, NJ 08077
Tel: 609-829-6315

Rockaways, Historical Society of
Faesch House
Mount Hope Road
Rockaway, NJ 07866
Mail:
P.O. Box 100
Hibernia, NJ 07842
Tel: 973-366-6730
http://www.gti.net/rocktwp/commdir.html#historical

Roebling Historical Society
140 Third Avenue
Roebling, NJ 08554

Roseland Historical Society
126 Eagle Rock Avenue
P.O. Box 152
Roseland, NJ 07068
Tel: 973-228-1812

Roselle Historical Society
116 E. 4th Avenue
Roselle, NJ 07203

Roselle Park Historical Society/Museum
9 West Grant Avenue
P.O. Box 135
Roselle Park, NJ 07204
http://www.rosellepark.org/upclose/history/
    museuminfo.htm

Roxbury Township Historical Society
P.O. Box 18
Succasunna, NJ 07876

Rumson Historical Society
Wilson Circle
Rumson, NJ 07760

Salem County Cultural & Heritage Commission
Salem Court House
92 Market Street
Salem, NJ 08079
Tel: 856-935-7510 ext. 292

Salem County Historical Society/
Museum & Research Library
79-83 Market Street
Salem, NJ 08079
Tel: 856-935-5004
http://www.salemcounty.com/schs/

Sayreville Historical Society
P.O. Box 66
Sayreville, NJ 08872
http://www.sayreville.com/historical_society.html

Scotch Plains & Fanwood, Historical Society of
P.O. Box 261
Scotch Plains, NJ 07076

Sewaren Historical Club
434 Cliff Street
Sewaren, NJ 07077

Shrewsbury Historical Society
419 Sycamore Avenue
P.O. Box 333
Shrewsbury, NJ 07702
Tel: 732-530-7974

Somers Point Historical Society
P.O. Box 517
Somers Point, NJ 08244

Somerset County Cultural & Heritage Commission
Historic Court House
P.O. Box 3000
Somerville, NJ 08876
Tel: 908-231-7110

Somerset County Historical Society
Van Veghten Drive
P.O. Box 632
Bridgewater, NJ 08807
Tel: 908-218-1281
http://home.att.net/~somersetcountyhistorical society/

Somerset Hills, Historical Society of
15 W. Oak Street
P.O. Box 136
Basking Ridge, NJ 07920
Tel: 908-221-1770

Somerville Historical Society
16 E. Summit Street
Somerville, NJ 08876

South Orange Historical & Preservation Society
P.O. Box 61
South Orange, NJ 07079
E-mail: calamander@mindspring.com

South Plainfield Historical Society
P.O. Box 11
South Plainfield, NJ 07080

South River Historical Society
129 Main Street
South River, NJ 08882

Southampton Historical Society
17 Mill
Vincentown, NJ 08088
Mail:
P.O. Box 2086
Southampton, NJ 08088
Tel: 609-859-9237
http://www.geocities.com/Heartland/Pointe/1495/
shshome.html

Spring Lake Historical Society
423 Warren Avenue
P.O. Box 703
Spring Lake, NJ 07762
Tel: 908-449-0772
http://www.springlake.org/historical/

Springfield Historical Society
126 Morris Avenue
Springfield, NJ 07081
Tel: 973-912-4464

Squan Village Historical Society
105 South Street
Manasquan, NJ 08736
Tel: 732-223-6770

Stillwater Township Historical Society
P.O. Box 23
Stillwater, NJ 07855

Summit Historical Society
100 Main Street #B
Newton, NJ 07860
Tel: 908-277-1747

Sussex County Arts & Heritage Council, Inc.
100 Main Street #B
Newton, NJ 07860
Tel: 973-383-0027

Sussex County Historical Society
82 Main Street
P.O. Box 913
Newton, NJ 07860
Tel: 973-383-6010
http://www.sussexcountyhistory.org/

Tabernacle Historical Society
162 Carranza Road
Tabernacle, NJ 08088

Tewsksberry Historical Society
P.O. Box 457
Oldwick, NJ 08858-0457
Tel: 908-832-2562

Toms River Seaport Society
78 Water Street
Toms River, NJ 08753
Tel: 732-349-9209

Trenton Historical Society
P.O. Box 1112
Trenton, NJ 08606-1112
Tel: 609-989-3111
E-mail: society@trentonhistory.org
http://trentonhistory.org/

Tuckerton Historical Society
P.O. Box 43
Tuckerton, NJ 08087

Union County Historical Society
116 E. Fourth Avenue
Roselle, NJ 07203

Union County Office of Cultural & Heritage Affairs
24-52 Rahway Avenue, 4th Floor
Elizabeth, NJ 07202

Union Landing Historical Society
P.O. Box 473
Brielle, NJ 08730

Union Township Historical Society
Caldwell Parsonage Museum
909 Caldwell Avenue
Union, NJ 07083

United Railroad Historical Society
158 Heights Terrace
Middletown, NJ 07748

Upper Saddle River Historical Society
245 Lake Street
Upper Saddle River, NJ 07458
http://www.uppersaddleriverlibrary.org/
Organizations/history.html

Van Harlingen Historical Society
33 Ludlow Avenue
Belle Mead, NJ 08502

Vernon Township Historical Society
173 Barrett Road
Highland Lakes, NJ 07422
Tel: 973-764-8554

Verona Historical Society
21 Grove Avenue
Verona, NJ 07044

Vineland Historical and Antiquarian Society/Library
108 S. 7th Street
P.O. Box 35
Vineland, NJ 08360
Tel: 856-691-1111

Voorhees Township Historical Society
820 Berlin Road
Voorhees, NJ 08043

Waldwick Historical Society
P.O. Box 273
Waldwick, NJ 07463

Wallpack Historical Society
3 Wallpack Center
P.O. Box 3
Branchville, NJ 07890
Tel: 973-948-6671

Warren County Cultural & Heritage Commission
Shippen Manor
8 Belvidere Avenue
Oxford, NJ 07863
Tel/Fax: 908-453-4981
E-mail: wcchc@nac.net
http://www.wcchc.org/

Warren County Historical & Genealogical Society/Museum & Library
313 Mansfield Street
P.O. Box 313
Belvidere, NJ 07823
Tel: 908-475-4246

Washington Township Historical Society
6 Fairview Avenue
P.O. Box 189
Long Valley, NJ 07853
Tel: 908-876-9696

Watchung Historical Society
105 Turtle Road
Watchung, NJ 07060

West Caldwell, Historical Society of
278 Westville Avenue
West Caldwell, NJ 07006

West Long Branch Historical Society
P.O. Box 151 West
Long Branch, NJ 07764

West Paterson Historical Society
Municipal Building
5 Brophy Land
West Paterson, NJ 07424

West Portal Historical Society
P.O. Box 134
Asbury, NJ 08802

West Windsor, Historical Society of
P.O. Box 38
Princeton Junction, NJ 08550

Westfield Historical Society/Library & Archives
Town Hall, 2nd Floor
425 E. Broad Street
P.O. Box 613
Westfield, NJ 07091
Tel: 908-789-4047
E-mail: history@westfieldnj.com
http://www.westfieldnj.com/history/

Wharton Historical Society
10 North Main Street
P.O. Box 424
Wharton, NJ 07885

White Township Historical Society/Museum
RD 3
Belvidere, NJ 07823

Wildwood Crest Historical Society
116 E. Heather Road
Wildwood Crest, NJ 08260
E-mail: KirkHastings2@aol.com
http://www.cresthistory.org/

Wildwood Historical Society
George F. Boyer Historical Museum
Holly Beach Mall
3907 Pacific Avenue
Wildwood, NJ 08260
Tel: 609-523-0277
http://www.the-wildwoods.com/history/ museum.html

Willingboro Historical Society
Municipal Complex
Willingboro, NJ 08046

Wyckoff Historical Society
P.O. Box 73
Wyckoff, NJ 07481
http://www.wyckoffhistory.org/

LDS FAMILY HISTORY CENTERS

For locations of Family History Centers in this state, see the Family History Center locator at FamilySearch.
http://www.familysearch.org/eng/Library/FHC/frameset_fhc.asp

ARCHIVES/LIBRARIES/MUSEUMS

Asbury Park Public Library
500 First Avenue
Asbury Park, NJ 07712
Tel: 732-774-4221
Fax: 732-988-6101
http://www.asburypark.lib.nj.us/

Atlantic City Free Public Library
1 North Tennessee Avenue
Atlantic City, NJ 08401
Tel: 609-345-2269
E-mail: brynk@library.atlantic.city.lib.nj.us
http://library.atlantic.city.lib.nj.us/

Atlantic County Historical Society/Library & Museum
907 Shore Road
P.O. Box 301
Somers Point, NJ 08244
Tel: 609-927-5218
http://www.aclink.org/achs/homepage.htm

Atlantic County Library/Mays Landing Branch
Reference Center/New Jersey Collection
40 South Farragut Avenue
Mays Landing, NJ 08330
Tel: 609-646-8699
    609-625-2776
Fax: 609-625-8143
http://www.aclink.org/aclibrary/branches/ aclszzz.htm

Barnegat Bay Decoy & Bayman's Museum
137 W. Main Street
P.O. Box 52
Tuckerton, NJ 08087
Tel: 609-296-8868
http://www.oceancountygov.com/decoy/default.htm

Belleville Public Library & Information Center
221 Washington Avenue
Belleville, NJ 07109
Tel: 973-450-3434
Fax: 973-450-9518
http://www.intac.com/~bpllibn/hpfront.htm

Bloomfield Public Library
90 Broad Street
Bloomfield, NJ 07003
Tel: 973-429-9292

Boonton/Holmes Public Library
621 Main Street
Boonton, NJ 07005
Tel: 973-334-2980
Fax: 973-334-3917
E-mail: boonton621library@hotmail.com
http://www.boonton.org/library/index.htm

Bridgeton Free Public Library
150 Commerce Street, E
Bridgeton, NJ 08302
Tel: 856-451-2620

Brookdale Community College
Learning Resource Center
765 Newman Springs Road
Lincroft, NJ 07738
Tel: 732-224-2706
http://www.brookdale.cc.nj.us/

Burlington County Library
Special Collections
5 Pioneer Blvd.
Westampton, NJ 08060
Tel: 609-267-9660
    609-298-0063
Fax: 609-267-4091
http://www.burlco.lib.nj.us/

Camden County Historical Society/Library
Park Blvd. & Euclid Avenue
Camden, NJ 08103-3697
Tel: 856-964-3333
http://www.cchsnj.com/

Camden County Library
203 Laurel Road
Voorhees, NJ 08043
Tel: 856-772-1636
Fax: 856-772-6105
E-mail: pagemaster@camden.lib.nj.us
http://www.camden.lib.nj.us/

Cape May County Library
30 West Mechanic Street
Mail:
DN2030, 4 Moore Road
Cape May Court House, NJ 08210
Tel: 609-463-6350
Fax: 609-465-3895
http://www.cape-may.county.lib.nj.us/

Cape May Historical & Genealogical Society/Library
504 Route 9
Cape May Courthouse, NJ 08210-3070
Tel: 609-465-3535
http://www.cmcmuseum.org/library.htm

Centenary College
Taylor Memorial Museum
400 Jefferson Street
Hackettstown, NJ 07840-2100
Tel: 908-852-1400
http://www.centenarycollege.edu/

Chathams, Library of the
214 Main Street
Chatham, NJ 07928
Tel: 973-635-0603
E-mail: obrien@main.morris.org
http://www.chatham-nj.org/coin/chatlib/library.html

Clark Public Library
303 Westfield Avenue
Clark, NJ 07066
Tel: 732-388-5999
Fax: 732-388-7866
E-mail: ref@clarklibrary.org
http://www.clarklibrary.org/

Clinton Historical Museum
56 Main Street
Clinton, NJ 08809
Tel: 908-735-4101

Drew University
United Methodist Archives
Madison, NJ 07940
Tel: 973-408-3590
E-mail: drewlib@drew.edu
http://www.depts.drew.edu/lib/uma.html

East Orange Public Library
21 South Arlington Avenue
East Orange, NJ 07018
Tel: 973-266-5600
Fax: 973-675-6128
E-mail: feedback@eopl.org
http://www.eopl.org/

Easton Area Public Library
Marx History Room
6th & Church Street
Easton, PA 18042
Tel: 610-258-2917
http://www.eastonpl.org/welcome.html

Eatontown Historical Committee/Museum
75 Broad Street
Eatontown, NJ 07724
Tel: 732-542-4026

Edison Public Library
340 Plainfield Avenue
Edison, NJ 08817
Tel: 732-287-2298
Fax: 732-819-9134

Ewing Township Historical Preservation Society/Library
27 Federal City Road
Ewing, NJ 08638
Tel: 609-530-1220
http://www.ethps.org/

Fairleigh Dickinson University
1000 River Road
Teaneck, NJ 07666
Tel: 201-692-2000
E-mail: globaleducation@fdu.edu
http://www.fdu.edu/studentsvcs/libraries.html

Gloucester County Historical Society/Library
17 Hunter Street
Woodbury, NJ 08096
Tel: 856-845-4771
http://www.rootsweb.com/~njglouce/gchs/

Hackettstown Public Library
110 Church Street
Hackettstown, NJ 07840
Tel: 908-852-4936
Fax: 908-852-7850
E-mail: hfplinfo@goes.com
http://www.goes.com/hfplinfo/

Haddonfield Public Library
60 Haddon Avenue
Haddonfield, NJ 08033
Tel: 856-429-1304
Fax: 856-429-3760
http://www.haddonfield.camden.lib.nj.us/

Hamilton Township Public Library
1 Municipal Drive
Trenton, NJ 08619
Tel: 609-581-4060
Fax: 609-581-4067

Hopewell Museum
28 E. Broad Street
Hopewell, NJ 08525
Tel: 609-466-0103
http://www.fieldtrip.com/nj/94660103.htm

Hunterdon County Historical Society
Hiram E. Deats Memorial Library
114 Main Street
Flemington, NJ 08822
Tel: 908-782-1091
http://members.aol.com/njysprez/hchs.htm

Hunterdon County Library
314 State Highway 12
Flemington, NJ 08822
Tel: 908-788-1444
http://www.hunterdon.lib.nj.us/

Indian Heritage Museum
730 Rancocas Road
P.O. Box 225
Rancocas, NJ 08073
Tel: 609-261-4747
E-mail: powhatan@powhatan.org
http://www.powhatan.org/museum.html

Irvington Public Library
346 16th Avenue
Irvington, NJ 07111
Tel: 973-372-6403

Jersey City Public Library
New Jersey Room
472 Jersey Avenue
Jersey City, NJ 07303
Tel: 201-547-4500
http://www.jclibrary.org/

Kinnelon Public Library
132 Kinnelon Road
Kinnelon, NJ 07405
Tel: 201-838-1321

Livingston/Ruth L. Rockwood Memorial Library
Livingston Memorial Park
10 Robert Harp Drive
Livingston, NJ 07039
Tel: 973-992-4600
Fax: 973-994-2346
http://www.bccls.org/livingston/library.html

Long Branch Historical Museum
1260 Ocean Avenue
Long Branch, NJ 07740
Tel: 732-222-9879

Long Branch Public Library
328 Broadway
Long Branch, NJ 07740
Tel: 732-222-3900
http://www.lmxac.org/longbranch/

Madison Public Library
39 Keep Street
Madison, NJ 07940
Tel: 973-377-0722

Maplewood Memorial Library
51 Baker Street
Maplewood, NJ 07040
Tel: 973-762-1622
Fax: 973-762-4573
http://www.maplewoodlibrary.org/

Meadowlands Museum
91 Crane Avenue
P.O. Box 3
Rutherford, NJ 07070
Tel: 201-935-1175
http://www.fieldtrip.com/nj/19351175.htm

Mercer County Public Library
2751 Brunswick Pike
Lawrenceville, NJ 08648
Tel: 609-989-6917
Fax: 609-538-1206

Metuchen Public Library
480 Middlesex Avenue
Metuchen, NJ 08840
Tel: 732-632-8526
Fax: 732-632-8535
http://www.metuchen.com/library.html

Middletown Public Library
55 New Monmouth Road
Middletown, NJ 07748
Tel: 732-671-3700
Fax: 732-671-5839
http://www.visitmonmouth.com/51000_library/ mdltn/

Monmouth County Archives
125 Symmes Drive
Manalapan, NJ 07726
Tel: 732-308-3772
Fax: 732-409-4888
http://www.visitmonmouth.com/archives/

Monmouth University
Guggenheim Library/Special Collections
Cedar Avenue
West Long Branch, NJ 07764
Tel: 732-571-3450
Fax: 732-263-5124
http://www.monmouth.edu/irs/library/special.html

Montclair Historical Society
Terhune Library
108 Orange Road
Montclair, NJ 07043
Tel: 973-744-1796
http://www.montclairhistorical.org/

Morris County Historical Society/Research Library
Acorn Hall
68 Morris Avenue
P.O. Box 170M Morristown, NJ 07960
Tel: 973-267-3465
http://www.acornhall.org/

Morris County Library
New Jersey Collection
30 East Hanover Avenue
Whippany, NJ 07981
Tel: 973-285-6930
E-mail: heagney@main.morris.org
http://www.gti.net/mocolib1/MCL.html

Morris Genealogical Library
228 Elberon Avenue
Allenhurst, NJ 07711

Morristown & Morris Township, Joint Free Public Library of
1 Miller Road
Morristown, NJ 07960
Tel: 973-538-6161
E-mail: gulick@main.morris.org
http://www.jfpl.org/

Neptune Public Library/Historical Society Museum
25 Neptune Blvd.
P.O. Box 1125
Neptune, NJ 07753
Tel: 732-775-8241 ext. 302
Fax: 732-774-1132
E-mail: library@neptunetownship.org
http://neptunepubliclibrary.org/

New Jersey Catholic Historical Records Commission
238 E. Blancke Street
P.O. Box 1246
Linden, NJ 07036
Tel: 908-486-1022

New Jersey Catholic Historical Records Commission
Seton Hall University
Walsh Library/Special Collections
South Orange, NJ 07079-2696
Tel: 973-761-9476
E-mail: somersma@lanmail.shu.edu
http://library.shu.edu/catholicrec/njhrc.htm

New Jersey Historical Commission
225 West State Street, Fourth Floor
P.O. Box 305
Trenton, NJ 08625-0305
Tel: 609-292-6062
Fax: 609-633-8168
http://www.state.nj.us/state/history/hisidx.html

New Jersey Historical Society/Library
230 Broadway
Newark, NJ 07104
Tel: 973-483-3939
Fax: 973-483-1988

New Jersey State Library
State Library Building
Level 4 (Genealogy & Local History Office)
185 West State Street
P.O. Box 520
Trenton, NJ 08625-0520
Tel: 609-292-6220 (General Information)
      609-292-6274 (Genealogy & Local History)
Fax: 609-984-7901
http://www.njstatelib.org/

New Jersey State Museum
205 West State Street
P.O. Box 530
Trenton, NJ 08625
Tel: 609-292-6464 (24 hour information)
      609-292-6308 (Mon-Fri, 8-4)
Fax: 609-599-4098
http://www.state.nj.us/state/museum/

New Jersey State Police Museum
River Road
P.O. Box 7068
West Trenton, NJ 08628
Tel: 609-882-2000 ext. 6400
http://www.fieldtrip.com/nj/98822000.htm

New Sweden Farmstead
50 E. Broad Street
Bridgeton, NJ 08302
Tel: 856-451-4802
http://www.fieldtrip.com/nj/94514802.htm

Newark Public Library
New Jersey Department
5 Washington Street
P.O. Box 630
Newark, NJ 07101-0630
Tel: 973-733-7784
http://www.npl.org/

Nutley Free Public Library
93 Booth Drive
Nutley, NJ 07110
Tel: 973-667-0405
Fax: 973-667-0408
E-mail: tropiano@bccls.org
http://www.bccls.org/nutley/

Ocean City Historical Museum
1735 Simpson Avenue
Ocean City, NJ 08226
Tel: 609-399-1801
Fax: 609-399-0544
http://www.ocnjmuseum.org/

Ocean County Historical Society
Strickler Research Library
26 Hadley Avenue
Toms River, NJ 08753
Tel: 732-341-1880
Fax: 732-341-4372
http://www.oceancountyhistory.org/Library/ library.html

Ocean County Library
Bishop Building
101 Washington Street
Toms River, NJ 08753
Tel: 732-349-6200 ext. 859
http://oceancountylibrary.org/Branches/Bishop/ bis.htm

Ocean Gate Historical Society/Museum
Cape May and Asbury Avenues
P.O. Box 895
Ocean Gate, NJ 08740
http://www.fieldtrip.com/nj/82693468.htm

Ocean Township Historical Museum
163 Monmouth Road
Oakhurst, NJ 07755
Tel: 908-531-2136

Paramus Public Library
116 E. Century Road
Paramus, NJ 07652
Tel: 201-599-1302
Fax: 201-599-0059
E-mail: pararef@bccls.org
http://www.bccls.org/paramus/

Passaic County Historical Society/Library
Lambert Castle
Valley Road
Paterson, NJ 07503
Tel: 973-881-2761
http://www.geocities.com/pchslc/library.html

Phillipsburg Free Public Library
200 Frost Avenue
Phillipsburg, NJ 08865
Tel: 908-454-3712
http://www.pburglib.com/

Princeton Historical Society/Library
158 Nassau Street
Princeton, NJ 08542
Tel: 609-921-6748
E-mail: PHS@injersey.com
http://www.princetonhistory.org/

Princeton Public Library
301 North Harrison Street
Princeton, NJ 08540
Tel: 609-924-9529
Fax: 609-924-7937
E-mail: pplwebmaster@princeton.lib.nj.us
http://www.princeton.lib.nj.us/

Princeton University
Firestone Library
One Washington Road
Princeton, NJ 08544
Tel: 609-258-1470
Fax: 609-258-0441
E-mail: web@library.princeton.edu
http://libweb.princeton.edu/

Ramsey Free Public Library
30 Wyckoff Avenue
Ramsey, NJ 07446
Tel: 201-327-1445
E-mail: rams1@bccls.org
http://www.bccls.org/ramsey/

Red Bank Public Library
84 West Front Street
Red Bank, NJ 07701
Tel: 732-842-0690
Fax: 732-842-4191
http://www.lmxac.org/redbank/

Richard Stockton College Library
Jim Leeds Road
Pomona, NJ 08240
Tel: 609-652-4343
http://library.stockton.edu/

Roselle Park Historical Society/Museum
9 West Grant Avenue
Roselle Park, NJ 07204
P.O. Box 135
Roselle Park, NJ 07204
http://www.rosellepark.org/upclose/history/
museum.htm

Roxbury Public Library
103 Main Street
Succasunna, NJ 07876
Tel: 973-584-2400
Fax: 973-584-5484
TDD: 800-852-7899
http://www.roxburylibrary.org/

Rutgers University
Archibald Stevens Alexander Library
Special Collections & Archives
169 College Avenue
New Brunswick, NJ 08903
Tel: 732-932-7510
Fax: 732-932-7012
http://www.libraries.rutgers.edu/rulib/spcol/
    spcol.htm

**Salem County Historical Society/Museum & Research
Library**
79-83 Market Street
Salem, NJ 08079
Tel: 856-935-5004
http://www.salemcounty.com/schs/

Sea Isle City Historical Museum
4208 Landis Avenue
Sea Isle City, NJ 08243
Tel: 609-263-2992
http://www.jerseyseashore.com/sic_museum/
    sic_museum.htm

Seton Hall University
Walsh Library/Special Collections
South Orange, NJ 07079-2696
Tel: 973-761-9476
E-mail: library@shu.edu
http://library.shu.edu/SpecColl.htm

Sparta Public Library
22 Woodport Road
Sparta, NJ 07871
Tel: 973-729-3101
http://www.sparta.lib.nj.us/

Sussex County Library
RD #3, Box
170 Newton, NJ 07860
Tel: 973-948-3660

Teaneck Public Library
840 Teaneck Road
Teaneck, NJ 07666
Tel: 201-837-4171
Fax: 201-837-0410
http://www.teaneck.org/

Tenafly Public Library
100 Riveredge Road
Tenafly, NJ 07670
Tel: 201-568-8680
E-mail: tenpubli@intac.com
http://www.bccls.org/tenafly/

Trenton Public Library/Main Branch
Trentoniana Dept.
120 Academy Street
Trenton, NJ 08608
Tel: 609-392-7188
Fax: 609-392-7655
E-mail: tplnj@pluto.njcc.com
http://www.princetonol.com/yo/data/tplml.html

Vineland Historical and Antiquarian Society/Library
108 South 7th Street
P.O. Box 35
Vineland, NJ 08360
Tel: 856-691-1111

**Warren County Historical & Genealogical
Society/Museum & Library**
313 Mansfield Street
P.O. Box 313
Belvidere, NJ 07823
Tel: 908-475-4246

Warren County Free Public Library/Main Branch
Court House Annex
199 Hardwick Street
Belvidere, NJ 07823
Tel: 908-475-6322

Washington Public Library
20 Carlton Avenue
Washington, NJ 07882
Tel: 908-689-0201

Wayne Public Library
Main Library
461Valley Road
Wayne, NJ 07470
Tel: 973-694-4272
Fax: 973-692-0907
http://www.waynepubliclibrary.org/index.shtml

Westfield Memorial Library
550 East Broad Street
Westfield, NJ 07090
Tel: 908-789-4090
http://www.wmlnj.org/

White Township Historical Society/Museum
RD 3
Belvidere, NJ 07823

Wildwood Historical Society
George F. Boyer Historical Museum
Holly Beach Mall
3907 Pacific Avenue
Wildwood, NJ 08260
Tel: 609-523-0277
http://www.the-wildwoods.com/history/ museum.html

Willingboro Township Library
1 Salem Road
Willingboro, NJ 08046
Tel: 609-877-6668

Woodbridge Free Public Library
George Frederick Plaza
Woodbridge, NJ 07095
Tel: 732-634-4450

Yesteryear Museum
Regina Place & Harriet Drive
Whippany, NJ 07981

NEWSPAPER REPOSITORIES

New Jersey State Archives
State Library Building
185 West State Street, Level 2
P.O. Box 520
Trenton, NJ 08625-0520
Tel: 609-530-3200
Fax: 609-984-7901
http://www.njstatelib.org/

Rutgers University
Archibald Stevens Alexander Library
Special Collections & Archives
169 College Avenue
New Brunswick, NJ 08903
Tel: 732-932-7510
Fax: 732-932-7012
http://www.libraries.rutgers.edu/rulib/spcol/
      spcol.htm

VITAL RECORDS

New Jersey State Dept. of Health
Health/Agriculture Building, Room 504
Front & Market Streets
Mail:
New Jersey State Department of Health
Vital Statistics Registration
P.O. Box 370
Trenton, NJ 08625-0370
Tel: 609-292-4087
      609-633-2860 (Vital Chek Operator)
Fax: 609-292-4292
http://www.vitalrec.com/nj.html

NEW JERSEY ON THE WEB

Descendants of Edward Ball of New Jersey
Gedcom Repository Site
http://www.altlaw.com/edball/biged1.htm

Horseneck Founders of New Jersey
http://www.rootsweb.com/~genepool/nj.htm

New Jersey GenWeb Project
http://www.rootsweb.com/~njgenweb/subindex.htm

New Jersey History
http://scils.rutgers.edu/~macan/nj.history.html

NEW MEXICO

ARCHIVES, STATE & NATIONAL

National Archives—Rocky Mountain Region
Bldg. 48, Denver Federal Center
West 6th Avenue and Kipling Street
Denver, CO 80225-0307
Mailing Address:
P.O. Box 25307
Denver, CO 80225-0307
Phone: 303-236-0817
Fax: 303-236-9297
E-mail: denver.archives@nara.gov
http://www.nara.gov/regional/denver.html

New Mexico State Records Center & Archives
1209 Camino Carlos Rey
Santa Fe, NM 87505
Mailing address:
1205 Camino Carlos Rey
Santa Fe, New Mexico 87505.
Tel: 505-476-7908
Fax: 505-476-7909
E-mail: archives@rain.state.nm.us
http://www.state.nm.us/cpr/

GENEALOGICAL SOCIETIES

Alamogordo Genealogy Society (AGeS)
P.O. Box 734
Alamogordo, NM 88310

Albuquerque, Genealogy Club of
Albuquerque Public Library
423 Central Avenue, NE
Albuquerque, NM 87102
http://abqgen.swnet.com/

Artesia Historical & Genealogical Society
P.O. Box 803
Artesia, NM 88211

Curry County Genealogy Society
Clovis-Carver Public Library
701 Main Street
Clovis, NM
Tel: 505-769-7840
Fax: 505-769-7842
E-mail: library@cityofclovis.org

Eddy County Genealogical Society
P.O. Box 461
Carlsbad, NM 88220

Grand Lodge of New Mexico
Ancient Free and Accepted Masons
P.O. Box 25004
Albuquerque, NM 87125-0004
E-mail: nmgndldg@juno.com
http://www.zianet.com/leon/gl.htm

Hispanic Genealogical Research Center—New Mexico
1331 Juan Tabo, NE
Suite P, No. 18
Albuquerque, NM 87112
Tel: 505-836-5438
E-mail: HGRC@HGRC-NM.ORG
http://www.hgrc-nm.org/

Las Vegas Genealogical Society
Las Vegas/Carnegie Public Library
729 Grand Avenue
Las Vegas, NM 87701

Lea County Genealogical Society
P.O. Box 1195
Lovington, NM 88260
Tel: 505-396-2608

Los Alamos Family History Society
P.O. Box 43
Los Alamos, NM 87544-0900

New Mexico Genealogical Society
P.O. Box 8283
Albuquerque, NM 87198-8283

New Mexico Jewish Historical Society
Genealogy & Family History Committee
5520 Wyoming Blvd. NE
Albuquerque, NM 87109
Tel: 505-348-4471
Fax: 505-821-3351
http://www.nmjewishhistory.org/

Roosevelt County Searchers
Tel: 505-359-0772

Roswell Genealogical Society
Roswell Adult Center
807 N. Missouri
P.O. Box 994
Roswell, NM 88201
Tel: 505-624-6718
Fax: 505-624-0538
http://www.roswellcvb.com/rac.htm

Sierra County Genealogical Society
Truth or Consequences Public Library
325 Library Lane
P.O. Box 311
Truth or Consequences, NM 87901
Tel: 505-894-3027
Fax: 505-894-2068
E-mail: torcpl@riolink.com
http://www.ci.truth-or-consequences.nm.us/library.htm

Southeastern New Mexico Genealogical Society/Library
P.O. Box 5725
Hobbs, NM 88240

Southern New Mexico Genealogical Society
P.O. Box 2563
Las Cruces, NM 88004-2563
E-mail: wheelerwc@zianet.com
http://www.zianet.com/wheelerwc/GenSSNM/

Totah Tracers Genealogical Society
Salmon Ruins
Bloomfield Highway
P.O. Box 125
Bloomfield, NM 87413

HISTORICAL SOCIETIES

Artesia Historical & Genealogical Society
P.O. Box 803
Artesia, NM 88211

Cimarron Historical Society
Old Mill Museum
NM 21
P.O. Box 58
Cimarron, NM 87714
http://www.nmculture.org/cgi-bin/
     instview.cgi?_recordnum=OMIL

Columbus Historical Society/Museum
Highway 9 & 11
P.O. Box 562
Columbus, NM 88029
Tel: 505-531-2620
http://www.nmculture.org/cgi-bin/
     instview.cgi?_recordnum=COLU

Historical Society for Southeast New Mexico/Museum & Archives
200 North Lea Avenue
Roswell, NM 88201
Tel: 505-622-8333
http://www.dfn.com/hssnm/

Los Alamos Historical Society/Museum & Archives
1921 Juniper Street
P.O. Box 43 VLA
Los Alamos, NM 87544
Tel: 505-662-6272 (Office & Archives)
     505-662-4493 (Museum & Shop)
E-mail: historicalsociety@losalamos.com
http://www.losalamos.com/historicalsociety/

Moriarty Historical Society/Museum
777 Old U.S. Route 66, SW
P.O. Box 1366
Moriarty, NM 87035
Tel: 505-832-4764
http://www.nmculture.org/cgi-bin/
     instview. cgi?_recordnum=MORI

New Mexico Jewish Historical Society
5520 Wyoming Blvd. NE
Albuquerque, NM 87109
Tel: 505-348-4471
Fax: 505-821-3351
http://www.nmjewishhistory.org/

Sacramento Mountains Historical Society/Museum
1000 U.S. Highway 82
P.O. Box 435
Cloudcroft, NM 88317
Tel: 505-682-2932
http://www.mountainmonthly.com/attractions/
     museum.htm

Santa Fe Trail Association
Santa Fe Trail Center
RR 3
Larned, KS 67550
Tel: 620-285-2054
Fax: 620-285-7491
E-mail: olsen_m@venus.nmhu.edu
http://www.santafetrail.org/

Socorro Historical Society/Hammel Museum
P.O. Box 923
Socorro, NM 87801
http://www.nmt.edu/~nmtlib/LOCAL/hammel.html

Tularosa Basin Historical Society/Museum
1501 White Sands Blvd.
P.O. Box 518
Alamogordo, NM 88310
Tel: 505-437-6120
http://www.nmculture.org/cgi-bin/
instview. cgi?_recordnum=TULA

Union County Historical Society/Museum
23 S. 2nd
Clayton, NM 88415
Tel: 505-374-2977

Valencia County Historical Society
Harvey House Museum
104 N. 1st Street
P.O. Box 166
Belen, NM 87002
Tel: 505-861-0581
http://www.nmculture.org/cgi-bin/
instview.cgi?_recordnum=HARV

LDS FAMILY HISTORY CENTERS

For locations of Family History Centers in this state, see
the Family History Center locator at FamilySearch.
http://www.familysearch.org/eng/Library/FHC/
frameset_fhc.asp

ARCHIVES/LIBRARIES/MUSEUMS

Acoma Pueblo Museum
NM 23
P.O. Box 309 Acoma Pueblo, NM 87034
Tel: 505-252-1139
http://www.nmculture.org/cgi-bin/
instview. cgi?_recordnum=ACOM

Alamogordo Public Library
920 Oregon Avenue
Alamogordo, NM 88310
Tel: 505-439-4140
Fax: 505-439-4108
TTY: 505-439-4149
E-mail: alamopl@wazoo.com
http://ci.alamogordo.nm.us/Library/libraryref.html

Albuquerque Public Library/Rio Grande Valley Library System
Special Collections Branch
423 Central Avenue, NE
Albuquerque, NM 87102
Tel: 505-848-1376
http://www.cabq.gov/rgvls/specol.html

Archdiocese of Santa Fe Museum
Historic Artistic Patrimony
223 Cathedral Place
Santa Fe, NM 87501-2028
Tel: 505-983-3811

Artesia Historical Museum & Arts Center
505 W. Richardson Avenue
Artesia, NM 88210
Tel: 505-748-2390
Fax: 505-746-3886 (Attn: Museum)
http://www.vpa.org/museumsnm.html

Artesia Public Library
306 W. Richardson
Artesia, NM 88210
Tel: 505-746-4252
E-mail: apublib@artesia.net
http://www.pvtnetworks.net/~apublib/

Aztec Museum/Archives & Pioneer Village
125 North Main Avenue
Aztec, NM 87410
Tel: 505-334-9829
http://www.aztecnm.com/museum/ museum_main.htm

Cimarron Historical Society
Old Mill Museum
NM 21
P.O. Box 58
Cimarron, NM 87714
http://www.nmculture.org/cgi-bin/
instview. cgi?_recordnum=OMIL

Clovis-Carver Public Library
701 Main Street
Clovis, NM
Tel: 505-769-7840
Fax: 505-769-7842
E-mail: library@cityofclovis.org

College of Santa Fe
Fogelson Library
1600 St. Michaels Drive
Santa Fe, NM 87505-7615
Tel: 505-473-6011
Fax: 505-473-6593
http://library.csf.edu/libhome.htm

Columbus Historical Society/Museum
Highway 9 & 11
P.O. Box 562
Columbus, NM 88029
Tel: 505-531-2620
E-mail: alnmarilyn@vtc.net
http://www.nmculture.org/cgi-bin/
instview. cgi?_recordnum=COLU

Deming Luna Mimbres Museum
301 S. Silver
Deming, NM 88030
Tel: 505-546-2382
    505-546-2677 (Archives)
E-mail: dlm-museum@ziznet.com
http://www.nmculture.org/cgi-bin/
    instview. cgi?_recordnum=MIMB

Deming/Marshall Memorial Library
301 S. Tin
Deming, NM 88030
Tel: 505-546-9202
Fax: 505-546-9649
E-mail: demingpl@nm-us.campus.mci.net
http://www.zianet.com/demingpl/

Eastern New Mexico University
Golden Library
Station 32
Portales, NM 88130
Tel: 505-562-2624
Fax: 505-562-2647
E-mail: powersd@golden.enmu.edu
http://www.enmu.edu/golden.html

Farmington Museum
302 N. Orchard
Farmington, NM 87401-6227
Tel: 505-599-1174
Fax: 505-326-7572
E-mail: alogan@fmtn.org
http://www.nmculture.org/cgi-bin/
    instview. cgi?_recordnum=FARM

General Douglas L. McBride Military Museum
New Mexico Military Institute
101 W. College Blvd.
P.O. Box J
Roswell, NM 88201
Tel: 505-624-8220
Fax: 505-624-8107
http://www.nmmi.cc.nm.us/

Hispanic Genealogical Research Center-New Mexico
1331 Juan Tabo, NE
Suite P, No. 18
Albuquerque, NM 87112
Tel: 505-836-5438
E-mail: HGRC@HGRC-NM.ORG
http://www.hgrc-nm.org/

Historical Society for Southeast New Mexico/Museum & Archives
200 North Lea Avenue
Roswell, NM 88201
Tel: 505-622-8333
http://www.roswell-usa.com/historic/

Kit Carson Home & Museums
Kit Carson Road
P.O. Drawer CCC
Taos, NM 87571
Tel: 505-758-0505
http://taoswebb.com/

Las Vegas/Carnegie Public Library
500 National Avenue
Las Vegas, NM 87701
Tel: 505-454-1403

Las Vegas City Museum & Rough Rider Memorial
725 Grand Avenue
Las Vegas, NM 87701
Tel: 505-454-1401 ext. 283
http://arco-iris.com/teddy/

Los Alamos Historical Society/Museum & Archives
1921 Juniper Street
Post Office Box 43
Los Alamos, NM 87544
Tel: 505-662-6272 (Office & Archives)
    505-662-4493 (Museum & Shop)
E-mail: historicalsociety@losalamos.com
http://www.losalamos.com/historicalsociety/

Lovington Public Library
113 S. Main
Lovington, NM 88260
Tel: 505-396-3144
Fax: 505-396-7189
http://www.elin.lib.nm.us/lpl/

Mescalero Apache Cultural Center
101 Central Avenue
P.O. Box 176
Mescalero, NM 88340
Tel: 505-671-4494

Million Dollar Museum
US-62/180 and Highway 7
Whites City, NM
http://www.bigwaste.com/photos/nm/million_dollar/

Moriarty Historical Society/Museum
777 Old U.S. Route 66, SW
P.O. Box 1366
Moriarty, NM 87035
Tel: 505-832-4764
http://www.nmculture.org/cgi-bin/
    instview. cgi?_recordnum=MORI

New Mexico Highlands University (NMHU)
Donnelly Library
Las Vegas, NM 87701
Tel: 505-425-7511 (University)
http://www.nmhu.edu/camplife/resources/
    library.htm

New Mexico State Library
1209 Camino Carlos Rey,
Santa Fe, NM 87507
Tel: 505-476-9700
Fax: 505-476-9701
http://www.stlib.state.nm.us/

New Mexico State University/Las Cruces
Branson Library
Box 30006, Dept. 3475
Las Cruces, NM 88003-8006
Tel: 505-646-6928
    505-646-2932
Fax: 505-646-1287 (Govt. Documents)
E-mail: library@lib.nmsu.edu
    or govdocs@lib.nmsu.edu
http://lib.nmsu.edu/

Palace of the Governors
Museum of New Mexico-History Library
105 W. Palace Avenue
P.O. Box 2087 Santa Fe, NM 87504-2087
Tel: 505-827-6483
Fax: 505-827-6521
http://palaceofthegovernors.org/

Portales Public Library
218 South Avenue B
Portales, NM 88130
Tel: 505-356-3940
Fax: 505-356-3964
E-mail ppl@yucca.net
http://www.portalesnm.org/library/home.htm

Pueblo Cultural Center
2401 12th Street, NW
Albuquerque, NM 87192
Tel: 505-843-7270
Fax: 505-842-6959
http://www.indianpueblo.org/

Raton Museum
216 S. First Street
Raton, NM 87740
Tel: 505-445-8979
http://www.nmculture.org/cgi-bin/
    instview. cgi?_recordnum=RATO

Roosevelt County Historical Museum
Eastern New Mexico University (ENMU)
Station No. 30
Portales, NM 88130
Tel: 505-562-2592
Fax: 505-562-2578
http://w3a.enmu.edu/academics/excellence/
    museums/roosevelt-county/

Roswell Public Library
301 North Pennsylvania Avenue
Roswell, NM 88201-4695
Tel: 505-622-7101
http://www.roswellpubliclibrary.org/

Sacramento Mountains Historical Society/Museum
1000 U.S. 82
P.O. Box 435
Cloudcroft, NM 88317
Tel: 505-682-2932
http://www.mountainmonthly.com/attractions/
    museum.htm

Santa Fe History Library
110 Washington Avenue
Santa Fe, NM 87501
Tel: 505-827-6470

Santa Fe Public Library
145 Washington Street
Santa Fe, NM 87501
Tel: 505-955-6780
E-mail: library@ci.santa-fe.nm.us
http://sfweb.ci.santa-fe.nm.us/sfpl/

Santa Fe Trail Historical Society/Museum
614 Maxwell Avenue
P.O. Box 323
Springer, NM 87747
Tel: 505-483-2682
http://www.nmculture.org/cgi-bin/
    instview. cgi?_recordnum=SFTM

Silver City Museum/Local History Research Library
312 W. Broadway
Silver City, NM 88061
Tel: 505-538-5921
Fax: 505-388-1096
http://www.silvercitymuseum.org/

Silver City Public Library
515 W. College Avenue Silver City, NM 88061
Tel: 505-538-3672
Fax: 505-388-3757

Socorro Historical Society/Hammel Museum
P.O. Box 923
Socorro, NM 87801
http://www.nmt.edu/~nmtlib/LOCAL/hammel.html

Socorro Public Library
401 Park Street
Socorro, NM 87801
Tel: 505-835-1114
E-mail: splcirc@sdc.org
http://www.sdc.org/~library/

Southeastern New Mexico Genealogical Society/Library
P.O. Box 5725
Hobbs, NM 88240

Thomas Branigan Memorial Library
200 E. Picacho Avenue
Las Cruces, NM 88001
Tel: 505-526-1045

Truth or Consequences Public Library
325 Library Lane
Truth or Consequences, NM 87901-2375
Tel: 505-894-3027
Fax: 505-894-2068
E-mail: torcpl@riolink.com
http://www.ci.truth-or-consequences.nm.us/ library.htm

Tularosa Basin Historical Society/Museum
1501 White Sands Blvd.
P.O. Box 518
Alamogordo, NM 88310
Tel: 505-437-6120
http://www.nmculture.org/cgi-bin/
        instview. cgi?_recordnum=TULA

Union County Historical Society/Museum
23 S. 2nd
Clayton, NM 88415
Tel: 505-374-2977

University of New Mexico
Center for Southwestern Research/Museum of New
Mexico General Library
Albuquerque, NM 87131
Tel: 505-277-6451
Fax: 505-277-6019
E-mail: libinfo@unm.edu
http://eLibrary.unm.edu/

Valencia County Historical Society
Harvey House Museum
104 N. 1st Street
P.O. Box 166
Belen, NM 87002
Tel: 505-861-0581
http://www.nmculture.org/cgi-bin/
        instview. cgi?_recordnum=HARV

Western New Mexico University Museum
1000 W. College Avenue
P.O. Box 680
Silver City, NM 88061
Tel: 505-538-6386
Fax: 505-538-6178
http://www.wnmu.edu/univ/museum.htm

NEWSPAPER REPOSITORIES

Santa Fe History Library
110 Washington Avenue
Santa Fe, NM 87501
Tel: 505-827-6470

University of New Mexico
General Library
Albuquerque, NM 87131
Tel: 505-277-6451
Fax: 505-277-6019
E-mail: libinfo@unm.edu
http://eLibrary.unm.edu/

VITAL RECORDS

New Mexico Department of Health
Bureau of Vital Records & Health Statistics
1105 St. Francis Drive
P.O. Box 26110
Santa Fe, NM 87504-6110
Tel: 505-827-2338 (Recorded Message)
http://dohewbs2.health.state.nm.us/VitalRec/
        Vital%20Records.htm

NEW MEXICO ON THE WEB

La Herencia Del Norte—Hispanic Heritage Magazine
http://www.herencia.com/

New Mexico Cultural Treasures
http://www.nmculture.org/

New Mexico GenWeb Project
http://www.rootsweb.com/~nmgenweb/

New York

Archives, State & National

National Archives—Northeast Region
201 Varick Street
New York, NY 10014-4811
Phone: 212-337-1300
Fax: 212-337-1306
E-mail: newyork.archives@nara.gov
http://www.nara.gov/regional/newyork.html

New York State Archives
Cultural Education Center Room 3043
Albany, NY 12230
Phone 518-474-8955
E-mail: archref@mail.nysed.gov
http://www.sara.nysed.gov/

Genealogical Societies

Adirondack Genealogical-Historical Society
Saranac Lake Free Library
100 Main Street
Saranac Lake, NY 12983
Tel: 518-891-4190
http://www.nc3r.org/slfl/

Afro-American Historical & Genealogical Society (AAHGS)
Jean Sampson Scott Chapter-Greater New York
P.O. Box 022340
Brooklyn, NY 11202

Amherst Museum Genealogy Society
Amherst Museum Colony Park
3755 Tonawanda Creek Road
Amherst, NY 14228
http://www.amherstmuseum.org/genealogy.htm

Ballston Spa Genealogy Club
c/o Ballston Spa Library
Ballston, NY 12020

Brooklyn Historical Society, Genealogy Workshop
128 Pierrepont Street
Brooklyn, NY 11201

Buffalo & Western New York Italian Genealogy Society
171 Fowler Avenue
Kenmore, NY 14217-1503

Capital District Genealogical Society
Empire State Plaza Station
P.O. Box 2175
Albany, NY 12220

Central New York Genealogical Society
P.O. Box 104, Colvin Station
Syracuse, NY 13205
http://www.rootsweb.com/~nycnygs/

Chautauqua County Genealogical Society
P.O. Box 404
Fredonia, NY 14063
http://www.netsync.net/users/djyj/CCGS.htm

Computer Genealogy Society of Long Island
c/o LDS Family History Center
160 Washington Avenue
Plainview, NY 11803
E-mail jbrower@optonline.net
http://freepages.genealogy.rootsweb.com/~cgsli/

Creole-American Genealogical Society, Inc.
Church Street Station
P.O. Box 2666
New York, NY 10008

Dutch Settlers Society of Albany
23 Dresden Court
Albany, NY 12203

Dutchess County Genealogical Society
P.O. Box 708
Poughkeepsie, NY 12602
http://www.dcgs-gen.org/

Finger Lakes Genealogical Society
P.O. Box 47
Seneca Falls, NY 13148

German Genealogy Group of Long Island
Post Office Box 1004
Kings Park, NY 11754
http://www.germangenealogygroup.com/

Heritage Hunters
P.O. Box 1389
Saratoga Springs, NY 12866
http://www.rootsweb.com/~nysarato/gwsarhh.html

Huntington Historical Society, Genealogy Workshop
209 Main Street
Huntington, NY 11743
Tel: 631-427-7045
Fax: 631-427-7056
http://www.huntingtonhistoricalsociety.org/ genealogy/

Irish Family History Forum, Inc.
P.O. Box 67
Plainview, NY 11803-0067

Italian Genealogical Group, Inc.
7 Grayon Drive
Dix Hills, NY 11746

Jefferson County New York Genealogical Society
P.O. Box 6453
Watertown, NY 13601
E-mail: jcnygs@imcnet.net
http://www.rootsweb.com/~nyjeffer/jeffsoc.htm

Jewish Genealogical Society, Inc.
P.O. Box 6398
New York, NY 10128
Tel: 212-330-8257
    212-294-8326
http://www.jgsny.org/

Jewish Genealogical Society of Capital District
P.O. Box 3850
Albany, NY 12208

Jewish Genealogical Society of Greater Buffalo
174 Peppertree Drive #7
Amherst, NY 14228

Jewish Genealogical Society of Long Island
37 West Cliff Drive
Dix Hills, NY 11746

Jewish Genealogical Society of Rochester
c/o Dr. Bruce Kahn
265 Viennawood Drive
Rochester, NY 14618
http://jgsr.org/

Kodak Genealogical Society
Eastman Kodak Company
Kodak Recreation Building 28
Rochester, NY 14652-3404

Livingston-Steuben County Genealogical Society
5 Elizabeth Street
Dansville, NY 14437-1719
http://www.rootsweb.com/~nyliving/lscgs.htm

National Society-Daughters of the American Revolution
New York State Chapter
http://www.nydar.org/

New York Genealogical & Biographical Society
122 East 58th Street
New York, NY 10022-1939
Tel: 212-755-8532
http://www.nygbs.org/

New York State Council of Genealogical Organizations
P.O. Box 2593
Syracuse, NY 13220-2593

Niagara County Genealogical Society
215 Niagara Street
Lockport, NY 14094
Tel: 716-433-1033
http://www.niagaracounty.org/
    genealogical_society_home.htm

Northeastern New York Genealogical Society
P.O. Box 4264
Queensbury, NY 12804
http://bfn.org/~ae487/nnygs.html

Northern New York American-Canadian Genealogical Society
P.O. Box 1256
Plattsburgh, NY 12901
http://www.rootsweb.com/~nnyacgs/

Nyando Roots Genealogical Society
P.O. Box 175
Massena, NY 13662

Oneida County Genealogical Club
c/o Oneida County Historical Society
318 Genesee Street
Utica, NY 13502

Ontario County Genealogical Society
55 North Main Street
Canandaigua, NY 14424
Tel: 716-394-4975
http://www.ochs.org/

Orange County Genealogical Society/Research Room
Historic Courthouse
101 Main Street
Goshen, NY 10924

Palatines to America, New York Chapter
9 Maple Street
Pittsford, NY 14534
Tel: 518-399-6187

Penfield Foundation, Inc.
Ironville Road
P.O. Box 126
Crown Point, NY 12928
Tel: 518-597-3804
http://www.penfieldmuseum.org/

Polish Genealogical Society of Western New York State (PGSWNY)
299 Barnard Street
Buffalo, NY 14206-3212
http://www.pgsnys.org/

Puerto Rican/Hispanic Genealogical Society
25 Ralph Avenue
P.O. Box 260118
Bellerose, NY 11426-0118
Tel: 516-834-2511
E-mail: prhgs@yahoo.com
http://www.linkdirect.com/hispsoc/

Queens Genealogy Workshop
1820 Flushing Avenue
Ridgewood, NY 11385
Tel: 718-456-1776
http://home.att.net/~CGohari/

Rochester Genealogical Society
P.O. Box 10501
Rochester, NY 14610-0501
E-mail: halsey@vivanet.com
http://www.rootsweb.com/~nyrgs/

Rockland County, Genealogical Society of
c/o Historical Society of Rockland County
20 Zukor Road
New City, NY 10956
Tel: 914-634-9629

St. Lawrence Valley Genealogical Society
P.O. Box 341
Colton, NY 13625-0341
http://www.rootsweb.com/~nystlawr/slvgs.htm

Southern Tier Genealogy Club
Location:
Vestal Public Library
320 Vestal Parkway East
Vestal, NY 13850
Mail:
P.O. Box 680
Vestal, NY 13851-0680
E-mail: ann@spectra.net
http://www.rootsweb.com/~nybroome/stgs/stgs.htm

Twin Tiers Genealogical Society
P.O. Box 763
Elmira, NY 14902
http://www.rootsweb.com/~nychemun/tths.htm

Ulster County Genealogical Society
P.O. Box 536
Hurley, NY 12443

Westchester County Genealogical Society
P.O. Box 518
White Plains, NY 10603-0518
http://www.rootsweb.com/~nywcgs/

Western New York Genealogical Society/Library & Museum
5859 South Park Avenue, Route 62
P.O. Box 338
Hamburg, NY 14075
http://www.pce.net/outram/wny.htm

Yates County Genealogical & Historical Society
200 Main Street
Penn Yan, NY 14527
Tel: 315-536-7318
http://www.yatespast.com/

HISTORICAL SOCIETIES

Adirondack Genealogical-Historical Society
100 Main Street
Saranac Lake, NY 12983

Afro-American Historical & Genealogical Society (AAHGS)
P.O. Box 022340
Brooklyn, NY 11202

Alabama Historical Society
Alabama Town Historian
Jean Richardson
7079 Maple Street Basom, NY 14013
Tel: 716-948-9886

Albany County Historical Association
Ten Broeck Mansion
9 Ten Broeck Place
Albany, NY 12210
Tel: 518-436-9826
http://www.tenbroeck.org/

Albany South End Historical Society
20 Second Avenue
Albany, NY 12202

Amagansett Historical Society
P.O. Box 7077
Amagansett, NY 11930
Tel: 516-267-3020

Amenia Historical Society
P.O. Box 22
Amenia, NY 12501
E-mail: Ameniahistorical@aol.com

American Baptist Historical Society
Samuel Colgate Historical Library
1106 South Goodman Street
Rochester, NY 14620-2532
Tel: 716-473-1740

Amityville Historical Society/Library
Lauder Museum
170 Broadway
P.O. Box 764
Amityville, NY 11701
Tel: 631-598-1486
Fax: 631-598-7399
E-mail: amityvillehistoricalsociety@juno.com
http://www.amityville.com/amhist.htm

Anderson Falls Heritage Society
P.O. Box 185
Keeseville, NY 12944

Ardsley Historical Society
9 American Legion Drive
Ardsley, NY 10502
Tel: 914-693-6027

Attica Historical Society
130 Main Street
P.O. Box 24
Attica, NY 14011
Tel: 716-591-2161

Babylon Village Historical and Preservation Society
117 West Main Street
Babylon, NY 11702

Baldwin Historical Society/Museum
1980 Grand Avenue
Baldwin, NY 11510
Tel: 516-223-6900

Beacon Historical Society
P.O. Box 89
Beacon, NY 12508

Bedford Historical Society
38 Village Green
Bedford, NY 10506
Tel: 914-234-9751
    914-234-9328

Beekman Historical Society
P.O. Box 165
Poughquag, NY 12570

Bellport-Brookhaven Historical Society/Museum
31 Bellport Lane
Bellport, NY 11713
Tel: 631-286-0888

Berne Historical Society
Berne Town Hall
P.O. Box 34
Berne, NY 12023
Tel: 518-768-2445
http://www.bernehistory.org/bhs.htm

Bethlehem Historical Association
1003 River Road
Selkirk, NY 12158
Tel: 518-767-9432

Bohemia Historical Society
P.O. Box 67
Bohemia, NY 11716
Tel: 631-244-2707

Bowdoin Park Historical & Archaeological Association
85 Sheafe Road
Wappingers Falls, NY 12590

Briarcliff Manor/Scarborough Historical Society
162 Macy Road
Briarcliff Manor, NY 10510
Tel: 914-941-4393

Bridge Line Historical Society
Historical Society for the Delaware & Hudson Railroad
Capitol Station
P.O. Box 7242
Albany, NY 12224
http://www.bridge-line.org/

Bridgehampton Historical Society/Museum
Montauk Highway
Bridgehampton, NY 11932
Tel: 631-537-1088

Brooklyn Historical Society
2 Metrotech Center
Brooklyn, NY 11201
Tel: 718-624-0890
Fax: 718-875-3869
http://www.brooklynhistory.org/

Broome County Historical Society
185 Court Street
Binghamton, NY 13901
Tel: 607-772-0660

Bronx County Historical Society
3309 Bainbridge Avenue
Bronx, NY 10467
Tel: 718-881-8900
http://www.bronxhistoricalsociety.org/index17.html

Brunswick Historical Society
P.O. Box 1776
Cropseyville, NY 12052
Tel: 518-279-4024
http://www.brunswickhistory.cjb.net/

Buffalo and Erie County Historical Society/Library
25 Nottingham Court
Buffalo, NY 14216
Tel: 716-873-9612
Fax: 716-873-8754
http://intotem.buffnet.net/bechs/

Castile Historical Society
17 Park Road
Castile, NY 14427
Tel: 716-493-5370

Cayuga-Owasco Lakes Historical Society
Luther Research Center and Archives
14 West Cayuga Street
P.O. Box 247
Moravia, NY 13118
Tel: 315-497-3206
http://www.rootsweb.com/~nycayuga/colhs.htm

Charlotte-Genesee Lighthouse Historical Society
70 Lighthouse Street
Rochester, NY 14612
Tel: 716-621-6179
http://www.frontiernet.net/~mikemay/

Chautauqua County Historical Society
P.O. Box 7
Westfield, NY 14787
Tel: 716-326-2977

Chautauqua Township Historical Society
15 Water Street
Mayville, NY 14757
Tel: 716-753-7535

Chemung County Historical Society
415 East Water Street
Elmira, NY 14901
Tel: 607-734-4167
http://www.rootsweb.com/~nychemun/cchsres.htm

Chenango County Historical Society/Museum
45 Rexford Street
Norwich, NY 13815
Tel: 607-334-9227
http://www.chenangocounty.org/chencohistso/

Clinton County Historical Association
48 Court Street
Plattsburgh, NY 12901
Tel: 518-561-0340

Colonie, Historical Society of the Town of
Memorial Town Hall
207 Old Niskayuna Road, Box 212
Newtonville, NY 12128
Tel: 518-783-1435
http://www.colonie.org/historian/historical/

Colton Historical Society
Main Street
P.O. Box 223
Colton, NY 13625
http://homepage.mac.com/clstph/coltonhist/
     Menu40.html

**Columbia County Historical Society/Museum &
Research Library**
5 Albany Avenue
P.O. Box 311
Kinderhook, NY 12106
Tel: 518-758-9265
http://www.berkshire.net/OnlineArchives/
     columbia/cchs.html

Conesus Historical Society
Town Hall
Conesus, NY 14435
Tel: 716-346-2201

Constable Hall Association, Inc.
Constable Hall
P.O. Box 36
Constableville, NY 13325

Cortland County Historical Society
Sugget House Museum
25 Homer Avenue
Cortland, NY 13045
Tel: 607-756-6071
http://www.rootsweb.com/~nycortla/chsfe.htm

Cow Neck Peninsula Historical Society
Sands Williet House
336 Port Washington Blvd.
Port Washington, NY 11050
Tel: 516-365-9074
E-mail: Curator@CowNeck.org
http://www.cowneck.org/

Cutchogue/New Suffolk Historical Council
Route 25
P.O. Box 575
Cutchogue, NY 11935
Tel: 631-734-7122

Dayton (Town of) Historical Society
P.O. Box 15
Dayton, NY 14041

Delaware County Historical Association/
Library & Archives
RD 2, Box 201C
Delhi, NY 13753
Tel: 607-746-3849
Fax: 607-746-7326
E-mail: dcha@catskill.net
http://www.rootsweb.com/~nydelaha/

DeWitt Historical Society of
Tompkins County Museum
401 East State Street
Ithaca, NY 14850
Tel: 607-273-8284
E-mail: dhs@lakenet.org
http://www.lakenet.org/dewitt/

Dobbs Ferry Historical Society
12 Elm
Dobbs Ferry, NY 10522
Tel: 914-674-1007

Dr. Asa Fitch Historical Society
E-mail: jchilds1@juno.com
http://www.salem-ny.com/histh13.html

Dutchess County Historical Society
Clinton House
549 Main Street
P.O. Box 88
Poughkeepsie, NY 12602
Tel: 845-471-1630

East Bloomfield, Historical Society of
Bloomfield Academy Museum
8 South Avenue
East Bloomfield, NY 14443
Tel: 585-657-7244

East Hampton Historical Society
101 Main Street
East Hampton, NY 11937
Tel: 631-324-6850
http://www.hamptonsweb.com/ehhs/

Eastchester Historical Society
Town Hall
40 Mill Road, Box 37
Eastchester, NY 10709
Tel: 914-771-3300

Egbert Benson Historical Society of Red Hook
P.O. Box 1813
Red Hook, NY 12571-0397

Esquatak Historical Society
P.O. Box 151
Castleton, NY 12033

Essex Community Heritage Organization, Inc.
P.O. Box 260
Essex, NY 12936
Tel: 518-963-7088

Essex County Historical Society
Adirondack Center Museum
Court Street
Elizabethtown, NY 12932
Tel: 518-873-6466

Fenton Historical Society
67 Washington Street
Jamestown, NY 14701
Tel: 716-664-6256
Fax: 716-483-7524
http://www.rootsweb.com/~nychauta/Fenton.htm

Fishkill Historical Society
Van Wyck Homestead Museum
Route 9 and I-84
P.O. Box 133
Fishkill, NY 12524
Tel: 845-896-9560

Franklin County Historical Society/Museum
51 Milwaukee Street
Malone, NY 12953
Tel: 518-483-2750

Freeport Historical Society/Museum
350 S. Main Street
Freeport, NY 11520
Tel: 516-623-9632

Frontenac Historical Society/Museum
State Route 90
Union Springs, NY 13160

Fulton, Historical Society of
177 South First Street
P.O. Box 157
Fulton, NY 13069
Tel: 315-598-4616

Geneva Historical Society
Prouty Chew House
543 South Main Street
Geneva, NY 14456-3194
Tel: 315-789-5151
Fax: 315-789-0314
http://www.rootsweb.com/~nyontari/genhist.htm

Genoa Historical Society
Rural Life Museum
Route 34B
Genoa, NY 13071
Tel: 315-364-7550

Goshen Historical Society
Goshen Public Library
203 Main Street
Goshen, NY 10924
Tel: 845-294-6606
Fax: 845-294-7158
http://www.rcls.org/gplhs/

Gouverneur Historical Association
30 Church Street
Gouverneur, NY 13642
Tel: 315-287-0570
http://northcountryguide.com/attractions/
    gouvmuseum.html

Greater Ridgewood Historical Society/Library
Onderdonk House
1820 Flushing Avenue
Ridgewood, NY 11385
Tel: 718-456-1776

Greece, Historical Society of
Greece Historical Center and Museum
595 Long Pond Road
Rochester, NY 14612
Tel: 716-225-7221

Greenbush Historical Society
P.O. Box 66
East Greenbush, NY 12061

Greenlawn/Centerport Historical Association
Harborfields Public Library Building
31 Broadway
P.O. Box 354
Greenlawn, NY 11740
Tel: 631-754-1180
E-mail: GCHA-Info@usa.net
http://gcha.suffolk.lib.ny.us/

Guilderland Historical Society
152 Main Street
P.O. Box 282
Guilderland Centr, NY 12085
Tel: 518-456-2400 (Library)

Hannibal Historical Society
P.O. Box 150
Hannibal, NY 13074
Tel: 315-564-5471
http://www.rootsweb.com/~nyoswego/towns/hannibal/
    hanhistsoc.html

Harmony Historical Society
1943 Open Meadows Road
P.O. Box 127
Ashville, NY 14710
http://c1web.com/local_info/artsed/

Harrisville/Bonaparte History Association
Gladys Van Wyck, Town Historian
High Street
P.O. Box 321
Harrisville, NY 13648

Hastings Heritage & History Club
Irene Meyers, Town & Village Historian
RR #3, County Rt. 33
Central Square, NY 13036
http://www.artshappening.org/Hastings.htm

Hastings-on-Hudson Historical Society
407 Broadway
Hastings On Hudson, NY 10706
Tel: 914-478-2249
http://www.hastingshistorical.org/society/home.htm

Henderson Historical Society
12581 County Rt 72
P.O. Box 322
Henderson, NY 13650
Tel: 315-938-7163

Heritage Foundation of Oswego
156 West 2nd Street
P.O. Box 405
Oswego, NY 13126
Tel: 315-342-3354

Herkimer County Historical Society
400 North Main Street
Herkimer, NY 13350
Tel: 315-866-6413
E-mail: herkimerhistory@yahoo.com
http://www.rootsweb.com/~nyhchs/

Historic Cherry Hill
523 1/2 South Pearl Street
Albany, NY 12202
Tel: 518-434-4791
Fax: 518-434-4806
E-mail:housemus@knick.net
http://www.historiccherryhill.org/

Holland Purchase Historical Society
131 West Main Street
Batavia, NY 14020
Tel: 716-345-0023

Holland Society of New York
122 E. 58th Street
New York, NY 10022
Tel: 212-758-1675
Fax: 212-758-2232
http://www.hollandsociety.com/

Hoosick Township Historical Society
166 Main Street
Hoosick Falls, NY 12090
E-mail: staff@hoosickhistory.com
http://www.hoosickhistory.com/

Hopkinton Historical Group
Hopkinton, NY 12965
Tel: 315-328-4684

Hudson Valley Railroad Society
34 River Road
P.O. Box 135
Hyde Park, NY 12538
Tel: 845-331-9233

Huguenot Historical Society
18 Broadhead Avenue
New Paltz, NY 12561
Tel: 845-255-1660
E-mail: hhsoffice@hhs-newpaltz.org
http://www.hhs-newpaltz.net/index.html

Huntington Historical Society/Resource Center & Archives
209 Main Street
Huntington, NY 11743
Tel: 631-427-7045
Fax: 631-427-7056
E-mail: hunthistory@juno.com
http://www.huntingtonhistoricalsociety.org/

Hyde Park Historical Society
4389 Albany Post Rd.
P.O. Box 182
Hyde Park, NY 12538
Tel: 845-229-2559
E-mail: patsyc97@aol.com

Interlaken Historical Society/Museum & Genealogical Res. Library
Main Street (Route 96)
Interlaken, NY 14847
Tel: 607-532-4341

Irvington Historical Society
P.O. Box 23
Irvington, NY 10533

Italian Historical Society of America
111 Columbia Hts
Brooklyn, NY 11201
Tel: 718-852-2929
E-mail: mail@italianhistorical.org
http://www.italianhistorical.org/

Jefferson County Historical Society
228 Washington Street
Watertown, NY 13601
Tel: 315-782-3491

Klyne-Esopus Historical Society/Museum
764 Route 9W P.O. Box 180
Ulster Park, NY 12487
Tel: 845-338-8109
E-mail: kehsm@ulster.net
http://www.ulster.net/~kehsm/about.htm

Knickerbocker Historical Society
P.O. Box 29
Schaghticoke, NY 12154
E-mail: Iseman7@aol.com
http://www.knic.com/historic.htm

Knox Historical Society
P.O. Box 11
Knox, NY 12107
Tel: 518-872-2551

LaGrange Historical Society
P.O. Box 112
LaGrange, NY 12540

Lake Placid/North Elba Historical Society
P.O. Box 189
Lake Placid, NY 12946
Tel: 518-523-1608

Lake Ronkonkoma Historical Society/Museum
328 Hawkins Avenue
P.O. Box 716
Lake Ronkonkoma, NY 11779
Tel: 631-467-3152

Lansing Historical Association
P.O. Box 100
Lansing, NY 14882
http://www.lightlink.com/dagra/lanhist/lanhist.htm

Lansingburgh Historical Society
P.O. Box 219
Lansingburgh, NY 12182

Larchmont Historical Society
740 West Boston Post Road
Mamaroneck, NY 10543
Tel: 914-381-2239
E-mail: lhs@savvy.net
http://members.savvy.net/~lhs/

Lewis County Historical Society
High Street
P.O. Box 277
Lyons Falls, NY 13368
Tel: 315-348-8089

Lindenhurst Historical Society
Old Village Hall Museum
215 S. Wellwood Avenue
P.O. Box 296
Lindenhurst, NY 11757
Tel: 631-957-4385

Little Nine Partners Historical Society
P.O. Box 243
Pine Plains, NY 12567
E-mail: LNPHS@hotmail.com

Little Red Schoolhouse Historical Society
P.O. Box 25
Coeymans Hollow, NY 12046

Livingston County Historical Society
30 Center Street
Geneseo, NY 14454
Tel: 716-243-9147
http://www.rootsweb.com/~nylchs/

Lloyd Harbor Historical Society
Lloyd Harbor Road
Lloyd Harbor, NY 11743
Tel: 631-424-6110

Lodi Historical Society
Main Street (Route 414)
Lodi, NY 14860

Madison County Historical Society/Library
Cottage Lawn House
435 Main Street
P.O. Box 415
Oneida, NY 13421
Tel: 315-363-4136

Mamaroneck Historical Society
P.O. Box 776
Mamaroneck, NY 10543
http://www.westchesterlibraries.org/libs/
    mamaroneck/histsoc.htm

Manlius Historical Society
109 Pleasant Street
Manlius, NY 13104
Tel: 315-682-6660
E-mail: Manliushistory@AOL.com
http://hometown.aol.com/manliushistory/
    myhomepage/business.html

Mannsville/Ellisburg, Historical Society of
108 Lilac Park Drive
P.O. Box 126
Mannsville, NY 13661
Tel: 315-465-4049

Massapequas, Historical Society of the
106 Toronto Avenue
Massapequa, NY 11758

Massena Historical Association/Town Museum
200 East Orvis Street
Massena, NY 13669
Tel: 315-769-8571

Mattituck Historical Society
Main Road, Rte. 25
P.O. Box 766
Mattituck, NY 11952
Tel: 631-298-5248

Maybrook Railroad Historical Society
Route 208E
Maybrook, NY 12543

Merricks, Historical Society of the
2279 South Merrick Avenue
Merrick, NY 11566
Tel: 516-379-3476

Mexico Historical Society
5319 South Jefferson
P.O. Box 331
Mexico, NY 13114
Tel: 315-963-8542

Middlebury Historical Society
1250 S. Academy Street
P.O. Box 198
Wyoming, NY 14591-0198
Tel: 716-495 6692

Middletown & Walkill Precinct, Historical Society of
25 East Avenue
Middletown, NY 10940
Tel: 845-342-0941

Miller Place/Mount Sinai Historical Society
William Miller House
North Country Road & Honey Lane
P.O. Box 651
Miller Place, NY 11764

Minisink Valley Historical Society
125-133 West Main Street
P.O. Box 659
Port Jervis, NY 12771
Tel: 845-856-2375
Fax: 845-856-1049
http://www.minisink.org/

Montauk Historical Society
Montauk Highway
RFD 2, Box 112
Montauk, NY 11954
Tel: 631-668-5340
Fax: 631-668-2546
E-mail: keeper@montauklighthouse.com
http://www.montauklighthouse.com/society.htm

Moriches Bay Historical Society
Haven's House Museum
Montauk Highway and Chet Sweezy Road
P.O. Box 31
Center Moriches, NY 11934
Tel: 631-878-1776

Mount Pleasant Historical Society
1 Town Hall Plaza
Valhalla, NY 10595

National Maritime Historical Society
5 John Walsh Blvd.
Peekskill, NY 10566
Tel: 845-737-7878
E-mail: nmhs@seahistory.org
http://www.seahistory.org/

National Railway Historical Society
Mohawk/Hudson Chapter
74 Brookline Avenue
Albany, NY 12203

New Scotland (Town of) Historical Association
Old New Scotland Road
P.O. Box 511
Slingerlands, NY 12159

New York Historical Society
170 Central Park West
New York, NY 10024
Tel: 212-873-3400
Fax: 212-875-1591
http://www.nyhistory.org/

New York State Historical Association
Fenimore House
Lake Road
P.O. Box 800
Cooperstown, NY 13326
Tel: 607-547-1400
Fax: 607-547-1404
E-mail: nyshal@aol.com
http://www.nysha.org/

Newfane (Town of) Historical Society
Van Horn Mansion
P.O. Box 115
Newfane, NY 14108-0115
E-mail: zeus@localnet.com
http://www.niagaracounty.org/ town_of_newfane_hs.htm

North Castle Historical Society
100 King Street
Chappaqua, NY 10514
Tel: 914-238-4666
http://www.town.new-castle.ny.us/nchs.html

Northern New York Agricultural Historical Society
P.O. Box 108
LaFargeville, NY 13656
Tel: 315-658-2353

Northport Historical Society
215 Main Street
Northport, NY 11768
Tel: 631-757-9859
Fax: 631-757-9398
E-mail: info@northporthistorical.org
http://www.northporthistorical.org/museum/

Norwood Historical Association/Museum
P.O. Box 163
Norwood, NY 13668

Old Brutus Historical Society
8943 N. Seneca Street
Weedsport, NY 13166
Tel: 315-834-9342
http://www.rootsweb.com/~nycayuga/obhs/

Onondaga County Historical Association/Research Center
321 Montgomery Street
Syracuse, NY 13202
Tel: 315-428-1864

Ontario & Western Railway Historical Society, Inc.
P.O. Box 713
Middletown, NY 10940

Ontario County Historical Society
55 North Main Street
Canandaigua, NY 14424
Tel: 716-394-4975
http://www.ochs.org/

Ossining Historical Society
196 Croton Avenue
Ossining, NY 10562
Tel: 914-941-0001
http://home.att.net/~ohsm/

Oswego County Historical Society
135 East 3rd Street
Oswego, NY 13126
Tel: 315-343-1342

Otego Historical Society
Harris Memorial Library
69 Main Street
Otego, NY 13825
Tel: 607-988-6661 (Library)
http://www.4cls.org/webpages/members/Otego/
    Otego.html

Oyster Bay Historical Society/Library & Museum
Earle-Wightman House
20 Summit Street
P.O. Box 297
Oyster Bay, NY 11771-0297
Tel: 516-922-5032
Fax: 516-922-6892
E-mail: OBHistory@aol.com
http://members.aol.com/OBHistory/index.html

Oysterponds Historical Society
Village Lane
Orient, NY 11957
Tel: 631-323-2480

Parishville Historical Association
P.O. Box 534
Parishville, NY 13672

Phelps Community Historical Society
66 Main Street
Phelps, NY 14532
Tel: 315-548-4940
    315-548-3522 (John M. Parmelee, Town Historian)
http://www.ochs.org/Preservation/phelps/
    phelpshistoricalsociety.html

Piseco Lake Historical Society
HC 1, Box 17
Piseco, NY 12139

Plattekill Historical Society
P.O. Box 357
Clintondale, NY 12515

Pleasant Valley Historical Society
P.O. Box 766
Pleasant Valley, NY 12569

Poestenkill Historical Society
P.O. Box 140
Poestenkill, NY 12140-0140

Port Jefferson Historical Society
Mather House Museum
115 Prospect Street
P.O. Box 586
Port Jefferson, NY 11777
Tel: 631-473-2665

Pulaski Historical Society
3428 Maple Avenue
Pulaski, NY 13142
Tel: 315-298-4650
http://www.artshappening.org/Pulaski/
    pulaskihist1.html

Pultneyville Historical Society
P.O. Box 92
Pultneyville, NY 14538
Tel: 315-589-9962 (Paula Carey, Archivist)

Putnam County Historical Society
Foundry Museum/Reference Library
63 Chestnut Street
Cold Spring, NY 10516
Tel: 845-265-4010
E-mail: PCHS@highlands.com

Quaker Hill and Pawling, Historical Society
P.O. Box 99
Pawling, NY 12564
Tel: 845-855-9316

Regional Council of Historical Agencies
P.O. Box 28
Cooperstown, NY 13326
Tel: 800-895-1648

Rensselaer (City of) Historical Society
Agents House
15 Forbes Avenue
Rensselaer, NY 12144

Rensselaer County Historical Society/Genealogy Library
Hart-Cluett Mansion
59 Second Street
Troy, NY 12180
Tel: 518-272-7232
Fax: 518-273-1264
http://www.rchsonline.org/

Rensselaerville Historical Society
P.O. Box 8
Rensselaerville, NY 12147

Rhinebeck Historical Society
P.O. Box 291
Rhinebeck, NY 12572

Richville Historical Association
170 Davis Road
Richville, NY 13681
Tel: 315-347-3221

Rochester Historical Society
485 East Avenue
Rochester, NY 14607
Tel: 716-271-2705

Rockland County Historical Society/History Center
20 Zukor Road
New City, NY 10956
Tel: 845-634-9629
     845-634-9645
Fax: 845-634-8690
E-mail: HSRockland@aol.com
http://www.planet-rockland.org/histsoc/

Rocky Point Historical Society
P.O. Box 1720
Rocky Point, NY 11778

Roe-Jan Historical Society/Museum
Route 344
Copake Falls, NY 12517

Rome Historical Society/Museum & Archives
200 Church Street
Rome, NY 13440
Tel: 315-336-5870
http://www.artcom.com/museums/nv/mr/13440-58.htm

Sag Harbor Historical Society
P.O. Box 1709
Sag Harbor, NY 11963
Tel: 631-725-5092
http://www.hamptons.com/shhs/

St. Lawrence County Historical Association
3 East Main Street
P.O. Box 8
Canton, NY 13617
Tel: 315-386-8133
http://slcha.org/

Sand Lake Historical Society
P.O. Box 492
West Sand Lake, NY 12196

Sayville Historical Society
Edwards Homestead
39 Edwards Street
P.O. Box 41
Sayville, NY 11782
Tel: 631-563-0186

Schenectady County Historical Society
32 Washington Avenue
Schenectady, NY 12305
Tel: 518-374-0263
Fax: 208-361-5305
E-mail: librarian@schist.org
http://www.schist.org/

Schroon-North Hudson Historical Society, Inc.
Main Street
P.O. Box 444
Schroon Lake, NY 12870
Tel: 518-532-7854

Schuyler County Historical Society/Library
108 North Catherine Street, Rte. 14
P.O. Box 651
Montour Falls, NY 14865
Tel: 607-535-9741

Scriba Town Historical Association
Scriba Municipal Building
RD #8
Oswego, NY 13126
Tel: 315-342-6420

Seaford Historical Society
Ross Plantation
Rt. 1, Box 393
Seaford, DE 19973
Tel: 302-628-9500

Shaker Heritage Society
1848 Shaker Meeting House
875 Watervliet Shaker Road, Suite 2
Albany, NY 12211
Fax: (518) 452-7348
E-mail: shakerwv@crisny.org
http://www.crisny.org/not-for-profit/shakerwv/

Shelter Island Historical Society
Old Havens House
16 S. Ferry Road
P.O. Box 847
Shelter Island, NY 11964
Tel: 631-749-0025
E-mail: sihissoc@hamptons.com
http://www.shelterislandhistsoc.org/

Skaneateles Historical Society/Archives
The Creamery
28 Hannum Street
Skaneateles, NY 13152
http://www.skaneateles.com/historical/index.shtml

Smithtown Historical Society/Library
Caleb Smith II House
North Country Road (Rte. 25A)
Smithtown, NY 11787
Tel: 631-265-6768

South Jefferson, Historical Association of
9 East Church Street
Adams, NY 13605
Tel: 315-232-2616
http://www.rootsweb.com/~nyjeffer/sjef.htm

Southampton Historical Society
17 Meeting House Lane
Southampton, NY 11968
Tel: 631-283-2494

Southold Historical Society
54325 Route 25
P.O. Box 1
Southold, NY 11971
Tel: 631-765-5500

Southport Historical Society
P.O. Box 146
Pine City, NY 14871

Spencer Historical Society/Museum
Center Street
P.O. Box 71
Spencer, NY 14883

Staten Island Historical Society
441 Clarke Avenue
Staten Island, NY 10306-1198
Tel: 718-351-1611
Fax: 718-351-6057
http://www.nychistory.org/SIHSPAGE.HTM

Steamship Historical Society of America
Hudson Valley Chapter
55 Indian Ledge Road
Voorheesville, NY 12186

Steamship Historical Society of America
Long Island Chapter
64 West Street
Northport, NY 11768

Stephentown Historical Society
P.O. Box 11
Stephentown, NY 12168

Sterling Historical Society
14352 Woods Road
Sterling, NY 13156
Tel: 315-947-6461
E-mail: sterlinghistory@lakeontario.net
http://www.lakeontario.net/sterlinghistory/

Steuben County Historical Society
P.O. Box 349
Bath, NY 14810

Stony Brook Historical Society
P.O. Box 802
Stony Brook, NY 11790

Suffolk County Historical Society/Library
300 West Main Street
Riverhead, NY 11901
Tel: 631-727-2881
http://www.riverheadli.com/rmuseum.html

Sullivan County Historical Society
265 Main Street
P.O. Box 247W
Hurleyville, NY 12747
Tel: 845-434-8044
E-mail: jmasten@citlink.net
http://www.sullivancountyhistory.org/

Taconic Valley Historical Society
P.O. Box 512
Berlin, NY 12022

Tarrytowns, Historical Society of the
1 Grove Street
Tarrytown, NY 10591
Tel: 914-631-8374

Three Village Historical Society
P.O. Box 76
East Setauket, NY 11733
http://members.aol.com/TVHS1/index.html

Ticonderoga Historical Association
Hancock House
1 Moses Circle
Ticonderoga, NY 12883
Tel: 518-585-7868
E-mail: ths2@capital.net
http://www.capital.net/~ths2/

Tioga County Historical Society/Museum
110 Front Street
Owego, NY 13827
Tel: 607-687-2460
Fax: 607-687-7788
E-mail: tiogamus@clarityconnect.com
http://www.tier.net/tiogahistory/

Tonawanda-Kenmore Historical Society
St. Peter's Church
100 Knoche Road
Tonawanda, NY 14150
Tel: 716-873-5774
http://freenet.buffalo.edu/~tot/htm/o_hsoc.htm

Ulster & Delaware Railroad Historical Society, Inc.
P.O. Box 404
Margaretville, NY 12455-0404
http://www.udrrhs.org/

Ulster County Historical Society/Museum
Route 209
Marbletown, NY 12401
Tel: 914-338-5614

Ulysses Historical Society
39 South Street
Trumansburg, NY 14886
Tel: 607-387-5659
http://www.ulysses.ny.us/history/

Union Vale Historical Society
Union Vale Town Hall
Duncan Rd.
LaGrangeville, NY 12540
Tel: 845-724-5600

Wading River Historical Society
North Country Road
Wading River, NY 11792
Tel: 631-929-4082

Walworth Historical Society/Museum
2257 Academy
Street Walworth, NY 14568
P.O. Box 142

Wappinger Historical Society
P.O. Box 174
Wappingers Falls, NY 12590

Warwick (Town of), Historical Society of
P.O. Box 353
Warwick, NY 10990

Waterloo Library & Historical Society
Terwilliger Museum
31 East Williams Street
Waterloo, NY 13165
Tel: 315-539-0533
http://www.waterloony.com/Library.html

Watervliet Historical Society
P.O. Box 123
Watervliet, NY 12189

Wayne County Historical Society
21 Butternut Street
Lyons, NY 14489
Tel: 315-946-4943

Westchester County Historical Society
2199 Saw Mill River Road
Elmsford, NY 10523
Tel: 914-592-4323
http://www.westchesterhistory.com/

Wheatland Historical Association
69 Main Street
P.O. Box 184
Scottsville, NY 14546
Tel: 716-889-4574
ULR:http://www.wheatland-ny.com/wha.htm

Woodbury Historical Society/Cemetery of the Highlands
Main Street
Woodbury, NY 11797
Tel: 845-928-6770
http://www.ci.woodbury.ny.us/historicalsociety.html

Woodstock, Historical Society of
Comeau Drive
81 Tinker Street
Woodstock, NY 12498

Wyoming Historical Pioneer Association
Walker Road
Perry, NY 14549

Yaphank Historical Society
Robert H. Hawkins House
P.O. Box 111
Yaphank, NY 11980
Tel: 631-924-3401
E-mail: Yaphankhistoric@aol.com
http://hometown.aol.com/yaphank%20historic/

Yates County Genealogical & Historical Society
Oliver House Museum & Research Room
200 Main Street
Penn Yan, NY 14527
Tel: 315-536-7318
http://www.yatespast.com/

MUNICIPAL AND COUNTY HISTORIANS/ARCHIVES

Albany (City of) Historian
Town Hall
Albany, NY 12207
Tel: 518-434-5100

Albany County Hall of Records
250 South Pearl Street
Albany, NY 12202
Tel: 518-447-4500
E-mail: achor@nyslgti.gen.ny.us
http://albanycounty.com/achor/

Albany County Historian
Mr. John Travis
112 State Street, Room 820
Albany, NY 12207
Tel: 518-447-7057

Allegany County Historian
Allegany County Museum
Court House
11 Wells Lane
Belmont, NY 14813
Tel: 716-268-9293
Fax: 716-268-9446

Brooklyn Historian
(See Kings County)

Broome County Historian
185 Court Street
Binghamton, NY 13901
Tel: 607-778-2076
Fax: 607-778-1441
http://www.geocities.com/bchistorian/histoff.htm
    #Broome Cty Historian

Bronx County Historian
Rev. William A. Tieck, Ph.D., Litt. D.
3930 Bailey Avenue
Bronx, NY 10463

Cattaraugus County Historian
Historical Museum
302 Court Street
Little Valley, NY 14755
Tel: 716-938-9111
http://www.co.cattaraugus.ny.us/

Cayuga County Historian
Historic Old Post Office Building, Main Floor
157 Genesee Street
Auburn, NY 13021
Tel: 315-253-1300
E-mail: historian@co.cayuga.ny.us
http://www.co.cayuga.ny.us/history/index.html

Chautauqua County Historian
131 Center Street
P.O. Box 170
Mayville, NY 14757
Tel: 716-753-4587
E-mail: henrym@co.chautauqua.ny.us

Chemung County Historian
1011 Lincoln Street
Elmira, NY 14901

Chenango County Historian
Chenango County Historical Society/Museum
45 Rexford Street
Norwich, NY 13815
Tel: 607-334-9227

Clinton County Historian/County Clerk
Clinton County Government Center
137 Margaret Street
Plattsburgh, NY 12901
Tel: 518-565-4749
    518-565-4700 (County Clerk)

Columbia County Historian
122 Main Street, Box 00
Philmont, NY 12565
Tel: 518-672-7032

Cortland County Historian
Cortland County Courthouse
P.O. Box 5590
Cortland, NY 13045-5590
Tel: 607-753-5360

Delaware County Historian
195 Main Street
Delhi, NY 13753

Dutchess County Historian
22 Market Street
Poughkeepsie, NY 12601

Erie County Historian
Buffalo & Erie County Historical Society
25 Nottingham Court
Buffalo, NY 14216
Tel: 716-873-9644
    716-873-9612
Fax: 716-873-8754
http://intotem.buffnet.net/bechs/

Essex County Historian
Adirondack Center Museum
Court Street
Elizabethtown, NY 12932
Tel: 518-873-6466

Franklin County Historian
Franklin County Historical Society
51 Milwaukee Street
Malone, NY 12953
Tel: 518-483-2750

Fulton County Historian
Lewis G. Decker
187 Bleeker Street
Gloversville, NY 12078
Tel: 518-725-0473

Genesee County History Department
Historian & Records Management Officer
3 West Main Street
Batavia, NY   14020
Tel: 716-344-2550
Fax: 716-344-2442
E-mail: conklins@nyslgti.gen.ny.us
http://www.sunygenesee.cc.ny.us/Library/
    gencohistdept.htm

Greene County Historian
RD 1 Box 10A
Coxackie, NY 12051
Tel: 518-731-1033
        581-731-6822 (Raymond Beecher)

Hamilton County Historian
Hamilton County Office Building, Route 8
Lake Pleasant, NY 12108
Voice: 518-548-5526
E-mail: pwilbur@superior.net

Herkimer County Historian
Herkimer County Historical Society
400 North Main Street
Herkimer, NY 13350
Tel: 315-866-6413
        315-866-1398 (James M. Greiner)
http://www.rootsweb.com/~nyhchs/

Jefferson County Historian
Jefferson County Planning Department
175 Arsenal Street
Watertown, NY 13601
Tel: 315-785-3144 ext. 5092
E-mail: llls3133@aol.com

Kings County Historian (Brooklyn)
John Manbeck, Brooklyn Borough Historian
16 Court Street
Brooklyn, NY 11241

Lewis County Historian
P.O. Box 277
Lyons Falls, NY 13368
Tel: 315-348-8089

Livingston County Historian
30 Center Street
Geneseo, NY 14454
Tel: 716-243-2311
        716-243-9147
http://www.rootsweb.com/~nylchs/societies.htm

Madison County Historian
Madison County Building, 2nd Floor
Wampsville, New York 13163
Tel: 315-366-2453
E-mail: historian@co.madison.ny.us

Monroe County Historian
Rochester Regional Library Council
Rundel Memorial Library, Room 230
115 South Avenue
Rochester, NY 14604
Tel: 716-428-7375
Fax: 716-428-7313

Montgomery County, Department of History & Archives
Old Court House
9 Park Street
P.O. Box 1500
Fonda, NY 12068-1500
Tel: 518-853-8187
Fax: 518-853-8392
E-mail:histarch@superior.net
http://www.amsterdam-ny.com/mcha/

Nassau County Historian
Nassau County Museum
1864 Muttontown
Road Syosset, NY 11791

New York City Municipal Archives
31 Chambers Street, Room 103
New York, NY 10007
Tel: 212-788-8580
Fax: 212-385-0984
http://www.ci.nyc.ny.us/html/doris/html/index.html

New York County Historian (Manhattan)
220 Manhattan Avenue #21
New York, NY 10025

Niagara County Historian
Niagara County Civil Defense Building
139 Niagara Street
Lockport, NY 14094-2740
Tel: 716-439-7324

Ontario County Historian
3051 County Complex Drive
Canandaigua, NY 14424
Tel: 716-396-4034
E-mail: PEP209@aol.com
http://www.raims.com/historian/

Ontario County Records & Archives Center
3051 County Complex Drive
Canandaigua, NY 14424
Tel: 716-396-4376
Fax: 716-396-4390
E-mail: hansjf@co.ontario.ny.us
http://www.raims.com/recordsmenu.html

Orange County Historian
101 Main Street
Goshen, NY 10924
Tel: 914-294-6644

Orleans County Historian
13925 State Route 31
Albion, NY 14411
Tel: 716-589-4174

Oswego County Clerk/Historian
46 E. Bridge Street
Oswego, NY 13126
Tel: 315-349-8385

Otsego County Historian
Nancy Milavec
RD #2, Box 297
Worcester, NY 12197

Putnam County Historian
Records Center
121 Main Street
Brewster, NY 10509
Tel: 845-278-7209
Fax: 845-278-1435

Queens County Historian
Queens Borough Hall
120-55 Queens Blvd.
Kew Gardens, NY 11424

Rensselaer County Historian
Rensselaer County Historical Society
57 Second Street, Troy, NY
518-272-7232
Fax: 518-273-1264
E-mail: info@rchsonline.org
http://www.rchsonline.org/

Richmond County Historian (Staten Island)
Staten Island Borough Hall
10 Richmond Terrace
Staten Island, NY 10301
Tel: 718-816-2137

Rochester (City of) Archives & Records Center
Historian's Office
414 Andrews Street
Rochester, N.Y. 14604
Telephone: (585) 428-7331
Fax: (585) 428-6092
E-mail: crarchiv@mcls.rochester.lib.ny.us
http://www.ci.rochester.ny.us/catalog.nsf/citysearch

Rochester City Historian
Historian's Office
115 South Avenue
Rochester, N.Y. 14604
Tel: 585-428-8095
Fax: 585-428-8098

Rockland County Historian
Thomas F.X. Casey
12 Ashwood Lane
Garnerville, NY 10923

Saratoga County Historical Office
Municipal Center
40 McMaster Street
Ballston Spa, NY 12020.
Tel: 518-884-4749

Schenectady City History Center Library
City Hall
105 Jay Street
Schenectady, NY 12305
Tel: 518-377-7061

Schenectady (City and County) Historian
Larry Hart
Schenectady City Hall - History Center
105 Jay Street
Schenectady, New York 12305
Tel: 518-399-3466

Schoharie County Historian
P.O. Box 449
Middleburgh, NY 12122

Schuyler County Historian
3460 County Rt. 28,
Watkins Glen, NY 14891

Seneca County Historian
Seneca County Office Building
1 DiPronia Drive
Waterloo, NY 13165

Staten Island Historian
(See Richmond County)

Steuben County Historian
Steuben County Office Building
3 E. Pulteney Square
Bath, NY 14810
Tel: 607-776-9631 ext. 3411
E-mail: Historian@co.steuben.ny.us
http://www.steubencony.org/hstorian.html

Suffolk County Historian
Suffolk County Vanderbilt Museum
180 Little Neck Road, Box 0605
Centerport, New York 11721
Tel: 631-854-5555

Sullivan County Historian
P.O. Box 185
Barryville, New York 12919
Tel: 845-557-6467

Tioga County Historian
16 Court Street
Owego, NY 13827
Tel: 607-687-8646

Tompkins County Historian
DeWitt Historical Society of
401 East State Street
Ithaca, NY 14850
Tel: 607-273-8284
E-mail: dhs@lakenet.org
http://www.lakenet.org/dewitt/gen.html

Ulster County Historian
11 Main Street
Saugerties, NY 12477
E-mail: karlynelia@aol.com

Warren County Historian
Warren County Municipal Center
1340 State Route 9
Lake George, NY 12845-9803
Tel: 518-761-6544

Washington County Historian/Archives
383 Broadway
Fort Edward, NY 12828
Tel: 518-746-2178 (Historian)
        518-746-2136 (Archivist)

Wayne County Historian
9 Pearl Street
Lyons, NY 14489
Tel: 315-946-5470

Westchester County Archives
2199 Saw Mill River Road
Elmsford, NY 10523
Tel: 914-592-4323
Fax: 914-592-5160
http://www.co.westchester.ny.us/wcarchives/

Westchester County Historian
Michaelian Building, Room 618
White Plains, NY 10601

Wyoming County Historian
26 Linwood Avenue
Warsaw, NY 14569
Tel: 716-786-8818

Yates County Historian
Yates County Building
110 Court Street
Penn Yan, NY 14527
Tel: 315-536-5147
Fax: 315-536-5545
E-mail: history@yatescounty.org

LDS FAMILY HISTORY CENTERS

For locations of Family History Centers in this state, see the Family History Center locator at FamilySearch. http://www.familysearch.org/eng/Library/FHC/frameset_fhc.asp

ARCHIVES/LIBRARIES/MUSEUMS

Adriance Memorial Library/Poughkeepsie Library District
93 Market Street
Poughkeepsie, NY 12601
Tel: 845-485-3445
        800-804-0092
Fax: 845-485-3789
http://www.poklib.org/html/adriance.php/

Ainsworth Memorial Library
6064 South Main Street
P.O. Box 69
Sandy Creek, NY 13145
Tel: 315-387-3732
http://www.tce.vcomm.net/library/

Akwesasne Library
RR #1, Box 14C
Hogansburg, NY 13655
Tel: 518-358-2240
Fax: 518-358-2649
E-mail: akwmuse@northnet.org

Albany Institute of History & Art/Museum & Library
125 Washington Avenue
Albany, NY 12210
Tel: 518-463-4478
E-mail: information@albanyinstitute.org
http://www.albanyinstitute.org/

Albany Public Library
161 Washington Avenue
Albany, NY 12210
Tel: 518-427-4300
Fax: 518-449-3386
http://www.albanypubliclibrary.org/

Albany South End Historical Society
20 Second Avenue
Albany, NY 12202

Alfred University
Herrick Memorial Library
Special Collections
Saxon Drive
Alfred, NY 14802
Tel: 607-871-2184
Fax: 607-871-2992
http://www.herr.alfred.edu/special/

Allegany County Museum
7 Court Street
Belmont, NY 14813
Tel: 585 268-9293
E-mail: historian@allegany.co.com

Altamont Archives/Museum
Village Hall
115 Main Street
Altamont, NY 12009
Tel: 518-861-8554

American Baptist Historical Society
Samuel Colgate Historical Library
1106 South Goodman Street
Rochester, NY 14620-2532
Tel: 716-473-1740
http://www.crds.edu/abhs/

American Merchant Marine Museum
U.S.M.M.A.
300 Steamboat Rd
Kings Point, NY 11024
Tel: 516-773-5515
http://www.usmma.edu/museum/

American Veterans Historical Museum
P.O. Box 115
Pleasantville, NY 10570
http://www.rootsweb.com/~amvethm/page1.html

Amherst Museum Colony Park
Nederlander Research Library/Archives
3755 Tonawanda Creek Road
Amherst, NY 14228
Tel: 716-689-1440
Fax: 716-689-1409

Amityville Historical Society/Library
Lauder Museum
170 Broadway
P.O. Box 764
Amityville, NY 11701
Tel: 631-598-1486
Fax: 631-598-7399
E-mail: amityvillehistoricalsociety@juno.com
http://www.amityville.com/amhist.htm

Ancient Order of Hibernians
1021 Ninth Avenue
Watervliet, NY 12189
Tel: 518-273-9725
http://www.aoh.com/

Ardsley Public Library
9 American Legion Drive
Ardsley, NY 10502
Tel: 914-693-6636
Fax: 914-693-6837
http://www.westchesterlibraries.org/libs/ardsley/

Babylon Public Library
24 S. Carll Avenue
Babylon, NY 11702-3403
Tel: 631-669-1624

Baldwin Historical Society/Museum
1980 Grand Avenue
Baldwin, NY 11510
Tel: 516-223-6900

Baldwinsville Public Library
Local History Room
33 East Genesee Street
Baldwinsville, NY 13027
Tel: 315-635-5631
Fax: 315-635-6760
E-mail: info@bville.lib.ny.us
http://www.bville.lib.ny.us/

Bayville Free Library
34 School Street
Bayville, NY 11709
Tel: 516-628-2765
Fax: 516-628-2738
http://www.516web.com/library/bayville/menu.htm

Bellport-Brookhaven Historical Society/Museum
31 Bellport Lane
Bellport, NY 11713
Tel: 631-286-0888

Bethlehem Public Library
451 Delaware Avenue
Delmar, NY 12054
Tel: 518-439-9314
Fax: 518-478-0901
http://www.uhls.org/bethlehem/

Binghamton University
Glenn G. Bartle Library
Vestal Parkway East
P.O. Box 6012
Binghamton, NY 13902-6012
Tel: 607-777-2800
http://library.lib.binghamton.edu/

Blauvelt Free Library
541 South Western Highway
Blauvelt, NY 10913
http://www.rcls.org/blv/

Bodman Memorial Library/Museum
8 Aldrich Street
Philadelphia, NY 13673
Tel: 315-642-3323

Brentwood Public Library
34 Second Avenue
Brentwood, NY 11717
Tel: 631-273-7883
http://www.suffolk.lib.ny.us/libraries/bren/

Bridgehampton Historical Society/Museum
Montauk Highway
Bridgehampton, NY 11932
Tel: 631-537-1088

Brighton Memorial Library
2300 Elmwood Avenue
Rochester, NY 14618
Tel: 585-784-5300
TDD: 585-784-5302
E-mail: kbolan@mcls.rochester.lib.ny.us
http://www.brightonlibrary.org/

Bronx County Historical Society
3309 Bainbridge Avenue
Bronx, NY 10467
Tel: 718-881-8900
Fax: 718-881-4827
ULR:http://www.bronxhistoricalsociety.org/index17.html

Bronx Public Library
Reference Center
2555 Marion Avenue
Bronx, NY 10458

Brooklyn College/City University of New York (CUNY)
Harry D. Gideonse Library
Brooklyn, NY 11210
Tel: 718-951-5336
http://www.brooklyn.cuny.edu/bc/fac/bclib.html

Brooklyn Museum/Wilbour Library & Archives
200 Eastern Parkway Brooklyn, NY 11238-6052
Tel: 718-638-5000
Fax: 718-638-3731

Brooklyn Public Library/Central Library
Grand Army Plaza
Brooklyn, NY 11238
Tel: 718-230-2100
E-mail: bplweb@bway.net
http://www.brooklynpubliclibrary.org/default.asp

Broome County Historical Society
30 Front Street
Binghamton, NY 13905
Tel: 607-772-0660
Fax: 607-771-8905
http://www.rootsweb.com/~nybroome/brcohis.htm
or
http://www.tier.net/broomehistory/

Broome County Public Library
185 Court Street
Binghamton, NY 13901
Tel: 607-778-6400
E-mail: bcpl@tier.net
http://www.tier.net/bcpl/

Bryant Library
Local History Collection
2 Paper Mill Road
Roslyn, NY 11576
Tel: 516-621-2240
Fax: 516-621-2542
E-mail: rnltech@lilrc.org
http://www.nassaulibrary.org/bryant/

Buffalo and Erie County Historical Society/Library
25 Nottingham Court
Buffalo, NY 14216
Tel: 716-873-9612
Fax: 716-873-8754
http://intotem.buffnet.net/bechs/

Buffalo and Erie County Public Library
1 Lafayette Square
Buffalo, NY 14203
Tel: 716-858-7113
Fax: 716-858-6211
http://www.buffalolib.org/

Canajoharie Library & Art Gallery
2 Erie Blvd.
Canajoharie, NY 13317
Tel: 518-673-2314
Fax: 518-673-5234
http://www.clag.org/

Canisius College
Andrew Bouwhuis Library
Archives Department
2001 Main Street
Buffalo, NY 14208-1098
Tel: 716-888-2530
E-mail: libweb@canisius.edu
http://www.canisius.edu/canhp/canlib/archives.html

Cape Vincent Historical Museum
175 N James Street
P.O. Box 302
Cape Vincent, NY 13618
Tel: 315-654-4400

Carthage Free Library
Heritage Room
412 Budd Street
Carthage, NY 13619
Tel: 315-493-2620

Cattaraugus County Memorial Historical Museum
302 Court Street
Little Valley, NY 14755

Cayuga Community College
Norman F. Bourke Memorial Library
Special Collections
197 Franklin Street
Auburn, NY 13021
Tel: 315-255-1743 ext. 290
E-mail: brownk@caylib.cayuga-cc.edu
http://www.cayuga-cc.edu/library/library/
	special.htm

Cayuga Museum of History & Art
203 Genesee Street
Auburn, NY 13021
Tel: 315-253-8051
Fax: 315-253-9829
E-mail: cayugamuseum@cayuganet.org
http://www.cayuganet.org/cayugamuseum/

Cayuga-Owasco Lakes Historical Society
Luther Research Center and Archives
14 West Cayuga Street
P.O. Box 247
Moravia, NY 13118
Tel: 315-497-3906
http://www.rootsweb.com/~nycayuga/colhs.htm

Central Islip Public Library
33 Hawthorne Avenue
Central Islip, NY 11722
Tel: 631-234-9333
http://www.suffolk.lib.ny.us/libraries/cisp/

Central Square Library
637 S. Main
P.O. Box 368
Central Square, NY 13036
Tel: 315-668-6104

Charles Dawson History Center
2 Park Lane
P.O. Box 1696
Harrison, NY 10528
Tel: 914-948-2550

Chautauqua Institution
Smith Memorial Library/Archives
21 Miller Avenue
P.O. Box 28
Chautauqua, NY 14722
Tel: 716-357-6332
Fax: 716-357-9014
http://www.chautauqua-inst.org/

Clinton House State Historic Site
Dutchess County Historical Society
P.O. Box 88
549 Main Street
Poughkeepsie, NY 12602
Tel: 845-471-1630
Fax: 845-471-8777

Coburn Free Library
275 Main Street
Owego, NY 13827
Tel: 607-687-3520

Columbia University
Journalism Library
203 Journalism
2950 Broadway
New York, NY 10027
Tel: 212-854-0390
E-mail: journalism@libraries.cul.columbia.edu
http://www.columbia.edu/acis/documentation/
	journ/journnew.html

Cornell University
Kroch Library
Ithaca, NY 14853-5302
Tel: 607-255-3530
Fax: 607-255-9524
http://rmc.library.cornell.edu/

Cornell University
John Henrik Clarke Africana Library
310 Triphammer Road
Ithaca, NY 14850
Tel: 607-255-3822
Fax: 607-255-0784
http://www.library.cornell.edu/africana/

Cornell University
John M. Olin Library
Ithaca, NY 14853
Tel: 607-255-5258
	607-255-9567 (Newspapers Dept.)
http://www.library.cornell.edu/okuref/oku/ okuhome.html

Cortland County Historical Society
25 Homer Avenue
Cortland, NY 13045
Tel: 607-756-6071
http://www.rootsweb.com/~nycortla/chsfe.htm

Crandall Library
Holden Room
251 Glen Street
Glen Falls, NY 12801
Tel: 518-792-6508
http://www.crandalllibrary.org/

Croghan Free Library
Main Street
P.O. Box 8
Croghan, NY 13327
Tel: 315-346-6521

Crown Point State Historic Site
739 Bridge Road
RD #1, Box 219, Bridge Road
Crown Point, NY 12928
Tel: 518-597-3666
Fax: 518-597-4668

Dansville Public Library
200 Main Street
Dansville, NY 14437
Tel: 716-335-6720
Fax: 716-335-6133
E-mail: dpl@servtech.com
http://dansville.lib.ny.us/

Darwin R. Barker Library/Museum
7 Day Street
Fredonia, NY 14063
Tel: 716-672-2114

Daughters of the American Revolution
Irondequoit Chapter, DAR
11 Livingston Park
Rochester, NY 14608
Tel: 716-232-4509
http://www.frontiernet.net/~adman/dar/dar.html

Daughters of Charity Archives
DePaul Provincial House
96 Menands Road
Albany, NY 12204
Tel: 518-462-5593

Dexter Free Library
120 East Kirby Street
P.O. Box 544
Dexter, NY 13634
Tel: 315-639-6785

Dodge Memorial Library
144 Lake Street
Rouses Point, NY 12979
Tel: 518-297-6242

Dunkirk Historical Museum
513 Washington Avenue
Dunkirk, NY 14048
Tel: 716-366-3797

Durham Center Museum/Research
Route 145
East Durham, NY 12433
Tel: 518-239-8461
      518-239-4081
E-mail: dougsancie@aol.com
http://www.rootsweb.com/~nygreen2/
      durham_center_museum.htm

East Bloomfield, Historical Society of
Bloomfield Academy Museum
8 South Avenue
East Bloomfield, NY 14443
Tel: 585-657-7244

East Hampton Free Library
Long Island Collection
159 Main Street
East Hampton, NY 11937
Tel: 631-324-0222
Fax: 631-324-5947
E-mail: ehamlib@suffolk.lib.ny.us
http://www.easthamptonlibrary.org/

Edmeston Free Library/Museum
6 West Street
P.O. Box 167
Edmeston, NY 13335-0167
Tel: 607-965-8208 (Library)
      607-965-8902 (Museum)
http://lib.4cty.org/dialups/edmeston.html

Ellenville Public Library/Museum
40 Center Street
Ellenville, NY 12428
Tel: 914-647-5530
http://www.rcls.org/epl/

Ellis Island Immigration Museum
American Family Immigration History Center
Liberty Island
New York, NY 10004
Tel: 212-363-3200
      212-269-5755 (Circle Line Ferry for schedules/rates)
http://www.ellisisland.org/

Elting Memorial Library
Haviland-Heidgerd Historical Collection
93 Main Street
New Paltz, NY 12561
Tel: 845-255-5030
Fax: 845-255-5818
E-mail: havilandheidgerd@yahoo.com
http://elting.newpaltz.lib.ny.us/

Emma Clark Library
120 Main Street
Setauket, NY 11733
Tel: 631-941-4080
E-mail: emsclib@suffolk.lib.ny.us
http://emma.suffolk.lib.ny.us/

Episcopal Church Home Archives
505 Mount Hope Avenue
Rochester, NY 14620
Tel: 716-546-8400
Fax: 716-325-6553
E-mail: ech@frontiernet.net
http://www.rahsa.com/episcpal/

Episcopal Diocese of Rochester Archives
935 East Avenue
Rochester, NY 14607
Tel: 585-473-2977
Fax: 585-473-3195
E-mail: dasisson@rochester.infi.net

Essex County Historical Society
Adirondack Center Museum
Court Street
Elizabethtown, NY 12932
Tel: 518-873-6466

Fenton Historical Center
67 Washington Street
Jamestown, NY 14701
Tel: 716-664-6256
http://www.rootsweb.com/~nychauta/Fenton.htm

Field Library
Peekskill Archives Collection
4 Nelson Avenue
Peekskill, NY 10566
Tel: 845-737-1212
Fax: 845-737-0714
http://www.peekskill.org/

First Unitarian Universalist Society of Albany
405 Washington Avenue
Albany, NY 12206
Tel: 518-463-7135
E-mail: fuusa@fuusalbany.org
http://www.fuusalbany.org/

Floral Park Public Library
17 Caroline Place
Floral Park, NY 11001
Tel: 516-326-6330
Fax: 516-437-6959
http://www.nassaulibrary.org/fpark/

Flower Memorial Library
Genealogical Committee
229 Washington Street
Watertown, NY 13601
Tel: 315-788-2352
http://www.rootsweb.com/~nyjeffer/flower.htm

Frank J. Basloe Library
245 Main Street
Herkimer, NY 13350-1918
Tel: 315-866-1733

Franklin County Historical Society/Museum
51 Milwaukee Street
Malone, NY 12953
Tel: 518-483-2750

Freeport Historical Society/Museum
350 S. Main Street
Freeport, NY 11520
Tel: 516-623-9632
http://www.freeportny.com/museum.htm

Fryer Memorial Museum
Rt. 46 & Williams St.
Munnsville, NY 13409
Tel: 315-495-6148
      315-495-5395 (Historian)
http://www.borg.com/~mcholli/fryer.htm

Fulton Public Library
160 South First Street
Fulton, NY 13069
Tel: 315-592-5159

Garden City Public Library
60 7th Street
Garden City, NY 11530-2800
Tel: 516-742-8405
http://www.nassaulibrary.org/gardenc/

Gates Public Library
1605 Buffalo Road
Rochester, NY 14624
Tel: 716-247-6446
Fax: 716-426-5733
E-mail: question@gateslibrary.org
http://www.gateslibrary.org/

Genesee County Library
Department of History
131 West Main Street
Batavia, NY 14020
Fax: 585-345-0023
E-mail: info@hollandlandoffice.com

Genesis HealthCare Library
218 Stone Street
Watertown, NY 13601
Tel: 315-782-7400 ext. 2152

Geneva Free Library
244 Main Street
Geneva, NY 14456
Tel: 315-789-5303
Fax: 315-789-9835
http://www.geneva.pls-net.org/

Gilbertsville Library
Local History Department
19 Commercial Street
P.O. Box 332
Gilbertsville, NY 13776
Tel: 607-783-2832
E-mail: glibrary@tri-town.net
http://lib.4cty.org/dialups/GI.HTML

Glen Cove Public Library
4 Glen Cove Avenue
Glen Cove, NY 11542-2885
Tel: 516-676-2130
Fax: 516-676-2788
E-mail: glencove@lilrc.org
http://www.nassaulibrary.org/glencove/

Goff Nelson Memorial Library
41 Lake Street
Tupper Lake, NY 12986
Tel: 518-359-9421
Fax: 518-358-2649
E-mail: goffnelson@adelphia.net
http://www.cefls.org/tupperlake.htm

Goshen Public Library
203 Main Street
Goshen, NY 10924
Tel: 845-294-6606
Fax: 845-294-7158
E-mail: gplhs@rcls.org (Electronic Reference)
http://www.rcls.org/gplhs/

Great Neck Library
139 Bayview Avenue at Gristmill
Great Neck, NY 11024
Tel: 516-466-8055
E-mail: gneck@nassaulibrary.org
http://www.nassaulibrary.org/gneck/

Greater Ridgewood Historical Society/Library
Onderdonk House
1820 Flushing Avenue
Ridgewood, NY 11385
Tel: 718-456-1776

Guernsey Memorial Library
Otis A. Thompson Local History Room
3 Court Street
Norwich, NY 13815
Tel: 607-334-4034
http://lib.4cty.org/NORWICH.HTML

Hamilton Public Library
13 Broad Street
Hamilton, NY 13346
Tel: 315-824-3060

Harris Memorial Library
Otego Historical Society
69 Main Street
Otego, NY 13825
Tel: 607-988-6661 (Library)

Haviland Records Room (Quaker)
New York Yearly Meeting
15 Rutherford Place
New York, NY 10016

Hawn Memorial Library
220 John Street
Clayton, NY 13624
Tel: 315-686-3762

Hempstead Public Library
115 Nichols Court
Hempstead, NY 11550
Tel: 516-481-6990
Fax: 516-481-6719
E-mail:hempstead@nassaulibrary.org
http://www.nassaulibrary.org/hempstd/

Henderson Free Library
Route 178
P.O. Box 302
Henderson, NY 13650
Tel: 315-938-5032

Henrietta Public Library
455 Calkins Road
Rochester, NY 14623
Tel: 716-359-7092
http://www.hpl.org/

Hepburn Library
P.O. Box 86
Lisbon, NY 13658
Tel: 315-393-0111

Hofstra University
Long Island Studies Institute
Axinn Library, 9th Floor
1000 Fulton Avenue
Hempstead, NY 11550
Tel: 516-463-6600
http://www.hofstra.edu/Libraries/Axinn/ index_axinn.cfm

Holland Land Office Museum
131 W. Main Street
Batavia, NY 14020
Tel: 585-343-4724
Fax: 585-345-0023
E-mail: info@hollandlandoffice.com
http://www.hollandlandoffice.com/

Holocaust Library & Research Center
557 Bedford Avenue
Brooklyn, NY 11211
Tel: 718-599-5833

Huntington Historical Society/Resource Center & Archives
209 Main Street
Huntington, NY 11743
Tel: 631-427-7045
Fax: 631-427-7056
E-mail: hunthistory@juno.com
http://www.huntingtonhistoricalsociety.org/

Huntington Memorial Library
New York State History Room
62 Chestnut Street
Oneonta, NY 13820
Tel: 607-432-1980
http://lib.4cty.org/oneonta/onnysr.html

Huntington Public Library
338 Main Street
Huntington, NY 11743-6956
Tel: 631-427-5165
http://www.suffolk.lib.ny.us/libraries/hunt/

Ilion Free Public Library
Municipal Building
78 West Street
Ilion, NY 13357-1725
Tel: 315-894-5028
Fax: 315-894-9980
http://www.midyork.org/LibraryList/LibraryInfo/
        Ilion.html

Institute for Jewish Research
The Center for Jewish History
15 West 16th Street
New York, NY 10011-6301
Tel: 212-246-6080
Fax: 212-292-1892
E-mail: yivomail@yivo.cjh.org
http://www.yivoinstitute.org/

Interlaken Historical Society/Museum & Genealogical Res. Library
Main Street (Route 96)
Interlaken, NY 14847
Tel: 607-532-4341

Irish American Heritage Museum
2267 Route 145
East Durham, NY 12423
Tel: 518-634-7497
OFFICE:
120 State Street
Albany, NY 12207
Tel: 518-432-6598
Fax: 518-449-2540
E-mail: irishamermuseum@cs.com
http://www.irishamericanheritagemuseum.org/

Irondequoit Public Library
Helen McGraw Branch
2180 E. Ridge Road
Rochester, NY 14622
Tel: 716-336-6060
http://www.irondequoit.org/library/program.htm

Jefferson Community College
Melvil Dewey Library
Outer Coffeen Street
Watertown, NY 13601
Tel: 315-786-2225
 www.sunyjefferson.edu/

Jericho Public Library
1 Merry Lane
Jericho, NY 11753-1792
Tel: 516-935-6790
Fax: 516-935-2693
http://www.nassaulibrary.org/jericho/

Jervis Library
613 N. Washington Street
Rome, NY 13440-4203
Tel: 315-336-4570
http://www.jervislibrary.org/

Johnstown Public Library
38 South Market Street
Johnstown, NY 12095
Tel: 518-762-8317
Fax: 518-762-9776
http://www.johnstown.com/city/library.html

Keene Public Library
P.O. Box 206
Keene, NY 12942
Tel: 518-576-2200
Fax: 518-576-2200

Keene Valley Library Archives
P.O. Box 86
Main Sreet
Keene Valley, NY 12943
Tel: 518-576-4335
Fax: 518-576-4693
E-mail: library@kvvi.net
http://www.kvvi.net/~library/

Klyne-Esopus Historical Society/Museum
Route 9W
Ulster Park, NY 12487
Tel: 845-338-8109
E-mail: kehsm@ulster.net
http://www.ulster.net/~kehsm/about.htm

Lake Placid Public Library
67 Main Street
Lake Placid, NY 12946
Tel/Fax: 518-523-3200
E-mail: lkp@northnet.org

Lake Ronkonkoma Historical Society/Museum
328 Hawkins Avenue
P.O. Box 2716
Lake Ronkonkoma, NY 11779
Tel: 631-467-3152

Lehman College Library/City University of New York
Special Collections
250 Bedford Park Blvd., West
Bronx, NY 10468
Tel: 718-960-8603
E-mail: libref@lehman.cuny.edu
http://www.lehman.cuny.edu/library/library2.htm

Leo Baeck Institute
German-Jewish Families
15 W 16th Street
New York, NY 10011
Tel: 212-744-6400
Fax: 212-988-1305
http://www.lbi.org/

Little Red Schoolhouse
Panama Rocks Road
Clymer Center, NY 14724
Tel: 716-355-6391
http://c1web.com/local_info/artsed/lrs.html

Lockport Public Library
23 East Avenue
Lockport, NY 14094
Tel: 716-433-5935
Fax: 716-439-0198
http://www.lockportlibrary.org/

Locust Valley Library
170 Buckram Road
Locust Valley, NY 11560
Tel: 516-671-1837
Fax: 516-676-8164
http://www.nassaulibrary.org/locustv/
    lvlchildrenshomepage.htm

Lorenzo-New York State Historic Site
RD #2
Cazenovia, NY 13035
Tel: 315-655-3200
http://cazenovia.com/lorenzo/index.html

Louise Adelia Read Memorial Library/Museum
104 Read Street
Hancock, NY 13783
Tel: 607-637-2519

Lower East Side Tenement Museum
97 Orchard Street (at Broome Street)
Mail:
66 Allen Street
New York, NY 10002
Tel: 212-431-0233
Fax: 212-431-0402
http://www.wnet.org/tenement/

Lyme Heritage Center
12165 Main Street
Chaumont, NY 13622
Tel: 315-649-5454
http://www.rootsweb.com/~nyjeffer/lyher.htm

Macsherry Public Library
112 Walton Street
Alexandria Bay, NY 13607
Tel: 315-482-2241

Madison County Historical Society/Library
Cottage Lawn House
435 Main Street
P.O. Box 415
Oneida, NY 13421
Tel: 315-363-4136

Mamaroneck Public Library
136 Prospect Avenue
Mamaroneck, NY 10543
Tel: 914-698-1250
     914-698-3751 (Children's Department)
http://www.westchesterlibraries.org/libs/mamaroneck/

Margaret Reaney Memorial Library/Museum
19 Kingsburg Avenue
St. Johnsville, NY 13452
Tel: 518-568-7822
E-mail: MRML@telenet.net

Montgomery Academy
Village Hall
133 Clinton Street
Maybrook, NY 12543
Tel: 845-457-9661
Fax: 845-457-5698
http://www.villageofmontgomery.com/

Montour Falls Memorial Library
406 W. Main Street
P.O. Box 486
Montour Falls, NY 14865
Tel: 607-535-7489
Fax: 607-535-5517
E-mail: montour@stls.org
http://www.stls.org/Schuyler_county/ Montour_Falls.htm

Moore Memorial Library
59 Genesee Street
Green, NY 13778
Tel: 607-656-9349
http://lib.4cty.org/greene/greene_r.html

Mount Vernon Public Library
Local History Room
28 S. First Avenue
Mount Vernon, NY 10550
Tel: 914-668-1840 ext. 32
Fax: 914-668-1018
http://www.wls.lib.ny.us/libs/mount_vernon/
    mtv.html

Nassau County Museum
1 Museum Drive
Roslyn Harbor, NY 11576
Tel: 516-484-9338
http://www.nassaumuseum.com/

Nazarene College of Rochester
Lorette Wilmot Library
4245 East Avenue
Rochester, NY 14610
Tel: 716-389-2129
Fax: 716-248-8766
http://www.naz.edu/dept/library/

New City Library
Rockland Room
220 North Main Street
New City, NY 10956
Tel: 845-634-4997
Fax: 845-634-0173
http://www.newcitylibrary.org/

New Netherland Project
New York State Library
Cultural Education Center, 8th Floor
Empire State Plaza
Albany, NY 12230
Tel: 518-474-6067
Fax: 518-473-0472
E-mail: cgehring@unix2.nysed.gov
http://www.nnp.org/

New York Division of Military & Naval Affairs
330 Old Niskayuna Road
Latham, NY 12110
Tel: 518-786-4828
Fax: 518-786-4521
http://www.dmna.state.ny.us/

New York Genealogical & Biographical Society
122 East 58th Street
New York, NY 10022-1939
Tel: 212-755-8532
http://www.nygbs.org/

New York Historical Society
170 Central Park West
New York, NY 10024
Tel: 212-873-3400
Fax: 212-875-1591
http://www.nyhistory.org/education/education.html

New York Public Library
U.S. History, Local History, and Genealogy Resources
5th Avenue and 42nd Street, Room 315S
New York, NY 10016
Tel: 212-340-0849
E-mail: histref@nypl.org
http://www.nypl.org/research/chss/lhg/genea.html

New York State Association of Museums
265 River Street
Troy, NY 12180
Tel: 518-273-3400

New York State Bureau of Historic Sites
Office of Parks, Recreation, & Historic Preservation
Peebles Island
P.O. Box 219
Waterford, NY 12188
Tel: 518-237-8643 ext. 200
Fax: 518-235-4248

New York State Library
Cultural Education Center
Empire State Plaza
Albany, NY 12230
Tel: 518-474-5355 (Information/Reference)
    518-474-6282 (Special Collections)
E-mail: nyslweb@unix2.nysed.gov
http://www.nysl.nysed.gov/

New York/Ulster County Library
(See Elting Memorial Library)

Newburgh Free Library
124 Grand Street
Newburgh, NY 12550
Tel: 845-561-1985
Fax: 845-561-2401
http://www.newburghlibrary.org/

Niagara County Community College
Library Learning Center, Special Collections
3111 Saunders Settlement Road
Sanborn, NY 14132
Tel: 716-614-6222
Fax: 716-614-6700
http://www.sunyniagara.cc.ny.us/library/
    special.html

Niagara County Genealogical Society/Library
215 Niagara Street
Lockport, NY 14094
Tel: 716-433-1033
http://www.niagaracounty.org/
    genealogical_society_research.htm

Niagara Falls Public Library
1425 Main Street
Niagara Falls, NY 14305
Tel: 716-286-4899
Fax: 716-286-4885
http://www.niagarafallspubliclib.org/

Norfolk Historical Museum
42 West Main Street
P.O. Box 643
Norfolk, N.Y. 13667
Tel: 315-384-4575

North Merrick Public Library
1691 Meadowbrook Road
North Merrick, NY 11566
Tel: 516-378-7474
http://www.nassaulibrary.org/nmerrick/

North Rockland History Museum
20 Oak Street
Garnerville, NY 10923

North Tonawanda Public Library
505 Meadow Drive
North Tonawanda, NY 14120
Tel: 716-693-4132
Fax: 716-693-0719
http://www.nioga.org/north_tonawanda/

Ogdensburg Dioceses Archives
622 Washington Street
P.O. Box 369
Ogdensburg, NY 13669
Tel: 315-393-2920

Ogdensburg Public Library
312 Washington Street
Ogdensburg, NY 13669
Tel: 315-393-4325
Fax: 315-393-4344
http://www.northnet.org/ogbpublib/

Oneida Library
220 Broad Street
Oneida, NY 13421
Tel: 315-363-3050
Fax: 315-363-4217
E-mail: on_circ@midyork.lib.ny.us
http://www.midyork.org/oneida/libwebdirectory.htm

Onondaga County Historical Association/Research Center
311 Montgomery Street
Syracuse, NY 13202
Tel: 315-428-1862

Onondaga County Public Library
Local History/Special Collections
447 South Salina Street
Syracuse, NY 13202-2494
Tel: 315-435-1900
http://www.ocpl.lib.ny.us/

Ontario County Historical Society
55 North Main Street
Canandaigua, NY 14424
Tel: 716-394-4975
http://www.ochs.org/

Orange County Genealogical Society/Research Room
1841 Court House
101 Main Street
Goshen, NY 10924
http://www.rootsweb.com/~nozell/ocgs/

Oswego City Library
120 East 2nd Street
Oswego, NY 13126
Tel: 315-341-5867

Otis A. Thompsom Local History Room
3 Court Street
Norwich, NY 13815

Paine Memorial Free Library
1 School Street
Willsboro, NY 12996
Tel: 518-963-4478
http://www.willsborony.com/PaineMemorialLibrary/

Patchogue Medford Library
Local History Room
54-60 E. Main Street
Patchogue, NY 11722
Tel: 631-654-4700
Fax: 631-289-3999
E-mail: ptchlib@suffolk.lib.ny.us
http://pml.suffolk.lib.ny.us/

Patterson Library
40 South Portage Street
Westfield, NY 14787
Tel: 716-326-2154
Fax: 716-326-2554
E-mail: wlibrary@epix.net

Penfield Public Library
1985 Baird Road
Penfield, NY 14526
Tel: 716-383-0500
      716-383-0800 (Hours & Programs)
TDD: 716-383-8712

Peru Free Library
N. Main Street
Tel: 518-643-8618

Pickering-Beach Museum
West Main Street
P.O. Box 204
Sackets Harbor, NY 13685
Tel: 315-646-2321 (Sackets Harbor Visitors Center)

Plattsburgh Public Library/Local History Room
19 Oak Street
Plattsburgh, NY 12901
Tel: 518-563-0921
Fax: 518-563-1681

Polish American Museum
16 Bellview Avenue
Port Washington, NY 11050
Tel: 516-883-6542
http://www.liglobal.com/t_i/attractions/
      museums/polish/

Port Chester Public Library
1 Haseco Avenue
Port Chester, NY 10573
Tel: 914-939-6710
http://www.portchesterlibrary.org/

Port Jervis Free Library
138 Pike Street
Port Jervis, NY 12771
Tel: 845-856-7313
Fax: 845-858-8710
http://www.rcls.org/ptj/

Port Leyden Museum
Lincoln & Main Street
P.O. Box 252
Port Leyden, NY 13433

Port Washington Library
One Library Drive
Port Washington, NY 11050
Tel: 516-883-4400
Fax: 516-883-7927
http://www.pwpl.org/

Potsdam Public Museum
Civic Center
Potsdam, NY 13676
Tel: 315-265-6910
http://www.potsdam.ny.us/museum/

Pulaski Public Library
4917 N Jefferson Street
Pulaski, NY 13142
Tel: 315-298-2717

Purchase Free Library
3093 Purchase Street
Purchase, NY 10577
Tel: 914-948-0550
http://westchesterlibraries.org/libs/purchase/

Queens Borough Public Library
89-11 Merrick Blvd.
Jamaica, NY 11432
Tel: 718-990-0770
http://www.queenslibrary.org/

Queens County Land Records
88-11 Sutphin Blvd.
Jamaica, NY 11435

Queens Genealogy Workshop
The Greater Ridgewood Historical Society
1820 Flushing Avenue
Ridgewood, NY 11385
Tel: 718-456-1776
http://home.att.net/~cgohari/

Rensselaer County Historical Society/Genealogy Library
57 Second Street
Troy, NY 12180
Tel: 518-272-7232
Fax: 518-273-1264
http://www.rchsonline.org/

Richmond Memorial Library
19 Ross Street
Batavia, NY 14020
Tel: 716-343-9550
http://www.nioga.org/batavia/

Roberts Wesleyan College
Kenneth B. Keating Library
Archives and Chesbrough-Roberts Historical Center
2301 Westside Drive
Rochester, NY 14624
Tel: 716-594-6016

Rochester Public Library
Local History Division
115 South Avenue
Rochester, NY 14604
Tel: 716-428-7300

Rochester Regional Research Library Council
Documentary Heritage Program
390 Packett's Landing
P.O. Box 66160
Fairport, NY 14450
Tel: 716-223-7570
Fax: 716-223-7712

Rogers Memorial Library
9 Jobs Lane
Southampton, NY 11968
Tel: 631-283-0774

Roman Catholic Diocese of Albany
40 North Main Avenue
Albany, NY 12203
Tel: 518-453-6633
www.rcda.org/

Roman Catholic Diocese of Rochester
1150 Buffalo Road
Rochester, NY 14624-1890
Tel: 585-328-3210
Fax: 585-328-3149
http://www.dor.org/

Rome Historical Society/Museum & Archives
200 Church Street
Rome, NY 13440
Tel: 315-336-5870
http://www.artcom.com/museums/nv/mr/ 13440-58.htm

Roxbury Library Association
Main Street
P.O. Box 186
Roxbury, NY 12474
Tel: 607-326-7901
http://www.4cls.org/webpages/members/Roxbury/
    Roxbury.html

St. Lawrence County Historical Association
3 East Main Street
P.O. Box 8
Canton, NY 13617
Tel: 315-386-8133
http://slcha.org/

St. Lawrence University
Owen D. Young Library
Special Collections
Canton, NY 13617
Tel: 315-229-5451
http://web.stlawu.edu/library/

Saint Mary's Hospital Library
89 Genesee Street
Rochester, NY 14611-3201

St. Peter's Armenian Church
100 Troy-Schenectady Rd
Watervliet, New York 12189
Tel: 518-274-3673
Fax: 518-274-3103
E-mail: STPETER.ARMCH@prodigy.net
http://pages.prodigy.net/stpeter.armch/

Saranac Lake Free Library
Adirondack Collection
100 Main Street
Saranac Lake, NY 12983
Tel: 518-891-4190
Fax: 518-891-5931
http://www.nc3r.org/slfl/

Saratoga Springs Public Library
49 Henry Street
Saratoga Springs, NY 12866
Tel: 518-584-7860
http://www.library.saratoga.ny.us/

Scarsdale Public Library
54 Olmsted Road
Scarsdale, NY 10583
Tel: 914-722-1300
http://www.scarsdalelibrary.org/

Schenectady County Historical Society
32 Washington Avenue
Schenectady, NY 12305
Tel: 518-374-0263
Fax: 208-361-5305
E-mail: librarian@schist.org
http://www.schist.org/

Schenectady County Public Library
99 Clinton Street
Schenectady, NY 12305-2083
Tel: 518-388-4500
E-mail: scpl@scpl.org
http://www.scpl.org/index.html

Schenectady Museum & Planetarium
Nott Terr Heights
Schenectady, NY 12308
Tel: 518-382-7890
Fax: 518-382-7893
http://www.schenectadymuseum.org/ planetarium.html

Schomburg Center for Research/Branch New York Public Library
515 Malcolm X Blvd.
New York, NY 10037-1801
Tel: 212-491-2200
http://www.nypl.org/research/sc/sc.html

Scottsville Free Library
Cox Room
28 Main Street
Scottsville, NY 14546
Tel: 585-889-2023
E-mail: lleo@mcls.rochester.lib.ny.us
http://www.rochester.lib.ny.us/scottsville/

Sea Cliff Village Museum
95 Tenth Street
Sea Cliff, NY 11579
Tel: 516-671-0090

Seymour Library
Local History Room
176 Genesee Street
Auburn, NY 13021
Tel: 315-252-2571
Fax: 315-252-7985
E-mail: serskine@adelphia.net
http://www.seymourlibrary.org/

Shandaken Historical Center
Academy Street
Pine Hill, NY 12465
Tel: 845-254-4460

Sherman Free Library
4 Church Street
Port Henry, NY 12974
Tel: 518-546-7461
http://www.porthenry.com/phframes/library.htm

Smithtown Historical Society/Library
Caleb Smith II House
North Country Road (Rte. 25A)
Smithtown, NY 11787
Tel: 631-265-6768

Smithtown Library
Long Island History Room
1 North Country Road
Smithtown, NY 11787
Tel: 631-265-2072
E-mail: tmadden@suffolk.lib.ny.us
http://www.smithlib.org/

South Central Regional Library Council
Documentary Heritage Program
215 North Cayuga Street Ithaca, NY 14850
Tel: 607-273-9106
Fax: 607-272-0740
E-mail: scrlc@lakenet.org
http://www.lakenet.org/

Southeastern New York Library Resources Council
220 Route 299
P.O. Box 879
Highland, NY 12528
Tel: 845-691-2734
Fax: 845-691-6987
http://www.senylrc.org/

Southold Free Library
Whitaker Historical Collection
Main Road
Southold, NY 11971
Tel: 631-765-2077
Fax: 631-765-2197
http://sohd.suffolk.lib.ny.us/

Spencer Historical Society/Museum
Center Street
P.O. Box 71
Spencer, NY 14883

Stamford Village Library
117 Main Street
Stamford, NY 12167
Tel: 607-652-5001
http://www.4cls.org/webpages/members/
Stamford/Stamford.html

State University of New York/Albany (SUNY)
University Library B-3
Special Collections & Archives
1400 Washington Avenue
Albany, NY 12222
Tel: 518-442-3544
http://library.albany.edu/speccoll/

State University of New York/Brockport (SUNY)
Drake Memorial Library
College Archives, Special Collections
Brockport, NY 14420
Tel: 716-395-5667
Fax: 716-395-5651
E-mail: archives@brockport.edu
http://cc.brockport.edu/~library1/archives.htm

State University of New York/Fredonia (SUNY)
Daniel E. Reed Library
Special Collections & Archives
Fredonia, NY 14063
Tel: 716-673-3183
Fax: 716-673-3185
http://www.fredonia.edu/library/archive.asp

State University of New York/Oswego (SUNY)
Penfield Library
Special Collections
Oswego, NY 13126
Tel: 315-341-3567
Fax: 315-341-3194
E-mail: osborne@oswego.oswego.edu
http://www.oswego.edu/library/collections/

Steele Memorial Library
101 E Church Street
Elmira, NY 14901
Tel: 607-733-9173
Fax: 607-733-9176
http://www.steele.lib.ny.us/downtown.htm

Strong Museum Library and Archives
One Manhattan Square
Rochester, NY 14607
Tel: 585-263-2700
Fax: 585-263-2493
http://www.strongmuseum.org/

Suffern Village Museum
61 Washington Avenue
Suffern, NY 10901
Tel: 845-357-2600

Suffolk County Historical Society/Library
300 West Main Street
Riverhead, NY 11901
Tel: 631-727-2881
http://www.riverheadli.com/rmuseum.html

Susan B. Anthony House National Historic Landmark
17 Madison Street
Rochester, NY 14608
Tel: 585-235-6124
http://www.susanbanthonyhouse.org/

Syosset Public Library
225 S. Oyster Bay Road
Syosset, NY 11791-5897
Tel: 516-921-7161
http://www.nassaulibrary.org/syosset/

Tarrytowns, Historical Society of the
1 Grove Street
Tarrytown, NY 10591
Tel: 914-631-8374

Theresa Free Library
301 Main Street
Theresa, NY 13691
Tel: 315-628-5972
http://humber.northnet.org/theresalibrary/ index2.html

Tioga County Historical Society/Museum
110 Front Street
Owego, NY 13827
Tel: 607-687-2460
Fax: 607-687-7788
E-mail: tiogamus@clarityconnect.com
http://www.tier.net/tiogahistory/

Tompkins County Museum
401 East State Street
Ithaca, NY 14850
Tel: 607-273-8284

Troy Public Library
Troy Room Collection
100 Second Street
Troy, NY 12180
Tel: 518-274-7071
Fax: 518-271-9154
http://www.uhls.org/troy/

Union College
Schaffer Library
807 Union St.
Schenectady, NY 12308
Tel: 518-370-6620
http://www.union.edu/PUBLIC/LIBRARY/

University of Rochester
Department of History
364 Rush Rhees Library
University of Rochester
Rochester, NY 14627
Tel: 585-275-2052
Fax: 585-756-4425
E-mail: rahz@mail.rochester.edu
http://www.rochester.edu/College/HIS/

University of Rochester
Rare Books & Special Collections-Local History &
    Archives Room
Rush Rhees Library
Rochester, NY 14627
Tel: 716-275-4477
Fax: 716-273-1032
http://www.lib.rochester.edu/rbk/rarehome2.htm

Utica Public Library
303 Genesee Street
Utica, NY 13501
Tel: 315-735-2279
http://www.uticapubliclibrary.org/

Vestal Public Library
320 Vestal Parkway East
Vestal, NY 13850
Tel: 607-754-4244
        607-754-4244   (Reference & Information)
Fax: 607-754-7936
http://lib.4cty.org/vestal/vestal_r.html

Voorheesvillle School District Public Library
51 School Road
Voorheesville, NY 12186
Tel: 518-765-2791

Waterloo Library & Historical Society
Terwilliger Museum
31 East Williams Street
Waterloo, NY 13165
Tel: 315-539-0533
http://www.waterloony.com/Library.html

Waterloo Memorial Day Museum
35 East Main Street
Waterloo, NY 13165
Tel: 315-539-5033
http://www.waterloony.com/MdayMus.html

Wead Library
64 Elm Street
Malone, NY 12953
Tel: 518-483-5251
Fax: 518-483-5255
E-mail: minnich@northnet.org

Wenrich Memorial Library
133 South Fitzhugh Street
Rochester, NY 14608
Tel: 716-546-7029
Fax: 716-546-4788

West Islip Public Library
3 Higbie Lane
West Islip, NY 11795
Tel: 631-661-7080
Fax: 631-661-7137
E-mail: wislip@suffolk.lib.ny.us
http://www.wipublib.org/

**Western New York Genealogical Society/Library &
Museum**
5859 South Park Avenue, Route 62
P.O. Box 338
Hamburg, NY 14075
http://www.pce.net/outram/wny.htm

Western New York Heritage Institute
495 Pine Ridge Road
Cheektowaga, NY 14225
Tel: 716-893-4011
Fax: 716-893-4013
E-mail: athcah@buffnet.net
http://wnyheritagepress.org/

Western New York Library Resources Council
Calspan Building, 2nd Floor
4455 Genesee Street
P.O. Box 400
Buffalo, NY 14225-0400
Tel: 716-633-0705
        716-633-1736
E-mail: hbamford@wnylrc.org (Heidi Bamford-Regional
        Archivist)
http://www.wnylrc.org/

Westport Library Association
P.O. Box 436
Washington Street
Westport, NY 12993-0436
Tel: 518-962-8219
E-mail: wptlib@nc3r.org
http://www.nc3r.org/wptlib/

William H. Bush Memorial Library
P.O. Box 141
Martinsburg, NY 13404
Tel: 315-376-7490
E-mail: whbml@nc3r.org
http://www.nc3r.org/whbml/

William K. Sanford Town Library
629 Albany-Shaker Road
Loudonville, NY 12211
Tel: 518-458-9274
http://www.colonie.org/library/

Wyckoff House Association
5816 Clarendon Road
P.O. Box 100-376
Brooklyn, NY 11210
Tel/Fax: 718-629-5400
http://www.wyckoffassociation.org/index.asp

Yivo Institute for Jewish Research
The Center for Jewish History
15 West 16th Street
New York, NY 10011-6301 Tel: 212-246-6080
Fax: 212-292-1892
E-mail: yivomail@yivo.cjh.org

NEWSPAPER REPOSITORIES

New York State Library
Cultural Education Center
Empire State Plaza
Albany, NY 12230
Tel: 518-474-5355 (Information/Reference)
      518-474-6282 (Special Collections)
E-mail: nyslweb@unix2.nysed.gov
http://www.nysl.nysed.gov/

New York State Newspaper Project
New York State Library
Cultural Education Center, 6th Floor
Empire State Plaza
Albany, NY 12220
Tel: 518-474-7491
Fax: 518-474-5786
E-mail: wvann@unix2.nysed.gov
http://www.nysl.nysed.gov/nysnp/

State University of New York/Albany (SUNY)
University Library B-3
Special Collections & Archives
1400 Washington Avenue
Albany, NY 12222
Tel: 518-442-3544
http://library.albany.edu/speccoll/

State University of New York/Oswego (SUNY)
Penfield Library
Special Collections
Oswego, NY 13126
Tel: 315-341-3567
Fax: 315-341-3194
E-mail: osborne@oswego.oswego.edu
http://www.oswego.edu/library/collections/

VITAL RECORDS

New York City Department of Health
Division of Vital Records
125 Worth Street New York, NY 10007
P.O. Box 3776, Church Street Station
New York, NY 10007
http://www.ci.nyc.ny.us/html/doh/html/vr/vr.html

New York City Municipal Archives
31 Chambers Street, Room 103
New York, NY 10007
Tel: 212-788-8580
http://www.ci.nyc.ny.us/html/doris/html/ archives.html

New York State Department of Health
Vital Records Section
Corning Tower Building, Empire State Plaza
Albany, NY 12237-0023
Tel: 518-474-3077
      518-486-1863
E-mail: nyhealth@health.state.ny.us
http://www.health.state.ny.us/nysdoh/consumer/ vr.htm

NEW YORK ON THE WEB

Eagle Byte Historical Research
http://home.eznet.net/~dminor/

Ed Nugent's Links to Links
http://www.geocities.com/Heartland/Plains/8622/
      gen_idx.html

History of Rochester
http://mcls.rochester.lib.ny.us/~rochhist/

Hudson Valley Network
http://www.hvnet.com/

Index of Marriages and Deaths in the New York Weekly Museum 1788-1817
http://freepages.family.rootsweb.com/~families/halsey/
      deaths2.html/

New York Addresses for Genealogy
http://www.geocities.com/~agiroux/

New York GenWeb Project
http://www.rootsweb.com/~nygenweb/

New York History Net
http://www.nyhistory.com/

New York State Archives
http://www.archives.nysed.gov/

New York State Library
http://unix2.nysed.gov/gengen.htm

New York State Newspaper Project
http://www.nysl.nysed.gov/nysnp/

Rochester Regional Library Council (RRLC)
http://www.rrlc.org/

North Carolina

Archives, State & National

National Archives—Southeast Region
1557 St. Joseph Avenue
East Point, GA 30344
Tel: 404-763-7474
Fax: 404-763-7059
E-mail: atlanta.center@nara.gov
http://www.nara.gov/regional/atlanta.html

North Carolina State Archives
Archives and History/State Library Building
109 East Jones Street
Raleigh, NC 27601-2807
Tel: 919-733-3952
Fax: 919-733-1354
E-mail: archives@ncsl.dcr.state.nc.us
http://www.ah.dcr.state.nc.us/archives/arch/ archhp.htm

Genealogical Societies

Alamance County Genealogical Society
P.O. Box 3052
Burlington, NC 27215-3052
Tel: 336-584-8381
E-mail: alamancecogen@yahoo.com
http://www.rootsweb.com/~ncacgs/

Albemarle Genealogical Society
142 Waterlily Road
Route 1, Box 15 Coinjock, NC 27923
http://pages.prodigy.net/mwise/AGS.html

Alexander County Ancesstry Association, Inc.
P.O. Box 241
Hiddenite, NC 28636

Alexander County Genealogical Society, Inc.
Route 2, Box 87A
Hiddenite, NC 28636

Alleghany Historical & Genealogical Society
P.O. Box 817
Sparta, NC 28675
http://www.ls.net/~ahgs/

Anson County, Genealogical Society of
108 Sunset Drive
Wadesboro, NC 28170

Beaufort County Genealogical Society
P.O. Box 1089
Washington, NC 27889-1089
http://www.beaufort-county.com/Genealogy/

Broad River Genealogical Society
P.O. Box 2261
Shelby, NC 28151-2261
http://www.rootsweb.com/~ncclevel/brgs.htm

Burke County Genealogical Society
P.O. Box 661
Morganton, NC 28680
http://www.rootsweb.com/~ncburke/burkegs.htm

Cabarrus Genealogical Society
P.O. Box 2981
Concord, NC 28025-2981
E-mail: cabgensoc@webkorner.com
http://www.rootsweb.com/~nccgs/index.htm

Caldwell County Genealogical Society
P.O. Box 2476
Lenoir, NC 28645-2476

Carolinas Genealogical Society
300 North Main Street
P.O. Box 397
Monroe, NC 28111
Tel: 704-289-6737
http://www.rootsweb.com/~ncunion/
　　　Genealogical_ society.htm

Catawba County Genealogical Society
P.O. Box 2406
Hickory, NC 28603-2406
http://www.co.catawba.nc.us/otheragency/ccgs/
　　　ccgsmain.htm

Coastal Genealogical Society
P.O. Box 1421
Swansboro, NC 28584
E-mail: rdhennon@coastalnet.com

Craven County Kinfolk Trackers
8375 HWY 306 South
Arapahoe, NC 28510
E-mail: cn1197@coastalnet.com
www2.always-online.com/kintracker/

Cumberland County Genealogical Society
P.O. Box 53299
Fayetteville, NC 28305

Davidson County, Genealogical Society of
P.O. Box 1665
Lexington, NC 27293-1665
http://www.rootsweb.com/~ncdavids/gsdcpub.htm

Davie County Historical & Genealogical Society
371 N. Main Street
Mocksville, NC 27028

Durham-Orange County Genealogical Society
P.O. Box 4703
Chapel Hill, NC 27515-4703
E-mail: allendrew@mindspring.com
http://www.rootsweb.com/~ncdogs

Eastern North Carolina Genealogical Society
P.O. Box 395
New Bern, NC 28563

Forsyth County Genealogical Society
P.O. Box 5715
Winston-Salem, NC 27113-5715
E-mail: ccasey@netunlimited.net
http://www.usgennet.org/alhnncus/ahncfors/

Gaston-Lincoln Genealogical Society
P.O. Box 584
Mount Holly, NC 28120
http://www.rootsweb.com/~ncglgs/Index.htm

Granville County Genealogical Society, Inc.
P.O. Box 1746
Oxford, NC 27565
http://www.gcgs.org/Default.asp

Guilford County Genealogical Society
P.O. Box 9693
Greensboro, NC 27429-0693
http://www.greensboro.com/gcgs/

Halifax County Genealogical Society
P.O. Box 447
Halifax, NC 27839

Hampstead Historical & Genealogical Society
P.O. Box 8
Hampstead, NC 28443

Harnett County Genealogical Society
P.O. Box 219
Buies Creek, NC 27506-0219

Haywood County Genealogical Society, Inc.
P.O. Box 1331
Waynesville, NC 28786
E-mail: hcgs_nc@yahoo.com
http://www.rootsweb.com/~nchcgs/

Henderson County Genealogical & Historical Society, Inc.
400 North Main Street
Hendersonville, NC 28792
Tel: 828-693-1531
E-mail:hcgenhis@brinet.com
www.brinet.com/~hcgenhis

Hyde County Historical & Genealogical Society
7820 Piney Woods Rd
Fairfield, NC 27826
www.rootsweb.com/~nchyde/HCHGS.HTM

Iredell County, Genealogical Society of
P.O. Box 946
Statesville, NC 28687
Tel: 704-878-5384

Jackson County Genealogical Society
P.O. Box 2108
Cullowee, NC 28723
www.main.nc.us/jcgs/

Johnston County Genealogical & Historical Society
P.O. Box 2373
Smithfield, NC 27577-2373

Lee County Genealogical & Historical Society, Inc.
P.O. Box 3216
Sanford, NC 27331-3216
E-mail: alvis@clegg.com

Loyalist Descendants, Society of
P.O. Box 848, Desk 120
Rockingham, NC 28379

Martin County Genealogical Society
P.O. Box 121
Williamston, NC 27892-0121
E-mail: shepjr@coastalnet.com

Moore County Genealogical Society
P.O. Box 1183
Pinehurst, NC 28374-1183

North Carolina Genealogical Society
P.O. Box 22
Greenville, NC 27835-0022
E-mail: ncgs@mail.com
http://www.ncgenealogy.org/

Northeastern North Carolina, Family Research Society of
410 E. Main Street, Suite 204
Elizabeth City, NC
Tel: 252-333-1640
http://www.geocities.com/Heartland/farm/7890/

Old Buncombe County Genealogical Society
Innsbruck Mall, Suite 22
85 Tunnel Road
P.O. Box 2122
Asheville, NC 28802
Tel: 828-253-1894
E-mail: obcgs@buncombe.main.nc.us
http://www.obcgs.com/

Old Dobbs County Genealogical Society
P.O. Box 617
Goldsboro, NC 27533

Old New Hanover Genealogical Society
P.O. Box 2536
Wilmington, NC 28402-2536
http://www.thedrake.org/ONH/

Old Tryon County, Genealogical Society of
P.O. Box 938
Forest City, NC 28043
Tel: 828-248-4010
http://www.blueridge.net/lds/nc/oldtryon.html

Olde Mecklenburg Genealogical Society
P.O. Box 32453
Charlotte, NC 28232-2453
E-mail: OMGS1775@yahoo.com
http://www.rootsweb.com/~ncomgs/

Onslow County Genealogical Association
P.O. Box 1739
Jacksonville, NC 28541-1739

Pasquotank Historical & Genealogical Society
P.O. Box 523
Elizabeth City, NC 27907

Personal Computer Club of Charlotte
Genealogy Special Interest Group
P.O. Box 114
Paw Creek, NC 28130-0114
http://www.pc3.org/

Pitt County Family Researchers
P.O. Box 20339
Greenville, NC 27858-0339
http://www.rootsweb.com/~ncpcfr/

Randolph County Genealogical Society
P.O. Box 4394
Asheboro, NC 27204

Richmond County Descendants, Society of
P.O. Box 848
Rockingham, N.C. 28380
Tel: 910-997-6641
E-mail: descendant@richmondcodescendants.org
http://www.richmondcodescendants.org/

Rockingham-Stokes Counties, Genealogical Society of
P.O. Box 152
Mayodan, NC 27027-0152
E-mail: DiginRoots@aol.com
Web: ns.netmcr.com/~lonabec/gsrsinfo.html

Rowan County, Genealogical Society of
P.O. Box 4305
Salisbury, NC 28145-4305
http://www.lib.co.rowan.nc.us/HistoryRoom/html/
    gsrc.htm

Scotland County Genealogical Society
P.O. Box 496
Laurel Hill, NC 28351
http://www.txdirect.net/~hpeele/ncgenweb/
    richscot/scgs.htm

Southeastern North Carolina Genealogical Society
P.O. Box 468
Chadbourn, NC 28431
http://www.spiritdesign.net/columbus/sencgs.htm

Southwestern North Carolina Genealogical Society
101 Blumenthal
Murphy, NC 28906

Stanly County Genealogical Society
P.O. Box 31
Albemarle, NC 28002-0031
http://www.eskimo.com/~lcsims/

Surry County Genealogical Association
P.O. Box 997
Dobson, NC 27017-0997
juliemorrison.com/surry/

Swain County Genealogical & Historical Society
P.O. Box 267
Bryson City, NC 28713

Tar River Connections Genealogical Society
P.O. Box 8764
Rocky Mount, NC 27804
E-mail: turn1104@aol.com
http://necn.ncwc.edu/TRCGS/TRCHP.HTML

Toe Valley Genealogical Society
491 Beaver Creek Road
Spruce Pine, NC 28777

Tyrell County Genealogical & Historical Society
P.O. Box 686
Columbia, NC 27825-0686
E-mail: jimmyfleming@coastalnet.com

VA-NC Piedmont Genealogical Society
P.O. Box 2272
Danville, VA 24541
http://www.rootsweb.com/~vancpgs/Index.htm

Wake County Genealogical Society
P.O. Box 17713
Raleigh, NC 27619-7713
E-mail: wcgs@pobox.com
http://www.rtpnet.org/wcgs/

Washington County Genealogical Society
P.O. Box 567
Plymouth, NC 27962

Watauga County, Genealogical Society of
P.O. Box 126 (DTS)
Boone, NC 28607

Wilkes Genealogical Society, Inc.
P.O. Box 1629
North Wilkesboro, NC 28659
http://www.angelfire.com/nc/wwwjmd/wgs.html

Wilson County Genealogical Society, Inc.
P.O. Box 802
Wilson, NC 27894
Tel: 252-243-1660
E-mail: ancestor@coastalnet.com
http://www.wcgs.org

Yadkin County Historical & Genealogical Society, Inc.
P.O. Box 1250
Yadkinville, NC 27055

HISTORICAL SOCIETIES

Alleghany Historical-Genealogical Society
P.O. Box 817
Sparta, NC 28675
http://www.ls.net/~ahgs/

Anson County Historical Society, Inc.
206 East Wade Street
Wadesboro, NC 28170
Tel: 704-694-6694
http://www.ghgcorp.com/sellers/html/socnews.htm

Apex Historical Society
P.O. Box 502
Apex, NC 27502
E-mail: thegrebings@worldnet.att.net
http://www.apexhs.freeservers.com/

Ashe County Historical Society
Route 1, 148 Library Drive
West Jefferson, NC 28694
http://www.ls.net/~newriver/nc/ashebook.htm

Avery County Historical Society
P.O. Box 266
Newland, NC 28657

Beaufort Historical Association
P.O. Box 1709
Beaufort, NC 28516-0363
E-mail: bha@bmd.clis.com
http://www.nccoastonline.com/AbtBHA.html

Black Creek Historical Society
P.O. Box 204
Black Creek, NC 27813

Bladen County Historical Society
P.O. Box 848
Elizabethtown, NC 28337

Brunswick County Historical Society
P.O. Box 874
Shallotte, NC 28459

Burke County Historical Society
P.O. Box 151
Morganton, NC 28655

Cabarrus, Historic
65 Union Street S
P.O. Box 966
Concord, NC 28025
Tel: 704-786-8515
E-mail: historiccabarrus@aol.com

Carteret County Historical Society, Inc.
P.O. Box 481
Morehead City, NC 28557
Tel: 252-247-7533

Cary Historical Society
P.O. Box 134
Cary, NC 27511

Caswell County Historical Association, Inc.
P.O. Box 278
Yanceyville, NC 27379

Catawba County Historical Association
P.O. Box 73
Newton, NC 28658
Tel: 828-465-0383
Fax: 828-465-9813
E-mail: inquiry@catawbahistory.org
http://www.catawbahistory.org/

431

Chapel Hill Historical Society, Inc.
P.O. Box 503
Chapel Hill, NC 27514-0503

Chatham County Historical Association, Inc.
P.O. Box 913
Pittsboro, NC 27312
Tel: 919-542-3603

Cherokee Historical Association
P.O. Box 398
Cherokee, NC 28719

China Grove, Historical Society of
113 N. Main Street
China Grove, NC 28023

Cleveland County Historical Association
P.O. Box 1335
Shelby, NC 28150

Cooleemee Historical Association
131 Church Street
P.O. Box 667
Cooleemee, NC 27014
Tel: 336-284-6040
Fax: 336-284-4983

Davie County Historical & Genealogical Society
371 N. Main Street
Mocksville, NC 27028

Duplin County Historical Society
P.O. Box 130
Rose Hill, NC 28458-0130

Edenton Historical Commission
505 S Broad Street
Edenton NC 27932-1937

Fair Bluff Historical Society
339 Railroad Street
P.O. Box 285
Fair Bluff, NC 28439
Tel: 910-649-7707

Federation of North Carolina Historical Societies
109 East Jones Street, Room 305
Raleigh, NC 27601
Tel: 919-733-7305

Gaston County Historical Society
P.O. Box 429
Dallas, NC 28034

Gates County Historical Society
P.O. Box 98
Gates, NC 27937

Halifax County Historical Association
P.O. Box 12
Halifax, NC 27839

Hampstead Historical & Genealogical Society
P.O. Box 8
Hampstead, NC 28443

Henderson County Genealogical & Historical Society, Inc.
P.O. Box 2616
Hendersonville, NC 28793-2616

Hillsborough Historical Society
P.O. Box 871
Hillsborough, NC 27278

Hyde County Historical & Genealogical Society
P. O. Box 159
Engelhard, NC 27824
Tel: 252-926-1955 (Library)
http://www.rootsweb.com/~nchyde/HCHGS.HTM

Jackson County Historical Association
P.O. Box 173
Sylva, NC 28779

Lee County Genealogical & Historical Society, Inc.
P.O. Box 3216
Sanford, NC 27331-3216

Lower Cape Fear Historical Society
126 S. 3rd Street
P.O. Box 813
Wilmington, NC 28402
Tel: 910-762-0492

Macon County Historical Society
36 W. Main Street
P.O. Box 822
Franklin, NC 28734
Tel: 828-524-9758
E-mail: historical@smnet.net
http://www.genealogybookstore.com/publishing/
        macon/historical/historicalsociety.htm

Malcolm Blue Historical Society
P.O. Box 603
Aberdeen, NC 28315-0603
Tel: 910-944-7558

Martin County Historical Society, Inc.
P.O. Box 468
Williamston, NC 27892

Mitchell County Historical Society
P.O. Box 651
Bakersville, NC 28705

Montgomery County Historical Society
P.O. Box 664
Troy, NC 27371
http://www.uwharrie-forest.org/chamber/ history.html

Murfreesboro Historical Association
116 E Main Street
P.O. Box 3
Murfreesboro, NC 27855
Tel: 252-398-5922
http://www.albemarle-nc.com/murfreesboro/
history/assoc.htm

Nash County Historical Association
100 Salem Court
Rocky Mt., NC 27804

New Bern Historical Society Foundation, Inc.
510 Pollock Street
P.O. Box 119
New Bern, NC 28536
Tel: 252-638-8558
Fax: 252-638-5773
E-mail: nbhistoricalsoc@coastalnet.com
http://www.pamlico-nc.com/historicnewbern/

North Carolina Afro-American Heritage Society
P.O. Box 26334
Raleigh, NC 27611

North Carolina Society of Historians
P.O. Box 848
Rockingham, NC 28379

Onslow County Historical Society
P.O. Box 5203
Jacksonville, NC 28540

Pasquotank Historical & Genealogical Society
P.O. Box 523
Elizabeth City, NC 27907

Pender County Historical Society
P.O. Box 1380
Burgaw, NC 28425

Person County Historical Society
P.O. Box 887
Roxboro, NC 27573
Tel: 336-597-3134
E-mail: pchs@esinc.net

Pitt County Historical Society
P.O. Box 5063
Greenville, NC 27834
Tel: 919-752-3129

Randolph County Historical Society
P.O. Box 4394
Asheboro, NC 27204

Richmond County Historical Society
P.O. Box 1041
Rockingham, NC 28379
http://www.rchs-nc.org/

Roanoke Island Historical Association
P.O. Box 40
Manteo, NC 27954

Robeson, Historic
P.O. Box 159
Lumberton, NC 28359

Rockingham County Historical Society
P.O. Box 84
Wentworth, NC 27375

Rockingham Society for Research and Preservation
P.O. Box 848
Rockingham, NC 28380-0848
Tel: 919-997-6641

Rutherford County Historical Society
P.O. Box 1044
Rutherfordton, NC 28139

Sampson County Historical Society
P.O. Box 1084
Clinton, NC 28328

Southport Historical Society
501 North Atlantic Avenue
Southport, NC 28461

Stokes County Historical Society
P.O. Box 250
Germantown, NC 27019
E-mail: StokesHistory@aol.com
http://journalnow.koz.com/servlet/wsj_ProcServ/
dbpage=page&gid=0121600115098627344797860l

Surry County Historical Society
P.O. Box 70
Siloam, NC 27047

Swain County Genealogical & Historical Society
P.O. Box 267
Bryson City, NC 28713

Tyrell County Genealogical & Historical Society
P.O. Box 686
Columbia, NC 27825

Union County Historical Society
P.O. Box 222
Monroe, NC 28110

Vance County Historical Society
P.O. Box 2284
Henderson, NC 27536

Wake County Historical Society
P.O. Box 17713
Raleigh 27619-7713

Warren County Historical Association
210 Plummer Street
Warrenton, NC 27589

Washington County Historical Society
P.O. Box 296
Plymouth, NC 27962
E-mail: Dav1207@aol.com
http://www.rootsweb.com/~ncwashin/wchs.htm

Watauga County Historical Society
P.O. Box 1306
Boone, NC 28607

Wayne County Historical Association, Inc.
P.O. Box 665
Goldsboro, NC 27533

Yancey History Association
108 Town Square
Burnsville, NC 28714

LDS FAMILY HISTORY CENTERS

For locations of Family History Centers in this state, see
the Family History Center locator at FamilySearch.
http://www.familysearch.org/eng/Library/FHC/
frameset_fhc.asp

ARCHIVES/LIBRARIES/MUSEUMS

Alamance County Historical Museum
4777 South NC Highway 62
Burlington, NC 27215
Tel: 336-226-8254

Appalachian State University
Carol Grotnes Belk Library, 2nd Floor
W.L. Eury Appalachian Collection
P.O. Box 32026
Boone, NC 28608-32026
Tel: 828-262-4041
Fax: 828-262-2553
E-mail: hayfj@appstate.edu
http://www.library.appstate.edu/appcoll/

Bladen County Public Library
Cypress Street
P.O. Box 1419
Elizabethtown, NC 28337
Tel: 910-862-6990
http://library.bladenco.org/default.asp

Blount-Bridgers House
Archives Room
130 Bridgers Street
Tarboro, NC 27886
Tel: 919-823-4159

Burke County Public Library
204 South King Street
Morganton, NC 28655
Tel: 828-437-5638
http://www.bcpls.org/

Caldwell County Public Library/Lenoir Headquarters
Local History Collection
120 Hospital Avenue
Lenoir, NC 28645
Tel: 704-757-1270
Fax: 704-757-1413
http://www.co.caldwell.nc.us/depart/library/ home.htm

Catawba County Main Library
Rhodes Room
115 West C Street
Newton, NC 28658
Tel/TDD: 828-465-8664
Fax: 828-465-8293
E-mail: cathyf@mail.co.catawba.nc.us
http://www.co.catawba.nc.us/depts/library/libmain.htm

Charles A. Cannon Memorial Library
27 Union Street, N
Concord, NC 28025-4726
Tel: 704-788-3167

Charlotte-Mecklenburg County Public Library
Robinson-Spangler Carolina Room
310 N. Tryon Street
Charlotte, NC 28202
Tel: 704-336-4140
       704-336-2980 (Carolina Room)
E-mail: infoserv@plcmc.org
http://www.plcmc.org/

Cherokee County Historical Museum
87 Peachtree Street
Murphy, NC 28906
Tel: 828-837-6792
E-mail: cchm@webworkz.com
http://www.tib.com/cchm/

Cleveland County Memorial Library
104 Howie Drive
Shelby, NC 28150
Tel: 704-487-9069
　　　704-481-1234
E-mail: jowens@ccml.org
http://www.ccml.org/

Cumberland County Library
Local & State History Room
300 Maiden Lane
Fayetteville, NC 28301-5000
Tel: 910-483-3745 (Local & State History Room)
TDD: 910-483-7878
http://www.cumberland.lib.nc.us/hisroom.htm

Currituck County Public Library
Joseph Palmer Knapp Section
4251 Caratoke Highway
Barco, NC 27917-9707
Tel: 252-453-8345
Fax: 252-453-8717
http://www.co.currituck.nc.us/Library/c_home.htm

Davidson County Public Library
602 South Main Street
Lexington, NC 27292
Tel: 336-242-2040
Fax: 336-248-4122
E-mail: bseuberling@co.davidson.nc.us
http://ils.unc.edu/nclibs/davidson/third.htm

Duke University
William R. Perkins Library
Special Collections
Durham, NC 27708
Tel: 919-660-5800
　　　919-660-5820 (Special Collections)
　　　919-660-5840 (Newspapers & Microforms)
Fax: 919-684-2855
http://www.lib.duke.edu/

Durham County Public Library
North Carolina Collection
300 North Roxboro Street
P.O. Box 3809
Durham, NC 27702
Tel: 919-560-0100
　　　919-560-0171 (North Carolina)
TTY: 919-560-0299
http://www.durhamcountylibrary.org/

East Carolina University
Joyner Library
North Carolina Collection
Greenville, NC 27858
Tel: 252-328-6671
Fax: 252-328-0268
http://www.lib.ecu.edu/

Eden Public Library
North Carolina Collection
598 S. Pierce Street
Eden, NC 27288
Tel: 336-623-3168
Fax: 336-623-1171

Edgecombe Community College
Learning Resource Center
North Carolina and Local History Collection
2009 W. Wilson Street
Tarboro, NC 27886
Tel: 252-823-5166
Fax: 252-823-6817
http://www.edgecombe.cc.nc.us/lrc/lrcframe.htm

Edgecombe County Memorial Library
Allsbrook Room
909 North Main Street
Tarboro, NC 27886-3800
Tel: 252-823-1141
Fax: 252-641-7004
http://www.edgecombelibrary.org/

Elbert Ivey Memorial Library
420 Third Avenue, NW
Hickory, NC 28601
Tel: 704-322-2905
Fax: 704-322-3479

Forsyth County Library
North Carolina Room
660 West 5th Street
Winston Salem, NC 27101
Tel: 336-727-8100
　　　336-727-2152 (North Carolina Room)
http://www.co.forsyth.nc.us/library/

Gaston County Public Library
North Carolina Collection
1555 E. Garrison Blvd.
Gastonia, NC 28054
Tel: 704-868-2164
Fax: 704-853-0609
http://www.glrl.lib.nc.us/

Greensboro Historical Museum
130 Summit Avenue
Greensboro, NC 27401-3004
Tel: 336-373-2043
Fax: 336-373-2204

Greensboro Public Library
219 N Church Street
Greensboro, NC 27401
Future Location:
NW Corner of Church Street & YMCA Place (Fall, 1998)
Tel: 336-373-2471
  336-373-2159
http://www.greensboro.com/library/central.htm

High Point Public Library
901 N. Main Street
P.O. Box 2530
High Point, NC 27261-2530
Tel: 336-883-3660
Fax: 336-883-3636
TDD: 336-883-3675
http://www.hipopl.org/body_index.html

Iredell County Public Library
James Iredell History & Genealogy Room
135 E. Water Street
Statesville, NC 28677
Tel: 704-878-3093
http://www.iredell.lib.nc.us/

Lawrence Memorial Public Library
204 Dundee Street
Windsor, NC 27983-1210
Tel: 252-794-2244

Lincoln County Public Library
Charles R. Jonas Public LIbrary
306 West Main Street
Lincolnton, NC 28092-2616
Tel: 704-735-8044
http://www.glrl.lib.nc.us/

Macon County Public Library
108 Wayah Street
Franklin, NC 28734
Tel: 828-524-3600

Madison Public Library
Genealogy Room
140 E. Murphy Street
Madison, NC 27025
Tel: 336-548-6553
Fax: 336-548-2010
http://www.rcpl.org/library/madison.htm

May Memorial Library
342 South Spring Street
Burlington, NC 27215
Tel: 336-229-3588
Fax: 336-229-3592
http://ils.unc.edu/nclibs/centralnc/may.htm

Murphy Public Library
9 Blumenthal Street
Murphy, NC 28906
Tel: 828-837-2417
Fax: 828-837-6416
E-mail: bstiles@grove.net
http://www.grove.net/~nrl/mpl.htm

New Bern-Craven County Public Library
400 Johnson Street
New Bern, NC 28560
Tel: 252-638-7800
http://www.newbern.com/library/

New Hanover County Public Library
State & Local History Department
North Carolina Collection
201 Chestnut Street
Wilmington, NC 28401
Tel: 910-341-4394
http://www.co.new-hanover.nc.us/lib/libmain.htm

North Carolina State Land Records Management Division
111 Hillsborough Street
Raleigh, NC 27601
Tel: 919-807-2206
http://www.secretary.state.nc.us/land/

North Carolina, State Library of
Archives and History/State Library Building
109 East Jones Street
Raleigh, NC 27601-2807
Tel: 919-733-3270 (Reference)
  919-733-7222 (Gen. Services)
Fax: 919-33-5679
http://statelibrary.dcr.state.nc.us/ncslhome.htm

Olivia Raney Local History Library
4016 Carya Drive
Raleigh, NC 27610
Tel: 919-250-1196
E-mail: oliviaraney@co.wake.nc.us
http://web.co.wake.nc.us/library/locations/orl/
  branches/orl/orl.htm

Onslow County Public Library
58 Doris Avenue, E
Jacksonville, NC 28540
Tel: 910-455-7350
Fax: 910-455-1661
E-mail: Library@co.onslow.nc.us
http://www.co.onslow.nc.us/library/

Pack Public Library
67 Haywood Street
Asheville, NC 28801
Tel: 828-255-5203
Fax: 828-255-5213
TDD: 828-250-4709
http://www.librarybuncombe.org/pack.html

Person County Public Library
319 S. Main Street
Roxboro, NC 27573
Tel: 336-597-7881
http://www2.person.net/person/library/

Reidsville Library
North Carolina Collection
204 W. Morehead Street
Reidsville, NC 27320
Tel: 336-349-8476
Fax: 336-342-4824
http://www.reidsville.net/library/

Richard H. Thornton Memorial Library
210 Main Street
P.O. Box 339
Oxford, NC 27565
Tel: 919-693-1121
http://www.rootsweb.com/~ncgranvi/thornton.htm

Robersonville Public Library
119 S Main Street
Robersonville, NC 27871
Tel: 252-795-3591
http://www.bhmlib.org/bhm/Robersonville.htm

Robeson County Public Library
101 North Chestnut Street
P.O. Box 988
Lumberton, NC 28359-0988
Tel: 910-738-4859

Rowan Public Library
Edith M. Clark History Room
201 West Fisher Street
P.O. Box 4039
Salisbury, NC 28145-4039
Tel: 704-638-3001
Fax: 704-638-3013
http://www.lib.co.rowan.nc.us/

Sandhill Regional Library
412 E. Franklin Street
Rockingham, NC 28379
Tel: 910-997-3388

Scotland County Memorial Library
312 W. Church Street
Laurinburg, NC 28352-3720
Tel: 910-276-0563
E-mail: rbusko@ncsl.dcr.state.nc.us

Scottish Tartans Museum/Heritage Center
86 E Main Street
Franklin, NC 28734
Tel: 828-524-7472
http://www.scottishtartans.org/

Stanly County Public Library/Main Branch
133 E. Main Street
Albemarle, NC 28001-4939
Tel: 704-983-6118
http://www.stanlylib.org/

Thomas Hackney Braswell Memorial Library
344 Falls Road
Rocky Mount, NC 27801
Tel: 252-442-1951

Union County Public Library
316 East Windsor
Monroe, NC 28112-4842
Tel: 704-283-8184
http://www.union.lib.nc.us/

University of North Carolina/Asheville
D. Hiden Ramsey Library
Special Collections/Southern Highlands Research Center
One University Heights
Asheville, NC 28804
Tel: 828-251-6336
E-mail: hwykle@unca.edu
http://bullpup.lib.unca.edu/library/

University of North Carolina/Chapel Hill
Louis Round Wilson Library
North Carolina Collection/Southern History
    Collection/Manuscripts
CB# 3914
Chapel Hill, NC 27514
Tel: 919-962-1301
    919-962-1345 (Manuscripts Dept.)
Fax: 919-962-4452
E-mail: webteam@www.lib.unc.edu
http://www.lib.unc.edu/wilson/index.html
or
http://www.lib.unc.edu/ncc/ (NC Collection)
or
http://www.lib.unc.edu/mss/ (Manuscripts)

University of North Carolina/Charlotte
J. Murrey Atkins Library, 10th Floor
Special Collections
Charlotte, NC 28223
Tel: 704-547-2449
Fax: 704-547-3050
E-mail: speccoll@e-mail.uncc.edu
http://libweb.uncc.edu/archives/

Wayne Count Public Library
1001 E. Ashe Street
Goldsboro, NC 27530
Tel: 919-735-1824
http://www.wcpl.org/

Wilkes Public Library
215 Tenth Street
North Wilkesboro, NC 28659
Tel: 336-838-2818
http://www.arlibrary.org/wilkes.htm

Wilson County Public Library
249 W. Nash Street
P.O. Box 400
Wilson, NC 27894-0400
Tel: 252-237-5355

NEWSPAPER REPOSITORIES

North Carolina Newspaper Project
North Carolina Department of Cultural Resources
109 E. Jones Street
Raleigh, NC 27601-2807
Tel/Fax: 919-733-2570
E-mail: jwelch@hal.dcr.state.nc.us
http://statelibrary.dcr.state.nc.us/ncnp/counties.htm

VITAL RECORDS

North Carolina Vital Records
P.O. Box 27687
Raleigh, NC 27611
Tel: 919-733-3526

NORTH CAROLINA ON THE WEB

North Carolina Genealogical Societies
http://www.ncgenealogy.org/local.html

North Carolina GenWeb Project
http://www.goldenbranches.com/nc-state/

North Carolina State Archives—Genealogy Page
http://statelibrary.dcr.state.nc.us/iss/gr/genealog.htm

North Carolina, State Library of
http://statelibrary.dcr.state.nc.us/ncslhome.htm

Traveller Southern Families
http://misc.traveller.com/genealogy/

North Dakota

Archives, State & National

National Archives—Central Plains Region
2312 East Bannister Road
Kansas City, MO 64131
Tel: 816-926-6920
Fax: 816-926-6982
E-mail: kansascity.archives@nara.gov
http://www.nara.gov/regional/kansas.html

National Archives—Rocky Mountain Region
Bldg. 48, Denver Federal Center
West 6th Avenue and Kipling Street
Denver, CO 80225-0307
Mailing Address:
P.O. Box 25307
Denver, CO 80225-0307
Phone: 303-236-0817
Fax: 303-236-9297
E-mail: denver.archives@nara.gov
http://www.nara.gov/regional/denver.html

State Archives and Historical Research Library
State Historical Society of North Dakota
North Dakota Heritage Center
612 East Boulevard Avenue
Bismarck, ND 58505-0830
Tel: 701-328-2091
E-mail: archives@state.nd.us
http://www.state.nd.us/hist/sal.htm

Genealogical Societies

Bismarck-Mandan Historical & Genealogical Society
P.O. Box 485
Bismarck, ND 58502-0485
E-mail: DEarlSmith@prodigy.net
http://www.rootsweb.com/~ndbmhgs/

Bowman County Genealogical Society
206 9th Avenue
NW Bowman, ND 58623

Bottineau Genealogical Society
614 West Pine Circle
Bottineau, ND 58318

Germans From Russia Heritage Society
1125 W. Turnpike Avenue
Bismarck, ND 58501
Tel: 701-223-6167
E-mail: grhs@btinet.net
http://www.teleport.com/nonprofit/grhs/

Griggs County Genealogical Society
Griggs County Court House
P.O. Box 237
Cooperstown, ND 58425

James River Genealogical Society
651 4th Street, N.
Carrington, ND 58421
http://www.rootsweb.com/~ndjrgc/

McLean County Genealogical Society
P.O. Box 84
Garrison, ND 58540

Minnkota Genealogical Society
P.O. Box 126
Grand Forks, ND 56721
http://www.rootsweb.com/~minnkota/

Mouse River Loop Genealogical Society
P.O. Box 1391
Minot, ND 58702-1391
E-mail: marockem@donnybrook.ndak.net
http://www.mrlgs-nd.org/

Red River Valley Genealogical Society/Library
Manchester Building, Suite L-116
112 N. University Drive
P.O. Box 9284
Fargo, ND 58106
E-mail: rrvgs@rrnet.com
Tel: 701-239-4129
http://www.fargocity.com/~rrvgs/htmls/publications.htm

Richland County, ND and Wilkin County, MN Genealogy Guild
Leach Public Library
417 2nd Avenue N.
Wahpeton, ND 58075

South Western North Dakota Genealogical Society
HCR 01, Box 321
Regent, ND 58650

Williams County Genealogical Society
703 West 7th Street
Williston, ND 58801-4908

HISTORICAL SOCIETIES

Barnes County Historical Society, Inc.
315 Central Avenue N
P. O. Box 661
Valley City, ND 58072
Tel: 701-845-0966

Bismarck-Mandan Historical & Genealogical Society
P.O. Box 485
Bismarck, ND 58502-0485
E-mail: DEarlSmith@prodigy.net
http://www.rootsweb.com/~ndbmhgs/

Cass County Historical Society
Bonanzaville, USA
1351 West Main Avenue (Interstate 94, Exit 85)
West Fargo, ND 58078
Tel: 701-282-2822

Divide County Historical Society and Pioneer Village
West of City
Crosby, ND 58730
Tel: 701-965-6705

Dunn County Historical Society
153 Museum Trail
P.O. Box 86
Dunn Center, ND 58626
Tel: 701-548-8111

Grand Forks Country Historical Society
2405 Belmont Road
Grand Forks, ND 58201-7505
Tel: 701-775-2216
E-mail: gfchs@infi.net
http://home.infi.net/~gfchs/

North Dakota, State Historical Society of
North Dakota Heritage Center
612 East Boulevard Avenue
Bismarck, ND 58505-0830
Tel: 701-328-2666
Fax: 701-328-3710
E-mail: E-mail: histsoc@state.nd.us
http://www.state.nd.us/hist/

Richland County Historical Society
11 7th Avenue, N.
Wahpeton, ND 58075-3931
Tel: 701-642-3075

Steele County Historical Society
Steele Avenue
P.O. Box 144
Hope, ND 58046
Tel: 701-945-2394

Turtle Mountain Indian Historical Society
Chippewa Heritage Center
P.O. Box 257
Belcourt, ND 58316
Tel: 701-477-6140
http://chippewa.utma.com/index2.html

LDS FAMILY HISTORY CENTERS

For locations of Family History Centers in this state, see the Family History Center locator at FamilySearch.
http://www.familysearch.org/eng/Library/FHC/frameset_fhc.asp

ARCHIVES/LIBRARIES/MUSEUMS

Bureau of Land Management
5001 Southgate Drive
P.O. Box 36800
Billings, MT 59107
http://www.mt.blm.gov/

Carnegie Regional Library
49 West 7th Street
Grafton, ND 58237-1409
Tel: 701-352-2754

Divide County Library
204 1st Street, NE
Crosby, ND 58730
Tel: 701-965-6305

Fargo Public Library
102 North 3rd Street
Fargo, ND 58102
Tel: 701-241-1491/2
TDD: 701-241-8809
http://www.fargolibrary.org/

Fort Totten State Historic Site
Pioneer Daughters Museum
P.O. Box 224
Fort Totten, ND 58335
Tel: 701-766-4441
    800-233-8048 (Devils Lake Convention and Visitors
    Bureau)
E-mail: jmattson@state.nd.us
http://www.state.nd.us/hist/totten/totten.htm

Grand Forks Public Library
2110 Library Circle
Grand Forks, ND 58201-6324
Tel: 701-772-8116
http://www.grandforksgov.com/library/

Leach Public Library
417 2nd Avenue, N
Wahpeton, ND 58075-4488
Tel: 701-642-5732

Minot Public Library
516 Second Avenue, SW
Minot, ND 58701-3792
Tel: 701-852-1045
www.minotlibrary.org

North Dakota, State Historical Society of
North Dakota Heritage Center
612 East Boulevard Avenue
Bismarck, ND 58505-0830
Tel: 701-328-2666
Fax: 701-328-3710
E-mail: histsoc@state.nd.us
http://www.state.nd.us/hist/

North Dakota State Library
State Capitol Grounds
604 E. Boulevard
Bismarck, ND 58505-0800
Tel: 800-472-2104
      701-328-4622
Fax: 701-328-2040
http://ndsl.lib.state.nd.us/

North Dakota State University
Germans from Russia Heritage Society Collection
NDSU Library
1201 Albrecht Blvd.
P.O. Box 5599
Fargo, ND 58105-5599
Tel: 701-231-8416
Fax: 701-231-7138
E-mail: mmmiller@badlands.nodak.edu
http://www.lib.ndsu.nodak.edu/grhc/

North Dakota State University
Institute for Regional Studies
NDSU Library, Lower Level, Room 6
Corner of 12th Avenue and Albrecht Blvd.
P.O. Box 5599
Fargo, ND 58105-5599
Tel: 701-231-8914
Fax: 701-231-7138
E-mail: nulibarc@plains.nodak.edu
http://www.lib.ndsu.nodak.edu/

Red River Valley Genealogical Society/Library
Manchester Building, Suite L-116
112 N. University Drive
P.O. Box 9284
Fargo, ND 58106
E-mail: rrvgs@rrnet.com
Tel: 701-239-4129
http://www.fargocity.com/~rrvgs/htmls/publications.htm

University of North Dakota
Chester Fritz Library
Elwyn B. Robinson Department of Special Collections
North Dakota Room and Family History/Genealogy Room
P.O. Box 9000
Grand Forks, ND 58202-9000
Tel: 701-777-4625
Fax: 701-777-3319
http://www.und.nodak.edu/dept/library/
      Collections/spk.html

NEWSPAPER REPOSITORIES

North Dakota, State Historical Society of
North Dakota Heritage Center
612 East Boulevard Avenue
Bismarck, ND 58505-0830
Tel: 701-328-2666
Fax: 701-328-3710
E-mail: E-mail: histsoc@state.nd.us
http://www.state.nd.us/hist/

VITAL RECORDS

Division of Vital Records, Dept. of Health
600 East Boulevard Avenue
Bismarck, ND 58505
Tel: 701-328-2360
E-mail: histsoc@state.nd.us
http://www.state.nd.us/hist/infvit.htm

NORTH DAKOTA ON THE WEB

Dakota Territory during the Civil War
Roster of the 1st Dakota Cavalry
http://www.rootsweb.com/~usgenweb/sd/military/cw.htm

North Dakota GenWeb Project
http://www.rootsweb.com/~ndgenweb/

State Historical Society of North Dakota,
Materials Available for Genealogical Research
http://www.state.nd.us/hist/infgen.htm

OHIO

ARCHIVES, STATE & NATIONAL

National Archives—Great Lakes Region
7358 Pulaski Road
Chicago, IL 60629
Tel: 773-581-7816
Fax: 312-886-7883
E-mail: chicago.archives@nara.gov
http://www.nara.gov/regional/chicago.html

Ohio State Archives
Ohio State Historical Society
1982 Velma Avenue
Columbus, OH 43211-2497
Tel: 614-297-2510
Fax: 614-297-2411
E-mail: ohswww@winslo.ohio.gov
http://www.ohiohistory.org/resource/archlib/

GENEALOGICAL SOCIETIES

Adams County Genealogical Society
P.O. Box 231
West Union, OH 45693
http://www.rootsweb.com/~ohacgs/

**African-American Historical & Genealogical
Society/Cleveland (AAHGS)**
P.O. Box 200382
Cleveland, OH 44120

Allen County Genealogical Society (OGS)
620 Market Street
Lima, OH 45801-4665

Alliance Genealogical Society (OGS)
P.O. Box 3630
Alliance, OH 44601
http://www.rootsweb.com/~ohags/

Arizona Chapter (OGS)
P.O. Box 677
Gilbert, AZ 85234-0677

Ashland County Genealogical Society (OGS)
P.O. Box 681 Ashland, OH 44805-0681

**Ashtabula County Genealogical Society
(OGS Chapter #83)**
Geneva Public Library
860 Sherman Street
Geneva, Ohio 44041-9101
E-mail: acgs@interlaced.net
http://www.ashtabulagen.org/

Athens County Genealogical Society (OGS)
65 N. Court Street
Athens, Ohio 45701-2506
Tel: 740-592-2280
E-mail: achsm@frognet.net
http://frognet.net/~achsm/

Auglaize County Genealogical Society (OGS)
P.O. Box 2021
Wapakoneta, OH 45895-0521
E-mail: acgsogs@rootsweb.com
http://www.rootsweb.com/~ohaugogs/

Belmont County Genealogical Society (OGS)
P.O. Box 285
Barnesville, OH 43713-0285
http://www.rootsweb.com/~ohbelogs/

Brown County Genealogical Society (OGS)
P.O. Box 83
Georgetown, OH 45121-0083
http://www.rootsweb.com/~ohbrown/

Butler County Genealogical Society (OGS)
P.O. Box 2011
Middletown, OH 45044-2011
E-mail: maxiney106@aol.com
http://www.rootsweb.com/~ohbutler/

Carroll County Genealogical Society (OGS)
24 Second St. N.E.
P.O. Box 36
Carrollton, Ohio 44615
Tel: 330-627-9411
http://www.rootsweb.com/~ohcarcgs/

Champaign County Genealogical Society (OGS)
P.O. Box 680
Urbana, OH 43078-0680
http://www.rootsweb.com/~ohchampa/society.htm

Clark County Genealogical Society (OGS)
P.O. Box 2524
Springfield, OH 45501-2524
Tel: 937-324-0657, ext. 235
E-mail : FHulsizer@aol.com
http://www.rootsweb.com/~ohcccogs/

Clermont County Genealogical Society (OGS)
P.O. Box 394
Batavia, OH 45103-0394
http://www.rootsweb.com/~ohclecgs/

Clinton County Genealogical Society (OGS)
149 E. Locust Street
P.O. Box 529
Wilmington, OH 45177
Tel: 937-382-4684
Fax: 937-382-5634
E-mail: info@clintoncountyhistory.org
http://www.clintoncountyhistory.org/

Colorado Chapter (OGS)
P.O. Box 1106
Longmont, CO 80502-1106

Columbiana County Genealogical Society (OGS)
P.O. Box 861, Dept. I
Salem, OH 44460-0861
E-mail: jackpike@hotmail.com
   or gikirt@neo.rr.com
http://www.rootsweb.com/~ohcolumb/

Coshocton County Genealogical Society (OGS)
P.O. Box 128
Coshocton, OH 43812-0128
E-mail: C05H0CT0N@aol.com
http://www.coshoctongenealogy.com/

Crawford County Genealogical Society (OGS)
P.O. Box 92
Galion, OH 44833-0092
http://www.rootsweb.com/~ohccgs/

Cuyahoga Valley Genealogical Society (OGS)
P.O. Box 41414
Brecksville, OH 44141-0414

Cuyahoga West Genealogical Society (OGS)
P.O. Box 26196
Fairview Park, OH 44126-0196

Darke County Genealogical Society (OGS)
P.O. Box 908
Greenville, OH 45331-0908
http://www.grandlake.net/darkegen/society.htm

Daughters of the American Revolution, Ohio Society
E-mail: ohiodar@yahoo.com
http://blake.prohosting.com/ohiodar/

Defiance County Genealogical Society (OGS)
P.O. Box 7006
Defiance, OH 43512-7006
http://www.rootsweb.com/~ohdcgs/

Delaware County Genealogical Society (OGS)/Library
157 E. William Street
P.O. Box 317
Delaware, OH 43015-8126
Tel: 740-369-3831
E-mail: dchsdcgs@midohio.net
http://www.midohio.net/dchsdcgs/

East Cuyahoga Genealogical Society (OGS)
P.O. Box 24182
Lyndhurst, OH 44124
Tel: 216-382-7297
E-mail: MorgaBD@MSN.COM
http://community.cleveland.com/cc/eastcuyahoga

Erie County Genealogical Society (OGS)
P.O. Box 1301
Sandusky, OH 44871-1301
http://www.rootsweb.com/~oheccogs/

Fairfield County Genealogical Society (OGS)
P.O. Box 1470
Lancaster, OH 43130-0570
E-mail: grwheel@juno.com
http://www.fairfieldgenealogy.org/

Fayette County Genealogical Society (OGS)
P.O. Box 342
Washington Court House, OH 43160-0342

Franklin County Genealogical Society (OGS)
570 West Broad Street
P.O. Box 2506
Columbus, OH 43216-2406

Fulton County Genealogical Society (OGS)
305 Chestnut St.
Swanton, OH 43558
http://www.rootsweb.com/~ohfulton/

Gallia County Genealogical Society (OGS)
430 Second Avenue
P.O. Box 295
Gallipolis, OH 45631-0295
Tel: 740-446-7200
http://www.zoomnet.net/~histsoc/

Geauga County Genealogical Society (OGS)
110 East Park St.
Chardon, OH 44024-1213
Tel: 440-285-7601

Greater Cleveland Genealogical Society (OGS)
P.O. Box 40254
Cleveland, OH 44140-0254
http://www.rootsweb.com/~ohgcgg/

Greene County Genealogical Society (OGS)
P.O. Box 706
Xenia, OH 45385-0706
E-mail: Blin4012@aol.com
http://www.rootsweb.com/~ohgccogs/

Guernsey County Genealogical Society (OGS)
8583 Georgetown Road
P.O. Box 661
Cambridge, OH 43725-0661

Hamilton County Genealogical Society (OGS)
P.O. Box 15851
Cincinnati, OH 45215-0851
Tel: 513-956-7078
E-mail: egan@fuse.net
http://members.aol.com/ogshc/index.htm

Hancock County Genealogical Society (OGS)
P.O. Box 672
Findlay, OH 45839-0672
E-mail:hancock_ogs@hotmail.com
http://www.rootsweb.com/~ohhccogs/

Hardin County Genealogical Society (OGS)
P.O. Box 520
Kenton, OH 43326-0520
http://hardincogenealogycenter.homestead.com/

Harrison County Genealogical Society (OGS)/Library
45507 Unionvale Road
Cadiz, OH 43907-9723

Henry County Genealogical Society (OGS)
P.O. Box 231
Deshler, OH 43516

Hocking County Genealogical Society (OGS)
P.O. Box 115
Rockbridge, OH 43149-0115

Holmes County Genealogical Society (OGS)
P.O. Box 136
Millersburg, OH 44654-0136
http://www.rootsweb.com/~ohholmes/hcgs.htm

Hudson Chapter (OGS)
Hudson Library & Historical Society
22 Aurora Street, #G
Hudson, OH 44236-2947
E-mail: hgsg@bigfoot.com

Huron County Genealogical Society (OGS)
P.O. Box 923
Norwalk, OH 44857-0923
http://www.rootsweb.com/~ohhuron/

International Society for British Genealogy & Family History
P.O. Box 20425
Cleveland, OH 44120

Jackson County Genealogical Society (OGS)
P.O. Box 807
Jackson, OH 45640-0807
http://www.scioto.org/OGS/Jackson/

Jefferson County Genealogical Society (OGS)
P.O. Box 4712
Steubenville, OH 43952-8712
http://www.rootsweb.com/~ohjefogs/

Johnstown Genealogy Society
P.O. Box 345
Johnstown, OH 43031

Knox County Genealogical Society (OGS)
P.O. Box 1098
Mount Vernon, OH 43050-1098

KYOWVA Genealogical Society
232 Main Street, Guyandotte
P.O. Box 1254
Huntington, WV 25715
Tel: 304-525-4367
http://www.rootsweb.com/~wvkgs/

Lake County Genealogical Society (OGS)
Morley Library
184 Phelps
Painesville, OH 44077-3927
http://131.187.173.99/genealogy_lcgs.htm

Lawrence County Genealogical Society (OGS)
P.O. Box 945
Ironton, OH 45638-0955

Logan County Genealogical Society (OGS)
521 East Columbus Avenue
P.O. Box 36
Bellefontaine, OH 43311
Tel: 937-593-7811
http://www.rootsweb.com/~ohlogan/soc.html

Lorain County Genealogical Society (OGS)
P.O. Box 865
Elyria, OH 44036-0865

Lucas County Genealogical Society (OGS)
325 N. Michigan Street
Toledo, OH 43624-1614
http://www.utoledo.edu/~gried/lcogs.htm

Madison County Genealogical Society (OGS)
P.O. Box 102
London, OH 43140-0102

Mahoning County Genealogical Society (OGS)
P.O. Box 9333
Boardman, OH 44513

Marion Area Genealogical Society (OGS)
Heritage Hall
169 E. Church Street
P.O. Box 844
Marion, OH 43301-0844
http://www.genealogy.org/~smoore/marion/

Medina County Genealogical Society (OGS)
P.O. Box 804
Medina, OH 44258-0804

Meigs County Genealogical Society (OGS)
P.O. Box 346
Pomeroy, OH 45769
http://www.meigscohistoricalsociety.com/index.htm

Mercer County Genealogical Society (OGS)
P.O. Box 437
Celina, OH 45822-0437
http://www.calweb.com/~wally/mercer/society.htm

Miami County Historical and Genealogical Society (OGS)
P.O. Box 305
Troy, OH 45373-0305
http://www.tdn-net.com/mchgs/

Miami Valley Genealogical Society (OGS)
P.O. Box 1364
Dayton, OH 45401-1364
http://www.tdn-net.com/mchgs/

Monroe County Genealogical Society (OGS)
P.O. Box 641
Woodsfield, OH 43793-0641
http://www.rootsweb.com/~ohmccogs/

Montgomery County Genealogical Society (OGS)
P.O. Box 1584
Dayton, OH 45401-1584
http://members.aol.com/ogsmont/

Morgan County Genealogical Society (OGS)
P.O. Box 418
McConnelsville, OH 43756-0418
http://www.rootsweb.com/~ohmorgs/

Morrow County Genealogical Society (OGS)
P.O. Box 401
Mount Gilead, OH 43338-0401
E-mail: b.j.gameier@juno.com
http://www.rootsweb.com/~ohmorrow/

Muskingum County Genealogical Society (OGS)
P.O. Box 2427
Zanesville, OH 43702-2427
http://www.rootsweb.com/~ohmuskin/mccogs/

National Capital Buckeye Chapter (OGS)
P.O. Box 105
Bladensburg, MD 20710

Noble County Genealogical Society (OGS)
P.O. Box 174
Caldwell, OH 43724-0174

Northwestern Ohio Genealogical Society
P.O. Box 17066
Toledo, OH 43615

Ohio Genealogical Society (OGS)
713 South Main Street
Mansfield, OH 44906-0625
Tel: 419-756-7294
Fax: 419-756-8681
E-mail: ogs@ogs.org
http://www.ogs.org/

Ottawa County Genealogical Society (OGS)
P.O. Box 193
Port Clinton, OH 43452-0193
http://www.rootsweb.com/~ohoccgs/

Palatines to America, Ohio Chapter
611 East Weber Road
Columbus, OH 43211-1097
Tel: 614-267-4700

Parma/Cuyahoga Genealogical Society (OGS)
6428 Nelwood Road
Parma Heights, OH 44130-3211

Paulding County Genealogical Society (OGS)
205 E. Main Street
Paulding, OH 45879-1492

Perry County Genealogical Society (OGS)
P.O. Box 275
Junction City, OH 43748-0275

Pickaway County Chapter (OGS)/Library
Pickaway County Historical Society
P.O. Box 85
Circleville, OH 43113
E-mail: pkwyhist@bright.net

Pike County Genealogical Society (OGS)
P.O. Box 224
Waverly, OH 45690-0224
http://www.rootsweb.com/~ohpcgs/

Polish Genealogical Society of Greater Cleveland
906 College Avenue
P. O. Box 609117
Cleveland, Ohio 44109-9117
E-mail: edjmendyka@aol.com
http://feefhs.org/pol/frgpgsgc.html

Portage County Genealogical Society (OGS)
6549 North Chestnut Street
Ravenna, Ohio 44266
Tel: 330-296-3523
E-mail:history@config.com
http://www.history.portage.oh.us/

Preble County Genealogical Society (OGS)
Preble County District Library
450 S. Barron Street
Eaton, OH 45320-1705
Tel: 937-456-4250
Fax: 937-456-6092
E-mail: pcroom@infinet.com
http://www.pcdl.lib.oh.us/pcgs/

Putnam County Genealogical Society (OGS)
P.O. Box 403
Ottawa, OH 45875-0403

Richland County Genealogical Society (OGS)
P.O. Box 3823
Mansfield, OH 44907-0823
http://www.rootsweb.com/~ohrichgs/

Richland County/Shelby Genealogical Society (OGS)
P.O. Box 766
Shelby, OH 44875-0766

Ross County Genealogical Society (OGS)
444 Douglas Avenue
P.O. Box 6352
Chillicothe, OH 45601-6352

Sandusky County Kin Hunters (OGS)
1337 Hayes Avenue
Fremont, OH 43420

Scioto County Genealogical Society (OGS)
P.O. Box 812
Portsmouth, OH 45662-0812

Seneca County Genealogical Society (OGS)
P.O. Box 157
Tiffin, OH 44883-0157
http://www.senecasearchers.org/

South Cuyahoga Genealogical Society (OGS)
13305 Pearl Road
Strongsville, OH 44136-3403
E-mail: gmtjaden@aol.com
http://members.aol.com/gmtjaden/

Southern California Chapter (OGS)
P.O. Box 5057
Los Alamitos, CA 90721-5057

Southern Ohio Genealogical Society (OGS)
229 Crestview Drive
P.O. Box 414
Hillsboro, OH 45133

Southwest Butler County Genealogical Society
P. O. Box 243
Hamilton, Ohio 45012
http://www2.eos.net/dajend/swbcgs.html

Stark County Genealogical Society (OGS)
7300 Woodcrest, NE
North Canton, OH 44721-1949
E-mail: dms@netcom.com

Summit County Genealogical Society (OGS)
P.O. Box 2232
Akron, OH 44309-2232

Trumbull County Genealogical Society (OGS)
P.O. Box 309
Warren, OH 44482-0309
http://www.rootsweb.com/~ohtrumbu/info/trumogs.htm

Tuscarawas County Genealogical Society (OGS)
307 Center Street
P.O. Box 141
New Philadelphia, OH 44663-0141
http://web1.tusco.net/tuscgen/society.htm

Union County Genealogical Society (OGS)
P.O. Box 438
Marysville, OH 43040-0438
http://www.rootsweb.com/~ohuniogs/

Van Wert County Genealogical Society (OGS)
P.O. Box 485
Van Wert, OH 45891-0485
http://www.rootsweb.com/~ohvanwer/

Vinton County Genealogical Society (OGS)
P.O. Box 306
Hamden, OH 45634-0306
http://www.rootsweb.com/~ohvinton/ogschapt.htm

Warren County Genealogical Society (OGS)/
Research Center
300 E. Silver Street
Lebanon, OH 45036-1800
Tel: 513-933-1144

Washington County Genealogical Society (OGS)
P.O. Box 2174
Marietta, OH 45750-2174

Wayne County Genealogical Society (OGS)
P.O. Box 856
Wooster, OH 44691
http://www.rootsweb.com/~ohwayne/wcgs.htm

Wellington Genealogical Workshop
P.O. Box 224
Wellington, OH 44090

West Augusta Historical & Genealogical Society
1510 Prairie Drive
Belpre. OH 45714

Williams County Genealogical Society (OGS)
P.O. Box 293
Bryan, OH 43506-0293
http://www.geocities.com/wmscogen/

Wood County Genealogical Society (OGS)
P.O. Box 722
Bowling Green, OH 43402-0722

Wyandot County Genealogical Society (OGS)
P.O. Box 414
Upper Sandusky, OH 43351-0414
http://www.udata.com/users/hsbaker/tracers.htm

HISTORICAL SOCIETIES

Adjutant General's Department Library
2825 W. Dublin Granville Road
Columbus, OH 43235-2712
Tel: 614-889-7038

Allen County Historical Society
Allen County Museum &
Elizabeth M. MacDonell Memorial Library
620 West Market Street
Lima, OH 45801
Tel: 419-222-9426

American West Research Center and Historical Society, Inc.
8614 Euclid Avenue
Cleveland, OH 44106
Tel: 216-721-9594

Amherst Historical Society
Quigley Museum
710 Milan Avenue
Amherst, OH 44001-1311
Tel: 440-988-7255

Athens County Historical Society
65 N. Court Street
Athens, OH 45701-2506
Tel: 614-592-2280
http://www.seorf.ohiou.edu/~xx023/

Auglaize County Historical Society
223 S. Main Street
Saint Marys, OH 45885-2208
Tel: 419-394-7069

Bedford Historical Society
30 South Park Avenue
Bedford, OH 44146
Tel: 216-323-0796

Berea Historical Society
Mahler Museum & History Center
118 E. Bridge Street
P.O. Box 173
Berea, OH 44017
Tel: 440-243-2541
http://home.earthlink.net/~bereahistorical/

Black River Historical Society
309 W. 5th Street
Lorain, OH 44052
Tel: 440-245-2563
http://www.loraincityhistory.org/

Botkins Historical Society
P.O. Box 256
Botkins, OH 45306
E-mail: BotkinsHS@aol.com
http://members.aol.com/BotkinsHS/history/
    bhshome.html

Brecksville Historical Association
P.O. Box 41403
Brecksville, OH 44141-0403
Tel: 440-526-7165
E-mail: BHA@Brecksville.oh.us
http://www.brecksville.oh.us/community/bha/

Brooklyn Historical Society
P.O. Box 44422
Cleveland, OH 44144
Tel: 216-749-2804

Brookville Historical Society/Library
P.O. Box 82
Brookville, OH 45309-0082

Centerville Historical Society
89 W. Franklin Street
Dayton, OH 45459-4735
Tel: 937-433-0123

Chagrin Falls Historical Society
21 Walnut Street
Chagrin Falls, OH 44022-3125
Tel: 216-247-4695

Champaign County Historical Society
809 East Lawn Avenue
Urbana, OH 43078

Chesterland Historical Foundation
P.O. Box 513
Chesterland, OH 44026-0513
Tel: 440-729-1830
http://www.geaugalink.com/adultorg/chistfnd.html

Cincinnati Historical Society/Library & Collections
Cincinnati Museum Center at Union Terminal
1301 Western Avenue
Cincinnati, OH 45203
Tel: 513-287-7094
E-mail: library@cincymuseum.org
http://www.cincymuseum.org/default3.asp

Cleveland Police Historical Society/Museum
1300 Ontario Street
Cleveland, OH 44113
Tel: 216-623-5055
E-mail: museum@stratos.net
http://www.clevelandpolicemuseum.org/

Clinton County Historical Society
149 E. Locust Street
P.O. Box 529
Wilmington, OH 45177-0529
Tel: 937-382-4684
E-mail: info@clintoncountyhistory.org
http://www.clintoncountyhistory.org/

Conneaut Historical Railroad Society
363 Depot Street
Conneaut, OH 44030-2468
Tel: 440-599-7878

Delaware County Historical Society/Library
157 E. William Street
P.O. Box 317
Delaware, OH 43015
Tel: 614-369-3831
E-mail: dchsdcgs@midohio.net
http://www.midohio.net/dchsdcgs/

Dover Historical Society
325 E. Iron Avenue
Dover, OH 44622-2105
Tel: 330-343-7040

East Liverpool Historical Society
305 Walnut Street
East Liverpool, OH 43920-3427
Tel: 330-385-2550

East Palestine Area Historical Society
555 Bacon Avenue
East Palestine, OH 44413-1530

Enon Community Historical Society
45 Indian Mound Drive
P.O. Box 442
Enon, OH 45323
Tel: 937-864-7080
E-mail: echs@erinet.com
http://www.enonhistory.org/

Fayette County Historical Society/Museum
517 Columbus Avenue
Washington Court House, OH 43160-1427
Tel: 740-335-2953

Firelands Historical Society
4 Case Avenue
P.O. Box 572
Norwalk, OH 44857-0572
Tel: 419-668-6038
http://www.topinteractive.com/free/firelandshistorical/

Franklin Area Historical Society
Harding Museum
302 Park Avenue
Franklin, OH 45005
Tel: 937-746-8295

Gahanna Historical Society
101 S. High Street
Columbus, OH 43230
Tel: 614-475-3342

Gallia County Historical Society
P.O. Box 295
Gallipolis, OH 45631-0295

Gates Mills Historical Society/Museum
7580 Old Mill Road
P.O. Box 249
Gates Mills, OH 44040-0249
Tel: 440-423-4808
Fax: 440-423-1363
http://clio1.cuyahoga.lib.oh.us/home/locations/
GAT.html

Geauga County Historical Society
14653 E. Park Street
Burton, OH 44021
Tel: 216-834-1492
http://www.geaugalink.com/geaugahistory/ghistfrm.html

Germantown, Historical Society of
47 W. Center Street
P.O. Box 144
Germantown, OH 45327-1341
Tel: 937-855-7951
http://home.earthlink.net/~barbwachter/
    histsocgermantown/

Granger Historical Society/Library
1261 Granger Road
Medina, OH 44256-7337
Tel: 330-239-1523

Highland County Historical Society
151 East Main Street
Hillsboro, OH 45133

Indian Hill Historical Society
8100 Given Road
Cincinnati, OH 45243
Tel: 513-891-1873
E-mail: ihhist@one.net
http://www.indianhill.org/

Jefferson County Historical Association/Library
426 Franklin Avenue
P.O. Box 4268
Steubenville, OH 43952
Tel: 740-283-1133
E-mail: cgreen@clover.net
http://www.rootsweb.com/~ohjcha/

Knox County Historical Society
P.O. Box 522
Mount Vernon, OH 43050
Tel: 740-393-5247

Lake County Historical Society
8610 King Memorial Road
Mentor, OH 44060-7959
Tel: 216-255-8979
Fax: 440-255-8980
http://www.lakehistory.org/

Lake Erie Islands Historical Society
441 Catawba Avenue
P.O. Box 25
Put-in-Bay, Ohio 43456
Tel: 419-285-2804
E-mail: history@leihs.org
http://www.leihs.org/

Lakewood Historical Society
14710 Lake Avenue
Lakewood, OH 44107
Tel: 216-221-7343
E-mail: lkwdhist@bge.net
http://www.lkwdpl.org/histsoc/

Licking County Historical Society/Museum
6 N. 6th Street
Newark, OH 43055-4902
Tel: 614-345-4898

Logan County Historical Society
521 E. Columbus Avenue
Bellefontaine, OH 43311-2401
Tel: 937-593-7557

Loghurst Western Reserve Historical Society
3967 Boardman Canfield Road
Canfield, OH 44406-9030
Tel: 330-533-4330

Lorain County Historical Society
509 Washington Avenue
Elyria, OH 44035
Tel: 440-322-3341
Fax: 440-322-2817
E-mail: thehickories@alltel.net
http://www.alltel.net/~thehickories/

Loveland Historical Society
201 E. Kemper Road
Loveland, OH 45140
Tel: 513-683-5692

Marion County Historical Society
Heritage Hall
169 E. Church Street
P.O. Box 844
Marion, OH 43301-0844
Tel: 740-387-4255
http://home1.gte.net/mchist/

Mayfield Township Historical Society
606 Som Center Road
Cleveland, OH 44143-2311
Tel: 440-461-0055

Miami County Historical and Genealogical Society (OGS)
P.O. Box 305
Troy, OH 45373-0305
http://www.tdn-net.com/mchgs/

Middlefield Historical Society
14979 S. State Street
P.O. Box 1100
Middlefield, OH 44062
Tel: 440-632-0400
http://www.geaugalink.com/mfldhist/

Middletown African-American Historical Society
4521 Poppy Drive
Middletown, OH 45044-5228
Tel: 513-424-1791

Middletown Historical Society/Canal Museum
1605 N. Verity Parkway
Middletown, OH 45042
Tel: 513-422-7161

Milford Area Historical Society
906 Main Street
Milford, OH 45150-1767
Tel: 513-248-0324

Mohican Historical Society/Museum
203 E. Main Street
Loudonville, OH 44842-1214
Tel: 419-994-4050

Montgomery County Historical Society
224 N Saint Clair Street
Dayton, OH 45402
Tel: 937-228-6271

Niles Historical Society
503 Brown Street
Niles, OH 44446
Tel: 330-544-2143

North Canton Heritage Society, Inc.
200 Charlotte Street
NW, Canton, OH 44720
Tel: 330-494-4791
http://www.northcantonheritage.org/

Oakwood Historical Society
1947 Far Hills Avenue
Dayton, OH 45419-2536
Tel: 937-299-3793
http://www.mvcc.net/Oakwood/ohistsoc.htm

Ohio Division of Veterans' Affairs
30 E. Broad Street, Room 1825
Columbus, OH 43266-0422
Tel: 614-466-5453

Ohio Historical Society
1982 Velma Avenue
Columbus, OH 43211-2497
Tel: 614-297-2300
    614-297-2510 (Archives/Library)
Fax: 614-297-2411
http://www.ohiohistory.org/

Perry County Historical Society
105 S. Columbus Street
P.O. Box 746
Somerset, OH 43783-0746
Tel: 740-743-2591
E-mail: pchs@netpluscom.com
http://www.netpluscom.com/~pchs/

Pickaway County Historical Society
P.O. Box 85
Circleville, OH 43113
E-mail: pkwyhist@bright.net
http://www.rootsweb.com/~ohpickaw/gen.html

Muskingum County, Pioneer and Historical Society of
115 Jefferson Street
Zanesville, OH 43701
Tel: 740-454-9500

Plymouth Area Historical Society
7 E. Main Street
Plymouth, OH 44865-1201
Tel: 419-687-5400

Portage County Historical Society
6549 N. Chestnut Street
Ravenna, OH 44266
Tel: 330-296-3523
E-mail: history@config.com
http://www.history.portage.oh.us/

Reynoldsburg Truro Historical Society
1399 Lancaster Avenue
Columbus, OH 43207
Tel: 614-863-6969

Salem Historical Society/Museum
208 S. Broadway
Salem, OH 44460
Tel: 216-337-8514

Sandusky County Historical Society
Rutherford B. Hayes Library
1337 Hayes Avenue
Fremont, OH 43420
Tel: 419-332 2081
Fax: 419-332-4952

Shelby County Historical Society
P.O. Box 376
Sidney, OH 45365-0376
Tel: 937-498-1653
E-mail: Info@ShelbyCountyHistory.org
http://www.shelbycountyhistory.org/

Stark County Historical Society
749 Hazlett Avenue, NW
Canton, OH 44708

Summit County Historical Society
550 Copley Road
Akron, OH 44320
Tel: 330-535-1120
E-mail: invision@interramp.com
http://www.neo.rr.com/
      Summit_County_ Historical_Society/

Twinsburg Historical Society
P.O. Box 7
Twinsburg, OH 44087
Tel: 330-487-5565
http://www.twinsburg.com/historicalsociety/

**Union Township Historical Museum/
Quaker Heritage Center**
47 N. Miami Street
West Milton, OH 45383-1831
Tel: 937-698-3820

Warren County Historical Society/Library & Museum
105 S. Broadway
P.O. Box 223
Lebanon, OH 45036-0223
Tel: 513-932-1817

Wayne County Historical Society
546 East Bowman Street
Wooster, OH 44691
Tel: 330-264-8856
Fax: 330-264-8823
http://www.waynehistorical.org/
E-mail: host@waynehistorical.org

Wellsville Historical Society
1003 Riverside Avenue
Wellsville, OH 43968
Tel: 330-532-1018

West Carrollton Historical Society
323 East Central Avenue
Dayton, OH 45449
Tel: 937-859-5912

Western Lake Erie Historical Society
2127 Evansdale Avenue
Toledo, OH 43607
Tel: 419-473-9534

Western Reserve Historical Society/Library
10825 East Boulevard
Cleveland, OH 44106
Tel: 216-721-5722
http://www.wrhs.org/sites/library.htm

Wood County Historical Society
13660 County Home Road
Bowling Green, OH 43402
Tel: 419-352-0967
Fax: 419-352-6220
E-mail: wchisctr@wcnet.org
http://www.woodcountyhistory.org/

Worthington Historical Society
50 W. New England Avenue
Columbus, OH 43085-3536
Tel: 614-885-1247
http://www.worthington.org/History/js2.htm

Wyandot County Historical Society
130 S. 7th Street
P.O. Box 372
Upper Sandusky, OH 43351
Tel: 419-294-3857
E-mail: wchs@udata.com
http://wyandotonline.com/wchs/

LDS FAMILY HISTORY CENTERS

For locations of Family History Centers in this state, see the Family History Center locator at FamilySearch.
http://www.familysearch.org/eng/Library/FHC/
frameset_fhc.asp

ARCHIVES/LIBRARIES/MUSEUMS

Akron/Summit County Public Library
1040 E. Tallmadge Avenue
Akron, OH 44310
Tel: 330-643-9000
Fax: 330-643-9033
E-mail: ascpl@acorn.net
http://ascpl.lib.oh.us/

American Jewish Archives
Hebrew Union College/Jewish Institute of Religion
3101 Clifton Avenue
Cincinnati, OH 45220-2488
Tel: 513-221-1875
Fax: 513-221-7812
http://www.huc.edu/

American West Research Center and Historical Society, Inc.
8614 Euclid Avenue
Cleveland, OH 44106
Tel: 216-721-9594

Amos Memorial Public Library
230 East North Street
Sidney, OH 45365-2733
Tel: 937-492-8354
Fax: 937-492-9229

Arms Family Museum of Local History
648 Wick Avenue
Youngstown, OH 44502-1215
Tel: 330-743-2589
Fax: 330-743-7210
E-mail: mvhs@mahoninghistory.org
        archives@mahoninghistory.org (Archives)
http://www.mahoninghistory.org/armhome.stm

Bellevue Public Library
224 E. Main Street
Bellevue, OH 44811
Tel: 419-483-4769
Fax: 419-483-0158
http://www.bellevue.lib.oh.us/

Bluffton/Richland Public Library
145 S. Main Street
Bluffton, OH 45817
Tel: 419-358-5016
Fax: 419-358-9653
E-mail: schirmsh@oplin.lib.oh.us
http://library.norweld.lib.oh.us/Bluffton/

Bowling Green State University
Jerome Library
Center for Archival Collections
Bowling Green, OH 43403-0175
Tel: 419-372-2411
http://www.bgsu.edu/colleges/library/cac/cac.html

Brookville Historical Society/Library
P.O. Box 82
Brookville, OH 45309-0082

Camp Dennison Civil War Museum (Scheduled to open Spring, 1998)
SR 126
Camp Dennison, OH 45111
For more information:
Mrs. Charles R. Wright
Museum Chairwoman, DAR
1779 Cottontail Drive
Milford, OH 45150
Tel: 513-575-9284
http://www.intcom.net/~tomt/dennison/dennison.html

Carnegie Public Library
127 South North Street
Washington Court House, OH 43160-2283
Tel: 740-335-2540
Fax: 740-335-8409
http://www.washington-ch.lib.oh.us/

Chagrin Falls Branch/Cuyahoga County Public Library
100 E. Orange Street
Chagrin Falls, OH 44022-2799
Tel: 440-247-3556
Fax: 440-247-0179
http://clio1.cuyahoga.lib.oh.us/home/locations/
        CHF.html

Champaign County Library
1060 Scioto Street
Urbana, OH 43078
Tel: 937-653-3811
Fax: 937-653-5679
http://www.champaign.lib.oh.us/

Chillicothe/Ross County Public Library
140-146 South Paint Street
Chillicothe, OH 45601-3214
Tel: 740-702-4145
Fax: 740-702-4156
E-mail: chillcot@oplin.lib.oh.us
http://www.chillicothe.lib.oh.us/

Cincinnati/Hamilton County, Public Library of
Library Square
800 Vine Street
Cincinnati, OH 45202-2071
Tel: 513-369-6900
        513-369-6905 (History and Genealogy)
Fax: 513-369-6067
http://www.cincinnatilibrary.org/

Cincinnati Historical Society/Library & Collections
Cincinnati Museum Center at Union Terminal
1301 Western Avenue
Cincinnati, OH 45203
Tel: 513-287-7094
E-mail: library@cincymuseum.org
http://www.cincymuseum.org/default3.asp

Clark County Public Library
201 South Fountain Avenue
P.O. Box 1080
Springfield, OH 45501-1080
Tel: 937-328-6901
Fax: 934-328-6908
http://www.ccpl.lib.oh.us/

Cleveland Police Historical Society/Museum
1300 Ontario Street
Cleveland, OH 44113
Tel: 216-623-5055
E-mail: museum@stratos.net
http://www.clevelandpolicemuseum.org/

Cleveland Public Library
325 Superior Avenue, N.E.
Cleveland, OH 44114-1271
Tel: 216-623-2800
Fax: 216-623-7015
E-mail: info@library.cpl.org
http://www.cpl.org/

Columbus/Franklin County, Public Library of
96 South Grant Avenue
Columbus, OH 43215
Tel: 614-645-2275
Fax: 614-645-2051
http://www.cml.lib.oh.us/

Croatian Heritage Museum & Library
34900 Lake Shore Blvd.
Willoughby, OH 44095-2043
Tel: 440-946-2044

Dayton/Montgomery County Public Library
215 E. Third Street
Dayton, OH 45402-2103
Tel: 937-227-9531
Fax: 937-227-9539
http://www.dayton.lib.oh.us/

Delaware County Genealogical Society (OGS)/Library
157 E. William Street
P.O. Box 317
Delaware, OH 43015-8126
Tel: 740-369-3831
E-mail: dchsdcgs@midohio.net
http://www.midohio.net/dchsdcgs/

Fairfield County District Library
219 N. Broad Street
Lancaster, OH 43130
Tel: 614-653-2745
http://www.fairfield.lib.oh.us/

Fairview Park Regional Library/Cuyahoga County Public Library
21255 Lorain Road
Cleveland, OH 44126
Tel: 440-333-4700
Fax: 440-333-4887
TDD: 440-333-4898
http://clio1.cuyahoga.lib.oh.us/home/locations/
    FPR.html

Fayette County Historical Society/Museum
517 Columbus Avenue
Washington Court House, OH 43160-1427
Tel: 740-335-2953

Firelands Historical Society Library
4 Case Avenue
P.O. Box 572
Norwalk, OH 44857-0572
Tel: 419-668-6038
http://www.topinteractive.com/free/firelandshistorical/

Garst Museum
205 N. Broadway
Greenville, OH 45331
Tel: 937-548-5250

Gates Mills Branch/Cuyahoga County Public Library and Gates Mills Historical Society/Museum
7580 Old Mill Road
P.O. Box 249
Gates Mills, OH 44040-0249
Tel: 440-423-4808
Fax: 440-423-1363
http://clio1.cuyahoga.lib.oh.us/home/locations/
    GAT.html

Geauga West Library
13455 Chillicothe Road
Chesterland, OH 44026
Tel: 440-729-4250
Fax: 440-729-7517
http://www.geauga.lib.oh.us/GCPL/newlibinfo/
    infogw.html

Geneva Public Library
860 Sherman Street
Geneva, OH 44041
Phone: 440-466-4521
Fax: 440-466-0162
http://www.ashtabula.lib.oh.us/geneva.htm

Grand Rapids Branch/Weston Public Library
17620 Bridge Street
P.O. Box 245
Grand Rapids, OH 43522
Tel: 419-832-5231
Fax: 419-832-8104
E-mail: dfroman@wcnet.org
http://library.norweld.lib.oh.us/weston/br.htm

Granville Public Library
217 E. Broadway
Granville, OH 43023-1398
Tel: 740-587-0196
Fax: 740-587-0197
http://www.granvillelibrary.org/

Greenville Public Library
Genealogy Department
520 Sycamore Street
Greenville, OH 45331-1438
Tel: 937-548-3915
Fax: 937-548-3837
E-mail: info@greenvillepublib.org
http://www.greenvillepublib.org/

Guernsey County District Public Library
800 Steubenville Avenue
Cambridge, OH 43725-2354
Tel: 740-432-5946
Fax: 740-432-7142
E-mail: hutcheca@oplin.lib.oh.us
http://www.gcdpl.lib.oh.us/

Harrison County Genealogical Society (OGS)/Library
45507 Unionvale Road
Cadiz, OH 43907-9723

Henderson Memorial Library Association
54 East Jefferson Street
Jefferson, OH 44047
Tel: 440-576-3761
Fax: 440-576-8402
http://www.henderson.lib.oh.us/

Hudson Library and Historical Society
22 Aurora Street
Hudson, OH 44236
Tel: 330-653-6658
http://www.hudsonlibrary.org/

Huron County Historical Library
Administration Building (Basement)
180 Milan Avenue
Norwalk, OH 44857
Tel: 419-668-8219
Fax: 419-663-4233

Huron Historical & Cultural Center
401 Williams Street
Huron, OH 44839-1642
Tel: 419-433-4660

Jefferson County Historical Association/Library
426 Franklin Avenue
P.O. Box 4268
Steubenville, OH 43952-4268
Tel: 740-283-1133
http://www.rootsweb.com/~ohjcha/

Kaubisch Library
205 Perry Street
Fostoria, OH 44830
Tel: 419-435-2813
Fax: 419-435-5350
E-mail: norrisdo@oplin.lib.oh.us
http://library.norweld.lib.oh.us/Kaubisch/

Lakewood Public Library
15425 Detroit Avenue
Lakewood, OH 44107-3890
Tel: 216-226-8275
Fax: 216-521-4327
E-mail: lpl@lkwdpl.org
http://www.lkwdpl.org/

Lorain Public Library
351 6th Street
Lorain, OH 44052-1770
Tel: 440-244-1192
Fax: 440-244-1733
E-mail: lor55@lorain.lib.oh.us

Mansfield/Richland County Public Library
John Sherman Room
43 West Third Street
Mansfield, OH 44902-1295
Tel: 419-521-3100
Fax: 419-525-4750
http://www.mrcpl.lib.oh.us/

McComb Public Library
Local History and Genealogy Dept.
113 S. Todd Street
P.O. Box 637
McComb, OH 45858
Tel: 419-293-2425
E-mail: grosede@oplin.lib.oh.us
http://library.norweld.lib.oh.us/McComb/

McKinley Museum/Ramsayer Research Library
800 McKinley Monument Drive, NW
Canton, OH 44708
Tel: 330-455-7043
http://www.mckinleymuseum.org/

Medina Branch/Medina County District Library
Franklin Sylvester Genealogy Room
210 S. Broadway
Medina, OH 44256
Tel: 330-725-0588
Fax: 330-725-2053
http://www.medina.lib.oh.us/

Middletown Public Library
125 S. Broad Street
Middletown, OH 45042
Tel: 513-424-1251
Fax: 513-424-6585
http://www.trentonlibrary.org/

Milan/Berlin Township Public Library
19 East Church Street
P.O. Box 1550
Milan, OH 44846
Tel: 419-499-4117
Fax: 419-499-4697
E-mail: steve.musgrave@milan.berlin.lib.oh.us

Minerva Public Library
677 Lynnwood Drive
Minerva, OH 44657
Tel: 330-868-4101
Fax: 330-868-4267
E-mail: minerva@oplin.lib.oh.us
http://www.minerva.lib.oh.us/

Monroeville Public Library
34 Monroe Street
Monroeville, OH 44847-9722
Tel: 419-465-2035

Morley Library
184 Phelps Street
Painesville, OH 44077
Tel: 440-352-3383
Fax: 440-352-1069
http://www.morleylibrary.org/

Mount Gilead Public Library
41 E High Street
Mount Gilead, OH 43338
Tel: 419-947-5866
Fax: 419-947-9252

New London Public Library
67 S. Main Street
New London, OH 44851
Tel: 419-929-3981
Fax: 419-929-0007
EMai: nwlondon@oplin.lib.oh.us
http://www.newlondonohio.com/library.htm

Norwalk Public Library
46 W. Main Street
Norwalk, OH 44857
Tel: 419-668-6063
Fax: 419-663-2190
E-mail: norwalk@oplin.blib.oh.us
http://library.norweld.lib.oh.us/norwalk/

Ohio Genealogical Society (OGS)
713 South Main Street
Mansfield, OH 44906-0625
Tel: 419-756-7294
Fax: 419-756-8681
E-mail: ogs@ogs.org
http://www.ogs.org/

Ohio Historical Society
1982 Velma Avenue
Columbus, OH 43211-2497
Tel: 614-297-2300
        614-297-2510 (Archives/Library)
Fax: 614-297-2411
http://www.ohiohistory.org/

Ohio Society of Military History Museum
316 Lincoln Way, E.
Massillon, OH 44646
Tel: 330-832-5553

Ohio State Land Office, Auditor
88 East Broad Street
Columbus, OH 43266-0040

Ohio State Library
274 E 1st Avenue
Columbus, OH 43201
Tel: 614-644-7061
Fax: 614-466-3584
http://winslo.state.oh.us/

Ohio University
Vernon R. Alden Library
Park Place
Athens, OH 45701-2978
Tel: 740-593-2699
Fax: 740-593-0138
http://www.library.ohiou.edu/

Paulding County Carnegie Library
Genealogy Department
205 South Main Street
Paulding, OH 45879
Tel: 419-399-2032
Fax: 419-399-2114
http://pauldingcountylibrary.org/

Pemberville Public Library
375 East Front Street
Pemberville, OH 43450
Tel: 419-287-4012
Fax: 419-287-4620
E-mail: pemlib@wcnet.org
http://www.pembervillelibrary.org/

Pike Heritage Museum
110 S. Market Street
Waverly, OH 45690-1317
Tel: 740-947-5281

Portsmouth Public Library
Local History Department
1220 Gallia Street
Portsmouth, OH 45662
Tel: 740-354-5304
Fax: 740-353-1249
http://www.portsmouth.lib.oh.us/

Preble County District Library
Preble County Room
450 S. Barron Street
Eaton, OH 45320-1705
Tel: 937-456-4250
Fax: 937-456-6092
E-mail: library@infinet.com
http://www.pcdl.lib.oh.us/

Reed Memorial Library
167 E. Main Street
Ravenna, OH 44266-3197
Tel: 330-296-2827
Fax: 330-296-3780

Rodman Public Library
Alliance Room
215 E. Broadway
Alliance, OH 44601
Tel: 330-821-2665
Fax: 330-821-5053
http://www.rodmanlibrary.com/

Rutherford B. Hayes Presidential Center
Library and Archives
Spiegel Grove
Fremont, OH 43420
Tel: 419-332-2081
Fax: 419-332-4952
E-mail: hayeslib@rbhayes.org
http://www.rbhayes.org/

Saint Paris Library
127 East Main Street
P.O. Box 740
St. Paris, OH 43072
Tel: 937-663-4349
Fax: 937-663-0297

Salem Public Library
821 E. State Street
Salem, OH 44460-2298
Tel: 330-332-0042
Fax: 330-332-4488
E-mail: library@salemohio.com
http://www.salemohio.com/library/

Schiappa Branch Library
4141 Mall Drive
Steubenville, OH 43952
Tel: 740-264-6166
Fax: 740-264-7397

Stark County District Library
715 Market Avenue, North
Canton, OH 44702-1080
Tel: 330-452-0665
Fax: 330-452-0403
E-mail: scdl@oplin.lib.oh.us
http://www.stark.lib.oh.us/

Toledo/Lucas County Public Library
Local History & Genealogy Department
325 Michigan Street
Toledo, OH 43624-1628
Tel: 419-259-5207
Fax: 419-255-1334
TTY: 419-259-5252
http://www.toledolibrary.org/

Ukrainian Museum/Archives
1202 Kenilworth Avenue
Cleveland, OH 44113-4417
Tel: 216-781-4329
http://www.umacleveland.org/

University of Akron Libraries
Polsky Building
Archival Services
225 S. Main, Room LL10
Akron, OH 44325-1702
Tel: 330-972-7670
Fax: 330-972-6170
E-mail: jvmiller@uakron.edu
http://www.uakron.edu/libraries/

University of Cincinnati
Archives and Rare Books Department
Cincinnati, OH 45221-0113
Tel: 513-556-1959
Fax: 513-556-2113
http://www.archives.uc.edu/

Warren County Genealogical Society (OGS)/Research Center
300 E. Silver Street
Lebanon, OH 45036-1800
Tel: 513-933-1144

Warren/Trumbull County Public Library
Local History & Genealogy Center
444 Mahoning Avenue
Warren, OH 44483
Tel: 330-399-8807 ext. 120
Fax: 330-395-3988
TDD: 330-393-0784
http://www.wtcpl.lib.oh.us/lh&g.htm

Washington County Public Library
615 Fifth Street
Marietta, OH 45750-1973
Tel: 740-373-1057
Fax: 740-373-2860
TDD: 740-374-0022
E-mail: joeller@state.lib.oh.us
http://www.wcplib.lib.oh.us/

Way Public Library
Local History Room
101 E. Indiana Avenue
Perrysburg, OH 43551
Tel/TDD: 419-874-3135
Fax: 419-874-6129
E-mail: kelleyna@oplin.lib.oh.us
http://www.way.lib.oh.us/

Wayne County Public Library
304 North Market Street
Wooster, OH 44691
Tel: 330-262-0916
Fax: 330-262-7313
http://www.wayne.lib.oh.us/newweb/

Wayne Public Library
Local History Room
137 E. Main Street
Wayne, OH 43466
Tel: 419-288-2708
Fax: 419-288-3766
E-mail: barnhate@oplin.lib.oh.us
http://library.norweld.lib.oh.us/Wayne/

Western Reserve Historical Society
Case Western Reserve University
History Library
10825 East Boulevard
Cleveland, OH 44106
Tel: 216-721-5722
http://www.wrhs.org/

Westerville Public Library
Ohio Room
126 S. State Street
Westerville, OH 43081-2095
Tel: 614-882-7277
http://www.wpl.lib.oh.us/

Wood County District Public Library
Local History Department
251 N. Main Street
Bowling Green, OH 43402
Tel: 419-352-5104
Fax: 419-354-0405
E-mail: WCDPL@wcnet.org
http://wcdpl.lib.oh.us/

Wright State University
Paul Laurence Dunbar Library, 4th Floor
Archives and Special Collections
Dayton, OH 45435-0001
Tel: 937-775-2092
E-mail: archive@library.wright.edu
http://www.libraries.wright.edu/

Xenia Community Library
Greene County Room, 2nd Floor
76 East Market Street
Xenia, OH 45385
Tel: 937-376-2995 ext. 221

Youngstown Historical Center of Industry and Labor
Archives and Library
151 W. Wood Street
P.O. Box 533
Youngstown, OH 44501-0533
Tel: 330-743-5934
E-mail: yhcillibrary@cisnet.com
http://www.ohiohistory.org/resource/archlib/

Youngstown/Mahoning County, Public Library of
305 Wick Avenue
Youngstown, OH 44503-1079
Tel: 330-744-8636
Fax: 330-744-3355
TDD: 330-744-7211
http://www.libraryvisit.org/

NEWSPAPER REPOSITORIES

Bowling Green State University
Jerome Library
Center for Archival Collections
Bowling Green, OH 43403-0175
Tel: 419-372-2411
http://www.bgsu.edu/colleges/library/cac/cac.html

Ohio Historical Society
1982 Velma Avenue
Columbus, OH 43211-2497
Tel: 614-297-2300
      614-297-2510 (Archives/Library)
Fax: 614-297-2411
http://www.ohiohistory.org/

Ohio University
Vernon R. Alden Library
Park Place
Athens, OH 45701-2978
Tel: 740-593-2699
Fax: 740-593-0138
http://www.library.ohiou.edu/

VITAL RECORDS

Ohio Department of Health
Division of Vital Statistics
P.O. Box 15098
Columbus, OH 43216-0118
Tel: 614-466-2531
E-mail: VitalStat@gw.odh.state.oh.us
http://www.odh.state.oh.us/

Ohio Historical Society
1982 Velma Avenue
Columbus, OH 43211-2497
Tel: 614-297-2300
    614-297-2510 (Archives/Library)
Fax: 614-297-2411
http://www.ohiohistory.org/

OHIO ON THE WEB

**African Americans in Southeastern Ohio
(AFROAMSEO)**
http://www.seorf.ohiou.edu/~xx057

Camp Dennison Civil War Museum
http://www.intcom.net/~tomt/dennison/dennison.html

Darke County Ohio Genealogical Researchers
http://php.ucs.indiana.edu/~jetorres/dco.html

Miami Valley Genealogical Index
http://www.pcdl.lib.oh.us/miami/miami.htm

Ohio Historical Society—Home Page
http://www.ohiohistory.org/

Ohio Historical Society
Ohio Online Death Certificate Index 1913-1937
http://www.ohiohistory.org/dindex/

Ohio in the Civil War
http://www.ohiocivilwar.com/

Ohio River Valley Families
http://orvf.com/

OKLAHOMA

ARCHIVES, STATE & NATIONAL

National Archives—Southwest Region
501 West Felix Street
Building 1, Dock 1
P.O. Box 6216
Fort Worth, TX 76115-0216
Tel: 817-334-5515
Fax: 817-334-5511
E-mail: ftworth.archives@nara.gov
http://www.nara.gov/regional/ftworth.html

Oklahoma State Archives
Allen Wright Memorial Library
200 NE 18th Street
Oklahoma City, OK 73105-3298
Tel: (405) 522-3579
Fax: (405) 522-3583
http://www.odl.state.ok.us/oar/index.htm

GENEALOGICAL SOCIETIES

Atoka County Genealogical Society
P.O. Box 245
Atoka 74525

Bartlesville Genealogical Society
c/o Bartlesville Public Library
600 S. Johnstone
Bartlesville, OK 74003
Tel: 918-337-5333

Beaver River Genealogical & Historical Society
Route 1, Box 79
Hooker, OK 73945

Broken Arrow Genealogical Society
P.O. Box 1244
Broken Arrow, OK 74013
http://www.city.broken-arrow.ok.us/gensoc.htm

Caddo County Genealogical Society
Anadarko Community Library
215 West Broadway
Anadarko, OK 73005-2841
Tel: 405-247-7351
Mail:
Route 1, Box 400
Fort Cobb, OK 73038
E-mail: ccgs73005@yahoo.com
http://www.rootsweb.com/~okcadcgs/

Canadian County Genealogical Society
P.O. Box 866
El Reno, OK 73036
Tel: 405-262-2409
E-mail: CANCOGEN@AOL.com
http://www.rootsweb.com/~okccgs/

Choctaw County Genealogical Society
P.O. Box 1056
Hugo, OK 74743-1056
Tel: 580-873-2301
Fax: 580-326-5556
http://www2.1starnet.com/choctaw/hsge_00.html

Cleveland County Genealogical Society
205 West Main Street
P.O. Box 6176
Norman, OK 73069
Tel: 405-329-9180
405-329-4481 (Library)
E-mail: ccgs@telepath.com
http://www.telepath.com/ccgs/

Coal County Historical & Genealogical Society
115 W Ohio Avenue
P. O. Box 436
Coalgate, OK 74538
Tel: 580-927-3103
http://www.rootsweb.com/~okcoalgs/

Craig County Genealogical Society
P.O. Box 484
Uinita, OK 74301-0484

Cushing Genealogical Society
Cushing Literacy Council
215 North Steele
P.O. Box 551
Cushing, OK 74023-1609
Tel: 918-225-4188
http://www.rootsweb.com/~okcgs/

Delaware County Genealogical Society
c/o Grove Public Library
206 South Elk
Grove, OK 74344
Tel: 918-786-2945
E-mail: dcgsinc@hotmail.com
http://www.rootsweb.com/~okdelawa/dcgs.htm

Federation of Oklahoma Genealogical Societies
P.O. Box 26151
Oklahoma City, OK 73126-0151

First Families of the Twin Territories
Oklahoma Genealogical Society
P.O. Box 12986
Oklahoma City, OK 73157
http://www.rootsweb.com/~okgs/fftt.htm

Fort Gibson Genealogical & Historical Society
P.O. Box 416
Fort Gibson, OK 74434

Garfield County Genealogists, Inc.
P.O. Box 1106
Enid, OK 73703
http://www.harvestcomm.net/org/
    garfield_genealogy/

Grady County Genealogical Society
P.O. Box 792
Chickasha, OK 73023
http://www.telepath.com/dataman/okgrady.html

Greer County Genealogical & Historical Society
240 W. Lincoln
Mangum, OK 73554
Tel: 580-782-3185
http://www.rootsweb.com/~okgcghs/

Haskell County Genealogy Society
P.O. Box 481
Stigler, OK 74462
Tel: 918-967-8681
http://www.rootsweb.com/~okhaskel/hasksoc.htm

Kiowa County Genealogical Society
P.O. Box 191
Hobart, OK 73651-0191

Latimer County Genealogical & Historical Society
c/o Hoyt Duncan
101 W. Durant
Wilburton, OK 74578
E-mail: lcghs@eosc.edu

Logan County Genealogical Society
P.O. Box 1419
Guthrie, OK 73044

Major County Genealogical Society
c/o Fairview City Library
P.O. Box 419
Fairview, OK 73737

Mayes County Genealogical Society
P.O. Box 924
Chouteau, OK 74337

McClain County Historical & Genealogical Society/Museum
203 W. Washington Street
Purcell, OK 73080-4227
Tel: 405-527-5894
http://www.rootsweb.com/~okmchgs/mchgs.htm

McCurtain County Genealogy Society
P.O. Box 1832
Idabel, OK 74745
http://members.tripod.com/~mccurtain_2/

Muldrow Genealogical Society
P.O. Box 1253
Muldrow, OK 74948

Muskogee County Genealogical Society
c/o Muskogee Public Library
801 West Okmulgee
Muskogee, OK 74401
Tel: 918-682-6657
http://www.rootsweb.com/~okmuscgs/

Noble County Genealogy Society
P.O. Box 785
Perry, OK 73077-0785
http://www.rootsweb.com/~oknoble/histsoci.htm

North Caddo Genealogical Society
P.O. Box 309
Hinton, OK 73047

Northwest Oklahoma Genealogical Society
P.O. Box 834
Woodward, OK 73801

Oklahoma Genealogical Society
P.O. Box 12986
Oklahoma City, OK 73157-2986
http://www.rootsweb.com/~okgs/

Okmulgee County Genealogical Society
314 West 7th Street
P.O. Box 904
Okmulgee, OK 74447
Tel: 918-756-0788

Ottawa County Genealogical Society
P.O. Box 1383
Miami, OK 74355-1383

Pawhuska Genealogical Society
P.O. Box 807
Pawhuska, OK 74056

Payne County Genealogical Society
Stillwater Public Library
P.O. Box 2708
Stillwater, OK 74076
E-mail: pcgsok@yahoo.com
http://www.pcgsok.org/

Pioneer Genealogical Society
P.O. Box 1965
Ponca City, OK 74602
E-mail: famfox@pcok.com
http://www.poncacitynews.com/community/localhistory/g
    enhis/pgs/frtpage.html/
    piogenhp.htm

Pittsburg County Genealogical & Historical Society
113 East Carl Albert Parkway
McAlester, OK 74501-5039
Tel: 918-426-0388
E-mail: tobucksy@osu-ext.pittsburg.ok.us
http://www.oil.tec.ok.us/tobucksy/history.htm

Pontotoc County Historical & Genealogical Society
221 West 16th Street
Ada, OK 74820
http://www.rootsweb.com/~okpontgs/

Poteau Valley Genealogical Society
P.O. Box 1031
Poteau, OK 74953
E-mail: dbrown@clnk.com
http://www.rootsweb.com/~okleflor/pvgs.htm

Rogers County Genealogical Society
P.O. Box 2493
Claremore, OK 74018

Sequoyah Genealogical Society
P.O. Box 1112
Sallisaw, OK 74955

Sons & Daughters of the Cherokee Strip Pioneers
P.O. Box 465
Enid, OK 73702
http://www.ok-history.mus.ok.us/mus-sites/16/sons.html

Southwest Oklahoma Genealogical Society
P.O. Box 148
Lawton, OK 73502-0148
E-mail: lgarris@sirinet.net
http://www.sirinet.net/~lgarris/swogs/

Stephens County Genealogical Society/Library
301 North 8th Street
Duncan, OK 73534

Texas-Oklahoma Panhandle Genealogical Society
c/o Perry Memorial Library
22 SE 5th Street
Perryton, OK 79070
Tel: 806-435-5801

Three Forks Genealogical Society
102 South State Street
Wagoner, OK 74467

Tulsa Genealogical Society
P.O. Box 585
Tulsa, OK 74101-0585
http://www.tulsagenealogy.org/

Western Plains Weatherford Genealogical Society
P.O.Box 1672
Weatherford, OK 73096

Western Trails Genealogical Society
P.O. Box 70
Altus, OK 73522
http://www.rootsweb.com/~okjackso/wtgs.htm

Woods County Genealogists
P.O. Box 234
Alva, OK 73717

HISTORICAL SOCIETIES

1889er Society/Museum
Harn Homestead
313 NE 16th Street
Oklahoma City, OK 73104
Tel: 405-235-4058
E-mail: info@harnhomestead.com
http://www.harnhomestead.com/

American Historical Society of Germans from Russia
Central Oklahoma Chapter
2133 NW 25th
Oklahoma City OK 73107
Tel: 405-525-3218
E-mail: lilarwig@swbell.net
http://www.ahsgr.org/okcentra.html

Arbuckle Historical Society
113 W. Muskogee Street
Sulphur, OK 73086

Atoka County Historical Society/Museum
Highway 69 North
P.O. Box 245
Atoka, OK 74525
Tel: 580-889-7192

Beaver River Genealogical & Historical Society
Route 1, Box 79
Hooker, OK 73945

Broken Arrow Historical Society
1800 S. Main Street
Broken Arrow, OK 74012-6503
Tel: 918-258-2616
http://www.city.broken-arrow.ok.us/museum.htm

Bryan County Heritage Society
P.O. Box 153
Calera, OK 74730-0153

Canadian County Historical Society
Canadian County Historical Museum
300 S Grand Avenue
El Reno, OK 73036
Tel: 405-262-5121

Cherokee Dixieland Historical Society/Museum
Downtown
Webbers Falls, OK 74470
Tel: 918-464-2728

Cherokee National Historical Society/Museum
Cherokee Heritage Center
P.O. Box 515
Tahlequah, OK 74465
Tel: 918-456-6007
      918-456-6165
Fax: 918-456-6165
http://www.powersource.com/heritage/default.html

Cheyenne Arapaho Cultural Preservation Committee
212 S. Rock Island Avenue
El Reno, OK 73036

Chickasaw Council
House Museum
Court House Square
P.O. Box 717
Tishomingo, OK 73460
Tel: 580-371-3351

Cleveland County Historical Society
508 N. Peters
P.O. Box 260
Norman, OK 73069
Tel: 405-321-0156
http://www.oknorman.org/historic.htm

Coal County Historical & Genealogical Society
111 West Ohio
Coalgate, OK 74538

Delaware County Historical Society
Jay, OK 74346
Tel: 918-253-4345

Drumright Community Historical Society
Broadway & Harley Streets
Mail:
118 S. Creek
Drumright, OK 74030

Eastern Oklahoma Historical Society
Kerr Museum
P.O. Box 111
Poteau, OK 74953
Tel: 918-647-8221

Edmond Historical Society/Museum
431 S. Boulevard
Edmond, OK 73034
Tel: 405-340-0078
Fax: 405-340-2771
E-mail:http://www.edmondhistory.org/

Fort Gibson Genealogical & Historical Society
P.O. Box 416
Fort Gibson, OK 74434

Grant County Historical Society/Museum
RR3, Box 301
Medford, OK 73759
Tel: 405-395-2822
      405-395-2888
Fax: 405-395-2343

Greer County Genealogical & Historical Society
240 W. Lincoln
Mangum, OK 73554
Tel: 580-782-3185

Haskell County Historical Society
P. O. Box 481
Stigler, OK 74462
Tel: 918-967-8681
http://www.rootsweb.com/~okhaskel/hasksoc.htm

Hughes County Historical Society
114 N. Creek Street
Holdenville, OK 74848
Tel: 405-379-6723

Lincoln County Historical Society
Museum of Pioneer History
717 Manvel Avenue
Chandler, OK 74834-2842
Tel: 405-258-2425

Logan County Historical Society
223 S. 1st Street
Guthrie, OK 73044-4707
Tel: 405-282-4446

Love County Historical Society
Pioneer Museum
101 SW Front Street
P.O. Box 134
Marietta, OK 73448
Tel: 405-276-5888

Major County Historical Society
P.O. Box 555
Fairview, OK 73737
Tel: 580-227-2265

Mayes County Historical Society
Coo-Y-Yah Country Museum
Old Depot
Pryor, OK 74361
Tel: 918-476-5473

McClain County Historical & Genealogical Society/Museum
203 W. Washington Street
Purcell, OK 73080-4227
Tel: 405-527-5894
http://www.rootsweb.com/~okmchgs/film.htm

Newkirk Community Historical Society
101 S. Maple Street
Newkirk, OK 73647
Tel: 405-362-3330

No Man's Land Historical Society/Museum
207 W. Sewell Street
Goodwell, OK 73939
Tel: 580-349-2670

North Central Oklahoma Historical Association
417 E. Grand Avenue
P.O. Box 2811 Dept. DP
Ponca City, OK 74602
Tel: 405-765-4600
    405-765-7169
E-mail: famfox@poncacity.net (Historian)
http://www.poncacitynews.com/community/localhistory/
    genhis/ncoha/ncoahafrt.htm

Nowata County Historical Society
121 S. Pine Street
Nowata, OK 74048-3413
Tel: 918-273-1191

Okfuskee County Historical Society
407 W. Broadway Street
Okemah, OK 74859-2401
Tel: 918-623-2027

Oklahoma Baptist Historical Society
1141 N. Robinson
Oklahoma City, OK 73103
Tel: 405-236-4341

Oklahoma Heritage Association
Oklahoma Heritage Center
201 NW 14th Street
Oklahoma City, OK 73103
Mail:
1500 N. Robinson
Oklahoma City, OK 73103
Tel: 405-235-4458
    888-501-2059
Fax: 405-235-2714
E-mail: gmc@oklahomaheritage.com
http://www.oklahomaheritage.com/

Oklahoma Historical Society/Library and Archives
2100 N. Lincoln Blvd.
Oklahoma City, OK 73105-4997
E-mail: libohs@ok-history.mus.ok.us
Archives & Manuscripts Division:
Tel: 405-522-5209
Fax: 405-521-2492
Library Resources Division:
Tel: 405-522-5225
Fax: 405-521-2492
http://www.ok-history.mus.ok.us/

Osage County Historical Society
700 N. Lynn Avenue
P.O. Box 267
Pawhuska, OK 74056
Tel: 918-287-9924

Piedmont Historical Society
Old Bank Building
Piedmont, OK 73078

Pittsburg County Genealogical & Historical Society
113 East Carl Albert Parkway
McAlester, Oklahoma 74501-5039
Tel: 918-426-0388
E-mail: tobucksy@osu-ext.pittsburg.ok.us
http://www.oil.tec.ok.us/tobucksy/

Pontotoc County Historical & Genealogical Society
221 West 16th Street
Ada, OK 74820
http://www.rootsweb.com/~okpontgs/

Pottawatomie County, Historical Society of
1301 East Farrall
Shawnee, OK 74801

Pushmataha County Historical Society
125 W. Main
P.O. Box 285
Antlers, OK 74523

Red River Valley Historical Association
Southeastern Oklahoma State University
P.O. Box 4014
Durant, OK 74701
Tel: 580-924-0121 ext. 203

Sacred Heart (Konawa) Historical Society
c/o Kennedy Library of Konawa
Konawa High School
Route 1, Box 3
Konawa, OK 74849
Tel: 580-925-3662
http://www.konawa.k12.ok.us/school/library/ library.html

Sapulpa Historical Society
100 E. Lee
P.O. Box 278
Sapulpa, OK 74066
Tel: 918-224-4871

Sayre Historical Society
106 E. Poplar Avenue
Sayre, OK 73662
Tel: 580-928-5757

Seminole Historical Society
1800 West Wrangler Blvd
Seminole, OK 74868
Tel: 405-382-1500
http://www.seminoleoklahoma.com/museum/

Seminole Nation Historical Society/Museum
524 S. Wewoka Avenue
Wewoka, OK 74884-3239
Tel: 405-257-5580

Shortgrass Country Historical Society/Museum
106 E. Poplar Avenue
Sayre, OK 73662-2933
Tel: 580-928-5757

Sod House Museum & Historical Society
RR 1
Aline, OK 73716
Tel: 580-463-2441

Southwestern Oklahoma Historical Society
P.O. Box 3693
Lawton, OK 73502

Sunbelt Railroad Historical Society
110 West A Street
Jenks, OK 74037
Tel: 918-298-7246

Tillman County Historical Society/Museum
201 N. 9th Street
Frederick, OK 73542
Tel: 405-335-2989
    405-335-2805
E-mail: bradbenson@pldi.net
http://www.frisco.org/msw/mswtil.htm

Tonkawa Historical Society
P.O. Box 336
Tonkawa, OK 74653

Top of Oklahoma Historical Society/Museum
303 S. Main Street
Blackwell, OK 74631-3347
Tel: 580-363-0209

Tulsa Historical Society
2445 South Peoria
Tulsa, OK 74114
Tel: 918-712-9484
E-mail: ths@tulsahistory.com
http://www.tulsahistory.org/index.htm

Turley Historical Society
6540 N. Peoria Avenue
Tulsa, OK 74126

Washington County Historical Society
P.O. Box 255
Bartlesville, OK 74003

Washita County Historical Society
105 East First
P.O. Box 440
Cordell, OK 73632
Tel: 405-343-2554

Waynoka Historical Society
103 Missouri
Waynoka, OK 73860
Tel: 580-824-1886
http://www.agweb.okstate.edu/woods/waynkhis.htm

Webbers Falls Historical Society/Museum
Commercial & Main Streets
Webbers Falls, OK 74470
Tel: 918-464-2728

Yukon Historical Society
Farm Museum
Third Street and Cedar Yukon, OK 73099

LDS FAMILY HISTORY CENTERS

For locations of Family History Centers in this state, see
    the Family History Center locator at FamilySearch.
http://www.familysearch.org/eng/Library/FHC/
    frameset_fhc.asp

ARCHIVES/LIBRARIES/MUSEUMS

Altus Library/Southern Prairie Library System
421 N. Hudson Street
Altus, OK 73521
Tel: 580-477-2890
Fax: 580-477-3626
http://www.spls.lib.ok.us/

Alva Public Library
504 Seventh Street
Alva, OK 73717
Tel: 405-327-1833

American Heritage Library
P.O. Box 176
Davis, OK 73030

Atoka County Library
215 East A Street
Atoka, OK 74525
Tel: 580-889-3555

Bartlesville Public Library/History Museum
600 S. Johnstone
Bartlesville, OK 74003
Tel: 918-337-5353
Fax: 918-337-5338
TDD: 918-337-5359
E-mail: webmaster@bartlesville.lib.ok.us
http://www.bartlesville.lib.ok.us/

Cherokee City/County Public Library
602 South Grand Avenue
Cherokee, OK 73728
Tel: 405-596-2366

Cherokee National Historical Society/Museum
Cherokee Heritage Center
P.O. Box 515
Tahlequah, OK 74465
Tel: 918-456-6007
        918-456-6165
Fax: 918-456-6165
http://www.powersource.com/heritage/default.html

Cherokee Strip Museum Association
901 14th Street
Alva, OK 73717
Tel: 580-327-2030

Cherokee Strip, Museum of
507 S. 4th Street
Enid, OK 73701
Tel: 580-237-1907
http://www.cherokee-strip-museum.org/

Chickasha Public Library
527 W. Iowa Avenue
Chickasha, OK 73018
Tel: 405-222-6075

Chisholm Trail Historical Museum
Highways 70 & 81
Waurika, OK 73573
Tel: 405-228-2166

Choctaw County Library
208 E. Jefferson
Hugo, OK 74743
Tel: 580-326-5591
Fax: 580-326-7388
E-mail: hugolib@1starnet.com
http://www2.1starnet.com/hugolib/

Cushing County Library
215 North Steele
P.O. Box 551
Cushing, OK 74023
Tel: 918-225-4188

El Reno Carnegie Library
Archives Room
215 E. Wade
El Reno, OK 73036
Tel: 405-262-2409

Enid Public Library
Great Plains Room
120 W. Maine Avenue
P.O. Box 8002
Enid, OK 73701
Tel: 580-234-6313
Fax: 580-233-2948
http://www.enid.org/library.htm

Fairview City Library
115 S. 6th Avenue
P.O. Box 419
Fairview, OK 73737
Tel: 580-227-2190

Five Civilized Tribes Museum
1019 Honor Heights Dr.
Muskogee, OK 74401
Tel: 918-683-1701
http://www.fivetribes.com/

Gilcrease Museum
1400 N. Gilcrease Museum Road
Tulsa, OK 74127
Tel: 918-596-2700
        888-655-2278
http://www.gilcrease.org/index2.html

Grove Public Library
206 South Elk
Grove, OK 74344
Tel: 918-786-2945
http://little.gcinet.net/

Idabel Public Library
2 SE Avenue D
P.O. Box 778
Idabel, OK 74745
E-mail: idabel@idabel.lib.ok.us
Tel: 405-286-6406
http://www.idabel.lib.ok.us/

John F. Henderson Memorial Library
116 North Williams
P.O. Box 580
Westville, OK 74965-0580
Tel: 918-723-5002
Fax: 918-723-3400
http://www.eodls.lib.ok.us/john_henderson.html

Lawton Public Library
Family History Room
110 SW Fourth Street
Lawton, OK 73501
Tel: 580-581-3450
http://www.cityof.lawton.ok.us/library/

Layland Museum
201 N Caddo Street
Cleburne, TX 76031
Tel: 817-645-0940

Martin East Regional Library
2601 S. Garnett Road
Tulsa, OK 74129
Tel: 918-669-6340

Metropolitan Library System/Downtown Library
Charles E. France Room, Oklahoma Collection
131 Dean McGee Avenue
Oklahoma City, OK 73102
Tel: 405-231-8650
http://www3.mls.lib.ok.us/index1.htm

Muldrow Public Library
City Hall Building
771 West Shawntel Smith Blvd.
P.O. Box 449
Muldrow, OK 74948
Tel: 918-427-6703
Fax: 918-427-7315

Museum of the Western Prairie
1100 N. Hightower
P.O. Box 574
Altus, OK 73522
Tel: 580-482-1044
Fax: 580-482-0128
http://members.staroffice.com/www/muswestpr/

Muskogee Public Library
801 West Okmulgee
Muskogee, OK 74401-6840
Tel: 918-682-6657
Fax: 918-682-9466
E-mail: muskpublib@eok.lib.ok.us
http://www.eok.lib.ok.us/

Norman Public Library
225 N. Webster
Norman, OK 73069
Tel: 405-321-1481
Fax: 405-360-7007

Northeastern State University
John Vaughan Library
711 N. Grand
Tahlequah, OK 74464
Tel: 918-456-5511 ext. 3233
        918-456-5511 ext. 3252 (Special Collections)
        918-456-5511 ext. 3220 (University Archives)
E-mail: library@nsuok.edu
http://www.nsuok.edu/jvl/

Oklahoma Department of Libraries
200 NE 18th Street
Oklahoma City, OK 73105-3298
Tel: 405-521-2502
Fax: 405-525-7804
http://www.odl.state.ok.us/

Oklahoma Heritage Association
Oklahoma Heritage Center
201 NW 14th Street
Oklahoma City, OK 73103
Mail:
1500 N. Robinson
Oklahoma City, OK 73103
Tel: 405-235-4458
        888-501-2059
Fax: 405-235-2714
E-mail: gmc@oklahomaheritage.com
http://www.oklahomaheritage.com/

Oklahoma Historical Society/Library and Archives
2100 N. Lincoln Blvd.
Oklahoma City, OK 73105-4997
E-mail: libohs@ok-history.mus.ok.us
Archives & Manuscripts Division:
Tel: 405-522-5209
Fax: 405-521-2492
Library Resources Division:
Tel: 405-522-5225
Fax: 405-521-2492
http://www.ok-history.mus.ok.us/

Oklahoma State University
204 Edmon Low Library
Stillwater, OK 74078
Tel: 405-744-6311
http://www.library.okstate.edu/

Oklahoma Territorial Museum
406 E. Oklahoma Avenue
Guthrie, OK 73044-3317
Tel: 405-282-1889
Fax: 405-282-7286
E-mail: guthriecomplex@ok-history.mus.ok.us

Old Greer County Museum & Hall of Fame
222 W. Jefferson Street
Mangum, OK 73554-4022
Tel: 580-782-2851

Pawnee Historical & Cultural Museum
657 Harrison Street
Pawnee, OK 74058-2520
Tel: 918-762-3706

Pioneer Museum & Art Center
2009 Williams Avenue
Woodward, OK 73801-5717
Tel: 580-256-6136

Pioneer Woman State Museum
701 Monument Road
Ponca City, OK 74604-3910
Tel: 580-765-6108
E-mail: piown@ok-history.mus.ok.us

Ponca City Cultural Center & Museum Library
1000 E. Grand Avenue
Ponca City, OK 74601
Tel: 580-767-0427

Ponca City Library
515 East Grand Avenue
P.O. Box 1450
Ponca City, OK 74601-5499
Tel: 580-767-0345
Fax: 580-767-0377
http://www.poncacity.com/ponca/attractions/ library.htm

Potawatomi Tribal Museum
1901 S. Gordon Cooper Drive
Shawnee, OK 74801-8604
Tel: 405-275-3119

Prague Historical Museum
1008 N. Broadway
Prague, OK 74864
Tel: 405-567-4750

Ralph Ellison Library
2000 North East 23rd
Oklahoma City, OK 73111
Tel: 405-424-1437
Fax: 405-424-1443
http://www.mls.lib.ok.us/Library/RE.htm

Rudisill North Regional Library
1520 N. Hartford
Tulsa, OK 74106
Tel: 918-596-7280

Sapulpa Public Library
27 West Dewey Avenue
Sapulpa, OK 74066-3909
Tel: 918-224-5624
http://www.rootsweb.com/~okcreek/sapulpa.html

Stanley Tubbs Memorial Library
101 East Cherokee Street
Sallisaw, OK 74955-4621
Tel: 918-775-4481
Fax: 981-775-4129
http://www.eodls.lib.ok.us/sallisaw.html

Stephens County Historical Museum
N Highway 81 & Beech
Duncan, OK 73533
Tel: 580-252-0717

Talbot Library & Museum
406 S. Colcord Avenue
P.O. Box 349
Colcord, OK 74338
Tel: 918-326-4532

Tillman County Historical Society/Museum
201 N. 9th Street
Frederick, OK 73542
Tel: 405-335-2989
     405-335-2805
E-mail: bradbenson@pldi.net
http://www.frisco.org/msw/mswtil.htm

University of Oklahoma Library
Western History Collection
Monnet Hall, Room 452
630 Parrington Oval
Norman, OK 73069
Tel: 405-325-3641
Fax: 405-325-2943
http://libraries.ou.edu/info/info.asp?id=22

University of Tulsa
McFarlin Library
2933 E. 6th Street
Tulsa, OK 74104-3123
Tel: 918-631-2873
Fax: 918-631-3791
http://www.lib.utulsa.edu/

Vinita Public Library
Maurice Haynes Memorial Bldg.
215 West Illinois Avenue
Vinita, OK 74301
Tel: 918-256-2115
Fax: 918-256-2309

Watonga Public Library
301 N. Prouty Avenue
Watonga, OK 73772
Tel: 405-623-7748
Fax: 405-623-7747
E-mail: bookwoman@watonga.lib.ok.us
http://www.watonga.lib.ok.us/

Weatherford Public Library
219 East Franklin Avenue
Weatherford, OK 73096
Tel: 580-772-3591

NEWSPAPER REPOSITORIES

Muskogee Public Library
801 West Okmulgee
Muskogee, OK 74401-6840
Tel: 918-682-6657
Fax: 918-682-9466
E-mail: muskpublib@eok.lib.ok.us
http://www.eok.lib.ok.us/

Oklahoma Department of Libraries
200 NE 18th Street
Oklahoma City, OK 73105-3298
Tel: 405-521-2502
Fax: 405-525-7804
http://www.odl.state.ok.us/

Oklahoma Historical Society/Library and Archives
2100 N. Lincoln Blvd.
Oklahoma City, OK 73105-4997
E-mail: libohs@ok-history.mus.ok.us
Archives & Manuscripts Division:
Tel: 405-522-5209
Fax: 405-521-2492
Library Resources Division:
Tel: 405-522-5225
Fax: 405-521-2492
http://www.ok-history.mus.ok.us/

VITAL RECORDS

Oklahoma Department of Health
Division of Vital Records
1000 Northeast 10th Street, Room 111
P.O. Box 53551
Oklahoma City, OK 73152-3551
Tel: 405-271-4040
http://www.health.state.ok.us/

OKLAHOMA ON THE WEB

Application for Search & Certified Copy of Birth Certificate
http://www.rootsweb.com/~okbits/birthform.htm

Application for Search & Certified Copy of Death Certificate
http://www.rootsweb.com/~okbits/deathform.htm

BJ's Place—Genealogy Home Page
http://www.harvestcomm.net/personal/bjsbytes/
    index.html

Electric Cemetery Home Page—Civil War Site
http://www.ionet.net/~cousin/index.html

Federal Tract Books of Oklahoma Territory (SWOGS)
http://www.sirinet.net/~lgarris/swogs/tract.html

History of the Cherokee—Genealogy
http://cherokeehistory.com/

Native American Resources
http://www.cowboy.net/native/

Oklahoma Department of Libraries/Archives— Genealogical Materials
http://www.odl.state.ok.us/oar/resources/genealogy.htm

Oklahoma GenWeb Project
http://www.rootsweb.com/~okgenweb/index.htm

Oklahoma Tribes and Officials
http://www.cowboy.net/native/tribes.html

OREGON

ARCHIVES, STATE & NATIONAL

National Archives—Pacific Northwest Region
6125 Sand Point Way, NE
Seattle, WA 98115-7999
Tel: 206-526-6501
Fax: 206-526-6575
E-mail: seattle.archives@nara.gov
http://www.nara.gov/regional/seattle.html

Oregon State Archives
8800 Summer Street, NE
Salem, OR 97310
Tel: 503-373-0701
Fax: 503-373-0953
E-mail: reference.archives@state.or.us
  (Reference requests welcome)
http://arcweb.sos.state.or.us/

GENEALOGICAL SOCIETIES

ALSI Historical & Genealogical Society
P.O. Box 822
Waldport, OR 97394

Baker County Genealogy Club
c/o Baker County Public Library
2400 Resort Street
Baker City, OR 97814

Belgian Researchers, Inc.
62073 Fruitdale Lane
LaGrande, OR 97850-5312

Bend Genealogical Society
P.O. Box 8254
Bend, OR 97708-8254
http://www.rootsweb.com/~ordeschu/BGS/
    bgsindex.htm

Blue Mountain Genealogical Society
P.O. Box 1801
Pendleton, OR 97801
Tel: 541-276-6000
http://www.ucinet.com/~sandral/index.htm

Clackamas County Family History Society/Library
211 Tumwater Drive
P.O. Box 995
Oregon City, OR 97045-2900
Tel: 503-655-5574
http://www.rootsweb.com/~genepool/ccfhs.htm

Clatsop County Genealogical Society
Astoria Public Library
450 10th Street
Astoria, OR 97103
http://home.pacifier.com/~karenl/

Columbia Gorge Genealogical Society
c/o The Dalles/Wasco County Public Library
722 Court Street
The Dalles, OR 97058
Tel: 541-296-2815
Fax: 541-296-4179
http://community.oregonlive.com/cc/genealogy

Coos Bay Genealogical Forum/Library
P.O. Box 1067
North Bend, OR 97459

Cottage Grove Genealogical Society/Library
Cottage Grove Community Building
P.O. Box 388
Cottage Grove, OR 97424
http://www.rootsweb.com/~orlane/links/cggs.htm

Crook County Genealogical Society
c/o A.R. Bowman Memorial Museum
246 North Main Street
Prineville, OR 97754-1852
Tel: 541-447-3715 (Museum)

Daughters of the American Revolution
Oregon State Society
http://www.teleport.com/~dareth/DAR/

Deschutes County Historical & Genealogical Society
P.O. Box 5252
Bend, OR 97708

Douglas County, Genealogical Society of
Douglas County Courthouse, Room 111
1036 SE Douglas
Roseburg OR 97470
Tel: 541-440-6178
E-mail: gsdc@co.douglas.or.us
http://www.rootsweb.com/~orgsdc/

Genealogical Council of Oregon
P.O. Box 2639
Salem, OR 97308-2639
http://www.rootsweb.com/~orgco/Index.htm

Genealogical Forum of Oregon/Library
1505 SE Gideon Street
P.O. Box 42567
Portland, OR 97202
Tel: 503-963-1932
Fax: 561-325-7676
E-mail: info@gfo.org
http://www.gfo.org/

Genealogical Heritage Council of Oregon
Room 111
P.O. Box 579
Roseburg, OR 97470
Tel: 541-440-6178

Grant County Genealogical Society
P.O. Box 418
Canyon City, OR 97820
Tel: 541-575-0362 (Museum)

Grants Pass Genealogical Society
P.O. Box 1834
Grants Pass, OR 97526

Juniper Branch of the Family Finders
P.O. Box 652
Madras, OR 97741
Tel: 541-475-9745
E-mail: jbff@madras.net
http://www.madras.net/~jbff/

Klamath Basin Genealogical Society
c/o Klamath Falls Public Library
126 S. 3rd Street
Klamath Falls, OR 97601
Tel: 541-882-8894 (library)

LaPine Genealogy Society
P.O. Box 1081
LaPine, OR 97739

Lebanon Genealogical Society
c/o Lebanon Public Library
626 2nd Street
Lebanon, OR 97355
Tel: 541-451-7461 (Library)
http://www.usgennet.org/usa/or/town/lebanon/

Linn Genealogical Society
P.O. Box 1222
Albany, OR 97321
http://www.rootsweb.com/~orlinngs/

Mid-Valley Genealogical Society
P.O. Box 1511
Corvallis, OR 97339

Oregon Genealogical Society
Oregon Research Room
955 Oak Alley
Eugene, OR
Mail:
P.O. Box 10306
Eugene, OR 97440-2306
Tel: 541-345-0399
http://www.rootsweb.com/~orlncogs/ogsinfo.htm

Polk County Genealogical Society
Katherine Johnson
535 SE Ash Street
Dallas, OR 97338

Rogue Valley Genealogical Society/Library
95 Houston Road
P.O.Box 1468
Phoenix, OR 97535-1468
Tel: 541-770-5848
E-mail: rvgs@grrtech.com
http://www.grrtech.com/rvgs/

Scandinavian Genealogical Society of Oregon
1123 7th Street, NW
Salem, OR 97304

Siuslaw Genealogical Society
P.O. Box 1540
Florence, OR 97439

Sons and Daughters of Oregon Pioneers
P.O. Box 6685
Portland, OR 97228

Sweet Home Genealogical Society
c/o Sweet Home Library
13th & Kalmia Streets
Sweet Home, OR 97386

Tillamook County Historical Society/Genealogy Study Group
P.O. Box 123
Tillamook, OR 97141

Willamette Valley Genealogical Society
P.O. Box 2083
Salem, OR 97308

Yamhill County Genealogical Society
P.O. Box 568
McMinnville, OR 97128
http://www.geocities.com/ycgsociety/index.html

Yaquina Genealogical Society
c/o Toledo Public Library
173 NW Seventh Street
Toledo, OR 97391

HISTORICAL SOCIETIES

Aurora Colony Historical Society
2nd. & Liberty Street
P.O. Box 202
Aurora, OR 97002
Tel: 503-678-5754
http://www.cdds.com/achs.htm

Bandon Historical Society/Museum
270 Filmore Avenue
P.O. Box 737
Bandon, OR 97411
Tel: 541-347-2164

Benton County Historical Society/Museum & Library
1101 Main Street
P.O. Box 35
Philomath, OR 97370
Tel: 541-929-6230
E-mail: bchm@peak.org
http://www.peak.org/~lewisb/Museum.html

Boston Mill Society
1132 30th Place SW
Albany, OR 97321-3419
http://www.bostonmill.org/

Clatsop County Historical Society
Clatsop County Heritage Museum
1618 Exchange Street
Astoria, OR 97103-3615
Tel: 503-325-2203
http://www.ohwy.com/or/c/clatcohs.htm

Big Butte Historical Society
432 Pine Street
P.O. Box 379
Butte Falls, OR 97522
Tel: 541-865-3332

Cannon Beach Historical Society
P.O. Box 1005
1387 S. Spruce
Cannon Beach, OR 97110
Tel: 503-436-9301
E-mail: cbhs@seasurf.net
www.cannon-beach.net/cbhs

Chetco Valley Historical Society/Museum
15461 Museum Road
Brookings, OR 97415-9519
Tel: 541-469-6651

Clatsop County Historical Society
Clatsop County Heritage Museum
1618 Exchange Street
Astoria, OR 97103-3615
Tel: 503-325-2203
http://www.clatsophistoricalsociety.org/

Coos County Historical Society/Museum
1220 Sherman Avenue
North Bend, OR 97459-3666
Tel: 541-756-6320

Crook County Historical Society
A.R. Bowman Memorial Museum
246 North Main Street
Prineville, OR 97754
Tel: 541-447-3715

Curry County Historical Society/Museum
P.O. Box 1598
Gold Beach, OR 97444-9705
Tel: 541-247-6113

Deschutes County Historical & Genealogical Society
129 NW Idaho Avenue
P.O. Box 5252
Bend, OR 97708
Tel: 541-389-1813

Gilliam County Historical Society
Highway 19 at Burns Park
P.O. Box 377
Condon, OR 97823
Tel: 541-384-4233
http://www.rootsweb.com/~orgillia/gchs.html

Gold Hill Historical Society
504 1st Street
Gold Hill, OR 97525-9609
Tel: 541-855-1182

Gresham Historical Society
410 North Main
P.O. Box 65
Gresham, OR 97030
Tel: 503-661-0347
E-mail: ghs@gorge.net
http://community.oregonlive.com/cc/ghs

Harney County Historical Society/Museum
18 West D Street
P.O. Box 388
Burns, OR 97720-1226
Tel: 541-573-5618

Josephine County Historical Society
508 SW Fifth Street
Grants Pass, OR 97526
Tel: 541-479-7827
E-mail: jchs@terragon.com
http://www.webtrail.com/jchs/index.html

Junction City Historical Society
Lee House
655 Holly Street
Junction City, OR 97448
Tel: 541-998-3657

Lake County Historical Society
35 South G Street
Lakeview, OR 97630

Lincoln County Historical Society/Library
545 SW 9th Street
Newport, OR 97365-4726
Tel: 541-265-7509

Marion County Historical Society/Museum
260 12th Street SE
Salem, OR 97301-4101
Tel: 503-364-2128
Fax: 503-391-5356
E-mail: mchs@open.org
http://www.open.org/~mchs/

North Santiam Historical Society
143 Wall, NE
Mill City, OR 97360
Tel: 503-897-4088
http://www.myfamilyjones.com/linncounty/ NSHS.htm

Oregon-California Trails Association
P.O. Box 1019
524 S Osage Street
Independence, MO 64051-0519
Tel: 816-252-2276
Fax: 816-836-0989
E-mail: octahqts@gvi.net
http://www.octa-trails.org/

Oregon Electric Railway Historical Society
P.O. Box 308,
Lake Oswego, OR 97034
Tel: 503-222-2226
E-mail: kavanaghtransit@home.com
http://www.trainweb.org/oerhs/

Oregon Historic Cemeteries Association
P.O. Box 802
Boring, OR 97009
E-mail: ohca@oregoncemeteries.org
http://www.oregoncemeteries.org/

Oregon Historical Society
1200 SW Park Avenue
Portland, OR 97205-2483
Tel: 503-222-1741
      503-306-5280 (Education & Outreach)
Fax: 503-221-2035
E-mail: orhist@ohs.org
http://www.ohs.org/

Polk County Historical Society
Robert Street East
Crookston, MN 56716
Dallas, OR 97338
Tel: 218-281-1038
http://crookston.net/Museum/

Santiam Historical Society
260 N. 2nd Avenue
Stayton, OR 97383-1710
Tel: 503-769-1406

Seaside Museum & Historical Society
570 Necanicum Drive
P.O. Box 1024
Seaside, OR 97138-6040
Tel: 503-738-7065

Sherman County Historical Society/Museum
200 Dewey Street
P.O. Box 173
Moro, OR 97039
Tel: 541-565-3232
Fax: 541-565-3080
E-mail: info@shermanmuseum.org
http://www.shermanmuseum.org/

South Umpqua Historical Society/Museum
421 W. Fifth
Canyonville, OR 97417
Tel: 541-839-4845

Southern Oregon Historical Society/Library
106 N. Central Avenue
Medford, OR 97501
Tel: 541-773-6536 ext. 238
Fax: 541-776-7994
E-mail: director@sohs.org
http://www.SOHS.org/

Umatilla County Historical Society
108 SW Frazer
P.O. Box 253
Pendleton, OR 97801
Tel: 541-276-0012
E-mail: uchs@oregontrail.net
http://www.umatillahistory.org/

Wasco County Historical Society
300 West 13th Street
The Dalles, OR 97058-2010
Tel: 541-296-1867
http://w3.gorge.net/dzopf/wchs.htm

Washington County Historical Society/Museum
PCC, Rock Creek Campus
17677 NW Springville Road
Portland, OR 97229-1743
Tel: 503-645-5353
Fax: 503-645-5650

LDS FAMILY HISTORY CENTERS

For locations of Family History Centers in this state, see
the Family History Center locator at FamilySearch.
http://www.familysearch.org/eng/Library/FHC/
frameset_fhc.asp

ARCHIVES/LIBRARIES/MUSEUMS

Albany Public Library/Main Branch
1390 Waverly Drive, SE
Albany, OR 97321
Tel: 541-967-4307

Astoria Public Library
450 10th Street
Astoria, OR 97103
Tel: 503-325-READ
Fax: 503-325-2017
http://www.crmm.org/pages/Library.html

Baker County Public Library
2400 Resort Street
Baker City, OR 97814
Tel: 541-523-6419
Fax: 541-523-9088

Benton County Historical Society/Museum & Library
1101 Main
P.O. Box 35
Philomath, OR 97370
Tel: 541-929-6230
E-mail: bchm@peak.org
http://www.peak.org/~lewisb/Museum.html

Clackamas County Family History Society/Library
211 Tumwater Drive
P.O. Box 995
Oregon City, OR 97045-2900
Tel: 503-655-5574
http://www.rootsweb.com/~genepool/ccfhs.htm

Clatsop County Historical Society
Clatsop County Heritage Museum
1618 Exchange Street
Astoria, OR 97103-3615
Tel: 503-325-2203
http://www.clatsophistoricalsociety.org/

Columbia River Maritime Museum Library
1792 Marine Drive
Astoria, OR 97103-3525
Tel: 503-325-2323
http://www.crmm.org/

Coos Bay Genealogical Forum/Library
P.O. Box 1067
North Bend, OR 97459

Coos Bay Public Library
Oregon Archives
525 W. Anderson
Coos Bay, OR 97420
Tel: 541-269-1101
Fax: 541-269-7567
E-mail: cblib@mail.coos.or.us
http://mail.coos.or.us/~cblib/

Crook County Historical Society
A.R. Bowman Memorial Museum
365 NW 2nd Street
Prineville, OR 97754
Tel: 541-447-3715
URLhttp://www.bowmanmuseum.org/

Dallas Public Library
Oregon Collection
950 Main Street
Dallas, OR 97338
Tel: 503-623-2633
E-mail: Library.Dir@ci.dallas.or.us
http://www.ci.dallas.or.us/library/Library.htm/

Douglas County Library System
County Courthouse
Roseburg, OR 97470
Tel: 541-440-4308
Fax: 541-440-4315
http://www.co.douglas.or.us/library/

Douglas County Museum of History and Natural History
123 Museum Drive
P.O. Box 1550
Roseburg, OR 97470
Tel: 541-957-7007
Fax: 541-440-6023
E-mail: museum@rosenet.net

Eastern Oregon Museum
610 3rd
P.O. Box 6
Haines, OR 97833
Tel: 541-856-3233

Eastern Oregon State University
Walter M. Pierce Library
1410 L Avenue
La Grande, OR 97850
Tel: 541-962-3579
    541-962-3605 (Reference)
Fax: 541-962-3335
http://lib-www.eou.edu/

Elgin Public Library
260 N 10th Avenue
P.O. Box 67
Elgin, OR 97827
Tel: 541-437-5931

Grant County Museum
P.O. Box 464
Canyon City, OR 97820
Tel: 541-575-0362

Hermiston Public Library/Archives
235 E. Gladys Avenue
Hermiston, OR 97838
Tel: 541-567-2882
http://www.hermiston.or.us/library/

Hillsboro Public Library
775 SE 10th Avenue
Hillsboro, OR 97123
Tel: 503-681-6115

Hudson's Bay Company Archives
Provincial Archives of Manitoba
200 Vaughan Street
Winnipeg, Manitoba R3C 1T5
Tel: 204-945-4949
Fax: 204-948-3236
E-mail: hbca@gov.mb.ca
http://www.gov.mb.ca/chc/archives/hbca/index.html

Hutson Museum
4967 Baseline Drive
Mount Hood Parkdale, OR 97041-9727
Tel: 541-352-6808

Independence Public Library
Local History
311 S. Monmouth Street
Independence, OR 97351
Tel: 503-838-1811
Fax: 503-838-4486
http://www.ccrls.org/independence/

Jackson County Public Library/Main Branch
413 W. Main Street
Medford, OR 97501
Tel: 541-774-8689
TTY: 541-776-7281

Josephine County Library System/Main Branch
200 NW C STreet
Grants Pass, OR 97526
Tel: 541-474-5482
http://www.co.josephine.or.us/library/

Klamath Falls Public Library
126 S. 3rd Street
Klamath Falls, OR 97601
Tel: 541-882-8894

Lake Oswego Public Library
706 4th Street
Lake Oswego, OR 97034
Tel: 503-636-7628
http://www.ci.oswego.or.us/library/library.htm

Lebanon Public Library
626 2nd Street
Lebanon, OR 97355
Tel: 541-451-7461

Lewis & Clark College
Aubrey R. Watzek Library
615 SW Palatine Hill Road
Portland, OR 97219
Tel: 503-768-7270
    503-768-7274 (Information)
    503-768-7285 (Reference)
E-mail: refdesk@lclark.edu
http://library.lclark.edu/

Lincoln County Historical Society/Library
545 SW 9th Street
Newport, OR 97365-4726
Tel: 541-265-7509

McMinnville Public Library
225 N. Adams
McMinnville, OR 97128
Tel: 503-435-5555
http://www.ci.mcminnville.or.us/service/library/

Monmouth Public Library
168 S Ecols
P.O. Box 10
Monmouth OR 97361
Tel: 503-838-1932
Fax: 503-838-3899
http://www.ccrls.org/monmouth/

Morrow County Museum
Genealogical Research Center
444 N. Main
P.O. Box 1153
Heppner, OR 97836
Tel: 541-676-5524
http://www.mcmuseum.org/

Multnomah County Library/Central Branch
John Wilson Room
801 SW 10th
Portland, OR 97205
Tel: 503-248-5123
http://www.multcolib.org/

North Bend Public Library
1800 Sherman Avenue
North Bend, OR 97459
Tel: 541-756-0400

Oregon City Public Library
362 Warner Milne Road
Oregon City, OR 97045
Tel: 503-657-8269
http://www.oregoncity.lib.or.us/

Oregon Genealogical Society/Library
Oregon Research Room
955 Oak Alley
Eugene, OR
Mail:
P.O. Box 10306
Eugene, OR 97440-2306
Tel: 541-345-0399
http://www.rootsweb.com/~orlncogs/ogsinfo.htm

Oregon Historical Society
1200 SW Park Avenue
Portland, OR 97205-2483
Tel: 503-222-1741
      503-306-5280 (Education & Outreach)
Fax: 503-221-2035
E-mail: orhist@ohs.org
http://www.ohs.org/

Oregon State Library
State Library Building
250 Winter Street, NE
Salem, OR 97310-0641
Tel: 503-378-4243 ext. 221
Fax: 503-588-7119
TTY/TDD: 503-378-4276
E-mail: websters@sparkie.osl.state.or.us
http://www.osl.state.or.us/home/

Oregon State University
Valley Library
Corvallis, OR 97331-4501
Tel: 541-737-3331
http://osulibrary.orst.edu/

Polk County Museum
650 S Pacific Highway W
Rickreall, OR 97371
Tel: 503-623-6251

Rogue Valley Genealogical Society/Library
95 Houston Road
P.O.Box 1468
Phoenix, OR 97535-1468
Tel: 541-512-2340
E-mail: rvgs@grrtech.com
http://www.grrtech.com/rvgs/

Schmidt House Museum
508 SW 5th Street
Grants Pass, OR 97526-2804
Tel: 541-479-7827

Schminck Memorial Memorial
128 S. East Street
Lakeview, OR 97630-1721
Tel: 541-947-3134

Sherman County Historical Society/Museum
200 Dewey Street
P.O. Box 173
Moro, OR 97039
Tel: 541-565-3232
Fax: 541-565-3080
E-mail: info@shermanmuseum.org
http://www.shermanmuseum.org/

Silverton Public Library
410 South Water
Street Silverton, OR 97381
Tel: 503-873-5173
Fax: 873-6227
E-mail: silvfals@ccrls.org
http://www.open.org/~silverpl/

Southern Oregon Historical Society/Library
106 N. Central Avenue
Medford, OR 97501
Tel: 541-773-6536 ext. 238
Fax: 541-776-7994
E-mail: director@sohs.org
http://www.SOHS.org/

Southern Oregon University Library
1250 Siskiyou Blvd.
Ashland, OR 97520-5076
Tel: 541-552-7672
Fax: 541-552-6429

The Dalles/Wasco County Library
722 Court Street
The Dalles, OR 97058
Tel: 541-296-2815
Fax: 541-296-4179

Tigard Public Library
13125 SW Hall Blvd.
Tigard, OR 97223
Tel: 503-684-6537
Fax: 503-598-7515
http://www.ci.tigard.or.us/library/

Tillamook County Library
210 Ivy Street
Tillamook, OR 97141
Tel: 503-842-4792
Fax: 503-842-1120
http://www.tbcc.cc.or.us/~library/

University of Oregon
Knight Library
Eugene, OR 97403-1299
Tel: 541-346-3053
Fax: 541-346-3485
E-mail: libref@oregon.uoregon.edu
http://libweb.uoregon.edu/

Washington County Historical Society
Washington County Museum
17677 NW Springville Road
Portland, OR 97229-1743
Tel: 503-645-5353
Fax: 503-645-5650

Western Oregon State College Library
345 N. Monmouth Avenue
Portland, OR 97229-1743
Tel: 503-838-8890
Fax: 503-838-8474
http://www.wou.edu/core/library.html

NEWSPAPER REPOSITORIES

Oregon Historical Society
1200 SW Park Avenue
Portland, OR 97205-2483
Tel: 503-222-1741
        503-306-5280 (Education & Outreach)
Fax: 503-221-2035
E-mail: orhist@ohs.org
http://www.ohs.org/

University of Oregon
Knight Library
Eugene, OR 97403-1299
Tel: 541-346-3053
Fax: 541-346-3485
E-mail: libref@oregon.uoregon.edu
http://libweb.uoregon.edu/

VITAL RECORDS

Oregon State Archives
800 Summer Street, NE
Salem, OR 97310
Tel: 503-373-0701
Fax: 503-373-0953
E-mail: reference.archives@state.or.us
        (Reference requests welcome)
http://arcweb.sos.state.or.us/

Oregon State Registrar
Oregon Center for Health Statistics, Suite 205
State Office Building
800 NE Oregon Street
P.O. Box 14050
Portland, OR 97293
Tel: 503-731-4108
Fax: 503-731-4084

OREGON ON THE WEB

Census of Overland Emigrant Documents (COED)
http://calcite.rocky.edu/octa/coed.htm

Gene Pool, by Joanne Todd Rabun
http://www.rootsweb.com/~genepool/

Oregon GenWeb Project
http://www.rootsweb.com/~orgenweb/

Oregon Pioneers, by Mike Ransom
http://www.peak.org/~mransom/pioneers.html

Oregon State Archives—Genealogical Name Database Search
http://arcweb.sos.state.or.us/banners/genealogy.htm

Oregon Trail
http://www.isu.edu/~trinmich/Oregontrail.html

Records of Interest to Genealogists at the Oregon State Archives
http://arcweb.sos.state.or.us/geneal.html

PENNSYLVANIA

ARCHIVES, STATE & NATIONAL

National Archives—Mid Atlantic Region
900 Market Street
Philadelphia, PA 19107-4292
Tel: 215-597-3000
Fax: 215-597-2303
E-mail: philadelphia.archives@nara.gov
http://www.nara.gov/regional/philacc.html

Pennsylvania State Archives
350 North Street
Harrisburg, PA 17120-0090
(717) 783-3281
http://www.phmc.state.pa.us/bah/dam/
     overview.htm?secid=31

GENEALOGICAL SOCIETIES

African-American Genealogy Group (AAGG)
P.O. Box 27356
Philadelphia, PA 19118
Tel: 215-572-6063
http://www.aagg.org/

Allegheny Regional Family History Society (ARFHS)
P.O. Box 1804
Elkins, WV 26241
http://www.swcp.com/~dhickman/arfhs.html

Armstrong County Historical Museum & Genealogical Society
300 North McKean Street
P.O. Box 735
Kittanning, PA 16201-1345
Tel: 724-548-5707
http://www.angelfire.com/pa2/acgs/

Beaver County Genealogical Society
c/o Carnegie Free Library
Beaver County Research Center
1301 Seventh Avenue
Beaver Falls, PA 15010
Tel: 724-846-4340 Ext. 5
Fax: 412-846-0370

Berks County Genealogical Society
3618 Kutztown Road
Laureldale, PA 19605
Tel: 610-921-4970
E-mail: beatagoose@aol.com
     genealogy@berkscounty.com
http://www.berksgenes.org/

Blair County Genealogical Society
431 Scotch Valley Rd.
Hollidaysburg, PA 16648
Tel: 814-696-3492
http://www.rootsweb.com/~pabcgs/

Bucks County Genealogical Society
P.O. Box 1092
Doylestown, PA 18901
Tel: 215-230-9410 ext. 41
E-mail: bucksgenpa@erols.com
     bucksgen@juno.com

Cameron County Genealogical Society
102 West 4th Street
Emporium, PA 15834

Capital Area Genealogical Society
P.O. Box 4502
Harrisburg, PA 17111-4502
Tel: 717-543-2622
http://maley.net/cags/

Carpatho/Rusyn Society
125 Westland Drive
Pittsburgh, PA 15217
E-mail: ggressa@carpatho-rusyn.org
http://www.carpathorusynsociety.org/

Central Pennsylvania Genealogical Pioneers
1150 North Front Street
Sunbury, PA 17801

Centre County Genealogical Society
P.O. Box 1135
State College, PA 16804-1135
http://www.rootsweb.com/~paccgs/

Columbia County Historical and Genealogical Society
225 Market Street
P.O. Box 360, Bloomsburg, PA 17815-0360
Tel: 570-784-1600
http://www.colcohist-gensoc.org/

Cornerstone Genealogical Society
311 N West Street
P.O. Box 547
Waynesburg, PA 15370
Tel: 724-627-5653
http://www.vicoa.com/cornerstone/

Elk County Genealogical Society
P.O. Box 142
Johnsonburg, PA 15845

Erie Society for Genealogical Research
P.O. Box 1403
Erie, PA 16512-1403
Tel: 814-454-1813
http://www.pa-roots.com/~erie/

Fayette County Genealogical Society
24 Jefferson Street
Uniontown, PA 15401-3699
http://www.fforward.com/gene/fcgene.htm

Genealogical Computing Association of Pennsylvania (GENCAP)
c/o M.A. Miller, Treas.
51 Hillcrest Road
Barto, PA 19504
BBS: 215-438-2858
E-mail: gencap@libertynet.org

Indiana County, Historical & Genealogical Society of
200 South 6th Street
Indiana, PA 15701
Tel: 724-463-9600
http://www.rootsweb.com/~paicgs/

Jefferson County Historical & Genealogical Society
232 Jefferson Street
P.O. Box 51
Brookville, PA 15825
Tel: 814-849-0077
http://www.pa-roots.com/~jefferson/jchgs/jchgs.html

Jewish Genealogical Society of Philadelphia
1279 June Road
Huntingdon Valley, PA 19006-8405
E-mail: priluki@voicenet.com
http://www.jewishgen.org/jgsp/

Jewish Genealogical Society of Pittsburgh
2131 Fifth Avenue
Pittsburgh, PA 15219
Tel: 412-471-0772
Fax: 412-471-1004

Lycoming County Genealogical Society
P.O. Box 3625
Williamsport, PA 17701
Tel: 717-326-3326
E-mail: LCGSgen@aol.com
http://members.aol.com/LCGSgen/lcgs.htm

McKean County Genealogical Society
P.O. Box 207A
Derrick City, PA 16727

Mercer County Genealogical Society
P.O. Box 812
Sharon, PA 16146-0812
Tel: 412-346-5117

Montgomery Area Genealogical Society
Montgomery Public Library
1 South Main Street
Montgomery, PA 17751
Tel: 570-547-6212

Montgomery County, Historical Society of
Library and Genealogy Study Group
1654 DeKalb Street
Norristown, PA 19401
Tel: 610-272-0297

North Hills Genealogists
Northland Public Library
300 Cumberland Road
Pittsburgh, PA 15237-5410
Tel: 412-366-8100
http://www.einetwork.net/ein/northland/textonly/
    texthome.htm

Northampton County Historical & Genealogical Society
107 South 4th Street
Easton, PA 18042
Tel: 610-253-1222
Fax: 610-253-4701
E-mail: director@northamptonctymuseum.org
http://www.northamptonctymuseum.org/index.html

Northeast Pennsylvania Genealogical Society
P.O. Box 1776
Shavertown, PA 18708-0776
http://www.rootsweb.com/~panepgs/

Northeastern Pennsylvania, Genealogical Research Society of
P.O. Box 1
Olyphant, PA 18447-0001
Tel: 570-383-7661
Fax: 570-383-7466
E-mail: genealogy@usnetway.com
http://www.cfrobbins.com/grsnp/

Old York Road Genealogical Society
1030 Old York Road
Abington, PA 19001
Tel: 215-885-5180

Palatines to America, Pennsylvania Chapter
P.O. Box 280
Strasburg, PA 17579-0280
Tel: 717-687-8234

Pennsylvania, Genealogical Society of
215 South Broad Street, 7th Floor
Philadelphia, PA 19107-5325
Tel: 215-545-0391
Fax: 215-545-0936
E-mail: gsppa@aol.com
http://www.libertynet.org/~gspa

Pennsylvania Society of Mayflower Descendants
c/o The Genealogical Society of Pennsylvania
215 S. Broad Street, 7th Floor
Philadelphia, PA 19107
http://www.sail1620.org/

Perry Historians/Genealogical Society
P.O. Box 73
Newport, PA 17074-0073

Punxsutawney Area Historical & Genealogical Society
Bennis House Museum
401 West Mahoning Street
P.O. Box 286
Punxsutawney, PA 15767
Tel: 814-938-2555
E-mail: mweimer@penn.com
http://users.penn.com/~mweimer/historcl.html

Slovenian Genealogy Society
52 Old Farm Road
Harrisburg, PA 17011-2604
Tel: 717-731-8804
E-mail: apeterlin@panetwork.com
http://feefhs.org/slovenia/frg-sgsi.html

Somerset County, Historical & Genealogical Society of
10649 Somerset Pike
Somerset, PA 15501
Tel: 814-445-6077

South Central Pennsylvania Genealogical Society
P.O. Box 1824
York, PA 17405
Tel: 717-843-6169

Southwestern Pennsylvania, Genealogical Society of
P.O. Box 894
Washington, PA 15301-0984

Swedish Colonial Society
371 Devon Way
West Chester, PA 19380
E-mail: DorineySeagers@ColonialSwedes.org
Tel: 610-688-1766
http://www.colonialswedes.org/
index.html# anchor1104877

Tarentum Genealogical Society
Community Library of Allegheny Valley
315 East 6th Avenue
P. O. Box 66
Tarentum, PA 15084
Tel: 412-226-0770
http://www.targensoc.homestead.com

Troy Genealogical Associates
10 Cherry Street
Brookville, PA 15825

Venango County Genealogical Club
2 Central Avenue
P.O. Box 811
Oil City, PA 16301-0811
Tel: 814-678-3077
E-mail: vengen@csonline.net
http://www.csonline.net/vengen/main.html

Warren County Genealogical Society
210 4th Ave., P.O. Box 427
Warren, PA 16365
Tel: 814-723-1795

Welcome Society of Pennsylvania
316 S. Juniper Street
Philadelphia, PA 19107

Western Pennsylvania Genealogical Society
4400 Forbes Avenue
Pittsburgh, PA 15213-4080
Tel: 412-687-6811
http://www.wpgs.org/wpgs.html

Windber-Johnstown Area Genealogical Society
1401 Graham Avenue
Windber, PA 15963
Tel: 814-467-4950
E-mail: wjags@aol.com
http://www.ccacc.cc.pa.us/library/genealogy.htm

HISTORICAL SOCIETIES

Adams County Historical Society
111 N. West Confederate Avenue
P.O. Box 4325
Gettysburg, PA 17325
Tel: 717-334-4723

Afro American Historical & Cultural Museum
701 Arch Street
Philadelphia, PA 19106
Tel: 215-574-0380
http://www.fieldtrip.com/pa/55740380.htm

Allegheny Foothills Historical Society
Pierson Run Road
Export, PA 15632
Tel: 412-325-4933

Allegheny-Kiski Historical Society
224 E. 7th Avenue
Tarentum, PA 15084-1513
Tel: 724-224-7666
E-mail: akvhs@salsgiver.com
http://www.akvhs.org/

Apollo Area Historical Society
P.O. Box 434
Apollo, PA 15613
Tel: 412-478-4214

Armstrong County Historical Museum & Genealogical Society
300 North McKean Street
P.O. Box 735
Kittanning, PA 16201-1345
Tel: 724-548-5707
http://www.angelfire.com/pa2/acgs/

Beaver County Historical Research & Landmarks Foundation
1235 3rd Avenue
Freedom, PA 15042
Tel: 724-775-1848

Beaver Falls Historical Society/Museum
Carnegie Public Library
Beaver County Research Center
1301 7th Avenue
Beaver Falls, PA 15010
Tel: 724-846-4340
Fax: 724-846-0370

Bedford County Historical Commission
231 S. Juliana Street
Bedford, PA 15522

Bedford County Pioneers Historical Society/Library
242 E. John Street
Bedford, PA 15522-1750
Tel: 814-623-2011
http://www.rootsweb.com/~paphsbc/

Bell Township Historical Preservation Society
RR 2
Saltsburg, PA 15681-9802
Tel: 724-697-4092

Bellefonte Historical Railroad Society
Train Station
Bellefonte, PA 16823
Tel: 814-355-0311
http://www.geocities.com/cprg44/00NP/bhr.html

Berks County, Historical Society of
Library and Museum
940 Centre Avenue
Reading, PA 19601
Tel: 610-375-4375
http://www.berksweb.com/histsoc.html

Berlin Historical Society
400 Vine Street
P.O. Box 35
Berlin, PA 15530
Tel: 814-267-5987

Berwick Historical Society
102 East Second Street
Berwick, PA 18603-4827
Tel: 570-759-8020

Blair County Historical Society
Baker Mansion Museum
3500 Baker Blvd.
P.O. Box 1083
Altoona, PA 16602-1828
Tel: 814-942-3916
Fax: 814-942-7078

Blairsville Area, Historical Society of the
116 E. Campbell Street
Blairsville, PA 15717
Tel: 724-459-0580
http://www.blairsvillehistoricalsociety.org/bhs/

Bloomingrove Historical Society
Dunkard Church Road
Cogan Station, PA 17728
Tel: 570-435-2997

Boyertown Area Historical Society
43 S. Chestnut Street
Boyertown, PA 19512-1508
Tel: 610-367-5255

Braddock Field Historical Society
419 Library Street
Pittsburgh, PA 15233
Tel: 412-351-5356

Bradford County Historical Society/Museum
109 Pine Street
Towanda PA 18848
Tel: 570-265-2240
http://www.rootsweb.com/~srgp/bchsmain.htm

Bristol Cultural & Historical Foundation
321 Cedar Street
P.O. Box 215
Bristol, PA 19007
Tel: 215-781-9895

Broad Top Area Coal Miners Historical Society
Main Street
Robertsdale, PA 16674
Tel: 814-635-3807
http://www.angelfire.com/pa3/btcoal/

Brownsville Historical Society
P.O. Box 24
Brownsville, PA 15417

Bucks County Historical Society
Spruance Library/Mercer Museum
84 S. Pine Street
Doylestown, PA 18901-4999
Tel: 215-345-0210
Fax: 215-230-0823
E-mail: info@mercermuseum.org
http://www.mercermuseum.org/

Butler County Historical Society
Butler County Heritage Center
119 W. New Castle Street
P.O. Box 414
Butler, PA 16003-0414
Tel: 412-283-8116
Fax: 412-283-2505
http://www.butlercounty.com/local/historical/

California Area Historical Society
429 Wood Street
P.O. Box 624
California, PA 15419-0624
Tel: 724-938-3250
http://www.geocities.com/mdonald318/californiahs.html

Cambria County Historical Society
615 N. Center Street
P.O. Box 278
Ebensburg, PA 15931
Tel: 814-472-6674
http://www.cambriacountyhistorical.com/

Cameron County Historical Society
102 East Fourth Street
Emporium, PA 15834

Carbondale Historical Society
1 North Main Street, 3rd Floor
P.O. Box 151
Carbondale, PA 18407-2356
Tel: 570-282-0385
E-mail: silasrobert@juno.cm

Carnegie, Historical Society of
140 E. Main Street
Carnegie, PA 15106
Tel: 412-276-7447

Centre County Historical Society
1001 East College Avenue
State College, PA 16801
Tel: 814-234-4779
http://centrecountyhistory.org/

Chadds Ford Historical Society
Route 100 North
1736 Creek Road
P.O. Box 27
Chadds Ford, PA 19317
Tel: 610-388-7376
Fax: 610-388-7480
E-mail: cfhs@voicenet.com
www.voicenet.com/~cfhs

Chester County Historical Society
225 North High Street
West Chester, PA 19380
Tel: 610-692-4800
Fax: 610-692-4357
E-mail: cchs@chestercohistorical.org
http://www.chesco.com/~cchs/

Clarion County Historical Society
17 South Fifth Avenue
Clarion, PA 16214-1501
Tel: 814-226-4450
Fax: 814-226-7106
E-mail: cchs@csonline.net
http://www.csonline.net/cchs/

Clearfield County Historical Society
104 East Pine Street
Clearfield, PA 16830-2517
Tel: 814-765-6125

Clinton County Historical Society
362 East Water Street
Lock Haven, PA 17745
Tel: 570-748-7254
http://www.kcnet.org/~heisey/

Cocalico Valley, Historical Society of
249 West Main Street
P.O. Box 193
Ephrata, PA 17522
Tel: 717-733-1616
http://www.fieldtrip.com/pa/77331616.htm

Cochranton Heritage Society
P.O. Box 598
Cochranton, PA 16314-0598
Tel: 814-425-7849

481

Columbia County Historical Society
225 Market Street
P.O. Box 360
Bloomsburg, PA 17815-0360
Tel: 570-784-1600

Conemaugh Township Historical Society
100 South Main Street
Davidsville, PA 15928
Tel: 814-479-2067

Conneaut Valley Area Historical Sociey (CVAHS)
1625 Main Street
P.O. Box 266
Conneatuville, PA 16406
Tel: 814-587-3782
http://cvahs.org/

Connellsville Area Historical Society
275 South Pittsburgh Street
Connellsville, PA 15425-3580
Tel: 724-628-5640

Corry Area Historical Society
945 Mead Avenue
Corry, PA 16407
Tel: 814-664-4749

Crawford County Historical Society
848 North Main Street
Meadville, PA 16335
Tel: 814-724-6080
E-mail: cchs@ccfls.org
http://ccfls.org/historical/

Croatian Fraternal Union of America
100 Delaney Street
Pittsburgh, PA 15235
Tel: 412-351-3909
Fax: 412-823-1594
http://www.croatianfraternalunion.org/

Cumberland County Historical Society
21 North Pitt Street
P.O. Box 626
Carlisle, PA 17013-0626
Tel: 717-249-7610
http://www.historicalsociety.com/

Dauphin County, Historical Society of
219 South Front Street
Harrisburg, PA 17104
Tel: 717-233-3462
Fax: 717-233-6059
http://www.visithhc.com/harrismn.html

Delaware County Historical Society
Room 208, Malin Road Center
Delaware County Community College
85 North Malin Road
Broomall, PA 19008-1928
Tel: 610-359-1148
http://www.delcohistory.org/dchs/

Derry Area Historical Society
P. O. Box 64
New Derry, PA 15671
Tel: 724-694-9564
E-mail: nquirer@juno.comg
http://www.derryhistory.org/

Derry Township Historical Society
50 North Linden Road
P.O. Box 316
Hershey, PA 17033
Tel: 717-520-0748

DuBois Area Historical Society
30 West Long Avenue
P.O. Box 401
DuBois, PA 15801-0401
Tel: 814-371-9006
http://home.wrkcs.net/history/

Elizabeth Township Historical Society
5811 Smithfield Street
Boston, PA 15135
Tel: 412-754-2030
Fax: 412.754.2036
E-mail: eths@icubed.com
http://www.15122.com/ETHS/

Elk County Historical Society
109 Center Street
P.O. Box 361
Ridgway, PA 15853-0361
Tel: 814-776-1032
http://www.elkcountyhistoricalsociety.org/

Erie County Historical Society
419 State Street
Erie, PA 16501-1106
Tel: 814-454-1813
E-mail: echs@velocity.net

Evangelical & Reformed Church, Historical Society of Archives
555 W James Street
Lancaster, PA 17604
Tel: 717-393-0654
Fax: 717-393-4254
E-mail: erhs@lts.org
http://www.erhs.info

Evans City Historical Society
220 Wahl Avenue
Evans City, PA 16033
Tel: 724-538-3629

Fairview Area Historical Society
4302 Garwood Street
P.O. Box 553
Fairview, PA 16415-0553
Tel: 814-474-5635

Fayette County Historical Society
P.O. Box 193
Uniontown, PA 15401-0193
Tel: 724-439-4422

Forest County Historical Society
206 Elm Street
Tionesta, PA 16353
Tel: 814-755-4422
http://members.tripod.com/forestchs/

Fort Loudon Historical Society
1720 Brooklyn Road
Fort Loudon, PA 17224
Tel: 717-369-3473
E-mail: fortloudoun@innernet.net

Fort Manson Historical Society
546 N. Main Street
Masontown, PA 15461
Tel: 724-583-9944

Fort Washintton, Historical Society of
473 Bethlehem Pike
Fort Washington, PA 19034
Tel: 215-646-6065

Frankford, Historical Society of
1507 Orthodox Street
Philadelphia, PA 19124
Tel: 215-743-6030

Fulton County Historical Society
P.O. Box 115
McConnellsburg, PA 17233-0115
http://www.fchs.tiu.k12.pa.us/

German Society of Pennsylvania
611 Spring Garden Street
Philadelphia, PA 19123
Tel: 215-627-2332
    215-627-4365 (Library)
Fax: 215-627-5297
E-mail: contact@germansociety.org
http://www.germansociety.org/

Germantown Historical Society
5501 Germantown Avenue (Market Square)
Philadelphia, PA 19144-2225
Tel: 215-844-0514 (Museum)
    215-844-8428 (Library/Archives)
http://www.libertynet.org/ghs/

Goschenhoppen Historians
Redmen's Hall
Route 29
Green Lane, PA 18054
Tel: 215-234-8953
E-mail: redmens_hall@goschenhoppen.org
http://www.goschenhoppen.org/

Governor Wolf Historical Society
6600 Jacksonville Road
Bath, PA 18014-8940
Tel: 610-837-9015

Green Tree, Historical Society of
10 West Manilla Avenue
Pittsburgh, PA 15220
Tel: 412-921-9292

Greene County Historical Society/Library & Museum
P.O. Box 127
Waynesburg, PA 15370-0127
Tel: 724-627-3204
http://www.greenepa.net/~museum/

Greenville Historical Society
94 College Avenue
Greenville, PA 16125
Tel: 724-588-7150

Hanover Area Historical Society
113 W. Chestnut Street
Hanover, PA 17331
Tel: 717-632-3207
Fax: 717-632-5199

Hazleton Historical Society
55 N. Wyoming Street
Hazleton, PA 18201
Tel: 570-455-8576
http://www.hazletonhistory.8m.com/home.htm

Hellertown Historical Society
150 W. Walnut Street
Hellertown, PA 18055
Tel: 610-838-1770

Heritage Society of Pennsylvania
P.O. Box 146
Laughlintown, PA 15655

Highlands Historical Society
7001 Sheaff Lane
Fort Washington, PA 19034
Tel: 215-641-2687

Historic Catasauqua Preservation Association
P.O. Box 186
Catasauqua, PA 18032
Tel: 610-266-2948

Historic Schaefferstown
P.O. Box 1776
Schaefferstown, PA 17088
Tel: 717-949-2244

Homestead Pennsylvania Historical Society
1110 Silvan Avenue
Homestead, PA 15120

Huguenot Society of Pennsylvania
1313 Spruce Street
Philadelphia, PA 19107

Hummelstown Area Historical Society
P.O. Box 252
Hummelstown, PA 17036
Tel: 717-566-6314

Huntingdon County Historical Society
100 4th Street
Huntingdon, PA 16652
Tel: 814-643-5449
E-mail: mail@huntingdonhistory.org
http://www.huntingdonhistory.org/

Indiana County, Historical & Genealogical Society of
200 South 6th Street
Indiana, PA 15701
Tel: 724-463-9600
http://www.rootsweb.com/~paicgs/

Jacobsburg Historical Society
402 Henry Road
Nazareth, PA 18064
Tel: 610-759-9029

Jamestown Area Historical Society
405 Summit Street
P.O. Box 243
Jamestown, PA 16134
Tel: 412-932-5997

Jefferson County Historical & Genealogical Society
232 Jefferson Street
P.O. Box 51
Brookville, PA 15825
Tel: 814-849-0077
http://www.pa-roots.com/~jefferson/jchgs/jchgs.html

Juniata County Historical Society
498 Jefferson Street
Mifflintown, PA 17059
Tel: 717-436-5152

Kittochtinny Historical Society
175 East Kint Street
Chambersburg, PA 17201
Tel: 717-264-1667
http://www.rootsweb.com/~pakhs/

Kutztown Area Historical Society
Normal & White Avenue
Kutztown, PA 19530
Tel: 610-683-7697

Lackawanna Historical Society
232 Monroe Avenue
Scranton, PA 18510
Tel: 717-344-3841

Lancaster County Historical Society/Library and Museum
230 North President Avenue
Lancaster, PA 17603
Tel: 717-392-4633
E-mail: lchs@ptd.net (Research requests)
        lchs@juno.com (Information)
http://lanclio.org/

Lancaster Mennonite Historical Society
2215 Millstream Road
Lancaster, PA 17602
Tel: 717-393-9745
http://www.lmhs.org/

Lansdale Historical Society
137 Jenkins Avenue
Lansdale, PA 19446
Tel: 215-855-1872

Latrobe Historical Society
1501 Ligonier Street
Latrobe, PA 15650
Tel: 724-539-8889

Lawrence County Historical Society
408 N. Jefferson Street
P.O. Box 1745
New Castle, PA 16101
Tel/Fax: 724-658-4022
E-mail: history@lcix.net
http://www.ilovehistory.com/

Lebanon County Historical Society
924 Cumberland Street
Lebanon, PA 17042
Tel: 717-272-1473

Lehigh County Historical Society
501 Hamilton Street
P.O. Box 1548
Allentown, PA 18105-1548
Tel: 610-435-1074
Fax: 610-435-9812
http://www.users.voicenet.com/~lchs/

Lenni Lenape Historical Society of Pennsylvania
2825 Fish Hatchery Road
Allentown, PA 18102
Tel: 610-797-2121

Levittown Historical Society
7200 New Falls Road
P.O. Box 1641
Levittown, PA 19058-1641

Ligonier Valley Historical Society
P.O. Box 167
Laughlintown, PA 15655
Tel: 412-238-6818
E-mail: info@compassinn.com
http://www.compassinn.com/lvhs.html

Limerick Township Historical Society
545 West Ridge Pike
Limerick, PA 19468
Tel: 610-495-5229

Lititz Historical Foundation
145 E. Main
Lititz, PA 17543
Tel: 717-627-4636
http://www.lititzmutual.com/historical/

Lower Macungie Township Historical Society
P.O. Box 3722
Wescosville, PA 18106
http://www.geocities.com/Heartland/3955/
      LMTHS.htm

Lycoming County Historical Society
858 West 4th Street
Williamsport, PA 17701
Tel: 570-326-3326
http://www.lycoming.org/lchsmuseum/

Manheim Historical Society
88 South Grant Street
P. O. Box 396
Manheim, PA 17545
Tel: 717-665-7989
http://www.manheimpa.com/board.html

Masontown Historical Society
P.O. Box 769
Masontown, PA 15461

Mauch Chunk Historical Society
14 W. Broadway
Jim Thorpe, PA 18229
Tel: 570-325-4439

McKean County Historical Society
Courthouse
Smethport, PA 16749
Tel: 814-887-5142

Mennonite Historians of Eastern Pennsylvania
Mennonite Heritage Center
565 Yoder Road
P.O. Box 82
Harleysville, PA 19438-0082
Tel: 215-256-3020
Fax: 215-256-3023
E-mail: info@mhep.org
http://www.mhep.org/

Mercer County Historical Society
119 South Pitt Street
Mercer, PA 16137
Tel: 724-662-3490

Mifflin County Historical Society
1 West Market Street, #1
Lewiston, PA 17044
Tel: 717-242-1022
http://www.mccoyhouse.com/

Military Order of the Loyal Legion of the United States
1805 Pine Street
Philadelphia, PA 19103
Tel: 215-546-2425
E-mail: YJNW42A@prodigy.com
http://suvcw.org/mollus.htm

Millersburg & Upper Paxton Township, Historical Society of
Center Street
Millersburg, PA 17061
Tel: 717-692-4084

Milton Historical Society
River Road
Milton, PA 17847
Tel: 570-742-7057

Monroe County Historical Association
900 Main Street
Stroudsburg, PA 18360
Tel: 570-421-7703
Fax: 570-421-9199
http://mcha.stroudsburg.com/

Monroeville Historical Society
2700 Monroeville Boulevard
Monroeville, PA 15146
Tel: 412-856-1000
Fax: 412856-3366

Montgomery County, Historical Society of
Library and Genealogy Study Group
1654 DeKalb Street
Norristown, PA 19401
Tel: 610-272-0297

Montour County Historical Society
Bloom Street
P.O. Box 8
Danville, PA 17821
Tel: 570-275-0228

Moravian Historical Society
214 E. Center Street
Nazareth, PA 18064
Tel: 610-759-5070
Fax: 610-759-2461
E-mail: morhistsoc@rcn.com
http://www.moravianhistoricalsociety.org/

Muncy Historical Society & Museum of History
40 N. Main Street
P.O. Box 11
Muncy, PA 17756
Tel: 570-546-5917
E-mail: muncyhistorical@aol.com
http://members.aol.com/LCGSgen/muncy.htm

National Historical Society
6405 Flank Drive
Harrisburg, PA 17112
Tel: 717-657-9555

National Railway Historical Society
100 N. 17th Street
P.O. Box 58547
Philadelphia, PA 19103
Tel: 215-557-6606
Fax: 215-557-6740
http://www.nrhs.com

New Hope Historical Society
45 South Main
New Hope, PA 18938
Tel: 215-862-5652
E-mail: newhopehistoricalso@msn.com
http://www.parrymansion.org/

Newtown Historic Association
Centre Avenue and Court Street
P.O. Box 303
Newtown, PA 18940
Tel: 215-968-4004
http://www.twp.newtown.pa.us/historic/nha.html

Newville Historical Society
Dougherty-Welch House
69 S. High Street
Newville, PA 17241
Tel: 717-776-6210
http://www.cumberlink.com/cumb/hist.groups.html

Northampton County Historical & Genealogical Society
101 South 4th Street
Easton, PA 18042
Tel: 610-253-1222
http://www.northamptonctymuseum.org/

Northumberland County Historical Society
1150 North Front Street
Sunbury, PA 17801
Tel: 570-286-4083
http://www.mahantongo.org/nchs.htm

Oil City Heritage Society
P.O. Box 962, Oil Creek Station
Oil City, PA 16301

Old York Road Historical Society
The Jenkintown Library
460 Old York Road
Jenkintown, PA 19046
Tel: 215-884-0593
Fax: 215-884-2243
http://www.jenkintown.com/library

Pennsylvania German Society
P.O. Box 244
Kutztown, PA 19530-0244
Tel: 610-894-9551

Pennsylvania, Historical Society of
Library & Museum (Closed 11/27/97 - 4/13/98)
1300 Locust Street
Philadelphia, PA 19107
Tel: 215-732-6200
Fax: 215-732-2680
E-mail: hsppr@aol.com
http://www.hsp.org/

Perry County Historical Society
P.O. Box 81
Newport, PA 17074

Phoenixville Area, Historical Society of
Main and Church
P.O. Box 552
Phoenixville, PA 19453
Tel: 610-935-7646
http://www.users.voicenet.com/~dstav/

Pike County Historical Society
608 Broad Street
Milford, PA 18337
Tel: 570-296-8126
E-mail: pchs1@pikeonline.net
http://www.pikehistory.org/

Pioneer Historical Society of Bedford County/Library
242 E. John Street
Bedford, PA 15522
Tel: 814-623-2011
http://www.rootsweb.com/~paphsbc/

Pittsburgh History & Landmarks Foundation
450 One Station Square
Pittsburgh, PA 15219
Tel: 412-471-5808
Fax: 412-471-1633
E-mail: info@phlf.org
http://www.phlf.org/

Plymouth Historical Society
115 Gaylord Avenue
Plymouth, PA 18651
Tel: 570-779-5840
http://www.rootsweb.com/~paplyhs/PHS/

Plymouth Meeting Historical Society
2130 Sierra Road
P.O. Box 167
Plymouth Meeting, PA 19462
Tel: 610-828-8111

Potter County Historical Society
308 North Main Street
P.O. Box 605
Coudersport, PA 16915-1626
Tel: 814-274-8124
www.pottercountypa.net/history

Presbyterian Historical Society
425 Lombard Street
Philadelphia, PA 19147
Tel: 215-627-1852
Fax: (215) 627-0509
E-mail: prehist@shrsys.hslc.org
http://www.history.pcusa.org/about/phila.html

Punxsutawney Area Historical & Genealogical Society
Bennis House Museum
401 West Mahoning Street
P.O. Box 286
Punxsutawney, PA 15767
Tel: 814-938-2555
E-mail: mweimer@penn.com
http://users.penn.com/~mweimer/historcl.html

Quakertown Historical Society
26 N. Main Street
Quakertown, PA 18951-1114
Tel: 215-536-3298

Radnor Historical Society
113 W. Beechtree Lane
Wayne, PA 19087-3212
Tel: 610-688-2668
http://www.delcohistory.org/rhs/

Reading Company Technical & Historical Society
P.O. Box 15143
Reading, PA 19612
Tel: 610-372-5513
E-mail: reading@vicon.net
http://www.readingrailroad.org/

Red Lion Area Historical Society
10 E. Broadway
Red Lion, PA 17356
Tel: 717-244-1912

St. Marys/Benzinger Township, Historical Society of
319 Erie Avenue
St. Marys, PA 15857
Tel: 814-834-6525

Schuylkill County, Historical Society of
14 N. Third Street
Pottsville, PA 17901-2905
Tel: 570-622-7540
http://www.rootsweb.com/~paschuyl/HSSC.html

Scotch-Irish Society of the U.S.A.
P.O. Box 181
Bryn Mawr, PA 19010

Scottish Historic & Research Society of the Delaware Valley
102 St. Paul's Road
Ardmore, PA 19003
Tel: 610-649-4144

Sewickley Valley Historical Society
200 Broad Street
Sewickley, PA 15143
Tel: 412-741-5315

Shippensburg Historical Society/Library
52 W. King Street
Shippensburg, PA 17257
Tel: 717-532-6727

Snyder County Historical Society
30 East Market Street
P.O. Box 276
Middleburg, PA 17842
Tel: 570-837-6191
Fax: 570-837-4282 (courthouse)
http://www.rootsweb.com/~pasnyder/historical.htm

Somerset County, Historical & Genealogical Society of
10649 Somerset Pike
RD 2, Box 238
Somerset, PA 15501-9802
Tel: 814-445-6077
http://www.somersetcounty.com/historicalcenter/
        index.html

South Bethlehem Historical Society
479 Brighton Street
Bethlehem, PA 18015
Tel: 610-758-8790

Springford Area Historical Society
200 South Fourth Avenue
Royersford, PA 19468
Tel: 610-948-7127

Stoneboro Community & Historical Society
11 Railroad Street
Stoneboro, PA 16153
Tel: 724-376-4190

Sullivan County Historical Society
Court House Square
Meylert Street
Laporte, PA 18626
Tel: 570-946-5020
http://www.rootsweb.com/~pasulliv/
        SullivanCountyHistoricalSociety/SCHS.html

Susquehanna County Historical Society
Susquehanna County Free Library
2 Monument Square, 2nd Floor
Montrose, PA 18801
Tel: 570-278-1881
E-mail: suspulib@epix.net
http://www.susqcohistsoc.org/

Susquehanna Depot Historical Society
P.O. Box 161
Susquehanna, PA 18847

Swedish Colonial Society
336 South Devon Avenue
Wayne, PA 19087
Tel: 610-688-1766
http://libertynet.org/~gencap/scs.html

Tamaqua Historical Society
118 W. Broad Street
Tamaqua, PA 18252
Tel: 570-668-5722

Tioga County Historical Society
Robinson House/Rhoda Ladd Genealogy Library
120 Main Street
P.O. Box 724
Wellsboro, PA 16901
Tel: 570-724-6116
http://www.rootsweb.com/~patioga/tchs.htm

Trappe Historical Society
201 Main Street
Trappe, PA 19426
Tel: 610-489-8883

Tri-County Heritage Society
8 Mill Road
Morgantown, PA 19543
Tel: 610-286-7477

Tulpehocken Settlement Historical Society
116 N. Front Street
P.O. Box 53
Womelsdorf, PA 19567
Tel: 610-589-2527
http://www.berksmuseums.org/tulpe/

Tuscarora Township Historical Society
RD 2, Box 105-C
Laceyville, PA 18623
Tel: 570-869-2184

Ukrainian Fraternal Association
440 Wyoming Avenue
Scranton, PA 18503
Tel: 717-342-0937
http://members.tripod.com/~ufa_home/

Union City Historical Society/Museum
11 South Main Street
Union City, PA 16438
Tel: 814-438-7573

Union County Historical Society
103 S. Second Street
Lewisburg, PA 17837
Tel: 570-524-8666
Fax:570-524-8743
E-mail: Hstoricl@ptd.net
http://www.rootsweb.com/~paunion/society.html

University City Historical Society
40th and Woodland Avenue
P.O. Box 31927
Philadelphia, PA 19104
Tel: 215-387-3019
E-mail: info@uchs.net
http://www.uchs.net/

Valley Forge Historical Society
P.O. Box 122
Valley Forge, PA 19481
Tel: 610-783-0535
E-mail: vfhs@ix.netcom.com
http://www.valleyforgemuseum.org/

Venango County Historical Society
301 S. Park Street
Franklin, PA 16323
Tel: 814-437-2275
http://www.rootsweb.com/~pavenang/venhistsc.htm

Victorian Vandergrift Museum and Historical Society
151 Lincoln Avenue
Vandergrift, PA 15690
Tel: 724-568-1990

Warren County Historical Society
210 Fourth Avenue
P.O. Box 427
Warren, PA 16365-0427
Tel: 814-723-1795

Washington County Historical Society
49 East Maiden Street
Washington, PA 15301
Tel: 724-225-6740
Fax: 724-225-8495
http://www.wchspa.org/

Wattsburg Area Historical Society
P.O. Box 240
Wattsburg, PA 16442

Wayne County Historical Society
810 Main Street
P.O. Box 446
Honesdale, PA 18431
Tel: 570-253-3240
E-mail: wchs@ptd.net~general

Waynesboro Historical Society
138 W. Main Street
Waynesboro, PA 17268
Tel: 717-762-1747

West Whiteland Township Historical Commission
222 North Pottstown Pike
Exton, PA 19341
Phone: 610-363-9525
Fax: 610-363-5099
http://www.westwhiteland.org

Western Pennsylvania, Historical Society of
Pittsburgh Regional History Center
1212 Smallman Street
Pittsburgh, PA 15222
Tel: 412-454-6000
Fax: 412-454-6031
E-mail: library@hswp.org
http://www.pghhistory.org/

Westmoreland County Historical Society
951 Old Salem Road
Greensburg, PA 15601
Tel: 724-836-1800
www.wchspa.com

Whitehall Historical Preservation Society
Mickley and Lenhart Roads
Whitehall, PA 18052
Tel: 610-776-7166

Wilkinsburg Historical Society
c/o Wilkinsburg Public Library
605 Ross Avenue
Pittsburgh, PA 15221
Tel: 412-244-2940
http://www.clpgh.org/ein/wlksbrg/

Wissahickon Valley Historical Society
Route 73 and School Road
Blue Bell, PA 19422
Tel: 215-646-6541

Wyoming County Historical Society
Harrison and Bridge Street
P.O. Box 309
Tunkhannock, PA 18657
Tel: 570-836-5303

Wyoming Historical & Geological Society
69 South Franklin Street
Wilkes-Barre, PA 18701
Tel: 570-822-1727

Yardley Historical Association
46 W. Afton Avenue
P.O. Box 212
Yardley, PA 19067
Tel: 215-493-9883
http://www.bucksnet.com/yardley/yha/histassn.html

York County, Historical Society of
250 East Market Street
York, PA 17403
Tel: 717-848-1587
http://www.yorkheritage.org

Zelienople Historical Society
243 S. Main Street
P.O. Box 45
Zelienople, PA 16063
Tel: 412-452-9457
http://www.fyi.net/~zhs/

LDS FAMILY HISTORY CENTERS

For locations of Family History Centers in this state, see the Family History Center locator at FamilySearch.
http://www.familysearch.org/eng/Library/FHC/frameset_fhc.asp

ARCHIVES/LIBRARIES/MUSEUMS

Afro American Historical & Cultural Museum
701 Arch Street
Philadelphia, PA 19106
Tel: 215-574-0380
http://www.fieldtrip.com/pa/55740380.htm

Allegheny Valley, Community Library of
315 East 6th Avenue
Tarentum, PA 15084
Tel: 724-226-0770
http://www.clpgh.org/ein/alvalley/

Altoona Area Public Library
1600 5th Avenue
Altoona, PA 16602-3621
Tel: 814-946-0417
Fax: 814-946-3230
E-mail: altpublib@aasdcat.com
http://www.altoonalibrary.org/

American-Swedish Historical Museum
(in Franklin Delano Roosevelt Park)
1900 Patterson Avenue
Philadelphia, PA 19102
Tel: 215-389-1776
E-mail: ashm@libertynet.org
http://www.libertynet.org/~ashm/

Annenberg Research Institute
420 Walnut Street
Philadelphia, PA 19106
Tel: 215-238-1290
Fax: 215-238-1540

Archives of the Moravian Church
41 W. Locust Street
Bethlehem, PA 18018
Tel: 610-866-3255
http://www.moravianchurcharchives.com/

Armstrong County Historical Museum & Genealogical Society
300 North McKean Street
P.O. Box 735
Kittanning, PA 16201-1345
Tel: 724-548-5707
http://www.angelfire.com/pa2/acgs/

Athenaeum of Philadelphia
219 S. Sixth Street
Philadelphia, PA 19106
Tel: 215-925-2688
Fax: 215-925-3755
E-mail: athena@libertynet.org
http://www.philaathenaeum.org/

Balch Institute for Ethnic Studies
18 South 7th Street
Philadelphia, PA 19106-3794
Tel: 215-925-8090
Fax: 215-925-4392
E-mail: info@balchinstitute.org
http://www.balchinstitute.org/

Bedford County Pioneers Historical Society/Library
242 E. John Street
Bedford, PA 15522-1750
Tel: 814-623-2011
http://www.rootsweb.com/~paphsbc/

Berks County, Historical Society of
Library and Museum
940 Centre Avenue
Reading, PA 19601
Tel: 610-375-4375
http://www.berksweb.com/histsoc.html

Bloomsburg Public Library
225 Market Street
Bloomsburg, PA 17815
Tel: 570-784-0883
Fax: 570-784-8541
E-mail: bloompl@earth.sunlink.net
townhall.bafn.org/library/bloom.htm

Bloomsburg University
Harvey A. Andruss Library
400 E. Second Street
Bloomsburg, PA 17815
Tel/TDD: 570-389-4204
Fax: 570-389-3895
http://library.bloomu.edu/

Bradford County Historical Society/Museum
109 Pine Street
Towanda PA 18848
Tel: 570-265-2240
http://www.rootsweb.com/~srgp/bchsmain.htm

Bucks County Historical Society
Spruance Library/Mercer Museum
84 S. Pine Street
Doylestown, PA 18901-4999
Tel: 215-345-0210
Fax: 215-230-0823
E-mail: info@mercermuseum.org
http://www.mercermuseum.org/

Butler Area Public Library
Weir Genealogy Room
218 N. McKean Street
Butler, PA 16001-4911
Tel: 724-287-1715
http://www.butler.library-online.org/

Cambria County Library
248 Main Street
Johnstown, PA 15901-1677
Tel: 814-536-5131
Fax: 814-536-6905
ILL Fax: 814-535-4140
E-mail: reference@ns.cclib.lib.pa.us
http://www.cclib.lib.pa.us/

Carnegie Free Library
Beaver County Research Center
1301 Seventh Avenue
Beaver Falls, PA 15010
Tel: 724-846-4340
Fax: 724-846-0370
E-mail: CFL2000@mailcity.com
http://www.co.beaver.pa.us/Library/bf.html

Carnegie Library of Pittsburgh
Pennsylvania Department
4400 Forbes Avenue
Pittsburgh, PA 15213
Tel: 412-622-3114
http://www.carnegielibrary.org/

Centre County Library/Historical Museum
203 N. Allegheny Street
Bellefonte, PA 16823-1601
Tel: 814-355-1516

Chester County Archives and Records Service
601 Westtown Road
West Chester, PA 19382-4527
Tel: 610-344-6760

Citizens Library
55 South College Street
Washington, PA 15301
Tel: 724-222-2400
Fax: 724-225-7303
Public Fax: 724-222-2606
E-mail: citlib@citlib.org
http://www.citlib.org/

Civil War Library and Museum
1805 Pine Street
Philadelphia, PA 19103
Tel: 215-735-8196
http://www.netreach.net/~cwlm/

Coyle Free Library
102 N. Main Street
Chambersburg, PA 17201
Tel: 717-263-1054
http://www.fclspa.org/coyle/coyle.htm

Cumberland County Historical Society
Hamilton Library
21 North Pitt Street
P.O. Box 626
Carlisle, PA 17013-0626
Tel: 717-249-7610
http://www.historicalsociety.com/

Darby Free Library
History Room
1001 Main Street
P.O. Box 164
Darby, PA 19023-0164
Tel: 610-586-7310
Fax: 610-586-2781
E-mail: darby@delco.lib.pa.us
http://www.darbylibrary.org/

David Library of the American Revolution
1201 River Road
P.O. Box 748
Washington Crossing, PA 18977
Tel: 215-493-6776
Fax: 215-493-9276
E-mail: dlar@dlar.org
http://www.dlar.org/

Easton Area Public Library
6th and Church Streets
Easton, PA 18042
Tel: 610-258-2917
http://www.eastonpl.org/welcome.html

Erie County Public Library/Blasco Library
160 East Front Street
Erie, PA 16509
Tel: 814-451-6900
    814-451-6927 (Heritage Room)
Fax: 814-451-6907
E-mail: reference@erielibrary.ecls.lib.pa.us
http://www.ecls.lib.pa.us/family.html

Eva K. Bowlby Public Library
311 N. West Street
Waynesburg, PA 15370-1238
Tel: 724-627-9776

Evangelical & Reformed Church, Historical Society of Archives
555 W James Street
Lancaster, PA 17604
Tel: 717-393-0654
Fax: 717-393-4254
E-mail: erhs@lts.org
http://www.erhs.info

Ford City Public Library
1136 4th Avenue
Fort City, PA 16226-1202
Tel: 724-763-3591

Franklin Public Library
Pennsylvania Room
421 12th Street
Franklin, PA 16323-1205
Tel: 814-432-5062

German Society of Pennsylvania
611 Spring Garden Street
Philadelphia, PA 19123
Tel: 215-627-2332
    215-627-4365 (Library)
Fax: 215-627-5297
E-mail: contact@germansociety.org
http://www.germansociety.org/

Germantown Historical Society
5501 Germantown Avenue (Market Square)
Philadelphia, PA 19144-2225
Tel: 215-844-0514 (Museum)
    215-844-8428 (Library/Archives)
http://www.libertynet.org/ghs/

Grand Army of the Republic War Museum/Ruan House Library
4278 Griscom Street
Philadelphia, PA 19124-3954
Tel: 215-289-6484
E-mail: GARMUSLIB@aol.com
http://suvcw.org/garmus.htm

Green Free Library
134 Main Street
Wellsboro, PA 16901-1489
Tel: 570-724-4876
Fax: 570-724-7605
http://home.epix.net/~greenlib/

Greene County Historical Society/Library & Museum
RR 2
P.O. Box 127
Waynesburg, PA 15370
Tel: 724-627-3204
E-mail: museum@greenepa.net
http://www.greenepa.net/~museum/

Hoenstine Rental Library
414 Montgomery
P.O. Box 208
Hollidaysburg, PA 16648
Tel: 814-695-0632

Holocaust Center of Greater Pittsburgh
242 McKee Place
Pittsburgh, PA 15213
E-mail: information@ujf.net

Independence Seaport Museum
211 S. Columbus Blvd. & Walnut Street
Philadelphia, PA 19106
Tel: 215-925-5439
http://phillyseaport.org/

James V. Brown Library
19 East 4th Street
Williamsport, PA 17701
Tel: 570-326-0536
http://www.jvbrown.edu/index.html

Juniata Mennonite Historical Center
HCR 63
Richfield, PA 17086
Tel: 717-694-3211

Lancaster County Historical Society/Library and Museum
230 North President Avenue
Lancaster, PA 17603
Tel: 717-392-4633
E-mail: lchs@ptd.net (Research requests)
    lchs@juno.com (Information)
http://lanclio.org/

Lancaster County Library
125 North Duke Street
Lancaster, PA 17602
Tel: 717-394-2651
http://www.lancaster.lib.pa.us/

Lancaster County Records and Archives Service
Old Courthouse
50 North Duke Street, Ground Floor
P.O. Box 3450
Lancaster, PA 17602
Tel: 717-299-8318

Lebanon Community Library
125 N. Seventh Street
Lebanon, PA 17046
Tel: 717-273-7624
Fax: 717-273-2719
E-mail: tremaine@lebanoncountylibraries.org
http://www.leblibrarysys.org/lebanon/

Library Company of Philadelphia
1314 Locust Street
Philadelphia, PA 19107
Tel: 215-546-3181
Fax: 215-546-5167
E-mail: refdept@librarycompany.org
http://www.librarycompany.org/

Martinsburg Community Library
201 South Walnut Street
Martinsburg, PA 16662
Tel: 814-793-3335
Fax: 814-793-9755
http://www.nbcsd.k12.pa.us/mar_lib.htm

Mechanicsburg Area Public Library
16 North Walnut Street
Mechanicsburg, PA 17055
Tel: 717-766-0171
Fax: 717-766-0152
E-mail: mechanicsburg@ccpa.net
http://www.ccpa.net/library/MCHhome.html

Media/Upper Providence Free Library
Upper Providence Room
Front and Jackson Streets
Media, PA 19063
Tel: 610-566-1918
http://www.medialibrary.org/

Mennonite Family History Library
10 W. Main Street
Elverson, PA 19520-0171
Tel: 610-286-0258
Fax: 610-286-6860
http://feefhs.org/men/frg-mfh.html

Mennonite Historians of Eastern Pennsylvania
Mennonite Heritage Center
565 Yoder Road
P.O. Box 82
Harleysville, PA 19438-0082
Tel: 215-256-3020
Fax: 215-256-3023
E-mail: info@mhep.org
http://www.mhep.org/

Mercer Area Library
143 N. Pitt Street
Mercer, PA 16137-1206
Tel: 724-662-4233
Fax: 724-662-8893
E-mail: mercerarealib@htol.net
http://206.180.110.12/mercer/

Methodist Historical Center
326 New Street
Philadelphia, PA 19106

Military Order of the Loyal Legion of the United States
1805 Pine Street
Philadelphia, PA 19103
Tel: 215-546-2425
E-mail: YJNW42A@prodigy.com
http://suvcw.org/mollus.htm

Monroe County Public Library
1002 N 9th Street
Stroudsburg, PA 18360
Tel: 570-421-0800

Montgomery County Archives
1880 Markley Street
Norristown, PA 19401
Tel: 610-278-3441

Montgomery County, Historical Society of Library and Genealogy Study Group
1654 DeKalb Street
Norristown, PA 19401
Tel: 610-272-0297
http://libertynet.org/~gencap/montcopa.html

Montgomery County/Norristown Public Library
1001 Powell Street
Norristown, PA 19401
Tel: 610-278-5100

Montgomery Public Library
1 South Main Street
Montgomery, PA 17751
Tel: 570-547-6212

Mount Lebanon Public Library
16 Castle Shannon Boulevard
Pittsburgh, PA 15228-2252
Tel: 412-531-1912
Fax: 412-531-1161
TTY: 412-531-5268
http://www.clpgh.org/ein/mtleb/

Myerstown Community Library
199 N. College Street
Myerstown, PA 17067
Tel: 717-866-2800
Fax: 717-866-5898
E-mail: llm@lebanoncountylibraries.org
http://www.leblibrarysys.org/myerstown/index.htm

National Museum of American Jewish History
55 North 5th Street
Philadelphia, PA 19102
Tel: 215-923-3811
Fax: 215-923-0763
E-mail: nmajh@nmajh.org
http://www.nmajh.org/

New Castle Public Library
207 East North Street
New Castle, PA 16101
Tel: 724-658-6659
http://www.newcastle.lib.pa.us/

Northland Public Library
300 Cumberland Road
Pittsburgh, PA 15237
Tel: 412-366-8100
E-mail: northland@einetwork.net
http://www.clpgh.org/ein/northland/home.htm

Oil City Library
2 Central Avenue
Oil City, PA 16301
Tel: 814-678-3072
E-mail: ocensle@csonline.net
http://www.csonline.net/oclibrary/

Osterhout Free Public Library
71 South Franklin Street
Wilkes-Barre, PA 18701
Tel: 570-823-0156
Fax: 570-823-5477
E-mail: dsuffren@osterhout.lib.pa.us
    Reference@osterhout.lib.pa.us
http://www.osterhout.lib.pa.us/

Pennsylvania German Cultural Heritage Center
Kutztown University
Weisenberger Alumni Center
Kutztown, PA 19530
Tel: 610-683-1330
http://www.kutztown.edu/community/pgchc/

Pennsylvania, Historical Society of
Library & Museum (Closed 11/27/97 - 4/13/98)
1300 Locust Street
Philadelphia, PA 19107
Tel: 215-732-6200
Fax: 215-732-2680
E-mail: hsppr@aol.com
http://www.hsp.org/

Pennsylvania, State Library of
Main Reading Room
Forum Building, Room 102
Walnut Street and Commonwealth Avenue
P.O. Box 1601
Harrisburg, PA 17105
Tel: 717-787-4440
    717-783-5950 (Reference)
Fax: 717-783-2070
TTY: 717-772-2863

Pennsylvania State University
Historical Collection and Labor Archives
104 Paterno Library
State Park, PA 16802
Tel: 814-863-2505
http://www.libraries.psu.edu/crsweb/speccol/
    spcoll.htm

Philadelphia Archdiocesan Historical Research Center
100 E. Wynnewood Road
Wynnewood, PA 19096-3001
Tel: 610-667-2125
E-mail: pahrc@ix.netcom.com
http://www.rc.net/philadelphia/pahrc/halvey.html

Philadelphia City Archives
401 North Broad Street, Suite 942
Philadelphia, PA 19108
Tel: 215-686-1580
Fax: 215-686-2283
http://libertynet.org/~gencap/philcity.html

Philadelphia, Free Library of
Central Library
Social Science and History Department
1901 Vine Street
Philadelphia, PA 19103
Tel: 215-686-5322
http://www.library.phila.gov/

Pioneer Historical Society of Bedford County/Library
242 E. John Street
Bedford, PA 15522
Tel: 814-623-2011
http://www.rootsweb.com/~paphsbc/

Polish American Cultural Center
308 Walnut Street
Philadelphia, PA 19106
Tel: 215-922-1700
E-mail: mail@polishamericancenter.org
http://www.polishamericancenter.com/index.htm

Pottsville Free Public Library
Reference Department
215 West Market Street
Pottsville, PA 17901
Tel: 570-622-8880
Fax: 570-622-2157
E-mail: potpublib@iu29.schiu.k12.pa.us
   or pot@iu29.schiu.k12.pa.us
http://www.schiu.k12.pa.us/potpl/library.html

Priestly-Forsythe Library
100 King Street
Northumberland, PA 17857
Tel: 570-473-8201
Fax: 570-473-8807
E-mail: pfml@ptdprolog.net
http://www.priestleyforsyth.org/

Punxsutawney Area Historical & Genealogical Society
401 West Mahoning Street
P.O. Box 286
Punxsutawney, PA 15767
Tel: 814-938-2555
E-mail: mweimer@penn.com
http://users.penn.com/~mweimer/historcl.html

Reading Public Library
100 South 5th
Reading, PA 19607
Tel: 610-655-6350
Fax: 610-478-9035
E-mail: webmaster@reading.lib.pa.us
http://www.reading.lib.pa.us/home

Ross Library
232 W. Main Street
Lock Haven, PA 17745-1241
Tel: 717-748-3321
Fax: 570-748-1050
http://www.rosslibrary.org/

St. Charles Borromeo Seminary
Ryan Memorial Library
100 East Wynnewood Road
Wynnewood, PA 19096
Tel: 610-785-6274
Fax: 610-664-7913
E-mail: libraryscs@adphila.org
http://www.scs.edu/library/

Schwenkfelder Theological and Historical Library
1 Seminary Street
Pennsburg, PA 18073
Tel: 215-679-3103

Sewickley Public Library
500 Thorn Street
Sewickley, PA 15143
Tel: 412-741-6920
http://www.einetwork.net/ein/sewickley/

Shenango Valley Community Library
11 N. Sharpsville Avenue
Sharon, PA 16146-2107
Tel: 724-981-4360
Fax: 724-981-5208

Shippensburg Historical Society/Library
52 W. King Street
Shippensburg, PA 17257
Tel: 717-532-6727

Susquehanna County Free Library
2 Monument Square
Montrose, PA 18801
Tel: 717-278-1881
E-mail: sctylibrary@stny.rr.com
http://www.epix.net/~suspulib/

Temple University
Paley Library/Special Collections
13th and Berks Streets
Philadelphia, PA 19122
Tel: 215-787-8230
Fax: 215-204-5201
http://www.library.temple.edu/speccoll/

Union City Historical Society/Museum
11 South Main Street
Union City, PA 16438
Tel: 814-438-7573

U.S. Army Military History Institute
22 Ashburn Drive, Carlisle Barracks
Carlisle, PA 17013-5008
Tel: 717-245-3611
http://carlisle-www.army.mil/usamhi/

University of Pennsylvania
Van Pelt Library
3420 Walnut Street
Philadelphia, PA 19104-6206
Tel: 215-898-7554/5
E-mail: librefer@pobox.upenn.edu
http://www.library.upenn.edu/vanpelt/

University of Pittsburgh
Hillman Library
3960 Forbes Avenue
Pittsburgh, PA 15260
Tel: 412-648-3330
    412-648-7800
http://www.library.pitt.edu/libraries/hillman/hillman.html

Upper Darby Township/Sellers Memorial Free Public Library
76 South State Road
Upper Darby, PA 19082-1999
Tel: 610-789-4440
http://www.geocities.com/udlib/
    Upper_Darby_ Library.html

Warren Library Association
205 Market Street
Warren, PA 16365
Tel: 814-723-4650
http://www.warrenlibrary.org/

West Chester University
Frances Harvey Green Library
University Avenue and High Street
West Chester, PA 19380
Tel: 610-436-3383
Fax: 610-436-2790
http://www.wcupa.edu/library.fhg/

Wilkinsburg Public Library
605 Ross Avenue
Pittsburgh, PA 15221
Tel: 412-244-2940
http://www.clpgh.org/ein/wlksbrg/

NEWSPAPER REPOSITORIES

Pennsylvania State Library
Main Reading Room
Forum Building, Room 102
Walnut Street and Commonwealth Avenue
P.O. Box 1601
Harrisburg, PA 17105
Tel: 717-787-4440
    717-783-5950 (Reference)
Fax: 717-783-2070
TTY: 717-772-2863

VITAL RECORDS

Philadelphia City Archives
401 North Broad Street, Suite 942
Philadelphia, PA 19108
Tel: 215-686-1580
Fax: 215-686-2283
http://libertynet.org/~gencap/philcity.html

Pittsburgh Registrar of Wills
City/County Building
Pittsburgh, PA 15219
Pittsburgh 1870-1905

State Department of Health
Division of Vital Statistics
101 S. Mercer Street
P.O. Box 1528
New Castle, PA 16103
Tel: 412-656-3100
Birth and Death 1906-present

PENNSYLVANIA ON THE WEB

Free Library of Philadelphia-Genealogy Pathfinder
http://www.library.phila.gov/

Kraig Ruckel's Palatine and Pennsylvania-Dutch Genealogy
http://www.geocities.com/Heartland/3955

Palatines to America-Online Immigrant Ancestor Registry Index
http://genealogy.org/~palam/ia_index.htm

Pennsylvania GenWeb Project
http://www.pagenweb.org/

Rhode Island

Archives, State & National

National Archives-Northeast Region (Boston)
Frederick C. Murphy Federal Center
380 Trapelo Road
Waltham, MA 02154-8104
Tel: 781-647-8104
Fax: 781-647-8088
E-mail: waltham.center@nara.gov
http://www.nara.gov/regional/boston.html

Rhode Island State Archives
337 Westminster Street
Providence, RI 02903
Tel: 401-222-2353
Fax: 401-222-3199
E-mail: reference@archives.state.ri.us
http://www.state.ri.us/archives/

Genealogical Societies

American-French Genealogical Society
(Library at the First Universalist Church
78 Earle Street
P.O. Box 830
Woonsocket, RI 02895-0870
Tel/Fax: 401-765-6141
E-mail: afgs@ids.net
http://www.afgs.org/

Italian Genealogy Society of America
P.O. Box 8571
Cranston, RI 02920-8571

New England Historical and Genealogical Society
(NEHGS)
101 Newbury Street
Boston, MA 02116-3007
Tel: 617-536-5740
   1-888-296-3447
   1-888-906-3447 (Library Circulation)
Fax: 617-536-7307
E-mail: nehgs@nehgs.org
http://www.nehgs.org/

Newport Genealogical Society
P.O. Box 4762
Middletown, RI 02842

Rhode Island Families Association
P.O. Box 1414
Ashburn, RI 20146-1414
E-mail: rigr@erols.com
http://www.erols.com/rigr/

Rhode Island Genealogical Society
507 Clarks Row
Bristol, RI 02809-1581

Rhode Island Mayflower Descendants
128 Massasoit
Warwick, RI 02888

Rhode Island Genealogical Society
P.O. Box 433
Greenville, RI 02828
E-mail: RIGenSociety@myfamily.com
http://users.ids.net/~ricon/rigs.html

Society of Mayflower Descendants
35 Hodsell Street
Cranston, RI 02910
http://www.mayflower-ri.org/

Sons of the American Revolution, Rhode Island Society
P.O. Box 137
East Greenwich, RI 02818

Historical Societies

Block Island Historical Society
Old Town Road
P.O. Box 79
Block Island, RI 02807
Tel: 401-466-2481 (July - Aug)
   401-466-5009 (all year, off season)

Bristol Historical and Preservation Society/
Library & Museum
48 Court Street
Bristol, RI 02809
Tel: 401-253-7223
   401-253-5705

Charlestown Historical Society
P.O. Box 100
Charlestown, RI 02813-0100
http://www.charlestown.com/ri/historicalsociety/
   index.htm

Coventry Historical Society
P.O. Box 401
Coventry, RI 02816

Cranston Historical Society
Sprague Mansion
1351 Cranston Street
Cranston, RI 02920
Tel: 401-944-9226
E-mail: RCarosi@aol.com rilydia@ix.netcom.com
http://www.geocities.com/Heartland/4678/ sprague.html

Jamestown Historical Society
Naragansett Avenue
Jamestown, RI 02835
Tel: 401-423-0784

Little Compton Historical Society
Wilbor House
548 West Main Road (Route 77)
P.O. Box 577
Little Compton, RI 02837
Tel: 401-635-4035
E-mail: lchistory@yahoo.com
http://www.rootsweb.com/~rinewpor/compton.html

Middletown Historical Society
Paradise Avenue
P.O. Box 1496
Middletown, RI 02842-0196
Tel: 401-849-1870

New England Historical and Genealogical Society (NEHGS)
101 Newbury Street
Boston, MA 02116-3007
Tel: 617-536-5740
    1-888-296-3447
    1-888-906-3447 (Library Circulation)
Fax: 617-536-7307
E-mail: nehgs@nehgs.org
http://www.nehgs.org/

Newport Historical Society
82 Touro Street
Newport, RI 02840
Tel: 401-846-0813
Fax: 401-846-1853

Rhode Island Black Heritage Society
202 Washington Street
Providence, RI 02903
Tel: 401-751-3490

Rhode Island Historical Preservation and Heritage Commission
150 Benefit Street
Providence, RI 02903
Tel: 401-277-2678
Fax: 401-277-2968
TDD: 401-277-3700
E-mail: info@rihphc.state.ri.us
http://www.rihphc.state.ri.us/

Rhode Island Historical Society/Library
110 Benevolent Street
Providence, RI 02906
Tel: 401-331-8575
Fax: 401-351-0127
http://www.rihs.org/index.shtml

Rhode Island Jewish Historical Association
130 Sessions Street
Providence, RI 02906
Tel: 401-331-1360
Fax: 401-728-5067

Westerly Historical Society
P.O. Box 91
Westerly, RI 02891

LDS Family History Center

For locations of Family History Centers in this state, see the Family History Center locator at FamilySearch.
http://www.familysearch.org/eng/Library/FHC/frameset_fhc.asp

Archives/Libraries/Museums

American-French Genealogical Society/Library
78 Earle Street
P.O. Box 830
Woonsocket, RI 02895-0870
Tel/Fax: 401-765-6141
E-mail: afgs@ids.net
http://www.afgs.org/

Barrington Public Library
281 Country Road
Barrington, RI 02806
Tel: 401-247-1920
http://www.barringtonlibrary.org/

Bristol Historical and Preservation Society/ Library & Museum
48 Court Street
Bristol, RI 02809
Tel: 401-253-7223
    401-253-5705

Brown University
Jay Hay Library
Providence, RI 02912
Tel: 401-863-2167
http://www.brown.edu/Facilities/
    John_Carter_Brown_Library/

Brown University
John Carter Brown Library
Box 1894
Providence, RI 02912
Tel: 401-863-2725
E-mail: JCBL_Information@Brown.edu
http://www.brown.edu/Facilities/
    John_Carter_Brown_Library/

Coventry Public Library
1672 Flat River Road
Coventry, RI 02816
Tel: 401-822-9100
    401-822-9105 (Reference)
Fax: 401-822-9133
TDD: 401-822-9105
E-mail: debbi@seq.clan.lib.ri.us
http://www.coventrylibrary.org/

Diocese of Providence
1 Cathedral Square
Providence, RI 02903
Tel: 401-278-4546
http://www.providiocese.com/

East Greenwich Free Library
82 Pierce Street
East Greenwich, RI 02818
Tel: 401-844-9510
Fax: 401-844-3790
http://www.eastgreenwichlibrary.org/

Jamestown Philomenian Library
Local History Collection
26 North Road
Jamestown, RI 02835
Tel: 401-423-7280
Fax: 401-423-7281
http://www.jamestownri.com/library/

Langworthy Public Library
24 Spring Street
P.O. Box 478
Hope Valley, RI 02832
Tel: 401-539-2851
http://www.langworthy.org/

Lincoln Public Library
145 Old River Road
Lincoln, RI 02865
Tel: 401-333-2422
Fax: 401-333-4154
E-mail: Linpub@ultranet.com
http://www.lincolnlibrary.com/

New England Historical and Genealogical Society (NEHGS)
101 Newbury Street
Boston, MA 02116-3007
Tel: 617-536-5740
    1-888-296-3447
    1-888-906-3447 (Library Circulation)
Fax: 617-536-7307
E-mail: nehgs@nehgs.org
http://www.nehgs.org/

Newport Historical Society/Library
82 Touro Street
Newport, RI 02840
Tel: 401-846-0813
Fax: 401-846-1853
http://www.newporthistorical.com/

Newport Public Library
Aquidneck Park
300 Spring Street
Newport, RI 02840
Tel: 401-847-8720
http://204.17.98.73/NptLib/

Providence City Archives
City Hall
25 Dorrance Street
Providence, RI 02903
Tel: 401-421-7740
TDD: 401-751-0203

Providence College
Phillips Memorial Library
549 River Avenue
Providence, RI 02918
Phone: 401-865-1252
Fax: 401-865-2823
http://www.providence.edu/library/

Providence Public Library
225 Washington Street
Providence, RI 02903
Tel: 401-455-8000
    401-455-8005 (Reference)
    401-455-8021 (Special Collections)
Fax: 401-455-8080
TDD: 401-455-8089
http://www.provlib.org/index.htm

Rhode Island Historical Society/Library
110 Benevolent Street
Providence, RI 02906
Tel: 401-331-8575
Fax: 401-351-0127
http://www.rihs.org/index.shtml

Rhode Island State Library
Office of the Secretary of State
337 Westminster Street
Providence, RI 02903
Tel: 401-277-2473
     401-277-2353
http://www.sec.state.ri.us/library/web.htm

Supreme Court Judicial Records Center
5 Hill Street
Pawtucket, RI 02860
Tel: 401-721-2640
E-mail: cmangual@courts.state.ri.us
http://www.judicial-records.state.ri.us/
Some early Court and Naturalization Records

United States Naval War College/Library
Code 1E3
686 Cushing Road
Newport, RI 02841
Tel: 401-841-3052
     401-841-4551
     401-841-4345 (Government Documents)
E-mail: libref@nwc.navy.mil
http://www.nwc.navy.mil/

University of Rhode Island
Library/Special Collections
Kingstown, RI 02881
Tel: 401-874-2594
     401-874-4632
Fax: 401-874-4608
E-mail: archives@etal.uri.edu
       dcm@uri.edu
http://www.uri.edu/library/special_collections/

Warwick Public Library
Greene Collection
600 Sandy Lane
Warwick, RI 02886
Tel: 401-739-5440
Fax: 401-732-2055
TDD: 401-739-3689
E-mail: warwickpl@ids.net
http://wpl.lib.ri.us/

West Warwick Public Library
1043 Main Street
West Warwick, RI 02893
Tel: 401-828-3750
Fax: 401-828-8493
http://www.ultranet.com/~wwpublib/

Westerly Public Library
44 Broad Street
P.O. Box 356
Westerly, RI 02891
Tel: 401-596-2877
Fax: 401-596-5600
http://www.clan.lib.ri.us/wes/index.htm

NEWSPAPER REPOSITORIES

Rhode Island Historical Society/Library
110 Benevolent Street
Providence, RI 02906
Tel: 401-331-8575
Fax: 401-351-0127
http://www.rihs.org/index.shtml

VITAL RECORDS

State of Rhode Island, Dept. of Health
Division of Vital Records
3 Capitol Hill, Rm. 101
Providence, RI 02908-5097
Tel: 401-222-2811
http://www.vitalrec.com/ri.html

RHODE ISLAND ON THE WEB

Rhode Island Cemeteries Database Home Page
http://members.tripod.com/~debyns/cemetery.html

Rhode Island GenWeb Project
http://www.rootsweb.com/~rigenweb/

SOUTH CAROLINA

ARCHIVES, STATE & NATIONAL

National Archives-Southeast Region
1557 St. Joseph Avenue
East Point, GA 30344
Tel: 404-763-7474
Fax: 404-763-7059
E-mail: atlanta.center@nara.gov
http://www.nara.gov/regional/atlanta.html

South Carolina Department of Archives and History
8301 Parklane Road
Columbia, SC 29223
Tele: (803) 896-6100
Fax: (803) 896-6198
http://www.state.sc.us/scdah/homepage.htm

GENEALOGICAL SOCIETIES

Aiken-Barnwell Chapter SCGS
P.O. Box 415
Aiken, SC 29802
E-mail: lhutto@home.ifx.net
http://www.ifx.net/~lhutto/page2.html

Anderson Chapter SCGS
Anderson County Chapter of SCGS
P.O. Box 74
Anderson, SC 29622-0074
http://www.rootsweb.com/~scanders/ andgensoc.html

Augusta Genealogical Society/Library
1109 Broad Street
P.O. Box 3743
Augusta, GA 30914-3743
Tel: 706-722-4073
http://www.augustagensociety.org/index.htm

Beaufort Chapter SCGS
P.O. Box 37
Ridgeland, SC 29936

Catawba-Wateree Chapter SCGS
c/o Camden Archives and Museum
1314 Broad Street
Camden, SC 29020
E-mail: CatawbaWatereeGS@aol.com
http://www.mindspring.com/~graysky1/page3.html

Charleston Chapter SCGS
P.O. Box 20266
Charleston, SC 29413
http://www.scgen.org/charlestonmain.htm

Chester District Genealogical Society
P.O. Box 336
Richburg, SC 29729

Columbia Chapter SCGS
P.O. Box 11353
Columbia, SC 29211-1353
E-mail: ozzie_29223@yahoo.com
http://www.rootsweb.com/~scccscgs/

Dutch Fork Chapter SCGS
P.O. Box 481
Chapin, SC 29036
http://www.dutchforkchapter.homestead.com/

Fairfield Chapter SCGS
P.O. Box 93
Winnsboro, SC 29180
http://www.rootsweb.com/~scfairfi/gensoc.html

Georgetown Chapter SCGS
P.O. Box 218
Georgetown, SC 29442

Greenville Chapter SCGS
P.O. Box 16236
Greenville, SC 29606-6236

Hilton Head Chapter SCGS
P.O. Box 5492
Hilton Head, SC 29938-5492

Huguenot Society of South Carolina/Library
138 Logan Street
Charleston, SC 29401-1941
Tel: 843-723-3235
Fax: 843-853-8476
http://www.huguenotsociety.org/

Laurens District Chapter SCGS
P.O. Box 1217
Laurens, SC 29360

Lexington County Genealogical Association
P.O. Box 1442
Lexington, SC 29071-1442
http://www.homestead.com/lexingtongenealogy/
main.html

Old 96 District Chapter SCGS
P.O. Box 3468
Greenwood, SC 29648
http://www.scgen.org/oldninetysix.htm

Old Darlington District Chapter SCGS
Old Train Depot
114 S. Fourth Street
P.O. Box 175
Hartsville, SC 29551-0175
http://www.geocities.com/Heartland/Estates/7212/

Old Edgefield District Chapter SCGS/Archives
104 Court House Square
P.O. Box 468
Edgefield, SC 29824

Old Newberry District Chapter SCGS
P.O. Box 154
Newberry, SC 29108
http://www.rootsweb.com/~scnewber/ncgs/

Old Pendleton District Chapter SCGS
1255 Corinth Road Seneca, SC 29678
http://oldpendleton.homestead.com/
or
http://freepages.genealogy.rootsweb.com/
~oldpend/

Old St. Bartholomew Chapter SCGS
104 Wade Hampton Ave.
Walterboro, SC 29488
http://patsabin.com/colleton/StBart.htm

Orangeburgh German-Swiss Genealogical Society
P.O. Box 974
Orangeburg, SC 29116-0974
E-mail: jeffries@netside.com
http://www.rootsweb.com/~scogsgs/

Pee Dee Chapter SCGS
P.O. Box 1428
Marion, SC 29571
E-mail: hbend65@aol.com

Pinckney District Chapter SCGS
385 Spring Street
P.O. Box 5281
Spartanburg, SC 29301

Savannah River Valley Genealogical Society
P.O. Box 895
Hartwell, GA 30643
http://www.nega.net/srvgs/

Sumter Chapter SCGS
P.O. Box 2543
Sumter, SC 29151-2543
Tel: 803-773-9144

Sumter County Genealogical Society
Sumter County Museum/Archives
219 W. Liberty Street
Sumter, SC 29151-2543
Tel: 803-773-9144
http://www.geocities.com/scgs2000/

HISTORICAL SOCIETIES

Bluffton Historical Preservation Society
P.O. Box 742
Bluffton, SC 29910

(Beaufort) Historic Beaufort Foundation
801 Bay Street
Beaufort, SC 29902
Tel: 803-524-6334
http://www.historic-beaufort.org/index.html

(Brattonsville) Historic Brattonsville
1444 Brattonsville Road
McConnells, SC 29726
Tel: 803-684-2327
E-mail: hbratton@rhtc.net
http://www.yorkcounty.org/brattonsville/bvilleinfo. html

(Camden) Historic Camden
222 Broad Street
Camden, SC 29020
Tel: 803-432-9841
Fax: 803-432-3815

Central Heritage Society
416 Church Street
Central, SC 29630
Tel: 864-639-2156

Charleston Library Society
164 King Street
Charleston, SC 29401
Tel: 843-723-9912
http://www.sciway.net/lib/cls_home.html

Chester County Historical Society/Museum
107 McAliley Street
Chester, SC 29706-1741
Tel: 803-385-2330

Confederation of Local Historical Societies
South Carolina Dept. of Archives & History
8301 Parklane Road
Columbia, SC 29223
Tel: 803-896-6100
Fax: 803-896-6198
E-mail: hornsby@history.scdah.sc.edu
http://www.state.sc.us/scdah/homepage.htm

Edisto Island Historic Preservation Society
2343 Highway 174
Edisto Island, SC 29438
Tel: 803-869-1954

Georgetown County Historical Commission
Front Street P.O. Box 902
Georgetown, SC 29440
Tel: 803-546-7423

Greenville Historical Society
211 East Washington Street
P.O. Box 10472
Greenville, SC 29603-0472
Tel: 864-233-4103

Horry County Historical Society
606 Main Street
Conway, SC 29526-4340
Tel: 843-488-1966
http://www.hchsonline.org/

Jewish Historical Society of South Carolina
College of Charleston
66 George Street
Charleston, SC 29424-0001
Tel: 843-953-5682
Fax: 843-953-7624
E-mail: jwst@cofc.edu
http://www.cofc.edu/~jwst/pages/jhssc.html

Kershaw County Historical Society
811 Fair Street
P.O. Box 501
Camden, SC 29020
Tel: 803-425-1123
E-mail: kchistory@mindspring.com
http://www.mindspring.com/~kchistory/

Pendleton District Historical Society
125 E. Queen Street
Pendleton, SC 29670
Tel: 864-646-3782

Piedmont Historical Society
P.O. Box 8096
Spartanburg, SC 29305-8096
http://www.angelfire.com/sc/piedmonths/

Richland County Historic Preservation Commission
1601 Blanding Street
Columbia, SC 29201
Tel: 803-252-1770

Saluda County Historical Society
Law Range Street
Box 22
Saluda, SC 29138
Tel: 864-445-8550
http://www.saludaschistorical.org/default.asp

South Carolina Historical Society/Library
100 Meeting Street
P.O. Box 5401
Spartanburg, SC 29304
Tel: 843-723-3225
Fax: 843-723-8584
http://www.schistory.org/

Spartanburg Historical Association
Regional Museum of Spartanburg County
501 Otis Boulevard
P.O. Box 887
Spartanburg, SC 29304
E-mail: scha@mindspring.com
http://www.spartanarts.org/history/index.html

Union County Historical Foundation
(Museum located above American Federal Bank)
P.O. Drawer 220
Union, SC 29379

University South Caroliniana Library Society
South Caroliniana Library
University of South Carolina
Columbia, SC 29208
http://www.sc.edu/library/socar/uscs/index.html

York County, Historical Center of
212 E. Jefferson Street
York, SC 29745
Tel: 803-684-7262
http://www.yorkcounty.org/historycenter/

LDS FAMILY HISTORY CENTERS

For locations of Family History Centers in this state, see
the Family History Center locator at FamilySearch.
http://www.familysearch.org/eng/Library/FHC/
frameset_fhc.asp

ARCHIVES/LIBRARIES/MUSEUMS

Abbeville/Greenwood Regional Library
106 North Main Street
Greenwood, SC 29646-2240
Tel: 864-941-4650
Fax: 864-941-4651
http://www.agrl.org/

Aiken County Historical Museum
433 Newberry Street, SW
Aidken, SC 29801
Tel: 803-642-2015
E-mail: acmuseum@scescape.net
http://www.scescape.com/aikenhistoricalmuseum/

Alexander Salley Archives
Middleton at Bull Street
Orangeburg, SC 29115

Avery Research Center for African American History & Culture
College of Charleston
125 Bull Street
Charleston, SC 29401
Tel: 843-953-7609
      843-953-7608 (Archives)
Fax: 843-953-7607
http://www.cofc.edu/%7Eaveryrsc/

Calhoun County Museum
303 Butler Street
St. Matthews, SC 29135
Tel: 803-874-3964
Fax: 803-874-1242
E-mail: ccm@scsn.net

Camden Archives and Museum
1314 Broad Street
Camden, SC 29020-3535
Tel: 803-425-6050
E-mail: camden@camden.net
http://www.camden-sc.org/Museum.asp

Charleston City Archives
701 E. Bay Street, Suite 348
Charleston, SC 29401
Tel: 803-724-7301

Charleston County Library
South Carolina Room
68 Calhoun Street
P.O. Box 22391
Charleston, SC 29413
Tel: 803-723-1165
      803-727-6720 (Voice)
Fax: 803-722-0429
http://www.ccpl.org/

Charleston Diocesan Archives
119 Broad Street
P.O. Box 818
Charleston, SC 29402
http://www.catholic-doc.org/archives/

Charleston Register of Mesne Conveyance
2 Courthouse Square
Charleston, SC 29401
Tel: 803-723-6780

Cherokee County Public Library
300 E. Rutledge Street
Gaffney, SC 29340
Tel: 864-487-2711
Fax: 864-487-2752

Citadel
Daniel Library
171 Moultrie Street
Charleston, SC 29409
Tel: 843-953-5116
      843-953-6845
Fax: 843-953-5190
E-mail: reichardtk@citadel.edu
http://www.citadel.edu/citadel/otherserv/
      library/index.htm

Francis Marion University
James A. Rogers Library-Arundel Room
P. O. Box 100547
Florence, South Carolina 29501-0547
Tel: 843-661-1300
      843-661-1319 (Archives)
http://library.fmarion.edu/

Greenville County Library
Stow South Carolina Historical Room
300 College Street
Greenville, SC 29601
Tel: 864-242-5000
Fax: 864-235-8375
E-mail: Betty_M@greenville.lib.sc.us
http://www.greenvillelibrary.org/

Laurens County Library
1017 West Main Street
Laurens, SC 29360
Tel: 864-984-0596
Fax: 864-984-0598
http://www.lcpl.org/

Old Edgefield District Chapter SCGS/Archives
104 Court House Square
P.O. Box 468
Edgefield, SC 29824

Orangeburg County Public Library
510 Louis Street, NE
Orangeburg, SC 29115
Tel: 803-531-4636
Fax: 803-533-5860

Richland County Public Library/Main Library
Local History Room
1431 Assembly Street
Columbia, SC 29201
Tel: 803-799-9084
http://www.richland.lib.sc.us/index.html

South Carolina State Library
1500 Senate Street
P.O. Box 11469
Columbia, SC 29211
Tel: 803-734-8666
Fax: 803-734-8676
http://www.state.sc.us/scsl/

Spartanburg Public Library
151 N. Church Street
Spartanburg, SC 29306
Tel: 864-596-3500
    864-596-3505 (Research Information)
Fax: 864-596-3518
http://www.spt.lib.sc.us/

Sumter County Genealogical Society
Sumter County Museum/Archives
219 W. Liberty Street
Sumter, SC 29151-2543
Tel: 803-773-9144
http://www.geocities.com/scgs2000/

University of South Carolina
South Caroliniana Library
Columbia, SC 29208
Tel: 803-777-3131
E-mail: cuthrellb@tcl.sc.edu
http://www.sc.edu/library/socar/index.html

York County Library
Post Office Box 10032
138 East Black Street
Rock Hill, SC 29731-0032
Tel: 803-324-3055
Fax: 803-328-9290
http://www.yclibrary.org/

NEWSPAPER REPOSITORIES

Charleston County Library
South Carolina Room
68 Calhoun Street
P.O. Box 22391
Charleston, SC 29413
Tel: 803-723-1165
    803-727-6720 (Voice)
Fax: 803-722-0429
http://www.ccpl.org/

South Carolina Department of Archives and History
1430 Senate Street
P.O. Box 11669, Capitol Station
Columbia, SC 29211-1669
Tel: 803-734-8577
    803-834-8596
Fax: 803-734-8820
http://www.state.sc.us/scdah/homepage.htm

University of South Carolina
South Caroliniana Library
720 College Street
Columbia, SC 29208
Tel: 803-777-3131/2
E-mail: rcopp@gwm.sc.edu
http://www.sc.edu/library/socar/
    books.html#newspapers

VITAL RECORDS

South Carolina Department of Archives and History
1430 Senate Street
P.O. Box 11669, Capitol Station
Columbia, SC 29211-1669
Tel: 803-734-8577
    803-834-8596
Fax: 803-734-8820
http://www.state.sc.us/scdah/homepage.htm
(Death starting 1915-50 years ago)

South Carolina Department of Health and Environment Control
Bureau of Vital Statistics
J. Marion Sims Building
2600 Bull Street
Columbia, SC 29201-1797
Tel: 803-734-4830
    803-898-3630
Fax: 803-898-3630
http://www.vitalrec.com/sc.html
(All Birth and Marriage, Death last 50 years)

SOUTH CAROLINA ON THE WEB

Charleston County Library/
South Carolina Room Home Page
http://www.ccpl.org/scr.html

Civil War @ Charleston
http://www.awod.com/gallery/

Confederate Corner (Kershaw and Lancaster Counties)
http://www.mindspring.com/~graysky1/page4.html

Genealogical Research at the South Carolina Archives
http://www.state.sc.us/scdah/research.htm

Roots and Branches-Genealogy from the Carolinas
http://angiesplace.behosting.com/roots/

South Carolina GenWeb Project
http://www.geocities.com/Heartland/Hills/3837

South Carolina Information
http://www.sciway.net/

South Carolina Information-Genealogy
http://www.sciway.net/hist/special/genealogy.html

Travellers Southern Families
http://misc.traveller.com/genealogy/

SOUTH DAKOTA

ARCHIVES, STATE & NATIONAL

National Archives-Central Plains Region
2312 East Bannister Road
Kansas City, MO 64131
Tel: 816-926-6920
Fax: 816-926-6982
E-mail: kansascity.archives@nara.gov
http://www.nara.gov/regional/kansas.html

National Archives-Rocky Mountain Region
Bldg. 48, Denver Federal Center
West 6th Avenue and Kipling Street
Denver, Colorado 80225-0307
Mailing Address:
P.O. Box 25307
Denver, Colorado 80225-0307
Phone: 303-236-0817
Fax: 303-236-9297
E-mail: denver.archives@nara.gov
http://www.nara.gov/regional/denver.html

South Dakota State Archives
Cultural Heritage Center
900 Governors Drive
Pierre, SD 57501-2217
Tel: 605-773-3804
Fax: 605-773-6041
E-mail: Archref@state.sd.us
http://www.sdhistory.org/archives.htm

GENEALOGICAL SOCIETIES

Aberdeen Area Genealogical Society (SDGS)
P.O. Box 493
Aberdeen, SD 57402-0493

Bennett County Genealogical Society (SDGS)
P.O. Box 483
Allen, SD 57714

Brookings Area Genealogical Society (SDGS)
524 Fourth Street
Brookings, SD 57006
http://www.rootsweb.com/~sdbags/index.html

Czech Heritage Preservation Society
P.O. Box 3
Tabor, SD 57063

East River Genealogical Forum (SDGS)
RR 2, Box 148
Wolsey, SD 57384

Family Tree Society (SDGS)
P.O. Box 202
Winner, SD 57580

Heritage Club-Platte (SDGS)
Route 2, Box 128
Platte, SD 57369

Hyde County Historical and Genealogical Society (SDGS)
P.O. Box 392
Highmore, SD 57345

Lake County Genealogical Society
c/o Karl Mundt Library
Dakota State College
Madison, SD 57042

Lyman-Brule Genealogical Society (SDGS)
Cozard Memorial Library
110 E. Lawler
P.O. Box 555
Chamberlain, SD 57325

Mitchell Area Genealogical Society (SDGS)
620 N. Edmunds
Mitchell, SD 57301

Moody County Genealogical Society (SDGS)
501 W. First Avenue
Flandreau, SD 57028-1003

Murdo Genealogical Society (SDGS)
P.O. Box 441
Murdo, SD 57559

North Central South Dakota Genealogical Society (SDGS)
178 Southshore Drive
Mina, SD 57462-3000
http://www.rootsweb.com/~sdgenweb/gensoc/
ncgensoc.html

Pierre-Ft. Pierre Genealogical Society (SDGS)
P.O. Box 925
Pierre, SD 57501

Rapid City Society for Genealogical Research, Inc. (SDGS)
(Library at Rapid City Public Library-
See Archives/Libraries/Museums)
P.O. Box 1495
Rapid City, SD   57709

Sioux Valley Genealogical Society (SDGS)
Siouxland Heritage Museum
200 West 6th Street
Sioux Falls, SD 57104-6001
Tel: 605-367-4210
Fax: 605-367-6004
http://www.rootsweb.com/~sdsvgs/

**South Dakota Genealogical Organization of Lyman Descendants
(SDGOLD)**
P.O. Box 145
Oacoma, SD 57365-0145
Tel: 605-734-6338
http://www.geocities.com/Heartland/Ridge/8591/ index.htm

South Dakota Genealogical Society
P.O. Box 1101
Pierre, SD 57501
http://www.rootsweb.com/~sdgenweb/gensoc/
        sdgensoc.html

Tri-State Genealogical Society (SDGS)
c/o Belle Fourche Public Library
905 5th Street
Belle Fourche, SD 57717-1705
http://scream.iw.net/~shepherd/

Watertown Genealogical Society (SDGS)
611 NE B Avenue
Watertown, SD 57201

Yankton Genealogical Society (SDGS)
1803 Douglas Avenue
Yankton, SD 57078

HISTORICAL SOCIETIES

Bennett County Historical Society
c/o Diana Nelson
HWC #1, Box 5
Martin, SD 57551

Brookings County Historical Society/Museum
Samara Avenue
Volga, SD 57071

Brookings Historic Preservation Commission
311 Third Avenue
Box 270, City Hall
Brookings, SD 57006
Tel:http://www.sdstate.edu/~wbhp/http/historic.html

Brown County Historical Society
Dacotah Prairie Museum
21 S. Main
Aberdeen, SD 57401
Tel: 605-626-7117
Fax: 605-626-4010
http://www.brown.sd.us/museum/default.html

Brule County Historical Society
P.O. Box 47
Kimball, SD 57355

Chamberlain Area Historical Preservation Association, Inc (CAHPA)
115 West Lawler Chamberlain, SD 57325
Tel/Fax: 605-734-6542
E-mail: barbara@easnet.net

Codington County Historical Society
Kampeska Heritage Museum
27 First Avenue, SE
Watertown, SD 57201
Tel: 605-886-7335
http://www.cchsmuseum.org/cchs.html

Czech Heritage Preservation Society
P.O. Box 3
Tabor, SD 57063

Deuel County Historical Society/Museum
Clear Lake, SD 57226

Douglas County Historical Society
710 Braddock
Armour, SD 57313
Tel: 605-724-2115

Fall River County Historical Society
Old Schoolhouse
300 N. Chicago St.
Hot Springs, SD 57747-1657
Tel: 605-745-5147

Garretson Area Historical Society
609 Main Avenue
Garretson, SD 57030
Tel: 605-594-6694

High Plains Heritage Society/Center Museum
825 Heritage Drive
P.O. Box 524h
Spearfish, SD 57783
Tel: 605-642-9378
http://www.members.mato.com/hpmuseum/

Hurley Historical Society
P.O. Box 302
Hurley, SD 57036
Tel: 605-238-5725

Hyde County Historical and Genealogical Society (SDGS)
P.O. Box 392
Highmore, SD 57345

Keystone Area Historical Society
410 3rd Street
Keystone, SD 57751
Tel: 605-666-4494

Lyman County Historical Museum
911 E. 9th Street
Presho, SD 57568
Tel: 605-895-9446

Menno Historical Society
150 Poplar
Menno, SD 57045

Minnehaha County Historical Society
Siouxland Heritage Museum
200 W. 6th Street
Sioux Falls, SD 57104-6001
Tel: 605-367-4210
Fax: 605-367-6004

Old Stanley County Historical Society
410 W. Main
P.O. Box 698
Fort Pierre, SD 57532

Potter County Historical Society
P.O. Box 1
Gettysburg, SD 57442
Tel: 605-765-5691

Prairie Historical Society
Prairie Village
P.O. Box 256
Madison, SD 57042
Tel: 605-256-3644
E-mail: Info@prairievillage.org
http://www.prairievillage.org/

Society of Black Hills Pioneers
c/o Adams Memorial Museum
54 Sherman Street
Deadwood, SD 57732-1364
Tel: 605-578-1714

South Dakota State Historical Society
Cultural Heritage Center
900 Governors Drive
Pierre, SD 57501-2217
Tel: 605-773-3458
Fax: 605-773-6041
E-mail: jeffm@chc.state.sd.us
http://www.sdhistory.org/

Tripp County Historical Society
East Highway 18
Winner, SD 57580
Tel: 605-842-0704

Union County Historical Society
124 E. Main Street
P.O. Box 552
Elk Point, SD 57025
http://www.acsnet.com/~jkjar/

Yankton County Historical Society
Dakota Territorial Museum
610 Summit Street
P.O. Box 1033
Yankton, SD 57078-1033
Tel: 605-665-3898

LDS FAMILY HISTORY CENTERS

For locations of Family History Centers in this state, see the Family History Center locator at FamilySearch.
http://www.familysearch.org/eng/Library/FHC/frameset_fhc.asp

ARCHIVES/LIBRARIES/MUSEUMS

Adams Memorial Museum
54 Sherman Street
Deadwood, SD 57732-1364
Tel: 605-578-1714
http://AdamsMuseumAndHouse.org/

Alexander Mitchell Public Library
Heritage Room, LL
519 South Kline Street
Aberdeen, SD 57401
Tel: 605-626-7097
http://ampl.sdln.net/history.htm

American Indian Culture Research Center
P.O. Box 98
Marvin, SD 57251-0098
Tel: 605-398-9200
Fax: 605-398-9201
E-mail: indian@bluecloud.org
http://www.bluecloud.org/dakota.html

Augustana College
Center for Western Studies
2001 S. Summit Avenue
Sioux Falls, SD 57197
Tel: 605-274-4007
　　　1-800-727-2844 (ext. 4007)
Fax: 605-274-4999
E-mail: hthomps@inst.augi.edu
http://inst.augie.edu/CWS/

Belle Fourche/Northwest Regional Public Library
905 5th Street
Belle Fourche, SD 57717-1705
Tel: 605-892-4407

Black Hills Mining Museum
323 W. Main Street
P.O. Box 694
Lead, SD 57754-1604
Tel: 605-584-1605
E-mail: bhminmus@mato.com
http://www.mining-museum.blackhills.com/

Brookings Public Library
515 Third Street
Brookings, SD 57006
Tel: 605-692-9407
Fax: 605-692-9386
http://www.sdstate.edu/~wbcg/http/library/
　　　library.html

Buechel Memorial Lakota Museum
St. Francis Mission
350 S. Oak Street
P.O. Box 499
St. Francis, SD 57572
Tel: 605-747-2745
Fax: 605-747-5057

Dacotah Prairie Museum
21 S. Main
Aberdeen, SD 57401
Tel: 605-626-7117
Fax: 605-626-4010
http://www.brown.sd.us/museum/

Deadwood Public Library
435 Williams Street
Deadwood, SD 57732-1113
Tel: 605-578-2821
Fax: 605-578-2170
E-mail: tdavis@sdln.net
http://dwdlib.sdln.net/

Eureka Pioneer Museum
P.O. Box 116
Eureka, SD 57437
Tel: 605-284-2711
http://www.glpta.org/eurekamuseum.htm

Grace Balloch Memorial Library
Spearfish Municipal Service Center
South Dakota History Room
625 Fifth Street
Spearfish, SD 57783
Tel: 605-642-1330
http://spflib.sdln.net/

High Plains Heritage Society/Center Museum
825 Heritage Drive
P.O. Box 524h
Spearfish, SD 57783
Tel: 605-642-9378
Fax: 605-642-8463
http://www.highplainsheritage.org

Huron Public Library
521 Dakota Avenue, S.
Huron, SD 57350
Tel: 605-353-8530
http://hpllib.sdln.net/

Kampeska Heritage Museum
27 First Avenue, SE
Watertown, SD 57201
Tel: 605-886-7335

North American Baptists Archives
1525 S. Grange Avenue
Sioux Falls, SD 57105-1599
Tel: 605-336-6588

Rapid City Public Library
610 Quincy Street
Rapid City, SD 57701
Tel: 605-394-4171
http://rcplib.sdln.net/

Rawlins Municipal Library
1000 E. Church Street
Pierre, SD 57501
Tel: 605-773-7421
Fax: 605-773-7423
http://www.dakotariver.com/rawlins/index.htm

Scotland Heritage Chapel & Museum
811 6th Street
P.O. Box 112
Scotland, SD 57059

Sioux Falls Public Library
201 North Main Avenue
Sioux Falls, SD 57102
Tel: 605-367-7081
http://www.siouxland.lib.sd.us/

Siouxland Heritage Museum
200 W. 6th Street
Sioux Falls, SD 57104-6001
Tel: 605-367-4210
Fax: 605-367-6004

Smith-Zimmerman Museum
Dakota State University Campus
221 NE Eighth Street
Madison, SD 57042
Tel: 605-256-5308
http://www.smith-zimmermann.dsu.edu/

South Dakota State Agricultural Heritage Museum
South Dakota State University
P.O. Box 2207C
Brookings, SD 57007-0999
Tel: 605-688-6226
Fax: 605-688-6303
E-mail: sdsu_agmuseum@sdstate.edu
http://web.sdstate.edu/sites/agmuseum/

South Dakota State Historical Society
Cultural Heritage Center
900 Governors Drive
Pierre, SD 57501-2217
Tel: 605-773-3804
Fax: 605-773-6041
E-mail: jeffm@chc.state.sd.us
http://www.sdhistory.org/

South Dakota State Library
Mercedes MacKay Memorial Building
800 Governors Drive
Pierre, SD 57501-2294
Tel: 605-773-3131
     800-423-6665
Fax: 605-773-4950
E-mail: library@state.sd.us
http://www.sdstatelibrary.com/

South Dakota State University
Hilton M. Briggs Library
Box 2115
Brookings, SD 57007
Tel: 605-688-5106
Fax: 605-688-6133
http://www3.sdstate.edu/academics/library/

University of South Dakota
I.D. Weeks Library
Vermillion, SD 57069
Tel: 605-677-5371
     605-677-5450 (Special Collections)
     605-677-5629 (Government Documents)
http://www.usd.edu/library/

Verendrye Museum/Archives
115 Deadwood Street
Fort Pierre, SD 57532

Vermillion Public Library
18 Church Street
Vermillion, SD 57069
Tel: 605-677-7060
http://www.usd.edu/vpl/

NEWSPAPER REPOSITORIES

South Dakota State Historical Society/Archives
South Dakota Newspaper Project
Cultural Heritage Center
900 Governor Drive
Pierre, SD 57501-2217
Tel: 605-773-3804
Fax: 605-773-6041
http://www.sdhistory.org/archives.htm/

VITAL RECORDS

Vital Records, Department of Health
600 E. Capitol
Pierre, SD 57501
Tel: 605-773-4961
E-mail: kathim@doh.state.sd.us
http://www.state.sd.us/doh/

SOUTH DAKOTA ON THE WEB

Homestead Records Information Page
http://members.aol.com/gkrell/homestead/home.html

Native American—SD GenWeb Project
http://www.geocities.com/Heartland/Plains/8430/
     index.htm

South Dakota GenWeb Project
http://www.rootsweb.com/~sdgenweb/

TENNESSEE

ARCHIVES, STATE & NATIONAL

National Archives—Southeast Region
1557 St. Joseph Avenue
East Point, GA 30344
Tel: 404-763-7474
Fax: 404-763-7059
E-mail: atlanta.center@nara.gov
http://www.nara.gov/regional/atlanta.html

Tennessee State Library and Archives
State Library and Archives Building
403 Seventh Avenue, North
Nashville, TN 37243-0312
Tel: 615-741-2764
    615-741-6471
E-mail: reference@mail.state.tn.us
http://www.state.tn.us/sos/statelib/tslahome.htm

GENEALOGICAL SOCIETIES

African American Historical & Genealogical Society (AAHGS)
Tennessee Chapter
P.O. Box 17684
Nashville, TN 37217

Blount County Genealogical & Historical Society
P.O. Box 4986
Maryville, TN 37802-4986

Delta Genealogical Society
Rossville Public Library
504 McFarland Avenue
Rossville, GA 30741
http://www.rootsweb.com/~gadgs/

Fentress County Genealogical Society
P.O. Box 178
Jamestown, TN 38556

First Families of Tennessee
East Tennessee Historical Society
P.O. Box 1629
Knoxville, TN 37901-1629
Tel: 423-544-5732
Fax: 423-544-4319
http://web.utk.edu/~kizzer/ethisctr/eths.htm

Greene County Genealogical Society
P.O. Box 1903
Greenville, TN 37744-1903

Hamblen County Genealogical Society
P.O. Box 1213
Morristown, TN 37816

Hancock County Historical & Genealogical Society
P.O. Box 307
Sneedville, TN 37869
E-mail: HCH&GS@xtn.net
http://www.korrnet.org/overhome/page3.html

Hawkins County Genealogical & Historical Society
P.O. Box 429
Rogersville, TN 37857
E-mail: hcghs@ hotmail.com
http://www.rootsweb.com/~tnhcghs/

Jefferson County Genealogical Society
P.O. Box 267
Jefferson City, TN 37760

Jonesborough Genealogical Society
c/o Washington County, Jonesborough Library
200 Sabin Drive
Jonesborough, TN 37659
Tel: 423-753-5000 (Library)
E-mail: Tenn-olina@naxs.com
http://www.rootsweb.com/~tncjones/JGS/

Lincoln County Genealogical Society
1508 West Washington Street
Fayetteville, TN 37334
Tel: 615-433-5991

McNairy County Genealogical Society
P.O. Box 1023
Selmer, TN 38375

Mid-West Tennessee Genealogical Society
P.O. Box 3343, Murray Station
Jackson, TN 38303-0343
http://www.jmcl.tn.org/Mid-West%20Tn.htm

Middle Tennessee Genealogical Society
P.O. Box 330948
Nashville, TN 37203-7507
E-mail: suesmith@bellsouth.net
http://www.mtgs.org/

Morgan County Genealogical & Historical Society
P. O. Box 684
Wartburg, TN 37887
Tel: 423-346-2479
http://www.tngennet.org/morgan/ genealogyroom.html

Obion County Genealogical Society
P.O. Box 241
Union City, TN 38261
E-mail: pghs@att.net
http://pghs.home.att.net/

Pellissippi Genealogical & Historical Society
c/o Clinton Public Library
118 South Hicks
Clinton, TN 37716
Tel: 615-457-5400
http://pghs.home.att.net/

Roane County Genealogical Society
P.O. Box 297
Kingston, TN 37763-0297

Signal Mountain Genealogical Society
103 Florida Avenue
Signal Mountain, TN 37377
Tel: 423-886-2956

Tennessee Genealogical Society/Library
9114 Davies Plantation Road
Memphis, TN 38133
P.O. Box 247
Brunswick, TN 38014-0247
Tel: 901-381-1447
E-mail: tngensociety@yahoo.com
http://www.rootsweb.com/~tngs/

Upper Cumberland Genealogical Association
P.O. Box 575
Cookeville, TN 38503-0575
E-mail: clark@blomand.net
http://www.clearwing.net/ucga/index.aspx

Watauga Association of Genealogists/Upper East Tennessee
P.O. Box 117
Johnson City, TN 37605-0117
Tel: 423-753-3116 (Secretary)

Weakley County Genealogical Society
P.O. Box 92
Martin, TN 38237

HISTORICAL SOCIETIES

African American Historical & Genealogical Society (AAHGS)
Tennessee Chapter
P.O. Box 17684
Nashville, TN 37217

Bedford County Historical Society
P.O. Box 165
Shelbyville, TN 37854

Blount County Genealogical & Historical Society
P.O. Box 4986
Maryville, TN 37802-4986

Bradley County Historical Society
c/o Cleveland Public Library
History Branch
795 Church Street, NE
Cleveland, TN 37311
Tel: 423-479-8367 (History Branch)
E-mail: info@clevelandlibrary.org

Campbell County Historical Society
167 E. Crestview Drive
LaFollette, TN 37766-4822
E-mail: mcdonald@campbellcounty.com
 www.campbellcounty.com/cchist

Chester County Historical Society
P.O. Box 721
Henderson, TN 38340-0721

Claiborne County Historical Society
P.O. Box 32
Tazewell, TN 37879

Coffee County Historical Society
Coffee County Courthouse
101 W. Fort Street
Manchester, TN 37355
Tel: 615-728-0145
E-mail: jlewis@cafes.com
http://www.cafes.net/jlewis/pubs.htm

East Tennessee Historical Society
(Library at East Tennessee Historical Center-See
 Libraries below)
600 Market Street (Museum)
P.O. Box 1629
Knoxville, TN 37901-1629
Tel: 423-544-5732
Fax: 423-544-4319
http://web.utk.edu/~kizzer/ethisctr/eths.htm

Franklin County Historical Society
P.O. Box 130
Winchester, TN 37398
Tel: 931-962-1476
http://www.tngenweb.org/franklin/society.htm

Giles County Historical Society
P.O. Box 693
Pulaski, TN 38478

Greene County Chapter, East Tennessee Historical Association
c/o Harry Roberts
105 Monument Avenue
Greeneville, TN 37743

Hancock County Historical & Genealogical Society
P O Box 307
Sneedville, TN 37869
http://www.korrnet.org/overhome/page3.html

Hardin County Historical Society
P.O. Box 1012
Savannah, TN 38372
Tel: 901-925-3106
E-mail: hcghs@ hotmail.com
http://www.hardinhistory.com/history/index.htm

Hawkins County Genealogical & Historical Society
P.O. Box 429
Rogersville, TN 37857
http://www.rootsweb.com/~tnhcghs/

Haywood County Historical Society/Museum
127 N. Grand Avenue
Brownsville, TN 38012
http://erc.jscc.cc.tn.us/jfn/libjmc/Haywood.html

Loudon County Heritage Association
P.O. Box 466
Loudon, TN 37774

Macon County Historical Society
c/o Macon County Public Library
294 Chaffin Road
Lafayette, TN 37083
Tel: 615-666-6030

Marshall County Historical Society
P 0 Box 1352
Lewisburg, TN 37091
E-mail: museum@tnweb.com

Maury County Historical Society
P.O. Box 147
Columbia, TN 38401
E-mail: reeco1@earthlink.net
http://historicmaury.org/

Morgan County Genealogical & Historical Society
P. O. Box 684
Wartburg, TN 37887
Tel: 423-346-2479
http://www.tngennet.org/morgan/ genealogyroom.html

Old James County Historical Society
P.O. Box 203
Ooltewah, TN 37363

Oliver Springs Historical Society
721 Main Street
Oliver Springs, TN 37840
http://www.oshistorical.com/

Pellissippi Genealogical & Historical Society
c/o Clinton Public Library
118 South Hicks
Clinton, TN 37716
Tel: 615-457-5400
http://pghs.home.att.net/

Smoky Mountain Historical Society
P.O. Box 5078
Sevierville, TN 37864
E-mail: smhs@SmokyKin.com
http://www.smokykin.com/smhs/

Tennessee Folklore Society
P.O. Box 529
Murfreesboro, TN 37133
Tel: 615-898-2576
Fax: 615-898-5098
http://www.middleenglish.org/tennfolk/

Union County Historical Society
P.O. Box 95
Maynardville, TN 37807
Tel: 423-687-2137

Van Buren County Historical Society
HC 69, Box 688
Burritt College Building
Spencer, TN 38585
Tel: 615-946-2121
http://www.rootsweb.com/~tnvanbur/vbchsoc.html

Washington County Historical Association
P.O. Box 205
Jonesborough, TN 37659
http://www.uriel.com/history/washco.htm

Wayne County Historical Society
P.O. Box 866
Waynesboro, TN 38450

LDS FAMILY HISTORY CENTERS

For locations of Family History Centers in this state, see the Family History Center locator at FamilySearch. http://www.familysearch.org/eng/Library/FHC/frameset_fhc.asp

ARCHIVES/LIBRARIES/MUSEUMS

Appalachian State University
Carol Grotnes Belk Library, 2nd Floor
W.L. Eury Appalachian Collection
Boone, NC 28608
Tel: 828-262-4041
Fax: 828-262-2553
E-mail: hayfj@appstate.edu
http://www.library.appstate.edu/appcoll/

Appalachian Studies Association
Regional Research Institute
West Virginia University
P.O. Box 6825
West Virginia University
Morgantown, WV 26506
Tel: 304-558-0220 ext. 35
http://www.appalachianstudies.org/

Art Circle Public Library
306 E. First Street
Crossville, TN 38555
Tel: 931-484-6790
Fax: 931-484-2350
http://www.artcircle.crossville.com/

Blount County Library
301 McGhee Street
Maryville, TN 37801
Tel: 865-982-0981
Fax: 865-977-1142
http://www.korrnet.org/bcpl/

Carroll County Library
625 High Street, Suite 102
Huntingdon, TN 38344-3903
Tel: 731-986-1919
Fax: 731-986-1335
E-mail: karen.pierce@state.tn.us

Center for Appalachian Studies and Services
East Tennessee State University (ETSU)
Johnson City, TN 37614-1707
Tel: 423-439-5348
Fax: 423-439-6340
E-mail: cass@etsu.edu
http://cass.etsu.edu/

Chattanooga/Hamilton County Bicentennial Library
Genealogy & Local History Department
1001 Broad Street
Chattanooga, TN 37402
Tel: 423-757-5310
    423-757-5316

Clarksville Montgomery County Museum
200 S. 2nd Street
Post Office Box 383
Clarksville, TN 37041
Tel: 931-648-5780

Cleveland Public Library
History Branch
795 Church Street, NE
Cleveland, TN 37311
Tel: 423-472-2163
    423-479-8367 (History Branch)
E-mail: info@clevelandlibrary.org
http://www.clevelandlibrary.org/

Clinton Public Library
118 South Hicks Street
Clinton, TN 37716-2826
Tel: 865-457-0519
E-mail: jgiles@usit.net

Dandridge Memorial/Jefferson County Public Library
P.O. Box 339
Dandridge, TN 37725
Tel: 423-397-9758

East Tennessee Historical Center
314 Clinch Avenue
Knoxville, TN 37902-1610
Tel: 423-544-5739
E-mail: kcplmccl@korrnet.org
http://www.knoxlib.org/ethc.htm
(Home to McClung Historical Collection, East Tennessee
    Historical Society, Sons of the American
    Revolution, and Knox County Archives)

East Tennessee State University
Sherrod Library
Archives of Appalachia and Special Collections
Lake Street & Seehorn Road
P.O. Box 70665
Johnson City, TN 37614-1701
Phone: 423-439-5308
http://cass.etsu.edu/archives/index.htm/

Fayetteville/Lincoln County Public Library
400 Rocky Knob Lane
Fayetteville, TN 37334-2558
Tel: 931-433-3286
Fax: 931-433-0063
E-mail: judy.pitts@state.tn.us

Greenville/Greene County Library
Tennessee Room
210 N. Main Street
Greeneville, TN 37745
Tel: 423-638-5034
Fax: 423-638-3841
E-mail: grv@ggcpl.org
http://ggcpl.org/

H.B. Stamps Memorial Library
407 E. Main Street
Rogersville, TN 37857
Tel: 423-272-8710
http://www.korrnet.org/hbslib/

Hardin County Library
1013 Main Street
P.O. Box 339
Savannah, TN 38372
Tel: 901-925-6397

Highland Rim Regional Library Center
2118 E. Main Street
Murfreesboro, TN 37130-4043
Tel: 615-893-3380
Fax: 615-895-6727
http://www.state.tn.us/sos/statelib/p&d/highrim/

Jackson/Madison County Public Library
Tennessee Room
433 East Lafayette
Jackson, TN 38301
Tel: 731-425-8600
http://www.jmcl.tn.org/

Jonesborough History Museum
117 Boone Street
Jonesborough, TN 37659
Tel: 423-753-1015
http://jonesborough.tricon.net/museum.html

Magness Memorial Library
118 W. Main Street
McMinnville, TN 37110
Tel: 615-473-2428
Fax: 615-473-6778
http://www.vision-x.com/library/

Maury County Public Library
211 W. 8th Street
Columbia, TN 38402
Tel: 931-388-6332
Fax: 931-388-6371
E-mail: maurylibrarysystem@yahoo.com

Memphis/Shelby County Public Library and Information Center
History and Travel Department
3030 Poplar Avenue
Memphis TN 38111-3527
Tel: 901-725-8821
E-mail: hisref@memphis.lib.tn.us
http://www.memphislibrary.org/about/

Memphis/Shelby County Public Library
Cossitt Branch
33 South Front Street
Memphis, TN 38103
Tel: 901-526-1712
http://www.memphislibrary.lib.tn.us/

Morristown/Hamblen Library
417 West Main Street
Morristown, TN 37814
Tel: 423-586-6410
http://www.tngenweb.org/hamblen/library.htm

Mount Pleasant Public Library
213 N. Madison
Mt. Pleasant, TN 75455
Tel: 903-575-4180
Fax: 903-577-8000

Museum of Appalachia
2819 Andersonville
Highway Clinton, TN 37716
Tel: 423-494-7680
Fax: 865-494-8957
http://www.andersoncountychamber.org/ musapp.html

Nashville/Davidson County Public Library
615 Church Street
Nashville, TN 37219
Tel: 615-862-5760
http://www.library.nashville.org/Index.html

Rossville Public Library
504 McFarland Avenue
Rossville, GA 30741
Tel: 706-866-1368
Fax: 706-858-0251
E-mail: roachm@mail.walker.public.lib.ga.us
http://www.walker.public.lib.ga.us/branches/
    rossville.html

Tennessee Genealogical Society/Library
9114 Davies Plantation Road
P.O. Box 247
Brunswick, TN 38014-0247
Tel: 901-381-1447
http://www.rootsweb.com/~tngs/

Tennessee State Library and Archives
State Library and Archives Building
403 Seventh Avenue, North
Nashville, TN 37243-0312
Tel: 615-741-2764
E-mail: reference@mail.state.tn.us
http://www.state.tn.us/sos/statelib/tslahome.htm

University of Memphis (Memphis State)
Brister Library, Special Collections
Mississippi Valley Collection
Memphis, TN 38104
Tel: 901-678-2210
http://www.lib.memphis.edu/speccoll.htm

University of Tennessee/Knoxville Library
Special Collections/Manuscripts
1015 Volunteer Blvd.
Knoxville, TN 37996-1000
Tel: 865-974-4351
http://www.lib.utk.edu/spcoll/

Vanderbilt University
Jean and Alexander Heard Library
Special Collections and University Archives
419 21st Avenue, S.
Nashville, TN 37240-0007
Tel: 615-322-2807
Fax: 615-343-9832
E-mail: archives@library.vanderbilt.edu
http://www.library.vanderbilt.edu/speccol/

Williamson County Public Library
Genealogy Room
611 West Main Street
Franklin, TN 37064
Tel: 615-794-3156
http://lib.williamson-tn.org/Index1.htm

NEWSPAPER REPOSITORIES

Tennessee State Library and Archives
State Library and Archives Building
403 Seventh Avenue, North
Nashville, TN 37243-0312
Tel: 615-741-2764
E-mail: reference@mail.state.tn.us
http://www.state.tn.us/sos/statelib/tslahome.htm

University of Tennessee/Knoxville Library
Special Collections/Manuscripts
1015 Volunteer Blvd.
Knoxville, TN 37996-1000
Tel: 865-974-4351
http://www.lib.utk.edu/spcoll/

VITAL RECORDS

Tennessee State Library and Archives
State Library and Archives Building
403 Seventh Avenue, North
Nashville, TN 37243-0312
Tel: 615-741-2764
E-mail: reference@mail.state.tn.us
http://www.state.tn.us/sos/statelib/tslahome.htm
Births for Nashville (1881-1908), Chattanooga (1879-
1908), and Knoxville (1881-1908)
Deaths for Memphis (1848-1908), Nashville (1874-1908),
Knoxville (1881-1908), and Chattanooga (1872-
1908)
Births and Deaths (1908-1912)

Tennessee Vital Records
Central Services Building, 1st Floor
421 Fifth Avenue, North
Nashville, TN 37247-0450
Tel: 615-741-1763
Fax: 615-741-9860
To order by phone with charge card:
Tel: 615-741-0778
Fax: 615-726-2559
http://www.segenealogy.com/tennessee/tn_vital.htm
Births (1914-Present) and Deaths (1914-50 Years ago)
No Birth or Death Records were recorded for the year
1913.

TENNESSEE ON THE WEB

8th Tennessee Cavalry, CSA
http://www.clearwing.net/8tncav/index.aspx

American Civil War Page
http://sunsite.utk.edu/civil-war/

Introduction to Tennessee Land History
http://www.ultranet.com/~deeds/tenn.htm

Smoky Mountain Ancestral Quest
http://www.smokykin.com/

Tennessee GenWeb Project
http://www.tngenweb.org/

Tennessee State Library and Archives
Historical & Genealogical Information
http://www.state.tn.us/sos/statelib/pubsvs/intro.htm

Tennessee State Library and Archives
Online Index to Acts of Tennessee 1796-1830 by Name
http://www.state.tn.us/sos/statelib/pubsvs/actintro.htm

TEXAS

ARCHIVES, STATE & NATIONAL

National Archives-Southwest Region
501 West Felix Street
Building 1, Dock 1
P.O. Box 6216
Fort Worth, TX 76115-0216
Tel: 817-334-5515
Fax: 817-334-5511
E-mail: ftworth.archives@nara.gov
http://www.nara.gov/regional/ftworth.html

Texas State Library and Archives Commission
Lorenzo de Zavala State Archives and Library Building
1201 Brazos Street
P.O. Box 12927
Austin, TX 78711
Tel: 512-463-5455
512-463-5463 (Genealogy Collection, Room 110)
512-463-5480 (Archives)
E-mail: archinfo@tsl.state.tx.us (archives)
        geninfo@tsl.state.tx.us (genealogy collection)
http://www.tsl.state.tx.us/

GENEALOGICAL SOCIETIES

Amarillo Genealogical Society
413 East Fourth Street
Amarillo, TX 79189
Tel: 806-378-3054
        806-378-4211 (Special Collections)
E-mail: reference@amarillolibrary.org
http://www.amarillolibrary.org/index.htm

Ancestor Club
P.O. Box 157
Anahuac, TX 77514

Anderson County Genealogical Society
c/o Palestine Public Library
1101 North Cedar
Palestine, TX 75801
E-mail: bonniew@e-tex.com
http://users.tvec.net/bonniew/acgs/acgs2.htm

Angelina County Genealogical Society
P.O. Box 150631
Lufkin, TX 75915
http://www.rootsweb.com/~txacgs/

Arlington Genealogical Society
101 East Abram Street
Arlington, TX 76010

Athens Genealogical Organization
121 South Prairieville Street
Athens, TX 75751
Tel: 903-675-2694

Austin Genealogical Society
P.O. Box 1507
Autsin, TX 78767-1507
E-mail: 70461.2144@compuserve.com
http://www.AustinTxGenSoc.org/

Baytown Genealogical Society
P.O. Box 2486
Baytown, TX 77522
Tel: 713-479-3244

Big Spring, Genealogical Society of
810 East 12th Street
Big Spring, TX 79720
Tel: 915-267-7236

Big Thicket Genealogical Club
P.O. Box 1260
Kountze, TX 77625

Brazos Genealogical Association
P.O. Box 5493
Bryan, TX 77805
E-mail: holt@cy-net.net
http://www2.cy-net.net/~bga/

Brazosport Genealogical Society
P.O. Box 813
Lake Jackson, TX 77566
E-mail: dpugh@brazosport.cc.tx.us
http://gator1.brazosport.cc.tx.us/~gensoc/

Burkburnett Genealogical Society
215 East Fourth Street
Burkburnett, TX 76354
Tel: 817-569-2991

Burnet County Genealogical Society
100 East Washington Street
Burnet, TX 78611
Tel: 512-756-2328

Caldwell County Genealogical and Historical Society
215 South Pecan Avenue
Luling, TX 78648
Tel: 830-875-9466
E-mail: ccg&hsoc@bcsnet.net
http://www.rootsweb.com/~txcaldwe/socpage.htm

Calhoun County Genealogical Society
P.O. Box 1150
Port Lavaca, TX 77979
Tel: 512-552-2588
E-mail: ccgs2002@yahoo.com
http://www.geocities.com/ccgs2002/home.html

Camp County Genealogical Society
P.O. Box 1083
Pittsburg, TX 75686
E-mail: Kinard75@cs.com
http://www.rootsweb.com/~txccgs/

Cass County Genealogical Society
P.O. Box 880, Dept. CCW
Atlanta, TX 75551-0880

Central Texas Genealogical Society
c/o Waco-McLennan County Library
1717 Austin Avenue
Waco, TX 76701
Tel: 254-750-5946 (Library Phone)
     254-750-5945 (Genealogy Librarian)
Fax: 254-750-5940
http://www.rootsweb.com/~txmclenn/interest.htm

Chaparral Genealogical Society/Library
310 N. Live Oak
P.O. Box 606
Tomball, TX 77375
Tel: 713-255-9081

Cherokee County Genealogical Society
P.O. Box 1332
Jacksonville, TX 75766-1332
E-mail: ccgs@tyler.net
http://www.tyler.net/ccgs/CCGS.html

Childress Genealogical Society
117 Avenue B, NE
Childress, TX 79201

Clayton Library Friends
P.O. Box 271078
Houston, TX 77277
http://www.hpl.lib.tx.us/clayton/clf.html

Coastal Bend Genealogical Society
P.O. Box 2711
Corpus Christi, TX 78403
http://www.rootsweb.com/~txcbgs/

Collin County Genealogical Society
P.O. Box 865052
Plano, TX 75086-5052
Tel: 214-596-3567
E-mail: Traceroots@aol.com
http://www.starbase21.com/PSGenealogy/

Comal County Genealogy Society
P.O. Box 310583
New Braunfels, TX 78130
Tel: 210-629-1900

Coryell County Genealogical Society
811 Main Street
Gatesville, TX 76528
Tel: 817-865-5367

Cottle County Genealogical Society
P.O. Box 1005
Paducah, TX 79248

Cross Timbers Genealogical Society
P.O. Box 197
Gainesville, TX 76240

Cypress Basin Genealogical Society
P.O. Box 403
Mount Pleasant, TX 75455
http://www.rootsweb.com/~txcypbgs/index.html

Dallas County East Genealogical Society
7637 Mary Dan Drive
Dallas, TX 75217

Dallas Genealogical Society
P.O. Box 12648
Dallas, TX 75225-0648
http://www.dallasgenealogy.org//

Daughters of the Republic of Texas/Library and Museum
Alamo Plaza
P.O. Box 1401
San Antonio, TX 78295-1401
Tel: 210-225-1071
Fax: 210-212-8514
E-mail: drtl@drtl.org
http://drtl.org/index.asp/

Deaf Smith County Genealogical Society
211 East Fourth Street
Hereford, TX 79045

Denison Library Genealogical Society
300 West Gandy
Denison, TX 75020

Denton County Genealogical Society
P.O. Box 424707
Denton, TX 76204

Donley County Genealogical Society
P.O. Box 116
Clarendon, TX 79226

East Bell County Genealogical Society
3219 Meadow Oaks Drive
Temple, TX 76502
Tel: 817-778-2073

East Texas Genealogical Society
P.O. Box 6967
Tyler, TX 75711
E-mail: everheart@tyler.net
http://www.rootsweb.com/~txetgs/

El Paso Genealogical Society
c/o El Paso Public Library
501 North Mesa Street
El Paso, TX 79901
Tel: 915-543-5474
E-mail: patrussb@juno.com
http://www.rootsweb.com/~txepgs/

Ellis County Genealogical Society
P.O. Box 479
Waxahachie, TX 75168

Erath County, Cross Timbers Genealogical Society
c/o Dublin Public Library
206 W. Blackjack St.
Dublin, TX 76446
E-mail: janice@htcomp.net

Fannin County Genealogical Society
65 Blanks Rd.
Whitewright, TX 75491
http://www.rootsweb.com/~txfcgs/

Fort Belknap Genealogical Association
Murray Route
Graham, TX 76046

Fort Bend County Genealogical Society
P.O. Box 274
Richmond, TX 77406-0274
Tel: 281-341-2608

Fort Brown Genealogical Society
608 East Adams
Brownsville, TX 78520
Tel: 512-542-4824

Fort Worth Genealogical Society (FWGS)
P.O. Box 9767
Fort Worth, TX 76147-2767
Tel: 817-457-3330
E-mail: joegrant@flash.net
http://www.rootsweb.com/~txfwgs/

Freestone County Genealogical Society
P.O. Box 14
Fairfield, TX 75840

Gainesville Genealogical Group
Cooke County College
Gainesville, TX 76240

Galveston County Genealogical Society
P.O. Box 1141
Galveston, TX 77553
http://www.rootsweb.com/~txgalves/gcgs.htm

Garland Genealogical Society
P.O. Box 461882
Garland, TX 75046
http://www.geocities.com/TheTropics/1926/
   society.html

Gilmer Genealogical Society
West Pine Street
Gilmer, TX 75644

Grand Prairie Genealogical Society
P.O. Box 532026
Grand Prairie, TX 75053

Grayson County Genealogical Society
421 North Travis
Sherman, TX 75090
Tel: 903-892-7240

Gregg County Genealogical Society
P.O. Box 2985
Longview, TX 75606-2985
http://www.rootsweb.com/~txgregg/gcgs.html

Guadalupe County Genealogical Society
707 East College Street
Sequin, TX 78155
Tel: 512-379-1531

Gulf Coast Ancestry Researchers
P.O. Box 16
Wallisville, TX 77597
Tel: 409-389-2486

Hamilton County Genealogical Society
209 W. Henry
Hamilton, TX 76531
Tel: 817-386-4566
E-mail: hcgs@htcomp.net
http://users.htcomp.net/hcgs/

Hardin County Genealogical Society
6699 Deer Park Lane
Lumberton, Tx 77657
E-mail: sstiles@ih2000.net
http://www.geocities.com/hardincounty/

Harris County Genealogical Society
P.O. Box 391
Pasadena, TX 77501
E-mail: jeffieb@hal-pc.org
http://www.hcgs.org/

Harrison County Genealogical Society
P.O. Box 597
Marshall, TX 75671
http://www.rootsweb.com/~txharris/hcgensoc.htm

Haskell County Genealogical Society
300 North Avenue E
Haskell, TX 79521

Hays County Genealogical Society
P.O. Box 503
San Marcos TX 78666

Heart of Texas Genealogical Society
P.O. Box 1837
Rochelle, TX 76872

Hemphill County Genealogical Society
Route 2
Canadian, TX 79014

Hi-Plains Genealogical Society
c/o Unger Memorial Library
825 Austin Street
Plainview, TX 79072-7235
Tel: 806-296-1148
http://www.texasonline.net/unger/geneal.htm

Hill Country Genealogical Society
Prairie Mt. Rt.
Llano, TX 78643

Hill County Genealogical Society
1019 E Elm
Hillsboro 76645

Hispanic Genealogical Society
P.O. Box 231271
Houston, TX 77223-1271
http://www.hispanicgs.com/

Hood County Genealogical Society
P.O. Box 1623
Granbury, TX 76048
E-mail: ancestor@GranburyDepot.org
http://www.granburydepot.org/

Hopkins County Genealogical Society
212 Main Street
P.O. Box 624
Sulphur Springs, TX 75483
Tel: 903-885-8523
http://gen.1starnet.com/hopkins/

Houston Area Genealogical Forum
Genealogical Record, Editor
P.O. Box 271466
Houston, TX 77277-1466
Tel: 713-827-4440

Humble Genealogical Society
P.O. Box 2723
Humble, TX 77347-2723
http://www.rootsweb.com/~txthags/

Hunt County Genealogical Society
P.O Box 398
Greenville, TX 75403
http://freepages.history.rootsweb.com/~huntnews/
   gensoc/

Hutchinson County Genealogical Society
625 Weatherly Street
Borger, TX 79007

Johnson County Genealogical Society
P.O. Box 1256
Cleburne, TX 76033
http://www.htcomp.net/jcgs/soc/soc.htm

Kaufman County Genealogical Society
P.O. Box 337
Terrell, TX 75160
Tel: 214-524-5605

Kendall County Genealogical Society
P.O. Box 623
Boerne, TX 78006
http://www.rootsweb.com/~txkendal/gskc.htm

Kent County Genealogical Society
P.O. Box 414
Jayton, TX 79528

Kerrville, Genealogical Society of
505 Water Street
Kerrville, TX 78028
Tel: 210-257-8422
http://www.ktc.net/kgs/about.htm

Kingsland Genealogical Society
P.O. Box 952
Kingsland, TX 78639
http://www.rootsweb.com/~txkinggs/

Lamar County Genealogical Society
Paris Junior College Campus-Jess B. Alford Center
2400 Clarksville Street
PJC Box 187
Paris, TX 75460
Tel: 903-782-0448
E-mail: betsym@stargate.1starnet.com
http://gen.1starnet.com/lamargen.htm

Lamesa Area Genealogical Society
P.O. Box 1264
Lamesa, TX 79331

Lancaster Genealogical Society
220 Main Street
Lancaster, TX 75146
http://www.rootsweb.com/~txlgs/

Lee County Genealogical Society
177 South Madison
Giddings, TX 78942

Leon County Genealogical Society
Old Courthouse
P.O. Box 400
Centerville, TX 75833
http://www.rootsweb.com/~txleon/lcgs.htm

Limestone County Genealogical Society
350 Rust Street
P.O. Box 1437
Mexia, TX 76667
Tel: 817-562-3231

Llano Estacado Genealogical Society
1313 West Ninth Street
Littlefield, TX 79339

Los Bexarenos Genealogical Society
P.O. Box 1935
San Antonio, TX 78297

Lower Gulf Coast Genealogical and Historical Society
E-mail: dsk@phoenix.net

Madison County Genealogical Society
P.O. Box 26
Madisonville, TX 77864

Marion County Genealogical Society
P.O. Box 224
Jefferson, TX 75657-0224

Matagorda County Genealogical Society
P.O. Box 264
Bay City, TX 77404
Tel: 409-245-6931
http://www.rootsweb.com/~txmatago/gensoc.htm

McAllen Genealogical Society
601 N. Main Street
P.O. Box 4714
McAllen, TX 78502-4714
Tel: 512-686-5669

Mesquite Historical and Genealogical Society
P.O. Box 850165
Mesquite, TX 75185-0165
Tel: 972-216-6229
http://members.aol.com/dstuart101/mesquite/
page1.htm

Mid-Cities Genealogical Society
P.O. Box 407
Bedford, TX 76095
E-mail: mmhay@home.com
http://www.geocities.com/Heartland/Ranch/3825/

Midland Genealogical Society
301 W. Missouri
P.O. Box 1191
Midland, TX 79702
Tel: 915-688-8991
http://www.rootsweb.com/~txmidlan/mgs.htm

Milam County Genealogical Society
c/o Lucy Hill Patterson Library
201 Ackerman Street
Rockdale, TX 76567
E-mail: lhpml@excite.com
http://www.geocities.com/milamco/milam-002.htm

**Montgomery County Genealogical and Historical
Society**
P.O. Box 867
Conroe, TX 77305-0867
Tel: 936-756-8625
http://www.rootsweb.com/~txmcghs/

Nacogdoches County Genealogical Society
P.O. Box 4634, SAF Station
Nacogdoches, TX 75962
http://www.rootsweb.com/~txngs/

Navarro County Genealogical Society
P.O. Box 2278
Corsicana, TX 75151
Tel: 903-654-4810
http://www.rootsweb.com/~txnavarr/genealogical_society/

New Boston Genealogical Society
P.O. Box 104
New Boston, TX 75570
http://www.rootsweb.com/~txbowie/nbgs.htm

North Collin County Genealogical Society
c/o McKinney Memorial Public Library
220 North Kentucky Street
McKinney, TX 75069
Tel: 972-529-9840
http://www.nccgs.org/

North Texas Genealogical Association
P.O. Box 4602
Wichita Falls, TX 76308
E-mail: fmaier@wf.net
http://www.wf.net/~fmaier/

Northest Texas, Genealogical Society Of
Paris Junior College Campus-Jess B. Alford Center
2400 Clarksville Street
PJC Box 187
Paris, TX 75460
Tel: 903-782-0448

Pacer-Hunt County Genealogical Society
P.O. Box 2306
Quinlan, TX 75474

Pampa Genealogical Society
430 North Summer Street
Pampa, TX 79065

Parker County Genealogical Society
1014 Charles Street
P. O. Box 201
Weatherford, TX 76086
http://www.rootsweb.com/~txpcgs/

Pecan Valley Genealogical Society
2018 Elizabeth Street
Brownwood TX 76801-4811

Permian Basin Genealogical Society
321 West Fifth Street
Odessa, TX 79761
Tel: 915-332-0634
http://www.odessahistory.com/geneolg.htm

Piney Woods Pioneer Genealogical Society
Route 1, Box 405
Kountze, TX 77625

Porciones Genealogical Society
P.O. Box 392
Edinburg, TX 78540

Randolph Area Genealogical Society
P.O. Box 2134
Universal City, TX 78148-1134
Tel: 210-659-7881

Red River County Genealogical Society
P.O. Box 516
Clarksville, TX 75426
Tel: 903-427-3991
http://www.red-river.net/rrcgs.htm

Rockwall County Genealogical Society
P.O. Box 471
Rockwall, TX 75087
http://www.rockwallroots.org/rcgs

Root Seekers Genealogical Society
Tri County Library
P.O. Box 1770
Mabank, TX 75147-1770
http://www.rootsweb.com/~txrsgs/rsgsweb/

Rusk County Genealogical Society
P.O. Box 1314
Henderson, TX 75653

San Angelo Genealogical and Historical Society
P.O. Box 3453
San Angelo, TX 76902
http://www.rootsweb.com/~saghs/index.htm

San Antonio Genealogical Society
401 Isom Road suite 540
P.O. Box 17461
San Antonio, TX 78216
Tel: 210 342-5242
Fax: 210 342-0386
http://saghs.home.texas.net/

San Marcos/Hays County Genealogy Society
P.O. Box 503
San Marcos, TX 78667

South Plains Genealogical Society
P.O. Box 6607
Lubbock, TX 79493
Tel: 806-775-3685
http://members.door.net/spgs/

South Texas Genealogical Society
P.O.Box 754
Beeville, Texas 78104-0754
E-mail: kpacheco@fnbnet.net

South East Texas Genealogical and Historical Society
c/o Tyrell Historical Library
P.O. Box 3827
Beaumont, TX 77704-3827
E-mail: fhallen@swbell.netÄ
http://www.rootsweb.com/~txsetghs/

Southwest Genealogical Society
1300 San Pedro Avenue
San Antonio, TX 78212

Southwest Texas Genealogical Society
P.O. Box 295
Uvalde, TX 78802

Stephens County Genealogical Society
P.O. Box 350
Breckenridge, TX 76424
Tel: 817-559-8471
http://www.rootsweb.com/~txscgs/

Texarkana USA Genealogy Society
P.O. Box 2323
Texarkana, TX 75504-2323
http://www.rootsweb.com/~txkusa/GenSoc.html

Texas State Genealogical Society
P.O. Box 110842
Carrollton, TX 75011

Texas City Ancestry Searchers
P.O. Box 3301
Texas City, TX 77592
Tel: 409-935-5343

Timpson Genealogical Society
P.O. Box 726
Timpson, TX 75975
Tel: 409-254-3344

Tip O'Texas Genealogical Society
c/o Harlingen Public Library
410 76 Drive
Harlingen, TX 78550
Tel: 210-430-6650

Tri-County Genealogical Society
P.O. Box 107
Leonard, TX 75452

TX-OK Panhandle Genealogical Society
2310 Texas Street
Perryton, TX 79070
Tel: 806-435-5801

Upton County Genealogical Society
P.O. Box 6
Rankin, TX 79778

Van Alstyne Genealogical Society
Van Alstyne Public Library
117 N. Waco
P.O. Box 629
Van Alstyne, TX 75495
Tel: 903-482-5991
Fax: 903-482-1316
E-mail: vanalstynepl@texoma.net
http://home.texoma.net/~vanalstynepl/gen1.html

Van Zandt County Genealogical Society
P.O. Box 716
Canton, TX 75103-0716
Tel: 903-567-5012
E-mail: sibyl@vzinet.com
http://www.rootsweb.com/~txvzcgs/vzgs.htm

Victoria County Genealogical Society
P.O. Box 413
Victoria, TX 77902
E-mail: cjbuttram@cox-internet.com
http://www.viptx.net/vcgs/vcgs.html

Walker County Genealogical Society
P.O. Box 1295
Huntsville, TX 77342-1295
Tel: 936-295-5551
E-mail: info@dickensonresearch.com
http://www.dickensonresearch.com/wcgen.htm

Winters High School, Genealogical Society of
P.O. Box 125
Winters, TX 79567

Wood County Genealogical Society
P.O. Box 832
Quitman, TX 75783
E-mail: woodco@cox-internet.com
http://www.rootsweb.com/~txwood/wcgs.htm/

HISTORICAL SOCIETIES

Bastrop County Historical Society
702 Main Street
P.O. Box 279
Bastrop, TX 78602
Tel: 512-321-6177

Beaumont Heritage Society
3025 French Road
Beaumont, TX 77706
Tel: 409-898-0348

Brazoria County Historical Society/Museum
Courthouse Square
100 East Cedar
Angleton, TX 77515
Tel: 409-849-5711 ext. 1208
E-mail: bchm@bchm.org

Caldwell County Genealogical and Historical Society
215 South Pecan Avenue
Luling, TX 78648
Tel: 830-875-9466
E-mail:
http://www.rootsweb.com/~txcaldwe/socpage.htm

Carson County Historical Survey Committee
Carson County Square House Museum
Highway 207
P.O. Box 276
Panhandle, TX 79068
Tel: 806-537-3524
Fax: 806-537-5628
E-mail: shm@squarehousemuseum.org

Collin County Historical Society/Museum
Old Post Office
105 Chestnut
McKinney, TX 75069
Tel: 972-542-9457
E-mail: Donhoke@msn.com
http://www.collincountyhistory.org/

Crockett County Historical Society/Museum
404 11th Street
P.O. Box 1444
Ozona, TX 76943
Tel: 915-392-2837

Dallas County Heritage Society
1717 Gano Street
Dallas, TX 75215
Tel: 214-421-5141

Dallas Historical Society
Hall of State, Fair Park
G.B. Dealey Library
P.O. Box 150038
Dallas, TX 75315
Tel: 214-421-4500
Fax: 214-421-7500
http://www.dallashistory.org/index.html

Dallas Jewish Historical Society
7900 Northaven Road
Dallas, TX 75230
Tel: 214-739-2737 ext. 261
E-mail: dvjcc@onramp.net
http://www.dvjc.org/history/

Denton County, Historical Society of
P.O. Box 50503
Denton, TX 76206-0503
Tel: 817-387-0995
E-mail: Mcochran@iglobal.net
http://www.mikecochran.net/HSDCPage.html

East Texas Historical Association
P.O. Box 6223, SFA Station
Nacogdoches, TX 75962
Tel: 409-468-2407
Fax: 409-468-2190
E-mail: AMcDonald@sfasu.edu
http://leonardo.sfasu.edu/etha/

Edgewood Historical Society
103 E. Elm Street
Edgewood, TX 75117-2519
Tel: 903-896-1940

German-Texan Heritage Society
507 East 10th Street
P.O. Box 684171
Austin, TX 78768-4171
Tel: 512-482-0927
Fax: 512-482-0636
E-mail: GermanTexans@aol.com
http://www.main.org/germantxn/

Gillespie County Historical Society
309 W. Main Street
Fredericksburg, TX 78624-3711
Tel: 210-997-2835
http://www.pioneermuseum.com/

Gonzales Historical Society/Archives and Records Center
1709 E Sarah Dewitt Drive
P.O. Box 114
Gonzales, TX 78629
Tel: 830-672-7970
E-mail: barney1@connecti.com

Henderson County Historical Society
217 N. Prairieville St.
P.O. Box 943
Athens, TX 75751
Tel: 903-677-3611

Jefferson Historical Society/Museum
223 Austin
Jefferson, TX 75657
Tel: 903-665-2775

Llano Estacado Heritage Society
1900 W. 8th Street
Plainview, TX 79072
Tel: 806-296-9599

Lower Gulf Coast Genealogical and Historical Society
E-mail: dsk@phoenix.net

Mesquite Historical and Genealogical Society
P.O. Box 850165
Mesquite, TX 75185-0165
Tel: 972-216-6229
http://members.aol.com/dstuart101/mesquite/
        page1.htm

Montgomery County Genealogical and Historical Society
P.O. Box 867
Conroe, TX 77305-0867
http://mcia.com/gsociety.htm

Newton County Historical Commission, Genealogy Division
213 Court Street
P. O. Box 1550
Newton, TX 75966
Tel: 409-379-2109
E-mail: newton@jas.net (Subject=Genealogy)
http://www.jas.net/~newton/

Panhandle-Plains Historical Museum
West Texas A & M University
2503 4th Avenue
Canyon, Texas
Tel: 806-651-2244
Fax: 806-656-2250
E-mail: wrdavis@wtpphmfs.wtamu.edu
http://www.panhandleplains.org/

Peters Colony Historical Society of Dallas County, Texas
P.O. Box 110846
Carrollton, TX 75011-0846

San Angelo Genealogical and Historical Society
P.O. Box 3453
San Angelo, TX 76902
http://www.rootsweb.com/~saghs/index.htm

Smithville Heritage Society
602 Main Street
Smithville, TX 78957
Tel: 512-237-4545

Somervell County Historical Society/Library
P.O. Box 669
Glen Rose, TX 76043

South East Texas Genealogical and Historical Society
c/o Tyrell Historical Library
P.O. Box 3827
Beaumont, TX 77704
http://www.rootsweb.com/~txsetghs/

Southwest Railroad Historical Society
Age of Steam Railroad Museum
Fair Park
P.O. Box 153259
Dallas, TX 75315
Tel: 214-428-0101
E-mail: railroad@startext.net
http://www.startext.net/homes/railroad/

Taylor Historical Commission
Tel: 915-673-4307
http://www.abilene.com/taylorhist/

Texas Historical Commission
P.O. Box 12276
Austin, TX 78711-2276
Tel: 512-463-6100
Fax: 512-475-4872
E-mail: thc@thc.state.tx.us
http://www.thc.state.tx.us/

Texas Military Historical Society
P.O. Box 2383
Bellaire, TX 77402-2383
E-mail: tog@io.com
http://members.aol.com/txmhs/

Texas State Historical Association
2306 Sid Richardson Hall
University Station
Austin, TX 78712
Tel: 512-471-1525
Fax: 512-471-1551
E-mail: rtyler@mail.utexas.edu
http://www.tsha.utexas.edu/

Texas Wendish Heritage Society/Museum and Research Library
Route 2, Box 155
Giddings, TX 78942-9769
Tel: 409-366-2441

Texian Heritage Society
15742 Fitzhugh Rd.
Dripping Springs, TX 78620
Tel: 512-264-2355
E-mail: ths@nabi.net
http://www.texianlegacy.com/

Weimar Heritage Society/Museum
125 E. Main Street
Weimar, TX 78962
Tel: 409-725-8203
http://www.rtis.com/reg/colorado-cty/weimar/
        museum/museum.htm

LDS FAMILY HISTORY CENTERS

For locations of Family History Centers in this state, see the Family History Center locator at FamilySearch. http://www.familysearch.org/eng/Library/FHC/ frameset_fhc.asp

ARCHIVES/LIBRARIES/MUSEUMS

Abilene Public Library
202 Cedar Street
Abilene, TX 79601
Tel: 915-677-2474
http://www.abilenetx.com/apl/

Amarillo Public Library
413 East 4th Avenue
P.O. Box 2171
Amarillo, TX 79189-2171
Tel: 806-378-3054
E-mail: Marykay@hlc.actx.edu
http://www.amarillolibrary.org/index.htm

Angelo State University
Porter Henderson Library
West Texas Collection
P.O. Box 11013, ASU Station
San Angelo, TX 76909
Tel: 915-942-2164
E-mail: Suzanne.Campbell@angelo.edu
http://www.angelo.edu/services/library/

Arlington Public Library
101 East Abram
Arlington, TX 76010
Tel: 817-459-6901
http://www.pub-lib.ci.arlington.tx.us/

Atlanta Public Library
Genealogy Section
101 W. Hiram Street
Atlanta, TX 75551
Tel: 903-796-2112

Austin History Center
9th and Guadalupe
P.O. Box 2287
Austin, TX 78768-2287
Tel: 512-499-7480

Austin Public Library
800 Guadalupe
Austin, TX 78701
Tel: 512-499-7300
E-mail: reference@ci.austin.tx.us
http://www.cityofaustin.org/library/

Bastrop Public Library
P.O. Box 670 Bastrop
Texas 78602-0670
Bastrop, TX 78602
Tel: 512-321-5441
Fax: 512-321-3163
E-mail: mickey@bastroplibrary.org
    genealogy@bastroplibrary.org (Genealogy)
http://www.bastroplibrary.org/

Bay City Public Library
1100 Seventh Street
Bay City, TX 77414
Tel: 979-245-6931
http://www.man-net.org/edu/library/bclibrary.html

Beaumont Public Library
801 Pearl Street
P.O. Box 3827
Beaumont, TX 77704
Tel: 409-838-6606

Belton City Library
301 East 1st Avenue
Belton, TX 76513
Tel: 254-933-5830
Fax: 254-933-5832
E-mail: library@ci.belton.tx.us

Blanco/James A. and Evelyn Williams Memorial Library
310 Pecan Street
P.O. Box 489
Blanco, TX 78606
Tel: 210-833-4280

Brazoria Branch Genealogical Library
620 South Brooks
Brazoria, TX 77422
Tel: 409-798-2372
Fax: 409-265-8496

Brazoria County Historical Society/Museum
Courthouse Square
100 East Cedar
Angleton, TX 77515
Tel: 409-849-5711 ext. 1208
E-mail: bchm@bchm.org

Brownwood Public Library
600 Carnegie Street
Brownwood, TX 76801-7038
Tel: 915-646-0155
http://www.ci.brownwood.tx.us/library.htm

Bryan Public Library
201 East 26th Street
Bryan, TX 77803
Tel: 409-361-3715

Cameron Public Library
P.O. Box 833
Cameron, TX 76520-3350
Tel: 817-697-2401

Carrollton Public Library
4220 N. Josey Lane
Carrollton, TX 75010
Tel: 972-466-3353
      972-466-3360
http://www.cityofcarrollton.com/leisure/library/
      home.html

Catholic Archives of Texas
1600 N. Congress
Austin, Texas
Tel: 512-476-6296
Fax: 512-476-3715
E-mail: cat@onr.com
http://www.onr.com/user/cat/

Catholic Museum Archives Building
2200 N. Spring Street
Amarillo, TX 79107
Tel: 806-381-9866

Center for Studies in Texas History
University of Texas/Austin
Austin, TX 78712
Tel: 512-471-1525
Fax: 512-471-1551
E-mail: rtyler@mail.utexas.edu
http://www.tsha.utexas.edu/

Chambers County Library
202 Cummings Street
Anahuac, TX 77514-M
Tel: 409-267-8261

Chaparral Genealogical Society/Library
310 N. Live Oak
P.O. Box 606
Tomball, TX 77375
Tel: 713-255-9081

Clayton Library
Center for Genealogical Research
5300 Caroline
Houston, TX 77004-6896
Tel: 832-393-2600
http://www.hpl.lib.tx.us/clayton/

Cleburne Public Library
302 West Henderson
P.O. Box 657
Cleburne, TX 76033-0657
Tel: 817-645-0934

Corpus Christi Public Library
805 Comanche
Corpus Christi, TX 78401
Tel: 512-880-7000
E-mail: library@ci.corpus-christi.tx.us
http://www.library.ci.corpus-christi.tx.us/

Corsicana Public Library
100 North 12th Street
Corsicana, TX 75110
Tel: 903-654-4810
Fax: 903-654-4814
E-mail: ref@corsicana.lib.tx.us; roots@corsicana.lib.tx.us
      (Genealogy)

Crockett/John H. Wooters Public Library
708 E. Goliad Avenue
P.O. Box 1226
Crockett, TX 75835
Tel: 409-544-3089
Fax: 936-544-4139

Dallas Historical Society
Hall of State, Fair Park
G.B. Dealey Library
P.O. Box 150038
Dallas, TX 75315
Tel: 214-421-4500
Fax: 214-421-7500
http://www.dallashistory.org/

Dallas Public Library/J. Erik Jonsson Branch
Genealogy Section
1515 Young Street
Dallas, TX 75201
Tel: 214-670-1400
Fax: 214-670-7839
http://dallaslibrary.org/home.htm

**Daughters of the Republic of Texas/
Library and Museum**
300 Alamo Plaza
San Antonio, Texas 78205-2606
Tel: 210-225-1071
Fax: 210-212-8514
E-mail: drtl@drtl.org
http://drtl.org/

Deer Park Public Library
3009 Center Street
Deer Park, TX 77536-5063
Tel: 281-478-7208

Denison Library Genealogical Society
300 West Gandy
Denison, TX 75020
Tel: 903-465-1797
Fax: 903-465-1130
http://www.barr.org/denison.htm

Denton Public Library/Emily Fowler Central Library
502 Oakland Street
Denton, TX 76201
Tel: 940-349-8558
E-mail: library@cityofdenton.com
http://www.dentonlibrary.com

Duncanville Public Library
201 James Collins Blvd.
Duncanville, TX 75116-4818
Tel: 972-780-5050
http://www.youseemore.com/duncanville/default.asp

Ector County Library
321 West 5th Street
Odessa, TX 79761
Tel: 915-333-9633
Fax: 915-337-6502
E-mail: library@ector.lib.tx.us

El Paso Public Library
501 North Oregon Street
El Paso, TX 79901
Tel: 915-543-5440

El Progreso Memorial Library
129 West Nopal
Uvalde, TX 78801
Tel: 830-278-2017
Fax: 830-278-2017
E-mail: letilibrary@hotmail.com

Euless Public Library
201 North Ector Drive
Euless, TX 76039
Tel: 817-685-1480
http://www.ci.euless.tx.us/library/library.html

Fort Bend County/George Memorial Library
1001 Golfview Drive
Richmond, TX 77469
Tel: 281-342-4455
http://www.fortbend.lib.tx.us/dept.html

Fort Worth Public Library
500 West Third Street
Fort Worth, TX 76102-7305
Tel: 817-871-7701
    817-871-7740 (Genealogy)
http://www.fortworthlibrary.org/

Gatesville Public Library
811 Main Street
Gatesville, TX 76528
Tel: 254-865-5367

Gibbs Memorial Library
305 East Rusk
Mexia, TX 76667
Tel: 254-562-3231
E-mail: Gibbs.Library@mexia.com
http://www.gibbslibrary.com

Gladys Harrington Public Library
1501 18th Street
Plano, TX 75074
Tel: 972-941-7175
http://www.ci.plano.tx.us/library/harlib.htm

**Gonzales Historical Society/
Archives and Records Center**
1709 E Sarah Dewitt Drive
P.O. Box 114
Gonzales, TX 78629
Tel: 830-672-7970
E-mail: barney1@connecti.com

Grand Prairie Memorial Library
901 Conover
Grand Prairie, TX 75051-1521
Tel: 972-264-1571

Grapevine Public Library
1201 Municipal Way
Grapevine, TX 76051-5545
Tel: 817-410-3403
Fax: 817-410-3080
http://www.grapevine.lib.tx.us/index.asp

Harlingen Public Library
410 - 76 Drive
Harlingen, TX 78550
Tel: 956-430-6650
http://webcat.harlingen.lib.tx.us/

Harrison County Historical Museum and Research Library
707 N Washington Avenue
Marshall, TX 756701
Tel: 903-938-2680
http://www.rootsweb.com/~txharris/newhome.htm

Hillsboro City Library
118 South Waco Street
Hillsboro, TX 76645
Tel: 254-582-7385
Fax: 254-582-7765

Hood County Library
222 North Travis
Granbury, TX 76048
Tel: 817-573-3569

Houston Public Library/Metropolitan Research Center
500 McKinney Street
Houston, TX 77002
http://www.hpl.lib.tx.us/hpl/hplhome.htm/

Huntsville Public Library
Genealogy/Texana/Local History Room
1216 14th Street
Huntsville, TX 77340
Tel: 409-291-5472

Irving Public Library
801 W. Irving Blvd.
P.O. Box 152288
Irving, TX 75015-2288
Tel: 972-721-2606
     972-721-2628
Fax: 972-259-1171
http://www.irving.lib.tx.us/

Kemp Public Library
1300 Lamar
Wichita Falls, TX 76301

Kurth Memorial Library
706 South Raguet
Lufkin, TX 75904
Tel: 936-634-7617
http://www.kurthmemoriallibrary.com/index.htm

Laredo Public Library
1120 San Bernardo Avenue
Laredo, TX 78040
Tel: 956-795-3035
Fax: 956-795-3039

Longview Public Library
222 West Cotton Street
Longview, TX 75601
Tel: 903-237-1350
http://www.longview.lib.tx.us/

Lubbock City/County Library
1306 9th Street
Lubbock, TX 79401
Tel: 806-775-2835

Lucy Hill Patterson Memorial Library
201 Ackerman Street
Rockdale, TX 76567
Tel: 512-446-3410
Fax: 512-446-5597
E-mail: pattersonlib@rockdalecityhall.com
http://www.main.org/patlib/library.htm

Luling Public Library
215 S. Pecan Avenue
Luling, TX 78648
Tel: 830-875-9466

McKinney Memorial Public Library
220 North Kentucky Street
McKinney, TX 75069
Tel: 972-542-4461
Fax: 972-542-1344

McMurry College Library
Scarborough Library of Genealogy
History and Biography of the South and Southwest
McMurry Station
Abilene, TX 79605
http://www.alc.org/www/mcm/mcm_library.html

Mesquite Public Library
300 Grubb Drive
Mesquite, TX 75149
Tel: 972-216-6220
     972-216-6229 (Genealogy)
Fax: 972-216-6740
http://www.cityofmesquite.com/library/

Montgomery County Library
104 I-45 North
P.O. Box 867
Conroe, TX 77301
Tel: 936-788-8361
     936-788-8363 (Genealogy)
http://www.countylibrary.org/

Moody Texas Ranger Library
P.O. Box 2570
Waco, TX 76702
Tel: 254-750-8631 254-750-5986
Fax: 254-750-8629
E-mail: trhf@eramp.net

Moore Memorial Library
1701 9th Avenue North
Texas City, TX 77590
Tel: 409-643-5979

Mount Pleasant Municipal Library
213 North Madison
Box 1285, 213 N, Madison
Mount Pleasant, TX 75455
Tel: 903-575-4180
Fax: 903-577-8000
E-mail: mppublib@stargate.1stargate.com
http://www2.1stargate.com/mppublib/

New Boston Public Library
127 North Ellis
New Boston, TX 75570
Tel: 903-628-5414

Nicholson Memorial Library
625 Austin Street
Garland, TX 75040
Tel: 972-205-2503
     972-205-2502 (Reference)
Fax: 972-205-2523
http://www.nmls.lib.tx.us/

Palestine Public Library
Special Collections
1101 North Cedar
Palestine, TX 75801
Tel: 903-729-4121
E-mail: reflib@palestine.lib.tx.us
     brenkay@palestine.lib.tx.us (Genealogy)
http://www.e-tex.com/personal/bonniew/
     acgs/gen.htm

Paris Junior College
A.M. Aikin Regional Archives
2400 Clarksville Street
Paris, TX 75460
Tel: 903-782-0411
E-mail: dharvill@paris.cc.tx.us
http://www.paris.cc.tx.us/archives/

Paris Junior College
Mike Rheudasil Learning Center
2400 Clarksville Street
Paris, TX 75460
Tel: 903-782-0215 (Director of Library Services)
http://www.paris.cc.tx.us/lrc/

Pilot Point Community Library
324 S. Washington Street
P.O. Box 969
Pilot Point, TX 76258-8906
Tel: 940-686-5004

Port Arthur Public Library
3601 Cultural Center Drive
Port Arthur, TX 77642
Tel: 409-985-8838
http://www.halan.lib.tx.us/ssetup.shtml

Quitman Library
202 East Goode Street
P.O. Box 1677
Quitman, TX 75783-0077
Tel: 903-763-4191
Fax (903) 763-2532
http://www.quitmanlibrary.org/

Richardson Public Library
900 Civic Center
Richardson, TX 75080-5298
Tel: 972-744-4350
Fax: 972-952-0870
http://www.cor.net/library/

Rosenberg Library
2310 Sealy Avenue
Galveston, TX 77550
Tel: 409-763-8854
Fax: 409-763-0275

Round Rock Public Library
216 East Main Street
Round Rock, TX 78664
Tel: 512-218-7000
Fax: 512-218-7061
E-mail: dale@round-rock.tx.us
     lindab@round-rock.tx.us
http://www.ci.round-rock.tx.us/library/library.html

San Antonio Central Library/Central Library
Texana/Genealogy Department
600 Soledad
San Antonio, TX 78205
Tel: 210-207-2500
E-mail: librarywebadmin@sanantonio.gov
http://www.sanantonio.gov/library/texana/

San Augustine Public Library
413 East Columbia
San Augustine, TX 75972
Tel: 936-275-5367
Fax: 936-275-5049
E-mail: kgamble1@qzip.net

Scurry County Library
1916 23rd Street
Snyder, TX 79549
Tel: 915-573-5572

Sherman Public Library
421 N. Travis
Sherman, TX 75090-5975
Tel: 903-892-7240
Fax: 903-892-7101
http://www.barr.org/sherman.htm

Somervell County Historical Society/Library
P.O. Box 669
Glen Rose, TX 76043

Southern Methodist University
Clements Center for Southwest Studies
3225 University Avenue, Room 356
Box 750176
356 Dallas Hall
Dallas, TX 75275-0176
Tel: 214-768-1233
Fax: 214-768-4129
E-mail: swcenter@mail.smu.edu
http://www2.smu.edu/swcenter/

Stephen F. Austin State University
Center for East Texas Studies
Ferguson Building 340
P.O. Box 6134, SFA Station
Nacogdoches, TX 75962
Tel: 409-468-1392
Fax: 409-468-2190
E-mail: CETS@SFASU
http://www.cets.sfasu.edu/ETRC/Index.html

Stephen F. Austin State University
Ralph W. Steen Library
Box 13055, SFA Station
Nacogdoches, TX 75962-3055
Tel: 409-468-4100
http://libweb.sfasu.edu/etrc/etrcbro.htm

Temple Public Library
100 W. Adams Ave.
Temple TX 76501 05
Tel: 254-298-5707
Fax: 254-298-5328
E-mail: cmaneice@ci.temple.tx.us

Texarkana Public Library
600 W. Third Street
Texarkana, TX 75501
Tel: 903-794-2149
Fax: 903-794-2139
http://www.txar-publib.org/home.htm/

Texas State General Land Office
Archives and Records Division
Stephen F. Austin Building
1700 North Congress Avenue
Austin, TX 78701
Tel: 512-463-5277
E-mail: archives@glo.state.tx.us
http://www.glo.state.tx.us/archives/

Texas State Library and Archives Commission
Lorenzo de Zavala State Archives and Library Building
1201 Brazos Street
P.O. Box 12927
Austin, TX 78711
Tel: 512-463-5455
    512-463-5463 (Genealogy Collection, Room 110)
E-mail: geninfo@tsl.state.tx.us
http://www.tsl.state.tx.us/index.html

Texas Wendish Heritage Society/
Museum and Research Library
Route 2, Box 155
Giddings, TX 78942
Tel: 409-366-2441

Tom Burnett Memorial Library
400 West Alameda
Iowa Park, TX 76367
Tel: 940-592-4981
Fax: 940-592-4664
E-mail: suern@wf.net

Tyler Public Library
Genealogy and Local History Dept.
201 S. College
Tyler, TX 75702
Tel: 903-593-7323
Fax: 903-531-1329
E-mail: library@tyler.net
http://www.cox-internet.com/library/

Tyrell Public Library
695 Pearl Street
P.O. Box 3827
Beaumont, TX 77704
Tel: 409-833-2759
    409-833-5069
Fax: 409-833-5828
http://www.rootsweb.com/~txjeffer/misc/library.htm

Unger Memorial Library
Local History and Genealogy Section
825 N Austin Street
Plainview, TX 79072-7235
Tel: 806-296-1148
E-mail: johnsigwald@texasonline.net
http://www.texasonline.net/unger/

University of Texas/Austin
The Center for American History
Eugene C. Barker Texas History Collections
Sid Richardson Hall 2.101
Austin, Texas 78712
Tel: 512-495-4515
Fax: 512-495-4542
http://www.lib.utexas.edu/Libs/CAH/

University of Texas/Austin
Perry Castaneda Library
Austin, TX 78712
Tel: 512-495-4250
http://www.lib.utexas.edu/

University of Texas/El Paso (UTEP)
C.L. Sonnichsen Special Collections Dept.
El Paso, TX 79968
Tel: 915-747-5683
Fax: 915-747-5345
http://libraryweb.utep.edu/

Van Alstyne Public Library
117 N. Waco
P.O. Box 629
Van Alstyne TX 75495
Tel: 903-482-5991
E-mail: vanalstynepl@texoma.net
http://www.vanalstynepl.lib.tx.us/

Van Zandt County Library of Genealogy and Local History
Van Zandt County Courthouse, Annex Building
Canton, TX 75103
Tel: 903-567-5012
http://www.rootsweb.com/~txvzcgs/vzgslib.htm

Waco/McLennan County Library
1717 Austin Avenue
Waco, TX 76701
Tel: 254-750-5941
http://www.waco-texas.com/city_depts/libraryservices/
    libraryservices.htm

Walworth Harrison Public Library
Genealogy Room
3716 Lee Street
Greenville, TX 75401
Tel: 903-457-2992
Fax: 903-457-2961
http://www.youseemore.com/harrison/default.asp

Weatherford Public Library
1014 Charles Street
Weatherford, TX 76086
Tel: 817-598-4150

Weimar Heritage Society/Museum
125 E. Main Street
Weimar, TX 78962
Tel: 409-725-8203
http://www.rtis.com/reg/colorado-cty/weimar/
    museum/museum.htm

West Texas A & M University
Panhandle-Plains Historical Museum
2403 4th Avenue
WTAMU Box 967
Canyon, TX 79015
Tel: 806-656-2244
Fax: 806-656-2250
E-mail: museum@wtamu.edu
http://www.wtamu.edu/museum/

Western Texas College
Learning Resource Center
6200 South College Avenue
Snyder, TX 79549
Tel: 915-573-8511
http://www.wtc.cc.tx.us/

Whitesboro Public Library
308 W. Main Street
Whitesboro, TX 76273
Tel: 903-564-5432

NEWSPAPER REPOSITORIES

Texas State Library and Archives Commission
Lorenzo de Zavala State Archives and Library Building
1201 Brazos Street
P.O. Box 12927
Austin, TX 78711
Tel: 512-463-5455
    512-463-5463 (Genealogy Collection, Room 110)
E-mail: geninfo@tsl.state.tx.us
http://www.tsl.state.tx.us/index.html

University of Texas/Austin
The Center for American History
Eugene C. Barker Texas History Collections
Sid Richardson Hall 2.101
Austin, Texas 78712
Tel: 512-495-4515
Fax: 512-495-4542
http://www.lib.utexas.edu/Libs/CAH/

VITAL RECORDS

Department of Health, Bureau of Vital Statistics
1100 W. 49th Street
P.O. Box 12040
Austin, TX 78756-3199
Tel: 512-458-7111
    512-458-4751
Fax: 512-458-7711
E-mail: register@stats.tdh.state.tx.us
http://www.tdh.state.tx.us/bvs/default.htm

TEXAS ON THE WEB

**Brazoria County Historical Museum–Old 300
Genealogical Database**
http://www.bchm.org/Gene/gene.html

**Brazos Genealogical Association–Links to Sites with
Searchable Databases**
http://user.txcyber.com/~bga/txlinks.html

Index to Confederate Pensions
http://www.tsl.state.tx.us/arc/pensions/

Texas Adjutant General Service Records 1836-1935
http://www.tsl.state.tx.us/arc/service/index.html

Texas GenWeb Project
http://www.rootsweb.com/~txgenweb/

**Welcome to Family History—Family History Radio
Show and The Family Historian magazine**
http://familyhistory.flash.net/

UTAH

ARCHIVES, STATE & NATIONAL

National Archives-Rocky Mountain Region
Bldg. 48, Denver Federal Center
West 6th Avenue and Kipling Street
Denver, CO 80225-0307
Mailing Address:
P.O. Box 25307
Denver, CO 80225-0307
Phone: 303-236-0817
Fax: 303-236-9297
E-mail: denver.archives@nara.gov
http://www.nara.gov/regional/denver.html

Utah State Archives
P.O. Box 141021
Salt Lake City, UT 84114-1021
Tel: 801-538-3013 (Research Center)
Fax: 801-538-3354
E-mail: research@das.state.ut.us
http://www.archives.state.ut.us/

GENEALOGICAL SOCIETIES

Cuban Genealogical Society
P.O. Box 2650
Salt Lake City, UT 84110-2650
E-mail: Mayra@Utah-Inter.Net
http://www.rootsweb.com/~utcubangs/INDEX.HTM

Genealogical Society of Utah
50 East North Temple
Salt Lake City, UT 84150
Tel: 801-538-2978
Fax: 801-240-1448
E-mail: society@gensocietyofutah.org
http://www.gensocietyofutah.org/

St. George Genealogy Club
P.O. Box 184
St. George, UT 84770

Utah Blue Chips (Utah Computer Society)
P.O. Box 510811
Salt Lake City, UT 84151
Tel: 801-281-8339
BBS: 801-281-8770
E-mail: sysop@ucs.org (BBS)
http://www.ucs.org/

Utah Genealogical Association
P.O. Box 1144
Salt Lake City, UT 84110
Tel: 888-INFO-UGA (Toll-free)
http://www.infouga.org/

Utah Valley PAF Users Group
Jay P. Markham, Pres.
490 East 600 South
Orem, UT 84058
Tel: 801-224-1167
http://www.uvpafug.org/

Utah Valley PC Users Group
P.O. Box 1834
Provo, UT 84603
E-mail: uvpcug@xmission.com
http://www.xmission.com/~uvpcug/

HISTORICAL SOCIETIES

Cache Valley Historical Society
290 West Center Street
Logan, UT 84321

Daughters of the Utah Pioneers
Pioneer Memorial Museum
300 North Main
Salt Lake City, UT 84103
Tel: 801-538-1050
http://www.northernutah.com/mayflower/dup.htm

Sons of the Utah Pioneers
3301 East 2920 South
Salt Lake City, UT 84109-4260
E-mail: editor@uvol.com
http://www.uvol.com/sup/

Utah State Historical Society/Library
300 Rio Grande
Salt Lake City, UT 84101
Tel: 801-533-3500
     801-533-3501 (Hours, Information)
Fax: 801-533-3502
TDD: 801-533-3503
E-mail: ushs@history.state.ut.us
        cehistry.ushs@e-mail.state.ut.us
http://www.dced.state.ut.us/history/

LDS FAMILY HISTORY CENTERS

For locations of Family History Centers in this state, see the Family History Center locator at FamilySearch.
http://www.familysearch.org/eng/Library/FHC/frameset_fhc.asp

ARCHIVES/LIBRARIES/MUSEUMS

Brigham City Library
26 E Forest
Brigham City, UT 84302-2198
Tel: 435-723-5891
    435-723-5850
Fax: 435-723-2813
Salt Lake Line: 544-2328 Ext 48
E-mail: susan@peachy.bcpl.lib.ut.us
http://bcpl.lib.ut.us

Brigham Young University (BYU)
Harold B. Lee Library
Utah Valley Regional Family History Center, 4th Floor
Provo, UT 84602
Tel: 801-378-6200 (Family History Center)
    801-378-2926 (Library Information)
http://www.lib.byu.edu/

Cedar City Public Library
136 W. Center Street
Cedar City, UT 84720-2597
Tel: 435-586-6661

Church of Jesus Christ of Latter-Day Saints
Historical Department
50 East North Temple
Salt Lake City, UT 84150

Everton's Genealogical Library
3223 South Main Street
P.O. Box 368
Nibley, UT 84323-0368
http://www.everton.com/

Family History Library
Church of Jesus Christ of Latter-Day Saints
35 North West Temple
Salt Lake City, UT 84150
Tel: 801-240-2331
    800-453-3860 x22331
Fax: 801-240-1584
E-mail: fhl@ldschurch.org
www.familysearch.org
Some Unofficial Sites:
http://www.genealogy.org/~uvpafug/fhlslc.html
or
http://www.aros.net/~drwaff/slcfhl.htm

Logan Public Library
Archives
255 North Main
Logan, UT 84321
Tel: 435-716-9123
Fax: 435-716-9145
http://www.logan.lib.ut.us/

Manti Public Library
2 South Main Street
Manti, UT 84642-1349
Tel: 801-835-2201
Fax: 435-835-2202

Ogden/Weber County Public Library
Special Collections
2464 Jefferson Avenue
Ogden, UT 84401-2404
Tel: 801-337-2617
Fax: 801-337-2615
http://www.weberpl.lib.ut.us/

Orem Public Library
58 N. State Street
Orem, UT 84057
Tel: 801-224-7050
Fax: 801-229-7130
http://168.177.93.4/html/orem_public_library.cfm

Provo City Library
550 North University Avenue
Provo, UT 84601-1618
Tel: 801-852-6650
    801-852-6661 (Reference Questions)
http://www.provo.lib.ut.us

Springville Public Library
50 South Main
Springville, UT 84663-1358
Tel: 801-489-2720
    801-489-2721
Fax: 801-489-2709
E-mail: lcathera@state.lib.ut.us

Southern Utah University Library
Special Collections
351 Center Street, Garden Level
Cedar City, UT 84720
Tel: 801-586-7933
    801-586-7945 (Special Collections)
E-mail: library@suu.edu
http://www.li.suu.edu/library/lispcoll.htm

University of Utah
Marriott Library
Special Collections, 5th Floor
295 S 1500 E
Salt Lake City, UT 84112-0860
Tel: 801-581-8558
Fax: 801-585-3464
E-mail: gthompso@alexandria.lib.utah.edu
http://www.lib.utah.edu/

Utah State Historical Society/Library
300 Rio Grande
Salt Lake City, UT 84101
Tel: 801-533-3500
        801-533-3501 (Hours, Information)
Fax: 801-533-3502
TDD: 801-533-3503
E-mail: ushs@history.state.ut.us
        cehistry.ushs@e-mail.state.ut.us
http://www.dced.state.ut.us/history/

Utah State University
Merrill Library
Special Collections and Archives, 1st Floor
Logan, UT 84322
Tel: 435-797-2663
E-mail: scweb@ngw.lib.usu.edu
http://www.usu.edu/~specol/index.html

Utah Valley State College (UVSC)
Library/Sparks Special Collection Room
800 West University Parkway
Orem, UT 84058-5999
Tel: 801-222-8000
        801-222-8265
        801-222-8173
http://www.uvsc.edu/studsvc/library/

NEWSPAPER REPOSITORIES

Family History Library
Church of Jesus Christ of Latter-Day Saints
35 North West Temple
Salt Lake City, UT 84150
Tel: 801-240-2331
        800-453-3860 x22331
Fax: 801-240-1584
E-mail: fhl@ldschurch.org
 www.familysearch.org
Some Unofficial Sites:
http://www.genealogy.org/~uvpafug/fhlslc.html
or
http://www.aros.net/~drwaff/slcfhl.htm

University of Utah
Marriott Library
Serials Department
295 S 1500 E
Salt Lake City, UT 84112-0860
Tel: 801-581-8558
Fax: 801-585-3464
http://www.lib.utah.edu/

Utah State Library
2150 South 300 West, Suite 16
Salt Lake City, UT 84115
Tel. 801-468-6777
E-mail: dslater@inter.state.lib.ut.us
http://www.state.lib.ut.us/

Utah State University
Merrill Library
Special Collections and Archives, 1st Floor
Logan, UT 84322
Tel: 435-797-2663
E-mail: scweb@ngw.lib.usu.edu
http://www.usu.edu/~specol/index.html

VITAL RECORDS

Utah Bureau of Vital Records
Bureau of Vital Records
Utah Department of Health
288 North 1460 West
P.O. Box 141012
Salt Lake City, UT 84114-1012
Tel: 801-538-3012
Fax: 801-538-3354
E-mail: archivesresearch@utah.gov
http://www.archives.state.ut.us/

Utah State Archives
P.O. Box 141021
Salt Lake City, UT 84114-1021
Tel: 801-538-3013 (Research Center)
Fax: 801-538-3354
E-mail: research@das.state.ut.us
http://www.archives.state.ut.us/
Births and Deaths 1898-1905

UTAH ON THE WEB

Pioneer-Utah's Online Electronic Library
http://pioneer.uen.org/

Utah GenWeb Project
http://www.rootsweb.com/~utgenweb/

Utah History Encyclopedia
http://www.media.utah.edu/UHE/

Utah Travel and Adventures
http://www.utah.com/

Utah Valley PAF Users Group
http://www.uvpafug.org/

VERMONT

ARCHIVES, STATE & NATIONAL

National Archives-New England Region
Frederick C. Murphy Federal Center
380 Trapelo Road
Waltham, MA 02154-8104
Tel: 781-647-8104
Fax: 781-647-8088
E-mail: waltham.center@nara.gov
http://www.nara.gov/regional/boston.html

Vermont State Archives
Redstone Building
26 Terrace Street
Drawer 09
Montpelier, VT 05609-1101
Tel: 802-828-2363
E-mail: gsanford@sec.state.vt.us
http://vermont-archives.org/

GENEALOGICAL SOCIETIES

Genealogical Society of Vermont
P.O. Box 1553
St. Albans, VT 05478-1006
E-mail: jtyler@sover.net
http://www.rootsweb.com/~vtgsv/

**New England Historical and Genealogical Society
(NEHGS)**
101 Newbury Street
Boston, MA 02116-3007
Tel: 617-536-5740
   888-296-3447 (Membership & Education)
   888-BY-NEHGS (Sales)
   1-888-906-3447 (Library Circulation)
Fax: 617-536-7307
E-mail: nehgs@nehgs.org
http://www.nehgs.org/

Vermont French-Canadian Genealogical Society
Library:
29 Ethan Allen Avenue
P.O. Box 65128
Burlington, VT 05406-5128
E-mail: mail@vt-fcgs.org
http://www.vt-fcgs.org/

HISTORICAL SOCIETIES

Barnet Historical Society
Goodwillie House
97 Old West Road
Barnet, VT 05821
Tel: 802-633-2611
   802-633-2563

Bellows Falls Historical Society
6 Chase Park
Bellows Falls, VT 05051
Tel: 802-463-3706

Bethel Historical Society
Church Street
Bethel, VT 05032
Tel: 802-234-9413

Bradford Historical Society
Academy Building
Main Street
P.O. Box 301
Bradford, VT 05033
Tel: 802-222-9026
E-mail: L_C_Coffin@kingcon.com

Braintree Historical Society
RFD 1, Thayer Brook Road
Randolph, VT 05060
Tel: 802-728-9291

Brattleboro Historical Society
230 Main Street, 3rd Floor
P.O. Box 6392
Brattleboro, VT 05302
Tel: 802-258-4957
E-mail: histsoc@together.net

Bridport Historical Society/Museum
Route 22-A
Mail:
2947 Basin Harbor Road
Bridport, VT 05734

Bristol Historical Society/Museum
Howden Hall Community Center
Main Street
Bristol, VT 05443
Tel: 802-453-6029

Brookfield Historical Society
Marvin Newton House
Ridge Road
P.O. Box 405
Brookfield, VT 05036
Tel: 802-276-3959
Fax: 276-3023

Cabot Historical Society/Museum
Main Street
Cabot, VT
Mail:
P.O. Box 63
Marshfield, VT 05658
E-mail: palmandan@aol.com

Canaan Historical Society
Alice Ward Memorial Library
27 Park St., Canaan, VT
Mailing Address:
P.O. Box 134, Canaan, VT 05903
Tel: 802-266-7135
Fax: 802-266-7867
E-mail: award_canaan@dol.state.vt.us

Castleton Historical Society/Museum
Main Street
P.O. Box 219
Castleton, VT 05735
Tel: 802-468-5523

Cavendish Historical Society/Museum
RFD 1, Box 171
Cavendish, VT 05142

Charleston Historical Society
RR 1, Box 840
West Charleston, VT 05872

Chelsea Historical Society
Main Street
P.O. Box 206
Chelsea, VT 05038

Chester Historical Society
Main Street
Chester, VT 05143
Tel: 802-875-3767

Chittenden County Historical Society
P.O. Box 1576
Burlington, VT 05402

Concord Historical Society/Museum
Concord Town Hall
Mail:
HCR 60, Box 40
North Concord, VT 05858

Crystal Lake Falls Historical Association
The Pierce House
Water Street
P.O. Box 253
Barton, VT 05822
Tel: 802-525-6251
    802-525-3703
E-mail: jfbmab@hotmail.com

Danville Historical Society/Archives
Pope Memorial Library
The Green
P.O. Box 260
Danville, VT 05828
Tel: 802-684-2256

Derby Historical Society
P.O. Box 357
Derby, VT 05829

Dorset Historical Society/Museum
P.O. Box 52
Dorset, VT 05251
Tel: 802-867-0331
E-mail: dorsethist@vermontel.net
http://www.dorsethistory.org

Enosburgh Historical Society
Main Street
P.O. Box 98
Enosburgh Falls, VT 05450

Essex Community Historical Society
Routes 15 and 128
Mail:
3 Browns River Road
Essex Junction, VT 05452
http://www.essex.org/esxhs/esxhsfindex.htm

Fairlee Historical Society
Fairlee Town Hall
P.O. Box 95
Fairlee, VT 05045
Tel: 802-333-4363
    802-333-9727

Georgia Historical Society/Museum
Georgia Center, VT
Mail:
RD 3
St. Albans, VT 05478

Glover Historical Society
Municipal Building, 2nd Floor
Glover, VT 05839
Tel: 802-525-6227 (Town Clerk)

Goodrich Memorial Library
70 Main Street
Newport, VT 05855
Tel: 802-334-7902
http://www.state.vt.us/libraries/n47/

Grafton Historical Society/Museum
Main Street
P.O. Box 202
Grafton, VT 05146
E-mail: grafhist@sover.net

Greensboro Historical Society/Museum
RR 1, Box 1290
Greensboro, VT 05841

Guilford Historical Society
RR 2, Box 18A
Brattleboro, VT 05301

Halifax Historical Society
RR 4, Box 531
Brattleboro, VT 05301

Hartford Historical Society
15 Bridge Street
P.O. Box 547
Hartford, VT 05047
Tel: 802-295-9353
Fax: 802-295-6382

Holland Historical Society
RD 1, Box 37, Derby Line
Holland, VT 05830
Tel: 802-895-4440

Huntington Historical Society
Lower Village
P.O. Box 147
Huntington, VT 05462

Island Pond Historical Society
Canadian Natl. Railway Station
P.O. Box 408
Island Pond, VT 05846
Tel: 802-482-3923

Isle La Motte Historical Society
1830 Schoolhouse
Isle La Motte, VT 05463
Tel: 802-928-3422

Jericho Historical Society
Old Red Mill, Route 15
P.O. Box 35
Jericho, VT 05465
Tel: 802-899-3225
http://snowflakebentley.com/jhs.htm

Lincoln Historical Society
Quaker Street
Lincoln, VT
Mail:
RD 1, Box 60
Bristol, VT 05443
Tel/Fax: 802-453-3628

Londonderry Historical Society
RR 1, Box 41
South Londonderry, VT 05155

Manchester Historical Society
P.O. Box 363
Manchester, VT 05254
Tel: 802-362-3747

Marlboro Historical Society/Museum
P.O. Box 131
Marlboro, VT 05344

Middletown Springs Historical Society
P.O. Box 1126
Middletown Springs, VT 05757
Tel: Jon Mathewson 802-235-2561
http://members.tripod.com/middletownspringshs/
index.html

Missisquoi Valley Historical Society/Museum
East Main Street
North Troy, VT 05859
http://www.vmga.org/essex/missiquoi.html

Montgomery Historical Society/Museum
P.O. Box 47
Montgomery, VT 05470
Tel: 802-326-4404

Morristown Historical Society
P.O. Box 1299
Morrisville, VT 05661
Tel: 802-888-7617

**New England Historical and Genealogical Society
(NEHGS)**
101 Newbury Street
Boston, MA 02116-3007
Tel: 617-536-5740
    888-296-3447 (Membership & Education)
    888-BY-NEHGS (Sales)
    1-888-906-3447 (Library Circulation)
Fax: 617-536-7307
E-mail: nehgs@nehgs.org
http://www.nehgs.org/

Norwich Historical Society
37 Church Street
P.O. Box 1680
Norwich, VT 05055
Tel: 802-649-0124

Orleans County Historical Society/Museum and Library
Old Stone House Museum
28 Old Stone House Road
Brownington, VT 05860
Tel: 802-754-2022
http://oldstonehousemuseum.org/

Peacham Historical Association
Peacham Corner, VT
104 Thaddeus Stevens Road
Peacham, VT 05862
http://www.peacham.net/historical/

Pittsford Historical Society/Museum
Eaton Hall, 3399 Route 7
Pittsford, VT
P.O. Box 423
Pittsford, VT 05763
Tel: 802-483-2040
E-mail: loisblitt@together.net
http://www.pittsford-historical.org/

Poultney Historical Society
RFD 1, Box 177
Poultney, VT 05764
http://www.rootsweb.com/~vtphs/

Putney Historical Society
Town Hall
P.O. Box 233
Putney, VT 05346
Tel: 802-387-5862
http://www.putneyvt.org/history/

Randolph Historical Society/Museum
P.O. Box 15
Randolph Center, VT 05061

Reading Historical Society/Museum
Reading, VT 05062

Readsboro Historical Society
P.O. Box 7
Rochester 05767

Rochester Historical Society
Town Library
Rochester, VT 05767

Royalton Historical Society/Museum
RR 1, Box 89D
Royalton, VT 05068
E-mail: jdumville@dca.state.vt.us

Rutland Historical Society
96 Center Street
Rutland, VT 05701
Tel: 802-775-2006

St. Albans Historical Society/Museum
Church Street
P.O. Box 722
St. Albans, VT 05478
Tel: 802-527-7933

Saxtons River Historical Society/Museum
P.O. Box 18
Saxtons River, VT 05154
E-mail: luring@sover.net

Shaftsbury Historical Society
Baptist Meeting House, Route 7-A
P.O. Box 401
Shaftsbury, VT 05262

Shoreham Historical Society
Route 22-A
Shoreham, VT 05770
http://steveworld.ksci.com/ShorehamHS/ SHShome.htm

Springfield Art and Historical Society
Miller Art Center
9 Elm Street
P.O. Box 313
Springfield, VT 05156

Stannard Historical Society
9 Willey Road
Greensboro Bend, VT 05842

Stowe Historical Society
Akeley Memorial Building/Stowe History Room
Main Street
Stowe, VT 05672

Thetford Historical Society/Museum
P.O. Box 33
Thetford, VT 05074
Tel: 802-785-2068

UVM Historic Preservation Program
Wheeler House
133 South Prospect Street
Burlington, VT 05405
Tel: 802-656-3180
Fax: 802-656-8794
E-mail: histpres@zoo.uvm.edu
http://www.uvm.edu/~histpres/index.html

Vermont Historical Society
Pavilion Office Building
109 State Street
Montpelier, VT 05602
Tel: 802-828-2291
E-mail: vhs@vhs.state.vt.us
http://www.state.vt.us/vhs/

Vermont Old Cemetery Association
c/o Charles Marchant
P.O. Box 132
Townshend, VT 05353
Tel: 802-365-7937
http://www.sover.net/~hwdbry/voca/

Vernon Historians
4201 Fort Bridgman Road
P.O. Box 282
Vernon, VT 05354

Wallingford Historical Society
P.O. Box 327
Wallingford, VT 05773
Tel: 802-446-2336

Waterbury Historical Society/Museum
28 North Main Street
Waterbury, VT 05676
Tel: 802-244-7036

Weathersfield Historical Society/Museum
Reverend Dan Foster House
Whed Center Road
Perkinsville, VT 05151
Tel: 802-263-5230

West Windsor Historical Society
Route 44
P.O. Box 12
Brownsville, VT 05037
Tel: 802-484-7474

Westminster Historical Society
Town Hall, Route 5
P.O. Box 2
Westminster, VT 05158
Tel: 802-387-5778
http://www.microserve.net/~rduffalo/wrhistsoc.html

Whitingham Historical Society
P.O. Box 125
Jacksonville, VT 05342

Williamstown Historical Society
2476 VT Rte. 14
P.O. Box 338
Williamstown, VT 05679

Williston Historical Society
688 Williston Road
P.O. Box 995
Williston, VT 05495

Windham County, Historical Society of
Route 30
P.O. Box 246
Newfane, VT 05345
Tel: 802-365-4148

Winooski Historical Society
73 East Allen Street (Location)
Winooski, VT 05404

Woodstock Historical Society
26 Elm Street
Woodstock, VT 05091
Tel: 802-457-1822
http://www.uvm.edu/~histpres/vtiana/
    woodstockhs.html

LDS FAMILY HISTORY CENTER

For locations of Family History Centers in this state, see
the Family History Center locator at FamilySearch.
http://www.familysearch.org/eng/Library/FHC/
frameset_fhc.asp

ARCHIVES/LIBRARIES/MUSEUMS

Aldrich Public Library
Vermont Room
6 Washington Street
Barre, VT 05641
Tel: 802-476-7550
    802-476-5118
E-mail: aldrich@helicon.net
http://www.state.vt.us/libraries/b27/
    orhttp://www.uvm.edu/~histpres/vtiana/aldrich.html

Bennington Museum/Genealogical Library
West Main Street
Bennington, VT 05201
Tel: 802-447-1571
Fax: 802-447-8305
http://www.benningtonmuseum.com/
   orhttp://www.uvm.edu/~histpres/vtiana/benningtonmu-
      seum.html

Bixby Memorial Library
258 Main Street
Vergennes, VT 05491
Tel: 802-877-2211
http://www.vergennes.org/bixby/
    orhttp://www.uvm.edu/~histpres/vtiana/bixby.html

Brooks Memorial Library
Vermontiana Collection
224 Main Street
Brattleboro, VT 05301
Tel: 802-254-5290
E-mail: brattlib@brooks.lib.vt.us
http://www.state.vt.us/libraries/b733/brookslibrary/

Castleton State College
Calvin Coolidge Library
Seminary Street
Castleton, VT 05735
Tel: 802-468-5611
Fax: 802-468-5237
http://www.csc.vsc.edu/library/index.htm

Danville Historical Society/Archives
Pope Memorial Library
The Green
P.O. Box 260
Danville, VT 05828
Tel: 802-684-2256

Fletcher Free Library
235 College Street
Burlington, VT 05401
Tel: 802-863-3403
      802-865-7217 (Reference)
Fax: 802-865-7227
http://www.fletcherfree.org/index.htm
or
http://www.uvm.edu/~histpres/vtiana/fletcher.html

Georgia Historical Society/Museum
Georgia Center, VT
Mail:
RD 3
St. Albans, VT 05478

Glover Historical Society
Municipal Building, 2nd Floor
Glover, VT 05839
Tel: 802-525-6227 (Town Clerk)

Goodrich Memorial Library
70 Main Street
Newport, VT 05855
Tel: 802-334-7902
http://www.state.vt.us/libraries/n47/

Greensboro Historical Society/Museum
RR 1, Box 1290
Greensboro, VT 05841

Ilsley Public Library
75 Main Street
Middlebury, VT 05753
Tel: 802-388-4095
Fax: 802-388-4367
E-mail: ilsley_midd@dol.state.vt.us
http://community.middlebury.edu/~ilsley/
or
http://www.uvm.edu/~histpres/vtiana/ilsley.html
or
http://www.middlebury.edu/~slse/VOPGuide/
      24%20-%20ILSLEY.htm

Lyndon State College
Samuel Read Hall Library
Northeast Kingdom Room
Lyndonville, VT 05851
Tel: 802-626-9371 ext. 147
Fax: 626-6331
E-mail: nelsong@mail.lsc.vsc.edu
http://www.lsc.vsc.edu/intranet/academics/library/

Martha Canfield Memorial Free Library
The Russell Vermontiana Collection
E Arlington Rd
Arlington, VT 05250
Tel: 802-375-6153
http://www.uvm.edu/~histpres/vtiana/arlington.html

Middlebury College
Starr Library
Meredith Wing, Level 4
Vermont Collection
Middlebury, VT 05753
Tel: 802-388-3711
Fax: 802-388-3467
http://www.middlebury.edu/~lib/index.html

Milton Museum
13 School Street
P.O. Box 2
Milton, VT 05468

New England Historical and Genealogical Society (NEHGS)
101 Newbury Street
Boston, MA 02116-3007
Tel: 617-536-5740
      888-296-3447 (Membership & Education)
      888-BY-NEHGS (Sales)
      1-888-906-3447 (Library Circulation)
Fax: 617-536-7307
E-mail: nehgs@nehgs.org
http://www.nehgs.org/

Norman Williams Public Library
10 S. Park Street
Woodstock, VT 05091
Tel: 802-457-2295
http://www.uvm.edu/~histpres/vtiana/nwilliams.html

Orleans County Historical Society/Museum and Library
Old Stone House Museum
28 Old Stone House Road
Brownington, VT 05860
Tel: 802-754-2022
http://oldstonehousemuseum.org/

Peacham Historical Association
Peacham Corner, VT
Mail: 104 Thaddeus Stevens Road
Peacham, VT 05862
http://www.peacham.net/historical/

Pittsford Historical Society/Museum
Eaton Hall, 3399 Route 7
Pittsford, VT
Mail: P.O. Box 423
Pittsford, VT 05763
Tel: 802-483-2040
E-mail: loisblitt@together.net
http://www.pittsford-historical.org/

Rockingham Free Public Library/Museum
65 Westminster Street
Bellows Falls, VT 05101
Tel: 802-463-4270
http://www.uvm.edu/~histpres/vtiana/
    rockingham.html

Rutland Free Library
10 Court Street
Rutland, VT 05701
Tel: 802-773-1860
http://www.uvm.edu/~histpres/vtiana/rutland.html

St. Albans Free Library
Vermont Room
39 Barlow St
Saint Albans, VT 05478
Tel: 802-524-1507
E-mail: stalbans@dol.state.vt.us
http://www.state.vt.us/libraries/s2/

St. Johnsbury Athenaeum
1171 Main Street
St. Johnsbury, VT 05819
Tel: 802-748-8291
Fax: 802-748-8086
http://www.stjathenaeum.org/

Saxtons River Historical Society/Museum
P.O. Box 18
Saxtons River, VT 05154
E-mail: luring@sover.net

Sheldon Museum
1 Park Street
Middlebury, VT 05753
Tel: 802-388-2117
E-mail: sheldon_mus@myriad.middlebury.edu
http://community.middlebury.edu/~shel-mus/

University of Vermont
Bailey/Howe Library
Special Collections
Burlington, VT 05405
Tel: 802-656-2138
Fax: 802-656-4038
http://bailey.uvm.edu/specialcollections/

Vermont Department of Libraries
Reference and Law Services
109 State Street
Montpelier, VT 05609
Tel: 802-828-3261
Fax: 802-828-2199
http://dol.state.vt.us/
    orhttp://www.uvm.edu/~histpres/vtiana/vtlib.html

Vermont Folklife Center
3 Court Street
P.O. Box 442
Middlebury, VT 05753
Tel: 802-388-4964
Fax: 802-388-1844
E-mail: vfc@sover.net
http://www.vermontfolklifecenter.org/

NEWSPAPER REPOSITORIES

University of Vermont
Bailey/Howe Library
Special Collections
Burlington, VT 05405
Tel: 802-656-2138
Fax: 802-656-4038
http://bailey.uvm.edu/specialcollections/

Vermont Department of Libraries
Reference and Law Services
109 State Street
Montpelier, VT 05609
Tel: 802-828-3261
Fax: 802-828-2199
E-mail: Questions@dol.state.vt.us
http://dol.state.vt.us/
    orhttp://www.uvm.edu/~histpres/vtiana/vtlib.html

VITAL RECORDS

Vermont General Services Center
Public Records Division
Route 2, Drawer 33
Middlesex, VT 05633-7601
Tel: 802-828-3286
Fax: 802-828-3710
http://www.bgs.state.vt.us/GSC/pubrec/referen/

VERMONT ON THE WEB

Middlebury College, Starr Library-Vermont Genealogy Page
http://www.middlebury.edu/library/genealogy.html

UVM Historic Preservation Program
http://www.uvm.edu/~histpres/index.html

Vermont GenWeb Project
http://home.att.net/~Local_History/VT_History.htm

Vermont Historical Society
http://www.state.vt.us/vhs/

VIRGINIA

ARCHIVES, STATE & NATIONAL

National Archives—Mid Atlantic Region
900 Market Street
Philadelphia, PA 19107-4292
Tel: 215-597-3000
Fax: 215-597-2303
E-mail: philadelphia.archives@nara.gov
http://www.nara.gov/regional/philacc.html

Library of Virginia, Archives Division
800 E. Broad Street
Richmond, VA 23219
Tel: 804-692-3888
Fax: 804-692-3556
http://www.lva.lib.va.us

GENEALOGICAL SOCIETIES

Afro-American Historical and Genealogical Society/Hampton Roads
(AAHGS)
P.O. Box 2448
Newport News, VA 23609-2448
E-mail: selinva@aol.com

Alleghany Highlands Genealogical Society
1011 North Rockbridge Avenue
Covington, VA 24426
http://www.rootsweb.com/~vaallegh/AHGS/

Allegheny Regional Family History Society (ARFHS)
P.O. Box 1804
Elkins, WV 26241
http://www.swcp.com/~dhickman/arfhs.html

Caroline County Genealogical Society
P.O. Box 9
Bowling Green, VA 22427

Central Virginia Genealogical Association
P.O. Box 5583
Charlottesville, VA 22905-5583
E-mail: cvga@avenue.org
http://monticello.avenue.gen.va.us/Community/
    Agencies/CVGA/

Fairfax Genealogical Society
P.O. Box 2290
Merrifield, VA 22116

Genealogical Research Institute of Virginia
P.O. Box 29178
Richmond, VA 23242
http://www.rootsweb.com/~vagriv/

Genealogy and History of the Eastern Shore (GHOTES)
E-mail: bgcox@ix.netcom.com
http://www.esva.net/ghotes/

Germanna Colonies in Virginia, Memorial Foundation of the
P.O. Box 693
Culpeper, VA 22701
Tel: 540-825-1496
Fax: 540-825-6572
E-mail: office@germanna.org
www.germanna.org

Holston Territory Genealogical Society
P.O. Box 433
Bristol, VA 24203
http://hometown.aol.com/Seesie260/ index.HTGS.html

Jewish Genealogical Society of Tidewater
Jewish Community Center
7300 Newport Avenue
Norfolk, VA 23505

Lee County Historical & Genealogical Society
P.O. Box 231
Jonesville, VA 24263

Loudoun County Genealogy Club
P.O. Box 254
Leesburg, VA 22075

Lower DelMarVa Genealogical Society
P.O. Box 3602
Salisbury, MD 21802-3602
Tel: 410-742-3501
    410-546-0314
http://bay.intercom.net/ldgs/index.html

National Genealogical Society/Library
4527 Seventeenth Street, North
Arlington, VA 22207-2363
Tel: 703-525-0050
     703-841-9065 (Library)
Fax: 703-525-0052
E-mail: 76702.2417@compuserve.com
Library E-mail: ngslibe@wizard.net
http://www.genealogy.org/~ngs/

Norfolk Genealogical Society
P.O. Box 12813, Thomas Corner Station
Norfolk, VA 23502

Page County, Genealogical Society of
100 Zerkel Street
P.O. Box 734
Luray, VA 228355651
E-mail: takelley@erols.com
http://www.rootsweb.com/~vagspc/pcgs.htm

Portsmouth Genealogical Society
Portsmouth Public Library
601 Court Street
Portsmouth, VA 23704
Mail:
3908 Turnpike Road
Portsmouth, VA 23701
Tel: 804-393-8501

Prince William County Genealogical Society
P.O. Box 2019
Manassas, VA 22110-0812
Tel: 888-927-9247
http://pwcgs.org/

Rockbridge Area Genealogical Society (RAGS)
P. O. Box 92
Rockbridge Baths, VA 24473
E-mail: reddog@rockbridge.net (RAGS in Subject field)
http://www.angelfire.com/va/rockbridge/index.html

Southwestern Virginia Genealogical Society
P.O. Box 12485
Roanoke, VA 24026

Tidewater Genealogical Society
P.O. Box 7650
Hampton, VA 23666
http://www.rootsweb.com/~vatgs/

Virginia Beach Genealogical Society
P.O. Box 62901
Virginia Beach, VA 23466-2901
http://www.rootsweb.com/~vavbgs/

Virginia Genealogical Society
5001 West Broad Street, Suite 115
Richmond, Virginia 23230-3023
Tel: 804-285-8954
E-mail mail@vgs.org
http://www.vgs.org/

VA-NC Piedmont Genealogical Society
P.O. Box 2272
Danville, VA 24541
Tel: 434-799-5195 ext. 8
E-mail: vancsoc@juno.com
http://www.rootsweb.com/~vancpgs/Index.htm

HISTORICAL SOCIETIES

Afro-American Historical and Genealogical Society/Hampton Roads
(AAHGS)
P.O. Box 2448
Newport News, VA 23609-2448
E-mail: sclinva@aol.com

Albemarle County Historical Society
200 Second Street, NE
Charlottesville, VA 22902-5245
Tel: 434-296-1492
Fax: 434-296-4576
http://monticello.avenue.org/achs/

Amelia County Historical Society/Library
P.O. Box 113
Amelia, VA 23002
Tel: 804-561-3180

Arlington Historical Society/Museum
1805 S. Arlington Ridge Road
Arlington, VA 22202-1628
Tel: 703-892-4204
http://www.arlingtonhistoricalsociety.org/

Association for the Preservation of Virginia Antiquities
204 W. Franklin Street
Richmond, VA 23220
Tel: 804-648-1889
E-mail: clong@apva.org
http://www.apva.org/

Augusta County Historical Society
P.O. Box 686
Staunton, VA 24401
Tel: 540-248-4151
E-mail: achsmail@augustacountyhs.org
http://www.augustacountyhs.org/achs/

Avoca Museums and Historical Society
1514 Main Street
Altavista, VA 24517-1132
Tel: 804-369-1076

Bath County Historical Society
P.O. Box 212
Warm Springs, VA 24484

Bedford Historical Society
P.O. Box 602
Bedford, VA 24523
E-mail: bedfordhs@aol.com
http://members.aol.com/bedfordhs/

Botetourt County Historical Society, Inc.
Courthouse Square
P.O. Box 468
Fincastle, VA 24090
E-mail: ehonts@aol.com

Catholic Historical Society/Museum
400 Campbell Ave SW
Roanoke, VA 24016
Tel: 540-982-0152

Chesterfield Historical Society
11001 Iron Bridge Road
P.O. Box 40
Chesterfield, VA 23832
Tel: 804-777-9663
Fax: 804-777-9643
http://leo.vsla.edu/reposit/sites/chsv.html

Claiborne County Historical Society
Route 1, Box 589
Jonesville, VA 24263

Clark County Historical Association/Museum and Archives
32 East Main Street
P.O. Box 306
Berryville, VA 22611
Tel: 540-955-2600
Fax: 540-955-0285
E-mail: archives@visuallink.com (Archives)
http://www.visuallink.net/ccha/

Culpeper Historical Society
P.O. Box 785
Culpeper, VA 22701

Cumberland County Historical Society
P.O. Box 88
Cumberland, VA 23040

Eastern Shore of Virginia Historical Society/Museum
Kerr Place
69 Market Street
P.O. Box 193
Onancock, VA 23417
Tel: 757-787-8012
http://www.esva.com/kerrplace.htm

Essex County Historical Society
Route 3, Box 498
Tappahannock, VA 22560
http://www.iocc.com/~swright/esxsoc.html

Fairfax County, Historical Society of
P.O. Box 415
Fairfax, VA 22030
Tel: 703-246-2123

Fauquier Historical Society
Court House Square and Ashby Street
Warrenton, VA 22186
Tel: 540-347-5525

Fort Eustis Historical and Archaelogical Association
P.O. Box 4408
Fort Eustis, VA 23604

Germanna Colonies in Virginia, Memorial Foundation of the
P.O. Box 279
Locust Grove, Va. 22508-0279
Tel: 540-423-1700
Fax: 540-423-1747
E-mail: office@germanna.org
http://www.germanna.org/

Giles County Historical Society
208 N. Main Street
P.O. Box 404
Pearisburg, VA 24134
Tel: 540-921-1050
E-mail: gileschs@i-plus.net

Goochland County Historical Society
P.O. Box 602
Goochland, VA 23063
Tel: 804-556-3966
Fax: 804-556-4617
http://www.goochlandhistory.org/

Grayson County Historical Society
P.O. Box 529
Independence, VA 24348-9529
Tel: 540-773-9041

Greene County Historical Society
P.O. Box 185
Stanardsville, VA 22973

Gum Springs Historical Society
8100 Fordson Road
Alexandria, VA 22306
Tel: 703-799-1198
http://www.gshsfcva.org/

Hanover County Historical Society
P.O. Box 91
Hanover, VA 23069

Harrisonburg-Rockingham Historical Society
Shenandoah Valley Folk Art and Heritage Center
Bowman Road and High Street
P.O. Box 716
Dayton, VA 22821
Tel: 540-879-2616
    540879-2681
http://www.heritagecenter.com/HRHS/abouthr.htm

King and Queen County Historical Society
"Canterbury"
Route 1, Box 18
Walkerton, VA 23177
http://www.iocc.com/~swright/k&qsoc.html

King George County Historical Society
P.O. Box 424
King George, VA 22485
URLhttp://www.rootsweb.com/~vakingge/HistSociety.htm

Lee County Historical & Genealogical Society
P.O. Box 231
Jonesville, VA 24263
http://www.rootsweb.com/~valee/lchgs.htm

Louisa County Historical Society/Library, Archives and Museum
Old Jail (next to courthouse)
Main Street
P.O. Box 1172
Louisa, VA 23093

Martinsville-Henry County Historical Society
P.O. Box Drawer 432
Martinsville, VA 24114

Mathews County Historical Society, Inc.
P.O. Box 855
Mathews, VA 23109

New River Historical Society
P.O. Box 373
Newbern, VA 24126
Tel: 540-674-4835
http://www.rootsweb.com/~vanrhs/

Norfolk County Historical Society
Chesapeake Public Library
298 Cedar Road
Chesapeake, VA 23320

Northern Neck of Virginia Historical Society
Westmoreland County Museum
Courthouse Square
P.O. Box 716
Montross, VA 22520
Tel: 804-493-8440

Northumberland County Historical Society
Heathsville, VA 22473
Tel: 804-580-8581

Nottoway County Historical Association
RDF 1, Box 56
Crewe, VA 23930

Orange County Historical Society/Library and Archives
130 Caroline Street
Orange, VA 22960-1533
Tel: 540-672-5366

Patrick County Historical Society/Museum
116 W. Blue Ridge St.
P.O. Box 1045
Stuart, VA 24171
Tel: 540-694-2840

Pittsylvania Historical Society
P.O. Box 1206
Chatham, VA 24531

Rappahannock Historical Society/Library
328 Gay Street
P.O. Box 261
Washington, VA 22747-0261
Tel: 540-675-1163

Roanoke Valley Historical Society
One Market Square, SE
P.O. Box 1904
Roanoke, VA 24008
Tel: 540-342-5770
Fax: 540-224-1238

Rockbridge Historical Society
101 E. Washington Street
Lexington, VA 24450
Tel: 540-464-1058

Rockingham County Historical Society
301 South Main Street
Harrisonburg, VA 22801

Salem Historical Society
801 E. Main Street
P.O. Box 201
Salem, VA 24153
Tel: 540-389-6760

Sergeant Kirkland's Historical Society/Museum
912 Lafayette Blvd.
Fredericksburg, VA 22401-5617
Tel: 540-899-5565

Shenandoah County Historical Society
Shenandoah County Library
514 Stoney Creek Blvd.
Edinburg, VA 22824
Tel: 540-984-8200
Fax: 540-984-8207
E-mail: scl@shentel.net

Smyth County Historical Society
P.O. Box 574
Marion, VA 24354
Tel: 276-783-7067

Tazewell County Historical Society
100 E. Main Street
P.O. Box 916
Tazewell, VA 24651-0916
Tel: 540-988-4069
http://www.cc.utah.edu/~pdp7277/taze-soc.html

Virginia Historical Society
428 North Boulevard
P.O. Box 7311
Richmond, VA 23221-0311
Tel: 804-358-4901
          804-342-9658 (Membership)
E-mail: kelly_winters@vahistorical.org
http://www.vahistorical.org

Washington County, Historical Society of
P.O. Box 484
Abingdon, VA 24210

Winchester-Frederick County Historical Society
c/o Handley Library
100 W. Piccadilly Street
Winchester, VA 22601

LDS FAMILY HISTORY CENTERS

For locations of Family History Centers in this state, see the Family History Center locator at FamilySearch.
http://www.familysearch.org/eng/Library/FHC/frameset_fhc.asp

ARCHIVES/LIBRARIES/MUSEUMS

Albemarle County Historical Society
200 Second Street, NE
Charlottesville, VA 22902-5245
Tel: 434-296-1492
Fax: 434-296-4576
http://monticello.avenue.org/achs/

Alexandria Black History Resource Center
638 N. Alfred Street
Alexandria, VA 22314-1823
Tel: 703-838-4356
http://oha.ci.alexandria.va.us/bhrc/

Alexandria Library
Kate Waller Barrett Branch
717 Queen Street
Alexandria, VA 22314-2420
703-838-4555
http://www.alexandria.lib.va.us/

Allen E. Roberts Masonic Library and Museum
4115 Nine Mile Road
Richmond, VA 23223-4926
Tel: 804-222-3110
Fax: 804-222-4253
http://www.grandlodgeofvirginia.org/library1.htm/

Amelia County Historical Society/Library
Jackson Building
P.O. Box 113
Amelia, VA 23002
Tel: 804-561-3180

Amherst County Public Library
380 S. Main Street
P.O. Box 370
Amherst, VA 24521
Tel: 804-946-9388
Fax: 804-946-9348
E-mail: lwilkins@leo.vsla.edu
http://www.amherstva.com/Library.htm

Arlington Central Public Library
1015 North Quincy Street
Arlington, VA 22201-4603
Tel: 703-228-5990

Bassett Branch Library
3969 Fairystone Park Highway
Bassett, VA 24055-6041
Tel: 540-629-2426
Fax: 540-629-3808
E-mail: bassettlib@hotmail.com

Blue Ridge Regional Library
310 East Church Street
P. O. Box 5264
Martinsville, VA 24115
Tel: 276-632-7125 ext. 224
Fax: 276-632-1660
http://www.brrl.lib.va.us/

Bridgewater College
Alexander Mack Memorial Library
East College Street
Bridgewater, VA 22812
Tel: 540-828-2501 ext. 510
Fax: 540-828-5482
E-mail: rgreenaw@bridgewater.edu
http://www.bridgewater.edu/departments/
    library/library.html

Bristol Public Library
701 Goode Street
Bristol, VA 24201
Tel: 276-645-8787
Fax: 276-669-5593
http://www.bristol-library.org/

Buchanan County Public Library
Poe Town Road
Route 2, Box 3
Grundy, VA 24614
Tel: 540-935-6581
Fax: 540-935-6292
E-mail: bcpl@mtinter.net
http://www.bcplnet.org/

Central Rappahannock Regional Library
1201 Caroline Street
Fredericksburg, VA 22401
Tel: 540-372-1160
    540-371-1144
Fax: 540-373-9411
TDD: 540-371-9165
http://www.librarypoint.org/

Charles Taylor Arts Center
4205 Victoria Boulevard
Hampton, VA 23669
Tel: 757-727-1490
Fax: 757-727-1167
E-mail: artscom@city.hampton.va.us
http://www.hampton.va.us/arts/

Chesapeake Public Library
William McGhee Wallace Memorial Room
298 Cedar Road
Chesapeake, VA 23320
Tel: 757-382-6717
Fax: 757-382-8301
http://www.chesapeake.lib.va.us/

Chesterfield Historical Society
11001 Iron Bridge Road
P.O. Box 40
Chesterfield, VA 23832
Tel: 804-777-9663
Fax: 804-777-9643
http://leo.vsla.edu/reposit/sites/chsv.html

Clark County Historical Association/Museum and Archives
32 East Main Street
P.O. Box 306
Berryville, VA 22611
Tel: 540-955-2600
Fax: 540-955-0285
E-mail: archives@visuallink.com (Archives)
http://www.visuallink.net/ccha/

College of William and Mary
P.O. Box 8794
College of William and Mary
Williamsburg, VA 23187-8794
Tel: 757-221-3050
Fax: 757-221-2635
http://swem.wm.edu/

Culpeper Town and County Library
271 Southgate Shopping Center
Culpeper, VA 22701-3215
Tre: 540-825-8691
Fax: 540-825-7486
http://tlc.library.net/culpeper/

Danville Public Library
511 Patton Street
Danville, VA 24541
Tel: 434-799-5195 ext. 7
Fax: 434-799-5221
E-mail: library5@ci.danville.va.usÄ
http://www.ci.danville.va.us/library/index.htm

Eastern Mennonite University
Menno Simons Historical Library/Archives
1200 Park Road
Harrisonburg, VA 22801
Tel: 540-432-4000
Fax: 540-432-4444
E-mail: lehmanjo@emu.edu
http://www.emu.edu/library/

Eastern Shore of Virginia Historical Society/Museum
Kerr Place
69 Market Street
P.O. Box 193
Onancock, VA 23417
Tel: 757-787-8012
http://www.esva.com/kerrplace.htm

Eastern Shore Public Library
23610 Front Street
P. O. Box 360
Accomac, VA 23301
Tel: 757-787-3400
Fax: 757-787-2241
http://www.espl.org/

Essex Public Library
117 North Church Lane
Tappahannock, VA 22560
Tel: 804-443-4945
Fax: 804-443-6444

Fairfax County Regional Library
Virginia Room
3915 Chain Bridge Road
Fairfax, VA 22030
Tel: 703-246-2281
Fax: 703-385-6977
     703-385-1911
E-mail: wwwlib@co.fairfax.va.us
http://www.co.fairfax.va.us/library/

Fluvanna County Library
P.O. Box 548
Fork Union, VA 23055
Tel/Fax: 804-842-2230
E-mail: mdrane@cfw.com
http://www.co.fluvanna.va.us/library.htm

Franklin County Public Library
Local History Room
120 East Court Street
Rocky Mount, VA 24151
Tel: 540-483-3098
Fax: 540-483-1568

Galax/Carroll Regional Library
608 W. Stuart Drive
Galax, VA 24333
Tel: 276-236-2042
Fax: 276-236-5153
E-mail: lbryant@leo.vsla.edu
http://galaxcarroll.lib.va.us

George Mason University
Fenwick Library-Special Collections
Fairfax, VA 22030-4444
Tel: 703-993-2220
Fax: 703-993-2229
E-mail: speccoll@osf1.gmu.edu
http://www.gmu.edu/library/specialcollections/

Gunston Hall Plantation/Library and Archives
10709 Gunston Road
Mason Neck, VA 22079-3901
Tel: 703-550-9220
Fax: 703-550-9480
E-mail: Historic@GunstonHall.org
http://www.gunstonhall.org/library/

Hampton Public Library
Virginiana Room
4207 Victoria Boulevard
Hampton, VA 23669
Tel: 757-727-1154
http://www.hamptonpubliclibrary.org/

Handley Library
100 W. Piccadilly Street
P.O. Box 58
Winchester, VA 22601
Tel: 540-662-9041
Fax: 540-722-4769
E-mail: reference@hrl.lib.state.va.us
http://leo.vsla.edu/reposit/sites/hrl.html

Heritage Library
P.O. Box 8
Providence Forge, VA 23140
Tel: 804-966-2480
Fax: 804-966-5982
http://www.developtg.net/hpl/

Historic Crab Orchard Museum
US 19/460
Mail:
Route 1, Box 194
Tazewell, VA 24651
Tel: 540-988-6755
Fax: 540-988-9400
http://histcrab.netscope.net/

Historic Fincastle, Inc.
James Early Cabin
121 E. Murray Street
P.O. Box 19
Fincastle, VA 24090
Tel: 540-473-3077

J. Robert Jamerson Memorial Library
106 Main Street
P.O. Box 789
Appomattox, VA 24522
Tel: 434-352-5340
http://65.169.41.33/Jamerson/default.asp

James Madison University
Carrier Library-Special Collections
Carrier Library MSC 1704
James Madison University
Harrisonburg, VA 228071
Fax: 540-568-3405
Tel: 540-568-3612
E-mail: bolgiace@jmu.edu
http://www.lib.jmu.edu/special/

James Monroe Museum and Memorial Library
908 Charles Street
Fredericksburg, VA 22401

Jefferson/Madison Regional Library
201 East Market Street
Charlottesville, VA 22903
Tel: 434-979-7151
Fax: 434-971-7035
E-mail: jmrlweb@avenue.org
http://jmrl.org/main/main.htm/

Jones Memorial Library
2311 Memorial Avenue
Lynchburg, VA 24501
Tel: 804-846-0501
Fax: 804-846-1572
http://www.jmlibrary.org/

Kenmore Association Library
1201 Washington Avenue
Fredericksburg, VA 22401
Tel: 540-373-3381
Fax: 540-371-6066

Kirn/Norfolk Public Library
301 East City Hall Avenue
Norfolk, VA 23510-1703
Tel: 757-664-7323
http://www.npl.lib.va.us/branches/kirn/kirn.html

Library of Virginia
800 E. Broad Street
Richmond, VA 23219
Tel: 804-692-3500 (Main)
    804-692-3777 (Library Reference)
    804-692-3600 (Records Management)
Fax: 804-692-3556
    804-692-3603 (Records Management)
http://www.lva.lib.va.us/

Louisa County Historical Society/
Library, Archives and Museum
Old Jail (next to courthouse)
Main Street
P.O. Box 1172
Louisa, VA 23093

Madison County Library
402 N. Main Street
P.O. Box 243
Madison, VA 22727
Tel: 540-948-4720
Fax: 540-948-4919

Manassas Museum
9101 Prince William Street
P.O. Box 560
Manassas, VA 22110
Tel: 703-368-1873
Fax: 703-257-8406
E-mail: Dbarker@ci.manassas.va.us
http://www.manassasmuseum.org/

Mariners Museum/Library and Archives
100 Museum Drive
Newport News, VA 23606
Tel: 757-591-7782
E-mail: library@mariner.org
http://www.mariner.org/library.html

Mary Ball Washington Museum and Library
8346 Mary Ball Road
Post Office Box 97
Lancaster, VA 22503
Tel: 804-462-7280
Fax: 804-462-6107
E-mail: history@rivnet.net
http://www.mbwm.org/

Massanutten Regional Library
174. S. Main St.
Harrisonburg, VA 22801
Tel: 540-434-4475
Toll Free: 1-800-594-BOOK
Fax: 540.434.4382
E-mail: mrl@mrlib.org
http://www.mrlib.org/

Montgomery/Floyd Regional Library
125 Sheltman Street
Christianburg, VA 24073
Tel: 540-382-6965
Fax: 540-382-6964
E-mail: christiansburg@mfrl.org
http://www.montgomery-floyd.lib.va.us/

Montgomery Museum and Lewis Miller Regional Art
Center
300 S. Pepper Street
P.O. Box 31
Christiansburg, VA 24073
Tel: 540-382-5644
http://leo.vsla.edu/reposit/sites/mmlm.html

Museum of American Frontier Culture Library
1250 Richmond Road
P.O. Box 810
Staunton, VA 24402
Tel: 540-332-7850
Fax: 540-332-9989
http://www.frontiermuseum.org/index.htm

National Genealogical Society/Library
4527 Seventeenth Street, North
Arlington, VA 22207-2363
Tel: 703-525-0050
    703-841-9065 (Library)
Fax: 703-525-0052
E-mail: 76702.2417@compuserve.com
Library E-mail: ngslibe@wizard.net

Newport News Public Library
Martha Woodroof Hiden Virginiana Collection
110 Main St.
Newport News, VA 23601
Tel: 757-591-4858
http://www.newport-
    news.va.us/library/virgrm/virgana.htm

Nottoway County Library
414 Tyler Street
Crewe, VA 23930
Tel: 434-645-9310
Fax: 434-645-8513
http://www.nottlib.org/nottoway/default.asp

Orange County Historical Society/Library and Archives
130 Caroline Street
Orange, VA 22960-1533
Tel: 540-672-5366
Main Library:
146A Madison Rd.
Orange, VA 22960
Tel: 540-672-3811
Fax: 540-672-5040
http://tlc.library.net/orange/default.asp

Page Public Library
100 Zerkel Street
P.O. Box 734
Luray, VA 22835
Tel: 540-743-6867
Fax 540-743-7661
http://home.rica.net/rpl/PagePublic.htm

Patrick County Historical Society/Museum
Blue Ridge Street
P.O. Box 1045
Stuart, VA 24171
Tel: 540-694-2840
http://leo.vsla.edu/reposit/sites/pchm.html

Pearisburg Public Library
209 Fort Branch Road
Pearisburg, VA 24134
Tel: 540-921-2556
Fax: 540-921-1708
http://library.pearisburg.org/

Petersburg National Battlefield Library
P.O. Box 549
Petersburg, VA 23804
Tel: 804-732-3531
Fax: 804-732-0835

Petersburg Public Library/William R. McKenney Branch
137 South Sycamore Street
Petersburg, VA 23803
Tel: 804-733-2387
http://www.ppls.org/

Portsmouth Public Library
601 Court Street
Portsmouth, VA 23704
Tel: 757-393-8501
    393-8973 (Reference)
Fax: 757-393-5107
http://www.portsmouth.va.us/ppl/ppl.html

Prince William Public Library System/Bull Run Regional Library
Ruth Emmons Lloyd Information Center (RELIC)
8051 Aston Avenue
Manassas, VA 22110
Tel: 703-792-4500
Fax: 703-792-4520
http://www.co.prince-william.va.us/ library/BR.asp#top

Radford Public Library
30 West Main Street
Radford, VA 24141
Tel: 540-731-3621
Fax: 540-731-4857
http://www.radford.va.us/library/

Rappahannock Historical Society/Library
P.O. Box 261
Washington, VA 22747-0261
Tel: 540-675-1163
Library Address:
4 Library Road
P. O. Box 55
Washington, VA 22747
Tel: 540-765-3780
Fax: 540-675-1290
http://www.rappahannocklibrary.org/

Roanoke City Public Library
Virginia Room
706 South Jefferson Street
Roanoke, VA 24016
Tel: 540-853-2475
Fax: 540-853-1781
http://www.co.roanoke.va.us/library/

Shenandoah County Library
514 Stoney Creek Blvd
Edinburg, VA 22824
Tel: 540-984-8200
Fax: 540-984-8207
E-mail: scl@shentel.net
http://www.shenandoah.co.lib.va.us/

Shenandoah Valley Folk Art and Heritage Center
Genealogy Research Library
Bowman Road and High Street
P.O. Box 716
Dayton, VA 22821
Tel/Fax: 540-879-2616
          540-879-2681 (Museum)
E-mail: heritag1@heritagecenter.com
http://www.heritagecenter.com

Southside Regional Library
316 Washington Street
P.O. Box 10
Boydton, VA 23917
Tel: 804-738-6580
Fax: 804-738-6070
http://www.srlib.org/

Suffolk Public Library System
443 W. Washington Street
Suffolk, VA 23434
Tel: 757-934-7686
Fax: 757-539-7155
E-mail: ref@suffolk.lib.va.us
http://www.suffolk.lib.va.us/

Thomas Balch Library
208 W. Market St.
Leesburg, VA 20176
Tel: 703-737-7195
Fax: 703-737-7150
E-mail: balchlib@leesburgva.org

Union Theological Seminary in Virginia/Library
3401 Brook Road
Richmond, VA 23227
Tel: 804-278-4310
Fax: 804-355-3919
http://www.loc.gov/rr/main/religion/uts.html

University of Virginia
Alderman Library
University of Virginia
P.O. Box 400114
Charlottesville VA 22904-4114
Tel: 434-924-3021
http://www.lib.virginia.edu/index.html

Virginia Beach Public Library
Local History Collection
4100 Virginia Beach Blvd.
Virginia Beach, VA 23452
Tel: 757-431-3001 (Reference)
Fax: 757-431-3018
http://www.vbgov.com/dept/library/

Virginia Commonwealth University (VCU)
James Branch Cabell Library
901 Park Avenue
Box 842033
Richmond, VA 23284-2033
Tel: 804-828-1110
Fax: 804-828-0151
http://www.library.vcu.edu/jbc/

Virginia Historical Society
428 North Boulevard
P.O. Box 7311
Richmond, VA 23221-0311
Tel: 804-358-4901
          804-342-9658 (Membership)
E-mail: kelly_winters@vahistorical.org
http://www.vahistorical.org

Virginia Military Institute Archives
Preston Library
Lexington, VA 24450
Tel: 540-464-7566
Fax: 540-464-7279
E-mail: Jacobdb@mail.vmi.edu
http://www.vmi.edu/archives/

Virginia Polytechnic Institute and State University
Newman Library-Special Collections and Manuscripts
P.O. Box 90001
Blacksburg, VA 24062-9001
Tel: 540-231-6308
Fax: 540-231-3694
E-mail: gailmac@vt.edu
http://spec.lib.vt.edu/specgen.html

Walter Cecil Rawls Library/Museum
22511 Main Street
P.O. Box 310
Courtland, VA 23837
Tel: 757-653-2821
Fax: 757-653-9374
http://www.rawlslib.net/rawls/default.htm

Washington and Lee University
James G. Leyburn Library
Special Collections
Lexington, VA 24450
Tel: 540-463-8640
Fax: 540-463-8640
E-mail: bbrown@wlu.edu
http://home.wlu.edu/~stanleyv/speccoll.html

Waynesboro Public Library
600 South Wayne Avenue
Waynesboro, VA 22980
Tel: 540-942-6746
http://www.waynesborova-online.com/ departments/
    publiclibrary/about.html

Wilderness Road Regional Museum
P.O. Box 373
Newbern, VA 24126
Tel: 540-674-4835
Wilderness Road Regional Museum

Wytheville Community College
F.B. Kegley Library
Genealogical and Local History Collection
1000 E. Main Street
Wytheville, VA 24382
Tel: 540-223-4742/3
Fax: 540-223-4778
E-mail: WCROBEA@WC.CC.VA.US
http://www.naxs.com/wcc/proud.htm

NEWSPAPER REPOSITORIES

College of William and Mary
Earl Gregg Swem Library
Williamsburg, VA 23187-8794
Tel: 757-221-3067
Fax: 757-221-2635
E-mail: sweref@wm.edu
http://swem.wm.edu/

Library of Virginia
800 E. Broad Street
Richmond, VA 23219
Tel: 804-692-3500 (Main)
    804-692-3777 (Library Reference)
    804-692-3600 (Records Management)
Fax: 804-692-3556
    804-692-3603 (Records Management)
http://www.lva.lib.va.us

University of Virginia
Alderman Library
University of Virginia
P.O. Box 400114
Charlottesville, VA 22904-4114
Tel: 434-924-3021
http://www.lib.virginia.edu/index.html

Virginia Historical Society
428 North Boulevard
P.O. Box 7311
Richmond, VA 23221-0311
Tel: 804-358-4901
    804-342-9658 (Membership)
E-mail: kelly_winters@vahistorical.org
http://www.vahistorical.org

Newspapers in Virginia Database
http://image.vtls.com/newspaper/

Virginia Newspaper Project
http://eagle.vsla.edu/newspaper/

VITAL RECORDS

Library of Virginia
800 E. Broad Street
Richmond, VA 23219
Tel: 804-692-3500 (Main)
    804-692-3777 (Library Reference)
    804-692-3600 (Records Management)
Fax: 804-692-3556
    804-692-3603 (Records Management)
http://www.lva.lib.va.us
Births and Deaths 1853-1896.
Marriages before 1936.

Virginia Department of Health
Office of Vital Records
James Madison Building
P.O. Box 1000
Richmond, VA 23208
Tel: 804-662-6200 (Recorded Message)
    804-786-6201
http://www.vdh.state.va.us/misc/f_08.htm
    http://www.vdh.state.va.us/misc/gene.htm
    (Genealogy Page)
Births and Deaths from 1913-present.
Marriages from 1936-present.
There was no law requiring registration of births and
    deaths between 1896 and 1912.

VIRGINIA ON THE WEB

Genealogy and History of the Eastern Shore (GHOTES)
http://www.esva.net/ghotes/

Library of Virginia
http://www.lva.lib.va.us

Library of Virginia, Archives Division
http://eagle.vsla.edu/bible/

Library of Virginia, Digital Collection
http://image.vtls.com/

Melungeon Ancestry Research and Information Page
http://www.bright.net/~kat/melung.htm

Order of Descendants of Ancient Planters
http://www.bbtyner.com/PLANTERS.HTM

Travellers Southern Families
http://misc.traveller.com/genealogy/othergen.htm

Virginia Colonial Records Database Project
http://eagle.vsla.edu/colonial/

Virginia GenWeb Project
http://www.rootsweb.com/~vagenweb/

VIVA–Virtual Library of Virginia
http://www.viva.lib.va.us/

Washington

Archives, State & National

National Archives—Pacific Northwest Region
6125 Sand Point Way, NE
Seattle, WA 98115-7999
Tel: 206-526-6501
Fax: 206-526-6575
E-mail: seattle.archives@nara.gov
http://www.nara.gov/regional/seattle.html

Washington State Archives
1129 Washington Street, SE
P.O. Box 40238
Olympia, WA 98504-0238
Tel: 360-753-5485 (Administration)
      360-586-1492 (Research)
E-mail: archives@secstate.wa.gov
http://www.secstate.wa.gov/archives/

Washington State Regional Archives
http://www.wa.gov/sec/archives/branches.htm

Central Regional Branch
Central Washington University
Bledsow-Washington Archives Building
400 E. 8th Ave., MS-7547
Ellensburg, WA 98926-7547
Tel: 509-963-2136
Fax: 509-963-1753
http://www.cwu.edu/~archives/home.htm
(Benton, Chelan, Douglas, Franklin, Grant, Kittitas,
      Klickitat, Okanogan, and Yakima Counties)

Eastern Regional Branch
Eastern Washington University
211 Tawanka
Cheney, WA 99004
Tel: 509-359-6900
Fax: (509) 359-6286
E-mail: era@mail.ewu.edu
http://www.ewu.edu/era/
(Adams, Asotin, Columbia, Ferry, Garfield, Lincoln, Pend
      Oreille, Spokane, Stevens, Walla Walla, and
      Whitman Counties)

Northwest Regional Branch
Western Washington University
Goltz-Murray Archives Building
Bellingham, WA 98225-9123
Tel: 360-650-3125
Fax: 360-650-3323
E-mail: state.archives@wwu.edu
(Clallam, Island, Jefferson, San Juan, Skagit, Snohomish,
      and Whatcom Counties)

Puget Sound Regional Branch
Pritchard-Fleming Building
3000 Landerholm Circle SE, MS-N100
Bellevue, WA 98007-6484
Tel: (425) 564-3940
Fax: (425) 564-3945
E-mail: Archives@bcc.ctc.edu
(King, Kitsap, and Pierce Counties)

Southwest Regional Branch
1129 Washington Street, SE
P.O. Box 40238
Olympia, WA 98504-0238
Tel: 360-753-1684 Fax: 360-664-8814
(Clark, Cowlitz, Grays Harbor, Lewis, Mason, Pacific,
      Skamania, Thurston, and Wahkiakum Counties)

Genealogical Societies

Camwood Genealogical Group
Stanwood Library
9701 271st Street NW
Stanwood, WA 98292
Tel: 360-629-3132

Chelan Valley Genealogical Society
P.O. Box Y
Chelan, WA 98816

Clallam County Genealogical Society
P.O. Box 1327
Port Angeles, WA 98362
Tel: 360-417-5000
E-mail: ccgs@olypen.com
http://www.olypen.com/ccgs/

Clark County Genealogical Society
Clark County Historical Museum
1511 Main Street
P.O. Box 2728
Vancouver, WA 98668-2728
E-mail: ccgswa@pacifier.com
http://www.ccgs-wa.org/

Columbia County Genealogical and Historical Society
P.O. Box 74
Dayton, WA 99328-0074

Douglas County Genealogical Society
P.O. Box 580
Waterville, WA 98858-0580

Eastern Washington Genealogical Society
Spokane Public Library
906 W. Main
Tel: 509-444-5336
http://www.rootsweb.com/~waewgs/index.html/

Eastside Genealogical Society
P.O. Box 374
Bellevue, WA 98009-0374
http://www.rootsweb.com/~wakcegs/

Fiske Genealogical Foundation/Library
1644 43rd Avenue E
Seattle, WA 98122-3222
Tel: 206-328-2716

Forks Genealogical Society
c/o Forks Memorial Library
Forks, WA 98331

Germans from Russia Heritage Society
Puget Sound Chapter
c/o Vi Sieler, Sec.
17956 W. Spring Lake Drive SE
Renton, WA 98058
Tel: 425-432-5627
http://www.teleport.com/nonprofit/grhs/
    pugetsnd.html

Grant County Genealogical Society
Ephrata Public Library
45 Alder Street, NW
Ephrata, WA 98823

Grays Harbor Genealogical Society
P.O. Box 867
Cosmopolis, WA 98537-0867

Jefferson County Genealogical Society
210 Madison Street
Port Townsend, WA 98368

Kitsap County Genealogical Society
4305 Lakeview Drive, SE
Port Orchard, WA 98366

Kittitas County Genealogical Society/Library
413 N. Maine, Suite D
P.O. Box 1342
Ellensburg, WA 98926

Lewis County Genealogical Society
P.O. Box 782
Chehalis, WA 98532

Lower Columbia Genealogical Society
P.O. Box 472
Longview, WA 98632-0472
http://www.rootsweb.com/~walcgs/

Mason County Genealogical Society
P.O. Box 1535
Shelon, WA 98584-1535

North Beach Genealogical Society
P.O. Box 2007
Ocean Shores, WA 98569

North Central Washington Genealogical Society
133 South Mission
P.O. Box 5280
Wenatchee, WA 98807-5280
Tel: 509-664-5989, ext. 20

Northeast Washington Genealogical Society
c/o Colville Public Library
195 South Oak Street
Colville, WA 99114
Tel: 509-935-6336

Northern Kittitas County Genealogical Society
P.O. Box 535
Cle Elum, WA 98922

Okanogan County Genealogical Society
Route 1, Box 323
Omak, WA 98841-0323

Olympia Genealogical Society
P.O. Box 1313
Olympia, WA 98507-1313
E-mail: OlympiaGenSoc@bigfoot.com
http://www.rootsweb.com/~waogs/

Pacific County Genealogical Society
P.O. Box 843
Ocean Park, WA 98640-0843

Pierce County, Genealogical Society of
P.O. Box 98634
Tacoma, WA 98498-0634

Puget Sound Genealogical Society
Givens Community Center
1026 Sidney Avenue, Suite 110
Port Orchard, WA 98366
Tel: 360-874-8813

Seattle Genealogical Society/Library
6200 Sand Point Way N. E. #101
Seattle, WA
Mail:
P.O. Box 75388
Seattle, WA 98125-0388
Tel: 206-522-8658
http://www.rootsweb.com/~waseags/main.html

Skagit Valley Genealogical Society
P.O. Box 715
Conway, WA 98238-0715
http://www.rootsweb.com/~wasvgs/

Sky Valley Genealogical Society
912 First Street
Salem, WA 98294

Sno-Isle Genealogical Society
P.O. Box 63
Edmonds, WA 98020-0063
http://rootsweb.com/~wasigs/index.htm

South King County Genealogical Society
P.O. Box 3174
Kent, WA 98032-3174
http://www.rootsweb.com/~waskcgs/

Stillaguamish Valley Genealogical Society/Library
135 N. Olympic, Arlington, WA
Mail:
P.O. Box 34
Arlington, WA 98223-0034
http://www.rootsweb.com/~wastvgs/

Sumner Genealogical Group
c/o Sumner Public Library
1116 Fryar Avenue
Sumner, WA 98390
Tel: 253-863-0441

Tacoma-Pierce County Genealogical Society
P.O. Box 1952
Tacoma, WA 98401-1952
Tel: 253-572-6650
http://www.rootsweb.com/~watpcgs/tpcgs.htm

Tonasket Genealogical Society
P.O. Box 84
Tonasket, WA 98855

Tri-City Genealogical Society
P.O. Box 1410
Richland, WA 98352-1410

Twin Rivers Genealogical Society
P.O. Box 386
Lewiston, ID 83501-2824

Walla Walla Valley Genealogical Society
P.O. Box 115
Walla Walla, WA 99362-0115

Washington State Genealogical Society
P.O. Box 1422
Olympia, WA 98507-1422
E-mail: jmccoy@attbi.com
http://www.rootsweb.com/~wasgs/

Wenatchee Area Genealogical Society
P.O. Box 5280
Wenatchee, WA 98807-5280
http://www.wagsweb.org/

Whatcom Genealogical Society
P.O. Box 1493
Bellingham, WA 98227-1493

Whidbey Island Genealogical Searchers
P.O. Box 627
Oak Harbor, WA 98277-0627

Whitman County Genealogical Society
P.O. Box 393
Pullman, WA 99163-0393
Tel: 509-332-2386
    509-334-1732
http://www.completebbs.com/simonsen/
    wcgsindex.html

Willapa Harbor Genealogical Society
507 Duryea
Raymond, WA 98577

Yakima Valley Genealogical Society
2609 River Road Yakima, Washington
P.O. Box 445
Yakima, WA 98907-0445
Tel: 509-248-1328
E-mail: fl635@nwinfo.net
http://www.rootsweb.com/~wayvgs/

HISTORICAL SOCIETIES

Adams County Historical Society/Museum
Phillips Building
P.O. Box 188
Lind, WA 99341
Tel: 509-677-3393

Anderson Island Historical Society
9306 Otso Point Road
Anderson Island, WA 98303
Tel: 206-884-2135

Bainbridge Island Historical Society/Museum
7650 NE High School Road
P.O. Box 11653
Bainbridge Island, WA 98110-2621
Tel: 206-842-2773

Benton County Historical Society/Museum
Prosser City Park
7th and Paterson
P.O. Box 591
Prosser, WA 99350
Tel: 509-786-3842

Black Diamond Historical Society/Museum
32627 Railroad and Baker Streets
P.O. Box 232
Black Diamond, WA 98010-9762
Tel: 360-886-2142

Camas-Washougal Historical Society/Museum
16th and Front
P.O. Box 204
Washougal, WA 98671
Tel: 360-835-2725

Chelan County Historical Society/Museum
600 Cottage Avenue
P.O. Box 22
Cashmere, WA 98815-1602
Tel: 509-782-3230

Clallum Historical Society/Museum
223 E. 4th Street
Port Angeles, WA 98362-3025
Tel: 360-417-2364

Cle Elum Historical Society/Museum
221 E. 1st Street
P.O. Box 43
Cle Elum, WA 98922-1103
Tel: 509-674-5702

Daughters of the Pioneers Association
Pioneer Hall
1642 43rd Avenue East
Seattle, WA 98112
Tel: 206-325-0888

East Benton County Historical Society/Museum
205 Keewaydin Drive
Kennewick, WA 99336-0602
Tel: 509-582-7704
E-mail: ebchs@gte.net
http://www.owt.com/ebchs/

Eastern Washington State Historical Society
2316 W. 1st Avenue
Spokane, WA 99204-1006
Tel: 509-456-3931

Edmonds-South Snohomish County Historical Society
118 5th Avenue, N.
Edmonds, WA 98020-3145
Tel: 425-774-0900
http://www.historicedmonds.org/index2.html

Fort Vancouver Historical Society
Clark County Historical Museum
1511 Main Street
P.O. Box 1834
Vancouver, WA 98663
Tel: 360-695-4681

Fox Island Historical Society/Museum
1017 9th Avenue
P.O. Box 242
Fox Island, WA 98333
Tel: 206-549-2461

Franklin County Historical Society/Museum
305 N. 4th Avenue
Pasco, WA 99301-5324
Tel: 509-547-3714

Gig Harbor Peninsula Historical Society
4218 Harborview Drive
P.O. Box 744
Gig Harbor, WA 98335
Tel: 253-858-6722
Fax: 253-853-4211
E-mail: info@gigharbormuseum.org

Island County Historical Society
908 NW Alexander St
P.O. Box 305
Coupeville, WA 98239
Tel: 360-678-3310

Issaquah Historical Society
P. O. Box 695
Issaquah, WA 98027
Tel: 425-392-3500
E-mail: info@issaquahhistory.org
http://issaquahhistory.org/default.htm

Jefferson County Historical Society/Museum
McCurdy Research Library
540 Water Street
Port Townsend, WA 98368
Tel: 360-385-1003
E-mail: jchsmuseum@olympus.net
http://www.jchsmuseum.org/

Lake Chelan Historical Society
204 Woodin Avenue
P.O. Box 1948
Chelan, WA 98816
Tel: 509-682-5644
http://www.chelanvalley.com/historicalsociety.htm

Lewis County Historical Society
599 NW Front Way
Chehalis, WA 98532
Tel: 360-748-0831

Lopez Island Historical Society/Museum
P.O. Box 361
Lopez Island, WA 98261
Tel: 360-468-2049

Maple Valley Historical Society
P.O. Box 123
Maple Valley, WA 98038
Tel: 425-432-3470

Mason County Historical Society
P.O. Box 1231
Shelton, WA 98584
Tel: 360-426-1020

Mukilteo Historical Society
304 Lincoln Avenue
Mukilteo, WA 98275
Tel: 425-355-2144

Okanogan Historical Society
1410 2nd Avenue North
P.O. Box 1299
Okanogan, WA 98840
Tel: 509-422-4272
http://www.omakchronicle.com/ochs/

Pacific County Historical Society
1008 W. Robert Bush Drive
South Bend, WA 98586
Tel: 360-875-5224

Pend Oreille County Historical Society
402 S. Washington Avenue
P.O. Box 1409
Newport, WA 99156
Tel: 509-447-5388

Puget Sound Maritime Historical Society
(Collection at Museum of History and Industry and
Univ. of WA)
P.O. Box 9731
Seattle, WA 98109-9731
Tel: 206-624-3028
E-mail: president@pugetmaritime.org
http://www.pugetmaritime.org/

Puget Sound Railway Historical Association
38625 SE King St
P.O. Box 459
Snoqualmie, WA 98065-0459
Tel: 425-888-3030
Fax: 425-888-9311
E-mail: visitorservices@trainmuseum.org
www.trainmuseum.org

Renton County Historical Society/Museum
235 Mill Avenue, South
Renton, WA 98055
Tel: 206-255-2330
Fax: 206-255-1570

San Juan Historical Society/Museum
405 Price
Friday Harbor, WA 98250
Tel: 360-378-3949
http://www.silverton.org/sjcm.html

Seattle-King County Historical Society
Museum of History and Industry
2700 24th East
Seattle, WA 98112
Tel: 206-324-1126
http://www.seattlehistory.org/

Skagit County Historical Museum
501 S. 4th
P.O. Box 818
La Conner, WA 98257
Tel: 360-466-3365

Snohomish County Historical Association
Heritage Center, Museum and Library
2817 Rockefeller Avenue
P.O. Box 5203
Everett, WA 98206
Tel: 425-259-2022
http://www.rootsweb.com/~wasnohom/

Snoqualmie Valley Historical Society/Museum
320 N. Bend Blvd. North
North Bend, WA 98045
Tel: 425-888-3200

Spanaway Historical Society
812 176th Street East
Spanaway, WA 98387
Tel: 253-536-6655

Stanwood Area Historical Society
P.O. Box 69
Stanwood, WA 98292
Tel: 360-629-6110
http://www.whidbey.com/sahs/

Stevens County Historical Society
700 N. Wynne Street
P.O. Box 25 Colville
Colville, WA 99114
Tel: 509-684-5968
http://homepage.plix.com/schs/

Swedish Finn Historical Society
6512 23rd Avenue, NW, #301
Seattle, WA 98117
Tel: 206-706-0738
http://home1.gte.net/SFHS/

Tacoma Historical Society
3712 S. Cedar Street, #101
P.O. Box 1865
Tacoma, WA 98401
Tel: 253-472-3738

Wahkiakum County Historical Society/Museum
65 River Street
P.O. Box 541
Cathlamet, WA 98612
Tel: 360-795-3954

Washington State Historical Society
Research Center
315 North Stadium Way
Tacoma, WA 98403
Tel: 253-272-WSHS
     888-BE-THERE (Toll-Free)
     253-798-5914 (Research Center)
http://www.wshs.org/

Washington State Railroads Historical Society
PO. BOX 552
Pasco, WA 99301
Tel: 509-543-4159
http://www.cbvcp.com/wsrhs/

White River Valley Historical Society
918 H Street, SE
Auburn, WA 98002
Tel: 253-939-2783

Whitman County Historical Society
623 N. Perkins Avenue
P.O. Box 67
Colfax, WA 99111
E-mail: epgjr@wsu.edu
http://www.wsu.edu/~sarek/wchs.html

Yakima Valley Museum and Historical Association
2105 Tieton Drive
Yakima, WA 98902
Tel: 509-248-0747
Fax: 509-453-4890
http://www.wolfenet.com/~museum/

LDS FAMILY HISTORY CENTERS

For locations of Family History Centers in this state, see the Family History Center locator at FamilySearch.
http://www.familysearch.org/eng/Library/FHC/frameset_fhc.asp

ARCHIVES/LIBRARIES/MUSEUMS

Anacortes Museum/Research Library
1305 8th Street
Anacortes, WA 98221-1833
Tel: 360-293-1915

Auburn Public Library
1102 Auburn Way S
Auburn WA 98002
Tel: 253-931-3018

Bellingham Public Library
210 Central Street
P.O. Box 1197
Bellingham, WA 98225
Tel: 360-676-6860
http://www.bellinghampubliclibrary.org/

Bellevue Regional Library
Special Collections
1111 110th Avenue, NE
Bellevue, WA 98004
Tel: 425-450-1765
http://www.kcls.org/brl/brlpage.html

Burlington Public Library
900 E. Fairhaven Street
Burlington, WA 98233
Tel: 360-755-0760
E-mail: janice@nwlink.com
http://www.ci.burlington.wa.us/library/index.htm

Clark County Museum
1511 Main
Vancouver, WA 98668
Tel: 360-695-4681

Colville Public Library
195 South Oak Street
Colville, WA 99114
Tel: 509-684-6620

Dupont Historical Museum
207 Barksdale Avenue
P.O. Box 173
Dupont, WA 98327
Tel: 206-964-2399
     206-964-8121

East Benton County Historical Society/Museum
205 Keewaydin Drive
Kennewick, WA 99336-0602
Tel: 509-582-7704
E-mail: ebchs@tcfn.org
http://www.owt.com/ebchs/

Ellensburg Public Library
209 N. Ruby Street
Ellensburg, WA 98926
Tel: 509-962-7250
http://epl.eburg.com/bookref.html

Ephrata Public Library
45 Alder Street, NW
Ephrata, WA 98823
Tel: 509-754-3971

Everett Public Library
Northwest Room
2702 Hoyt Avenue
Everett, WA 98201
Tel: 425-257-8000
E-mail: libref@ci.everett.wa.us
http://www.epls.org/

Fiske Genealogical Foundation/Library
1644 43rd Avenue E
Seattle, WA 98122-3222
Tel: 206-328-2716

Forks Memorial Library
171 N. Forks Avenue
P.O. Box 1817
Forks, WA 98331
Tel: 360-374-6402

Forks Timber Museum
1421 S. Forks Avenue
Forks, WA 98331
Tel: 360-374-9663

Fort Vancouver Regional Library
1007 East Mill Plain Blvd.
Vancouver, WA 98663
Tel: 360-695-1561
        360-695-1566 (Reference)
http://www.fvrl.org/

Grant County Historical Museum
742 Basin Street, NW
P.O. Box 1141
Ephrata, WA 98823
Tel: 509-754-3334

Heritage Quest Genealogy Research Library
909 Main Street, Suite 5
Sumner, WA 98390
Tel: 253-863-1806
Fax: 253-863-0577
E-mail: research@hqrl.com.

Highline Community College Library
Special Collections
2400 S. 240th Street
Des Moines, WA 98198-9800
Tel: 206-878-3710 ext. 3232 (Reference Desk)
Fax: 206-870-3776
E-mail: tpollard@hcc.ctc.edu
http://flightline.highline.edu/library/

Hudson's Bay Company Archives
Provincial Archives of Manitoba
200 Vaughan Street
Winnipeg, Manitoba R3C 1T5
Tel: 204-945-4949
Fax: 204-948-3236
E-mail: hbca@gov.mb.ca
http://www.gov.mb.ca/chc/archives/hbca/index.html

Jefferson County Historical Society/Museum
McCurdy Research Library
210 Madison Street
Port Townsend, WA 98368
Tel: 360-385-1003
http://www.jchsmuseum.org/libraryinfo.html

King County Law Library
W621 King County Courthouse
516 3rd Avenue
Seattle, WA 98104
Tel: 206-296-0940
Fax: 206-205-0513
E-mail: kcll@metrokc.gov
http://www.kcll.org/

Kitsap Regional Library/Poulsbo Branch
700 NE Lincoln Road
Poulsbo, WA 98370
Tel: 360-779-2915
http://www.krl.org/branches/NewPO.htm

Kittitas County Genealogical Society/Library
413 N. Maine, Suite D
P.O. Box 1342
Ellensburg, WA 98926

Kittitas County Museum
114 E. Third Avenue
P.O. Box 265
Ellensburg, WA 98926
Tel: 509-925-3778

Makah Cultural and Research Center
P.O. Box 160
Neah Bay, WA 98357
Tel: 360-645-2711

Marymoor Museum
6046 W. Lake Sammamish Parkway, NE
P.O. Box 162
Redmond, WA 98073
Tel: 425-885-3684
Fax: 425-885-3684 (call before sending)
E-mail: marymoormuseum@hotmail.com
http://www.lcss.net/marymoor/

Mid-Columbia Library
405 South Dayton
Kennewick, WA 99336
Tel: 509-586-3156
http://www.mcl-lib.org/employment_opportunities. htm

Mount Vernon City Library
315 Snoqualmie Street
Mount Vernon, WA 98273
Tel: 360-336-6209
E-mail: lib@sos.net

Museum of History and Industry
McCurdy Park
2700 24th Avenue, East
Seattle, WA 98112
Tel: 206-324-1126
Fax: 206-324-1346
E-mail: information@seattlehistory.org
http://www.seattlehistory.org/

Neill Public Library
North 210 Grand Avenue
Pullman, WA 99163
Tel: 509-334-4555 (Weekdays)
     509-334-3595 (Evenings and Weekends)
E-mail: library@neill-lib.org
http://www.neill-lib.org/

Nordic Heritage Museum
3014 NW 67th Street
Seattle, WA 98117
Tel: 206-789-5707
Fax: 206-789-3271
http://www.ohwy.com/wa/n/nordichm.htm

North Central Washington Museum
127 S. Mission Street
Wenatchee, WA 98801
Tel: 509-664-3340

Northwest Seaport Maritime Heritage Center
1002 Valley Street
Seattle, WA 98109-4332
Tel: 206-447-9800
Fax: 206-447-598
E-mail: seaport@oz.net
http://www.nwseaport.org/

Olympia Timberland Library
313 8th Avenue
Olympia, WA 98501-1307
Tel: 360-352-0595
http://www.timberland.lib.wa.us/olympia.htm

Orcas Island Historical Museum
P.O. Box 134
Eastsound, WA 98245
Tel: 360-376-4849
http://www.orcasisland.org/historicalmuseum/

Pacific Lutheran University
Robert A.L. Mortvedt Library
Tacoma, WA 98447
Tel: 253-535-7586
http://www.plu.edu/libr/services.html
Scandinavian Immigrant Experience Collection
http://www.plu.edu/~lib/

Richland Public Library
955 Northlake Drive
Richland, WA 99352
Tel: 509-943-7457
Fax: 509-942-7447
E-mail: referenc@richland.lib.wa.us
http://www.richland.lib.wa.us/

Seattle Genealogical Society/Library
6200 Sand Point Way N. E. #101
Seattle, WA
Mail:
P.O. Box 75388
Seattle, WA 98125-0388
Tel: 206-522-8658
http://www.rootsweb.com/~waseags/main.html

Seattle Pacific University Library
3307 Third Avenue West
Seattle, WA 98119-1997
Tel: 206-281-2124
http://www.spu.edu/depts/library/

Seattle Public Library
Humanities Department
1000 4th Avenue
Seattle, WA 98104
Tel: 206-386-4625
http://www.spl.org/humanities/genealogy/
     genealogy.html

Seattle Public Schools Archives and Records Management Center
Frank B. Cooper Elementary School, Room 20
901 SW Genesee St
Seattle, WA 98106
Phone: 206-252-8170
E-mail: etoews@seattleschools.org
http://www.seattleschools.org/area/archives/ index.xml

Seattle University
Lemieux Library
900 Broadway
Seattle, WA 98122
Tel: 206-296-6228 (Hours)
     206-296-6230 (Reference)
Fax: 206-296-2572
E-mail: libref@seattleu.edu
http://www.seattleu.edu/lemlib/index.htm

Shoreline Historical Museum
749 N. 175th Street
Seattle, WA 98133
Tel: 206-542-7111

Snohomish County Historical Association
Heritage Center, Museum and Library
2817 Rockefeller Avenue
P.O. Box 5203
Everett, WA 98206
Tel: 425-259-2022

Spokane Public Library
Genealogy Room
906 West Main Avenue
Spokane, WA 99201
Tel: 509-444-5300
Fax: 509-444-5365
http://www2.spokanelibrary.org/

Stanwood Library
9701 271st Street, NW
P.O. Box 247
Stanwood, WA 98292
Tel: 206-629-3132
Fax: 360-629-3516

Steilacoom Historical Museum
112 Main Street
Steilacoom, WA 98388
Tel: 253-584-4133

Steilacoom Tribal Cultural Center/Museum
1515 Lafayette Street
Steilacoom, WA 98388
Tel: 253-584-6308

Stillaguamish Valley Genealogical Society/Library
20325 71st Avenue, NE
P.O. Box 34
Arlington, WA 98223-0034

Stillaguamish Valley Pioneer Museum
20722 67th Avenue, NE
Arlington, WA 98223
Tel: 360-435-7289
http://www.ohwy.com/wa/s/stillvpm.htm

Suquamish Museum
Port Madison Indian Reservation
15383 Sandy Hook Road
Suquamish, WA 98392
Tel: 360-598-3311 ext. 422
http://www.suquamish.nsn.us/museum/

Tacoma Public Library
Northwest Room
1102 S. Tacoma Way
Tacoma, WA 98402
Tel: 253-591-5622
Fax: 253-627-1693
E-mail: webfoot@tpl.lib.wa.us
http://www.tpl.lib.wa.us/

Toppenish Museum
1 S. Elm Street
Toppenish, WA 98948
Tel: 509-865-4510

University of Puget Sound
Collins Memorial Library/Archives
1500 North Warner
Tacoma, WA 98416
Tel: 253-756-3100
E-mail: libref@ups.eduê
http://library.ups.edu/

University of Washington
Suzzallo Library
Special Collections
Box 352900
Seattle, WA 98199
Tel: 206-543-0140 (Hours)
     206-543-0242 (Information)
http://www.washington.edu/

Washington State Historical Society
Heritage Research Center
315 North Stadium Way
Tacoma, WA 98403
Tel: 253-272-WSHS
     888-BE-THERE (Toll-Free)
     253-798-5914 (Research Center)
http://www.wshs.org/

Washington State Library
Point Plaza East
6880 Capitol Blvd S
P.O. Box 42460
Olympia, WA 98504-2460
Tel: 360-704-5200
Fax: 360-586-7575
http://www.statelib.wa.gov/

Washington State University
Holland Library
Manuscripts, Archives, and Special Collections
Pullman, WA 99164-5610
Tel: 509-3335-6691
http://www.wsulibs.wsu.edu/holland/masc/masc.htm

Whatcom Museum Archives
Syre Education Center
201 Prospect Street
Mail:
121 Prospect Street
Bellingham, WA 98226
Tel: 360-676-6981
360-738-7397
Fax: 360-738-7409
http://www.whatcommuseum.org/index.html

Whitman County Library
102 S. Main Street
Colfax. WA 99111
Tel: 509-397-4366

Yakima Indian Nation Cultural Center
Highway 97
Toppenish, WA 98948
Tel: 509-865-2800

NEWSPAPER REPOSITORIES

Washington State Library
Point Plaza East
6880 Capitol Blvd S
P.O. Box 42460
Olympia, WA 98504-2460
Tel: 360-704-5200
Fax: 360-586-7575
http://www.statelib.wa.gov/

VITAL RECORDS

Department of Health
Center for Health Statistics
1112 SE Quince Street
P.O. Box 47814
Olympia, WA, 98504-7814
Tel: 360-753-4379
360-352-2586
http://www.doh.wa.gov/ehsphl/chs/cert.htm

WASHINGTON ON THE WEB

East Benton County Historical Society/1910 Benton County Census
http://www.owt.com/ebchs/ebchs/census.htm

Puget Sound Maritime Historical Society/Kitsap County Indexes
http://www.psmaritime.org/

Tacoma-Pierce County Genealogical Society
http://www.rootsweb.com/~watpcgs/tpcgs.htm

Tacoma Public Library's Northwest History Databases
http://www.tpl.lib.wa.us/v2/nwroom/nwroom.htm

Washington State Genealogical Society
http://www.rootsweb.com/~wasgs/

Washington GenWeb Project
http://www.rootsweb.com/~wagenweb/

West Virginia

Archives, State & National

National Archives-Mid Atlantic Region
900 Market Street
Philadelphia, PA 19107-4292
Tel: 215-597-3000
Fax: 215-597-2303
E-mail: philadelphia.archives@nara.gov
http://www.nara.gov/regional/philacc.html

West Virginia State Archives and History Library
West Virginia Division of Culture and History
Cultural Center, Capitol Complex
1900 Kanawha Boulevard, East
Charleston, WV 25305-0300
Tel: 304-558-0230
Fax: 304-558-2779
http://www.wvculture.org/history/index.html

Genealogical Societies

Allegheny Regional Family History Society (ARFHS)
P.O. Box 1804
Elkins, WV 26241
Tel: 304-636-1958
     304-636-1959
http://www.swcp.com/~dhickman/arfhs.html

Boone County Genealogical Society
P.O. Box 295
Madison, WV 25130

Braxton County Genealogical Society
228 Braxton St.
Gassaway, WV 26224

Brooke County Genealogical Society
P.O. Box 144
Beech Bottom, WV 26030-0144

Calhoun County Historical and Genealogical Society
Board of Education Plaza
High Street
P.O. Box 242
Grantsville, WV 26147
Tel: 304-354-7614
http://www.rootsweb.com/~wvcalhou/society.htm

Daughters of American Pioneers, Centennial Chapter
2334 Broad Street
Parkersburg, WV 26101

Fayette and Raleigh Counties, Genealogical Society of
P.O. Box 68
Oak Hill, WV 25901-0068

Hacker's Creek Pioneer Descendants
Central West Virginia Genealogy and History Library
45 Abbott's Run Road
Horner, WV 26372-0056
Tel: 304-269-7091
Fax: 304-269-4430
E-mail: hcpd.lewisco@westvirginia.com
http://www.rootsweb.com/~hcpd/

Harrison County Genealogical Society
P.O. Box 387
Clarksburg, WV 26301

Kanawha Valley Genealogical Society/Library
P.O. Box 8555
South Charleston, WV 25303

KYOWVA Genealogical Society
Keenan House (Library)
232 Main Street
Guyandotte, WV
Mail:
P.O. Box 1254
Huntington, WV 25715
Tel: 304-525-4367

Lincoln County Genealogical Society
7999 Lynn Avenue
Hamlin, WV 25523
http://www.rootsweb.com/~wvlincol/LCGS.html

Logan County Genealogical Society
Southern West Virginia Community College Library
P.O. Box 1959
Logan, WV 25601

Marion County Genealogical Club
Marion County Library, Genealogy Room
321 Monroe Street
Fairmont, WV 26554
Tel: 304-287-2411
http://www.hhs.net/sss/preston/mcgc.htm

Mineral County Genealogical/Historical Society
107 Orchard Street
Keyser, WV 26726

Mining Your History Foundation
P.O. Box 6923
Charleston, WV 25362-0923
Tel: 304-345-3808
E-mail: hcpd.lewisco@westvirginia.com
http://www.rootsweb.com/~myhf/

Mingo County Genealogical Society
P.O. Box 2581
Williamson, WV 25661
http://www.rootsweb.com/~wvmingo/mingogs.htm

Morgan County Historical and Genealogical Society
P.O. Box 52
Berkeley Springs, WV 25411

Nicholas County Historical and Genealogical Society
P.O. Box 443
Summersville, WV 26651
http://svis.org/shirley/Nicholas.htm

Palatines to America, West Virginia Chapter
1283 Kings Road
Morgantown, WV 26508-9189
Tel: 304-284-9278

Taylor County Historical and Genealogical Society
P.O. Box 522
Grafton, WV 26354
Tel: 304-265-5015

Tri-State Genealogical and Historical Society
P.O. Box 454
Newell, WV 26050
Tel: 304-387-2467
http://www.rootsweb.com/~wvtsghs/indext.htm

West Augusta Historical and Genealogical Society
P.O. Box 266
Mannington, WV 26582

West Virginia Genealogical Society/Library
5238 Elk River Road, N.
P.O. Box 249
Elkview, WV 25071
http://members.aol.com/edeaj/wvgenealogicalsociety.html

Wetzel County Genealogical Society, Inc.
P.O. Box 464
New Martinsville, WV 26155-0464
http://www.ovis.net/~billcham/

Wheeling Area Genealogical Society
P. O. Box 6450
Wheeling, WV 26003-6450
http://www.rootsweb.com/~wvwags/

Wyoming County Genealogical Society
P.O. Box 1186
Pineville, WV 24874-1186
Tel: 304-732-8394
   304-294-6108
   304-732-9472

HISTORICAL SOCIETIES

Barbour County Historical Society
146 N. Main
Philippi, WV 26416
Tel: 304-457-4846
   304-457-3349

Berkeley County Historical Society
Belle Boyd House
126 East Race Street
P.O. Box 1624
Martinsburg, WV 25402
Tel: 304-267-4713

Braxton County Historical Society
Route 1, Box 14
Exchange, WV 26619
Tel: 304-765-2415

Brooke County Historical Society/Library
10th and Main
Mail:
1200 Pleasant Avenue
Wellsburg, WV 26070

Buffalo Historical Society
P.O. Box 144
Buffalo, WV 25033
Tel: 304-937-2241

Cabell-Wayne County Historical Society
P.O. Box 9412
Huntington, WV 25704

Calhoun County Historical and Genealogical Society
Board of Education Plaza
High Street
P.O. Box 242
Grantsville, WV 26147
Tel: 304-354-7614
http://www.rootsweb.com/~wvcalhou/society.htm

Clay County Landmarks Commission and Historical Society
P.O. Box 523
Clay, WV 25043

Doddridge County Historical Society
P.O. Box 23
West Union, WV 26456

Elk/Blue Creek Historical Society
P.O. Box 649
Elkview, WV 25071

Fayette County Historical Society
P.O. Box 463
Ansted, WV 25812-0463
Tel: 304-469-9505

Gilmer County Historical Society
P.O Box 235
Glenville, WV 26351

Grant County Historical Society
P.O. Box 665
Petersburg, WV 26847
Tel: 304-257-1444

Greenbrier Historical Society/Library
North House Museum
301 West Washington Street
Lewisburg, WV 24901
Tel: 304-645-3398
E-mail: info@greenbrierhistorical.org
http://www.greenbrierhistorical.org/

Hampshire County Historical Society
170 East Birch Lane
Rommney, WV 26757
Tel: 304-822-3185 (Hampshire County Public Library)

Hancock County Historical Society of West Virginia
Swaney Library
New Cumberland, WV 26047
mailing address:
2669 Main Street
Weirton, WV 26062
Tel: 304-748-4829

Hardy County Historical Society
P.O. Box 644
Moorefield, WV 26836

Harpers Ferry Historical Association
Harpers Ferry National Historic Park
Shenandoah Street
P.O. Box 197
Harpers Ferry, WV 25425
Tel: 304-535-6881
   800-821-5206
E-mail: hfha@intrepid.net

Harrison County Historical Society
Stealy Goff Vance House
123 West Main Street
P.O. Box 2074
Clarksburg, WV 26302-2074

Helvetia, Historical Society of
General Delivery
Helvetia, WV 26224

Historic Shepherdstown Commission/Museum
Entler Hotel, Room 200
P.O. Box 1786
Shepherdstown, WV 25443
Tel: 304-876-0910

Jackson County Historical Society
P.O. Box 22
Ripley, WV 25271
Tel: 304-372-2541

Jefferson County Historical Society
P.O. Box 485
Charles Town, WV 25414

Lewis County Historical Society
252 Main Avenue
Weston, WV 26452

Kanawha Valley Historical and Preservation Society
P.O. Box 2283
Charlestown, WV 25328

Marion County Historical Society
P.O. Box 1636
Fairmont, WV 26555-1636

Marshall County Historical Society
P.O. Box 267
Moundsville, WV 26041
http://www.rootsweb.com/~wvmarsha/hist1.htm

Mason City Historical Society
P.O. Box 165
Mason, WV 25260
Tel: 304-773-5557

Mason Historical Society
P.O. Box 125
Hartford, WV 25247

McDowell Historical Society
P.O. Box 369
War, WV 24892
Tel: 304-875-2841

Mercer County Historical Society, Inc.
P.O. Box 5012
Princeton, WV 24740
Tel: 304-425-2697

Mineral County Genealogical/Historical Society
107 Orchard Street
Keyser, WV 26726

Mingo County Historical Society
P.O. Box 2581
Williamson, WV 25661

Monongalia Historical Society
P.O. Box 127
Morgantown, WV 26505

Monroe County Historical Society
P.O. Box 465
Union, WV 24983

Morgan County Historical and Genealogical Society
P.O. Box 52
Berkeley Springs, WV 25411

Mountain State Railroad and Logging Historical Association
P.O. Box 89
Cass, WV 24927

National Railway Historical Society
C.P. Huntington RR Historical Society
P.O. Box 451
Kenova, WV 25530-0451
Tel: 304-453-1641
http://www.serve.com/cphrrhs/

Nicholas County Historical and Genealogical Society
P.O. Box 443
Summersville, WV 26651
http://svis.org/shirley/Nicholas.htm

Pendleton County Historical Society
1 South Main Street
Franklin, WV 26807

Pleasants County Historical Society/Museum
Jim Spence Community Building
Pleasants County Park
605 Cherry Street
Mail:
P.O. Box 335
Saint Marys, WV 26170
Tel: 304-684-7621

Pocahontas County Historical Society/Archives
810 Second Avenue
Marlinton, WV 24954
Tel: 304-799-6659 (Summer)
304-799-4973 (Year Round)

Preston County Historical Society
215 Jackson Street
Kingwood, WV 26537
Tel: 304-329-1468

Raleigh County Historical Society
Wildwood House
Beckley, WV
Mail:
P.O. Box 897
Skelton, WV 25919-0897

Randolph County Historical Society/Library
P.O. Box 1164
Elkins, WV 26241
Tel: 304-636-0841
304-636-1958/9

Ritchie County Historical Society
200 South Church Street
Harrisville, WV 26362
Tel: 304-643-2738

Roane County Historical Society
P.O. Box 161
Spencer, WV 25276

Saint Albans Historical Society
2745 Lincoln Avenue
Saint Albans, WV
Mail:
919 Lee Street
Saint Albans, WV 25177
Tel: 304-727-5972

Summers County Historical Society
P.O. Box 1300
Hinton, WV 25951

Taylor County Historical and Genealogical Society
P.O. Box 522
Grafton, WV 26354

Tri-State Genealogical and Historical Society
P.O. Box 454
Newell, WV 26050
Tel: (304) 387-2467
http://www.rootsweb.com/~wvtsghs/indext.htm

Tucker County Historical Society
Town Building
P.O. Box 13
Hambleton, WV 26269

Tyler County Heritage and Historical Society
P. O. Box 317
Dodd Street
Middlebourne, WV 26149
http://www.rootsweb.com/~wvtyler/SOCIETY.htm

Upper Vandalia Historical Society
P.O. Box 517
Poca, WV 25159

Upshur County Historical Society
History Center
81 West Main Street
P.O. Box 2082
Buckhannon, WV 26201
http://www.msys.net/uchs/

Webster County Historical Society
P.O. Box 1012
Summersville, WV 26651

West Augusta Historical and Genealogical Society
P.O. Box 266
Mannington, WV 26582

West Virginia and Regional History Association
West Virginia University Libraries
Colson Hall, WVU
P.O. Box 6464
Morgantown, WV 26506-6464
Tel: 304-293-3536
Fax: 304-293-3981

West Virginia Baptist Historical Society
Conference Center
Route 2, Box 304
Ripley, WV 25271

West Virginia Historical Society
P.O. Box 5220
Charleston, WV 25305-0300
Tel: 304-348-2277
      304-348-0230
http://www.wvlc.wvnet.edu/history/wvhssoc.html

Wheeling Area Historical Society
136 North 19th Street
Ohio County
Wheeling, WV 26003

Wood County Historical and Preservation Society, Inc.
P.O. BOx 617
Parkersburg, WV 26101

LDS FAMILY HISTORY CENTERS

For locations of Family History Centers in this state, see the Family History Center locator at FamilySearch.
http://www.familysearch.org/eng/Library/FHC/frameset_fhc.asp

ARCHIVES/LIBRARIES/MUSEUMS

Alderson-Braddus College
Pickett Library
College Hill
Philippi, WV 26416
Tel: 304-457-1700 ext. 306
      304-457-6229
Fax: 304-457-6239
http://ab.edu/ab/catalog/facilities.html

Beckley Exhibition Coal Mine
Drawer AJ
Beckley, WV 25802

Bethany College
T.W. Phillips Library
Alexander Campbell Archives
Bethany, WV 26032
Tel: 304-829-7321
Fax: 304-829-7333
http://www.bethanywv.edu/library/

Boone-Madison Public Library
375 Main Street
Madison, WV 25130
Tel:304-369-7842
Fax: 304-369-2950

Brooke County Historical Society/Library
10th and Main
Mail:
1200 Pleasant Avenue
Wellsburg, WV 26070

Brooke County Public Library
945 Main Street
Wellsburg, WV 26070
Tel/Fax: 304-737-1551
http://brooke.lib.wv.us/

Burnsville Public Library
Kanawha Street
Burnsville, WV 26335
Tel/Fax: 304-853-2338

Cabell County Public Library/Huntington Branch
455 Ninth Street Plaza
Huntington, WV 25701
Tel: 304-528-5700
Fax: 304-528-5701
http://cabell.lib.wv.us/index.html

Central West Virginia Genealogy and History Library
23 Abbotts Run Road
Horner, WV 26372
Tel: 304-269-7091
Fax: 304-269-4430
E-mail: hcpd.lewisco@westvirginia.com
http://www.hackerscreek.com/library1.htm/

Clarksburg-Harrison Public Library
West Virginia Collections
404 West Pike Street
Clarksburg, WV 26301
Tel: 304-627-2236
http://129.71.125.8/clark/clarksburg1.html

Davis and Elkins College
Booth Library
100 Campus Drive
Elkins, WV 26241
Tel: 304-637-1200
Fax: 304-637-1415
http://www.dne.edu/library/index.htm

Doddridge County Public Library
117 Court Street
West Union, WV 26456
Tel/Fax: 304-873-1941

Dora B. Woodyard Memorial Library
Box 340 Mulberry Street
Elizabeth WV 26143
Tel/Fax: 304-275-4295
http://raleigh.lib.wv.us/wirt/dbwoodyard/

Elkins/Randolph County Public Library
416 Davis Avenue
Elkins, WV 26241
Tel: 304-636-1121
Fax: 304-636-6073

Fairmont State College
Ruth Ann Musick Library
Fairmont, WV 26554-2491
Tel: 304-367-4123
Fax: 304-367-4589
http://www.fscwv.edu/library/

Family Research Library and Archives
Wilma Myers
805 State Street
Gassaway, WV 26624

Fort New Salem
Salem-Teikyo University
Salem, WV 26426
Tel: 304-782-5336
     800-283-4562
http://www.salem-teikyo.wvnet.edu/

Gassaway Public Library
536 Elks
Gassaway, WV 26624
Tel/Fax: 304-364-8292

Gilmer County Public Library
214 Walnut Street
Glenville, WV 26351
Tel/Fax: 304-462-5620

Greenbrier Historical Society/Library
North House Museum
301 West Washington Street
Lewisburg, WV 24901
Tel: 304-645-3398
E-mail: info@greenbrierhistorical.org
http://www.greenbrierhistorical.org/

Hamlin/Lincoln County Public Library
7999 Lynn Ave
Hamlin WV 25523-1494
Tel: 304-824-5481
Fax: 304-824-7014

Hampshire County Historical Society
170 East Birch Lane
Romney, WV 26757
Tel: 304-822-3185 (Hampshire County Public Library)

Hampshire County Public Library
153 West Main Street
Romney, WV 26757
Tel: 304-822-3185
Fax: 304-822-3955

Hardy County Public Library
102 North Main Street
Moorefield, WV 26836
Tel: 304-538-6560
Fax: 304-538-2639

Harpers Ferry National Historical Park
P.O. Box 65
Harpers Ferry, WV 25425
Tel: 304-535-6020
     304-535-6441
http://www.nps.gov/hafe/

Harrison County Historical Society
Stealy Goff Vance House
123 West Main Street
P.O. Box 2074
Clarksburg, WV 26302-2074
Tel: 304-842-3073

Henderson Hall
Henderson Hall Historic District
Route 2, Box 103
Williamstown, WV 26187
Tel: 304-375-2129
        304-295-4772

Hinton Railroad Museum
217 7th Avenue
Hinton, WV 25951
Tel: 304-466-1433

Kanawha Valley Genealogical Society/Library
P.O. Box 8555
South Charleston, WV 25303
http://www.rootsweb.com/~wvkvgs/

Kanawha County Public Library
123 Capitol Street
Charlestown, WV 25301
Tel: 304-343-4646

KYOWVA Genealogical Society
Keenan House (Library)
232 Main Street
Guyandotte, WV
Mail:
P.O. Box 1254
Huntington, WV 25715
Tel: 304-525-4367

Lee Cabin Museum
Lost River State Park
Route 2, Box 24
Mathias, WV 26812

Marion County Library
Genealogy Room
321 Monroe Street
Fairmont, WV 26554
Tel: 304-366-1210/1

Marshall University
Special Collections, Morrow Library, Marshall University
400 Hal Greer Blvd.
Huntington, WV 25755
Tel: 304-696-2343
Fax: 304-696-2361
http://www.marshall.edu/speccoll/wvcoll.html

Martinsburg-Berkeley County Public Library
Public Square
101 West King Street
Martinsburg, WV 25401
Tel: 304-267-8933
Fax: 307-267-9720

Mary H. Weir Public Library
3442 Main Street
Weirton, WV 26062-4590
Tel: 304-797-8510

Mason City Public Library
8 Brown Street
P.O. Box 609
Mason City, WV 25260
Tel: 304-773-5580

Mason County Public Library
508 Viand Street
Point Pleasant, WV 25550
Tel: 304-675-2913
Fax: 304-675-2943

Miracle Valley City/County Public Library
700 Fifth Street
Moundsville, WV 26041
Tel: 304-845-6911
Fax: 304-845-6912

Monroe County Public Library
Route 219
P.O. Box 558
Union, WV 24983
Tel: 304-772-3038
Fax: 304-772-4052

Moomau Public Library
One North Main Street
Petersburg, WV 26847
Tel/Fax: 304-257-4122

Morgantown Public Library
West Virginia Collection and Archives
373 Spruce Street
Morgantown, WV 26505
Tel: 304-291-7425
Fax: 304-291-7437
http://clark.lib.wv.us/morg/morg.html

Ohio County Public Library
52 16th Street
Wheeling, WV 26003
Tel: 304-232-0244
Fax: 304-232-6848
http://wheeling.weirton.lib.wv.us/

Old Charles Town Library
200 East Washington Street
Charles Town, WV 25414
Tel: 304-725-2208

Parkersburg and Wood County Public Library
3100 Emerson Avenue
Parkersburg, WV 26104
Tel: 304-485-6564
Fax: 304-485-6580

Pendleton County Public Library
P.O. Box 519
Franklin, WV 26807
Tel/Fax: 304-358-7038

Philippi Public Library
102 South Main Street
Philippi, WV 26416
Tel: 304-457-3495

Pleasants County Historical Society/Museum
Jim Spence Community Building
Pleasants County Park
605 Cherry Street
Mail:
P.O. Box 335
Saint Marys, WV 26170
Tel: 304-684-7621

Pleasants County Public Library
101 Lafayette Street
St. Marys, WV 26170-1025
Tel/Fax: 304-684-7494

Pocahontas County Historical Society/Archives
810 Second Avenue
Marlinton, WV 24954
Tel: 304-799-6659 (Summer)
    304-799-4973 (Year Round)

Pricketts Fort Memorial Foundation
Pricketts Fort State Park
Route 3, Box 407
Fairmont, WV 26554
Tel: 304-363-3030

Putnam County Library
4219 State Route 34
Hurricane, WV 25526
Tel: 304-757-7308
Fax: 304-757-7307

Quinwood Public Library
P.O. Box 157
Quinwood, WV 25981
Tel/Fax: 304-438-6741

Randolph County Historical Society/Library
P.O. Box 1164
Elkins, WV 26241
Tel: 304-636-0841
    304-636-1958/9

Ritchie County Public Library
130 N. Court Street
Harrisville, WV 26362
Tel/Fax: 304-643-2717

Roane County Public Library
Parking Plaza
Spencer, WV 25276
Tel: 304-927-1130
Fax: 304-927-1196

Shepherdstown Public Library
P.O. Box 278
Shepherdstown, WV 25443
Tel: 304-876-2783

Summers County Public Library
201 Temple Street
Hinton, WV 25951
Tel: 304-466-4490
Fax: 304-466-5260

Sutton Public Library
450-C Fourth Street
Sutton, WV 26601
Tel/Fax: 304-765-7224

Taylor County Public Library
200 Beech Street
Grafton, WV 26354
Tel/Fax: 304-265-5015

Upshur County Public Library
RR 6, Box 480
Buckhannon, WV 26201
Tel: 304-472-5475
Fax: 304-472-0106

West Huntington Public Library
901 West 14th Street
Huntington, WV 25704
Tel: 304-528-5697
Fax: 304-528-5697

West Virginia Baptist Historical Society
Rt. 2 Box 304
Jackson County
Ripley, WV 25271

West Virginia Genealogical Society/Library
5238 Elk River Road, N.
P.O. Box 249
Elkview, WV 25071

West Virginia State Archives and History Library
West Virginia Division of Culture and History
Cultural Center, Capitol Complex
1900 Kanawha Boulevard, East
Charleston, WV 25305-0300
Tel: 304-558-0230
Fax: 304-558-2779
http://www.wvlc.wvnet.edu/history/wvsamenu.html

West Virginia State Farm Museum
Route 1, Box 479
Point Pleasant, WV 25550
Tel: 304-675-5737

West Virginia University Library
Special Collections
Colson Hall, WVU
P.O. Box 6464
Morgantown, WV 26506-6464
Tel: 304-293-3536/7
Fax: 304-293-6638
http://www.wvu.edu/~library/collect.htm

Williamson Public Library
Court House Annex
Williamson, WV 25661
Tel/Fax: 304-235-2402

Wyoming County Public Library
Castle Rock Avenue
P.O. Box 130
Pineville, WV 24874
Tel: 304-732-6899
http://wyoming.lib.wv.us

NEWSPAPER REPOSITORIES

West Virginia State Archives and History Library
West Virginia Division of Culture and History
Cultural Center, Capitol Complex
1900 Kanawha Boulevard, East
Charleston, WV 25305-0300
Tel: 304-558-0230
Fax: 304-558-2779
http://www.wvlc.wvnet.edu/history/wvsamenu.html

West Virginia University Library
Special Collections
Colson Hall, WVU
P.O. Box 6464
Morgantown, WV 26506-6464
Tel: 304-293-3536
Fax: 304-293-6638
E-mail: hforbes@wvu.edu
http://www.wvu.edu/~library/wvarhc.htm

VITAL RECORDS

Division of Health, Vital Registration
Vital Registration Office
Division of Health State
350 Capitol Street, Rm. 157
Charleston, WV 25301-3701

WEST VIRGINIA ON THE WEB

Civil War in West Virginia
http://www.wvculture.org/history/cwmenu.html

Don Norman's West Virginia Family Histories
http://www.rootsweb.com/~hcpd/norman/norman.htm

West Virginia GenWeb Project
http://www.rootsweb.com/~wvgenweb//

West Virginia Historical Resources Guide-Marshall University
http://www.marshall.edu/speccoll/rg-title.html

West Virginia Histories Homepage (A Bibliography)
http://www.clearlight.com/~wvhh/

West Virginia Infomine
http://129.71.160.4/

West Virginia Military Research from the WV GenWeb
http://www.rootsweb.com/~wvgenweb/military/

West Virginia State Archives Civil War Medals Homepage
http://www.wvculture.org/history/medals.html

West Virginia State Archives Genealogy Surname Exchange
http://www.wvculture.org/history/surintro.html

West Virginia State Archives History Databases
http://www.wvculture.org/history/wvah.html

WISCONSIN

ARCHIVES, STATE & NATIONAL

National Archives—Great Lakes Region
7358 Pulaski Road
Chicago, IL 60629
Tel: 773-581-7816
Fax: 312-886-7883
E-mail: chicago.archives@nara.gov
http://www.nara.gov/regional/chicago.html

State Historical Society of Wisconsin/Archives Division
816 State Street
Madison, WI 53706
Tel: 608-264-6460
E-mail: Archives.Reference@CCMAIL.ADP.WISC.EDU
http://www.shsw.wisc.edu/archives/

Area Research Centers
http://www.shsw.wisc.edu/archives/arcnet/
For individual homepages with more information on
    each Area Research Center, see the section on
    Archives/Libraries/Museums

Madeline Island Historical Museum
P.O. Box 9
La Pointe, WI 54850
Tel: 715-747-2415
http://www.shsw.wisc.edu/sites/madisle/
(Original Materials for Ashland, Bayfield, and Iron
    Counties—See Vaughn Public Library for Microfilm)

Superior Public Library
1530 Tower Avenue
Superior, WI 54880
Tel: 715-394-8860
http://www.wisc.edu/shs-archives/arcnet/
    superior.html
(Douglas County)

University of Wisconsin/Eau Claire
William D. McIntyre Library
Special Collections Department
Eau Claire, WI 54702-4004
Tel: 715-836-3715
http://www.uwec.edu/library/
(Buffalo, Chippewa, Clark, Eau Claire, Price, Rusk,
    Sawyer, and Taylor Counties)

University of Wisconsin/Green Bay
Cofrin Library, 7th Floor
2420 Nicolet Drive
Green Bay, WI 54311-7001
Tel: 920-465-2303
http://www.shsw.wisc.edu/archives/arcnet/greenbay.html
(Brown, Calumet, Door, Florence, Kewaunee, Manitowoc,
    Marinette, Menominee, Oconto, Outagamie, and
    Shawano Counties)

University of Wisconsin/La Crosse
Murphy Library Resource Center
University of WI - La Crosse
1631 Pine Street
La Crosse, WI 54601
http://www.shsw.wisc.edu/archives/arcnet/ lacrosse.html
(Jackson, La Crosse, Monroe, Trempealeau, and Vernon
    Counties)

University of Wisconsin/Milwaukee
Golda Meir Library, Room W250
Milwaukee Urban Archives
P.O. Box 604
Milwaukee, WI 53201-0604
Tel: 414-229-4785
http://www.shsw.wisc.edu/archives/arcnet/milwauke.html
(Milwaukee, Ozaukee, Sheboygan, Washington, and
    Waukesha Counties)

University of Wisconsin/Oshkosh
Forrest R. Polk Library
800 Algoma Boulevard
Oshkosh, WI 54901
Tel: 920-424-0828
http://www.uwosh.edu/library/
(Dodge, Fond du Lac, Green Lake, Marquette, and
    Winnebago Counties)

University of Wisconsin/Parkside
D276 Wyllie Library Learning Center
University Archives and Area Research Center
900 Wood Road
Kenosha, WI 53141-2000
Tel: 262-595-2077
    262-595-2411
http://www.shsw.wisc.edu/archives/arcnet/parkside.html
(Racine and Kenosha Counties)

University of Wisconsin/Platteville
Elton S. Karrmann Library
Southwest Wisconsin Room
Platteville, WI 53818-3099
Tel: 608-342-1719
http://www.shsw.wisc.edu/archives/arcnet/ plattvil.html
(Crawford, Grant, Green, Iowa, Lafayette, and Richland
Counties)

University of Wisconsin/River Falls
Chalmer Davee Library
120 Cascade Avenue
River Falls, WI 54022
Tel: 715-425-3567
http://www.shsw.wisc.edu/archives/arcnet/ riverfls.html
(Burnett, Polk, St. Croix, Pierce, and Washburn
Counties)

University of Wisconsin/Stevens Point
Learning Resources Center
Stevens Point, WI 54481
Tel: 715-346-2586
http://www.shsw.wisc.edu/archives/arcnet/ stevens.html
(Adams, Forest, Juneau, Langlade, Lincoln, Marathon,
Oneida, Portage, Vilas, Waupaca, Waushara, and
Wood Counties)

University of Wisconsin/Stout
Library Learning Center
Menomonie, WI 54751
Tel: 715-232-2300
http://www.shsw.wisc.edu/archives/arcnet/ stout.htm
(Barron, Dunn, and Pepin Counties)

University of Wisconsin/Whitewater
Harold Anderson Library
800 West Main Street
Whitewater, WI 53190
Tel: 414-472-5520
http://www.shsw.wisc.edu/archives/arcnet/ whitewtr.html
(Jefferson, Rock, and Walworth Counties)

Vaughn Public Library
502 West Main Street
Ashland, WI 54806
Tel: 715-682-7060
Fax: 715-682-7185
(Microfilmed Materials for Ashland, Bayfield, and Iron
Counties-See Madeline Island for Original Material)

GENEALOGICAL SOCIETIES

Bay Area Genealogical Society
P.O. Box 283
Green Bay, WI 54305

Bayfield County Genealogical Society
Route 1, Box 139
Mason, WI 54856

Chippewa County Genealogical Society
123 Allen Street
Chippewa Falls, WI 54729-1920

Daughters of the American Revolution, Wisconsin State Society
http://www.execpc.com/~drg/wisdar.html

Dodge/Jefferson Counties Genealogical Society
P.O. Box 91
Watertown, WI 53094-0091

Dunn County Genealogical Society
P.O. Box 633
Menomonie, WI 54751
Tel: 715-235-0770

Eau Claire, Genealogical Research Society of
c/o Chippewa Valley Museum
Carson Park Drive
P.O. Box 1204
Eau Claire, WI 54702
Tel: 715-834-7871

Fond du Lac County Genealogical Society
P.O. Box 1264
North Fond du Lac, WI 54935-1056

Forest County Historical and Genealogical Society/Museum
P.O. Box 432
Crandon, WI 54520
Tel: 715-478-3559

Fox Valley Genealogical Society
P.O. Box 1592
Appleton, WI 54913-1592

French-Canadian/Acadian Genealogists of Wisconsin
P.O. Box 414
Hales Corners, WI 53130-0414
http://www.fcgw.org/

German Interest Group of Southern Wisconsin
P.O. Box 2185
Janesville, WI 53547-2185
Tel: 608-757-2777
http://www.rootsweb.com/~wigig/index.html

Grant County Genealogical Society
P.O. Box 281
Dickeyville, WI 53808-0281
E-mail: reese@mwci.net
http://www.rootsweb.com/~wigrant/gcgensoc.htm

Hartford Genealogical Society
Hartford Public Library
109 North Main Street
Hartford, WI 53027

Heart O' Wisconsin Genealogical Society
MacMillan Memorial Library
490 East Grand Avenue
Wisconsin Rapids, WI 54494
http://www.rootsweb.com/~wiwood/HeartOWi/
   h-master.htm

Irish Genealogical Society of Wisconsin
P.O. 13766
Wauwatosa, WI 53213-0766
Fax: 414-251-5564
E-mail: igsw@execpc.com/~igsw
http://www.execpc.com/~igsw/

Jackson County Footprints (Genealogy Club)
W11770 County Road P
Black River Falls, WI 54615-5926

Kenosha County Genealogical Society
4902 52nd Street
Kenosha, WI 53142

Lafayette County Genealogical Workshop
P.O. Box 443
Shullsburg, WI 54305

LaCrosse Area Genealogical Society
P.O. Box 1782
LaCrosse, WI 54602

Manitowoc County Genealogical Society
P.O. Box 1745
Manitowoc, WI 54221-1745

Marathon County Genealogical Society
P.O. Box 1512
Wausau, WI 54402-1512

Marshfield Area Genealogy Group
P.O. Box 337
Marshfield, WI 54449
http://marshfieldgenealogy.homestead.com/
   indexmagg. html

Milwaukee County Genealogical Society
P.O. Box 27326
Milwaukee, WI 53227
http://www.execpc.com/~mcgs/

Milwaukee PAF Users Group (MPAFUG)
P.O. Box 268
Muskego, WI 53150
E-mail: akoes24194@aol.com
http://www.mpafug.org/

Monroe, Juneau, Jackson County Wisconsin Genealogy Workshop
Route 3, Box 253
Black River Falls, WI 54615

Northern Wisconsin Genealogists
912 Zingler
P.O. Box 321
Shawano, WI 54166

Northwoods Genealogical Society
P.O. Box 1132
Rhinelander, WI 54501

Oconomowoc Genealogical Club of Waukesha County
37189 East Washington
Oconomowoc, WI 53066

Polish Genealogical Society of Wisconsin
P. O. Box 342341
Milwaukee, WI 53234-2341
http://feefhs.org/pol/frgpgswi.html

Pomeranian Society of Freistadt
(Pommerscher Verein Freistadt Rundschreiben)
P.O. Box 204
Germantown, WI 53022
http://feefhs.org/ger/pvf/frg-pvf.html

Plymouth Genealogical Society
Plymouth Public Library
317 East Main
Plymouth, WI 53073

Rock County Genealogical Society
10 S. High Street
P.O. Box 711
Janesville, WI 53547
Tel: 608-756-4509
http://www.rootsweb.com/~wircgs/index.html

Saint Croix Valley Genealogical Society
P.O. Box 396
River Falls, WI 54022
http://www.pressenter.com/~scvgs/

Sheboygan County Genealogical Society
518 Water Street
Sheboygan Falls, WI 53085

Sons of the American Revolution, Wisconsin State Society
http://www.execpc.com/~drg/srwi.html

Stevens Point Area Genealogical Society
Portage County Library
1001 Main
Stevens Point, WI 54481

Twin Ports Genealogical Society
P.O. Box 16895
Duluth, WI 55816-0895

Walworth County Genealogical Society
P.O. Box 159
Delavan, WI 53115-0159
http://www.rootsweb.com/~wiwalwor/wcgs.html

Washburn County Genealogical Society
P.O. Box 366
Shell Lake, WI 54871
http://www.rootsweb.com/~wiwashbu/wcgs.htm

Waukesha County Genealogical Society
P.O. Box 1541
Waukesha, WI 53186

White Pine Genealogical Society
P.O. Box 512
Marienette, WI 54143

Winnebagoland Genealogical Society
Oshkosh Public Library
106 Washington Avenue
Oshkosh, WI 54901-4985

Wisconsin Jewish Genealogical Society
9180 North Fairway Drive
Milwaukee, WI 53217

Wisconsin State Genealogical Society
2109 20th Avenue
P.O. Box 5106
Madison, WI 53705-0106
http://www.wsgs.org

HISTORICAL SOCIETIES

Ashland County Historical Society
Genealogy Department
P.O. Box 433
Ashland, WI 54806

Bayfield Heritage Association
P.O. Box 137
Bayfield, WI 54814
Tel: 715-779-5958

Beloit Historical Society/Library
845 Hackett Street
Beloit, WI 53511
Tel: 608-365-7835
Fax: 608-365-5999
E-mail: beloiths@ticon.net

Berlin Historical Society
P.O. Box 21
Berlin, WI 54923-0021
Tel: 920-361-1274

Burlington Historical Society/Museum
W. Jefferson & N. Perkins Blvd.
Burlington, WI 53105
Tel: 262-539-2935

Chippewa County Historical Society
100 North Bridge St.
Chippewa Falls, WI 54729
Tel: 715-723-4399

Clark County Historical Society
215 E. 5th Street
Neillsville, WI 54456-1942

Cliff High Historical Society
N7526 Lower Cliff Road
Sherwood, WI 54169-9703
Tel: 920-989-1636

Dartford Historical Society
P.O. Box 638
Green Lake, WI 54941
Tel: 920-294-6194

Dodge County Historical Society
105 Park Avenue
Beaver Dam, WI 53916
Tel: 414-887-1266

Dunn County Historical Society
P.O. Box 437
Menomonie, WI 54751
Tel: 715-232-8685
http://discover-net.net/~dchs/

Fennimore Railroad Historical Society/Museum
610 Lincoln Avenue
Fennimore, WI 53809
Tel: 608-822-6144
http://www.fennimore.com/railmuseum/

Fond du Lac County Historical Society
P.O. Box 1284
Fond du Lac, WI 54935

Forest County Historical and Genealogical Society/Museum
P.O. Box 432
Crandon, WI 54520
Tel: 715-478-3559

Headwaters Historical Society
P.O. Box 2011
Eagle River, WI 54521

Iron County Historical Society/Museum
303 Iron Street
Hurley, WI 54534
Tel: 715-561-2244

Jackson County Historical Society
13 South 1st Street
Black River Falls, WI 54615

Kenosha County Historical Society/Museum
6300 3rd Avenue
Kenosha, WI 53143
Tel: 262-654-5770

LaCrosse County Historical Society
P.O. Box 1272
La Crosse, WI 54602-1272
Tel: 608-782-1980
http://www.lchsonline.org/

Madeline Island Historical Preservation Association
P.O. Box 250
LaPointe, WI 54850
Tel: 715-747-2415

Manitowoc County Historical Society
P.O. Box 574
Manitowoc, WI 54221
Tel: 920-684-4445

Marathon County Historical Society/ Museum and Library
504 McIndoe St
Wausau, WI 54403
Tel: 715-848-6143

Mazomanie Historical Society/Museum
130 Brodhead Street
Mazomanie, WI 53560
Tel: 608-795-4733

Menomonee Falls Historical Society
P.O. Box 91
Menomonee Falls, WI 53051

Mercer Historical Society
P.O. Box 638
Mercer, WI 54547
Tel: 715-476-2714

Middleton Area Historical Society
7426 Hubbard Avenue
Middleton, WI 53562

Milwaukee County Historical Society
910 North Old World Third Street
Milwaukee, WI 53203
Tel: 414-273-8288
http://www.milwaukeecountyhistsoc.org/

Milton Historical Society
P.O. Box 245
Milton, WI 53563
Tel: 608-868-7772
http://www.miltonhouse.org

Neenah Historical Society
P.O. Box 343
Neenah, WI 54957-0343
Tel: 920-729-0244

New Glarus Historical Society
Sixth Ave. and 7th St.
New Glarus, WI 53574

North Wood County Historical Society
P.O. Box 142
Marshfield, WI 54449
Tel: 715-389-2916

Oak Creek Historical Society
P.O. Box 243
Oak Creek, WI 53154

Oconomowoc Historical Society/Museum
P.O. Box 969
103 W. Jefferson Street
Oconomowoc, WI 53066

Oconto County Historical Society
4295 Cty J
Oconto, WI 54153
Tel: 920-834-3860

Omro Area Historical Society
P.O. Box 133
Omro, WI 54963
Tel: 920-685-6123

Ozaukee County Historical Society
P.O. Box 206
Cedarburg, WI 53012
Tel: 262-377-5213

Pewaukee Area Historical Society
P.O. Box 104
Pewaukee, WI 53072
Tel: 608-224-5140
http://www.execpc.com/~jthorson/phs/phs0.html

Pierce County Historical Association
P.O. Box 148
Ellsworth, WI 54011
Tel: 715-273-6611

Portage County Historical Society
P.O. Box 672
Stevens Point, WI 54481
Tel: 715-344-5752

Racine County Historical Society and Museum
Local History and Genealogical Library
701 S. Main Street
P.O. Box 1527
Racine, WI 53401
Tel: 262-636-3926

Rhinelander Historical Society/Museum
9 S. Pelham Street
Rhinelander, WI 54501
Tel: 715-282-6120

Rock County Historical Society/Museum and Library
P.O. Box 8096
Janesville, WI 53547-8096
Tel: 608-756-4509
http://www.lincolntallman.org/

St. Croix County Historical Society
1051 Golden Oaks Dr
Hudson, WI 54016
Tel: 715-386-6194

Sauk County Historical Society/Museum
531 Fourth Avenue
P.O. Box 651
Baraboo, WI 53913
Tel: 608-356-9479
http://www.saukcounty.com/schs.htm

Seventh Day Baptist Historical Society
P.O. Box 1678
Janesville, WI 53547

Stanley Area Historical Society
228 Helgerson
Stanley, WI 54768
Tel: 715-644-5880
http://timbertrails.com/sahsm1.htm

State Historical Society of Wisconsin
816 State Street
Madison, WI 53706
Tel: 608-264-6534
http://www.shsw.wisc.edu/

Two Rivers Historical Society
1622 Jefferson Street
Two Rivers, WI 54241
Tel: 920-793-2490

Wauwatosa Historical Society
7406 Hillcrest Drive
Wauwatosa, WI 53213
Tel: 414-774-8672
http://www.wauwatosahistoricalsociety.org/

Webster House Historical Society
9 E. Rockwell Street
Elkhorn, WI 53121
Tel: 414-723-4248

Winnebago County Historical/Archaelogical Society
Morgan House
234 Church Street
Oshkosh, WI 54901
Tel: 920-235-3091

Winneconne Historical Society
P.O. Box 262
Winneconne, WI 54986
Tel: 920-582-7887

Wisconsin Black Historical Society
2620 W. Center Street
Milwaukee, WI 53206
Tel: 414-372-7677

Wisconsin Marine Historical Society
814 W. Wisconsin Avenue
Milwaukee, WI 53233-2385
Tel: 414-286-3074
E-mail: wmhs@execpc.com
http://www.execpc.com/~wmhs/

Wisconsin State Old Cemetery Society
1562 N 119th St
Wauwatosa, WI 53226
Tel: 414-771-7781

LDS FAMILY HISTORY CENTERS

For locations of Family History Centers in this state, see
the Family History Center locator at FamilySearch.
http://www.familysearch.org/eng/Library/FHC/
frameset_fhc.asp

ARCHIVES/LIBRARIES/MUSEUMS

Appleton Public Library
225 N. Oneida Street
Appleton, WI 54911
Tel/TDD: 920-832-6170
Fax: 920-832-6182
E-mail: apl@apl.org
http://apl.org/

Beaver Dam Community Library
311 South Spring Street
Beaver Dam, WI 53916
Tel: 920-887-4631
Fax: 920-887-4633
E-mail: bdref@mwfls.org
http://www.beaverdam.lib.wi.us/

Beloit Historical Society/Library
845 Hackett Street
Beloit, WI 53511
Tel: 608-365-7835
Fax: 608-365-5999
E-mail: beloiths@ticon.net

Beloit Public Library
409 Pleasant Street
Beloit, WI 53511
Tel: 608-364-2905
Fax: 608-364-2907
http://als.lib.wi.us/BPL/

Brown County Library
Local History and Genealogy Dept.
515 Pine Street
Green Bay, WI 54301
Tel: 920-448-4400
http://www.co.brown.wi.us/Library/libinfo/
    genealogy.html

Chippewa Falls Public Library
105 W. Central Street
Chippewa Falls, WI 54729
Tel: 715-723-1146
Fax: 715-720-6922
http://www.chippewalibrary.org/

Chippewa Valley Museum
Carson Park Drive
P.O. Box 1204
Eau Claire, WI 54702
Tel: 715-834-7871
http://timbertrails.com/cvm1.htm

Cudahy Public Library
4665 South Packard Avenue
Cudahy, WI 53110
Tel: 414-769-2246
Fax: 414-769-2252

Darlington Public Library
131 E. Catherine St.
Darlington, WI 53530-1359
Tel: 608-776-4171
Fax: 608-776-3365

Door County Library
107 S. 4th Avenue
Sturgeon Bay, WI 54235-2203
Tel: 414-743-6578

Fond du Lac Public Library
32 Sheboygan Street
Fond du Lac, WI 54935
Tel: 920-929-7085
Fax: 920-929-7082

Hartford Public Library
115 North Main Street
Hartford, WI 53027
Tel: 262-673-8240
Fax: 262-673-8300
http://www.mcfls.org/LCOMM/ml.htm

Hartland Public Library
110 E. Park Avenue
Hartland, WI 53029
Tel: 262-367-3350
Fax: 262-369-2251

Kenosha Public Library
812 56th Street
P.O. Box 1414
Kenosha, WI 53141-1414
Tel: 262-605-2160
Fax: 262-605-2170

LaCrosse Public Library
Archives and Local History
800 Main Street
LaCrosse, WI 54601
Tel: 608-789-7100
Fax: 608-789-7106

Madeline Island Historical Museum
P.O. Box 9
La Pointe, WI 54850
Tel: 715-747-2415

Madison Public Library
201 W. Mifflin Street
Madison, WI 53703
Tel: 608-266-6363
Fax 608-266-4338
http://elink.scls.lib.wi.us/madison/index2.html

Manitowoc County Historical Society
707 Quay St.
Manitowoc, WI 54220-4539
Tel: 920-684-4445
Fax: 920-683-4657

**Marathon County Historical Society/Museum and
Library**
504 McIndoe St
Wausau, WI 54403
Tel: 715-848-6143

Marathon County Public Library
300 First Street
Wausau, WI 54401
Tel: 715-261-7200
http://www.mcpl.lib.wi.us/

Maude Shunk Public Library
W156 N8446 Pilgrim Road
Menomonee Falls, WI 53051
Tel: 262-532-8900
http://www.mf.lib.wi.us/

McMillan Memorial Library
490 East Grand Avenue
Wisconsin Rapids, WI 54494
Tel: 715-423-1040
Fax: 715-423-2665
TDD: 715-422-5138
E-mail: mcmweb@scls.lib.wi.us
http://www.scls.lib.wi.us/mcm/

Milwaukee County Historical Society
910 North Old World Third Street
Milwaukee, WI 53203
Tel: 414-273-8288
http://www.milwaukeecountyhistsoc.org/

Milwaukee Public Library
814 West Wisconsin Avenue
Milwaukee, WI 53233
Tel: 414-286-3000
E-mail: Webmaster@mpl.org
http://www.mpl.org/

Monroe County Local History Room/Research Library
200 W. Main Street
Sparta, WI 54656
Tel: 608-269-8680
E-mail: MCLHR@centurytel.net
http://www.spartan.org/historyroom/

Neenah Public Library
240 E. Wisconsin Avenue
P.O. Box 569, Neenah
WI 54957-0569
Tel: 920-751-4722
http://www.focol.org/~npl/

North Fond du Lac Village Public Library
719 Wisconsin Avenue
North Fond Du Lac, WI 54935
Tel: 920-929-3771
Fax: 920-929-3669
www.northfonddulaclibrary.org

Northland College
Dexter Library Area Research Center
1411 Ellis Avenue
Ashland, WI 54806
Tel: 715-682-1279
Fax: 715-682-1693

Oconomowoc Public Library
200 South Street
Oconomowoc, WI 53066
Tel: 262-569-2193
Fax: 262-569-2176
http://www.wcfls.lib.wi.us/opl/

Oshkosh Public Library
106 Washington Avenue
Oshkosh, WI 54901
Tel: 920-236-5205
    920-236-5226 (Genealogy and Local History)
http://www.oshkoshpubliclibrary.org/

Oshkosh Public Museum Library
1331 Algoma Blvd.
Oshkosh, WI 54901
Tel: 920-424-4730

Plymouth Public Library
130 Division
Plymouth, WI 53073
Tel: 715-647-2373
Fax: 715-647-2373

Portage County Library
1001 Main Street
Stevens Point, WI 54481
Tel: 715-346-1544
http://library.uwsp.edu/pcl/

Racine County Historical Society and Museum
Local History and Genealogical Library
701 S. Main Street
P.O. Box 1527
Racine, WI 53401
Tel: 262-636-3926

Racine Public Library
75 Seventh Street
Racine, WI 53403
Tel: 262-636-9170
Fax: 262-636-9260

Sheboygan County Historical Research Center
518 Water Street
Sheboygan Falls, WI 53085
Tel: 920-467-4667
Fax: 920-467-1395
E-mail: schrc@execpc.com
http://www.schrc.org/

State Historical Society of Wisconsin/Library Division
816 State Street
Madison, WI 53706
Tel: 608-264-6534
    608-264-6535 (Reference)
    608-264-6525 (Government Publications Reference)
http://www.shsw.wisc.edu/

Superior Public Library
1530 Tower Avenue
Superior, WI 54880
Tel: 715-394-8860
Fax: 715-394-8870

University of Wisconsin/Eau Claire
William D. McIntyre Library
Special Collections Department
Eau Claire, WI 54702-4004
Tel: 715-836-3715
E-mail: lynchld@uwec.edu
http://www.uwec.edu/library/

University of Wisconsin/Green Bay
Cofrin Library, 7th Floor
2420 Nicolet Drive
Green Bay, WI 54311-7001
Tel: 920-465-2303
http://www.shsw.wisc.edu/archives/arcnet/greenbay.html

University of Wisconsin/La Crosse
D276 Wyllie Library Learning Center
University Archives and Area Research Center
900 Wood Road
Kenosha, WI 53141-2000
Tel: 262-595-2077
    262-595-2411
http://www.uwlax.edu/murphylibrary/

University of Wisconsin/Milwaukee
Golda Meir Library, Room W250
Milwaukee Urban Archives
P.O. Box 604
Milwaukee, WI 53201-0604
Tel: 414-229-4785
http://www.uwm.edu/Library/arch/

University of Wisconsin/Oshkosh
Forrest R. Polk Library
800 Algoma Boulevard
Oshkosh, WI 54901
Tel: 920-424-0828
http://www.uwosh.edu/home_pages/departments/llr/

University of Wisconsin/Parkside
D276 Wyllie Library Learning Center
University Archives and Area Research Center
900 Wood Road
Kenosha, WI 53141-2000
Tel: 414-595-2411

University of Wisconsin/Platteville
Elton S. Karrmann Library
Southwest Wisconsin Room
Platteville, WI 53818-3099
Tel: 608-342-1719
http://vms.www.uwplatt.edu/~library/

University of Wisconsin/River Falls
Chalmer Davee Library
120 Cascade Avenue
River Falls, WI 54022
Tel: 715-425-3567
http://www.uwrf.edu/library/welcome.html

University of Wisconsin/Stevens Point
Learning Resources Center
Nelis R. Kampenga University Archives
Stevens Point, WI 54481
Tel: 715-346-2586
http://library.uwsp.edu/depts/archives/archives.htm

University of Wisconsin/Stout
Library Learning Center
Menomonie, WI 54751
Tel: 715-232-2300
http://www.uwstout.edu/lib/

University of Wisconsin/Whitewater
Harold Anderson Library
800 West Main Street
Whitewater, WI 53190
Tel: 414-472-5520
http://library.uww.edu/

Vaughn Public Library
502 West Main Street
Ashland, WI 54806
Tel: 715-682-7060

Vesterheim Genealogical Center and Naeseth Library
415 W. Main Street
Madison, WI 53703-3116
Tel. 608-255-2224
Fax: 608-255-6842
E-mail: vesterheim@juno.com
http://www.library.wisc.edu/local/memorial/
    libraries/Memorial/vesterhe.htm

Waukesha Public Library
321 Wisconsin Avenue
Waukesha, WI 53186
Tel: 262-524-3680
http://www.waukesha.lib.wi.us/

Wauwatosa Public Library
7635 W. North Avenue
Wauwatosa, WI 53213
Tel: 414-471-8484
E-mail: shawn.duffy@mcfls.org
http://tpublib.fp.execpc.com//

Whitefish Bay Public Library
5420 N. Marlborough Drive
Whitefish Bay, WI 53217
Tel: 414-964-4380
Fax: 414-964-5733
http://www.mcfls.org/wfbay/

Wisconsin Marine Historical Society
814 W. Wisconsin Avenue
Milwaukee, WI 53233-2385
Tel: 414-286-3074
E-mail: wmhs@execpc.com
http://www.execpc.com/~wmhs/

NEWSPAPER REPOSITORIES

State Historical Society of Wisconsin
816 State Street
Madison, WI 53706
Tel: 608-264-6534
http://www.shsw.wisc.edu/

VITAL RECORDS

Wisconsin State Department of Health and Family Services
Vital Records
P.O. Box 309
Madison, WI 53701-0309
Tel: 608-266-1371
E-mail: VitalRecords@dhfs.state.wi.us
http://www.dhfs.state.wi.us/

WISCONSIN ON THE WEB

Wisconsin GenWeb Project
http://www.rootsweb.com/~wigenweb/

Wisconsin Land Records—Interactive Search
http://searches.rootsweb.com/cgi-bin/wisconsin/
    wisconsin.pl

WYOMING

ARCHIVES, STATE & NATIONAL

National Archives-Rocky Mountain Region
Bldg. 48, Denver Federal Center
West 6th Avenue and Kipling Street
Denver, CO 80225-0307
Mailing Address:
P.O. Box 25307
Denver, CO 80225-0307
Phone: 303-236-0817
Fax: 303-236-9297
E-mail: denver.archives@nara.gov
http://www.nara.gov/regional/denver.html

Wyoming State Archives and Historical Department
Barrett Building
2301 Central Avenue
Cheyenne, WY 82002
Tel: (307) 777-7826
FAX: (307) 777-7044
E-mail:WYARCHIVE@STATE.WY.US
http://spacr.state.wy.us/cr/archives/index.htm

GENEALOGICAL SOCIETIES

Albany County Genealogical Society
P.O. Box 6163
Laramie, WY 82070

Cheyenne Genealogical Society
Laramie County Library
2800 Central Avenue
Cheyenne, WY 82001
Tel: 307-634-3561

Converse County Genealogical Society
119 North Ninth Street, 2418
Douglas, WY 82633

Fremont County Genealogical Society
Riverton Branch Library
1330 West Park Avenue
Riverton, WY 82501
Tel: 307-856-5310

Laramie Peekers Genealogy Society of Platte County
1108 21st Street
Wheatland, WY 82201

Natrona County Genealogical Society
P.O. Box 9244
Casper, WY 82601

Park County Genealogy Society
P.O. Box 3056
Cody, WY 82414

Powell Valley Genealogical Club
830 North Day
P.O. Box 184
Powell, WY 82435

Sheridan Genealogical Society, Inc.
Sheridan County/Fulmer Public Library
Wyoming Room
335 West Alger Street
Sheridan, WY 82801
Tel: 307-674-8585

Sublette County Genealogy Society
P.O. Box 1186
Pindale, WY 82941

HISTORICAL SOCIETIES

Albany County Historical Society
E-mail: amyml@uwyo.edu
http://www.uwyo.edu/ahc/achs/index.html

Fort Phil Kearney/Bozeman Trail Association
P.O. Box 5013
Sheridan, WY 82801
Tel: 307-684-7687

Lincoln County Historical Society
P.O. Box 242
Afton 83110

State Historic Preservation Office
Barrett Building
2301 Central Avenue, 3rd Floor
Cheyenne, WY 82002
Tel: 307-777-7697
Fax: 307-777-6421
http://wyoshpo.state.wy.us/

Union Pacific Historical Society
P.O. Box 4006
Cheyenne, WY 82003
http://www.uphs.org/uphs.html

Wyoming State Historical Society
PMB #184, 1740H Dell Range Blvd.
Cheyenne, WY 82009

LDS FAMILY HISTORY CENTERS

For locations of Family History Centers in this state, see
the Family History Center locator at FamilySearch
http://www.familysearch.org/eng/Library/FHC/
frameset_fhc.asp

ARCHIVES/LIBRARIES/MUSEUMS

Albany Public Library
310 S. 8th Street
Laramie, WY 82070-3969
Tel: 307-721-2580
E-mail: ssimpson@will.state.wy.us
http://www-wsl.state.wy.us/wyld/libraries/alby/

Buffalo Bill Historical Center
Harold McCracken Research Library
720 Sheridan Avenue
Cody, WY 82414
Tel: 307-587-4771
E-mail: hmrl@wave.park.wy.us
http://www.bbhc.org/

Casper College
Goodstein Foundation Library
Special Collections
125 College Drive
Casper, WY 82601
Tel: 307-268-2100
Fax: 307-268-2682
E-mail: cspcbibman@wyld.state.wy.us
http://www.caspercollege.edu/library/

Goshen County Public Library
2001 East A Street
Torrington, WY 82240
Tel: 307-532-3411

Laramie County Library
2800 Central Avenue
Cheyenne, WY 82001
Tel: 307-635-1032
Fax: 307) 634-2082
TDD: 307-634-0105
http://www.lclsonline.org/

Laramie Plains Museum
603 Ivinson Avenue
Laramie, WY 82070
Tel: 307-742-4448

National Historic Trails Interpretive Center
(Still in the planning stages)
500 N. Center Street
P.O. Box 399
Casper, WY 82601
Tel: 307-265-8030
http://w3.trib.com/~rlund/NHTIC.html

National U.S. Marshals Museum
Wyoming Territorial Prison and Old West Park
975 Snowy Range Road
Laramie, WY 82070
Tel: 800-845-2287
       307-745-6161
Fax: 307-745-8620
E-mail: info@wyoprisonpark.org
http://www.wyoprisonpark.org/

Park County Library
1057 Sheridan Avenue
Cody, WY 82414
Tel: 307-527-8820
http://will.state.wy.us/park

Platte County Public Library
Wyoming Room
904 9th Street
Wheatland, WY 82201
Tel: 307-322-2689
       1-888-841-0964
Fax: 307-322-3540
http://www-wsl.state.wy.us/wyld/libraries/plat/

Riverton Branch Library
1330 West Park Avenue
Riverton, WY 82501
Tel: 307-856-3556
Fax: 307/857-3722

Riverton Museum/Research Library
700 E. Park Avenue
Riverton, WY 82501
Tel: 307-856-2665
E-mail: ljost@wyoming.com
http://www.wyoming.com/~rivmus/

Rock River Museum
131 Avenue C
P. O. Box 52
Rock River, WY 82058
Tel: 307-378-2386

Sheridan County/Fulmer Public Library
Wyoming Room
335 West Alger Street
Sheridan, WY 82801
Tel: 307-674-8585
Fax: 307-674-7374
http://www.sheridanwyolibrary.org/

Sweetwater County Historical Museum
3 East Flaming Gorge Way
Green River, WY 82935
Tel: 307-872-6435
Fax: 307-872-3234
http://www.sweetwatermuseum.org/

Teton County Historical Center
1005 Mercell Avenue
P.O. Box 1005
Jackson, WY 83001
Tel: 307-733-9605

Teton County Library
125 Virginian Lane
P.O. Box 1629
Jackson, WY 83001
Tel: 307-733-2164
Fax: 307-733-4568
E-mail: tetnref@wyld.state.wy.us
http://will.state.wy.us/teton/home/

Uinta County Library
701 Main Street
Evanston, WY 82930
Tel: 307-789-2770

University of Wyoming
American Heritage Center
Centennial Complex
2221 Willett Drive
P.O. Box 3924
Laramie, WY 82070
Tel: 307-766-2574
Fax: 307-766-5511
http://www.uwyo.edu/ahc/ahcinfo.htm

Western Wyoming Community College Library
2500 College Drive
Rock Springs, WY 82901
Tel: 307-382-1600
Fax: 307-382-7665
http://www.wwcc.cc.wy.us/college/library/

Wyoming State Library
Division of the Department of Administration and
    Information
Supreme Court and State Librarty Building
2301 Capitol Avenue
Cheyenne, WY 82002-0060
Tel: 307-777-7283
Fax: 307-777-6289
http://www-wsl.state.wy.us/

Yellowstone National Park Museum
P.O. Box 168
Yellowstone National Park, WY 82190
Tel: 307-344-2262
http://www.nps.gov/yell/technical/museum/

NEWSPAPER REPOSITORIES

University of Wyoming Library
P.O. Box 3334, University Station
Laramie, WY 82071
Tel: 307-766-2070
http://www-lib.uwyo.edu/

VITAL RECORDS

Division of Health and Medical Services
Vital Records
117 Hathaway Building
Cheyenne, WY 82002
Tel: 307-777-7656
Fax: (307) 777-7327
http://wdhfs.state.wy.us/WDH/index.htm

WYOMING ON THE WEB

Oregon/California Trails Association (OCTA)
http://www.octa-trails.org/

**Oregon/California Trails Association (OCTA)/
Wyoming Chapter**
http://w3.trib.com/~rlund/treks.html

Stannary of Wyoming
http://plains.uwyo.edu/~lcurtis/index.htm

Wyoming GenWeb Project
http://www.rootsweb.com/~wygenweb/

THE
ANCESTRY
FAMILY HISTORIAN'S
ADDRESS
BOOK

2ND EDITION

A Comprehensive List of Local, State, and Federal
Agencies and Institutions and Ethnic and
Genealogical Organizations